International Environmental Law, Fourth Edition

International Environmental Law

Series Editor

Makane Moïse Mbengue

VOLUME 22

The titles published in this series are listed at *brill.com/iel*

International Environmental Law, Fourth Edition

By

Dinah Shelton

Edited by

Makane Moïse Mbengue
Elena Cima
Brian McGarry

BRILL | NIJHOFF

LEIDEN | BOSTON

Library of Congress Cataloging-in-Publication Data

Names: Shelton, Dinah, editor.
Title: International environmental law / edited by Dinah Shelton.
Description: Fourth edition. | Boston, Massachusett : Brill, 2026. | Series: International environmental law, 18736599 ; 22 | Previous edition classed in K3585.3–xg09 | Includes bibliographical references and index. | Summary: "Dinah Shelton's International Environmental Law provides a comprehensive and updated analysis of international environmental frameworks, offering insights into the triple planetary crisis-climate change, biodiversity loss, and pollution. This edition further develops the intersection of environmental law with human rights, trade, and other international legal fields, while examining the role of global institutions, treaties, and customary law in addressing today's most pressing environmental issues. The book provides an essential guide to the legal frameworks that underpin efforts to protect the environment and ensure sustainable development in the 21st century"– Provided by publisher.
Identifiers: LCCN 2025014909 (print) | LCCN 2025014910 (ebook) | ISBN 9789004178458 (hardback) | ISBN 9789047440802 (ebook)
Subjects: LCSH: Environmental law, International.
Classification: LCC K3585 .I577 2026 (print) | LCC K3585 (ebook) | DDC 344.04/6–dc23/eng/20250401
LC record available at https://lccn.loc.gov/2025014909
LC ebook record available at https://lccn.loc.gov/2025014910

Typeface for the Latin, Greek, and Cyrillic scripts: "Brill". See and download: brill.com/brill-typeface.

ISSN 1873-6599
ISBN 978-90-04-17845-8 (hardback)
ISBN 978-90-47-44080-2 (e-book)
DOI 10.1163/9789047440802

This book is printed on acid-free paper and produced in a sustainable manner.

We fondly dedicate this edition to Alex Kiss and, like the first edition, to all who have given their lives to protect the environment for present and future generations.

•••

To see the World in a Grain of Sand
And a Heaven in a Wild Flower
Hold Infinity in the Palm of your Hand
And Eternity in an Hour

William Blake, Auguries of Innocence

Contents

PART 3
Inclusive Environmental Protection

Authors' Preface

The field of international environmental law has rapidly expanded in recent decades to encompass many issues of fundamental concern to international law scholars and practitioners, environmental lawyers, public officials and civil society. To serve these various audiences, this treatise introduces the major international legal rules, institutions, and procedures concerned with protecting the environment in an epoch increasingly referred to as the Anthropocene (a time in which the old conceptual divide between humans and the natural world has lost its accuracy and utility because human action now shapes everything).

Along these lines, in this book we canvass the theories, objectives, and historical evolution of international environmental law, as well as the principles of general international law that are particularly important in the environmental field. The text reviews the norms applicable to each sector or milieu of the environment, as well as developments concerning sources of transboundary environmental harm, such as chemicals, toxic waste and global warming. The book further describes and analyses the contemporary moves towards integrated protection and ecosystem management. We also treat important areas of international activity – such as international trade, human rights protection, and the use of force – that have significant environmental bearing, as well as efforts to include environmental considerations in cognate international legal regimes.

The first edition of the book was published in 1991, before the landmark United Nations Conference on Environment and Development, held in Rio de Janeiro in June 1992. The second edition included developments that took place in the subsequent five years. The third edition appeared in 2003, a decade after the Rio Conference and shortly after the conclusion of the World Summit on Sustainable Development, held in Johannesburg, South Africa, in September 2002. The fourth edition takes account of significant developments since, including the outcomes of Rio +20 (or Stockholm +40) in 2012 and continuing efforts to meet the challenge of climate change. The new edition comes a decade after the sad loss of the original co-author and brilliant international environmental law pioneer Alex Kiss in 2007. It is current through May 2024 (and in a few instances beyond).

Very few fields have burst on the scene with as much fecundity and fervor as contemporary international environmental law. In response to emerging environmental problems and continuing environmental decline, an impressive corpus of international environmental law has been negotiated and brought into force following the 1972 Stockholm U.N. Conference on the Human Environment, the world's first major conference on the environment. By the late-1990s, it was estimated that over 1000 different international environmental legal instruments (hard and soft)[1] and 139 different major multilateral

---

1 Edith Brown Weiss, Understanding Compliance with International Environmental Agreements: The Baker's Dozen Myths, *University of Richmond Law Review*, 1999, vol. 32, p. 1555. The normative proliferation of international environmental law was contemporaneously chronicled in an array of helpful treaty collections. See W. E. Burhenne, ed. & Robert Muecke, comp., *International Environmental Law: Multilateral Treaties*, 9 loose-leaf vols, Berlin: E. Schmidt, 1974–onwards; Bernd Rüster and Burno Simma, eds, *International Protection of the Environment: Multilateral Treaties*, 30 vols [1754-1981], Dobbs Ferry, NY: Oceana Publications, 1975–1983. In 1990 the publication, with a slightly modified title, but with the same editors and publisher, continued in a second series Bernd Rüster and Burno Simma, eds., *International Protection of the Environment: Treaties and Related Documents, Second Series* [1981-], Dobbs Ferry, NY: Oceana Publications, 1989–[]. A six volume third series also appeared specifically for the proceedings of the 1992 United Nations Conference on Environment and Development. See Nicholas A. Robinson, ed., *Agenda 21 & The UNCED Proceedings*, New York: Oceana Publications, Inc., 1992. A host of other environmental treaty collections of treaties and instruments also proliferated. See Alexandre Charles Kiss, ed., *Selected Multilateral Treaties in the Field of the Environment*, Nairobi, Kenya: United Nations Environment Programme, 1983; Philippe Sands, *Chernobyl: Law and Communication*, Cambridge: Grotius Publications, 1988; Peter Sand, *Marine Environmental Law in the United Nations Environment Programme*, Dublin: Tycooly, 1988; United Nations Environment Programme, *Register of International Treaties and Other Agreements in the Field of the Environment*, Nairobi, Kenya, 1989 and updated regularly, currently U.N. Doc. UNEP/Env.Law/2005/3 (2005); Iwona Rummel-Bulska and Seth Osafo, eds, *Selected Multilateral Treaties in the Field of the Environment*, vol. 2, Nairobi: United Nations Environment Programme, 1991; Paul R. Molitor, ed., *International Environmental Law: Primary Materials*, Deventer/Boston: Kluwer Law and Taxation Publishers, 1991; Edith Brown Weiss, Paul C. Szasz & Daniel B. Magraw, eds, *International Environmental Law: Basic Instruments and References*, Dobbs Ferry, NY: Transnational Publishers, Inc., 1992; Harold Hohmann, ed., *Basic Documents of International Environmental Law*, 3 vols, London/Dordrecht/Boston: Graham & Trotman/Martinus Nijhoff, 1992; Preparatory Committee for the United Nations Conference on Environment and Development, *Report of the Secretary-General of the Conference on the Survey of Existing Agreements and Instruments and its Follow-up*, U.N. Doc. A/CONF.151/PC/103 and Add.1 (30 April 1992); Barbara Kwiatkowska & Alfred H.A. Soons, eds, *Transboundary Movements and Disposal of Hazardous Wastes in International Law: Basic Documents*, Dordrect/Boston/London: Martinus Nijhoff/Graham & Trotman, 1993; Günter Hoog & Angela Steinmets, eds, *International Conventions on Protection of Humanity and Environment*, Berlin/New York: Walter de Gruyter, 1993; Wolfgang Burhenne & Marlene Jahnke, eds, *International Environmental Soft Law: Collection of Relevant Instruments*, looseleaf service, Dordrecht/Boston: Martinus Nijhoff Publishers, 1993–2003; Philippe Sands, Richard Tarasofsky, and Mary Weiss, eds, *Documents in International Environmental Law*, 2 vols., Manchester, UK: Manchester Univ. Press, 1994; Patricia W. Birnie & Alan Boyle, eds, *Basic Documents on International Environmental Law*, Oxford: Clarendon Press, 1995; Wolfgang Burhenne & Nicholas Robinson, eds, *International Protection of the Environment: Conservation in Sustainable Development*, looseleaf service, 1995–present (Dobbs Ferry, NY:

international environmental treaties[2] were in existence. In the years between 1972 and 1992 alone, it was said that more than 50 multilateral treaties relating to the protection of the environment were concluded.[3] This rapid development of the law has had a number of consequences, but two should be mentioned here. First of all, the sheer volume has proved to be a challenge to the student and practitioner alike. Keeping up to date and conversant with all the normative developments across the field requires intellectual commitment and substantial time. And even then, it is still possible to be overwhelmed by substance. One of our main aims in this book is to distil this large content in order to highlight fundamentals and provide a sophisticated pathfinder for either the tyro or the initiate.

A second consequence of international environmental law's rapid development has been the growth of a perception of the law's ineffectiveness. With the rapid development a large body of international environmental law, it is natural to think that we would see tangible environmental improvement. In the end, the law's worth must be gauged on how well (or not) it achieves its purposes. If international environmental law is designed to halt and reverse transboundary environmental degradation, then it may be judged accordingly. Agenda 21, the Program of Action adopted at the Rio Conference, created widespread hope for improving environmental conditions throughout the world by way of the application of the concept of sustainable development. The idea was that economic and social priorities would be balanced with the

---

Oceana Publications); United States National Oceanic and Atmospheric Administration, *1998 Year of the Ocean: A Survey of International Agreements*, Washington, DC: NOAA, 1998; Edith Brown Weiss, Daniel Barstow Magraw & Paul C. Szasz eds, *International Environmental Law: Basic Instruments and References 1992–1999*, Dobbs Ferry, NY: Transnational Publishers, Inc., 1999; Mark Austen & Tamara Richards, *Basic Legal Documents on International Animal Welfare and Wildlife Conservation*, The Hague/London/Boston: Kluwer Law International, 2000. See also the extensive document supplements that have accompanied the various editions of major casebooks on International Environmental Law: Lakshman D. Guruswamy, Geoffrey W.R. Palmer, Burns H. Weston, Jonathan C. Carlson, eds, *Supplement of Basic Documents to International Environmental Law and World Order*, St Paul: West Group, 1994 and 1999; David Hunter, James Salzman & Durwood Zaelke, eds, *International Environmental Law and Policy Treaty Supplement*, New York: Foundation Press, 2002, 2007 and 2011; Donald K. Anton, Jonathan I. Charney, Philippe Sands, Thomas J. Schoenbaum & Michael K. Young, eds, *International Environmental Law: Cases, Materials, Problems: Document Supplement*, Newark: LexisNexis, 2007.

2 United Nations Environment Programme, *Register of International Treaties*, U.N. Doc. UNEP/GC.15/Inf.2 (1989).

3 Andronico O. Adede, *International Environmental Law Digest: Instruments for International Responses to Problems of Environment and Development 1972–1992*, Amsterdam: Elsiver, 1992, p. 14.

legal measures to protect the environment in order to stem environmental degradation. The anticipated progress continues to be slow. In 2002, the United Nations University and the Institute of Advanced Studies provided a sobering overview of the global environment in their report to the World Summit on Sustainable Development:

> There are at least 1.1 billion people who still lack access to safe drinking water and 2.4 billion who lack adequate sanitation. Two thirds of the world's population will live in 'water-stressed' areas by the year 2025. In some cases groundwater levels are falling by one to three meters each year. 75 percent of the world's energy is being produced by burning fossil fuels, increasing CO_2 emission levels by 1 percent each year, despite reduction targets being established since the adoption of the United Nations Framework Convention on Climate Change. The fourteen hottest years since 1860, when systematic measuring began, have all occurred in the past two decades. More than 8 percent of children in developing countries still die before the age of five, and in some of the poorest countries, one in five children die before their first birthday. More than 113 million school-age children in developing countries are not in school, over 60 percent of them girls. About 815 million people in the world are undernourished. Hunger in South Asia, where it is most prevalent, is declining, while in Africa, about one third of the population is undernourished and the numbers are increasing. In many developing countries, poor health conditions prevail as a result of contaminated water, poor sanitation, severe indoor air pollution, malaria and other infectious diseases, and the spread of HIV/AIDS. The loss of 2.5 percent of forests globally each year, along with the threat of extinction of 24 percent of mammals and 12 percent of birds, leads experts to the estimation that we are losing one major drug every two years, whilst only one percent of the world's tropical plants have been screened for potential pharmaceutical application. If this current development continues, biodiversity will be threatened on up to 74 percent of the land area by 2032.[4]

In this growing environmental crisis, international environmental law and policy take on added urgency and there is evident need to place environmental considerations at the center of social and economic issues. In addition,

4 United Nations University/Institute of Advanced Studies, *International Sustainable Development Governance* (Aug. 2002) 8.

international institutions and civil society need to play an increasing role in developing international obligations and monitoring compliance with them.

The potential for law and policy to improve the environment can be seen in some of the positive developments of recent years. Water quality has generally improved in developed countries. After decades of absence, salmon have returned to the Rhine River. European forests that were dying decades ago due to environmental stresses are again healthy and expanding. In other regions of the world, species that were once threatened or endangered have recovered. These successes, however, are largely overshadowed by the scope of the current problems.

In taking needed action, states and other actors are increasingly mainstreaming or integrating environmental protection into other subject areas of international regulation, such as human rights, armed conflict, and trade. The expansion and maturing of international environmental law is also reflected in the large number of treaties adopted in the past two decades, the development of customary international norms, and the increasing utilization of international dispute settlement mechanisms to address environmental problems.

Without analyzing in detail each of the hundreds of agreements and other normative instruments in the field, this volume attempts a comprehensive overview of the development of international environmental law, its current status and emerging trends. The book is divided into three parts. Part I examines the structure, basic concepts, and institutions of international environmental law. The second part turns to the regulation of each environmental sector or milieu (soil, water, air, living organisms) and the sources of environmental harm. Part III concerns integrated approaches to environmental protection, such as ecosystem management, and the mainstreaming of environmental issues into the international legal regimes of human rights, armed conflict, and international economic law. Due to the increased availability of primary texts, no international instrument is reproduced herein. Print and electronic resources are indicated in the bibliographies that follow each chapter.

We hope the book will prove a useful resource not only for those persons studying and actively involved in environmental protection, but also those who have a general interest in the subject.

Acknowledgements

The authors wish to thank the following Research Assistants for their dedicated efforts to bring this new edition up to date: Ms. Roos de Kraker, Ms. Zoë Knijff, Ms. Loeva Georges, Ms. Nolwen Guilleman, and Ms. Agata Szczepańska. We also thank the following Editorial Assistants for their excellent support during the publication process: Ms. Elena Graham, Ms. Teodora Blaga, Ms. Eva Canavan, Ms. Calypso Ruë Simon, Ms. Courtney Lynch, and Ms. Rebecca Walker.

Abbreviations

ASEAN	Association of Southeast Asian Nations
ATCM	Antarctic Treaty Consultative Meeting
ATCP	Antarctic Treaty Consultative Parties
A.T.S.	Antarctic Treaty System
B.F.S.P.	British and Foreign State Papers
CBD	Convention on Biological Diversity
CCAMLR	Commission for the Conservation of Antarctic Marine Living Resources
CDM	Clean development mechanism
CFC	Chlorofluorocarbons
CIEL	Center for International Environmental Law
CITES	Convention on International Trade in Endangered Species
Cmd.	United Kingdom Command Papers
COP	Conference of the Parties
CSD	Commission on Sustainable Development
CTE	World Trade Organization Committee on Trade and Environment
C.T.S.	Canadian Treaty Series
ECOSOC	United Nations Economic and Social Council
EC	European Community
EEZ	Exclusive Economic Zone
EIA	Environmental Impact Assessment
EMEP	Environmental Management
EMuT	International Law: Multilateral Agreements
Envtl L.	Environmental Law
E.P.L.	Environmental Policy and Law
E.T.S.	European Treaty Series
EU	European Union
FAO	Food and Agriculture Organization
GATT	General Agreement on Tariffs and Trade
GEF	Global Environment Facility
GEMS	Global Environment Monitoring System
GHG	Greenhouse gases
IAEA	International Atomic Energy Agency
I.C.J.	International Court of Justice Reports
ICRC	International Committee of the Red Cross

ICZM	Integrated coastal zone management
ILC	International Law Commission
I.L.M.	International Legal Materials
ILO	International Labor Organization
IMF	International Monetary Fund
IMCO	International Maritime Consultative Organizations
IMO	International Maritime Organization
IPCC	Intergovernmental Panel on Climate Change
IRPTC	International Register of Potentially Toxic Chemicals
ITLOS	International Tribunal on the Law of the Sea
IUCN	World Conservation Union
IWC	International Whaling Commission
JI	Joint implementation
LMO	Living modified organism
L.N.T.S.	League of Nations Treaty Series
LRTAP	Convention on Long-Range Transboundary Air Pollution
MARPOL	International Convention on the Prevention of Pollution by Ships
MOU	Memorandum of understanding
NAFTA	North American Free Trade Agreement
NGO	Non-governmental organization
O.J.E.C.	Official Journal of the European Communities
OAS	Organization of American States
OAU	Organization of African Unity
OECD	Organization of Economic Cooperation and Development
OSCE	Organization for Security and Cooperation in Europe
PCBS	polychlorinated biphenyls
PIC	Prior informed consent
POPS	Persistant organic pollutants
stat.	Statute
T.I.A.S.	U.S. Treaties and Other International Agreements
TOMAS	Tropospheric Ozone Management Areas
U.K.T.S.	United Kingdom Treaty Series
UNCED	United Nations Conference on Environment and Development
UNCLOS	United Nations Convention on the Law of the Sea
UNCTAD	United Nations Conference on Trade and Development
UNDP	United Nations Development Program
UNECE	United Nations Economic Commission for Europe
UNEP	United Nations Environment Program

UNESCO	United Nations Educational, Scientific and Cultural Organization
UNFCCC	United Nations Framework Convention on Climate Change
UNGAOR	United Nations General Assembly Official Records
UNRIAA	United Nations Reports of International Arbitral Awards
U.N.T.S.	United Nations Treaty Series
U.S.T.	United States Treaty Series
VOCs	Volatile organic compounds
WHO	World Health Organization
WMO	World Meteorological Organization
WSSD	World Summit on Sustainable Development
WTO	World Trade Organization
WWF	Worldwide Fund for Nature

Chronological Table of Treaties and Other International Instruments

29 Nov. 1868	Declaration of St. Petersburg Renouncing the Use, in Time of War, of Explosive Projectiles, AJIL 1 (Supp.) 95.
19 May 1900	Convention for the Preservation of Wild Animals, Birds and Fish in Africa, 188 Parry 418
19 March 1902	Convention for the Protection of Birds Useful to Agriculture (Paris), 30 Martens (2d) 686; 102 B.F.S.P. 969
21 May 1906	United States-Mexico Convention Concerning the Equitable Distribution of the Waters of the Rio Grande for Irrigation Purposes, UN DOC/ST/LEG/Ser. 8/12 p.232; 34 Stat. 2953, T.S. 455; 9 Bevans 924
18 October 1907	Convention (No. IV) Respecting the Laws and Customs of War on Land (The Hague), 36 Stat. 2277, T.S. No. 539
11 January 1909	Treaty between the United States and Great Britain Respecting Boundary Waters Between the United States and Canada (Washington), 36 Stat. 2448, T.S. No. 548, 12 Bevans 319; 4 AM.J.INT'L.L. 239 (1920 Supp.)
7 February 1911	Treaty for the Preservation and Protection of the Fur Seals (Washington), 104 B.F.S.P. 175
22 March 1923	U.S. - Great Britain Convention for the Preservation of the Halibut Fishery (Washington D.C.)
17 June 1925	Geneva Protocol for the Prohibition of the Use in War of Asphyxiating, Poisonous or Other Gases and of Bacteriological Methods of Warfare (Geneva), 26 U.S.T. 571, T.I.A.S. No. 8061, 14 I.L.M. 49 (1975)
24 September 1931	Convention for the Regulation of Whaling, 155 L.N.T.S. 349; 49 Stat. 3079, T.S. 880, 3 Bevans 26
8 November 1933	Convention Relative to the Preservation of Fauna and Flora in their Natural State (London), 172 L.N.T.S. 241; U.K.T.S. 27 (1930), Cmd. 5280; 137 B.F.S.P. 254; 6 Hudson 504; Kiss 57
15 April 1935	Convention for the Settlement of Difficulties arising from Operations of Smelter at Trail, B.C. (Ottawa), 162 L.N.T.S. 73; 49 Stat. 3245, T.S. No. 893, 6 Bevans 60; C.T.S. 1935, No. 20, 30 AJIL 163 (Supp.).

12 October 1940	Convention on Nature Protection and Wild-Life Preservation in the Western Hemisphere (Washington), 161 U.N.T.S. 193; 56 Stat. 1354, T.S. No. 981, 3 Bevans 630
3 February 1944	U.S.-Mexico Treaty Relating to the Utilization of Waters of the Colorado and Tijuana Rivers and of the Rio Grande, 3 U.N.T.S. 313, 59 Stat. 1219, T.S. No. 994.
2 December 1946	International Convention for the Regulation of Whaling (Washington), 161 U.N.T.S. 72, U.K.T.S. 5 (1949), Cmd. 7604; 62 Stat. 1716, T.I.A.S. No. 1849, 4 Bevans 248
30 October 1947	General Agreement on Tariffs and Trade, 55 U.N.T.S. 187, A.T.S. 23 (1948), 1947 Can. T.S. 27, T.I.A.S. 1700; 4 WESTON IV.C.1.
26 February 1948	Indo-Pacific Fisheries Commission (Baguio, The Philippines)
2 May 1948	American Declaration of the Rights and Duties of Man, Res. XXX, Ninth Conference of American States, 3 WESTON III.B.23.
30 April 1948	Charter of the Organization of American States, 119 U.N.T.S. 3, 2 U.S.T. 2416, T.I.A.S. No. 2361; *amended* Feb. 27, 1967, 721 U.N.T.S. 326, 21 U.S.T. 607, T.I.A.S. No. 6847; *amended* Dec. 5, 1985, O.A.S.T.S. 1-D, OEA/Ser.A/2 Rev. 2.
10 December 1948	Universal Declaration of Human Rights, G.A. Res. 217A(III), U.N.DOC A/810
31 May 1949	Convention for the Establishment of an Inter-American Tropical Tuna Commission (Washington D.C.), , 1 U.S.T. 230, T.I.A.S. 2044
12 August 1949	Convention Relative to the Protection of Civilian Persons in Time of War, 6 U.S.T. 3516, T.I.A.S. No. 3365, 75 U.N.T.S. 287
8 April 1950	Protocol to Establish a Tripartite Standing Committee on Polluted Waters (Brussels) 66 U.N.T.S. 285
18 October 1950	International Convention for the Protection of Birds (Paris), 638 U.N.T.S. 185; Kiss 84, 5 WESTON V.H.3
4 November 1950	European Convention for the Protection of Human Rights and Freedoms (Rome), 213 U.N.T.S. 221; E.T.S. 5; U.K.T.S. 71 (1953), Cmd. 8969; 156 B.F.S.P. 915
9 May 1952	Convention for the High Seas Fisheries of the North Pacific Ocean (Tokyo), EMuT 52:35.

12 May 1954	International Convention for the Prevention of Pollution of the Sea by Oil (London), 327 U.N.T.S. 3; U.K.T.S. 54 (1958), Cmd. 595; A.T.S. 7 (1962); C.T.S. 31 (1958); 12 U.S.T. 2989, T.I.A.S. No. 4900, Kiss 101. Amended 1962: 600 U.N.T.S. 332; U.K.T.S. 59 (1967), Cmd 3354; 17 U.S.T. 1523, T.I.A.S. No. 6109. Amended 1969: U.K.T.S. 21 (1978), Cmd. 7094; 28 U.S.T. 1205, T.I.A.S. 8508, 5 WESTON V.F.2.
26 October 1956	Statute of the International Atomic Energy Agency, 276 U.N.T.S. 3; U.K.T.S. 19 (1958), Cmd. 450; 8 U.S.T. 1043, T.I.A.S. 3873; A.T.S. 11 (1957)
27 October 1956	Convention on the Canalization of the Mosel (Luxembourg) J.O.R.F. 1 Jan. 1957, p. 534.
9 February 1957	Interim Convention on Conservation of North Pacific Fur Seals (Washington), 314 U.N.T.S. 105; 8 U.S.T. 2283, T.I.A.S. No 3948
22 November 1957	Agreement between Norway and the U.S.S.R. on Measures Regulating the Catch and Conserving Stocks of Seal in the North-Eastern Part of the Atlantic Ocean (Oslo), 309 U.N.T.S. 280
29 April 1958	Convention on Fishing and Conservation of the Living Resources of the High Seas, 559 U.N.T.S. 285; U.K.T.S. 39 (1966), Cmd. 3028; 17 U.S.T. 138, T.I.A.S. No. 5969; A.T.S. 12; 52 AM.J.INT'L.L. 851; 5 WESTON V.H.5;
29 April 1958	Convention on the High Seas, 450 U.N.T.S. 82; U.K.T.S. 5 (1963), Cmd. 1929; 13 U.S.T. 2312, T.I.A.S. No. 5200; A.T.S. 12 (1963); 52 AM.J.INT'L.L. 842; Kiss 129; 5 WESTON V.H.3;
29 April 1958	Convention on the Continental Shelf (Geneva), 499 U.N.T.S. 311, 15 U.S.T. 471
7 July 1959	Convention concerning Fishing in the Black Sea (Varna), 377 U.N.T.S. 220
1 December 1959	The Antarctic Treaty (Washington), 402 U.N.T.S. 71; U.K.T.S. 97 (1961), Cmd. 1535; 12 U.S.T. 794, T.I.A.S. 4780; 52 AM.J.INT'L.L. 477 (1960); 5 WESTON V.D.1;
8 April 1960	General Treaty for the Settlement of Frontier Questions Between the Netherlands and the Federal Republic of Germany, 508 U.N.T.S. 14
29 July 1960	Convention on Third Party Liability in the Field of Nuclear Energy (Paris), 8 E.Y.B. 203; U.K.T.S. 69 (1968), Cmd. 3755, 55 Am.J.Int'l.L. 1082 (1961); Kiss 159

27 October 1960	Agreement on the Protection of Lake Constance Against Pollution (Steckborn), UN Legislative Series, ST/LEG/SER.B/12 p. 438
25 May 1962	Convention on the Liability of Operators of Nuclear Ships (Brussels), 57 AM.J.INT'L.L. 268 (1963)
16 November 1962	Convention Between France and Switzerland Concerning the Protection of Lake Leman Against Pollution (Paris), 922 U.N.T.S. 49
14 December 1962	G.A. Res. 1803 (XVII) on Permanent Sovereignty over Natural Resources
29 April 1963	Agreement Concerning the International Commission for the Protection of the Rhine Against Pollution (Bern), 994 U.N.T.S. 3; Kiss 176
21 May 1963	Convention on Civil Liability for Nuclear Damage (Vienna), Misc. 9 (1964), Cmd. 2333; 2 I.L.M. 727 (1963); Kiss 179; 5 WESTON V.J.3;
5 August 1963	Treaty Banning Nuclear Weapon Tests in the Atmosphere, in Outer Space and Under Water, Moscow, 480 U.N.T.S. 43; U.K.T.S. 3 (1964), Cmd. 2245; 14 U.S.T. 1313, T.I.A.S. 5433; A.T.S. 26 (1963); 57 AM.J.INT'L.L. 1026; Kiss 185; 2 WESTON II.C.14;
17 October 1963	Nordic Mutual Emergency Assistance Agreement in Connection with Radiation Accidents, 525 U.N.T.S. 75
26 October 1963	Act Regarding Navigation and Economic Cooperation Between the States of the Niger Basin, 567 U.N.T.S. 9;
22 August 1964	Statute of the Lake Chad Basin, III I.U.W.R.
25 November 1964	Agreement Concerning the River Niger Commission and the Navigation and Transport on the River Niger (Niamey), 587 U.N.T.S. 19;
14 May 1966	International Convention for the Conservation of Atlantic Tuna (Rio de Janeiro), 20 U.S.T. 2887, 673 U.N.T.S. 63
16 December 1966	UN Covenant on Civil & Political Rights, G.A. Res. 2200 (XXI)(Annex); 6 I.L.M. 368 (1967)
16 December 1966	UN Covenant on Economic, Social & Cultural Rights, G.A. Res. 2200 (XXI)(Annex); 6 I.L.M. 360 (1967)
27 January 1967	Treaty on Principles Governing the Activities of States in the Exploration and Use of Outer Space, Including the Moon and Other Celestial Bodies, 610 U.N.T.S. 205;

	U.K.T.S. 10 (1968), Cmd. 3519; 18 U.S.T. 2410, T.I.A.S. No. 6347, A.T.S. 24 (1967); 6 I.L.M. 386; 5 WESTON V.E. 21;
14 February 1967	Treaty for the Prohibition of Nuclear Weapons in Latin America (Tlatelolco), 634 U.N.T.S. 281, 22 U.S.T. 762; T.I.A.S. No. 7137;
8 March 1968	European Declaration of Principles on Air Pollution Control, Committee of Ministers, Council of Europe Res. (60) 4;
6 May 1968	European Water Charter, in "Legal Problems Relating to Non-navigational Use of International Watercourses," Supp. Rep. of the Secretary-General, U.N. Doc. A/CN.4/274, 2 Y.B. I.L.C. 342 (1974)
13 December 1968	European Convention on the Protection of Animals during International Transport (Paris), EMuT 968:92
1 July 1968	Treaty on the Non-Proliferation of Nuclear Weapons, 72 U.N.T.S. 161, 21 U.S.T. 483, T.I.A.S. No. 6839.
15 September 1968	African Convention on the Conservation of Nature and Natural Resources (Algiers), 1001 U.N.T.S. 3, EMuT 968:68; 5 WESTON V.H.7;
16 September 1968	European Agreement on the Restriction of the Use of Certain Detergents in Washing and Cleaning Products (Brussels), 788 U.N.T.S. 181; E.T.S. 64, U.K.T.S. 23 (1971), Cmd. 4646
27 September 1968	Convention on Jurisdiction and Enforcement of Judgments in Civil and Commercial Matters (Brussels), O.J.E.C. L 304/77 1978; EC 46 (1978), Cmd. 7395; 8 I.L.M. 229 (1969)
23 May 1968	Convention on the Law of Treaties (Vienna), 1155 U.N.T.S. 205
9 June 1969	Agreement for Cooperation in Dealing with Pollution of the North Sea by Oil (Bonn), 704 U.N.T.S. 3; U.K.T.S. 78 (1960), Cmd. 4205; 9 I.L.M. 359 (1970)
22 November 1969	American Convention on Human Rights (San José), O.A.S.T.S. No. 36, 9 I.L.M. 673 (1970);
29 November 1969	International Convention on Civil Liability for Oil Pollution Damage (Brussels), 973 U.N.T.S. 3; U.K.T.S. 106 (1975), Cmd. 6183; 9 I.L.M. 45 (1970); Kiss 235; 5 WESTON V.J.5;
29 November 1969	International Convention Relating to Intervention on the High Seas in Cases of Oil Pollution Casualties

	(Brussels), U.K.T.S. 77 (1975), Cmd. 6056; 26 U.S.T. 765, T.I.A.S. 8068; 9 I.L.M. 25 (1970); Kiss 230; 5 WESTON V.F.7;
2 February 1971	Convention on Wetlands of International Importance (Ramsar), 996 U.N.T.S. 245; U.K.T.S. 34 (1976), Cmd. 6465; 11 I.L.M. 969 (1972); 5 WESTON V.F.33;
15 July 1971	Agreement Between Canada and Norway on Sealing and the Conservation of the Seal Stock in the North-West Atlantic (Ottawa), 870 U.N.T.S. 71
16 September 1971	Agreement Concerning Frontier Rivers Between Finland & Sweden, 825 U.N.T.S. 191
16 September 1971	Agreement Concerning Cooperation in Taking Measures Against Pollution of the Sea by Oil (Copenhagen), 822 U.N.T.S. 311
17 December 1971	Convention Relating to Civil Liability in the Field of Maritime Carriage of Nuclear Material, EMuT 971:93
18 December 1971	Convention on the Establishment of an International Fund for Compensation for Oil Pollution Damage (Brussels), U.K.T.S. 95 (1978), Cmd. 7383; 11 I.L.M. 284 (1972); Kiss 255. Amended 1976, 16 I.L.M. 621 (1977); 5 WESTON V.F. 12
15 February 1972	Convention for the Prevention of Marine Pollution by Dumping from Ships and Aircraft (Oslo), 932 U.N.T.S. 3; U.K.T.S. 119 (1975), Cmd. 6228; 11 I.L.M. 262 (1972); Kiss 266; EMuT 972:12/A
29 March 1972	Convention on International Liability for Damage Caused by Space Objects, 961 U.N.T.S. 187; U.K.T.S. 16 (1974), Cmd. 5551; 24 U.S.T. 2389, T.I.A.S. 7762
10 April 1972	Convention on the Prohibition of the Development, Production and Stockpiling of Biological and Toxic Weapons and Their Destruction, 1015 U.N.T.S. 163
26 May 1972	OECD Recommendation C(72)128, Guiding Principles concerning International Economic Aspects of Environmental Policies.
30 May 1972	European Soil Charter, Council of Europe, Res. (72) 19
1 June 1972	Convention for the Conservation of Antarctic Seals (London), 29 U.S.T. 441, T.I.A.S. 8826; 11 I.L.M. 251 (1972); 5 WESTON V.D.3;
16 June 1972	Stockholm Declaration on the Human Environment, U.N. Doc. A/Conf. 48/14/Rev. 1 (U.N. Pub. E.73, II.A.14) (1973); 5 WESTON V.B.3; 11 I.L.M. 1416 (1972)

3 July 1972	Action Plan for the Human Environment, U.N. Doc. A/Conf.48/14.
23 November 1972	UNESCO Convention Concerning the Protection of the World Cultural and Natural Heritage, U.K.T.S. 2 (1985), Cmd. 9424; 27 U.S.T. 37, T.I.A.S. 8225; 11 I.L.M. 1358 (1972); Kiss 276; 5 WESTON V.B.4;
15 December 1972	General Assembly Res. 2995 (XXVII) Concerning Cooperation Between States in the Field of the Environment, 27 G.A.O.R., Supp. No. 30 (A/8730) at 42 (1973)
29 December 1972	Convention on the Prevention of Marine Pollution by Dumping of Wastes and other Matter (London), 26 U.S.T. 2403, T.I.A.S. 8165. Amended Oct. 12, 1978, T.I.A.S. No. 8165; 18 I.L.M. 510 (1979); 5 WESTON V.F.14;
13 February 1973	OECD Decision on the Protection of the Environment by Control of Polychlorinated Biphenils (PCB), C(73)1(Final);
3 March 1973	Convention on International Trade in Endangered Species of Wild Fauna and Flora (Washington), 993 U.N.T.S. 243; U.K.T.S. 101 (1976), Cmd. 6647; 12 I.L.M. 1085 (1973); Kiss 289; 5 WESTON V.H.10;
4 July 1973	Treaty Establishing the Caribbean Community, 12 I.L.M. 1033 (1973).
13 September 1973	Convention on Fishing and Conservation of the Living Resources in the Baltic Sea and Belts (Gdansk)
19 September 1973	OECD Recommendation C(73)172 on Measures to Reduce all Man-made Emissions of Mercury to the Environment
2 November 1973	International Convention for the Prevention of Pollution by Ships (MARPOL) (London), U.N. Legislative Series ST/LEG/SER.B/18, at 461; U.K.T.S. 27 (1983), Cmd. 8924; 12 I.L.M. 1319 (1973); Kiss 400; 5 WESTON V.F.15;
15 November 1973	Agreement on the Conservation of Polar Bears (Oslo), 27 U.S.T. 3918, T.I.A.S. 8409; 13 I.L.M. 13 (1974); Kiss 401
19 February 1974	Nordic Environmental Protection Convention (Stockholm), U.N. Legislative Series, ST/LEG/SER.B/18, at 397; 13 I.L.M. 511 (1974); 5 WESTON V.C.1;
22 March 1974	Convention on the Protection of Marine Environment of the Baltic Sea Area (Helsinki), U.N. Legislative Series, ST/LEG/SER.B/18, at 518; 13 I.L.M. 546 (1974); Kiss 405; 5 WESTON V.F. 17; EMuT 974:23

4 June 1974	Convention for the Prevention of Marine Pollution from Land-Based Sources (Paris), U.K.T.S. 64 (1978), Cmd. 7251; 13 I.L.M. 352 (1974); Kiss 430; 5 WESTON V.F. 18;
19 June 1974	United States-Canada Agreement Relating to the Establishment of Joint Pollution Contingency Plans for Spills of Oil and Other Noxious Substances, 25 U.S.T. 1280, T.I.A.S. 7861
1 November 1974	International Convention for the Safety of Human Life at Sea, 1184 U.N.T.S. 2 (EC Texts); U.K.T.S. 46 (1980), Cmd. 7874; T.I.A.S. 9700
14 November 1974	OECD Principles Concerning Transfrontier Pollution, C(74)224, 14 I.L.M. 234 (1975)
14 November 1974	OECD Recommendation on the Assessment of the Potential Environmental Effects of Chemicals, C(74)215
14 November 1974	OECD Recommendation on Air Poluution Control C(74)219
12 December 1974	UN Charter of Economic Rights and Duties of States, G.A. Res. 3281, Dec. 12, 1974, 29 U.N.G.A.O.R. Supp. No. 31, (A/9631) at 50
1 August 1975	Final Act of the Helsinki Conference on Security and Cooperation in Europe, 14 I.L.M. 1292 (1975)
16 February 1976	Convention for the Protection of the Mediterranean Sea Against Pollution (Barcelona), U.N. Legislative Series, ST/LEG/SER.B/19 at 459; 15 I.L.M. 290 (1976), Kiss 448; EMuT 976:14
16 February 1976	Protocol for the Prevention of Pollution of the Mediterranean Sea by Dumping from Ships and Aircraft, 15 I.L.M. 300 (1976); Kiss 454; EMuT 976:15
16 February 1976	Protocol Concerning Cooperation in Combating Pollution of the Mediterranean Sea by Oil and Other Harmful Substances in Cases of Emergency, U.N. Legislative Series, ST/LEG/SER.B/19 at 468; 15 I.L.M. 306 (1976), Kiss 457
11 May 1976	OECD Recommendation on Equal Right of Access in Relation to Transfrontier Pollution, C(76)55(Final)
12 June 1976	Convention on Conservation of Nature in the South Pacific, (Apia) Kiss 463, EMuT 976:45
28 September 1976	OECD Recommendation on a Comprehensive Waste Management Policy, C(76)155(Final)

12 October 1976	OECD Principles Concerning Coastal Management, C(76)161(Final)
19 November 1976	Protocol to the Brussels Convention on Civil Liability for Oil Pollution Damage, U.K.T.S. 26 (1981), Cmd. 8238; 16 I.L.M. 617; 5 WESTON V.J.6a;
3 December 1976	Convention for the Protection of the Rhine Against Chemical Pollution (Bonn), 1124 U.N.T.S. 375; 16 I.L.M. 242 (1977)
3 December 1976	Convention for the Protection of the Rhine from Pollution by Chlorides (Bonn), 16 I.L.M. 265 (1977)
10 December 1976	Convention on the Prohibition of Military or Any Other Hostile Use of Environmental Modification Techniques (Geneva), 31 U.S.T. 333; T.I.A.S. 9614; 16 I.L.M. 88 (1977); Kiss 479;
17 December 1976	Convention on Civil Liability for Oil Pollution Damage Resulting from Exploration for and Exploitation of Seabed Mineral Resources (London), 16 I.L.M. 1450 (1977); 5 WESTON V.J. 7;
17 May 1977	OECD Recommendation on the Implementation of a Regime of Equal Right of Access and Non-discrimination in Relation to Transfrontier Pollution, OECD Doc. C(77)28(Final); 16 I.L.M. 977 (1977); 5 WESTON V.E.2;
8 June 1977	Protocol Additional to the Geneva Conventions of 12 August 1949 and Relating to the Protection of Victims of International Armed Conflicts, 1125 U.N.T.S. 3 (P. I); 1125 U.N.T.S. 609 (P. II); 16 I.L.M. 1391
7 July 1977	OECD Recommendation on Procedures and Requirements for Anticipating the Effects of Chemicals on Man and in the Environment, C(77)97(Final)
22 July 1977	OECD Decision on Multilateral Consultation and Surveillance Mechanism for Sea Dumping of Radioactive Waste, 17 I.L.M. 445 (1978)
3 February 1978	OECD Recommendation on the Re-Use and Recycling of Beverage Containers, C(78)8(Final)
17 February 1978	Protocol Relating to the Convention for the Prevention of Pollution from Ships (MARPOL), 17 I.L.M. 546 (1978); 5 WESTON V.F.20
5 April 1978	OECD Recommendation C(78)4, Water Management Policies and Instruments

24 April 1978	Kuwait Regional Convention for Cooperation on the Protection of the Marine Environment from Pollution, 1140 U.N.T.S. 133; 17 I.L.M. 511 (1978); Kiss 486
24 April 1978	Protocol Concerning Regional Cooperation in Combating Pollution by Oil and Other Harmful Substances in Cases of Emergency, 17 I.L.M. 526 (1978)
19 May 1978	UNEP, Principles of Conduct in the Field of the Environment for the Guidance of States in the Conservation and Harmonious Utilization of Natural Resources shared by Two or More States, U.N.Doc. UNEP/1G 12/2 (1978); 17 I.L.M. 1097 (1978); 5 WESTON V.B.8;
30 June 1978	Convention Relating to the Status of the River Gambia, Natural Resources/Water Series No. 134 ST/ESA/141 (1984) at 39;
3 July 1978	Treaty for Amazonian Cooperation (Brasilia), 17 I.L.M. 1045 (1978)
21 September 1978	OECD Recommendation for Strengthening International Cooperation on Environmental Protection in Transfrontier Regions, C(78)77(Final); 17 I.L.M. 1530 (1978)
22 November 1978	United States-Canada Agreement on Great Lakes Water Quality with Annexes, 30 U.S.T. 1383, T.I.A.S. 9257. Amended October 16, 1983, T.I.A.S. 10798
23 June 1979	Convention on the Conservation of Migratory Species of Wild Animals (Bonn), 19 I.L.M. 15 (1980), Kiss 500; 5 WESTON V.H.11
19 September 1979	Convention on the Conservation of European Wildlife and Natural Habitats (Bern), E.T.S. 104; U.K.T.S. 56 (1982), Cmd. 8738; Kiss 509
13 November 1979	Convention on Long-Range Transboundary Air Pollution (Geneva), U.K.T.S. 57 (1983), Cmd. 9034; T.I.A.S. No. 10541; 18 I.L.M. 1442 (1979), Kiss 519; 5 WESTON V.E.3;
5 December 1979	Agreement Governing the Activities of States on the Moon and Other Celestial Bodies, G.A. Res. 34/68; U.N.G.A.O.R. Supp. No. 46 at 77, U.N. Doc.(A/34/46); 18 I.L.M. 1434 (1979); 5 WESTON V.E.23;
20 December 1979	Convention for the Conservation and Management of the Vicuna, Lima, EMuT 979:94

30 January 1980	OECD, Recommendation on Waste Paper Recovery, C(79)218(Final)
17 May 1980	Protocol for the Protection of the Mediterranean Sea against Pollution from Land-Based Sources (Athens), 19 I.L.M. 869 (1980); 5 WESTON V.F.21; EMuT 976:13/1
20 May 1980	Convention on the Conservation of Antarctic Marine Living Resources, Canberra, U.K.T.S. 48 (1982), Cmd. 8714; T.I.A.S. 10240; A.T.S. 3 (1982); 19 I.L.M. 837 (1980); 5 WESTON V.D.4;
21 May 1980	European Outline Convention on Transfrontier Cooperation Between Territorial Communities or Authorities, E.T.S. 106
5 August 1980	Memorandum of Intent Between Canada and the United States Concerning Transboundary Air Pollution, 32 U.S.T. 2521, T.I.A.S. 9856; 20 I.L.M. 690 (1981)
18 November 1980	Convention for the Future Multilateral Cooperation in North-East Atlantic Fisheries (London), 1284 U.N.T.S. 130
21 November 1980	Convention Creating the Niger Basin Authority, EMuT 980:86
19 January 1981	African Charter on Human Rights and Peoples' Rights, 21 I.L.M. 59 (1982), 7 H.R.L.J. 403 (1986)
23 March 1981	Convention and Protocol for Cooperation in the Protection and Development of the Marine and Coastal Environment of the West and Central African Region (Abidjan), U.N. Doc. UNEP/1G, 22/7; 20 I.L.M. 746 (1981)
23 March 1981	Protocol Concerning Cooperation in Combating Pollution in Cases of Emergency (Abidjan), EMuT 981:24
2 April 1981	Protocol between the Government of Canada and the Government of the U.S.S.R. on Settlement of Canada's Claim for Damage Caused by COSMOS 954, 20 I.L.M. 689 (1981)
12 May 1981	OECD Decision on the Mutual Acceptance of Data in the Assessment of Chemicals, C(81)30(Final)
12 November 1981	Agreement on Regional Cooperation in Combating Pollution of the South-East Pacific by Hydrocarbons or Other Harmful Substances in Cases of Emergency (Lima), EMuT 981:85
20 November 1981	Convention for the Protection of the Marine Environment and Coastal Area of the South-East Pacific (Lima), U.N. Doc. UNEP-CPPS/IG. 32/4

25 November 1981	World Soil Charter, 5 WESTON V.G.2
24 January 1982	Protocol on the Conservation of Common Natural Resources (Khartoum), EMuT 982:10
26 January 1982	Memorandum of Understanding on the Surveillance of Ships by Port States, 21 I.L.M. 1 (1982)
14 February 1982	Regional Convention for the Conservation of the Red Sea and of the Gulf of Aden Environment (Jeddah), 9 EPL 56 (1982)' EMuT 982:13
14 February 1982	Protocol Concerning Regional Cooperation in Combating Pollution by Oil and Other Harmful Substances in Cases of Emergency (Jeddah), EMuT 982:14
3 April 1982	Protocol Concerning Mediterranean Specially Protected Areas (Geneva), EMuT 982:26
28 October 1982	World Charter for Nature, G.A. Res. 37/7, 37 U.N.G.A.O.R. Supp. (No. 51) at 17, U.N. Doc. A/37/51 (1982)
8 November 1982	OECD Decision on the Minimum Pre-Marketing Set of Data in the Assessment of Chemicals, C(82)196(Final)
10 December 1982	UN Convention on the Law of the Sea (Montego Bay), U.N. Doc. A/Conf 62/122 (1982); Misc. 11 (1983), Cmd. 8941; 21 I.L.M. 1261 (1982); 5 WESTON V.F.22;
24 March 1983	Convention for the Protection and Development of the Marine Environment of the Wider Caribbean Region (Cartegena de Indias), U.K.T.S. 38 (1988), Cmd. 391; 22 I.L.M. 227 (1983); EMuT 983:23
24 March 1983	Protocol Concerning Cooperation in Combating Oil Spills in the Wider Caribbean Region, 22 I.L.M. 240 (1983); EMuT 983:24
22 July 1983	Protocol for the Protection of South-East Pacific Against Pollution from Land-Based Sources (Quito), EMuT 983:54
22 July 1983	Supplementary Protocol to the Agreement on Regional Co-operation in Combating Pollution of the South-Pacific by Hydrcarbons or Other Harmful Substances (Quito), EMuT 983:55
26 July 1983	OECD Recommendation on Good Laboratory Practices, C(83)95(Final)
6 August 1983	Agreement Between Canada and Denmark on Cooperation Relating to the Marine Environment, 23 I.L.M. 269 (1984)

14 August 1983	United States-Mexico Agreement for Cooperation for the Protection and Improvement of the Environment of the Border Area, T.I.A.S. 10827, 23 I.L.M. 1025 (1983)
23 August 1983	Memorandum of Understanding Between Canada and the United States on the Cross Appalachian Tracer Experiment, 22 I.L.M. 1017 (1983)
13 September 1983	Agreement for Cooperation in Dealing with Pollution of the North Sea by Oil and Other Harmful Substances, Misc. 26 (1983), Cmd. 9104; EMuT 983:68
1 October 1983	Convention for the Conservation of Salmon in the North Atlantic (Reykavik)
18 November 1983	International Tropical Timber Agreement, UNCTAD Doc TD/Timber/11; Misc. 11 (1984), Cmd. 9240; 5 WESTON V.H.14;
1 February 1984	OECD Decision and Recommendation on Transfrontier Movements of Hazardous Waste, C(83)180(Final), 23 I.L.M. 214 (1984)
28 September 1984	Protocol to the Convention on Long-range Transboundary Air Pollution on Long-Term Financing of Cooperative Program for Monitoring and Evaluation of the Long Range Transmission of Air Pollutants in Europe (EMEP), EMuT 979:84A
22 March 1985	Vienna Convention for the Protection of the Ozone Layer, UNEP Doc. IG. 53/5; Misc. 13 (1985), Cmd. 9652; 26 I.L.M. 1529 (1987); 5 WESTON V.E.5;
20 June 1985	OECD Guidelines for action to reduce emission of sulfur oxides and particulates from stationary fuel combustion sources, C(85)101;
21 June 1985	Convention for the Protection, Management and Development of the Marine and Coastal Environment of the Eastern African Region (Nairobi), EMuT 985:46
21 June 1985	Protocol concerning Protected Areas and Wild Fauna and Flora in the Eastern African Region (Nairobi), EMuT 985:47;
8 July 1985	Protocol to LRTAP on the Reduction of Sulphur Emissions (Helsinki), U.N. Doc. ECE/EB. AIR/12; 27 I.L.M. 707 (1988); 5 WESTON V.E.6;
9 July 1985	ASEAN Agreement on the Conservation of Nature and Natural Resources (Kuala Lumpur), 15 EPL 64 (1985), EMuT 985:51; 5 WESTON V.C.5;

6 August 1985 Treaty Establishing a South Pacific Nuclear Free Zone, EMuT 985:58

26 September 1986 Vienna Convention on Early Notification of a Nuclear Accident, Misc. 2 (1989), Cmd. 565; IAEA INFCIRC 335; 25 I.L.M. 1370 (1986); 5 WESTON V.I.2;

26 September 1986 Vienna Convention on Assistance in the Case of a Nuclear Accident or Radiological Emergency, Misc. 3 (1989), Cmd. 566; IAEA INFRIRC 336, 25 I.L.M. 1377 (1986); 5 V.I.3;

28 October 1986 Agreement Between Canada and the United States on Transfrontier Movements of Hazardous Waste (Ottawa), T.I.A.S.

12 November 1986 Agreement Between Mexico and the United States on Cooperation for the Protection and Improvement of the Environment in the Border Area, 26 I.L.M. 16 (1987)

24 November 1986 Convention for the Protection of the Natural Resources and Environment of the South Pacific Region (Nouméa), 26 I.L.M. 38 (1987); 5 WESTON V.C.6; EMuT 986:87

25 November 1986 Protocol for the Prevention of Pollution of the South Pacific Region by Dumping (Nouméa), EMuT 986:87A

25 November 1986 Protocol Concerning Cooperation in Combating Pollution Emergencies in the South Pacific Region (Nouméa), 26 I.L.M. 58 (1987); EMuT 986:87B

29 January 1987 United States-Mexico Agreement of Cooperation Regarding Transboundary Air Pollution Caused by Copper Smelters Along the Common Border, T.I.A.S.

2 April 1987 South Pacific Fisheries Treaty, EMuT 987:26

28 May 1987 Agreement on the Action Plan for the Environmentally Sound Management of the Common Zambezi River System (Harare), available at <http://faolex.org>

16 September 1987 Montreal Protocol on Substances that Deplete the Ozone Layer, Misc. 1 (1988), Cmd. 283; 26 I.L.M. 1541 (1987); 5 WESTON V.E.9;

8 July 1988 OECD Council Decision on the Exchange of Information concerning Accidents Capable of Causing Transfrontier Damage, C(88)84(Final) 28 I.L.M. 249 (1989)

31 October 1988 Protocol to the 1979 Convention on Long Range Transboundary Air Pollution Concerning the Control of Emissions of Nitrogen Oxides or Their Transboundary

	Fluxes (Sofia), Misc. 16 (1989), Cmd. 885; 27 I.L.M. 698 (1988), 5 WESTON V.E.10;
17 November 1988	Protocol to the American Convention on Human Rights in the Area of Economic, Social & Cultural Rights (Protocol of San Salvador), O.A.S.T.S. 69; 28 I.L.M. 156 (1989)
6 December 1988	General Assembly Resolution on Protection of the Global Climate for Present and Future Generations of Mankind, A/Res/43/53, 28 I.L.M. 1326 (1989)
8 December 1989	European Charter on the Environment and Health (WHO), 20 E.P.L. 57 (1990).
22 March 1989	Convention on the Control of Transboundary Movements of Hazardous Wastes and Their Disposal (Basel), UNEP/WG.190/4 28 I.L.M. 657 (1989); 5 WESTON V.I.11
29 March 1989	Protocol Concerning Marine Pollution Resulting from Exploration and Exploitation of the Continental Shelf (Kuwait), EMuT 989:24
31 March 1989	OECD Recommendation on Water Resource Management Policies, C(89)12(Final)
6 May 1989	The Amazon Declaration, 28 I.L.M. 1303 (1989); 5 WESTON V.C.8;
27 June 1989	ILO Convention (169) concerning Indigenous and Tribal Peoples in Independent Countries, 72 ILO Off. Bull. 59 (1989); 28 I.L.M. 1382 (1989)
21 September 1989	Protocol for the Protection of the South-East Pacific against Radioactive Pollution (Paipa), EMuT 989:70
21 September 1989	Protocol for the Conservation and Management of Protected Marine and Coastal Areas of the South-East Pacific (Paipa), EMuT 989:71
20 November 1989	Convention on the Rights of the Child, 28 I.L.M. 1457 (1989)
24 November 1989	Convention for the Prohibition of Fishing with Long Driftnets in the South Pacific (Wellington), 29 I.L.M.1449 (1990); 5 WESTON V.H.18;
15 December 1989	Fourth ACP - EEC Convention (Lome IV) 29 I.L.M. 783 (1990); EMuT 989:93
22 December 1989	General Assembly Resolution on Protection of the Global Climate for Present and Future Generations of Mankind, UN GA//Res/44/207; 5 WESTON V.H.19;

18 January 1990	Protocol Concerning Specially Protected Areas and Wildlife to the 1983 Convention for the Protection and Development of the Marine Environment of the Wider Caribbean Region (Kingston), EMuT 990:85.
21 February 1990	Protocol for the Protection of the Marine Environment against Pollution from Land-Based Sources (Kuwait), EMuT 990:14
29 June 1990	Adjustment and Amendment to the Montreal Protocol on Substances that Deplete the Ozone Layer (London); 30 I.L.M. 537 (1991); 5 WESTON V.E.9;
8 October 1990	Convention on the International Commission for the Protection of the Elbe (Magdeburg), EMuT 990:75
16 October 1990	Agreement on the Conservation of Seals in the Wadden Sea, (Bonn), EMuT 990:77.
17 October 1990	Accord of Cooperation for the Protection of the Coast and Waters of the Northeast Atlantic Against Pollution Due to Hydrocarbons or Other Harmful Substances (Lisbon), EMuT 990:79; 30 I.L.M. 1227 (1991).
20 October 1990	Protocols I and II to the Convention for the Prohibition of Fishing with Long Driftnets in the South Pacific (Nouméa), 29 I.L.M. 1449 (1990).
30 November 1990	International Convention on Oil Pollution Preparedness, Response and Cooperation (London), EMuT 990:88; 30 I.L.M. 733 (1991); 5 WESTON V.F.28;
29 January 1991	Convention on the Ban of the Import into Africa and the Control of Transboundary Movement and Management of Hazardous Wastes within Africa with Annexes (Bamako), EMuT 991:08; 30 I.L.M. 773 (1991), 31 I.L.M. 163 (1992); 5 WESTON V.I.14;
31 January 1991	OECD Regulation on the Use of Economic Instruments in Environmental Policy;
25 February 1991	Convention on Environmental Impact Assessment in a Transboundary Context (Espoo), EMuT 991:15; 30 I.L.M. 800 (1991); 5 WESTON V.B.15;
13 March 1991	Canada - United States Agreement on Air Quality; 30 I.L.M. 676 (1991).
14 March 1991	World Bank Resolution on the Global Environmental Facility, Exec. Dir. Res. No. 91-5; 30 I.L.M. 1758 (1991).
17 March 1991	Summit of Central African Heads of State on the Conservation and Sustainable Management of Tropical Forests, Yaounde Declaration, 38 ILM 783 (1999)

26 March 1991	Treaty of Asuncion, South American Quadripartite Common Market, Argentina, Brazil, Paraguay and Uruguay, 30 I.L.M. 1041 (1991.
3 April 1991	Security Council Resolution 687E (1991) on the Iraqi Invasion of Kuwait, S/RES/687 (1991); 30 I.L.M. 847, 852 (1991).
3 June 1991	Treaty Establishing the African Economic Community (Abuja), 30 I.L.M. 1241 (1991).
14 June 1991	Arctic Environmental Protection Strategy, 30 I.L.M. 1624 (1991)
20 June 1991	Agreement for the Establishment of Southern African Center for Ivory Marketing (Lilongwe, Malawi), EMuT 991:46.
13 September 1991	Agreement on the Conservation of Small Cetaceans of the Baltic and North Sea (New York, opened for signature 17 March 1992), EMuT 992:21.
4 October 1991	Protocol on Environmental Protection to the Antarctic Treaty of 1 December 1959 (Madrid), EMuT 991:74; 30 I.L.M. 1455 (1991); 5 WESTON V.D.6;
7 November 1991	Convention Concerning the Protection of the Alps (Salzburg), EMuT 991:83; 31 I.L.M. 767 (1992).
18 November 1991	Protocol to the 1979 Convention on Long-Range Transboundary Air Pollution Concerning the Control of Emissions of Volatile Organic Compounds or Their Transboundary Fluxes (Geneva); 31 I.L.M. 568 (1992); 5 WESTON V.E.18;
4 December 1991	Agreement on the Conservation of Bats in Europe, EMuT 991:90
6 December 1991	Resolution on General and Complete Disarmament, A/RES/46/36, A-K; 31 I.L.M. 470 (1992).
11 December 1991	Regional Agreement on the Transboundary Movement of Hazardous Waste (Panama), EMuT 992:91
20 December 1991	Resolution on Large-scale Pelagic Driftnet Fishing and its Impact on Living Marine Resources of the World's Oeans and Seas, A/RES/46/215, 10 Feb. 1992; 31 I.L.M.241 (1991); 5 WESTON V.H.21;
11 February 1992	Convention for the Conservation of Anadromous Stocks in the North Pacific Ocean, EMuT 992:13
17 March 1992	Convention on the Protection and Use of Transboundary Watercourses and International Lakes (Helsinki), U.N. Doc. E/ECE/1267; EMuT 992:20; 31 I.L.M. 1312 (1992); 5 WESTON V.F.36;

17 March 1992	Convention on the Transboundary Effects of Industrial Accidents (Helsinki), U.N. Doc. E/ECE/1268; EMuT 992:22; 31 I.L.M. 1330 (1992); 5 V.I.14A;
9 April 1992	Convention on the Protection of the Marine Environment of the Baltic Sea (Helsinki), EMuT 992:28
21 April 1992	Convention on the Protection of the Black Sea against Pollution (Bucharest) 32 I.L.M. 1101 (1993); EMuT 992:20
9 May 1992	Framework Convention on Climate Change (New York), EMuT 992:35; 31 I.L.M. 849 (1992); 5 WESTON V.E.19;
5 June 1992	Convention on Biological Diversity (Rio de Janeiro), EMuT 992:42; 31 I.L.M. 818 (1992); 5 WESTON V.H.22;
5 June 1992	Convention for the Conservation of Biodiversity and the Protection of Wilderness Areas in Central America (Managua), EMuT 992:43
13 June 1992	Statement of Principles for a Global Consensus on the Management, Conservation and Sustainable Development of All Types of Forests (Rio de Janeiro), A/CONF.151/26 (Vol. I); 31 I.L.M. 881 (1992) 5 WESTON V.H.23;
13 June 1992	Agenda 21, A/CONF.151/26 (Vols. I, II, III) (1992); 5 WESTON V.B.17;
14 June 1992	Rio Declaration on Environment and Development, A/CONF.151/26 (Vol. I), 8; 31 I.L.M. 874 (1992); 5 WESTON V.B.16;
9 July 1992	Treaty on Cooperation in Fisheries Surveillance and Law Enforcement in the South Pacific Region (Niue); 32 I.L.M.136 (1993).
17 August 1992	Treaty of the South African Development Community (Windhoek), 32 I.L.M. 116 (1993).
14 September 1992	Namibia-South Africa, Agreement on the Establishment of a Permanent Water Commission (Noordoewer), 32 I.L.M. 1147(1993); EMuT 992:55
22 September 1992	Convention for the Protection of the Marine Environment of the North-East Atlantic (Paris), 32 I.L.M. 1069 (1993); EMuT 992:71.
25 November 1992	Protection of the Environment in Times of Armed Conflict, G.A. Res. 47/37, U.N. Doc. A/47/591.
27 November 1992	Protocol to the 1971 Convention on the Establishment of an International Fund for Compensation for Oil Pollution Damage, 5 WESTON V.F.30;

12 December 1992	Treaty on Sharing of the Ganges Waters at Farakka Between Bangladesh and India, 36 I.L.M. 519 (1997); EMuT 992:91
17 December 1992	North American Free Trade Agreement (Washington, 8 and 17 Dec.; 11 and 17 Dec., Ottawa; 14 and 17 Dec. Mexico City); 32 I.L.M. 289; 32 I.L.M. 605 (1993).
21 December 1992	Central European Free Trade Agreement (Krakow), 34 I.L.M. 3 (1995).
22 December 1992	UN G.A. Res.47/191creating the Commission on Sustainable Development, 5 WESTON V. A.7.
22 December 1992	UN G.A. Res. 47/443, Decision on Large-scale Pelagic Driftnet Fishing and its Impact on the Living Marine Resources of the World's Oceans and Seas
13 January 1993	Convention on the Prohibition of the Development, Production, Stockpiling and Use of Chemical Weapons and on their Destruction (Paris), 32 I.L.M. 800 (1993).
26 March 1993	Agreement on Joint Activities in Addressing the Aral Sea and the Zone around the Sea Crisis, Improving the Environment, and Ensuring the Social and Economic Development of the Aral Sea Region, UNEP/DEWA/DPDL/RS.02/4.
7 April 1993	Hungary-Slovak Republic Special Agreement for Submission to the International Court of Justice of the Differences Between them Concerning the Gabcíkovo-Nagymaros Project (Brussels), 32 I.L.M. 1293 (1993).
10 May 1993	Convention for the Conservation of Southern Bluefin Tuna (Canberra)
16 June 1993	Agreement Establishing the South Pacific Regional Environment Program (SPREP), EMuT 993:45.
21 June 1993	Convention on Civil Liability for Damage Resulting From Activities Dangerous to the Environment (Lugano), 32 I.L.M.1228 ((1993), EMuT 993:19
1 July 1993	Memorandum of Understanding concerning Conservation Measures for the Siberian Crane
13 September 1993	North American Agreement on Environmental Cooperation, EMuT 993:68; 5 WESTON V.C.13
29 October 1993	Convention on the Management and Conservation of Natural Forest Ecosystems and Forest Plantation Development (Guatemala), EMuT 993:80

5 November 1993	Treaty Establishing the Common Market for Eastern and Southern Africa (Kampala), 33 I.L.M. 1067 (1994).
29 November 1993	Agreement to Promote Compliance with International Conservation and Management Measures by Fishing Vessels on the High Seas, EMuT 993:89
21 December 1993	U.N.G.A. Res. 48/445, Decision on Large-scale Pelagic Driftnet Fishing and its Impact on the Living Marine Resources of the World's Oceans and Seas
26 January 1994	International Tropical Timber Agreement (Geneva), EMuT 994:07
16 March 1994	Instrument Establishing the Restructured Global Environment Facility (Geneva), 33 I.L.M. 1273 (1994); 5 WESTON V.A.8
14 April 1994	GATT, Final Act Embodying the Results of the Uruguay Round of Multilateral Trade Negotiations (Marrakesh), 33 I.L.M. 1125 (1994)
26 April 1994	Agreements on the Protection of the Rivers Meuse and Scheldt (Charleville Mezieres) 34 I.L.M. 851 (1995)
14 June 1994	Protocol to LRTAP on Further Reduction of Sulphur Emissions (Oslo), 33 I.L.M. 540 (1994); EMuT 979: 84/E; 5 WESTON V.E.20a;
16 June 1994	Convention on the Conservation and Management of Pollack Resources in the Central Bering Sea (Washington D.C.)
17 June 1994	UN Convention to Combat Desertification in those Countries Experiencing Serious Drought and/or Desertification, Particularly in Africa (Paris), UNGA Doc. A/AC.241/15/Rev.7, 33 I.L.M. 1328 (1994); 5 WESTON V.G.4; EMuT 994:76
29 June 1994	Agreement on Cooperation for the Protection and Sustainable Use of the Danube River (Sofia), EMuT 994:49.
5 August 1994	Agreement on the Preparation of a Tripartite Environmental Management Program for Lake Victoria, EMuT 994:59
19 August 1994	IBRD/IDA (World Bank) Inspection Panel Operating Procedures, 34 I.L.M. 503 (1995)
8 September 1994	Agreement on Cooperative Enforcement Operations Directed at Illegal Trade in Wild Fauna and Flora, EMuT 994:67

10 September 1994	Memorandum of Understanding concerning Conservation Measures for the Slender-billed Curlew
29 September 1994	IAEA Convention on Nuclear Safety (Vienna), INFCIRC/449 of July 5, 1994, 33 I.L.M. 1514 (1994); 5 WESTON V.I.6
14 October 1994	Protocol to Protect the Mediterranean Sea against Pollution resulting from the Exploration and Exploitation of the Continental Shelf, the Seabed and its Subsoil (Madrid), EMuT 976:13E
17 December 1994	Energy Charter Treaty and Protocol on Energy Efficiency and Related Environmental Aspects, EMuT 994:93, 994:93A
19 December 1994	U.N. G.A. Res. 49/436, Decision on Large-scale Pelagic Driftnet Fishing and its Impact on the Living Marine Resources of the World's Oceans and Seas
20 December 1994	Protocol for the Implementation of the Alpine Convention in the Field of Town and Country Planning and Sustainable Development, EMuT 991:83/B
20 December 1994	Protocol for the Implementation of the Alpine Convention in the Field of Mountain Agriculture, EMuT 991:93/C
20 December 1994	Protocol for the Implementation of the Alpine Convention in the Field of Nature Protection and Landscape Conservation, EMuT 991:83/D
17 January 1995	ILO/UNEP/FAO/WHO Memorandum of Understanding Concerning Establishment of the Inter-Organization Program for the Social Management of Chemicals, 34 I.L.M. 1311 (1995)
9 February 1995	Agreement constituting the Three-National Commission for the Development of the Riverbed Rio Pilamayo, La Paz, EMuT, 995:12.
5 April 1995	Agreement on the Cooperation for the Sustainable Development of the Mekong River Basin (Chiang Mai), 34 I.L.M. 864 EMuT 995:26
10 June 1995	Protocol Concerning Specially Protected Areas and Biological Diversity in the Mediterranean (Barcelona), EMuT 976:13/F
16 June 1995	Agreement on the Conservation of African-Eurasian Migratory Waterbirds, EMuT 995:45

29 June 1995	OSCOM Decision 95/1 on the Disposal of Offshore Installations
4 August 1995	Agreement for the Implementation of the Provisions of the United Nations Convention on the Law of the Sea relating to the Conservation and Management of Straddling Fish Stocks and Highly Migratory Fish Stocks, EMuT 982:92B, 34 I.L.M. 1542 (1995)
28 August 1995	Protocol on Shared Watercourse Systems in the Southern African Development Community Region, EMuT 992:62A
16 September 1995	Convention to Ban the Importation into Forum Island Countries of Hazardous Wastes and Radioactive Wastes and to Control the Transboundary Movement and Management of Hazardous Wastes within the South Pacific (Waigani), EMuT 995:69
28 September 1995	Interim Agreement on the West Bank and Gaza Strip (Washington), 36 I.L.M. 551 (1997)
4 November. 1995	ACP-EEC Convention Revising the Fourth Lome Convention (Mauritius)
5 December 1995	G.A. Res. 50/25 Decision on Large-scale Pelagic Driftnet Fishing and its Impact on the Living Marine Resources of the World's Oceans and Seas
15 December 1995	Treaty on the Southeast Asia Nuclear Weapon-Free Zone, EMuT 995:94
27 February 1996	Protocol for the Implementation of the Alpine Convention in the Field of Mountain forests, EMuT 992:83/E
7 March 1996	Amendments to the Protocol for the Protection of the Mediterranean Sea against Pollution from Land-Based Sources (Syracuse), EMuT, 976:13/I.
27 March 1996	Agreement for the Establishment of the Indian Ocean Tuna Commission (FAO)
11 April 1996	Convention on the International Commission for the Protection of the Oder (Wroclaw), EMuT, 996:28.
11 April 1996	The African Nuclear-Weapon-Free Zone Treaty, EMuT 996:28/2
2 May 1996	Protocol to amend the Convention on Limitation of Liability for Maritime Claims (London), EMuT 976:85/A
3 May 1996	International Convention on Liability and Compensation for Damage in Connection with the

	Carriage of Hazardous and Noxious Substances by Sea, EMuT 996:34
3 May 1996	Protocol II to the Convention on Prohibitions on the Use of Certain Conventional Weapons which may be Deemed to be Excessively Injurious or to Have Indiscriminate Effects, 35 I.L.M. 1206
9 September 1996	Convention on the Collection and Disposal of Waste in the Navigation of the Rhine (Strasbourg), EMuT 996:68
19 September 1996	Joint Communique and Declaration on the Establishment of the Arctic Council (Ottawa), 35 I.L.M. 1382 (1996).
24 September 1996	Comprehensive Nuclear Test Ban Treaty, EMuT 996:71, with Protocol, EMuT 996:71/A
1 October 1996	Protocol on the Prevention of Pollution of the Mediterranean Sea by Tansboundary Movements of Hazardous Wastes and Their Disposal (Izmir), UNEP(OCA) ED/IG.4/4.11
7 November 1996	Protocol to the Convention on the Prevention of Marine Pollution by Dumping of Wastes and Other Matter, 1972, EMuT 972:96/D
24 November 1996	Agreement on the Conservation of Cetaceans of the Black Sea, Mediterranean Sea and Contiguous Atlantic Area, EMuT 979:55C
1 December 1996	Inter-American Convention for the Protection and Conservation of Sea Turtles (Caracas), EMuT 996:90
9 December 1996	U.N. Res. 51/36 Decision on Large-scale Pelagic Driftnet Fishing and its Impact on the Living Marine Resources of the World's Oceans and Seas
6 February 1997	Agreement on Environmental Cooperation between Canada and Chile (Ottawa), 26 I.L.M. 1193 (1997)
4 April 1997	Convention for the Protection of Human Rights and Dignity of the Human Being with Regard to the Application of Biology and Medicine (Oviedo), 36 I.L.M. 817 (1997).
21 May 1997	Convention on the Law of the Non-Navigational Uses of International Watercourses (New York), EMuT 997:39, 36 I.L.M. 700 (1997), 5 WESTON V.F.37
5 September 1997	Joint Convention on the Safety of Spent Fuel Management and on the Safety of Radioactive Waste Management, EMuT 997:67

12 September 1997	Protocol to Amend the Vienna Convention on Civil Liability for Nuclear Damage (Vienna), EMuT, 963:40/A, 608 ftnote.
12 September 1997	Convention on Supplementary Compensation for Nuclear Damage (Vienna) EMuT, 997:92.
17 September 1997	Amendment to the Montreal Protocol on Substances that Deplete the Ozone Layer (Montreal), EMuT, 985:D.
18 September 1997	Convention on the Prohibition of the Use, Stockpiling, Production, and Transfer of Anti-Personnel Mines and on their Destruction (Oslo), EMuT 997:70; 36 I.L.M. 1507 (1997)
17 November 1997	International Plant Protection Convention (Revised), EMuT 951:90/B
26 November 1997	U.N. G.A. Res. 52/29 Decision on Large-scale Pelagic Driftnet Fishing and its Impact on the Living Marine Resources of the World's Oceans and Seas
11 December 1997	Kyoto Protocol to the United Nations Framework Convention on Climate Change, EMuT 992:35/A, 5 WESTON V.E.20d
17 March 1998	Agreement between the Government of the Republic of Kazakhstan, the Government of the Kyrgyz Republic, and the Government of the Republic of Uzbekistan on Cooperation in the Area of the Environment and Regional Nature, UNEP/DEWA/DPDL/RS.02/4.
17 March 1998	Agreement on the Use of Water and Energy Resources of the Sry Darya Basin, UNEP/DEWA/DPDL/RS.02/4.
24 June 1998	Protocol to the Convention on Long-Range Transboundary Air Pollution on Heavy Metals (Aarhus), EMuT 979:84/F
24 June 1998	Protocol to the Convention on Long-Range Transboundary Air Pollution on Persistent Organic Pollutants (Aarhus), EMuT 979:84/G; 5 WESTON V.E.20e;
25 June 1998	Convention on Access to Information, Public Participation in Decision-Making and Access to Justice in Environmental Matters (Aarhus), EMuT 998:48
19 July 1998	Statute of the International Criminal Court (Rome), 37 I.L.M. 999 (1998).
10 September 1998	Convention on the Prior Informed Consent Procedure for Certain Hazardous Chemicals and Pesticides in International Trade, 30 I.L.M.1 (1999); EMuT 998:6; 2244 UNTS 337.

16 October 1998	Protocol for the Implementation of the Alpine Convention in the Field of the Protection of Soils, EMuT 991:83/F
16 October 1998	Protocol for the Implementation of the Alpine Convention in the Field of Energy, EMuT 991:83/G
16 October 1998	Protocol for the Implementation of the Alpine Convention in the Field of Tourism, EMuT 991:83/H
22 October 1998	Memorandum of Understanding between the Republic of Kenya, the United Republic of Tanzania and the Republic of Uganda for Cooperation on Environment Management (Nairobi), EMuT, 998:79.
4 November 1998	Convention on the Protection of the Environment through Criminal Law, (Strasbourg), E.T.S. No. 172
13 December 1998	Memorandum of Understanding concerning Conservation Measures for the Siberian Crane (Ramsar), EMuT, 979:55/G.
6 January 1999	U.N.G.A. Res. 53/33 Decision on Large-scale Pelagic Driftnet Fishing and its Impact on the Living Marine Resources of the World's Oceans and Seas
12 March 1999	International Convention on Arrest of Ships (Geneva), EMuT, 999:20.
12 April 1999	Convention on the Protection of the Rhine (Bern), EMuT, 999:28.
7 May 1999	Protocol to the Agreement on the Use of Water and Energy Resources of the Syr Darya Basin, UNEP/DEWA/DPDL/RS.02/4
29 May 1999	Memorandum of Understanding Concerning Conservation Measures for Marine Turtles of the Atlantic Coast of Africa (Abidjan), 39 ILM 1 (2000)
17 June 1999	Protocol on Water and Health to the 1992 Helsinki Convention on the Protection and Use of Transboundary Watercourses and International Lakes (London); UNECE, MP/WAT/AC.1/1999/1, EMuT 992:20/A.
13 August 1999	Protocol on Wildlife Conservation and Law Enforcement (Maputo) EMuT, 992:62/E.
6 October 1999	Protocol concerning Pollution from Land-Based Sources and Activities to the Convention for the Protection and Development of the Marine Environment of the Wider Caribbean Region (Oranjestad, Aruba), EMuT, 983:23/C.

11 November 1999	Agreement for the Establishment of the Eastern African Community (Arusha), EMuT, 999:88.
19 November 1999	OSCE, Charter for European Security, Instanbul.
30 November 1999	Protocol to the 1979 Convention on Long-Range Transboundary Air Pollution to Abate Acidification, Eutrophication and Ground-Level Ozone (Gothenburg), EMuT, 979:84/H.
3 December 1999	Amendment to the Montreal Protocol on Substances that Deplete the Ozone Layer (Beijing), EMuT, 985:22/E.
10 December 1999	Basel Protocol on Liability and Compensation for Damage Resulting from Transboundary Movements of Hazardous Wastes and their Disposal (Basel), EMuT 989:22/B.
29 January 2000	Cartagena Protocol on Biosafety to the Convention on Biological Diversity (Montreal), 39 I.L.M.1027 (2000).
15 March 2000	Protocol on Preparedness, Response and Cooperation to Pollution by Hazardous and Noxious Substances
7 April 2000	MOU on Port State Control in the Black Sea (Istanbul)
23 May 2000	Agreement for the Establishment of the International Organisation for the Development of Fisheries in Eastern and Central Europe (Copenhagen) (FAO)
27 June 2000	OECD Guidelines for Multinational Enterprises, 40 ILM 237 (2000)
13 July 2000	International Seabed Authority, Regulations on Prospecting and Exploration for Polymetallic Nodules in the Area, 30 EPL 174 (2000)
7 August 2000	Revised Protocol on Shared Watercourses in the Southern African Development Community (SADC) (Windhoek), 40 I.L.M. 321 (2001).
14 August 2000	Convention on the Conservation of Living Marine Resources on the High Seas of the South Pacific (Santiago).
5 September 2000	Convention on the Conservation and Management of Highly Migratory Fish Stocks in the Western and Central Pacific Ocean, (Honolulu) 40 I.L.M. 278 (2001).
11 October 2000	Recommendations of IUCN's Second World Conservation Congress, Amann, 30 EPL 285 and 313 (2000).
16 October 2000	Agreement on the Conservation and Management of the Alaska-Chukotka Polar Bear Population (United States-Russia) (Washington), 40 I.L.M. 397 (2001).

20 October 2000	European Landscape Convention (Florence), EMuT, 2000:78.
8 November 2000	UN CESCR, General Comment No. 14, "Substantive Issues Arising in the Implementation of the International Covenant on Economic, Social and Cultural Rights" (Art. 12), U.N. Doc. E/C.12/2000/4 (2000).
14 November 2000	Convention on the Conservation and Management of High Seas Fishery Resources in the South Pacific Ocean (Auckland).
2 February 2001	Agreement on the Conservation of Albatrosses and Petrels (Capetown).
9 February 2001	UNEP Governing Council, Program for the Development and Periodic Review of Environmental Law for the First Decade of the 21th Century (Montevideo III), (Nairobi), 30 EPL 309 (2000) and 31 EPL 121 (2001).
27 February 2001	Amendment to the Convention on Environmental Impact Assessment in a Transboundary Context (Sofia) UN/ECE.
23 March 2001	International Convention on Civil Liability for Bunker Oil Pollution Damage (London).
20 April 2001	Convention on the Conservation and Management of Fishery Resources in the South-East Atlantic Ocean (Windhoek), 41 I.L.M. 257 (2002).
22 May 2001	Convention on Persistent Organic Pollutants (Stockholm), EMuT, 2001:3, 40 I.L.M. 532 (2001).
21 June 2001	ILO Convention on Safety and Health in Agriculture.
14 August 2001	IAEA, Guidelines on Physical Protection Objectives and Fundamental Principles, 41 ILM 737 (2002).
11 September 2001	OAS Inter-American Democratic Charter (Lima), 40 I.L.M. 1289 (2001).
5 October 2001	International Convention on the Control of Harmful Anti-Fouling Systems (London).
3 November 2001	FAO, International Treaty on Plant Genetic Resources for Food and Agriculture, (Rome), EMuT 2001:28.
14 November 2001	Declaration of the World Trade Organization (Doha), 41 ILM 746 (2002).
12 December 2001	G.A. Res. 56/83 approving Draft Articles on Responsibility of States for Internationally Wrongful Acts, in Report of the International Law Commission on

	the Work of Its Fifty-third Session, UNGAOR, 56th Sess., Supp. No. 10, at 45, UN Doc. A/56/10 (2001).
18 February 2002	Convention for Cooperation in the Protection and Sustainable Development of the Marine and Coastal Environment of the Northern Pacific (Antigua).
22 May 2002	OAS General Assembly Resolution "Human Rights and the Environment in the Americas, OEA/Ser.P, June 2, 2002, AG/doc.4118/02.
28 may 2022	Charter of the Senegal River Waters.
10 June 2002	ASEAN Agreement on Transboundary Haze Pollution (Kuala Lumpur), EMuT, 2002:44.
4 September 2002	Declaration on Sustainable Development and Plan of Implementation of the World Summit on Sustainable Development (Johannesburg), A/CONF.199/CRP/7 and A/CONF/L/6/Rev.2.
26 November 2002	UN CESCR, General Comment No. 15 on the Right to Water, Arts. 11 and 12, UN Doc. E/C.12/2002/11.
16 May 2003	Protocol to the International Convention on the Establishment of an International Fund for Compensation for Oil Pollution Damage.
23 May 2003	Protocol to the Aarhus Convention establishing a Pollutant Release and Transfer Register (Kiev).
23 May 2003	Framework Convention on the Protection and Sustainable Development of the Carpathians (Kiev).
21 July 2003	African Convention on the Conservation of Nature and Natural Resources (Maputo).
4 November 2003	Framework Convention for the Protection of the Marine Environment (Tehran)
29 November 2003	Protocol for the Sustainable Development of Lake Victoria Basin (Arusha)
13 February 2004	International Convention for the Control and Management of Ships' Ballast Water and Sediments
13 July 2004	Agreement on the Establishment of the Zambezi Watercourse Commission (Kasane)
20 April 2005	Human Rights Council Resolution 2005/60 on Human rights and the environment as part of sustainable development
18 May 2007	Nairobi International Convention on the Removal of Wrecks
30 April 2008	Niger Basin Water Charter (Niamey)

25 March 2009	Human Rights Council Resolution 10/4 on Human Rights and Climate Change
15 May 2009	Honk Kong International Convention for the Safe and Environmentally Sound Recycling of Ships
22 November 2009	Agreement on Port State Measures to Prevent, Deter and Eliminate Illegal, Unreported and Unregulated Fishing
26 July 2010	G.A. Res. 64/292 on the Human Right to Water and Sanitation
29 October 2010	Nagoya Protocol on Access to Genetic Resources and the Fair and Equitable Sharing of Benefits Arising from their Utilization to the Convention on Biological Diversity (Nagoya)
12 May 2011	Agreement on Cooperation on Aeronautical and Maritime Search and Rescue in the Arctic
27 May 2011	Sustainable Tourism Protocol to the Convention on the Protection and Sustainable Development of the Carpathians
12 August 2011	Protocol Concerning Regional Preparedness, Response and Co-operation in Combating Oil Pollution Incidents
8 June 2012	Convention on the Determination of the Minimal Conditions for Access and Exploitation of Marine Resources within the Maritime Areas under the Jurisdiction of the Member States of the Sub-Regional Fisheries Commission
11 September 2012	G.A. Res. 66/288 The Future We Want, A/RES/66/288
13 March 2013	G.A. Res. 67/251 on Change of the designation of the Governing Council of the United Nations Environment Programme
15 May 2013	Agreement on Cooperation on Marine Oil Pollution Preparedness and Response in the Arctic
11 July 2013	Revised African Nature Convention
10 October 2013	Minamata Convention on Mercury
16 September 2014	Agreement between the Government of the Republic of Angola and the Government of the Republic of Namibia on the Establishment of Cuvelai Watercourse Commission (Windhoek)
21 November 2014	International Code for Ships Operating in Polar Waters
25 September 2015	G.A. Res. on Transforming Our World: the 2030 Agenda for Sustainable Development, UN GA/Res/70/01

12 December 2015	UN Framework Convention on Climate Change (Paris)
27 September 2018	Regional Agreement on Access to Information, Public Participation and Justice in Environmental Matters in Latin America and the Caribbean (Escazú)
18 December 2019	G.A. Res. on Strengthening the United Nations crime prevention and criminal justice programme, in particular its technical cooperation capacity, UN Doc A/RES/74/177
1 July 2020	United States – Mexico – Canada Agreement (USMCA)
23 July 2021	G.A. Res. on Tackling Illicit Trafficking in Wildlife, UN Doc A/RES/75/311
8 October 2021	Human Rights Council Resolution on the Human Right to a Clean, Healthy and Sustainable Environment, A/HRC/RES/48/13
31 October 2021	Agreement for the establishment of the Commission of Small Island States on Climate Change and International Law
28 July 2022	G.A. Res. on the Human Right to a Clean, Healthy and Sustainable Environment, A/RES/76/300
7 December 2022	G. A. Res. on the Protection of the Environment in Relation to Armed Conflict, UN. Doc. A/RES/77/104
29 March 2023	G.A. Res. on the Request for an advisory opinion of the International Court of Justice on the obligations of States in respect of climate change, UN Doc A/77/L.58
19 June 2023	Agreement under the United Nations Convention on the Law of the Sea on the Conservation and Sustainable Use of Marine Biological Diversity of Areas beyond National Jurisdiction

European Union Law

Treaties

18 April 1951	Treaty Establishing the European Coal and Steel Community (Paris), 261 U.N.T.S. 140; U.K.T.S. 16 (1979), Cmd. 7461, 158 B.F.S.P. 630
25 March 1957	Treaty Establishing the European Economic Community (Rome) 298 U.N.T.S. 11; U.K.T.S. 15 (1979), Cmd. 7480
25 March 1957	Treaty Establishing the European Atomic Energy Community (Euratom) (Rome) 298 U.N.T.S. 167; U.K.T.S. 15 (1979), Cmd. 7480
17 February 1986	Single European Act, EC 12 (1986), Cmd. 9758; U.K.T.S. 31 (1988), Cmd. 372; 25 I.L.M. 506 (1986)
7 February 1992	Treaty on European Union (Maastricht), EMuT 992:11; 31 I.L.M. 247 (1992)
12 May 1992	European Economic Area Agreement (Oporto), 1 C.M.L.R. 921 (1992)
2 October 1997	Treaty of Amsterdam amending the Treaty on European Union, Consolidated Versions O.J. C 32 (12/24/02).
9 May 2008	Consolidated Version of the Treaty on European Union (2008) O.J. C115/13

Regulations, Directives, and Decisions

18 March 1967	Directive Relating to the Classification, Packaging and Labelling of Dangerous Substances, 67/548/EEC O.J. No. L 196 of 8/16/67. Amended: March 13, 1969 (O.J. L 68 of 3/19/69); March 6, 1970 (O.J. L 59 of 3/14/70); March 22, 1971 (O.J. L 74 of 3/29/71); May 21, 1973 (O.J. L. 167 of 6/25/73); June 24, 1975 (O.J. L 183 of 7/14/75); and Sept. 18, 1979, (O.J. L 98 of 7/22/78)
22 November 1973	Directive Relating to Detergents, 73/404/EEC, O.J. 347 (1973)
16 June 1975	Directive Concerning the Quality Required of Surface Water Intended for Abstraction of Drinking Water, 75/440/EEC, O.J. L 194 (7/15/75)

15 July 1975	Directive on Waste, 75/442/EEC, O.J. L 194 (7/25/75)
8 December 1975	Directive Concerning the Quality of Bathing Water, 76/160/EEC, O.J. L 31 (2/5/76)
6 April 1976	Directive on Disposal of Polychlorinated Biphenyls (PCB), and Polychlorinated Terphenyl (PCT), O.J. L 108 (4/26/76)
4 May 1976	Directive on Pollution Caused by Certain Dangerous Substances Discharged in the Aquatic Environment of the Communities, 1976 76/464/EEC, O.J. L 129 (5/18/76)
18 July 1977	Directive on the Protection of Animals During International Transport, 77/489/EEC, O.J. No. L 200 (8/8/77)
7 November 1977	Directive 77/728 on paints, varnishes, printing inks, glues and related products, O.J. L 303 (11/28/77), modified by Directive 82/265 of May 16, 1983, O.J. L 147 (6/6/83)
20 February 1978	Directive on Waste from Titanium Dioxide Industry, 78/176/EEC, O.J. L 54 (2/25/78)
20 March 1978	Directive on Toxic and Dangerous Waste, 78/319/EEC, O.J. L 84 (3/31/78)
26 June 1978	Directive 78/631 on pesticides, O.J. L 206 (7/29/78), modified by directive 81/187 of May 16, 1983, O.J. L 88 (4/2/81)
18 July 1978	Directive on the Quality of Fresh Water Needing Protection or Improvement in Order to Support Fish Life, 78/659/EEC, O.J. L 222 (8/14/78)
21 December 1978	Directive prohibiting Plant Protection Products Containing Certain Active Substances, 79/117/EEC, O.J. No. L 33.
2 April 1979	Directive on the Conservation of Wild Birds, 79/409/EEC, O.J. L 103 (4/2/79) Amended: 85/411/EEC
9 October 1979	Directive on Drinking Water, 79/869/EEC, O.J. L 271 (10/29/79)
30 October 1979	Directive on the Quality Required of Shellfish Waters, 79/923/EEC, O.J.281 (11/10/79)
17 December 1979	Directive on the Protection of Groundwater Against Pollution Caused by Certain Dangerous Substances, 80/68/EEC, O.J.L 20 (1/26/80)
15 July 1980	Directive Relating to the Quality of Water Intended for Human Consumption, 80/778/EEC, O.J.L 229 (8/30/80)

20 January 1981	Regulation on Common Rules for Imports of Whales or Other Cetecean Products, 348/881/EEC, O.J. L 39 (2/12/81)
22 March 1982	Directive on Mercury Discharges, 82/176/EEC, O.J. L. 81 (27/3/82);
24 June 1982	"Seveso" Directive on the Major Accident Hazards of Certain Industrial Activities, 82/501/EEC, 1982 O.J. L 230 (8/5/82), amended by 87/216/EEC of 19 March 1987, O.J. L 85 (3/28/87)
28 March 1983	Directive Concerning the Importation of Skins of Certain Seal Pups, 3/129/EEC, O.J. L 19 (4/9/83). Extended by 85/444/EEC, O.J.L 259 (10/1/85)
26 September 1983	Directive on Limit Values and Quality Objectives for Cadmium Discharges, 83/513/EEC, O.J. L 191 (10/24/83)
8 March 1984	Directive on Limit Values and Quality Objectives for Mercury Discharges, 84/156/EEC, O.J. L 47 (3/17/84)
28 June 1984	Directive on Combating Air Pollution from Industrial Plants, 84/360/EEC, O.J. L 188 (7/16/84)
13 December 1984	Directive 84/631 on the Supervision and Control Within the European Community of the Transfrontier Shipment of Hazardous Waste, O.J. L 326, (12/13/84)
7 March 1985	Directive on Air Quality Standards for Nitrogen Dioxide, 85/203/EEC, O.J. L 87 (3/27/85)
27 June 1985	Directive on the Assessment of the Effects of Certain Projects on the Environment, 85/337/EEC, O.J. L 175 (5/7/85)
12 June 1986	Directive on Sewage Sludge Used in the Agriculture, 86/278/EEC, O.J. L 181 (7/4/86)
12 June 1986	Directive on Limit Values and Quality Objectives for Discharges of Certain Dangerous Substances, 86/280/EEC, O.J. L 181 (7/4/86)
12 June 1988	Directive 88/609 on installations of combustion of 50 megawatts or more, O.J. L 336 (12/7/88)
23 April 1990	Directive 90/219/EEC on Good Microbiological Practices, O.J. no. L 117, (8/5/90)
23 April 1990	Directive 90/220/EEC on Voluntary Release of Genetically Modified Organisms, O.J. no. L 117, (5/8/90) *repealed by EC/2001/18/EC*
7 June 1990	Directive 90/313/EEC on the Freedom of Access to Information on the Environment, O.J. no. L 158/56 (23/6/90)

18 March 1991	Directive 91/156/EEC on Management, O.J.L 78 of (3/26/91)
20 December 1991	Directive 91/676/EEC on Toxic and Dangerous Wastes, O.J. L 377 (31/12/91)
22 March 1992	Regulation 880/92 on a Community Eco-label Award Scheme, O.J. no. L 99/1 (4/11/92)
21 May 1992	Directive 92/43/EC on the Conservation of Natural Habitats and of Wild Fauna and Flora, O.J. no. L 206 (22/7/92)
27 January 1992	Regulation No. 345/92 on driftnet fishing *O.J. L 42 of 18 February 1992*
1 February 1993	Regulation 259/93 on the Supervision and Control of Shipments of Waste within, into and out of the E.C., O.J. L 30 (6/2/93)
23 March 1993	Regulation 793/93/EEC on the Evaluation and Control of the Risks of Existing Substances, O.J. L 083 (05/04/93)
29 June 1993	Regulation 1836/93 Concerning Eco-Managment and Audit Schemes, O.J.L. 168/1 (10/7/93)
20 June 1994	Regulation 1467/94/EC on the Conservation, Characterization, Collection and Utilization of Genetic Resources in Agriculture, O.J. no. L 159/1 of 28 June 1994
	Regulation 1488/94 laying down the principles for the assessment of risks to man and the environment of existing substances in accordance with Council Regulation 793/93
24 September 1996	Directive 96/61 Governing Integrated Pollution Prevention and Control, O.J.E.C. L 257/26 (10/10/96)
7 October 1997	Council Resolution on Environmental Agreements, O.J. C 321 (22/10/97)
7 October 1997	Council Resolution on the Drafting, Implementation and Enforcement of Community Environmental Law, O.J. C 321 (22/10/97)
December 1998	Directive 98/81/EC revising Directive 90/212/EEC on the contained use of genetically-modified organisms, O.J. L. 330 (12/12/98)
15 December 1998	Council Resolution on a Forestry Strategy for the European Union, O.J. C 56 (26/02/99)
12 October 1999	Regulation 2161/1999/EC Imposing Further Testing Requirements on the Importers or Manufacturers of a Certain Priority Substance as Foreseen under Council

	Regulation (EEC) No. 793/93 on the Evaluation and Control of the Risks of Existing Substances, O.J. L 265 (13/10/1999)
21 October 1999	Regulation 2278/1999/EC Laying Down Certain Detailed Rules for the Application of Council Regulation 3528/86 on the Protection of the Community's Forests against Atmospheric Pollution, O.J. L 279 (29/10/99)
8 May 2000	Directive 2000/14/EC on the Approximation of the Laws of Member States relating to the Noise Emission in the Environment by Equipment for Use Outdoors, O.J. L 162 (03/07/20)
22 May 2000	Directive 2000/25/ED on Action to be Taken against the Emission of Gaseous and Particular Pollutants by Engines Intended to Power Agricultural or Forestry Tractors and Amending Council Directive 74/150/EEC, O.J. L 173 (12/07/00)
22 June 2000	Decision 1753/2000/EC Establishing a Scheme to Monitor the Average Specific Emissions of CO_2 from New Passenger Cars, O.J. L 2020 (10/08/2000)
23 June 2000	Cotonou Partnership Agreement between EC-ACP States
17 July 2000	Regulation 1980/2000/EC on a Revised Community Eco-label Award Scheme, O.J. L. 237 (21/09/00)
23 October 2000	Directive 2000/60/EC Establishing a Framework for Community Action in the Field of Water Policy, O.J. L 327 (22/12/00)
31 October 2000	Protocol for the Implementation of the Alpine Convention of 1991 in the Field of Transport (Lausanne) EMuT 991:83/I
31 October 2000	Protocol on Dispute Settlement to the Alpine Convention of 1991, EMuT 991:83/J
16 November 2000	Directive 2000/69/EC Relating to Limit Values for Benzene and Carbon Monoxide in Ambient Air, O.J. L 313 (13/12/00)
4 December 2000	Directive 2000/76/EC on the Incineration of Waste, O.J. L 332 (28/12/00)
7 November 2000	Regulation 2493/2000/EC on Measures to Promote the Full Integration of the Environmental Dimension in the Development Process of Developing Countries

7 November 2000	Regulation 2494/2000/EC on Measures to Promote the Conservation and Sustainable Management of Tropical Forests and Other Forests in Developing Countries, O.J L 288 (15/11/00)
20 December 2000	Decision 2850/2000/EC Setting up a Community Framework for Cooperation in the Field of Accidental or Deliberate Marine Pollution, O.J. L 332 (28/12/00)
12 March 2001	Directive 2001/18/EC on the Deliberate Release into the Environment of Genetically Modified Organisms and Repealing Council Directive 90/220/EEC, OJ L 106 (17/04/01)
19 March 2001	Regulation 761/2001/EC Allowing Voluntary Participation by Organizations in a Community Eco-Management and Audit Scheme (EMAS), O.J. L114 (24/04/01)
27 June 2001	Directive 2001/42/EC on the Assessment of the Effects of Certain Plans and Programmes on the Environment, O.J. L 197 (21/07/01)
30 August 2001	Regulation 1808/2001 Laying Down Detailed Rules Concerning the Implementation of Council Regulation 338/97 on the Protection of Species of Wild Fauna and Flora by Regulating Trade Therein, O.J. L 250 (19/09/01)
2 September 2001	Recommendation on Guidance for the Implementation of Reg. 761/2001 of the European Parliament and of the Council, O.J. L. 247 (9/17/01)
23 October 2001	2001/792/EC, Euratom; Establishing a Community Mechanism to Facilitate Reinforced Cooperation in Civil Protection Assistance Interventions, O.J. L 297 (15/11/01)
23 October 2001	Directive 2001/80/EC on the Limitation of Emissions of Certain Pollutants into the Air from Large Combustion Plants, O.J. L 309 (27/11/01)
23 October 2001	Directive 2001/81/EC on National Emission Ceilings for Certain Atmospheric Pollutants, O.J. L 309 (27/11/01)
24 October 2001	Regulation 2087/2001/EC Suspending the Introduction into the Community of Specimens of Certain Species of Wild Fauna and Flora
20 November 2001	Decision 2455/2001/EC Establishing the List of Priority Substances in the Field of Water Policy, O.J. L 331 (15/12/01)

12 February 2002	Directive 2002/3/EC Relating to Ozone in Ambient Air, O.J. L 067 (09/03/02)
18 February 2002	Regulation 417/2002/EC on the Accelerated Phasing-in of Double Hull or Equivalent Design Requirements for Single Hull Oil Tankers, O.J. L 64, 7 March 2002
1 March 2002	Decision 466/2002/EC Laying Down a Community Action Programme Promoting Non-Governmental Organizations Primarily Active in the Field of Environmental Protection, O.J. L 075 (16/03/02)
26 March 2002	Directive 2002/30/EC on the Establishment of Rules and Procedures with Regard to the Introduction of Noise-Related Operating Restrictions at Community Airports, O.J. L 85 (28/03/02)
25 June 2002	Directive 2002/49/EC Relating to the Assessment and Management of Environmental Noise, O.J. 189 (18/07/02)
19 July 2002	EC Directive 2002/51/EC on the Reduction of the Level of Pollutant Emissions from Two- and Three-wheel Motor Vehicles, O.J. L 252 (9/20/02)
22 July 2002	Decision No. 1600/2002/EC Laying Down the Sixth Community Action Programme, O.J. L. 242 (9/10/02)
3 October 2002	Decision 2002/812/EC establishing pursuant to Directive 2001/18/IC the Summary Information Format Relating to the Placing on the Market of Genetically Modified Organisms as or in Products, O.J. L280 (18/10/02)
3 October 2002	Decision 2002/813/EC establishing pursuant to Directive 2001/18/EC the Summary Notification Information Format for Notifications Concerning the Delierate Release into the Environment of Genetically Modified Organisms for Purposes other than for Placing on the Market, O.J. L 280 (18/10/02)
16 December 2002	Directive 2002/91/EC on the Energy Performance of Buildings, O.J. L 001 (04/01/03)
16 December 2002	Regulation 2347/2002/EC Establishing Specific Access Requirements and Assoicated Conditions Applicable to Fishing for Deep-Sea Stocks, O.J> L351 (28/12/02)
19 December 2002	Council Decision 26/2003/EC Establishing Criteria and Procedures for the Acceptance of Waste at Landfills Pursuant to Directive 199/31/EC, O.J. L 011 (16/01/03)
20 December 2002	Council Regulation 2371/2002/EC on the Conservation and Sustainable Exploitation of Fisheries Resources

	under the Common Fisheries Policy, O.J. L 358 (31/12/02)
27 January 2003	Framework Decision 2003/80/JHA on the Protection of the Environment through Criminal Law, O.J. L. 029 (05/02/03)
28 January 2003	EC Directive 2003/4/EC on Public Access to Environmental Information
21 April 2004	Directive 2004/35/CE of the European Parliament and of the Council on environmental liability with regard to the prevention and remedying of environmental damage, OJ L 143/0056
15 February 2006	Directive 2996/7/EC of the European Parliament and of the Council concerning the management of bathing water quality and repealing Directive 76/160/EEC
12 June 2006	Regulation (EC) No 1013/2006 of the European Parliament and of the Council on shipments of waste
19 October 2007	Communication from the Commission COM(2007)621 on the Agenda for a sustainable and competitive European tourism
23 October 2007	Directive of the European Parliament and of the Council on the assessment and management of flood risks
19 November 2008	Directive 2008/98/EC of the European Parliament and of the Council on waste and repealing certain Directives
16 September 2009	Regulation (EC) No 1007/2009 of the European Parliament and of the Council on trade in seal products
25 November 2009	Regulation (EC) No 66/2010 of the European Parliament and of the Council on the EU Ecolabel
30 November 2009	Directive 2009/147/EC of the European Parliament and of the Council on the conservation of wild birds
24 November 2010	Directive 2010/75/EU of the European Parliament and of the Council on industrial emissions (integrated pollution prevention and control)
13 December 2011	Directive 2011/92/EU of the European Parliament and of the Council on the assessment of the effects of certain public and private projects on the environment
4 July 2012	Directive 2012/18/EU of the European Parliament and of the Council on the control of major-accident hazards involving dangerous substances, amending and subsequently repealing Council Directive 96/82/EC

24 August 2013	Directive 2013/39/EU of the European Parliament and the Council amending Directives 2000/60/EC and 2008/105/EC as regards priority substances in the field of water policy
20 November 2013	Council Decision 1386/2013/EU on a General Union Environment Action Programme to 2020 'Living Well, within the Limits of our Planet'
16 April 2014	Directive 2014/52/EU of the European Parliament and of the Council amending Directive 2011/92/EU on the assessment of the effects of certain public and private projects on the environment
15 May 2014	Regulation (EU) No 508/2014 of the European Parliament and of the Council on the European Maritime and Fisheries Fund
23 July 2014	Directive 2014/89/EU of the European Parliament and of the Council establishing a framework for maritime spatial planning
11 December 2019	Communication from the Commission COM(2019)640 on The European Green Deal
30 June 2021	Regulation (EU) 2021/1119 of the European Parliament and of the Council establishing the framework for achieving climate neutrality and amending Regulations (EC) No 401/2009 and (EU) 2018/1999 ('European Climate Law')
14 December 2022	Directive (EU) 2022/2464 of the European Parliament and of the Council amending Regulation (EU) No 537/2014, Directive 2004/109/EC, Directive 2006/43/EC and Directive 2013/34/EU, as regards corporate sustainability reporting
18 October 2023	Directive (EU) 2023/2413 of the European Parliament and of the Council amending Directive (EU) 2018/2001, Regulation (EU) 2018/1999 and Directive 98/70/EC as regards the promotion of energy from renewable sources, and repealing Council Directive (EU) 2015/652
11 April 2024	Regulation (EU) 2024/1157 of the European Parliament and of the Council of on shipments of waste, amending Regulations (EU) No 1257/2013 and (EU) 2020/1056 and repealing Regulation (EC) No 1013/2006
11 April 2024	Directive (EU) 2024/1203 of the European Parliament and of the Council on the protection of the

	environment through criminal law and replacing Directives 2008/99/EC and 2009/123/EC (April 11, 2024) OJ L 2024/1203
24 April 2024	Council Directive 2024/0628 amending Directive (EU) 2019/1937 on Corporate on Sustainability Due Diligence

Table of Cases

January Term, 1829	*Foster and Elam v. Nielson*, 27 U.S. (2 Pet. 253), 7 L.Ed 415 (1829)
7 April 1902	*Kansas v. Colorado*, 185 U.S. 125 (1902)
19 Feburary 1906	*Missouri v. Illinois*, 200 U.S. 496 (1906)
13 May 1907	*State of Georgia v. Tennessee Copper Company and Ducktown Sulphur, Copper and Iron Company, Ltd.*, 206 U.S. 230 (1907)
2 May 1921	*New York v. New Jersey*, 256 U.S. 296 (1921)
30 August 1924	PCIJ, *Mavrommatis Case*, Ser. A, No. 2 p. 12
13 September 1928	PCIJ, *Chorzow Factory (Indemnity) Case*, Ser. A, No. 17, p. 29
28 June 1937	*Diversion Of Water from the Meuse* (Neth. v. Belg. 1937 P.C.I.J. (Ser. A/B) No. 70 at 4
11 March 1941	Arbitral Award, *Trail Smelter Case*, 3 U.N.R.I.A.A. 1905, 1938 (1949)
10 March 1949	*Gulf Oil v. Gilbert*, 330 U.S. 501, 67 S.Ct. 839, 91 L.Ed. 1055 (1947)
10 March 1949	*Koster v. Lumbermends Mut.Case. Co*, 330 U.S. 518, 67 S.Ct. 828, 91 L.Ed. 1067 (1947)
3 April 1949	*Corfu Channel Case* (U.K. v. Albania), Merits, 1949 I.C.J. Rep. 4
28 May 1951	*Reservations to the Convention on Genocide (Advisory Opinion)*, 1951 I.C.J. Rep. 23
6 April 1955	*Nottebohm Case* (Liechtenstein v. Guatemala) [1955] I.C.J. Rep. 4
19 November 1957	*Lake Lanoux Case* (France v. Spain), 12 U.N.R.I.A.A. 281 (1957)
5 February 1970	*Barcelona Traction, Light and Power Company, Ltd.* (Bel. v. Spain), 1970 I.C.J. Rep. 32
20 December 1974	*Nuclear Tests in the Pacific* (Australia v. France), [1974] I.C.J. Rep. 253; (New Zealand v. France), [1974] I.C.J. Rep. 457
21 February 1975	*Golder v. United Kingdom*, 18 Eur.Ct.H.R. (ser.A)(1975);
12 May 1975	Handelskwkerij G.J. Bier et al v. Mines de Potasse d'Alsace S.A.(Rotterdam municipal court, 6th chamber, Judgment of May 12, 1975), 1976 Rev. Jur. Env 71

30 November 1976	Eur.Court of Justice, *S.A. Handelskwekerij Bier et Fondation Reinwater v. Mines de Potasse d'Alsace*, 1976 E.Ct.J. Rep. 1735
18 January 1978	*Ireland v. United Kingdom*, 25 Eur. Ct. Hum. Rts. (Ser. A.) (1978)
6 September 1978	*Klass v. Germany*, 28 Eur.Ct.H.R. (ser.A)(1978)
August 18, 1978	*Sierra Club v. Adams*, 578 F.2d 389 (D.C. Cir. 1978)
15 July	1980 Eur. Comm'n Hum. Rts, Application 7889/77, *Arrondelle v. United Kingdom*, 19 D. & R. 186 (1980) and 26 D. & R. 5 (1982)
8 December 1981	*Piper Aircraft Co. v. Reyno*, 454 U.S. 235, 102 S.Ct. 252, 70 L.Ed.2d 419
23 November 1982	*Macedo v. Boeing Co.*, 693 F.2d 683 (7th Cir. 1982)
13 July 1983	*Zimmerman and Steiner v. Switzerland*, 66 Eur. Ct. Hum. Rts. (Ser. A)(1993)
16 December 1983	District Court of Rotterdam, Decision in *Handelskwekerij G.J. Bier et Fondation Reinwater v. Mines de Potasse d'Alsace*
16 October 1985	Eur. Comm'n Hum. Rts, Application 9310/81, *Baggs v. United Kingdom*, 44 D. & R. 13 (1985); 52 D. & R. 29 (1987). *Benthem v. Netherlands*, 97 Eur.Ct.H.R.(ser.A) (1985)
27 June 1986	*Military and Paramilitary Activities in and Against Nicaragua* (Nicaragua v. USA), 1986 I.C.J. Rep. 14
13 January 1987	*In re Union Carbide Corp. Gas Plant Disaster at Bhopal, India in December 1984*, 809 F.2d 195 (2d Cir. 1987)
24 March 1987	*Amoco Production Co. v. Village of Gambell, Alaska*, 107 S.Ct. 1396 (1987)
26 March 1987	*Leander v. Sweden*, 116 Eur.Ct.H.R. (ser.A)(1987)
7 July 1987	*Gaskin v. United Kingdom*, 160 Eur.Ct.H.R. (ser.A)(1987)
20 November 1987	WTO, *Report of the Panel, Canada – Measures Affecting Exports of Unprocessed Herring and Salmon*
11 January 1988	*In Re Oil Spill by Amoco Cadiz off the Coast of France on May 16, 1978*, (N.D. Ill. 1988) 1988 U.S. Dist. Lexis 16832, M.D.L. Docket No. 376
21 February 1990	*Powell and Rayner v. United Kingdom*, 172 Eur. Ct. Hum. Rts (ser. A)(1990)
18 January 1989	Application 1281/87, *Vearncombe et al. v. United Kingdom and Federal Republic of Germany*, 59 D. & R. 186 (1989)

9 March 1989	*Braunerheilm v. Sweden*, App. NO. 11764/85, Eur. Comm'n Hum. Rts.
16 October 1989	US-Canada FTA, *Final Report of the Panel in the Matter of Canada's Landing Requirement for Pacific Coast Salmon and Herring*
17 March 1991	Eur.Court of Justice, *Commission v. Council*, Case C-155/91
27 November 1991	*Oerlemans v. Netherlands*, 219 Eur.Ct.H.R. (ser.A)(1991)
3 September 1991	GATT Dispute Settlement Panel, Report on United States Restrictions on Imports of Tuna; 30 I.L.M. 1594 (1991)
30 July 1993	Supreme Court of the Philippines, *Minors Oposa v. Secretary of the Department of Environment and Natural Resources*, 33 I.L.M. 173
25 November 1993	*Zander v. Sweden*, 279B Eur. Ct. Hum. Rts (Ser. A)(1993)
23 March 1994	*O.S. et al v. Finland*, CCPR Comm. No. 431/1990
20 May 1994	GATT, Dispute Settlement Panel Report on United States Restrictions on Imports of Tuna, DS 29/R (1994), 33 I.L.M. 839 (1994)
11 October 1994	GATT, Dispute Settlement Panel Report on United States Taxes on Automobiles, 33 I.L.M. 1397 (1994)
9 December 1994	*López Ostra v. Spain*, 303-C Eur. Ct. Hum. Rts. (1994)
29 April 1996	WTO, *United States – Standards for Reformulated and Conventional Gasoline*, WT/DS2/AB/R
20 May 1996	*United States – Standards for Reformulated and Conventional Gasoline*, WTO Doc. WT/DS/2/AB/R
8 July 1996	*Legality of the Threat or Use by a State of Nuclear Weapons in Armed Conflict* (Advisory Opinion), 1996 I.C.J. 226
28 August 1996	*Vellore Citizens' Welfare Forum v. Union of India and Others*, Sup. Ct. India
30 October 1996	*Jouni E. Lansmann et al v. Finland*, CCPR Comm. 671/1995
18 August 1997	*European Communities – Measures Concerning Meat and Meat Products (Hormones)*, WTO Doc. WT/DS/26/AB/R and WT/DS/48/AB/R
25 September 1997	*Case Concerning the Gabfikovo Nagymaros Project*, 1997 I.C.J. Rep. 7
19 February 1998	*Guerra v. Italy*, 1998-I Eur. Ct. Hum. Rts.

15 May 1998	WTO Panel, *United States – Import Prohibition of Certain Shrimp and Shrimp Products*, WTO Doc. WT/DS/58/R
19 May 1998	Case C-3/96, *Commission of the European Communities v. The Netherlands*, [1998] ECR I-3031
25 September 1998	*Association Greenpeace France*, Counseil d'Etat, France
12 October 1998	WTO Appellate Body, *United States – Prohibition of Shrimp and Certain Shrimp Products*, WTO Doc. WT/DS58/AB/R
20 October 1998	WTO Appellate Body, *Australian Measures Affecting the Importation of Salmon*, WTO Doc. WT/DS18/AB/R
5 October 1998	*Jota v. Texaco Inc.*, 157 F.3d 153 (2d Cir. 1998)
6 November 1998	WTO Appellate Body, *United States- Import Prohibition of Certain Shrimp and Shrimp Products*, AB Report, WT/DS58/AB/R, modifying the WTO Panel established Feb. 25, 1997, WT/DS58/R and Corr.1
22 February 1999	WTO Appellate Body, *Japan – Varietals, Measures Affecting Agricultural Products*, WT/DS76/AB/R
29 April 1999	ECJ, Standley and Others, [1999] ECR I-2603
29 April 1999	*Chassagnou, Petit and Lasgrezas v. France*, Eur. Ct. Hum. Rts., 29 EHRR 525 (1999)
20 May 1999	Bladet Tromso and Stensaas v. Norway, Eur. Ct. Hum. Rts., 29 EHRR 125 (2000)
27 August 1999	*Southern Bluefin Tuna Cases*, ITLOS Order of 27 August 1999 on Provisional Measures
13 December 1999	*Case Concerning Kasilili/Sedudu Island (Botswana v. Namibia)*, (Dec. 13, 1999) 1999 I.C.J. Rep. 98, 39 I.L.M. 310 (2000)
17 February 2000	*Compañía del Desarrollo de Santa Elena S.A. v. Republic of Costa Rica*, ICSID Case No ARB/96/1, Award
13 April 2000	*In the Matter of the People of Enewetak*, NCT No. 23-0902, 39 I.L.M. 1214 (2000)
30 August 2000	*Metalclad Corporation v. The United Mexican States*, ICSID Case No ARB(AF)/97/1, Award
14 Sept. 2000	*Wiwa v. Royal Dutch Petroleum*, 226 F.3d 88 (2d. Cir. 2000)
13 November 2000	*S.D. Myers v. Canada* (Nov. 13, 2000), NAFTA
16 November 2000	*Communication No. 547/1992, Apriana Mahuika et al v. New Zealand*, CCPR/C/70/D/547/1993
18 January 2001	*Chapman v. The United Kingdom*, 33 EHRR 18 (2001)

6 February 2001	*In the Matter of Cross-border Trucking Services*, NAFTA
15 February 2001	*Pialopoulos and Others v. Greece.*, 33 EHRR 39 (2001)
13 March 2001	WTO Appellate Body, *European Communities. – Measures Affecting Asbestos and Asbestos-Containing Products*, WT/DS135/AB/R
29 March 2001	*Thoma v. Luxembourg*, Eur. Ct. Hum. Rts.
5 April 2001	Case E-3/00 *EFTA Surveillance Authority v. Norway* (2001)
10 April 2001	*Pope and Talbot v. Canada, Award on the Merits of Phase 2*, NAFTA
15 June 2001	WTO Panel, *United States – Import Prohibition of Certain Shrimp and Shrimp Products. Recourse to Article 21.5 by Malaysia*, WT/DS58/RW
30 August 2001	*Awas Tingni Mayagna (Sumo) Indigenous Community v. Nicaragua*, Inter-Am. Ct. Hum. Rts.
22 October 2001	*United States – Import Prohibition of Certain Shrimp and Shrimp Products, Report of the Appellate Body*, WT/DS58/AB/RW, 41 I.L.M. 149 (2002)
3 December 2001	*The MOX Plant Case*, ITLOS, Order of 3 December 2001 on Provisional Measures
27 February 2002	Case C-6/00, *Abfall Service AG (ASA) v. Bundeminister fur Umwelt, Jugend und Familie*, [2002] ECR-I 1961
18 April 2002	Case C-9/00 *Palin Granit Oy and Vehmassalon kansanterveystyon kuntayhtyman hallitus*, [2002] ECR-I 3533
18 September 2002	*Doe v. Unocal*, __ F.3d __, 2002 WL 31063976, RICO Bus. Disp.Guide 10,336, 2 Cal. Daily Op. Serv. 9585, 2002 Daily Journal D.A.R. 10,794, 9th Cir.(Cal.)
27 May 2002	*Social and Economic Rights Action Center/Center for Economic and Social Rights v. Nigeria*, Case No. ACHPR/COMM/A044/1 (Afr. Comm'n Hum. & Peoples' Rts)
11 September 2002	Case T-13/99 *Pfizer Animal Health SA v Council* (2002)
2 July 2003	OSPAR Arbitral Tribunal, *Dispute Concerning Access to Information under Article 9 of the OSPAR Convention* (Ireland v. United Kingdom)
8 July 2003	*Hatton v. United Kingdom*, Eur. Ct. Hum. Rts (Grand Chamber)
4 December 2003	*Taşkın and Others v. Turkey*, Eur. Ct. Hum. Rts., App. NO. 49517/99

30 April 2004	*Waste Management, Inc. v United Mexican States,* ICSID Case No ARB(AF)98/2, Award
30 November 2004	*Oneryildiz v. Turkey*, App. NO. 48939/99, Eur. Ct. Hum. Rts., Judgment
24 May 2005	*Iron Rhine Arbitration (Belgium v. Netherlands)* (Award)
9 June 2005	*Fadayeva v. Russia*, App. no. 55723/00, Eur. Ct. Hum. Rts., Judgment
3 August 2005	*Methanex Corporation v. United States of America*, UNCITRAL, Final Award of the Tribunal on Jurisdiction and Merits
19 December 2005	*Armed Activities on the Territory of the Congo* (DRC *v. Uganda*), ICJ, Judgment
29 March 2006	*Case of the Sawhoyamaxa Indigenous Community v. Paraguay* (Judgement) Inter-Am. Ct. Hum. Rts.
29 September 2006	WTO Panel, *European Communities – Measures Affecting the Approval and Marketing of Biotech Projects*, WT/DS291, 292, 293/R
12 April 2007	*Case of Zeleni Balkani v. Bulgaria*, Eur. Ct. Hum. Rts., Judgment
11 September 2007	*Parkerings-Compagniet AS v. Republic of Lithuania*, ICSID Case No. ARB/05/8, Award
17 September 2007	*Guyana v. Suriname*, PCA Case No. 2004-04, Award
28 November 2007	*Case of the Saramaka People v Suriname* (Judgement) Inter-Am. Ct. Hum. Rts.
3 December 2007	WTO Appellate Body, *Brazil – Measures Affecting Imports of Retreaded Tyres*, WT/DS332/AB/R
20 March 2008	*Budayeva and Others v. Russia*, App. NOS. 15339/02, 21166/02, 20058/02, 11673/02 and 15343/02 Eur. Ct. Hum. Rts., Judgement
3 April 2008	*Koretsky and Others v. Ukraine,* Eur. Ct. Hum. Rts., Judgement
27 January 2009	*Tatar v. Romania*, Eur. Ct. Hum. Rts. (Chamber Judgment)
25 November 2009	*Center for Minority Rights Development (Kenya) and Minority Rights Group International on Behalf of Endoris Welfare Council v. Kenya*, Afr. Comm. Hum. Rts.
30 March 2010	*Bacila v. Romania*, Eur. Ct. Hum. Rts., Judgment
20 April 2010	*Case Concerning Pulp Mills on the River Uruguay,* 2010 I.C.J. Rep. 14

29 November 2010	WTO Appellate Body, *Australia – Measures Affecting the Importation of Apples from New Zealand,* WT/DS367R/AB/R
1 February 2011	*Responsibilities and Obligations of States sponsoring Persons and Entities with Respect to Activities in the Area* (Advisory Opinion) Case No. 17, ITLOS (Seabed Dispute Chamber)
10 February 2011	*Dubetska and Others v Ukraine*, Eur. Ct. Hum. Rts., Judgment
22 February 2012	WTO Panel, *China – Measures Related to the exportation of Various Raw Materials*, WT/DS394/R
16 may 2012	WTO Appellate Body, *United States – Measures Concerning the Importation, Marketing and Sale of Tuna and Tuna Products*, WT/DS381/AB/R
23 July 2012	WTO Appellate Body, *United States – Certain Country of Origin Labelling (COOL) Requirements*, WT/DS384/AB/R
13 September 2013	*Case concerning Aerial Herbicide Spraying (Ecuador v. Colombia)*, Order, ICJ Rep 2013
5 December 2013	*Vilnes and others v. Norway,* App. No. 52806/09, Eur. Ct. Hum. Rts., Judgment
20 December 2013	*Indus Waters Kishenganga Arbitration (Pakistan v. India)*, PCA, Final Award
31 March 2014	*Whaling in the Antarctic (Australa v. Japan: New Zealand intervening)*, Judgement, ICJ Rep 2014
22 May 2014	WTO Appellate Body, *European Communities – Measures Prohibiting the Importation and Marketing of Seal Products*, WT/DS401/AB/R
7 August 2014	WTO Appellate Body, *China – Measures related to the Exportation of Rare Earths, Tungsten, and Molybdenum*, WT/DS431, 432, 433/AB/R
18 March 2015	*Chagos Marine Protected Area Arbitration (Mauritius v. UK)*, Award
1 April 2015	*Request for an advisory opinion submitted by the Sub-Regional Fisheries Commission (SRFC)*, ITLOS
25 April 2015	*Dispute Concerning Delimitation of the Maritime Boundary between Ghana and Côte d'Ivoire in the Atlantic Ocean (Ghana/Côte d'Ivoire)* ITLOS Case No. 23
3 November 2015	*Adel A Hamadi Al Tamimi v. Sultanate of Oman*, ICSID Case No. ARB/11/33, Award

17 November 2015	*Özel and others v. Turkey*, App. Nos. 14350/05, 15245/05, and 16051/05, Eur. Ct. Hum. Rts., Judgment
25 November 2015	*Kaliña and Lokono People v. Suriname* (Judgement) Inter-Am. Ct. Hum. Rts.
16 December 2015	*Certain Activities Carried Out by Nicaragua in the Border Area (Costa Rica v. Nicaragua)* (Judgement) 2015 I.C.J. Rep. 15
12 July 2016	*South China Sea Arbitration (The Republic of Philippines v. The People's Republic of China)* Award
24 March 2016	*The Prosecutor v. Ahmad Al Faqi Al Mahdi*, Decision on the confirmation of charges against Ahmad Al Faqi Al Mahdi, Case no ICC-01/12-01/15, ICC-01/12-01/15-84-Red, International Criminal Court
15 November 2017	*Human Rights and the Environment*, Advisory Opinion OC-23/17 Inter-Am. Ct. Hum. Rts.
25 January 2018	*Leghari v. Federation of Pakistan*, Lahore High Court, W.P. No. 25501/2015
4 April 2019	Case T-108/17 *ClientEarth v. European Commission* (2019)
27 September 2019	*Perenco Ecuador Ltd. V. Republic of Ecuador and Empresa Estatal Petróleos del Ecuador (Petroecuador)*, ICSID Case No ARB/08/6, Award
20 December 2019	*Urgenda Foundation v. The State of the Netherlands* (Dutch Supreme Court)
14 October 2020	*Tsama William and Others v. Uganda's Attorney General and Others*, High Court of Uganda at Mbale, Miscellaneous Case No. 024 of 2020
26 May 2021	*Milieudefensie and Others v. Royal Dutch Shell PLC and Others*, The Hague District Court, Case No. C/09/571932, Judgment
3 November 2022	*PSB et al. v. Brazil (on Amazon Fund)*, Federal Supreme Court of Brazil, ADO 59/DF
1 December 2022	*Dispute over the Status and Use of the Waters of the Silala (Chile v. Bolivia)* Merits, ICJ Rep. 22
9 April 2024	*Verein Klimaseniorinnen Schweiz and Others v. Switzerland* Eur. Ct. Hum. Rts. [GC] 53600/20 Judgment
21 May 2024	*Request for an Advisory Opinion submitted by the Commission of Small Island States on Climate Change and International Law* (Advisory Opinion) ITLOS

Introduction

International environmental law is complex and vast, comprising hundreds of global and regional norms aimed at conserving the earth's living and non-living elements and protecting its ecological processes from anthropogenic harm. This relatively recent body of law emerged from growing public awareness, informed by warnings of scientists, that our survival on this planet is endangered by the activities of an ever-increasing number of humans utilizing destructive technology, rapidly consuming the earth's resources, and generating more waste than the planet can absorb. Environmental degradation is evident in the pollution of rivers and lakes, deterioration of the marine environment, desertification, mass extinction of species, as well as climate change. Many problems stem from but also contribute to widespread and extreme poverty.

The globalization of markets and the emergence of transnational civil society present new challenges and opportunities. While access to media makes possible more rapid knowledge of the existence and scope of environmental problems, global movements of persons and products are accompanied by the introduction of alien species and the spread of new pollutants and disease vectors. Over-production and consumption in wealthy countries threatens to exhaust living and non-living resources while also producing greenhouse gas emissions that alter the global climate. New problems resulting from technological advances are constantly being identified, such as the environmental impacts of industrial-scale farming and endocrine disruption due to the introduction of unprocessed pharmaceuticals in wastewater. Studies are also confirming the harmful effects of noise pollution on human and animal health. Such developments emphasize the constant need to develop and revise the national and international legal framework of environmental protection.

Concern for at least some aspects of the environment has long been evident. National laws enacted as early as the fourteenth century aimed to combat a specific pollutant such as smoke or to protect a particular forest or a body of water.[1] The first international agreements, dating from the beginning of the nineteenth century, sought to conserve endangered species of domesticated or wild flora or fauna: for example, the 1900 Convention for the Protection of Wild Animals, Birds and Fish in Africa, the 1902 Convention 'for the protection

1 In 1306, an ordinance of Edward I prohibited the use of coal in open furnaces in London. Other early laws can be found in Belgium, France, and the Netherlands. *See* C.A. Colliard, *La Pollution Atmospherique En Droit Francais et En Droit Comparé* (1976), pp. 22, 90, 101, 139.

 | DOI:10.1163/9789047440802_002

of birds useful to agriculture',[2] and a 1911 treaty protecting fur seals. These instruments concerned shared resources and approached the subject primarily from a utilitarian perspective, seeking to maximize and preserve the economic exploitation of the designated species.[3]

The approach to conservation changed fundamentally near the end of the 1960s. Under growing pressure from international public opinion, governments began to demonstrate concern over the general state of the environment and introduced legislation to combat pollution of inland waters, ocean, and air, and safeguard certain cities or areas. Simultaneously, they established special administrative organs, ministries or environmental agencies, to preserve more effectively the quality of life of their citizens. As discussed in Chapter 2, developments in international environmental law paralleled the evolution of law and policy within states.

1 The 'Environment' and 'Environmental Law'

A legal definition of the 'environment' is important to delineate the scope of the subject, determine the application of legal rules, and establish the extent of liability when harm occurs. Most languages borrowed or invented new terms when concern emerged about the potential destruction of natural resources and processes on which life depends.[4] The English word 'environment' is borrowed from an ancient French word "environner", meaning to encircle. A program of the United Nations Educational, Scientific and Cultural Organization (UNESCO)[5] uses the term 'biosphere' to designate the part of the universe where, according to present knowledge, all life is concentrated. *Webster's Dictionary* begins with a general definition of the environment, reflecting the original French meaning: 'the circumstances, objects, or conditions by which one is surrounded'.[6] It continues with a more precise meaning: 'the complex of physical, chemical, and biotic factors (such as climate, soil, and living things) that act upon an organism or an ecological community and ultimately determine its form and survival' to which it adds 'the aggregate of social and cultural

2 For further discussion of these instruments, see Chapter 8 on protection of living organisms and ecosystems.

3 The history of international environmental law is discussed in more detail in Chapter 2.

4 New words have emerged in many languages to express the concept of the environment: 'Umwelt'(German), 'milieu' (Dutch), 'medio ambiente' (Spanish), 'meio ambiente' (Portuguese), 'Al'biah' (Arabic), 'okruzhauchhaia sreda' (Russian) and 'kankyo' (Japanese).

5 UNESCO, *Man Belongs to the Earth: Unesco's Man and the Biosphere Program* (1988).

6 'Environment' defined in *Webster's Ninth New Collegiate Dictionary* (1983).

conditions that influence the life of an individual or community'. The last definition is broad and includes problems such as traffic congestion, crime, and noise within the field of environmental protection.

In law, 'environment' can refer to a limited area or encompass the entire planet, including the atmosphere and stratosphere. Often a broad approach is taken, given the understanding that the total surroundings determine the form and survival of each organism and community; thus national, regional, and international efforts must be taken to ensure the continued viability of the planet and the sustainability of its species. Yet, there is often tension between a focus on the 'human' environment, that is, those parts of the environment necessary or useful to human health and well-being, and the broader 'natural environment' whose deterioration may be less direct, but in the long term more harmful.[7] This tension was reflected in debates during the 1977 treaty negotiations for Protocol I to the 1949 Geneva Conventions on the Law of Armed Conflict, where the term human environment was invoked to refer to 'the immediate surroundings in which the civilian population lives'[8] to distinguish it from the natural environment. A further category the drafters developed was that of 'cultivated environment', meaning crops and agricultural land, specifically protected by Protocol I, Article 54.[9]

Few international instruments define 'environment'. An early directive of the European Community included 'water, air and land and their inter-relationship as well as relationships between them and any living organism'.[10] The Espoo Convention on Environmental Impact Assessment in a Transboundary Context[11] and the European Convention on Civil Liability for Damage Resulting

---

7 Human rights approaches to environmental protection are anthropocentric by definition. See *Fadeyeva v. Russia*, Eur. Ct. H.R. (2005), para. 68 ("no right to nature preservation is as such included among the rights and freedoms guaranteed by the [European] Convention [of Human Rights and Fundamental Freedoms]").

8 Report of the Chairman of the Group 'Biotope' (1975), Official Records of the Diplomatic Conference on the Reaffirmation and Development of International Humanitarian Law Applicable in Armed Conflicts, Additional (1974–77), CDDH/III/GT/35, para. 5.

9 As discussed in Chapter 16, the natural environment is protected by Protocol I, Article 35(3). It is unclear what level of protection and which article would apply to co-mingled areas, those in which wild flora and fauna are present in agricultural areas. See: Hulme, K., 'Natural Environment', in E. Wilmshurst and S. Breau (eds.), *Perspectives on the ICRC Customary International Humanitarian Law Study* (Cambridge University Press 2007), 204–37.

10 Article 2, Council Directive of June 27, 1967, O.J. L 196 (7/16/67).

11 Espoo, Feb. 25, 1991.

from Activities Dangerous to the Environment[12] contain comprehensive definitions. The latter provides:

For the purpose of this Convention …

'Environment' includes:

- natural resources both abiotic and biotic, such as air, water, soil, fauna and flora and the interaction between the same factors;
- property which forms part of the cultural heritage; and
- the characteristic aspects of the landscape.

Thus, the man-made environment, including structures and landscapes, can be considered a part of the environment to be protected. The International Court of Justice (ICJ) has gone further to encompass a social dimension, stating that 'the environment is not an abstraction, but represents the living space, the quality of life, and the very health of human beings, including generations unborn'.[13] These broad definitions and the fact that all human activities affect the environment make it difficult to establish the limits of environmental law as an independent legal field; indeed they imply the integration of environmental protection into all areas of law and policy.

The breadth of the definitions entails that in some cases law and policy will respond to environmental deterioration produced by natural events, such as volcanic eruptions or tsunamis, as well as those caused by human actions. Even though law cannot affect the natural processes causing environmental changes, law can and does regulate human behavior, including behavior in response to natural disasters. Thus, the fact of a natural disaster does not modify a state's international legal duty to notify and cooperate with other states in response to an environmental emergency, or excuse a lack due diligence in preventing and responding to the consequences of such disasters on those persons within the state's jurisdiction.[14]

Due to the inevitable environmental impact of human actions, rules having other objectives sometimes provide important indirect protection. Early international conventions concerning fishing, for example, were enacted primarily to allocate marine living resources and to assure their management in order to protect local economies and prevent conflicts between fishermen. Implementation and enforcement of the economic goal of the sustainable exploitation of

12 Lugano, June 21, 1993.

13 *Legality of the Threat or Use of Nuclear Weapons,* Advisory Opinion, I.C.J. Rep. 1996, pp. 241–242, para. 29.

14 See *Budayeva v. Russia*, [2008] ECtHR 15339/02 & Ors (20 March 2008); Andrej Zwitter et al (eds.) *Humanitarian Action: Global, Regional and Domestic Legal Responses* (Cambridge University Press 2015).

living resources nonetheless benefitted the environment, permitting the maintenance and renewal of stocks.

Environmental protection is thus sometimes advanced through rules adopted with another motivation. The severe ecological consequences of marine accidents such as the 1988 grounding of the Alaskan oil tanker *Exxon Valdez*, the 1999 breakup of the tanker *Erica*, and the similar disaster caused by the *Prestige* in 2002, demonstrated the importance of international maritime rules governing the construction of ships and training of vessel crews. Similarly, norms that standardize the performance of internal combustion engines, originally adopted in order to facilitate international trade, have supported clean technology leading to a reduction in engine noise and the emission of noxious gases.

In its own domain, environmental law prescribes and prohibits specific activities and processes, adopts economic incentives and disincentives, and creates management tools. Economic measures such as taxes on polluting emissions or on fuel, subsidies for clean technology and ecologically-sound land management, tradable permits for pollution, eco-auditing, and eco-labels generally require legal instruments. Local and national authorities must not only adopt laws and regulations, but they must organize and ensure the functioning of public institutions to ensure their compliance.

2 The Necessity of International Law

The need and desire to protect the environment presents a challenge for international law because it is now widely recognized that environmental problems are often transboundary, regional or global in scope. The 1968 European Water Charter, one of the first modern international instruments relating to the environment, expressed the natural reality: water knows no boundaries. Experience since then have made it obvious that neither the ocean, nor the atmosphere, nor living resources in general know political boundaries. Any significant impact on the environment can produce effects outside national territory, as evidenced by the consequences of long-range transboundary air pollution,[15] the widespread impact of ozone-depleting substances, and anthropogenic climate change.

15 In the 1980s an estimated 50 percent of atmospheric acidity deposited in eastern Canadian aquatic and terrestrial ecosystems was 'imported' from the United States, with levels in some areas exceeding 80 percent. John M. Sibley, 'A Canadian Perspective on the North American Acid Rain Problem' (1983) 4 N.Y.L.S. J. Int'l & Comp. L. 529–30. The 1990 U.S.

Modern economics and trade relations also play a role in internationalizing efforts to safeguard the environment. A state that enacts environmental measures must count the increased costs that are borne by its economy. In the long term, 'green' investments are advantageous, because it is more costly and in some cases impossible to repair environmental damage by, for example, cleaning up rivers or groundwater, rehabilitating the countryside, or reintroducing wildlife species. In the short term, however, environmental protection costs are borne by the producers, consumers or public authorities of the enacting state. The national economy feels the consequences, because the costs usually are reflected in the export prices of national products and services. The state that protects its environment thus risks a competitive disadvantage in the marketplace unless international legal measures harmonize the environmental protection requirements for all competitors.

Controlling the international transfer of polluting products, wastes, installations and environmentally-harmful activities also requires international cooperation and the adoption of common standards. In some instances, there is a risk that activities regulated by one country will move to a state where legislation or enforcement is less rigorous. In recent decades, the latter often have been developing countries which accept the risks involved in order to welcome less expensive or otherwise unavailable foreign products and investment. Widely reported deaths due to the use of exported pesticides banned in the country of origin, as well as industrial catastrophes such as the 1984 disaster in Bhopal, India, which killed 2500 people and injured thousands of others,[16] demonstrate the dangers. International agreements based on prior informed consent of the importing states[17] or a ban on the transfer of certain substances[18] address some of these problems, but some national regulatory efforts may be challenged as incompatible with international policies that emphasize free trade and investment. Unilateral measures to block environmentally-harmful products have run afoul of the obligations

Clean Air Act Amendments and the 1991 U.S.-Canada Bilateral Agreement on Air Quality took steps to remedy the problem. See *US-Canada Air Quality Progress Report*, 2–3 (2000).

16 See Marc Galanter, 'Bhopals Past and Present: The Changing Legal Response to Mass Disaster' (1990) 10 Windsor Y.B. of Access to Justice 151.

17 See e.g. Convention on the Prior Informed Consent Procedure for Certain Hazardous Chemicals and Pesticides in International Trade (Sept. 10, 1998); Protocol on Biosafety to the Convention on Biological Diversity (Montreal, Jan. 29, 2000).

18 See e.g., Montreal Protocol on Substances that Deplete the Ozone Layer (Sept. 16, 1987); Convention on the Ban of the Import into Africa and the Control of Transboundary Movement and Management of Hazardous Wastes Within Africa (Bamako, Jan. 20, 1991).

contained in the General Agreement on Tariffs and Trade, as interpreted by the organs of the World Trade Organization.[19]

Finally, the dimensions of some existing phenomena require regional or global action: desertification, reduction of the world genetic heritage, ozone-depletion, global warming – the catalogue lengthens as our understanding of the biosphere's life-supporting systems and processes improves. None of these problems can be resolved by a single state or even a small group of states, but instead require broad international cooperation.

International regulation thus becomes a basic requirement of environmental protection, but standard-setting to prevent environmental harm is insufficient by itself to assure effective environmental protection. An indispensable corollary to international regulation is the creation of supervisory institutions and the maintenance of cooperation between states, especially where continuity of action is necessary. International law must ensure compliance and provide redress for harm to those injured. The following chapters in Part I discuss the foundations and sources of international environmental law, its history, the general principles of law applicable today, implementation techniques and procedures, the international institutional framework and civil society, and, finally, compliance and enforcement.

Bibliography

Beyerlin, U. & Marauhn, Th., *International Environmental Law* (Oxford: Hart Publishing, 2011).

Birnie, P., Boyle, A. & Redgewell, C., *International Law and the Environment* (3d edn, Oxford: OUP, 2012).

Bodansky, D., *The Art and Craft of International Environmental Law* (Cambridge, Mass: Harvard University Press, 2011).

Bodansky, D., et al (eds), *The Oxford Handbook of International Environmental Law* (Oxford: OUP, 2007).

Desai, B.H., *Institutionalizing International Environmental Law* (Ardsley: Transnational Pub. 2004).

Dupuy, P.M. & Vinuales, J., *International Environmental Law: A Modern Introduction* (Cambridge: CUP, 2015).

Fitzmaurice, M., Ong, D., and Merkouris, P, *Research Handbook on International Environmental Law* (Cheltenham: Edward Elgar, 2010).

19 See Chapter 17.

Gillespie, Alexandre, *International Environmental Law, Policy and Ethics* (2d edn. Oxford: OUP, 2014).

Harris, P.G., *Routledge Handbook of Global Environmental Politics* (New York: Routledge, 2014).

Leary, D. & Pisupati, B., *The Future of International Environmental Law* (Tokyo: UNU, 2010.

Louka, E., *International Environmental Law: Fairness, Effectiveness and World Order* (Cambridge: CUP, 2006).

Palmer, G., *Environment: the International Challenge* (1995).

Sands, Ph. & Peel, J., *Principles of International Environmental Law* (3d edn, Cambridge: CUP, 2012).

Singh, G., *Environmental Law: International and National Perspectives* (1995).

PART 1

Structure and Basic Concepts

CHAPTER 1

Foundations of International Environmental Law

International environmental law aims to protect the biosphere from major deterioration that could endanger its present or future functioning. This objective provokes the fundamental questions: why protect the biosphere and for whose benefit? Who has legal obligations in this field and on what bases do such obligations exist? The present chapter addresses these questions, as well as the characteristics of international environmental law deriving from scientific, economic, political and legal realities. It begins with an overview of the religious, philosophical and ethical foundations of environmental protection.

1 Religion and Philosophy

Religious and philosophical concepts are crucial to understanding views about nature and humankind's relationship to it that have helped shape environmental law. These views have ranged from exploitive and dominating to holistic and cognizant of the intrinsic value of nature. They are relevant to understanding current law and creating new approaches to environmental protection.

1.1 *Religious Sources*

Religious texts and doctrine provide conceptual foundations for environmental protection, but also have been invoked to justify human use and abuse of nature.[1] Judeo-Christian religious traditions contain both elements. A prevalent view in the past claimed human supremacy and ownership over all creation based on the 'dominion' given humans in the first of the Creation stories in Genesis.[2] This perspective, which has by no means disappeared, regards humanity as the centre of existence, with the only justification for conservation being human self-interest or utility. More recent interpretations argue

1 For an overview of the Judeo-Christian sacred texts, see Dinah Shelton, 'Nature in the Bible' in *Man and the Environment: Essays in Honor of Alexandre Kiss* (Frison-Roche 1998).

2 'Be fruitful, and multiply, and replenish the earth, and subdue it; and have dominion over the fish of the sea, and over the fowl of the air, and over every living thing that moveth upon the earth' (*Gen.* 1:28).

 | DOI:10.1163/9789047440802_003

that the relevant passages do not grant ownership to humans,[3] but rather establish human power over other creatures and the right to beneficial use of them, imposing a type of guardianship or a trust.[4] Reflecting this notion of responsibility, Jewish laws provided for conservation of birds[5] and protection of trees during wartime,[6] and regulated the disposal of human waste.[7]

In the *Summa Theologica*, Thomas Aquinas argued that man's dominion over nature includes a competence to use and manage the world's resources, not selfishly, but in the interests of all, being ready to help others in case of necessity.[8] Individual title imposes a responsibility and a trust. In an address on 1 January 1990, the World Day of Peace, Pope John Paul II reflected on the consequences of failing to fulfil that trust:

> In our day, there is a growing awareness that world peace is threatened not only by the arms race, regional conflicts and continued injustices among people and nations, but also by a lack of due respect for nature, by the plundering of natural resources and by a progressive decline in the quality of life.[9]

3 Cf 'for the earth is the Lord's and the fullness thereof' (I *Cor.* 10:26). In speaking of the desolation of Egypt, God says 'the river is mine and I have made it' (*Ezek.* 29:9).

4 In Revelation, the twenty-four elders worship God by saying 'Thou art worthy, O Lord, to receive glory and honour and power: for thou hast created all things, and for thy pleasure they are and were created' (*Rev.* 7); 'All things being created for God's pleasure, humans err in extinguishing any of them. In Revelation the angels are commanded not to hurt the earth, the sea, the grass of the earth, nor any green thing including any tree' (*Rev.* 9); 'Only humans are marked and judged, at which judgment God will destroy them which destroy the earth' (*Rev.* 11:18).

5 'Those coming upon a bird's nest either in a tree or on the ground may not take the mother bird, although the eggs and the young may be taken'. (*Deut.* 22:6–7).

6 'When thou shalt besiege a city a long time, in making war against it to take it, thou shalt not destroy the trees thereof by forcing an axe against them: for thou mayest eat of them, and thou shalt not cut them down (for the tree of the field is man's life) to employ them in siege'. (*Deut.* 20:19).

7 Places outside camps were to be established for human waste. 'And thou shalt have a paddle upon thy weapon; and it shall be, when thou wilt ease thyself abroad, thou shalt dig therewith, and shalt turn back and cover that which cometh from thee'. (*Deut.* 23:13)

8 30 *Summa Theologica* (Blackfriars, 1975), 2a2ae, 66, 2. The commentary notes that this 'contains the nub of the teaching that individuals should be only trustees and stewards of the world's resources – and, presumably, on behalf of future generations of the human race as well as of the living'. p. 69.

9 Quoted in *Environment and the World of Work*, Report of the Director-General of the ILO (1990), 4.

In June 2015, Pope Francis issued a lengthy encyclical devoted to 'Our Common Home'.[10] The message is intended to be a universal one, not limited to all Catholics or even all Christians, but to 'every person living on this planet'.[11] The encyclical begins by reviewing the present ecological crisis, then considers some principles drawn from the Judaeo-Christian tradition which can render commitment to the environment more coherent. The initial overview reveals 'that our common home is falling into serious disrepair' and 'things are now reaching a breaking point, due to the rapid pace of change and degradation' as a consequence of which 'the present world system is certainly unsustainable from a number of points of view'.[12]

Most importantly, the encyclical rejects the idea of 'dominion' often put forward to justify harming or destroying nature:

> The earth was here before us and it has been given to us. This allows us to respond to the charge that Judaeo-Christian thinking, on the basis of the Genesis account which grants man 'dominion' over the earth (cf. Gen 1:28), has encouraged the unbridled exploitation of nature by painting him as domineering and destructive by nature. *This is not a correct interpretation of the Bible as understood by the Church.* Although it is true that we Christians have at times incorrectly interpreted the Scriptures, nowadays we must forcefully reject the notion that our being created in God's image and given dominion over the earth justifies absolute domination over other creatures .... Each community can take from the bounty of the earth whatever it needs for subsistence, but it also has the duty to protect the earth and to ensure its fruitfulness for coming generations. 'The earth is the Lord's' (Ps 24:1); to him belongs 'the earth with all that is within it' (Dt 10:14). Thus God rejects every claim to absolute ownership: 'The land shall not be sold in perpetuity, for the land is mine; for you are strangers and sojourners with me' (Lev 25:23).
>
> This responsibility for God's earth means that human beings, endowed with intelligence, must respect the laws of nature and the delicate equilibria existing between the creatures of this world .... Clearly, the Bible has no place for a tyrannical anthropocentrism unconcerned for other creatures.[13]

---

10 Encyclical Letter of Pope Francis, *'Laudato Si' On Care For Our Common Home*, June 18, 2015.

11 ibid, para. 3.

12 ibid, para. 61.

13 ibid, paras. 67–69 (emphasis added).

The encyclical thus expressly recognizes the intrinsic value of other species and the mutual dependence of all living things. In sum, '[t]he natural environment is a collective good, the patrimony of all humanity and the responsibility of everyone'.[14]

In 1983, Muslim experts undertook a study of the relationship between Islam and environmental protection. The results underscored that 'Islam presents a way of life that encompasses an overall view of the universe, life, man and the interrelationships existing between them and also combines conviction, belief, legislation and enforcement of this legislation'.[15]

Humans are seen as forming part of the universe, whose elements are complementary to one another in an integrated whole, but humankind has a special relationship to the other parts of nature, a relationship of utilization and development. The basic principle of the biosphere is that:

> God's wisdom has ordained to grant man inheritance on earth. Therefore, in addition to being part of the earth and part of the universe, man is also the executor of God's injunctions and commands. And as such he is a mere manager of the earth and not a proprietor; a beneficiary and not a disposer or ordainer. Man has been granted inheritance to manage and utilize the earth for his benefit, and for the fulfilment of his interests. He therefore has to keep, maintain and preserve it honestly, and has to act within the limits dictated by honesty.[16]

Accordingly, each generation is entitled to use nature to the extent that it does not disrupt or upset the interests of future generations. Islamic principles thus envisage the protection and conservation of basic natural elements, making protection, conservation and development of the environment and natural resources a mandatory religious duty of every Muslim.[17] Any deliberate or intentional damage to the natural environment and resources is forbidden. In conclusion, the study proposes Islamic legislative rules to serve as the foundation of procedures and measures necessary for the protection and conservation of the environment.

Ancient Buddhist chronicles, dating to the third century B.C., record a sermon on Buddhism in which the son of the Emperor Asoka of India stated that

---

14 ibid, para. 95.

15 'Islamic Principles for the Conservation of the Natural Environment', IUCN Environmental Policy and Law Paper No. 20 (1983), p. 9.

16 ibid at 45.

17 ibid at 20.

'the birds of the air and the beasts have as equal a right to live and move about in any part of the land as thou. The land belongs to the people and all living beings; thou art only the guardian of it'.[18] Subsequently, the King initiated a legal system which continued to provide sanctuaries for wild animals into the eighteenth century.

The religious beliefs of indigenous peoples also contain precepts on respect for all life and impose duties on individuals and the community to avoid waste or harm.[19] According to one commentator, 'indigenous peoples unanimously emphasize the spiritual nature of their relationship with the land or earth, which is basic to their existence and to their beliefs, customs, traditions, and culture'.[20] The special relationship (of both material and spiritual nature) between indigenous peoples and their land has been reaffirmed by regional human rights courts in a number of instances where the integrity of their surrounding environment was at stake (see later Chapter 15).[21]

1.2 *Utilitarianism*

Alongside the traditions just discussed, strong anthropocentric approaches can be found in the majority of cultural traditions. In antiquity, Protagoras proclaimed '[m]an is the measure of all things'.[22] Even enlightenment philosophers such as Kant asserted that '[m]an is the ultimate purpose of creation here on Earth'.[23] From this perspective, human self-interest is the sole justification for environmental protection.

Many early treaties had a utilitarian or anthropocentric orientation based on the centrality of human dominance and humankind's unlimited right to exploit nature, found in some religious doctrines and philosophy. Utilitarianism

---

18 The Mahavamsa, or the Great Chronicle of Ceylon, Chap. 14, quoted in I.C.J., *Case Concerning the Gabçikovo-Nagymaros Project* (Hungary/Slovakia), Sep. Op. of Judge C. Weeremantry, n. 41.

19 See J. Baird Callicott, 'Traditional American Indian and Western European Attitudes Toward Nature: An Overview' (1982) 4 Envtl Ethics 293; Johnson D. Hughes, *American Indian Ecology* (Texas Western 1983).

20 Hurst Hannum, 'New Developments in Indigenous Rights' (1988) 18 Va J Int'l L. 649, 666.

21 See e.g. *Case of the Mayagna (Sumo) Awas Tingni Community v Nicaragua* (Judgement) [2001] IACHR Series C No. 79, para. 149; *Case of the Saramaka People v Suriname* (Judgement) [2007] IACHR Series C No. 185, paras. 85–96; *Case of the Indigenous People Kichwa of Sarayaku v. Ecuador* (Judgement) [2012] IACHR Series C No. 145 para. 145; *Case of the Kuna Indigenous People of Madungandí and the Emberá Indigenous People of Bayano and their members v. Panama* (Judgement) [2014] IACHR Series C No. 284 paras. 111–13; *Kaliña and Lokono People v. Suriname* (Judgement) [2015] IACHR Series C No. 328 paras. 129–32.

22 Quoted in John Rodman, 'The Dolphin Papers' (1974) 259 North American Review 12, 16.

23 Immanuel Kant, *Critique of Judgment* (Macmillan 1916) 92.

grounds environmental protection on the well-being of humans, seeing nature primarily or only as a means to enhance the quality of human life and the satisfaction of human needs. Some early environmental agreements thus stressed the protection of resources 'useful' to man and the destruction of non-useful living creatures. A notable example is the 1902 Convention on the Protection of Birds Useful to Agriculture, which was designed to protect only those species of birds that were instrumental to protecting crops.[24] The same utilitarian approach characterized the first international environmental disputes, such as the *Fur Seals Bering Sea* Arbitration and the *Trail Smelter* Arbitration.[25] In fact, economic interests, rather than genuine environmental concerns, underpinned both disputes: the economic exploitability of fur seals (rather than their conservation) in the former and the impact of sulphur dioxide emissions on crops and cattle (rather than on air quality) in the latter. Early environmental laws also tended to focus on pollution, because of its impact on human health, and only later addressed issues of endangered species and protection of biological diversity. Even today, air pollution agreements express the idea that the negative effects of such pollution on humans is the reason why action must be taken.[26]

One of the central texts of international environmental law, the 1972 Stockholm Declaration 'on the Human Environment', reflects a utilitarian approach. As a matter of fact, its preamble emphasizes that 'Man is both creature and moulder of his environment, which gives him physical sustenance and affords him the opportunity for intellectual, moral, social and spiritual growth' while its first principle incorporates an early formulation of what would later become known as the right to a healthy environment.[27] The 1992 Rio Declaration

---

24 Other examples include the 1900 Convention Designed to Ensure the Conservation of Various Species of Wild Animals in Africa, which are Useful to Man or Inoffensive and the 1946 International Convention for the Regulation of Whaling.

25 *Bering Sea Fur Seals Arbitration* (*United Kingdom v. United States*) (Award) [1983] RIAA Vol XXVIII 263–76. *Trail Smelter Arbitration* (*United States v. Canada*) (Award) [1941]3 RIAA 1905.

26 This is not to minimize the detrimental effects of air pollution on human health. According to the United Nations Environment Programme (UNEP), 'Air pollution is the most important environmental contributor to the global burden of disease, leading to an estimated 6 million to 7 million premature deaths annually'. UNEP, *Global Environmental Outlook* 6 (2019) 108. These estimates are confirmed by the World Health Organisation (WHO). See WHO, *WHO Global Air Quality Guidelines* (2021). See also UNECE, 'The 2004 Substantive Report on the Review and Assessment of Air Pollution Effects and their Recorded Trends' UN Doc. EB.AIR/WG.1/2003/14, Rev. 1.

27 Stockholm Declaration, G. A. Res. 2994/XXVII UN Doc A/CONF.48/14/Rev 1 (Dec. 15, 1972), Preamble and Principle 1.

on Environment and Development, adopts a similar approach as it attempts to merge the goal of economic development with environmental protection. Its first principle proclaims that 'Human beings are at the centre of concerns for sustainable development. They are entitled to a healthy and productive life in harmony with nature'.[28] This approach was reinforced by the Political Declaration of the World Summit on Sustainable Development (WSSD), which emphasizes the importance of economic and social development, especially combating poverty,[29] as well as by the World Health Organization (WHO), on providing every individual with sufficient water of adequate quality by 2012. The 2030 Agenda for Sustainable Development, which was adopted in 2015 and established the Sustainable Development Goals (SDGs), goes in the same direction: the Agenda itself is defined as a '*people-centred* set of universal and transformative goals and targets' and recognizes that 'eradicating poverty in all its forms and dimensions, including extreme poverty, is the greatest global challenge and an indispensable requirement for sustainable development'.[30] In parallel to these developments, the right to a clean, healthy and sustainable environment, first formulated at Principle 1 of the Stockholm Declaration, found its way in more than 100 national constitutions, several regional human rights instruments, and was finally recognized as a universal human right by the Human Rights Council (HRC) and the United Nations General Assembly (UNGA) (see Chapter 15).

Part of the self-interest that humans see in environmental protection lies in the economic value of resources to humans. Whether it is a matter of monetizing the ecological services of honey bees or undertaking a cost-benefit analysis of combatting climate change, 'green' economists insist that natural resources should be considered according to their total economic value – that is, the cumulative economic value for humans of all aspects of a resource, not just its immediate consumptive value.

1.3 *Equity*[31]

It may be argued that equity plays a more important role in international environmental law than in any other area of international law. Issues of equity have

28 Rio Declaration, G. A. Res. 47/190 UN Doc A/CONF.151/26 (Dec. 22, 1992), Principle 1.

29 Political Declaration of the World Summit on Sustainable Development, G. A. Res. 1 A/CONF.199/20 (Sept. 2, 2002).

30 G. A. Res. 70/1 Transforming Our World: The 2030 Agenda for Sustainable Development (Sept. 25, 2015), para 2 (emphasis added).

31 For a fuller discussion of the role of equity in international environmental law, see Dinah Shelton, 'Equity' in Daniel Bodansky et al (eds), *Oxford Handbook of International Environmental Law* (Oxford University Press 2010).

become prominent in international environmental law for two main reasons. First, international environmental law involves limits on the use of resources – that is, how to conserve and allocate increasingly scarce or threatened shared natural resources and public goods, such as commercial fish stocks or international rivers and lakes. Assuming that states sharing resources form a community, conditions of scarcity within a community – where it is agreed that all are entitled to a share of the resource, and none is entitled to all of it – give rise to questions of equity as distributive justice. While all may agree that there should be a fair distribution, it is far more difficult, as discussed below, to attain agreement on what constitutes the fair method of allocation. The second reason for the prominence of equity is that environmental law imposes burdens and costs as it seeks to reduce the pollution that is the major cause of environmental degradation. It must allocate this burden among countries whose emission levels and capacities to reduce them differ greatly (intra-generational equity), as well as among present and future generations (inter-generational equity).

As a result, environmental ethicists construct environmental protection around concepts of equity and justice, as seen in three sets of relationships: among existing persons, between present and future generations, and between humans and other species.[32] In international law, equity is often used as a synonym for fairness or justice in both substance and procedures.[33] The procedural aspect is concerned with reaching decisions by the 'right process', while the substantive dimension aims at distributive justice.[34] The procedural and substantive dimensions of equity are often perceived as inter-related, based on the assumption that fairer proceedings lead to fairer outcomes.[35]

1.3.1 Intra-Generational Equity

The first ethical requirement is to assure justice among existing human beings. Beyond the protections of human rights law, discussed in Chapter 15, states and the international community must fairly allocate scarce resources to ensure

32 See Klaus Bosselman, *When Two World's Collide: Society and Ecology* (Rsvp Pub 1995); Christopher D. Stone, *The Gnat is Older Than Man: Global Environment and the Human Agenda* (Princeton University Press 1993); Roderick Nash, *The Rights of Nature: A History of Environmental Ethics* (University of Wisconsin Press 1989).

33 Thomas M. Franck, *Fairness in International Law and Institutions* (Clarendon Press 1995) 7–9.

34 ibid at 7.

35 Franck argues that the two dimensions are more likely to be in tension because procedural fairness favours stability and order while distributive justice strives for change to achieve a fair outcome. ibid.

that the benefits of environmental resources, the costs associated with protecting them, and any degradation that occurs (i.e. all the benefits and burdens) are equitably shared by all members of society. In this regard, environmental justice is an application of the principles of distributive justice as it seeks to reconcile competing social and economic policies in order to obtain equitable sharing of resources.

At the international level, some developing countries argue that they are bearing a disproportionate environmental burden due to the export of pollution from wealthier countries, while they are unable to share in the benefits derived from the activities producing the pollution. While developing states have the legal right to exercise their sovereignty to exclude hazardous enterprises, waste, and products, in practice they often lack clean substitutes or the material and human resources necessary to enforce their environmental laws, or to reject foreign investment activities that are harmful to the environment. In addition, some of these countries assert that they may be injured by future climate change to which they have largely not contributed and which is due to industrial and other processes from which they have not benefited. In their view, it is equitable for the cost of clean-up or reduction of pollution to be borne by those who were responsible for the origin of the problems.

At least since the 1972 Stockholm Conference on the Human Environment, international environmental law has sought to fairly allocate the benefits and burdens involved in natural resources and their protection, based on historic responsibility, capacity, and need. At Stockholm, poorer states asserted the greater responsibility of industrialized countries to remedy the environmental problems that the latter states were charged with creating. The Stockholm Declaration recognized that environmental protection is a major issue that affects the well-being of people and economic development throughout the world, affirming that environmental problems in developing countries are caused by a lack of development.[36] Principle 5 calls for sharing among all mankind the benefits from the use of non-renewable resources, while Principle 9 calls for the transfer of 'substantial quantities' of financial and technological assistance to supplement the domestic effort of developing countries to remedy environmental deficiencies. Several other principles call for particular attention to the needs of developing countries in meeting the costs of environmental safeguards (Principles 11 and 12).

Twenty years later, the Rio Declaration on Environment and Development echoed many of these principles and developed others in its effort to balance

36 On the causative link between underdevelopment and environmental degradation, see *Founex Report on Development and Environment* (1971).

the two elements in its title. The term 'sustainable development' itself can be seen as encompassing an international understanding of intra-generational (as well as inter-generational) equity in its effort to strike a fair balance between the often-conflicting goals of economic development and environmental protection. Indeed, many of the principles in the Rio Declaration on Environment and Development reflect this balance. Principle 3 of this declaration refers to the 'right to development', which is to be fulfilled so as to equitably meet the developmental and environmental needs of present and future generations. Principle 6 calls for giving special priority to the situation and needs of developing countries, particularly the least developed and those most environmentally vulnerable. While these principles focus on elements of need as a basis for distributive justice, Principle 7 shifts to take into account responsibility and capacity:

> In view of the different contributions to global environmental degradation, States have common but differentiated responsibilities. The developed countries acknowledge the responsibility that they bear in the international pursuit of sustainable development in view of the pressures their societies place on the global environment and of the technologies and financial resources they command.[37]

Thus, the declaration identifies at least three factors that could be taken into account in the equitable allocation of benefits and burdens: need, responsibility, and capacity.

The principle of common but differentiated responsibilities (CBDR) deserves special attention when discussing intra-generational equity. It should be first noted that this principle does not result in a specific outcome in weighing the different factors relevant to equity. Instead, it reflects a multifaceted approach, with most formulations referring to different historical responsibilities, capacities, and needs. Given this, states may plead for recognition of acquired rights or prior uses. In response, other states could stress the polluter pays principle, the principle of good neighbourliness, or the needs of its population as a basis for limiting activities, even when there are acquired rights. Where such conflicts arise in negotiations, states may agree upon priorities or select one or

37 Lavanya Rajamani, *Differential Treatment in International Environmental Law* (Oxford University Press 2006). Philippe Cullet, 'Principle 7: Common but Differentiated Responsibilities', in Jorge E. Viñuales (ed.), *The Rio Declaration on Environment and Development* (Oxford University Press 2015).

more of the factors to be the basis of decisions. Failure to agree may lead to long-term disputes over determining a fair allocation of resources or burdens.

All of the texts adopted at Rio include some formulation of the principle of CBDR. Principles 6 and 7 of the Rio Declaration are particularly important in affording priority to the needs of the least developed and most environmentally vulnerable states while expressing the general principle of common but differentiated responsibilities. The latter principle was especially controversial, with neither developed nor developing countries satisfied with the result.[38] The United States issued an interpretive statement indicating its view that the principle does not 'imply a recognition ... of any international obligations'.[39] The legal status of CBDR is, in fact, not entirely clear. It is referred to explicitly and applied in several multilateral environmental agreements, but whether it is a fundamental principle of international environmental law, a bundle of some or all of the above factors that lead to equitable decision-making, or itself a rule of equity remains debated. Its formulation could encompass, and in some formulations has encompassed, the notion of the historic responsibility of the North for most environmental degradation used to achieve its wealth. In this sense, the principle of CBDR appears as a legal concept involving redistribution of wealth because the North took a disproportionate amount of the Earth's environmental goods. Principle 7 of the Rio Declaration, however, speaks not of historical responsibility but rather of the responsibility of developed countries for the present and future pursuit of sustainable development in view of the pressures their societies are placing on the global environment and on the resources they command.

In the context of the Montreal Protocol, negotiator Richard Benedick observed at least three possible interpretations of the principle: (1) a justifiable effort to achieve equity (distributive justice) between richer and poorer states in general; (2) a formula for balancing the performance of developing countries according to the technological and financial assistance given to them; and (3) an opportunity for developing countries to extract the maximum

38 The Group of 77 had proposed a stronger formulation: 'The major cause of the continuing deterioration of the global environment is the unsustainable patterns of production and consumption, particularly in developed countries ... In view of their main historical and current responsibility for global environmental degradation and their capability to address the common concern, developed countries shall provide adequate, new, and additional financial resources and environmentally sound technologies on preferential and concessional terms to developing countries to enable them to achieve sustainable development.' UN Doc. /CONF.151/PC/WG.III/L.20/REV.1 (1992).

39 UN Doc. A/CONF.151/26 (Vol. IV) (1992) 20.

possible transfer of wealth as a precondition for accepting responsibility for protecting the environment (potentially because of historical responsibility).[40] Given the many factors involved in determining equity, it is not surprising that when developing countries look at past actions of the developed states, they see historical responsibility for the harm done, while developed countries see prior entitlement (this debate could be considered to fall within the scope of inter-generational equity). Looking forward, developing countries assert their present and future needs, while developed countries point to the wealth of biological resources predominately found in the developing world. The ambiguities involved in the principle of common but differentiated responsibilities make it essential to observe how it and other equitable principles can be implemented in practice to reduce disagreements in these perspectives of the North and the South. The CBDR principle plays a critical role in the climate change regime (see Chapter 12).[41] Not only is this principle enshrined in several provisions of the key climate law instruments, but it informs the overall architecture of the regime. The United Nations Framework Convention on Climate Change (UNFCCC) clearly states that the Parties 'should protect the climate system … on the basis of equity and in accordance with their common but differentiated responsibilities and respective capabilities' (Preamble).[42] Accordingly, the UNFCCC provides for common commitments (Article 4.1), shared by all Parties to the convention, and differentiated commitments (Article 4.2) in that only Parties included in Annex I commit to reduce their emissions. Further differentiation exists within Annex I countries and within non-Annex I countries (Arts. 4.3 and 4.8). The Paris Agreement remains faithful to the principle of CBDR but constructs it in a different way, by allowing each country to determine its own emission reduction targets on the basis of their responsibilities and capabilities (Art. 3).

40 Richard E. Benedick, *Ozone Diplomacy: New Directions in Safeguarding the Planet* (Harvard University Press 1998) 24.

41 Lavanya Rajamani, 'The Principle of Common but Differentiated Responsibilities and Respective Capabilities in the International Climate Change Regime' in Rosemary Lyster & Robert R.M. Verchick (eds), *Research Handbook on Climate Disaster Law* (Edward Elgar 2019).

42 See also United Nations Framework Convention on Climate Change (May 9, 1992) (hereinafter UNFCCC), Art. 3.1. See Paris Agreement (Dec. 12, 2015), Preamble, Arts. 2.2, 4.3, and 4.19.

1.3.2 Inter-Generational Equity: Rights of Future Generations

Humanity's concern with long-term human survival underlies legal and social norms and may be grounded in a genetic or biological imperative.[43] Interest in survival of the human species requires that 'humanity' be seen to include not only present but also future generations.[44] As UN Secretary-General Ban-Ki Moon observed in 2015, 'dedication to future generations is a universal value, visible across countries and cultures'.[45]

Concern for future generations can thus be seen as implicit in all that touches environmental protection and the preservation of natural resources, reflected in the requirement that development be sustainable. Inter-generational equity is based on the recognition of two key facts: (1) that human life emerged from, and is dependent upon, the Earth's natural resource base, including its ecological processes, and is thus inseparable from environmental conditions; and (2) that human beings have a unique capacity to alter the environment upon which life depends.

From these facts emerges the notion that humans who are alive today have a special obligation as custodians or trustees of the planet to maintain its integrity to ensure the survival of the human species. Those living have received a heritage from their forbearers in which they have beneficial rights of use that are limited by the interests and needs of future generations. This limitation requires each generation to maintain the corpus of the trust and pass it on in no worse condition than it was received. Another way to consider the issue is to view current environmental goods, wealth, and technology as owing to the progress of prior generations. This debt cannot be discharged backward, so it is projected forward and discharged in the present on behalf of the future.

The concept of trust involves understanding the relationships between the trust corpus, the trustees and beneficiaries, and the obligations imposed on the latter. Generally, these obligations require conserving and maintaining the trust resources, thus placing constraints on the present generation of beneficiaries. Meeting the obligation does not mean that no change is possible, but it does call for minimizing or avoiding long-term and irreversible damage to the environment. The implications of the principle of inter-generational equity

---

43 See Margaret Gruter, 'The Origins of Legal Behavior' (1979) 2(1) J. Social Biol. Struct. 43; Elliott White, *Sociobiology and Human Politics* (Lexington Brooks 1981); Margaret Gruter & Paul Bohannan (eds), *Law, Biology & Culture* (Ross Erikson 1983).

44 For further elaboration see Edith Brown Weiss, *In Fairness to Future Generations* (Brill 1988).

45 Intergenerational Justice Crucial to Post-2015 Development Agenda, Secretary-General Tells Law Conference, https://www.un.org/press/en/2014/sgsm15959.doc.htm (last accessed 14 April 2025).

are three: first, that each generation is required to conserve the diversity of the natural and cultural resource base so that it does not unduly restrict the options available to future generations to satisfy their own values and needs. Second, the quality of ecological processes passed on should be comparable to that enjoyed by the present generation. Third, the past and present cultural and natural heritage should be conserved so that future generations will have access to it. These rights and obligations derive from a notion of human society that extends beyond the totality of the current planetary population, giving it a temporal dimension.

International environmental texts have referred to the need to conserve the natural heritage of humankind for the benefit of present and future generations, at least since the International Convention for the Regulation of Whaling. Principle 2 of the 1972 Stockholm Declaration on the Human Environment endorsed a concern with future generations, stating: 'The natural resources of the earth, including the air, water, and flora and fauna and especially representative samples of natural ecosystems, must be safeguarded for the benefit of present and future generations through careful planning or management, as appropriate'. The same year, the UNESCO World Heritage Convention included a reference to future generations.[46] Particularly significant is Article 3 (1) of the UNFCCC which declares that '[t]he parties should protect the climate system for the benefit of present and future generations of humankind'.

More broadly, inter-generational equity is inherent in the concept of sustainable development. The 1987 Report of the Brundtland Commission, which introduced the concept of sustainable development, defined it as a development that 'meets the needs of the present without compromising the ability of

46 Other recent texts mentioning future generations include the 1973 Convention on International Trade in Endangered Species of Wild Fauna and Flora; 1976 Convention for the Mediterranean Sea; 1976 Convention on the Conservation of Nature in the South Pacific; 1977 Convention on the Prohibition of Military or Any Other Hostile Use of Environmental Modification Techniques; 1978 Kuwait Regional Convention; 1979 Convention on the Conservation of European Wildlife and Natural Habitats; 1979 Convention on the Conservation of Migratory Species of Wild Animals; 1983 Convention for the Wider Caribbean Region; 1985 ASEAN Agreement on the Conservation of Nature and Natural Resources; 1992 Convention on Biological Diversity; 1992 UN Framework Convention on Climate Change; 1994 UN Convention to Combat Desertification; and 1997 United Nations Convention on the Law of the Non-Navigable Uses of International Watercourses. The same concept appears in United Nations General Assembly resolutions. See, e.g., Protection of global climate for present and future generations of mankind, G.A. Res. 43/53, Dec. 6, 1988, U.N. Doc. A/Res/43/53 of Jan. 27, 1989.

future generations to meet their own needs'.[47] The 1992 Rio Declaration echoed this approach to sustainable development by declaring, at Principle 3, that 'the right to development must be fulfilled so as to equitably meet developmental and environmental needs of present and future generations'. Concretely, the rights of future humanity may be encompassed in the concept of sustainable development, deemed to include the attainment of economic, social and cultural rights. The realization of such rights requires the availability of natural resources over an indefinite period of time and includes not only material resources that are essential to the survival of humankind and those that serve to enrich it, but also ecosystems, life-support processes, and biological diversity. The enjoyment of cultural rights necessarily includes the conservation of basic elements of civilization, including wild flora and fauna, landscapes and natural sites. This broad interpretation of economic, social and cultural rights reflects the interests of present and future humanity.

This principle of inter-generational equity has been also recognized in the case law of international courts. The International Court of Justice (ICJ), for instance, in its *Advisory Opinion on the Legality of the Threat or Use of Nuclear Weapons*, specified that the environment 'is not an abstraction but represents the living space, the quality of life and the very health of human beings, *including generations unborn*'.[48] Similarly, in the *Gabčikovo-Nagymaros Project* case, the Court acknowledged that 'new [environmental] norms and standards have been developed' precisely to address the risks that human activities pose for the environment for both 'present and future generations'.[49]

On the basis of these treaty provisions, declarations, resolutions and judicial decisions, it is possible to conclude that each generation may benefit from and develop the natural and cultural patrimony inherited from previous generations, but then must pass it on to future generations in no worse condition than it was received. This is not a completely satisfactory approach, however, over the long term. It is not clear how the same amount of space, wilderness, clean water, and biological diversity can be guaranteed to endless generations of increasingly larger numbers of individuals. It is also impossible to anticipate the preferences of future generations.

---

47 Report of the World Commission on Environment and Development: Our Common Future, UN Doc. A/42/427, Annex, 4 August 1986, para. 27.

48 *Legality of the Threat or Use of Nuclear* Weapons (Advisory Opinion) [1996] ICJ Rep 226, para. 29 (emphasis added).

49 *Gabčikovo-Nagymaros Project (Hungary v. Slovakia)* (Judgement) [1997] ICJ Rep 3, para. 140.

A recognition of the rights of future generations also raises the problems of defining a generation and means of implementing such rights. The concept of a generation is not clear. Based on average life expectancy and reproductive patterns, the time-span of a human generation has been taken to be thirty years, but there are significant differences in both of these elements between individuals and between industrialized and developing countries. In fact, there are no distinct generations, because at each moment hundreds of human beings born and die, with the result that some eight billion people co-exist. In law, therefore, it is perhaps more logical to speak of future humanity (rather than future generations), as the holder of rights, and to recognize humanity, including its present and future members, as a collective legal person. National and international law already recognize various entities as legal persons, from the state and other levels of government to corporations. The same capacity could be afforded humanity as a whole, although this does raise the problem of who might represent it.

International instruments provide little guidance on representation and implementation of the rights of future humanity, but domestic legal systems offer some guidance. Indeed, pleading the concept of intergenerational equity before domestic courts has at times yielded substantive developments beyond its 'important rhetorical role'.[50] One of the most notable examples is the Philippine Supreme Court decision in *Minors Oposa v. Secretary of the Department of Environment and Natural Resources*.[51] Nearly three dozen minors, represented by their parents and an association, sought an order requiring the government to discontinue existing timber licenses, and restraining it from issuing new licenses. Their petition was based on the allegation that deforestation was causing environmental damage. The Court ruled that the plaintiffs had standing to represent their as yet unborn progeny and that they had adequately asserted a right to a balanced and healthy ecology. It also declared that 'the minors' assertion of their right to a sound environment constitutes, at the same time, the performance of their obligation to ensure the protection of that right for the generations to come'.[52] The decision provides an example of how rights of future generations might be enforced in practice. Internationally, the task of ensuring the rights of future humanity could be conferred upon an independent international authority, such as an international environmental

50 Lydia Slobodian, 'Defending the Future: Intergenerational Equity in Climate Litigation' (2020) 32 Georgetown Environmental Law Review 569, 577.

51 *Minors Oposa v. Secretary of the Department of Environment and Natural Resources* (Supreme Court of the Philippines) 33 I.L.M. 168 (1994).

52 ibid.

agency or ombudsman. More recently, the Colombian Supreme Court in *Future Generations v. Ministry of Environment* ordered 'the construction of an "inter-generational pact for the life of the Colombian Amazon"', to be formulated by the Colombian government in consultation with affected communities and scientific organizations.[53] Finally, as affirmed by the Dutch Supreme Court in its 2019 *Urgenda* judgment, climate change is an example of an environmental threat which demonstrates that 'the current generation of Dutch nationals, in particular but not limited to the youngest individuals in this group, will have to deal with the adverse effects of climate change in their lifetime if global emissions of greenhouse gases are not adequately reduced'.[54]

1.3.3 Inter-Species Equity

Inter-species equity emerges from and enhances respect for the intrinsic value of nature independently of its utility to humans. It posits a non-hierarchical view of human relations with other species. Precursors of this concept can be seen in those constitutions, laws, and international instruments that require the humane treatment of living creatures.[55]

Since the beginning of the 1970s, some theorists have suggested that the legal personality of certain components of the environment, such as trees or animals, could be recognized.[56] Movements for recognition of 'animal or biotic rights' are increasingly evident, motivated by ethical considerations and concerns about the continued decline of biological diversity at an alarming rate.[57] The comprehensive philosophical worldviews encompassed by the 'deep ecology' and the animal rights movements could imply profound changes in law and policy.

---

53 Radicación n.° 11001-22-03-000-2018-00319-01; STC4360-2018, 5 April 2018 ("3. Decision"), (unofficial English translation).

54 *Urgenda Foundation v. The State of the Netherlands* (Dutch Supreme Court) Dec. 20, 2019, para 4.7.

55 See e.g. Art. 32 of the Constitution of the German Land of Thuringen, 'Animals are to be respected as living beings and fellow creatures. They will be protected from treatment inappropriate to the species and from avoidable suffering'. International and national legal texts have long protected species from inhumane treatment. See the 1968 European Convention on the Protection of Animals during International Transport, and the 1979 Convention on the Conservation of European Wildlife and Natural Habitats, E.T.S. 104.

56 Christopher D. Stone, 'Should Trees Have Standing? Towards Legal Rights for Natural Objects' (1974) 45 S.Cal. L.Rev. 450; Christopher D. Stone, 'Should Trees Have Standing Revisited: How Far Will Law and Morals Reach? A Pluralist Perspective' (1985) 59 S.Cal L. Rev. 1. See also Justice William O. Douglas' dissenting opinion in the landmark environmental law case *Sierra Club v. Morton*, 405 U.S. 727 (USSC 1972), at 741–43.

57 See David S. Favre, 'Wildlife Rights: The Ever-Widening Circle' (1979) 9 Envtl. L. 279.

The concept of nature's rights and legal personality has been proposed in a variety of formulations, from legally enforceable rights, to 'biotic rights' as moral imperatives, to human responsibilities and duties towards nature.[58] Giving legal recognition to the intrinsic value of nature, by adding new 'subjects' of law, is one far-reaching proposal. Some argue that this has already occurred,[59] while others object that the ascription of rights to nature anthropomorphizes it to its detriment.[60] Still others view rights-conferring as one tool to enhance the value of nature. All recognize that legal personality is a policy decision, not a biological one.[61] In international law, states and intergovernmental organizations have legal personality; in domestic law, business and charitable organizations, municipalities and other government bodies are recognized as legal persons.[62] One basis for personhood rests on the interests of the entity in question. Another basis consists of the interests of human persons.[63]

A number of different factors have been proposed as a basis for according legal status.[64] Characteristics that have been used, either singly or in combination, include: biological life, genetic humanness, brain development, ability to feel pain, consciousness/sentience, ability to communicate, ability to form relationships, higher reasoning ability, and rationality. According to the prominent legal philosopher Joel Feinberg, an entity must have interests to have moral status.[65] Steinbock adds that 'interests' is a term of art which refers to the capacity of an entity to have a stake in things, and this capacity is contingent

58 Dinah Shelton, 'Nature as a Legal Person' (2015) OpenEdition Journals 22 (September). Daniel P. Corrigan & Markku Oksanen, *Rights of Nature: A Re-Examination* (Routledge 2021).

59 See Anthony D'Amato & Sudhir Chopra, 'Whales: Their Emerging Right to Life' (991) 85 AJIL 21.

60 See Cynthia Giagnocavo & Howard Goldstein, 'Laws Reform or World Re-Form' (1990) 35 McGill L. J. 346.

61 Byrn v. N.Y. City Health & Hosp. Corp., 286 N.E.2d 887, 889 (N.Y. 1972) ('It is not true … that the legal order necessarily corresponds to the natural order …; it is a policy determination whether legal personality should attach and not a question of biological or "natural" correspondence').

62 Jessica Berg, 'Of Elephants and Embryos: A Proposed Framework for Legal Personhood' (2007) 59 Hastings L.J. 369.

63 ibid.

64 Jane English, 'Abortion and the Concept of a Person' (1975) V(2) Canadian Journal of Philosophy, 234–35 (noting that no single criterion can capture the concept of a person but that a '"person" is a cluster of features, of which rationality, having a self-concept and being conceived of humans are only part').

65 Joel Feinberg, *Harm to Others* (Oxford University Press 1984) 34.

on the entity being sentient, or consciously aware.[66] In this sense, 'interests' refers to an entity having 'a sake or welfare of its own' and 'the expression ... is intended to emphasize the stake that conscious, sentient beings have in their own well-being'.[67]

The recognition of the rights of nature has taken various forms over the years, including constitutional provisions, national laws, municipal ordinances, and judicial decisions.[68] In 2008, Ecuador became the first country in the world to declare in its constitution that nature is a legal person.[69] Articles 10 and 71–74 of this constitution recognize the inalienable rights of ecosystems, give individuals the authority to petition on the behalf of ecosystems, and require the government to remedy violations of nature's rights, including 'the right to exist, persist, maintain and regenerate its vital cycles, structure, functions and its processes in evolution'.[70] Many of these provisions have been tested in court. In a 2011 case involving a highway construction project that damaged the Vilcabamba River, 'the court found that the river's constitutional rights had been violated, and ordered the government to carry out restoration activities'.[71] Ecuador subsequently incorporated the rights of nature in many of

66 Bonnie Steinbock, *Life Before Birth: The Moral and Legal Status of Embryos and Fetuses* (Oxford University Press 1992) 40–41.

67 ibid 18–20.

68 David R. Boyd, 'Recognizing the Rights of Nature: Lofty Rhetoric or Legal Revolution?' (2018) 32(4) Natural Resources & Environment 1, 13. Several American municipalities (including Pittsburgh, Pennsylvania; Santa Monica, California; Mora County, New Mexico; Athens, Ohio; and Mountain Lake Park, Maryland) have passed ordinances recognizing that nature has rights, and many of such ordinances have been tested in court. See e.g. Pa. Gen. Energy (PGE) v. Grant Twp., Case No. 1:14-cv-00209-JFM (W.D. Pa., Aug. 8, 2014); Pa. Gen. Energy (PGE) v. Grant Twp., 139 F. Supp. 3d 706 (W.D. Pa. 2015); Pa. Gen. Energy (PGE) v. Grant Twp., Case No. 1:14-cv-00209-SPB, 2017 WL 1215444 (W.D. Pa. Mar. 31, 2017); Seneca Resources Corp. v. Highland Twp., Case No. 1:16-CV-289 (W.D. Pa.).

69 2008 Constitution of the Republic of Ecuador. Political Database of the Americas (PDBA), http://pdba.georgetown.edu/Constitutions/Ecuador/english08.html. *Wheeler c. Director de la Procuraduria General Del Estado de Loja* was the first case to invoke the Ecuadoran constitutional provisions. See Erin Daly, 'Ecuadorian Exemplar: The First Ever Vindications of Constitutional Rights' (2012) 21(1) Review of European Community & International Environmental Law 63.

70 Ecuador Constitution, Article 71.

71 Boyd, 'Recognizing the Rights of Nature' (n 68) 15. R.F. Wheeler and E.G. Huddle v. Attorney Gen. of the State of Loja, (2011) Judgment No. 11121-2011-0010 (Loja Provincial Court of Justice Mar. 30, 2011). See Daly, 'The Ecuadorian Exemplar' (n 69). Craig M. Kauffman & Pamela L. Martin, 'Can Rights of Nature Make Development More Sustainable? Why Some Ecuadorian Lawsuits Succeed and Others Fail' (2017) 92 World Development 130.

its laws including its criminal code and its environmental code.[72] Bolivia followed Ecuador in 2009 by similarly giving Constitutional protection to natural ecosystems, in order to override the immediate interests of residents. The constitutional amendment gives nature equal rights to humans. The 2010 Law of Mother Earth (*Ley de Derechos de la Madre Tierra,* Law 071) first implemented the amendment by redefining the country's mineral deposits as 'blessings' and establishing new rights for nature. The law proclaimed the creation of the *Defensoría de la Madre Tierra* a counterpart to the human rights ombudsman office (the *Defensoría del Pueblo*). Nature's rights include: the right to life and to exist; the right to continue vital cycles and processes free from human alteration; the right to pure water and clean air; the right to ecological balance; the right to the effective and opportune restoration of life systems affected by direct or indirect human activities; and the right for preservation of Mother Earth and any of its components with regards to toxic and radioactive waste generated by human activities. In October 2012, Bolivia enacted an expanded version of the 2010 law. The *Framework Law on Mother Earth and Integral Development for Living Well* recognizes Mother Earth as a 'living dynamic system', and grants it comprehensive legal rights that are comparable to human rights.

While Ecuador and Bolivia recognize the rights of 'Mother Earth', other countries, such as Bangladesh, Colombia, India and New Zealand recognize the rights of specific ecosystems, rivers and forests. A case report and agreement (*Tutohu Whakatupua*) from the New Zealand Whanganui Tribunal concerning the Whanganui River established legal personhood for the river, with the river's rights to be enforced through judicial action by appointed guardians.[73] The law based on the agreement reflects that the river is 'a living entity in its own right … incapable of being "owned" in an absolute sense'.[74]

The legal status of animals continues to evolve. During the Middle Ages in Europe, it was widely accepted that animals could be held responsible for the commission of crimes.[75] Several hundred trials are recorded of pigs, donkeys, dogs, and other animals that lived in close proximity to humans. Recent scholarly and activist attention has been devoted to questioning whether some or

72 National Assembly, Republic of Ecuador, Comprehensive Criminal Code, Feb. 3, 2014; National Assembly, Republic of Ecuador, Environmental Code, Dec. 21, 2016.

73 Whanganui River Management Trust Board, Record of Understanding in Relation to Whanganui River Settlement – Whanganui Iwi and the Crown (signed Oct. 13, 2011).

74 Tutohu Whakatupua, Aug. 30, 2012, para. 2.7.1.

75 Katie Sykes, 'Human Drama, Animal Trials: What The Medieval Animal Trials Can Teach Us About Justice For Animals' (2011) 17 Animal L. 273; Jen Girgen, 'The Historical and Contemporary Prosecution and Punishment of Animals' (2003) 9 Animal L. 97.

all living species should be recognized as legal persons.[76] The international 'Great Ape Project' seeks to imbue non-human primates with attributes of legal personhood – specifically 'protections of the right to life, the freedom from arbitrary deprivation of liberty, and protection from torture'.[77] Spain responded when its parliament's environmental committee voted in 2008 to approve principles committing Spain to the Great Ape Project.[78] Proposals and lawsuits have also sought to confer personhood on cetaceans. A few recent judicial decisions in a number of jurisdictions (including Argentina and Germany) have begun to acknowledge animal rights.[79] A notable example is a 2014 decision of the Indian Supreme Court, which recognized fundamental animal rights under the Indian Constitution.[80]

Among international instruments, the preamble of the 1979 Bern Convention on the Conservation of European Wildlife and Natural Habitats was one of the first to express a basis of environmental protection in the intrinsic value of nature: 'Recognizing that wild flora and fauna constitute a natural heritage of aesthetic, scientific, cultural, recreational, economic, and intrinsic value that needs to be preserved and handed on to future generations'.[81] The text demonstrates an integrated approach: the natural heritage presents a certain number of qualities important for humanity, but these do not diminish nature's inherent value. Just one year prior, in 1978, The Universal Declaration of Animal Rights was solemnly proclaimed in Paris at the UNESCO headquarters, and later made public in 1990.[82] The contracting parties to the 1992

76 See e.g. Tom Regan. *Defending Animal Rights* (University of Illinois Press 2001). Gary E. Varner, *In Nature's Interests? Interests, Animal Rights, and Environmental Ethics*. Environmental Ethics and Science Policy Series (Oxford University Press 1998). Anne Peters, *Animals in International Law* (Brill Nijhoff 2021). Saskia Stucki, 'Towards a Theory of Legal Animal Rights: Simple and Fundamental Rights' (2020) 40(3) Oxford Journal of Legal *Studies* 533.

77 See GAP: Great Ape Project, The Great Ape Project: An Idea, A Book, An Organization, http://www.greatapeproject.org (last visited 14 April 2025).

78 Thomas Catan, 'Apes Get Legal Rights in Spain, to Surprise of Bullfight Critics' *The Times* (London, 27 June 2008).

79 Argentina: Tercer Juzgado de Garantías Mendoza, case no. P-72.254/15, 3 November 2016 – Chimpanzee Cecilia. LG Magdeburg, Az. 28 Ns 182 Js 32201/14 (74/17), 28 Ns 74/17, judgment of 11 October 2017.

80 Supreme Court of India, Animal Welfare Board of India v. Nagaraja and others, Civil appeal no. 5387, 7 May 2014. See most recently also High Court of Punjab and Haryana at Chandighar, CRR 533–2013, judgment of 31 May 2019.

81 Preamble, para. 3, Convention on the Conservation of European Wildlife and Natural Habitats (Bern, Sept. 19, 1979), E.T.S. 104; U.K.T.S. 56 (1982), Cmd. 8738.

82 Jean-Marc Neumann, 'The Universal Declaration of Animal Rights or the Creation of a New Equilibrium Between Species' (2013) 19 Animal L. 91.

Convention on Biological Diversity similarly profess that they are '[c]onscious of the intrinsic value of biological diversity and of the ecological, genetic, social, economic, scientific, educational, cultural, recreational and aesthetic values of biological diversity and its components'.[83] Given the lack of legal status for components of the environment despite recognition of their intrinsic and independent value, an integrated approach best creates a foundation for environmental protection. The first phrases of the preamble of the World Charter for Nature set out such an approach: 'Mankind is a part of nature and life depends on the uninterrupted functioning of natural systems which ensure the supply of energy and nutrients …'.

The intrinsic value of the biosphere is not rejected but is integrated with an understanding that humans make up part of the universe and cannot exist without conservation of the biosphere and the ecosystems comprising it. In this perspective, all components of the environment have a value not only in their short-term utility to humans, as the earlier exclusively utilitarian approach would have it, but also as indispensable elements of an interrelated system which must be protected.[84] While the aim of human survival remains anthropocentric, humans are not viewed as apart from or above the natural universe, but as a linked and interdependent part of it. It follows that because all parts of the natural web are linked, they must all be protected and conserved. It is in this sense that 'intrinsic value' may be understood.[85]

1.3.4 The Application of Equity in Practice: Some Concluding Remarks

The International Court of Justice has applied equity primarily within rules that call for its application or to interpret or fill in gaps in existing law (*praeter legem*). Most of these cases concern resource allocation, where it is clear that the international community has determined that elements of distributive justice should play a role. In the *Case Concerning the Continental Shelf*

---

83 Preamble, para. 1, Convention on Biological Diversity (Rio de Janeiro, June 5, 1992), 31 I.L.M. 818 (1992). Other international treaties that take into account the intrinsic value of nature include the 1980 Convention for the Conservation of Antarctic Marine Living Resources, the 1991 Protocol to the Antarctic Treaty on Environmental Protection, and the 1973 CITES.

84 See Laurence H. Tribe, 'Ways not to Think About Plastic Trees: New Foundations for Environmental Law' (1974) 83 Yale L.J. 1315.

85 There are no doubt other philosophical and ethical foundations to the conservation movement, some of which may lead to conflicting approaches. Similar problems exist in other areas of the law. During the drafting of the Universal Declaration of Human Rights, Jacques Maritain confessed that agreement could be reached on a catalogue of human rights so long as no attempt was made to agree on *why* human rights should be protected.

(*Tunisia/Libya*), the ICJ called equity a legal concept that is a direct emanation of the idea of justice, which it is bound to apply as a general principle of law in achieving an equitable or just solution to a case.[86] In delimiting maritime boundaries, the ICJ has indicated that tribunals 'will always have regard to equity *infra legem*, that is, that form of equity which constitutes a method of interpretation of the law in force, and is one of its attributes'.[87]

The ICJ aims to avoid purely subjective views of justice between the parties when it makes use of equitable principles in a case. The ICJ decided the *North Sea Continental Shelf* case, 'in accordance with equitable principles' as a matter of customary international law.[88] Subsequently, it described

> the justice of which equity is an emanation is [...] justice according to the rule of law: which is to say that its application should display consistency and a degree of predictability; even though it looks with particularity to the more peculiar circumstances in an instant case, it also looks beyond it to principles of more general application.[89]

This passage suggests that the court seeks a degree of legal certainty in its choice and application of norms, but it must take into account the facts, the situations, and the specific interests or claims of the parties. Equitable norms themselves provide no guidance in selecting among the various facts or factors that could weigh in the decision. Thus, an element of subjectivity is probably present in all efforts to achieve an equitable result.

In general, equity suggests that imposing equal obligations on subjects of law that are unequal in relevant ways may be unjust if they exacerbate inequalities or impose unfair burdens on those least able to bear them. Legal systems often seek therefore to base the distribution of goods and the burdens of society according to the principle of distributive justice, seeking substantive equality by treating like alike and unlike differently according to various

---

86 *Case Concerning the Continental Shelf* (*Tunisia/Libya*), Judgment of 24 February 1982, [1982] I.C.J. 18.

87 *Case Concerning the Frontier Dispute* (*Burkina Faso/Republic of Mali*), Judgment of 22 December 1986, [1986] I.C.J. 554 at 567. For the use of equity in maritime boundary cases, see also *North Sea Continental Shelf Cases* (*FRG/Den./Neth.*), Judgment of 20 February 1969, [1969] I.C.J. 3; *Case Concerning Delimitation of the Maritime Boundary in the Gulf of Maine* (*Canada/United States of America*), Judgment of 12 October 1984, [1984] I.C.J. 246; and *Case Concerning the Continental Shelf* (*Libya/Malta*), Judgment of 3 June 1985, [1985] I.C.J. 13.

88 *North Sea Continental Shelf Cases*, at 3 and 53.

89 *Case Concerning the Continental Shelf* (*Libya/Malta*), at para. 45.

criteria such as prior entitlement, just desserts, or need. International law has allocated both shared resources and environmental burdens through the equitable principle of distributive justice. Such an equitable approach may call for accommodating pervasive inequalities of economic development or lack of capacity to tackle a given problem, by imposing differential obligations or providing preferential treatment. These unequal relationships seek to foster true equality, largely through favouring the least developed or most affected states. One application of this notion of equity is in the principle of equitable utilization of shared natural resources, most frequently applied in the context of international watercourses. Another overarching application is the principle of CBDR.

The implementation of environmental equity calls for appropriate or fair benefit and burden sharing among all those who have an interest in a shared resource, which implies distributive justice and participatory processes to manage the shared resources. Equity thus has both substantive and procedural aspects. In practice, several important multilateral environmental agreements set forth a general objective or objectives to be achieved with a set of general obligations applicable to all states parties, followed by differentiated specific duties imposed on different categories of states. Determining the factors that are relevant for differentiating obligations is difficult, and substantive measures of equity may be applied in one of several ways. The principle of equitable burden-sharing between legally equal parties can involve allocating costs on the basis of ability to pay, or the party's contributions to the problem, per unit or per capita. Emissions can be allocated on the basis of past or current emission levels, promoting stability in the international economic order by maintaining current practices, and limiting the entry of new polluters. This approach, however, constitutes an entitlement approach that benefits neither the environment nor the most disadvantaged countries, rewarding those who have done the least to curb emissions. In the climate change regime, differentiated responsibilities to attain emission reductions reflect a variety of factors, including different starting points, economic structures and resources, past and present contributions to atmospheric pollution, and capacity to perform.

2 Science

Environmental law has several characteristics deriving from the need to take into consideration the 'laws of nature' basic to biology, chemistry and physics. Few legal disciplines require the same consideration of scientific knowledge.[90] Most areas of law attempt to regulate variable and often unpredictable human interrelationships. In contrast, environmental law uses science to predict and regulate the consequences of human behavior on natural phenomena.

The need for environmental law to take into consideration the 'laws of nature' inevitably leads to an interdisciplinary approach to environmental problems. Law-makers and jurists must rely upon and utilize scientific expertise. Scientists themselves must share knowledge. In efforts to understand global climate change, for example, atmospheric scientists trained in meteorology and chemistry produce climate change models, while biologists and ecologists are needed to analyze the impact of these changes on biotopes and ecological systems.[91] These models are collected in the Assessment Reports prepared by the Intergovernmental Panel on Climate Change (IPCC), which play a critical role in the development of international climate law.[92] The close link between science and law can be seen in most multilateral environmental agreements. In the context of the Stockholm Convention on Persistent Organic Pollutants (POPs), for instance, a detailed scientific assessment of proposed new chemicals represents the first step in the procedure to add new chemicals to the Convention.[93]

Environmental law and policy also must take into account the interdependence of different sectors of the environment. Ocean pollution taints the shore, as recognized in the 1982 UN Convention on Law of the Sea (UNCLOS) and a number of regional instruments.[94] In turn, a large proportion of marine pollution derives from land-based sources. Atmospheric pollution also can

---

90 See e.g. David Fisk, 'Environmental Science and Environmental Law' (1998) 10 Journal of Environmental Law 3; Eric Biber, 'Which Science? Whose Science? How Scientific Disciplines Can Shape Environmental Law' (2012) 79(2) The University of Chicago Law Review 471–552; Makane M. Mbengue & Iga J. Józefiak, 'To Know Without Knowing? Reinforcing the Science-Policy Interface in Global Environmental Governance' Pathway to the 2022 Declaration (29 April 2021).

91 See e.g. Ronald D. Brunner, 'Science and the Climate Change Regime' (2001) 34(1) Policy Sciences 1; Thomas Hickmann, 'Science–Policy Interaction in International Environmental Politics: An Analysis of the Ozone Regime and the Climate Regime' (2014) 16(1) Environmental Economics and Policy Studies 21.

92 Kari De Pryck & Mike Hulme (eds), *A Critical Assessment of the Intergovernmental Panel on Climate Change* (Cambridge University Press 2022).

93 Stockholm Convention on Persistent Organic Pollutants (POPs Convention) (Stockholm, May 22, 2001), U.N.T.S. 119, Article 8. Daniel Bodansky, *The Art and Craft of International Environmental Law* (Harvard University Press 2010) 188.

94 United Nations Convention on the Law of the Sea (Montego Bay, Dec. 10, 1982), Art. 211, U.N. Doc. A/CONF 62/122 (1982); Misc 11 (1983), Cmd. 8941, 21 I.L.M. 1261 (1982) (hereinafter UNCLOS). The regional seas conventions are discussed in Chapter 11.

affect the earth and imperil forests and buildings. The UNFCCC recognizes that climate change due to emissions of certain gases into the air can have significant deleterious effects on the composition, resilience or productivity of natural and managed ecosystems, on the operation of socio-economic systems, and on human health and welfare.[95] Freshwaters receive a large part of their pollution from the soil, whose pollutants may seep into the underground water table. Obviously, all pollutants endanger biodiversity. Such interrelationships necessarily have international consequences, because the transfer of pollution from one milieu to another will frequently result in transboundary impacts. International instruments, notably UNCLOS, stress the need to avoid substituting injury or risk to one sector of the environment with injury to another, as well as replacing one type of pollution with another.[96]

Another scientific reality with which environmental law and policy must grapple is the lack of scientific certainty about many aspects of the physical world. Although there is unprecedented scientific knowledge available today, no one knows the ecological processes over the five billion year history of the earth with sufficient detail and understanding to be able to predict all the consequences and causal relationships of various human interventions and activities. Debates over the time and full impact of anthropogenic climate change are but one aspect of this uncertainty.[97] Even the concept of 'balance of nature', i.e., that nature generally remains in a state of stable equilibrium, has been challenged by some studies which see nature ruled by flux and perpetual disturbances.[98]

Scientific uncertainty thus often attends issues of the nature and scope of the adverse environmental impacts of human activities. Exacerbating the uncertainty, damage often is measurable only years after the causative actions have occurred. Given this situation, questions arise over how to develop environmental policy and how to allocate risk between the present and the future. Many decisions cannot await scientific certainty, assuming something

---

95 UNFCCC, Art. 1(1).

96 UNCLOS, Art. 195.

97 While most scientists predict severe ecological disruption from global warming attributable to unchecked pollution, others reach different conclusions or find that the data are insufficient to reach any conclusions. One study concluded that more than half the global temperature increases of recent years are due to warm ocean currents known as El Nino, but acknowledged that it is not known whether the currents themselves are affected by the rise in carbon dioxide, methane, and other heat-trapping gases. See generally David L. Bazelon, 'Science and Uncertainty: A Jurist's View' (1981) 5 Harv. Envtl. L. Rev. 209.

98 William K. Stevens, 'Scientists Rethinking Balance of Nature' *San Francisco Chronicle* (31 July 1990) A5.

approaching certainty can ever be achieved. Therefore, debate centres on whether a policy should be adopted to assume harmful consequences will occur unless activities or products are proven safe or whether to take a less cautious approach, knowing that many environmental processes and changes may be irreversible and ultimately life-threatening.[99] To address scientific uncertainty, the precautionary approach (or principle) was included in the 1992 Rio Declaration and was later incorporated in many multilateral environmental agreements (see Chapter 4).

In addition to uncertainty and irreversibility, environmental law must recognize the fact that the environment is dynamic and constantly evolving. This characteristic requires flexible laws and policies that are capable of rapid alteration in response to new circumstances. This result can be achieved with a number of instruments and techniques, such as the use of technical annexes, amendments, or even soft law instruments.[100] At the same time, and perhaps paradoxically, the legal framework must look long term in its efforts to maintain life and the ecological balance in an unseeable future.

Finally, it is notable that as early as 1962, Rachel Carson demonstrated that the combined effect of substances can be very different than the environmental impact of each substance released separately.[101] A chemical innocuous in isolation may be polluting or even highly toxic when combined with other substances in the environment. Industrial emissions, for example, change their characteristics in the atmosphere, creating acid rain. Synergistic interactions have been observed in mixtures of up to twenty or more chemicals, with some effects 10,000 times more harmful that would be expected from adding the toxicities of the individual chemicals.[102] The need for precaution and an integrated or holistic approach thus emerges from the science of ecology.

---

99 On occasion, scientific uncertainty has been invoked as a reason for refusing to take costly environmental action. One author notes that the United States as a recipient of acid rain exported from Mexico does not debate the scientific certainty of the causal link between pollutants and acid rain damage. However, when the United States is exporting similar pollutants towards Canada, scientific uncertainty is cited as a reason to delay adopting measures. See Jutta Brunnée, *Acid Rain and Ozone Layer Depletion: Law and Regulation* (Brill 1988). The United States government has also refused to ratify the Kyoto Protocol on Climate Change based upon its claims of scientific uncertainty about fact of anthropogenic global climate change.

100 Laurence Boisson de Chazournes, 'Environmental Treaties in Time' (2009) 39(6) Environmental Policy and Law 293.

101 Rachel Carson, *Silent Spring* (Houghton Mifflin 1962) 195–196.

102 Davis Hunter, James Salzman & Durwood Zaelke, *International Environmental Law and Policy* (2nd ed., Foundation Press 2002) 22.

3 Economics

The current economic system presents numerous challenges to environmental protection. First, if the earth's resource base is considered as a whole, the structure and functioning of the marketplace can produce what has long been referred to as the 'tragedy of the commons'.[103] In addition, the emphasis on free trade in goods and services in the international economic system raises problems of competitive disadvantage and opposition to trade barriers resulting from regulations to protect the environment. Finally, the north-south disparity in economic development and resources creates difficulties for the traditional legal technique of imposing uniform norms and standards through international agreements.

The tragedy of the commons is a consequence of the market of supply and demand, a fundamental principle of liberal economic theory. In an open market, the pressure of demand leads to higher prices as goods become scarce. Prices that are too high deter further purchasers leading to a fall in demand. For many environmental amenities, however, the market system does not work because such resources are considered 'public goods' that are free and in principle shared by all. No one legally can prevent another from using air. The lack of a market for public goods means that no price rise signals scarcity due to, *inter alia*, environmental degradation. Each consumer continues to maximize use until the resource is exhausted. The consequences of this system are perhaps most apparent in regard to exhaustible living resources, such as fish. Unregulated fishing on the high seas leads each vessel to try to obtain the maximum possible catch, leading fisheries to 'crash'.[104]

The same profit motivation likewise produces environmental degradation from pollution. The harmful introduction of substances into the environment results from each person deciding that her or his short-term advantage involves discharging pollutants into the commons, rather than bearing the cost of purifying emissions before release. If the sole objective of the market is to

---

103 See Garrett Hardin, 'Tragedy of the Commons' (1968) 168 Science 243. The article describes a common pasture in which everyone in a village has unlimited grazing rights for sheep. It is to each person's advantage in the short run to maximize the grazing of her or his own sheep. Within a short time, the pasture is destroyed through over-grazing.

104 See FAO, *The State of World Fisheries and Aquaculture* (2022) 46, stating that the proportion of assessed marine fish stocks fished within biologically sustainable levels declined from 90 percent in 1974 to 64.6 percent in 2019, when 35.4 percent of fish stocks were estimated as fished at a biologically unsustainable level and, therefore, overfished. Of the stocks assessed in 2019, fully fished stocks accounted for 57.3 percent and underfished stocks 7.2 percent.

maximize the wealth of each individual, a system of open and non-regulated access to the commons will invariably result in environmental degradation. The environmental law response has been to formulate the 'polluter pays' principle that converts the economic externalities of commons degradation into costs for the polluter.[105] Market instruments, such as environmental taxes (or carbon taxes in the context of climate change mitigation) have been introduced in many jurisdictions for the same purpose, and are increasingly addressed in international instruments (see Chapter 17).

The second economic issue is competitive disadvantage: a state taking measures to protect the environment must count the increased costs which are borne by its economy. Distortions are especially felt in an interstate system founded on free trade. The former European Economic Community, now incorporated in the European Union (EU), initially based its environmental protection measures on Article 100 of the Treaty of Rome, which promoted the approximation of national legislation that has a direct effect on the establishment or functioning of the common market. The purpose of approximation is 'to eliminate disparities between the legislative or administrative provisions of the Member States which distort the conditions of competition in the Common Market'.[106] The preoccupation with conditions of competition is evident also in the work of the Organization of Economic Cooperation and Development (OECD)[107] and the environmental side agreement to the North American Free Trade Agreement (NAFTA). The latter called for cooperation to better conserve, protect, and enhance the environment, while avoiding the creation of trade distortions or new trade barriers.[108] Such provisions would later be integrated into the text of that treaty's successor instrument, the US-Mexico-Canada Trade Agreement (USMCA).[109] Chapter 17 of the present volume describes the current efforts to protect the environment in the context of the international market.

105 According to Principle 16 of the Rio Declaration on Environment and Development, '[n]ational authorities should endeavour to promote the internalization of environmental costs and the use of economic instruments, taking into account the approach that the polluter should, in principle, bear the cost of pollution, with due regard to the public interest and without distorting international trade and investment'.

106 Article 101(1), Treaty Establishing the European Economic Community (Rome, March 25, 1957), 298 U.N.T.S. 11, U.K.T.S. 15 (1979), Cmd. 7480. For further discussion see later Chapter 5.

107 See Chapter 5.

108 North American Agreement on Environmental Cooperation (Sept. 8, 1993), Art. 1, 32 I.L.M. 1480 (1993).

109 United States-Mexico-Canada Agreement (USMCA) (entered into force July 1, 2020), Chapter 24.

Thirdly, the solidarity imposed by global problems necessitates better cooperation between industrialized and developing countries, between the North and the South. Full collaboration involves assisting poor countries to face the burden of implementing environmental measures that serve to safeguard the biosphere as a whole. In addition, it is now understood that global poverty threatens human existence through its impact on the environment. The result is an increased emphasis on partnership and mutuality in multilateral environmental protection, as well as on the interrelationship of environmental protection and development.

While these economic challenges are complex and difficult, the field of economics offers possible means to quantify the value of the environment to society, important when decisions are based a cost-benefit analysis. Direct valuation can compute the revenues generated by products extracted from nature, including food, medicine, petroleum and minerals. Indirect methods of estimating substitute markets may measure ecosystem services, which are probably of even greater value. These include the value of coral reefs in protecting shorelines from storm surges and mangroves services in slowing erosion and preventing siltation of coastal waters. Soil provides important ecological services by purifying groundwater and supporting agriculture, honeybees contribute through pollination. Harder to measure are the life-supporting services provided by the ozone layer, for example, or Antarctica's contribution to regulating the global climate, or even the carbon content of products throughout a global supply chain. Even less quantifiable are such aspects as the aesthetic enjoyment of landscapes and the inherent contribution of each species to the ecosystem in which it lives.[110] Nonetheless, various initiatives are attempting to provide better valuation of the environment. The United Nations Statistical Office has developed a System of Environmental and Economic Accounting (SEEA). It includes environmental functions and natural resources as assets of production and records depletion of a resource as capital depreciation. The SEEA contains the internationally agreed standard concepts, definitions, classifications, accounting rules and tables for producing internationally comparable statistics on the environment and its relationship with the economy. The World Bank uses SEEAs in its economic analyses. Some economists suggest an alternative method to directly value the ecological functions that serve to meet human needs from subsistence to identity and freedom, rather than measuring

110 For discussions about valuing ecological services, see Gretchen C. Daily (ed), *Nature's Services: Societal Dependence on Natural Ecosystems* (Island Press 1997); Dana Clark & David Downes, *What Price Biodiversity?* (CIEL 1995); Robert Costanza et al., *An Introduction to Ecological Economics* (2nd ed, CRC Press 2015).

production and consumption.[111] Finally, the development of the Environmental Sustainability Index (ESI) and the Environmental Performance Index (EPI) provides a basis for assessing the ability of states to meet the environmental needs of their society in a sustainable manner. The ESI looks at core indicators based on a larger set of underlying variables. It measures five key components of environmental sustainability: natural systems; environmental stresses and risks; human exposure and risks (vulnerability to harm); societal capacity to respond to environmental challenges; and transboundary equity issues (contributions to harm and to solutions of environmental problems).[112] The EPI uses 40 performance indicators across 11 issue categories, ranking countries on climate change performance, environmental health and ecosystem vitality.[113]

4 International Law

International law, as traditionally defined, governed relations among juridically equal states, once considered the sole subjects of international law.[114] International law has regulated interstate relations through rules based on the consent of states, primarily expressed in the adoption of treaties and the development of customary international law through state practice viewed as obligatory (*opinio juris*).[115] While the contours of this classic system remain intact, it has undergone fundamental changes in the past half century. International environmental law is both a product and a partial cause of this transformation that affects the processes of law-making and the role of consent, as well concepts of sovereignty.[116] Many aspects of modern international environmental law are linked to the concepts of the common concern of humanity and common heritage of mankind.

111 See Robert Costanza (ed), *Ecological Economics* (Columbia University Press 1991).

112 Daniel C. Esty et al, '2005 Environmental Sustainability Index: Benchmarking National Environmental Stewardship' (2005) Yale Center for Environmental Law & Policy.

113 See https://epi.yale.edu/ (last accessed 14 April 2025).

114 James Crawford, *The Creation of States in International Law* (2nd edn, Oxford University Press 2006); Nico Schrijver, 'The Changing Nature of State Sovereignty' (1999) 70 BYIL 65.

115 Clive Parry, *The Sources and Evidences of International Law* (Cambridge University Press 1965); Alan Boyle & Christine Chinkin, *The Making of International Law* (Oxford University Press 2007).

116 Edith Brown-Weiss, 'The Evolution of International Environmental Law' (2011) 54 Japanese Yearbook of International Law 1.

4.1 *Sovereignty*

State sovereignty, one of the oldest principles of international law, means that each state has exclusive jurisdiction within its territory to adopt laws and enforce them, administer the territory, and judge disputes that arise therein. A State's supreme authority over its territory includes its sovereignty over the natural resources located within it.[117] This principle first appeared in the 1962 United Nations General Assembly (UNGA) Resolution 1803 on Permanent Sovereignty over Natural Resources (PSNR)[118] and it has been recognized as a principle of customary international law.[119] This principle is established in a number of key international environmental law instruments, such as the 1972 Stockholm Declaration at Principle 21, which affirms that '[s]tates have, in accordance with the Charter of the United Nations and the principles of international law, the sovereign right to exploit their own resources pursuant to their own environmental policies …'. The same formulation has been reproduced in other binding and non-binding international instruments. Principle 2 of the Rio Declaration uses the same wording, but enlarges its scope by referring to 'environmental *and developmental* policies', reflecting the Rio Conference's focus on both environment and development.[120]

A tension between traditional notions of state sovereignty and environmental concerns can be seen in the evolution of legal texts regarding permanent sovereignty over natural resources. Early formulations mainly focused on rights of states over these resources, responding to concerns about neo-colonialism and economic development. The Stockholm Declaration was the first international document to balance state sovereignty with 'the responsibility to ensure that activities within their jurisdiction or control do not cause damage to the environment of other States or of areas beyond the limits of national jurisdiction'. This formulation, which finds its origin in the 1941 *Trail Smelter* Arbitration, is repeated in the Rio Declaration and in the Convention on Biological Diversity and other international texts. Repetition of the principle, its invocation in state practice, and its widespread acceptance led the ICJ to declare that 'the general obligation of States to ensure that activities within their jurisdiction and control respect the environment of other States or of areas beyond national control is now part of the corpus of international law relating

117 Alexander Kiss & Dinah Shelton, 'Systems Analysis of International Law: A Methodological Inquiry' (1986) Neth. Y.B. Int'l L. 45.

118 Permanent Sovereignty over Natural Resources, G.A. Res. 3171 of Dec. 17, 1973.

119 *Mayagna Awas Tigni Community v. Nicaragua* and *Armed Activities on the territory of the Congo* (*DRC v. Uganda*).

120 Emphasis added. The same formulation can be found in the preamble of the UNFCCC.

to the environment'.[121] The principle of no-harm, as it is generally referred to, has been codified in many multilateral environmental agreements, as well as treaties that feature environmental chapters or provision. A notable example is Article 194 of UNCLOS, which provides that:

> States shall take, individually or jointly as appropriate, all measures consistent with this Convention that are necessary to prevent, reduce and control pollution of the marine environment from any source, using for this purpose the best practicable means at their disposal and in accordance with their capabilities, and they shall endeavour to harmonize their policies in this connection.[122]

Some environmental issues raise serious problems for the application of state sovereignty, since the environment knows no boundary. Migratory species of wild animals, birds, and fish as well as pollution of oceans, rivers, lakes and the air, do not stop at the limits of territorial jurisdiction. Environmental harm can even occur in areas beyond a country's jurisdiction, where the principle of no harm continues to apply.[123] Such situations can lead to conflicts between sovereign rights which can only be solved by international law. Treaties to which a state becomes a contracting party limit its sovereignty, but such limitations are self-imposed. Each state is now involved in a large web of international treaty obligations concerning environmental protection that must be executed on its territory, including agreements to protect species of wild fauna and flora, prohibit the dumping of harmful substances into rivers, lakes or the sea, and prevent atmospheric pollution by constraints imposed upon industries. The general trend toward integrated protection of the environment requires that states exercise broad control over activities which can harm the environment and this necessarily limits their freedom of action.

4.2 *Cooperation*

An obligation to cooperate with other states derives from the very essence of general international law, and finds reflection in the existence and proliferation

---

121 *Legality of the Threat or Use of Nuclear Weapons*, Advisory Opinion, I.C.J. Rep. 1996, pp. 241–242, para. 29.

122 UNCLOS, Art. 194.

123 Principle 2 of the Rio Declaration clearly states that States have the States have the 'responsibility to ensure that activities within their jurisdiction or control do not cause damage to the environment of other States or of *areas beyond the limits of national jurisdiction'* (emphasis added).

of international institutions.[124] In the field of environmental protection, international cooperation is necessary to conserve the environment in its totality, as much for states within their territorial jurisdiction as for areas outside territorial limits. The general need to cooperate to conserve the environment is expressed in several texts, starting with Principle 24 of the Stockholm Declaration:

> International matters concerning the protection and improvement of the environment should be handled in a cooperative spirit by all countries, big and small, on an equal footing. Cooperation through multilateral or bilateral arrangements or other appropriate means is essential to effectively control, prevent, reduce and eliminate adverse environmental effects resulting from activities conducted in all spheres, in such a way that due account is taken of the sovereignty and interests of all states.

The UN General Assembly reaffirmed the same principle in Resolution 2995 (XXVII) of 1972,[125] and in the 1982 World Charter for Nature. According to the latter instrument, states shall cooperate in the conservation of nature through common activities and other relevant actions, including information exchanges and consultations. They must also establish standards for products and manufacturing processes that may have adverse effects on the environment, as well as methods to assess these effects. The Rio Declaration on Environment and Development is also largely based on the principle of cooperation, in particular between industrialized and developing countries.

The principle of cooperation underlies most treaty obligations. Nevertheless, several texts make it explicit, such as Article 197 of UNCLOS:

> States shall cooperate on a global basis and, as appropriate, on a regional basis, directly or through competent international organizations, in formulating and elaborating international rules, standards and recommended practices and procedures consistent with this Convention, for the protection and preservation of the marine environment, taking into account characteristic regional features.

---

124 Declaration on Principles of International Law concerning Friendly Relations and Cooperation among States in accordance with the Charter of the United Nations, G.A. Res. 2625 (XXV) of Oct. 26, 1970.

125 Cooperation between States in the Field of the Environment, G.A. Res. 2995 (XXVII) of Dec. 15, 1972.

An example of regional co-operation is provided by the Memorandum of Understanding (MOU) between Kenya, Tanzania and Uganda for Co-operation on Environment Management.[126] Its aim is the development and harmonization of national framework environmental laws on environmental impact assessment, management of non-hazardous and hazardous wastes, toxic and hazardous chemicals, wildlife and forest resources, laws for the management of the Lake Victoria ecosystem and formulation of environmental standards. Co-operation shall include continued consultations, capacity building and networking on environmental policies, laws and strategies, undertaking joint programs and the development and implementation of environmentally sound principles, agreements, instruments and strategies for environment and natural resources management. The MOU provides for the establishment of an Interim Sectoral Committee as well as interim national focal points.

Different legal instruments specify the fields of international cooperation. According to Principle 5 of the Rio Declaration, all states and peoples shall cooperate in the essential task of eradicating poverty as an indispensable requirement for sustainable development. In 1995, during a World Summit for Social Development, 117 Heads of State agreed to an integrated approach to poverty eradication based on the concept of partnership, within societies as well as between developed and developing countries. As noted in the 2030 Agenda for Sustainable Development, the UN Sustainable Development Goals reflect an increasingly broad and urgent pledge of partnership among world leaders 'collectively to the pursuit of global development and of "win-win" cooperation'.[127]

The concept of partnership emerged during preparations for the Rio Conference as an expression of closer and more systematic cooperation. Principle 27 of the Rio Declaration adds that cooperation shall be conducted in good faith and shall include further development of international law in the field of sustainable development.[128] The 2002 World Summit on Sustainable Development extended the concept of partnership to encompass non-state actors as well as states. The Johannesburg Declaration on Sustainable Development recognizes that sustainable development requires a long-term perspective and

126 Nairobi, October 22, 1998.

127 'Transforming our world: the 2030 Agenda for Sustainable Development,' G.A. Res. 70/1 of Oct. 21, 2015, para 18. Connecting this partnership to past and future generations, see further Preamble, and paras 50, 53.

128 See also Rio Declaration, Principle 7. Peter H. Sand, 'Principle 27: Cooperation in a Spirit of Global Partnership' in Jorge E. Viñuales (ed), *The Rio Declaration on Environment and Development. A Commentary* (Oxford University Press 2015) 617–32.

'stable partnerships with all major groups'.[129] The Johannesburg Plan of Implementation also calls for enhanced partnerships between governmental and non-governmental actors.

The Rio Declaration also insists on cooperation to strengthen endogenous capacity-building for sustainable development, by improving scientific understanding through exchange of scientific and technological knowledge, and by enhancing the development, adaptation, diffusion and transfer of technologies, including new and innovative technologies (Principle 9). Similar clauses related to the transfer of knowledge, information, and technology form an important part of most global environmental treaties. Article 4(5) of the UNFCCC, for example, provides that the developed country parties shall take all practicable steps to promote, facilitate and finance, as appropriate, the transfer of, or access to, environmentally sound technologies and know-how, in particular to developing countries. Moreover, they are to support the development and enhancement of endogenous capacities and technologies of developing countries. The Paris Agreement further recognizes 'the importance of support for and international cooperation on adaptation efforts' to address the disparate effects of climate change (Art. 7(6)).

Another designated area of international cooperation in the Rio Declaration is in regard to the relocation and transfer to other states of any activities and substances that cause severe environmental degradation, or which are found to be harmful to human health. Principle 14 requires, *inter alia*, that if a state chooses to ban or restrict the importation of hazardous substances or the relocation of hazardous activities, the ban or restriction should be respected by other states. The Basel Convention on the Control of Transboundary Movements of Hazardous Wastes and their Disposal (March 22, 1989) supports this principle.

Cooperation is also needed for the rational and equitable use of shared resources, such as in regards to transboundary watercourses and international lakes, as well as natural resources in the sea and seabed.

Another essential part of cooperation is providing financial assistance to countries to enable them to comply with their obligations, especially in the relations between industrialized and developing countries. Article 20(2) of the 1982 Convention on Biological Diversity, and Articles 20 and 21 of the Convention to Combat Desertification in those Countries Experiencing Serious Drought and/or Desertification, Particularly in Africa, provide that the developed country parties shall provide new and additional financial resources

129 Johannesburg Declaration on Sustainable Development, para. 23.

to developing or affected country parties. In the climate change regime, the Paris Agreement states that 'Developed country Parties shall provide financial resources to assist developing country Parties with respect to both mitigation and adaptation in continuation of their existing obligations under the Convention' (Art. 9(1)).

Finally, the principle of cooperation encompasses the duty to cooperate 'in a transboundary context', which reflects customary international law and includes *inter alia* the duty of notification and consultation with States potentially affected by an activity or an event having consequences on the environment.[130] This procedural duty, which has been codified in many multilateral environmental agreements, has been addressed in the 2001 order on provisional measures issued by the International Tribunal on the Law of the Sea (ITLOS) in the *Mox Plant* case (Ireland v. United Kingdom).[131] Ireland invoked article 123 of UNCLOS, concerning enclosed or semi-enclosed seas, which requires states to cooperate in exercising their rights and performing their duties. Ireland also relied upon article 206 which requires assessment of the potential effects of planned activities that may cause substantial pollution or significant and harmful changes to the environment. The Tribunal enunciated in its order that the duty to cooperate is a fundamental principle in the prevention of pollution of the marine environment, according to UNCLOS Part XII, and in general international law and that rights arise therefrom which the tribunal may consider appropriate to preserve under Article 290 of the Convention (on provisional measures).[132] Judge Wolfrum's separate opinion questioned whether the customary international obligation to cooperate for environmental protection creates corresponding legal rights, but he did find that UNCLOS creates a legally protected right to cooperation for its contracting parties. The *Mox Plant* tribunal's findings have been more recently affirmed by ITLOS in the *SRFC* Advisory Opinion, which extended the customary duty to cooperate to cases of alleged illegal, unreported and unregulated fishing activities.[133]

4.3 *Common Concern of Humankind*

The cohesion of every society and community is based upon and maintained by a value system such as a common religion, philosophy, ideology or ethics. The system may demand respect for the human person, propriety, patriotism,

130 Rio Declaration, Principle 19.

131 *MOX Plant Case (Ireland v. United Kingdom)*, ITLOS Case No. 10, Order (Dec. 3, 2001).

132 ibid, para 82.

133 *Request for an advisory opinion submitted by the Sub-Regional Fisheries Commission* (*SRFC*), Case No. 21 (Apr. 1, 2015) para 140.

respect for cultural values, or adherence to a particular social order. The protection of such fundamental values is generally recognized as a common concern of the community and is ensured through law, especially constitutional law.

The common concern of a society thus leads to the creation of a legal system whose rules impose duties on society as a whole and on each individual member of the community. Almost all national constitutions proclaim fundamental human rights and freedoms and require the government to respect and ensure those rights. Increasingly, similar provisions are included to secure environmental protection. Article 66 of the 1976 Portuguese Constitution is illustrative. It proclaims an obligation on the state through its agencies to prevent and control pollution and its effects and harmful forms of erosion, to organize territorial space so as to establish biologically balanced landscapes, and to create and develop natural parks and reserves. As a counterpart, this constitution recognizes that all persons have the right to a human, healthy and ecologically balanced environment and the duty to protect it. The national regulatory system is built upon this foundation.

International law lacks a constitutional text and central authority to determine the common concern of all humankind because states individually and jointly draft and adopt legal regulations governing international relations. During the second half of the twentieth century states aimed to create a universal political organization to maintain international peace and security and improve the well-being of all humanity. This ambitious effort could only proceed by defining domains of common concern. The international recognition of human rights and fundamental freedoms constituted a first step of paramount importance in developing the concept of an international community built upon the fundamental values of humanity. Similarly, knowledge that the biosphere is the only known place in the universe where life is possible led to the emergence of another universal value, protection of the human environment as a common concern of humankind.[134] The global environment, an interdependent ecological system, can only be protected at the global level, making it a common concern for all humanity. Transboundary and domestic environmental issues that cannot be managed effectively by national or regional efforts also are common concerns. The modalities of protection and preservation are formulated in law and policy and enforced by national and international institutions. A large number of international instruments

---

134 Thomas Cottier (ed), *The Prospects of Common Concern of Humankind in International Law* (Cambridge University Press, 2021).

recognize the common concern of humankind.[135] The term 'common interest' appeared early in international treaties concerning the exploitation of natural resources. The International Convention for the Regulation of Whaling recognizes in its preamble the 'interest of the world in safeguarding for future generations the great natural resources represented by the whale stocks',[136] and that it is in the common interest to achieve the optimum level of whale stocks as rapidly as possible. The depletion of fish resources, which began as a local problem, took on much larger dimensions in the second half of the twentieth century. States then recognized that it was in their common interest to take conservation measures. The 1952 Tokyo Convention for the High Seas Fisheries of the North Pacific Ocean expresses the conviction of the parties that it will best serve the common interest of mankind, as well as the interests of the contracting parties, to ensure the maximum sustained productivity of the fishery resources of the North Pacific Ocean.

A major step in international recognition of the common concern of humankind was the conclusion of the 1959 Antarctic Treaty. Its preamble affirms that 'it is in the interest of all mankind that Antarctica shall continue forever to be used exclusively for peaceful purposes'.[137] Article IX authorizes the adoption of measures for the preservation and conservation of living resources in Antarctica 'in furtherance of the principles and objectives of the Treaty'.[138] The Antarctic Treaty system further developed with the adoption of the Canberra Convention on the Conservation of Antarctic Marine Living Resources (CCAMLR), which made express reference to the 'interest of all mankind to preserve the waters surrounding the Antarctic continent for peaceful purposes only'.[139] The most recent addition to the Antarctic Treaty system, the 1991 Madrid Protocol on Environmental Protection to the Antarctic Treaty,[140] achieved full recognition of the common interest. Its preamble expresses the conviction that the development of a comprehensive regime for the protection of the Antarctic environment and dependent and associated ecosystems

---

135 See e.g. UNFCCC, Preamble, para 1; CBD, Preamble, para 3.

136 Feb. 12, 1946, 161 U.N.T.S. 72, Preamble, para 2.

137 Dec. 1, 1959, 402 U.N.T.S. 71, Preamble.

138 ibid, Article IX.

139 May 20, 1980, preamble, 19 I.L.M. 837 (1980). See also Daniel Vignes, 'Protection of the Antarctic Marine Fauna and Flora, The Canberra Convention and the Commission Set up by It' in Francesco Francioni & Tullio Scovazzi (eds), *International Law for Antarctica* (Martinus Nijhoff Publishers 1996) 159.

140 Oct. 4, 1991, 30 I.L.M. 1461 (1991). See also Laura Pineschi, 'The Madrid Protocol on the Protection of the Antarctic Environment and its Effectiveness' in Francioni & Scovazzi (n 139) 261.

is in the interest of mankind, and for this purpose it denominates Antarctica a nature reserve, devoted to peace and science.[141]

Such evolution must be seen as reflecting awareness of the general depletion of natural resources and of the threats to the environment, awareness that is increasing the pressure to adopt broad measures in the interest of present and future generations. Even before the 1972 Stockholm Conference, the 1968 African Convention on the Conservation of Nature and Natural Resources had expressed the desire of the contracting states to undertake individual and joint action for the conservation, utilization and development of natural resources by establishing and maintaining their rational utilization for the present and future welfare of mankind.[142] With the words 'future welfare' the temporal dimension of the common interest of humanity has appeared.

Other international environmental treaties similarly recognize the common concern of humankind. The 1979 Bonn Convention on the Conservation of Migratory Species of Wild Animals recognizes in its preamble that

> wild animals in their innumerable forms are an irreplaceable part of the earth's natural system which must be conserved for the good of mankind [...]. [E]ach generation of man holds the resources of the earth for future generations and has an obligation to ensure that this legacy is conserved and, where utilized, is used wisely.[143]

The Convention on the Conservation of European Wildlife and Natural Habitats, adopted several months after the Bonn Convention joins the concepts of general interest and future humanity by recognizing that wild flora and fauna constitute a natural heritage that 'needs to be handed on to future generations'.[144] Similarly, the World Charter for Nature states that the preservation of the species and of the ecosystems should be ensured 'for the benefit of present and future generations'.[145] The World Charter opened the door for the 1992 Convention on Biological Diversity, which explicitly proclaims the principle of common concern of humanity,[146] by stating 'the importance of

141 See also the UN General Assembly Resolution on the Question of Antarctica, Dec. 6, 1991, G.A. Res 46/41, UN GAOR, 46th Sess. Supp. No 49 at 83, UN Doc. A/46/49 (1992) which implicitly expresses that Antarctica constitutes a common concern for all the states.

142 Algiers, Sept. 15, 1968, 1001 U.N.T.S. 3.

143 June 23, 1979, 19 I.L.M. 15 (1980).

144 Bern, Sept. 19, 1979, E.T.S. 104.

145 Oct. 28, 1982, Res. 37/7, UN Doc. A/37/51.

146 On the replacement of the concept of 'common heritage of mankind' by 'common concern', see Nico Schrijver, *Sovereignty over Natural Resources, Balancing Rights and Duties* (Cambridge University Press 1997) 246, 389.

biological diversity for evolution and for maintaining life sustaining systems in the biosphere', and 'affirming that the conservation of biological diversity is a common concern of humankind [...]'. The UNFCCC similarly affirms in the first paragraph of its preamble that 'change in the Earth's climate and its adverse effects are a common concern of humankind'. The same is reiterated in the 2015 Paris Agreement (Preamble).

The inclusion of smaller areas in the common concern is seen in the Paris Convention for the Protection of the Marine Environment of the North-East Atlantic, adopted several months after the Convention on Biological Diversity. It recognizes that 'the marine environment and the fauna and flora which it supports are of vital importance to all nations'.[147] More recently, the UN Convention to Combat Desertification in those Countries Experiencing Serious Drought and/or Desertification, Particularly in Africa refers to 'the urgent concern of the international community, including states and international organizations, about the adverse impacts of desertification and drought,' although only some parts of the world are directly concerned.[148]

As within states, the common concern (*l'intérêt général*) is a general concept which does not connote specific rules and obligations, but establishes the general basis for the concerned community to act. The conventions cited imply a global responsibility to conserve disappearing or diminishing wild fauna and flora, ecosystems, and natural resources in general in danger. Language to this effect can be found in the 1980 resolution of the UN General Assembly on the draft World Charter for Nature, which asserts the 'supreme importance of protecting natural systems, maintaining the balance and quality of nature and conserving natural resources, in the interests of present and future generations'.[149]

The right and duty of the international community to act in matters of common concern must be balanced with respect for national sovereignty. States retain sovereignty subject to the requirements of international law developed to ensure the common interest. Other domains of international law, including trade and diplomatic relations, are instrumental to achieving this common interest of humanity. They do not constitute in themselves the ultimate goals of international society, but are means to improve the moral and economic well-being of humanity as a whole. The terms of the United Nations Charter indicate that international peace and security must be coupled with economic and social advancement of all peoples and individuals in order to

147 September 22, 1992, 32 I.L.M. 1069 (1993).

148 Paris, June 17, 1994, 33 I.L.M. 1328 (1994).

149 G.A.Res. 35/7 on the Draft World Charter for Nature, UN GAOR, 35th Sess., Supp.No 48 at 15, UN Doc. A/35/7, Nov. 5, 1980, 20 I.L.M. 462 (1981).

ensure overall advancement of humanity. Respect for human rights, economic development and environmental protection have been unified in the concept of sustainable development as a common concern of humanity.

4.4 *Common Heritage of Mankind*

The common heritage of mankind is a concept that emerged at the end of the 1960s to challenge older concepts of *res nullius* and *res communis* in legal approaches to common resources. *Res nullius,* which in most systems included wild animals and plants, belong to no one and can be freely used and appropriated when taken or captured. The concept of *res communis* implies the reverse: common ownership that precludes individual appropriation but allows common use of the resources, *e.g.* navigation on the high seas. The concept of common heritage of mankind is distinct from both earlier concepts, in part because of its inclusion of the word 'heritage', connoting a temporal aspect in the communal safeguarding of areas incapable of national appropriation. Special legal regimes have been created for the deep seabed and its subsoil,[150] Antarctica, the Moon, the geostationary orbit of satellites, and areas, sites and monuments that form essential parts of the cultural heritage of humanity.

The nature of the common heritage is a form of trust whose principal aims are exclusive use for peaceful purposes, rational utilization in a spirit of conservation, good management or wise use, and transmission to future generations. As noted by the ILC in its work on the protection of the atmosphere, some domestic courts have admitted lawsuits in this field on the basis of the 'public trust doctrine', in which governments are held accountable as trustees for the management of common environmental resources.[151]

Benefits of the common heritage may be shared in the present through equitable allocation of revenue, but this is not the essential feature of the concept. Benefit-sharing can also mean sharing scientific knowledge acquired in common heritage areas – such as Antarctica or the Moon – or sharing use, as with cultural heritage or the orbit of geostationary satellites.

Whether the trustee is the international community through the intermediary of an international body – or one or more states acting on the community's

150 See: UN, Division for Ocean Affairs and the Law of the Sea, *The Law of the Sea, Concept of the Common Heritage of Mankind* (1996).

151 Report of the International Law Commission, Sixty-ninth session (1 May–2 June and 3 July–4 August 2017), Fourth Report on the Protection of the Atmosphere, A/CN.4/705, 2017.01.31, para 88. See further Edith Brown Weiss, *In Fairness to Future Generations: International Law, Common Patrimony, and Intergenerational Equity* (United Nations University Press 1989) 96; Klaus Bosselmann, *Earth Governance: Trusteeship of the Global Commons* (Edward Elgar Publishing 2015).

behalf – is a policy decision. The common heritage of mankind can be administered by a special authority, like the International Seabed Authority created by UNCLOS, amended by agreement in 1994. It also can be administered in common by a group of states, as in Antarctica. Finally, it can remain under state sovereignty and be administered by individual states under the supervision of an international body, as with the cultural and natural heritage designated by the 1972 UNESCO Convention for the Protection of the World's Cultural and Natural Heritage. The last example shows that, in contrast to the concept of *res communis,* the common heritage of mankind can remain under national sovereignty, like protected cultural areas in Egypt or nature reserves in Kenya, and even can be owned by private persons.

During the drafting of the Convention on Biological Diversity, some states criticized the concept of common heritage of mankind. States having rich biological diversity opposed considering such resources as parts of the common heritage of mankind. These views demonstrated a lack of understanding of the concept of common heritage, which does not necessarily include the present sharing of material benefit. The Convention on Biological Diversity, by entrusting the contracting states with the conservation and sustainable use of biological diversity on their territories (Arts. 6–10), incorporates the main elements of the concept of common heritage.

Conclusions

The foundations of international environmental law presented here can be summarized by highlighting several key characteristics. Policies emerge from religious and philosophical beliefs, but also must be based on scientific and economic realities that require an integrated and interdisciplinary approach. At the international level, the emergence of environmental protection as a common interest of humanity alters the traditional role of state sovereignty. A lack of reciprocity in most environmental obligations necessitates new forms of law-making, compliance techniques and enforcement. Other consequences, to be discussed further, include the importance of participation by non-state actors and management of environmental resources at all levels of governance.

One approach that brings together many of these ideas is the notion of subsidiarity. Subsidiarity means making decisions and implementing them at the lowest effective level of government or other organization. Each higher level of governance is subsidiary to the level below it, serving as a safety net when problems cannot be resolved. This idea appears to be woven throughout the entire United Nations Desertification Convention. At the regional level, we may conclude by noting that in addition to the European legal order's use of subsidiarity as a fundamental principle, the 2000 European Landscape Convention embodies the principle in Article 4:

> Each Party shall implement this Convention, in particular Articles 5 and 6, according to its own division of powers, in conformity with its constitutional principles and administrative arrangements, and respecting the principle of subsidiarity, taking into account the European Charter of Local Self-government. Without derogating from the provisions of this Convention, each Party shall harmonize the implementation of this Convention with its own policies.[152]

Bibliography

Anand, R., *International Environmental Justice: A North-South Dimension* (Aldershot: Ashgate, 2004).

Anderson, T. & Libecap, G.D., *Environmental Markets: A Property Rights Approach* (Cambridge: CUP, 2014).

Bavikatte, S.K, *Stewarding the Earth* (New Delhi: OUP India, 2014).

Bohannan, R., *Religions and Environments* (London: Bloomsbury Academic, 2014).

Dimitrov, R., *Science and International Environmental Policy: Regimes and Nonregimes in Global Governance* (Lanham, MD: Rowman & Littlefield, 2005).

Lenzerini, F. & Vrdoljak, A.F., *International Law for Common Goods: Normative Perspectives on Human Rights, Culture and Nature* (Oxford: Hart Publishing, 2014).

Mushkat, R., *International Environmental Law and Asian Values: Legal Norms and Cultural Influences* (Vancouver: UBC Press, 2005).

Rajamani, L, *Differential Treatment in International Environmental Law* (Oxford: OUP, 2006).

Soltau, F., *Fairness in International Climate Change Law and Policy* (Cambridge: CUP, 2011).

Stone, C., *Should Trees Have Standing* (3d rev. edn, Oxford: OUP, 2010).

Tanner, R., *Religion and the Environment* (Basingstoke: Palgrave MacMillan, 2002).

Taylor, P., *An Ecological Approach to International Law* (London: Routledge, 1998).

Tucker, C.M., *Nature, Science and Religion: Intersections Shaping Society and the Environment* (Santa Fe NM: SAR Press, 2012).

152 Florence, Oct. 10, 2000.

CHAPTER 2

Origin and Evolution of International Environmental Law

The present ecological era began at the end of the 1960s, after post-World War II reconstruction led to unprecedented global economic development. This development was unequal, accentuating differences in wealth between countries of the Northern and Southern hemispheres as well as within countries. It also required unprecedented use of exhaustible natural resources such as clean water, air, flora and fauna, and minerals. As it became clear that limited resources would ultimately become incapable of satisfying the various needs of industrial and developing countries, public opinion increasingly demanded action to protect the quantity and quality of the components of the environment.

During preceding centuries, sporadic efforts were made to remedy specific local forms of pollution or nuisances, such as smoke, noise, and water pollution. The first international agreements appeared in the nineteenth century with the conclusion of international fishing treaties and agreements to protect various plant species, but their primary purpose was to sustain the harvesting of economically valuable species. Genuine measures of international environmental protection appeared only during the second half of the twentieth century. A brief glance at the period prior to the development of modern international environmental law indicates the significance of current international legal norms.

1 International Environmental Law before the Stockholm Conference

The 1902 Convention for the Protection of Birds Useful to Agriculture[1] was the first global convention to enter into force for the protection of designated species of wildlife.[2] Its title reveals the perspective of those who adopted it.

1 International Convention for the Protection of Birds Useful to Agriculture (Paris, March 19, 1902), 30 Martens (2d) 686; 102 BFSP 969.

2 An even earlier Convention for the Preservation of Wild Animals, Birds and Fish in Africa, May 19, 1900, 188 Parry 418, never entered into force. It was motivated by the desire to halt the

 | DOI:10.1163/9789047440802_004

The Convention concerned *useful* birds, especially insectivores, and aimed to enhance agricultural production. Annex 2 numbered among 'non-useful birds' the majority of hunting birds, including some eagles and falcons which are strictly protected today. The criterion was short-term utility, the immediate usefulness of protected species. The role of other birds in ecosystems, particularly hunters of small rodents, was completely ignored. The same utilitarianism characterizes the 1911 United States-Great Britain Treaty Relating to the Preservation and Protection of Fur Seals[3] and the subsequent Washington Convention joining each of these states with Japan and Russia.[4] However, these early treaties also called for national quotas and regulating international trade in objects produced from seal hunting, both progressive conservation techniques.

Several early boundary waters treaties contain measures against water pollution. The 1909 agreement respecting boundary waters between the United States and Canada[5] was considered a model. It is still in force and has been amended and expanded periodically since the 1970s.[6] The treaty instituted an international joint commission which continues to play a significant role in water quality control.[7]

Some genuinely ecological approaches emerged in the 1930s, with the adoption of two regional instruments that can be seen as precursors to present-day environmental law. First, the 1933 London Convention Relative to the Preservation of Fauna and Flora in their Natural State, applied to an Africa then largely colonized. It excluded from its scope the metropolitan areas of the colonial

---

massacre of diverse animal species deemed useful or inoffensive to man. The treaty simultaneously encouraged the destruction of creatures deemed harmful to human interests, including lions, leopards, crocodiles, and poisonous snakes.

3 Treaty for the Preservation and Protection of the Fur Seals (Washington, DC, 7 Feb. 1911), 104 BFSP 175.

4 Interim Convention on Conservation of North Pacific Fur Seals (Washington, 9 Feb. 1957), 314 UNTS 105, 5 Martens (3rd) 720.

5 Washington, 11 Jan. 1909, AJIL 239 (1910 Supp.).

6 See United States-Canada Agreement relating to the Establishment of Joint Pollution Contingency Plans for Spills of Oil and Other Noxious Substances (June 19, 1974), 25 UST 1280; TIAS 7861; United States-Canada Agreement on Great Lakes Water Quality with Annexes (Nov. 22, 1978), 30 UST 1383, TIAS No. 9257; amended Oct. 16, 1983, TIAS No. 10798; Great Lakes Water Quality Agreement of 2012, Protocol Amending the Agreement Between Canada and the United States of America on Great Lakes Water Quality, 1978, as Amended on October 16, 1983 and on November 18, 1987, available at http://www.ijc.org/en_/Great_Lakes_Water_Quality.

7 See Chapter 10 for a discussion of the International Joint Commission.

powers.[8] Within the territories to which it applied, it provided for the creation of national parks and strict protection for some species of wild animals. It also included measures regulating the export of hunting trophies and banned certain methods of hunting. The Convention remained fundamentally utilitarian, however, adopting these measures in part for the purpose of preserving big game hunting (Art. 4(2)); it also specifically called for measures to be taken to domesticate wild animals susceptible of economic utilization (Art. 7(8)) and allowed additional measures to be taken to protect species of animals or plants 'which by general admission are useful to man or of special scientific interest' (Art. 8(4)). The second instrument, the Convention on Nature Protection and Wildlife Preservation in the Western Hemisphere,[9] remains in force and envisages the establishment of reserves and the protection of wild animals and plants, especially migratory birds; however, the main provisions of the Convention are less restrictive than those of the London agreement.

Increasingly during the twentieth century, states entered into boundary water agreements that included provisions on the problem of water pollution. Some states concluded a network of bilateral agreements to regulate the utilization of waters through the creation of international commissions, while other states entered into regional agreements. In 1950, Belgium, France and Luxembourg concluded the first treaty entirely dedicated to countering freshwater pollution, one part of which created a tripartite standing committee to tackle the problems.[10] Similar treaties followed for the Mosel (1956),[11] Lake Constance (1960),[12] Lake Leman (1962),[13] and the Rhine (1963).[14] Although in the majority of instances these treaties established international commissions, the agreements did not set water quality standards nor adopt norms against pollution.[15]

---

8 Convention Relative to the Preservation of Fauna and Flora in their Natural State, Art. 1 (London, 8 Nov. 1933), 172 LNTS 241; UKTS 27, Cmd. 5280; 137 BFSP 254.

9 Convention on Nature Protection and Wildlife Preservation in the Western Hemisphere (Washington DC, 12 Oct. 1940), 161 UNTS 193; 56 Stat. 1354, TS No. 981; 3 Bevans 630.

10 Protocol to Establish a Tripartite Standing Committee on Polluted Waters (Brussels, 8 Apr. 1950), 66 UNTS 285.

11 Convention on the Canalization of the Mosel (Luxembourg, Oct. 27, 1956) *J.O.R.F*, 1 Jan. 1957, 534.

12 Agreement on the Protection of Lake Constance against Pollution (Steckborn, 27 Oct. 1960), UN Doc. ST/LEG/SERB/12 p.458.

13 Convention between France and Switzerland Concerning the Protection of Lake Leman against Pollution (Paris, 16 Nov. 1962), 922 UNTS 49.

14 Agreement concerning the International Commission for the Protection of the Rhine against Pollution (Bern, 29 Apr. 1963), 994 UNTS 3.

15 For more on freshwater pollution and its legislation, see Chapter 10.

Efforts to combat marine pollution appeared during the 1950s. The 1954 London Convention for the Prevention of the Pollution of the Sea by Oil[16] was the first rather tentative step in this direction. The Convention was later modified and reinforced, then replaced in 1973 by a much more detailed and effective convention.[17] New technologies, in particular the utilization of nuclear energy, led to further international regulation. A 1963 treaty addressed military use of radioactive materials, banning nuclear weapons testing in the atmosphere, in outer space and under water.[18]

During this period, environmental concerns increasingly appeared in general international legal texts. The 1959 Antarctic Treaty forbade all nuclear activity on the sixth continent and envisaged the adoption of measures to protect animals and plants.[19] Two of the four 1958 conventions relating to the law of the sea prohibited ocean pollution by oil or pipelines and by radioactive waste, as well as damage to the marine environment caused by drilling operations on the continental shelf.[20] The third of the four 1958 conventions was entirely dedicated to fishing and the conservation of marine living resources.[21] For the other commons area, the 1967 Treaty on Principles Governing the Exploration and Use of Outer Space declared that states should avoid contamination as well as harmful modifications of the earth through the introduction of extraterrestrial substances.[22]

Thus, incrementally, the first elements emerged of international norms for the protection of the environment. International jurisprudence contributed by introducing the fundamental principles which dominate this area of law. In as early as 1893, the *Bering Sea* arbitration set forth the principle that the

16 International Convention for the Prevention of Pollution of the Sea by Oil (London, 12 May 1954), 327 UNTS 3; 12 UST 2989, TIAS No. 4900; UKTS 54 (1958), Cmd. 595.

17 International Convention for the Prevention of Pollution by Ships (London, 2 Nov. 1973) 12 ILM 1319 (1973).

18 Treaty Banning Nuclear Weapons in the Atmosphere, in Outer Space, and Underwater (Moscow, 5 Aug. 1963), 480 UNTS 43; 14 UST 1313.

19 The Antarctic Treaty (Washington DC, 1 Dec. 1959, 402 UNTS 71; UKTS 97 (1961), Cmd. 1535; 12 UST 794, TIAS 4780.

20 Convention on the High Seas, Arts. 24–25 (Geneva, 29 Apr. 1958), 450 UNTS 82, UKTS 5 (1963), Cmd. 1929, 13 UST 2312, TIAS No. 5200, 52 AJIL 842. Convention on the Continental Shelf, Art. 5(7) (Geneva, 29 Apr. 1958), 499 UNTS 311, 15 UST 471.

21 Convention on Fishing and Conservation of the Living Resources of the High Seas (Geneva, 29 Apr. 1958), 559 UNTS 285, UKTS 39 (1966), Cmd. 3028, 17 UST 138, TIAS No. 5969, 52 AJIL 851.

22 Treaty on Principles Governing the Activities of States in the Exploration and Use of Outer Space, Including the Moon and Other Celestial Bodies, Art. IX (27 Jan. 1967), 610 UNTS 205; UKTS 10 (1968), Cmd. 3519; 18 UST 2410, TIAS No. 6347.

protection of species outside of territorial waters requires international regulation and state cooperation.[23] With regard to transboundary pollution, the *Trail Smelter* arbitration of March 11, 1941,[24] affirmed that no state has the right to use its territory or permit it to be used to cause serious damage by emissions to the territory of another state or to the property of persons found there. In 1949, the International Court of Justice (ICJ), in the *Corfu Channel* case, more generally affirmed that no state may utilize its territory contrary to the rights of other states.[25] Finally, in the *Lake Lanoux* decision of November 19, 1956,[26] the arbitral panel alluded to the invasion of the rights of states that may result from pollution of boundary waters. These precedents furnished the first legal principles from which present environmental law has evolved.

At the end of the 1960's, scientific studies raised general public awareness of dangers threatening the biosphere.[27] The resulting mobilization of public opinion was unprecedented in two ways. First, it was a grass roots phenomenon, only later finding a power base when several governments officially adopted environmental laws and policies. Second, the movement was transnational from the beginning. The global grass roots efforts emerged from a changing philosophical and ethical consensus, incorporating new individual and social values in reaction to the post-war 'consumer society'. Rejecting traditional ideologies to the degree that they were seen as materialistic, the ecological movement spanned across political factions and parties. As a consequence, many environmental laws were adopted unanimously by national legislatures. International organizations also began to recognize the emergence of a new problem. The United Nations Economic Commission for Europe,[28] for example, made studies beginning in 1956 about pollution of inland waters and later the dumping of wastes.

The year 1968 marked a turning point with the United Nations, the Council of Europe and the Organization of African Unity all taking decisive steps. The Council of Europe became the first international organization to adopt texts on environmental protection: a March 8 Declaration on Air Pollution Control,[29] and the European Water Charter, proclaimed May 6, 1968.[30] Today

23 *Bering Sea Case* (US v UK) (Aug. 15, 1893).

24 Arbitral Award in the *Trail Smelter Case*, (March 11, 1941), 3 UNRIAA 1905.

25 *Corfu Channel Case* (UK v Albania) (Apr. 3, 1949), Merits, ICJ Rep. [1949] 4.

26 *Lake Lanoux Case* (France v Spain) (Nov. 19, 1957), 12 UNRIAA 281 (1957).

27 Rachel Carson's classic *The Silent Spring* (Houghton Mifflin 1962) is often credited with bringing environmental concerns to public awareness.

28 See Chapter 5.

29 Res. 60(4) of March 8, 1968, Committee of Ministers, Council of Europe.

30 Published as a separate sheet, without number.

the principles they affirm appear obvious. At that time, however, even the transboundary dimensions of protecting freshwaters and air were generally not perceived. During the same year, the Council of Europe also adopted the first European regional environmental treaty: the European Agreement on the Restriction of the Use of Certain Detergents in Washing and Cleaning Products.[31]

Africa produced the second major initiative despite a widely-held view in the region that environmental deterioration was due to industrial pollution and was thus primarily a problem of the northern hemisphere. On September 15, 1968, the heads of states and governments of the Organization of African Unity signed an African Convention on the Conservation of Nature and Natural Resources,[32] replacing the 1933 London Convention. The 1968 Convention is a model of comprehensiveness: it concerns the conservation and utilization of soil, water, plant and animal resources, virtually the entire environment. This breadth of objectives means that some provisions in the Convention announce only general principles, but those that concern the conservation of plant and animal resources adopt precise rules, including the creation of reserves, regulation of hunting, capturing and fishing and protection of specific species. Two important environmental innovations appear in the African Convention: the recognized need to protect the habitat of endangered species as well as the species itself, and the proclaimed special responsibility of the state whose territory is the sole locale of a rare species.[33]

2 The Stockholm Conference on the Human Environment

The United Nations joined the actions during 1968 directed at protecting the environment when the General Assembly convened a world conference on the human environment to be held in Stockholm in 1972.[34] The decision gave rise to diverse activities, particularly within inter-governmental organizations whose mandate could extend to environmental issues. Numerous non-governmental environmental organizations and governments also engaged in preparatory work.

31 European Agreement on the Restriction of the Use of Certain Detergents in Washing and Cleaning Products (Brussels, 16 Sept. 1968), 788 UNTS 181; ETS No. 64; UKTS 23 (1971), Cmd. 4646.

32 African Convention on the Conservation of Nature and Natural Resources (Algiers, 15 Sept. 1968), 1001 UNTS 3.

33 Art. VIII(1).

34 G. A. Res. 2398 (XXIII) of December 3, 1968.

Ecological catastrophes such as the 1967 'black tides' off the coasts of France, England and Belgium, caused by the shipwreck of the oil tanker *Torrey Canyon* incited governments to take action immediately, without waiting for the Stockholm meeting. These efforts focused on international cooperation to counter marine oil pollution through measures of prevention and establishment of liability. Several steps also were taken to conserve wild animals, notably with the conclusion of the 1971 Ramsar Convention on Wetlands of International Importance[35] and the 1972 London Convention for the Conservation of Antarctic Seals.[36]

While these actions responded to urgent environmental problems, ambitious preparations for the Stockholm Conference continued, based on the work of a special committee of twenty-seven states advising the United Nations Secretary General. When the Stockholm meeting took place June 5–16, 1972, it brought together some 6,000 persons, including delegations from 113 states, representatives of every major intergovernmental organization, 700 observers sent by 400 non-governmental organizations, invited individuals, and approximately 1,500 journalists. While the participation was global, the priorities and concerns were not shared equally. Many developing countries considered environmental protection to be a problem resulting from the pollution produced by industrialized countries. Poorer nations were far more focused on development and the alleviation of poverty. They also were concerned about competitive disadvantage for their goods and skeptical of the motivations of wealthier nations. The perceived tension between environmental protection and economic development may have emerged at Stockholm, but it remains visible if not more prevalent today.

The Conference nonetheless achieved an internationally-recognized significance, enhanced by the texts adopted during a closing plenary session. Most notable are the Stockholm Declaration on the Human Environment,[37] adopted by acclamation, an 'Action Plan' containing 109 recommendations, and a resolution on institutional and financial measures to implement the Action Plan within the United Nations.

The Stockholm Declaration on the Human Environment begins with the preambular statement that man is at once the creature and molder of his

---

35 2 Feb. 1971, 996 UNTS 245, UKTS 34 (1976), Cmd. 6465, 11 ILM 969 (1972). The initial aim of the Ramsar Convention was to protect the habitat of migratory waterbirds.

36 1 June 1972, 29 UST 441, TIAS 8826; 11 ILM 251 (1972).

37 Stockholm Declaration on the Human Environment (June 16, 1972), UN Doc. A/Conf.48/14/Rev.1 (UN Pub. 73.II.A.14) (1973), 11 ILM 1416 (1972).

environment; the natural element and the man-made are essential to human well-being and the full enjoyment of basic human rights, including the right to life. Protecting the human environment is also viewed as a major issue for economic development, a recognition that subsequently has come to dominate global action respecting the environment. The Declaration recognizes that the continuous natural growth of world population poses problems for preserving the environment, but expresses a conviction that with social progress and the evolution of production, science, and technology, human ability to improve the environment strengthens each day.

The principles contained in the second part of the Declaration translate the preamble into more concrete language, while reflecting the various political preoccupations of the meeting's participants. The first principle, for example, affirms the fundamental human right to liberty, equality and adequate conditions of life in an environment of a quality that permits a life of dignity and well-being, adding that man bears a solemn responsibility to protect and improve the environment for present and future generations. The principle concludes by condemning apartheid, racial segregation and discrimination, colonialism, and other forms of oppression and foreign domination. Significantly, Principle 1 establishes a fundamental link between environmental protection and human rights, setting the stage for rights-based approaches in environmental law, despite the conflation of ideas and themes.

Principles 2 to 7 constitute the ecological heart of the Declaration. They proclaim that the natural resources of the globe are not only oil and minerals, but also air, water, earth, plants and animals as well as representative samples of natural ecosystems. These should be preserved in the interest of present and future generations. Man has a particular responsibility to safeguard the heritage of wildlife and its habitats. Renewable resources must maintain their ability to replenish themselves and nonrenewable resources should not be wasted. In all cases the Declaration emphasizes the necessity of adequate resource management. This section concludes by calling for a halt to the production of toxic wastes or other matter that cannot be absorbed by the environment and in particular to prevent marine pollution.

Principles 8 to 25 address implementation of environmental protection. Four provisions concern the particular situation of developing countries. After stating that economic and social development is indispensable if an environment favorable to the existence and work of man is to be sought, Principle 9 affirms that the best means to remedy underdevelopment is to enhance financial and technical assistance. National environmental policies should assist the potential progress of poorer countries and they should be accorded supplementary international assistance. Principles 10 to 12 concern international trade and economic consequences of environmental protection, particularly for developing countries. Principle 10 provides that the stability of prices and an adequate remuneration for primary products and goods is essential for the management of the environment. Principles 13 to 15 underline the necessity of integrated, coordinated and rational development planning. Demographic issues produced a simple recommendation in Principle 16 in favor of policies which respect fundamental human rights and are judged adequate by the governments concerned. Principles 18–20 mention other instruments of environmental policy: recourse to science and technology, exchange of information, and finally, teaching and information about environmental matters.

The last group of principles, 21 to 26, is of particular importance in the development of international law. Principle 21 codifies the no-harm principle, which was introduced in the 1941 *Trail Smelter Arbitration*. It has thus been widely recognized as expressing a basic norm of customary international environmental law:

> States have, in accordance with the Charter of the United Nations and the principles of international law, the sovereign right to exploit their own resources pursuant to their own environmental policies, and the responsibility to ensure that the activities within their jurisdiction or control do not cause damage to the environment of other states or of areas beyond the limits of national jurisdiction.

The Declaration further affirms that states should cooperate to develop international law regarding liability and compensation for victims of pollution and other environmental damage produced outside their boundaries (Principle 22). They should define criteria and norms in environmental matters, taking into consideration the system of values prevailing in each country, in particular in developing countries (Principle 23). States should cooperate to protect and improve the environment and ensure that international organizations play a coordinated, effective and dynamic role in this field (Principles 24–25). The final principle condemns nuclear weapons and all other means of mass destruction.

The 'Action Plan for the Human Environment',[38] another major outcome of the Stockholm Conference, did not always follow an operational order but can be re-grouped around three themes: a global environmental assessment program, environmental management activities, and supporting measures. The

38 UN Doc. A/Conf.48/14, July 3, 1972 at 10.

assessment program, christened 'Earthwatch', included evaluation and review, research, monitoring and information exchanges. Understandably, international cooperation was given an important place.

The chapter on environmental management, which concerns both human establishments and natural resources, contains most of the provisions concerning pollution. The Plan addresses the problem of dumping toxic or dangerous substances, elaboration of norms to limit noise, control of contaminants in food, and measures for controlling pollution. The Plan's authors give particular attention to protection of the marine environment, understandable in light of the preparations for the Third United Nations Conference on the Law of the Sea that had already begun. Finally, the Plan addresses wildlife and natural spaces, with the accent again strongly placed on international cooperation through the conclusion of treaties, coordinated action by governments, and exchange of information on national legislation. The text stresses the importance of planning, including the development of international plans of action.

Measures of support contained in the Stockholm Action Plan focus on information and public education as well as training of specialists in environmental matters. They include institutional aspects, in effect providing that anticipated actions should be coordinated at the international level. For this, the Plan recommends creation of a central organ to be charged with environmental matters. In addition, the Action Plan recommends a division of duties among specialized agencies of the United Nations (FAO, WHO, UNESCO, etc.) and among regional organizations. On the basis of the recommendations of the Stockholm Conference, the United Nations General Assembly in 1972 created a specialized subsidiary organ, the United Nations Environment Program (UNEP).[39] The UNEP is headquartered in Nairobi, and it functions as a central organ for environmental matters as intended by the Stockholm Conference, on their website being named as 'the leading global authority on the environment'.[40]

3 From Stockholm to Rio

The Stockholm Conference had immense value in drawing attention to the problem of environmental deterioration and methods to prevent or remedy it. The Conference was global both in its planetary conception of the

39 See Chapter 5 for a discussion of UNEP.

40 For more on the UNEP, visit their website: <https://www.unep.org/>.

environment, and in its view of institutional structures and world policies. It was also global in addressing all the major environmental themes of the time.

The vision and divisions emerging from Stockholm dominated the evolution of international environmental law until the Rio Conference and produced a spike in national and international laws and policies during the 1970s. The usual approach during this decade concentrated on separately protecting specific sectors of the environment: oceans, inland waters, atmosphere, outer space, wild plants and animals. The living components of the environment were given added attention in 1982 when the General Assembly adopted the World Charter for Nature.[41]

During the 1980s, it became increasingly evident that the prevailing sectoral approach was insufficient to address environmental deterioration because it often failed to regulate the causes or sources of harm that could affect more than one or several sectors. Thus, a second approach, which aimed to reduce the sources and risks of harm, became a common complement to sectoral regulation. This led eventually to some common management of shared resources and an ecosystem approach, but by the end of the 1980s, global problems emerged that required comprehensive cooperation among all states, in particular the need to address anthropogenic climate change and the extensive loss of biological diversity.

3.1 *Global Instruments*

The Stockholm Conference had a major impact on the development of new legal texts. First, the third United Nations Conference on the Law of the Sea, which began meeting the same year as the Stockholm Conference, produced the United Nations Convention on the Law of the Sea (UNCLOS)[42] in 1982, after ten years of negotiations. As a comprehensive code of the oceans, UNCLOS encompasses marine environmental protection, providing an integrated legal framework for formerly widely dispersed standards. UNCLOS reaffirms and gives detail to global and regional norms to combat vessel-source and land-based pollution as well as pollution caused by dumping of wastes and other matter. UNCLOS also adopted significant new rules, in particular the fundamentally important principle that states have a general obligation to protect

41 World Charter for Nature, 28 Oct. 1982, GA Res. 37/7, 37 UNGAOR Supp. (No. 51), at 17, UN Doc. A/37/51 (1982). For the legislative history and a commentary on the Charter, see: European Council for Environmental Law, *The World Charter for Nature* (1986).

42 Montego Bay, 10 Dec. 1982. For a detailed discussion of the environmental aspects of UNCLOS, see Chapter 11.

and preserve the totality of the marine environment,[43] including areas within the sovereignty and jurisdiction of the states themselves.

Several weeks before the adoption of UNCLOS, the United Nations General Assembly solemnly proclaimed the World Charter for Nature.[44] The preamble expresses fundamental concepts and international values, affirming that mankind itself is part of nature, civilization is rooted in nature, and every form of life is unique and merits respect regardless of its worth to man. Thus, all human conduct that could affect nature is to be guided and judged according to the twenty-four proclaimed principles. As the preamble indicates, this text breaks away from the earlier anthropocentric approach that sought to protect only those parts of nature deemed useful to man. It is a document for all of nature.

The principles operationalize this *pro natura* ethic by insisting that nature shall be respected and its essential processes shall not be impaired, the genetic viability of the earth shall not be compromised, and the population levels of all life forms, wild and domesticated, shall be at least sufficient for their survival. In addition, special protection shall be afforded to the unique areas of the globe, both land and sea. Ecosystems, organisms and other natural resources shall be managed to achieve and maintain their optimum sustainable productivity and continuity. The Charter envisages the integration of nature conservation into social and economic development planning and implementation. Nearly half of the principles concern the application of the Charter and foresee incorporation of its principles in the law and practice of each state, the broadest dissemination possible of knowledge of nature and efforts to increase that knowledge, as well as monitoring of the status of nature. Funds, programs and administrative structures necessary to achieve the objective of conserving nature should be provided.

The principles of the World Charter of Nature were not elaborated in a binding legal instrument, but they have influenced the direction of international environmental law, particularly in regard to preservation of biological diversity. Moreover, they have been incorporated in conventions such as the 1985 South-East Asian Agreement on the Conservation of Nature and its Resources.[45] Other noteworthy conventions on nature protection were concluded even prior to the World Charter for Nature. Three of them, the 1971 Ramsar

43 Art. 192, UNCLOS.

44 *Supra* n 41.

45 South-East Asian Agreement on the Conservation of Nature and its Resources, 9 July 1985, Kuala Lumpur (1985).

Convention on Conservation of Wetlands of International Importance,[46] the fundamentally important UNESCO Convention on the Protection of the World Cultural and Natural Heritage,[47] and the 1979 Bonn Convention on the Conservation of Migratory Species of Wild Animals,[48] envisage the protection of nature in designated natural zones. The fourth treaty, the 1973 Washington Convention on International Trade in Endangered Species of Wild Fauna and Flora,[49] tackles the protection of species by regulating the particular threat posed by trade in endangered plants and animals.

Following the Stockholm Conference, new problems emerged that had not been perceived earlier, such as long-range air pollution and depletion of the ozone layer. The multilateral Vienna Convention, adopted March 22, 1985 and its 1987 Montreal Protocol[50] created an effective international system to reduce emissions of stratospheric ozone-depleting substances. The effective compliance mechanisms these instruments introduced have become a potential model for other environmental treaties. If awareness of stratospheric ozone depletion emerged due to years of study, the nuclear catastrophe at Chernobyl, April 26, 1986, suddenly raised awareness of another problem. The event led to an almost immediate adoption of two conventions, the first requiring rapid notification of nuclear accidents, the second covering assistance in the case of a nuclear accident or radioactive emergency.[51]

The regulation of other potential sources of environmental harm became more common beginning in the 1980s as it became clear that toxic or dangerous products and processes threatening most or all parts of the environment must be regulated during their whole lifetime. A 'cradle to grave' approach brought regulations covering production, transport, marketing, and waste elimination, although the highly technical aspects of regulating production require applying different methods to different groups of products. UNEP established an International Register of Potentially Toxic Chemicals containing detailed information on substances of international importance, available for consultation.

---

46 Ramsar, 2 Feb. 1971, 996 UNTS 245, UKTS 34 (1976), Cmd. 6465, 11 ILM 969 (1972).

47 23 Nov. 1972, UKTS 2 (1985), Cmd. 9424, 27 UST 37, TIAS No. 8225, 11 ILM 1358 (1972).

48 Bonn, 23 June 1979, 19 ILM 15 (1980).

49 Washington, 3 March 1973, 993 UNTS 243, UKTS 101 (1976), Cmd. 6647, 27 UST, TIAS No. 8249.

50 Convention for the Protection of the Ozone Layer, (Vienna, 22 March 1985), 1513 UNTS 293; Misc. 13 (1987), Cmd. 9652, 26 ILM 529 (1985); Montreal Protocol, 16 Sept. 1987,1522 UNTS 3, 26 ILM 1541 (1987).

51 Convention on Early Notification of a Nuclear Accident and Convention on Assistance in the Case of a Nuclear Accident or Radiological Emergency (Vienna, 26 Sept. 1986) 1457 UNTS 133 / [1987] ATS 14, 25 ILM 1369 (1986).

The Convention on the Control of Transboundary Movements of Hazardous Wastes and their Disposal[52] and regional treaties on the topic concluded for Africa,[53] Central America[54] and the South Pacific[55] contributed significantly to regulating the sources of environmental harm.

Stockholm stimulated a variety of international organizations and institutions to consider environmental issues. New rules concerning the environment were included in instruments concerned with human rights,[56] humanitarian law,[57] and economic law.[58] Article 30 of the Charter of Economic Rights and Duties of States, adopted by the United Nations General Assembly in 1974,[59] for example, proclaims that the protection, preservation and management of the environment for present and future generations is the responsibility of all states; they should strive to halt any detrimental policies in environmental matters and develop programs conforming to this responsibility. More generally, on October 30, 1980, the United Nations General Assembly proclaimed the responsibility of states for the preservation of nature in the interest of present and future generations.[60]

Continuing north-south divisions over how to integrate environmental protection into programs for needed economic development led the General Assembly in 1983 to create the World Commission on Environment and Development, an independent body linked to but outside the United Nations system. More commonly known as the Brundtland Commission,[61] its mandate was to examine critical environment and development issues and formulate realistic proposals; propose new forms of international cooperation on these issues to influence policies in the direction of needed changes; and raise the levels of understanding and commitment to action of individuals, organizations, businesses and governments. The conclusions of the Brundtland Report stressed the need for an integrated approach to development policies and projects which, if environmentally sound, should lead to sustainable economic development in both developed and developing countries. The report emphasized

52 Basel, March 22, 1989.
53 Bamako, Jan. 29, 1991.
54 Panama, Dec. 11, 1991.
55 Waigani, Sept. 16, 1995.
56 See Chapter 15.
57 See Chapter 16.
58 See Chapter 17.
59 G. A. Res. 3281 (XXIX) of December 12, 1974, UNGAOR, 29th Sess., Supp. No. 31, UN Doc. A/9631, p. 50.
60 G. A. Res/35/7, 20 I.L.M. 462 (1981).
61 See Brundtland Commission, *OUR COMMON FUTURE* (Oxford University Press 1987).

the need to give higher priority to anticipating and preventing problems. It adopted the term 'sustainable development' and defined it as development that meets present and future environment and development objectives. It concluded that without an equitable sharing of the costs and benefits of environmental protection within and between countries neither social justice nor sustainable development can be achieved.

The Brundtland Report led the United Nations to convene a second global conference on the environment, held in 1992 in Rio de Janeiro, under the title United Nations Conference on Environment and Development (UNCED). The name of the conference reflected a change of approach from that of the Stockholm Conference on the Human Environment, bringing to the forefront concerns of countries struggling with poverty.

3.2 *Regional Instruments*

At the regional level, an equally important evolution occurred following the Stockholm Conference. Immediately after, in 1972, the Conference of Heads of State and Governments of the European Economic Community met in Paris and adopted a Declaration stating that economic expansion is not an end in itself, but that the quality of life should be improved, with particular attention given to intangible values and protecting the environment.[62] The European Community adopted its first Action Program on the Environment the following year. It declared that economic activities could no longer be imagined in the absence of an effective campaign to combat pollution and nuisance and protect the environment.[63] The EC thus began taking action in the environmental field, principally but not exclusively against pollutants and nuisances, adopting Programs of Action followed by directives and regulations.[64]

In 1975, at the conclusion of the Helsinki Conference on Security and Cooperation in Europe,[65] all European countries, Canada and the United States adopted a Final Act that contained an entire chapter on cooperation in the environmental field. The declaration envisaged international studies of environmental problems, increased effectiveness of national and international measures, in particular procedures for evaluating environmental accidents, and efforts to reconcile or harmonize environmental policies and legislation. The chosen institutional structure was the United Nations Economic Commission

62 EC Commission, 6th General Report (1972) 8.

63 First Action Programme on the Environment, OJ 1983, No. C 112. See also Chapter 5.

64 To this day, the EU works with Environment Action Programmes. The current, 8th Programme guides European environmental policy until 2030.

65 Helsinki, Aug. 1, 1975, 14 I.L.M. 1292 at 1307 (1975).

for Europe. In 1979, the Geneva Convention on Long Range Trans-Boundary Air Pollution was adopted within this framework.[66] Subsequent protocols have created a general system to regulate the emissions of air pollutants.

The importance of regional institutions to international environmental law was demonstrated by the Nordic Council when concluding the 1974 Nordic Convention on the Protection of the Environment,[67] which is considered a model on the subject of environmental cooperation between neighboring states and an inspiration for OECD's principles on transboundary environment cooperation. The Council of Europe also adopted measures for the protection of nature, elaborating the 1979 Bern Convention on the Conservation of Wildlife and Natural Habitats in Europe.

Global institutions also undertake actions concerning specific regions of the world. UNEP has drafted a series of conventions concerning regional seas, sometimes in collaboration with other institutions such as the Food and Agriculture Organization. Treaty systems now exist for most maritime and coastal zones of the world, most of them adopted under UNEP auspices.[68]

Regional regulations, like those adopted on the global level, address sources of harm as well as environmental milieu. The OCDE adopted recommendations concerning methods of assessing the potential environmental effects of activities. Regional transport of dangerous or toxic materials became regulated by separate international conventions relating to rail, road, and river transport. The EC regulated the marketing of chemical products, mainly by harmonizing the classification, packaging and handling of dangerous substances. The OECD and the European Union also adopted regulations governing specific hazardous substances, such as mercury and phytopharmaceutical products. Cooperation to prevent industrial accidents or minimize their effects also progressed, in particular through a 1992 Convention on the Transboundary Effects of Industrial Accidents drafted in the framework of the UN Economic Commission for Europe.

4 The United Nations Conference on Environment and Development

UNCED emerged from the Brundtland Report.[69] The UN General Assembly resolution accepting the Report[70] convened a world conference on environment

66 Geneva, Nov. 13, 1979, UKTS 57 (1983), Cmd. 9034, TIAS No. 10541, 18 ILM 1442 (1979).

67 Stockholm, Feb. 19, 1974, 13 ILM 511 (1974).

68 See Chapter 11.

69 See the end of subsection 3.1 above for a discussion of the Brundtland Commission and its report.

70 Resolution 44/228 of December 22, 1989.

and development to be held in Brazil in 1992. To achieve this, it created a preparatory committee (PREPCOM) open to all United Nations member states, as well as members states of specialized agencies, and accredited observers. The three PREPCOM sessions negotiated legal, institutional and financial questions. The initial goal was to proclaim an Earth Charter, i.e. principles containing general environmental obligations of states. After difficult negotiations, the idea was abandoned in favor of adopting a declaration of principles, a compromise between the developing countries (Group of 77) who sought only political commitments, and industrialized countries, mainly OECD member states, who insisted on legal norms. In addition, there were competing views on the Declaration's contents: the industrialized countries considered it essential to include principles on public information and participation, precaution, and the polluter pays principle, while developing countries demanded inclusion of the rights to development, poverty alleviation, and recognition of CBDR.

The debate over institutions centered on the necessity of creating new organs as opposed to revitalizing and restructuring existing bodies. The delay in raising this issue limited the degree of innovation possible. Ultimately, the participating states agreed to create a Commission on Sustainable Development under the authority of the UN Economic and Social Council. The question of its composition and functioning was left to the UN General Assembly.[71]

UNCED met in Rio de Janeiro from June 3 to 14, 1992. One hundred seventy-two states (all but six members of the United Nations) were represented by close to 10,000 participants, including 116 heads of state and government; Japan alone sent 300 delegates. 1,400 non-governmental organizations were accredited as well as nearly 9000 journalists.

Five texts emerged from the meeting. Two conventions, drafted and adopted before the Conference, were opened for signature at Rio: the UN Framework Convention on Climate Change and the Convention on Biological Diversity. The Conference also adopted a declaration whose title reflects the difficulties of reaching agreement on it: Non-legally binding authoritative statement of principles for a global consensus on the management, conservation and sustainable development of all types of forests.[72]

The remaining two texts adopted at UNCED have a general scope: the Rio Declaration on Environment and Development and an action program called Agenda 21. The Declaration, a statement of twenty-seven principles, has a composite character which its legislative history can explain. It reaffirms the Stockholm Declaration of 1972 on which it seeks to build, but its approach and

71 See Chapter 5.

72 See Chapter 8.

philosophy shift away from a central focus on the environment. The organizing concept is instead sustainable development, derived from the Brundtland Report. Principle 4 is the main affirmation, stating that in order to achieve sustainable development, environmental protection shall constitute an integral part of the development process and cannot be considered in isolation from it. Whether intentional or not, the language of this Principle and the thrust of the Rio meeting as a whole began a trend towards viewing environmental protection as an instrument to achieve development rather than as a goal of intrinsic value. This view is also reflected in Principle 1, whose anthropocentric approach can be contrasted with the Stockholm Declaration and the World Charter of Nature: 'Human beings are at the center of concerns for sustainable development. They are entitled to a healthy and productive life in harmony with nature'.

Despite its more limited view of the need for environmental protection, the Rio Declaration contains important innovations, including several principles of an unambiguous, general legal character. It reinforces some existing principles and proclaims new ones. The first category includes Principle 2, which concerns the transboundary effects of activities. It is similar to Principle 21 of the Stockholm Declaration, but adds the word 'developmental'. Other legal norms can be found in Principle 10, affirming rights of access to public information, participation, and remedies, Principle 13, which calls for the development of liability rules, and Principles 18 and 19 which require notifying other states about emergencies and projects that may affect their environment. The formulation of then-emerging principles includes the precautionary principle (Principle 15), the 'polluter pays' principle requiring internalization of environmental costs (Principle 16) and the obligation to perform an environmental impact assessment (Principle 17). Principle 11 stresses the importance of enacting effective environmental legislation, although it notes that standards applied by some countries may not be appropriate to others because of the economic and social costs involved.

Other principles are more in the nature of policy guidelines, although the line between law and policy is not always clear. A distinction can be made between three groups of policy provisions. The first group expresses concern for development: Principle 5 aims at the eradication of poverty, Principle 6 claims special priority for the needs of developing countries, and Principle 9 relates to the strengthening of endogenous capacity-building for sustainable development by improving scientific understanding. All these provisions use the term 'shall', while the other groups of policy principles substitute 'should' for 'shall'.

A second and related group of principles addresses the world economic order. Principle 7 proclaims CBDR, including the special responsibility of developed countries 'in view of the pressures their societies place on the global environment'. Principle 8 adds that states should reduce and eliminate unsustainable patterns of production and consumption and promote demographic policies. Although it is not made explicit, the first part of this principle mainly concerns industrialized states, while the second part concerns situations in developing countries. Economic aspects are treated in Principle 12 which advocates a 'supportive and open economic system' and international consensus, and condemns discriminatory trade measures or disguised restrictions on international trade, as well as unilateral actions. Finally, Principle 14 aims to discourage or prevent the relocation and transfer to other states of activities and substances that cause severe environmental degradation or are harmful to human health.

A last group of principles concerns national governance, especially public participation in decision-making. Principle 10 recognizes the rights to information, to participation and to remedies in environmental matters. Principles 20 to 22 stress the importance of the participation of women, youth and indigenous peoples.

Agenda 21, the second general document adopted by the Rio Conference, supplemented the Declaration in an 800 page program of action consisting of forty chapters with 115 specific topics. The four main parts address:

- socio-economic dimensions (*e.g.* habitats, health, demography, consumption and production patterns);
- conservation and resource management (*e.g.* atmosphere, forest, water, waste, chemical products);
- strengthening the role of non-governmental organizations and other social groups such as trade unions, women, youth;
- measures of implementation (*e.g.* financing, institutions).

The chapters concerning different sectors such as the atmosphere (chapter 9), biological diversity (chapter 15), the oceans (chapter 17), and freshwater resources (chapter 18), as well as discussion of specific problems such as biotechnology (chapter 15), toxic chemicals (chapter 19), and waste (chapters 20–22) are of particular interest to the development of international environmental law. Also important are the two chapters dedicated to international institutional arrangements (chapter 38) and international legal instruments and mechanisms (chapter 39).

The chapter on international legal instruments has implications for international law in general because it designates specific means that should be used to develop the substance of international environmental law and its procedural dimensions. It insists on the legal aspects of sustainable development and on the adoption of environmental standards. It calls for the integration of environment and development policies in international treaties and emphasizes the participation in and the contribution of all countries to the further elaboration of international environmental law in the context of sustainable development. It refers to the relationship between existing national instruments and relevant social and economic agreements and calls for improvement in the efficacy of international environmental law, in particular by procedures and mechanisms to promote and review the implementation of treaties, such as efficient and practical reporting systems.

Agenda 21 pays particular attention to the adoption of national law and policy. It makes frequent reference to national laws, measures, plans, programs, and standards. Chapter 8, Integrating Environment and Development in Decision-Making, advocates the use of legal and economic instruments for planning and management, seeking incorporation of efficiency criteria in decisions. It recognizes the importance of laws and regulations suited to country-specific conditions for transforming environment and development policies into action, adding that not only 'command-and-control' methods should be used, but also a normative framework for economic planning and market instruments. Such methods can be useful for the implementation of obligations resulting from international treaties.

Governments should regularly assess the laws and regulations enacted and the related institutional or administrative machinery to render them effective; integrated strategies should be developed to maximize compliance with law and regulations relating to sustainable development. Finally,

> Governments and legislators (...) should establish judicial and administrative procedures for legal redress and remedy of actions affecting environment and development that may be unlawful or infringe on rights under the law, and should provide access to individuals, groups and organizations with a recognized legal interest.[73]

In sum, the Rio documents join environmental protection and economic development in the concept of sustainable development. All components of society are called upon to participate towards the achievement of this goal.

---

73 Agenda 21, para. 8.18.

Although at first some contested the importance of the Rio Conference legal texts, the two Conventions and the Declaration represent milestones in international environmental law. Several principles of the Declaration, such as those related to public participation, the prior assessment of environmental impacts, precaution, notification of emergencies, and prior information and consultation on projects potentially affecting the environment of other states, have been included in numerous binding and non-binding international instruments since Rio and constitute emerging customary law rules. At the same time, the shift from taking up the topic of environmental protection as a value on its own, to subsuming it in the concept of sustainable development, presented new challenges.

5 From Rio to Johannesburg

As was the case after the Stockholm Conference, the Rio meeting stimulated a decade of normative development in the field of international environmental law. In addition to the texts adopted at Rio itself, the 1990s produced *inter alia* the UN Convention to Combat Desertification,[74] the Kyoto Protocol to the UNFCCC,[75] the Fish Stocks agreement,[76] and the Rotterdam Convention on Prior Informed Consent.[77] Moreover, in the aftermath of Rio, virtually every major new international convention on multilateral cooperation included environmental protection as one of the goals of the states' parties. The result has been an infusion of environmental norms into nearly every branch of international law.

In the area of trade relationships,[78] the 1994 Marrakesh Agreement Establishing the World Trade Organization[79] and regional economic and trade agreements mention sustainable development and environmental protection

---

74 United Nations Convention to Combat Desertification in those Countries Experiencing Serious Drought and/or Desertification, Particularly in Africa, UN Doc. A/AC.241/15/Rev. 7 (1994), 17 June 1994, 33 ILM 1328.

75 Kyoto Protocol to the United Nations Framework Convention on Climate Change, Kyoto, 11 December 1997, 2303 UNTS 148.

76 Agreement for the Implementation of the Provisions of the United Nations Convention on the Law of the Sea of 10 December 1982 Relating to the Conservation and Management of Straddling Fish Stocks and Highly Migratory Fish Stocks, 4 August 1995, 2167 UNTS 88.

77 Convention on the Prior Informed Consent Procedure for Certain Hazardous Chemicals and Pesticides in International Trade, 10 September 1998, 2244 UNTS 337.

78 See further, Chapter 17.

79 Marrakesh, 14 April 1994.

and preservation as an aim. Regional examples include: the 1992 Treaty establishing the South African Development Community;[80] 1993 Treaty Establishing a Common Market for Eastern and Southern Africa;[81] 1992 Agreement on the North American Free Trade Area;[82] 1994 Tropical Timber Agreement[83] and 1994 European Energy Charter.[84] All of them call for respect for the environment.

Institutions concerned with human rights law and humanitarian law also began examining the impact of international environmental conditions on the exercise of the rights they guarantee.[85] Increasingly, the human rights community came to accept environmental protection as part of the human rights agenda and began to address environmental concerns. The humanitarian protections afforded during periods of armed conflict emerged as increasingly affected by environmental harm, due to changes in technology and the means and methods of warfare, including the use of natural resources to finance conflicts. The Rio Declaration, Principle 24, took up this concern in declaring that warfare is inherently destructive of sustainable development and insisting that states are to respect international law providing for the environment in times of armed conflict and cooperate in its further development, as necessary. The IAEA General Conference adopted a resolution on September 21, 1990, which recognized that attacks or threats of attack on nuclear facilities devoted to peaceful purposes could jeopardize the development of nuclear energy, affirmed the importance and reliability of its safeguard procedures, and emphasized the need for the Security Council to act immediately should such a threat or attack occur.[86] The Security Council in turn affirmed the liability of Iraq for environmental harm resulting from its invasion of Kuwait in 1991.

Regulation of weapons systems causing indiscriminate effects or excessive injuries expanded. Chemical and nuclear weapons and anti-personnel land mines, in particular, have been targeted by the international community. A Convention on the Prohibition of the Development, Production, Stockpiling and Use of Chemical Weapons and on their Destruction was signed in Paris, January 15, 1993. In 1996, the conference of state parties to the Convention on Prohibitions or Restrictions on the Use of Certain Conventional Weapons

80 Windhoek, 17 Aug. 1992.
81 Kampala, 5 Nov. 1993.
82 Washington DC, Ottawa, Mexico City, 17 Dec. 1992.
83 26 Jan. 1994.
84 17 Dec. 1994.
85 See further Chapters 15 and 16.
86 IAEA GC (XXXIV)RES/533 (21 September 1990).

adopted a protocol regulating the use of mines, booby-traps and other devices.[87] Finally, the Convention on the Prohibition of the Use, Stockpiling, Production and Transfer of Anti-Personnel Mines and on Their Destruction[88] mentions the environment, although its purpose is to end the casualties caused by land mines.

Technological developments brought other emerging issues to the forefront in the development of international environmental law in order to avoid potentially disastrous consequences to humanity. On September 29, 1994, the IAEA adopted a Convention on Nuclear Safety that obliges all contracting parties to establish and maintain a legislative and regulatory framework to govern the safety of nuclear installations. Biotechnology provoked concern about biosafety centered on two related issues: first, the handling of living modified organisms (LMOs) in the laboratory to protect workers and prevent the accidental liberation of such organisms into the surrounding ecosystem ('contained use'); second, the need for regulatory systems to govern the deliberate release of LMOs into the environment for testing or commercial purposes. The OECD first issued recommendations concerning the deliberate release of LMOs into the environment during field testing. Subsequently, the EC issued revised directives containing a lengthy series of control procedures both for laboratory research and for the release of LMOs. States parties to the Convention on Biological Diversity adopted a protocol on biosafety on January 29, 2000 after years of negotiations.[89]

The importance of controlling substances which can harm the environment necessitates an active role for states engaged in international trade. As early as the 1973 Washington Convention on International Trade in Endangered Species of Wild Fauna and Flora,[90] states parties introduced a double authorization procedure by the exporting and the importing states. The technique became a fundamental part of the 1989 Basel Convention on the Control of Transboundary Movements of Hazardous Wastes and Their Disposal[91] and the 1991 Bamako Convention on the Ban of the Import into Africa and the Control

87 Protocol II to the Convention on Prohibitions on the Use of Certain Conventional Weapons which may be Deemed to be Excessively Injurious or to have Indiscriminate Effects (Geneva, 3 May 1996), 35 ILM 1206 (1996).

88 Oslo, 18 Sept. 1997, 36 ILM 1507 (1997).

89 Protocol on Biosafety to the Convention on Biological Diversity (Cartagena, 29 January 2000), 39 ILM 1027.

90 Convention on International Trade in Endangered Species of Wild Fauna and Flora (Washington, 3 March 1973), 983 UNTS 243.

91 Basel Convention on the Control of Transboundary Movements of Hazardous Wastes and Their Disposal, (Basel, 22 March 1989) 1673 UNTS 57.

of Transboundary Movement and Management of Hazardous Wastes within Africa.[92] It has been further developed by the 1998 Rotterdam Convention on the Prior Informed Consent Procedure for Certain Hazardous Chemicals and Pesticides in International Trade and by the 2000 Cartagena Protocol on Biosafety to the Convention on Biological Diversity. Such procedures allow states parties to determine the goods and substances they accept to be introduced into or exploited from their environments, with the aim of making the treaty regimes more effective.

In sum, after Rio there was increased recognition of the international and multidimensional character of environmental problems and potential remedies for them. Most states came to accept that global efforts are required to solve many aspects of environmental deterioration, such as ocean pollution, depletion of stratospheric ozone, anthropogenic climate change, and threats to biodiversity. Such problems especially require cooperation between industrialized and developing countries. The June 17, 1994 International Convention to Combat Desertification in Those Countries Experiencing Serious Drought and/or Desertification, particularly in Africa is one of the most significant results of such cooperation, strongly reflecting the concept of common but differentiated responsibilities. In addition, it takes the principle of cooperation and melds it with the right of public participation, emphasizing the need for all levels of governance and civil society to be involved in actions to combat desertification.

Concern for ecosystems broadened and deepened as well, due to the adoption of integrated approaches to safeguarding the planet's environment. The earlier sectoral aim of protecting wild fauna and flora is now incorporated in the comprehensive goal of maintaining biological diversity. This expanded and integrated vision includes efforts to reverse the trend towards monocultural agriculture and stockbreeding, as well as to combat the overuse of pesticides and fertilizers. The latter problem is addressed through the technique of prior informed consent in the Convention on the Prior Informed Consent Procedure for Certain Hazardous Chemicals and Pesticides in International Trade.[93] An integrated approach also appears in the growing number of instruments addressing large ecosystems: Antarctica (Madrid Protocol of 1991),

92 Convention on the Ban of the Import into Africa and the Control of Transboundary Movement and Management of Hazardous Wastes within Africa (Bamako, 30 January 1991), 2101 UNTS 177.

93 Convention on the Prior Informed Consent Procedure for Certain Hazardous Chemicals and Pesticides in International Trade (Rotterdam, 10 Sept. 1998).

mountain ranges such as the Alps and Carpathians,[94] and the Arctic region (1996 Declaration).

The same trend has been seen in the shift to protecting freshwater resources as hydrographic units rather than as individual watercourses. The unity of water resources in a hydrographic basin and a consequent ecosystem approach to regulating such resources is now generally accepted. The 1987 Agreement on the Action Plan for the Environmentally Sound Management of the Common Zambezi River System[95] was one of the first to adopt a holistic approach to water resources management through the entire river system. The U.N. Convention on the Non-navigational Uses of International Watercourses[96] which unified the international legal status of surface and subsurface water, hastened recognition of the need to regulate freshwaters within the entire catchment basin, mainly a regional task calling for shared management of water resources by those who are concerned.

The crucial role of economic and other non-state actors in environmental protection became increasingly recognized during this period. Public opinion represented by civil society organizations emerged as a powerful new factor in the international lawmaking process during the preparations for the Rio Conference and in the negotiation of treaties. Civil society groups have contributed to the elaboration of the legal regime for the global environment by participating in the meetings as observers, sharing information and taking part in the drafting of important international agreements, assisting official state delegations and on occasion, being included in them. Enterprises have become more responsive to public pressure and the demands of insurance companies, leading to voluntary codes of corporate social responsibility and other initiatives. Parallel to this evolution, states and intergovernmental organizations have utilized innovative economic incentives in environmental protection, such as labeling, standardization, environmental auditing, use of the best available techniques and environmental practices, and emissions trading.

With the proliferation of international environmental instruments, there is an inevitable overlap in goals and subject area. Some relatively comprehensive conventions, like the 1992 Convention on Biological Diversity (CBD), address the entire range of human activities in an effort to protect natural systems. Other agreements are more specialized, directed either at particular activities or particular areas or species. Global and regional agreements may reinforce each other on the same or similar issues. Rarely does a convention specifically

---

94 See Chapter 14 infra.

95 Harare, 28 May 1987, available at <http://faolex.fao.org/docs/texts/bot15888.doc>.

96 New York, 21 May 1997.

indicate its relationship to other agreements. The Convention on Biological Diversity is one of the few instances where a specific hierarchy is established; it provides in Article 22 that the CBD shall not affect the rights and obligations of any contracting party deriving from any existing international agreement *except where the exercise of those rights and obligations would cause a serious damage or threat to biological diversity.* It adds that the Convention is to be implemented consistent with the rights and obligations of states under the law of the sea.

One avenue to resolve conflicts in international obligations is through the jurisprudence of the ICJ and other international tribunals. The ICJ has given several opinions and judgments in which it has recognized the importance of environment protection. Starting with the 1996 *Nuclear Weapons* advisory opinion and the 1997 *Gabçikovo-Nagymaros* judgment, the ICJ has affirmed that the duty not to cause transboundary environmental harm is an obligation of general international law. Other tribunals, including ITLOS and human rights bodies, have also contributed to normative development in this field.

By the end of the 1990s, the proliferation of instruments and jurisprudence on international environmental law led the international community to consider how it could ensure national implementation and compliance with international environmental commitments. In the five-year review following the Rio Conference, the UN General Assembly in 1997 lamented the continued deterioration of the state of the global environment. It noted that some progress had been made in institutional development, international consensus-building and public participation, but found that the overall trends were worsening.[97] The elusive goal of implementing Agenda 21 seemed to call for new initiatives, including greater integration of the private sector through public-private partnerships (perhaps also reflecting a recognition that the political will was lacking for governments to take stronger action).

The Millennium Development Goals (MDGs)[98] adopted at the conclusion of the Millennium Summit of 2000, also signaled a shift, moving economic development to the forefront of the international agenda. UN member states expressed their commitment to achieving eight major development goals by 2015, beginning with eradicating extreme poverty and hunger. Other goals addressed promoting gender equality and improving maternal health, achieving universal primary education, reducing child mortality and combatting

97 G. A. Res. S/19/2, 28 June 1997, Annex, 'Programme for the Further Implementation of Agenda 21'.

98 United Nations Millennium Declaration (Sept. 13, 2000), UN Doc. A/RES/55/2.

diseases, and developing a global partnership for development. The seventh goal called for ensuring environmental sustainability. Specific targets and indicators were tied to each goal to allow for assessment of progress.[99]

6 The World Summit on Sustainable Development

As the MDGs demonstrated, in the decade after the Rio Conference, environmental concerns encountered increasing competition on the international agenda from economic globalization, with its emphasis on free trade and the development crises of poor countries. Exemplifying this, the Doha Declaration of the World Trade Organization, adopted by a Ministerial Meeting on November 14, 2001, appeared to give priority to WTO norms in addressing the relationship and potential conflict between existing free trade rules and the restrictions on trade set out in several important multilateral environmental agreements. As another visible example, the United Nations convened a conference to mark the tenth anniversary of the Rio meeting, but failed to mention the environment in its name. Instead, it was convened as the World Summit on Sustainable Development (WSSD). Organized after the adoption of the MDGs, the WSSD's agenda appeared to emphasize social and economic development over the environmental pillar of sustainable development.

Between August 26 and September 4, 2002 the representatives of more than 190 countries met in Johannesburg, South Africa, in order to 'reaffirm commitment to the Rio Principles, the full implementation of Agenda 21 and the Programme for the Further Implementation of Agenda 21'.[100] At the end of the conference the participating governments adopted a Declaration on Sustainable Development affirming their will to 'assume a collective responsibility to advance and strengthen the interdependent and mutually reinforcing pillars of sustainable development – economic development, social development and environmental protection – at local, national, regional and global levels'.[101] While recognizing that 'the global environment continues to suffer,' and acknowledging the loss of biodiversity, the depletion of fish stocks, the progress of desertification, the evident adverse effects of climate change as well as the pollution of air, water and the sea,[102] the Declaration aimed

99 See the annual Millennium Development Goals Reports published by the United Nations.

100 Plan of Implementation of the World Summit on Sustainable Development, A/CONF.199/CRP.7, 1.

101 A.CONF./L.6/Rev.2, para. 5.

102 Para. 13.

its focus on development and poverty eradication, especially in the poorest countries. Despite proposals advocating the creation of a specialized global institution for environmental protection, the Declaration less ambitiously expressed support for the leadership role of the UN and proposed more effective, democratic and accountable international and multilateral institutions to achieve the goals of sustainable development.[103]

The lengthy WSSD Plan of Implementation provides concrete suggestions of measures to implement the Declaration. The Plan reaffirms the principle of CBDR and declares that '(p)overty eradication, changing unsustainable patterns of production and consumption, and protecting and managing the natural resource base of economic and social development are overarching objectives of and essential requirements for sustainable development'.[104] As this statement suggests, the economic pillar dominates the Declaration and Plan of Implementation.

Care for environmental protection appears in Part III of the Plan which advocates changing unsustainable patterns of consumption and production towards sustainability within the carrying capacity of ecosystems, de-linking economic growth and environmental degradation and reducing resource degradation, pollution and waste. It also recommends application of the polluter-pays principle, increasing eco-efficiency, the use of cleaner production programs, enhancing corporate environmental responsibility, environmental management systems, use of economic instruments and of environmental impact assessment procedures. The text also calls for sustainable energy production and use, an integrated approach to policy-making for transport services, and the sound management of chemicals and of hazardous wastes. Part IV of the Plan on Protecting and Managing the Natural Resource Base of Economic and Social Development is particularly important for environmental protection, although its legal content is rather weak. Given the threatening shortage of freshwater, the text proposes to mobilize international and domestic financial resources at all levels, transfer technology and support capacity-building for water and sanitation infrastructure and services development (paras. 24–28).

Paragraphs 29–35 of the Plan contain lengthy discussions of issues related to oceans, seas, islands and coastal areas, inviting states to ratify or accede to and implement existing international treaties to achieve sustainable fisheries, and maintaining or restoring stocks to levels that can produce the maximum sustainable yield. Paragraphs 36 and 37 address the atmosphere and confirm

---

103 Paras. 27 and 28.

104 A/CONF.199/CRP.7, para. 2.

the determination of governments to embark on the required reduction of emissions of greenhouse gases.

The Plan has only one paragraph devoted to biodiversity. It invited the governments to comply with the Convention on Biological Diversity and to achieve by 2010 a significant reduction in the current rate of loss of biological diversity, adding that such effort will require the provision of new and additional financial resources to developing countries.[105] The problems of forests were similarly treated.[106]

Part IX, on Means of Implementation, gives financial and trade aspects a major role, but some recommendations concern access to environmentally sound technologies, along with their development, transfer and diffusion.[107] Recommendations on education only speak of sustainable development, but one paragraph proposes to ensure access, at the national level, to environmental information and judicial and administrative proceedings in environmental matters, as well as public participation in decision-making. The section on institutional development proposes to strengthen collaboration within and between the UN system, international financial institutions, the Global Environmental Facility and the WTO, mainly in the perspective of sustainable development. A short paragraph at the end of the Plan invites partnerships between governmental and non-governmental actors, including all major groups, as well as volunteer groups, on programmes and activities for the achievement of sustainable development at all levels.[108]

In sum, economic development, international trade and corporations, many of which are more powerful than small states, prevailed. An opportunity to further discuss the link between human rights and environmental protection was missed. Despite these lacunae, the instruments adopted at the World Summit did not affect the on-going relevance of Agenda 21. Indeed, the WSSD reaffirmed the texts adopted at Rio and called for priority attention to two matters: the implementation of, and compliance with, international environmental agreements by contracting states and the coordination among the secretariats of multilateral environmental agreements.[109]

105 Para. 42.
106 Para. 43.
107 Para. 99.
108 Para. 151.
109 See the Report of the Executive Director of UNEP to the Governing Council, December 16, 2002, UNEP/GC.22/4.

7 Rio+20 and the Post-2015 Development Agenda

The trend towards subordinating environmental protection to the global development agenda continued in texts adopted after the WSSD. The 2012 global conference known as Rio+20 produced an outcome document on global environmental governance entitled *The Future We Want*.[110] Critics found the text disappointing and the conference itself a missed opportunity.[111] Indeed, while reaffirming commitments to sustainable development, the concluding document affirms that eradicating poverty is the greatest global challenge facing the world and expresses the need to mainstream sustainable development, integrating economic, social and environmental aspects. While mentioning all three 'pillars' of sustainable development, the focus is clearly on 'sustained inclusive and equitable economic growth'.[112] This is represented by adoption of a new term, the 'green economy', the elements of which 'should' include various policies, but whose implementation defers to national priorities, recognizing 'that each country can choose an appropriate approach in accordance with national sustainable development plans, strategies and priorities'. In sum, the text seems to adopt an impossible goal of maintaining or enhancing economic growth or business as usual while also managing natural resources sustainably.[113]

No new environmental instruments emerged from the meeting; its main contribution was to strengthen UNEP by transforming the Governing Council to an Assembly open to all states and agreeing to enhance UNEP's budget. The focus remained on implementation, with a call for developing measurable sustainable development goals for the period beginning after 2015, to be assessed on a regular basis. The three pillars of sustainable development envisaged at Rio further shifted towards a predominant, if not exclusive focus on social and economic development at the expense of environmental protection.

The 2030 Sustainable Development Agenda[114] is intended to continue and further develop the Millennium Development Goals, due to expire at the end of 2030. Although it adds the word sustainable to the MDG title, it continues the emphasis on development rather than balancing development with sustainability. There are 17 SDGs, divided up into 169 targets. The new Agenda places

---

110 *The Future We Want*, 11 September 2012, UN Doc. /RES/66/288.

111 See Karen Morrow, 'Rio+20: a critique – The global is personal: the personal is global' (2013) 4 (1) JHRE 1.

112 *The Future We Want*, *supra* n 110, para. 4.

113 See Sam Adelman, 'Rio+20: sustainable injustice in a time of crises,' (2013) 4 (1) JHRE 6.

114 G. A. 'Transforming Our World: The 2030 Agenda for Sustainable Development' (2015) UNGA/Res/70/1.

poverty eradication as the first goal, to be achieved by 2030.[115] It also includes a commitment to end hunger and ensure access by all people, in particular the poor and people in vulnerable situations, including infants, to safe, nutritious and sufficient food all year. It seeks, by 2030, to double the agricultural productivity and incomes of small-scale food producers, in particular women, indigenous peoples, family farmers, pastoralists and fishers, including through secure and equal access to land, other productive resources and inputs, knowledge, financial services, markets and opportunities for value addition and non-farm employment. The dangers of unsustainable practices are address by seeking to ensure sustainable food production systems and implement resilient agricultural practices that increase productivity and production, that help maintain ecosystems, that strengthen capacity for adaptation to climate change, extreme weather, drought, flooding and other disasters and that progressively improve land and soil quality.[116]

The Agenda aims to ensure healthy lives and promote well-being for all at all ages, putting emphasis on maternal and child mortality.[117] The SDGs also include the aim to ensure equitable quality education, and achieve gender equality (Goals 4 and 5). Goal 6 is about the availability of water and sanitation, as well as the sustainable management of these resources. It aims to reduce pollution, eliminate dumping and minimize release of hazardous chemicals and materials, and to combat water scarcity by substantially increasing water-use efficiency, as well as implementing integrated water resources management including through transboundary cooperation.[118] Under the same goal, it aimed to protect and restore all water-related ecosystems by 2020.[119] Goal 7 aims to ensure access to affordable, reliable, sustainable and modern energy for all. Goal 8 focuses on the promotion of sustained, inclusive and sustainable economic growth, and employment and decent work for all. Goal 9 is aimed at infrastructure, and sustainability and innovation on this front. Goal 10 broadly aims to reduce inequality within and among countries, and Goal 11 promises to strive for cities and human settlements to be inclusive, safe, resilient and sustainable. Goal 12 aims to ensure sustainable consumption and production patterns. This goal includes the target to achieve by 2020 the environmentally sound management of chemical and all wastes, and to have significantly

115 ibid, goal 1.
116 ibid, goal 2.
117 ibid, goal 3.
118 ibid, paras. 6.3–6.5.
119 ibid, para. 6.6.

reduced their release to air, water and soil.[120] Goal 13 is the goal most concerned with the environment, promising to take urgent action to combat climate change and its impacts. It has special focus on climate-related hazards and natural disasters, aims to integrate climate change measures into national policies, strategies and planning, and improve education on climate change mitigation and adaptation.[121] It is immediately followed by the goal to conserve and sustainably use the oceans, seas and marine resources for sustainable development (Goal 14). This goal gives attention to the prevention and reduction of marine pollution, minimizing and addressing ocean acidification, regulating harvesting and ending overfishing.[122] Goal 15 is also concerned with the environment, aiming to protect, restore and promote sustainable use of terrestrial ecosystems, sustainably managed forests, combat desertification, and halt and reverse land degradation and halt biodiversity loss. This strong focus on the environment is again lost in Goal 16, which aims to promote peaceful and inclusive societies for sustainable development, and provide justice for all. Goal 17 is concerned with the implementation of all preceding goals.

As this summary suggests, environmental issues other than climate change have a limited place in the Agenda, suggesting a certain retrenchment despite the environmental crises of global dimension. Although there are a few goals specifically focused on the environment, in most of them the environmental component takes a back-seat compared to the development aspect. The relatively few treaties and other instruments adopted in the past decade reinforces concerns about the apparent reduction in political will to conserve the planet and its resources. However, the fact that there are few instruments adopted does not mean that the decade has been void of any: the Paris Agreement proves this, and so do the efforts since 2017 for drafting a Global Pact for the Environment.[123]

---

120 ibid, para. 12.4.

121 ibid, paras. 13.1–13.3.

122 ibid, paras. 14.1–14.4.

123 Paris Agreement at the Conference of the Parties (adopted 12 December 2015) UN Doc. FCCC/CP/2015/L.9/Rev/1; The Global Pact for the Environment has currently not left the stages of drafting yet, but for more on the topic, visit the website of the organization: <https://globalpactenvironment.org/en/>; see also, Jasmin Raith, 'The "Global Pact for the Environment" – A New Instrument to Protect the Planet?' (2018) 15 (1) JEEPL 3 and Maria Antonia Tigre, *Gaps in International Environmental Law: Toward a Global Pact for the Environment* (Environmental Law Institute 2020).

Bibliography

Calster, G. van & Reins, L., *The Paris Agreement on Climate Change: A Commentary* (Elgar 2021).

Campiglio, L., et al (eds.), *The Environment after Rio: International Law and Economics* (Martinus Nijhoff, 1994).

Carson, R., *The Silent Spring* (1962).

Chasek, P., and Wagner, L.M., *The Roads from Rio: Lesson Learned from Twenty Years of Multilateral Environmental Negotiations* (Routledge 2012).

Dodds, F., Strauss, M., and Strong, M.F., *Only One Earth: The Long Road via Rio to Sustainable Development* (Routledge 2012).

Gutman, M. and Gorman, D., *Before the UN Sustainable Development Goals: A Historical Companion* (OUP 2022).

Scotford, E., *Environmental Principles and the Evolution of Environmental Law* (2017).

Sohn, L., *The Stockholm Declaration on the Human Environment*, 14 Harv. Int'l L. J. 423 (1971).

Viñuales, J.E., *The Rio Declaration on Environment and Development: A Commentary* (Oxford University Press 2015)

World Commission on Environment and Development, *Our Common Future* (1987).

CHAPTER 3

Emergence of Georgian Secular Literature: Shota Rustaveli

Environmental law-making is a complicated process, not only due to economic and political disagreements and disparities, but because of the fluid boundaries of the topic and its highly technical nature. It depends on scientific expertise, both in identifying and describing issues the law can and should address. Science is also important in providing definitions for terms that must be incorporated into the law, such as biological diversity, climate change, and habitat. Science identifies safe methods to dispose of toxic substances as well as what levels of substances are hazardous or toxic. Scientists also identify sources of pollution and gaps in compliance. Given these important roles in a continuous dialogue between the legal community and scientists, difficult issues are faced by law-makers, judges, and regulators where scientific consensus is lacking or uncertainties remain, which can arise where scientific research is funded by economic interests seeking a particular outcome.

Despite the difficulties in law-making, the international legal community has concluded many agreements and adopted other texts aimed at protecting the environment both within and outside the limits of state jurisdiction. The process of law-making has led international environmental law to develop several characteristics that differ from those of other international regimes. In particular, states have adopted innovative treaty practices and made frequent use of so-called 'soft law,' meaning formally non-binding expressions of commitment, such as the Stockholm and Rio Declarations, or general directions or guidelines in treaties. From the many texts supported by state practice, norms of customary international law have emerged. These and other aspects of environmental law are described in this chapter.

Traditional international law identifies its sources in Article 38(1) of the Statute of the International Court of Justice, initially drafted in 1920 for the predecessor Permanent Court of International Justice. Although applying only to the Court, Article 38 represents the authoritative listing of processes that states identified at the time as capable of creating rules binding on them; it remains the only such listing ever made. It sets out in order general or specialized international conventions (treaties), international custom as evidence of a general practice accepted as law, general principles of law recognized by civilized nations, and, as subsidiary sources, international judicial decisions and doctrine. This enumeration is the accepted minimum, but does not wholly

 | DOI:10.1163/9789047440802_005

reflect either the current international practice or the diverse activities that contribute to the development of a new rule of law. In particular, it omits all non-treaty texts adopted by international organizations, although they play more than a nominal role in the formation of international law in general and environmental law in particular.

This chapter will review environmental norms derived from the traditional sources of international law, then turn to rules stemming from acts of international organizations and conferences. Finally, it considers the development of codes of conduct and other norms by non-state actors, which can influence the content of international environmental law. It is important to keep in mind that the sources of law are not mutually exclusive but are interrelated and often apply simultaneously. Thus, the law used to interpret treaties is largely customary international law, codified in the Vienna Convention on the Law of Treaties (VCLT). Further, the adoption of a treaty does not extinguish rules of custom, but provides an independent source of obligation unless the treaty expressly modifies a prior customary norm.[1]

1 International Conventions

The first source of international environmental law is 'conventional norms,' which now number more than one thousand in this field, although many agreements contain only a few provisions concerning the environment.[2] Article 2.1(a) of the 1969 VCLT (May 23, 1969) defines a 'treaty' as 'an international agreement concluded between states in written form and governed by international law, whether embodied in a single instrument or in two or more related instruments and whatever its particular designation.' This definition omits all international agreements to which intergovernmental or non-governmental organizations are parties as well as agreements concluded

1 See Philippe Sands, 'Treaty Custom and the Cross-Fertilization of International Law' (1998) 1 Yale Human Rights and Development L. J. 85.

2 The 1967 Outer Space Treaty, for example, contains only one relevant provision, Article IX, which relates to protecting the earth against pollution from outer space and, in turn, protecting outer space from earth-source contamination: '... States Parties to the Treaty shall pursue studies of outer space, including the moon and other celestial bodies, and conduct exploration of them so as to avoid their harmful contamination and also adverse changes in the environment of the Earth resulting from the introduction of extraterrestrial matter and, where necessary, shall adopt appropriate measures for this purpose.' Article IX, Treaty on Principles Governing the Activities of States in the Exploration and Use of Outer Space, including the Moon and Other Celestial Bodies, 610 UNTS 205, 18 UST 2410. A large number of treaties concerning boundary waters similarly contain one or a few provisions on water pollution.

by internal agents not entitled to bind the state, for example port authorities or customs bureaus. Yet, all these entities increasing enter into agreements intending to cooperate for environmental protection.

The geographic coverage of environmental treaties varies widely. Some instruments contain norms regulating the entire international community. Article 35(3) of Protocol I to the 1949 Geneva Conventions, for example, prohibits all states involved in non-international armed conflicts from employing methods or means of warfare which are intended, or may be expected to cause widespread, long-term and severe damage to the natural environment.[3] The London conventions of 1972 and 1973 concerning pollution of the high seas[4] and the CITES regulation of trade in endangered species[5] similarly address global problems. In fact, a broad global framework of international law has been established for each of the four 'traditional' sectors of the environment: water, soil, air and biological diversity.

Principles and norms adopted for the whole community of nations often are more effective when implemented and enforced regionally, as has been experienced in the field of human rights. UNEP aims at regional application of international environmental law through conventions for different maritime regions around the globe, including the Mediterranean, Persian Gulf, West Africa, South-East Pacific, Red Sea, Gulf of Aden, Caribbean, and East Africa.[6] These conventions rely on the same principles and generally adopt the same norms, often incorporating those previously articulated in global instruments, including some not yet in force. The regional approach is motivated by the similarity of the geography and environment among neighboring states bordering regional seas and is enhanced in many cases by similar economic, cultural, and political conditions. At the same time, the agreements take into consideration the different ecological conditions in the regional seas.

Apart from UNEP's systematic regional seas program, specific environmental problems of geographically-limited areas are often regulated by the small number of affected states. Efforts to combat pollution of rivers and lakes and the depletion of regionally-endemic species of plants or animals have benefitted from organizations such as the Council of Europe or the OECD, which frequently initiate the development of conventional solutions to these problems among their member states. In addition, the trend towards

3 See Chapter 16.
4 See below, Chapter 11.
5 See below, Chapter 8.
6 See Chapter 11.

ecosystem protection allows a holistic approach to the problems of a single geophysical space.

Despite their variety in subject matter and geographic scope, environmental treaties have common characteristics, use similar legal techniques, and often are interrelated. The main features they share are: an absence of reciprocity of obligations; interrelated or cross-referenced provisions from one instrument to another; adoption of a core framework followed by protocols or annexes; frequent interim application; the creation of new institutions or the utilization of already existing ones to promote continuous cooperation; innovative compliance and non-compliance procedures; and simplified means of modification or amendment. Some of these points will be explored below in more detail.

1.1 *The Nature of Obligations*

Each international environmental agreement contains legally binding rules, although in many treaties there are few precise duties created. Instead, the provisions indicate areas of cooperation, and, in some cases, set forth the means states parties should adopt to achieve the goals of the treaty. Environmental treaties often invade traditional spheres of government activities by requiring states to limit pollution emissions, establish licensing systems, regulate and monitor waste disposal, control the export and import of endangered species and hazardous products, and enact penal legislation. Such treaties usually set forth the obligations in general terms and require completion through internal legislative or executive action. For countries like the United States that distinguish between self-executing and non-self-executing treaties – those capable of immediate judicial application and those that require implementing measures – such treaties fall within the latter category,[7] although it is more common to find treaties containing a mixture of self-executing and non-self-executing obligations. Thus, individual treaty provisions must be analyzed, rather than the agreement as a whole.

Non-self-executing provisions of treaties encompass obligations to enact the necessary legislation or regulations. The Bonn Convention on the Conservation of Migratory Species of Wild Animals (June 23, 1979), for example, requires that states in the migratory areas of animals listed in Convention

7 For the distinction between self-executing and non-self-executing treaties in U.S. courts, see *Foster v. Nielson*, 27 US (2 Pet. 253, 314 (1829)). This structure also resembles a type of domestic French legislation, known as 'lois-cadre.' Such a law establishes legislative goals and principles, leaving to the executive the duty to take the necessary implementing measures. See Law No. 76–676 relating to Nature Protection, Dalloz 1976.308.

Annex I forbid the taking of any of these animals.[8] States also may be called upon to designate or create organs to be entrusted with certain functions, such as maintaining contacts with the authorities of other states parties,[9] or issuing licenses or authorizations for regulated activities.[10] Some treaty provisions oblige states parties to enact and enforce penal sanctions against persons who violate its terms. For example, Article 8 of CITES provides:

1. The Parties shall take appropriate measures to enforce the provisions of the present Convention and to prohibit trade in specimens in violation thereof. These shall include measures:
   a. to penalize trade in, or possession of such specimens, or both; and
   b. to provide for the confiscation or return to the State of export of such specimens.[11]

International environmental treaties often cross-reference other international instruments or contain savings clauses indicating priority of application. Marine environmental treaties, for example, often cite the rules of MARPOL or UNCLOS, sometimes incorporating their rules by reference. This can result in extending the legal effect of these instruments to states that have not ratified them but which ratify the later texts. The Convention on the Protection of the Black Sea against Pollution (April 21, 1992) states in its preamble that the Contracting Parties are

> taking into account the relevant provisions of the Convention on Prevention of Marine Pollution by Dumping of Wastes and Other Matter of 1972 as amended; the International Convention on Prevention of Pollution from Ships of 1973 as modified by the Protocol of 1978 relating thereto as amended; the Convention on Control of Transboundary Movement of Hazardous Wastes and Their Disposal of 1989 and the International Convention on Oil Pollution Preparedness, Response and Cooperation of 1990.

---

8 Art. 3(5).

9 Nordic Convention for Environmental Protection (Feb. 19, 1974), Art. 4.

10 Convention on International Trade in Endangered Species of Wild Fauna and Flora, Art. 9 (Washington, March 3, 1973).

11 Similarly, Article 4 of the International Convention for the Prevention of Pollution from Ships (MARPOL) London, November 2, 1973, requires states parties to prohibit and sanction any violation of the requirements of the Convention and to bring proceedings against any ship which commits a violation, or furnish evidence to the state administering the ship. The penalties adopted by the State 'shall be adequate in severity to discharge violations of the present Convention and shall be equally severe irrespective of where the violations occur.'

In some cases, specific treaties or provisions may be affirmed as customary international law. The preamble of the Convention for the Protection of the Marine Environment of the North-East Atlantic (Paris, September 22, 1992), for example, refers to 'the relevant provisions of customary international law reflected in Part XII of the UN Law of the Sea Convention and, in particular, Article 197 on global and regional cooperation for the protection and preservation of the marine environment.'

Some treaties even incorporate 'soft law' texts, especially using global instruments in regional or bilateral agreements. The May 27, 2011 Sustainable Tourism Protocol to the Convention on the Protection and Sustainable Development of the Carpathians (Kyiv, May 22, 2003) calls on each state party to promote the integration of the CBD Guidelines on Biodiversity and Tourism Development in its own strategies and plans for tourism development. Similarly, the Namibia-South Africa Agreement on the Establishment of a Permanent Water Commission provides that the parties have agreed to the text 'wishing to consolidate their existing friendly relations by promoting regional water resource development on the basis of the rules relating to the uses of the waters of international rivers approved in 1966 at Helsinki by the 52nd Conference of the International Law Association.' The cumulating of instruments through repeated cross-referencing can be seen as a movement toward consolidation of a global environmental code.

Examples of savings clauses or statements of priority can be found in Article 22 of the Convention on Biological Diversity and its 2010 Nagoya Protocol on Benefit-Sharing. The former provides for priority to be given to the law of the sea on issues relating to the marine environment, while for other instruments, 'the provisions of th[e CBD] shall not affect the rights and obligations of any Contracting Party deriving from any existing international agreement, except where the exercise of those rights and obligations would cause a serious damage or threat to biological diversity.' Article 4 of the Nagoya Protocol repeats this provision while adding that the provision is not intended to create a hierarchy of instruments. Article 4 also provides that parties can adopt other specialized access and benefit-sharing agreements *supportive* of the Convention and Protocol. As states are always free to adopt subsequent treaties, the intent seems to be to suggest that the Convention and Protocol would override subsequent agreements contrary to the aims of the Convention and Protocol. The preamble to the Protocol expresses a further recognition of other law, affirming that nothing in the Protocol shall be construed as diminishing or extinguishing the existing rights of indigenous and local communities.

The rights and obligations of states parties to environmental agreements can be contrasted with nearly all conventions of the nineteenth and early twentieth centuries, including treaties of commerce and alliance, and instruments regulating diplomatic and consular relations; agreements that were governed by the principle of reciprocity. Characterized in Roman law by the adage *do ut des*, the principle requires a legal equilibrium between the obligations accepted by one state and the advantages it obtains from the other contracting party or parties. Exceptions to this construct existed, however, even during the dominant period of positivist international law, as states began to establish rules of general obligation, including freedom of navigation on international rivers and canals, prohibition of slave trading,[12] protection of religious liberty,[13] and restrictions on the means and methods of warfare.[14] States subscribing to these treaties accepted their obligations without receiving any immediate demonstrable advantage from the other states parties.

Other exceptions to the principle of reciprocity emerged after World War I, primarily in international labor conventions.[15] Suppressing phenomena such as exploitation of child labor or inhuman and dangerous conditions of work appealed in a systematic fashion to the international community. Following World War II, non-reciprocal obligations expanded further to include the international protection of human rights, regulations on the use of Antarctica and its surrounding seas, codes governing activities in outer space and on celestial bodies, and reaffirmation of freedom of the high seas with an obligation to respect its environment.

These non-reciprocal rules of international law, adopted in the common interest of humanity, include norms of international environmental law. They generally do not bring immediate reciprocal advantages to contracting states in obliging them to protect species of wild plant and animal life, the oceans, the air, the soil, and the countryside from destructive human activities, often

---

12 Treaty of Paris, March 30, 1856.

13 In 1878, Western powers agreed at the Berlin Congress that the Balkan States would be recognized only under the condition that they did not impose any religious disabilities on their subjects. Treaty of Berlin, July 13, 1878. See Louis Sohn & Thomas Buergenthal, *International Protection Of Human Rights* (1973) 143–92.

14 Conventions to protect medical personnel, wounded and sick combatants and to restrict certain means of warfare were adopted in 1864 (Geneva), 1899 and 1907 (The Hague). See Pierre Boissier, *History Of The International Committee Of The Red Cross: From Solferino To Tsushima* (1985).

15 Since 1919, the International Labor Organization has engaged in standard-setting and supervision of international labor standards. See Clarence W. Jenks, *Human Rights and International Labor Standards* (1960). Summaries of the work of the ILO can be found in the Report of the Director-General to the 77th International Labor Conference (1990) and the Report of the Committee of Experts on the Application of Conventions and Recommendations (Report III, Part 4A) (1990). On the ILO and the Environment *see below*, Chapter 4.

economically-productive ones. For coastal states, the general direction of winds and ocean currents may cut against the equality of the parties in rights and obligations. Assessing these norms, some international jurists have posited the existence in international law of 'treaty-laws,' distinguished from 'treaty-contracts.' The distinction may have meaning in the sense that 'treaty-laws' are concluded in the common interest of humanity, while 'treaty-contracts' are based on the principle of reciprocity. In its *Advisory Opinion on Reservations to the Convention on Genocide*, the ICJ distinguished conventions adopted in the common interest from those based on reciprocal rights. States parties to conventions in the former category

> do not have any interests of their own; they merely have, one and all, a common interest, namely, the accomplishment of those high purposes which are the *raison d'être* of the convention. Consequently, in a convention of this type one cannot speak of individual advantages or disadvantages to states, or of the maintenance of a perfect contractual balance between rights and duties. The high ideals which inspired the convention provide, by virtue of the common will of the parties, the foundation and measure of all its provisions.[16]

In municipal law, a similar distinction is made between public law legislated in the general interest and private contract law based on consensual offer, acceptance, and consideration. Most importantly, properly enacted public laws apply whether or not a particular individual disagrees with the substance of the norm. The roles of reciprocity and of consent become altered in the shift from contract to legislation. Common interests shared by the international community may be protected as obligations *erga omnes*. In the *Case of Barcelona Traction, Light and Power Company, Limited* the ICJ recognized the distinction between reciprocal contractual norms and other more public norms:[17]

> [A]n essential distinction should be drawn between the obligations of a State towards the international community as a whole, and those arising vis-à-vis another State in the field of diplomatic protection. By their very nature the former are the concern of all States. In view of the importance of the rights involved, all States can be held to have a legal interest in their protection; they are obligations *erga omnes*.

---

16 1951 ICJ Rep. 15.

17 *Barcelona Traction, Light and Power Company*, Limited (New Application: 1962) (Belgium v. Spain, Second Phase) 1970 ICJ. Rep. 4, 32.

The Court included in the category of obligations *erga omnes* the international laws prohibiting aggression, genocide, slavery and racial discrimination. In the *Gabçikovo-Nagymaros* case, the ICJ cited with approval the view of the International Law Commission that safeguarding the earth's ecological balance has come to be considered an essential interest of all states, to protect the international community as a whole.[18] This factor, plus the absence of reciprocity, characterizes much of international environmental law. Thus, many of the codified norms and customary standards in the environmental field may be viewed as obligations *erga omnes*.

International environmental obligations also differ from other international laws in calling upon the state to regulate the behavior of non-state actors which is the source of most harm to the environment. The obligations must be implemented in national law to control non-state actors within the state's territory and jurisdiction. In contrast, treaties to establish diplomatic relations, or to lower trade barriers, generally impact only the state and its agents. Human rights law also primarily applies to the conduct of state authorities.

Non-reciprocity often leads to differential rights and obligations. Principle 7 of the Rio Declaration provides an example, proclaiming that

> States shall cooperate in a spirit of global partnership to conserve, protect and restore the health and integrity of the Earth's ecosystem. In view of the different contributions to global environmental degradation, States have common but differentiated responsibilities. The developed countries acknowledge the responsibility that they bear in the international pursuit of sustainable development in view of the pressures their societies place on the global environment and of the technologies and financial resources they command.

Principle 8 adds that states should reduce and eliminate unsustainable patterns of production and consumption and promote appropriate demographic policies, implicitly referring both to industrialized states and developing ones.

The character of differentiated responsibility refers to general legal and political obligations rather than the formal concept of state responsibility which is the consequence of harm caused to another state in violation of law. The acceptance by an industrialized state of its differentiated responsibility

---

18 *Case Concerning the Gabçikovo-Nagymaros Project* (Hungary/Slovakia), 1996 ICJ Rep. 7, para. 53, citing the International Law Commission, Commentary to Art. 33 of the Draft Articles on the International Responsibility of States, *See Yearbook of the ILC*, 1980, Vol. II, Part 2, 39, para. 14.

results in increased participation, often financial, in the effort to enhance sustainable development. Some treaties establish links between fulfillment by one group of their responsibilities and reciprocal compliance by the other group of states to their differential duties.

The concept of CBDR has been incorporated in all global environmental conventions adopted since the end of the 1980s. In particular, the 1989 Basel Convention on the Control of Transboundary Movements of Hazardous Wastes and Their Disposal (Article 10(2)), the 1987 Montreal Protocol on the Protection of the Ozone Layer as amended in 1992, the 1992 Convention on Biological Diversity (Articles 16, 20, and 21), and the 1992 UN Framework Convention on Climate Change all provide for transfer of technology or for financial assistance.

The 1994 Convention to Combat Desertification in those Countries Experiencing Serious Drought and/or Desertification, particularly in Africa (Paris, October 14, 1994) contains detailed provisions on the obligations of developed country parties. It calls on them to mobilize substantial financial resources, including additional funding from the Global Environmental Facility in order to support the implementation of programs to combat desertification and mitigate the effects of drought (Articles 21, 22).

Three remaining characteristics of international environmental agreements are significant. The first is the deliberate reference to non-party states. To the extent that international environmental agreements impact international trade, it is necessary to include measures to discourage free-riders or provide incentives to compliance. CITES and the Montreal Protocol, for example, seek to influence the behavior of non-parties by requiring parties to restrict imports from them unless they effectively comply with the provisions of the agreement. The Antarctic Treaty also contains an obligation on states parties to see that 'no one' acts inconsistent with the principles of the treaty (Article X).

Second, several international environmental agreements respond to urgent problems that must be confronted in the shortest possible time. Taking this into account, negotiating states have adopted the technique of approving interim application of the agreements pending their entry into force. This technique was used with the 1998 FAO Convention on Prior Informed Consent and the August 4, 1995 Agreement for the Implementation of the Provisions of UNCLOS relating to the Conservation and Management of Straddling Fish Stocks and Highly Migratory Fish Stocks (Article 41).[19]

---

19 Article 41(1) provides: 'This Agreement shall be applied provisionally by a State or entity which consents to its provisional application by so notifying the depositary in writing.

Finally, many environmental agreements and larger law-making treaties such as UNCLOS prohibit reservations, requiring states to accept them in their entirety. This is understandable in treaties that codify independently-binding customary international law, but most environmental agreements cannot claim to be codifications of customary law. Instead, the absence of reservations may reflect the give and take of a multilateral negotiating process where decisions are based upon consensus and bargains. The process would unravel if states could pick and choose their obligations.

1.2 *Framework Conventions*

Since the beginning of the 1970s an increasing number of international treaties have been adopted by procedures that include several phases. The technique of 'framework conventions' means that a convention of general scope is adopted, proclaiming basic principles on which consent can be achieved. The parties foresee the elaboration of additional protocols containing more detailed obligations.

This method first was used in regional seas agreements, beginning with the 1976 Convention for the Protection of the Mediterranean Sea against Pollution (Barcelona, February 16, 1976). Regional seas conventions state the basic principles which the contracting parties are to apply. Detailed regulations are set forth in additional protocols, some of which are signed at the same time as the principal instrument. Others are elaborated later. Most regional seas treaty systems include development plans for the concerned region.

In a different realm, the 1979 Geneva Convention on Long-Range Transboundary Air Pollution created a legal structure for subsequent negotiations. The Convention has been completed by a series of protocols establishing the detailed content of the general obligation contained in the main treaty. The 1985 Convention for the Protection of the Ozone Layer (Vienna, March 22, 1985) and the Montreal Protocol followed this pattern as well. Among UNCED texts, the Framework Convention on Climate Change adopted this approach. Later on, the same approach was used in creating the 1997 Kyoto Protocol and the 2015 Paris Agreement.

Framework agreements are advantageous in that it is generally easier to reach a consensus on basic principles and on the need for action which will follow than it is to negotiate the details of the action itself, which often have

---

Such provisional application shall become effective from the date of receipt of the notification.' Article 41(2) adds that provisional application terminates upon entry into force of the agreement or upon notification by the state that it intends to terminate provisional application.

a technical character. Further negotiations, sometimes taking place in subsidiary bodies of experts with the participation of civil society, can determine the necessary measures. New elements can be incorporated as well, as exemplified by the Montreal Protocol on the Protection of the Ozone Layer which reflects the discovery of the ozone 'hole' above Antarctica after the Vienna Convention was adopted. Changes in knowledge and even basic concepts make framework treaties particularly well-adapted to the needs of environmental protection.

1.3 *Mechanisms and Organs of Cooperation*

The previous considerations lead to a need for permanent international organs of cooperation among states parties to environmental treaties. Eighty years ago, the *Trail Smelter* arbitration, the first case of transboundary pollution and a principal source of customary international law in this field, concluded that the two contending states should cooperate to jointly examine questions concerning damage caused by the smelter's air pollution. Today, the importance of acquiring new knowledge, disseminating information and observing the biosphere makes international cooperation even more necessary and, clearly, permanent. It is not surprising, therefore, that most environmental treaties contain institutional provisions, granting specific powers and competence to international organs. Sometimes new functions are confided to organs of already-existing international organizations. The MARPOL Convention, for example, gives the International Maritime Organization (IMO) competence to receive information from governments on action taken regarding any violation of the Convention by a ship (Articles 4(3) and 6(4)), obtain reports on incidents involving harmful substances (Article 8), as well as details of laws, procedures, and national authorities concerned with implementation of the Convention (Article 11), and the results of investigations on polluting accidents (Article 12). The IMO also plays a role in the administration of the Convention, in the amendment procedure, and in the promotion of technical cooperation.[20] These numerous functions can be regrouped under three headings: managing the Convention, gathering and diffusing information, and supervising enforcement of the Convention's norms by states parties.

Authority also may be confided to new organizations created by environmental treaties to serve the special needs of the agreement, particularly in the field of regional or sub-regional cooperation.[21] Conferences of the Parties (COPs) and international commissions have been created to assure permanent cooperation among contracting parties to treaties concerning e.g. inland

20 Arts. 13–19.

21 See Chapter 5.

waters,[22] the oceans,[23] and the protection of wildlife.[24] As a general rule these organizations are lightly structured; many do not have permanent secretariats or the secretariat functions are handled by another existing inter-governmental or non-governmental organization.[25]

1.4 *Compliance Procedures*

A fundamental obligation of international law is that treaties must be observed and their obligations performed in good faith.[26] Generally, each state party to a treaty monitors whether or not other states parties comply with the requirements of the agreement. This approach remains basic to environmental agreements, but such conventions often also establish international supervisory mechanisms.

A treaty may delegate supervision to states parties. UNCLOS Article 218 provides, for example, that when a ship voluntarily enters a port or offshore installation, the port state can investigate and, where the evidence warrants, institute proceedings regarding any discharge from that vessel outside the state's internal waters, territorial sea or exclusive economic zone in violation of applicable international rules and standards established through the competent international organization or general diplomatic conference. The Basel Convention on Transboundary Movement of Hazardous Wastes delegates supervision generally: each party suspecting a breach is to inform the Secretariat and the offending party. The Secretariat, in turn, informs other parties.

Procedures overriding state domestic jurisdiction are rare. As discussed in Chapter 7, the most accepted supervisory technique remains a state reporting system that obliges treaty parties to address periodic reports to an organ established or designated by the treaty, indicating the implementing measures which they have taken. Article 16 of the African Convention on the Conservation of Nature and Natural Resources (Algiers, September 15, 1968) designates the Organization of African Unity as the organ to which states should address the texts of laws, decrees, regulations and instructions in force in their

---

22 The International Commission for Protection of the Rhine against Pollution, created by the Bern Convention of April 29, 1963.

23 The 1974 Helsinki Convention on the Protection of the Baltic Sea Area created a commission.

24 An International Commission and a Scientific Committee were created by the 1980 Canberra Convention on the Conservation of Antarctic Marine Living Resources.

25 UNEP is often invested with the secretariat function of the regional seas conventions, e.g., Barcelona Convention of Feb. 16, 1976, Art. 13; Abidjan Convention of March 23, 1987, Art. 16; Cartegena Convention of March 24, 1983, Art. 15.

26 Convention on the Law of Treaties (Vienna, May 23, 1969), Art. 26.

territories and aimed at ensuring the application of the Convention. They must also report on the results obtained in applying the Convention's terms. In addition, on request, they should provide all information required to permit review of matters treated by the Convention.

International conventions based on the common interest of humanity, distinguished by the restricted role of reciprocity in their provisions, pose particular problems of enforcement. In a decentralized international society, bilateral reciprocity has provided an essential guarantee of compliance with treaty obligations. A state violating the treaty rights of another state under an agreement that contains reciprocal rights and duties risks losing its corresponding benefits. Such results are inconceivable in a conventional system aimed at the common interest: violation of human rights by one state cannot be sanctioned by another state engaging in similar violations. It is the same for international environmental law: norms against pollution of the sea or the air cannot be enforced by reciprocal pollution. Enforcement must be by other means, especially by international control mechanisms that supervise the implementation of international environmental law by states.

Experience indicates that compliance with multilateral environmental agreements (MEAs) and even non-binding norms is best ensured at the international level when there is institutional support. Many international environmental agreements create their own institutional framework rather than relying on existing international organs, as discussed in Chapter 5. Over time, the states drafting international environmental agreements have created a now widely-used pattern of institutions. As agreements have proliferated, so have the institutions and the compliance mechanisms, raising problems of coordination and possible conflict. Increasingly, communities of scientists, government officials, and non-governmental organizations are involved. As a rule, the costs of international administration (secretariat, meetings, programs) are financed by contributions of states parties, either voluntary or agreed at each meeting of the Conference for a fixed subsequent period.

1.5 *Adaptation and Evolution of Obligations*

One of the principal challenges of environmental law, both internal and international, is to adapt to changes in conditions or knowledge altering the requirements of environmental protection. Environmental needs may change rapidly: marine or river pollution may increase due to the appearance of new substances or new means of production or consumption, or a species of wildlife may risk extinction due to new threats which develop before international rules can be adopted or existing rules amended. The ICJ has recognized that as a supplemental means of interpreting treaties, nothing in the Vienna Convention prevents the Court 'from taking into account the present-day state of scientific knowledge.'[27]

Knowledge of the biosphere, its deterioration, renewal and the effects of pollution, can evolve quickly. Most authorities viewed atmospheric pollution as a local phenomenon until, during the 1970s, acidity in the lakes of Scandinavia showed that long-range damage could occur. After 1980, the destruction of forests demonstrated that sulfur dioxide (SO_2) was not the only agent responsible for atmospheric pollution, because nitrogen oxide (NO_2) emitted from automobiles may also play a major role in causing damage. Subsequently, discovery that the stratospheric ozone layer is damaged added yet another element to the problem of protecting the atmosphere from pollution. Thus, international action to address one problem necessarily changed directions during the space of a dozen years.

This is well-illustrated by discussing the influence the Intergovernmental Panel on Climate Change (IPCC) has had on climate policy. The IPCC is tasked with researching and examining the science behind climate change, and during its years of existing it has published six 'assessment reports' in which it has published its major findings.[28] These reports have been of great importance to the formation of international legislation on the topic, providing a trustworthy scientific source. It is no simple coincidence that major framework conventions on climate change in the past thirty years have consistently been established shortly after the publishing of these assessment reports to be able to incorporate the most up-to-date facts in the considerations. For example, the process that eventually led to the creation of the UNFCCC was started just after the publishing of the IPCC Assessment Report 1 in 1990, and the Paris Agreement was established at the COP 21, which was purposefully planned after the release of IPCC Assessment Report 5. It is thus without doubt that the continuous updates from the IPCC have significant influence on the course of action taken politically.

The challenge is how law, which is based upon predictability and the constancy of rules, can respond to these changing demands of environmental protection. In addition to the using the technique of framework conventions, states have developed an effective response by drafting treaties that establish stable general obligations but also add flexible provisions, especially those

27 ICJ, *Case Concerning Kasilili/Sedudu Island* (*Botswana v. Namibia*), (Dec. 13, 1999) 1999 ICJ Rep. 98, 39 ILM 310 (2000).

28 See IPCC Assessment Reports 1 to 6, published in 1990, 1995, 2001, 2007, 2013/2014 and 2021/2022. The IPCC has also published smaller reports in between on more specific issues. They can all be found on their website: <www.ipcc.ch/>.

prescribing technical norms. The latter may designate the specific products that cannot be dumped or discharged in a given area or may identify the endangered species needing additional protection. The general obligations are set forth in the treaty, which remains stable, while the detailed listing of products or species is reserved to annexes that can be modified easily without amending the principal treaty. The annexes form an integral part of the treaty and thus the modification procedure is expressly included in the treaty's provisions.

Agreements of this type include many wildlife treaties, such as the 1979 Bern Convention on the Conservation of European Wildlife and Natural Habitats (September 19, 1979). Its Article 16 allows for amendment of the treaty according to generally recognized international rules codified in Articles 39 and 40 of the Vienna Convention on the Law of Treaties. In other words, any amendment must be accepted by all the contracting parties according to their internal constitutional requirements. In contrast, the treaty's annexes listing protected species may be modified pursuant to the procedure set forth in Article 17 which allows changes to be proposed by a permanent Committee established by the Convention. Proposals are communicated to the contracting parties and at the expiration of three months each modification enters into force for all states that have not filed objections. This process of formal approval followed by automatic entry into force after a certain period of time for states that have not voiced opposition is also foreseen by Article 15 of the London Convention on the Prevention of Marine Pollution by Dumping of Wastes and Other Matter December 29, 1972). States thus must opt out of obligations, rather than having the task of expressing their approval and agreement to be bound.

Other treaties require express formal approval rather than tacit acceptance. Article 9 of the 1972 London Convention for the Conservation of Antarctic Seals (June 1, 1972) is one example. In both models, the treaties establish a bifurcated modification process, in which the structural parts of the treaties are subject to traditional, rather difficult, amendment processes, while the technical details may be altered quickly and less formally.

2 Customary International Law

Despite the relatively recent emergence of international environmental law, it is still possible to discern among current norms 'evidence of a general practice, accepted as law' as the definition of customary international law requires. The UN Conference on the Law of the Sea, which met between 1973 and 1982, adopted one of the most important of modern international treaties. During the long process of its elaboration by states of the world, a certain number of existing rules were codified, but there also arose a consensus on several new norms. On the basis of this consensus an international practice formed, even before adoption of the treaty. This was particularly the case with the creation of the 'exclusive economic zone,' now codified in Part v of the Convention.[29] During the negotiations, it was clearly recognized that coastal states have sovereign rights for the purpose of conserving and managing living and non-living natural resources and have jurisdiction to preserve the marine environment.[30] It also became accepted that coastal state jurisdiction to legislate regarding ships in innocent passage through the territorial sea includes measures to conserve marine biological resources and preserve the marine environment and to prevent, reduce and control marine pollution.[31]

Other rules of customary international law can be observed emerging and at different stages in their evolution. The formulation of non-binding principles undoubtedly plays an important role in this process, as does the repetition of specific rules in numerous international texts. It is also possible that the process of formulating a rule creates a rather rapid consensus which leads to general acceptance of the rule in state practice. The follow-up to the nuclear accident at Chernobyl illustrates this development. Although the Soviet government evacuated nearly 50,000 persons in the days immediately following the incident, it failed to inform other states until much later and did not give a complete explanation of the event until a specially organized meeting of the International Atomic Energy Agency (IAEA) took place between August 25 and 29, 1986. One of the general principles repeated in numerous conventions and declarations was the duty of a state to urgently notify other states at risk of having their environment adversely affected by any situation or any event. The non-application of this principle by the USSR after Chernobyl made it necessary to formulate the norm in more detail, based on the parallel conventional provisions. Thus, fifty-eight states signed an agreement in Vienna on early notification of a nuclear accident and the treaty entered into force with unusual speed one month later. As its title indicates, it requires states to give notification without delay of any nuclear accident which will or might lead to radioactive consequences for another state.[32] The information to be transmitted is specified in the Convention.[33] The speed of codification of this rule

29 UNCLOS Arts. 55–75.
30 ibid, Art. 56(a).
31 ibid, Art. 21.
32 Convention on Early Notification of a Nuclear Accident, Art. 1.
33 ibid, Art. 5.

can only be explained by the circumstances and by the recognition of a prior international duty to notify.

Several other customary rules of international environmental law have emerged. Most widely recognized is the norm that no state may cause or allow its territory to be used to cause significant damage to the environment of other states. This norm, the no-harm principle, first arose in international jurisprudence, in the *Trail Smelter Arbitration*.[34] It was later formulated in Principle 21 of the Stockholm Declaration before being adopted and reaffirmed in numerous other binding and nonbinding international instruments. The duty to cooperate, announced by Principle 24 of the Stockholm Declaration, also appears to have acquired this status, as well as reflecting a fundamental norm of the entire United Nations system.[35] It merits underscoring that the precise legal status of principles of environmental law can be difficult to discern and that the status of some of them in particular have remained subject to debate.[36] In sum, it is possible to speak of a body of customary international environmental law composed of fundamental principles underlying the entire system and applicable to all environmental subjects.

The number of treaties and other international instruments reproducing the same legal norms concerning the environment continues to grow. The work of the International Law Commission shows that repetition of the same norms in numerous international instruments can be considered as giving birth to new customary rules. In this regard, it is worth noting that several international instruments have declared that Part XII of UNCLOS, relating to protection of the marine environment, is part of customary international law.

3 General Principles of Law

The third source of international law provoked much discussion in scholarly writings. The underlying concept seeks to identify those principles that are common to the major legal systems of the world, if not to all of them. The global proliferation of national norms concerning the environment, whose number is exceedingly high, can permit discovery of numerous such rules

34 *Trail Smelter Arbitration*, RIAA, vol. III 1905–82 at 1965.

35 The ICJ has also identified as customary international law the requirement of conducting an environmental impact assessment to prevent transboundary harm. See Chapter 4.

36 The status of the precautionary principle is an example of this, see Ole W. Pendersen, 'From Abundance to Indeterminacy: The Precautionary Principle and Its Two Camps of Custom' (2014) Vol.3, Transnational Environmental Law.

after a period of consolidation. Even now certain principles may be considered as an established part of the common law of environmental protection. Many of them originate from the inter-penetration of legal rules at all levels of governance from the global to the municipal. Laws and policies adopted at the global, regional, and national levels influence each other. Initiatives begun at one level of governance often lead to similar approaches being adopted in other legal orders. A few examples demonstrate this widespread practice.

As discussed above, the 1941 arbitral decision resolving a long-standing dispute between the United States and Canada over air pollution originating in a Canadian smelter found no applicable international law on the topic and turned to norms articulated in the case law of federal states – the United States and Switzerland, in particular – to establish the principle that states have a duty not to cause significant transboundary air pollution.[37] Principle 21 of the Stockholm Declaration made this a general obligation not to cause transboundary environmental harm. The Rio Declaration reiterated the duty and it has been incorporated since then into numerous environmental treaties and other texts, reflecting both a general principle of law and a norm of customary international law.

International norms similarly can formulate new principles that pass into regional and national laws. Most states traditionally had few rules protecting wildlife, which was freely available for capture, killing, or other use. From hunting safaris in Africa to whaling on the open seas and plant collectors in Latin America, unregulated access was the general rule. Many of the norms that now protect wildlife developed first in international agreements to protect migratory species and resources of the commons. The international regulations were incorporated into the national law of states parties to treaties and influenced other states. The Convention on Biological Diversity was more protective of flora and fauna than the laws of most states at the time it was adopted and required new domestic laws and regulations.

Substantive obligations are not the only aspect of environmental law that has benefitted from the mutual influence of national, regional and international law. The tools and techniques to implement environmental law also reflect the trend towards borrowing from the experience of different levels of governance. The environmental impact assessment procedure (EIA), for example, was first mandated in the United States at the end of the 1960s in the State of Michigan. Its aim was and remains to ensure that adequate and early

---

37 *Trail Smelter Arbitration.*

information is obtained on the likely environmental consequences of projects and possible alternatives and measures to mitigate harm. United States federal legislation adopted the EIA in 1969, following which it was introduced into the laws of many other countries. It became part of regional law initially with the 1978 Kuwait Regional Convention for Co-operation on the Protection of the Marine Environment from Pollution (April 24, 1978). From the regional seas agreements, it was introduced at the global level in UNCLOS, Article 206 of which proclaims the principle of assessment of potential effects of environment-harming activities. Several years later, a Directive of the European Communities obliged member states to adopt national EIA legislation by July 1988. In 1991, the EIA procedure became the subject of a specific agreement drafted by the UN Economic Commission for Europe: the Convention on Environmental Impact Assessment in a Transboundary Context (Espoo, February 25, 1991). The procedure is the cornerstone of another 1991 agreement, the Madrid Protocol to the Antarctic Treaty on Environmental Protection (October 4, 1991). It also appears in Article 4(1)(f) of the 1992 UN Framework Convention on Climate Change.

In sum, the EIA, having started as the law of a component unit of a federal state, was progressively adopted at the federal level, then by other countries, regional organizations and regional treaty systems. Finally, it became a major part of global environmental regulation, proposed to countries whose domestic legislation has not adopted it as yet. In the *Pulp Mills* judgment,[38] the ICJ declared that EIA has become a customary international obligation in a transboundary context. Although the specific obligations in question arose pursuant to a bilateral treaty, the Court described EIA as:

> a practice, which in recent years has gained so much acceptance among States that it may now be considered a requirement under general international law to undertake an environmental impact assessment where there is a risk that the proposed industrial activity may have a significant adverse impact in a transboundary context, in particular, on a shared resource. Moreover, due diligence, and the duty of vigilance and prevention which it implies, would not be considered to have been exercised, if a party planning works liable to affect the régime of the river or the quality of its waters did not undertake an environmental impact assessment on the potential effects of such works.[39]

38 *Case Concerning Pulp Mills on the River Uruguay (Arg. v. Urug)*, 2010 ICJ Rep. 14 (20 Apr.).
39 ibid, para. 204.

Another example traverses the legal orders in the opposite direction, showing the effects that international law and policy can have on national law. Principle 15 of the 1992 Rio Declaration formulated the precautionary approach, according to which lack of full scientific certainty shall not be used as a reason for postponing measures to prevent environmental degradation where there are threats of serious or irreversible damage. During the same period the precautionary principle appeared in regional texts as well: e.g., in the 1991 Bamako Convention on the Ban of the Import into Africa and the Control of Transboundary Movement and Management of Hazardous Wastes within Africa (January 29, 1991) and the Treaty on European Union (Article 130R, para. 2). It spread rapidly during the following years in regional seas treaties. The legal system of different countries also adopted it either by introducing it into laws or regulations or by applying it in judicial decisions.[40] By 2009, the European Court of Human Rights could declare that the precautionary principle had become a binding legal norm within Europe.[41]

As these examples demonstrate, the various levels of the legal order interact as initiatives move among them to provide models for action, adapting and evolving as necessary. Certain principles, techniques and practices are or could be extended from one level to others providing dynamic and creative solutions to environmental problems.

4 Judicial Decisions and Doctrine

Although the Statute of the ICJ refers to jurisprudence as a subsidiary source for determining rules of law, judgments and advisory opinions of the World Court and arbitral or other international tribunals have been quite important from the first landmark case, the 1893 *Fur Seals* arbitration.[42]

---

40 See, e.g. the judgment of the Supreme Court of India handed down on 28 August 1996 in *Vellore Citizens' Welfare Forum v. Union of India and Others* and the decision of the French high administrative court, the Conseil d'Etat of Sept. 25, 1998 in *Association Greenpeace France.*

41 Judgment, *Tatar v. Romania*, Application No. 67021/01, Chamber Judgment, ECtHR, 27 January 2009 (declaring that the precautionary principle has moved, on the European level, from being a philosophical concept to being a juridical norm requiring the government to adopt reasonable and adequate measures capable of respecting the rights of individuals against serious risks to their health and well-being, even where scientific certainty is lacking).

42 *Rights of Jurisdiction of the United States in the Bering Sea and the Preservation of Fur Seals* (US-UK), Arbitral Award of August 15, 1893.

International decisions often are considered as the affirmation or the revelation of customary international rules. The arbitral award of March 11, 1941 in the *Trail Smelter* case is considered as having laid the foundations of international environmental law, at least regarding transboundary pollution. Confirmed by a more general principle enunciated in the *Corfu Channel* case[43] and referred to in the 1956 *Lake Lanoux* arbitration in the context of transboundary water pollution,[44] the announced rule forms part of positive international law today. The number of judicial and arbitral decisions has been expanding with the proliferation of international tribunals, each of which is experiencing a rising caseload. Many environmental cases now come before specialized tribunals like the International Tribunal on the Law of the Sea, the WTO's dispute settlement and Appellate Body, and human rights courts and commissions. It should be noted that in 1993, the ICJ created a Chamber for Environmental Matters, for which it had authority under Article 26 paragraph 1 of its Statute. However, in the thirteen years that the Chamber was in existence, not one case was put before it. It was therefore dissolved in 2006.

Scholarly writings in international environmental law continue to expand rapidly in quantity and improve in quality. While books entirely devoted to international environmental law remained exceptional until the end of the 1980s, a mass of articles began appearing after the 1972 Stockholm Conference. Other significant sources are the legal texts adopted by scientific and professional associations, such as the 1979 Athens resolution of the International Law Institute on pollution of rivers and lakes in international law,[45] and the numerous texts of the International Law Association, including the Helsinki rules on the uses of the waters of international rivers (1966),[46] principles concerning land-based marine pollution (1972),[47] the relations between international water resources and other natural resources and the environment (1980),[48] and transboundary pollution in general (1980).[49] Of considerable importance has been the work of the UN's International Law Commission, which has addressed, *inter alia*, the marine environment, international watercourses,

43 ICJ, April 3, 1949 ('No state may utilize its territory contrary to the rights of other States').

44 12 UNRIAA 285 at 303.

45 'Annuaire Français de Droit International' (1979) 1233.

46 ILA, The Helsinki Rules with Commentaries, (1967). See E.J. Manier, 'The Present State Of International Water Resources Law', ILA, 1873–1973.

47 ILA, Report of the Fifty-fifth Conference, New York, 1972, 97 at 98.

48 ILA, Report of the Fifty-ninth Conference, Belgrade, 1980, 373.

49 ibid 531.

transboundary aquifers, state responsibility and liability for environmental harm, and protection of the environment during armed conflict. This work is discussed in more detail in Chapter 5. Scholarly writings on international environmental law have come a long way since the 1970s, and it is by now a well-developed field of law with extensive literature devoted to it.[50]

5 The Role of Legally Non-Binding Norms

In international practice, instruments that are not treaties and thus not legally binding nonetheless serve important roles in the development of international environmental law. First, the careful negotiating process can lead to a consensus about the appropriate conduct of states and a political commitment to achieve the articulated goals. States on occasion have even established compliance control mechanisms for soft law instruments, as happened with the creation of the Commission on Sustainable Development tasked with overseeing implementation of Agenda 21. Each text must therefore be examined for its language, process of adoption (whether unanimous or by divided vote), and follow-up to determine its normativity.

States often choose to set forth their understandings in these so-called 'soft law'[51] texts for several reasons. First, states can avoid serious domestic legal or political obstacles to treaty ratification by adopting common rules of conduct in non-binding form. The negotiating period of such instruments generally is shorter and because the texts are not subject to national ratification, they can take instant effect. Second, states feel less constrained about accepting norms and goals that are not legally binding,[52] especially where their capacity to comply is not certain. Third, non-legally binding instruments may be more appropriate to the substance under consideration than formal agreements.

---

50 For examples and literature regarding the interaction between international environmental law and other fields of international law, see Part III of this book.

51 Soft law can also refer to weak conventional obligations, such as many of the provisions in the Convention on Biological Diversity which begin with 'Each contracting party shall, as far as possible, and where appropriate …' or 'Each contracting party shall, in accordance with its particular conditions and capabilities …'

52 The participation in the Memorandum of Understanding related to the Siberian Crane, a formally non-binding instrument, drafted under the 1979 Bonn Convention on the Conservation of Migratory Species of Wild Animals, 19 ILM 15 (1980) is particularly high: seven out of the nine known range states accepted it, including four states which are not parties to the Bonn Convention. Similarly, another soft law instrument, the Memorandum of Understanding concerning Conservation Measures for the Slender-billed Curlew was signed by 17 range states out of 30. Only six of these are party to the Bonn Convention.

Examples are action plans outlining desirable approaches or orientations, rather than commitments that may be difficult to fulfil when contracting parties are at different stages of development. Fourth, the negotiation of non-binding instruments more easily allows the participation of international institutions and of non-state actors in the process of creating and complying with environmental rules. The IUCN prepared the first draft of the World Charter of Nature which was sent out by the UN General Assembly to the member states for comments and later adopted and solemnly proclaimed on October 28, 1982.[53] NGOs also participated in the adoption and continue to be involved in monitoring memoranda of understanding complementing the 1979 Bonn Convention on the Conservation of Migratory Species of Wild Animals. Finally, resolutions and similar non-binding instruments may be more appropriate where there is uncertainty about the scope of the problem or the appropriate solution. The codes of good practices and guides relating to safety of nuclear facilities adopted by the International Atomic Energy Agency indicate how soft law regulations evolve with the development of knowledge in a given domain. Recommended measures adopted under the 1959 Antarctic Treaty by the Consultative Parties also show that governments are more willing to be innovative when the text is not legally binding.

In sum, soft law rules have the necessary flexibility to enable the international community to progress in the new domain, especially for approaching problems which are new for international co-operation.

Compliance with formally non-binding norms is affected by the authority of the text on which the instruments is based and many are related to binding agreements. In becoming parties to the Antarctic Treaty, for example, states bind themselves to carry out the Treaty's purposes and principles. Recommendations that become effective in accordance with Article IX of the Treaty are 'measures in furtherance of the principles and objectives of the Treaty' and thus have a high degree of authority. Legitimacy also can be conferred on non-binding texts by the fact that they have been adopted with an overwhelming majority or by consensus by an inter-governmental institution or under the aegis of such a body.

The legitimacy of the adoptive process of a recommended measure and the perceived fairness of the norm also favor compliance: the adoption of the 1989 Convention for the Prohibition of Fishing with Long Driftnets in the South Pacific (Wellington, November 24, 1989) was a major incentive for the

53 G.A. Res. 37/7, 37 UNGAOR, Supp (No 51) at 17, UN Doc. A/37/51 (1982).

resolutions of the UN General Assembly[54] generally prohibiting this means of fishing as part of a much larger effort to address concerns over the environment and resource implications at a time when the concept of sustainable development became influential.

Scientific evidence and media publicity can enhance compliance with non-binding instruments by raising public awareness of a problem and the need for it to be addressed. Meetings of the Parties to the 1987 Montreal Protocol on Substances that Deplete the Ozone Layer successively adjusted their obligations to accelerate the phasing out of ozone-depleting substances. This upward revision was the consequence of a Declaration adopted in Helsinki in May 1989 where eighty-two countries called for a complete CFC phase-out by the end of the century.

Incentives enhance compliance, from technical and financial assistance for institutional strengthening and specialized training to the sharing of experience. At the opposite extreme, the absence of enforcement measures, sanctions for non-compliance, and mechanisms for dispute resolution are not conducive to enhancing compliance among reluctant states. The development of legal rules concerning driftnet fishing shows, however, that monitoring compliance with non-binding texts constitutes a useful tool for exercising pressure upon states, especially when monitoring is ensured not only by individual states but by intergovernmental organizations and independent NGOs.

In sum, soft law may be a source of obligation. As the Arbitral Tribunal in the *Iron Rhine Arbitration* stated, the fact that a relevant text is not, as a matter of international law, a binding instrument, does not mean it is 'without legal relevance.'[55]

5.1 *Resolutions and Decisions of International Organizations*

One of the principal characteristics of international organizations is that very few have the power to adopt legally binding texts. Only three have such power among all the organizations which are concerned with matters of environmental protection: the UN Security Council, the OECD and the UN General Assembly. Thus, since their beginning in the nineteenth century, international organizations have adopted non-binding resolutions addressed to member

54 Resolutions on Large-Scale Pelagic Driftnet Fishing and its Impact on the Living Marine Resources of the World's Oceans and Seas, Dec. 22, 1989, Dec. 21, 1990 and Dec. 20, 1991. See Chapter 11.

55 *Iron Rhine Railway between the Kingdom of Belgium and the Kingdom of Netherlands*, Arbitral Award of May 24, 2005, paras. 156–57.

states. This procedure has taken on increased importance over the years, particularly for new fields of international regulation such as environmental protection. Recommendations and declarations of principles of conferences such as Stockholm or meetings of the United Nations Environmental Program (Vancouver 1976, Mar del Plate 1977, Nairobi 1978) have had great impact on the evolution of international environmental law. Moreover, the multiplication of intergovernmental organizations has considerably augmented the number and diversity of non-binding texts because they are the principal means of expression for most organizations. With many resolutions adopted by consensus and implemented and invoked in practice, it may be argued that they constitute a now-recognized source of international law not foreseen by the Statute of the ICJ, or a new technique for creating international juridical norms. This technique is particularly effective in establishing law for new fields where rapid decisions are needed, like human rights, exploration and exploitation of outer space and the deep seabed, and environmental law.

The Security Council of the United Nations, by virtue of its peace-keeping functions and other roles conferred on it, is one of the few organizations that can adopt binding decisions. Its actions in regard to environmental destruction in the Persian Gulf in the aftermath of the Iraqi invasion of Kuwait indicate a heightened concern for environmental protection during armed conflict.[56] In addition, according to Article 5 of the Convention on the Prohibition of Military or Any Other Hostile Use of Environmental Modification Techniques,[57] each state party that has reason to believe another state party is violating its obligations can file a complaint with the Security Council. The latter may undertake an inquiry with the power to decide that the state bringing the complaint has been or might be harmed due to a violation of the Convention. However, the consequences of such a decision are not discussed. No doubt they would include the application of Articles 36 and 37 of the United Nations Charter, which recommend dispute-settlement procedures.

The Organization for Economic Cooperation and Development (OECD) has wider competence in the field of environmental protection. In order to achieve its objectives, this organization of market-economy industrial states can take decisions which, unless otherwise stated, bind all its members.[58] The nature of this organization as an agency of study and consultation, however, means that in practice binding environmental decisions are infrequent. When taken, they

56 See Chapter 16.

57 Geneva, Dec. 10, 1976.

58 Art. 5(a), Convention on the Organization for Economic Co-operation and Development, 12 UST 1928.

generally treat narrow, technical subjects, such as the exchange of information on polychlorinated biphenils (PCBS),[59] the mutual acceptance of data in the assessment of chemicals,[60] and the institution of a multilateral organ for consultation and surveillance of marine dumping of radioactive waste.[61]

Directive recommendations concerning environmental protection have played an important role in the activities of most intergovernmental organizations and in the general development of international environmental law. The UN General Assembly has adopted resolutions on global climate change, Antarctica, driftnet fishing, sustainable development, and, indeed, nearly all the subjects of international concern. On the regional level, the OECD has adopted recommendations on such subjects as hazardous products,[62] transboundary pollution,[63] tourism,[64] waste management,[65] the relationship between the environment and economy,[66] the management of natural resources,[67] and the management of coastal zones.[68]

Declarations of principles differ from directive recommendations in that they do not envisage precise action to be undertaken, but they may fix general guidelines for states to follow and they may exercise considerable influence on the development of subsequent legal rules.[69] Another function of principles is to set forth a fundamental societal consensus on the underlying rationale for a body of law. In this respect, principles serve one of the fundamental objectives of any legal system, which is to recognize and formulate the emergence of new social values recognized as essential within the society. At the international level, this can be achieved through declarations adopted and proclaimed by global organizations or international conferences. All the major soft law texts

---

59 Decision C(73)1 of Feb. 13, 1973.

60 Decision C(81)30, of May 12, 1981.

61 Decision C(77)115, of July 22, 1977.

62 E.g., Recommendation C(73)172, Sept. 19, 1973, Measures to Reduce all Man-made Emissions of Mercury to the Environment.

63 Recommendation C(74)224, Nov. 14, 1974; Principles Concerning Transfrontier Pollution, 14 ILM 234 (1975).

64 Recommendation C(79)115, Environment and Tourism.

65 Recommendation of C(76)155, Sept. 28, 1976, A Comprehensive Waste Management Policy.

66 Recommendation C(72)128, May 26, 1972, Guiding Principles concerning International Economic Aspects of Environmental Policies.

67 E.g., Recommendation C(78)4, April 5, 1978, Water Management Policies and Instruments.

68 Recommendation C(76)161, Oct. 1976, Principles Concerning Coastal Management.

69 See, generally, Nicolas De Sadeleer, *Environmental Principles: From Political Slogans To Legal Rules* (2002).

contain principles that are then taken up, defined and given concrete meaning in international treaties and jurisprudence.

A principle and its juridical value, if any, can change from one legal system to another. Principles can be descriptive and indicate the essential characteristics of legal institutions, designate fundamental legal norms, or fill gaps in positive law by assigning a value to rules not yet contained in formal legal instruments, although they are considered important. Principles can be foundational (equality and legal certainty) or technical (proportionality). They may appear in constitutions and basic laws, as in European continental legal traditions, or they may be of judicial construction. According to some, a principle provides the general orientation and direction to which positive law must conform, a rationale for the law, without itself constituting a binding norm. Another definition of a principle is a rule of indeterminate conduct where the degree of abstraction is so great that it is not possible to deduce obligations with a degree of certainty, thus leaving a wide margin of appreciation or discretion to the actor.[70]

Most environmental principles proclaimed in declarations have reappeared in one form or another in conventional texts, the mandate given to international institutions, and the practice of states. The influence of the principles contained in the Stockholm Declaration, the World Charter for Nature, and the 1992 Rio Declaration on Environment and Development is substantial. Other declarations of principles have directly led to the creation of obligatory norms, including the European Water Charter,[71] the 1974 OECD recommendation containing principles relative to transboundary pollution,[72] and the 1978 UNEP statement of principles of conduct in the field of environment for the guidance of states in the conservation and harmonious utilization of natural resources shared by two or more states.[73] Finally, even where declarations of principles are not directly transformed into binding rules, they may serve to guide states in adopting legislation. Without the Stockholm Declaration, it is likely that national environmental laws would have been fewer and weaker.

5.2 *Decisions of COPs/MOPs*

The requirements of environmental protection mean that effective instruments must be dynamic and responsive to changing conditions. Thus, although MEAs can set out the basic framework of rights and obligations,

70 ibid at 309.
71 See Chapter 10.A.1.b.
72 ibid.
73 UNEP/IG.12/2, May 19, 1978; 17 ILM 1091 (1978).

there must be on-going interaction by the states parties to ensure currency, consistency and implementation of the agreement. In this respect, the VCLT, Article 31, makes clear that the states parties to international agreements may interpret the agreement or define its terms through subsequent state practice.

For many MEAs, the Conference of the Parties (COP) or Meeting of the Parties (MOP) is the plenary organ that governs the continuous operation of the agreement. COPs or MOPs are not part of any international organization but act autonomously,[74] holding regular meetings, reviewing periodic reports from states and subsidiary bodies, establishing permanent secretariats, and setting budgets. In fact, commentators and official organizations have recognized COPs as a new form of intergovernmental organization.[75]

The earliest COP was introduced by the 1971 Ramsar Convention on Wetlands of International Importance. Initially it had advisory powers only under Article 6 of the Convention, but in 1987, the states parties amended Article 6 to provide for the establishment of a new COP to review and promote implementation of the Convention, without reference to any advisory character in the work undertaken. Following the Ramsar Convention, in 1972, the London Dumping Convention established a COP with greater powers than the Ramsar COP originally had, although it did not expressly refer to the creation of subsidiary bodies. CITES, in 1973, was the first treaty to use the term Conference of the Parties, granting the COP extensive powers that were expanded further in 1979 to include financial provisions. Later conventions negotiated under the auspices of UNEP, like CITES, all contain similar provisions for COPs.

The powers of COPs are set out in the treaty articles and generally provide for the adoption of rules of procedure, financial arrangements, establishment of subsidiary bodies, the powers of the secretariat, and the process for amendments and protocols. COPs also are usually tasked with supervising implementation of and compliance with the treaty obligations of states parties. These functions result in developing the law and providing authoritative interpretation of various treaty provisions. General powers may also be granted, such as

74 For further information, see Philippe Sand, 'The Role of Environmental Agreements' Conferences of the Parties,' in Y. Kerbrat and S. Maljean-Dubois, *The Transformation Of International Environmental Law* (Pedone & Hart 2011).

75 ibid 90.

to 'consider any additional action that may be required'[76] or fulfil other functions as appropriate to achieve the objective of the Convention.[77]

The COPs and MOPs created by MEAs are increasingly adopting interpretive decisions, recommendations and guidelines for action. The decisions and recommendations can have considerable juridical value when they express the common understanding of the States parties concerning the norms and obligations contained in the agreement.[78] The Kyoto Protocol Article 17 in fact enabled the COP to adopt 'rules' for emissions trading, perhaps suggesting an intent that they be considered binding, although in this instance and in respect to other COPs the legal nature of the measures taken is ambiguous and debated. The Paris Agreement gave the COP the power to create rules, modalities and procedures for a newly established mechanism to contribute to the mitigation of greenhouse gas emissions and support sustainable development.[79]

Another place where a COP adopted guidelines, was the CBD COP15 in 2022.[80] At the COP, global goals and targets for 2030 were set to address loss of biodiversity and restore natural ecosystems in the Kunming-Montreal Global Biodiversity Framework (GBF).[81] Besides this, it approved multiple agreements concerned with implementation such as a Special Trust Fund for the Global Environment Facility. This 'GBF Fund' has the purpose of supporting the implementation of the new Global Diversity Framework. 188 governments were represented at the COP, including two non-members (the Vatican and the US), showing that there is a great common understanding between state parties of the importance and legitimacy of the agreements established.

In practice, the Agreed Measures adopted by the Antarctic Treaty Consultative Parties constitute a veritable code of conduct for all activities in the Antarctic region and themselves are supplemented by decisions and

---

76 London Dumping Convention, Art. XIV(4)(f).

77 See, e.g., Convention on Long-Range Transboundary Air Pollution, Art. 10(2)(c) and UNFCCC, Art. 7(2)(m).

78 The delegation of law-making or regulatory powers to COP s can raise constitutional problems in domestic legal systems, as seen in a judgment of the U.S. Court of Appeals for the D.C. Circuit, which refused to apply a decision of the COP of the Montreal Protocol on Ozone-Depleting Substances. See: *Natural Resources Defence Council* (*NRDC*) *v. Environmental Protection Agency* (*EPA*), 464, f.2RD 1 (D.C. Cir., 2006). For a commentary see Alice Bodnar, 'Testing the Waters of the Constitutionality of Delegation to International Organizations' (2007) 34 Ecology L. Q. 895.

79 Paris Agreement at the Conference of the Parties (adopted December 12, 2015) UN Doc. FCCC/CP/2015/L.9/Rev/1 art. 6(4) and (7).

80 This is the COP associated with the Convention on Biological Diversity (May 22, 1992).

81 Decision Adopted by the Conference of the Parties to the Convention on Biological Diversity (Montréal, Dec. 19, 2022) CBD/COP/DEC/15/4.

resolutions of more hortatory value. During the 1960s alone, some 74 agreed measures were adopted. Similarly, the Ramsar, CBD, and CITES meetings have produced numerous and lengthy guidelines, recommendations and decisions, such as the Bonn Guidelines on Access to Genetic Resources and Fair and Equitable Sharing of the Benefits Arising out of their Utilization adopted by the sixth conference of the parties to the Convention on Biological Diversity. In the last-mentioned instance, as well as in regard to a decision of the COP to the 1989 Basel Convention, later COPs have either rescinded or supplemented the earlier decision by adopting a formal treaty amendment or Protocol to the agreement.

At least one COP, that of the CITES, undertakes to sanction infringements of the primary treaty as well as the secondary norms generated by the COP. Continuous practice of the COP seeks to settle disputes over compliance by direct communications between the state concerned and the secretariat or the Standing Committee created by the COP. If the matter is not resolved, the COP or the Standing Committee may recommend countermeasures in the form of an embargo of one or more CITES-listed species.[82] This has been done in at least 40 cases since 1985, with six states subject to a total trade ban with regard to all species protected under the Convention.

5.3 *Action Plans and Programs*

While directive recommendations are addressed to states members of an international organization, programs of action often are aimed at the organizations which draft them, setting forth the activities to be undertaken within a given period of time. The European Community, for example, has adopted programs of action for successive four-year periods since 1973. Similarly, the IUCN in 1980 proposed its global program of action, the 'World Conservation Strategy.'

Treaties normally require states parties to undertake or refrain from specific conduct, but the nature of environmental problems often makes it impossible to define the exact content of obligations, especially when long-range pollution or long-term problems are addressed. The result is more programmatic, even vague obligations. The 1979 Geneva Convention on Long-Range Transboundary Air Pollution (November 13, 1979), for example concerns pollution 'at a distance where it is generally not possible to distinguish the source or sources of emission.'[83] Rather than fix precise duties, the obligations of states parties are to cooperate in the field of research and to implement a common program

82 Guide to CITES Compliance Procedures, Art. 30 (adopted by Res. Conf. 14.3, 2007).
83 Art. 1(b).

of continuous observation and evaluation of long range air pollution.[84] States parties also agree to elaborate policies and strategies to combat the dumping of pollutants into the atmosphere. The Paris Convention to Combat Desertification in those Countries Experiencing Serious Drought and/or Desertification, particularly in Africa (June 17, 1994) provide for action programs at the national, sub-regional and regional levels to be supported by intergovernmental and non-governmental bodies.

Treaties referring to action programs may be completed by more precise obligations for contracting parties through the conclusion of additional protocols to the original text. The 1979 Geneva Convention on Long-Range Transboundary Air Pollution, for example, has been supplemented by a series of protocols that give greater precision to the obligations of its states parties.[85] Similar arrangements exist for many of the regional seas treaties.[86]

The first well-known action plan is no doubt the Action Plan for the Human Environment, adopted by the 1972 Stockholm Conference on the Human Environment. The text is composed of 109 recommendations, sometimes addressed to governments, sometimes to international organizations, sometimes to both. It contains not only an indication of actions to be taken, but also directive recommendations. It has served as the basis for a large number of international measures taken since its adoption, including the global environmental assessment plan (Earthwatch) to survey the state of the environment. It also has been the foundation of global conventions, studies sponsored by various intergovernmental organizations, and UNEP's regional seas program begun in 1974. Agenda 21, adopted by the 1992 Rio Conference succeeded to it as a global program for sustainable development. It added to each chapter an evaluation of the cost of the proposed measures.

The role of non-binding texts expanded in the follow-up to UNCED. The UN General Assembly created the Commission on Sustainable Development (CSD) 'in order to ensure the effective follow-up of the Conference' and 'to examine the progress of the implementation of Agenda 21 at the national, regional and international levels, fully guided by the principles of the Rio Declaration on Environment and Development.' Thus, an institution created by a non-binding General Assembly resolution reviews state compliance with two other non-binding international instruments. The periodic reporting procedure foreseen for the CSD is a technique widely used in monitoring state

84 Arts. 8 and 9.

85 Such Protocols were adopted in Geneva, Sept. 28, 1984; in Helsinki, July 8, 1985; in Sofia, Oct. 31, 1988 and in Oslo, June 14, 1994.

86 See Chapter 11.

compliance with international legal obligations, but until now has been based upon treaty provisions obliging states to file reports. The CSD, however, seeks information based upon 'the commitments' and 'agreed objectives' contained in Agenda 21, including those related to the provision of financial resources and transfer of technology. The import of these provisions is to further blur the line between binding and non-binding international instruments.

5.4 *Standardization*

International norms may be developed not only by states, but by organizations in which private actors are dominant. The standards developed may apply directly to private organizations or states. The International Organization for Standardization is one such organization. It is a federation of over 100 national standardization bodies, one from each represented country. It was formed in 1946 to harmonize technical requirements and standards. Each national body establishes the composition of its delegations, which should include a mix of producer, consumer and other relevant interests. It often includes government officials. International meetings adopt the standards. By the late 1980s the standards included a global standard for quality control management, one source of emerging environmental management standards. Other inputs came from corporate codes of conduct. Similar, sometimes competing, environmental management standards developed in Europe and in national law.

Environmental management standards require the company management to define the organization's environmental policy and ensure that it is appropriate to the nature, scale and environmental impacts of its activities. Each registered facility must commit to continual improvement, to comply with relevant laws, and to the prevention of pollution. The commitment must be publicly available and the organization must set up procedures to identify the environmental effects of its activities, create and maintain procedures to document these activities, identify individual responsibilities, train appropriate personnel, and prepare an emergency response plan. These activities must be periodically monitored and corrective action taken in cases of noncompliance. Environmental audits, whether internal or external, are required.

5.5 *Codes of Conduct and Guidelines*

During the preparations for the 1992 Rio Conference, a group of companies formed the World Business Council for Sustainable Development, now consisting of more than 200 businesses. It continues to promote the goal of sustainable development through 'corporate social responsibility.' One outcome has been increased publication of corporate environmental reports based on new methodologies to measure the impact of business activities.

There also has been a growing number of guidelines or codes of conduct developed within industry. There is, for example, the OECD Guidelines for Multinational Enterprises on Responsible Business Conduct, which contains a chapter on the environment, in which it emphasizes that enterprises 'should conduct their activities in a manner that takes due account of the need to protect the environment, (...) avoids and addresses adverse environmental impacts and contributes to the wider goal of sustainable development.'[87] Other examples include the World Industry Council for the Environment, the FAO International Code of Conduct on the Distribution and Use of Pesticides, the Responsible Care Initiative of the Chemical Manufacturers Association, the CERES/Valdez Principles, the ICC Business Charter on Sustainable Development (2015) which draws from the ICC Green Economy Roadmap, and the Royal Dutch/Shell Group General Business Principles. The latter enunciates the responsibility 'to conduct business as responsible corporate members of society, to comply with applicable laws and regulations, to support fundamental human rights in line with the legitimate role of business, and to give proper regard to health, safety, security and the environment.'[88] Principle 5 states that Shell promises to 'continually look for ways to reduce the environmental impact of our operations, products and services.'[89]

Private regulation may constrain behavior by exercising a moral or practical (sanctioning) influence as effective as that of law. Breach of private codes may be evidence of malpractice or negligence, providing a relatively inexpensive means of evaluating conduct in case of a dispute. On the other hand, private codes may involve monopolistic professional regulation that is contrary to the public interest, less precise than legislation, and with standards below those that would be adopted through the normal law-making process. Where standards are stringent, the code may be ignored unless there is strong public pressure for compliance. The 1990 Valdez Principles on corporate environmental conduct may be debated within these terms. The Valdez Principles were adopted by the Coalition for Environmentally Responsible Economies, a group of investors and environmental organizations. The intent was to create corporate self-governance 'that will maintain business practices consistent with

87 OECD, *OECD Guidelines for Multinational Enterprises on Responsible Business Conduct* (OECD 2023) 33.

88 Shell International Limited, *General Business Principles* (2014) 3.

89 ibid 7.

the goals of sustaining our fragile environment for future generations, within a culture that respects all life and honors its independence.'[90]

Whether they are strong or weak, non-state codes may become the de facto minimum requirements for non-state actors. Corporate codes of conduct, industry standards, guidelines, recommendations, backed by informal or formal pressures, sometimes may effectively regulate the conduct of the community. Where norms are drafted by one community to regulate another, the results may be less pronounced, although the expertise and disinterestedness of the drafters may make the rules influential. The authority and legitimacy of the body adopting a normative text is no doubt important to the impact of the standards adopted. Both may be enhanced when the target community participates in the formulation of the norm. Although self-regulation may be self-serving and produce minimal constraints, it is also likely to produce a high degree of compliance. A process that is not wholly self-regulatory, but which allows meaningful participation of the regulated community and other interested communities may be most effective.

5.6 *State/Private Contracts*

Negotiated agreements between government and industry can serve to implement environmental standards. Pioneering instances of relevant transboundary contracts between public and private bodies should thus be noted. For example, on August 21, 1991, the Municipality of Rotterdam and the German Association of Chemical Industries concluded a contract to improve water quality and to reduce contaminated mud in the Rotterdam harbor.[91] The so-called 'Rhine Contract' ensured that certain categories of listed substances would be reduced by 2010. The Association issued reports on the achieved reduction of the substances in the waste water. Rotterdam would submit a report on the quality improvement of the harbor and the reduction in mud every two years. Significantly, according to Article 3 of the contract, Rotterdam waived any prior claims to compensation that it might have had against the subscribing companies. In case of non-performance

90 Valdez Principles in Daniel H. Pink, 'The Valdez Principles: Is What's Good for America Good for General Motors?' (1990) 8 Yale L. And POL'Y REV. 180. See also Valerie Ann Zondorak, '*A New Face in Corporate Environmental Responsibility: The Valdez Principles*' (1991) 18 B.C. ENVTL AFF. L. REV. 457.

91 See further European Union Research Network, 'Voluntary Approaches', Policy Research Series on Market-Based Instruments for Sustainable Development (1997) No. 1 <www.ucd.ie/t4cms/pb-ep-01.pdf>.

by the companies, Rotterdam could withdraw from the contract after three months' notice.

6 Conclusions

An increasing number of concepts, principles and norms appear repeatedly in national, regional and global instruments, usually following an initial formulation in a non-binding instrument. Principles such as public participation, EIA, notification of environmental emergencies, prevention, precaution and polluter pays are examples of principles that have been incorporated into treaties and given greater specificity. In many cases this can result in greater agreed specification, such as when the same definition of a term appears from one treaty to another.[92] In some instances, however, the effort to detail obligations leads to divergences from one instrument or region to another. For example, the duty not to cause transboundary harm has been variously qualified as 'significant' 'measurable' 'serious' or 'appreciable' harm. As with the institutional proliferation discussed in Chapter 5, normative proliferation leads to a need for coordination and reconciliation of obligations.

Bibliography

Bodansky, D., 'Customary (and not so Customary) International Environmental Law', 3 *Ind. J. Global Legal Studies* 105 (1995).

Drumbl, M, 'Actors and Law-Making in International Environmental Law', in Fitzmaurice, M., Ong, D. And Merkouris, P, *Research Handbook On International Environmental Law* (Edward Elgar, 2010).

Dupuy, P., 'Soft Law and The International Law of the Environment', 12 *Mich. J.Int'l L.* 420 (1991).

Ebbesson, J., *Compatibility Of International And National Environmental Law* (1996).

Kerbrat, Y. & Maljean-Dubois, S, *The Transformation Of International Environmental Law* (Pedone, 2011).

Sadeler, N. De, *Environmental Principles* (2002).

92 See e.g. the definition of pollution in the 1974 OECD Principles Concerning Transfrontier Pollution, Art. 1 of the Convention on Long-Range Transboundary Air Pollution, art. 1(4) of UNCLOS and Art. 1(c) of the 1992 Paris Convention for the Protection of the Marine Environment of the Northeast Atlantic.

Sand, P., 'UNCED and the Development of International Environmental Law', 3 *YBIEL* 3 (1992).

Shelton, D. (Ed.) *Commitment And Compliance: The Role Of Non-Binding Norms In The International Legal System* (1999).

Susskind, L., Ed., *International Environmental Treaty-Making* (1992).

Szasz, P., 'International Norm-Making', in Weiss, E.B., Ed., *Environmental Change In International Law* (1995).

CHAPTER 4

Customary International Law and Environmental Principles

Customary international law, general principles of law, and normative instruments have advanced a kind of a common law of the environment. Environmental norms and principles have become widely accepted and repeated consistently in treaties and national laws concerned with environmental protection. National and international jurisprudence further develops these norms and principles and may formulate new concepts as international environmental law evolves to meet new challenges.

International law first faced issues of environmental protection in two contexts: bilateral disputes resulting from transboundary pollution and over-exploitation of shared resources, especially migratory species. The international community subsequently realized that environmental problems are often global in origin and consequences, and that approaching environmental protection through rules designed to resolve isolated or local problems provides only limited solutions and often results in transferring environmental harm elsewhere.

The integrated nature of the biosphere signifies that international rules must be concerned with the full range of human activities within states, even when they produce no obvious or immediate detrimental effects outside the national territory. International law also must protect areas that are outside national jurisdiction, including the high seas and sea bed, the atmosphere and climate, Antarctica, outer space and objects therein. In sum, general rules and principles are necessary to guide states in environmental matters. Principle 21 of the Stockholm Declaration on the Human Environment first expressed the global nature of this requirement by affirming that 'States have the responsibility to ensure that activities within their jurisdiction or control do not cause damage to the environment of other States or of areas beyond the limits of national jurisdiction'.[1] Over the years, several treaty norms have been providing further detail on the modalities of performing this duty and express the major characteristics and values of international environmental law.[2] These

1 G.A. Res. 2994/XXVII U.N. Doc. A/CONF.48/14/Rev 1 (Dec. 15, 1972), Principle 21.

2 The United Convention on the Law of the Sea (UNCLOS), for instance, provides that 'States have the obligation to protect and preserve the marine environment' and to take all measures

 | DOI:10.1163/9789047440802_006

principles, as well as others that are emerging, play an important role in national as well as international approaches to environmental protection. This chapter assesses the customary international law of the environment and the general principles that have emerged to govern environmental protection in all its dimensions.

1 Responsibility for Transboundary Pollution

1.1 *Definition of Transboundary Pollution*

States first agreed on the meaning of pollution in a recommendation adopted after several revisions by the Organization for Economic Cooperation and Development (OECD) Council on November 14, 1974.[3] The same definition has since appeared, with minor modifications, in all major texts concerning pollution.[4]

> pollution means the introduction by man, directly or indirectly, of substances or energy into the environment resulting in deleterious effects of such a nature as to endanger human health, harm living resources and ecosystems, and impair or interfere with amenities and other legitimate uses of the environment.[5]

Several aspects of the definition are notable. First, pollution can result only from human activities; naturally occurring events such as lightning, floods, and earthquakes are excluded. Of course, human activities may trigger or exacerbate harm from natural events and cause pollution, such as would occur from a

'prevent, reduce and control pollution of the marine environment'. United Nations Convention on the Law of the Sea (Montego Bay, Dec. 10, 1982), Art. 211, U.N. Doc. A/CONF 62/122 (1982); Misc 11 (1983), Cmd. 8941, 21 I.L.M. 1261 (1982) (hereinafter UNCLOS), Arts. 192 and 194. The United Framework Convention on Climate Change (UNFCCC) reiterates that States have the 'responsibility to ensure that activities within their jurisdiction or control do not cause damage to the environment of other States or of areas beyond the limits of national jurisdiction.' United Nations Framework Convention on Climate Change (May 9, 1992), 1771 U.N.T.S. 107 (hereinafter UNFCCC), Preamble.

3 Council Recommendation C(74)219 of Nov. 14, 1974.

4 See, for example, Art. 2(a) of the 1976 Convention for the Protection of the Mediterranean Sea against Pollution (Feb. 17, 1976); Art. 1, EC Council Directive concerning Pollution caused by Certain Dangerous Substances Discharged in the Marine Environment of the Community, O.J. L 129 (5/18/76); Art. 1, Geneva Convention on Long-Range Transboundary Air Pollution (Nov. 13 1979); and Art. 1(1)(4) UNCLOS (Dec. 10, 1982).

5 OECD, Recommendation on Principles Concerning Transfrontier Pollution, Annex.

flood of contaminated water caused by upland deforestation. Where pollution results from human activities set in motion through natural events – a chemical factory that burns because it is struck by lightning or radioactive fallout from a nuclear installation damaged during an earthquake – authorities may at least have a duty to inform those who might suffer harm from the pollution. The reference to 'substances or energy' means that pollution includes not only solid, liquid or gaseous material objects, but also noise, vibrations, heat, and radiation.

The clauses concerning the introduction of pollution 'directly or indirectly' 'into the environment' pose the difficult problem of delimiting the environment.[6] Most international texts seem to suggest that 'environment' means areas outside industrial installations and habitations.[7] Thus, the 'introduction' of pollutants from the discharge of liquid waste, dumping of solid waste, emission of air pollutants or of dust, is the act through which such substances are directly placed in the natural milieu. Indirect introduction covers situations where an intermediary element occurs between the original human act and the arrival of polluting substances in the environment. For example, discharge of pollutants into a sewage system that directly leads into a watercourse or the sea would be within the definition.[8]

The requirement of 'deleterious effects' raises the problem of determining the proper threshold and criteria for labeling a substance or act polluting, because all human activity alters the environment to some extent. The definition requires that the activity attain a requisite level of importance in light of the stated relevant consequences: endangerment of human health and

---

6 There is no single definition of the 'environment' in international law. The International Court of Justice (ICJ), in its *Nuclear Weapons* Advisory Opinion, has defined the environment not as an abstraction but as representing 'a living space, the quality of life and the very health of human beings, including generations unborn.' *Legality of the Threat or use of Nuclear* Weapons (Advisory Opinion) [1996] ICJ Rep. 226. The *Iron Rhine* arbitral tribunal has offered a different definition of the environment: 'Environment is broadly referred to as including air, water, land, flora, and fauna, natural ecosystems and sites, human health and safety, and climate'. *Iron Rhine Arbitration (Belgium v Netherlands)* (2005) Award ICGJ 373, para. 58.

7 However, ILO efforts have extended international concern over environmental pollution into the workplace. See Chapter 5. World Bank Operation Policy 4.01 provides that: 'Environmental Assessment takes into account the natural environment (air, water, and land); human health and safety; social aspects (involuntary resettlement, indigenous peoples, and physical cultural resources); and transboundary and global environmental aspects. EA considers natural and social aspects in an integrated way'. Reproduced in David Freestone, *The World Bank and Sustainable Development* (Brill 2012).

8 This is very important for the definition of land-based marine pollution.

harm to resources. Many international texts refer to 'significant' environmental impact.[9] Although the term 'significant' generally is not defined, it would clearly exclude *de minimis* damage.[10] The phrase 'of such a nature as to endanger' greatly enlarges the scope of the definition by including risk or possible risk of damage. The phrase 'to endanger' signifies the risk and 'of such a nature' adds to it a second more comprehensive element. Applying these terms, an industrial installation may be deemed dangerous because of its inherently risky nature as well as because of its activities at any particular time. The definition thus encompasses the notion of ultra-hazardous activities and recalls various national laws requiring prior authorization for dangerous installations.[11]

'Human health' is designated as the primary reason to combat pollution. This anthropocentric approach is reinforced in protecting human 'amenities' and 'other legitimate uses of the environment' from interference. 'Impair or interfere with amenities' can cover aesthetic nuisances such as pollution of lake waters or beaches, or harming tourist activities through deterioration of sites by smoke or waste. Even the reference to 'living resources' shows that other creatures are envisaged in light of their service to humans. 'Other legitimate uses of the environment' are sometimes specified in conventions,

9 See, e.g., G.A. Res. 2995 (XXVII) concerning cooperation between states in the field of the environment, U.N.G.A.O.R. Supp. No. 30, at 42 (1973); Art. 7, Mexico-United States Agreement to Cooperate in the Solution of Environmental Problems in the Border Area, 23 I.L.M. 1025 (Aug. 14, 1983); Art. 6, OECD Principles Concerning Transfrontier Pollution, Council Recommendation C(74)224 of Nov. 14, 1974; Art. 21 (2) of the UN Convention on the Law of the Non-Navigational Uses of International Watercourses (May 21, 1997), speaks of 'significant harm to other watercourse States or to their environment, including harm to human health or safety, to the use of the waters for any beneficial purpose or to the living resources of the watercourse'. The ICJ in *Pulp Mills* talks about 'significant damage', and so do the 2001 International Law Commission (ILC) Draft Articles on Prevention of Transboundary Harm from Hazardous Activities (PTHHA). Other instruments use terms such as 'appreciable', 'measurable', 'serious' or 'substantial'.

10 According to the ILC Special Rapporteur on liability for transboundary harm, some discussions in the ILC have suggested that 'significant' harm is more than *de minimis*, 'negligible', 'detectable', or 'appreciable' but need not be at the level of 'serious' or 'substantial'. Further, the harm must lead to real detrimental effects on such aspects as human health, industry, property, the environment or agriculture in other states, measured by factual and objective standards. Pemmaraju Sreenivasa Rao, *First Report on the Legal Regime for Allocation of Loss in Case of Transboundary Harm Arising out of Hazardous Activities, International Law Commission*, 55th sess., 5 May-6 June and 7 July-8 August 2003, U.N. Doc. A/CN.4/531, March 21, 2003, citing YBILC, 1996, vol. II (Part Two), U.N. Doc. A/51/10, annex I, paras. (4) and (5) of the commentary to Article 2.

11 E.g., French law of July 19, 1976, which defines the activities submitted to previous authorization for their dangerous or polluting character. See Michel Prieur, *Droit De L'environnement* 578 (1985).

including the 1982 UN Convention on the Law of the Sea (UNCLOS), which speaks of 'hindrances to marine activities, including fishing and other legitimate uses of the sea'.[12]

'Ecosystem' may be understood as the totality of the physical-chemical environment and the living things which populate it,[13] characterized as a system by the dynamic relations of its constituting elements and processes. Pollutants act to disturb these relations and such processes as the water cycle and the biological food chain.

The term 'transboundary' or 'transfrontier' may be understood to refer to spatial or territorial limits. Concern about transboundary pollution initially extended to a zone only 15–20 miles on each side of an international border.[14] This led to a mistaken identification of the border region with 'transfrontier' pollution, when in fact many pollutants, especially those transported by air, have their origin and impact separated by considerable distances. A second OECD recommendation, this one relating to the implementation of a regime of equality of access and non-discrimination in matters of transfrontier pollution,[15] reflects a broader approach:

> 'Transfrontier pollution' means any intentional or unintentional pollution whose physical origin is subject to, and situated wholly or in part within the area under the national jurisdiction of one Country and which has effects in the area under the national jurisdiction of another Country.

An even greater expansion is found in the 1979 Geneva Convention on Long-Range Transboundary Air Pollution which defines 'long-range transboundary air pollution' as 'air pollution whose physical origin is situated wholly or in part within the area under the national jurisdiction of one state and which has adverse effects in the area under the jurisdiction of another state at such

12 UNCLOS, Art. 1(4). See the similar definition in the Convention for Cooperation in the Protection and Sustainable Development of the Marine and Coastal Environment of the Northern Pacific (Antigua, Feb. 18, 2002).

13 François Ramade, *Eléments d'écologie – écologie appliqueé* (Dunod 1982) 425.

14 Bilateral agreements on transboundary pollution continue to establish geographic limits to their application. For example, the 1983 Mexico-United States Agreement to Cooperate in the Solution of Environmental Problems in the Border Area defines the border area as 'the area situated 100 kilometers on either side of the inland and maritime boundaries'. 23 ILM 1025 (1983).

15 Annex, Council Recommendation for the Implementation of a Regime of Equal Right of Access and Non-Discrimination in Relation to Transfrontier Pollution, C(77)28(Final), May 17, 1977.

a distance that it is not generally possible to distinguish the contribution of individual emission sources or groups of sources'.

It should be noted that both the above definitions of the transfrontier phenomena require the presence of two states, although the causative agent may be physically located outside the territorial limits of the responsible state as long as that agent is subject to the state's jurisdiction. Other formulations extend potential liability or responsibility for harm to areas outside national jurisdiction such as Antarctica, the high seas, or even the climate system.[16] As a consequence, environmental harm can be deemed 'transboundary' when it is caused by activities within a state's jurisdiction but the harm itself occurs outside of the jurisdiction of said state – whether on the territory of another state or in areas that do not belong to the jurisdiction of any state.

1.2 *Historic Approaches*

Traditional international law acknowledges each state's exclusive jurisdiction over its territory. Yet, acts which take place or originate on the territory of one state may cause damage or infringe upon the sovereignty of another state, giving rise to conflict between the rights of the two states. The conflict can be looked at from two perspectives: that of the state on whose territory the pollution originates and that of the state whose territory is affected by the pollution. The *polluter* state might argue the theory of 'absolute territorial sovereignty', while the *polluted* state may rely on the theory of 'absolute territorial integrity'. However, both approaches have been discarded in a world where states are increasingly obliged to cooperate and it became therefore necessary to search for more useful international legal principles.

1.2.1 Theories of Absolute Territorial Sovereignty and Absolute Territorial Integrity

The claim of absolute territorial sovereignty is identified with the so-called 'Harmon Doctrine', named for a nineteenth century United States (US) Attorney General. In 1895, during a conflict between the United States and Mexico, Harmon expressed his official opinion through the State Department that the Mexican government had no right to protest water pollution affecting the boundary Rio Grande River, although the pollution had lowered water quality in Mexico and damaged Mexican agriculture. Harmon contended that the rules, principles, and precedents of international law imposed no obligation

16 See e.g. Sandrine Maljean-Dubois, 'The No-Harm Principle as the Foundation of International Climate Law', in Benoit Mayer & Alexander Zahar (eds), *Debating Climate Law* (Cambridge University Press 2021).

or responsibility on the United States to protect Mexico from pollution originating from lawful activities in the United States where it had full sovereignty over the waters therein. Therefore, any harm to Mexico was a political rather than a legal question.[17] Although there are rare instances in the modern period of states invoking the Harmon Doctrine,[18] international practice is virtually unanimous in condemning this extreme view of state sovereignty, which offers no legal solutions capable of reconciling the rights of two opposing and equal states, especially when the conflict is over use of a shared natural resource.

The reverse of the Harmon Doctrine of absolute territorial sovereignty is the theory or doctrine of absolute territorial integrity, sometimes asserted by downstream states who argue that they are entitled to an undiminished and unpolluted natural volume of water entering their territory.[19] According to this theory, upstream utilization of the resource cannot adversely affect the quantity or quality of the water entering the downstream state. This was the argument advanced, for instance, by Spain in the 1957 *Lake Lanoux* arbitration.[20] Just like claims to absolute territorial sovereignty, this claim has also been resisted. In fact, over the years, the development of international law on shared natural resources, especially watercourses, has produced a firm rejection of claims of absolute sovereignty or integrity, emphasizing instead a community of interests among the riparian states.

1.2.2. The Concept of Abuse of Rights and the Principle of Equitable and Reasonable Utilization

The doctrine of abuse of rights recognizes the sovereignty and territorial jurisdiction of a polluting state, but subordinates the exercise of jurisdiction to a superior rule of international law which forbids sovereignty to be wielded in an abusive manner. Abuse of rights means the arbitrary exercise of a right, i.e., the absence of an acceptable motivation for action when the activity prejudices another state. It can also be applied to disproportionate acts, those whose benefits are negligible when compared to the harmful consequences produced in another state. Taking a concrete example, if dumping chemicals

---

17 21 OP. Att'y GEN. 274, at 280–83 (1895). See Stephen McCaffrey, 'The Harmon Doctrine One Hundred Years Later: Buried, Not Praised' (1996) 36 Natural Resources Journal 549.

18 Authorities cite examples of upstream riparian states citing the Harmon Doctrine to support their uses of international watercourses, including Canada, Ethiopia, India, and Turkey. See Patricia Wouters, 'Dynamic cooperation' – The Evolution of Transboundary Water Cooperation,' in Michael Kidd et al (eds), *Water and the Law: Towards Sustainability* (Edward Elgar 2014)31, 76. See also McCaffrey, supra n 17, 549.

19 See L. Oppenheim, *International Law* (8th edn by Hersch Lauterpacht, Longmans 1955).

20 *Lake Lanoux Arbitration* (*Spain v. France*) (Award) [1957] 12 RIAA 281.

from an installation of relatively small importance would pollute an international watercourse and thereby deprive another state of its source of drinking water, the state on whose territory the installation is located should deny permission for the dumping. An agreement between Finland and Sweden concerning boundary waters incorporates this concept:

> Where the construction would result in a substantial deterioration in the living conditions of the population or cause a permanent change in natural conditions such as might entail substantially diminished comfort for people living in the vicinity or a significant nature conservancy loss or where significant public interests would be otherwise prejudiced, the construction shall be permitted only if it is of particular importance for the economy or for the locality or from some other public standpoint.[21]

This principle requires balancing the interests of the two states and respecting proportionality in conduct.[22] The OECD Principles on Transfrontier Pollution explicitly refer in the introduction to 'a fair balance of the rights and obligations among countries concerned by transfrontier pollution'[23] and subsequently state that 'countries should seek, as far as possible, an equitable balance of their rights and obligations as regards the zones concerned by transfrontier pollution'.[24]

Today it is generally accepted that the principle forbidding abuse of right, whose origin lies in Roman law (*sic utere iure tuo ut alterum no laedas*) and which exists in all legal systems, forms part of international law. Treaties and judicial decisions apply the abuse of right principle to transboundary pollution.[25] According to Article 5(1) of the UN Convention on the Law of the Non-Navigational Uses of International Watercourses,[26]

---

21 Art. 3(2), Agreement Concerning Frontier Rivers between Finland and Sweden (Sept. 16, 1971).

22 The legal principles drafted by the panel of independent experts for the Brundtland Commission reflect this concept. See Art. 12, p. 28.

23 OECD, Principles Concerning Transfrontier Pollution, C(74)224 of Nov. 14, 1974, Introduction.

24 ibid.

25 As early as 1911, in reference to international watercourses, the Institute of International Law stated that neither state bounded by a river may 'on its own territory, utilize or allow the utilization of the water in such a way as seriously to interfere with its utilization by the other State or by individuals, corporations, etc., thereof'. James Brown Scott, *Resolutions of the Institute of International Law Dealing with the Law of Nations* (Oxford University Press 1916) 169.

26 New York, May 21, 1997.

> Watercourse States shall in their respective territories utilize an international watercourse in an equitable and reasonable manner. In particular, an international watercourse shall be used and developed by watercourse States with a view to attaining optimal and sustainable utilization thereof and benefits therefrom, taking into account the interests of the watercourse States concerned, consistent with adequate protection of the watercourse.

The widespread adoption of the concept of equitable utilization of shared resources in treaty law and state practice could be deemed to create a specific rule of international law directly forbidding significant transboundary pollution of such resources, without further recourse to the theory of abuse of rights, if transboundary pollution is viewed as inherently inequitable. However, not all transboundary pollution concerns shared resources and the concept of abuse of rights continues to serve as a basis for limiting activities with harmful transboundary consequences.

1.2.3 Jurisprudence on the Prohibition of Transboundary Environmental Harm

In balancing the equal and competing rights to sovereignty of different states, the International Court of Justice (ICJ), in its judgment in the 1949 *Corfu Channel* case, announced a fundamental principle of general international law. The Court referred to 'every State's obligation not to allow knowingly its territory to be used contrary to the rights of other states'.[27] The same year as this decision, the United Nations Survey of International Law concluded that there is 'general recognition of the rule that a State must not permit the use of its territory for purposes injurious to the interests of other States in a manner contrary to international law'.[28] Within this framework several international precedents directly address the issue of transboundary pollution.

The first case is the arbitral decision between the United States and Canada resulting from the activities of a Canadian smelter of zinc and lead ores, located in Trail, British Columbia, known as the *Trail Smelter* case.[29] From the beginning of its operations in 1896, American farmers suffered damage due to emissions of sulphur dioxide by the plant. In 1903, the record year, these emissions exceeded 10,000 tons a month. In 1930, 300 to 350 tons of sulphur, in addition to other chemical residues, poured into the

27 I.C.J. Rep. (1949) p. 22.

28 U.N. Doc. A/CN.4/1/Rev.1 (U.N. Pub. 1948. V.1(1)), at 34 (1949).

29 3 U.N.R.I.A.A. 1938, 1965.

air. Initially, the smelter company paid indemnities to those suffering from the pollution, either following American court procedures or as a result of bilateral accords. In 1925, the case was reopened after the smelter added two 409-foot stacks to the plant to increase production, resulting in greater pollution. An association of injured persons was formed in order to obtain general damages in the place of individual recoveries. In 1927, the US government officially took up the case and presented a claim to the government of Canada. After various efforts to settle the case by other means, the two governments submitted the matter to arbitration, signing a Convention to this effect April 15, 1935.[30]

The Convention settled the issue of responsibility. Its first article obligated the Canadian government to pay the US government $350,000 to settle damage claims arising out of smelter activity before January 1, 1932. For periods after this date, the arbitral commission was asked to respond to four questions:

1. Did the Trail Smelter cause damage after January 1, 1932, and if so, what indemnity should be paid as a consequence?
2. If the first question is answered affirmatively, should the Trail Smelter be required to refrain from causing damage in the State of Washington in the future, and if so, to what extent?
3. In light of the preceding question, what measures or regime, if any, should be adopted or maintained by the Trail Smelter?
4. What indemnity or compensation should be paid on account of the decision of the arbitral tribunal?[31]

While in an interim decision, dated April 16, 1938, the arbitral tribunal responded to the first question,[32] the final decision of the arbitral tribunal, issued March 11, 1941, detailed the facts and topographical, meteorological, and economic conditions of the region subjected to pollution. On the merits, it applied the principle of *res judicata*, calling it 'an essential and settled rule of international law' and thus refused to review its previous opinion concerning damage occurring before October 1, 1937. It also refused to allow an indemnity to the US government for damage to crops, trees or otherwise during the

30 Convention for the Settlement of Difficulties arising from Operations of Smelter at Trail, B.C. (Ottawa, April 15, 1935), 162 L.N.T.S. 73; 49 Stat. 3245, T.S. No. 893, 6 Bevans 60; C.T.S. 1935, No. 20, 30 AJIL 163 (Supp.).

31 ibid, Art III.

32 For the period between that date and October 1, 1937, the tribunal awarded $78,000 for damage to cleared and uncleared land. The tribunal also decided that the Trail Smelter should be subject to a temporary regime to continue until October 1, 1940, including abstention from causing damage and installation of equipment to control pollution.

following period, judging that the government had failed to provide sufficient evidence.

On the question of whether or to what extent the Trail Smelter must refrain from causing damages on the American territory, the tribunal defined the applicable principles in referring to Article IV of the arbitration Convention. It decided that it should take into consideration not only international law and practice but the law and practice existing in federal states. It deemed US and Swiss law to confer on their constituent units rights analogous to those of states under international law. The arbitrators found the air pollution law of the United States in dealing with the quasi-sovereign rights of the states of the union conformed to the general rules of international law while providing more detail.

On the international plane, the tribunal established for the first time what would later be known as the 'no-harm' principle, as it asserted a general duty on the part of a state to protect other states from injurious acts by individuals within its jurisdiction. It also noted the difficulty of determining what constitutes an injurious act. In this regard it referred to two decisions of the Federal Court of Switzerland concerning the Cantons of Soleure and Argovia related to a military shooting range which endangered the border between the two cantons. Despite claims for absolute prohibition of the harmful activity, the Court concluded, and this tribunal agreed, that precautions taken by a state should be the same as those it would take to protect its own inhabitants.

The arbitral tribunal discovered no international precedent concerning pollution of the atmosphere or water, but found guidance in decisions of the US Supreme Court that concerned both sectors. Several are cited, in particular an air pollution decision concerning Georgia and the Tennessee Copper Co. and Ducktown Sulphur, Copper and Iron Co. Ltd.[33] The Tribunal quoted approvingly a judgment of the US Supreme Court for the proposition that a state has an interest in all the earth and air within its domain, and that it is a fair and reasonable demand that the air over its territory should not be polluted on a grand scale by sulphurous acid gas by acts of persons beyond its control. Thus,

> [t]he Tribunal, therefore, finds that the above decisions, taken as a whole, constitute an adequate basis for its conclusions, namely, that, under the principles of international law, as well as of the law of the United States,

33 *State of Georgia v. Tennessee Copper Company and Ducktown Sulphur, Copper and Iron Company, Ltd.*, 206 U.S. 230 (May 13, 1907). The Tribunal also cited *Missouri v. Illinois*, 200 U.S. 496 (Feb. 19, 1906); *Kansas v. Colorado*, 185 U.S. 125 (April 7, 1902); and *New York v. New Jersey*, 256 U.S. 296 (May 2, 1921).

> no State has the right to use or permit the use of its territory in such a manner as to cause injury by fumes in or to the territory of another or the properties or persons therein, when the case is of serious consequence and the injury is established by clear and convincing evidence.[34]

For the arbitral tribunal, Canada's liability for the Trail Smelter derives from its duty to ensure that the Smelter's activities conform to the obligations that international law places on each state. The Trail Smelter itself should refrain from causing damage by emission of fumes on the territory of the State of Washington. The damage which did occur should be repaired by the governments, in conformity with Article XI of the arbitral Convention.

The third question posed to the tribunal concerned the future, asking what measures or what regime should be adopted or maintained by Canada. In responding, the tribunal elaborated a complete system based studies previously made on its initiative and setting out control measures. The latter included the right to inspect the installations of the Smelter and visit each property which allegedly suffered damage because of pollution. Notably, the regulatory scheme by its own terms allowed modification or suspension conforming to the decisions of a scientific commission to be constituted. The regime thus foreseen aimed to eliminate future damage on US territory by air pollution from Canada. Should the Smelter fail to conform to the order given it to refrain from causing further damage, the tribunal, in response to the fourth question regarding future damages, approved the principle of indemnity, leaving the extent and amount to the agreement between the governments involved.

It is difficult to overestimate the importance of the *Trail Smelter* arbitration.[35] The arbitral Convention itself constitutes a noteworthy precedent, insofar as it announces two principles. First, it recognized the responsibility of a state for acts of pollution having their origin on its territory and causing damage on the territory of other states, even if the polluting acts are not imputable to the state itself or its organs. Thus, the state may be responsible for not enacting necessary legislation, for not enforcing its laws against those within its jurisdiction or control, for not preventing or terminating an illegal activity, or for not sanctioning the person responsible for it. Second, the Convention transcends international responsibility to resolve the conflict before it, aiming towards a

34 3 U.N.R.I.A.A. 1938, 1965.

35 The case continues to be invoked. In 1972, Canada referred to the judgment when an oil spill in Washington polluted beaches in British Colombia. See 11 *Can YB Int'l L* 333–34 (1973).

common regulation of the issue. The award itself affirms the existence of a rule of international law forbidding significant transboundary pollution, a fact of fundamental importance. The Tribunal also elaborated a framework for the future, perhaps exceeding its mandate, in recognizing the necessity of further cooperation between the interested states. In requiring regulation, the award identifies what is now seen as a general requirement of environmental law: the rules adopted should be flexible and adaptable according to the evolution of the situation and knowledge of it.

The enlightened approach of the *Trail Smelter* arbitrators is also seen in the last sentence of the decision, which sums up a fundamental aspect of international environmental law: 'The Tribunal expresses the strong hope that any investigations which the Governments may undertake in the future, in connection with the matters dealt with in this decision, shall be conducted jointly'.

Some fifteen years after the *Trail Smelter* award, the *Lake Lanoux* arbitral decision also alluded to the problem of transboundary pollution in holding that France could use the waters of the lake for French public works, restoring the waters to the River Carol which crosses the Spanish frontier to join the Segre River. No water pollution was alleged, but the arbitral tribunal nonetheless addressed the matter:

> It could have been argued that the works would bring about a definitive pollution of the waters of the Carol or that the returned waters would have a chemical composition or a temperature or some other characteristic which could injure Spanish interests. Spain could then have claimed that her rights had been impaired in violation of the Additional Act.[36]

The Tribunal later indicated the consequences which would occur from such pollution:

> Thus, while admittedly there is a rule prohibiting the upper riparian State from altering the waters of a river in circumstances calculated to do serious injury to the lower riparian State, such a principle has no application to the present case, since it was agreed by the Tribunal ... that the French project did not alter the waters of the Carol.[37]

Another transboundary pollution case arose in the Netherlands in 1974, stemming from some twelve million tons of salt dumped annually into the Rhine

36 12 U.N.R.I.A.A. at 303.

37 Yearbook of the ILC 1974, Vol. II (Part Two), p. 197, U.N. Doc. A/5409, para. 1066.

River, most of it from potassium mines in Alsace, France. The pollution made the production of drinking water expensive and adding to the constant problem of combating salt water infiltration into Dutch agricultural fields. Diplomatic efforts to resolve the problem failed. A Dutch association, 'Reinwater', intervened in a case brought in Rotterdam by a grower who claimed damages from the Alsatian company for his salt-damaged crops. A Rotterdam court addressed the merits of the case in several decisions. The first, issued in 1979,[38] held that Dutch courts should apply international law which is part of Dutch law. Finding no treaty between France and the Netherlands containing an applicable rule and no relevant rule of customary international law, it referred to general principles of law, according to Article 38(1)(c) of the Statute of the ICJ. It cited the *Trail Smelter* decision as a case concerning abuse of right. After it was established by clear and convincing evidence that the grower's damage was caused by the dumped salt, the Court found the dumping constituted a violation of the abuse of right principle.

More evidence was needed on several points, including the scope of the damages and apportionment of liability. On the basis of an expert report subsequently prepared, the court issued a second decision in 1983 holding the mines responsible for an average of 37.5 percent of the salt transported by the Rhine to the Netherlands.[39] The second Rotterdam judgment held that international custom did not forbid the dumping of wastes in an international waterway. However, international law did recognize the principle that an upstream country's rights to utilize the waters requires that it take into account the equitable uses of downstream states. In addition, states must respect the principle announced in the *Trail Smelter* arbitration which forbids causing damage to the territory or inhabitants of another state, confirmed in the *Lake Lanoux* arbitration.

The two judgments were upheld by the Hague Court of Appeal in 1986. However, the Court moved away from international law, deciding that international law applies only in relations between states, and thus the only ground for judging the case was internal Dutch law. It still held the Mines de Potasse negligent and therefore liable for failing to take into consideration the damage resulting downstream from their dumping of salt into the Rhine.[40] The case

38 *Handelskwekerij G.-J. Bier B.V., Stichting Reinwater c. Mines de potasse d'Alsace* S.A. (in Dutch only).

39 Rotterdam Tribunal, *Handelskwekerij G.-J. Bier et autres v. Mines de Potasse d'Alsace* (Dec. 16, 1983) 15 Neth YB Int'l L (1984).

40 Judgment of September 10, 1986. The Potassium Mines lodged a further appeal. On September 23, 1988, the Supreme Court of the Netherlands denied the appeal, indicating that transboundary pollution is not a matter of international law. It applied the Dutch law of

was finally settled in 1988, with the Mines de Potasse agreeing to pay the plaintiffs 11,250,000 French francs (approximately $2,000,000).

More recent litigation, following ample codification of the principle against causing significant transboundary harm, includes judgments and advisory opinions of the ICJ[41] and the International Tribunal for the Law of the Sea (ITLOS)[42] reaffirming this basic norm. The ICJ recognized in its Advisory Opinion on the *Legality of Nuclear Weapons*, for example, that '[t]he existence of the general obligation of states to ensure that activities within their jurisdiction and control respect the environment of other states or of areas beyond national control is now part of the corpus of international law relating to the environment'.[43] This statement was repeated in the judgment concerning the *Gabçikovo-Nagymaros Project*, in which the Court also 'recall[ed] that it has recently had occasion to stress … the great significance that it attaches to respect for the environment, not only for states but also for the whole of mankind'.[44]

1.3 *Current Rules*

1.3.1 Respect for the Environment of Other States and Commons Areas

Case law precedents and the application of general rules of international law have led to development of the fundamental norm of international environmental law concerning transboundary pollution: the no-harm principle. The 1972 Stockholm Declaration formulated it in Principle 21 as follows:

> States have, in accordance with the Charter of the United Nations and the principles of international law, the sovereign right to exploit their own resources pursuant to their own environmental policies, and the

---

nuisance, where the gravity of the harm inflicted and the weighing of interests are the central issues.

41 See: *Advisory Opinion on the Legality of the Threat or Use of Nuclear Weapons*, ICJ Reports 1996, para. 36; *Gabcikovo-Nagymaros Project* (*Hungary v. Slovakia*) Judgment, ICJ Reports 1997, 7, para. 140; *Pulp Mills over the River Uruguay* (*Argentina v. Uruguay*), Judgment, ICJ Reports 2010, paras. 101 and 185; *Certain Activities Carried Out by Nicaragua in the Border Area* (*Costa Rica v. Nicaragua*) (Judgement) ICJ Reports 2015, 15, paras. 104, 118.

42 Advisory Opinion of the ITLOS Seabed Chamber, *Responsibilities and Obligations of States sponsoring Persons and Entities with respect to Activities in the Area*, paras. 115–120. *Dispute Concerning Delimitation of the Maritime Boundary between Ghana and Côte d'Ivoire in the Atlantic Ocean* (*Ghana/Côte d'Ivoire*) ITLOS Case No. 23, Order of 25 April 2015, paras. 68–73.

43 *Legality of the Threat or Use of Nuclear Weapons*, pp. 241–242, para. 29.

44 Sept. 25, 1997, para. 53.

> responsibility to ensure that activities within their jurisdiction or control do not cause damage to the environment of other States or of areas beyond the limits of national jurisdiction.

The rule was reiterated in Principle 2 of the 1992 Rio Declaration, adding the adjective 'developmental' between the words 'environmental' and 'policies' and was again confirmed in the 2002 World Summit on Sustainable Development. The norm contains two elements. First, it reaffirms the sovereign right of states over their natural resources, pronounced in numerous resolutions of the General Assembly[45] as well as international instruments relating to the protection of human rights.[46] However, the allusion to national environmental policies gives a more ecological color to this norm, inviting states to develop a coherent policy for environmental protection. The addition of the term 'developmental' in the Rio Declaration corresponds to the emergence of and emphasis on the concept of sustainable development.[47]

In its second aspect, Principle 21 affirms the duty of states 'to ensure' that activities within their jurisdiction or control do not cause damage to the environment of other states or of areas beyond the limits of national jurisdiction. In the first place, this means that states are responsible not only for their own activities, but also that they have a due diligence obligation to regulate all public and private activities within their jurisdiction or control. This implies a duty to regulate activities that could harm the environment of other states or areas outside the limits of their jurisdiction. In numerous countries, this regime takes the form of a licensing of installations which could prejudice the environment.[48] Second, states should apply the same rules not only in places

45 E.g. Permanent Sovereignty over Natural Resources, G.A. Res. 1803(XVII) of December 14, 1962; The New International Economic Order, G.A. Res. 3201(S-VI) of May 1, 1974; Charter of Economic Rights and Duties of States, G.A. Res. 3281(XXIX) of December 12, 1974, G.A.O.R. 29th Sess., Supp. No. 31 (A/9631), p. 50. See Nico Schriver, *Sovereignty over Natural Resources, Balancing Rights and Duties* (Cambridge University Press 1997) 231–251.

46 E.g. common Art. 1, United Nations Covenants on Civil and Political Rights, 999 U.N.T.S. 171, and Economic, Social, and Cultural Rights, 993 U.N.T.S. 3 (Dec. 16, 1966); Art. 21, African Charter on Human and Peoples' Rights, 7 *Hum. Rts. L.J.* 403 (1986), 21 I.L.M. 58 (1982).

47 This focus emerges clearly from the title of Rio Declaration itself: United Nations Declaration on Environment and Development.

48 In the United States, both the Clean Water Act, 33 USC. sec 1251–76, and the Clean Air Act, 42 USC sec 7401–7642, apply to transboundary pollution on condition of reciprocity where there is reason to believe that pollution is occurring that endangers the health or welfare of persons in a foreign state. Hearings may be held with the participation of the foreign country that may be adversely affected by the pollution. Another form of regulation is found in an Executive Order on Environmental Effects Abroad of Major Federal

where they exercise territorial jurisdiction ('within their jurisdiction'), that is on land, in the territorial sea, on the continental shelf and within the exclusive economic zone, but everywhere they exercise 'control'. In other words, the obligation exists for ships, airplanes and spacecraft having the nationality of the state, as well as for missions to Antarctica, troops stationed in foreign territories, and any occupied or dependent territories.

Principle 21 fundamentally derives from the obligations that states assume towards the international community. Thus, the duty to not cause damage to the environment exists not only towards other states, but also towards the 'areas beyond the limits of national jurisdiction:' the high seas and the airspace above them, the deep seabed, outer space, the Moon and other celestial bodies, as well as Antarctica. In part, it is the control over activities in these regions that engages the obligations of states, together with the duty to combat any pollution coming directly from their territory that affects these regions.

Principle 21 of the Stockholm Declaration, although part of a non-binding text, is nonetheless recognized as a rule of customary international law.[49] It has been reaffirmed in resolutions and declarations adopted by the United Nations, including the Charter of Economic Rights and Duties of States and the World Charter for Nature, and has been adopted by other international organizations and conferences.[50] Its content is codified in UNCLOS;[51] Article 20 of the ASEAN Convention on the Conservation of Nature and Natural Resources;[52] the 1979 Geneva Convention on Long Range Transboundary Air Pollution (stating that the Principle 'expresses the common conviction that States have' on this matter); the 1992 the preamble of the United Nations Framework Convention on Climate Change (UNFCCC); Article 3 of the Convention on Biological Diversity; and the UN Convention on the Law of Non-Navigational Uses of International Watercourses. The duty not to harm the environment has also been discussed

Actions, which requires federal agencies to take into consideration environmental impact statements and relevant international environmental studies when approving major federal actions significantly affecting the environment of the global commons outside the jurisdiction of any nation. US Exec Order No 12114 (4 January 1979), sec 3–4, 44 Fed Reg 1957 (1979).

49 *Corfu Channel,* 22.

50 See e.g., Preliminary Declaration of a Program of Action of the European Communities in respect to the Environment, O.J. C 112/1, Dec.20, 1973; Final Act, Conference on Security and Cooperation in Europe, Helsinki, Aug. 1976.

51 UNCLOS, Art. 194(2).

52 ASEAN Agreement on the Conservation of Nature and Natural Resources (Kuala Lumpur, July 9, 1985), 15 EPL 64 (1985).

at length and in depth by the International Law Commission (ILC) in its work of the prevention of significant transboundary harm from hazardous activities.

Although the Stockholm/Rio Principles seem to establish an unlimited duty not to cause harm, it is generally accepted that the international obligation is in fact to refrain from 'significant' environmental damage and not any and all harm. This is recognized in treaty law[53] and in jurisprudence,[54] as well as in the ILC articles on the duty to prevent harm.[55] According to the ILC commentary, the term significant means more than detectable but need not arrive at the level of serious or substantial.[56] As for the required conduct, the obligation of due diligence is one of conduct and not one of result. In the *Pulp Mills* case, the ICJ indicated that the requirement to prevent harm requires conduct and cooperation to implement and apply appropriate measures to protect the environment[57] and a duty to conduct an environmental impact assessment (EIA) prior to activities that may have a significant adverse transboundary impact.[58] For its part, the Seabed Chamber of the International Tribunal on the Law of the Sea has advised that the due diligence obligation encompasses: the obligation to adopt appropriate measures and ensure that they are reasonably enforced; the obligation to conduct an EIA; and the obligation to apply the precautionary approach.[59] The *South China Sea* arbitral tribunal partly based its decision in that case on the general obligation of States to 'ensure that activities within their jurisdiction and control respect the environment of other States or of areas beyond national control' (as codified in UNCLOS).[60] According to the tribunal, this obligation gives rise to several of the principles discussed in the present chapter, such as a positive 'duty to prevent, or at least

53 See, e.g. Convention for the Protection of the Ozone Layer, Art. 1(2); the Espoo Convention, Art. 2(1); Helsinki Convention on the Protection and Use of Transboundary Watercourses and International Lakes, Art. 1(2); UNFCCC, Art. 1(1); Convention on Biological Diversity, Art. 14(1)(a); and New York Convention on International Watercourses, Art. 7.

54 See, e.g., *Iron Rhine Railway (Belgium v. Netherlands)* PCA (2005), 27 RIAA 35, para. 222; *Pulp Mills*, ICJ Rep. 14, para. 101; *Indus Waters Kishenganga Arbitration (Pakistan v. India)*, PCA, Partial Award, 18 Feb. 2013, para. 451 and Final Award, 20 Dec. 2013, para. 112.

55 ILC, Draft Articles on Prevention of Transboundary Harm from Hazardous Activities (with Commentaries) (2001) YB of the ILC, vol. II, part 2, 148.

56 ILC Draft Articles, Commentary to Article 2, para. 4.

57 *Pulp Mills*, paras. 101–2 and 181–9.

58 *Pulp Mills*, para. 204.

59 *Responsibilities and Obligations of States sponsoring Persons and Entities with Respect to Activities in the Area,* Case No. 17, ITLOS (Seabed Dispute Chamber), Advisory Opinion of 1 February 2011, paras. 115, 145, and 125–35.

60 UNCLOS, Art. 194.

mitigate, significant harm to the environment' when pursuing large-scale construction activities.[61]

1.3.2 Notification of Imminent Harm

International environmental law requires states to immediately inform other states likely to be affected by any sudden situation or event (natural or man-made) that could cause harm to their environment and to provide those states with all pertinent information. Principle 18 of the Rio Declaration provides that 'States shall immediately notify other States of any natural disasters or other emergencies that are likely to produce sudden harmful effects on the environment of those States'. The foundation of this rule appears in general international law. In the *Corfu Channel* case, the ICJ held that Albania, in the interest of navigation in general, had a duty to make known the existence of a mine field in Albanian territorial waters and to alert warships of the British navy at the moment when they approached imminent danger from the mines. This obligation, said the Court, derives from certain general and well-known principles, including elementary considerations of humanity.[62] On the basis of analogous considerations a duty is imposed to alert states of any serious transboundary risk to their environment.[63]

Several non-binding texts affirm the duty to notify those at risk, beginning with the OECD Principles concerning Transfrontier Pollution,[64] later developed by the OECD in a decision on the exchange of information concerning accidents capable of causing transfrontier damage.[65] This decision requires members to exchange information, consult to prevent accidents causing transfrontier damage, and reduce the damage caused. Practical measures in Annex I include arrangements or agreements on the means of exchanging information on hazardous installations and hazardous substances, defined in appendices.

---

61 *South China Sea Arbitration* (*The Republic of Philippines v. The People's Republic of China*) (2016) Award, para. 941 and n. 1095.

62 I.J.C. Rep. (1949) at 22.

63 Comment (e) to section 601 of the Third Restatement of Foreign Relations Law of the United States, finds within the general environmental responsibilities of states an obligation to warn another state promptly of any situation that may cause significant pollution damage in that state.

64 Principle 9, OECD, 'Principles Concerning Transfrontier Pollution', C(74)224 (November 14, 1974): 'Countries should promptly warn other potentially affected countries of any situation which may cause any sudden increase in the level of pollution in areas outside the country of origin of pollution, and take all appropriate steps to reduce the effects of any such sudden increase'.

65 C(88)84(Final), July 8, 1988.

A particularly complete formulation is contained in the 1978 United Nations Environment Programme (UNEP) Principles on Shared Resources:

States have a duty urgently to inform other states which may be affected:

a. Of any emergency situation arising from the utilization of a shared natural resource which might cause sudden harmful effects on their environment;
b. Of any sudden grave natural events related to a shared natural resource which may affect the environment of such states.[66]

While the notion of 'shared natural resource' is difficult to define, boundary waters or contiguous seas and air to a certain distance can be considered as included. The duty to notify is expressed even in regard to remote sensing. Principle 10 of a resolution adopted June 13, 1986 by the UN Committee on Peaceful Uses of Outer Space, provides that states conducting remote sensing activities should transmit to the states concerned any information they acquire indicating harmful environmental phenomena on earth.[67]

The customary duty to notify environmental crises has developed in a general fashion and is spelled out more concretely in numerous international treaties. UNCLOS Article 198, for instance, sums up the provisions contained in various conventions relating to marine pollution, both in general and in regard to regional seas:[68]

> When a State becomes aware of cases in which the marine environment is in imminent danger of being damaged or has been damaged by pollution, it shall immediately notify other States it deems likely to be affected by such damage, as well as the competent international organizations.

Articles 4 and 5 of the 1990 London Convention on Oil Pollution Preparedness, Response and Co-operation[69] develop this obligation by setting specific procedures for providing the relevant information. Principle 18 of the Rio Declaration formulates the same obligation in the following way: 'States shall immediately notify other States of any natural disasters or other emergencies

66 UNEP Principles of Conduct in the Field of the Environment for the Guidance of States in the Conservation and Harmonious Utilization of Natural Resources Shared by Two or More States (1978), Principle 9(1).

67 June 13, 1986, 25 I.L.M. 1334 (1986).

68 For example, see Art. 5, Agreement for Cooperation in Dealing with Pollution of the North Sea by Oil (June 9, 1969); Art. 8, International Convention for the Prevention of Pollution from Ships (Nov. 2, 1973); the series of agreements concerning regional seas concluded under the auspices of UNEP.

69 Nov. 30, 1990.

that are likely to produce sudden harmful effects on the environment of those States'.

The duty to notify is often inserted in treaties relating to rivers. It is included, for example, in Article 11 of the Convention for the Protection of the Rhine against Chemical Pollution, which also established an international alert system.[70] It must be noted, however, that this system did not perform well during the 1986 Sandoz factory chemical spill near Basel, Switzerland, which caused serious pollution of the Rhine.[71] The system has since been reviewed and corrected.[72] The model in this regard is Article 14 of the 1992 Helsinki Convention on the Protection and Use of Transboundary Watercourses and International Lakes:

> The Riparian States shall without delay inform each other about any critical situation that may have transboundary impact. The Riparian Parties shall set up, where appropriate, and operate coordinated or joint communication, warning and alarm systems with the aim of obtaining and transmitting information. These systems shall operate on the basis of compatible data transmission and treatment procedures and facilities to be agreed upon by the Riparian Parties. The Riparian Parties shall inform each other about competent authorities or points of contact designated for this purpose.[73]

Finally, Article 28 of the UN Convention on the Law of the Non-Navigational Uses of International Watercourses requires states parties to notify without delay, and by the most expeditious means available, potentially affected states and competent international organizations of any emergency originating within its territory.[74]

Provisions on notification are also included in more general agreements, as exemplified by Article 20(d) of the ASEAN Agreement on the Conservation of

70 Art. 11, Bonn Convention on Protection of the Rhine (Dec. 3, 1976). A duty to notify of pollution emergencies is also contained in Arts. 6(1)(i) and 10 of the 1978 Great Lakes Water Quality Agreement between Canada and the United States.

71 See Aaron Schwabach, 'The Sandoz Spill: The Failure of International Law to Protect the Rhine from Pollution' (1989) 16 Ecology Law Quarterly 443.

72 See later Chapter 10.

73 Art. 16 of the Convention on Cooperation for the Protection and Sustainable Use of the Danube River (Sofia, June 29, 1994), can be considered as a further development of this provision.

74 New York, May 21, 1997.

Nature and Natural Resources,[75] Article 10 of the 1992 Helsinki Convention on Transboundary Effects of Industrial Accidents,[76] Article 15(2)(b) of the Madrid Protocol on Environmental Protection to the Antarctic Treaty,[77] Article 14(1)(d) of the Convention on Biological Diversity,[78] and Article 6 of the Agreement on Cooperation on Marine Oil Pollution Preparedness and Response in the Arctic.[79] Similarly, the duty to notify is found in several bilateral conventions regarding environmental disasters along shared borders[80] and in numerous agreements concerning nuclear accidents.[81] Among the latter, particular attention is due the Vienna Convention on Early Notification in the Case of Nuclear Accident or Radiological Emergency.[82] Article 2 requires that each state on whose territory a nuclear accident occurs notify other states which are or could be physically affected, of the accident, its nature, the moment when it occurred and its exact location. It thus must rapidly furnish available relevant information in order to limit as much as possible the radioactive consequences to the exposed state or states. The International Atomic Energy Agency (IAEA) and the World Meteorological Organization (WMO) announced on February 26, 1988 the development of a worldwide early warning network which would alert states of the possibility of pollution resulting from a nuclear power plant accident.[83]

1.3.3 Assistance in Emergencies

It is less clear whether or not there is a legal obligation to assist a state in an environmental emergency. In its Declaration of Principles on Transfrontier Pollution, the OECD couples the duty to warn with a principle that for incidents that could result in transfrontier pollution, 'countries should assist each other, whenever necessary, in order to ... minimize, and if possible eliminate,

---

75 Kuala Lumpur, July 9, 1985.

76 Helsinki, March 17, 1992.

77 Madrid, Oct. 4, 1991.

78 Rio de Janeiro, June 5, 1992.

79 Kiruna Norway, May 13, 2013.

80 See the German-French Agreement of September 20, 1973, *Bulletin d'information du Gouvernement federal allemand*, 21 Sept. 1973, No. 115, p. 1141.

81 Such agreements sometimes extend to nuclear weapons. See e.g. the 1978 agreement between France and the Soviet Union regarding prevention of accidental or unauthorized use of nuclear weapons. The treaty requires each state to notify the other party immediately 'of any accidental occurrence or any other unexplained incident that could lead to the explosion of one of their nuclear weapons which may have harmful effect on the other party.' 1036 U.N.T.S. 299.

82 IAEA INFCIRC 335, 25 I.L.M. 1370 (1986).

83 Int'l Env. Rptr. 161, March 3, 1988.

the effects of such incidents, and should develop contingency plans to this end'.[84] Principle 18, in its second part states that '[e]very effort shall be made by the international community to help States' affected by disaster. The language and the drafting history both suggest that this was not intended to create binding obligations on states, but as an incentive to develop new rules and mechanisms. In 2016, the UN International Law Commission adopted a set of principles on the protection of persons in the event of disasters, which indicate the duty of the affected state to seek assistance, a requirement that it not withhold its consent to external assistance arbitrarily, and that it facilitate external assistance.[85]

A general duty of assistance, or, at least of cooperation, has been inserted in the majority of conventional provisions establishing an obligation to notify. However, notification does not per se necessitate a special procedure, although it can be useful to establish communications systems and know which authorities of the foreign state should be alerted. In contrast, assistance usually implies operations on the territory of a foreign state and necessitates specific arrangements between the states requesting and supplying assistance. States may hesitate because assistance, while sometimes necessary, is also inherently more intrusive. UNCLOS Article 199 summarizes the situation well, foreseeing that in case of imminent risk of damage or of actual damage from pollution to the marine environment

> … States in the areas affected, in accordance with their capabilities, and the competent international organizations shall cooperate, to the extent possible, in eliminating the effects of pollution and preventing or minimizing the damage. To this end, States shall jointly develop and promote contingency plans for responding to pollution incidents in the marine environment.

The 1990 International Convention on Oil Pollution Preparedness, Response and Cooperation[86] provides that, upon the request of any party affected by oil pollution, the parties will cooperate according to their capabilities and the availability of relevant resources, by providing advisory services, technical

84 Principle 10.

85 Protection of persons in the event of disasters, Texts and titles of draft articles 10 and 11 provisionally adopted by the Drafting Committee on 19 July 2011, 20 July 2011, A/CN.4/L/794; Protection of persons in the event of disasters, Texts and titles of draft articles 5bis, 12, 13, 14 and 15, provisionally adopted by the Drafting Committee from 5 to 11 July 2012, 12 July 2012, U.N. Doc. A/CN.4/L. 812.

86 London, November 30, 1990, 30 I.L.M. 733 (1991).

support, and equipment for the purpose of responding to the incident. An annex to the Convention concerns the reimbursement of costs of assistance.

A growing number of contingency arrangements do exist. The earliest of these agreements aimed at providing emergency assistance and mutual cooperation in combating oil spills or nuclear accidents, such as the Nordic Mutual Emergency Assistance Agreement in Connection with Radiation Accidents,[87] the International Convention Relating to Intervention on the High Seas in Case of Oil Pollution Casualties,[88] and the Bonn Agreement for Cooperation in Dealing with Pollution of the North Sea by Oil.[89]

In many cases, common emergency plans have been elaborated on a bilateral basis. For example, a common emergency plan is in effect between Canada and Denmark concerning ocean pollution caused by ships, annexed to their Agreement on Cooperation Relating to the Marine Environment (Aug. 6, 1983).[90] A 1977 agreement between France and Germany provides for mutual assistance in case of catastrophe or serious accidents. The 1990 International Convention on Oil Pollution Preparedness, Response and Co-operation provides that the parties will cooperate and provide advisory services, technical support and equipment for the purpose of responding to an oil pollution accident, when the severity of such incident so justifies, upon the request of any party affected or likely to be affected.[91] Several of the UNEP regional seas treaty systems include protocols on emergencies and provide for cooperation in cases of grave and imminent danger to the marine environment and the establishment in this regard of joint contingency plans.[92]

Generally, cooperation arrangements should detail action required prior to any accident and action to be taken in case of an accident. Prior action consists of exchanges of information regarding the competent organs which should be notified, the plans or national programs applicable in case of an emergency, and the applicable legal rules. The information may include the means available to combat the consequences of any accident, the means of communication, and the relevant measures concerning security. The surveillance of specified zones can be organized, as is seen in the Bonn Agreement for Cooperation in Dealing with Pollution of the North Sea by Oil[93] and in the

87 October 17, 1963, 525 UNTS 75.
88 November 29, 1969.
89 June 9, 1969.
90 23 I.L.M. 269 (1984).
91 Art. 7, London Convention, November 11, 1990.
92 See Chapter 11.
93 June 9, 1969.

1990 Cooperation Agreement for the Protection of the Coasts and Waters of the North-East Atlantic against Pollution.[94]

For action during emergencies, plans should focus on the organization of assistance and the scope and division of authority. Material aspects must not be ignored, including arrangements for financing of assistance and customs formalities concerning the border passage for aid personnel and supplies. The 1990 Lisbon Agreement concerning Cooperation for the North East Atlantic provides for the establishment of an International Center with the aim of assisting the parties to react swiftly and effectively to pollution accidents.[95]

After the Chernobyl accident, along with the convention on early notification, a second treaty was concluded focusing on assistance in the case of a nuclear accident or radiological emergency.[96] Due to the complexity of the subject, the measures adopted were in the nature of a framework treaty necessitating further agreements between states. Article 1 requires only that the states parties cooperate 'to facilitate assistance', without truly imposing an obligation to assist a state which is the victim of significant environmental deterioration because of nuclear accident or radioactive emergency.

Treaties relating to inland waters also provide for mutual assistance. According to Article 15 of the 1992 Helsinki Convention on the Protection and Use of Transboundary Watercourses and Lakes[97] riparian states parties shall provide mutual assistance upon request and establish procedures for doing so. These should address issues such as the direction, control, coordination and supervision of assistance, the existence of local facilities and services, the facilitation of border-crossing formalities, the indemnification and/or compensation of the assisting party and/or of its personnel and the methods of reimbursing assistance services. The UN Convention on the Law of the Non-navigational Uses of International Watercourses[98] also prescribes the joint development of contingency plans for responding to emergencies, in cooperation, where appropriate, with other potentially affected states and competent international organizations. A similar framework exists to ensure technical and advisory support for responding to oil pollution incidents in the Arctic region,

94 Lisbon, Oct. 17, 1990.

95 Arts. 18–21. Annex 2 to the Agreement defines the functions of the Center.

96 Convention on Assistance in the Case of a Nuclear Accident or Radiological Emergency (Vienna, Sept. 26, 1986).

97 March 17, 1992. Art. 17 of the Convention on Cooperation for the Protection and Sustainable Use of the Danube River (Sofia, June 26, 1994) reproduces this provision.

98 New York, May 21, 1997, Art. 28(3) and (4).

under Article 8 of the Agreement on Cooperation on Marine Oil Pollution, Preparedness and Response in the Arctic.[99]

After the Indian Ocean tsunami of 2004, the Association of South-East Asian Nations (ASEAN) adopted the ASEAN Agreement on Disaster Management and Emergency Response (AADMER) (Vientiane, Laos, 26 July 2005). All ten ASEAN Member States ratified the agreement, which entered into force on 24 December 2009. The text provides a regional framework for cooperation, coordination, technical assistance, and resource mobilization in all aspects of disaster management. It establishes policies and operational mechanisms within the region to allow member states to seek and extend assistance in times of disaster. It also enables member states to carry out collaborative undertakings on disaster mitigation, prevention, preparedness, response, recovery and rehabilitation. Although an affected member-country still has the primary responsibility to respond to disasters within its territory, offers of assistance need not be based on a request from the affected country. In any disaster, the member-state still has the overall control and command with external assistance. The treaty requires each member-country to cooperate in developing and implementing measures to reduce disaster losses. This entails identification of disaster risks, monitoring, assessment and putting in place early warning systems, standby arrangements for disaster relief and emergency response, exchange of information and technology, and the provision of mutual assistance. It also seeks that each member-country immediately responds to a disaster occurring within its territory. Meanwhile, AADMER also obliges each member-state to respond to a request for assistance. Member-countries must also take legislative, administrative and other measures as necessary to implement their obligations under this agreement. This requires all member-countries to look into their policies to support and facilitate the effective implementation of AADMER. In 2011, member-countries adopted the Agreement on the Establishment of the ASEAN Co-ordinating Centre for Humanitarian Assistance on Disaster Management,[100] followed by several declarations, action plans, and work programs.[101]

In 2015, during the Third UN World Conference on Disaster Risk Reduction held in Sendai, Japan, the Sendai Framework for Disaster Risk Reduction was

99 Kiruna Norway, May 13, 2013.

100 Agreement on the Establishment of the ASEAN Co-ordinating Centre for Humanitarian Assistance on Disaster Management (Nov. 17, 2011).

101 See e.g. the 2015 Declaration on Institutionalizing the Resilience of ASEAN and its Communities and Peoples to Disasters and Climate Change, the 2016 ASEAN Vision 2025 on Disaster Management and the 2015 Regional Framework and Action Plan to Implement the ASEAN Declaration on Strengthening Social Protection.

adopted.[102] It sets out a 15-year plan to reduce disaster risk and improve disaster resilience globally. The framework aims to guide countries in implementing strategies to prevent or mitigate the impacts of disasters on communities, infrastructure, and economies. Some of its key aspects include the promotion of multi-sectoral collaboration, coordination, and partnerships among governments, communities, and other stakeholders to enhance disaster resilience, as well as the emphasis on investing in disaster-resilient infrastructure, early warning systems, and community-based disaster preparedness measures to minimize the impacts of disasters and ensure swift recovery.

1.3.4 Advance Notification and Prior Consultation

Apart from emergency situations, a state that plans to undertake or authorize activities capable of having significant impact on the environment of another state must inform the latter and should transmit to it the pertinent details of the project, to the extent that no national legislation or applicable international treaty prohibits or restricts such transmission. Principle 19 of the 1992 Rio Declaration formulates the obligation as follows: 'States shall provide prior and timely notification and relevant information to potentially affected States on activities that may have a significant adverse transboundary environmental effect and shall consult with those States at an early stage and in good faith'. The aim is to avoid disputes and liability that could arise once transboundary harm occurs.

The requirement of prior notification of activities or projects that could cause transboundary pollution was first included in bilateral treaties, notably concerning the construction of nuclear installations.[103] It is also included in many watercourse agreements, including the 1997 UN Watercourses Convention (Article 12). A series of non-binding texts also proclaim the norm. The obligation is included in a 1973 resolution of the United Nations[104] and in Article 3 of the Charter of Economic Rights and Duties of States.[105] It is most developed in a series of OECD resolutions, beginning with Title E of the 1974 Principles concerning Transfrontier Pollution.[106] Several OECD texts insist

102 Sendai Framework for Disaster Risk Reduction 2015–2030, A/CONF.224/L.2 (Apr. 7, 2015).

103 See e.g. the French-Belgian agreement on protection from radioactivity concerning construction of the nuclear power station at Ardennes, Sept. 26, 1966, Art. 2.

104 G. A. Res. 3139(XXVIII) Dec. 13, 1973.

105 G. A. Res 3281(XXIX) Dec. 12, 1974.

106 Title E, Art. 6, provides that 'prior to the initiation in a country of works or undertakings which might create a significant risk of transfrontier pollution, this country should provide early information to other countries which are or may be affected. It should provide these countries with relevant information and data, the transmission of which

on the transmission of information to persons who risk being exposed to the harmful consequences of a project.[107]

The duty to consult often accompanies the duty to inform.[108] Principle 6 of the 1978 UNEP Principles of Conduct in the Field of the Environment for the Guidance of States in the Conservation and Harmonious Utilization of Natural Resources Shared by Two or More States is particularly explicit in this regard. It stresses the necessity to notify in advance the other state or states of the pertinent details of plans to initiate activities which can reasonably be expected to significantly affect the environment in the territory of the other state or states, and upon request of the other state or states, to enter into consultations concerning the above-mentioned plans.

The number of international treaties requiring prior notification increased during the 1970s and the first half of the 1980s. The agreements mainly concern air pollution or water pollution, but the norm can also be found in more general instruments like the Nordic Environmental Protection Convention[109] which effectively integrates the territories of the contracting parties in regard to the authorization of environmentally-harmful activities; any activity that could cause harm in another state is equated with a nuisance in the state where the activity is carried out. Other conventions of the same period include a more modestly drafted duty to inform. The regional Kuwait Convention on the Protection of the Marine Environment from Pollution,[110] for instance, provides in Article 11 for the dissemination of information containing an evaluation

---

is not prohibited by legislative provisions or prescriptions or applicable international conventions, and should invite their comments'. Council Recommendation C(74)224, Nov. 14, 1974.

107 OECD, Implementation of a Regime of Equal Right of Access and Non-Discrimination in Relation to Transfrontier Pollution, Recommendation C(77)28(Final), May 17, 1977, part C; Strengthening International Cooperation on Environmental Protection of Transfrontier Regions, Recommendation C(78)77(Final) of Sept. 21, 1978, para. 3.

108 In the 1974 OECD Principles Concerning Transfrontier Pollution, the Title E obligation to provide information is coupled with a duty to consult: '7. Countries should enter into consultation on an existing or foreseeable transfrontier pollution problem at the request of a country which is or may be directly affected and should diligently pursue such consultations on this particular problem over a reasonable period of time'. In addition, Article 8 provides that countries should refrain from carrying out projects or activities which might create a significant risk of transfrontier pollution until they have informed and provided a reasonable amount of time for diligent consultation with countries which are or may be affected. Such consultations 'held in the best spirit of cooperation and good neighborliness' should not entail unreasonable delay or impediments to the activities or projects.

109 Stockholm, Feb. 19, 1974.

110 Kuwait, April 24, 1978.

of the possible effects of planned activities on the environment. Similarly, Article 20 of the ASEAN Agreement on the Conservation of Nature and Natural Resources[111] provides that the contracting parties will notify in advance the other contracting parties of the pertinent details of proposed activities which 'can reasonably be expected to have' significant impact outside the limits of their national jurisdiction. Article 20 also provides for consultation on a project or activity at the request of a state whose environment could be affected by it. States parties to the 1979 Geneva Convention on Long-Range Transboundary Pollution are required to institute exchanges of information not so much on specific activities as on national policies and industrial development in general and the effects that changes in these areas could produce regarding long-range air pollution.[112]

In a bilateral example, the 1980 United States-Canada air quality agreement includes a rather detailed commitment to continue and expand the long-standing practice of advance notification and consultations on proposed actions involving a significant or potential risk of causing or increasing transboundary air pollution, including: (a) proposed major industrial development or other actions which may cause significant increases in transboundary air pollution: and (b) proposed changes of policy, regulations or practices which may significantly affect transboundary air pollution.[113]

In the 1990s the same norm appears almost regularly in treaties relating to transboundary issues, generally linked with an environmental impact assessment procedure. The entire Espoo Convention on Environmental Impact Assessment in a Transboundary Context[114] is based upon the obligation to notify other states of proposed activities which are listed in Appendix I to the Convention. Appendix III sets general criteria to assist in the determination of the environmental significance of activities not listed in Appendix I. Article 5 and Appendix II specify the information to be transmitted. Other conventions do not give such lists, but leave the requirement to inform and consult open-ended.

The obligation to notify is imposed on the state where the project is to take place and regardless of whether the project is a public or private one. The ICJ reaffirmed this in the *Pulp Mills* case, responding to Uruguay's contention that

111 Kuala Lumpur, July 9, 1985.

112 Arts. 4 and 8, Geneva Convention on Long-Range Transboundary Air Pollution (Nov. 13, 1979). A similar obligation is found in the 1980 Memorandum of Intent between Canada and the U.S. concerning Transboundary Air Pollution.

113 Memorandum of Intent between Canada and the U.S. Concerning Transboundary Air Pollution, Aug. 5, 1980.

114 Espoo, Feb. 25, 1991.

the private company involved had notified the relevant administrative body set up pursuant to a bilateral agreement between the parties. According to the Court, information submitted from non-governmental sources 'cannot substitute for the obligation to inform' laid down in the relevant agreement.[115]

The related obligation to enter into consultation signifies that the state which is the potential polluter must be willing to discuss the information which it has forwarded to the potentially-affected state, which in turn may make observations concerning the project. However, the observations need not be fully accepted by the state which proposes to act; otherwise the potentially-affected state would have an effective veto over planned projects.

Part III of the 1997 UN Convention on the Law of the Non-Navigational Uses of International Watercourses[116] describes the procedure to be applied. Watercourse states are to exchange information and consult each other and, if necessary, negotiate on the possible effects of planned measures on the condition of an international watercourse. This includes timely notification concerning planned measures with possible adverse effects. The notified state has a period of six months to answer, but the period can be extended in exceptional cases for another six months. During this period the planned measures shall not be implemented without the consent of the notified state. If a notified state finds that implementation of the planned measures would be inconsistent with the norm of equitable and reasonable utilization, the reply to notification shall include a documented explanation in this regard. If the notified state does not reply within the period applicable, the notifying state may proceed with the implementation of the planned measures. If the notification is made, the concerned states shall enter into consultations and, if necessary, negotiations, conducted in good faith with a view to arriving at an equitable resolution of the situation.[117] Special procedures are provided for the absence of notification and in the event that the implementation of planned measures is of the utmost urgency to protect public health, public safety or other equally important interests.

The procedure of information and consultation has been applied in a different context in the Protocol Concerning Mediterranean Specially Protected Areas.[118] Article 6 provides that when one contracting party proposes to create

115 *Pulp Mills*, para. 110.

116 New York, May 21, 1997, Arts. 11–19.

117 A similar procedure is required by the World Bank Operational Policy 7.50 for Projects on International Waterways. Freestone, supra n 7 *and Salman M.A. Salman, The World Bank Policy for Projects on International Waterways* (World Bank 2009).

118 Geneva, April 3, 1982.

a protected zone contiguous to the frontier or limits of a zone of national jurisdiction of another party, the competent authorities of the two shall consult to arrive at an agreement on the measures to take and, among other things, examine the possibility for the second state to create a corresponding protected zone or to adopt any other appropriate measure.

In the end, the obligation to inform and consult is a product of the obligation to cooperate for improving the protection of the environment. The ICJ in *Costa Rica/Nicaragua* acknowledged that if 'there is a risk of significant transboundary harm, a State planning an activity that carries such a risk is required, in order to fulfil its obligation to exercise due diligence in preventing significant transboundary harm, to notify, and consult with, the potentially affected State in good faith, where that is necessary to determine the appropriate measures to prevent or mitigate that risk'.[119] In treaty instruments, this is evidenced in Article 5 of the 1979 Geneva Convention on Long-Range Transboundary Pollution, which provides for consultations between any state affected by long-range transboundary air pollution or exposed to a significant risk of such pollution and the state on whose territory and within whose jurisdiction a substantial part of such pollution is created because of existing or proposed activities. The mechanism for consultations, like other aspects of cooperation, is governed by the principle of good faith. It imposes an obligation on the parties to conduct themselves so that the consultations and negotiations are meaningful.[120] Moreover, it is clear now that the requirements of notification and consultations go beyond the context of transboundary pollution. Treaties for the protection of wildlife, access to and benefit-sharing from genetic resources, and other conservation agreements increasingly impose these obligations.

1.3.5 Equality of Access to Administrative or Judicial Procedures

This norm emerged principally in non-binding international texts[121] and in some judicial opinions. It specifies that if the activities taking place within the limits of jurisdiction or control of one state cause or threaten deterioration to the environment of another state, the residents of the latter who are or risk being affected should have access to administrative or judicial procedures in the state causing the environmental harm, under the same conditions as the

---

119 *Certain Activities Carried Out by Nicaragua in the Border Area* (*Costa Rica v. Nicaragua*) *and Construction of a Road in Costa Rica along the San Juan River* (*Nicaragua v. Costa Rica*), Judgment, I.C.J. Reports 2015, p. 665, para. 168.

120 *Pulp Mills*, at para. 146, citing the *North Sea Continental Shelf* (*Federal Republic of Germany/Denmark; Federal Republic of Germany/Netherlands*) Judgment, ICJ Rep. 1969, p. 47, para. 85.

121 See e.g. OECD, C(76)55(Final) of May 11, 1976.

residents of the latter state. If the persons residing elsewhere have already suffered damage, the same remedies should be available to them as to residents of the country. This includes application of the same substantive law and the same measures of compensation as are available to persons injured within the polluting state's territory. Throughout these procedures, nonresidents are entitled to the same treatment as residents.[122]

Equality of access concerns not only the nationals of the state that experiences transboundary pollution, but all those inhabiting its territory, even if they possess another nationality. There are, however, particular problems concerning nonprofit organizations, principally nature protection associations, which do not always have access to procedures and remedies. An OECD Council recommendation on equality of access regarding transboundary pollution[123] proposes that when the national law of a state permits such entities to engage in actions for the furtherance of their environmental purposes, the country should also permit the same actions by comparable groups domiciled in the country threatened with harm.

The norm of equality of access contains four elements: informing nonresidents, allowing their participation in decision-making procedures, permitting the possibility of appeal in case of inadequate application of relevant rules during the procedures, and providing remedies in case of damage.

Information is required on projects, activities and new developments which could engender a risk of damage to the environment of nonresidents. Also, access to information that the competent national authorities make available to interested local persons may be included. This aspect of transboundary cooperation resembles the interstate duty to inform of projects that could cause transboundary pollution.

According to a 1977 OECD recommendation, the authorities of the country of origin should take appropriate measures to provide persons exposed to a significant risk of transfrontier pollution with sufficient information to enable them to exercise their rights in a timely manner. This information should be equivalent to that provided in the country of origin in cases of comparable domestic pollution. However, it is also provided that exposed countries should

122 National laws sometimes implement this norm on a basis of reciprocity. See the US Comprehensive Environmental Response, Compensation and Liability Act of 1980 (CERCLA), 42 USC sec. 9601. CERCLA provides that a foreign claimant may assert a claim to the same extent as a United States claimant if there is a treaty or executive agreement with the foreign country involved, or if the Secretary of State certifies that such country provides a comparable remedy for United States claimants. Sec. 9611(1).

123 C(76)55(Final) of May 11, 1976.

designate one or more authorities which will have the duty to receive this information and disseminate it.[124]

The participation of nonresidents implies that they have the right to make oral or written observations or manifest their opinion in any other manner under the same conditions as residents. Where existing procedures in the state of origin have not been respected, nonresidents should have at their disposition the same remedies as residents.

Finally, the right of nonresidents to demand compensation for damage they have suffered due to transboundary pollution is undoubtedly the most accepted norm of equality of access. Leaving aside questions of jurisdiction, the statutes and case law of various countries recognize the right of nonresidents to claim damages.[125]

Early texts such as OECD Recommendations of 1974 concerning Transfrontier Pollution[126] and the 1977 Recommendation on Implementation of a Regime of Equal Right of Access in Relation to Transfrontier Pollution, as well as Principle 13 of the UNEP principles relating to shared resources, contain a separate rule on non-discrimination. According to this norm a state may not discriminate in its legislation according to the source of environmental harm, by applying its laws less rigorously to activities which produce harmful effects only outside the territorial limits.

Some treaty provisions support the existence of a norm of non-discrimination which is separate from the principle of equality of access. According to Article 227 of UNCLOS when exercising their rights and performing their duties under Part XII of the Convention, which relates to the marine environment, states shall not discriminate in form or in fact against vessels of another state. Article 32 of the 1997 UN Convention on the Law of Non-Navigational Uses of International Watercourses however, makes no distinction between the two:

> Unless the watercourse States concerned have agreed otherwise for the protection of the interests of persons, natural or juridical, who have

---

124 OECD Council Recommendation C(77)28(Final), May 17, 1977.

125 E.g., the 1977 OECD recommendation for implementation of equal access and non-discrimination, was accepted by the United States and Canadian Bar Associations. In the absence of a treaty, a private Joint Working Group from the two countries prepared a draft Uniform Transfrontier Pollution Reciprocal Access Act, subsequently incorporated into the state and provincial laws of Colorado (Colo.Rev.Stat. sec. 13–1.5.101, 1984), Montana (Mont.Code Ann. sec. 75–16-101, 1987), New Jersey (N.J.Stat.Ann. 2A:58A-1, 1984), Wisconsin (Wis.Stat.Ann. sec. 144.995, 1987), Manitoba (Man.Stat.1985,ch.11), and Ontario (Ont. Stat.35 Eliz.II, c.10, 1986).

126 Principle 4.

suffered or are under a serious threat of suffering significant transboundary harm as a result of activities related to an international watercourse, a watercourse State shall not discriminate on the basis of nationality or residence or place where the injury occurred, in granting to such persons, in accordance with its legal system, access to judicial or other procedures, or a right to claim compensation or other relief in respect of significant harm caused by such activities carried on in its territory.

2 General Legal Principles

Principles are widely used in international environmental law, perhaps more than in any other field of international law. Principles can indicate the essential characteristics of legal institutions, designate fundamental legal norms, or fill gaps in positive law by assigning a value to rules not yet formally set in legal instruments, although they are considered important. Principles can be foundational (e.g. equality and legal certainty) or technical (e.g. proportionality). They may appear in constitutions and basic laws or they may be of judicial construction. According to some, a principle provides the general orientation and direction to which positive law must conform, a rationale for the law, without itself constituting a binding norm. Principles can also be defined as 'rules of indeterminate content', having a degree of abstraction so great that it is not possible to deduce obligations from them with any degree of certainty. Principles as such therefore can be defined and applied in varying, even competing ways. Even the concept of 'principle' and the juridical value, if any, of a principle can change from one legal system to another.[127]

All the major non-binding normative instruments contain principles, taken up, defined and given concrete meaning in international treaties and jurisprudence. Notable examples include the Stockholm and Rio Declarations. The latter, in particular, contains nearly all the key principles that are relevant in the context of environmental protection.

It is precisely the complexity of many environmental issues that makes specific regulation so difficult at the international level and why principles play such an important role in setting forth the general approach of anticipation rather than reaction. The anticipatory model is necessary because 'our

127 Nicolas de Sadeleer, *Environmental Principles: From Political Slogans to Legal Rules* (Oxford University Press 2002).

understanding of the environment is no longer able to keep pace with our ability to modify it'.[128] Prevention thus leads to precaution.

2.1 *Prevention*

Experience and scientific expertise demonstrate that prevention must be the Golden Rule for the environment, for both ecological and economic reasons. It is frequently impossible to remedy environmental injury: the extinction of a species of fauna or flora, erosion, and the dumping of persistent pollutants into the sea create irreversible situations. Even when harm is remediable, the costs of rehabilitation are often prohibitive. The duty of prevention also clearly emerges from the international obligation not to cause significant damage to the environment extra-territorially, codified in the Stockholm and Rio Declarations, but the preventive principle seeks to avoid harm irrespective of whether or not there are transboundary impacts. As such it is a component of the exercise of sovereignty[129] over natural resources.[130] The Rio Declaration places an emphasis, in this context, on the need to adopt domestic environmental laws and policies.

The requirement of prevention is complex owing to the number and diversity of the legal instruments in which it occurs. It can perhaps better be considered an overarching aim that gives rise to a multitude of legal mechanisms, including prior assessment of environmental harm, licensing or authorizations that set out the conditions for operation and the consequences for violation of the conditions.[131] Emission limits and other product or process standards, the use of best available techniques (BAT) and similar techniques can all be seen as applications of the principle of prevention. The preventive approach also can involve the elaboration and adoption of strategies and policies.

The principle of prevention requires each state to exercise *due diligence*, which means to act reasonably and in good faith and to regulate public and private activities subject to its jurisdiction or control that are possibly harmful

128 ibid.

129 On the concept of 'functional' sovereignty, see e.g. Franz X. Perrez, *Cooperative Sovereignty: From Independence to Interdependence in the Structure of International Environmental Law* (Kluwer 2000).

130 See G. A. Res. 523 (VI) of 12 January 1952 (States have the 'right to determine freely the use of their natural resources'); G. A. Res. 626 (VII) of 21 Dec. 1952; G. A. Res. 1314 (XIII) of 12 Dec. 1958 and G. A. Res. 1803 (XVII) of 14 Dec. 1962, Permanent Sovereignty over Natural Resources.

131 For a discussion of legal mechanisms of prevention, including EIA, see the ICJ judgment in *Pulp Mills*, paras. 101–02, 181–9 and 203–04, which gave an implied 'seal of approval' to the World Bank EA Policy.

to any part of the environment.[132] As the ITLOS observed in its *Sub-Regional Fisheries Commission* (*SRFC*) Advisory Opinion, this is an obligation of conduct – not of result – leading the Tribunal to find that each State has a 'due diligence obligation' to take all necessary measures to ensure compliance and prevent illegal, unregulated and unreported fishing by vessels flying its flag.[133]

The principle of due diligence does not impose an absolute duty to prevent all harm, but rather an obligation on each state to prohibit activities that could cause significant harm to the environment, for instance, the dumping of toxic waste into an international lake. The state should also regulate to minimize the detrimental consequences of permissible activities, by imposing limits, for example, on the discharges of sulphur dioxide (SO^2) in the atmosphere, or by imposing rigorous licensing requirements for entities it sponsors to engage in seabed mining,[134] or for vessels it permits to fish in the exclusive economic zone of another state.[135]

The primary procedural obligation that flows from the principle of prevention and the duty of due diligence is prior assessment of potentially harmful activities, with continuous monitoring of its effects on the environment throughout the life of the project.[136] Whether an activity carries a risk of significant harm for the purpose of triggering an obligation of prevention may be a contentious issue. In *Costa Rica/Nicaragua*, the ICJ assessed Nicaragua's dredging activities in the Lower San Juan. In this case, the principal risk cited by Costa Rica was the potential adverse impact of those dredging activities on the flow of the Colorado River, and its potential effects on Costa Rica's wetland. Noting that both parties' experts agreed with an earlier Nicaraguan study that the dredging program would not have a significant impact on the flow of the river, the Court found an absence of risk of significant transboundary harm,

---

132 *Pulp Mills*, paras. 101–2; *Costa Rica v. Nicaragua*, paras. 104, 118; *Responsibilities in the Area*, para. 117; *SRFC Advisory Opinion*, para. 131; *Indus Waters Kishenganga Arbitration* (Partial Award), para. 451; *South China Sea Arbitration*, para. 941.

133 *SRFC Advisory Opinion*, para. 129.

134 *Responsibilities in the Area.*

135 *SRFC Advisory Opinion.*

136 *Pulp Mills*, paras. 204–05. The EIA duty is expressed in the Rio texts: Principle 17 of the Rio Declaration, Chapter 22 of Agenda 21, Article 8(h) of the Statement on Forests, and Article 14(1)(a) and (b) of the Convention on Biological Diversity treat both the national and international aspects of the issue. See also Article 206 of UNCLOS ('When states have reasonable grounds for believing that planned activities under their jurisdiction or control may cause substantial pollution of or significant and harmful changes to the marine environment, they shall, as far as practicable, assess the potential effects of such activities on the marine environment and shall communicate reports of the results of such assessments'.)

and concluded on this basis that Nicaragua had not been required to carry out a formal environmental impact assessment of this transboundary harm.[137]

Many multilateral environmental agreements provide for the duty to conduct an environmental impact assessment. These include, among others, the 1991 Espoo Convention on Environmental Impact Assessment in a Transboundary Context,[138] the 1992 Convention on Transboundary Effects of Industrial Accidents,[139] and the 1993 North American Agreement on Environmental Co-operation.[140] Others, such as UNCLOS,[141] the Convention on Biological Diversity (CBD),[142] and the Madrid Protocol[143] indicate the applicability of EIA to those specific environmental issues – respectively the protection of the marine environment, biological diversity and the Antarctic environment.[144] Since the failure to exercise due diligence to prevent significant transboundary harm can lead to international responsibility, it may be considered that properly done environmental impact assessments can serve as one standard for determining whether or not due diligence was exercised.

Preventive mechanisms also include monitoring, notification, and exchange of information,[145] all of which are general obligations in nearly all environmental agreements. The International Tribunal for the Law of the Sea, in the *MOX Plant* case, considered the duty to cooperate in exchanging information concerning environmental risks a 'fundamental principle in the prevention of pollution of the marine environment' under UNCLOS and general international law.[146] Many other international environmental treaties provide for such duty to cooperate in exchanging information concerning environmental risks. This is especially true in the context of transboundary watercourses,[147]

137 *Costa Rica v. Nicaragua,* para. 105.

138 Espoo, Feb. 25, 1991.

139 Helsinkii, March 17, 1992, Annexes IV and V.

140 Sept. 13, 1993, Art. 2(1)(e).

141 UNCLOS, Arts. 204–6.

142 CBD, Art. 14.

143 Protocol on Environmental Protection to the Antarctic Treaty, Art, 8 and Annex I.

144 Neil Craik, 'Principle 17', in Jorge E. Viñuales, *The Rio Declaration on Environment and Development: A Commentary* 451 (Oxford University Press 2015) 463–4.

145 Laurence Boisson de Chazournes & Komlan Sangbana, 'Principle 19' in Viñuales, supra n 144, 493.

146 ITLOS, *The MOX Plant Case (Ireland v. U.K.),* Order No. 10 of 3 December 2001 on Provisional Measures, para. 84, *reprinted in* 47 ILM 405 (2002).

147 See e.g. Convention on the Law of Non-Navigational Uses of International Watercourses, Arts. 8 and 9.

but also in areas such as long-distance air pollution,[148] marine pollution,[149] nature conservation[150] and protection of biodiversity.[151]

The duty of prevention extends to combating the introduction of exogenous species into an ecosystem. The 1976 Convention on Conservation of Nature in the South Pacific[152] provides that the contracting parties must carefully examine the consequences of such introduction (Art. 5(4)). More stringently, Article 22 of the UN Convention on the Law of the Non-Navigational Uses of International Watercourses requires watercourse states to 'take all measures necessary to prevent the introduction of species, alien or new, into an international watercourse which may have effects detrimental to the ecosystem of the watercourse resulting in significant harm to other watercourse States'.

In fact, the objective of almost all international environmental instruments is to prevent environmental deterioration, whether the texts concern pollution of the sea, inland waters, the atmosphere or the protection of living resources. On the regional level, prevention is referred to in the 1993 North American Agreement on Environmental Co-operation, the 2003 African Convention on the Conservation of Nature, and in Protocols to the 1979 United Nations Economic Commission for Europe (UNECE) Convention on Long-Range Transboundary Air Pollution.[153] Only a few international instruments use other approaches, such as the traditional principle of state responsibility or direct compensation of the victims.

In jurisprudence, the ICJ recognized the principle of prevention as a customary rule in the *Advisory Opinion on the Legality of Nuclear Weapons*,[154] the *Gabcikovo-Nagymaros Case* judgment,[155] the *Pulp Mills* judgment,[156] and the *Costa Rica/Nicaragua* judgment.[157] In the last-mentioned case, the Court indicated that the due diligence duty to prevent harm entails not only the adoption

---

148 See e.g. LRTAP, Arts. 3, 4 and 8.

149 See e.g. UNCLOS, Arts. 123 and 197.

150 See e.g. Revised African Nature Convention (July 11, 2013), Art. XVI(1).

151 See e.g. CBD, Art. 5.

152 Apia, June 12, 1976.

153 These include the Protocol on Persistent Organic Pollutants (June 24, 1998), the Heavy Metals Protocol (24 June 1998), and the Protocol to Abate Acidification, Eutrophication and Ground-Level Ozone (Nov. 30, 1999).

154 *Nuclear Weapons Advisory Opinion*, para. 29.

155 *Gabčíkovo-Nagymaros*, para. 140 (emphasizing the importance of prevention over reparation).

156 *Pulp Mills*, para. 101 (recognizing the origin of prevention 'in the due diligence that is required of a state in its territory' to avoid significant damage to the environment outside its jurisdiction).

157 *Costa Rica v. Nicaragua*, paras. 104 and 118.

of appropriate rules and measures, but also 'a certain level of vigilance in their enforcement and the exercise of administrative control' over public and private operators with respect to all activities which take place under the jurisdiction and control of the state. In the *Iron Rhine* arbitration of 2005 the tribunal noted that the duty of prevention is now 'a principle of general international law' that applies in the implementation of specific treaties.[158] Similarly, the arbitral tribunal in the 2013 *Indus Waters Kishenganga* case referred to the prevention principle as 'a foundational principle of customary international environmental law'[159] and in the Final Award reaffirmed that customary international law imposes a duty to prevent or at least mitigate significant harm to the environment when pursuing large-scale construction activities.[160]

The principle of prevention is partly linked to the notion of deterrence and the idea that disincentives such as penalties and civil liability will cause actors to take greater care in their behavior to avoid the increased costs. To the extent that the activity causing the harm is lawful, resulting e.g. from societal choice to destroy habitats by deliberate conversion of land to other uses, there is no liability. Little empirical work has been done, but there is some evidence for the preventive effect of a liability regime. One study examined the relationship between the imposition of strict liability for environmental damages and emissions of toxic chemicals into the environment and found that 'strict liability has little obvious effect on annual emission levels'.[161] As a matter of economic analysis, in a perfect market, those responsible for harm would be expected to invest in prevention when the cost of prevention is likely to avoid damage that would be more costly to restore than to prevent. The market is not perfect, however, in part because of the complexity of regulation. For example, prevention may require new equipment that tax regulations demand be capitalized and depreciated over time, while the costs of restoration can be deducted immediately as expenses, giving an economic incentive for the latter. Permit requirements may make changes to installations more difficult and costly, even if the result is greater prevention. The uncertainty of harm, its scale or likelihood may also contribute to a decision that the costs of prevention are greater than the potential costs of liability.

158 *Iron Rhine Arbitration*, para. 59.

159 *Indus Waters Kishenganga Arbitration*, (Partial Award) para. 454.

160 *Indus Waters Kishenganga Arbitration*, (Final Award) para. 112.

161 David Austin & Anna Alberini, *An Analysis of the Preventive Effect of Environmental Liability: Environmental Liability, Location and Emissions Substitution: Evidence from the Toxic Release Inventory* (Resources for the Future 2001).

2.2 *Precaution*

The proclamation of the precautionary approach can be considered one of the most important additions to the Rio Declaration when compared to the earlier Stockholm Declaration. Rio Principle 15 provides:

> In order to protect the environment, the precautionary principle shall be widely applied by States according to their capabilities. Where there are threats of serious or irreversible damage, lack of full scientific certainty shall not be used as a reason for postponing cost effective measures to prevent environmental degradation.

There were few precedents, as formulations of the precautionary principle are relatively recent and derive from national law.[162] The World Charter for Nature indicated the thrust of the principle in Article 11(b):

> Activities which are likely to pose a significant risk to nature shall be preceded by an exhaustive examination; their proponents shall demonstrate that expected benefits outweigh potential damage to nature, and where potential adverse effects are not fully understood, the activities should not proceed.

The term itself first appeared in international environmental law in a declaration adopted by a conference on the North Sea in 1987.[163] In 1990, the ministers of the thirty-four member states of UNECE and the representative of the EC adopted the Bergen Declaration which included a broad formulation of the precautionary principle foreshadowing the Rio text.[164] The first treaty to refer to precaution was the 1985 Vienna Convention for the Protection of the Ozone

162 The Federal Republic of Germany formulated a principle of *Versorgeprinzip* in the early 1970s to limit threats to the environment.

163 See David Freestone, 'The Precautionary Principle' in Robin Churchill & David Freestone (eds), *International Law and Global Climate Change* (Graham & Trotman 1991) 21–40.

164 'In order to achieve sustainable development, policies must be based on the precautionary principle. Environmental measures must anticipate, prevent and attack the causes of environmental degradation. Where there are threats of serious or irreversible damage, lack of full scientific certainty should not be used as a reason for postponing measures to prevent environmental degradation'. Bergen Declaration, Principle 7, May 15, 1990, 20 E.P.L. 200 (1990).

Layer (22 March). Since then, the precautionary principle has appeared in almost all international instruments related to environmental protection.[165]

Precaution is also one of the bases of the European Union (EU)'s environmental policy according to the 1992 Maastricht Treaty,[166] but the term is not defined by the treaty. In February 2000, the European Commission produced a Communication to inform all institutions and member states of the manner in which the Commission intends to apply the principle when faced with risks of environmental harm.[167] Seeking a common position on the application of the principle, the Communication describes precaution as a risk management tool which is part of a risk analysis framework rather than an overall guide to implementation. Precautionary action should only be taken after experts prepare an objective quantitative risk assessment. Moreover, the Communication

165 See e.g., the Bamako Convention on the Ban of the Import of Hazardous Wastes into Africa and on the Control of their Transboundary Movements within Africa, Art. 4(3)(f) (Jan. 29, 1991); Helsinki Convention on the Protection of the Marine Environment of the Baltic Sea, Art. 3(2) (Apr. 9, 1992); UNFCCC, Art. 4(1)(f); Convention on Biological Diversity, Preamble (June 5, 1992); 1995 Agreement for the Implementation of the Provisions of the UN Convention on the Law of the Sea of 10 December 1982, Relating to the Conservation and Management of Fish Stocks and Highly Migratory Fish Stocks (August 4, 1995); Amendments to the Protocol for the Protection of the Mediterranean Sea against Pollution from Land-Based Sources, Preamble (Syracuse, March 7, 1996); Protocol to the 1979 Convention on Long-Range Transboundary Air Pollution to Abate Acidification, Eutrophication and Ground-Level Ozone (Gothenburg, Nov. 30, 1999); the Cartagena Protocol on Biosafety (Jan. 29, 2000); Convention on the Conservation and Management of Highly Migratory Fish Stocks in the Western and Central Pacific Ocean (Honolulu, Sept. 5, 2000); Convention on the Conservation and Management of Fishery Resources in the South-East Atlantic Ocean (April 20, 2001); the Stockholm Convention on Persistent Organic Pollutants (May 22, 2001); and the European Energy Charter Treaty, Art. 19(1) (Lisbon, Dec. 17, 1994).

166 'Community policy on the environment shall aim at a high level of protection ... It shall be based on the precautionary principle and on the principles that preventive action should be taken, that environmental damage should as a priority be rectified at source ...' Treaty of Maastricht [1992] OJ C325/5, Art. 130*r*. Other regional instruments that include the precautionary principle are: Amendments to the Protocol for the Protection of the Mediterranean Sea against Pollution from Land-Based Sources, Preamble (Syracuse, March 7, 1996); Protocol to the 1979 Convention on Long-Range Transboundary Air Pollution to Abate Acidification, Eutrophication and Ground-Level Ozone (Gothenburg, Nov. 30, 1999); Convention on the Conservation and Management of Fishery Resources in the South-East Atlantic Ocean (April 20, 2001); Convention on the Conservation and Management of Highly Migratory Fish Stocks in the Western and Central Pacific Ocean (Honolulu, Sept. 5, 2000); and the ASEAN Agreement on Transboundary Haze Pollution (Kuala Lumpur, June 10, 2002).

167 See Communication from the Commission COM(2000)1 on the Precautionary Principle [2000].

clarifies that '[t]he implementation of an approach based on the precautionary principle should start with a scientific evaluation, as complete as possible, and where possible, identifying at each stage the degree of scientific uncertainty'.[168] It is thus a temporary measure pending further scientific information. The Communication mentions the need to incorporate qualitative as well as quantitative scientific evidence, acknowledging that protection of human health and the environment should have priority over economic concerns. It also encourages a transparent and open decision-making process with the participation of all interested parties as early as possible. According to the Communication, the determination of what constitutes an 'acceptable' level of risk is eminently a political responsibility and that the Commission thus has the right to fix levels of protection of the environment, within the limits of proportionality and non-discrimination, cost-benefit analysis and review. The Council endorsed the broad lines of the Communication during the Nice Summit in December 2000.

The European Court of Justice (ECJ) has adopted the precautionary principle, particularly in respect to environmental risks that pose dangers to human health. The Court held that the Commission had not committed manifest error when banning the export of beef during the so-called 'mad cow' crisis.[169] The ECJ said: 'At the time when the contested decision was adopted, there was great uncertainty as to the risks posed by live animals, bovine meat and derived products. Where there is uncertainty as to the existence or extent of risks to human health, the institutions may take protective measures without having to await the reality and seriousness of those risks to become fully apparent'.[170] In the *European Free Trade Association* case, the Court held that proper application of the precautionary principle presupposes an identification of potentially negative consequences and a comprehensive evaluation of the risk based upon the most recent scientific information.[171] Where the insufficient, inconclusive or imprecise nature of the conclusions make it impossible to determine risk or hazard with any certainty, but the likelihood of harm

---

168 ibid, para. 4.

169 Case C-180/96 P *United Kingdom v. Commission* [1996] ECR I-3903, para. 93; Case T-76/96 R *National Farmers' Union* (*NFU*) [1996] ECR II-815, para. 88.

170 *NFU*, para 63. See also Case T-199/96 *Bergaderm* [1998] ECR II-2305; Case T-79-99P *Alpharma* [1999] ECR II-2027; Case C-514/99 *France v. Commission* [2000] ECR I-4705. Case C-355/90, *Commission v. Spain* [1993] ECR I-6159, para. 28; Case C-405/92 *Armand Mondiet* [1993] ECR I-6176, paras. 31–36.

171 Case E-3/00 *EFTA Surveillance Authority v. Norway* [2001], paras. 16, 21.

persists, the precautionary principle would justify taking restrictive measures.[172] The Court has identified non-discrimination, proportionality and objectivity as the relevant criteria for the adoption of such restrictive measures.[173] The latter 'must be non-discriminatory and objective, and must be applied within the framework of a policy based on the best available scientific knowledge at any given time. The precautionary principle can never justify the adoption of arbitrary decisions, and the pursuit of the objective of "zero risk" only in the most exceptional circumstances'.[174]

Concrete application of the precautionary principle is often found in treaties for the management of living resources, especially those concerning fishing. The 1995 Agreement for the Implementation of the Provisions of the UN Convention on the Law of the Sea of 10 December 1982, Relating to the Conservation and Management of Fish Stocks and Highly Migratory Fish Stocks declares that states shall apply the precautionary principle (Art. 5(c)). Article 6 adds that such application includes the precautionary approach to conservation, management and exploitation of straddling fish stocks and highly migratory fish stocks, *inter alia*, by improving decision-making in this field, by taking into account uncertainties relating to the size and productivity of the stocks, by developing knowledge, by not exceeding reference points, by enhanced monitoring and by adopting, if necessary, emergency measures. Annex II to the Agreement sets out the detailed methodology for such a precautionary approach. Similarly, the Convention on the Conservation and Management of Highly Migratory Fish Stocks in the Western and Central Pacific Ocean (Honolulu, Sept. 5, 2000) provides that the Commission created by this instrument shall apply the precautionary approach (Art.5 (c)). EC Regulation 2371/2002 of December 2002 on the Conservation and Sustainable Exploitation of Fisheries Resources under the Common Fisheries Policy also foresees that the Community 'shall apply the precautionary approach in

---

172 Case T-13/99 *Pfizer Animal Health SA v. Council* [2002]; Case T-108/17 *ClientEarth v. European Commission* [2019], para. 284.

173 See Case C-77/09 *Gowan Comércio Internacional e Serviços* [2010] ECR I-13533, para. 76; T-429/13 *Bayer CropScience AG and Others v. European Commission* [2018], para. 117; C-192/01 *Commission v. Denmark* [2003] ECR I-09693, para. 53; T-392/02 *Solvay Pharmaceuticals v. Council* [2003] ECR II-04555, para. 125; C-333/08 *Commission v. France* [2010] ECR I-00757, para. 93; C-446/08 *Solgar Vitamin's France an Others* [2010] ECR I-03973, para. 67; T-71/10 *Xeda International and Pace International v. Commission* [2012], para. 76; T-817/14 *Zoofachhandel Züpke and Others v. Commission* [2016], para. 51; C-477/14 *Pillbox 38* [2016], para. 48; C-78/16 *Pesce and Others* [2016], para. 48; C-282/15 *Queisser Pharma* [2017], para. 57; T-584/13 *BASF Agro and Others v. Commission* [2018], para. 68.

174 *EFTA Surveillance Authority v. Norway*, para. 2.3.

taking measures designed to protect and conserve living aquatic resources, to provide for their sustainable exploitation and to minimize the impact of fishing activities on marine ecosystems' (Art. 2(1)).[175] In this respect, notable recent instruments focusing on specific threats to marine living resources include UNEP's work in respect of marine plastic debris and microplastics, which has stressed that 'lack of full scientific certainty should not be used for postponing cost-effective measures to prevent environmental degradation, where there are threats of serious or irreversible damage'.[176]

The Cartagena Biosafety Protocol to the Convention on Biological Diversity is based upon the precautionary principle. It is contained in Article 1 on the objectives of the Protocol which refers explicitly to Rio Principle 15. Articles 10 and 11 contain the key provisions on the principle. Article 10(6) says that 'lack of scientific certainty due to insufficient relevant information and knowledge regarding the extent of the potential adverse effects of an LMO shall not prevent the party from taking a decision on the LMO in order to avoid or minimize such potential adverse effects.' Article 11 uses similar language. Thus, a country may reject an import even in the absence of scientific certainty that it will potentially cause harm. These provisions are broader than Rio Principle 15 because they lack reference to 'serious or irreversible damage' or to cost-effectiveness.

The precautionary approach is included in the Regulations on Prospecting and Exploration for Polymetallic Nodules (Mining Code) which the International Seabed Authority (ISA) approved on 13 July 2000: 'In order to ensure effective protection for the marine environment from harmful effects which may arise from activities in the Area, the Authority and sponsoring States shall apply a precautionary approach, as reflected in Principle 15 of the Rio Declaration, to such activities. The Legal and Technical Commission shall make recommendations to the Council on the implementation of this paragraph'.[177] The Recommendations for the Guidance of Contractors for the Assessment of Possible Environmental Impacts Arising from Exploration for Polymetallic Nodules in the Area, approved by the Legal and Technical Commission of the ISA adopts this approach as well.[178]

---

175 Other EC instruments use the term 'precautionary principle' which appears in the Amsterdam Convention on the European Union. EC practice considers that the two expressions are equivalent. The variations in terminology may also reflect a degree of uncertainty or controversy surrounding the contents and requirements of the principle. Notably, the 1991 Bamako Convention calls precaution both a principle and an approach.

176 United Nations Environment Assembly of the United Nations Environment Programme, 1st session, Nairobi, June 27, 2014, 1/6 'Marine plastic debris and microplastics'.

177 Document ISBA/6/A/18, 4 October 2000, Reg. 31, para. 2.

178 Document ISBA/7/LTC/1/Rev.1 of July 10, 2001.

In litigation outside the European Union, one finds reliance on the precautionary principle as a general matter in an increasing range of domestic litigation. The courts of Brazil, for example, emphasized the critical value of groundwater quality when observing that '[i]n terms of the environment, the precautionary principle must always prevail'.[179] The courts of Pakistan have considered the precautionary principle as 'a settled part of our domestic jurisprudence'.[180]

International courts and tribunals, on the other hand, have at times shown reluctance to rely directly upon the precautionary principle despite its inclusion in nearly all recent environmental agreements. In *Gabçikovo Nagymaros*, the ICJ did not accept Hungary's argument that a state of necessity could arise from application of the precautionary principle.[181] In *Pulp Mills*, the ICJ considered that while a precautionary approach may be relevant to interpreting and applying a treaty, 'it does not follow that it operates as a reversal of the burden of proof'.[182] Nonetheless, Australia based its claim in the *Whaling in the Antarctic* Case largely on the precautionary principle.[183] Regional human rights courts have been more accepting of the principle. The European Court of Human Rights (ECHR), in a chamber judgment delivered on 27 January 2009 in the case of *Tatar v. Romania*,[184] declared that the precautionary principle has moved, on the European level, from being a philosophical concept to being a juridical norm with content to be applied. This means the government must take action to adopt reasonable and adequate measures capable of respecting the rights of individuals against serious risks to their health and well-being, even where scientific certainty is lacking. In its 2017 Advisory Opinion on *The Environment and Human Rights*, the Inter-American Court of Human Rights (IACHR) recognized that 'States must act in keeping with the precautionary principle in order to protect the right to life and to personal integrity in cases where there are plausible indications that an activity could result in sever and irreversible damage to the environment, even in the absence of scientific

179 *Suspension of the Ponta Grossa Ambiental Ltda license in view of precautionary principle* (2015) Superior Tribunal de Justiça.

180 *Sheikh Asim Farooq vs. Federation of Pakistan etc.* (2019) Lahore High Court para. 29.

181 See *Gabčikovo-Nagymaros*, paras. 54–56.

182 *Pulp Mills*, para. 164.

183 *Whaling in the Antarctic*, Memorial of Australia, submitted 9 March 2011, para. 4.87-4.90. See also the separate opinion of Judge Cancado Trindade, para. 64.

184 *Tătar v. Romania* App No 67021/01, ECtHR (Jan. 27, 2009)).

certainty' and that they must therefore adopt 'effective measures' to prevent such severe or irreversible damage.[185]

In the context of the World Trade Organization (WTO) and the General Agreement on Tariffs and Trade (GATT), dispute settlement panels have agreed that in cases where it is not possible to conduct a proper risk assessment,[186] Article 5(7) of the Sanitary and Phytosanitary (SPS) Agreement allows members to adopt and maintain a provisional or precautionary SPS measure. According to both the Panel and the Appellate Body, this provision incorporates the precautionary principle to a limited extent, when four cumulative criteria are met: (1) the relevant scientific information must be insufficient; (2) the measure should be adopted on the basis of available pertinent information; (3) the member must seek to obtain the additional information necessary for a more objective assessment of risk;[187] (4) the member must review the measure accordingly within a reasonable period of time established on a case by case basis depending on the specific circumstances, including the difficulty of obtaining additional information needed for review and the characteristics of the SPS measure.[188] At the same time, in the *Hormones* case, the WTO Appellate Body has expressed skepticism about whether the precautionary principle or approach has become customary international law.[189]

In the *Southern Bluefin Tuna* Case, the International Tribunal on the Law of the Sea seemed to view the precautionary principle more favorably than does the WTO Appellate Body or the ICJ. ITLOS could not conclusively assess the scientific evidence regarding the provisional measures sought by New Zealand and indeed, the latter requested the measures on the basis of the precautionary principle, pending a final settlement of the case. ITLOS found that in the face of scientific uncertainty regarding the measures, action should be taken as a measure of urgency to avert further deterioration of the tuna stock. In

185 *Human Rights and the Environment*, Advisory Opinion OC-23/17 Inter-American Court of Human Rights (Nov. 15, 2017) para. 180.

186 On risk assessment, see Chapter 6.

187 Report of the Appellate Body, *Japan – Varietals, Measures Affecting Agricultural Products* (Feb. 22, 1999) WT/DS76/AB/R, para. 92.

188 ibid, para. 93.

189 In the *Hormones Case*, the Appellate Body observed that: 'The precautionary principle is regarded by some as having crystallized into a general principle of customary international environmental law. Whether it is widely accepted by Members as a principle of general or customary international law appears less than clear. We consider, however, that it is unnecessary and probably imprudent, for the Appellate Body in this appeal to take a position on this important, but abstract, question'. Report of the Appellate Body, *European Communities – Measures Concerning Meat and Meat Products (Hormones)* (Jan. 16, 1998) WT/DS26/AB/R, para. 123.

its *consideratum*, the tribunal said that in its view, 'the parties should in the circumstances act with prudence and caution to ensure that effective conservation measures are taken to prevent serious harm to the stock of southern bluefin tuna'.[190] It prescribed a limitation to experimental fishing to avoid possible damage to the stock.[191] In its 2011 Advisory Opinion in *Responsibilities in the Area*, the ITLOS Seabed Disputes Chamber went further, observing:

> The precautionary approach has been incorporated into a growing number of international treaties and other instruments, many of which reflect the formulation of Principle 15 of the Rio Declaration. In the view of the Chamber, this has initiated a trend towards making this approach part of customary international law.[192]

Despite this trend, the formulations of the precautionary principle contain certain limitations. First, it may apply only when there are threats of 'serious or irreversible damage', according to Rio Principle 15 although some treaties have a lower threshold of 'significant' harm[193] or 'reasonable grounds for concern'.[194] It is also unclear how uncertain the science may be, although it may be presumed that some scientific basis for concern must be present. The European Court of Justice has taken a liberal view of this issue, allowing that the precautionary principle justifies the adoption of non-discriminatory and objective restrictive measures, even when it is impossible to determine with certainty the existence or extent of an alleged risk because of the insufficiency, inconclusiveness or imprecision of the results of studies conducted, but the likelihood of real harm to public health persists if the risk materializes.[195] A further limit is that economic considerations are taken into account,

190 *Southern Bluefin Tuna Case* (*Australia and New Zealand v Japan*) (Order of Aug. 27, 1999) ITLOS Reports 1999, para. 77.

191 In the MOX plant case, ITLOS responded to Irish demands for provisional measures on the basis of the precautionary principle. Ireland argued that the latter required Britain to prove no harm. Using again the terms 'prudence and caution', the Tribunal rejected the request for provisional measures but called on the parties to cooperate in exchanging information concerning risks or effects of the operation of the plant and devising ways to deal with them, as appropriate. *MOX Plant*, para. 84.

192 Advisory Opinion on *Responsibilities And Obligations Of States Sponsoring Persons And Entities With Respect To Activities In The Area*, para. 135.

193 See e.g. CBD, Preamble.

194 E.g. Convention for the protection of the Marine Environment of the North-East Atlantic (Paris, 22 Sept. 1992), Art. 2(2)(a).

195 Case C-77/09 *Gowan Comercio Internacional e Servicos Ltd, v. Ministero della Salute* [2010] ECR 1–13533, para. 76.

meaning the measures to be taken must be cost-effective. Finally, Principle 15 seems to accept a differentiated approach, providing that the approach shall be applied by States only 'according to their capabilities'.

The principle of precaution has played an important role in the climate change regime (see Chapter 12). Due to the fact that the causes and impacts of climate change were initially characterized by a strong scientific uncertainty, the UNFCCC incorporated this principle at Article 3(3): 'The Parties should take precautionary measures to anticipate, prevent or minimize the causes of climate change and mitigate its adverse effects. Where there are threats of serious or irreversible damage, lack of full scientific certainty should not be used as a reason for postponing such measures ...'. The importance of precaution in the adoption of climate change mitigation measures has been emphasized by national courts as well as by regional human rights courts. In *Urgenda*, the Dutch Supreme Court concluded that taking precautionary measures is part of the duty that the state needs to comply with in order to respect the right to life – as enshrined in Article 2 of the European Convention of Human Rights and Fundamental Freedoms (ECHR) – and the right the respect of private and family life (Article 8 of the ECHR).[196] Concretely, as explained by the Dutch Supreme Court, the precautionary principle requires a certain level of ambition from states in their climate change mitigation efforts, as it means that 'more far-reaching measures should be taken to reduce greenhouse gas emissions, rather than less far-reaching measures.'[197]

In general, and to conclude, the precautionary principle can be considered as a logical extension of prevention which remains the general basis for environmental protection measures. Precaution means preparing for potential, uncertain even hypothetical threats, when there is no irrefutable proof that damage will occur. It is prevention based on probabilities or contingencies but it cannot involve eliminating all claimed risks, even those without any basis, such as astrological predictions or psychic visions. Precaution particularly applies when the consequences of non-action could be serious. The problems of irreversibility and scientific uncertainty are thus brought into international law. Policy-makers must consider the circumstances of a given situation and decide which scientific opinion is based upon the most credible evidence and most reliable scientific methodology. Such a development expands the important role of scientists in the protection of the environment: decision-makers must adopt measures based upon a general knowledge of the environment

196 *Urgenda Foundation v. The State of the Netherlands* (2019) Dutch Supreme Court, para. 2.3.2.

197 ibid, para. 7.2.10.

and the problems its protection raises. Like in all environmental matters, the public must support the decision. The role of scientists thus includes a general environmental education of the public as well as of those who take the formal decision.

2.3 *The Polluter Pays Principle*

The polluter pays principle seeks to impose the costs of environmental harm on the party responsible for the pollution. This principle was set out by the OECD as an economic principle and as the most efficient way of allocating costs of pollution prevention and control measures introduced by the public authorities in member countries. It is intended to encourage rational use of scarce environmental resources and avoid distortions in international trade and investment.

The Rio Declaration includes it in rather abstract terms, stating in Principle 16 that

> National authorities should endeavor to promote the internalization of environmental costs and the use of economic instruments, taking into account the approach that the polluter should, in principle, bear the cost of pollution, with regard to the public interest and without distorting international trade and investment.

Prior to the Rio Conference on Environment and Development, the polluter pays requirement was included in different EC documents such as the 1986 Single European Act,[198] the 1992 Maastricht Treaty[199] (Art.130R(2)) and in the successive Programs of Action on the Environment. The Convention on the Protection of the Marine Environment of the Baltic Sea Area[200] states the principle as an obligatory norm, while the 1992 Helsinki Convention on the Protection and Use of Transboundary Watercourses and International Lakes[201] includes it as a guiding principle.

On the global level, the International Convention on Oil Pollution Preparedness, Response and Cooperation states in its preamble that the polluter pays principle is 'a general principle of international environmental law'.[202] More recent examples of reference to it are found in the Amendments to the

198 Feb. 17, 1986.
199 Treaty of Maastricht, Art. 130*r*(2).
200 Helsinki, April 9, 1992, Art. 3(4).
201 March 17, 1992, Art. 2(5).
202 Preamble.

Protocol for the Protection of the Mediterranean Sea against Pollution from Land-Based Sources,[203] and the Stockholm Convention on Persistent Organic Pollutants.[204]

The content of the polluter pays principle can be seen in the 1992 Convention for the Protection of the Marine Environment of the North-East Atlantic. According to Article 2(2)(b) '[t]he contracting parties shall apply:... the polluter pays principle, by virtue of which the costs of pollution prevention, control and reduction measures are to be borne by the polluter'. This can be interpreted in different ways depending upon the extent of prevention and control and whether compensation for damage is included in the definition of reduction. Further, the concept of the 'polluter' varies, and can range from the producer of merchandise to the consumer who uses it and who pays the higher price resulting from anti-pollution production measures. International practice thus far, mainly that of the European Union, seems to aim at eliminating public subsidies for pollution abatement by companies.

In fact, pollution control costs can be borne either by the community, by those who pollute, or by consumers. Community assumption of the costs can be demonstrated using the example of an industry that discharges pollutants into a river. There are at least three possibilities: (1) the river can remain polluted and rendered unsuitable for certain downstream activities, causing the downstream community to suffer an economic loss; (2) the downstream community can build an adequate water treatment plant at its own cost; (3) the polluter may receive public subsidies for controlling the pollution. In all these hypotheses, the affected community bears the cost of the pollution and of the measures designed to eliminate it or to mitigate its effects. The polluter pays principle avoids this result by obliging the polluter to bear the costs of pollution control, to 'internalize' them. In most cases the enterprise will in fact incorporate the costs in the price of the products and pass them on to the consumer.

'Polluter pays' thus is a method for internalizing externalities.[205] Those who benefit from air made cleaner have a positive externality if they do not pay for the cleanup. Where air is fouled by producer who bears no cost it is a negative externality; those who buy the product also are free riders if the fouling is not reflected in the price of the goods. Internalization requires that all

203 Syracuse, March 7, 1996, Preamble.

204 Stockholm, May 22, 2001, Preamble.

205 See e.g. E. Donald Elliott & Daniel C. Esty, 'The End Environmental Externalities Manifesto: A Rights-Based Foundation for Environmental Law' (2021) 29 NYU Environmental Law Journal 505.

the environmental costs be borne by the producer/consumer instead of the community as a whole. Prices will reflect the full cost if regulatory standards require or if taxes on the production or product correspond to the true cost of environmental damage. Coase's theorem posits an alternative, that from an economic perspective it is just as efficient to allow the victim of pollution a right to compensation as it is to recognize the polluter's right to pollute.[206] In this view, both the polluter and the victim compete for the same limited natural resource, and there is no a priori right to prefer one over the other. If each is ready to pay for use of a resource, they will be inclined to conclude a transaction to reduce pollution in order to reach optimal economic efficiency. So, it is most efficient to attribute ownership rights over natural resources. If the polluter holds a right to pollute, the victims must pay for cessation or reduction of the activity. Conversely the polluter will have to compensate any party suffering from pollution. This rejects the intervention of public authorities in favor of free negotiation. It only works, however, where the rights of the parties are clearly defined, information is complete and there are few if any transaction costs. This rarely happens. Further, this ignores the role of prevention and the common interests in natural resources, now and in the future.

Often, the market fails to tackle specific externalities and government intervention may therefore be preferable. A classic example of market failure is represented by climate change (see Chapter 12), as

> The full costs of GHG emissions, in terms of climate change, are not immediately – indeed they are unlikely ever to be – borne by the emitter, so they face little or no economic incentive to reduce emissions. Similarly, emitters do not have to compensate those who lose out because of climate change. In this sense, human-induced climate change is an externality, one that is not 'corrected' through any institution or market, unless policy intervenes.[207]

This explains the vast array of domestic measures aimed either at taxing those activities that produce negative externalities or at supporting and incentivizing those that create positive externalities (see Chapter 17).

The polluter pays principle can be applied most easily in a geographic region subject to uniform environmental law, such as within a state or in the European Union. In fact, the polluter pays principle has been well-defined in EU

---

206 See Ronald Coase, 'The Problem of Social Cost' (1960) 3 J. L. & Econ 1.

207 Nicholas Stern, *The Economics of Climate Change: Stern Review* (Cambridge University Press, 2007), p. 24.

law. An EC Council recommendation of November 7, 1974 defined 'polluter' as 'someone who directly or indirectly damages the environment or who creates conditions leading to such damage'. The breadth of the definition has been criticized because it can apply to automobile drivers, farmers, factory owners and community sewage treatment plants. The recommendation provides alternatives if identifying the polluter proves impossible or too difficult, and hence arbitrary, because the pollution arises from several simultaneous causes, (cumulative pollution), or from several consecutive causes. In such instances, the pollution-abatement cost should be borne at the point and by the legal or administrative means which offer the best solution administratively, economically, and environmentally. Thus, in the case of pollution 'chains', costs should be charged at the point at which the number of economic operators is least and control is easiest or at the point where the most effective contribution is made towards improving the environment, and where distortions to competition are avoided.

Polluters should pay for the cost of pollution control measures, such as the construction and operation of anti-pollution installations, investment in anti-pollution equipment and new processes, so that a necessary environmental quality objective is achieved. An important application of the principle is found in an EC Directive of December 6, 1984 on the control within the European Community of the transboundary shipment of hazardous waste. It instructs the member states to impose the costs of waste control on the holder of the waste and/or on prior holders or the waste generator. Also, Article 9 of EC Directive 2000/60 on water requires member states to take account of the principle of recovery of the costs of water services, including environmental and resource costs. Water pricing policies by 2010 are to provide adequate incentives for the efficient use of water resources. In sum, the polluter pays principle has to be taken into account by all the EU institutions and the European Court of Justice must ensure respect for the principle in the cases it decides.

In fact, the ECJ applied the principle in the *Standley Case*,[208] when a British High Court asked for a preliminary ruling on Directive 91/676/EEC of December 12, 1991 concerning the protection of waters against pollution caused by nitrates from agricultural sources. Farmers argued that the directive violated the polluter pays principle because they were asked to bear the cost of reducing the concentration of nitrates into waters, below the threshold level set, even though agriculture is only one source of nitrates. According to the ECJ,

208 C-293/97, *Standley and Others*, judgment of April 29, 1999, [1999] ECR I-2603.

however, 'the Directive does not mean that farmers must take on burdens for the elimination of pollution to which they have not contributed;... the Member States are to take account of the other sources of pollution when implementing the Directive and, having regard to the circumstances, are not to impose on farmers costs of eliminating pollution that are unnecessary. Viewed in that light, the polluter pays principle reflects the principle of proportionality'.[209]

The global economic system does not similarly impose the polluter pays principle, although it permits a state to apply it. In the *US Chemicals case*, the EC argued before a GATT panel that a US tax on certain chemicals was not eligible for border tax adjustment because the regime would only finance environmental programs of benefit to US producers. Since the US production was causing pollution in North America, the EC said that the polluter pays principle required the US to tax domestic products only. The Panel found that since the tax was directly imposed on products, it was eligible for border tax adjustment independent of its purpose. According to the panel, GATT rules on tax adjustment 'give the contracting party ... the possibility to follow the polluter-pays principle, but they do not oblige it to do so'.[210] The application of the polluter pays principle in international trade law remains at the heart of heated debates, as many countries have started adopting border tax adjustments on carbon, as part of their efforts to reduce global emissions and contribute to climate change mitigation (see Chapter 17).

2.4 *Sustainable Development*

Since the end of the 1980s the term sustainable development has dominated international discourse on environmental protection,[211]without any consensus on its meaning or operational consequences. It was defined in the 1987 Report of the World Commission on Environment and Development as 'development that meets the needs of the present without compromising the ability of future

---

209 ibid, paras. 51–2.

210 *United States – Taxes on Petroleum and Certain Imported Substances* (1987) GATT BISD 34S/136.

211 Although the term was not used at the Stockholm Conference, the basics of the concept were reflected in Principle 13 of the Stockholm Declaration, which states that: 'In order to achieve a more rational management of resources and thus to improve the environment, States should adopt an integrated and coordinated approach to their development planning so as to ensure that development is compatible with the need to protect and improve the environment for the benefit of their population'. The Helsinki Final Act of 1975 opined that environmental protection is a task of major importance for the economic development of all countries.

generations to meet their own needs'.[212] Building on this, Principle 4 of the Rio Declaration states that 'in order to achieve sustainable development, environmental protection shall constitute an integral part of the development process and cannot be considered in isolation from it'. Agenda 21, chapter 8, confirmed that development embodies both economic and social pillars.

In *Gabčikovo-Nagymaros*, the ICJ characterized the essence of sustainable development as the need 'to reconcile economic development with protection of the environment'.[213] The Court, however, limited itself to defining sustainable development as a *concept* and not a *principle*.[214] Almost ten years later, in 2005, the Arbitral Tribunal in the *Iron Rhine* Arbitration acknowledged that certain 'emerging principles now integrate environmental protection into the development process' and continued stating that 'where development may cause significant harm to the environment there is a duty to prevent, or at least mitigate, such harm', a duty which, in the opinion of the Tribunal 'has now become a principle of general international law.'[215] In *Pulp Mills*, the ICJ reaffirmed the conception of sustainable development expressed in *Gabčikovo-Nagymaros*, by stating that the 'essence' of sustainable development is a balance between economic development and environmental protection; any utilization of a shared watercourse, for example, that did not take into account environmental protection could not be considered to be equitable and reasonable.[216]

Sustainable development quickly became the cornerstone of international cooperation on environmental matters. As its title shows, the *Johannesburg World Summit on Sustainable Development* focused on sustainable development with particular emphasis on eradicating poverty.[217] This focus was already expressed in Principle 5 of the Rio Declaration which called on the international community to cooperate on 'the essential task of eradicating poverty as an indispensable requirement for sustainable development'.

---

212 *Our Common Future: Report of the World Commission on Environment and Development* (1987) U.N. Doc. A/42/427, 43.

213 *Gabčikovo-Nagymaros*, para. 140.

214 In his Separate Opinion, Judge Weeramantry considers sustainable development 'to be more than a mere concept, but as a principle with normative value.' 85.

215 *Iron Rhine Arbitration*, para. 59.

216 *Pulp Mills*, para. 177. See also *Indus Waters Kishenganga*, Partial Award, paras. 448–52.

217 In 2005, the World Bank defined the poverty line as subsistence on $1.25 a day. See Martin Ravallion et al, *Dollar a Day Revisited, World Bank (2008) Policy Research Working Paper* 4620.

Poverty is also seen as a human rights problem.[218] General Assembly Resolution A/69/183, adopted on December 18, 2014 and titled 'Human rights and extreme poverty' recognized the links between extreme poverty, inability to exercise human rights, and environmental conditions, encouraging the international community 'to strengthen its efforts to address challenges that are contributing to extreme poverty, including those derived from the ongoing impact of the financial and economic crisis, the food crisis and ongoing concerns over food security, as well as the increasing challenges posed by climate change and the loss of biodiversity in all parts of the world, especially in developing countries, by enhancing cooperation to help to build national capacities'.[219]

In 2000, the UN General Assembly adopted the Millennium Development Goals (MDGs)[220] to provide the international community with a framework for development priorities, including poverty alleviation. The MDGs called for achieving eight quantifiable goals, including ensuring environmental sustainability (MDG 7). Progress was achieved in respect to several of the goals, in particular cutting in half the number of persons in extreme poverty, providing of safe drinking water, improving access to education and political participation for girls and women, and reducing in cases of malaria and tuberculosis. In regard to other goals, the picture was less positive.[221] Of particular concern was the fact that the number of newly displaced persons tripled between 2010 and 2013. Concerning MDG 7, the 2014 report noted that carbon emissions continue to rise, increasing almost 50 percent since 1990. Also pointed out as challenges are increasing water scarcity and the massive loss of biological diversity. On the positive side, global consumption of ozone-depleting substances (ODS) decreased by over 98 per cent between 1986 and 2013.

As the MDGs reached the conclusion of their 15-year term, the UN turned to the post-2015 development agenda, which builds on the MDGs and also on the Rio+20 outcome document *The Future We Want*. The latter proclaims poverty eradication as the greatest global challenge facing the world[222] and indicates a process of elaborating Sustainable Development Goals for the post-2015

---

218 Statement on Poverty and the International Covenant on Economic, Social and Cultural Rights, UN Doc E/2002/22-E/C.12/2001/17 (10 May 2001). See also *Guiding Principles on Extreme Poverty and Human Rights*, adopted by the Human Rights Council, September 2012. The principles are contained in UN Doc. A/HRC/21/39 (July 18, 2012).

219 G. A. Res. 69/183, Dec. 18, 2014), para. 16.

220 G. A. Res. 55/2, Sept. 18, 2000.

221 United Nations, *The Millennium Development Goals Report 2014*.

222 G.A. Res. 66/288, *The Future We Want*, U.N. Doc. A/RES/66/288, Sept. 11, 2012, para. 2.

agenda.[223] The UN General Assembly Resolution 'Transforming our World: The 2030 Agenda for Sustainable Development', adopted in 2015, continues to recognize that poverty eradication is an indispensable requirement for sustainable development. The 2030 Agenda sets out 17 Sustainable Development Goals (SDGs) – 16 of which are of a substantive nature and one, SDG 17, which focuses on implementation. The Preamble recognizes that 'eradicating poverty in all its forms and dimensions, including extreme poverty, is the greatest global challenge and an indispensable requirement for sustainable development' and the first Goal, SDG 1, focuses precisely on ending poverty in all its forms everywhere.

Treaties now refer to the principle of sustainable development or the right to development. The UNFCCC, at Article 3(4), for example states that

> The Parties have a right to, and should, promote sustainable development. Policies and measures to protect the climate system against human-induced change should be appropriate for the specific conditions of each Party and should be integrated with national development programmes, taking into account that economic development is essential for adopting measures to address climate change.

The Paris Agreement, which enhances the implementation of the UNFCCC, aims to 'strengthens the global response to the threat of climate change, *in the context of sustainable development and efforts to eradicate poverty*.'[224]

According to Article 3(1)(a) of the Convention for Cooperation in the Protection and Sustainable Development of the Marine and Coastal Environment of the Northeast Pacific:

> For the purpose of this Convention sustainable development means the process of progressive change in the quality of life of human beings, which places it as the center and primordial subject of development, by means of economic growth with social equity and the transformation of methods of production and consumption patterns, and which is sustained in the ecological balance and vital support of the region. This pro-

223 On the Sustainable Development Goals, see: Ban Ki-Moon, *The road to dignity by 2030: ending poverty, transforming all lives and protecting the planet: Synthesis report of the Secretary-General on the post-2015 sustainable development agenda*, U.N. Doc. A/69/700 (Dec. 4, 2014), paras. 23, 34–36; see also the 2015 Sustainable Development Agenda, *Transforming our World: The 2030 Agenda for Global Action*, adopted at the World Summit, September 2015.

224 Art. 2 (emphasis added).

> cess implies respect for regional, national and local ethnic and cultural diversity, and full participation of people in peaceful coexistence and in harmony with nature, without prejudice to and ensuring the quality of life of future generations.

The process of integrating environment and development has both procedural and substantive dimensions and means more than simply taking into account environmental considerations during the process of making decisions.[225] States have agreed that achieving sustainable development requires policies aimed at the eradication of poverty, the general improvement of economic, social and cultural conditions, the conservation of biological diversity, and the maintenance of essential ecological processes and life-support systems. Environmental conservation should be treated as an integral part of the planning and implementation of activities at all stages and at all levels, giving full and equal consideration to environmental, economic, social and cultural factors. To this end, states should conduct regular national reviews of environmental and developmental policies and plans, enact effective laws and regulations which use, where appropriate, economic instruments and establish and strengthen institutional structures and procedures to fully integrate environmental and developmental issues in all spheres of decision-making. Also necessary are approaches that take into account long-term strategies and that include the use of environmental and social impact assessment, risk analysis, cost-benefit analysis and natural resources accounting. The integration of environmental, social and economic policies also requires transparency and broad public participation in governmental decision-making.

The concept of 'environmental services' has also become linked with sustainable development. According to the 2002 Antigua Convention it means the services provided by the functions of nature itself, such as the protection of soil by trees, the natural filtration and purification of water, and the protection of habitat for biodiversity (Art. 3(1)(c)). Nonetheless, overall, the global trend in elaborating the meaning of sustainable development has been to focus on development and not on sustainability. The risks for further development and implementation of environmental law are significant ones.

The principle of sustainable development has played a key role in ensuring the mutual supportiveness between international environmental and

225 'Environmental law and the law on development stand not as alternatives but as mutually reinforcing, integral concepts, which require that where development may cause significant harm to the environment there is a duty to prevent, or at least mitigate, such harm'. *Iron Rhine Arbitration*, para. 59.

international economic law. According to Principle 12 of the Rio Declaration, 'States should cooperate to promote a supportive and open international economic system that would lead to economic growth and sustainable development in all countries, to better address the problems of environmental degradation.' Adopted just a few years later, in 1995, the Agreement Establishing the WTO clearly indicates 'sustainable development' as one of the core objectives of the newly-created organization.[226] This reference to sustainable development has then been used by the WTO Appellate Body (*US-Shrimp*) to ensure the mutual supportiveness between trade liberalization and environmental policy considerations and to ensure an evolutionary interpretation of WTO rules, in a way that would take into account sustainable development and the importance of protecting the environment through trade (see Chapter 17).[227]

2.5 *Protection, Preservation and Conservation: Non-Regression?*

General international legal norms for the protection of the environment continue to emerge. For the most part, these norms appear piecemeal but regularly in texts and in international practice. They apply within the territory of states whether or not there are transboundary environmental impacts and in zones outside national jurisdiction.[228]

The most fundamental norm to appear is the obligation of all states to conserve the environment and the earth's natural resources. It designates a specific objective in the framework of interstate cooperation. Although all international environmental instruments have this aim, clear statements of the duty are rare. Article 192 of the UN Convention on the Law of the Sea, however, explicitly proclaims the duty of states to protect and preserve the marine environment. Article 20 of the 1997 UN Convention on the Non-Navigational Uses of International Watercourses affirms the same duty for international freshwater. The 1992 Convention on Biological Diversity lists the measures which should be taken to ensure conservation and sustainable use of biological resources, while the 1992 UNFCCC declares, in Article 3(1), that the parties should protect the climate system. The Paris Agreement builds on the UNFCCC

226 Marrakech Agreement establishing the World Trade Organization (Apr. 15, 1994) 1867 U.N.T.S. 154, Preamble.

227 Report of the Appellate Body, *United States – Import Prohibition of Certain Shrimps and Shrimp Products*, WT/DS58/AB/R (Oct. 12, 1998).

228 The US Restatement of Foreign Affairs Law, sec 601, refers to the obligation of states 'to conform to generally accepted international rules and standards for the prevention, reduction, and control of injury to the environment of another state or of areas beyond the limits of national jurisdiction'.

and declares the importance of 'the conservation and enhancement ... of sinks and reservoirs of ... greenhouse gases' and 'of ensuring the integrity of all ecosystems, including oceans, and the protection of biodiversity.'[229]

There is no treaty definition of the terms 'protect', 'preserve' or 'conserve'. The first two terms are used in Article 192 of the Convention on the Law of the Sea, suggesting that their meaning differs. *Protection* can be seen as abstaining from harmful activities and taking affirmative measures to ensure that environmental deterioration does not occur.[230] Increasingly, the concept of protection includes comprehensive ecological planning and management, with substantive regulations, procedures, and institutions on a national scale. *Preservation* could be considered as including long-time perspectives which take into account the rights and interests of future generations for whom natural resources should be safeguarded.[231] The term *conserve* or '*conservation*' has a narrower scope, but falls under the heading of protection. It generally is used in the field of living resources and is based upon the status quo, mainly demanding maintenance of the conditions necessary for continued resource existence. The IUCN World Conservation Strategy demonstrates the conservation principle in establishing as its objectives: (1) maintaining essential ecological processes and life-support systems; (2) preserving genetic diversity; and (3) achieving sustainable utilization of species and ecosystems.

When applied to exploited species of flora and fauna, conservation often meant establishing 'optimal sustainable yields', signifying exploitation of the resource without exceeding the limits that guarantee its renewal and thus its sustainability. In recent texts 'conservation' has been supplemented or replaced by reference to 'sustainable development', assuring the on-going productivity of exploitable natural resources and conserving all species of fauna and flora. A relatively recent and related concept is the 'favorable state of conservation', based not on the idea of exploitation or of yield but on that of maintaining living resources. In its 2015 *SRFC* Advisory Opinion, ITLOS examined the concept of 'sustainable management' as applied to straddling and migratory fish stocks. The Tribunal noted that 'the overarching objectives of sustainable management of fish stocks are to preserve and cultivate them as a viable

229 Paris, Dec. 12, 2005, 3156 U.N.T.S. 79, Preamble.

230 The American Heritage Dictionary defines 'to protect' as 'to keep from being damaged, attacked, stolen, or injured; guard'.

231 The American Heritage Dictionary defines 'to preserve' as 'to maintain in safety from injury, peril, or harm; protect', and adds 'to keep in perfect or unaltered condition; maintain unchanged'. In relation to food it has the meaning of preparing for future use, supporting the implication that it refers to more long-term approaches.

and enduring resource.'[232] The term 'sustainable management' was therefore interpreted by ITLOS as to encompass 'conservation and development', as articulated in Article 63(1) of UNCLOS. Terms such as 'essential ecological processes', 'genetic diversity' and even 'sustainable development' are abstract and relatively new, making it difficult for a state to comply with its legal obligations without the close collaboration of several scientific disciplines. The legal principles adopted by the World Commission on Environment and Development provide details on some terminology. They provide that states shall:

a. maintain ecosystems and related ecological processes essential for the functioning of the biosphere in all its diversity, in particular those important for food production, health and other aspects of human survival and sustainable development;
b. maintain maximum biological diversity by ensuring the survival and promoting the conservation in their natural habitat of all species of fauna and flora, in particular those which are rare, endemic or endangered;
c. observe, in the exploitation of living natural resources and ecosystems, the principle of optimum sustainable yield.[233]

The same concerns are evident in various international conventions aimed at protecting living species threatened with extinction and those concerned with the natural heritage. One of the earliest such international instruments is the Ramsar Convention on Wetlands of International Importance.[234] Article 2(6) speaks of the responsibility of each contracting party for the conservation, management, and wise use of migratory stocks of waterfowl, notably in designating wetlands in its territory which should receive a special protection. More extensive duties exist in the UNESCO Convention Concerning the Protection of the World Cultural and Natural Heritage.[235] Article 4 of this treaty proclaims the obligation of states to ensure the identification, protection, conservation, presentation and transmission to future generations of the cultural and natural heritage which is situated on its territory. Similarly, the preamble to the 1979 Bonn Migratory Species Convention recognizes that states are and must be the protectors of the migratory species of wild animals that live within the limits of their national jurisdiction or which cross these boundaries.[236] On June 19, 2023, the Agreement on the Conservation and Sustainable Use of Marine Biological Diversity of Areas beyond National Jurisdiction (BBNJ Agreement) was

232 *SRFC* Advisory Opinion, para. 190.
233 ibid.
234 Ramsar, Feb. 2, 1971.
235 Nov. 23, 1972.
236 Bonn, June 23, 1979.

adopted.[237] The agreement, which is aimed at the 'conservation and sustainable use of marine biological diversity of areas beyond national jurisdiction',[238] defines 'sustainable use' as 'the use of components of biological diversity in a way and at a rate that does not lead to a long-term decline of biological diversity, thereby maintaining its potential to meet the needs and aspirations of present and future generation'.[239]

On the regional level such provisions appear even more frequently. The 1976 Convention on the Conservation of Nature in the South Pacific contains numerous expressions of the duty to protect the environment, without explicitly speaking of the responsibility of states. The 1979 Bern Convention on the Conservation of European Wildlife and Natural Habitats leaves few doubts about the obligation to preserve and transmit to future generations the natural heritage of wild plant and animal species. The 1985 ASEAN Convention on the Conservation of Nature and Natural Resources recognizes the importance of natural resources for present and future generations and imposes clear duties on the south-east Asian states parties, and finally the 1990 Kingston Protocol on Specially Protected Areas and Wildlife to the 1983 Cartagena Convention for the Protection and Development of the Marine Environment in the Wider Caribbean Region provides in Article 3(3) that each Party, *to the extent possible, consistent with each Party's legal system*, shall manage species of fauna and flora with the objective of preventing species from becoming endangered or threatened. All these formulations make clear that one of the foundations of all environmental law, protecting the interests of future generations, is a primary motivation for conserving nature and natural resources.

Monitoring the state of the environment is a corollary of the duty of conservation. Logically, measures of conservation cannot be taken without knowledge of the environmental conditions nor can the impact of certain activities be evaluated. Principle 19 of the World Charter for Nature recommends monitoring in all sectors of the environment for all forms of environmental deterioration, not only by states, but also by international organizations, individuals and groups. The status of natural processes, ecosystems and species shall be closely monitored to enable early detection of degradation or threat, ensure timely intervention and facilitate the evaluation of conservation policies and methods.

---

237 Agreement under the United Nations Convention on the Law of the Sea on the Conservation and Sustainable Use of Marine Biological Diversity of Areas beyond National Jurisdiction (BBNJ) (June 19, 2023).

238 ibid, Art. 2.

239 ibid, Art. 1(13).

Permanent monitoring and international cooperation are closely linked in several international conventions, especially those concerning regional seas. Thus, Article 10 of the 1976 Convention for the Protection of the Mediterranean Sea Against Pollution provides for the institution by contracting states, in close cooperation with competent international organizations, of complementary or common continuous monitoring systems against pollution in the Mediterranean Sea.[240] Similarly, in international treaties relating to conservation of wildlife, states frequently undertake to furnish information concerning the status of protected species or their activities aimed at conserving or managing specific species.[241] Under Article 7 of the Agreement on Cooperation on Marine Oil Pollution, Preparedness and Response in the Arctic, States must not only monitor activities to identify oil pollutions incidents in areas under their respective jurisdictions, but also 'to the extent feasible, in adjacent areas beyond the jurisdiction of any State'.

Some governments and commentators argue from the duties to protect, preserve and conserve, for an emerging principle of non-regression, advocating that environmental laws must be maintained without regression, interpreted and applied in favour of ecological integrity, unless compelling reasons of public interest require otherwise. While absolute application of the principle is probably unattainable, the necessity of any measures of regression should be revisited and re-examined on a periodic basis in order to restore or enhance pre-existing levels of environmental conservation.

The principle emerges from belief that environmental law has an immutable core content closely linked to the right to life, which is an inalienable human right. Sustainable development means that this right and the right to health of future generations must not be ignored and measures that would be detrimental to them, such as imposing a more degraded environment, must be avoided. Human rights law itself condemns regression. In its General Comment 3 of December 14, 1990, the UN Committee for Economic Social and Cultural Rights (CESCR) repudiates the legality of 'any deliberately retrogressive measures'.

Universal and regional international environmental conventions all aim at 'improving the environment'. Among declarative texts, the 1992 Rio Declaration

---

240 See also Art. 10(1), Kuwait Regional Convention for Cooperation in Combating Pollution by Oil and other Harmful Substances in Cases of Emergency (Apr. 24, 1978); Art. 14, Convention for Cooperation in the Protection and Development of the Marine and Coastal Environment of the West and Central African Region (March 23, 1981); and Art. 10, Regional Convention for the Conservation of the Red Sea and of the Gulf of Aden Environment (Feb. 14, 1982).

241 E.g., Art. 20 of the 1980 Convention on the Conservation of Antarctic Marine Living Resources.

on Environment and Development includes an undertaking to 'conserve, protect and restore the health and integrity of the Earth's ecosystem' (Principle 7). A number of conventions state expressly that it is prohibited to reduce the level of environmental protection. In the 1940 Convention on Nature Protection and Wildlife Preservation in the Western Hemisphere, for example, the Contracting Governments agree that *the boundaries of national parks shall not be altered, or any portion thereof be capable of alienation, except by the competent legislative authority*. Further, the resources of these reserves shall not be subject to exploitation for commercial profit and the Contracting Governments agree to prohibit hunting, killing and capturing of members of the fauna and destruction or collection of representatives of the flora in national parks except by or under the direction or control of the park authorities, or for duly authorized scientific investigations. In 2011, the European Parliament adopted resolution 29/9/2011 which unhesitatingly stated: 'international law forbids repeal or amendment by nations of laws designed to protect the environment' (para. 97). Other political statements include the Rio + 20 outcome statement *The Future We Want* which states that '… it is critical that we do not backtrack from our commitment to the Earth Summit' (para. 20). The principle of non-regression plays a key role in the climate regime, where the Paris Agreement requires the Contracting Parties to periodically communicate their Nationally Determined Contributions (NDCs) every five years to the UNFCCC Secretariat and clarifies that 'the efforts of all Parties will represent a progression over time'.[242]

Among bilateral agreements, a duty of non-regression is expressly contained in Article 41 of the 1975 Statute of the River Uruguay (Argentina/Uruguay).[243] Article 41(a) establishes a general obligation to protect and preserve the aquatic environment of the river, adding in paragraph (b) an explicit undertaking by the parties 'not to reduce in their respective legal systems: (1) the technical requirements in force for preventing water pollution, and (2) the severity of the penalties established for violations …'. The duty to protect and preserve the river includes adopting measures in accordance with applicable international agreements and in keeping, where relevant, with the guidelines and recommendations of international technical bodies. As the ICJ indicated in the *Pulp Mills* judgment, this means keeping abreast of developments in international law (para. 204).

Regression can occur when states denounce treaties in order to escape environmental obligations or enact legislation that rolls back environmental

242 Art. 3, Paris Agreement.

243 Statute of the River Uruguay (26 Feb. 1975) 1295 UNTS 340.

conservation and protection measures. Legal support for a principle of non-regression is found in some national constitutions and laws. Jurisprudence supports it as well.[244] The principle of non-regression has also been incorporated in free trade agreements (FTAS) ever since the adoption of the North-American Free Trade Agreement (NAFTA) in 1994. In its 'Investment' Chapter, Article 1114 of NAFTA STATES THAT '[t]he Parties recognize that it is inappropriate to encourage investment by relaxing domestic health, safety or environmental measures'. Following NAFTA's example, most FTAS feature a similar provision, often with reference to both trade and investment, where the Parties commit not to lower their environmental standards to encourage trade or investment (See Chapter 17).

Clearly, the principle of non-regression allows for exceptions, so long as they do not contravene fundamental environmental policy objectives. For instance, under the Convention on International Trade in Endangered Species of Wild Fauna and Flora (CITES), species that are no longer endangered could be removed from the list without a regression in the level of protection. The ban on a particular pollutant could be lifted when it is demonstrated that it no longer poses a health hazard. Non-regression thus does not prohibit repealing or amending existing texts, provided the environmental quality does not deteriorate.

3 Conclusions

Taken as a whole, the common law of the environment is rapidly developing to include a general obligation to protect and conserve the global environment. Recent environmental agreements demonstrate the widespread acceptance of this notion and the principles discussed above. The Framework Convention on the Protection and Sustainable Development of the Carpathians, adopted in Kiev May 22, 2003, provides an example in its Article 2. The objective of

244 I/A Court H.R., *Acevedo Buendia et al.*, Judgment of July 1, 2009, Series C, No. 198, para. 103; S.T.J., REsp No. 176.753/SC (2d Panel), Relator: Min. Antonio Herman Benjamin, 07.02.2008 (Nov. 11, 2009) (Braz.); S.T.J., REsp No. 418.565/SP (1st Section), Relator: Min. Teori Albino Zavascki, 29.09.2010 (Oct. 13, 2010) (Braz.); Constitutional Chamber of the Supreme Court of Costa Rica, sentencia 2014–18836 del 18 de noviembre de 2014; and 2012–13367 of 21 September 2012. See: Marta Franch I Saguer, « Le principe de non-régression dans la jurisprudence récente du Tribunal Suprême espagnol: commentaire des décisions du 22 février 2012 (STS 3774/2009) et du 29 mars 2012 (STS 2000/2012) », 39(2) *Revue juridique de l'environnement* 219 (2014).

the treaty is articulated as 'the protection and sustainable development of the Carpathians with a view to *inter alia* improving quality of life, strengthening local economies and communities, and conservation of natural values and cultural heritage'. In order to achieve the stated objectives, Article 2(2) provides that the parties are to utilize the principles of precaution and prevention; the polluter pays principle; public participation and stakeholder involvement; transboundary cooperation; integrated planning and management of land and water resources; a programmatic approach; and the ecosystem approach. The integrated and ecosystem approaches reflect the on-going evolution of international environmental law and are discussed in Chapter 14.

Bibliography

Barral, V., 'Sustainable Development in International Law: Nature and Operation of an Evolutive Legal Norm' (2012) 23 EJIL 377.

Boyle, A., and Freestone, D. (eds), *International Law and Sustainable Development. Past Achievements and Future Challenges* (Oxford University Press, 1999).

Bratspies, R., and Miller, R. (eds.) *Transboundary Harm in International Law: Lessons from the 'Trail Smelter' Arbitration* (Cambridge University Press, 2006).

De Guttry, A., Gestri, M., Venturini, G. (eds), *International Disaster Response Law* (The Hague: TMC Asser Press, 2012).

Foster, C.E., *Science and the Precautionary Principle in International Courts and Tribunals: Expert Evidence, Burden of Proof and Finality* (Cambridge University Press, 2011).

Freestone, D., and E. Hey, *The Precautionary Principle and International Law: the Challenge of Implementation* (Kluwer Law International, 1996).

Freestone, D. *The World Bank and Sustainable Development – Legal Essays* (Brill, 2012).

Koivurova, T., 'Due diligence,' *Max Planck Encyclopedia of Public International Law* (Oxford University Press, 2008).

Perrez, F.X., 'The Relationship between 'Permanent Sovereignty' and the Obligation not to Cause Transboundary Environmental Damage,' (1996) 26 *Environmental Law* 1190.

Plakokelafos, I., 'Prevention Obligations in International Environmental Law' (2012) 23 *YbIEL* 3.

Sadeleer, N., de, *Environmental Principles: From Political Slogans to Legal Rules* (Oxford University Press, 2002).

Schrijver, N., 'The Evolution of Sustainable Development in International Law: Inception, Meaning and Status' (2007) 329 *Recueil de Cours* 217.

Schwartz, P., 'Polluter Pays Principle', in Fitzmaurice, M., Ong, D., and Merkouris, P. (eds), *Research Handbook on International Environmental Law* (Edward Elgar 2010), 243.

Vessey, J., 'The Principle of Prevention in International Law' (1998) 3 *Austrian Review of International and European Law* 181.

Wiener, J. "Precaution" in Bodansky, D., Brunee, J., and Hey, E. (eds), *The Oxford Handbook of International Environmental Law* (Oxford University Press 2007), 597.

CHAPTER 5

International Institutions and Actors

Protecting the environment necessitates action at all governance[1] levels; international institutions play an important role for several reasons. First, scientists and policy-makers are far from having complete knowledge about the environment, its current and potential deterioration, and the measures which should be adopted in response to the problems identified. New issues arise needing relatively quick and coordinated attention, from the depletion of the stratospheric ozone layer, to deforestation, desertification, global climate change, and the loss of biological diversity. Rapid evolution in knowledge makes necessary permanent assessment of the environment, but information is not equally accessible or disseminated throughout the world. In this regard international organizations are indispensable in providing a permanent mechanism for effective assessment through environmental monitoring, with the participation of researchers and policy-makers from many countries. Second, although adoption of international norms and standards is indispensable to protect the environment, adherence to and entry into force of agreements usually does not alone ensure short- or long-term effectiveness. Changes in environmental conditions require virtually constant revisions of the rules through adapting existing instruments or concluding new ones. In addition, there must be mechanisms to supervise implementation of the agreed rules. These tasks demand sustained cooperation and an institutional framework. Third, the solutions to

1 The term governance, now common in international policy, can be defined as the rational organization of society in order to achieve the objectives emerging from its common concerns. It is based on material, economic, historical and cultural foundations and needs. Governance includes the creation and the functioning of institutions and of norms at various levels from the local to the global. It also should determine the place and role of non-state actors and of stakeholders in public life. A particular aspect of governance is the designation and organization of basic services ensuring personal security, the supply of energy, food, transport systems, health, education, the conservation and management of natural resources. Art. 2(2) of EC Reg. 2371/2002 on the Conservation and Sustainable Exploitation of Fisheries Resources under the Common Fisheries Policy contains the following principles of good governance: '(a) clear definition of responsibilities at the Community, national and local levels; (b) a decision-making process based on sound scientific advice which delivers timely results; (c) broad involvement of stakeholders at all stages of the policy from conception to implementation; (d) consistence with other Community policies, in particular with environmental, social, regional, development, health and consumer protection policies'. EC Reg. No 2371/2002 of Dec. 20, 2002, O.J. L 358 (12/31/02).

 | DOI:10.1163/9789047440802_007

environmental problems often require a structure to manage natural resources across international boundaries and in commons areas. For this, international organizations are crucial. Finally, international organizations with general mandates can best integrate and respond to the interdependent issues of environmental quality, economic development, peace and human rights. Global and regional intergovernmental and non-governmental organizations have participated from the beginning in the development and implementation of international environmental law. Over time, institutional proliferation has accompanied the on-going adoption of multilateral treaties. No single institution exists to coordinate the activities of these organizations, which work together with treaty bodies and new international actors such as businesses, scientific and professional associations, and civil society generally. In addition to having grown in number, international institutions have seen their functions expand in response to demands for solutions to environmental problems.

Prior to the 1972 Stockholm Conference, no United Nations (UN) body had an express mandate to address issues of environmental protection. Principle 25 of the Stockholm Declaration expressed the desire of the participating states for dedicated action among existing bodies: 'States shall ensure that international organizations play a coordinated, efficient and dynamic role for the protection and improvement of the environment'. The creation of the United Nations Environment Program (UNEP) following the Stockholm Conference emerged from the desire for dedicated international action: the UN General Assembly conferred on UNEP a role as catalyst and coordinating agency for environmental matters, as discussed in more detail below. Two decades later, when the 1992 Rio Conference on Environment and Development shifted from addressing environmental protection as a separate matter to a focus on its relationship with economic development, the Conference called for the creation of a high-level UN commission to monitor the implementation of Agenda 21. The UN General Assembly accepted the recommendation and created the Commission on Sustainable Development (CSD), which operated until its replacement two decades later following the Rio+20 conference.

Concerns about the respective mandates and coordination of work between UNEP and the CSD, among other institutions, led many scholars and activists to propose the creation of a single World Environment Organization or Agency, akin to the World Trade Organization.[2] This proposal gained

2 See e.g. Frank Biermann & Steffen Bauer (eds), *A World Environmental Organization: Solution or Threat for Effective International Environmental Governance* (Ashgate 2005); Steve Charnovitz, 'A World Environmental Organization' (2002) 27 Columbia Journal of Environmental Law 323.

considerable attention prior to the 2002 World Summit on Sustainable Development (WSSD), but the WSSD declined to act; governments instead continued to support UNEP as the 'principal United Nations body in the field of the environment'. No new institution emerged from the meeting.

A new body did emerge from the 2012 Rio+20 conference. The Rio+20 outcome document, *The Future We Want*, shifted the focus of the international community further towards economic development and away from environmental protection, stating that 'eradicating poverty is the greatest global challenge facing the world today and an indispensable requirement for sustainable development' (para. 2). Consistent with this focus, the document placed greater emphasis than previously on international financial institutions, recognizing their contributions to sustainable development and the importance of cooperation among them and with the United Nations, in particular in mobilizing resources for sustainable development.[3]

Chapter IV of the outcome document specifically addressed the institutional framework for sustainable development, calling for international bodies to integrate the three dimensions of sustainable development (environmental, social and economic) in a balanced manner and to enhance implementation. As part of this mainstreaming effort, the participating states, while recognizing the preeminence of the UN General Assembly, decided to establish a universal intergovernmental high level political forum, to replace the widely-criticized Commission on Sustainable Development. The ambitious aims of the high level forum are set forth in paragraph 84 of the outcome document and affirmed in GA Res. 67/290 (Aug. 23, 2013): (a) provide political leadership, guidance, and recommendations for sustainable development; (b) enhance integration of the three dimensions of sustainable development in a holistic and cross-sectoral manner at all levels; (c) provide a dynamic platform for regular dialogue, and stocktaking and agenda setting; (d) ensure the appropriate consideration of new and emerging sustainable development challenges; (e) follow up and review progress in the implementation of sustainable development commitments contained in the outcomes of UN summits and conferences; (f) encourage high-level system-wide participation of UN bodies and multilateral financial and trade institutions, and treaty bodies; (g) improve cooperation and coordination within the UN system; (h) promote transparency and implementation through further enhancing the consultative role and participation of major groups and other relevant stakeholders; (i) promote the sharing of best practices and experiences, including successes, challenges, and

3 G.A. Res. 66/288 'The Future We Want', para. 54.

lessons learnt; (j) promote system-wide coherence and coordination of sustainable development policies; (k) strengthen the science-policy interface; and (l) enhance evidence-based decision-making and contribute to ongoing efforts of capacity-building for data collection and analysis in developing countries. UNEP in turn remained identified as the focus of environmental action.

In addition to the institutions emerging from the four UN Conferences, new institutions have been created as a result of concluding multilateral environmental agreements. Most major global and regional treaties establish a governing structure, generally consisting of a conference or meeting of the parties, a secretariat, and often a scientific and other subsidiary committee. While these institutions have taken on considerable importance, problems of coordination and duplication have been exacerbated, particularly among United Nations organs.

In addition to institutions created with a very specific environmental mandate, many other institutions are active in environmental matters, despite having a wider or even a different mandate, thus contributing to a key feature of global environmental governance: its fragmentation and decentralization. These include international organizations such as the World Health Organization (WHO), the World Meteorological Organization (WMO), the Food and Agriculture Organization (FAO) and the International Maritime Organization (IMO), just to name a few. While these organizations are not strictly speaking *environmental*, coordinating the efforts of States on certain environmental issues is essential to fulfil their respective mandates.

Finally, several non-state actors – such as private sector organizations, organizations from civil society, the scientific community and others – play a pivotal role in shaping the development of international environmental law and are key actors of global environmental governance.

The present Chapter addresses the governance structure of international environmental law and provides a comprehensive overview of the institutions and actors concerned with environmental protection.

1 Functions

There are many structural and functional parallels among international institutions that lead to similar and sometimes overlapping activities in addressing environmental protection.

1. *Research* plays a particularly important role in the activities of international organizations. While they rarely carry out their own scientific research, organizations often undertake comparative legal studies of

national or international measures prior to drafting international treaties, recommendations, directives, and model laws. In this regard the work of the FAO and the Organization for Economic Cooperation and Development (OECD) can be cited. Where research programs require scientific analysis, the member states often undertake the research, with international organizations coordinating the tasks delegated to one or more states and disseminating the results. In certain cases, institutions like the EU Commission may give financial assistance or may conclude research contracts with experts or groups, a practice also followed by United Nations Educational, Scientific and Cultural Organization (UNESCO) and the OECD.

2. *Exchange of information* based on national and international studies, research and projects is another important aspect of cooperation within and among international organizations. Nearly all international organizations concerned with environmental protection collect and exchange information with member states. Some international organizations also prepare a synthesis of information received. The synthesis may concern a given problem, such as reports prepared by the United Nations Economic Commission for Europe (UNECE), or may address the whole state of the environment, as does the annual report of the United Nations Environment Program.
3. *Regulatory functions* may be exercised by international organizations. Various bodies adopt new norms for member states, either recommendations or, more rarely, obligatory decisions or draft treaties. Many binding texts follow a common path before being adopted as international instruments, i.e., elaboration by a group of experts followed by submission to a diplomatic conference, without this necessarily leading to adherence by every member state.[4] Another means of standard-setting may occur when an environmental agreement creates its own supervisory or executive organ. In such instances, the organ is often given responsibility for elaborating rules for implementation or application of the treaty or for modification of existing norms, sometimes contained in detailed appendices. When such power is conferred, participating states generally maintain their right to object to the changes and thus to withhold acceptance of them. Some regulatory regimes are characterised by considerable complexity, as is the case with the Stratospheric Ozone treaty and its Montreal Protocol. Another notable example is provided by the climate change regime,

4 An example is the 1979 Bern Convention on Protection of Wildlife and Nature in Europe, developed within the Council of Europe and discussed in Chapter 8.

where the Conferences of the Parties (COPs) periodically adopt decisions that clarify the content and scope of the obligations contained in the initial treaty – the United Nations Framework Convention on Climate Change (UNFCCC) – and that sometimes result in binding agreements for the Contracting Parties, as in the case of the Paris Agreement.[5]

4. *Supervising implementation* of the norms generally does not extend to coercive action, such as policing the high seas to catch polluters, but such power may be granted either to the organization or, more commonly, to its member states. The use of such coercive measures may be increasing in respect to resources of the global commons. Article 24 of the Canberra Convention on the Conservation of Antarctic Marine Living Resources establishes an international system of 'observation and inspection'. The 1995 UN Convention on Straddling Stocks[6] also provides for boarding, inspecting, and even potential seizure of vessels illegally fishing in regulated high seas fishing areas. Supervision is much more commonly conducted, however, through reviews of periodic state reports about national implementation of international norms.
5. *Management of natural resources* by an international organization is the most ambitious measure of international cooperation in the field of environmental protection. Article V(2) of the 1957 Interim Convention on the Conservation of North-Pacific Fur Seals confers on its Commission power to recommend to states parties appropriate measures concerning the size, sex, and age composition of the seals taken each year. There is also a management system for mineral resource activities on the deep seabed created by Part XI of the 1982 United Convention on the Law of the Sea (UNCLOS), in which protection of the marine environment holds a high place. In fact, under Part XI of UNCLOS, the Parties established the International Seabed Authority, which is in charge with organizing and controlling activities in the Area, particularly with a view to administering its resources.[7] Shared natural resources are increasingly coming under international management agreements, such as those governing international fisheries, rivers, and lakes. Management of fish

5 Adoption of the Paris Agreement, Decision 1/CP.21, 12 December 2015, FCCC/CP/2015/L.9. See Chapter 12.

6 The full title is Agreement for the Implementation of the Provisions of the United Nations Convention on the Law of the Sea of Dec. 10, 1982 relating to the Conservation and Management of Straddling Fish Stocks and Highly Migratory Fish Stocks (Dec. 4, 1995). See Chapter 8.

7 United Nations Convention on the Law of the Sea (Dec. 10, 1982) (hereinafter UNCLOS) 1833 U.N.T.S. 397, part XI.

stocks is often ensured by international bodies created by treaties, such as the 2000 Convention on the Conservation and Management of Highly Migratory Fish Stocks in the Western and Central Pacific.[8] Similarly, international watercourses are often managed by basin organizations and commissions, which provide the riparian States with an institutional framework for interaction, exchange and cooperative activity.

2 Division of Tasks

Efforts to protect the environment impact most activities of public agencies and institutions, generating concerns about efficiency and conflicting norms or policies. Some allocation of authority arises naturally as a consequence of the specific functions and powers conferred upon each organization: the World Health Organization's mandate extends to problems affecting human health, the IMO is concerned with ocean pollution, and the Food and Agriculture Organization addresses problems of water and soil. At the same time, the treaty mandates of international organizations are often written in broad terms and permit many subject areas and powers to be implied.[9] The FAO considers fisheries within its food mandate, for which it must cooperate with UNEP and the IMO. The FAO also regulates pesticides and other hazardous chemicals. Coordination of the activities of international organizations with each other and with the growing number of treaty bodies established by international environmental agreements is difficult but essential.[10] The problem is similar to that faced by national governments in determining whether to grant an agency or organ primary responsibility over all aspects of environmental protection or whether a specific agency should simply coordinate the many and varied activities of other organs concerned with specific aspects of the issue. In the international field the last solution is the only one possible in the absence of a global environmental agency.

---

8 Convention on the Conservation and Management of Highly Migratory Fish Stocks in the Western and Central Pacific (Sept. 5 2000). For further discussion, see Chapter 8.

9 Henry G. Schermers & Niels Blokker, *International Institutional Law* (5th ed, Martinus Nijhoff 2011) 180, 184–6.

10 An example of synergetic relationship between COPs established by different treaties is provided by the cooperation between the Stockholm, Rotterdam and Basel Conventions. Decision SC-2/15 'Synergies' May 15, 2006, UNEP/POPS/COP.4/38; Decision RC-3/8 'Cooperation and Coordination between the Basel, Rotterdam and Stockholm Conventions' Jan. 5, 2007, UNEP/CHW.8/16.

Another potential basis for allocating responsibility is geographic. Certain environmental questions can be dealt with either on a global level, essentially by institutions within the United Nations system, on a regional basis by regional organizations, or, even on a sub-regional level, when a few states are concerned with the solution to a concrete problem of limited geographic scope. The latter include addressing the pollution of a watercourse or a lake, establishing protected areas in a border zone, and protecting endemic species of wild fauna or flora. The principle of subsidiarity, applied within the European Union, may be generalized to express a preference for decision-making at the lowest effective level of governance. Decisions made at a local level may be more likely to take account of local conditions and allow the participation of those directly affected. While the principle of subsidiarity will decentralize much decision-making, the requirement of effectiveness to resolve a problem will still require many regional and global regulations.

There follows a survey of the principal international organizations concerned with environmental matters. The primary focus is on the legal aspects of the organizations' environmental activities.

3 Global Organizations

Many environmental problems are recognized to affect the entire biosphere and call for measures to be taken by United Nations organs or specialized agencies. Several global non-governmental or mixed[11] organizations also undertake important activities in the field.

3.1 *The United Nations*

The United Nations became involved in environmental matters in 1968 when the General Assembly, upon a proposal by the Economic and Social Council, recommended convening what became the Stockholm Conference on the Human Environment.[12] Since then, the General Assembly has taken other major initiatives in the field of environmental protection. It created the United Nations Environment Program,[13] which changed its name to 'UN Environment'

11 Mixed organizations are those whose membership includes states as well as non-governmental entities or individuals.

12 G. A. Res. 2398 (XXIII), Dec. 3, 1968.

13 G. A. Res. 2995 on Institutional and Financial Arrangements for International Environmental Cooperation (establishing UNEP), Dec. 15, 1972.

in 2016, and the United Nations Development Program (UNDP);[14] it adopted the World Charter for Nature,[15] set up the Brundtland Commission,[16] and established, then replaced, the Commission on Sustainable Development.[17] It also convened the 1992 Rio Conference on Environment and Development,[18] the 2002 World Summit on Sustainable Development,[19] the 2012 Rio+20 Conference on Sustainable Development,[20] and the 2015 Sustainable Development Summit.[21] It has convened the negotiations of the UNFCCC,[22] the Convention on Drought and Desertification,[23] and the 1995 Fish Stocks Agreement.[24] It has adopted important treaties such as the 1997 UN Convention on the Law of the Non-navigational Uses of International Watercourses.[25] Finally, the General Assembly regularly adopts recommendations and resolutions with varying juridical or normative content, including its series of resolutions banning 'large-scale pelagic drift-net fishing; unauthorized fishing in zones of national jurisdiction; and fisheries by-catch and discards'. These resolutions included calls for minimizing pollution, waste, discards, catch by lost or abandoned gear, catch of non-target species and impacts on associated

14 G. A. Res. 2029 (XX) on Consolidation of the Special Fund and the Expanded Programme on Technical Assistance in United Nations Development Programme, Nov. 22, 1965.

15 G. A. Res. 37/7, Oct. 28, 1982.

16 G. A. Res. 38/161 on Process of Preparation of the Environmental Perspective to the Year 2000 and Beyond, Dec. 19, 1983.

17 G. A. Res. 47/49 on Institutional Arrangement to Follow up the UN Conference on Environment and Development (creating the Commission on Sustainable Development), Dec. 22, 1992.

18 G. A. Res. 44/228 on United Nations Conference on Environment and Development, Dec. 22, 1989.

19 G. A. Res. 55/199 on Ten-year review of progress achieved in the implementation of the outcome of the United Nations Conference on Environment and Development, Dec. 20, 2000.

20 G. A. Res. 64/236, Dec. 24, 2009.

21 G. A. Res. 68/6 on Outcome document of the special event to follow up efforts made towards achieving the Millennium Development Goals, Sept. 25, 2013.

22 G. A. Res. 45/212 on Protection of global climate for present and future generations of mankind, Dec. 21, 1990.

23 G. A. Res. 47/188 on the Establishment of an intergovernmental negotiating committee for the elaboration of an international convention to combat desertification in those countries experiencing serious drought and/or desertification, particularly in Africa, Dec. 22, 1992.

24 G. A. Res. 48/194 on United Nations Conference on Straddling Fish Stocks and Highly Migratory Fish Stocks, Dec. 21, 1993.

25 G. A. Res. 51/229, May 21, 1997.

or dependent species.[26] Other important resolutions have addressed climate change,[27] the protection of the marine environment,[28] the relationship between environment and development,[29] cooperation on shared natural resources,[30] and have declared a human right to safe drinking water and sanitation,[31] as well as the right to a clean, healthy and sustainable environment.[32]

Other UN bodies have also taken action. As a consequence of the Gulf War, the UN Security Council adopted a series of resolutions concerning the Iraqi occupation of Kuwait, some of which addressed the environmental consequences of the conflict. In Resolution 687(1991) the Security Council affirmed that Iraq '… is liable under international law for any direct loss, damage, including environmental damage and the depletion of natural resources …'[33] The Council also established a UN Compensation Commission in April 1991 to hear claims of environmental damage and depletion of natural resources caused by military activities.[34] In April 2007 the Security Council held its first debate on the impact of climate change on peace and security. While some speakers praised the initiative, there were reservations from developing countries, which saw climate change as a socio-economic development issue to be dealt with by the more widely representative General Assembly. Influenced by the debate, the General Assembly adopted two years later, in 2009, the

26 See e.g., G.A. Decision on Large-scale Pelagic Driftnet Fishing and its Impact on the Living Marine Resources of the World's Oceans and Seas, UN Resolutions 44/207 (Dec. 22, 1989), 45/197 (Dec. 21, 1990), 46/215 (Dec. 20,1991), 47/443 (Dec. 22, 1992); 48/445 (Dec. 21, 1993), 49/436 (Dec. 19, 1994), 50/25 (Dec. 5, 1995), 51/36 (Dec. 9, 1996), 52/29 (Nov. 26, 1997), 53/33 (Jan. 6, 1999). For further discussion, see Chapter 8.

27 See, e.g., A/RES/43/53 of 6 Dec. 1988, A/RES/54/222 of 22 Dec. 1999, A/RES/61/201 of 20 Dec. 2006, A/RES/62/86 of 10 Dec. 2007, A/RES/62/32 of 26 Nov. 2008, A/RES/64/73 of 7 Dec. 2009 and A/RES/65/159 of 4 March 2011, A/RES/66/200 of 22 Dec. 2011, A/RES/67/210 of 21 Dec. 2012, A/RES/68/212 of 20 Dec. 2013, A/RES/69/220 of 19 Dec. 2014, A/RES/70/205 of 22 Dec. 2015, A/RES/71/228 of 21 Dec. 2016, A/RES/72/219 of 20 Dec. 2017, A/RES/73/232 of 20 Dec. 2018, A/RES/74/219 of 19 Dec. 2019, A/RES/75/217 of 21 Dec. 2020, A/RES/76/205 of 17 Dec. 2021, A/RES/77/165 of 14 Dec. 2022, A/RES/78/153 of 19 Dec. 2023. See also G. A. Res. 77/276 on the Request for an advisory opinion of the International Court of Justice on the obligations of States in respect of climate change, March 29, 2023.

28 See e.g. G.A. Res. 2566 (XXIV) on Promoting effective measures for the prevention and control of marine pollution, Dec. 13, 1969.

29 See e.g. G. A. Res. 2849 (XXVI) on Development and environment, Dec. 20, 1971.

30 See e.g. G. A. Res. 3129 (XXIX) on Co-operation in the field of the environment concerning natural resources shared by two or more States, No. 22, 1974.

31 G. A. Res. 64/292 on The Human Right to Water and Sanitation, July 28, 2010.

32 G. A. Res. 76/300 on The human right to a clean, healthy and sustainable environment, July 28, 2022.

33 UN Security Council Res. 687 (1991) (April 8, 1991).

34 See Chapter 16.

Resolution 63/281, 'Climate Change and its possible Security Implications'.[35] General Assembly Resolution 63/281 recognized the respective responsibilities of the principal organs of the United Nations. These included the primary responsibility for the maintenance of international peace and security conferred upon the Security Council and the responsibility for sustainable development issues, including climate change, conferred upon the General Assembly and the Economic and Social Council. In 2011, the UN Security Council held its second thematic debate on 'Maintenance of international peace and security: the impact of climate change'.[36] This debate concluded with a Presidential Statement from the Security Council which, among other issues, recognized the responsibility for climate change and other sustainable development issues conferred upon the General Assembly and ECOSOC and reaffirmed the UNFCCC as the key instrument for addressing climate change. At the same time, it noted that the context of climate change was relevant to the Security Council's responsibility for international peace and security. A further discussion took place in 2015, on the role of climate change as a threat multiplier for global security and on the problems of small island states, and another one took place in 2018 on 'Understanding and addressing climate-related security risks'.[37] These debates highlighted the security dimensions of climate change, but also revealed the divisions among states about which institutions are most appropriate for addressing the issue.

3.1.1 United Nations Environment Program (UNEP)

The United Nations General Assembly created UNEP, which changed its name to 'UN Environment' in 2016, by Resolution 2997 (XXVII) of December 15, 1972 as a subsidiary body. UNEP's secretariat is the central organ of action and coordination for environmental matters within the United Nations system as well as for regional organizations outside the United Nations. Its role is generally that of a catalyst for action by other institutions. It studies environmental problems and elaborates programs, but implementation is undertaken by the United Nations as a whole, with the aid, if appropriate, of regional governmental and non-governmental organizations as well as individual states. Specific

35 G. A. Res. 63/281 on Climate change and its possible security implications, June 11, 2009.

36 UN Security Council 'Maintenance of peace and security. Impact of climate change' (July 20, 2011). On the impact of climate change on peace and security, see also UN Security Council Res. 2349 (2017) (March 31, 2017).

37 UN Security Council 'Understanding and addressing climate-related security risks' (July 11, 2018).

projects are encouraged by utilizing the Environment Fund[38] to contribute to the cost of the program or operation. Persuasion, based on information relating to environmental threats, is another means of stimulating action.

The outcome document of the Rio+20 meeting expressed commitment to strengthening the role of UNEP as the leading global environmental authority that sets the global environmental agenda, promotes the coherent implementation of the environmental dimension of sustainable development, and serves as an authoritative advocate for the global environment. The document invited the United Nations General Assembly, in its 67th Session, to adopt a Resolution strengthening and upgrading UNEP by establishing universal membership in UNEP's Governing Council. The outcome document also requested more financial resources for UNEP and an increased mandate.[39]

In response to the recommendations, member states formally called on the UN General Assembly to transform UNEP's Governing Council, its 58-member governing body, to make it a United Nations Environment Assembly of the United Nations Environment Program with universal membership. In March 2013, General Assembly Resolution 67/251 formally approved the establishment of the United Nations Environment Assembly (UNEA).[40] All United Nations member and observer states and other stakeholders participate in discussions and decision-making on issues that affect the state of the environment and global sustainability.

UNEA has the mandate to take strategic decisions, provide political guidance for UNEP's work, and promote a strong science-policy interface. Supported by a 10-member bureau, UNEA meets biennially in Nairobi and concludes with a two-day high-level segment that serves to replace the Global Ministerial Environment Forum, convened since 2000 alongside the Governing Council sessions. Where appropriate, UNEA can also recommend draft resolutions for adoption at the United Nations General Assembly. A subsidiary inter-sessional body called an 'open-ended Committee of Permanent Representatives' (CPR) provides policy advice to its governing body, contributes to the preparation of the agenda and decisions to be adopted by UNEA and oversees their implementation. The UN Secretary-General appoints the Executive Director of

38 The operational financing of UNEP comes from the general United Nations budget but specific UNEP actions are financed by the Environment Fund, established by G. A. Res. 2997(XXVII). States make voluntary contributions, which vary considerably over time, to the Fund.

39 G. A. Res. 67/251 on Change of the designation of the Governing Council of the United Nations Environment Programme, March 13, 2013.

40 ibid.

UNEP, who heads the staff, most of them based at the headquarters in Nairobi. UNEP also has regional bureaus around the world.

One of the first issues taken up by the UNEA at its inaugural session in June 2014 was the environmental rule of law. Violations of environmental law were seen to undermine the achievement of all dimensions of sustainable development and environmental sustainability. A Global Symposium on Environmental Rule of Law invited Chief Justices, Attorneys General, Judges, Chief prosecutors, Auditors General, leading legal scholars, practitioners and experts to discuss the ways and means by which the further development and implementation of the environmental rule of law can help ensure just and sustainable development outcomes, including adequate and implementable laws, access to justice and information, public participation, accountability, transparency, liability for environmental damage, fair and just enforcement, and human rights.

UNEP's mandate as far as the management of the environment is concerned includes the regulation of human activities that have any measurable impact on the environment and has led it to play a major role in the development of international environmental law. First, UNEP developed its program on regional seas. The program has drafted treaties and action plans for different maritime regions of the world in order to combat pollution and contribute to the best management of the environment as a whole in the regulated areas.[41] Second, UNEP provides the secretariat of important multilateral environmental conventions, including the 1973 Washington Convention on the International Trade of Endangered Species, the 1979 Bonn Convention on the Conservation of Migratory species of Wild Animals, the 1985 Vienna ozone treaty and its 1987 Montreal Protocol, the 1989 Basel Convention on Transboundary Movements of Hazardous Wastes, the 1992 Convention on Biodiversity, and the 1994 Convention on Desertification. UNEP activities thus have global dimensions and include a large range of tasks.

A third activity devoted to the development of international environmental law is the Montevideo Program begun in 1982.The Program provides a framework for most of UNEP's normative activities and has led to the creation of a special unit dedicated to promoting environmental law. The Environmental Law Unit prepares draft treaties which are reviewed and revised by ad hoc expert working groups. Drafts are then submitted to the Governing Council (now Assembly) for debate and adoption or UNEP may convene a diplomatic conference to adopt the text, as it did with the 1985 Vienna Convention for the

---

41 See Chapter 11.

Protection of the Ozone Layer and the 1987 Montreal Protocol on Substances that Deplete the Ozone Layer. Over the last fifty years more than forty multilateral environmental treaties have been negotiated under UNEP's guidance, including, *inter alia*, the 1973 Washington Convention on the International Trade in Endangered Species, the 1989 Basel Convention on the Control of Transboundary Movements of Hazardous Wastes, the 1992 Convention on Biological Diversity, the 1994 Paris Convention to Combat Desertification in those Experiencing Serious Drought and/or Desertification particularly in Africa, the 2000 Biosafety Protocol, the 2001 POPs Convention, the 2003 Carpathians Convention, the 2010 Nagoya Protocol, the 2013 Minamata Mercury Convention, as well as the regional seas treaty systems. In co-operation with FAO, UNEP facilitated the development of the 1998 Convention on the Prior Informed Consent Procedure for Certain Hazardous Chemicals and Pesticides in International Trade. It provided substantive support and expertise for the development of sub-regional treaties such as the Agreement on the Action Plan for the Environmentally Sound Management of the Common Zambezi River System and for the Lusaka Agreement on Cooperative Enforcement Operations Directed at Illegal Trade in Fauna and Flora. In 2024, UNEP is mid-way through its fifth Montevideo program for law.

UNEP has been active also in the development of non-binding instruments in the field of the environment. The Governing Council of UNEP or intergovernmental meetings convened by UNEP adopted such instruments as the Principles of Conduct in the Field of the Environment for the Guidance of States in the Conservation and Harmonious Utilization of Natural Resources Shared by Two or More States; the Conclusions of the Study of Legal Aspects concerning the Environment Related to Offshore Mining and Drilling within the Limits of National Jurisdiction; the Montreal Guidelines for the Protection of the Marine Environment Against Pollution from Land-Based Resources; the Cairo Guidelines and Principles for the Environmentally Sound Management of Hazardous Wastes; the Goals and Principles of Environmental Impact Assessment; the London Guidelines for the Exchange of Information on Chemicals in International Trade; the Code of Ethics on the International Trade in Chemicals; the Global Program of Action for the Protection of the Marine Environment from Land-based Activities; and the International Technical Guidelines for Safety in Biotechnology.

Finally, UNEP assists governments of developing countries with drafting national environmental laws and with training judges[42] on the enforcement of

---

42 UNITAR, the United Nations Institute for Training and Research, has also conducted numerous training programs in international environmental law directed at government officials including judges.

international environmental norms. Through its activities, UNEP has exerted a marked influence on the development of environmental protection throughout the world.

3.1.2 Commission on Sustainable Development and High-Level Political Forum

The United Nations General Assembly created the Commission on Sustainable Development (CSD) as a functional commission of the Economic and Social Council (ECOSOC) following UNCED.[43] It was composed of fifty-three UN member states serving three-year terms, with its activities funded through the UN's regular budget. The CSD was set up to examine progress in implementing Agenda 21 at the national, regional and international levels, explicitly guided by the principles of the Rio Declaration. In could make recommendations through ECOSOC to the General Assembly. At its first session in 1993, the CSD adopted a framework program for nine areas. Five related to economic development and related procedures were considered on an annual basis. Environmental matters were relegated to a three-year cycle. Criticism of the CSD grew as its impact was seen to be minimal in its first ten years of existence. Some accused the CSD of becoming an avenue of complaint or reconsideration for governments unhappy with the decisions or outcomes of discussions in meetings of environmental treaty bodies.

At the 2012 Rio+20 conference, participating states decided to replace the CSD with a high-level political forum on sustainable development. The new forum convenes Heads of State and Government every four years, under the auspices of the UN General Assembly, to promote the implementation of sustainable development and address new challenges. The first session convened by the General Assembly met in September 2013. Each meeting is intended to produce a negotiated declaration to provide policy guidance for action and more effective results. The high-level forum also meets annually for three days at the ministerial level, under the auspices of ECOSOC. As one of its most important functions, the High- Level Political Forum is the central UN platform for the follow-up and review of the 2030 Agenda for Sustainable Development adopted at the United Nations Sustainable Development Summit on September 25, 2015. Since then, UN Member States have been reviewing the format and organizational aspects of the High-Level Political Forum and, in June 2021, the UN General Assembly has adopted Resolution 75/290 B, outlining the scope of the remainder of the High-Level Political Forum's mandate.[44]

43 G. A. Res. 47/191 on Institutional arrangements to follow up the United Nations Conference on Environment and Development, Dec. 22, 1992.

44 G. A. Res. 75/290 B, June 30, 2021.

3.1.3 International Law Commission

The thirty-four member International Law Commission (ILC), established by the United Nations General Assembly,[45] was created to undertake the codification and progressive development of international law. Within its mandate it has considered issues of international environmental law since its early work on the law of the sea.[46] A survey of its work program in 1971 reflected emerging ecological views, stating that greater attention would have to be paid in the future to problems of protecting the environment.[47] Entering the 1990s, a large number of subjects on the agenda of the ILC directly involved the development and codification of international environmental law. In 1997, the Commission submitted to the UN General Assembly a draft Convention on the Non-Navigational Uses of International Watercourses, a treaty that the General Assembly adopted on May 21, 1997.[48] In 2001 the ILC completed work on its articles on the law of state responsibility and presented its draft to the General Assembly.[49] The ILC has long distinguished the issue of state responsibility for wrongful conduct from the issue of international liability for injurious consequences arising out of acts not prohibited by international law.[50] The major focus of the latter study, which started in 1978, became transboundary environmental harm. In 2001, the ILC completed Draft articles on Prevention of Transboundary Harm from Hazardous Activities.[51] The General Assembly requested the ILC to resume consideration of the liability aspects of the topic 'bearing in mind the interrelationship between prevention and liability, and taking into account the developments in international law and comments by Governments'.[52] The ILC draft on prevention of harm recommended that a convention be adopted on the topic, something not done in the articles on state responsibility. Other environmental issues taken up in recent years include international aquifers, shared natural resources, sea-level rise in

---

45 G. A. Res. 174(II), Nov. 21, 1947.

46 See Stephen C. McCaffrey, 'The Work of the International Law Commission Relating to the Environment' (1983) 11 Ecol. L. Q. 189.

47 A/CN.4/245, II-2 YBINT'L L COMM'N 1100 (1971).

48 UN Doc. A/51/869, 36 I.L.M. 700 (1997).

49 Draft Articles on Responsibility of States for Internationally Wrongful Acts, in Report of the International Law Commission on the Work of Its Fifty-third Session, UNGAOR, 56th Sess., Supp. No. 10, at 45, U.N. Doc. A/56/10 (2001), approved by the General Assembly in G. A. Res. 56/83, Dec. 12, 2001. For a history of the ILC's work and commentary on the articles, see James Crawford, *The ILC's Articles on State Responsibility* (Cambridge University Press 2002).

50 International Law Commission, A/CN.4/450, April 5, 1993.

51 See Report of the ILC, United Nations 53rd Sess. at 370 (2001), UN Doc. A/56/10 (2001).

52 G. A. Res. 56/82 of Dec. 12, 2001.

relation to international law, protection of the atmosphere and protection of the environment during armed conflicts.

3.1.4 UNECE

The UN Economic and Social Council created the Economic Commission for Europe in 1947, in the perspective of postwar European reconstruction. Since the 1950s, UNECE has been active in questions concerning the environment, even though this was not its initial aim. It supplies governments with analyses and economic, technological and statistical information. Its method of work is to assemble experts, prepare and publish analyses and statistics and organize exchanges of technical information. In appropriate cases it elaborates texts announcing action principles or draft conventions. UNECE then submits such drafts to diplomatic conferences for adoption.

UNECE first addressed an environmental problem in 1956 when its committee on transportation examined the issue of water pollution during its work on inland navigable waterways. Over time, other committees also faced questions of environmental deterioration. In 1963, the committee on coal production took up the problem of air pollution by coal factories, after which the committee on electric energy became interested in pollution caused by heating plants and thermal pollution of inland waters. In 1967, it looked at environmental protection for the first time in a larger perspective, leading to a 1969 decision that intergovernmental cooperation in the environmental field should constitute one of the four principal objectives of the organization's overall waste program.

The Committee on Environmental Policy plays a key role within UNECE as do the Ministers of Environment who regularly meet in the framework of the Ministerial Conferences on Environment for Europe. The Conference of 1995, held in Sofia, adopted a Pan-European Biological and Landscape Strategy which envisages five-year Action Plans to provide a framework for a common European response to the Convention on Biodiversity. The Strategy entrusts the Committee on Environmental Policy with specific tasks to assess and report on progress made in the implementation of an Environmental Program for Europe.

International conventions elaborated within UNECE have made important contributions to the development of environmental law. One of the first environmental agreements adopted by UNECE, in 1958, concerned uniform standards and recognition of standards for equipment and parts for motor vehicles and included, in an annex, norms concerning polluting gasoline emissions. Another 1958 agreement, relating to international road transport of dangerous merchandise, acted to prevent soil and water pollution. The most important conventions drafted in the context of UNECE are the 1979 Convention on Long-range Transboundary Air Pollution and its Protocols, the 1991 Convention on Environmental Impact Assessment in a Transboundary Context, the 1992 Convention on Transboundary Effects of Industrial Accidents, the 1992 Convention on the Protection and Use of Transboundary Watercourses and International Lakes, and the 1998 Convention on Access to Information, Public Participation in Decision-Making and Access to Justice in Environmental Matters. The five conventions have been supplemented by a number of protocols, including the Protocol on Water and Health, the Protocol on Strategic Environmental Assessment, the Protocol on Pollutant Release and Transfer Registers, and the Protocol on Civil Liability and Compensation for Damage Caused by the Transboundary Effects of Industrial Accidents on Transboundary Waters (not in force).

3.1.5 Other UN Bodies

Another institutional child of UNCED is the High Level Advisory Board on Sustainable Development. The twenty-one members were appointed in July 1993 by the UN Secretary General. The Board formulates policy proposals and identifies emerging issues for the attention of relevant intergovernmental bodies, particularly the Commission on Sustainable Development and the Economic and Social Council. Many of its members are environmental experts. The UN also created an Inter-Agency Committee on Sustainable Development, made up of nine members, representing UNEP, FAO, the International Atomic Energy Agency (IAEA), the International Labor Organization (ILO), UNDP, UNESCO, WHO, WMO, and the World Bank.[53] Established in October 1992, it is one of the main bodies concerned with implementing Agenda 21, ensuring cooperation and coordination within the United Nations. It is charged with allocating competence and tasks within the system, as well as with evaluating financial and material needs. It is the link between technical UN working groups and agency heads. Its role is to prepare policy recommendations to improve cooperation and coordination among different UN organs. Its two initial sub-committees (the Sub-committee on Water Resources and the Sub-committee on Oceans and Coastal Areas) were replaced in 2003 by two organizations: UN Oceans and UN Water.

Other organs of the United Nations addressed the environment as the issue became integrated throughout the system. The former Human Rights Commission and Sub-Commission on Human Rights took up environmental issues

53 G. A. Res. 47/191, para. 25.

in the late 1980s. In 1988 the Sub-Commission first considered the relationship between the environment and human rights, in the context of the trans-boundary movement of toxic and dangerous products and wastes. It adopted a resolution referring to the right of all peoples to life and the right of future generations to enjoy their environmental heritage. It called for a ban on the export of toxic and dangerous wastes and a global convention on that subject. As discussed in detail in Chapter 15, before their demise, the Commission and Sub-Commission added to their agendas topics related to human rights and the environment, appointing a special rapporteur to undertake a study of the relationship of human rights and the environment, the impact on human rights of international movements of toxic and hazardous substances, the right to food, and the right to water.[2] The Human Rights Committee (HRC), established under the 1966 International Covenant on Civil and Political Rights (ICCPR) and the Committee on Economic, Social and Cultural Rights (CESCR), established under the International Covenant on Economic, Social and Cultural Rights (ICESCR) have addressed several matters at the interface of environmental protection and the protection and promotion of human rights. For instance, in November 2002, the CESCR issued a General Comment recognizing access to safe drinking water and sanitation as a human right.[54] Similarly, the Human Rights Council and the Office of the High Commissioner for Human Rights (OHCHR) have contributed in a significant way to the development of the environment/human rights interface, most notably on the issue of the recognition of the right to a clean, healthy and sustainable environment as a human right (see Chapter 15).

Finally, the work of the United Nations Development Program is increasingly concerned with environmental issues. Created in 1965 to administer technical assistance for developing countries, it has now incorporated principles of sustainable development throughout its program. In response to Agenda 21, UNDP created the Sustainable Energy and Environment Division which consolidated into one office all the operations at UNDP headquarters with responsibility for environmental issues. The mandate of the Division is 'to help developing countries successfully design and carry out programs which integrate the protection and regeneration of the environment and the use of natural resources to reduce poverty, generate sustainable livelihoods, and advance the status of women'. The Division therefore seeks to ensure that all aspects of UNDP's activities are considered from an environmental perspective. In the area of energy and the environment, UNDP's work is supported by

54 UN Committee on Economic, Social and Cultural Rights, General Comment No 15 (Nov. 26, 2002).

the Environment and Energy Thematic Trust Fund. The UNDP participates in the management of a number of programs and institutions, such as the UN-REDD Porgramme and the Global Environment Facility (GEF).

3.2 *UNESCO*

The mandate of the United Nations Education, Science and Culture Organization (UNESCO) may appear rather far from matters concerned with the environment. However, influenced by public opinion concerned with ecological problems, UNESCO launched the Man and Biosphere Program (MAB) in 1970, commissioning a study on the interactions between man and the environment. Fourteen principal themes were included in the framework of this project, including the impact of human activities on different sectors of the environment and the conservation of natural areas and the genetic resources they contain. A 'world bank' of biosphere reserves was proposed and adopted with the aim of conserving and utilizing resources, including characteristic examples of ecosystems and human habitats. One of the objectives of the biosphere reserves is to establish management models of space and water, combining the satisfaction of human needs with the necessities of conservation. In 2016, under the MAB Program, the Lima Action Plan for UNESCO's Man and the Biosphere Program and its World Network of Biosphere Reserves 2016–2025 were adopted. As of 2024, 748 sites have been recognized as biosphere reserves in 134 countries, with 23 transboundary sites. UNESCO has incorporated the World Network of Biosphere Reserves into two non-binding instruments: the Seville Strategy and the Statutory Framework.

UNESCO also has elaborated two major global conventions, the Ramsar Convention on Wetlands of International Importance and the 1972 World Cultural and Natural Heritage Convention. As of late 2024, 1199 properties were on the World Heritage list established by the World Heritage Convention, including more than 227 natural and 39 mixed natural and cultural sites; 48 sites are transboundary. Other UNESCO treaties touch upon environmental issues, such as the 2001 Convention on Underwater Cultural Heritage and the 1954 Convention for the Protection of Cultural Property in the Event of Armed Conflict.

3.3 *Food and Agriculture Organization (FAO)*

According to its statute, signed October 16, 1945, the mission of FAO is to promote investment in agriculture, promote better soil and water management, improve yields of crops and livestock, incite the transfer of technology to, and the development of, agricultural research in developing countries.[55] It is not

55 FAO Constitution, Art. I.

surprising, therefore, to find it concerned with the conservation of natural resources. The mandate of the FAO Commission on Plant Genetic Resources, for example, includes all components of biodiversity relevant to food and agriculture, including animal, plant, forestry and fishery genetic resources.[56]

Representatives of members meet at the biennial FAO Conference to review global governance policy issues and international frameworks, as well as to evaluate work carried out and to approve the budget for the next biennium. The Conference elects Council Members, to serve three-year rotating terms to carry out executive oversight of programs and budgetary activities. The Conference also elects a Director-General to a four-year term of office, renewable once. FAO is composed of eight departments: (i) Agriculture and Consumer Protection; (ii) Climate, biodiversity, land and water department; (iii) Economic and Social Development; (iv) Fisheries and Aquaculture; (v) Forestry; (vi) Corporate Services, Human Resources and Finance; (vii) Technical Cooperation; and (viii) Programme management. Since 1996, the FAO has added five regional and nine sub-regional offices as part of a restructuring and decentralization. The principal duty of the offices is to assist countries in the region to reinforce their agricultural sectors.

The FAO has contributed significantly to the development of international environmental law. Even before the Stockholm Conference, it adopted measures to protect fisheries and plants from environmental harm. Later it drafted the 1981 World Soil Charter[57] (which was later revised in 2015), the 1985 International Code of Conduct on the Distribution and Use of Pesticides (updated in 2013 and renamed 'International Code of Conduct on Pesticide Management'), and the 1993 Agreement to Promote Compliance with International Conservation and Management Measures by Fishing Vessels on the High Seas.[58] On November 3, 2001, it completed and opened for signature the International Treaty on Plant Genetic Resources for Food and Agriculture. The FAO also participated in drafting other international texts, for example the 1976 Barcelona Convention for the Protection of the Mediterranean, and its Protocols, the 1987 London Guidelines for the Exchange of Information on Chemicals in International Trade, the 1995 Code of Conduct for Responsible Fisheries prepared by the Committee on Fisheries and approved by the FAO Conference (Resolution 4/95), the 1998 Convention on the Prior Consent Procedure for certain Hazardous Chemicals and Pesticides in International Trade, and the 2013 Global Plan of Action for the Conservation, Sustainable Use and Development of Forest Genetic Resources. Often, it cooperates with UNEP in the drafting or updating

56 Resolution 3/95 of the FAO Conference.

57 FAO Doc. C81/27, October 1981, reprinted in 8 E.P.L. 63 (1982).

58 33 I.L.M. 968 (1994).

of such texts. The Codex Alimentarius establishing food standards is the result of cooperation between FAO and WHO. In 2007, all 119 countries at FAO's Committee on Fisheries in Rome agreed on a proposal to develop a legally binding measure to tackle illegal, unreported and unregulated fishing practices.

The FAO is the source of domestic legislation in numerous countries, above all developing ones, regarding agriculture, forests, fishing and soil conservation, subjects closely linked to environmental protection. For this purpose, the FAO publishes a series of legislative studies that contain national and international legal texts, for example on the law of water, fishing regulations, and evaluations of the environmental impact of agricultural development. Food security is a major issue and in 1996 the FAO issued Legislative Study No. 59, entitled The Legal Framework for Food Security.

The working methods of FAO enhance the role of environmental considerations in its projects. On the one hand, states or parties are assisted by the collection and dissemination of information, the opinions of experts, training courses and the implementation of pilot projects. On the other hand, FAO supports the integrated development of agriculture, including monitoring of soil, inventory of water resources, development of hydrographic basins, and implementation of particularly adapted agricultural systems. An example of the work of FAO's legal office is the technical assistance provided to the Lake Chad Basin Commission. The office prepared a draft agreement on water utilization and conservation in the Lake Chad Basin. Article IV of the draft requires states to take every reasonable measure to ensure the conservation of the water resources of the Basin, maintain their natural flow and quality, prevent their misuse, waste or pollution, and plan and implement projects conducive to the integrated development of the Basin.[59]

In 2013, the Reviewed Strategic Framework of the FAO was adopted, and included several new environmental strategic objectives, such as increasing and improving the provision of goods and services from agriculture, forestry and fisheries in a sustainable manner and enabling more inclusive and efficient agricultural and food systems at local, national and international levels.[60]

3.4 *World Health Organization* (WHO)

Given its name, it is not surprising that the principal mandate of the World Health Organization, created July 22, 1946, is international cooperation in the interests of human health. By virtue of Article 2 of its Constitution, the WHO has, in particular, the task of seeking to eliminate epidemic, endemic and other

59 International Law Commission, U.N. Doc. A/CN.4/412 Add 1, 30.

60 FAO, 'Reviewed Strategic Framework', C2013/7 (June 2013).

illnesses, and improve housing and hospitals. All these objectives are linked to environmental protection. As such, the WHO collects and disseminates information, publishes manuals and guides, furnishes technical assistance, organizes courses and seminars, establishes centers for information, conducts research, and monitors particular pollutants harmful to health.

The WHO developed a Global Strategy for Health and Environment as a response to Agenda 21. Implementation of the Strategy is guided by action plans for WHO's programs, including The Program for the Promotion of Environmental Health and the Program for the Promotion of Chemical Safety. The problem of the supply of drinking water is a crucial issue of concern to the WHO and it requires a favorable environmental context. WHO has established a Community Water Supply and Sanitation Unit to monitor and report on progress in improving health in this sector. It also has drafted Guidelines for Drinking Water Quality, whose fourth edition was published in 2022. The WHO has a Food Safety Program concerned with protecting human health from unsafe or potentially unsafe food through the prevention of health hazards associated with biological and chemical contamination and additives, and has adopted several resolutions on the matter.[61] WHO with FAO established the Codex Alimentarius Commission to implement a joint FAO/WHO Food Standards Program. Its current membership represents over 98 per cent of the world's population. The Prevention of Environmental Pollution Unit of WHO's Division of Environmental Health provides support to member states in the development of national programs for control of environmental health hazards, whether chemical, physical, or biological and monitors environmental quality and human exposure.

In the field of law, the WHO has established binding and non-binding health standards. On December 8, 1989, a WHO regional conference of ministers of health and environment concluded a European Charter on the Environment and Health.[62] The Charter, recognizing that a clean and harmonious environment exercises a beneficial influence on health and well-being, provides that every individual is entitled to an environment conducive to the highest attainable level of health and well-being, to information and consultation on the state of the environment and on plans, decisions and activities likely to affect both the environment and health, and to participation in the decision-making process. In turn, every individual has a responsibility to contribute to the protection of the environment, in the interests of his or her own health and the health of others. The Charter adopts as a preferred approach 'prevention is

61 WHO Res WHA63.3 'Advancing food safety initiatives' (20 May 2010); WHO Res. WHA73.5 'Strengthening efforts on food safety' (Aug. 3, 2020).

62 WHO Doc. ICP/RUD 113/Conf.Doc./1, reprinted in 20 EPL 57 (1990).

better than cure', application of which requires that new policies, technologies and initiatives should be adopted only after prior assessment demonstrating that they will have no negative impact on the environment and health. The Charter also provides that environmental standards should be constantly revised in light of new knowledge relating to the environment and health as well as new economic conditions. Further, it is necessary to apply the 'polluter-pays' principle, whereby any public or private entity causing or likely to cause damage to the environment is financially responsible for preventive or restorative measures. To implement these principles, the Charter calls for clearly defined responsibility, adoption and application of norms, standards, and strategies based upon the best scientific evidence, and elaboration of emergency plans regarding environmental accidents.

In 2003 the WHO sponsored an Anti-Tobacco Convention which, although its principal aim is health, has obvious consequences for air pollution, particularly in contained environments. The WHO also collects, edits, and disseminates information, particularly through the trimestral publication 'International Digest of Health Legislation'.

Starting in 2008, the WHO has been engaged in addressing the impacts of climate change on human health. On May 24, 2008, a Resolution was adopted on the matter, highlighting, among other things, the importance of working 'on promoting consideration of the health impacts of climate change by the relevant United Nations bodies in order to help developing countries to address the health impacts of climate change'.[63] A number of initiatives have been introduced and workplans adopted, focusing *inter alia* on the health impacts of climate change in vulnerable countries, in particular small island developing states.

3.5 *World Meteorological Organization* (*WMO*)

Created in 1947, the WMO aims to establish a system of monitoring and rapid exchange of meteorological information, standardize observations, encourage applications of meteorological science, including prediction and modification of weather, and encourage and coordinate research. These activities permit the observation of pollution and its persistence in the atmosphere. In addition, the WMO is clearly placed to assess reduction in the stratospheric ozone layer. Overall, the WMO is particularly equipped to undertake global monitoring. It actively participated in the creation of a world system of continuous monitoring of the environment (GEMS). The legal office of the WMO has contributed

63 WHO Res. WHA61.19 'Climate change and health' (May 24, 2008).

to the elaboration of international instruments on artificial weather modification, protection of the ozone layer, and long-range atmospheric pollution.

In 1988, the WMO and UNEP jointly established the Intergovernmental Panel on Climate Change (IPCC), charged with providing scientific, technical and socio-economic advice on all issues related to climate change (see Chapter 12). On the issue of climate change, the WMO operates a number of programs, such as the World Climate Programme, the World Climate Research Programme, the Global Atmospheric Watch Programme, and the Disaster Risk Reduction Programme.[64] The World Climate Programme, in particular, supports the Global Climate Observing System, co-sponsored with UNESCO's International Oceanographic Commission, UNEP and the International Council for Science.

3.6 *International Atomic Energy Agency* (IAEA)

The IAEA was created in 1956 in order to hasten and increase 'the contribution of atomic energy to peace, health and prosperity in the entire world'. Its functions also include the task of establishing and overseeing implementation of norms designed to protect health and reduce to a minimum the dangers to which persons and property are exposed from radiation. Thus, for projects which the Agency assists or for any other arrangement where interested parties invite the Agency to apply its standards, the Agency seeks to ensure that the projects conform to its norms and it can require application of any safety measures it prescribes.

As discussed in more detail in Chapter 13, the Agency adopts norms for nuclear safety and codes of proper procedure which it proposes to member states, including radioactive waste management. It has adopted guidelines for monitoring and preventing radiological contamination of personnel and the environment, safe handling and the transport of radioactive materials, treatment and disposal of radioactive wastes, and containment and safety of nuclear power plants. In 1961, it published a regulation on transportation of radioactive materials which has been revised several times. In 1984 it proposed directives for the conclusion of arrangements between member states for mutual emergency assistance in case of nuclear accident or radioactive crisis. However, not all nuclear states have fully implemented these directives, which as recommendations are not legally binding. In fact, only one

64 These programs are in addition to the World Weather Watch Programme, which was established in 1963.

of the recommended arrangements was signed, providing for mutual assistance between the Nordic countries in case of accidents implying radioactive damage.[65]

After the Chernobyl nuclear accident of April 26, 1986,[66] the IAEA was asked to examine the consequences of Chernobyl and furnish the framework necessary to elaborate international standards regarding future accidents having international implications. Two international conventions, one on Early Notification of a Nuclear Accident, the other on Assistance in the Case of Nuclear Accident or Radiological Emergency were adopted September 26, 1986 by the IAEA general conference meeting in extraordinary session. The organization continues to be involved in standard-setting and in verification of nuclear safeguards. The latter role has become particularly important with concerns about international terrorism and in response to the 2011 Fukushima accident. The impact of nuclear accidents on the environment has become the object of several initiatives, such as the establishment if the IAEA Task Force created to conduct a safety review of Japan's discharge of treated water into the sea at the Fukushima Daiichi Nuclear Power Station.

Over the years, several treaties were concluded under the auspices of the IAEA, including the Convention on Nuclear Safety, the Joint Convention on the Safety of Spent Fuel Management and on the Safety of Radioactive Waste Management, the Convention on the Physical Protection of Nuclear Material, the Convention on Supplementary Compensation for Nuclear Damage, as well as a number of regional agreements on technical cooperation.

3.7 *International Maritime Organization* (IMO)

In 1948 states meeting at an international conference in Geneva agreed to establish an institution for the regulation of international commercial navigation. The founding treaty entered into force in 1958 and the new organization, originally called the International Maritime Consultative Organization, met for the first time the following year. The IMO's first important responsibility was safety at sea and it adopted a number of legal instruments on this topic, most importantly, the 1960 International Convention for the Safety of Life at Sea (SOLAS).[67] By the late 1960s, however, the increasing amount of oil being

65 IAEA Doc. INFCIRC/310 'Guidelines for mutual emergency assistance arrangements in connection with a nuclear accident or radiological emergency' (Jan. 1984).

66 See Chapter 13.

67 June 17, 1960, replaced Nov. 1, 1974. The first version of the SOLAS Convention was adopted in 1914, in response to the Titanic disaster, the second in 1929, the third in 1948 and the fourth in 1960. The 1960 Convention was the first major task for the IMO after the Organization's creation and was adopted to modernize regulations and keep pace with technical

transported by sea in ever-larger oil tankers became a particular concern, especially after a number of major tanker accidents.

The IMO has introduced a series of measures designed to prevent accidents and to minimize marine pollution due to oil. It also has tackled the environmental threats caused by routine operations such as the cleaning of oil cargo tanks and the disposal of engine room wastes – a bigger menace than accidents in terms of tonnage. Measures introduced by the IMO are concerned with the safety of containers, bulk cargoes, liquefied gas tankers and other ship types. Special attention has been paid to ship crews, including the adoption of a convention on standards of training, certification and watch-keeping.

IMO's mandate includes establishing a system to ensure redress for those who suffer financially as a result of pollution. It adopted treaties in 1969 and 1971 to enable victims of oil pollution to obtain compensation simply and quickly, later followed by conventions on liability and compensation for other shipping hazards.

The IMO has benefitted from technological advances that allowed major improvements to the maritime distress system. In the 1970s it initiated a global search and rescue system and began use of the International Mobile Satellite Organization (INMARSAT) which greatly improved radio and other ship communications. In 1992 the Global Maritime Distress and Safety System became operative. With it, a ship in distress anywhere in the world can be guaranteed assistance even if its crew does not have time to radio for help, because the distress signal is transmitted automatically.

The adoption of maritime legislation is still IMO's most visible responsibility. The Organization has sponsored a large number of conventions and protocols, most of which have been amended on several occasions to ensure that they keep up with changes in world shipping. The most important treaties for environmental protection are the 1954 Convention for the Prevention of Pollution of the Sea by Oil (OILPOL); the 1972 Convention on the Prevention of Marine Pollution by Dumping of Wastes and Other Matter; the 1973/78 Convention for the Prevention of Pollution by Ships (MARPOL); the 1969 Convention Relating to Intervention on the High Seas in Cases of Oil Pollution Casualties; the 1990 Convention on Oil Pollution Preparedness, Responses and Co-operation; the

developments in the shipping industry. The IMO intended to adopt periodic amendments to maintain the Convention, but in practice the amendments procedure proved to be very slow. As a result, a completely new Convention was adopted in 1974 which included not only the amendments agreed up until that date but a new amendment procedure – the tacit acceptance procedure – designed to ensure that changes could be made within a specified (and acceptably short) period of time.

1969 Convention on Civil Liability for Oil Pollution Damages; the 1971 Convention on the Establishment of an International Fund for Compensation for Oil Pollution Damage; the 1971 Convention relating to Civil Liability in the Field of Maritime Carriage of Nuclear Materials (Nuclear); the 1976 Convention on Limitation of Liability for Maritime Claims; the 1996 Convention on Liability and Compensation for Damage in connection with the Carriage of Hazardous and Noxious Substances by Sea; the 2001 International Convention on the Control of Harmful Anti-Fouling Systems on Ships; the 2001 International Convention on Civil Liability for Bunker Oil Pollution Damage; the 2004 International Convention for the Control and Management of Ships' Ballast Water and Sediments; the 2007 Nairobi International Convention on the Removal of Wrecks; and the 2009 Honk Kong International Convention for the Safe and Environmentally Sound Recycling of Ships (see Chapter 11)

The IMO has created a Marine Environment Protection Committee that discusses the on-going issues of revising MARPOL annexes and other environmental problems such as harmful aquatic organisms in ballast water. The question of IMO's constitutional competence has arisen with the adoption of the Global Program of Action for the Protection of the Marine Environment from Land-Based Activities (GPA). UN General Assembly Resolution 51/189, on Institutional Arrangements for the Implementation of the GPA, adopted in December 1996, called upon the IMO to develop a clearing-house mechanism for oils and litter in the marine environment that originate from land-based sources. The IMO Assembly responded that the IMO had a mandate to prevent marine pollution from sea-based sources only and that the subject matter of the request lay outside its constitutional responsibilities. When no voluntary resources were provided by member states, the Assembly concluded that the IMO should not undertake the work.

3.8 *International Labor Organization* (ILO)

The ILO has a constitutional mandate to assist countries in improving the working environment. Since 1919, the ILO has devoted a significant proportion of its efforts in that direction, especially through standard-setting activities. The ILO has adopted more than 40 standards specifically dealing with occupational safety and health, as well as over 40 Codes of Practice. Nearly half of ILO instruments deal directly or indirectly with occupational safety and health issues. The extensive list of ILO instruments that concern occupational safety and health include the Working Environment (Air Pollution, Noise and Vibration) Convention (No. 148) and Recommendation (No. 156)(1977) as well as the Safety and Health in Construction Convention (No. 167) and Recommendation (No. 175), adopted in June 1988. The ILO also adopted conventions on indigenous peoples (1989), chemicals in the workplace (1990), and agricultural work (2002), which contain provisions directly concerned with environmental protection. On January 17, 1995, the ILO signed a Memorandum of Understanding Concerning Establishment of the Inter-Organization Program for the Social Management of Chemicals which created a framework for coordinating chemicals-related policies and activities with UNEP, the FAO, the WHO, the UN Industrial Development Organization, and OECD.[68] An action program on the use of chemicals at work was completed in 1996, involving assistance in designing and implementing national programs for the environmentally sound management of hazardous chemicals and their waste in five countries. An ILO technical working group has been established to elaborate a set of harmonized hazard communication tools, such as labeling, chemical safety data sheets and training. The ILO also contributed to the elaboration of the FAO convention on prior informed consent and has worked with the IMO on maritime standards.[69]

In 1994, the ILO launched an Interdepartmental Project on Environment and the World of Work. Since that time, environmental issues have become integrated in all programs and activities of the organization in keeping with the goals set by Agenda 21. In 2003, the ILO adopted a global strategy to improve occupational safety and health which included the introduction of a preventive safety and health culture, the promotion and development of relevant instruments, and technical assistance. In addition to standard-setting activities, the ILO aims to promote and support efforts at the international, regional and national levels to reduce occupational accidents and diseases and to improve the working environment.[70] The Occupational Safety and Health Branch within the Working Conditions and Environment Department has prepared a draft code to prevent major hazards, a training manual on the use of chemicals at work, and dissemination of information.

68 See 34 I.L.M. 1311 (1995). The MOU was revised in 1996 to add ethical considerations as an integral part of the IPCS's work.

69 In 1996, the ILO held a maritime session that adopted three new international conventions, three recommendations and a Protocol to the Merchant Shipping (Minimum Standards) Convention No. 147. The major focus of Convention 147 is accident prevention and a key feature is port state control.

70 There are more than 35 ILO instruments directly relevant to the health and safety of workers at work, linked to the following three ILO Conventions: the Convention on Occupational Safety and Health (No. 155) and its Recommendation (No. 164); the Occupational Health Services Convention (No. 161) and its Recommendation (No. 171); and the Promotional Framework for Occupational Safety and Health Convention (No. 187) and its Recommendation (No. 197).

In 2015, *decent work*, one of the key areas of work of the ILO, has become an integral part of the 2030 Agenda for Sustainable Development. Goal 8, in fact, calls for the achievement of 'full and productive employment and decent work for all women and men, including for young people and persons with disabilities, and equal pay for work of equal value' by 2030, and has been fully integrated in the ILO's 'Decent Work Agenda'.

3.9 *International Civil Aviation Organization (ICAO)*

The first nuisance the public experienced from civil aviation was aircraft noise and the International Civil Aviation Organization (ICAO) initially focused its efforts on securing quieter aircraft. The ICAO also insists on the importance of compatible land-use planning and control, in order to avoid offsetting the gains of reduced engine noise with further residential developments around airports.

In 1983, the ICAO replaced two committees that had dealt with noise and emissions, creating a single Committee on Aviation Environmental Protection. At this time, in response to concerns regarding air quality in the vicinity of airports, the organization began to establish standards to control aircraft engine emissions through an engine certification scheme. These standards, contained in Volume II of Annex 16 to the Convention on International Civil Aviation, establish limits for emissions of oxides of nitrogen (NO_x), carbon monoxide, and unburned hydrocarbons from new engines during an aircraft's landing and take-off. The NOx standards were tightened periodically over the years. In 2010, the ICAO began developing a standard on particulate matter and a new standard on non-volatile Particulate Matter (nvPM) mass and number was adoped by the ICAO Council in March 2020, marking a groundbreaking achievement, as this standard closes the full circle on noise, local air quality and CO_2 standards for subsonic aeroplanes.

Recent concerns about climate change, depletion of the ozone layer, and long-range air pollution have led to questions about the contribution of aircraft and space shuttle launch emissions to these problems. ICAO coordinates its activities on these issues with other UN bodies, but scientific information is lacking on aviation's impact on the global atmosphere. The development of a new emissions parameter that would take into account technical performances, climb and cruise emissions, new communications, navigation, surveillance and air traffic management could be an effective means to reduce fuel burning and avoiding unnecessary emissions. In 2022, the ICAO Assembly adopted Resolution A41-21, which endorsed the long-term global aspirational goal (LTAG) for international aviation, aiming for net-zero carbon emissions by 2050. This commitment aligns with the temperature goal outlined in the Paris Agreement. In order to realize these global aspirations and encourage sustainable development in international aviation, ICAO is actively pursuing a set of measures. These include advancements in aircraft technology, improvements in operational practices, the utilization of sustainable aviation fuels, and the implementation of market-based measures such as CORSIA (Carbon Offsetting and Reduction Scheme for International Aviation) (see later Chapter 12).

3.10 *World Trade Organization* (*WTO*)

The international community first envisaged an international organization governed by a comprehensive code governing all aspects of trade at the end of the Second World War. Negotiations for the organization did not succeed but produced a General Agreement on Tariffs and Trade (GATT) in 1947.[71] The GATT evolved as a set of normative standards and eventually developed some institutional elements through a series of eight multilateral rounds of negotiations. The Uruguay Round, which ended in December 1994, led to formation of the World Trade Organization (WTO) on January 1, 1995.

The Agreement Establishing the WTO, signed in Marrakesh (Marrakesh Agreement), incorporates the original GATT and adds new undertakings on five main subject matters that have impacts on environmental protection. They are the Agreement on Technical Barriers to Trade, Agreement on Sanitary and Phytosanitary Measures, Agreement on Subsidies and Countervailing Measures, Agreement on Trade-Related Aspects of Intellectual Property, and General Agreement on Trade in Services. Moreover, the preamble to the Marrakesh Agreement clearly recognizes sustainable development as one of the key objectives of the Organization.[72] The WTO Dispute Settlement Understanding is another important feature of the organization; it establishes procedures for resolving trade disputes and creates a Dispute Settlement Body consisting of panels and an Appellate Body, which stopped functioning in 2019. The WTO also has a Trade and Environment Division (TED) as part of its Secretariat, and a Committee on Trade and the Environment (CTE) whose mandate is to identify the trade-related aspects of environmental measures and, if necessary, make recommendations for modification of the rules of the multilateral trading system or attempt to resolve problems of policy coordination while upholding the principles of the

71 General Agreement on Tariffs and Trade (adopted Oct. 30, 1947, entered into force Jan. 1, 1948) 55 U.N.T.S. 194.

72 Agreement Establishing the World Trade Organization (adopted Apr. 15, 1994, entered into force Jan. 1, 1995) 1867 U.N.T.S. 154.

multilateral trading system. In particular the CTE looks at the relationship between the trade rules and the use of trade measures for environmental purposes; the use of environmental charges and taxes, and environmental standards for packaging, labeling and recycling; the effect of environmental measures on developing country's market access and the environmental benefits of removing trade restrictions and distortions. Recently, a number of new initiatives on the trade/environment interface have been launched, such as the Trade and Environmental Sustainability Structured Discussions (TESSD), the Informal Dialogue on Plastics, and the Fossil Fuels Subsidies Reform (FFSR) Initiative (see Chapter 17).

4 Regional Organizations

Almost all regional organizations have become engaged in activities in the environmental field. Organizations within Europe have the most comprehensive regulation, for several reasons. First, the process of political and legal integration is most developed in Europe. Second, Europe is densely populated and highly industrialized, leading to greater risks of pollution. Finally, cooperation in environmental matters is facilitated by the homogeneity of economic structures and the similarity of political conceptions.

'European organizations' includes entities that are different from one another. Pan-European organizations such as the Organization on Security and Cooperation in Europe (OSCE) and the Organization for Economic Cooperation and Development are not limited to European member states; the OECD, for example, also has among its member states the United States, Canada, Mexico, Japan, Korea, Australia, and New Zealand.[73] The 46 member states of the Council of Europe now range from Iceland to Turkey. Twenty-eight members of the Council of Europe also form the European Union. The United Nations Economic Commission for Europe could also be included here, but as a UN entity is discussed above.

The first section discusses the Council of Europe, the OECD, the European Union, and the OSCE. The work of organizations in other regions follows: the Organization of American States (OAS), the African Union (AU), and the organizations of Asia and the South Pacific. Finally, mention will be made of the increasingly important sub-regional and bilateral institutions.

73 T.I.A.S. No. 4891, entered into force Sept. 30, 1961.

4.1 *The Council of Europe*

The oldest of the existing European institutions, the Council of Europe, was created in London on May 5, 1949 and is based in Strasbourg. Today it consists of 46 states, nearly all the European countries except Belarus, Russia and the Asian republics of the former Soviet Union. The Council of Europe has jurisdiction to address environmental issues, because Article 1 of its statute permits it to consider all regional questions except those relating to national defense. Its broad competence is not accompanied by equally expansive powers, however. The Committee of Ministers, its executive organ, can only adopt recommendations addressed to member states. The other principal organ, the Parliamentary Assembly, has few powers but carries considerable weight with European public opinion. In fact, Assembly debates and the resolutions it addresses to the Committee of Ministers largely reflect European political consensus and often set forth solutions which are adopted subsequently either at the European or national level.

Even prior to Stockholm, the Council of Europe took action and approved several basic texts proclaiming principles to protect the environment. In 1962 the Council created a European Committee for the Protection of Nature and Natural Resources. Since that time, nature conservation has remained one of the principal concerns of the Council. Between 1968 and 1974 the Council adopted numerous declaratory texts, including the European Water Charter (1968), the Declaration of Principles on Air Pollution Control (1968), and the European Soil Charter (1972). In addition, the European Conference of Local Authorities, created at the initiative of the Parliamentary Assembly, adopted in 1970 a European Declaration regarding Conservation of Nature. The same year, a conference meeting to celebrate the European Year of Nature Conservation proclaimed a Declaration on the Management of the Natural Environment in Europe. The Council actively participated in the elaboration and adoption, in 1995, of the Pan-European Biological and Landscape Diversity Strategy and serves as its Secretariat and coordinator. In addition, it is responsible for several action themes of the Strategy, such as the establishment of the Pan-European Ecological Network and the Protection of Threatened Species.

Several landmark regional environmental treaties have been concluded under the auspices of the Council of Europe, beginning with the European Agreement on the Restriction of the Use of Certain Detergents in Washing and Cleaning Products (Sept. 16, 1968). Notable are the Convention for the Protection of Animals during International Transport (Dec. 13, 1968) and the Bern Convention on the Conservation of European Wildlife and Natural Habitats (Sept. 19, 1979). The latter, a particularly important contribution in this field, created a permanent supervisory committee which functions within the

Council of Europe. In addition, the Council of Europe drafted and adopted the 1993 Lugano Convention on Civil Liability for Damage Resulting from Activities Dangerous to the Environment, the 1998 Convention on the Protection of the Environment through Criminal Law, and the 2000 European Landscape Convention.

The Council of Europe also promotes transnational cooperation. Its efforts have produced a European Outline Convention on Transfrontier Cooperation between Territorial Communities or Authorities (Madrid, May 21, 1980). The Convention explicitly designates environmental protection and mutual assistance in case of accidents among the topics which may be the object of joint action between local or territorial authorities from different states. The Convention annexes models agreements on questions such as mutual transfrontier urban development and protection of nature, water and air.

The Council of Europe addressed regional planning initially at a 1970 European Conference of Ministers Responsible for Regional Planning. In January 2002, the Council's Committee of Ministers adopted Recommendation Rec(2002)1 on the guiding principles for sustainable spatial development of the European continent. The Guiding Principles recommend to member states to take account of the needs of all who presently live in Europe's regions without jeopardizing the fundamental rights and development prospects of future generations. The objectives of the Principles include the conservation, enhancement and management of landscapes and of the natural, cultural and landscape heritage, as well as environmental protection, resource management and risk prevention. The text especially stresses the need to reduce environmental damage and enhance and protect natural resources and the cultural heritage.

The European Convention on Human Rights and the European Social Charter have been adopted under the auspices of the Council of Europe and have proven critical in advancing the debate on the positive interrelationship between environmental protection and the promotion of human rights (see Chapter 15). The former contains several provisions that have allowed the European Court of Human Rights to integrate environmental considerations in its decisions, while the latter expressly guarantees the right to a healthy environment as part of the right to protection of health.

4.2 *Organization for Economic Cooperation and Development* (OECD)

The OECD, successor to the former Organization for European Economic Cooperation founded in 1948 to administer the Marshall Plan, took its current form in 1960. Its membership consists of all Western and Central European countries, Australia, Canada, Costa Rica, Chile, Colombia, Israel, Japan, Korea,

Mexico, New Zealand, and the United States. The Commission of the European Community participates in the work of the organization.

The executive organ of the OECD is a Council composed of the representatives of member states, but the OECD secretariat is particularly important because the OECD is primarily an organ of study and economic reflection, responsible for making an inventory of resources, analyzing and elaborating measures for the future. The OECD can take decisions that are binding for all the member states who participate in their adoption, not including states abstaining. Resolutions adopted by the Council are binding for the organization itself. Recommendations addressed to the member states are not binding, but do reflect the general views and intentions of the governments which vote in favor of them.

In 1970, the OECD created a Committee on the Environment to take over the work of some twenty other committees. Its purpose is to aid the governments of OECD member states to define their policies in regard to environmental problems, taking into account pertinent information, especially economic and scientific, and reconcile their environmental policies with economic and social development. The Committee is also entitled to review the state of the environment in member countries. Reports on the environmental performances of OECD countries are regularly published. In 1991, with the creation of the Joint Session on Trade and Environment Experts, the OECD became the first international organization to examine, on a regular basis, the integration of trade and environmental policies.

The OECD has made major contributions to the development of international environmental law. OECD recommendations, sometimes accompanied by declarations of principles, formulated the first legal definition of pollution and enunciated the basic standards applicable to transfrontier pollution.[74] It also enunciated the obligation to inform and consult, to notify of emergency situations, the principle of equality of access between residents and nonresidents, non-discrimination in the application of legislative rules,[75] and the polluter-pays principle.[76] Other recommendations have been adopted on the

74 Recommendation on Principles Concerning Transfrontier Pollution (1974) C(74)224.

75 Recommendation on Equal Right of Access in Relation to Transfrontier Pollution (1976) C(76)55. Recommendation on Implementation of a Regime of Equal Right of Access and Non-Discrimination in Relation to Transfrontier Pollution (1977) C(77)28.

76 See e.g. Recommendation on the Implementation of the Polluter-Pays Principle (1974) C(74)223.

issues of water quality,[77] air quality,[78] transboundary movement of wastes,[79] energy,[80] chemicals,[81] tourism,[82] and multinational enterprises.[83] Moreover, the OECD has adopted precise regulations concerning some types of air and water pollution. Its standard-setting has been decisive in the regulation of chemical substances as well as toxic and dangerous wastes, including radioactive wastes. In more recent action, the OECD drafted voluntary principles and standards for responsible business conduct.[84] Section V of the text affirms that enterprises should take due account of the need to protect the environment and recommends good environmental management, communication with the public and the adoption of preventive and precautionary approaches. Thus, despite its essentially economic focus, the OECD has been a pioneer in international environmental law.

4.3 *Organization for Security and Cooperation in Europe (OSCE)*

The OSCE has 57 participating states and can claim to be the largest existing regional security organization. Its area includes continental Europe, the Caucasus, Central Asia, and North America, and it co-operates with Mediterranean and Asian partners. The OSCE brings together the Euro-Atlantic and the Euro-Asian communities 'from Vancouver to Vladivostok'. It succeeded to the Conference on Security and Cooperation in Europe,[85] more widely known as the Helsinki Conference, which has met regularly since the first session of all Western, Central and Eastern European states, together with the United States and the Soviet Union, opened in Helsinki in 1973.[86] The Helsinki Final Act adopted at the close of the Conference on August 1, 1975, contained a

---

77 See e.g. Recommendation on Water Management Policies and Instruments (1978) C(78)77; Recommendation on Water (2016) C(2016)16.

78 See e.g. Recommendation on Guidelines for Actions to Reduce Emissions of Sulphur Oxides and Particular Matter from Fuel Combustion in Stationary Sources (1974) C(74)219.

79 See e.g. Decision and Recommendation on Transfrontier Movement of Hazardous Waste (1984) C(83)180; Decision on the Control of Transboundary Movements of Wastes Destined for Recovery Operations (2021).

80 See e.g. Recommendation on Energy and the Environment (1974) C(74)222.

81 See e.g. Recommendation on the Assessment of the Potential Environmental Effects of Chemicals (1974) C(74)215.

82 Recommendation on Environment and Tourism (1979) C(79)115.

83 Recommendation of the Council on Principles of Corporate Governance (2015) C(2015)84.

84 Guidelines for Multinational Enterprises, June 27, 2000, 40 ILM 237 (2000).

85 The 1994 participating states changed the name of the body from the Conference on Security and Cooperation in Europe to the Organization for Security and Cooperation in Europe.

86 The first follow-up meetings were held in Belgrade (1977–78); Madrid (1980–83); Vienna (1989) and Copenhagen (1990).

section specifically devoted to the environment. The text emphasizes cooperation, based on a conviction stated at the outset that many environmental problems, particularly in Europe, can be solved effectively through close international cooperation.

The OSCE approach to security is comprehensive and cooperative. It deals with a wide range of issues, including environmental security, because it sees the various aspects of security as interconnected and interdependent. A continuous effort is made by the OSCE participating States to enhance the complementarity of the various dimensions of security. The Organization is thus active in all phases of the conflict cycle, from early warning and conflict prevention to conflict management and post-conflict rehabilitation.

The OSCE has no legal status as a formal organization under international law and its decisions are politically but not legally binding. Nevertheless, it possesses most of the normal attributes of an international organization: standing decision-making bodies, permanent headquarters and institutions, permanent staff, regular financial resources and field offices. Most of its instruments, decisions and commitments are framed in legal language and their interpretation requires an understanding of the principles of international law and of the standard techniques of the law of treaties.

The OSCE's economic dimension involves monitoring economic and environmental developments among participating states, with the aim of alerting them to any threat of conflict; and facilitating the formulation of economic and environmental policies and initiatives to promote security in the OSCE area. A Charter for European Security, adopted in Istanbul on November 19, 1999, addressed the economic and environmental dimensions of OSCE's common response to the challenges it faces. Recalling the risk to security from environmental degradation and the depletion of natural resources, the Declaration stresses that economic liberty, social justice and environmental responsibility are indispensable for prosperity. Affirming the intention of the signatories to 'help build vibrant civil societies' it proclaims adhesion to the 1998 Aarhus Convention on Access to Information, Public participation in Decision-Making and Access to Justice in Environmental Matters.

In 2003, the Environment and Security initiative was launched concurrently at the Fifth Environment for Europe Ministerial Conference and the 11th Economic and Environmental Forum of the OSCE in Prague. Initially established by the OSCE, UNDP, and UN Environment, this collaboration later welcomed the participation of additional organizations. Presently, it stands as a partnership involving the OSCE, UNDP, UN Environment, and the UNECE. The primary goal is to address risks to both the environment and security by fostering cooperative environmental efforts among and within countries in four regions: Eastern Europe, South-Eastern Europe, the South Caucasus, and Central Asia.

4.4 *European Union*

A distinction is often made between the preceding organizations, which are generally organizations of cooperation, and the European Union, a unique agent of economic and political integration. The European Union benefits from a true transfer of sovereignty from member states which have abandoned in its favor some of their national powers.

The European Union, originally consisting of six western European countries and as of 2024 having a membership of 27 states, began as a set of three economic communities, which merged into a single entity that was transformed into the Union. The main institutions of the European Union are the Council of the European Union, the European Commission, the European Parliament and the European Court of Justice. The legal instruments that progressively integrated the member states also gradually strengthened the provisions concerning the environment. The 1951 Paris Treaty creating the European Coal and Steel Community, the 1957 Treaty of Rome establishing the European Economic Community (Rome Treaty) and the 1957 Euratom Treaty initially had no mention of environmental matters.[87] The first initiative was a political decision taken outside the statutory organs of the Communities. The heads of state or government of the then-nine member countries, meeting in Paris on October 19–20,1972, adopted a declaration proclaiming the need to improve the quality of life, paying particular attention to non-material values and to protection of the environment. The declaration called for development of an environmental policy and invited the Community institutions to establish, before July 31, 1973, an action program setting forth a precise calendar. The Commission elaborated a Program of Action of the European Communities on the Environment to cover the years 1974–1976 and other action plans have followed.

Article 100 of the Rome Treaty provided the initial legal basis for action. It authorized the European Economic Community to adopt directives[88] for the

87 Wolfgang E. Burhenne & Thomas J. Shoenbaum, 'The European Community and Management of the Environment: A Dilemma' (1973) 13 Natural Resources Journal 494.

88 Directives, the only form of instrument authorized by Article 100, bind every member state to achieve the stated result, but leave to national authorities the choice of means. Regulations, binding in all their elements and directly applicable in every member state, are adopted in the field of environmental protection generally when the provisions con-

approximation of legislative and administrative provisions that had a direct impact on the establishment or the functioning of the Common Market, particularly when disparities among the provisions distorted conditions of competition in the Common Market. Article 235 of the Rome Treaty also could be used as it permitted action by the Community when necessary to achieve one of the aims in the functioning of the Common Market.

The Community adopted over one hundred legal texts under this regime. Environmental measures dating from this period based exclusively on Article 100 include directives concerning the lead content of petrol, detergents, and the permissible sound level and exhaust system of motor cycles.[89] The European Court of Justice (ECJ) confirmed the appropriateness of legislative reliance on Article 100 in a decision in which the validity of Directive 75/716, relating to the maximum sulphur content of liquid fuel was at issue. The judgment reflects an understanding of the potential for competitive disadvantage from environmental protection measures:

> It is by no means ruled out that provisions on the environment may be based upon Article 100 of the Treaty. Provisions which are made necessary by considerations relating to the environment and health may be a burden upon undertakings to which they apply and if there is no harmonization of national provisions on the matter, competition may be appreciably distorted.[90]

Most of the Community's environmental legislation during this period is based, however, both on Article 100 and Article 235, including the directives on pollution caused by certain dangerous substances discharged into the aquatic environment of the Community; combating of air pollution from industrial plants; the major accident hazards of certain industrial plants; and regulation of toxic and dangerous waste.

The joint use of both Articles 100 and 235 for environmental protection was confirmed by the ECJ in a decision that marks the first time the Court recognized environmental protection as one of the Community's essential objectives. It was an important step for the further development of Community

---

cern external trade of the Community, for example, banning the importation of certain hazardous substances.

89 All EU legal texts and summaries of environmental laws are available at http://eur-lex.europa.eu/.

90 Case 92/79 *Commission v. Italy* (1980) E.C.R. 1115.

action in this field. In the case, concerning the validity of a directive on the disposal of waste oils, the Court held:

> In the first place it should be observed that the principle of freedom of trade is not to be viewed in absolute terms but is subject to certain limits justified by the objectives of general interest pursued by the Community, provided that the rights in question are not substantively impaired. There is no reason to conclude that the directive has exceeded those limits. The directive must be seen in the perspective of environmental protection, which is one of the Community's essential objectives.[91]

During this period the EC became a contracting party to the major international treaties on nature protection and biological diversity, including the Convention on International Trade in Endangered Species of Wild Fauna and Flora (CITES),[92] the Bonn Convention on Migratory Species,[93] and the Bern Convention on the Conservation of European Wildlife and Natural Habitats.[94] It also adopted directives of general scope relating to the assessment of the effects of certain public and private projects on the environment,[95] integrated pollution prevention and control, the freedom of access to information on the environment,[96] and to eco-labeling.[97]

An important change in the action of the Community in the field of environmental protection resulted from the adoption, on February 27, 1986, of the Single European Act (SEA), which superseded the original founding treaties. The SEA instrument settled the issue of Community competence in respect to environmental protection. Later the SEA was replaced by the Maastricht Treaty on European Union (TEU) of February 7, 1992 which was modified in turn by the Treaty of Amsterdam adopted on October 2, 1997 and the Treaty of Lisbon (2007). A consolidated version of the Treaty on European Union was published in 2012.[98]

The TEU includes provisions designed specifically to confirm the Union's task in developing an environmental policy. TEU Article 3 sets forth the objectives of the EU and includes a policy to work for a high level of protection and improvement of the quality of the environment (Art. 3(3)). Title XX concerns

---

91 Case 240/83, ABDHU (1985) ECR 531.

92 Regulation 3626/82 of December 3, 1982, O.J. L. 384 (12/31/82).

93 O.J. L.210 of July 19, 1982.

94 O.J. L 38 of February 10, 1982.

95 Directives 85/337, O.J. L.175, July 7, 1985 and 97./11, O.J. L.5 (3/13/97).

96 Directive 90/313, O.J. L.158 (6/21/90).

97 Regulation 880/92, O.J. L.58 (2/27/97).

98 Consolidated Version of the Treaty on European Union [2008] O.J. C115/13.

the environment and repeats that the Union policy on the environment shall aim at a high level of protection taking into account the diversity of situations in the various regions of the Union. Article 191 designates the four aims of Union policy: (1) preserving, protecting and improving the quality of the environment, (2) protecting human health, (3) prudent and rational utilization of natural resources, and (4) prompting measures at international level to deal with regional or worldwide environmental problems.

Article 191(2) proclaims that the Union's environmental policy shall be based on the precautionary principle and on the principles that preventive action should be taken, that environmental damage should as a priority be rectified at the source and that the polluter should pay. According to Article 191(3), in preparing its policy on the environment, the Union shall take account of available scientific and technical data; environmental conditions in the various regions of the Union; the potential benefits and costs of action or lack of action; the economic and social development of the Union as a whole and the balanced development of its regions.

Problems may arise in reconciling the conditions which must be taken into account on the one hand and the basic principles proclaimed on the other. The precautionary principle implies that there can be lack of full scientific certainty, which means that taking account of available scientific and technical data will not always afford a solution. Similarly, the 'polluter pays principle' should be reconciled with the economic and social development of the Union and, in particular, with the balanced development of its regions. The latter could imply the appropriateness of subsidies in order to help polluters suppress or minimize the pollution they cause. Article 192(5) may help. It provides that without prejudice to the principle that the polluter should pay, if a measure based on a decision of the Council taken in conformity with the usual procedure involves costs deemed disproportionate for the public authorities of a Member State, the Council shall, in the act adopting that measure, lay down appropriate provisions in the form of either temporary derogations and/or financial support from a special fund of the EC

While the TEU confers specific powers upon the Union in the field of environmental protection, it also establishes limits on those powers. In particular:

a. Such powers are to be exercised only if the Union's environmental objectives can be attained better at the Community level than at the level of the individual Member States. This flows from the principle of subsidiarity, one of the basic principles of the Community.[99]

---

99 According to Article 3 B of the Amsterdam Treaty, 'In areas which do not fall within its exclusive competence, the Community shall take action, in accordance with the principle of subsidiarity, only if and in so far as the objectives of the proposed action cannot be

b. According to Article 191(2), harmonization measures for environmental protection shall include, where appropriate, a safeguard clause allowing Member States to take provisional measures, for non-economic environmental reasons, subject to a Community inspection procedure.
c. The protective measures adopted pursuant to the environmental principles proclaimed by the Treaty do not prevent any Member State from maintaining or introducing more stringent protective measures. Such measures must be compatible with the Treaty and notified to the Commission (Art. 193). Concerns about the impact of environmental measures on free trade are evident and arise not only inside the European Community but also in the large context of globalization.
d. Finally, while Article 191(4) recognizes the capacity and the authority of the Community to conclude arrangements with non-member States or other international institutions in the field of environmental protection, it also affirms that such authority does not deprive the Member States of the right to negotiate in international bodies and to conclude international agreements.

Further limitations are found in a Protocol on the application of the principles of subsidiarity and proportionality of the Treaty of Amsterdam. It requires the European Commission to justify the relevance of its proposals with regard to the principle of subsidiarity and take due account of the need for any burden, whether financial or administrative, imposed upon government or industry.[100] The European Commission' actions cannot go beyond what is necessary to achieve the objectives of the Treaty, must be as simple as possible, and leave as much scope for national decisions as possible. Framework directives are preferred over detailed measures.

At the institutional level, on May 7, 1990, the Council created a European Environmental Agency. Its main objective is to provide technical and scientific support to the Community and Member States regarding environmental protection. Unlike other organs of the Community, the Agency is open to countries non-members of the Community who share the environmental concerns of the Member States. The Agency is directed by a management board consisting of one representative of each Member State and two representatives from the Commission. In addition, the European Parliament designates two

---

sufficiently achieved by the Member States and can therefore, by reason of the scale or effects of the proposed action, be better achieved by the Community'.

100 Protocol on the application of the principles of subsidiarity and proportionality, Treaty of Amsterdam, Protocols annexed to the Treaty establishing the European Community, consolidated version O.J. C 340 (11/10/97).

'scientific personalities' to the Board. The Agency, the functions of which are mainly non-political, is based in Copenhagen.

During its existence, the European Commission has developed comprehensive legislation in environmental matters. Following the general trend in domestic as well as in international environmental legislation, its policy shifted from indirect approaches towards distinct measures aiming at the protection of water, or of air or of wildlife. During the 1990s the European Commission demonstrated a general trend towards integrated protection and most human activities which can have an impact on the environment enter the scope of European Commission's environmental legislation. At the same time economic aspects of the proposed measures as well as the generally proclaimed need for sustainable development are increasingly taken into account. The European Charter of Fundamental Rights and Freedoms of the European Union, which falls short of proclaiming a human right to environment, expresses well this trend. Its Article 37 affirms that 'a high level of environmental protection and the improvement of the quality of the environment must be integrated into the policies of the Union and ensured in accordance with the principle of sustainable development'.

By Decision No 1386/2013/EU of the European Parliament and of the Council of November 20, 2013, the EU adopted its 7th General Environment Action Program, entitled 'Living well, within the limits of our planet.' It applies to the year 2020, but to give more long-term direction, it sets out a vision of where it wants the Union to be by 2050: 'In 2050, we live well, within the planet's ecological limits. Our prosperity and healthy environment stem from an innovative, circular economy where nothing is wasted and where natural resources are managed sustainably, and biodiversity is protected, valued and restored in ways that enhance our society's resilience. Our low-carbon growth has long been decoupled from resource use, setting the pace for a safe and sustainable global society'. The Program identifies three key objectives: to protect, conserve and enhance the Union's natural capital; to turn the Union into a resource-efficient, green, and competitive low-carbon economy; and to safeguard the Union's citizens from environment-related pressures and risks to health and wellbeing. Four so called 'enablers' are described as helping Europe deliver these goals: better implementation of legislation; better information by improving the knowledge base; more and wiser investment for environment and climate policy; and full integration of environmental requirements and considerations into other policies. Two other objectives complete the program: to make the Union's cities more sustainable and to help the Union address international environmental and climate challenges more effectively.

In 2019, the European Green Deal was adopted.[101] This initiative, presented by the European Commission, outlines a comprehensive set of policy measures and goals to make the EU climate-neutral by 2050 and transform its economy into a more sustainable one. The policy areas covered by the European Green Deal include renewable energy, energy efficiency, circular economy, biodiversity, sustainable mobility, and green innovation and research. On July 29, 2021, another important piece of EU legislation, the European Climate Law, entered into force. It enshrines in legal terms the objective outlined in the European Green Deal, aiming for the climate neutrality of Europe's economy and society by 2050. Additionally, the European Climate Law establishes a milestone target, calling for a minimum 55% reduction in net greenhouse gas emissions by 2030, relative to 1990 levels.

The same year, the 8th General Environment Action Programme was adopted, which entered into force in May 2022 and guides the EU's environmental policy until 2030. It reaffirms the EU's enduring vision until 2050, centered on achieving a high quality of life while staying within the Earth's ecological limits. It outlines key objectives for 2030 and the necessary conditions to attain them. Building upon the principles of the European Green Deal, the 8th Environmental Action Programme emphasizes the active involvement of all stakeholders across governance levels to ensure the effective implementation of EU climate and environmental laws. It serves as the EU's framework for realizing the United Nations' 2030 Agenda and its Sustainable Development Goals.

4.5 *Organization of American States* (OAS)

The Organization of American States (OAS) is the oldest regional political organization in the world, dating back to the First International Conference of American States held in Washington DC in 1890. Today, the OAS is made up of 34 independent states of the Western Hemisphere. Although the OAS Charter does not mention the environment and, as amended, places heavy emphasis on economic development, the Organization has long undertaken environmental activities, particularly concerning nature protection.

The Eighth International Conference of American States, meeting in Lima, Peru, in December 1938, recommended the establishment of a committee of experts to study problems relating to nature and wildlife in the American republics and called for preparation of a draft convention for nature and

101 Commission, 'The European Green Deal' (Communication) COM(2019)640.

wildlife protection.[102] The Executive Council of the Pan American Union (today the Permanent Council of the OAS) convened the recommended meeting of experts which prepared the Convention on Nature Protection and Wildlife Preservation in the Western Hemisphere.[103] The Convention was adopted in Washington on June 4, 1940. States parties agree to adopt certain measures of mutual cooperation to preserve nature by establishing parks, reserves and protected areas and to take all steps necessary to administer and conserve wildlife and nature and to protect threatened species. The OAS Secretariat is depository of the Convention.

Since enactment of the 1940 Convention, the OAS has convened several inter-American meetings on environmental protection, including the 1965 Mar Del Plata Conference on Problems Related to the Conservation of Renewable Natural Resources of the Continent, the periodical Inter-American Congresses on the Environment, and the 2006 Inter-American Meeting of Ministers and High-Level Authorities on Sustainable Development. Several subregional multilateral agreements and numerous bilateral treaties also have been concluded. Since 1977, the Secretariat has been instrumental in encouraging oil spill contingency planning in the wider Caribbean region, leading to adoption of the First Protocol of the Cartagena Convention for the Protection of the Marine Environment.

In 1988, the Inter-American Juridical Committee (IJC) called for creation of an Inter-American System of Nature Conservation.[104] The IJC resolution recommended the creation of a permanent inter-American mechanism utilizing the existing institutions of the OAS to identify environmental problems common to the countries of the Americas, link the numerous multilateral and bilateral agreements that cover various geographic and subject areas, and coordinate efforts to optimize regional management of natural resources. Because of this broad focus, the IJC recommended the creation of a 'system' and not the adoption of a 'treaty'. The General Assembly considered the report and instructed the Secretariat to conduct a multidisciplinary study aimed at creating the proposed system.[105]

The Secretariat study, completed in November 1989, was presented to the Permanent Council of the OAS.[106] The study analyzes the Americas' natural and

102 Resolution XXVIII 'Protection of Nature and Wildlife' Eighth International Conference of American States (Dec. 1938).

103 161 U.N.T.S. 193, 56 Stat. 1354, T.S. No. 981, 3 Bevans 630.

104 AG/doc.2282/88.

105 AG/RES.948 (XVIII-O/88).

106 OEA/Ser.G, CP/doc. 2036/89, Nov. 3, 1989.

developmental features and reviews prior regional action. It then discusses the objectives, functions, alternative structures and courses of action necessary to establish the Inter-American System of Nature Conservation. The alternatives considered are the 1) adoption of a convention; 2) adoption of a program of action and the subsequent establishment of a permanent commission; and 3) creation of a technical office to implement the 1940 Convention. In June 1990, the OAS General Assembly instructed the Permanent Council as a priority matter to establish a special working group to review the Secretariat study and present its conclusions and recommendations by December 31, 1990. The Working Group report proposed establishment of the first OAS environmental program of action and subsequent establishment of a permanent commission on the environment. It did not recommend adoption of a new regional convention, at least at first. There was concern that the process of drafting a new agreement could delay effective measures which are currently needed. In addition, the lack of political will among some states in the region, reflected in a few key OAS officials, could prevent adoption of effective conventional norms.

In June 1996, the OAS created a Unit of Sustainable Development and Environment within the Office of the Secretary General. It is the principal entity within the General Secretariat responsible for matters directly related to sustainable development and the environment and for providing technical and administrative support to the Organization's efforts to become the principal inter-American forum for formulating regional policy in this field. The Unit has four basic functions: 1) to provide support, in the areas of its expertise, to the fora and organs of the OAS, and to participate in the pertinent technical dialogue in hemispheric and subregional conferences, workshops, and seminars; 2) to formulate and selectively execute technical cooperation projects within its field of technical competence, including the integrated development of water resources, especially international river basins; sustainable development of border areas; coastal-zone management; biodiversity and conservation; environmental management in emerging trade corridors; and the mitigation of natural disasters; 3) to facilitate the exchange of information related to sustainable development and environment in the region; and 4) to support efforts to promote coordination and cooperation among agencies in the pursuit of goals established by the member states of the OAS. The Unit of Sustainable Development and Environment has undertaken major projects in the region and within the OAS Secretariat has been assigned the primary responsibility for the follow-up of the Summit on Sustainable Development, which took place in Bolivia in December of 1996.

An important step forward was made with the Declaration of Santa Cruz de la Sierra and the Plan of Action for the Sustainable Development of the

Americas adopted by the Heads of State and Government of the American States on December 9, 1996. The declaration was based on the Rio Declaration and on Agenda 21. The signatories confirmed their intention to assess the environmental impact of their policies, strategies, programs and projects nationally and in the framework of international agreements to ensure that adverse environmental effects are identified, prevented, minimized or mitigated as appropriate. They stated their intent to enhance the progress of international environmental law and promote the reform and modernization of national laws, as appropriate, to reflect sustainable development concepts. Accordingly, the Plan of Action listed a series of initiatives which the Governments pledge to take concerning fields such as sustainable agriculture and forests, water resources and coastal areas management, mining, and energy production. Despite these commitments, deforestation, pollution, and gross wealth disparities in the region continue largely unabated.

In 2001, the Department of Sustainable Development (DSD) was created within the OAS to promote sustainable development across the Americas. Its mandate includes supporting member states in implementing policies and practices that integrate environmental, economic, and social dimensions of development. The DSD focuses on key areas such as biodiversity conservation, climate change adaptation and mitigation, sustainable energy, water resource management, and disaster risk reduction. It provides technical assistance and capacity-building support, collaborates with international organizations and various stakeholders, and advocates for sustainable development policies at regional and international forums. Through initiatives like the Inter-American Biodiversity Information Network (IABIN) and partnerships with entities such as UNEP, the DSD works to enhance the region's resilience to environmental challenges and promote sustainable resource use.

In 2022, in the context of the Ninth Summit of the Americas, the Heads of State and Government of the Americas adopted *Our Sustainable Green Future*, which outlines commitments to combat climate change and promote environmental sustainability. It emphasizes goals from the Paris Agreement, forest and land conservation, emission reduction, ocean conservation, climate adaptation, regional cooperation, and responsible production and consumption. Overall, it aims for comprehensive action, emphasizing cooperation and innovation for a sustainable future in the Americas.

4.6 *South Pacific Regional Organizations*

The South Pacific region contains about 10,000 small islands scattered through a hemispheric ocean. The region may contain major sources of non-renewable resources and is among the largest source of renewable marine living resources.

It is also an area which has been harmed by nuclear tests and is further threatened by the dumping of radioactive waste. Another major concern is the prevention or mitigation of the greenhouse effect. In this context, there are two major regional organizations which separately and cooperatively have elaborated legal instruments to protect the vast Pacific territory.

The former South Pacific Commission (SPC), now the Pacific Community, was founded in Australia in 1947 under the Canberra Agreement by the six 'participating governments' that then administered territories in the Pacific: Australia, France, New Zealand, the Netherlands, the United Kingdom and the United States of America. As Pacific islands became independent or largely self-governing, they joined the organization. The name, South Pacific Commission, was changed to the Pacific Community at the 50th anniversary conference in 1997 to reflect the organisation's Pacific-wide membership. As of 2023, SPC's 27 members include the 22 Pacific Island countries and territories along with five of the original founders (the Netherlands and United Kingdom withdrew in 1962 and 2004 respectively when they relinquished their Pacific interests but the Netherlands rejoined as a member in 2016). The SPC is a consultative and advisory body which studies, formulates and recommends measures regarding, *inter alia*, fisheries and forestry.

The Conference of the Pacific Community, which is held every two years, is the governing body of SPC with each member entitled to one vote on decisions. However, debates are usually resolved in the Pacific way by consensus. The Committee of Representatives of Governments and Administrations (CRGA) meets annually, and in the years that the conference does not meet, is empowered to make decisions on the governance of SPC. Environmental issues have become an increasingly important part of the agenda, especially as regards fisheries and climate change. The Commission launched a Special Project on Conservation of Nature and Natural Resources in July 1974, working with IUCN and UNEP. The project resulted in the 1976 Convention on Conservation of Nature in the South Pacific (Apia) and the Comprehensive Environmental Management Program. Later, the members adopted a Climate Change Engagement Strategy for SPC 2011–2015, providing an overarching framework for SPC's climate change work, setting organizational objectives and identifying key result areas against which progress can be monitored.

In 1971, another Pacific group was formed, the South Pacific Forum, now known as the Pacific Islands Forum. Initially, the Forum had no formal structure or permanent secretariat. However, it has since evolved to include a permanent secretariat based in Suva, Fiji. The Forum, which now comprises eighteen member states,[107] meets annually in different capitals throughout the region to discuss and coordinate regional policies and initiatives.

Both the South Pacific Commission and the Forum have been involved in adopting recent regional instruments concerning the Pacific region. Based on a suggestion of the South Pacific Commission, a coordinating body began work with UNEP in 1980 to prepare a regional Conference on the Human Environment in the South Pacific, held in 1982. Part of UNEP's regional seas program, the Conference adopted a South Pacific Declaration on Natural Resources and the Environment, an action plan for resource management, and an agreement on administrative and financial arrangements to implement the action plan.

After four years of work on the action plan known as the South Pacific Regional Environment Program, a 1986 conference in Noumea adopted the Convention for the Protection of the Natural Resources and Environment of the South Pacific Region[108] and two protocols, one relating to pollution emergencies and the other the prevention of pollution by dumping. Administration of the Convention and protocols is assigned to the South Pacific Commission.

On the issue of nuclear testing and dumping of radioactive wastes, the South Pacific Forum has taken the lead. Australia introduced the idea of a Pacific nuclear-free zone at the fourteenth meeting of the Forum in 1983. The fifteenth Forum in 1984 adopted the proposal leading to the South Pacific Nuclear Free Zone Treaty, signed in Raratonga, Cook Islands, August 6, 1985.[109] The Treaty of Raratonga prohibits the testing, manufacture, acquisition and stationing of nuclear weapons in the territory of the state parties, as well as the dumping of nuclear wastes at sea.[110]

Another concern of the South Pacific states is the depletion of fishing stocks due to unregulated driftnet fishing. During 1989 the South Pacific Forum and South Pacific Conference met to develop a response to the problem. In

107 Australia, the Cook Islands, the Federated States of Micronesia, Fiji, French Polynesia, Kiribati, Marshall Islands, Nauru, New Caledonia, New Zealand, Niue, Palau, Papua New Guinea, Solomon Islands, Tonga, Tuvalu, Vanuatu, and Western Samoa.

108 Noumea, Nov. 25, 1986, 26 I.L.M. 38.

109 24 I.L.M. 1440 (1985).

110 Arts. 3, 5, 6–7. The geographic scope of the Inter-American Treaty for the Prohibition of Nuclear Weapons in Latin America, known as the Treaty of Tlatelolco extends outwards to meet the area covered by the Raratonga Treaty. The two treaties plus the Antarctic Treaty make the entire area of the south Pacific a nuclear-free zone. However, the Treaty of Tlatelolco does not prohibit the dumping of nuclear wastes within the area it covers. Treaty for the Prohibition of Nuclear Weapons in Latin America (Feb. 14, 1967), 634 U.N.T.S. 281, 22 U.S.T. 762, T.I.A.S. No. 7137.

November 1989, twenty Pacific states and territories adopted a Convention for the Prohibition of Fishing with Long Driftnets in the South Pacific.[111] Two protocols containing implementation and enforcement measures were adopted on October 20, 1990.[112] Protocol I is open to countries which fish in the South Pacific region, while Protocol II is open to all Pacific rim states. In 2004, the Western and Central Pacific Fisheries Commission (WCPFC) was established by the Convention for the Conservation and Management of Highly Migratory Fish Stocks in the Western and Central Pacific Ocean.

On climate change, in 2019, the Pacific Islands Forum adopted the Kainaki II Declaration for Urgent Climate Change Action Now, which calls for urgent and immediate actions to address climate change and its impacts on Pacific Island nations.

On the other side of the Pacific, Peru, Ecuador, Chile and Colombia are members of the South Pacific Permanent Commission. Created in 1954,[113] the Commission acts with regard to common interests in the states' exclusive economic zones and also takes common action to protect the marine environment from pollution. In 1987, the Ministers of Foreign Affairs of the four countries declared the Commission to be the appropriate regional organization to implement measures required by UNCLOS regarding conservation and utilization of marine living resources.

4.7 *The Organization of African Unity/African Union*

The Organization of African Unity (OAU), established in large part to bring an end to colonialism in Africa, considered environmental concerns from the time it was founded. Africa is home to extraordinary wildlife and the OAU took action to protect this resource through the conclusion of the 1968 African Convention on the Conservation of Nature and Natural Resources.[114] The Convention calls on states parties to protect natural resources by all necessary measures to ensure conservation, utilization and development in the best interests of the people. Article IX calls for regulation of trade in certain species.

In 1964, the OAU adopted a Declaration on the Denuclearization of Africa. Three decades later, in 1996, in cooperation with the United Nations and the

---

111 Wellington, November 24, 1989, 29 I.L.M. 1449 (1990).

112 ibid at 1462.

113 The South Pacific Permanent Commission was created by agreement between Chile, Ecuador, and Peru at the Second Conference on the Exploitation and Conservation of Marine Resources of the South Pacific, December 4, 1954, in Lima, Peru. Law and Regulations on the Regime of the Territorial Sea, U.N. Doc. ST/LEG/SER.B/6, U.N. Sales No. 1957.V.2 (1957). Colombia became a member in 1979.

114 Sept. 15, 1968, 1001 U.N.T.S. 3.

IAEA, it adopted the Treaty of Pelindaba[115] establishing an African Nuclear Weapons Free Zone. Article 1 establishes the zone as comprising the African continent, island state members of the OAU and islands considered by the OAU to be part of Africa. The Treaty bans nuclear testing and regulates the dumping of radioactive wastes within the zone. In a more general agreement concerning wastes, the best known of the African agreements on pollution is the Bamako Convention on the Ban of Import into Africa and the Control of Transboundary Movement and Management of Hazardous Wastes Within Africa,[116] signed by all OAU member states. The Convention generally bans the import of hazardous waste generated outside Africa, calling unauthorized and illegal dumping a crime against the African continent.

Taking another approach to environmental protection, the 1981 African Charter on Human and Peoples Rights, adopted under the auspices of the OAU, was the first international human rights instrument to include the right 'to a general satisfactory environment' among its guarantees.

In 2002, the OAU was transformed into the African Union (AU) on July 9, 2002, through the adoption of the Constitutive Act of the African Union. The AU aims to accelerate the process of integration and sustainable development, promote peace, security, and stability on the continent, and strengthen Africa's position in the global economy. The AU has been actively engaged in environmental issues, recognizing the critical importance of environmental sustainability for the continent's development and well-being.[117] In 2014, it adopted the African Strategy on Climate Change, which provides a unified approach to addressing climate change across the continent, emphasizing adaptation and mitigation measures. In 2015, it adopted Agenda 2063, a strategic framework for the socio-economic transformation of the continent over 50 years, emphasizing sustainable development and environmental protection.

In addition to the overall strategy of the AU for the whole continent, an increasingly important role is played by sub-regional and ecosystem approaches seen in the Congo Basin initiative, the Lusaka Agreement on criminal enforcement of wildlife treaties in East Africa, and the Southern African Center for Ivory Marketing.

115 April 11, 1996, UNGA A/50/426.

116 Bamako, Jan. 29, 1991, 30 I.L.M. 773 (1991); 31 I.L.M. 163 (1992).

117 See e.g. Namira Negm, *An Introduction to the African Union Environmental Treaties* (Brill 2023).

5 Sub-Regional and Bilateral Organizations

Sub-regional and bilateral treaties that are partly or wholly devoted to environmental protection frequently establish permanent agencies to assure equitable sharing and efficient utilization of resources. Generally, their features are similar to those of other international organizations: governmental participation, permanent secretariats or organs, specified functions and powers. The number of such treaties is extremely high: for water resources alone there are perhaps 600 international treaties concerning over 200 river basins shared by two or more states.[118] Examples of bilateral and sub-regional agencies are discussed in various chapters, especially those concerning the protection of inland waters, atmospheric pollution, and integrated protection.

In Africa, the Niger River Commission was created in 1964 between the nine riparian countries to promote and coordinate all matters related to exploitation of the basin resources. Its functions were expanded in 1980 when it became the Niger River Authority. It now insures an integrated developmental program for all Niger basin water resource activities.[119] The functions of the Authority include collecting, centralizing, standardizing, disseminating and exchanging data, coordinating and considering plans and projects, making recommendations, monitoring research and works of member states, and formulating coordinated plans.[120] Article 4 of the 1963 agreement[121] requires riparian states to closely cooperate with regard to the study and execution of any project likely to have an appreciable effect on features of the river, its tributaries and sub-tributaries, including the sanitary conditions of their waters and the biological characteristics of their fauna and flora. To achieve this cooperation, the riparian states agree to inform the Commission at the earliest stage, of all studies and works upon which they propose to embark and to abstain from carrying out any works likely to pollute the waters, or any modification likely to

118 See Joanne Linnerooth, 'The Danube River Basin: Negotiating Settlements to Transboundary Environmental Issues' (1990) 30 Nat Res. J. 629.

119 Convention creating the Niger Basin Authority, Nov. 21, 1980, reprinted in *U.N. Treaties Concerning the Utilization of International Water Courses for Other Purposes than Navigation*, 13 Nat. Res. Water Ser. 56, U.N. Sales No. E/F.84.II A.7.

120 Other African Commissions include the Senegal River Basin Management Organization, created in 1972, the Lake Chad Basin Commission and the Organization for the Development of the Gambia River Basin. In Asia, there is a Committee for the Lower Mekong River and the Permanent Indus Commission, established in 1960. For a description of these Commissions, *see* Dante A. Caponera, 'Patterns of Cooperation in International Water Law: Principles and Institutions' (1985) 25(3) Nat. Res. J.

121 Niamey Act regarding Navigation and Economic Cooperation between the States of the Niger Basin, 587 U.N.T.S. 9.

affect biological characteristics of its fauna and flora without adequate notice to and consultation with the Commission.[122]

On a bilateral level, numerous boundary commissions exist which exercise jurisdiction over shared natural resources.[123] For example, the United States and Mexico created an International Boundary Commission in 1889 to examine and settle boundary demarcation disputes. This Commission was replaced and its functions expanded in 1944 upon adoption of the Water Utilization Treaty,[124] which established the International Boundary and Water Commission (IBWC). It is responsible for the application of the treaty, the regulation and exercise of the rights and obligations which the two governments assume under the treaty and the settlement of all disputes between the parties. However, the Commission is authorized to act as an arbitral tribunal to settle disputes only with the permission of both nations, which seldom occurs; thus, the Commission acts primarily as an administrative body. The IBWC is composed of two national sections of technical engineers and legal advisors. Each section reports directly to its nation's foreign office for policy guidance. Since 1944, the IBWC has primarily been concerned with construction of flood control and municipal sewage treatment works along the border, including joint waterway management projects. The treaty contains no substantive obligations or principles for water quality protection and the role of the Commission has been limited; however, recent agreements have expanded its functions.

The US and Canada also set up an International Joint Commission under the terms of the 1909 treaty for the protection of boundary waters between the two countries. The Commission is composed of six members, three named by each government. It takes its decisions by majority vote. The Commission's jurisdiction consists of a power of prior authorization for certain works, a function of consultation or inquiry, and even an arbitral role for disputes which the states agree to submit to it. However, to date the latter power has never been utilized. In practice, the most important function of

122 Niamey Agreement concerning the River Niger Commission and the Navigation and Transport on the River Niger, Art. 12 (Nov. 25, 1964), 587 U.N.T.S. 19.

123 In addition to those discussed, there are bilateral commissions established between Argentina-Paraguay, Agreement Concerning a Study on the Parana River, June 15, 1971, OEA Rios y Lagos Internacinales 5119 (1971); Ecuador-Peru, Agreement on the Use of Binational Basins Puyango-Tumbes and Catamayo Chire, September 27, 1971, 385 Registro Oficial (Ecuador) 1 (1972); Finland-Sweden, Treaty Concerning Frontier Waters, 825 U.N.T.S. 191; Finland-U.S.S.R., Treaty Concerning Frontier Watercourses, April 2, 1964, 537 U.N.T.S. and nearly all central and eastern European States. See Caponera, *supra n 120* at 19.

124 Treaty Relating to the Utilization of Waters of the Colorado and Tijuana Rivers and of the Rio Grande, February 3, 1944, 59 Stat. 1219, T.S. No. 994, 3 U.N.T.S. 313. See also Chapter 10.

the Joint Commission has been to serve as a consultative organ. Its action led to the conclusion of the November 22, 1972 agreement on water quality in the Great Lakes. In addition, the Canada-United States Agreement on Air Quality (Ottawa, March 13, 1991), establishes a bilateral Air Quality Committee composed of an equal number of members representing each party. The Committee reviews progress made in the implementation of the agreement, including general and specific objectives; prepares and submits to the Parties a progress report every two years; and refers each progress report to the International Joint Commission for action. The Air Quality Committee releases the progress report to the public after its submission to the parties. The pre-existing International Joint Commission may hold hearings on the progress reports, but shall in any case, invite comments on the reports and synthesize these for the parties. The synthesis is also released to the public after its submission to the Parties.

Finally, the environmental side agreement of the North American Free Trade Agreement (NAFTA) set up a Commission on Environmental Cooperation (CEC), consisting of one high-level representative from each of the three parties.[125] It also created a 15-member Joint Public Advisory Committee, with equal national representation. The United States-Mexico-Canada Agreement (USMCA) has replaced the NAFTA but the environmental side agreement continues through the revised CEC. The CEC Secretariat reports regularly to the commission on the state of the environment in the three countries and on efforts to make improvements, particularly in enforcement of each country's own environmental standards. The public as well as governmental and non-governmental organizations may file complaints that such standards are not being applied. If the Secretariat decides that complaints show a 'consistent pattern of failure' of enforcement it can require a response from the government involved and submit a report to the commission. If the dispute is not settled within 60 days, the commission by two-thirds vote will appoint a five-member panel, drawn from a roster of 45 environmental experts to conduct public hearings. The panel can call for the government involved to submit an action plan to fix the problem. To enforce its decisions, the panel can impose fines on the offending government. If the fines are not paid, the other parties may impose sanctions of pre-USMCA tariffs.

125 Canada-Mexico-United States : *North American Agreement on Environmental Cooperation*, 8–14 September 1993, 32 I.L.M. 1480 (1993).

6 Institutions Established by Multilateral Environmental Conventions

A common feature of multilateral environmental agreements can be observed in the institutional structures and procedures they establish. The pattern of institutions includes a plenary Conference or Meeting of the Parties (COP or MOP), a secretariat, and scientific committees or other subsidiary commissions. Article 7(2) of the UNFCCC is typical in providing the mandate for its COP: 'The Conference of the Parties, as the supreme body of this Convention, shall keep under regular review the implementation of the Convention and any related legal instruments that the Conference of the Parties may adopt, and shall make, within its mandate, the decisions necessary to promote the effective implementation of the Convention'. Article 7 goes on to grant a number of specific powers to the COP: periodically examine the Convention and institutions to keep them current; promote and facilitate the exchange of information on and coordinate implementation of the Convention by parties; promote development and refinement of scientific methodologies relevant to the Convention; undertake compliance review; adopt and publish reports on implementation; mobilize financial resources; establish subsidiary bodies and review their reports; adopt rules of procedure for all bodies; seek and utilize appropriate services and cooperate with other international organizations and non-governmental bodies; and 'exercise such other functions as are required for the achievement of the objective of the Convention as well as all other functions assigned to it under the Convention'.

Treaty organs thus serve as compliance monitoring bodies, but also in a quasi-legislative capacity, making decisions, interpreting the principal agreement, and adopting recommendations, plans of action, amendments and protocols to achieve the goals of the instrument. They set the policy for most treaty regimes, act as information clearing-houses, and promote scientific research. It is these bodies that maintain the flexibility and responsiveness of international environmental treaties and they are thus of crucial importance to the effectiveness of the agreements.

The crucial function of reviewing implementation of a convention is normally conducted by discussing reports submitted by states parties as well as other public information concerning measures that the contracting parties have taken in order to ensure the effectiveness of the provisions of the agreement. In some cases, COPs discuss information provided by NGOs or individuals. COPs can adopt recommendations for the guidance of all the contracting parties and in some cases address recommendations to individual states parties.

Several conventions invest their COPs with the power to adopt amendments to the convention according to a special procedure, allowing the convention to be adapted to new circumstances to enhance its effectiveness. In addition, the COP often may draft and adopt additional protocols; this function may constitute one of the most important contributions of COPs to achieving the goals of the concerned treaty. The role of the 1987 Montreal Protocol in the implementation of the 1985 Vienna Ozone Convention is the most developed example. When such protocols are adopted, the instruments can have separate plenary bodies, as is the case with the Conference of the Parties of the Vienna Ozone Convention and the separate Meeting of the Parties of the Montreal Protocol.

The meetings of COPs are often open to participants other than representatives of the contracting parties and the trend is towards greater openness. This is an important feature to ensure the transparency of the work of COPs and cooperation with intergovernmental bodies as well as with non-state actors. The 1989 Basel Convention on Transboundary Movement of Hazardous Wastes is particularly progressive in this regard; it foresees that the UN, its specialized agencies, as well as states not party to the Convention may participate as observers at COP meetings. Any other body or agency, whether international or national, governmental or non-governmental, such as industry associations, that are qualified in the matter of hazardous wastes or other wastes, and having given notice of their interest in attending the COP can participate as observer unless one-third of the state parties objects.

COPs usually create subsidiary bodies to ensure the functioning of the treaty between sessions and to facilitate state implementation of the convention. The most developed body in the latter respect is the Montreal Protocol's Implementation Committee of the Non-Compliance Procedure. Scientific bodies are particularly important in environmental protection and they have a key role in many treaty regimes. The Biodiversity Convention, for example, has a Subsidiary Body on Scientific, Technical and Technological Advice (SBSTTA) whose members meet annually to draft proposals for adoption by the COP. Each party to the Convention may designate a governmental representative, but it must have expertise in one or more of the relevant fields. The SBSTTA has drafted many important guidelines that the COPs have adopted, such as on access to genetic resource, and integrated coastal management. Similar bodies exist for the Ramsar Convention (Scientific and Technical Review Panel), the Antarctic Treaty System (Scientific Council on Antarctic Research), CITES, the UNESCO World Heritage Convention, and others.

Secretariats, in most cases either designated or created by the basic convention, assist the COPs. Their services may be provided by existing international bodies like UNEP which provides the secretariat for the Convention on Biological Diversity, CITES and the Basel Convention. The ozone treaties refer to other international bodies such as UNDP, the World Bank, WMO, and GEF. More frequently, however, environmental agreements establish their own secretariat, sometimes after a transitory period. Secretariats can play an important role in supporting the implementation of the relevant conventions by collecting national reports on compliance by domestic authorities. In some cases they can also accept information on compliance submitted by other governments, NGOs and/or individuals. They transmit to the COP such reports and information but sometimes they elaborate a synthesis of the national reports and information on implementation.

Sometimes a secretariat, such as that of the CBD, can act as an information clearing house. In the ozone treaty system, the secretariat receives data reported by the parties on production, imports and exports of each substance controlled by the Montreal Protocol, analyses the data and submits a report to the Implementation Committee and to the Meeting of the Parties. It also can initiate the non-compliance procedure of the Montreal Protocol by transmitting the information with the corroborating data to the Implementation Committee.

Secretariats may assist states parties to implement the Convention. The secretariat of the CBD, for example, facilitates technology and information transfer and the development of cross-border projects, and in certain cases works to enhance the capacity of officials regarding implementation. The secretariat of the Basel Convention on Hazardous Wastes contributes to capacity-building and development of appropriate legislation by states in order to prevent and monitor illegal traffic. For this purpose, the secretariat has compiled existing national legislation of contracting parties and drawn up a draft model law on the management of hazardous wastes and other wastes and their disposal. It also has prepared a manual for the implementation of the Convention and a number of technical guidelines on related issues for the practical management of wastes. The UNEP-administered secretariat for CITES has published Guidelines for Legislation to Implement CITES. It undertakes technical assistance and analysis of national implementing legislation.

Capacity-building also can be enhanced by regional workshops organized by convention secretariats or by UNEP or UNITAR, in consultation with governments. Voluntary contributions from contracting parties may allow the reimbursement of expenses for participating representatives from developing countries or countries in transition. In 1994, UNEP opened an International Environmental Technology Center (IETC) whose main function is to facilitate the transfer of environmentally sound technologies to developing countries and countries with economies in transition.

COPs/MOPs also can facilitate compliance by creating financial bodies. The Multilateral Fund was established by a decision of the Second Meeting of the Parties to the Montreal Protocol (London, June 1990) and began operation in 1991. The main objective of the Multilateral Fund is to assist developing country parties to the Montreal Protocol whose annual consumption and production of ozone depleting substances (ODS) is less than 0.3 kg per capita to comply with the control measures of the Protocol. As of 2024, 147 of the 197 Parties to the Montreal Protocol meet these criteria. They are referred to as Article 5 countries. Contributions to the Multilateral Fund from the industrialized countries, or non-Article 5 countries, are assessed according to the United Nations scale of assessment. The Fund has been replenished nine times: US $240 million (1991–1993), US $455 million (1994–1996), US $466 million (1997–1999), US $440 million (2000–2002), US $474 million (2003–2005), US $400.4 million (2006–2008), US $400 million (2009–2011), US $400 million (2012–2014), US $437.5 million (2015–2017), US $540 million (2018–2020), and US $540 million (2021–2023). On October 27, 2023, during the Thirty-Fifth Meeting of the Parties to the Montreal Protocol (35th MOP), it was decided to replenish the Multilateral Fund for the triennium 2024–2026 with a budget of US $965 million, marking a record amount. As of November 8, 2023, contributions to the Multilateral Fund from developed countries, or non-Article 5 countries, have exceeded US $4.7 billion. Additionally, the Fund has received additional voluntary contributions totaling US $25.5 million from a group of donor countries to support fast-start activities for implementing the HFC phase-down.

The Fund is managed by an Executive Committee assisted by the Fund Secretariat. Projects and activities supported by the Fund are implemented by four international implementing agencies. Responsibility for overseeing the operation of the Fund rests with an Executive Committee, comprising seven members each from Article 5 and non-Article 5 countries. The term of office of the Executive Committee is one calendar year. The Chair and Vice-Chair of the Executive Committee alternate each year between the two groups. The functions of the Committee include developing operational policies, criteria for project eligibility, and other guidelines and administrative arrangements, monitoring the implementation of these policies, approving implementing agencies' business plans and work programs, approving expenditures for investment projects and other activities, allocating and disbursing resources, and monitoring and evaluating performance. The Executive Committee holds three meetings per year, each of three days duration. The meetings are preceded by two day meetings of the Executive Committee's two standing Sub-Committees on Monitoring, Evaluation and Finance and on Project Review, which are held in parallel.

The Fund Secretariat was established in 1991 in Montreal, Canada. It assists the Executive Committee in the discharge of its functions. Its activities include: development of the three-year plan and budget and a system for fund disbursement; management of the business planning cycle of the Multilateral Fund; monitoring the expenditures and activities of the implementing agencies; preparation of policy papers and other documents; review and assessment of investment projects, country programs and the business plans and work programs of the implementing agencies; liaison between the Committee, governments and implementing agencies; and servicing meetings of the Executive Committee. Monitoring and evaluation were added to the secretariat's functions by the Executive Committee in May 1997.

UNEP, UNDP, the World Bank and the United Nations Industrial Development Organization (UNIDO) have contractual agreements with the Executive Committee to assist Article 5 countries by preparing country programs, feasibility studies and project proposals, providing technical assistance for project development and implementation, as well as information dissemination. Additionally, several developed countries provide similar assistance on a bilateral basis. With the assistance of these four implementing agencies as well as the bilateral agencies, recipient enterprises prepare project proposals and ODS phase-out related activities which are reviewed by the Fund secretariat and considered by the Executive Committee.

The proliferation of environmental agreements and new treaty bodies combined with the generalized attention to environmental matters within international organizations result in a vast array of international entities working on similar issues, raising the problem of coordination and cooperative action. While by no means resolved, several actions have been taken to increase coordination. The secretariats of some treaty bodies have concluded Memoranda of Understanding to provide mutual assistance. In some instances, state-adopted Memoranda of Understanding invite intergovernmental and non-governmental organizations to become signatories (e.g. MOUs concluded under the Bonn Convention on Migratory Species). The Ramsar secretariat has been particularly pro-active in seeking cooperation with other treaty bodies like the secretariat of the Convention on Biological Diversity.

In other actions, the complex problems raised by hazardous substances in international trade led to the establishment of an Inter-organizational

Programme for the Sound Management of Chemicals (IOMC), whose participating members are the WHO, ILO, UNEP, FAO, UNIDO, OECD and UNITAR. Particular areas of coordination include harmonizing the classification of chemicals, information exchange on toxic chemicals and chemical risks, pollutant release and transfer registers, and chemical accident prevention and response. The General Assembly also has acted, creating by Res. 53/242 an overarching Environmental Management Group that includes specialized agencies, funds and programs of the UN system and the secretariats of MEAs.

7 International Financial Institutions

The legal instruments creating international financial institutions do not mention environmental protection but it has become an issue in their lending policies. Today, nearly all international financial institutions support sustainable development and condition funding of development projects on respect for the environment. Since the beginning of the 1990s most of them have created specific procedures for selecting environmentally-friendly projects and also instituted mechanisms to revise projects considered as not respecting environmental conditions.

7.1 *The World Bank*

The World Bank and the International Monetary Fund (IMF) were created in 1944 to assist in the reconstruction of Europe and Asia after the Second World War, although the Bank has since turned its attention to the economic problems of developing countries. The IMF works closely with the Bank on economic policy, but is more concerned with financial markets and stability than with development and poverty. The Bank is founded on Articles of Agreement supplemented with by-laws approved by the member states. A Board of Governors meets once a year to set policy for the Bank while on-going operations are handled by a 24-member Board of Executive Directors that meets weekly. The Bank President acts as the Chair of the Board of Executive Directors. Voting in the Bank is weighted and based upon financial shares that correspond in large part to the global economic rank of the member state. The seven largest industrial states (G–7) hold about 40% of the voting shares at the Bank. Generally, however, decisions are taken by consensus.

The World Bank Group is comprised of five associated institutions: the International Bank for Reconstruction and Development, the International Development Association, the International Finance Corporation, the Multilateral Investment Guarantee Agency, and the International Center for the

Settlement of Investment Disputes. The Group uses financial instruments to promote sustainable development, including by loan arrangements, long-term low-interest concessional credits and grants made to the poorest countries, partial risk guarantees, and private sector debt and equity.[126] The World Bank also acts as implementing agency for the Global Environmental Facility (GEF), the Montreal Protocol Multilateral Fund, the Rain Forest Trust Fund, the Prototype Carbon Fund and the Critical Ecosystem Partnership Fund, the Climate Investment Funds and the Green Climate Fund.

The World Bank's Articles of Agreement do not mention the environment. During the past three decades, however, the World Bank has addressed social and environmental issues through the development of 'Safeguard Policies' and through the work of the Inspection Panel established in 1993. In doing so, the Bank recognized the connection between economic issues and environmental degradation. In 1998 the Bank decided to reorganize its Operational Manual around related themes. Ten key environmental social and legal policies were grouped together, covering Environmental Assessment (OP 4.01, Jan. 1999), Natural Habitats (OP 4.04, Sept. 1995), Forestry (OP 4.36 Sept. 1993), Pest Management (OP 4.09, Dec. 1998), Involuntary Resettlement (OP 4.12, Dec. 2001), Indigenous Peoples (OD 4.20, Sept. 1991), Cultural Property (OP 11.03, Sept. 1986), Safety of Dams (OP 4.37, Sept. 1996), International Waterways (OP 7.50, Oct. 1994), and Projects in Disputed Areas (OP 7.60, Nov. 1994). Disclosure of Information applies to all ten safeguard policies according to the new Disclosure Policy which came into effect in January 2002. During the 1980s, environmental concerns also were integrated into the World Bank's activities through establishing an environmental department in all four of the regional divisions of the Bank.

The World Bank launched a new Environment Strategy in 2012 which focuses on nurturing more inclusive growth, while protecting biodiversity and ecosystems. The Strategy seeks to enhance countries' decision-making through the Wealth Accounting and Valuation of Ecosystem Services global partnership that supports valuing countries' natural capital assets and incorporating them into their systems of national accounts. It also aims to restore the world's oceans to health and economic productivity through a cooperative broad coalition of governments, international agencies, non-governmental

126 IBRD and IDA provide loans for public-sector projects, with IDA providing concessional or low-cost loans to the poorest countries, while IBRD provides loans to other developing countries and to countries in transition. The IFC finances private sector projects and MIGA provides insurance against the risks of loss private investors face in developing countries.

organizations and private companies. Third, it began testing the market's willingness to encourage protection of critical habitat areas while also providing carbon storage benefits through continuing work on forests and land use linked to the Reducing Emissions from Deforestation and Forest Degradation program. One focus is on support to countries to find low pollution and low-emission development paths. There is also a resilience agenda aimed at reducing vulnerability to climate risks.

The World Bank has since transitioned to a new Environmental and Social Framework (ESF), which was launched in October 2018 and which replaced the previous set of policies. The ESF includes ten Environmental and Social Standards (ESS) that set out the requirements for borrowers to manage environmental and social risks: (1) Assessment and Management of Environmental and Social Risks and Impacts (ESS1); (2) Labor and Working Conditions (ESS2); (3) Resource Efficiency and Pollution Prevention and Management (ESS3); (4) Health and Safety (ESS4); (5) Land Acquisition, Restrictions on Land Use and Involuntary Resettlement (ESS5); (6) Biodiversity Conservation and Sustainable Management of Living Natural Resources (ESS6); (7) Indigenous Peoples/Sub-Saharan African Historically Underserved Traditional Local Communities (ESS7); (8) Cultural Heritage (ESS8); (9) Financial Intermediaries (ESS9); (10) Stakeholder Engagement and Information Disclosure (ESS10).

With such changes, Bank lending for environmental projects has grown substantially in recent years. Over the past few decades, the Bank committed funding for over US$33 billion to support investment in environment and natural resource management, with climate change becoming the fastest growing area where the Bank is supporting client countries. Shortly after the global community united for the landmark 2015 Paris Agreement on climate change, the World Bank Group introduced its Climate Change Action Plan. This plan committed to increasing the share of climate finance from 20 percent of total lending in 2016 to 28 percent by 2020, aiming to support countries in achieving their climate objectives. The World Bank Group's climate finance totaled over $83 billion during the five-year period of the Climate Change Action Plan from 2016 to 2020. Other areas that have significantly expanded in the last 15 years are environmental policy and institutions, and water resource management. In addition to funding environmental projects, the Bank provides technical and legal environmental assistance to developing countries, in particular by helping in the development of Country Environmental Strategies and planning coordinated responses to address regional environmental problems, mainly in Central and Eastern Europe.

The World Bank established an Inspection Panel in 1993 because of growing concerns about the accountability of it and other international development agencies in supporting projects and programs. The Panel is an independent investigatory body receiving and investigating complaints issuing from those in the territory of a borrower whose rights or interests have been adversely affected by the Bank's failure to comply with its policies and procedures in the design, appraisal and implementation of a Bank-financed project. The Panel may investigate complaints upon authorization by the Bank Board of Executive Directors, and assess to what extent the Bank has complied with its standards. At the first stage, the Panel registers the request and asks Management to respond to the concerns expressed in it. The Panel then assesses whether or not the request meets the eligibility requirements, in particular, whether prima facie the Bank has engaged in a serious violation of its operational policies and procedures resulting or likely to result in material and adverse harm to those making the request and to which Management has failed to respond adequately. On the basis of this assessment, the Panel recommends to the Executive Directors whether or not to authorize an investigation. If authorized, the Panel investigates the merits and reaches findings. The process can result in a remedial action plan requiring management to take actions in response to Bank failures.

Several outside reviews have led to clarifications and changes in the operation of the Inspection Panel. The first review, done in 1996, focused on procedure. The Second Inspection Panel Review, completed in 1999,[127] added to and revised the 1996 conclusions. The results clarify that the initial (admissibility) stage of the procedure must focus on assertions of non-compliance and resulting potential or material harm; it is not a decision on the merits involving a true finding of harm. The issue of non-compliance is antecedent to the issue of harm and supports the notion of the Inspection Panel as a mechanism of accountability rather than a true remedial procedure. Other aspects of the conclusions similarly focus on the Panel's role to monitor the Bank non-compliance with its own policies and procedures.

The 1999 review of the panel paid particular attention to the relatively small number of full reviews that had been undertaken by the Panel. The 1999 Clarifications prevent management from short-cutting the procedure. The Clarifications make clear that the Board will authorize an investigation the Panel recommends without making any judgment on the merits or without discussion except in relation to 'technical eligibility criteria' or admissibility requirements. The latter define 'affected party' as two or more persons with common interests in the borrower's territory. In addition, they require: that the request

127 Conclusions of the Second Review of the World Bank Inspection Panel, 39 I.L.M. 243 (2000).

allege a serious violation by the Bank of its operational policies and procedures resulting in or likely to have a material adverse effect on the requesting party; that the matter be submitted to Management without adequate response; that the matter not relate to procurement and that the related loan not be closed or substantially disbursed. The matter also must be a new matter or raise new evidence or circumstances. The Panel when established is authorized to collect all pertinent bank records, interview bank staff, the requesters and others in the territory who may be able to provide information about the issue. The 1999 Clarifications emphasize the non-judicial function of the Panel and its absence of authority to interpret the legal instruments involved in the request. If issues of interpretation arise, the Panel is to seek the advice of the Legal Department.

Efforts to extend the Inspection Panel to private sector funding were opposed by the relevant institutions (International Finance Corporation or IFC / Multilateral Investment Guarantee Agency or MIGA) who instead appointed a Compliance Adviser/Ombudsman with different terms of reference, a more flexible confidential procedure and emphasis on mitigating damage. The cooperation of the Bank and the private International Finance Corporation means that in some instances both procedures may apply to a single project, e.g. the Chad/Cameroon Pipeline and the Bujagali Hydropower Project in Uganda.

In 2012, the World Bank began reviewing and updating its safeguards policies. The policies under review are the eight environmental and social safeguard policies – OP 4.01 Environmental Assessment, OP 4.04 Natural Habitats, OP 4.09 Pest Management, OP 4.10 Indigenous Peoples, OP 4.11 Physical Cultural Resources, OP 4.12 Involuntary Resettlement, OP 4.36 Forests, OP 4.37 Safety of Dams – as well as the Policy on Piloting the Use of Borrower Systems for Environmental and Social Safeguards ('Use of Country Systems'), OP 4.00.

The stated goals of the review are to enhance protections for the poor and the environment through modernized standards; provide inclusive access to development benefits through the introduction of a non-discrimination principle; strengthen partnerships with borrowing countries through closer cooperation and increased use of borrower frameworks; and strengthen the World Bank's leadership through a modernized safeguards framework. Consultations on the first draft Environmental and Social Framework showed a wide range of views among shareholder governments and civil society groups. When the Committee on Development Effectiveness (CODE) of the World Bank's Board of Executive Directors discussed the second draft of the proposed Framework, consensus emerged on the overall architecture and some of the proposed provisions. However, many issues remained open and CODE authorized consultations in order to continue efforts to find solutions. In particular, it was considered that further discussion was required on various aspects – notably the Vision statement, some Standards, and sensitivity/ambition of language. Equally, further clarity was needed on implementation and potential impact on borrowers. Executive Directors requested the preparation of an indicative list of outstanding issues to guide discussions throughout the consultation process.

A third consultation phase on the second draft of a proposed new Environmental and Social Framework (ESF) opened on August 4, 2015. The Bank held consultations in 16 countries during the rest of the year and scheduled further meetings in 2016 in another 17 states. The feedback from these meetings provides the basis for analysis and revisions to the second draft framework. As part of the review and update process the Bank is also considering if and how it could address emerging areas that are not covered by the current safeguard policies. These include climate change; disability; free, prior and informed consent of indigenous people; gender; human rights; labor and occupational health and safety; and land tenure and natural resources.

In August 2017, the Board initiated an External Review of the Inspection Panel Toolkit to assess whether any updates were necessary for the Panel to continue functioning effectively under the new ESF. At the conclusion of this review, the World Bank Accountability Mechanism was established, which aims to strengthen the Panel's role, improve its procedures, and ensure better responsiveness to stakeholders' concerns.

7.2 *The Global Environmental Facility*

The Global Environmental Facility (GEF) is the primary mechanism providing developing countries with 'new and additional grants and concessional funding to meet the agreed full incremental cost of measures to achieve global benefits', as required by various global environmental agreements.[128] In particular, funding is intended to address six environmental issues: climate change, stratospheric ozone depletion, loss of biological diversity, pollution of international waters, land degradation and persistent organic pollutants. The GEF operates as the interim financial mechanism under the UNFCCC, the Convention on Biological Diversity, the POPs Convention, the Convention to Combat Desertification and the Minamata Convention.

THE GEF, launched in 1991 for a three-year pilot phase with an initial sum of $1.2 billion,[129] was restructured and made permanent in 1994. It is governed by an Assembly, a Council and a Secretariat. The Assembly consists of

128 See *Instrument for the Establishment of the Restructured Global Environment Facility* (1994), 33 I.L.M. 1273 (1994).

129 By 1999, GEF grants totaled $2.7 billion. E <http://www.gefweb.org>.

representatives of 186 countries; it meets every three years to review and revise the GEF's general policy and operations. The Council consists of thirty-two members representing constituency groups; it has primary authority for developing, adopting and evaluating the operational policies and programs for GEF-financed activities. It also reviews, approves and monitors the implementing agencies' work program. The Secretariat is located at the World Bank which provides administrative support, but the GEF is supposed to be functionally independent. Funds are transferred through 18 GEF Agencies: Asian Development Bank (ADB), African Development Bank (AfDB), European Bank for Reconstruction and Development (EBRD), FAO, Inter-American Development Bank (IDB), International Fund for Agricultural Development (IFAD), UNDP, UNEP, UNIDO, WB Group, Conservation International, Development Bank of Latin America, Development Bank of Southern Africa, Foreign Economic Cooperation Office Ministry of Environmental Protection of China, Brazilian Biodiversity Fund, IUCN, West African Development Bank, and World Wildlife Fund (WWF). They are accountable to the Council for their GEF-funded activities.

Over the past three decades, the GEF has allocated over $25 billion in financing and mobilized $145 billion for priority projects driven by country needs. The family of funds includes the Global Environment Facility Trust Fund, Global Biodiversity Framework Fund (GBFF), Least Developed Countries Fund (LDCF), Special Climate Change Fund (SCCF), Nagoya Protocol Implementation Fund (NPIF), and Capacity-building Initiative for Transparency Trust Fund (CBIT).

7.3 *The International Finance Corporation*

The International Finance Corporation (IFC) is the private sector part of the World Bank group, providing loans to private companies for projects in developing countries. It shares an almost identical Board of Executive Directors with the World Bank. The IFC published in September 1993 a document providing guidance to its staff in conducting an environmental review of proposed projects.[130] This document is similar in many respects to the World Bank's OP 4.01 (Environmental Assessment) and has identical goals, but there are some significant differences between the two texts. The procedure of the International Finance Corporation addresses project sponsors who approach the institution much later in the project development cycle, often after feasibility studies, site selection, and preliminary design work have been completed. In such cases,

130 *Environmental Analysis and Review of Projects*, Sept. 8, 1993.

the sponsor may be required to do the environmental analysis concurrently with the appraisal of other aspects of the project. Thus, IFC's procedure is designed for flexibility, to accommodate projects brought to the IFC in various stages of development. The IFC, however, does not require the project sponsor to consult with local interested parties and affected groups during the preparation of the environmental assessment or to make the draft EA publicly available for review and comment, including release to relevant national agencies and institutions. The procedure of the World Bank Inspection Panel does not apply to IFC-funded projects.

7.4 *The European Bank for Reconstruction and Development*

The European Bank for Reconstruction and Development (EBRD) adopted its first Environmental Policy in 1991 at the initial meeting of its Board of Directors. The scope of the Policy has evolved over time and it is now an Environmental and Social Policy. On May 7, 2014, the EBRD Board of Directors approved revisions to three major governance policies: the Environmental and Social Policy, Public Information Policy, and Project Complaint Mechanism Rules of Procedure. The revisions followed consultations with civil society organizations, industry associations, clients, other international financial institutions, and international organizations.

The Environmental and Social Policy, which was revised in 2019, includes a comprehensive set of specific Performance Requirements that projects are expected to meet to manage the environmental and social issues associated with them over a reasonable period of time. The EBRD aims to ensure through its environmental and social appraisal and monitoring processes that projects are designed, implemented and operated in compliance with applicable regulatory requirements and good international practice. The EBRD is a signatory to the European Principles for the Environment,[131] and seeks to have them applied at the project level, regardless of their geographical location. When host country regulations differ from EU substantive environmental standards, projects will be expected to meet whichever is the more stringent. Furthermore, the EBRD will not knowingly finance projects that would contravene country obligations under relevant international treaties and agreements, as identified

131 The European Principles for the Environment were adopted by the Council of Europe Development Bank, the EBRD, European Investment Bank, Nordic Environment Finance Corporation and Nordic Investment Bank. The EPE is an initiative launched in response to the drive for increased harmonization of environmental principles, practices and standards associated with the financing of projects.

during the project appraisal, or that would result in forced evictions.[132] All proposed projects undergo environmental and social appraisals reviewed by the EBRD Board of Directors. Performance is monitored through the life of the project.

The EBRD's Sustainable Resource Initiative (SRI) was launched in 2006 to promote sustainable energy, climate change resilience and resource efficiency. As well as tackling water and materials efficiency, it supported energy efficiency, renewable energy and climate change adaptation. Until 2015, the EBRD invested €16.4 billion more than 926 projects under the SRI.

In 2014, the EBRD established a Project Complaint Mechanism (PCM) to assess and review complaints about Bank-financed projects. The PCM gives local individuals, organizations and local groups that perceive harm from a Bank project, a means of raising complaints and seeking assistance through an independent review. It can also be used by individuals or groups to file a complaint if they believe that the Bank has not complied with this Policy or project-specific components of the policy. In 2021, the EBRD adopted the Green Economy Transition (GET) 2021–25, which represents its latest strategy to assist economies in its operational areas in developing environmentally sustainable, low-carbon, and resilient economies.

7.5 *The European Investment Bank*

The European Investment Bank (EIB) is the organ of the European Union that funds long-term development projects outside the Union, in the ACP countries, in the Mediterranean region and in Central and Eastern European countries. Although it has an autonomy within the EU, it functions in close co-operation with other institutions, mainly the EU Commission. It also acts in conformity

132 Other projects excluded from finance are those that directly or indirectly involve: the production of or trade in any product or activity deemed illegal under host country (national) laws or regulations, or international conventions and agreements, or subject to international phase out or bans, such as production of or trade in products containing PCBs15 or production of or trade in ozone depleting substances or pharmaceuticals, pesticides/herbicides and other hazardous substances subject to international phase-outs or bans; trade in wildlife or production of or trade in wildlife products regulated under CITES; transboundary movements of waste prohibited under international law; production or use of or trade in unbonded asbestos fibers or asbestos-containing products; activities prohibited by host country legislation or international conventions relating to the protection of biodiversity resources or cultural heritage; drift net fishing in the marine environment using nets in excess of 2.5 km in length; shipment of oil or other hazardous substances in tankers which do not comply with IMO requirements; trade in goods without required export or import licenses or other evidence of authorization of transit from the relevant countries of export, import and, if applicable, transit.

with the environmental legislation of the EU, especially Directives 85/337 and 2014/52/EU relating to the environmental impact assessment.

The Bank takes an active part in identifying the potential risks of projects and the necessary or appropriate mitigation measures. The borrower must prepare an environmental impact assessment which must be combined with public consultation. When screening the project, the Bank can require the insertion in the loan contract of appropriate provisions for guaranteeing environmental protection. The Bank also can intervene as a consultant in environmental issues and fund the identification and the preparation of projects improving the environment.

7.6 *The Inter-American Development Bank*

The Inter-American Development Bank (IDB) first adopted a document on Environmental Policy in 1979. During the late 1980s and early 1990s the IDB supported the principles of sustainable development and the 1994 Eighth Replenishment of Resources declared the environment, together with poverty reduction and social equity, as priority areas for Bank support, including a number of specific environmental mandates that have guided Bank work since then. These mandates included provisions for: (i) strengthening environmental legal and regulatory frameworks; (ii) strengthening environmental institutions; (iii) improving the environmental quality of operations financed by the Bank; (iv) promoting the conservation and efficient use of energy in the Bank's projects; (v) improving the urban environment; (vi) promoting sustainable management of natural resources with specific references to environmentally sustainable practices for water resources, forestry, biological diversity, marine resources, and agriculture; (vii) addressing issues of transparency and access to environmental information, and stakeholder consultation; (viii) quality control and environmental impact assessments (EIAs); and (xi) fostering environmental education and training.

In 2003, the Board of Executive Directors endorsed a new Environment Strategy (GN-2208-4, 2003) to enhance sustainability outcomes, particularly by mainstreaming environment as a cross-cutting dimension of social and sustainable development. The Environment and Safeguards Compliance Policy is intended to provide the necessary directives to put into operation and reinforce key priorities stated in the IDB's Environment Strategy and the Eighth Replenishment. The Policy, replacing the IDB's Environment Policy (OP–703), takes into account current changes and realities that influence environmental sustainability, which include the positive development of institutional capacities among borrowing member countries; the increased role of civil society participation in the context of democratic processes; the process of convergence of policies and harmonization among multilateral and bilateral development institutions; the need to enhance development effectiveness; the increased role of private sector investments and public/private partnerships; the sustainability commitments of leading private-sector financial institutions to the Equator Principles; and the growing importance of global and regional challenges and opportunities. This Policy also considers the links that exist between poverty and environmental management. It recognizes the need to enhance conditions for social and economic development and the important role that sound management of natural resources and the environment plays in this process.

The operational standards and guidelines as well as decisions of its Board require that all operations financed by the IDB be environmentally and socially sustainable. The focal point of environmental quality and social impact management within the Bank is the Committee on Environment and Social Impact (CESI) which attempts to address the root causes of environmental deterioration and the institutional framework that determines the success of measures to prevent and mitigate harm. Project review includes e.g. the promotion of adequate environmental regulatory and management frameworks; the adoption of environmental protection, management, mitigation and enhancement measures in specific operations; indigenous rights and community development issues; involuntary resettlement matters; and issues of social impact and sustainability. In this context, the objective of the procedures is to assure and enhance the quality of Bank operations. Such procedures are applicable to all Bank operations, including sector loans, investment loans, technical co-operations, small projects, private sector operations and any major reformulation of those operations.

In 2021 the IDB approved over US$4.5 billion in lending, as well as additional non-reimbursable grant resources, to projects targeting environmental sustainability and climate change mitigation and adaptation. All projects require the assessment of the risks that may affect the success of the project, such as environmental and social capacity, track record, local sensitivities or reputational risks. The implementation of the project is monitored to ensure that it complies with IDB safeguards as well as specific national and international standards. The IDB reviews the adequacy of the environmental and social impact assessments, management plans and procedures, and institutional arrangements for mitigating and managing impacts and risks, and determines what additional measures need to be included in the project design and operation to ensure that environmental and social impacts and risks are mitigated and managed. In 1994 the IDB created an independent investigation mechanism to receive complaints about IDB-funded projects, a mechanism strengthened in 2010 and again in 2014.

7.7 *African Development Bank*

The African Development Bank (AfDB) adopted its first Environmental Policy in 1990, a set of Environmental and Social Assessment Procedures (ESAPS) in 2001, the Involuntary Resettlement Policy in 2003 and a revised Policy on the Environment in 2004. These policies have provided the basis for the Bank's current environmental and social safeguards, which set out the requirements for an appropriate level of environmental and social assessment and management measures to mitigate project-related risks. The Bank also has other cross-cutting and sector policies that contain commitments to promote environmental and social sustainability in Bank operations: policies on health (1996), integrated water resources management (2000), agriculture and rural development (2000), gender (2001), co-operation with civil society organisations (2001), involuntary resettlement (2003), poverty reduction (2004), and the environment (2004), as well as the Civil Society Engagement Framework (2012).

Taking all these into account, in 2013 the Bank published an Integrated Safeguards System (ISS). Part of this Integrated Safeguards System is a set of five safeguard requirements that Bank clients are expected to meet when addressing social and environmental impacts and risks. Bank staff review and supervise projects to ensure that clients comply with these requirements during project preparation and implementation. The five safeguards include requiring that all proposed projects undertake an integrated social and environmental impact assessment. Others concern issues of land acquisition and resettlement, biodiversity and ecosystem services, pollution prevention and control, including the use of hazardous substances, and labor conditions, health and safety. The ISS makes it mandatory to apply Strategic Environmental and Social Assessment to address the environmental and social issues arising from 'upstream' operations, such as budget support and investment programs managed by the client. It also makes it mandatory for clients implementing regional or sector-wide programs to develop Environmental and Social Management Frameworks identifying, appraising, and financing individual investments under the program.

The Bank monitors implementation through quarterly reports by borrowers and clients and during its own supervision missions, using proportionality and adaptive management principles to differentiate projects on the basis of the nature and category of the risks. For projects presenting high environmental and social risks, the Bank may, at its own discretion, perform compliance audits. The Bank's Compliance and Safeguards Division monitors the environmental and social performance of Bank's projects in consultation with borrowers and/or clients. For complex projects or when conflicts with host communities arise, the Bank uses independent third parties – independent environmental and social advisers, consultants, monitors and auditors – to monitor compliance. The Bank ensures that the reports of these monitoring exercises are publicly available to all parties in line with the Bank's Disclosure and Access to Information policy. From such reports, the relevant Bank department prepares, and agrees with the client on, an implementable action plan, with measurable indicators. The Bank's efforts to strengthen the capacity of country systems do not alter the role and function of the Bank's accountability mechanisms.

To enhance its efforts and align more closely with the Sustainable Development Goals, the AfDB has taken several significant steps since 2015. These include introducing the five operational priorities known as 'the High 5s, the Gender Strategy (2021–2025), and the Climate Change and Green Growth Strategic Framework (2021). Additionally, in recent years, the AfDB has developed new lending and investment instruments, such as the revised Policy on Non-sovereign Operations in 2018 and the Private Sector Development Strategy for 2021–2025.

The Bank has a grievance and redress mechanism comprising five elements: (i) policies and procedures established by the Bank on addressing requests for dispute resolution in the environmental and social context; (ii) public access to the process through the Bank country office or through the Compliance Review and Mediation Unit (CRMU); iii) country-level responsibility for receiving and responding to requests for redress; (iv) the CRMU, which provides a corporate window for receiving requests for dispute resolution and mediation process; and (v) tracking and monitoring grievances and their resolutions. The mandate of the Bank's Independent Review Mechanism (IRM) is to provide people who are, or are likely to be, adversely affected by a project financed by the Bank Group as a result of violation of the Bank Group's policies and procedures with an avenue to request the Bank to comply with its own policies and procedures. The requestors first seek to resolve their complaints with Bank Management; but if in their opinion, Bank Management has not adequately handled their complaints, they may submit their requests to IRM. The IRM comprises two separate, but related, phases: (i) a grievance or problem-solving phase, led by the CRMU reporting directly to the Bank President, to assist project-affected people in finding solutions to their problems; and (ii) a compliance review phase, led by a three-member panel drawn from the IRM roster of experts.

7.8 *The Asian Development Bank*

The Asian Development Bank (ADB) has expressed its commitment to promoting environmentally sustainable economic development in its member countries. The ADB's Office of the Environment categorizes all projects listed in country operational program papers according to their type, location, sensitivity and the nature and magnitude of their potential impact and availability of cost-effective mitigation measures. If a significant impact is expected, an EIA or an initial environmental examination is required for the project, according to the importance of the impact. When an impact assessment is mandated, the procedure starts with the submission of a summary environmental assessment by the Projects department to the Board. The full EIA should be made available to a member of the Board upon request. The ADB requires the borrower to take the views of affected groups and local NGOs into account in the preparation of environmental assessment reports. The assessment reports may also be made available to them. Specific rules govern program loans, sector loans and private sector operations.

For all projects that can have a potential impact on the environment, the project staff should carry out an initial environmental examination. On the return of the fact-finding mission, the report will be reviewed and the terms of reference for the special study or EIA will be prepared with the active assistance of the Office for the Environment. The loan fact-finding mission analyzes the results of the assessment and identifies probable additional environmental concerns not addressed in the study or resulting from changes in project scope. Towards the end of each calendar year a report is published listing all projects requiring specific environmental treatment during the implementation phase.

A review mission is dispatched periodically to discuss with concerned executing agencies the implementation of environmental mitigation measures agreed upon by both the borrower and the Bank. It verifies that environmental safeguards built into the project design are satisfactorily implemented during the construction and the operation of the project. At the end of the operations a project completion report should include a general assessment of any significant environmental impact experienced during project implementation.

In addition to the specific practices described above, several international lending institutions have established formal channels through which local communities, organizations and other groups, and, in special cases members of the Board of Directors, can request independent review or 'inspection' of the bank's role in specific bank-financed projects.[133]

133 See the World Bank rules governing the inspection panels adopted on August 19, 1994; the Asian Development Bank Inspection Procedures approved by the Board of Directors on

The environmental practices of international financial institutions display several general trends. The first is the creation of special procedures for introducing environmental conditions in the banks' decision-making processes. Such procedures involve the prior assessment of potential environmental impacts of planned activities, a factor that has become important in selecting projects for funding. In some cases the environmental impact is understood in a large manner, taking into account the broad environmental and social effects. The legislative and institutional capacity of the borrowing state to fulfil the environmental conditions of the loan generally are considered as well. The information and the participation of local groups and NGOs at different stages of the procedure is always required. The importance of the intervention of local groups and of NGOs is also reflected in the possibility afforded them to ask for the review of a decision they consider as contrary to environmental protection. The special procedures that the financial institutions have established for this purpose generally combine expertise and independence.

8 Non-Governmental Organizations and Civil Society

During much of international legal history, states were considered as the sole subjects of international law, leaving other entities without legal competence and with few roles to play. A transformation of the international system occurred in the twentieth century with the emergence of non-state actors, from the international organizations described in the preceding sections to non-governmental organizations, multinational companies, and individual participants. The role of transnational civil society has been particularly important in the evolution of international environmental law.

The communications revolution that introduced faxes, the Internet, and electronic mail has allowed environmental activism to move beyond formal NGOs to create grass-roots networks and campaigns that may be limited to a single project or may form around a larger issue. This dynamic process can result in powerful movements that force governments to consider public opinion beyond their borders, creating change in many parts of the world.[134] The notion of an international civil society is now widely recognized[135] and seen as a process of directly channeling public participation to private actors in

October 9, 1996 and for the Inter-American Development Bank the document on Independent Investigation Mechanism (no date is available).

134 See Jessica Tuchman Matthews, 'Power Shift' (1997) Foreign Affairs 50.

135 See e.g., J. Smith, 'Global Civil Society' (1998) 42 AM. Behavioral Scientist 93.

policy-making and implementation. Political discourse across borders helps shape common interests and the identities of societies. The interaction also lends legitimacy and increases accountability when compared to many traditional decision-making processes and structures.

Non-governmental organizations formed to advance the interests of their groups have long existed[136] but their numbers have grown considerably along with their ability to participate in international events. Three decades ago, it was estimated that 275,000 NGOs operated in the United Kingdom alone.[137] Environmental groups emerged due to frustration with governments' lack of initiative to address the extent of environmental degradation, while the communications revolution has made it possible to connect the global community efficiently and inexpensively. In the past two decades, environmental NGOs have developed scientific expertise and lobbying skills that allow them to effectively participate in negotiations for environmental agreements. Some of the environmental NGOs have become well-known for their work on a global basis: IUCN, Friends of the Earth, Greenpeace International, and the WWF. Thousands more work nationally or transnationally, sometimes on single issues, at other times with broad mandates. Because of their importance, the Brundtland Commission recommended that governments establish official consultation with NGOs to share information, strategies and resources, and to permit meaningful participation in all aspects of environmental matters.

Many NGOs act within international institutions, seeking to influence international decision-making, as well as within states, where they promote positive environmental policies. They represent their members in advancing their common values. Like individual members of the public, NGOs may compile data, seek to influence legislation, intervene in decisions on licensing or permitting projects, and monitor compliance with environmental laws. With these roles and because of their greater means, expertise, and organized efforts, NGOs often can effectively assert public rights of information and participation. They have a variety of assets, including access to funds, ability to attract media attention, and the ability to acquire, communicate and disseminate expert information. Most importantly, they possess a legitimacy and transnationalism that gives them influence and permits them to push the transparency of international institutions as they frame issues, build communities, and set examples, at their best becoming moral agents of change. Increasingly, too, they have become aware of their own needs for transparency

136 See Lyman C. White, *International Non-Governmental Organizations: Their Purposes, Methods and Accomplishments* (1951).

137 See Lester M. Salamon, 'The Rights of the Non-Profit Sector' (1994) 75 Foreign Affairs 109, 111.

and are becoming more public about funding sources, membership and other governance issues.

The strength of NGOs is often necessary to counterbalance powerful business interests,[138] but the industry itself can contribute to the implementation of international environmental law, as is discussed in more detail in Chapter 17. Chemical companies supported the ozone regime by rapidly developing chemical alternatives to ozone-depleting substances. The insurance sector has undertaken advanced research on climate change and supported action to curb greenhouse gas emissions. Representatives of the tourist industry have participated in consultative meetings of the Antarctic Treaty system.

To strengthen the international role of NGOs, Agenda 21 called on the UN system, including international finance and development agencies, and all intergovernmental organizations and forums, in consultation with NGOs, to take measures to:

a. Review and report on ways of enhancing existing procedures and mechanisms by which NGOs contribute to policy design, decision-making, implementation and evaluation at the individual agency level, in inter-agency discussions and in UN conferences;
b. On the basis of subparagraph(a) above, enhance existing or, where they do not exist, establish mechanisms and procedures within each agency to draw on the expertise and views of NGOs in policy and program design, implementation and evaluation;

   …
c. design open and effective means of achieving the participation of NGOs in the processes established to review and evaluate the implementation of Agenda 21 at all levels; and …
d. provide access for NGOs to accurate and timely data and information to promote the effectiveness of their programs and activities and their roles in support of sustainable development.[139]

NGOs, and civil society at large, played an important role in the adoption in 2015 of the 2030 Agenda for Sustainable Development. In fact, the Sustainable Development Goals (SDGs), were the result of more than two years of extensive public consultation and engagement with civil society and various stakeholders worldwide. Moreover, NGOs and civil society are also seen as instrumental to the implementation of the 2030 Agenda: 'We acknowledge the role of the

138 As part of the private sector, business groups may also form NGOs. At COP-7 of the Framework Convention on Climate Change, held in Marrakesh at the end of 2001, the overwhelming majority of accredited NGOs represented the energy sector, coal and steel producers, the chemical industry, and other business interests.

139 Agenda 21, Chapter 27.9.

diverse private sector, ranging from micro-enterprises to cooperatives to multinationals, and that of civil society organizations and philanthropic organizations in the implementation of the new Agenda' (para. 41).

Many NGOs obtain formal status in international institutions. Article 71 of the UN Charter provides that the Economic and Social Council may extend 'consultative status' to international NGOs that satisfy criteria established by the United Nations. Such status entitles an NGO to access to UN meetings and conferences, and, in some instances, the right to intervene orally and submit written statements. NGOs were prominent at the Stockholm and Rio Conferences. At UNCED, some 1500 NGOs were accredited to attend formal meetings and some informal meetings. They were permitted to lobby, present documents and meet among themselves. NGOs also were present at negotiations for the Kyoto Protocol and at COP21 in Paris at the end of 2014. Many have been afforded observer status in international environmental treaties[140] and they increasingly have a role in launching international inquiries.[141]

Several environmental agreements recognize a formal role for NGOs. The Convention for the Protection of the Marine Environment of the North-East Atlantic (September 22, 1992) granted observer status to NGOs along with non-party states and inter-governmental organizations. Article 4.1 of the UNFCCC (June 4, 1992) provides that all parties shall 'promote and cooperate in education, training and public awareness related to climate change and encourage the widest participation in this process, including that of non-governmental organizations'. Article 7.2.1 addresses the issue of supervising the implementation of the Convention by the Conference of the Parties and states that it shall 'seek and utilize, where appropriate, the services and cooperation of, and information provided by, competent international organizations and intergovernmental and non-governmental bodies'. CITES (Washington, March 3, 1973), Article 11(7), similarly provides them a role. The Montreal Protocol (September 16, 1987) establishes a relatively open process for NGOs. It states that

> Any body or agency, whether national or international, governmental or non-governmental, qualified in fields relating to the protection of the ozone layer which has informed the secretariat of its wish to be represented at a meeting of the Parties as an observer may be admitted unless at least one third of the parties present object. (Article 11.5).

140 *See e.g.* Convention on Biological Diversity, Art. 23(5), 31 I.L.M. 818 (1992); Convention for the Protection of the Marine Environment of the North East Atlantic, Sept. 22, 1992.

141 *See e.g.* the discussion of the World Bank Inspection Panel and NAAEC in Chapters 4 and 17.

The rules of procedure of the Executive Committee for the Multilateral Fund established by the Protocol provide for notification to qualified NGOs of meetings where they may participate as observers without the right to vote, upon invitation of the Chairman and if there is no objection from Committee members present. The language of the 1992 Biodiversity Convention is nearly identical to that of the Montreal Protocol. The UN Desertification Convention (June 17, 1994) speaks in its preamble of 'the special role of non-governmental organizations and other major groups in programs to combat desertification and mitigate the effects of drought'. Finally, during the drafting of the 1998 Rotterdam Convention on Prior Informed Consent, a number of representatives strongly advocated that the Chemical Review Committee should be open not only to the participation of observers from Governments, but to international organizations and non-governmental organizations. In the end, the adopted treaty allows such participation unless one-third of the parties objects.

In addition to their formal role, NGOs act to inform public opinion, exposing environmental harm and setting environmental agendas. Globalization may enhance the power of NGOs to mobilize effective consumer actions. Non-governmental organizations also may draft or develop norms either for their own governance, or for submission to states for adoption. They perform monitoring, information gathering and other functions related to compliance with binding and non-binding norms. In practice, most non-binding international norms – indeed most binding international norms – are not drafted by one type of international actor independently of all others but, instead, are adopted through a complex interplay of state and non-state actors. The relatively homogenous character of the international order at the beginning of this century has given way to an international system comprised of a highly diverse and enlarged group of states, international institutions, and non-state actors. All of them increasingly take part in making and applying national and international norms. Today, purely inter-state development of norms is probably non-existent in most fields of international law. It is also rare to find purely private standard-setting. The modes of interaction between state and non-state actors may be particularly important to achieving compliance with soft law norms, as a participatory process enhancing the legitimacy and authority of the norms adopted.

The important role of NGOs in the development of and compliance with international norms and standards is indicated by several examples. IUCN was instrumental in elaborating and pressing for UN adoption of the World Charter for Nature. The International Law Association adopted the 1966 Helsinki Rules on the Uses of the Waters of International Rivers that provided the basis for several treaties on international waterways, such as the agreement between Namibia and South Africa to establish a permanent water commission.[142]

An NGO sometimes serves as the secretariat for an inter-governmental treaty, *e.g.* IUCN in regard to the Ramsar Convention on Wetlands of International Importance. Other non-governmental bodies serve as expert bodies in treaty administration, such as the Scientific Committee on Antarctic Research of the International Council of Scientific Unions in regard to the Antarctic Treaty system. On occasion, NGOs may take on an official role in regard to monitoring and compliance. Unofficially, most of them serve as 'watchdogs' in the process of adoption and implementation of international environmental law.

The role of NGOs is expanding, both in numbers and in functions. The expanded functions of NGOs can be seen in the Rules of Procedure of the Permanent Committee of the Bern Convention. It authorizes oral declarations and written submissions by NGOs; their propositions may be the subject of a vote if requested by a delegation (Art. 9 Rules of Procedure). Going further, the Mediterranean Commission on Sustainable Development, created in 1995, comprises thirty-six delegates, of which twenty-one represent states and fifteen come from environmental NGOs. They sit on a basis of equality. It is, however, only a consultative organization in which there is no vote.

Given the expanded functions, NGOs sometimes form alliances among themselves and with inter-governmental organizations to help implement international environmental law. In the early 1980s, the WWF, IUCN and UNEP formed the World Conservation Monitoring Center to collect and provide information services on conservation and sustainable use of biological resources. The Monitoring Center now provides data management services for the CITES Secretariat, the World Heritage Convention, the Convention on Biological Diversity, the Convention on Migratory Species and the Ramsar Convention. Centralizing conservation data allows the Center to work with the secretariats of the five major biodiversity treaties to harmonize reporting and management of information.

Finally, NGOs may be able to participate in dispute settlement procedures, either as parties, or as amicus curiae. In the *US-Shrimp* case at the World Trade Organization, NGO briefs were attached as exhibits to the US submission, but a revised version of one of the briefs was submitted independently by a group of NGOs and was accepted by the panel, despite protests of some governments. In recent years, NGOs have increasingly turned to domestic courts

142 Agreement between the Government of the Republic of Namibia and the Government of the Republic of South Africa on the Establishment of a Permanent Water Commission, done at Noordoewer, Sept. 14, 1992, 32 ILM 1147 (1993).

to hold states and multinational enterprises accountable for environmental degradation and climate change impacts. These legal actions seek to enforce national and international environmental laws, compelling governments and corporations to adopt more sustainable practices and reduce greenhouse gas emissions. By leveraging litigation, NGOs aim to fill regulatory gaps, push for stricter enforcement of existing laws, and promote greater environmental responsibility. High-profile cases, such as those against major oil companies (e.g. *Milieudefensie v. Shell*) and government agencies (e.g. *Urgenda v. The Netherlands*) highlight the growing role of judicial systems in addressing global environmental and climate crises. This trend underscores the vital role of civil society in advocating for environmental justice and sustainable development through legal channels.

Bibliography

Axelrod, R. And Van Deveer, S.D., The Global Environment: Institutions, Law and Policy (4th Edn, 2015).

Bartlett, R.V., Kurian, P.A. And Malik, M. (Eds.), *International Organizations and Environmental Policy* (1995).

Bodansky, D., 'The Legitimacy of International Governance: A Coming Challenge for International Environmental Law', 93 *AJILl* 614 (1999).

Conca, Ken, *An Unfunished Foundation: The United Nations and Global Environmental Governance* (2015).

Desombre, E.R., *Global Environmental Institutions* (2006).

Gunthur, Konrad et al (Eds), *Sustainable Development and Good Governance* (1995).

Haas, Peter et al (Eds), *Institutions for the Earth – Sources of Effective Environmental Protection* (1993).

Keohane R. et al., *Institutions for the Earth* (1993).

Kimball, L. A., *Forging International Agreement: Strengthening Inter-Governmental Institutions for Environment and Development* (1992).

Potter, D., *NGOs and Environmental Policies: Asia and Africa* (1996).

Raustiala, K., 'States, NGOs and International Environmental Institutions', 41 *Int'l Studies Q.* 719–49 (1997).

Rolen, M., Sjoberg, H. & Svedin, U. (Eds.), *International Governance on Environmental Issues* (1997).

Sands, Ph., 'The Role Of Environmental NGOs in International Environmental Law', 2 *Development* 28 (1992).

Shihata, I. *The World Bank Inspection Panel* (1994).

Turlock, A. D., 'The Role of Non-Governmental Organizations in the Development of International Environmental Law', 68 *Chi-Kent L. Rev.* 61 (1992).

CHAPTER 6

Implementing International Environmental Law: Techniques and Procedures

1 Introduction

International environmental instruments often suggest or mandate the use of specified techniques and procedures to achieve the aims of the agreement. While most instruments call for the adoption of legislation or regulation, some also detail the specific content of the measures to be taken[1] and others permit or recommend particular techniques.[2]

The variety, complexity and acceptance of these legal mechanisms have increased in recent years through the mutual influence of national and international environmental law. International environmental agreements today usually require states parties to adopt environmental impact or risk assessment procedures, licensing, and monitoring. Environmental auditing, product labeling, use of best available techniques and practices, and prior informed consent also commonly appear in global and regional instruments. States often enact and implement several techniques and procedures simultaneously, in response to treaty mandates as well as to particular threats to the environment, national and local conditions, traditions and cultural norms, and the economic situation specific to each country. This chapter will discuss the legal techniques and procedures that commonly appear in international environmental instruments.

1 United Nations Convention on the Law of the Sea (Dec. 10, 1982) (hereinafter UNCLOS), Art. 210 requires states parties to adopt laws and regulations to prevent, reduce and control pollution of the marine environment by dumping. The third paragraph of the article specifies that the measures 'shall ensure that dumping is not carried out without the permission of the competent authorities' of the state.

2 UNCLOS, Art. 62, for example, allows that the laws and regulations of a state party concerning fishing in the Exclusive Economic Zone (EEZ) 'may relate' to licensing of fishermen and fishing vessels, payment of fees, setting fishing quotas and seasons, and similar measures.

 | DOI:10.1163/9789047440802_008

Environmental agreements and national laws often regulate a single environmental milieu, e.g. water,[3] air,[4] soil,[5] biological diversity[6] due to the particular environmental problems facing a given area, political or economic priorities, or the ease of achieving consensus on a specific environmental issue. A more comprehensive approach seeks integrated pollution prevention and control, i.e. protection against pollution of all natural systems necessary to support the biosphere. The 1994 United Nations Convention to Combat Desertification in those Countries Experiencing Serious Drought and/or Desertification, Particularly in Africa requires states parties to adopt an integrated approach addressing the physical, biological and socio-economic aspects of the processes of desertification and drought (Art. 4(2)(a)). Other international agreements mandate broad national action plans, with targets and time-tables.[7] This is for instance the case of the other two framework conventions adopted at the Rio Conference in 1992: the United Nations Framework Convention on Climate Change (UNFCCC) and the Convention on Biological Diversity (CBD).

Texts calling for integrated pollution prevention and control exist also on the regional level, for example in the European Union (EU) and the Organization for Economic Co-operation and Development (OECD). An OECD Council Recommendation of January 31, 1991 expresses the purpose of integrated pollution prevention and control: to prevent or minimize the risk of harm to the environment as a whole, recognizing the integrated nature of the environment by taking account of the effects of substances or activities on all environmental media.

The focus of 'integrated pollution prevention and control' is thus on eliminating or at least reducing the polluting substance, noting its origin and geographic target. Integrated pollution prevention and control involves a 'cradle to grave' approach that considers the whole life cycle of substances and products, anticipates the effects of substances and activities on all environmental media, minimizes the quantity and harmfulness of waste, uses a single method such as risk assessment for estimating and comparing

---

3 UNCLOS; United Nations Economic Commission for Europe (UNECE) Transboundary Watercourses Convention (March 17, 1992), UN Convention on the Law of the Non-Navigational Uses of International Watercourses (May 21, 1997).

4 Convention on Long-Range Transboundary Air Pollution (Nov. 13, 1979) (hereinafter LRTAP) and the Protocols thereto; Vienna Convention on the Ozone Layer (March 22, 1985) and the Montreal Protocol (Sept. 16, 1987); United Nations Framework Convention on Climate Change (May 9, 1992) (hereinafter UNFCCC).

5 Food and Agriculture Organization (FAO) Soil Charter (Nov. 25, 1981), the European Soil Charter (May 30, 1972) and the Desertification Convention (Oct. 14, 1994).

6 Convention on Biological Diversity (June 5, 1992) (hereinafter CBD).

7 See e.g. Montreal Protocol (Sept. 16, 1987), UNFCCC and CBD. See also Agenda 21 and Principle 3 of the Forest Principles (1992).

environmental problems, and involves complementary use of objectives and limits. Certain policies are essential to an effective integrated approach. They include sustainable development, clean technologies, and use of less harmful substances. In addition, it requires application of the precautionary principle and public information and participation during the evaluation of the effects of new substances and proposed activities. The negotiations on a treaty to end plastic pollution, initiated through a Resolution of the United Nations Environment Assembly (UNEA) in 2022, adopt this approach and aim to eliminate the negative environmental impacts of plastics throughout their whole life cycle.

2 Regulatory Measures

The duty to prevent environmental harm implies the application of measures to avoid harm and reduce or eliminate the risk of harm. Many international agreements require or suggest the adoption of implementing laws and regulations and specify measures such as those discussed below. Overall, states must make efforts to prevent environmental damage that is foreseeable through the normal operations of an activity or the use of a product and mitigate or prevent accidental transboundary harm. International law also is concerned with environmental protection within states, due to the inherently integrated nature of the environment and its problems. Laws and regulations generally should apply to all activities and products within the state, whether of foreign or domestic origin, to comply with international trade rules.

Recent treaties often contain a general obligation to apply the best available technology (BAT) or use the best practicable means.[8] This requirement can be seen as deriving in part from the customary international obligation of 'due diligence' to prevent environmental harm. In determining whether a particular technology is the best available, several factors are to be taken into account, including the nature and volume of the pollution and the economic feasibility of the technology in question.

Several international texts define best available technology or related terms. The Convention on the Protection and Use of Transboundary Watercourses

8 See e.g. Art. 2(3)(b), Convention for the Protection of the Marine Environment of the North-East Atlantic (Sept. 22, 1992); Art. 3(3), Convention on the Protection of the Baltic Environment (Apr. 9, 1992); Art. 3(1)(f), UNECE Convention on the Protection and Use of Transboundary Watercourses and International Lakes (March 17, 1992); Art. 194(1), UNCLOS; Art. 6, LRTAP and Art. 2(2) of its 1988 Protocol; and Amendments to the Protocol for the Protection of the Mediterranean Sea against Pollution from Land-Based Sources, Annex IV (March 7, 1996).

and International Lakes (Helsinki, March 17, 1992) defines 'best available technology' in Annex I as:

> the latest stage of development of processes, facilities or methods of operation which indicate the practical suitability of a particular measure for limiting discharges, emissions and waste.

The Convention for the Protection of the Marine Environment in the North-East Atlantic defines the similar term 'best available techniques' as

> the latest stage of development (state of the art) of processes, of facilities or of methods of operation which indicate the practical suitability of a particular measure for limiting discharges, emissions and waste.

The same instrument defines the term 'best environmental practice' as the application of the most appropriate combination of environmental control measures and strategies ranging from education and information to establishing a system of licensing. The Minamata Convention is even more precise in its definition of 'best available technique':

> 'Best available techniques' means those techniques that are the most effective to prevent and, where that is not practicable, to reduce emissions and releases of mercury to air, water and land and the impact of such emissions and releases on the environment as a whole, taking into account economic and technical considerations for a given Party or a given facility within the territory of that Party. In this context:
>
> i. 'Best' means most effective in achieving a high general level of protection of the environment as a whole;
> ii. 'Available' techniques means, in respect of a given Party and a given facility within the territory of that Party, those techniques developed on a scale that allows implementation in a relevant industrial sector under economically and technically viable conditions, taking into consideration the costs and benefits, whether or not those techniques are used or developed within the territory of that Party, provided that they are accessible to the operator of the facility as determined by that Party; and
> iii. 'Techniques' means technologies used, operational practices and the ways in which installations are designed, built, maintained, operated and decommissioned.[9]

9 Minamata Convention (Oct. 10, 2013), Art. 2.

Other treaties use related terms. The Convention on the Protection of the Elbe calls on the contracting parties to develop work programs providing proposals for the application of state of the art techniques for the reduction of emissions and reduction of pollution (Art. 1(3)). The United Nations Convention on the Law of the Sea (UNCLOS) requires states to take measures to prevent, reduce and control marine pollution using for this purpose the best practicable means at their disposal.[10]

To aid states in determining what is the best available technology, techniques or practices, some international agreements specify the criteria to which special consideration shall be given. These include: comparable processes, technological advances and changes, economic feasibility, time limitations, the nature and volume of the discharges and effluents concerned, low and non-waste technology. The Stockholm Convention on Persistent Organic Pollutants[11] (POPs), in its Annex C Part V on unintentional production of POPs, provides general guidance on best available techniques and best environmental practices. It describes general measures to prevent the formation and release of its listed chemicals, such as using low-waste technology and less hazardous substances, promoting the recovery and recycling of waste, improving waste management programs, adopting preventive maintenance programs and avoiding the use of certain substances.

The Paris Agreement on climate change refers to the concept of 'best available science', on which climate action should be based.[12] This reference underscores the importance of utilizing the most current, reliable, and peer-reviewed scientific research to guide and inform global climate action. This principle ensures that climate policies and measures are based on the most accurate and up-to-date scientific understanding, which is crucial for effectively addressing climate change. In the Advisory Opinion rendered by the International Tribunal of the Law of the Sea (ITLOS) in May 2024 on *Climate Change and International Law*, the ITLOS found that 'with regard to climate change and ocean acidification, the best available science is found in

10 See also the regional seas agreements, e.g. Convention for the Protection, Management and Development of the Marine and Coastal Environment of the Eastern African Region, Art. 4 (June 21, 1985); Convention for the Protection and Development of the Marine Environment of the Wider Caribbean Region, Art. 4 (March 24, 1983; Convention for the Protection of the Natural Resources and Environment of the South Pacific Region, Art. 5 (Nov. 24, 1986).

11 May 22, 2001.

12 Paris Agreement (Dec. 12, 2015), Arts. 4(1), 7(5) and 14(1).

the works of the [Intergovernmental Panel on Climate Change] IPCC which reflect the scientific consensus'.[13]

Public authorities may require activities within their jurisdiction to apply the best available technology or techniques and verify its application through authorization, permits, licenses and monitoring, or through other administrative or judicial enforcement.

2.1 *Standard-Setting*

International agreements sometimes call on states parties to establish standards for products and processes that impact the environment. Standards are prescriptive norms that govern products or processes or set limits on the amount of pollutants or emissions produced. Four categories of standards may be distinguished according to the subjects they regulate.

2.1.1 Process Standards

Process standards specify design requirements or operating procedures applicable to fixed installations such as factories or may designate permissible means and methods of activities like hunting or fishing. Sometimes, a particular production process or technique is imposed on operations, such as the installation of purification or filtration systems in production facilities. International process standards include the requirement that hazardous waste be incinerated (1991 Antarctic Environment Protocol), the ban on driftnet fishing (1989 Driftnet Convention), and operating procedures for biotechnology (EC Directives).

Process standards often are used to regulate the operations of hazardous activities posing a risk of accidents or other dangers. The Montreal Protocol on the Ozone Layer calls on states parties to determine the feasibility of banning or restricting the import from non-state parties of products produced with, but not containing, ozone-depleting substances. UNCLOS requires states parties to adopt measures to prevent pollution from installations and devices used in exploration or exploitation of the natural resources of the sea-bed, in particular measures to prevent accidents and emergencies, including regulation of the operation and manning of such installations or devices (Art. 194(3)(c)).

As discussed in Chapter 17, process standards that apply to imported products pose particular problems in respect to their compatibility with the international trading regime set up under the General Agreement on Tariffs and Trade (GATT) and the World Trade Organization (WTO).

---

13 *Request for an Advisory Opinion submitted by the Commission of Small Island States on Climate Change and International Law* (Advisory Opinion) (May 21, 2024) para. 208.

2.1.2 Product Standards

Product standards are used for items that are created or manufactured for sale or distribution. Such standards may regulate:

1. The physical or chemical composition of items such as pharmaceuticals or detergents. Examples include regulations that control the sulphur content of fuels or list substances whose presence is forbidden in certain products, for instance, mercury in pesticides.
2. The technical performance of products, such as maximum levels of pollutant or noise emissions from motor vehicles, or specifications of required product components such as catalytic converters.
3. The handling, presentation and packaging of products, particularly those that are toxic. Packaging regulations may focus on waste minimization and safety. Labeling requirements are used to ensure that consumers are aware of the contents and permissible uses of products. In addition, the 'green label' is increasingly used to identify environmentally-safe products. Labeling is discussed further in the context of legislated market incentives to environmental protection. While most product standards are based on normal uses of the product, labeling requirements often aim to avoid accidental environmental harm through misuse, spills, or improper disposal of the product.

For economic reasons, product standards usually are adopted for an entire industry. In general, standards for new products are drafted to reflect the best available pollution control technology, in some cases requiring a percentage reduction of pollutants emitted in comparison with older sources. International product standards include the 1991 Amendments to the International Convention for the Prevention of Pollution from Ships (MARPOL 73/78) requiring construction of new oil tankers with 'double hulls', the ban on trade in products containing ozone-depleting substances (1987 Montreal Protocol, Art. 4(3) as amended), and the requirement to provide unleaded fuel for motor vehicles (Sofia Protocol to the 1979 Convention on Long-Range Transboundary Air Pollution, Art. 4).

2.1.3 Emission Standards

Emission standards specify the quantity or concentration of pollutants that can be emitted in discharges from a specific source. As a general rule, emission standards apply to fixed installations, such as factories or homes; mobile sources of pollution are more often regulated by product standards. Emission standards establish obligations of result, leaving to the polluter the free choice of means to conform to the norm.

Often the environmental sector of the discharge, such as groundwater, air, soil, is a variant factor. Emission standards may also vary according to the number of polluters and the capacity of the sector to absorb pollutants. Different standards may be imposed in response to particular climatic conditions, for example persistent fog or inversion layers. Emission standards are the type of standard most commonly required by international agreements and are mandated by the Protocols to the 1979 Convention on Long-Range Transboundary Air Pollution (LRTAP), the 1985 Association of Southeast Asian Nations (ASEAN) Agreement on the Conservation of Nature and Natural Resources, the regional seas agreements, the Rhine Conventions on Chemicals and Chlorides, MARPOL, and the UNFCCC.

Emission standards are often applied to protect a specific environmental resource. The Convention for the Protection of the Marine Environment in the North-East Atlantic (Paris, September 22, 1992) partly uses this approach. Annex I states that the Parties shall strictly authorize or regulate point source discharges from land-based sources to the maritime area and releases into water or air which reach and may affect the maritime area, implementing relevant decisions of the PARCOM Commission foreseen by the agreement. The Commission plans for the reduction and phasing out of hazardous substances and for the reduction of inputs of nutrients from urban, municipal, industrial and other sources.

Emission standards are based on several assumptions. First, that a certain level of some contaminants will not produce any undesirable effect, second, that there is a finite capacity of each environment to accommodate substances without unacceptable consequences (the assimilative capacity) and, third, that the assimilative capacity can be quantified, apportioned to each actor and utilized. Each of these assumptions has been questioned because in all cases chemicals discharged into the environment are likely to lead to statistically significant deterioration. Pollution occurs when the effects of the contamination on biological systems can be measured. Emission standards most often reflect a political decision about the amount of pollution that is deemed acceptable. Reflecting these concerns, the Bamako Convention on Waste in Africa is rare in opposing emissions standards based on assumptions about assimilative capacity, calling instead for application of clean production methods (Art. 3(3)(f)).

2.1.4 Quality Standards

Quality standards fix the maximum allowable level of pollution in an environmental sector or target during normal periods. A quality standard may set the level of mercury permissible in rivers, the level of sulfur dioxide in the air, or noise level of airplanes in the proximity of residential areas. Quality standards often vary according to the particular use made of the environmental resource. For example, different water quality standards may be set for drinking water and waters used for bathing and fishing. Quality standards also can vary in geographic scope, covering national or regional zones, or a particular resource, such as a river or lake, but each quality standard establishes base norms against which compliance or deviance are measured. The 1992 UN Convention on the Protection and Use of Transboundary Watercourses and International Lakes calls on each party to define, where appropriate, water-quality objectives and to adopt water-quality criteria, setting forth guidelines for this purpose in Annex III. Some bilateral and regional agreements on freshwaters and air foresee or mandate water-quality objectives.

2.2 *Restrictions and Prohibitions*

If an activity, product or process presents a risk of environmental harm, strict measures can be imposed in an effort to reduce or eliminate the harm. When the likelihood of risk is too great, the measure may call for a total product or process ban. The numbers and types of restrictions are almost unlimited, but certain ones are more commonly used.

2.2.1 Limits or Bans

Some environmental instruments call for restricting or banning hazardous products, processes or activities.[14] Controlled substances or activities frequently are named in easily-amended lists appended to the regulation. Such lists permit individualizing situations and give the regulation some flexibility. Lists also avoid too much technical detail being included in the basic legislative or regulatory text. The use of lists is very common in combating pollution by dumping of wastes, discharge of hazardous substances during normal operations, and the protection of wild flora and fauna, especially endangered species.

Lists have been widely employed in protocols to environmental treaties, beginning with the Convention on the Prevention of Marine Pollution by Dumping of Wastes and Other Matter (London, Nov. 13, 1972). The model of 'black', 'grey' and 'white' lists it establishes was subsequently employed in the United Nations Environment Programme (UNEP) regional seas agreements for

14 See e.g. Convention and Montreal Protocol on the Ozone Layer (March 22, 1985, Sept. 16, 1987); Convention on the Prevention of Marine Pollution by Dumping of Wastes (Dec. 29, 1972); Antarctic Treaty (Dec. 1, 1959) and Environmental Protocol (Oct. 4, 1991); Sofia Protocol to the 1979 Convention on Long-Range Transboundary Air Pollution concerning the Control of Emissions of Nitrogen Oxides (Oct. 31, 1988).

controlling land-based sources of pollution.[15] Substances are classified and limits established on the basis of their toxicity, persistence, and bioaccumulation.

Critics of the listing approach claim that its utility is limited because it is inherently responsive to previously identified problems, is often based upon uncertain dose-response relationships, and is not specific or flexible enough to be truly protective. Several hundred new substances are introduced each year that may cause considerable harm before their environmental impacts are known, especially given the possibilities of transformation of pollutants coming into contact with others after release. Setting legal limits for the acceptable concentration of substances requires a judgment on the amount of damage which is acceptable as a consequence of human activities and how much the population is willing to pay for reducing or lowering the risks of such damage.

Recent work has sought to estimate the 'lowest-observed-effect level' and 'no-observed-effect level'. The first is defined as the lowest test dose at which the response is significantly different from the control group. The second is the dose at which the difference with the control group is not statistically significant. Both are highly dependent upon the size and conditions of the test populations and on the effects being monitored. A safety factor may then be added. Similar concepts are the 'critical loads' and 'critical levels' of pollutant concentrations, as developed in the context of the LRTAP. Critical load is defined in Article 1(7) of its NOx Protocol as 'a quantitative estimate of the exposure to one or more pollutants below which significant harmful effects on specified sensitive elements of the environment do not occur according to present knowledge'. Article 1(8) of the Volatile Organic Compounds (VOC) Protocol defines the related notion of critical level as 'concentrations of pollutants in the atmosphere for a specified exposure time below which direct adverse effects on receptors, such as human beings, plants, ecosystems or materials do not occur according to present knowledge'.

Lists of polluting substances whose discharge is prohibited or submitted to prior authorization raise practical problems in enforcement. A substance such as mercury or cadmium usually is discharged in the environment as a component of many different compounds rather than in its pure form. The Minamata Convention on Mercury relies on the 'lists' approach. According to Article 4(1), for instance, Parties 'shall not allow … the manufacture, import or export of mercury-added products listed in Part I of Annex A', while according to Article 5(2), they 'shall not allow the use of mercury or mercury compounds in the manufacturing processes listed in Part I of Annex B'.

---

15 See e.g. Protocol for the Protection of the Mediterranean Sea Against Pollution from Land-based Sources (May 17, 1980).

Implementing the 1976 Convention related to the Protection of the Rhine against Pollution by Chemicals required an investigation into the use of most of the listed substances and it was estimated that the number of listed substances and materials had to be multiplied by hundreds. As a result, some conventions have moved to 'reverse listing', specifying in annexes those substances or activities that are permitted rather than those that are prohibited. The 1989 Basel Convention on Transboundary Movements of Hazardous Wastes adopted this approach, prohibiting all discharges except those which are explicitly authorized in individual cases. Its annexes list categories of wastes not only according to constituent substances and materials, but also according to the generating activities (e.g. clinical wastes, wastes from the production, formulation and use of organic solvents) and hazardous characteristics (e.g. explosive, flammable, poisonous). The 1992 Convention on Protection of the Baltic Marine Environment also uses reverse listing. The precautionary approach suggests that the method of reverse listing is justified, because it requires those seeking to act or to release a new substance or product to prove that it will cause no significant harm.

Banning the import/export of certain products or substances raises some possible issues from an international trade law perspective. Multilateral Environmental Agreements (MEAS) that adopt this approach usually clarify that there should be mutual supportiveness between them and trade agreements, and that nothing in their texts 'shall be interpreted as implying in any way a change in the rights and obligations of the Contracting Parties under other international agreements'. However, a conflict between the domestic measures adopted by a State Party to an MEA and WTO rules may arise. These questions are addressed in Chapter 17.

2.2.2 Taking and Trade Restrictions

Treaties for the protection of biological diversity frequently mandate the use of trade restrictions or require the imposition of limits on taking specimens of protected living or non-living resources.[16] The types of restrictions vary and include:

Hunting and Collecting Restrictions. Hunting and collecting restrictions are used to protect biological diversity by prohibiting non-selective means of

---

16 See e.g. Convention on International Trade in Endangered Species of Fauna and Flora (March 3, 1973) (hereinafter CITES), the Basel (March 22, 1989) and Bamako (Jan. 29, 1991) Conventions on Hazardous Waste; the Montreal Protocol (Sept. 16, 1987), the Regional Seas Agreements concerning Protected Areas and Wild Fauna and Flora, MARPOL (Feb. 17, 1978), the International Convention for the Regulation of Whaling (Dec. 2, 1946), UNCLOS (Arts. 61–65, 119), and the Convention on the Conservation of Migratory Species of Wild Animals (June 23, 1979).

killing or capturing specimens of wildlife. The Bern Convention on the Conservation of European Wildlife and Natural Habitats includes a special Appendix listing hunting means prohibited for mammals and for birds.

More generally, protective measures may restrict injury to and destruction or taking of some or all wild plants and animals. The revised African Convention on the Conservation of Nature and Natural Resources requires adoption of adequate legislation to regulate hunting, capture and fishing, and to prohibit certain means of hunting and fishing.[17] Annexes specify measures to be taken regarding threatened or endangered species, which benefit from the most stringent protective legal measures.

Migratory species are also subject to special protection by treaties such as the Bonn Convention on the Conservation of Migratory Species of Wild Animals, which is aimed at all states through which such species transit and in which they spend part of their lives. States parties to the Bonn Convention are obliged to ban or regulate the taking of these animals in cases where the conservation status of such animals – the sum of influences on their long-term distribution and abundance – is unfavorable.

Taking restrictions and prohibitions may apply to non-living as well as living resources, although they are imposed more frequently for flora and fauna. Principle 5 of the Stockholm Declaration states that 'the non-renewable resources of the earth must be employed in such a way as to guard against the danger of their future exhaustion and to ensure that benefits from such employment are shared by all mankind'. International agreements regulate the taking of non-living resources in international commons areas (the deep-seabed, Antarctica and outer space), and to shared freshwater resources. Within states, the Desertification Convention calls for long-term integrated strategies that focus on improved productivity of land and the rehabilitation, conservation and sustainable management of land and water resources (Art. 2(2)).

Import/export restrictions, both temporary and permanent suspensions, are commonly utilized for the protection of wild flora and fauna. The 1973 Convention on International Trade in Endangered Species of Wild Fauna and Flora (CITES), for example, uses trade restrictions and trade bans as means of protecting threatened and endangered species. The Convention lists in a first appendix all species threatened with extinction that are or may be affected by trade. Trade in these species is virtually prohibited, requiring prior grant

---

17 Maputo, July 11, 2003, Art. 9. See also the ASEAN Convention on the Conservation of Nature and Natural Resources (July 9, 1985), Art. 4(2), the Convention on Nature Protection and Wild Life Preservation in the Western Hemisphere (Oct 12, 1940), and the CBD, Art. 8.

and presentation of export and import permits issued under stringent conditions. Two additional appendices list those species that may become threatened with extinction unless trade is regulated. The European Commission has issued additional regulations banning the importation of cetacean and fur seal products.

Trade regulations also are used to prohibit or regulate transport and dumping of toxic and dangerous wastes. The Basel Convention of 1989 regulates the transfer of toxic or dangerous wastes and particularly requires informed consent of the countries concerned prior to any transfer.

In this context as well, most MEAs clarify that they are mutually supportive with other relevant international agreements. When a conflict arises between a domestic measure and international trade rules, the dispute settlement mechanism of the WTO is the forum where such conflict is resolved (see Chapter 17).

2.2.3 Land Use Regulation

The Convention on Biological Diversity, the regional seas protocols on specially protected areas, and other global and regional nature protection agreements call for land use regulation. Land use controls play a major role in environmental law for both urban and rural areas, through zoning, physical planning, and the creation of protected areas. Zoning helps distribute activities harmful to the environment in order to limit potential damage and allows application of different legal rules from zone to zone for more effective protection. The broader approach of physical planning merges provisions for infrastructure and town and country planning in order to integrate conservation of the environment into social and economic development.[18] Generally, once a planning scheme for the relevant land and water areas is approved by the state or local government, special procedures must be used to obtain exceptions. Regional planning procedures may classify a city, a region or the entire territory of a country into broad land use categories such as residential, industrial, agricultural, forest, or nature conservation. Designated geographical areas may be given special legal protection for purposes such as health care or nature conservation, including national parks, reserves, and sanctuaries.

Land use planning and zoning regulations are normally expressed in negative terms, as prohibitions or restrictions on any undesirable utilization or change in utilization of the area. Modern planning also may encourage and promote economic land uses that are considered beneficial or compatible with environmental objectives and special land use management plans. Because of

18 See Chapter 10, Agenda 21 (1992). See also Art. 3(1), Ramsar Convention (Feb. 2, 1971); Art. 6(b), CBD; (June 5, 1992); Art. 12 of the ASEAN Agreement (July 9, 1985).

the evolution of environmental protection schemes and the numerous levels of government involved, land use regulations can become extremely complex.

Protected Areas. International environmental instruments require states parties to set aside areas for specific management and the *in situ* conservation of biological diversity as well as to protect monuments and sites of outstanding importance for geological, physiographical, paleontological or other scientific reasons, or for aesthetic purposes.[19] There are many kinds of protected areas and flexibility is necessary to design appropriate ones to ensure their effectiveness in conserving biological diversity. 'Buffer zones' are special areas surrounding protected areas, designed to preserve them from harmful outside influences. Activities which do not have adverse effects on the protected area may be allowed to continue. 'Interconnected corridors', created through land use regulations or private contracts and other incentives, are necessary to allow genetic exchanges to occur between protected areas. If the gene flow is impeded, protected areas soon lose a part of their biological diversity. Corridors can be linear, such as along river banks if natural vegetation is maintained, or may consist of strings or patches of natural vegetation from which animals (and plants) can move. Effective use of protected areas requires development and application of comprehensive conservation and management plans.

3 Environmental Impact Assessment

Environmental impact assessment (EIA) is a procedure that seeks to ensure the acquisition of adequate and early information on likely environmental consequences of development projects, on possible alternatives, and on measures to mitigate harm. It is generally a prerequisite to decisions to undertake or to authorize designated construction, processes or activities. EIA procedure requires that a developer or business owner submit a written document to a designated agency or decision-making body, describing the probable or possible future environmental impact of the intended action. The procedure may be integrated into licensing schemes or land use planning.

19 CBD (June 5, 1992); Convention on Nature Protection and Wildlife Preservation in the Western Hemisphere (Oct. 12, 1940); African Convention on the Conservation of Nature and Natural Resources (Sept. 15, 1968); ASEAN Agreement on the Conservation of Nature and Natural Resources (July 9, 1985); Ramsar Convention on Wetlands of International Importance (1971); World Heritage Convention (Feb. 2, 1972) and the Convention on Migratory Species of Wild Animals (Sept. 19, 1979).

Throughout the 1970s and early 1980s, international agreements began imposing EIA requirements that were increasingly broad in their scope and detailed in their requirements and provisions. At present, environmental impact assessment is singularly important in both domestic and international environmental law. International instruments commonly provide that states should not undertake or authorize activities without prior consideration, at an early stage, of their environmental effects.[20]

Some of the early EIA provisions were written into regional seas agreements, beginning with the 1978 Kuwait Regional Convention for Cooperation on the Protection of the Marine Environment from Pollution. Article 11 says that each contracting state shall endeavor to include an assessment of the potential environmental effects in any planning activity entailing projects within its territory, particularly in the coastal areas, which may cause significant risks of pollution in the Sea Area. The term 'significant risks' is not defined. The Sea Area includes the high seas, the territorial seas, and the exclusive economic zones within the limits fixed by the Convention.[21]

An obligation to assess activities risking significant harm also is found in UNCLOS at Article 206:

> When states have reasonable grounds for believing that planned activities under their jurisdiction or control may cause substantial pollution of or significant and harmful changes to the marine environment, they shall, as far as practicable, assess the potential effects of such activities on the marine environment and shall communicate reports of the results of such assessments....

This obligation clearly applies to any part of the marine environment, including marine waters under national jurisdiction.[22] Similarly, Article 4 of the

20 Espoo Convention (Feb. 25, 1991); Art. 14(1)(a), CBD (June 5, 1982); Art. 4(1)(f), UNFCCC (May 9, 1992); Art. 206, UNCLOS (Dec. 10, 1982); Art. I, Kuwait Regional Convention (Apr. 24, 1978); Art. 13, West and Central African Marine Environment Convention (March 23, 1981); Art. 10, South-East Pacific Marine Environment Convention (Nov. 20, 1981); Art. 14, ASEAN Agreement (July 9, 1985); Preamble, Amendments to the Protocol for the Protection of the Mediterranean Sea against Pollution from Land-Based Sources, (Syracuse, March 7, 1996); Art. III(3), Agreement on the Conservation of Albatrosses and Petrels (Feb. 2, 2001). See also Principle 17 of the Rio Declaration (1992) and Principle 11 of the World Charter for Nature (Oct. 28, 1982).

21 See also the Convention on the Protection of Nature in the South Pacific (June 12, 1976).

22 The Montreal Guidelines for the Protection of the Marine Environment Against Pollution from Land-Based Sources (1985) is similarly broad: 'States should assess the potential effects/impacts, of proposed major projects under their jurisdiction or control,

UNFCCC calls for using EIAs as a tool to minimize adverse effects on the environment. Principle 17 of the Rio Declaration more generally extends the rule of prior assessment of potentially harmful activities to include activities whose impacts are felt solely within a state. Chapter 22 of Agenda 21 similarly proclaims the necessity to assess the environmental impact of certain planned activities. Article 14(1)(a) and (b) of the CBD concerns both the national and international aspects of the issue.

Environmental impact assessment is required in a transboundary context by the Espoo Convention (February 25, 1991). The treaty requires that states parties establish an environmental impact assessment procedure with regard to listed activities that are 'likely to cause significant adverse transboundary impact'. Impact is defined to mean any effect caused by a proposed activity on the environment, including human health and safety, flora, fauna, soil, air, water, climate, landscape and historical monuments or other physical structures or the interaction among these factors; it also includes effects on cultural heritage or socioeconomic conditions resulting from alterations to those factors. For these activities, the party of origin must prepare an EIA.

The list of seventeen activities subject to the EIA requirement includes crude oil refineries, thermal and nuclear power stations, treatment, storage and disposal of radioactive waste, smelting, asbestos factories, chemical installations, road and rail construction, oil and gas pipelines, ports, toxic and dangerous waste disposal, large dams and reservoirs, groundwater abstraction, pulp and paper manufacturing, major mining, offshore oil production, storage of petroleum and chemicals, and major deforestation. Non-listed activities may be subject to the Convention requirements if the party of origin and the affected party or parties agree.

To determine the significance of the activity to the environment, criteria are provided in Appendix III of the treaty: size, location, and effects, including those giving rise to serious effects on humans or on valued species or organisms, those which threaten the existing or potential use of an affected area and those causing additional loading which cannot be sustained by the carrying capacity of the environment.

The Espoo Convention sets out in detail the procedural and substantive requirements of an environmental impact assessment. First, any proposed, listed activity likely to cause significant adverse transboundary impact shall be notified to any potentially affected Party as early as possible. The latter has the right to participate in the environmental impact assessment procedure if it

---

particularly in coastal areas, which may cause pollution from land-based sources, so that appropriate measures may be taken to prevent or mitigate such pollution'. (Art. 12).

wishes. The public in the affected area – both inside the country of origin and in other states – also has the right to be informed of and to participate in the assessment procedure.

The environmental impact assessment documentation submitted by the originator must contain at a minimum:

1. a description of the proposed activity and its purpose;
2. a statement of the reasonable alternatives including a no-action alternative;
3. information on the environment likely to be significantly affected and alternative sites;
4. the potential environmental impact of the proposed activity and its alternatives and an estimation of its significance;
5. a description of mitigation measures to keep adverse environmental impact to a minimum;
6. an explanation of predictive methods and underlying assumptions as well as the relevant environmental data used;
7. an identification of gaps in knowledge and uncertainties encountered in compiling the required information;
8. where appropriate, an outline for monitoring and management programs and plans for post-project analysis, and
9. a non-technical summary, including a visual presentation.

Article 6(1) delineates the manner in which a final decision should be reached, requiring the party of origin to take 'due account' of the environmental impact assessment documentation, as well as the comments thereon received, and the outcome of the consultations as referred to in Article 5. The party of origin should consider possible alternatives to the proposed activity and measures to mitigate significant adverse impacts. Once the final decision is reached, the party of origin must notify the affected party of the decision, along with the considerations which form its basis. Finally, Article 6 anticipates the situation where new information is obtained which was not available when the final decision was made, but before work on the project has begun. In this situation, Article 6(3) requires the parties to consult to determine if the decision should be revised.

The last step in the procedure is post-project analysis, an important innovation of the Convention. Article 7(1) states that the concerned parties should determine what manner of post-project analysis needs to occur, suggesting surveillance of the project as a preferred method. If either the party of origin or the concerned party determines that there is a significant adverse transboundary impact, the parties then consult to determine what measures should be taken to eliminate the adverse impact. This includes monitoring compliance with the conditions of approval of the activity and the effectiveness of mitigation measures, as well as verification of past predictions in order to utilize the results in regard to future activities of the same type.

The Espoo Convention was amended twice, at the second and third meeting of the Parties. The First amendment was adopted in order to clarify that the public entitled to participate in procedures under Articles 2(6) and 3(8) of the Convention, includes civil society and, in particular, non-governmental organizations. The amendment also allows states situated outside the United Nations Economic Commission for Europe (UNECE) region to become Parties to the Convention. It entered into force on August 26, 2014.

A second international agreement providing a model for EIAs is the Madrid Protocol on Environmental Protection of the Antarctic (Oct. 4, 1991). Article 3 sets forth the general environmental principles which apply to all Antarctic activities, while Article 8 and Annex I detail the requirements for prior impact assessment. All activities for which advance notice is required under the Antarctic Treaty, pursuant to scientific research programs, tourism and all other governmental and non-governmental activities in the Treaty area, shall be subject to national assessment 'in the planning processes leading to decisions' to undertake them and when there is any proposed change in the activities.

The need for an EIA depends on whether the activity has: (a) less than a minor or transitory impact; (b) a minor or transitory impact; or (c) more than a minor or transitory impact. If the impact is found to have less than a minor or transitory impact it may proceed forthwith. In every other case there must be Initial Environmental Evaluation (IEE) which shall include sufficient details to assess whether the activity may have more than a minor or transitory impact. If the IEE indicates that no more than such minor impact is likely, the activity may proceed, but appropriate procedures, including monitoring must be put into place. In cases where more than a minor impact is indicated, a Comprehensive Environmental Evaluation (CEE) must be undertaken, with procedures for public comments and consideration by the Committee for Environmental Protection.

The CEE is governed by the provisions of Annex I Article 3.[23] Once a draft of the CEE is complete, it is made publicly available and circulated to all parties

23 Art. 3(2) lists the information that should be included in the Comprehensive Environmental Evaluation:

a. description of the proposed activity including its purpose, location, duration, and intensity, and possible alternatives to the activity, including the alternatives of not proceeding, and the consequences of those alternatives;

for 90 days in order to allow comment. The final CEE should include any comments which are made during the 90-day period. Article 4 requires that decisions on the proposed activity be based on the CEE.

Other provisions of the Treaty require monitoring the impacts of any activity that proceeds after the CEE is considered (Annex I, Art. 5), and annually circulating to the parties, the Committee, and the public any information about any Initial Assessments and other information obtained as a result of the assessment process (Annex I, Art. 6). The Treaty also contains an emergency provision in Annex I, Art. 7 that allows parties to bypass the EIA process in the case of certain emergencies, provided notice is later circulated describing the emergency actions which were taken.

No final decision may be taken to proceed with the proposed activity until a Consultative Meeting has had an opportunity to consider the Evaluation and comments, for a period of up to fifteen months. A final Evaluation, on which any decision to proceed must be based, is then prepared and must be made public for 60 days before activity can begin.

---

b. a description of the initial environmental reference state with which predicted changes are to be compared and a prediction of the future environmental reference state in the absence of the proposed activity;
c. a description of the methods and data used to forecast the impacts of the proposed activity;
d. estimation of the nature, extent, duration, and intensity of the likely direct impacts of the proposed activity;
e. consideration of possible indirect or second order impacts of the proposed activity;
f. consideration of cumulative impacts of the proposed activity in the light of existing activities and other known planned activities;
g. identification of measures, including monitoring programs, that could be taken to minimize or mitigate impacts of the proposed activity and to detect unforeseen impacts and that could provide early warning of any adverse effects of the activity as well as deal promptly and effectively with accidents;
h. identification of unavoidable impacts of the proposed activity;
i. consideration of the effects of the proposed activity on the conduct of scientific research and on other existing uses and values;
j. an identification of gaps in knowledge and uncertainties encountered in compiling the information required under this paragraph;
k. a non-technical summary of the information provided under this paragraph; and
l. the name and address of the person or organization which prepared the Comprehensive Environmental Evaluation and the address to which comments thereon should be directed.

3.1 *Criteria and Procedures*

As the examples indicate, not every proposed activity is subject to assessment, only those that may be or are likely to cause a stated level of harm to the environment. While the customary international law duty to conduct an EIA gets triggered by the risk of causing 'significant damage to the environment of another state',[24] the threshold differs in the many treaty references to EIA, with some referring to 'measurable' effects, others 'appreciable' or 'significant' harm. The most frequently stated formulation requires a comprehensive EIA where the extent, nature, or location of a proposed activity is such that it is likely to significantly affect the environment.[25] The Espoo Convention requires an EIA for all activities which could cause 'significant adverse transboundary harm.' The procedure to determine whether an EIA is necessary in the 1991 Environmental Protocol to the Antarctica Treaty refers to activities 'with the potential to cause environmental harm in Antarctica'. Article 14 of the 1985 Association of Southeast Asian Nations (ASEAN) Convention on the Conservation of Nature and Natural Resources provides that all proposed activities which 'could have significant effects on the natural environment' are to be evaluated before they are adopted and the results of this evaluation taken into account in the decision-making process. The obligation applies without regard to the place where the effects on the environment might take place.

The requirement to conduct EIAs may be based upon

a. lists of categories of activities that by their nature are likely to have significant effects;[26]
b. lists of areas that are of special importance or sensitivity (such as national parks); the impact of any activity within or affecting such areas must be assessed;[27]
c. lists of categories of resources or environmental problems which are of special concern;
d. an initial environmental evaluation of all activities, a quick and informal assessment to determine whether the effects are likely to be significant;
e. defined and listed criteria which make an impact 'significant.'

---

24 *Pulp Mills on the River Uruguay* (*Argentina v. Uruguay*) 2010 ICJ Rep. 14, para. 101.

25 Rio Declaration, Principle 17; Espoo Convention, Art. 2(2) (Feb. 25, 1991); ASEAN Agreement, Art. 14(1) (July 5, 1985); Agreement on the Caribbean Marine Environment, Art. 12(2) (March 24, 1983).

26 EC Council Directive on the assessment of the effects of certain public and private projects on the environment (June 27, 1985).

27 Art. 1(2) of Appendix III of the Espoo Convention (Feb. 25, 1991).

Consultation and dissemination of information to the public are important objectives of EIAs. For example, the 1986 Convention for the Protection of the Natural Resources and Environment of the South Pacific Region, Article 16(3), requires that the information gathered in the assessment be shared with the public and affected parties. In Africa, the Memorandum of Understanding of October 22, 1998 between Kenya, Tanzania and Uganda[28] contains the agreement of the three states to develop technical guides and regulations on environmental impact assessment procedures, including enabling public participation at all stages of the process and to enact corresponding legislation (Art. 14). The CBD also emphasizes public participation as a goal of environmental assessment in Article 14(1)(a), and includes a notification and consultation requirement in Article 14(1)(c). Additionally, each contracting party is required to 'ensure that the environmental consequences of [their] programmes and policies that are likely to have significant adverse impacts on biological diversity are duly taken into account' (Art. 14(1)(b)). This Convention also requires assessment of national policies as well as of proposed projects. In Article 14(1)(d), the Convention contains emergency clauses, typically found in the more comprehensive EIA regimes, which allow immediate emergency action when there is grave danger to biological diversity.

3.2 *European Union Law*

Within Europe, Directive 85/337/EEC of June 27, 1985,[29] obliged member states to have national EIA legislation by July 1988. Some non-member European States have developed legislation based on the EC Directive which has a very broad scope, requiring assessment, prior to consent being given, of the effects of those public and private projects likely to have significant impact on the environment due to the nature, size or location of the project. Assessment must be made of both the direct and indirect effects of a project on (1) human beings, fauna and flora; (2) soil, water, air, climate, and landscape; (3) the interactions between the factors mentioned in (1) and (2); and (4) material assets and the cultural heritage. Member states retain power to exempt a specific project from the assessment requirement in exceptional cases, but must inform the Commission. The Directive (Annex I) and some national laws list classes of projects that require impact assessments, thus presuming that they risk substantial environmental impact. The Directive also lists in Annex II the classes of projects subject to an assessment procedure if national law deems it necessary.

28 Nairobi, Oct. 22, 1998.

29 Community Directive 85/337 of June 27, 1985, O.J. L 175 (7/5/85).

The EIA is integrated into the procedure introduced by Directive 96/61/EC of September 24, 1996 concerning Integrated Pollution Prevention and Control. This instrument establishes a system of permits for new installations listed in an annex to the directive, such as energy industries, production and processing of metals, mineral and chemical industrial plants, and waste management. An application to the competent authority for a permit must include a description of the major elements of an EIA (Art. 6), but the requirement may be fulfilled by submitting information obtained in accordance with the 1985 EIA Directive or other information produced in response to legislation fulfilling the requirements of the new directive.

Directive 85/337/EEC has undergone four updates to align with the EU's international obligations and other legal advancements. In 2011, Directive 85/337/EEC, along with its amendments, was consolidated into a single new act, Directive 2011/92/EU, which was amended by 2014/52/EU. Under this Directive, major building or development projects must undergo an EIA before they can begin. This requirement applies to projects such as nuclear power stations, long-distance railways, motorways, express roads, hazardous waste disposal installations, and large dams. For other projects, such as urban or industrial developments, roads, tourism projects, and canalization and flood relief works, individual EU Member States determine the need for an EIA on a case-by-case basis or by specific criteria like location, size, or type of project. The EIA evaluates both direct and indirect significant impacts on various environmental factors, including population and human health, biodiversity, land, soil, water, air, climate, landscape, material assets, and cultural heritage. The project developer must submit a report to the approval authority detailing the project's description, potential significant effects, reasonable alternatives, and measures to mitigate significant environmental impacts. There are stringent rules for informing the public about the project and the EIA process, enabling public participation in decision-making. The public is also informed of the final decision and has the right to challenge it in court.

3.3 *Procedures of International Financial Institutions*

3.3.1 World Bank

In October 1991 the World Bank issued an Operational Manual including Operational Directives[30] that describe its procedure of environmental assessment during project preparation and before appraisal, closely linked to a feasibility study of the project. The environmental assessment covers project-specific and

30 OD 4.01.

other environmental impacts in the area influenced by the project. Its purpose is to ensure that the project options under consideration are environmentally sound and sustainable.[31] All environmental consequences should be recognized early in the project cycle and taken into account in project selection, siting, planning and design. The environmental assessment should also identify ways of improving projects, by preventing, minimizing or compensating for adverse environmental impacts.

The Operational Directive distinguishes types of environmental assessment: project-specific, regional, and sectoral, where similar but significant development activities are planned for a localized area, for sector investment loans and loans through intermediaries, emergency recovery projects, and larger issues such as ozone depletion or pollution of international waters. The preparation of the environmental assessment is the responsibility of the borrower, but the Bank's task manager assists and monitors the project and screens it in order to determine the nature and extent of the environmental work required. After the screening the project is assigned in one of three categories:

Category A: A full environmental assessment is required;
Category B: Environmental analysis is required, but not a full one;
Category C: No environmental assessment is required.

The Operational Directive includes checklists of potential issues for an environmental assessment. It also proposes outlines and models for the assessment and prescriptions for the assessment and the screening procedures. It has been revised and updated over the years, with the current version known as Operational Policy (OP) 4.01.

The Bank expects the borrower to ensure coordination among government agencies and to take the views of affected groups and local non-governmental organizations (NGOs).[32] It also requires the borrower to provide relevant information to affected groups and local NGOs and hold meaningful consultations with them. The environmental assessment should form part of the overall feasibility study or project preparation and be submitted to the Bank which decides on the loan.

3.3.2 International Finance Corporation

The International Finance Corporation (IFC) published in September 1993 a document providing guidance to its staff in conducting an environmental review of proposed projects.[33] This document is similar in many respects to

31 Guidance on sustainability is provided in OMS 2.36, *Environmental Aspects of Bank Work.*
32 See OD 14.70 *Involving Non-governmental Organizations in Bank-Supported Activities.*
33 *Environmental Analysis and Review of Projects*, Sept. 8, 1993.

the World Bank's OP 4.01 (Environmental Assessment) and has identical goals, but there are some significant differences between the two texts. The procedure of the International Finance Corporation addresses project sponsors who approach the institution much later in the project development cycle, often after feasibility studies, site selection, and preliminary design work have been completed. In such cases, the sponsor may be required to do the environmental analysis concurrently with the appraisal of other aspects of the project. Thus, IFC's procedure is designed for flexibility to accommodate projects brought to the IFC in various stages of development. The IFC also does not require the project sponsor to consult with local interested parties and affected groups during the preparation of the environmental assessment or to make the draft EA publicly available for review and comment, including release to relevant national agencies and institutions. The 1993 IFC guidelines were revised multiple times. The most significant revisions occurred in 1998, 2006, and 2012. The initial revision in 1998 led to the introduction of new procedures that focused on environmental and social reviews, incorporating more detailed requirements for project evaluations. In 2006, the IFC introduced new environmental and social standards that further expanded the scope and depth of the guidelines, emphasizing sustainability and comprehensive risk management. The last major update, which occurred in 2012, known as the IFC Sustainability Framework, included updated Performance Standards that applied to all investment and advisory clients whose projects underwent IFC's credit review process starting on January 1, 2012. This revision also integrated a broader range of social and environmental risk management practices.

3.3.3 Regional Banks

The Environmental Policy document of the European Bank for Reconstruction and Development (EBRD) requires that all of its investment and technical cooperation activities undergo environmental appraisal as part of an overall financial, economic, legal and technical due diligence. The environmental appraisal must be initiated at an early stage. The Bank determines the type of appraisal needed and provides guidance on how it should be conducted,[34] but the Project Sponsor is responsible for providing sufficient environmental information to the Bank, by preparing an environmental action plan that forms part of the legal documents of the Bank's investment. On behalf of the Bank, an Operation Leader has the overall responsibility for the environmental aspects of the operation. Together with the Office of the General Counsel,

34 See the *Principles of Action* adopted by the E.B.R.D. in March 1992, document ML057.

the Operation Leader incorporates environmental requirements in legal documentation. The environmental appraisal by the EBRD includes not only prior environmental impact assessment, but also an environmental audit which identifies past or present concerns and potential environmental and health and safety risks and liabilities associated with the project. A generic environmental audit protocol for manufacturing facilities and specific questionnaires for various sectors have been developed by the Bank.

The policy was subsequently updated and expanded over the years to incorporate evolving environmental and social standards and requirements. The EBRD's Environmental and Social Policy (ESP) was last revised in 2019, and provides a comprehensive framework for assessing and managing the environmental and social impacts of the projects it finances. This policy is accompanied by ten Performance Requirements (PRS) that set out specific standards and expectations for clients and projects, covering areas such as environmental protection, community health and safety, and labor standards.

The European Investment Bank (EIB), an organ of the European Union, funds long-term development projects in African, Caribbean and Pacific countries, in the Mediterranean region and in Central and Eastern Europe.[35] Although it has an autonomy within the EU, it acts in conformity with the environmental legislation of the EU and thus applies EU Directives relating to the environmental impact assessment. The Bank takes an active part in identifying the potential risks of projects and the necessary or appropriate mitigation measures. The borrower must prepare an environmental impact assessment which must be combined with public consultation. When screening the project, the Bank can require the insertion in the loan contract of appropriate provisions for guaranteeing environmental protection. The Bank also can intervene as a consultant in environmental issues and fund the identification and the preparation of projects improving the environment.

The Inter-American Development Bank (IDB) first adopted a document on Environmental Policy in 1979. These guidelines have evolved over time and the last update is the Environmental and Social Policy Framework (ESPF), approved in 2020 and effective from October 2021. This framework includes comprehensive standards for environmental and social sustainability, aligning with international best practices and addressing a broader range of issues than before, such as gender equality and the rights of indigenous peoples. It requires that all operations financed by the Bank be environmentally and socially sustainable. The Bank's Committee on Environment and Social Impact

35 See Art. 198 E of the Maastricht Treaty (Feb. 2, 1992).

(CESI) reviews projects for e.g. the promotion of adequate environmental regulatory and management frameworks; the adoption of environmental protection, management, mitigation and enhancement measures in specific operations; indigenous rights and community development issues; involuntary resettlement matters; and issues of social impact and sustainability. Review procedures apply to all Bank operations, including sector loans, investment loans, technical co-operations, small projects, private sector operations and any major reformulation of those operations. The CESI relies on the Bank's country environmental strategy, when available, an environmental and social impact brief and, in specific cases, on an environmental and social report. The environmental and social impact brief, required only for projects above US $10,000,000, establishes the environmental assessment requirements to be met in preparing the project and identifies the environmental quality and social impact issues that must be resolved to ensure that the project is viable and eligible for Bank support. The evaluation stage includes an environmental impact assessment prepared, as a rule, by the borrower or the project sponsor, who has to take into account recommendations contained in the environmental and social impact brief. In addition to the usual elements, the EIA must include a record of the process and a summary of the results of consultations with affected groups; monitoring, reporting and evaluation requirements during the execution of the operation and thereafter; a description and, when possible, quantification of the environmental and social benefits as well as of the costs of any unmitigated environmental and social impacts. The data and information thus gathered are analyzed and the Project Team prepares an environmental and social impact report which is the Bank's final impact statement after review and discussion by the CESI. The draft loan contract contains the recommended environmental quality and social impact management measures. After approval, the full environmental and social impact report is made available to the public. For projects that include environmental quality and social impact management components or conditions, regular project reporting is required.

The Board of Directors of the African Development Bank (AfDB) adopted an Environment Policy Paper in 1990, with the overall objective of ensuring environmental viability of investment projects in the Bank Group's Operation Program. In 1991, the Bank initiated action for the preparation of Environmental Assessment Guidelines and environmental assessment procedures which were finalized in 1992. The guidelines are based on the principles that environmental assessment procedures should be linked as much as possible with existing procedures in the Bank Group and that loans and project officers will identify further action to be taken at the earliest stage. Environmental screening is carried out during the identification of projects that need further attention due to their impacts on the environment. The Environmental Assessment Guidelines compare this initial environmental examination to an early warning system. It determines whether a project will be assigned to a category requiring detailed field review and an environmental impact assessment, specific measures or changes in the project design, or no environmental assessment. It also determines whether the selected project site is located in an environmentally sensitive area, characterized by ecosystems with high species diversity, by the presence of endangered or endemic species, or the presence of unique historical or archeological sites. The impact assessment should envisage, if necessary, mitigating measures and should take into consideration the priorities and concerns of the local population, by working in close consultation with NGOs and local institutions at all stages of the project cycle.

Once the project is approved, the Bank undertakes environmental monitoring to ensure that the planned mitigating measures are implemented, that legal standards for pollutants are not exceeded, and to provide early warning of environmental damage. After project completion, the actual impacts of project operations, the accuracy of the predictions, the effectiveness of the mitigating measures and the functioning of the established monitoring program are determined and evaluated through auditing.

In 2013, the Integrated Safeguards System (ISS) was adopted, setting out policies and guidelines to ensure that projects financed by the African Development Bank are environmentally and socially sustainable. The ISS includes Operational Safeguards (OS) covering environmental and social assessments, biodiversity, pollution prevention, labor conditions, community health, and safety. In 2024, the Board of Directors of the African Development Bank approved further updates to the ISS, reflecting new priorities and improved frameworks for environmental and social issues.

Finally, the Asian Development Bank (ADB) has expressed its commitment to promoting environmentally sustainable economic development in its member countries. The 2001 Environmental and Social Assessment Procedures for public sector operations by the ADB were designed to ensure that projects are environmentally sustainable and socially responsible. These procedures were articulated in detail in the Environmental Assessment Guidelines issued in 2003 and continue to evolve to address emerging environmental and social challenges. These procedures have been updated over time to incorporate new insights and best practices. The ADB's 2009 Safeguard Policy Statement further strengthened these requirements, integrating environmental and social considerations more robustly into the project cycle.

The Bank's Office of the Environment categorizes all projects listed in country operational program papers according to their type, location, sensitivity and the nature and magnitude of their potential impact and availability of cost-effective mitigation measures. If a significant impact is expected, an EIA or an initial environmental examination is required for the project, according to the importance of the impact. When an impact assessment is mandated, the procedure starts with the submission of a summary environmental assessment by the Projects department to the Board. The full EIA should be made available to a member of the Board upon request. The Bank requires the borrower to take the views of affected groups and local NGOs into account in the preparation of environmental assessment reports. The assessment reports may also be made available to them. Specific rules govern program loans, sector loans and private sector operations.

For all projects that can have a potential impact on the environment, the project staff should carry out an initial environmental examination. On the return of the fact-finding mission, the report will be reviewed and the terms of reference for the special study or EIA will be prepared with the active assistance of the Office for the Environment. The loan fact-finding mission analyzes the results of the assessment and identifies probable additional environmental concerns not addressed in the study or resulting from changes in project scope. Towards the end of each calendar year a report is published listing all projects requiring specific environmental treatment during the implementation phase.

A review mission is dispatched periodically to discuss with concerned executing agencies the implementation of environmental mitigation measures agreed upon by both the borrower and the Bank. It verifies that environmental safeguards built into the project design are satisfactorily implemented during the construction and the operation of the project. At the end of the operations a project completion report should include a general assessment of any significant environmental impact experienced during project implementation.

In addition to the specific practices described above, several international lending institutions have established formal channels through which local communities, organizations and other groups, and, in special cases members of the Board of Directors, can request independent review or 'inspection' of the bank's role in specific bank-financed projects.[36] These are discussed in Chapter 7. The environmental practices of international financial institutions show

36 See the World Bank rules governing the inspection panels adopted on Aug. 19, 1994; the Asian Development Bank Inspection Procedures approved by the Board of Directors on Oct. 9, 1996 and for the Inter-American Development Bank the document on Independent Investigation Mechanism (no date is available).

several general trends. The first is the creation of special procedures for introducing environmental conditions in the banks' decision-making processes. Such procedures always involve the prior assessment of potential environmental impacts of planned activities, a factor that has become important in selecting projects for funding. In some cases, the environmental impact is understood in a large manner, taking into account the broad environmental and social effects. The legislative and institutional capacity of the borrowing state to fulfil the environmental conditions of the loan generally are considered as well. The information and the participation of local groups and NGOs at different stages of the procedure is always required. The importance of the intervention of local groups and of NGOs is also reflected in the possibility afforded them to ask for the review of a decision they consider as contrary to environmental protection. The special procedures that the financial institutions have established for this purpose generally combine expertise and independence.

4 Risk Assessment

The concept of risk is a predominant factor of modern environmental law. Risk means the possibility or likelihood of adverse consequences from a given action. All human actions involve some risk and interaction with nature itself features risks. Managing and reducing risk is a basic objective of many governmental policies, legislation and regulation. Activities posing certain known risks are highly regulated: industrial activities, airline, rail, and automobile transportation, products containing mercury or lead.

The concept of risk is inherently uncertain, however, because if a given result is certain or it is impossible there is no risk. It is a question of the probabilities in between these two extremes. Ignorance can pose the greatest risks, e.g. not knowing that asbestos causes mesothelioma cancers, or that CFCs deplete the ozone layer. The first goal thus is to understand what is known and not known about the impacts of substances and actions. Risk assessment is thus a specific application of the precautionary principle,[37] because it attempts to evaluate the probabilities of various harms resulting from a proposed activity. From a

37 See Art. 3(3), UNFCCC (May 9, 1992) (states should adopt policies that are 'comprehensive, cover all relevant sources, sinks and reservoirs of greenhouse gases and ... comprise all economic sectors'.)

legal perspective, once a *prima facie* case is made that a risk exists, the burden may be placed on the polluter to minimize or eliminate the risk.[38]

The criteria for assessing the need to regulate risk involve the probability and magnitude of harm. For many industrial activities both the likelihood and the nature of harm are well understood. Other risks can only be estimated because there is no prior human experience with them: Living Modified Organisms (LMOs,) ozone depletion, anthropogenic climate change, and endocrine disrupting substances, for example, are all governed by uncertainty about the quantity and quality of risk associated with them, i.e., the likelihood of harm, the geographic range of the harm, and the character of damage (duration, reversibility, etc.). The reliability of any prediction will be affected by the complexity of the problem and the number of factors it is necessary to take into account.

Once the factors are assessed, policy-makers must determine the acceptable level of risk, knowing that zero risk is an impossibility if actions are allowed to proceed. Some legal definitions speak of the 'likely' or 'evident' risks, based on technical knowledge of 'serious or irreversible' harm. Proportionate measures may be required to avoid the harm. Other legal instruments set the threshold for responsive action at harms that are 'non-negligible', 'appreciable' or 'significant'.

When policy-makers or societies differ about the appropriate level of risk, providing information may be the primary legal obligation imposed. The Cartagena Biosafety Protocol requires that risk be assessed prior to the first intentional transboundary movement of an LMO for intentional introduction into the environment of the importing country. The treaty then leaves it to the importing state to decide whether or not to accept the risk. Risk assessment and informed consent thus form the heart of the Protocol's regulatory process. Article 15 establishes the basic obligation to carry out risk assessment in a scientifically sound manner, in accordance with Annex III and taking into account recognized risk assessment techniques and risks to human health. Developing countries may encounter difficulties complying with this obligation due to lack of scientific data, technical bases, financial resources or biological experts. The Protocol accepts that these factors may require the party

38 See the Prior Justification Procedure adopted by the Oslo Commission. OSCOM Decision 89/1. EC law applies the same approach in prohibiting the introduction of new substances on the market until they have been proven to be safe. Art. 7 of Directive 67/548/EEC on the Approximation of the Laws, Regulations and Administrative Provisions of the Member States Relating to the Classification, Packaging, and Labeling of Dangerous Substances, O.J. L 96/1 (1967), amended inter alia by Directive 93/21/EEC, O.J. L 110/20 (1993).

of import to shift the costs of risk assessment to the notifying party, an application of the principle of common but differentiated responsibilities. Article 16 of the Protocol requires parties to establish and maintain a system to control the risks identified through the assessment procedure.

The application of risk assessment to products in international trade implicates the international trading regime. WTO cases show that the identification of real risks is generally required as a condition *sine qua non* for trade barriers to be compatible with the GATT/WTO regime and especially with bans permitted by the Sanitary and Phytosanitary (SPS) Agreement. In various cases, the dispute settlement panels and the Appellate Body have established the contours of a WTO-acceptable risk assessment procedure: (1) risk assessments should set out both the prevailing view and opinions taking a divergent view; (2) there is no requirement to establish a minimum threshold level of risk and states may set zero risk as the level it will accept; (3) risk must be ascertainable and not theoretical, but ascertainable potential is enough; (4) the criteria used by the state must include all risks and their origin with a degree of specificity. Perhaps most importantly, there must be a rational or objective relationship between the SPS measure and the scientific evidence.[39]

In cases where it is not possible to conduct a proper risk assessment, Article 5(7) of the SPS Agreement allows members to adopt and maintain a provisional SPS measure. According to WTO Panels and the Appellate Body, this provision incorporates the precautionary principle to a limited extent, when four cumulative criteria are met: (1) the relevant scientific information must be insufficient; (2) the measure should be adopted on the basis of available pertinent information; (3) the member must seek to obtain the additional information necessary for a more objective assessment of risk; (4) the member must review the measure accordingly within a reasonable period of time established on a case by case basis depending on the specific circumstances, including the difficulty of obtaining additional information needed for review and the characteristics of the SPS measure.

Environmental agreements require states to act once there is a 'likelihood of' or a 'reasonable concern for' harm.[40] Cost/benefit analysis is not included

---

39 See e.g., Report of the Appellate Body, *Australia – Measures Affecting the Importation of Salmon*, WT/DS18/AB/R (Oct. 20, 1998); Report of the Appellate Body, *Japan – Varietals, Measures Affecting Agricultural Products*, WT/DS76/AB/R (Feb. 22, 1999).

40 See Art. 4(3), Convention on the Ban of Import into Africa and the Control of Transboundary Movement and Management of Hazardous Wastes within Africa (Jan. 29, 1991); Art. 2(5), Convention on the Protection and Use of Transboundary Watercourses and International Lakes (March 17, 1992); Art. 3(2), Convention on the Protection of the Baltic Sea Area (Apr. 9, 1992); Art. 3(3), UNFCCC (May 9, 1992).

in the treaty formulations; for example, states are not allowed to consider the costs of regulation in determining whether transboundary water pollution is likely to cause significant adverse transboundary effects and thus crosses the threshold where action is required. However, in practice, states often weigh the benefits of the proposed activity against the magnitude and probability of occurrence of the risks identified, in determining what actions to take. States must still assess how serious a given risk is in relation to other risks and allocate resources accordingly. Consideration may be given to extended latency periods that may exist between exposure and effects, with potential cumulative impacts, and irreversibility of harm. As a result, abatement may be required of relatively remote dangers.

Risk assessment thus addresses the issues of scientific uncertainty in a procedural manner, documenting each part of a process that is accessible or transparent to all key parties. There are several key steps, beginning with hazard identification (the possible consequences of the proposed action) and risk characterization (estimating the magnitude and distribution of risks based on assessments of the qualities of the substance or action under review and the extent and nature of exposure). Alternatives to the action must be identified and compared as must risk management strategies, on the basis of costs, technical and administrative feasibility, and distributive consequences. Once a risk management strategy is chosen, it must be implemented, reviewed and, if necessary, adjusted.

5 Strategic Environmental Evaluation

Strategic Environmental Evaluation (SEE) or strategic environmental assessment (SEA) is an advanced form of impact assessment procedure that was developed by the World Bank. It is a comprehensive and integrated process for evaluating environmental plans, policies and programs along with the social and economic impacts of a project early in the decision-making. The process can and should be adapted to the specific circumstances of different regions. Some of the characteristics of a SEE are:

- Its perspective is more general than that of an EIA, not targeting a specific project but rather a broader sector of human activities and developing general guidelines for the sector (e.g. transport, energy, poverty reduction);
- It should influence the macro level of decision-making to develop policies that could become law in the future;
- It should easily adapt to different activities and projects in the sector for which it is elaborated and allow for combination with programs and policies for other sectors;

- SEE normally includes consultation with the potential stakeholders on a long-term basis, including individuals, NGOs, indigenous or local communities;
- SEE sector guidelines can be cost effective in evaluating future projects, especially in the public domain.

Within Europe, the European Commission adopted a Directive on strategic environmental assessment.[41] The Directive is supplementary to existing EIA requirements. It calls for adequate transboundary consultations where the implementation of a plan or program being prepared in one member state is likely to have significant effects on the environment of another member state. 'Significant' is not defined, but Annex II sets out criteria for determining the likely significance of effects. Consultations and their results are deemed part of the assessment, which also includes preparation of an environmental report, taking it into account, and the provision of information on the decision. (Art. 2(b)). Articles 6 and 7 further detail the requirements of consultations and their importance.

About the same time as the European Commission adopted its directive, the second Meeting of the Parties to the Espoo Convention, held February 26–27, 2001, established a working group to develop a protocol on strategic environmental assessment. The Protocol on Strategic Environmental Assessment (SEA) to the UNECE Convention on Environmental Impact Assessment in a Transboundary Context was adopted in Kiev in June 2003. The Protocol clearly differentiates between assessment of two kinds of decision-making instruments: plans and programs (Arts. 12, 14) and policies and legislation (Art. 13). The assessment of plans and programs is binding, while for policies and legislation it is only recommended. On the whole the Protocol follows the EC SEA Directive that is based on project-related environmental impact assessment. Annex IV lists elements to be contained in the environmental report which must be made publicly available. Article 12 also requires the results of monitoring to be made available to the public. Article 13 on strategic environmental assessment of policies and legislation includes a substantive obligation to consider and integrate environmental and health policies into proposed policies and legislation. Its drafting is, however, weak and only requires the parties to 'endeavor to ensure … to the extent appropriate …' the assessment of such policies and legislation. Significantly, the Protocol addresses health consequences in the same way as the environmental effects of planned activities. It requires health effects to be examined together with environmental effects, which is an important step toward the integration of the two major concerns.

---

41 EC Directive 2001/42 of June 27, 2001, O.J. L 197 (7/21/01) on the Assessment of the Effects of Certain Plans and Programs on the Environment.

The SEE process corresponds to the three pillars of sustainable development – the social, the economic, and the environmental dimensions – developed by the World Summit on Sustainable Development (WSSD). As such, it is likely to be influential at the international level in future law and policy. It also should be noted, finally, that EIA, risk assessment and SEE are not mutually exclusive. Indeed, the Framework Convention on the Protection and Sustainable Development of the Carpathians (Kiev, May 22, 2003) requires its parties to apply, where necessary, 'risk assessments, environmental impact assessments, and strategic environmental assessments, taking into account the specificities of the Carpathian mountain ecosystems, and shall consult on projects of transboundary character in the Carpathians, and assess their environmental impact, in order to avoid transboundary harmful effects' (Art. 12(1)).

6 Licensing and Permitting

One of the most widely used techniques to prevent environmental harm is government authorization through permits, certification, or licensing.[42] Each activity or establishment considered environmentally hazardous is defined or listed and made subject to formal licensing procedures. Another purpose of licensing or permitting is to ensure the sustainable use of environmental resources. In addition to laws containing general licensing measures, it is common to find norms that regulate directly or indirectly only specific aspects of environmental protection, such as air pollution, drinking water, noise, chemicals, and taking of wildlife. In this regard, hazardous installations such as nuclear plants, mines, natural gas or petroleum works are likely to have more stringent licensing requirements.

6.1 *Purpose and Goals*

Most licensing controls are not designed to eliminate all pollution or risk, but rather to control serious pollution and to reduce its level as much as possible.

42 See e.g. the Oslo Convention for the Prevention of Marine Pollution by Dumping from Ships and Aircraft (Feb. 15, 1972); the Paris Convention for the Prevention of Marine Pollution from Land-Based Sources (June 4, 1974), the Bonn Convention on Protection of the Rhine against Chemical Pollution (Dec. 3, 1976), CITES (March 3, 1973), the Basel (March 22, 1989) and Bamako (Jan. 29, 1991) Conventions on Hazardous Waste, the London Dumping Convention (Dec. 20, 1972), MARPOL (Feb. 17, 1978), UNCLOS (Dec. 10, 1982), the regional seas agreements, the Whaling Convention (Dec. 2, 1946), the Antarctic Treaty (Dec. 1, 1959), and the African (Sept. 15, 1968) and ASEAN (July 9, 1985) Agreements on Conservation of Nature and Natural Resources.

Pollution-control licenses represent a middle ground between unregulated industrial practices and absolute prohibition. As such, they provide an alternative to zoning as a means to site installations and allow experimentation through the granting of temporary licenses. Where environmentally hazardous products are present, such as industrial chemicals, pesticides or pharmaceuticals, authorizations may be required at each step for the manufacture, use, marketing, importation or exportation of the product. Taking permits allow the government to regulate the numbers of wild plants or animals that may be appropriate for private use.

The requirement that installations acquire a license is often given broad application. Most licensing systems operate on the basis of a list, or an inventory of activities necessitating a license because of their foreseeable potential harm to the environment. These lists may constitute part of the law or be contained in a supplementary legal instrument, as in the Annexes to the London Dumping Convention. Most laws make no distinction between profit-making and non-profit-making enterprises, except as to public bodies where they often exempt military operations. Retroactivity is also a problem because in principle laws are not given retroactive effect, but exemption for existing installations arguably grants them a *de facto* subsidy. The gradual trend favors requiring licenses for the continued operation of pre-existing facilities.

An essential condition for initial and continuing authorization is compliance with certain environmental standards. These conditions are reviewed at least once every four years and require, for example, use of the best available techniques; compliance with obligations under national or international law relating to environmental protection; compliance with limits or requirements and achievement of quality standards or objectives prescribed by legislation; imposition of emission limits; and a requirement of advance notification of any proposed change in the operations of the activity or process.

Conditions often are based upon environmental impact assessments whose preparation may be incorporated into the licensing process and form part of the decision for or against issuing the license. In many cases, particularly in regard to chemicals and pharmaceuticals, elaborate testing procedures according to accepted laboratory practices serve the same purpose and may replace environmental impact assessments.

6.2 *Procedures*

Initial control consists of an examination of the installations and an assessment of the foreseeable results of their operations; licensed activities generally also are subject to measures of ongoing special supervision. The existence of several different licensing systems may result in similar functions being confided to different bodies in respect to the same installation. In practice, several licenses may be required for a single project, but in some cases multiple license applications may be merged. Provision then is made for a more detailed investigation, incorporating the procedures of the different licensing systems. The decision is based on information supplied by the applicant and, in most cases, an environmental impact assessment. In general, the costs of the procedure are borne by the public authorities, but in some cases, costs are paid by the applicant.

EU Directives, such as Directive 85/337/EEC and the subsequent Directive 2011/92/EU, play a significant role in licensing procedures in Europe. The former provides in Article 6 that any demand for authorization of a public or private project which could have effect on the environment, as well as information received on this subject, should be made public. States also should ensure that opportunity is given to concerned members of the public to express an opinion before the project is approved. States members should establish the means to provide this information and allow consultation. The particular characteristics of the projects or sites concerned may determine what sector of the public is affected, control the location where the information can be consulted and establish the particular methods of information (poster, newspapers, displays). States also may determine the manner according to which the public should be consulted, whether it is by written submission, public inquiry or other, and fix the appropriate time limits for the various stages of the procedure. Once the inquiry is closed, the authority may grant a license, if appropriate with conditions, give partial or temporary authorization, or refuse a license entirely. If the license is refused, there may be grounds for appeal to a judicial body for review of the decision. In most cases, there are both time limits and restrictions on who may take the appeal.

International requirements for licensing are increasing, part of the strong trend toward transparency attending the movement and use of substances, products and activities which might have a negative impact on the environment. In international trade, the delivery of *export* licenses and permits are often subject to the prior authorization of the *importing* state. Such consent is required by the Basel Convention on the Control of Transboundary Movements of Hazardous Wastes. The 1998 Convention on Prior Informed Consent, derived from non-binding principles established by UNEP and the Food and Agriculture Organization (FAO), extends the system of double authorization to hazardous substances and products others than wastes. It also represents a step towards inter-state recognition of national permits. Such a practice is already found in the acceptance by other states of flag state certification that marine vessels conform to international legal standards. The 1977 International

Convention for the Safety of Fishing Vessels was one of the first to establish that certificates issued by one party according to the provisions of the Convention shall be accepted by other parties as having the same validity as one issued by them (Art. 4). In 1989, the OECD similarly mandated the mutual recognition of data on chemical hazards provided by states that assure that test data have been generated in accordance with good laboratory practices.

7 Prior Informed Consent

Like environmental impact assessment, prior informed consent (PIC) is a procedural mechanism utilized in advance of activities in order to avoid potential conflict and reduce the risks of environmental or social harm. PIC requires obtaining and disseminating the decisions of importing countries on whether they wish to receive shipments of restricted or banned products after they have been fully informed about the hazards posed by the products. In most instances, the products to which the procedure applies are those that pose serious or irreversible risks to health or the environment. The procedure also applies, however, to mediate access to a state's biological resources, in order to obtain disclosure of potential benefits arising from the access. The importance of PIC was recognized as early as 1983 in General Assembly resolution 37/137 which states:

> Products that have been banned from domestic consumption and/or sale because they have been judged to endanger health and the environment should be sold abroad by companies, corporations or individuals only when a request for such products is received from an importing country or when the consumption of such products is officially permitted in the exporting country.[43]

In 1989 the FAO Conference introduced the principle of PIC when amending the International Code of Conduct on the Distribution and Use of Pesticides. The Governing Council of UNEP also adopted it for incorporation in the London Guidelines for the Exchange of Information on Chemicals in International Trade.[44] A 1992 Memorandum of Understanding (MOU) between the two organizations led to guidelines on the PIC principle. In 1994 and 1995, the two organizations agreed on the need for a legally binding instrument for the

43 G. A. Res. 37/137 para. 1 (1983).

44 UNEP/GC.14/17, annex IV.

application of the PIC procedure for certain hazardous chemicals and pesticides in international trade. The Convention was adopted in Rotterdam in 1998.

UNEP's 1987 London Guidelines for the Exchange of Information on Chemicals in International Trade define prior informed consent as

> the principle that international shipment of a chemical that is banned or severely restricted in order to protect human health or the environment should not proceed without the agreement, where such agreement exists, or contrary to the decision, or the designated national authority in the importing country.

Four global environmental agreements rely on a form of PIC: the Convention on Transboundary Movements of Hazardous Wastes,[45] the Convention on Prior Informed Consent Procedure for Certain Hazardous Chemicals and Pesticides in International Trade,[46] the Biosafety Protocol[47] to the 1992 CBD and the Minamata Convention on Mercury.[48] The CBD itself calls for access to genetic resources on agreed terms and requires that such access be subject to the prior informed consent of the provider country of such resources (Art. 15(5)). According to the Minamata Convention, Parties shall not allow the export of mercury except *inter alia* 'to a Party that has provided the exporting Party with its written consent' and only for limited purposes (Art. 3.6(a)). UNCLOS suggests a similar procedure for scientific research within a state's exclusive economic zone, specifying that foreign vessels obtain prior state consent.

The modalities of the PIC process as applied to access to genetic resources were elaborated through the Bonn Guidelines adopted by Decision VI/24 of the sixth Conference of the Parties in April 2002. Guideline VI/24 sets forth basic principles of a prior informed consent system for access to genetic resources. The principles set forth that the system should include: (1) legal certainty and clarity; (2) accessibility, in that access to genetic resources should be facilitated at minimum cost; (3) transparency: restrictions on access to genetic resources should be transparent, based on legal grounds, and not run counter to the objectives of the Convention; (4) consent of the relevant competent national authority(ies) in the provider country and the consent of relevant

45 Basel, March 22, 1989.
46 Rotterdam, Sept. 10, 1998.
47 Montreal, Jan. 29, 2000.
48 Oct. 10, 2013.

stakeholders, such as indigenous and local communities should be obtained as appropriate and according to domestic law.

The 1998 Rotterdam Convention has a broad scope, requiring PIC for any product or substance subject to final regulatory action, so that it includes chemicals refused permission to enter the market as well as those which have been withdrawn or banned. All information on such substances is channeled through the secretariat (UNEP/FAO) to a subsidiary body, the Chemicals Review Committee. The final listing decision rests with the conference of the parties which takes such decisions by consensus. Unlike the Basel and Cartagena agreements, the Rotterdam Convention does not require shipments made without consent to be taken back by the exporting state. The Cartagena Protocol is unique among the treaties in requiring a risk assessment as part of the process.

8 Economic Measures

As an alternative to the regulatory approach, some international instruments recommend that states make efforts to influence the decisions of individual state and non-state actors who choose their activities by comparing the benefits and costs of the available and perceived options. Decisions can be influenced by limiting the options, altering the cost and/or benefits or altering the priorities and significance agents attach to environmental change (preferences). Economic measures can act as incentives or disincentives to behavior. Yet a third approach relies on education, information, and training, as well as social pressure, negotiation and moral arguments.

Economists in general see pollution as an externality that leads to an inefficient or sub-optimal allocation of scarce resources. Corrective devices are necessary to establish an optimal solution, one that maximizes the benefits to society. Polluters need to be confronted with a tax or charge equal to the marginal external costs or damage of their pollution in order to induce them to take account of the full social costs of their activities. Alternatively, an environmental agency could issue permits for emissions, the total number of which equals the optimal emission level, and allow sources to bid for them. Another market device sets the overall pollution limits and allows emission rights to be traded.

The use of economic measures is an application of the polluter pays principle. International environmental texts show a trend towards use of economic instruments and market mechanisms for environmental protection. Principle 16 of the Rio Declaration calls on national authorities to promote the internalization of environmental costs and the use of economic instruments, taking into account the approach that the polluter should, in principle, bear the cost of pollution, 'with due regard to the public interest and without distorting international trade and investment'. Agenda 21 also calls for the effective use of economic instruments, as does the Convention on Biological Diversity, in which the parties undertake to provide financial support and incentives for national activities intended to achieve the objectives of the Convention.

Most international instruments do not attempt to define what is meant by 'economic instruments', but instead enumerate the major categories considered relevant. The OECD addressed the subject of economic instruments in a general regulation on their use in environmental policy, adopted January 31, 1991.[49] The regulation recommends that member countries make greater and more consistent use of economic instruments, such as charges and taxes, marketable permits, deposit-refund systems, and financial assistance, to complement other policy instruments, on both national and international levels. An Annex provides guidelines for the use of economic instruments, establishing five sets of criteria:

- environmental effectiveness, determined by the ability of polluters to react to the incentives provided;
- economic efficiency, achieved by an optimal allocation of resources. It implies that the economic cost of complying with environmental requirements is minimized;
- equity in regard to the distributive consequences;
- administrative feasibility and cost, including the ease and cost of monitoring given the existing legal and institutional arrangements;
- acceptability. It is of crucial importance that target groups be informed and consulted on the economic instruments imposed on them. In general, the success of any (economic) instrument requires certainty and stability over time with respect to their basic elements.

Economic instruments play a key role in the climate change regime. The Intergovernmental Panel on Climate Change (IPCC) explicitly lists a number of economic instruments among efficient climate change mitigation policies countries have been adopting or considering, including 'import bans, standards and labelling schemes, border carbon adjustments, renewable energy support measures, fossil fuel subsidy reform, and the use of international market mechanisms'.[50] Economic incentives can either (1) coerce or apply

49 OECD Council Regulation on the Use of Economic Instruments in Environmental Policy (Jan. 31, 1991).

50 IPCC. (2022) Climate Change 2022: Mitigation of Climate Change: Synthesis Report.

disincentives; (2) provide incentives or (3) allow participants to negotiate the level of benefits they receive by providing, e.g. tradable emissions. The first group includes 'governmental interventions which impose a net burden or disadvantage on economic agents for the purpose of inducing environment-friendly behavior'.[51] Incentives can be applied not only internally, but internationally to encourage participation in a multilateral treaty regime. The 1987 Montreal Protocol on Substances that Deplete the Ozone Layer, for example, granted a ten-year implementation period to developing countries and EU members were allowed to aggregate their national consumption limits. On a national level, economic incentives not only include direct investment subsidies, but preferential loans, accelerated depreciation allowances, tax differentials, tax exemptions, credits and other promotional measures. Often such measures aim to include the cost of environmental damage, as well as the cost of raw materials, production, marketing, and so on. in the price of a product. Even the concept of 'product' changes, as the consumption of fresh air and clean water becomes priced and polluters pay, through fees or taxes, for causing deterioration to these resources. Some of the most widely used economic measures are discussed below.

8.1 *Taxation*

Charges are the 'price' paid for pollution, a disincentive to environmentally damaging behavior. Polluters have to pay for their implicit claim on environmental services. This enters into their cost/benefit analysis, but because environmental charges and taxes set an artificial price on pollution their actual impact on behavior is uncertain. Charges also may have a revenue-raising impact, intended for collective treatment, rather than being high enough to be a disincentive. Taxes can finance environmental investments and provide incentives to reduce pollution and waste. The state must monitor and if necessary correct the tax rate in order to ensure the goal is achieved.

Effluent charges are charges that are levied according to the quantity and/or quality of discharge of polluting substances into the environment. Emissions charges may take the form of user charges, payments for the costs of collective or public treatment of effluent. Tariffs may be uniform or may differ according to the amount of effluent treated.

Product charges are levied on products that are polluting in the manufacturing or in the consumption phase or that are obsolete and for which a disposal system is introduced. The charges can be based on some characteristic of the

51 Peter Sand, 'International Economic Instruments for Sustainable Development: Sticks, Carrots and Games' (1996) 36(2) Indian Journal of International Law 1.

product (mercury content) or the product itself (paint). Tax differentiation is one aspect, leading to more favorable prices for environmentally friendly products.

Tax differentiation may result in subsidizing a relatively clean product by introducing a product charge on a polluting substitute. The differentiation results in more favorable prices for clean products.

User charges are payments, either at a uniform rate or based on amounts involved, for the costs of collective treatment of wastes.

Administrative charges are control and authorization fees, paid for government services, such as the registration of chemicals or for implementation and enforcement of certain regulations.

Taxes on polluting industries or products are a common mechanism used to induce environmental improvement. Though opposed by industry, many countries have enacted some form of environmental tax or other fiscal incentives. This is in line with the generally accepted 'polluter pays' principle. Both the United Nations and the OECD are in favor of greater use being made of environmental taxes and charges. An increasing number of States have been adopting carbon taxes as part of their climate change mitigation efforts as shown in many Nationally Determined Contributions (NDCs) (see later Chapter 12). Carbon taxes are a type of environmental tax levied on the carbon content of fossil fuels, with the aim of reducing greenhouse gas emissions by discouraging their use. These taxes are typically applied at a fixed rate per ton of carbon dioxide (CO_2) emitted or per unit of fuel consumed. By internalizing the social cost of carbon emissions, carbon taxes create a financial incentive for businesses and individuals to reduce their carbon footprint and transition towards cleaner energy sources.

Revenues from collected taxes usually go into the general fund from which government expenditures are financed. Earmarking introduces inefficiencies and constraints. If environmental taxes are earmarked for expenditure on environmental investments, the level of those investments will be dictated by the tax revenues or the tax rates will be dictated by the abatement expenditure requirements and not be estimates of the environmental damage. On the other hand, earmarking may increase political support for environmental taxes. Moreover, environmental taxes can be seen as charges for the use of specific environmental services and the revenues appropriately used to maintain the quality of the same services. Earmarking also can play an important role in funding environmental protection in a declining economy.

8.2 *Loans*

In some countries, government financial assistance and incentives, taking the form of low-interest loans, aid the construction and operation of more environmentally-safe installations and recycling systems. International instruments do not often refer to loans, but speak of grants and 'concessional' access to funds.[52] From the perspective of WTO law, these measures often belong to the broader 'subsidies' category.

8.3 *Insurance*

Governments can impose an obligation on those whose activities present a risk for the environment to be insured against any responsibility for damage to third parties, the state, or the local authorities which may result from an ecological accident. Some multilateral treaties include provisions that require the maintenance of insurance or other financial security for the payment of damages in the case of liability. These are often found in agreements imposing strict liability on hazardous activities, such as the 1962 Convention on the Liability of Operators of Nuclear Ships; the 1963 Vienna Convention on Civil Liability for Nuclear Damage; the 1960 Convention on Third Party Liability in the Field of Nuclear Energy; the 1969 International Convention on Civil Liability for Oil Pollution Damage; and the 1993 Convention on Civil Liability for Damage Resulting from Activities Dangerous to the Environment.

Insurance can have a positive influence on the behavior of companies by putting pressure on them to act in an environmentally sound way; insurance companies may exercise influence to avoid high payouts for environmental accidents. In the same way, investor concerns may impact company behavior.

The law and practices governing insurance coverage of pollution-related claims vary from one jurisdiction to another. However, a general principle is that insurance only covers fortuitous events. Therefore, if damage results from pollution caused by deliberate acts or omissions of the insured, there usually is no coverage.

Disputes over the application of exceptions, especially over broad interpretations of 'accidental pollution' clauses, led to the introduction of pollution exclusion in the 1980s, completely eliminating coverage for pollution, whether or not the source was sudden and accidental. As an alternative, the insurance industry began offering, on a limited basis, Environmental Impairment Liability (EIL) coverage at premiums several times higher than the average policy. Coverage is narrowly drawn, often excluding the cleanup of hazardous waste dump sites and including only gradual escape of pollutants from the insured's own property. In addition, policies typically cover tangible property loss or damage, but exclude such consequences as loss of use of a facility

52 CBD and UNFCCC.

caused by toxic air pollution in the area. Several environmental regulatory programs require insurance coverage as a precondition to licensing or issuance of required permits. In some cases, letters of credit, trust funds or solvency tests may be substituted for insurance.

In recent years, insurance companies in several countries have formed pools. These pools underwrite new and relatively unknown pollution risks under a controlled regime of environmental legislation. Unlike earlier policies, there is a tendency to extend coverage to gradual pollution risk. Generally, there is no coverage for expenses incurred for the restoration and reconstruction of the insured's operating equipment or installation grounds.

8.4 *Grants and Subsidies*

Environmental funds, which have been created in several countries, often directly finance environmental protection. Subsidies can include fiscal measures such as reduced taxes on anti-pollution activities, accelerated depreciation allowances, and favorable interest rates for anti-pollution investments. Such subsidies should not create significant distortions in international trade and investment. Subsidies to new polluting installations are generally prohibited. However, public authorities may aid research and development for the purpose of stimulating experimentation with new pollution control technologies, and development of new pollution abatement equipment. They also may subsidize anti-pollution investment in the framework of regional, industrial, social, agricultural and scientific policies, or whenever new environmental protection measures would create serious economic dislocations.

Subsidies are a particular problem when dealing with exploitation of living resources. Among the issues on the agenda of the Doha round of trade negotiations are subsidies, tariffs and access to fisheries resources. During discussions of the WTO Committee on Trade and Environment (CTE) in 1997–98, governments disagreed over the impact of subsidies on the status of fish stocks and whether subsidies should be singled out for special treatment. Several major countries argued that subsidies have a negative impact from a conservation standpoint. Other participants disagreed and argued that fisheries management should be dealt with in a comprehensive manner. In 1999 some twenty countries expressed support for an Icelandic proposal for a WTO agreement on subsidy removal in the fisheries sector. In preparation for the 1999 multilateral trade round, states calling themselves 'Friends of the Fish' (Australia, Iceland, New Zealand, Peru, Philippines and United States) formed a group to promote conservation and sustainability of fish stocks. Jurisdiction became an issue, with some states arguing for return of the matter to the FAO. The Friends of the Fish sought to obtain an agreement to form a negotiating group on fisheries subsidies, but debate continued without achieving a result throughout the next year. In the meantime, various organizations studied the impact of subsidies on overfishing. The OECD confirmed that subsidies contributed to overfishing and overexploitation in several regions of the world, although many other factors influence the health of fish stocks.

In late 2000, FAO convened an Expert Consultation on Economic Incentives and Responsible Fishing which reviewed and reported on the impacts of subsidies on fishery resources and on trade. Subsidies can allow the expansion of fishing fleets by e.g. supporting the building of new, larger ships or allowing purchase of new equipment; or it can simply hinder the reduction of fleets by supporting economically unsustainable capacity. Subsidies have the effect of slowing the exit of capital from the fishing industry even when it is in difficulty because of overcapacity and declining catches.[53]

Resolving the problem is difficult in part because it is not easy to determine what is a subsidy. It may be considered, for example, that states who pay foreign countries to cover any significant part of the effective costs of access to a foreign fishery are in effect subsidizing the entry of their fishing fleet. Such indirect subsidies are imbedded in international fishing access agreements through an agreed level of compensation for distant water fishing fleets to have a specific level of access to a fishery. From the perspective of conservation, the problem is that access is sometimes granted to already fully exploited or even over-exploited fisheries. Japan has argued that the negative impacts of subsidies 'can be minimized if appropriate management and conservation measures are taken'.[54] One economic model suggests that as long as the Total Allowable Catch does not change, subsidies have minimal impact. The subsidy simply transfers resources among industry. The problem is that for most fisheries, especially high seas ones, there is no established Total Allowable Catch. Due to the conservation problems raised by various mechanisms that have the effect of subsidizing fishing fleets, the Doha round of negotiations of GATT/WTO parties placed the matter on its agenda.

Virtually every major fishing state has used a decommissioning scheme over the past four decades to reduce overcapacity in its fishing fleet. The question of whether these can be considered as environmental subsidies given a special

53 For further information on fishing subsidies, see: APEC Fisheries Working Group, *Study into the Nature and Extent of Subsidies in the Fisheries Sector of APEC Member Economies* (2000); FAO, *Government Financial Transfers to Fishing Industries in OECD* (2000); FAO, *Report Of The Expert Consultation on Economic Incentives and Responsible Fisheries* (2001). OECD, *Transition to Responsible Fisheries: Economic and Policy Implications* (2000).

54 See Gareth Porter, *Fisheries and the Environment* (UNEP 2001).

status within a fisheries subsidies regime remains open. Many states strongly assert that aid to decommission fishing vessels should be considered a benefit to the industry and the environment, because by reducing the fishing fleet it in all likelihood reduces the total catch and improves profits for those who continue to fish. Transfers aimed at capacity reduction, combined with other conservation measures, can reduce pressures on fish stocks. But unless those who remain are discouraged from expanding vessel capacity or more efficient gear to take more fish, the result can be at best neutral. Indeed, decommissioning can be overwhelmed by 'input stuffing' to expand take among those who remain in the industry. Problem: with decommissioning, the value of a license becomes more valuable to those who remain, making vessels more valuable and stimulating increased investment in fishing capacity. Decommissioning funds may be used to buy bigger, faster and better equipped vessels. Some decommissioned vessels simply reappear as reflagged ships. Some stricter measures have been taken, such as limits on 'days at sea' or prohibitions on re-entry of decommissioned vessels. The problem is to ensure that the catching power of vessel does not increase to equal or surpass the loss occasioned by decommissioning.

The need to introduce multilateral discipline prohibiting certain harmful fisheries subsidies became all the more compelling after the adoption of the 2030 Agenda for Sustainable Development in 2015. SDG 14.6 calls on countries to prohibit, by 2020

> certain forms of fisheries subsidies which contribute to overcapacity and overfishing, eliminate subsidies that contribute to illegal, unreported and unregulated fishing and refrain from introducing new such subsidies, recognizing that appropriate and effective special and differential treatment for developing and least developed countries should be an integral part of the World Trade Organization fisheries subsidies negotiation.

In 2022, the negotiations of the WTO Fisheries Subsidies Agreement were concluded. The agreement prohibits subsidies that contribute to Illegal, Unreported and Unregulated (IUU) fishing, thus marking a significant milestone in global efforts to promote sustainable fisheries management and conserve marine resources. The agreement also recognizes the special needs and circumstances of developing and least developed countries, providing them with flexibility and technical assistance to transition towards sustainable fisheries practices.

The 2030 Agenda for Sustainable Development refers also to the importance of phasing out subsidies to the fossil fuels industry. According to SDG 12.c, countries committed to

> Rationalize inefficient fossil-fuel subsidies that encourage wasteful consumption by removing market distortions, in accordance with national circumstances, including by restructuring taxation and phasing out those harmful subsidies, where they exist, to reflect their environmental impacts, taking fully into account the specific needs and conditions of developing countries and minimizing the possible adverse impacts on their development in a manner that protects the poor and the affected communities

The Conference of the Parties (COP) of the UNFCCC has repeatedly stressed the importance of phasing out subsidies to the fossil fuels industry. At COP28, which took place in Dubai in December 2023, the Parties to the UNFCCC adopted the *Decision on the outcome of the first global stocktake,* which underlined the importance of 'Transitioning away from fossil fuels in energy systems, in a just, orderly and equitable manner, accelerating action in this critical decade, so as to achieve net zero by 2050 in keeping with the science'.[55]

8.5 *Negotiable Permits and Joint Implementation*

A system of negotiable permits, sometimes referred to as 'bubbles', fixes total amount of pollution permissible within an area. Each company is required to obtain an emission permit from local authorities conforming to emission standards. Companies investing in processes that reduce pollution may exchange or sell their permits to other companies located in the same geographic area. Emissions trading allows discharges to operate under a multi-source emission limit and trade is allowed in permits adding up to that limit. Resource extraction concessions can be issued and traded.

The idea underlying tradeable permits is to leave the decisions on allocating permission to pollute and actual pollution behavior to the market. The initial distribution of permitted levels may be based on historic levels of emissions which raises the question of how market allocation can be controlled so that regionally disproportionate distribution of pollution does not arise and present an unacceptable risk of harm to those in that area. In the case of carcinogens for which safe concentration levels cannot be determined, very low levels may be unacceptable and a tradeable permit system inappropriate.

Tradeable permits may provoke objections if the system is not coupled with requirements to use and maintain the best available technology. A periodic devaluation or phasing out of tradable permits may be appropriate with incentives for technological innovations.

55 Outcome of the First Global Stocktake. Draft Decision -/CMA.5 (Dec. 13, 2023), para. 28(d).

The Kyoto Protocol, for instance, introduced three flexible mechanisms, including 'emission trading', which allows countries with emission reduction targets to trade emission allowances or credits among themselves. The EU Emissions Trading System (EU ETS) was launched in 2005. It operates on a 'cap and trade' principle, setting a cap on the total greenhouse gases emitted by covered installations and aircraft operators. This cap decreases annually to meet the EU's climate targets, leading to a 37% reduction in emissions from power and industry plants since 2005. Emission allowances, each permitting the emission of one tonne of CO_2 equivalent, are distributed within this cap. Companies must surrender enough allowances annually to cover their emissions or face heavy fines. Companies primarily buy allowances on the EU carbon market, though some are received for free. They can trade allowances, selling surplus if they reduce emissions. The steadily decreasing cap ensures the long-term scarcity of allowances, maintaining their market value and incentivizing cost-effective emissions reductions. This system has generated over 152 billion Euros in revenues since 2013. Most revenues from the EU ETS go into national budgets, funding renewable energy, energy efficiency, and low-carbon technologies. The sale of allowances also supports the Innovation Fund and Modernisation Fund, which finance low-carbon innovation and the energy transition. The legislative framework for the EU ETS is outlined in the ETS Directive, which has been revised multiple times to align with the EU's climate goals. The Directive for phase 4 was initially revised in 2018 to match the 2030 climate and energy framework. However, in response to the European Green Deal and the EU's heightened climate ambitions, another revision began in 2021. On July 14, 2021, the European Commission introduced the 'Fit for 55' package to reform EU climate and energy policies, including the EU ETS.

Another flexible mechanism introduced with the Kyoto Protocol is Joint Implementation (JI), which is related to the idea of negotiable permits. It allows industrialized countries to meet their obligations by financing or undertaking activities in other countries. Many states and scholars favor joint implementation for addressing anthropogenic climate change, where the issue lends itself to global trading markets for pollution because reduction in carbon dioxide emissions anywhere in the world should produce a positive effect in mitigating climate change.

Article 4(2) of the UNFCCC also endorses the general concept of joint implementation. It provides that, for the purpose of meeting its commitments, any developed country may transfer to or acquire from any other party 'emission reduction units' for projects aimed at reducing emissions or enhancing anthropogenic removals by sinks of greenhouse gases in any sector of the economy. The condition is that any such project reduce emission by sources or enhance removal by sinks beyond the amount that would otherwise occur. The acquisition of emission reduction units should be supplemental to domestic actions for the purposes of meeting commitments under Article 3. A developed country may authorize legal entities to participate, under its responsibility, in actions leading to the generation, transfer or acquisition of emission reduction units (Art. 6(3)).

The argument in favor of such trading is that it lowers the overall cost of reducing emissions and may increase the amount of abatement that can be achieved. Those who are concerned about this technique focus on the technical difficulty of assessing the climate benefits resulting from joint implementation because assessment requires estimating the amount of greenhouse gas emissions that would have occurred in the absence of the joint implementation project or activity. It will be difficult, if not impossible, to accurately measure, monitor and verify actual benefits. In addition, some countries fear that joint implementation will distort development in favor of projects that 'count' for climate change and that they will not receive a fair price, including transfer of technology, for their carbon offset actions. On a theoretical level, it may be questioned whether joint implementation violates the polluter pays principle by allowing polluters to continue their activities without paying full costs. In spite of these concerns, some developing countries have actively sought joint implementation projects with developed countries and have benefitted therefrom.

The third mechanism introduced by the Kyoto Protocol is the Clean Development Mechanism (CDM), which differs from JI for one key element: the type of countries involved (as well as the nature of the project). In fact. while JI is between developed (Annex I) countries, CDM involves developed (Annex I) and developing (non-Annex I) countries (see later Chapter 12).

8.6 *Deposits*

Another market mechanism is mandatory deposits on glass, plastic or metal containers to encourage their return or recycling. Deposit refund systems add a surcharge to the price of potentially polluting products. The surcharge is refunded when the product or residual is returned to a collection agent.

8.7 *Labeling*

Labeling requirements are not new. They have been used to detail the nutritional content of foods, the proper use and hazards of cleaning products, and the dangers of cigarettes. However, broader environmental concerns recently have led to adapting the use of labels to promote environmentally 'friendly' products. The 'ecolabel' is an increasingly popular incentive to environmental protection. It is part of a gradual trend away from 'end of the pipe' reactive solutions, which can be extremely costly, toward identifying and avoiding environmental problems before they occur. Environmental labeling programs constitute an economic instrument promoting pro-environmental purchasing on the side of the public and a precautionary approach on the side of industry.

Environmental labeling can involve regulations that insist upon accurate reporting of all the contents and dangers involved in a product. International instruments concerned with hazardous substances and products often call for adequate labeling of the dangers involved in the use of the substance or product. These instruments include the London Guidelines for the Exchange of Information on Chemicals in International Trade and the FAO Code of Conduct on the Distribution and Use of Pesticides. MARPOL, Annex III requires adequate labeling of harmful substances carried by sea.

The second method involves a public or private body awarding positive labels to inform consumers that the products are less destructive of the environment than similar competitive products, based on a holistic, overall judgment of the product's environmental quality. As such, it differs from 'negative' labels that warn of particular dangers, and specific matters such as the use of recycled materials.

Labeling programs are very difficult to administer due to the need to comprehensively assess the entire life-cycle of the product, provide financing and establish product categories and criteria. However, their use continues to spread. The EC adopted Regulation 880/92 on March 22, 1992[56] to create a Community system for awarding the ecology label, based on voluntary participation of manufacturers. The determination of product groups and ecological criteria would be ensured by the Commission, assisted by a committee composed of representatives from the Member states. Initially, the regulation would not apply to food, beverages and pharmaceutical products. In 2010, the European Parliament and Council adopted Regulation 66/2010, amending Regulation 880/92 to modernize and expand the EU Ecolabel framework. The EU Ecolabel can be awarded to products and services that demonstrate a lower environmental impact compared to others in the same category. The criteria for the label are based on scientific data covering the entire life cycle of a product, from development to disposal. This label is available for any goods or services distributed, consumed, or used in the EU market, whether sold or provided for free, as long as the established ecological criteria are met. However, it does not apply to medicinal products for human or veterinary use, nor to medical devices.

56 O.J. L 99/1 of April 11, 1992.

Labeling schemes can be equated to technical regulations or standards, depending on their mandatory or voluntary nature, and as such they fall under the WTO disciplines on technical barriers to trade (see Chapter 17).

In conclusion, like all forms of environmental regulation, economic incentives must be studied to evaluate their effectiveness in protecting the environment. Effectiveness requires analysis of the changes of producer and/or consumer behavior and the costs of the measures taken. Some procedures may have only small effects while being administratively cumbersome and thus do not meet the requirements of efficiency or effectiveness. On the other hand, efforts at environmental protection also can provide a degree of economic growth.

9 Monitoring and Surveillance

The implementation, as well as the formulation, of environmental laws and policies must be based on the collection of reliable information and on its continuous assessment. The techniques adopted in international and national environmental laws to ensure this are surveillance, reporting, and monitoring. International environmental instruments generally require the acquisition of data through surveillance, mainly a scientific activity, on which further action such as monitoring may be based.[57] Surveillance includes taking samples of the affected environments. It can be done by individual enterprises, by associations or by local or national authorities. Once the information is gathered, it must be assembled, organized and analyzed by an appropriate agency or institution to which the information is sent. It is common to find environmental laws requiring reporting by enterprises or state institutions.

Monitoring is the continuous assessment of information, comparing it to mandated parameters. The 1992 OSPAR Convention, Annex IV, Article 1 defines monitoring as the 'repeated measurement' of three separate, but related, factors: (a) the quality of the environment and each of its compartments; (b) activities or natural and anthropogenic inputs which may affect the quality of the environment; (c) the effects of such activities.

Monitoring is a necessary foundation for giving effect to all environmental obligations. Generally, the monitoring organ can intervene based on reports and other means of surveillance that make it possible to assess the effectiveness of legislation or action taken. Monitoring provides constant feedback for

57 See e.g. UN Straddling Stocks Convention (Aug. 4, 1995), CBD (June 5, 1992), UNFCCC (May 9, 1992), the regional seas agreements, MARPOL (Feb. 17, 1978), UNCLOS (Dec. 10, 1982), and the Rhine Chemicals Convention (Dec. 3, 1976).

decision-making, from long-term protection to rapid guidance in emergency situations. To ensure progress, the effectiveness of surveillance and monitoring must itself be monitored and assessed.

Principle 19 of the World Charter for Nature recommends that states, international organizations, and private actors monitor all sectors of the environment for all forms of environmental deterioration 'to enable early detection of degradation or threat, ensure timely intervention and facilitate the evaluation of conservation policies and methods'. Some international agreements contain explicit surveillance and monitoring obligations. The United Nations Convention on the Law of the Sea in Article 204 mandates that:

> 1. States shall, consistent with the rights of other States, endeavor, as far as practicable, directly or through the competent international organizations, to observe, measure, evaluate and analyse, by recognized scientific methods, the risks or effects of pollution of the marine environment.
> 2. In particular, States shall keep under surveillance the effects of any activities which they permit or in which they engage in order to determine whether these activities are likely to pollute the marine environment.

Notably, this obligation extends to all areas of the marine environment.

Permanent monitoring and international cooperation are also required by other international conventions, including the regional seas agreements and those governing the dumping of wastes at sea, international watercourses, ozone-depleting substances, air pollution, climate change, biological diversity, fisheries, and desertification. Article 7 of the Convention on Biological Diversity is an example:

Each Contracting Party shall, as far as possible and as appropriate, in particular for purposes of Articles 8 to 10 [*in situ* and *ex situ* conservation]:

a. Identify components of biological diversity important for its conservation and sustainable use having regard to the indicative list of categories set down in Annex I;
b. Monitor, through sampling and other techniques, the components of biological diversity identified pursuant to sub-paragraph (a) above, paying particular attention to those requiring urgent conservation measures and those which offer the greatest potential for sustainable use;
c. Identify processes and categories of activities which have or are likely to have significant adverse impacts on the conservation and sustainable use of biological diversity, and monitor their effects through sampling and other techniques; and

d. Maintain and organize, by any mechanism data, derived from identification and monitoring activities pursuant to subparagraphs (a), (b) and (c) above.

The 1979 Convention on Long-Range Transboundary Air Pollution contains one of the most detailed monitoring systems. It establishes a cooperative program for the monitoring and evaluation of the long-range transmission of air pollutants in Europe (EMEP), to monitor sulphur dioxide and related substances and develop and use comparable or standardized monitoring procedures, and establish monitoring stations as part of an international program (Art. 9). A 1984 Protocol provides for Long-Term Financing of EMEP.

Monitoring or inspection of record books is required by treaties relating to the carriage of oil, carriage by sea of hazardous substances, imported species and goods, worker health, air quality of the working environment, the composition of waste to be dumped, discharge of harmful substances, and fisheries conservation levels. In some circumstances UNCLOS allows the physical inspection of foreign vessels as do many Memoranda of Understanding on Port State Control. Monitoring systems have been established by several international organizations and the use of it to identify trends and patterns is now well-established.

10 Environmental Management and Audits

The environmental audit or independent review, sometimes referred to as the eco-audit, has come to serve two purposes. First, it is a legislative control mechanism of growing popularity. Second, it is a device of importance to business in sales, acquisitions and other transactions involving assets, where the risk of liability for environmental non-compliance can be a crucial element in negotiations and contracts. It differs from environmental monitoring because it is not a continuous process, but an overall evaluation at a specific moment.

With increasingly complex technology, company structures and environmental regulations, it is sometimes difficult for management and authorities to remain fully informed about the environmental consequences of company operations. This can result in hidden problems, leading to accidents as well as to violation of environmental laws and regulations. Environmental management and auditing are the systematic investigation of the procedures and work methods of a company or institution, as they are relevant to its environmental responsibilities. It is designed to determine to what degree these procedures and methods are consistent with legal regulations and generally-accepted practices. Both the 1991 Espoo Convention on Environmental Impact Assessment in a Transboundary Context and EC regulations refer to environmental audits.

The main elements of the environmental audit are the introduction of a systematic approach by companies to setting environmental standards; self-assessment by companies of their performance; an independent body to audit companies; and companies' right to use a certified statement of their participation in the scheme. The regulation includes criteria for accrediting environmental verifiers and a listing of their functions.

Eco-auditing can be part of the legal-administrative procedure for decision-making or part of the role of the judiciary. There can be parliamentary commissions of inquiry or studies by non-governmental environmental organizations, which play an important review role. Often research is undertaken by independent experts in the field. Environmental audits add an element of external quality control to the administrative system.

In 1993, the EC adopted an Eco-Management and Audit Scheme (EMAS).[58] EMAS is intended to be a management tool to encourage companies to apply high standards of environmental management and to evaluate the environmental impact of their activities. Although it is voluntary, participating companies must conform to the requirements of the Regulation's Annex I. The Annex requires the company policy to be in writing, to be regularly reviewed, in particular in the light of environmental audits, and revised if necessary, and to be publicly available. Company policy must aim to provide for compliance with all relevant environmental requirements and to continually improve environmental performance. The company policy is also to include specific environmental objectives to be achieved over defined time-scales.

Annex II sets forth the requirements of environmental auditing, referencing other international standards including those of the International Standards Organization (ISO). The objectives of each audit, which must take place at least once every three years, must include assessing the management systems in place and determining compliance with relevant environmental regulatory requirements. Environmental audits, including on-site discussions, inspections and reviews, must be performed by independent persons with appropriate knowledge of the sectors and fields audited. Written audit reports are submitted to the top company management and culminate in the preparation and implementation of a plan of appropriate corrective action. Appropriate mechanisms must be in place and in operation to ensure follow-up to the audit.

58 Council Regulation No. 1836/93 of June 29, 1993 allowing voluntary participation by companies in the industrial sector in a Community eco-management and audit scheme, O.J. L 168/1 (7/10/93).

A 2001 Recommendation contains guidance on the EMAS environment statement intended to assist organizations in producing the environmental statement required by the scheme. It identifies issues to be considered in preparing the statement. Its Annex III stresses that significant environmental aspects must be at the center of attention of an organization's environmental management system. The organization must evaluate and improve its environmental performance by setting objectives and targets maintaining an ongoing review process.[59]

The EMAS has undergone significant amendments over the years to enhance its framework and effectiveness. In 2009, the EMAS Regulation was revised and modified for the second time, leading to the publication of Regulation (EC) No 1221/2009 on December 22, 2009. This revision also introduced the EMAS Global Mechanism, making EMAS available worldwide. In 2013, the EMAS User's Guide was developed as a user-oriented tool to translate the EMAS Regulation into practical steps. In 2017, revisions of the new ISO 14001:2015 standard were integrated into Annexes I to III of the EMAS Regulation, making it easier for ISO 14001-certified organizations to upgrade their environmental management system to EMAS. Lastly, Annex IV to the EMAS Regulation was amended by EU Commission Regulation (EU) 2018/2026.

Apart from its function as a regulatory mechanism, environmental audits form a growing part of business transactions. Purchasers of businesses may seek to have environmental representations and warranties, or a determination whether they will be assuming liabilities for environmental damage. This can involve physical inspection of property and assets, including any disposal site used in the processes carried out on the property; examination of documents, including all operating licenses and permissions; and physical and scientific analysis of processes, by-products, and waste streams. Specific investigation usually is made for any signs of past environmental misconduct that would lead to a claim for liability for environmental damage in the future. The results of the audit can govern the nature and extent of protection built into the contract covering acquisition of the company or asset.

11 Conclusions

While the techniques designed to promote sustainable development, including environmental protection, are many and varied, all depend upon some degree of legal regulation. While law in and of itself is not sufficient to ensure

59 Recommendation of September 2, 2001 on guidance for the implementation of Regulation (EC) No 761/2001 of the European Parliament and of the Council, O.J. L.247 (9/17/01).

improvement, good laws and effective institutions contribute to security and provide incentives to environmental protection. Despite the variations in international agreements and national strategies and legal systems, certain common issues arise in deciding upon the adoption of specific techniques. First, the law should be predictable, understandable and enforceable, adopted with the participation of relevant stakeholders. Rules should concern access to, and management of, public goods and natural resources. At the same time, regulatory obstacles can increase costs and create disincentives to compliance. It is also important to coordinate various agencies and departments concerned with different aspects of legal regulation. In this regard, methods of integrated and ecosystem protection, discussed in Chapter 14, can be especially useful. Finally, a strong judiciary can not only enforce the law, but also ensure access to justice for communities and individuals seeking to protect their environmental rights, powers and responsibilities.

Bibliography

Boyle, A., & Freestone, D., Eds., *International Law and Sustainable Development – Past Achievements and Future Challenges* (1999).

Freestone, D., *The Burden of Proof in Natural Resources Legislation: Some Critical Issues for Fisheries Law* (1998).

Freestone, D. & Hey, E., *The Precautionary Principle and International Law: The Challenge of Implementation* (1996).

Glowka, L., *The Role of Law in Realising the Potential and Avoiding the Risks of Modern Biotechnology: Selected Issues of Relevance to Food and Agriculture* (2002).

Helfer, L.R., *Intellectual Property Rights in Plant Varieties: An Overview of Options for National Governments* (FAO, 2002).

CHAPTER 7

Compliance and Dispute Settlement

International environmental law is largely a system to coordinate national legal responses to unsustainable behavior by state and non-state actors. The proliferation of international environmental agreements arouses concern over the extent to which states can and do implement and comply with the multitude of obligations imposed by such instruments. The potential for competitive advantage through non-compliance, due to the incremental costs of environmental protection, requires a credible monitoring system to deter free-riders. The greater the cost of compliance, the greater the disincentive to comply. There is also an incentive to violate or refrain from joining some agreements as they become more effective. This is the case, in particular, with agreements that call for a ban on production or trade in substances for which there is a market. Increased compliance leads to greater scarcity which drives up the price of the substance. The potential for profit thus increases the incentive to holdout or violate the agreement.

International environmental law thus places emphasis on national measures of enforcement, complemented by international compliance and enforcement procedures, from state reporting to judicial proceedings based on state responsibility. The number and variety of mechanisms created to supervise national implementation compliance have increased steadily. As in other fields of international law, the progress of states in meeting treaty obligations is monitored largely through international institutions.

Prevention is the Golden Rule for the environment, both for ecological and economic reasons. It is frequently impossible to remedy environmental injury and even if the damage is reparable, the costs of rehabilitation may be prohibitive.[1] Moreover, prevention cannot be assured solely by reliance on the principle of state responsibility because there are significant procedural hurdles to obtaining a remedy for breaches of international law, as well as problems of proving causation and injury. These factors, plus relatively low damage

1 Damage to the French coastline from the *Amoco Cadiz* oil spill was estimated at $2.2 billion. The need for preventive measures increases the availability of equitable judicial remedies. As the US Supreme Court noted in *Amoco Production Co. v. Village of Gambell, Alaska*, 107 S.CT. 1396 (1987): 'Environmental injury, by its nature, can seldom be adequately remedied by money damages and is often permanent or at least of long duration, i.e., irreparable. If such injury is sufficiently likely, therefore, the balance of harms will usually favor the issuance of an injunction to protect the environment'.

 | DOI:10.1163/9789047440802_009

awards, indicate that, in the present state of international law, imposition of liability cannot be relied upon as the primary means of halting environmental harm. Instead, treaty regimes focus on other means to enforce international obligations.

1 National Enforcement of International Environmental Norms

International environmental law requires implementation and enforcement at the national level. Many of the environmental principles discussed thus far in the present book have been identified and directly enforced at the domestic level, such as concern requirements of public participation during the environmental impact assessment process,[2] intergenerational equity,[3] and the precautionary principle.[4]

Treaties and other agreements call on states to take appropriate action in domestic legal systems to enforce the laws they enact pursuant to international obligations. UNCLOS,[5] for example, requires states parties to enforce their laws and regulations and take the other measures necessary to implement applicable international rules and standards.[6] In particular, flag states of ships violating international norms are to take enforcement actions, including conducting an immediate investigation and, where appropriate, instituting proceedings. Penalties are required to be adequate in severity to discourage violations wherever they occur.[7]

National remedies should be provided as well for transboundary environmental harm. Procedures can include administrative remedies, civil actions

2 See e.g. *Save Lamu et al. vs. National Environmental Management Authority and Amu Power Co., Ltd.*, National Environmental Tribunal, Kenya, Tribunal Appeal No. Net 196 of 2016 (Judgement, 2019), 2019.06.26, https://www.ecolex.org/details/court-decision/save-lamu-et-al-vs-national-environmental-management-authority-and-amu-power-co-ltd-e6f6526d-6f2b-4e44-82d3-0727c09b6140/?type=court_decision.

3 See e.g. *Sheikh Asim Farooq vs. Federation of Pakistan etc*, Lahore High Court, 192069 of 2018, 2019.08.30, https://www.ecolex.org/details/court-decision/sheikh-asim-farooq-vs-federation-of-pakistan-etc-08bc8e44-c0d4-453f-89df-5ee8d5135f9d/?type=court_decision.

4 See e.g. *Suspension of the Ponta Grossa Ambiental Ltda license in view of precautionary principle*, Superior Tribunal de Justiça, 46913523, 2015.06.05, https://www.ecolex.org/details/court-decision/suspension-of-the-ponta-grossa-ambiental-ltda-license-in-view-of-precautionary-principle-26ee9e74-44ea-4784-ac18-2a097764ac6d/?q=precautionary+principle&type=court_decision&xdate_min=&xdate_max=.

5 United Nations Convention on the Law of the Sea (December 10, 1982) 1833 UNTS 3.

6 ibid, arts 213–220.

7 ibid, art 217 (8).

and criminal prosecution of persons who violate norms and standards of environmental law. Some treaty obligations specify particular national measures, such as a civil liability regime to hold liable the polluter or 'the operator or owner of a facility'.[8] If no remedies are available or the remedies provided are inadequate, the case may become an inter-state dispute engaging state responsibility or liability.

In recent years, national environmental litigation has developed to invoke international norms which go beyond pure environmental regulation. In the *Urgenda* case, for example, the Dutch Supreme Court required the government of the Netherlands to reduce greenhouse gas emissions.[9] In so doing, the court relied not only upon the State's obligations under the UNFCCC, but also the rights of Dutch nationals to a right to family life and other protections enshrined in the European Convention of Human Rights. The same sources were more recently considered by the Irish Supreme Court in the *Friends of the Irish Environment* climate litigation, though the court found that the claimant – as a corporate entity – lacked standing to rely specifically upon human rights instruments for this purpose.[10] Rights-based environmental litigation has also developed outside of Europe, with, among others, the *PSB et al. v. Brazil* cases on the Amazon Fund, on the Climate Fund and on Deforestation and Human Rights respectively,[11] the case *Tsama William and Others v. Uganda's Attorney General and Others* filed against the Ugandan government for failure to implement landslide adaptation measures,[12] or the case *Shrestha v. Office of the Prime Minister et al.* where Nepal's Supreme Court held that climate change

8 Convention on the Marine Environment of the South-East Pacific (November 10, 1981) art 11; Convention on Third Party Liability in the Field of Nuclear Energy (Paris Convention) (July 29, 1960) 1519 UNTS 329, art 3; International Convention on Civil Liability for Oil Pollution Damage (London, November 27, 1992), 973 UNTS 3, art III.

9 *Urgenda Foundation v. The State of the Netherlands*, 19/00135, 2019.12.20, <https://www.urgenda.nl/wp-content/uploads/ENG-Dutch-Supreme-Court-Urgenda-v-Netherlands-20-12-2019.pdf> 4.7-4.8.

10 *Friends of the Irish Environment v Government of Ireland*, Supreme Court of Ireland, Appeal No: 205/19, 2020.07.31, <https://www.bailii.org/ie/cases/IESC/2020/2020IESC49.html> 9.5.

11 *PSB et al. v. Brazil* (*on Amazon Fund*), Federal Supreme Court of Brazil, ADO 59/DF, 2022.11.03, https://climatecasechart.com/non-us-case/psb-et-al-v-brazil/; *PSB et al. v. Brazil* (*on Climate Fund*), Federal Supreme Court of Brazil, ADPF 708, 2022.07.01, https://climatecasechart.com/non-us-case/psb-et-al-v-federal-union/; *PSB et al. v. Brazil* (*on Deforestation and Human Rights*), Federal Supreme Court of Brazil, ADPF 760, 2022.04.06, https://climatecasechart.com/non-us-case/brazilian-socialist-party-and-others-v-brazil/.

12 *Tsama William and Others v. Uganda's Attorney General and Others*, High Court of Uganda at Mbale, Miscellaneous Case No. 024 of 2020, 2020.10.14, https://climatecasechart.com/non-us-case/tsama-william-and-others-v-ugandas-attorney-general-and-others/.

impaired the petitioner's constitutional right to a dignified life and a clean and healthy environment and ordered the government of Nepal to enact a new climate change law.[13]

1.1 *Administrative Procedures*

The breach of a statutory environmental duty, even without measurable harm, can result in sanctions or remedies, just as infraction of speeding laws can result in a traffic citation and fine even if no accident occurs. Proceedings usually can be initiated either by the authorities, concerned individuals or companies, or by associations. In some states, administrative procedures are the primary means of a quasi-judicial character for enforcing environmental laws. The courts of Pakistan, for example, have held the government of Pakistan responsible for failing to uphold its own national laws on climate change, finding that the State's 'delay and lethargy' in implementing such laws 'offend the fundamental rights of the citizen'.[14] National environmental laws also may permit agencies to impose fines on violators.[15]

The range of remedies may include fines, confiscation of machinery and tools, closure of the installation, prohibitions on exercise of a profession or activity, and depriving a company or individual of the right of public competition. There also exists an obligation to restore the environment that can be undertaken by the state and charged to the company if the latter fails to carry out its duty. Other sanctions may include a denial of government contracts or blacklisting of harmful products. Lending institutions may refuse loans or other benefits to projects failing to meet environmental standards or those scheduled for establishment in areas not attaining quality objectives. For example, the European Investment Bank may reject projects for areas not attaining the European Union's air quality objectives.[16]

---

13 Shrestha v. Office of the Prime Minister et al, Supreme Court of Nepal, Order 074-WO-0283, 2018.12.25, https://climatecasechart.com/non-us-case/shrestha-v-office-of-the-prime-minister-et-al/.

14 *Leghari v. Federation of Pakistan*, Lahore High Court, W.P. No. 25501/2015, 2018.01.25, <http://climatecasechart.com/non-us-case/ashgar-leghari-v-federation-of-pakistan/>

15 Examples of environmental agencies that may impose fines include England's Environment Agency under the Regulatory Enforcement and Sanctions Act 2008, the United States' Environmental Protection Agency or state environmental agencies notably under the Clean Water Act and the Clean Air Act, the Peruvian Agency for Environmental Assessment and Enforcement under Law No. 29325, amended by Law N°30011.

16 Directive 2008/50/EC of the European Parliament and of the Council on ambient air quality and cleaner air for Europe (May 21, 2008).

1.2 *Civil Liability*

Despite efforts to prevent pollution and protect the environment, human activities and accidents both give rise to environmental damage. To deter harmful acts and remedy damage, legal consequences are attached to those acts that cause injury. International agreements and domestic law may refer liability issues for determination between the actor and the injured parties, or may provide for both inter-state and/or private actions. The increasingly accepted solution is to transfer the question from the inter-state level to the inter-personal level, that is from public to private international law where the polluter and victim are brought directly before the competent domestic authorities. A transnational element is present in all these cases, creating potential jurisdictional problems. It is not surprising, therefore, that states have sought to overcome the difficulties by prior agreement, concluding treaties or adopting other international texts to resolve at least some of the problems.

Civil liability refers to the liability of any legal or natural person under rules of national law adopted pursuant to international treaty obligations which establish harmonized minimum national standards. Several treaties establish rules on civil liability for environmental or related damage. These regimes usually have developed regarding specific activities, such as nuclear installations and oil transport.[17] Recent regional treaties in Europe apply more generally to industrial operations.[18] Civil liability agreements generally define the activities or substances covered and the harm covered, channel liability, establish a standard of care and exceptions, set limitations on the amount of liability, and provide for enforcement of judgments. Most include a provision for mandatory insurance or other financial guarantees.[19] In addition to civil liability agreements, the EU Directive on environmental liability adopted in 2004 requires Member States of the EU to impose liability on the operator of an occupational activity that has caused environmental damage or the imminent threat of environmental damage.[20]

---

17 See e.g. Convention relating to Civil Liability in the Field of Maritime Carriage of Nuclear Material (December 17, 1971) 11 ILM 277; International Convention on Civil Liability for Bunker Oil Pollution Damage (March 23, 2001) IMO Doc LEG/CONF.12/DC/1; Protocol on Liability and Compensation for Damage resulting from Transboundary Movements of Hazardous Wastes and their Disposal (Basel, December 10, 1999).

18 See e.g. Convention on Civil Liability for Damages Resulting from the Exercise of Activities Dangerous for the Environment (Lugano, June 21 1993) ETS No. 150, 21.VI.1993.

19 ibid, art 12.

20 Directive 2004/35/CE of the European Parliament and of the Council on environmental liability with regard to the prevention and remedying of environmental damage (April 21, 2004) OJ L 143/0056.

The concept of liability generally implies that damage or harm has occurred to something. Normally, civil actions are commenced by those who have suffered harm to themselves or their property. They seek to halt further damage and repair that which has been done. Liability is most often imposed on the principal owner or manager of a polluting enterprise, in accordance with the 'polluter-pays' principle.[21] Remedies can be sought if the damage results from the breach of law and the damage is not too remote from the wrongful action. Some national laws permit consumers or even those with no direct injury to sue. While the international law of strict liability is less developed than is national law, the concept applies in most of the treaties concerned with hazardous activities and substances. In civil liability, as in state responsibility, the fundamental problems are to establish causation, identify the polluter, and prove damage. To these difficulties are added three issues particular to the field of private international law: jurisdiction, choice of law and execution of judgments.

1.2.1 Adjudicative Jurisdiction

Adjudicative jurisdiction can exist in the state where the pollution occurs or the state where the polluter is found. As a general rule, private international law favors jurisdiction in the defendant's domicile, sometimes under principles of *forum non conveniens*.[22] Several factors support this approach: the accused is able to defend itself in local tribunals, the evidence of harmful activity is more readily available, witnesses more easily may be called, and execution of a judgment in favor of the plaintiff will be more easily enforced. Conversely, it can be argued that the victim of the pollution should have the benefit of local courts to obtain compensation, especially because evidence of damage is more readily available in plaintiff's domicile where experts can evaluate and establish the scope of injury. Moreover, the innocent victim should not have to bear

---

21 Philippe Sands and others, *Principles of International Environmental Law* (3 ed., Cambridge: Cambridge University Press 2012) 228.

22 In United States federal courts and most state courts, there is a presumption in favor of plaintiff's choice of forum which the defendant must overcome by showing that the chosen forum would be unnecessarily burdensome. *Piper Aircraft Co. v. Reyno*, 454 US 235, 102 S.Ct. 252, 70 L.Ed.2d 419 at n. 19. In various cases, often involving international litigation, the United States Supreme Court has stated that a plaintiff's choice of forum should rarely be disturbed. *Piper Aircraft v. Reyno, supra* n 22; *Gulf Oil v. Gilbert*, 330 U.S. 501, 67 S.Ct. 839, 91 L.Ed. 1055 1947); *Koster v. Lumbermens Mut.Case.* Co, 330 U.S. 518, 67 S.Ct. 828, 91 L.Ed. 1067 (1947). See also *Macedo v. Boeing Co.*, 693 F.2d 683 (7th Cir. 1982) (reversing dismissal that would require resort to foreign forum) and *In re Union Carbide Corp. Gas Plant Disaster at Bhopal, India in December 1984*, 809 F.2d 195 (2d Cir. 1987) (upholding dismissal on forum non conveniens grounds).

the additional expenses of litigation in a foreign country. Whatever solution is taken, the basic principle applies of equality of access and equal treatment of aliens and nationals.

State practice has evolved in this field. German courts have accepted cases brought by resident victims against non-resident defendants since 1957, when the Sarrebrucken Court of Appeal permitted suit by a German restaurateur located on the German side of the Mosel against a French power station in Lorraine for damage caused by smoke and dust.[23] The plaintiff complained that the smoke had destroyed his gardens, made his houses unrentable and rendered his outdoor terrace unusable. The Court applied French law and awarded damages. However, there was no guarantee that the judgment would be enforced in France. The parties had to rely on comity and French cooperation due to the lack of an international text requiring mutual recognition of judgments.

Subsequently, EC countries adopted a Convention concerning Jurisdiction and the Enforcement of Judgments in Civil and Commercial Matters (1968 Brussels Convention).[24] Unfortunately, the Convention did not settle the jurisdictional issue. According to Article 3, the contracting parties agree that a defendant can be sued in tort before the courts of the place where the harmful event occurred, but, in reality, the harmful event could be deemed to occur in the place where the wrongful act is committed or the place where the harm is suffered. The first interpretation gives jurisdiction to courts in the state where the polluter acts; the second interpretation favors the state of the victim.

Several tribunals deciding claims based on environmental damage have utilized the Brussels Convention, with conflicting results. A trial court in Freiburg, Germany, awarding damages on a complaint by German farmers against a French chemical factory, held that jurisdiction lies in the court of the place where the damage is felt.[25] In contrast, a Rotterdam court, in a Rhine pollution case, initially held it had no jurisdiction because the action had to be brought where the polluting acts originated.[26] On appeal, plaintiffs argued that interpretation of the jurisdictional clause in the treaty should be referred

---

23 *Poro v. Houilleres du Bassin de Lorraine*, 11 Oberlandesgericht (OLG) Saarbrucken 752 (1958), summarized at 1973 R.C.A.D.I 161.

24 European Convention on Jurisdiction and the Enforcement of Judgments in Civil and Commercial Matters, 8 ILM 229 (1968), amended in 1978, 21 OJ L 304 (1977), 18 ILM 81(1979).

25 Unpublished opinion, 1975.

26 See *Handelskwkerij G.J. Bier et al v. Mines de Potasse d'Alsace S.A.* (Rotterdam municipal court, 6th chamber, Judgment of May 12, 1975), 1976 Rev. Jur. Env 71.

to the European Court of Justice.[27] The appellate court agreed and submitted the question for determination. The European Court of Justice judgment of November 30, 1976, supported the plaintiffs.[28] The Court declined to adopt a preference for one jurisdiction over another, finding too close a link between the two elements of liability (wrongful polluting activities, subsequent damages suffered). In the Court's view, the circumstances of every transboundary pollution case give rise to factors of proof and procedure which support the jurisdiction of both courts. According to the Court, the authors of the Convention deliberately created the ambiguity in Article 3, no doubt having in mind the interests of the injured party, for whom it is advantageous to be able to choose the best forum. Moreover, the nature of the wrong in question, international pollution, might require that the choice of forum be left to the plaintiff. Thus, the provision should be read to encompass both locations. This meant that the Dutch plaintiffs could choose freely to bring the case either before Dutch or before French courts.[29]

1.2.2 Choice of Law

Choice of law in the demand for compensation is determined by the court with jurisdiction. Generally, tribunals apply local law, but public policy concerns and the principle of non-discrimination may affect the choice. The latter rule requires that in no case may the plaintiff's complaint be judged according to rules less favorable than those which would be used to judge the matter in the state where the activities took place. This norm is included in Article 3(2) the 1974 Nordic Environmental Protection Convention and should lead judges to apply foreign law when its substance is more favorable than local law.[30] German courts have chosen to apply the law most favorable to the victim in two cases involving transfrontier pollution coming from France

27 The amendments to the Brussels Convention, adopted by Protocol, conferred jurisdiction on the European Court of Justice to interpret the terms of the Brussels agreement.

28 *G.J. Bier v. Mines de Potasse*, Judgment No. 21/76, 1976 Com. Mkt Rep. 7816.

29 Following the Rhine case, the first application of the European Court judgment on jurisdiction was by the Tribunal of Bastia (France). In its December 8, 1976, judgment the tribunal upheld its jurisdiction to decide a complaint by Bastia fishermen against the Italian company Montedison, based on the dumping of sludge into the Mediterranean causing harm to the fishing off Corsica. The decision was upheld on appeal February 28, 1977. The appellate judgement expressly referred to the decision of the European Court of Justice. 8 REV. JUR. ENV. 331 (1977).

30 Convention on the Protection of the Environment between Denmark, Finland, Norway and Sweden (February 19, 1974) 1092 UNTS 279.

to cause harm to German plaintiffs. Each time the more favorable French law was applied.[31]

1.2.3 Assessing Damages

Providing compensation for environmental harm requires a consideration of the amount of damage that has occurred. The concept of harm to the environment is often viewed as a property concept, where economic value is placed on the lost or damaged object. This may include market value, loss of income, and damage to moral, aesthetic and scientific interests.[32] The economic approach poses problems for protection of species of wild fauna and flora that are not exploited and thus have no market value, as well as for ecosystems or landscapes the economic value of which cannot be assessed. Evaluating the economic value of the intangible aspects of the environment, such as biological diversity, balanced ecosystems, and environmental services, is difficult. The situation is similar for areas that are under common ownership, and even more for those areas that are for common use but not capable of ownership, such as the high seas and outer space. Measurement or evaluation of harm for the purpose of damage awards also involves important questions of the threshold or *de minimis* level of harm, proximity of harm, especially for long-term, long-distance, multiple-authored actions and, finally, the possible irreversibility of the harm caused. The last issue is something that is thus far largely ignored in law.

One of the most difficult issues in environmental litigation is the scope of damage. The key question is whether damage extends beyond persons and properties to include damage to the environment itself. Increasingly, relevant civil liability conventions are addressing damage to the environment but generally limit recovery to the costs of reasonable measures of reinstatement and the costs of preventive measures. The UNECE Task Force on Responsibility and Liability regarding Transboundary Water Pollution has proposed a definition of damage that includes 'detrimental changes in ecosystems'. For this there

31 The *Poro* plaintiff sought and was awarded damages for business losses which were not recoverable under German law, but were permitted by the French Civil Code. *Poro v. Houilleres du Bassin de Lorraine, Sarrebrucken, supra* n 23.

32 For an assessment of valuation methodologies, see Lucas Bergkamp, 'Liability and Environment: Private and Public Law Aspects of Civil Liability for Environmental Harm in an International Context' in *Liability and Environment*. Brill Nijhoff (2021), 337; Van Den Bergh CIM (editor), *Handbook of Environmental and Resource Economics*, Cheltenham: Edward Elgar (2000); Jason Rudall, 'Economic and Philosophical Approaches to Valuing Environmental Damage' in Jason Rudall, *Compensation for Environmental Damage Under International Law,* Routledge (2020) 95.

may be awarded the equivalent costs of reasonable measures of reinstatement actually undertaken and further damages exceeding those provided for under the first measure, i.e. there may be substitute damages where reinstatement is impossible because of the irremediable nature of the harm.[33]

Courts and tribunals use a variety of methods to assess the scope of damage to the environment. The most common approaches applied in environmental litigation are based on the (economic) value of environmental goods or services to human beings, such as the contingent valuation, restoration cost method, or the ecosystem services approach.[34] These methods, however, may not accurately represent the intrinsic value of the environment which exists independently of the value that it provides to humans. They are predicated on an anthropocentric understanding of the environment that emphasizes the benefits or utility that humans derive from it.[35] Although taking into account the value of the intrinsic environment in assessing environmental damage is challenging, certain methods may more accurately reflect it than others, such as the habitat equivalency analysis (HEA) and resource equivalency analysis (REA), which measure the amount of resources required to compensate for losses in an ecosystem.[36]

The *Amoco Cadiz* case illustrates the current problems in the civil liability regime, especially in regard to the assessment of damages. The *Amoco Cadiz* tanker ran aground on March 16, 1978, due to damage to its navigational equipment. The accident occurred two miles from the small port of Portsall on the coast of Brittany. During the following three weeks, nearly all the 219,617 tons of crude oil cargo as well as its fuel, together totaling nearly 230,000 tons of oil,

---

33 See Alfred Rest, *New Tendencies in Environmental Responsibility/Liability Law: The Work of the UNECE Task Force on Responsiblity and Liability regarding Transboundary Water Pollution*, 21 EPL 137 (1991).

34 For further details on the ecosystem services approach, see Millennium Ecosystem Assessment, "Ecosystems and Human Well-being" (2005) 38.

35 Jason Rudall, 'Economic and Philosophical Approaches to Valuing Environmental Damage' in Jason Rudall, *Compensation for Environmental Damage Under International Law*, (Routledge 2020) 96–106; Peter Gailhofer, 'National Civil Liability and Transboundary Environmental Damage' in *Corporate Liability for Transboundary Environmental Harm: An International and Transnational Perspective*, edited by Peter Gailhofer, David Krebs, Alexander Proelss, Kirsten Schmalenbach, and Roda Verheyen, 177, (Cham: Springer International Publishing 2023), 206.

36 Jason Rudall, 'Economic and Philosophical Approaches to Valuing Environmental Damage' in Jason Rudall, *Compensation for Environmental Damage Under International Law*, (Routledge 2020) 96–106; William Nicholas Desvousges Gard, Holly Micheal and Anne Chance, 'Habitant and Resource Equivalency Analysis: A Critical Assessment', 143 *Ecological Economics* (2018) 74.

escaped into the sea creating an oil slick eighteen miles wide and eight miles long. Part of the oil evaporated, another part broke down by natural means, but the rest filtered to the seabed or reached the coastline, creating ecological disaster.

Three hundred seventy-five kilometers of coast was polluted by 50–60,000 tons of oil. Of this, 15–20,000 tons were cleaned up by volunteers and the military. In the affected zone, in the sea and on the coast, a total of 30 percent of the animal life and 5 percent of the plant life was destroyed. Approximately 20,000 birds died, the shellfish industry suffered damage, and the fishermen lost 45–60 days of fishing. There was also indirect damage, notably to tourism.

In 1983, multiple lawsuits filed in the United States were consolidated in the United States District Court for the Northern District of Illinois. The claimants included the French government, various French administrative departments, numerous towns, businesses, associations, individuals, and the insurers of the cargo. The defendant Amoco parties included Astilleros Espanoles, the Spanish company that designed and constructed the *Amoco Cadiz*; Amoco Transport Company, the Liberian company which was the registered owner of the ship and whose principal place of business was in Bermuda; Standard Oil Company, the owner of Amoco Transport Company, incorporated in Indiana, with its principal office in Illinois; Amoco International Oil Company, also owned by Standard Oil, incorporated in Delaware; Bugsier Reederei und Bergungs A.G., the German salvage tug company that sought to assist the *Amoco Cadiz*; and the American Bureau of Shipping, which approved the design of the supertanker.

Normally, the pollution victims would have been able to bring an action in French court for damages under the Brussels Liability Convention, discussed infra, which France had ratified. However, their damages substantially exceeded the limits of 77 million francs which would have been due under the original Liability Convention formula. According to estimates prepared at the time, the cleanup alone cost some 450 million francs, the damage caused to fish and shellfish was 140 million, and the losses caused by the reduction in tourism were more than 400 million. In these circumstances the victims sought to escape the limits of the Liability Convention by taking the case to the United States courts because the United States is not a party to the Liability Convention. The complaint sought $2.2 billion damages for environmental harm suffered due to the negligence of the companies in the construction, maintenance, and operations of the *Amoco Cadiz*.

In a judgment of April 18, 1984, the Court determined it had jurisdiction over the action and that United States law would apply, finding that local law was not proved to be different from French law which should govern because of the place of the harm.[37] The Court seemingly ignored the fact that France was a party to the Liability Convention and the latter thus formed part of French law. The Court could have reached the same result by conceding the difference in law and concluding that United States law should apply for policy reasons or on an interest analysis.

This ruling was sufficient to escape the limits of the Brussels Convention, which would have limited the liability of Amoco to under $20 million. If the Convention had been applied, the provisions of Article 9, according to which no claim may be presented except before the tribunal of the state victim of the pollution, would likely have required dismissal of the action. Even if this were not the case, the choice of French law including the Liability Convention would have bolstered Amoco's arguments for dismissal on grounds of *forum non conveniens*.

On the merits, the court held liable Standard Oil and its two subsidiaries.[38] Amoco International Oil Company, the American corporation responsible for the organization and administration of transportation for all of Standard Oil, was found negligent in its obligation to maintain the *Amoco Cadiz* in a state of navigability. In particular, there was a negligent breakdown in the steering mechanism of the tanker which was one of the immediate causes of the grounding of the tanker and the resulting damage. Moreover, the crew of the tanker was not sufficiently trained to maintain, utilize, inspect and repair the steering system, a supplementary cause of the grounding. Finally, the company using the *Amoco Cadiz* was negligent in leaving the ship without any backup steering system and without any other means of controlling the direction of the ship in case of failure. There was no limitation set on liability for any of the defendants.

Four years later the court examined the question of damages, awarding the plaintiffs $85.2 million. The court's 435-page opinion addressed the claims made by France,[39] the harmed cities and towns, individuals, farmers,

37 Elsewhere in the opinion, the Court does seem to recognize that ratification of the Liability Convention by France creates differences in substantive law: 'The [Liability Convention] is the law of France and not the United States; it thus does not apply …' 20 Env't Rep Case (BNA) at 2076.

38 The plaintiffs failed to show the required gross negligence or willful misconduct necessary to hold the German salvage tug company liable. The Spanish design and construction company defaulted.

39 *In re Oil Spill by Amoco Cadiz off the Coast of France on March 16, 1978*, No. MDL376 (N.D.Ill. 1988), 1988 U.S.Dist. LEXIS 16832.

fishermen and environmental protection groups,[40] discussing several categories of damages:

1. Cleanup operations by public employees. The court accepted the claim for costs of the cleanup to the extent that public employees, including elected officials and the military, took time from their regular duties or put in overtime to assist. Travel costs incurred in the cleanup were also reimbursed. The time of volunteers was not compensated because their efforts were donated, but the proven costs of transportation, food and lodging could be claimed.
2. Gifts made by local communities in money or goods to volunteers or military officials were found to be inappropriate for inclusion in the damage claim, being in the nature of recognition of and gratitude for the services rendered.
3. Costs of material and equipment purchased for the cleanup. The court allowed recovery, less the residual value of purchased items, provided the acquisition was reasonable and the equipment was used during the cleanup and that a residual value could be proven. As for previously-owned equipment, depending on the evidence the claimants were found entitled to recover either the difference between the value of the equipment before its use commenced and the value thereafter, or a reasonable rental value for the equipment during the term of its use.
4. Costs of using public buildings. The damage suffered by buildings during the cleanup operations was compensated and reimbursement was awarded for the extra costs arising from use of the buildings during the cleanup, such as increased water, power, and telephone usage.
5. Coastline and harbor restoration. The expenses for these purposes were included.
6. Lost enjoyment. The court applied French law and rejected this claim, which it viewed as a claim for damage to the quality of life and public services.
7. Loss of reputation and public image of the towns. This claim assumed that tourists who would normally have visited the communes for vacation and other recreational purposes went elsewhere due to deterioration of the beaches. The court rejected the claim, finding that it was more precisely covered and measurable in individual claims brought by hotels, restaurants, campgrounds and other businesses.

---

40 The various claimants initially demanded $2.2 billion in damages. See Business Insurance, April 30, 1984, at 1. *Final Cost of Amoco Cadiz*, 14 MAR POLLUTION BULL. 12 (1983).

8. Individual claims. The court accepted some of the numerous individual claims, applying as a general rule the loss of income for one year. A claim by the Departmental Union of Family Associations was rejected as tenuous and not grounded in French law.
9. Ecological harm. This part of the decision was awaited with the greatest interest and it produced the greatest disappointment. The court did not award damages for injury to the biomass, the totality of life in the sea and on the bottom in the affected zone, deeming the matter complex, attenuated, speculative and based on a chain of assumptions. The court also found it did not have to reach this issue, because the damage was to *res nullius* and no one had standing to claim compensation. French arguments that the state could assert a legal interest in protecting the maritime public domain were found unpersuasive. In addition, the court decided that damage caused to the ecosystems already had been fully recognized in the claims of fishermen and fishing associations, based on the reduction in their catches and their resultant profits. In respect to French governmental programs to restore the ecosystems, the Court allowed only expenses incurred to reintroduce species that suffered from the pollution and its consequences, finding that if the initial experiments were useful, the program should not be financed further by the defendants.

Ecologists, in particular, deplored the judge's failure to attach importance to the deterioration of ecosystems. An opportunity was lost to progress towards solving the difficult problem of evaluating ecological damage, that is, damage to the environment itself apart from any harm suffered by those who exploit its resources.

In addition to the *Amoco Cadiz* case, another domestic dispute relevant to the issue of assessing environmental damages is the Texaco/Chevron litigation in Ecuador. Between 1964 and 1992, Chevron, and Texaco after its acquisition by Chevron in 2001, carried out petroleum exploration and exploitation activities in the Ecuadorian Amazon region. For approximately twenty years, victims of environmental contamination sought compensation from Chevron/Texaco through arbitration and judicial proceedings in different jurisdictions, including the United States and Ecuador. In 2003, they filed a class action suit through the Amazon Defence Coalition against Chevron/Texaco in Ecuador, alleging serious environmental contamination of the areas where Texaco exploited petroleum. An expert designated by the judge found the presence of hydrocarbons and heavy metals in the analysed water samples at levels considered to be unsafe according to national standards and recommended the Court of Lago Agrio to order Texaco/Chevron to pay 27 billion dollars as compensation. However, due to Chevron's accusation of collusion with the plaintiffs and motions to revoke the expert's nomination, the Court omitted to consider this expert's report in its judgement.[41] A new evaluation of damages ranging from 90 to 113 billion dollars was presented by the plaintiffs in 2010. On February 14, 2011, the Court of Lago Agrio gave a judgement in favor of the plaintiffs.[42] Based on the evidence presented before the Court, including over one hundred expert reports, it found that: '1. Contamination attributable to the scheme of petroleum operations in the concession exists, since it was designed to take advantage of the dumping of effluents into the environment, in spite of the existence of other available alternative technologies; 2. The contamination reported can be considered as hazardous, because of the admitted possibility that the dumping of fluids such as those that Texaco has admitted to have dumped, under the name of Texpet, causes damage to agriculture and to the health of persons'.[43] With respect to reparations, the Court distinguished between the following three types of reparation measures:

> (1) primary measures, focused upon restoration of the natural resources to their original state to the extent possible and as soon as possible; (2) compensatory measures, created in recognition that the principal measures could be delayed or may not be performed in their entirety, and the objective of which is to compensate for the fact that the primary reparation does not achieve full restitution of the natural resources and to compensate for the time that passes without reparation; and (3) measures for mitigation, designated to reduce and attenuate the effect of damages impossible to repair[44]

The Court of Lago Agrio ordered a total amount of reparation of 8.646 billion dollars to be distributed as follows: 600 million for cleaning up subterranean waters; 5.396 billion for cleaning up contaminated soils, 200 million (10 million per year for 20 years) for recuperation of the flora and fauna and the aquatic life native to the area; 150 million to create a system to bring potable water to the region; 1.4 billion to create a health system to address the health-related needs created by the public health problems; 100 million for the creation of

---

41 Antoni Pigrau, 'The Texaco-Chevron Case in Ecuador: Law and Justice in the Age of Globalization' 2014, 13.

42 Ruling, Trial No 2003–0002, Judge: Nicolas Zambrano Lozada, Provincial Court of Justice of Sucumbios – Single Chamber of the Provincial Court of Justice of Sucumbios, Nueva Loja (February 14, 2011).

43 ibid 172.

44 ibid 177–178.

a community reconstruction and ethnic reaffirmation program for the indigenous peoples; 800 million to provide funds for a health plan.[45] In order to implement the judgement, the Court requested the creation of a trust to be administered by the Amazon Defence Coalition on behalf of those affected.[46] The Court also imposed a punitive sanction equivalent to an additional 100 percent 8.646 billion dollars if Chevron/Texaco did not present a public apology.[47] Petitions of appeal were subsequently brought against this judgement respectively by each party. The plaintiffs argued that the reparations awarded had omitted reparations for the economic impact on the persons affected by the contamination, as well as for the damages caused by the loss of territory suffered by the ethnic groups in the area.[48] The Provincial Court of Sucumbíos confirmed the judgement of the Court of Lago Agrio in all aspects.[49] A petition of appeal was filed by Chevron/Texaco to the Supreme Court of Ecuador. In its judgment of November 12, 2013, the Supreme Court noted that neither the imposition of punitive damage, nor the requirement for public apology, had basis in Ecuadorian law. The Supreme Court therefore cancelled the judgement in second instance with respect to punitive damage and confirmed the rest of the judgment.[50]

1.2.4 Execution of Foreign Judgments

Execution of foreign judgments in tort matters is not guaranteed in the absence of treaty protection, although the state of the polluter may consent to respect the judgment on the basis of comity. Uncertainty on this question may induce plaintiffs to choose the courts of the state where the polluter is found rather than their own national courts.

Within the EC, the question is regulated by Article 31 of the 1968 Brussels Convention, according to which the decisions rendered in one contracting state may be executed in another contracting state on request of any interested party. This guarantee of the execution of judgments complements the

45 ibid 179–184.

46 ibid 186–187.

47 ibid 185–186.

48 Trial No 2011–0106, Judge: Dr. Milton Toral Zevallos. Provincial Court of Justice of Sucumbíos, Single Chamber of the Provincial Court of Justice of Sucumbíos, Nueva Loja Trial No 2011–0106, Judge: Dr. Milton Toral Zevallos. Provincial Court of Justice of Sucumbíos, Single Chamber of the Provincial Court of Justice of Sucumbíos, Nueva Loja (January 3, 2012); Pigrau, Antoni, 19.

49 ibid.

50 National Justice Court, Trial No 174–2012, Dr. Wilson Andino Reinoso, National Court of Justice, Civil and Merchant Court Room, Quito (November 12, 2013).

European Court of Justice decision permitting victims of transfrontier pollution to choose the jurisdiction to which to bring cases by ensuring that even judgments rendered in local courts will be effective in the state of the polluter.

1.2.5 Treaty Regimes of Liability and Compensation

Given the myriad uncertainties and risks of litigation, a plaintiff could become involved in a legal steeplechase where one hurdle after another must be overcome in order to receive compensation for environmental harm. States have agreed on special procedures in an effort to reduce the hurdles in two fields where the effects of environmental harm may be the most serious: the transportation of hazardous substances by sea and the production and use of nuclear energy.

Current treaties on civil liability number about one dozen,[51] nearly all of them concerned with one type of hazardous activity such as nuclear energy generation or oil transport. Only the regional Lugano Convention on Civil Liability for Damages Resulting from the Exercise of Activities Dangerous for the Environment applies to all harmful activities.[52] Apart from it, there are several conventions on marine pollution from shipping and on nuclear damage, and one each on pollution from offshore oil and gas exploitation, carriage of dangerous goods by various means of transport, and transboundary movements of hazardous wastes.

1.2.5.1 *Marine Oil Pollution*

Marine oil pollution, in particular compensation for environmental injury caused by it, is regulated by an entire system based on the 1969 International Convention on Civil Liability for Oil Pollution as modified in 1971, 1976, 1984 and replaced by a protocol in 1992.[53] To this must be added the 1971 Convention

---

51 This approximate number of civil liability treaties comprises treaties that establish a comprehensive civil liability regime within their specific areas of application, along with protocols that make important additions to an existing civil liability regime. However, it does not include protocols or conventions setting liability limitations, establishing international funds, and governing conflicts of application between liability conventions. See further Kirsten Schmalenbach, 'International Standards for National Environmental Liability Regimes', in Peter Gailhofer and others (eds), *Corporate Liability for Transboundary Environmental Harm* (Springer 2023), 131.

52 June 21, 1993.

53 Protocol to amend the International Convention on Civil Liability for Oil Pollution (London, November 27, 1992). In contrast to the treaty system, some states, notably the US, have held out and enacted national legislation with much higher limits of liability, including some contexts in which liability is unlimited. See Oil Pollution Act of 1990, Public Law 101–380, enacted following the Exxon Valdez disaster of 1989.

on the Establishment of an International Fund for Compensation for Oil Pollution Damage,[54] also modified by the protocols. The 1969 Convention establishes the liability of the owner of a ship for pollution damage caused by oil escaping from the ship as a result of an incident on the territory of a party and covers preventive measures to minimize such damage.[55] Other marine liability conventions include the 1976 International Convention on Civil Liability for Oil Pollution Damage Resulting from the Exploration for or Exploitation of Submarine Mineral Resources,[56] the 1996 Convention on Carriage of Hazardous and Noxious Substances,[57] and the 2001 Convention on Civil Liability for Bunker Oil Pollution Damage.[58]

The 1992 Protocol to the 1969 International Convention on Civil Liability for Oil Pollution defines pollution damage as 'loss or damage caused outside the ship carrying oil by contamination resulting from the escape or discharge of oil from the ship, wherever such escape or discharge may occur' and includes 'the cost of preventive measures and further loss or damage caused by preventive measures'.[59] While the Convention applies to incidents wherever occurring, Article 3 of the 1992 Protocol specifies that the Convention covers only damage suffered in the territory, the territorial sea or the EEZ of a Contracting State. The Convention also applies to preventive measures, wherever taken, to prevent or minimize such damage.[60] The 1992 Liability Protocol makes clear that this

---

54 December 18, 1971, 1110 UNTS 57.

55 The owner of the ship is not responsible if he can prove that the damage resulted from an act of war, hostilities, civil war, insurrection or a natural phenomenon of an exceptional, inevitable and irresistible character. The same is true if the damage results from an act or omission of a third party done with intent to cause damage or results from the negligence or other wrongful act of any government or other authority responsible for the maintenance of lights or other navigational aids.

56 December 17, 1976, 16 ILM 1451 (1977). Due to dissatisfaction with limits of liability, there are no ratifications as of 2003.

57 May 3, 1996, 35 ILM 1406 (1996). The HNS treaty system of liability is similar to the 1992 oil pollution agreement, imposing strict liability for damage caused. It has a wide definition of hazardous and noxious substances, excluding nuclear materials. Insurance is required and liability is limited on a sliding scale depending on the size of the ship. A second tier of compensation applies when ship owner not liable because the incident falls within the treaty's exceptions or the owner has no reason to know of the nature of the substances being transported, or where the claim exceeds the liability limits. A fund is created, financed by levies on the importation of HNS cargoes.

58 International Convention on Civil Liability for Bunker Oil Pollution Damage (March 23, 2001), IMO Doc LEG/CONF.12/DC/1, available at http://www.imo.org.

59 Protocol to amend the International Convention on Civil Liability for Oil Pollution (London, November 27, 1992) art 2(3).

60 ibid, art 3(b).

includes environmental harm. It states that compensation for impairment of the environment other than loss of profit from such impairment shall be limited to costs of reasonable measures of reinstatement actually undertaken or to be undertaken.[61] The owner may limit liability except in case of actual fault and must maintain insurance or other financial security to cover its liability.[62]

The structure of oil pollution liability was extended to other hazardous substances in 1996 with the adoption of the International Convention on Liability and Compensation for Damage in Connection with the Carriage of Hazardous and Noxious Substances at Sea (HNS Convention).[63] The treaty covers claims for damage arising from the carriage of such substances at sea, i.e. that period during which the substances are on the ship or ship's equipment. Article 1(6) of the HNS Convention defines 'damage' to include, in addition to loss of life or personal injury or the loss of or damage to property, 'loss or damage by contamination of the environment caused by hazardous and noxious substances, provided that compensation for impairment of the environment other than loss of profit from such impairment shall be limited to the costs of reasonable measures of reinstatement actually undertaken or to be undertaken', and 'the costs of preventive measures and further loss or damage caused by preventive measures'.

The marine pollution system balances strict liability with limitations on liability. Article 2 of the 1996 Protocol to amend the 1976 Convention on Limitation of Liability for Maritime Claims established a ceiling defined by IMF special withdrawal rights.[64] The Protocol differentiates between claims for loss of life or personal injury in respect of which the minimum limit is 2 million

61 Article 8(2) of the Antarctic Mineral Resource Activities Convention also provides for strict liability for damages 'in the event that there has been no restoration to the *status quo ante*'. The Council of Europe rules on compensation for damage caused to the environment include among the definitions given in Rule 2: (9) 'Measures of reinstatement' means any appropriate and reasonable measures aiming to reinstate or restore damaged or destroyed natural resources or where appropriate or reasonable to introduce the equivalent of these resources into the environment. In all cases, restoring the environment to its status quo ante is the preferred remedy and this is especially true where it is difficult to assess the harm and the corresponding compensation. Only when restoration is not possible would it then be necessary to measure the damages.

62 Protocol to amend the International Convention on Civil Liability for Oil Pollution (London, November 27, 1992) art 15; ibid, art 7(1).

63 LEG/CONF.10/8/2 (May 9, 1996), modified by the Protocol of 2010 to the Convention (not entered into force). For a similar strict liability regime, see the earlier Convention on Civil Liability for Damage Caused During Carriage of Dangerous Goods by Road, Rail and Inland Navigation Vessels of October 10, 1989.

64 November 19, 1976, 16 ILM 606 (1977).

Units of Account (Art. 6(1) of the 1976 Convention). That limit increases with the tonnage of the involved ship. In respect of any other claim the minimum is 1 million which is augmented following the same method.[65] For states which are not members of the IMF the corresponding amounts are respectively 30 million and 15 million monetary units.[66]

Under the 1992 Protocol replacing the 1969 International Convention on Civil Liability for Oil Pollution, any claim for compensation for pollution damage may be brought directly against the insurer or other persons providing financial security for the owner's liability for pollution damage.[67] When an action is brought, to benefit from the limitation on liability, the owner must deposit the total sum representing the limit of his liability with the court or other authority with jurisdiction, either by direct deposit of the sum or producing a bank guarantee or another guarantee considered adequate by the legislation and national authority of the state. If liability is found, the fund is then distributed among the claimants in proportion to their established claims.[68] The owner of a ship registered in a contracting state and carrying more than 2000 tons of oil in bulk as cargo must maintain insurance or other financial guarantee of compensation in case of liability for pollution damage.[69] An insurance or guarantee certificate must be issued to each ship by the appropriate national authority and contracting states are obliged to prevent a ship from trading unless the appropriate certificate has been issued. Each state must recognize the certificates issued by other contracting states.[70]

Before its amendments, the 1969 Convention threatened to become obsolete because the damages ceiling was far too low to compensate for the harm that could occur. As a result, a 1971 Convention established an International Fund for Compensation for Oil Pollution Damage.[71] Basing itself on the 1969 Convention, this treaty also has been amended by two protocols in 1992, respectively referred to as the 1992 Civil Liability Convention and the 1992 Fund Convention supplementary to the 1992 Civil Liability Convention,[72] that together establish a new regime for the compensation of oil pollution damage.

65 ibid, art 6(1).

66 ibid, art 8(2).

67 London, November 27, 1992, art VI(8).

68 ibid, arts V(3) and 5(4).

69 ibid, art VI(2).

70 ibid, art VI.

71 December 18, 1971.

72 International Convention on Civil Liability for Oil Pollution Damage (London, November 27, 1992), 973 UNTS 3; International Convention on the Establishment of an International Fund for Compensation for Oil Pollution Damage (London, November 27, 1992).

These two conventions respectively replace the 1969 Liability Convention and the 1971 Fund Convention. Following concerns about the failure to secure full and timely compensation for serious oil pollution incidents such as that involving the *Erica* in 1999, a Supplementary Fund Protocol was adopted in 2003 to provide an optional third tier level of compensation above the prior conventions.[73] The aim of the International Funds for Compensation of Oil Pollution Damage is to assure payment of compensation for pollution damage to the extent that protection afforded by the 1992 Civil Liability Convention proves inadequate.[74] The 1992 Civil Liability Convention applies to pollution damage caused on the territory of a state, in its territorial waters and its exclusive economic zone.[75] Damages are defined in Article III of the 1992 Civil Liability Convention to include measures taken to prevent or minimize pollution damage.

The Fund established by the 1992 Fund Convention is required by Article 4 of the 1992 Fund Convention to pay compensation to any person suffering pollution damage if the person is unable to obtain full and adequate compensation for the damage under the terms of the 1992 Civil Liability Convention, either because no liability arises under the Convention, because the owner is financially incapable of payment, or because the damage exceeds the owner's liability under the Convention. However, the total amount of damages that the Fund will pay is limited, also, to 203 million Special Drawing Rights. This ceiling can be raised to 300.74 million for certain polluting accidents.[76]

The Fund created by the 1992 Fund Convention is an international organization, made up of an Assembly composed of all Contracting States, an independent secretariat headed by a Director[77] and an Executive Committee.[78] The latter consists of 15 Contracting States elected by the Assembly taking into account an equitable geographical distribution ensuring adequate

73 Protocol to the International Convention on the Establishment of an International Fund for Compensation for Oil Pollution Damage (May 16, 2003).

74 International Convention on the Establishment of an International Fund for Compensation for Oil Pollution Damage (London, November 27, 1992) art 2.

75 International Convention on Civil Liability for Oil Pollution Damage (London, November 27, 1992) art II.

76 International Convention on the Establishment of an International Fund for Compensation for Oil Pollution Damage (London, November 27, 1992, as amended in 2000) art 6(3). The liability limitations were increased pursuant to two resolutions adopted by the Legal Committee of the IMO in 2000, with the amendment entering into force on November 1, 2003.

77 ibid, arts 16–30.

78 Resolution N°5 (Establishment of the Executive Committee) adopted by the Assembly of the International Oil Pollution Compensation Fund (October 1997).

representation of Contracting States particularly exposed to the risks of oil pollution and those having large tanker fleets. Contributions to the Fund are made by any person who has received total quantities of oil in excess of 150,000 tons during the prior calendar year.[79] The amount of the contributions is fixed by the Assembly for each of these persons on the basis of a sum fixed by ton of oil.

The system has been active. Hundreds of claims have been brought against ship owners and the Funds and between 1978 and 2023, the Funds paid out nearly 766 million British pounds sterling with respect to over 150 incidents.[80]

Environmental damage or threat of damage to the coastline or a related interest may raise maritime claims and lead to the arrest of a ship. The 1999 International Convention on Arrest of Ships allows and regulates such arrest by the state within whose jurisdiction the ship is found,[81] irrespective of the flag the ship is flying.[82] A ship may be arrested or released only under the authority of a court of the state party in which the arrest is effectuated.[83] Maritime claims can include compensation for environmental damage, measures taken to prevent, minimize, or remove such damage, costs of reasonable measures of reinstatement of the environment undertaken or to be undertaken, and loss incurred or likely to be incurred by third parties in connection with such damage. The courts of the state in which an arrest has been effectuated shall have jurisdiction to determine the merits of the case.[84]

The 2001 International Convention on Civil Liability for Bunker Oil Pollution Damage is one of the latest IMO Conventions on civil liability for marine pollution.[85] The amount of oil carried as fuel by vessels that are not transporting oil as cargo was estimated at around 14 million tons of oil.[86] These vessels are responsible for the majority of oil spills but are not covered by the 1971/1992 Civil Liability Convention. Hence the new treaty, which acts like the tanker treaties.

In contrast to earlier conventions dealing with damage caused by the cargo of relatively small and well-defined categories of vessels, the Bunker

79 International Convention on the Establishment of an International Fund for Compensation for Oil Pollution Damage (London, November 27, 1992) art 10.

80 See International Oil Pollution Compensation Fund, Annual Report for 2023, 12.

81 Geneva, March 12, 1999.

82 ibid, art 8.

83 ibid, art 2.

84 ibid, art 7.

85 March 23, 2001; Since 2001, the International Convention on the Removal of Wrecks was adopted in Nairobi on May 18, 2007 and entered into force on April 14, 2015.

86 See IMO LEG 75/5/1.

Convention potentially applies to all ships, defined as 'any seagoing vessel and seaborne craft whatsoever'.[87] Bunker oil means 'any hydrocarbon mineral oil, including lubricating oil, used or intended to be used for the operation or propulsion of the ship, and any residues of such oil'.[88] The definition of 'pollution damage' is identical to that of the 1992 Convention on Civil Liability.[89] It is also subject to the same limitation in that it does not cover damage to the environment in itself, but only clean-up costs and the loss of profit suffered by victims such as fishermen and local industries dependent on ocean resources and the tourist trade. Actions for compensation may only be brought in the courts of the states where damage was suffered. Ships must carry certificates attesting to their financial security and claims for compensation may be made directly against the insurer or other provider of financial security.[90]

Unlike other treaties, the Bunker Oil Convention does not channel liability to a single person but defines ship owner to include others who have joint and several liability.[91] However, only the registered owner of a ship over 1000 gross tonnage is required to provide financial security.[92] The regulation of mutual liability is left to national law. Article 6 provides that the ship owner may limit liability 'under any applicable national or international regime', such as the 1976 Convention on Limitation of Liability for Maritime Claims.[93] Under this convention, the limits of liability are on a sliding scale depending on the size of the ship. The 1996 Protocol to the 1976 Convention on Limitation of Liability for Maritime Claims, entered into force in 2004, raised the limits of liability for claims. In any case, the reference to national and international law means a lack of uniformity in liability limits for oil spills from non-tanker vessels. While it was proposed to exclude from liability any person taking reasonable measures to prevent or minimize the effects of oil pollution, no agreement was reached to include such a provision. Instead, the conference recommended legal provisions for such persons in domestic laws.[94]

---

87 art 1(1).
88 art 1(5).
89 art 1(9).
90 art 7.
91 art 1(3).
92 art 7(1).
93 November 19, 1976, 16 ILM 606 (1977).
94 See IMO Resolution on the Protection of Persons Taking Measures to Prevent or Minimize the Effects of Oil Pollution, IMO/LEG/CONF.12/18. The International Convention on Civil Liability for Bunker Oil Pollution Damage (London, March 23, 2001) would include no such provision excluding from liability persons taking reasonable measures to prevent or minimize the effects of oil pollution.

1.2.5.2 *Nuclear Operations*

The three nuclear liability treaties adopted in the 1960s concern civilian uses of nuclear power. Their aim is partly to protect potential victims and partly to insulate nuclear industry from devastating claims. The first agreement, the 1960 Convention on Third Party Liability in the Field of Nuclear Energy (Paris Convention) is a regional agreement concluded in the context of OECD. It was intended to provide unified rules for adequate and equitable compensation while still supporting development of nuclear energy. As of May 2024, the Paris Convention has obtained only 14 ratifications, less than half the OCED member states. Non-members may ratify but only one has done so. There are no known transnational claims brought to date based on the Paris Convention, although some national claims are based on legislation implementing the Paris Convention. The Paris Convention was later enhanced in 1963 with a Supplementary Convention (Brussels).[95]

The Paris Convention is linked to the second agreement, the Vienna Convention on Civil Liability for Nuclear Damage of 1963,[96] by a Joint Protocol adopted in 1988 and the 1997 Protocol to Amend the 1963 Vienna Convention on Civil Liability for Nuclear Damage.[97] These conventions are based on the civil liability and share the following main principles:

- 'Liability is channeled exclusively to the operators of the nuclear installations;
- Liability of the operator is absolute, i.e. the operator is held liable irrespective of fault;
- Liability is limited in amount. Under the Vienna Convention, it may be limited to not less than US$ 5 million (value in gold on April 29, 1963), but an upper ceiling is not fixed. The Paris Convention sets a maximum liability of 15 million Special Drawing Rights (SDRs) provided that the installation State may provide for a greater or lesser amount but not below 5 million SDRs taking into account the availability of insurance coverage. The Brussels Supplementary Convention established additional funding beyond the amount

95 E.g. *Merlin v. British Nuclear Fuels*, (1990) 3 All ER 711; Convention supplementary to the Paris Convention of July 29, 1960 (Brussels, January 31, 1963). The Supplementary Convention allows compensation beyond the liability limits of the Paris Convention. All claims must be brought in the state where the incident occurred if there is one and if not then the territory of the installation or the operator liable. Claims must normally be brought within ten years of the date of the incident and awards are enforceable in any state party. Eleven states are parties to the supplementary convention.

96 Vienna, May 21, 1963, 1063 UNTS 266.

97 Vienna, September 21, 1988; Vienna, September 12, 1997.

available under the Paris Convention up to a total of 300 million SDRS, consisting of contributions by the installation state and contracting parties;
- Liability is limited in time. Compensation rights are extinguished under both Conventions if an action is not brought within ten years from the date of the nuclear incident. Longer periods are permissible if, under the law of the installation State, the liability of the operator is covered by financial security. National law may establish a shorter time limit, but not less than two years (the Paris Convention) or three years (the Vienna Convention) from the date the claimant knew or ought to have known of the damage and of the liable operator;
- The operator must maintain insurance of other financial security for an amount corresponding to his liability; if such security is insufficient, the installation State is obliged to make up the difference up to the limit of the operator's liability;
- Jurisdiction over actions lies exclusively with the courts of the Contracting Party in whose territory the nuclear incident occurred;
- A guarantee of non-discrimination of victims on the grounds of nationality, domicile or residence'.

Following the Chernobyl accident, the IAEA initiated work on all aspects of nuclear liability with a view to improving the basic conventions and establishing a comprehensive liability regime. In 1988, as a result of joint efforts by the IAEA and OECD/NEA, the Joint Protocol Relating to the Application of the Vienna Convention and the Paris Convention was adopted.[98] The Joint Protocol established a link between the Vienna and Paris Conventions combining them into one expanded liability regime. Parties to the Joint Protocol are treated as though they were Parties to both Conventions and a choice of law rule is provided to determine which of the two Conventions should apply to the exclusion of the other in respect of the same incident.

The 1997 Protocol to the Vienna Convention set the possible limit of the operator's liability at not less than 300 million Special Drawing Rights (SDRS) (equivalent to US$400 million).[99] The 1997 Convention on Supplementary Compensation defines additional amounts to be provided through contributions by States Parties on the basis of installed nuclear capacity and the UN

98 Vienna, September 21, 1988.

99 Two instruments were in fact signed in Vienna on September 12, 1997: the Protocol to Amend the Vienna Convention, 36 ILM 1462 and a Convention on Supplementary Compensation for Nuclear Damage, 36 ILM 1473; Protocol to Amend the Vienna Convention (Vienna, September 12, 1997) art V.

rate of assessment.[100] The Convention is open for adherence regardless of whether the state is party to any existing nuclear liability conventions or has nuclear installations on its territories. The 1997 Protocol to the Vienna Convention redefines nuclear damage to include the concept of environmental damage and preventive measures, extends the geographical scope of the Vienna Convention, and extends the period during which claims may be brought for loss of life and personal injury. It also provides for jurisdiction of coastal states over actions incurring nuclear damage during maritime transport.

Finally, the 1971 Convention relating to Civil Liability in the Field of Maritime Carriage of Nuclear Material provides that the ship owner is liable if the ship owner committed or omitted to do an act with intent to cause damage.[101]

1.2.5.3 *Hazardous Wastes*

The 1999 Protocol on Liability and Compensation to the Basel Convention on the Control of Transboundary Movements of Hazardous Wastes and their Disposal has further developed the regime of civil liability for environmental damage.[102] Its purpose is to provide a comprehensive regime for liability and for adequate and prompt compensation for damage resulting from transboundary waste movements, including illegal traffic. It defines damage broadly to include not only loss of life or personal injury and loss of or damage to property, but also loss of income directly deriving from an economic interest in any use of the environment incurred as a result of impairment of the environment. It also includes recovery of the costs of measures of reinstatement of the impaired environment, limited to the costs of measures actually taken or to be undertaken and the costs of preventive measures, including any loss or damage caused by such measures.[103] Preventive measures are defined as any reasonable measures taken by any person in response to an incident to prevent, minimize, or mitigate loss or damage, or to affect environmental clean-up.[104] The Protocol applies to damage due to an incident occurring during a transboundary movement of hazardous wastes and other wastes and their disposal, including illegal traffic, in particular in relation to movements

100 Convention on Supplementary Compensation for Nuclear Damage (Vienna, September 12 1997) art IV.

101 December 17 1971.

102 Protocol on Liability and Compensation for Damage Resulting from Transboundary Movements of Hazardous Wastes and their Disposal (Basel, December 10, 1999); 1673 UNTS 57 (Basel, March 22, 1989).

103 Protocol on Liability and Compensation for Damage Resulting from Transboundary Movements of Hazardous Wastes and their Disposal (Basel, December 10, 1999) art 2(2)(c).

104 ibid, art 2 (2)(e)).

destined for disposal operations specified in Annex IV of the 1989 Basel Convention.[105] Similar to other treaties related to environmental liability, the Basel Protocol imposes strict liability on, first, the person who provides notification of a proposed transboundary movement according to Article 6 of the Basel Convention, and, thereafter, the disposer of the wastes. Liability for damage is subject to financial limits specified in Article 12(1) and Annex B to the Protocol. During the ten year-period of liability, those potentially liable shall establish and maintain insurance or other financial guarantees.[106] Liability limits are removed if the responsible person causes or contributes to causing damage by failure to comply with the provisions implementing the Basel Convention, or due to wrongful intentional, reckless, or negligent acts or omissions.[107] Any person in operational control of hazardous wastes and other wastes at the time of an incident shall take all reasonable measures to mitigate damage arising therefrom.[108]

The 1999 Protocol to the Basel Convention imposes upon the Contracting Parties the obligation to adopt the legislative, regulatory and administrative measures necessary to implement the Protocol and to inform the Secretariat of the Protocol of the measures it has taken.[109] For the rest, the Protocol shall not affect the rights and obligations of the Contracting Parties under the rules of general international law with respect to state responsibility.[110] The competent jurisdictions are the courts of the state where the damage was suffered or the incident occurred or the defendant has his habitual residence or has his principal place of business.[111] All matters of substance or procedure regarding claims before the competent court shall be governed by the law of that court.[112] Enforceable judgments thus handed down shall be mutually recognized and enforced.[113]

1.2.5.4 *The Lugano Convention*

A regional model for civil liability is the Lugano Convention on Civil Liability for Damages Resulting from the Exercise of Activities Dangerous for the

105 Basel, March 22, 1989, art 3.

106 Protocol on Liability and Compensation for Damage Resulting from Transboundary Movements of Hazardous Wastes and their Disposal (Basel, December 10, 1999) art 14.

107 ibid, arts 5 and 12(2).

108 ibid, art 6.

109 ibid, art 10.

110 ibid, art 16.

111 ibid, art 17.

112 ibid, art 19.

113 ibid, art 21.

Environment.[114] It establishes general standards for indemnification of those injured by hazardous activities and products. The Convention broadly imposes responsibility on all persons and companies and state and all agencies exercising control over dangerous activities, irrespective of the place of the harm. However, if the damage occurs in a non-contracting state, the Convention permits reservations to be filed demanding reciprocity of remedies.[115]

The Convention applies to dangerous activities and substances, including living modified organisms. The quality of dangerousness is largely based upon assessment of the risk of harm to human beings, the environment or property. Nuclear damage is excluded if the incident is regulated by the Paris Convention on Civil Liability of 1960 or by the Vienna Convention of 1963 with its amendments, or by national legislation at least as favorable to the plaintiffs as the Conventions. Workplace accidents covered by social security and automobile accidents in places inaccessible to the public as well as assimilated to other activities within the installation also are excluded.[116]

In addition to compensation for death, bodily harm, and injury to property other than that found on the site or within the installation where the dangerous activity has taken place, recovery can be had for environmental harm,[117] limited to the costs of reasonable measures taken to restore or rehabilitate the environment to its prior state. Recovery is also possible for the costs of mitigating measures and any losses or damage caused by such measures after an incident or event. The maximum amount of liability may be fixed by local law, which should also insist upon adequate insurance coverage taking into account the risks associated with the activity.

Anyone who is in control of a dangerous activity is responsible for damages caused by that activity.[118] The problem of multiple or long-term sources is solved by imposing joint responsibility and placing the burden of proof on the various persons who were in control of the activity or activities to prove they were not responsible. In cases where the activity has ceased when the damage

114 Lugano, June 21, 1993.

115 ibid, art 35.

116 ibid, art 4.

117 ibid, art 2(7). For these purposes, environment is broadly defined under Article 2(10) of the Lugano Convention to include biotic and abiotic natural resources, such as air, water, soil, fauna and flora, the interaction between them, cultural property and characteristic aspects of the countryside.

118 Lugano, June 21, 1993, art 2(5); States parties may reserve to the basic principle of liability to the extent of allowing the defendant to escape liability if it can show that the state of scientific and technical knowledge at the moment of the incident was insufficient to indicate the dangerous properties of the substance or the organism.

occurs, the last person in control will be liable unless he can show that the causative event took place before he was in control.

Liability is not imposed if damage occurs as a result of armed conflict, a natural disaster, an intentional act of a third party, a state command, 'pollution at tolerable levels under local relevant circumstances', or if the activity was taken for the benefit of the person damaged, to the extent it was reasonable for the latter to be exposed to the risks of the dangerous activity, or if the injured party was at fault.[119]

From the perspective of the plaintiff, there are several favorable provisions. Article 10 provides that in examining the proof of causality, a judge in any case falling within the terms of the Lugano Convention should take into account the probable risk of damage inherent in the dangerous activity in question. Moreover, the statute of limitations is rather long. According to Article 17, actions for compensation should be brought within three years of the date on which the plaintiff knew or reasonably should have known of the damage and of the identity of the person in control. No action may be brought more than 30 years after the causative event or the last in a series of causative events. For waste disposal sites, the final date is 30 years from the closure of the site. Article 19 permits the action to be filed either in the courts of a state party where the damage occurred, where the dangerous activity took place, or where the defendant has its permanent residence.

Injunctive relief may be sought by environmental associations in the courts where the dangerous activity takes place, on conditions set by internal law.[120] States may declare at signature, ratification, or accession that this possibility will be open to non-governmental organizations based in other states parties. Environmental groups may demand prohibition of any illegal dangerous activity threatening serious environmental harm as well as injunctions against the person in control of dangerous activity, in order to require preventive or remedial actions be taken. Where remedial action is sought, the courts of the state where the action should be taken also have jurisdiction over the case. Public authorities have the right to intervene when environmental groups bring actions. Article 19 is explicitly subject to reservations.

All judgments rendered by a tribunal with jurisdiction according to the Lugano Convention are entitled to be recognized in other states parties unless they are contrary to public order, the defendant was not properly notified of

119 ibid, art 8.

120 ibid, art 18.

the action in time to prepare a defense, or if the decision is irreconcilable with a decision rendered between the same parties (*res judicata*).[121]

In sum, several common traits are found in the liability agreements:

a. 'Identification of the polluter is assured through a presumption which channels responsibility. Thus, in case of damage, the responsibility automatically is imputed to the exploiter or the ship owner.
b. The system of liability is settled by imposing strict liability for damage, but specifying a limited set of excuses.
c. Jurisdictional competence is determined by designating the proper forum, in some cases that of the plaintiff, in other cases that of the polluter or in permitting the victim the free choice of tribunal.
d. Time limits are imposed. The Lugano Convention makes it three years from the date of knowledge or the time when the plaintiff reasonably should have known of the damage and the identity of the operator. An absolute bar to suit is imposed after thirty years.
e. Liability limits are coupled with mandatory insurance requirements.
f. The execution of judgments is assured'.

Civil liability and compensation procedure require that there be identifiable victims with standing to bring an action, something that may not exist in all cases of all environmental harm, for example, that was caused on the high seas, Antarctica, or in outer space. Damage in these places risks escaping protection if no specific norms are adopted, making regulation and international cooperation to implement and supervise enforcement of the rules essential. Within the Antarctic system, efforts to conclude a liability Annex to the 1991 Madrid Protocol were unsuccessful until 2003,[122] and efforts turned to reaching a more limited agreement on environmental emergencies, as a step towards complying with the Article 16 of the Madrid Protocol.[123] The emergency regime establishes rules on liability for the failure to provide for response action as well as rules related to the prevention of damage, contingency planning and response action. There is broad support for imposing liability on an operator for the costs of response action taken by other parties to the protocol and payments to an environmental fund if such action has not been taken by the operator.

It must be noted, in conclusion, that only four of the dozen major liability treaties are in force because many states oppose the limits on liability that these

121 ibid, art 23.

122 Protocol on Environmental Protection to the Antarctic Treaty (Madrid, October 4, 1991) 2941 UNTS.

123 Annex VI to the Protocol on Environmental Protection to the Antarctic Treaty Liability Arising from Environmental Emergencies (2005) (not entered into force).

agreements contain.[124] The Lugano Convention has not been ratified by any state to date. The existence of certain holdout states in turn discourages others from accepting what becomes an unequal burden-sharing. While limited liability derives from maritime law existing for several centuries in recognition of the value of maritime transport and the extant dangers, some see it as an unwarranted subsidy at the expense of other interests and as undermining the polluter pays principle.[125] Those favoring limited liability respond that unlimited damage awards could drive responsible ship owners out of business.[126] It is also argued that unlimited liability will mean maritime transport will become uninsurable. In fact, liability limits have been set in large part according to insurance industry indications, rather than degree of risk and needs of victims. The problems are political and practical rather than principled.

1.3 *Penal Law*

The function of penal law is to protect the most important values of society by creating and enforcing penalties, including those involving deprivation of liberty. Increasingly, national law is imposing criminal liability on those who pollute and perform other acts damaging to the environment.

In most states, not only the company, but also directors and other senior managers may be held responsible. Normally, a company will be guilty of an offense if the offense-relevant conduct involves instructions or other acts of a 'directing mind' of the company. Conversely, the director's position as a directing mind will not always produce criminal liability on his part, but may do so.

A resolution adopted by the UN Economic and Social Council in 1994 insists on the importance of environmental criminal law and, *inter alia*, recommends that states seriously consider enacting legislation prohibiting and sanctioning the export of products that have been banned from domestic use, as well as the production and import of specific dangerous materials, unless sufficient precautionary measures can be taken in respect of their use, treatment or disposal

124 The four liability treaties in force are the 1960 Convention on Third Party Liability in the Field of Nuclear Energy (July 29, 1960), the 1963 Vienna Convention on Civil Liability for Nuclear Damage (Vienna, May 21, 1963), the 1969 Convention on Civil Liability for Oil Pollution Damage (London, November 27, 1992), and the 2001 Bunker Oil Convention (March 23, 2001).

125 See Gotthard Gauci, 'Limitation of Liability in Maritime Law: An Anachronism?' (1995) Marine Policy 65 (1995).

126 See Robin R. Churchill, '*Facilitating (Transnational) Civil Liability Litigation for Environmental Damage by Means of Treaties: Problems and Progress*' (2001) 12 YBIEL 1, 35–36.

in their countries.[127] It also recommends giving support to the idea of imposing criminal or non-criminal fines or other measures on corporations. The General Assembly also recognizes crime that affect the environment as a form of transnational organized crime falling under the UN Convention against Transnational Organized Crime and calls upon states to make crimes that affect the environment a serious crime in accordance with their national legislation.[128]

There are elements of environmental offenses that distinguish them from other areas of criminal law. Most criminal law is based upon a direct individual relation between a perpetrator and a victim who has been harmed. Environmental protection can involve perpetrators and victims who can only be identified statistically where harm results from long term multiple causes. To regulate, two possibilities exist. The first is to assume the existence of danger or harm to public interests that are traditionally protected by penal law, such as life, health and property. The other is to develop new offenses against the environment, protecting independent natural elements without requiring an element of provable harm to specific victims. Both approaches can be found in existing provisions of penal law.

Penal sanctions can range from fines for petty offenses to imprisonment for more serious offenses. Criminal liability may be primary, accomplice, or conspiracy. In many countries, accomplice liability is imposed on those who give help, support or assistance to a person committing an offense, or who incite, encourage, or counsel such a person. The lesser offense of conspiracy involves a decision by two or more parties to perpetrate an unlawful act.

Several existing international agreements call for penalties adequate to deter violations. UNCLOS,[129] the Paris Convention for the Prevention of Land-Based Pollution,[130] the Basel Convention on Transboundary Movement of Hazardous Wastes,[131] and CITES require contracting parties to ensure compliance by taking appropriate measures to not only prevent but also to punish conduct

127 Based on a recommendation of the Commission on Crime Prevention and Criminal Justice, Third Session, Vienna, April 26 – May 6, 1994, 24 EPL 286 (1994).

128 United Nations Convention against Transnational Organized Crime (New York, November 15, 2000) 2225 UNTS 209; UN General Assembly, 'Strengthening the United Nations crime prevention and criminal justice programme, in particular its technical cooperation capacity' (December 18, 2019) UN Doc A/RES/74/177. See also Resolution 10/6 adopted by the Conference of the Parties to the United Nations Convention against Transnational Organized Crime 'Preventing and combating crimes that affect the environment falling within the scope of the United Nations Convention against Transnational Organized Crime'.

129 UNCLOS, arts 213–222.

130 Convention for the Prevention of Marine Pollution from Land-Based Sources (June 4, 1974) 1546 UNTS 103, art 12.

131 Basel, March 22, 1989, art 9.

in contravention of the provisions of the agreement.[132] The Bamako Convention on Waste Trade in Africa goes further in requiring that the penalties be sufficiently high to both punish and deter illegal traffic.[133] The 1994 Lusaka Agreement on Cooperative Enforcement Operations directed at Illegal Trade in Wild Fauna and Flora supplements earlier provisions regarding the illegality of such trade by requiring States Parties to investigate and prosecute such cases.[134]

The Council of Europe drew attention to the important role that criminal law can play towards effective protection of the environment as early as in 1977.[135] On November 4, 1998, it adopted the first treaty to generally criminalize acts causing or likely to cause environmental damage, the Convention on the Protection of the Environment through Criminal Law.[136] However, the threshold of three ratifications required for its entry into force has not been reached, and this convention has therefore not entered into force. Pursuant to renewed engagement and efforts to use criminal law as a means to protect the environment, the Council of Europe mandated a Committee of experts on the protection of the environment through Criminal Law (PC-ENV) in 2022 to elaborate a new Council of Europe Convention on the Protection of the Environment through Criminal Law replacing the 1998 Convention.[137] The draft of this new Convention is currently under discussion.[138] The aim of this Convention is to set out a general framework for European environmental criminal law to prevent and combat environmental crime. The draft provisions of this Convention call for non-criminal sanctions for less serious offenses,[139] while

132 Convention on International Trade in Endangered Species of Wild Fauna and Flora (Washington, March 2, 1973) 1976 UNTS 244, art VIII.1.

133 Bamako Convention on the Ban of the Import into Africa and the Control of Transboundary Movement and Management of Hazardous Wastes within Africa (Bamako, January 30, 1991) 2101 UNTS 177.

134 Lusaka Agreement on Co-operative Enforcement Operations directed at Illegal Trade in Wild Fauna and Flora (Lusaka, September 8, 1994) 1977 UNTS 502.

135 Council of Europe, Committee of Ministers, Resolution (77) 28 on the Contribution of Criminal Law to the Protection of the Environment (September 28, 1977).

136 Convention on the Protection of the Environment through Criminal Law (Strasbourg, November 4, 1998) ET.S. No. 172.

137 Pursuant to the Terms of reference of the Committee of Experts on the protection of the environment through criminal law (PC-ENV) adopted by the Committee of Ministers of the Council of Europe on November 23, 2022, PC-ENV has been created and mandated to draft a new Convention on the Protection of the Environment through Criminal Law.

138 As of June 2024, the Committee of experts on the protection of the environment through Criminal Law (PC-ENV) has had four meetings, respectively held on April 3-4, 2023, October 16-18, 2023, February 27-29, 2024, and June 4.7, 2024.

139 The present analysis of the draft convention is based on the last publicly available draft dated May 17, 2023.

serious offenses should result in imprisonment or fines and may call for reinstatement of the environment or disqualification from exercising commercial activity (Art. 31 of the draft Convention dated May 17, 2023). Articles 17 to 27 of the draft Convention lay down categories of intentional offenses that the States Parties must declare criminal, including:

- 'unlawful discharge, emission or introduction of a quantity of materials or substances or ionising radiation into air, soil or water;
- unlawful collection, transport, recovery or disposal of waste, including hazardous waste;
- unlawful operation or closure of an installation in which a dangerous activity is carried out or in which dangerous substances or mixtures are stored or used;
- unlawful disposal or recycling of ships or ship-source discharges of polluting substances;
- unlawful abstraction of surface water or groundwater;
- trading of unlawfully harvested timber;
- unlawful fishing;
- unlawful killing or trading of wild fauna or flora;
- unlawful deterioration of habitats or disruption of ecosystems;
- unlawful mining and trafficking in minerals and metals;
- ecocide'.

The criminalization of 'ecocide' is aimed to cover offenses with a high degree of seriousness and accordingly attract stricter sanctions. The working definition of ecocide under the draft Convention dated May 17, 2023 comprises two options (Art. 27 of the draft Convention). The first option defines ecocide as 'any conduct which causes or is likely to cause death or serious injury to any person or substantial damage to the quality of air, the quality of soil or the quality of water, biodiversity, ecosystem services and functions, or to animals or plants, when such conduct causes severe and widespread, or severe and long-term, or severe and irreversible damage'. The second option constitutes a narrower definition of ecocide and is set out as follows: 'any action covered by the scope of the offences established in accordance with this Convention, when such action results in, and is committed with the knowledge that there was a substantial likelihood that it could result in severe and widespread, or severe and long-term, or severe and irreversible damage to human health or to the environment'.

Under the draft provisions of the Convention on the Protection of the Environment through Criminal Law, jurisdiction over offenses established under the draft Convention can be based on territory, flag, and nationality (Art. 29 of the draft Convention). Corporate liability does not exclude individual liability (Art. 30(4) of the draft Convention) and states parties should cooperate in investigations and judicial proceedings (Art. 36 of the draft Convention). States Parties shall also consider granting any group, foundation or association which, according to its statutes, aims at the protection of the environment, the right to participate in criminal proceedings concerning offences established in accordance with this Convention (Art. 35 of the draft Convention).

Following the example of the Council of Europe, the EC adopted a Framework Decision on the protection of the environment through criminal law on January 27, 2003 inviting Member States to establish criminal jurisdiction with respect to environmental offences.[140] One of the aims is to avoid physical or legal persons escaping prosecution by the simple fact that the offence was not committed in the territory of a state. The Framework Decision was annulled by the Court of Justice for failure to provide a valid legal basis,[141] but its content was largely replicated in the Directive on the protection of the environment through criminal law adopted in 2008 by the Council and the European Parliament ('Environmental Crime Directive').[142] Under the 2008 Environmental Crime Directive, Member States are required to criminalize nine categories of conduct when unlawful and committed intentionally, or at least with serious negligence.[143] Moreover, the Directive on ship-source pollution ('Ship-Source Pollution Directive') was adopted in 2009 to provide for the criminalization of conduct relating to ship-source pollution.[144] As part of the European Commission's 'European Green Deal' and its commitment to promote action 'to step up efforts against environmental crime', a new Directive on the protection of the

140 Council Framework Decision 2003/80/JHA of January 27, 2003 on the protection of the environment through criminal law (January 27, 2003) OJ L 29 (2/5/03).

141 Case C-176/03, *Commission of the European Communities v Council of the European Union* (13 September 2005).

142 Directive 2008/99/EC of the European Parliament and of the Council on the protection of the environment through criminal law (November 19, 2008) OJ L 328/28.

143 Directive 2008/99/EC (November 19, 2008) art 3. The covered categories of conduct include, but are not limited to, the discharge, emission or introduction of a quantity of materials or ionising radiation into air, soil or water; the collection, transport, recovery or disposal of waste; the production, processing, handling, use, holding, storage, transport, import, export or disposal of nuclear materials or other hazardous radioactive substances; the killing, destruction, possession or taking of specimens of protected wild fauna or flora species; any conduct which causes the significant deterioration of a habitat within a protected site.

144 Directive 2009/123/EC of the European Parliament and of the Council amending Directive 2005/35/EC on ship-source pollution and on the introduction of penalties for infringements (October 21, 2009) OJ L 280/52.

environment through criminal law was adopted on March 13, 2024, replacing the 2008 Environmental Crime Directive and the 2009 Ship-Source Pollution Directive.[145] This new Environmental Crime Directive increases the number of categories constituting a criminal offense from nine to twenty, with new offenses including timber trafficking and serious breaches of legislation on chemicals. Article 3(3) of this Directive introduces a 'qualified offense' clause according to which:

> Member States shall ensure that criminal offences relating to conduct listed in paragraph 2 constitute qualified criminal offences if such conduct causes:
> a. the destruction of, or widespread and substantial damage which is either irreversible or long-lasting to, an ecosystem of considerable size or environmental value or a habitat within a protected site, or
> b. widespread and substantial damage which is either irreversible or long-lasting to the quality of air, soil or water.

The fact that a given offense has caused the destruction of, or irreversible or long-lasting substantial damage to, an ecosystem shall be regarded as an aggravating circumstance, and shall therefore lead to more severe penalties.[146] For natural persons, a qualified offense is punishable by a maximum term of imprisonment of eight years, while other offenses generally result in imprisonment of up to five years, or up to ten years if they cause the death of a person. Accessory penalties may also include fines, the withdrawal of permits and authorizations to pursue activities that resulted in the relevant criminal offence, and an obligation to restore the environment, if the damage is reversible, or pay compensation, if the damage is irreversible or the offender is not in a capacity to carry out such restoration.[147] Corporate or entity liability is included in Article 6 of this Directive, according to which Member States must ensure the liability of legal persons where criminal offenses covered by this Directive have been committed for the benefit of those legal persons by any

---

145 The 'European Green Deal' is a global strategy announced by the European Commission in December 2019 which aims at transforming the EU into 'a fair and prosperous society, with a modern, resource-efficient and competitive economy where there are no net emissions of greenhouse gases in 2050 and where economic growth is decoupled from resource use', as stated by the European Commission in the Communication 'The European Green Deal' on December 11, 2019; European Commission, 'Commission Staff Working Document Evaluation of the Directive 2008/99/EC' (October 28, 2020) 63; Directive (EU) 2024/1203 of the European Parliament and of the Council of April 11, 2024 on the protection of the environment through criminal law and replacing Directives 2008/99/EC and 2009/123/EC (April 11, 2024) OJ L 2024/1203.

146 ibid, art 8.

147 ibid, art 5.

person who has a leading position within the legal person concerned, acting either individually or as part of an organ of that legal person. For legal persons, the sanctions shall include fines and may include other measures such as obligating it to establish due diligence schemes for enhancing compliance with environmental standards, imposing on it an obligation to restore or compensate for the damage to the environment, disqualifying the entity from business activities, placing it under judicial supervision, or ordering it to cease operations.[148]

Each member state shall take the necessary measures to establish its jurisdiction with regard to offences committed fully or in part in its territory, even if the effects of the offence occur elsewhere. Jurisdiction also extends on board a ship or an aircraft registered in the state or flying its flag, or to the state's nationals. Member States may also decide to extend their jurisdiction to criminal offenses 'committed outside its territory where: (a) the offender is a habitual resident in its territory; (b) the offence is committed for the benefit of a legal person established in its territory; (c) the offence is committed against one of its nationals or its habitual residents; (d) the offence has created a severe risk for the environment on its territory'.[149] These rules should have a major impact on the international protection of the environment if properly enforced. EU Member States shall adopt the measures necessary to comply with the provisions of the 2024 Environmental Crime Directive before May 21 2026.[150]

Effective enforcement of criminal law may require international cooperation, particularly when the offenses concern illicit trade. Recognizing this, twelve of the thirteen member states of the Southern African Development Community (SADC) adopted a Protocol on Wildlife Conservation and Law Enforcement which aims to ensure regional conservation and sustainable use of wildlife and the enforcement of wildlife conservation laws.[151] As all the Contracting States are members of the International Criminal Police Organization (Interpol), enforcement measures include coordinating the designated Interpol National Central Bureaus. The Bureaus exchange information concerning the illegal taking of, and trade in, wildlife and wildlife products, coordinate efforts to apprehend illegal traders and takers and to recover and dispose of illegal wildlife products. The Bureaus may request from each other any assistance or

148 ibid, art 7.

149 ibid, art 12.

150 ibid, art 28.

151 Declaration and Treaty of the Southern African Development Community (Windhoek, August 17, 1992); Maputo, August 18, 1999.

information which may be required to locate, apprehend or extradite an individual charged with violating the wildlife laws of a State Party. States Parties to the Protocol on Wildlife Conservation and Law Enforcement are to provide all available data on the location and movement of illegal takers and traders and the location of routes for illegal transfrontier trafficking in wildlife and wildlife products.[152] Institutional arrangements provide for the establishment of different committees and of a Wildlife Sector Technical Coordinating Unit. The Protocol is unusual in foreseeing that sanctions can be imposed against any State Party that persistently fails, without good reason, to fulfil its obligations assumed under the Protocol or that implements policies which undermine the treaty's objectives and principles.[153] The States Parties also recognize that compliance with wildlife conservation laws depends on the perceptions and development needs of people living with wildlife. The Protocol on Wildlife Conservation and Law Enforcement thus affirms that regional management of wildlife products will promote awareness of the socio-economic value of wildlife and enable equitable distribution of the benefits derived from the sustainable use of it.[154] The State Parties signal their intention to promote 'community based wildlife management', allowing a community or group of communities to manage wildlife and to receive the benefits from managing wildlife.[155] The Protocol also aims at ensuring co-operation at the national level among government authorities, non-governmental organizations and the private sector.

In conclusion, principles of international environmental law and more precise obligations found in international agreements give guidance to states in their drafting of national and local environmental laws and procedures. The array of techniques and procedures discussed serves to direct the implementation of international norms and standards; the actual techniques and procedures adopted in each legal system will reflect local priorities and conditions as well as international law. Careful choices and legal drafting will assist in making law an effective tool to protect and preserve the environment.

2 International Compliance Mechanisms

International environmental agreements often include provisions pertaining to monitoring, implementation review, compliance verification, and

152 ibid, art 9.
153 ibid, art 12.
154 ibid, art 7.
155 ibid, art 1.

non-compliance mechanisms. It is increasingly clear that the effectiveness of such procedures and institutions should be evaluated to determine whether they require reform and harmonization. It is also important to evaluate the underlying normative framework of each agreement to understand whether, if fully implemented, it is capable of producing the desired improvement in the status of the environment. Good compliance with rules that do not go beyond existing practice or that represent an inadequate goal will not prevent further environmental deterioration.

Environmental problems often require long-term solutions, making supervision of international agreements difficult. Scientific uncertainty or political disagreement over the required solutions can lead to international environmental obligations that are vague and indeterminate, constituting obligations of comportment rather than of result. An example is found in framework conventions that establish broad guidelines which are difficult to evaluate. If the nature of the norm has an impact on compliance review, according to one view, the less precise the obligation, the more important the review.[156]

The process is dynamic and ongoing, requiring periodic review of national laws to implement agreed goals that shift over time. The Protocol to the Convention on Long-Range Transboundary Air Pollution on Persistent Organic Pollutants expresses the need for constant updating of laws and policies. Annex V, para 4 notes that 'Experience with new plants incorporating low-emission techniques, as well as with retrofitting of existing plants, is constantly growing. The regular elaboration and amendment of the annex will therefore be necessary. Best available techniques (BAT) identified for new plants can usually be applied to existing plants provided there is an adequate transition period and they are adapted'.

International environmental law places great emphasis on mechanisms and procedures that are non-coercive or non-contentious. The objective is to prevent any violation of an environmental norm and to assure respect and promotion. Control mechanisms are considered primarily as forums for observing the behavior of the parties and only secondly as a means of resolving conflicts through discussion and negotiation. They are considerably different from the judicial institutions and procedures that have developed in other fields of international law.

156 Jean Charpentier, 'Le contrôle par les organisations internationales de l'exécution des obligations des Etats', (1983-IV) 182 RCADI 172.

2.1 *Reporting Obligations*

International environmental agreements rely heavily on reporting by states parties in order to monitor implementation. The most accepted supervisory technique in international law generally, it obliges states parties to a treaty to address periodic reports to an organ established or designated by the treaty, indicating the implementing measures they have taken. It also applies within international organizations in regard to some non-binding instruments. The Commission on Sustainable Development created following UNCED examines the progress in implementing Agenda 21 largely through review of periodic state reports, along with information provided by non-governmental organizations.[157]

Most environmental agreements expressly require parties to report certain information to the international organization designated by the agreement. States parties are required to report, for example, on national measures to halt trade in endangered species (CITES, Art. VIII(7)),[158] to reduce greenhouse gas emission (UNFCCC, Art. 12) and levels of ozone-depleting substances (Montreal Protocol, Art. 7),[159] to implement nationally determined contributions to mitigate and adapt to climate change (Paris Agreement,[160] Art. 13), to conserve biological diversity (Convention on Biological Diversity, Art. 26),[161] to control transboundary movements of hazardous wastes (Basel Convention, Art. 13(3)) and to halt marine dumping (Convention on the Prevention of Marine Pollution by Dumping of Wastes and Other Matter, Art. 9).[162] Article 12 of the UNF-

157 UNCED, 'Agenda 21' (Rio de Janerio, June 3–14, 1992).

158 CITES (March 3, 1973) requires that each state keep records of all transactions involving protected species, including the types of permits authorized, and file annual reports with the Secretariat under articles VIII (6) and (7). With such reports the Secretariat and the parties can determine the volume of trade in a given species as well as monitor the quantity and type of permits granted.

159 United Nations Framework Convention on Climate Change (May 9, 1992) 1771 UNTS 107; The Montreal Protocol on the Ozone Layer (September 16, 1987) contains precise reporting requirements relating to annual production and imports and exports of controlled substances. Article 7 requires that parties notify the Secretariat of any allowed transfer of production between parties and of any addition to calculated production levels allowed by the Protocol. With this data the Secretariat and the parties may determine that other parties are meeting their consumption level under the defined baselines.

160 UNFCCC COP 21, Report of the Conference of the Parties on its twenty-first session, held in Paris from November 30 to December 13, 2015. Addendum. Part two: Action taken by the Conference of the Parties at its twenty-first session, FCCC/CP/2015/10/Add.1, Annex 'Paris Agreement' (December 12, 2015).

161 Convention on Biological Diversity (Rio de Janeiro, June 5, 1992), 1760 UNTS 79.

162 The Basel Convention (March 22, 1989) on hazardous wastes requires parties to report annually information relating to the amount and types of wastes governed by the

CCC is indicative. It requires each state party to conduct a national inventory, in this case containing estimates of the party's greenhouse gas emissions and removals by sinks. The inventories are to be developed, periodically updated, published and made available to the Conference of the Parties. The Kyoto Protocol supplemented this obligation in Article 8, setting out a system of implementation review based on expert review teams. It also set up a means of establishing guidelines for the review.

As the UNFCCC illustrates, the text of the treaty sets forth the general reporting requirements. These are usually supplemented by guidelines drafted by the international body. The Convention on Biological Diversity, also, states that '[e]ach Contracting Party shall, at intervals to be determined by the Conference of the Parties, present to the Conference of the Parties, reports on measures which it has taken for the implementation of the provisions of this Convention and their effectiveness in meeting the objectives of this Convention'.[163] Further standards or guidelines establish the periodicity of the reports, the contents of the reports, and the procedures to be followed in submitting and reviewing the reports. The information to be submitted may include the texts of relevant laws or regulations, statistical data on matters covered by the agreement (e.g. production, imports and exports, consumption, numbers of permits issued), decisions taken by national authorities, scientific reports, and enforcement actions.

A major issue in designing reporting systems concerns the methods for critically examining the contents of state reports and the question of follow-up. Experience indicates that the role of non-governmental organizations is often crucial to the effectiveness of the procedure. NGOs may comment on, or supplement, information given by states about compliance with international obligations. Agenda 21, Chapter 27 suggests a formal role for NGOs in committees of control, given their expertise and concrete knowledge.[164] Recent conventions institute scientific and technical committees independent of the parties and such committees also may have a role in the review of compliance

Convention which are exported and imported. Information is required on disposal operations and efforts to reduce the amount of waste subject to transboundary movements; Convention on the Prevention of Marine Pollution by Dumping of Wastes and Other Matter (December 29, 1972) 1046 UNTS 120. The MARPOL Convention (November 2, 1973), Article 11 also requires the communication of information, including a statistical report, on an IMO-prepared standardized form, of penalties imposed for infringement of the Convention.

163 Convention on Biological Diversity (June 5, 1992) art 26.

164 UNCED, "Agenda 21" (Rio de Janerio, June 3–14, 1992).

reports.[165] The UNESCO World Heritage Convention and the Ramsar Convention allow verification of the information furnished by the state reports.[166]

Regional agreements also require reporting. Article XXIX of the revised African Convention on the Conservation of Nature and Natural Resources is particularly complete.[167] It specifies as follows:

1. The Parties shall present, through the Secretariat, to the Conference of the Parties reports on the measures adopted by them in the implementation of this Convention and the results thereof in applying its provisions in such form and at such intervals as the Conference of the Parties may determine. This presentation shall be accompanied by the comments of the Secretariat, in particular regarding failure to report, adequacy of the report and of the measures described therein.
2. The Parties shall supply the Secretariat with:
    a. the texts of laws, decrees, regulations and instructions in force which are intended to ensure the implementation of this Convention;
    b. any other information that may be necessary to provide complete documentation on matters dealt with by this Convention;
    c. the names of the agencies or coordinating institutions empowered to be focal points in matters under this Convention; and
    d. information on bilateral or multilateral agreements relating to the environment and natural resources to which they are parties.

A United Nations study setting forth the objectives of international reporting procedures,[168] although undertaken in the context of human rights reporting, conveys that the procedure should ensure that states parties undertake a comprehensive initial review of national legislation, administrative rules, and procedures and practices either before or soon after ratification and regularly monitor the actual situation with respect to each of the obligations, to become aware of the extent to which the various duties are, or are not, being fulfilled. The reporting procedure itself should provide a basis for the elaboration of clearly stated and carefully targeted policies, including the establishment of

165 See e.g. Madrid Protocol on Antarctica (October 4, 1991), Convention on Biological Diversity (June 5, 1992), UNFCCC (May 9, 1992) the Paris Agreement (December 12, 2015) arts 9, 10, 13(11).

166 Convention for the Protection of the World Cultural and Natural Heritage (Paris, November 16, 1972) 152 UNTS 1977; Convention on Wetlands of International Importance especially as Waterfowl Habitat (Ramsar, 2 February 1971) 246 UNTS 1976.

167 Maputo, July 21, 2003.

168 *Report of the 3rd Session of the UN Committee on Economic, Social and Cultural Rights*, E/1989/22, Annex III.

priorities that reflect the provisions of the treaty in question. It also should facilitate public scrutiny of relevant government policies, encouraging the involvement of various sectors of society in the formulation, implementation, and review of national policies. On the international level, the procedure should provide a basis for the state party as well as the supervisory body effectively to evaluate the progress made in the realization of the obligations contained in the treaty, giving the state party a better understanding of the problems and shortcomings encountered in its efforts to comply. Among the states parties, the procedure can facilitate the exchange of information and develop a better understanding of the common problems faced.

One may be skeptical of the effectiveness of reporting systems, expecting that states will be less than forthcoming about problems and defects. Even the fact of having to write a report is useful, however, and exercises an influence on state behavior. Often state reports are discussed in the supervisory organs where independent experts or representatives of other states can address questions to, or request information from, the state authoring the report.[169] The strength of the system is both psychological and political. States may not always protect the environment as they should, but they seek to maintain a good reputation in this field where public opinion is particularly sensitive. Thus, they make efforts to avoid or mitigate damage that could result in condemnation or criticism during review of their reports.

In addition to assisting in determining treaty compliance, reporting requirements serve to provide information on whether the objectives of the agreement are being met or whether new policies need be developed or amendments proposed. Effective reporting systems depend, however, upon the willingness and capacity of parties to gather and report data accurately and objectively, and on the existence of well-resourced secretariats that can process the information into accessible formats in order to track the implementation process.

The proliferation of reporting obligations raises a problem of capacity and overburdening of states parties. Many states have fallen behind in reporting, making supervision of implementation difficult. The Convention on Biological Diversity, the UNFCCC, and the Paris Agreement attempt to respond to this problem by making financial resources available to developing countries to

169 For example, under CITES (March 3, 1973), the Secretariat is empowered to study reports of the parties and request any information it deems necessary to ensure the implementation of the convention and to focus the attention of the parties on any pertinent matter. Articles XII, 2(d) and (e). In addition, the Secretariat may notify a party directly if it believes that the Convention is not being effectively implemented and the party is obliged to respond (art XIII).

meet the incremental costs of fulfilling their reporting obligations.[170] Consolidation of reporting obligations also could ease the burden, allowing states to file a single report with core environmental data, to which specific information relevant to the particular instrument could be added.

2.2 *Verification and Non-Compliance Procedures*

International environmental agreements and international organizations have established a variety of innovative compliance verification procedures to supplement or substitute for reporting procedures. Some regional organizations are undertaking full compliance review. The OECD, for example, has engaged in independent review of the environmental performance of each of its thirty-eight member states. It publishes a country report, together with recommendations for improvement. Treaties that link the environment with other issues or provide financial benefits, e.g. the North American Free Trade Agreement (NAFTA) and UNESCO World Heritage Convention,[171] can stimulate compliance by the threat of withdrawing benefits.

The implementation of the Ramsar Convention on Wetlands of International Importance especially as Waterfowl Habitat is enhanced by a Monitoring Procedure created to address specific problems that may arise in maintaining the ecological character of a designated wetland of international importance.[172] The Monitoring Procedure may take the form of a mission to the Contracting Party concerned, with the consent of that state. The mission generally is composed of one secretariat representative and two international experts with expertise appropriate to the technical circumstances. The mission undertakes field visits and holds office-based discussions with local experts and government representatives. A detailed report, with recommendations for action, then is compiled and submitted to the government concerned.

A different method is established in the Bern Convention on the Conservation of European Wildlife and Natural Habitats.[173] To improve compliance, a special supervisory procedure has been set up using 'case-files'. The procedure may be initiated by a complaint of non-compliance from a state party, an NGO, or an individual. The Secretariat of the Convention refers the complaints to the

170 See e.g., Paris Agreement (December 12, 2015) art 13(14) which provides that support shall be provided to developing countries for the implementation of their reporting obligations.

171 North American Free Trade Agreement (December 17, 1992); Paris, November 16, 1972.

172 Ramsar, February 2, 1971; Ramsar Convention Standing Committee, Fourth Meeting, Recommendation C.4.7.

173 Convention on the Conservation of European Wildlife and Natural Habitats (Bern, September 19, 1979).

relevant party for details and clarification. The latter should answer within a reasonable period of time. After the response, the Secretariat decides whether the case should be placed on the agenda of the Standing Committee, which by consensus after discussions can open a case-file and make recommendations. If any doubt or difficulties arise regarding implementation measures, on-the-spot appraisals by an independent expert also are possible with the consent of the concerned parties. The courts of Liechtenstein have cited the Bern Convention in administrative proceedings requiring the government to repeal and reconsider a decision allowing for capture and killing of beavers in a flood protection area.[174]

A common method of supervision is through the delegation of specific monitoring powers to the states parties. Coastal states, for example, may exercise prescriptive and enforcement jurisdiction over vessel-source pollution that affects their internal waters and territorial seas. Port state jurisdiction is perhaps even more common. Under the International Convention for the Prevention of Pollution from Ships (MARPOL),[175] port and coastal states have a responsibility to detect violations and the right to inspect vessels in their ports and offshore terminals. If a ship reveals significant violations then the ship may be held in port until the repairs are made.[176] UNCLOS, Article 218 provides that when a ship voluntarily enters a port or offshore installation, the coastal state can investigate and, where the evidence warrants, institute proceedings regarding any discharge from that vessel outside the internal waters, territorial sea or exclusive economic zone of that state in violation of applicable international rules and standards established through the competent international organization or general diplomatic conference. UNCLOS, Article 220(6) also provides authority for a coastal state to detain foreign ships and institute legal proceedings for violation of international rules concerning the prevention, reduction, or control of pollution from vessels if that violation causes 'major damage or threat of major damage to the coastline or related interests of the coastal state or to any resources of its territorial sea or exclusive economic zone'.

Some treaties, particularly those involving resource use in the commons areas, specify monitoring by designated observers. The Antarctic Treaty

---

174 Administrative Court of the Principality of Liechtenstein, Decision of the Appeals Commission for Administrative Affairs, 2017.06.28, VBK 2017/22 ON 16, https://www.ecolex.org/details/court-decision/decision-of-the-appeals-commission-for-administrative-affairs-of-28-june-2017-vbk-201722-on-16-7067abc7-683d-403d-b8f4-6fc9c2523014/?q=Animal+welfare&type=court_decision&xdate_min=2015&xdate_max=2020.

175 November 2, 1973.

176 ibid, arts 5 and 6.

system has used this method of supervising compliance with obligations since it began. Supplementing the original mandate, the Canberra Convention on Conservation of Antarctic Marine Living Resources (CCAMLR) includes procedures relating to on-site visits to, and inspections of, ships operating in the applicable zone.[177] The inspections are undertaken by observers and inspectors designated by members of an international Commission established by the Convention.[178] The August 4, 1995 Agreement for the Implementation of the Provisions of the UN Convention to the Conservation and Management of Straddling Fish Stocks and Highly Migratory Fish Stocks delegates to parties in regional fishing agreements the power to monitor the activities of other parties fishing in the region. Any member state may board and inspect fishing vessels flying the flag of another member state. Inspectors may inspect the vessel itself and its license, gear, equipment, records, facilities, fish and fish products, and any relevant documents needed to verify compliance.[179] Similar provisions are found in the Convention on Antarctic Marine Living Resources and the Convention for the Conservation of Anadromous Stocks in the North Pacific Ocean.[180] Physical inspection may be unnecessary to monitor compliance with many of these obligations. Remote sensing from satellites can monitor national emissions of specific pollutants, the loss of forest resources and the activities of fishing vessels.

Verification is a central part of the Chemical Weapons Convention (CWC).[181] Even states parties with no chemical weapons to destroy must comply with the verification measures. The CWC creates the Organization for the Prohibition of Chemical Weapons (OPCW) as an independent international body to monitor CWC States Parties and ensure that their activities comply with the CWC. The Technical Secretariat, consisting of a Director-General appointed for a four-year term as well as inspectors and other personnel, carries out the CWC verification measures which include on-site inspections.[182]

Many non-compliance procedures instituted by international environmental agreements aim to provide assistance to the defaulting state. In the

177 Convention on Conservation of Antarctic Marine Living Resources (May 20, 1980) 48 UNTS 1983.

178 ibid, art XXIV.

179 Agreement for the Implementation of the Provisions of the UN Convention to the Conservation and Management of Straddling Fish Stocks and Highly Migratory Fish Stocks (August 4, 1995) arts 18 and 19.

180 May 20, 1980, Article XXIV; February 11, 1992, art V.

181 Convention on the Prohibition of the Development, Production, Stockpiling and Use of Chemical Weapons and on their Destruction (January 13, 1993) 1975 UNTS 45.

182 ibid, art VIII(D) and Verification Annex.

Montreal Protocol to the Ozone Convention, for example, a party that cannot meet its obligations may report its compliance problems to the Implementation Committee.[183] In addition, any party or parties that has concerns about another party's implementation of its obligations under the Protocol may communicate the concerns in writing, supported by corroborating information, to the secretariat.

The Implementation Committee can request further information or, upon the invitation of the party concerned, it can undertake information gathering on site. At the end of the procedure, the Committee reports to the Meeting of the Parties. Any recommendation it considers appropriate can be included in the report, which is made available to the parties six weeks before the meeting. The Meeting of the Parties may decide upon steps to bring about full compliance with the Protocol. Any state involved in a matter under consideration by the Implementation Committee cannot take part in the elaboration and adoption of recommendations concerning it. The parties subject to the procedure must subsequently inform the Meeting of the Parties of the measures they have taken in response to the report.

Annex V of Decision IV/18 of the Meeting of Parties to the Montreal Protocol contains an indicative list of measures that might be taken by the Meeting of the Parties in respect of non-compliance with the Protocol. The first consists in providing assistance, for, *e.g.*, the collection and reporting of data, technology transfer, financing, information transfer and training. At the second level 'cautions' or warnings are issued. The third level involves the suspension of specific rights and privileges under the Protocol. Such rights and privileges can concern industrial rationalization, production, consumption, trade, transfer of technology, financial mechanisms, and industrial arrangements.

In May 1995, the Russian Federation, Belarus, Bulgaria, Poland, and Ukraine, in a joint statement, expressed concern about their capability to be in full compliance with the obligations under the Protocol in 1996, due to the severe situation of their economies. The Implementation Committee took this statement as a submission under the non-compliance procedure of the Protocol. After consultations a draft decision was submitted to the Meeting of the Parties.[184] The report noted that the Russian Federation was in compliance with

183 Ozone Convention (March 22, 1985); Montreal Protocol (September 16, 1987). In accordance with paragraph 3 of Annex III, 'Non-compliance procedure' to the report of the Second Meeting of the Parties to the Montreal Protocol, the Implementation Committee consists of ten parties elected by the Meeting of the Parties for two years, based on equitable geographical distribution.

184 26 EPL.68 (1996).

its obligations under the Montreal Protocol in 1995 but would likely not be in non-compliance in 1996. The draft decision recommended that international assistance should be considered in consultation with the relevant Montreal Protocol Secretariats and the Implementation Committee. It said that the Russian Federation should submit annual reports on progress in phasing out ozone depleting substances in line with the schedule included in its submission to the parties. Disbursement of the international assistance should be contingent on the settlement of problems related to the reporting requirements and the action of the Russian Federation.[185] It is worth noting that the decision concerning the Russian Federation was adopted without its consent and may indicate the limits of the non-compliance procedure.

The Kyoto Protocol compliance regime was developed pursuant to Article 18 of the UNFCCC by the Conference of the Parties (COP) serving as the meeting of the Parties (MOP) to the Kyoto Protocol.[186] A Joint Working Group elaborated a draft regime on compliance which the COP 7 approved in 2001 as part of the Marrakesh Accords. The objective of the regime is to 'facilitate, promote and enforce compliance with the commitments under the Protocol'.[187] The Marrakech Accords contain an innovative, unprecedented compliance mechanism. It foresees a Compliance Committee with two branches, a facilitative branch and an enforcement branch.[188] The facilitative branch supports efforts by parties to comply. The enforcement branch is to monitor compliance with the most important obligations. The enforcement branch has several tools available to bring about compliance: a party may be prohibited from selling under the emissions trading regime and for every ton of emissions by which a party exceeds its target, 1.3 tons will be deducted from its assigned among for the subsequent commitment period. The party will be required to submit a compliance action plan for review by the committee. An appeals procedure provides for a review of decisions by the UNFCCC COP serving as the Protocol's Meeting of the Parties. During the procedure the decisions by the Compliance Committee remain in force. Overturning the decision requires a three-fourth's majority of the COP/MOP. Both branches of the Committee are composed of

185 Draft Decision VII/16. See 26 EPL 120 (1996).

186 May 9, 1992.

187 UNFCCC COP 7, 'Implementation of the Buenos Aires Plan of Action: Adoption of the decisions giving effect to the Bonn Agreements. Procedures and mechanisms relating to compliance under the Kyoto Protocol. Draft decision -/CP.7. Procedures and mechanisms relating to compliance under the Kyoto Protocol' (November 7, 2001), Document FCCC /CP/2001/L.21, Annex on Procedures and Mechanisms relating to Compliance under the Kyoto Protocol, art I.

188 UNFCCC COP 7, November 7, 2001, art II.

ten members, one each from the five regions, one small island developing state and two from Annex I and two from non-Annex I countries. A double majority vote is required for decisions: three-fourths of all members including a simple majority of Annex I and non-Annex I countries.

While the compliance procedure was not adopted as an amendment to the Kyoto Protocol and thus is not legally binding as part of the treaty, it has the advantage of being applicable to all parties to the protocol upon adoption.

The UNFCCC parties also agreed in 2001 to establish three new funds to promote compliance by developing countries, two under the UNFCCC and one under the Kyoto Protocol: the Special Climate Change Fund, the Least Developed Countries Fund, and the Adaptation Fund. Decision 7/CP.7 creates a Special Climate Change Fund complementary to the Global Environment Facility (GEF) funding to provide finances for the adaptation, technology transfer, and the mitigation of greenhouse gases.[189] The Special Climate Change Fund also aims to encourage and assist countries that are heavily dependent on the export of fossil fuels shall be encouraged and assisted in diversifying their economies. The second special fund created under the UNFCCC is reserved for the least developed countries to assist financially in the preparation of national programs.[190] Third, an Adaptation Fund under the Kyoto Protocol is financed by voluntary contributions and by a share of two percent of proceeds from certified emissions reductions generated by the clean development mechanism under Article 12 of the Kyoto Protocol.[191] It marks the first time that a levy is foreseen on business transactions to finance environmental and developmental activities. In 2011, the Parties to the UNFCC established a Green Climate Fund as an operating entity of the financial mechanism of the Convention.[192] A new Fund on Loss and Damage was agreed upon in 2022 at COP 27 and operationalized in 2023 at COP 28.[193] This fund seeks to assist developing countries that are particularly vulnerable to the adverse effects of climate

189 UNFCCC COP 8, Decision 7/CP.7, 'Funding under the Convention', Document FCCC /CP/2001/13/Add.1 (November 10, 2001) [2].

190 UNFCCC COP 8, Decision 7/CP.7 [6].

191 See UNFCCC COP 8, Decision 10/CP.7, 'Funding under the Kyoto Protocol', FCCC /CP/2001/13/Add.1; UNFCCC COP 8, Decision 17/CP.7, "Modalities and procedures for a clean development mechanism as defined in Article 12 of the Kyoto Protocol", FCCC /CP/2001/13/Add.2..

192 UNFCCC COP 16, Decision 1/CP.16, 'The Cancun Agreements: Outcome of the work of the Ad Hoc Working Group on Long-term Cooperative Action under the Convention', FCCC /CP/2010/7/Add.1 [102].

193 UNFCCC COP 27, Decision 2/CP.27, 'Funding arrangements for responding to loss and damage associated with the adverse effects of climate change, including a focus on addressing loss and damage', FCCC/CP/2022/10/Add.1 [2].

change in responding to loss and damage, including with a focus on addressing loss and damage.

The Paris Agreement, which was adopted by the Parties to the UNFCCC on December 12, 2015, lays down the framework under which the Parties voluntarily bind themselves to implement actions, referred to as 'Nationally Determined Contributions' (NDCs), to reduce their greenhouse gas emissions and adapt to the effects of climate change.[194] Given the voluntary approach to commitments taken by the Paris Agreement, the implementation and compliance procedures of this treaty are central to the realization of its goal to hold 'the increase in the global average temperature to well below 2°C above pre-industrial levels' and pursue efforts 'to limit the temperature increase to 1.5°C above pre-industrial levels'.[195] In order to facilitate implementation and promote compliance with the Paris Agreement, the Parties have established an 'enhanced transparency framework' (EFT) under which they are required to report transparently on a biennial basis on actions taken in relation to mitigation, adaptation, and financial support provided or received.[196] The aggregated information from the EFT then feeds into the 'Global Stocktake', where the collective progress towards the long-term climate goals is assessed.[197] The biennial transparency reports submitted by the Parties are subject to technical expert review.[198] The UNFCCC Conference of Parties serving as the meeting of the Parties to the Paris Agreement (CMA) oversees the implementation of the Paris Agreement, together with the Implementation and Compliance Committee, which reports annually to the CMA.[199] Although states climate action is currently well below what is needed to meet the goals of the Paris Agreement, the innovative implementation and compliance regime set up by the Paris Agreement has demonstrated some benefits, prompting states to set ambitious climate targets and to take steps to meet them, while providing financial assistance to those that are less endowed and more vulnerable to climate change.

On a regional level, NAFTA's Environmental Side Agreement, the North American Agreement on Environmental Cooperation (NAAEC),[200] created a trilateral commission, the Commission for Environmental Cooperation, to investigate and report on allegations of a consistent pattern of lack of enforcement of environmental laws and agreements. The NAAEC was originally

194 Paris Agreement (December 12, 2015).
195 ibid, art 2.
196 ibid, art 13.
197 ibid, art 14.
198 ibid, art 13(11) and (12).
199 ibid, art 15(1) and (2).
200 September 13, 1993.

designed to complement the existing environmental provisions of NAFTA. While the NAFTA was replaced by the Agreement between the United States of America, Mexico, and Canada (USMCA) as of July 1, 2020,[201] the NAAEC is still in force and its compliance procedures remain active. The NAAEC creates a mechanism that allows individuals and non-governmental organizations to make submissions alleging that a state party is failing to effectively enforce its environmental law (Art. 14 on Submissions on Enforcement Matters). The procedure is not designed to provide a remedy for individual environmental harm; instead, its purpose is to enlist the public to help ensure that the parties abide by their obligation to enforce their respective environmental laws. Anyone residing or established in North America can bring a submission. The identity of the submitter must be established, although privacy and confidentiality can be protected, and the party must have been given prior notice of the matters alleged in the submission. Sufficient facts must be alleged to allow the Secretariat to review the submission.

The Secretariat determines if the submission merits making a request for a response from a party based on criteria in Article 14(2). The Secretariat should decide whether:

a. 'the submission alleges harm to the person or organization making the submission;
b. the submission, alone or in combination with other submissions, raises matters whose further study in this process would advance the goals of the NAAEC;
c. private remedies available under the law of the party concerned have been pursued; and
d. the submission is drawn exclusively from mass media reports'.

A complaint must aim to promote enforcement rather than harass industry.[202] According to Article 14, the Secretariat will solicit a response from a party if the complaint raises matters whose further study in the process would advance the goals of the Agreement. The party must provide a response, which may consist of responding to the complaint, referring the matter to relevant judicial proceedings, or advising that private remedies are available. The Secretariat may dismiss the submission on the basis of the response or may recommend to the Council the creation of a Factual Record of the submission and the response. The Council must approve the recommendation by a two-thirds vote, after which the Secretariat is authorized to create the Factual

201 Agreement between the United States of America, Mexico, and Canada (USMCA) (November 30, 2018).

202 NAAEC (September 13, 1993) art 14(1)(d).

Record (Art. 15(2)). In preparing the Factual Record, the Secretariat is mandated to consider information furnished by a party and any relevant technical, scientific or other information that is (a) publicly available; (b) submitted by interested non-governmental organizations or persons; (c) submitted by the Joint Public Advisory Committee; or (d) developed by the Secretariat or by independent experts. No judgment issues nor are remedies directly afforded.

Since NAAEC came into force on January 1, 1994, the Secretariat has received one hundred and sixteen submissions from NGOs and private persons and prepared twenty-seven Factual Records, seventeen involving Mexico, eight for Canada, and two for the United States. The first of the Factual Records prepared on Mexico,[203] known as the 'Comuzel' case, is typical. It was based on a submission filed by Mexican environmental groups alleging that the government had failed to enforce its environmental law by not requiring the preparation of an environmental impact assessment in connection with a port and related works on the island of Cozumel near the Paraiso coral reef. The submission was accompanied by extensive factual documentation. Among the points raised in response, Mexico challenged the jurisdiction of the CEC because the acts complained of occurred prior to NAAEC's entry into force and because the submitters had not alleged that they suffered any harm. The Secretariat adopted the notion of 'continuing effects', well known in human rights jurisprudence, and decided that the submission was admissible in regard to lack of enforcement that continued after January 1, 1994, date the treaty entered into force. The Secretariat took a broad view on the issue of standing, rejecting the argument that national tests for standing should be applied to the international procedure. While the Secretariat noted that the submitters 'may not have alleged the particularized, individual harm required to acquire legal standing to bring suit in some civil proceedings' in domestic courts, it found that the matter should go forward given 'the especially public nature of marine resources'. It found that the submitters' concerns were within the 'spirit and intent' of the NAAEC. Looking at the submission as a whole, the Secretariat affirmed that the object and purpose of the Agreement is the overriding consideration in deciding on whether or not to recommend the preparation of a Factual Record. The Council concurred and ordered the preparation of the Record.

The Council approved the Guidelines for Submissions on Enforcement Matters under Articles 14 and 15 of NAAEC (October 13, 1995) and revised them by

---

203 Commission for Environmental Cooperation, Secretariat, Final Factual Record Prepared in Accordance with Article 15 of the North American Agreement on Environmental Cooperation in relation to the 'Cruise Ship Pier Project in Cozumel, Quintana Roo', SEM-96-001 (October 25, 1997).

adopting Resolution 99–06 on June 28, 1999, in order to improve transparency and fairness consistent with the Agreement. Council Resolution 01–06 of June 29, 2001 further amended Section 10.2 of the Guidelines in order to provide a more speedy and open process. The provision now specifies that five days after the Secretariat notifies the Council of its opinion that a Factual Recorded is needed, both the notice and the Secretariat's reasoning will be placed in the public registry. If the Council decides not to authorize the preparation of a factual record the reasons for that decision will be made public. The NAAEC registry contains summary information of all proceedings so that any interested non-governmental organization or person, as well as the JPAC, may follow the status of any given submission during the submission process envisaged under Articles 14 and 15 of the Agreement. The registry is accessible to the public. In addition, the Secretariat maintains a file on each submission at its headquarters in Montreal that is available for public access, inspection and photocopying, subject to confidentiality requirements.[204]

The Canada-Chile side Agreement on Environmental Cooperation,[205] very similar to the NAAEC led to the creation of the Canada-Chile Commission for Environmental Cooperation. The main objectives are to strengthen environmental cooperation and ensure effective enforcement of environmental laws and regulations. Like the NAAEC, it allows citizens and non-governmental organizations to file submissions if one of the participating countries fails to effectively enforce its environmental legislation.

The Convention for the Protection of the Marine Environment of the North-East Atlantic (OSPAR Convention) contains other types of non-compliance procedures.[206] The Commission it establishes has the duty to review the condition of the marine area, the effectiveness of the measures being adopted and the need for any additional or different measures and to supervise the implementation of the Convention as a whole.[207] The Contracting parties report to the Commission at regular intervals on the legal, regulatory, or other measures taken by them to implement the provisions of the Convention and decisions and recommendations of the Commission, as well as on their effectiveness. They also shall report on measures taken to prevent and punish conduct in

204 Information on activities of the North American Commission on Environmental Cooperation and on citizen submissions is available at <http://www.cec.org>.

205 Agreement on Environmental Cooperation between the Government of Canada and the Government of the Republic of Chile (Ottawa, February 6, 1997).

206 Convention for the Protection of the Marine Environment of the North-East Atlantic (September 22, 1992) 2354 UNTS 67.

207 ibid, art 10(2).

contravention of those provisions.[208] The Commission assesses the conformity of national measures with the obligations under the Convention. When appropriate, it decides upon and calls for steps to bring about full compliance including measures to assist a state to carry out its obligations.[209] The impact of this procedure may be increased by the presence of observers at the meetings of the Commission. Any non-party State and any international governmental or non-governmental organization can be admitted as an observer by unanimous vote of the Commission. Such observers may present any information or reports relevant to the objectives of the Convention.[210]

Customary international law traditionally allowed the use of proportional countermeasures and other forms of self-help in response to an illegal act by another state. Such a system does not work well in its classic form in the field of environmental law. A state cannot reasonably respond to another state's illegal environmental harm by similarly injuring its own environment. In this regard, environmental obligations are similar to humanitarian obligations which the Vienna Convention on the Law of Treaties excepts from the system of counter-measures in kind.[211]

A different and often unilateral approach to non-compliance links environmental protection and trade. It is a controversial approach to non-compliance, as is reflected in the Rio Declaration, Principle 12, which says that 'unilateral actions to deal with environmental challenges outside the jurisdiction of the importing country should be avoided'.[212] Yet, trade sanctions are used by some states in an attempt to enforce international environmental norms. United States law bans the importation of shrimp products caught by methods that endanger turtles and took action to bar the importation of tuna caught by methods that excessively killed dolphins.[213] The primary controversy is over measures that seek to protect resources located outside the jurisdiction of the country imposing the restriction. As discussed herein and in Chapter 17, the World Trade Organization's dispute settlement panels have condemned most unilateral trade sanctions when they concern the environment outside national jurisdiction. The issue of multilateral trade measures also must be considered.

---

208 ibid, art 22.

209 ibid, art 23.

210 ibid, art 11. See, Ellen Hey, Ton Ijlstra, André Nollkaemper, 'The 1992 Paris Convention for the Protection of the Marine Environment of the North-East Atlantic: a Critical Analysis' (1983), 8(1) INT'L J. MARINE AND COASTAL L. 1. The text of the Convention is annexed, 50–76.

211 Vienna Convention on the Law of Treaties (May 23, 1969) 1155 UNTS 331, art 60(5).

212 UN General Assembly, 'Report on the United Nations Conference on the Environment and Development', Resolution No. A/CONF.151/26, Vol. I (1992) principle 12.

213 Public Law 101–162, Title VI, Section 609 (November 21, 1989).

2.3 *Bank Inspection Panels*

After criticism of its support for major environmentally damaging projects, such as the construction of a dam and reservoir in Java between 1985 and 1993 and the Sardar Sarovar dam in India, the World Bank began to play an increasing role in the field of the international protection of the environment. The World Bank established its Inspection Panel in 1993 because of growing concerns about the accountability of it and other international development agencies in supporting projects and programs.[214] The Inspection Panel was complemented in 2020 by the Dispute Resolution Service, which together form the World Bank Accountability Mechanism, established in 2020 and supported by the Accountability Mechanism Secretary.[215] The Inspection Panel is an independent investigatory body receiving and investigating complaints issuing from those in the territory of a borrower whose rights or interests have been, or are likely to be, adversely affected by the World Bank's failure to comply with its own policies and procedures in the design, appraisal and implementation of a Bank-financed project.[216] The Inspection Panel may investigate complaints upon authorization by the World Bank's Board of Executive Directors and assess to what extent the World Bank has complied with its standards. At the first stage, the Inspection Panel registers the request and asks Management to respond to the concerns expressed in it.[217] The Inspection Panel then assesses whether or not the request for inspecting meets the eligibility requirements, in particular, whether *prima facie* the World Bank has engaged in a serious violation of its operational policies and procedures resulting or likely to result in material and adverse harm to those making the request and to which Management has failed to respond adequately.[218] On the basis of this assessment, the Inspection Panel recommends to the Executive Directors whether or not to authorize an investigation. Following the authorization of an investigation, the requester(s) and the borrower(s) may decide to engage in a voluntary and independent dispute resolution process facilitated by the Dispute Resolution Service. If the requester(s) and the borrower(s) do not agree to do so and if the Executive Directors decide to investigate the request, the Inspection Panel investigates the merits and reaches findings. The process can result

---

214 The World Bank's Inspection Panel was originally established by the Resolution No. IBRD 93–10 and Resolution No. IDA 93–6 (1993). Its current role and functions are set out in Resolution No. IBRD 2020–0004/IDA2020-0003, (September 8, 2020).

215 Resolution No. IBRD 2020–0005/IDA 2020–0004 (September 8, 2020).

216 ibid 13.

217 ibid 19–21.

218 ibid 22–27.

in a remedial action plan requiring management to take actions in response to World Bank failures.[219]

Between 1995 and 2022, the Accountability Mechanism received one hundred and fifty-eight requests for inspection. The main policies issues raised in requests are environmental assessment, consultation/disclosure, investment project financing, involuntary resettlement, and access to information. Investigations have been recommended in forty-nine cases and actually conducted in forty-one cases. Since the Dispute Resolution Service became operational in 2021, two cases have led to a dispute resolution process.[220]

The 1993 Resolution establishing the Inspection Panel has been reviewed twice,[221] leading to clarifications and changes in the operation of the Inspection Panel. The first review, done in 1996, focused on procedure. The second review, completed in 1999, added to and revised the 1996 conclusions.[222] The results clarify that the initial (admissibility) stage of the procedure must focus on assertions of non-compliance and resulting potential or material harm; it is not a decision on the merits involving a true finding of harm. The issue of non-compliance is antecedent to the issue of harm and supports the notion of the Inspection Panel as a mechanism of accountability rather than a true remedial procedure. Other aspects of the conclusions similarly focus on the Inspection Panel's role to monitor the World Bank's non-compliance with its own policies and procedures. The review of the Inspection Panel carried out between 2017–2020 led to the adoption of a two Resolutions on September 8, 2020, which respectively established the Accountability Mechanism and revised the functions of the Inspection Panel.[223] The Accountability Mechanism constitutes an independent complaints mechanism, with the Inspection Panel performing compliance reviews and the Dispute Resolution Service facilitating a dispute resolution process.

Other banks have developed similar procedures with some minor differences.[224] At the World Bank, the Inspection Panel consists of three members, while the Compliance Review Panel of the Asian Development Bank comprises three

---

219 ibid 28–58.

220 Annual Report of the Accountability Mechanism, 2021–2022.

221 Resolution No. IBRD 93–10 and Resolution No. IDA 93–6 (1993).

222 Conclusions of the Second Review of the World Bank Inspection Panel, 39 ILM 243 (2000).

223 Resolution No. IBRD 2020–0005/IDA 2020–0004 (September 8, 2020); Resolution No. IBRD 2020–0004/IDA2020-0003, (September 8, 2020).

224 The procedures for these compliance mechanisms are laid down under the following documents: for the World Bank, under the Inspection Panel at the World Bank, Operating Procedures (December 2022); for the Asian Bank, under the Accountability Mechanism

members of the board, including two regional members. The Inter-American Development Bank maintains a permanent roaster of independent experts to exercise an independent investigation mechanism triggered by requests for investigation.

Requests for inspection of bank-financed projects generally can be made by communities, organizations or other groups residing in the borrowing country where the project is being implemented or is proposed to be implemented (Asian Bank, Inter-American Bank) or in another member country adjacent to that country if the group is affected by the project (Asian Development Bank). Requesters need not have independent legal status (Asian Bank). The World Bank's panel can receive requests from groups of at least two persons.

The request must describe the project and explain how the rules, procedures and the agreed provisions of the bank have been violated (World Bank). It must present reasonable evidence that their rights or interests of the requesting party have been or are likely to be directly, materially and adversely affected by an action or omission of the bank (World Bank, Asian Bank, Inter-American Bank). A request for inspection must assert that the bank has failed, in formulating, processing or implementing a project, to follow its operational policies or procedures (World Bank, Asian Bank, Inter-American Bank) and the failure was brought to the attention of the bank's management, which failed within a determined period to demonstrate that the bank had followed, or was taking adequate steps to follow, its operational policies and procedures (Asian Bank).

The inspection process starts with a written complaint to the President of the bank (World Bank, Asian Bank). In the mechanism of the Asian Bank, the management responds to the complaint, but if the complaining party is unsatisfied with this response, it can make a written request to the Board Compliance Review Committee for an inspection of the project. The Committee will recommend to the Board whether an inspection is warranted. If the Board authorizes an inspection, it will select a panel of experts from the roster to inspect the project and make a report to the Board Compliance Review Committee. The World Bank's procedure provides that the Inspection Panel recommends within twenty-one days whether or not to proceed to an inspection. The procedure of the Inter-American Bank prescribes that the request for investigation is forwarded to the Independent Consultation and Investigation Mechanism (MICI) which recommends to the Board of Executive Directors (or the Donors Committee) of the Inter-American Bank whether or not to proceed to an investigation. If such investigation is recommended, the MICI Director

Policy (March 2012); and for the Inter-American Bank, under the Policy of the Independent Investigation and Consultation Mechanism, MI-47-6 (December 16, 2015).

names a three-person panel from the permanent roster. The investigation report of the panel shall address all relevant facts and shall conclude with findings on the Inter-American Bank's compliance with all its relevant operational policies and norms. On the basis of such investigations, the Board of Executive Directors (or the Donors Committee) shall determine what preventive or corrective action, if any, should be taken.

At the conclusion of the Asian Bank procedure, the Board takes a decision which can ask for changes in the scope or implementation of an approved project. Any remedial changes in project scope or implementation are processed in accordance with standard Bank procedures and the relevant legal documents. At the World Bank, the panel adopts conclusions to be submitted to the management, which addresses recommendations to the Board of Executive Directors. The final decision is taken by the Board. In all the procedures, the conclusions and decisions taken by the banks generally are made available to the public.

3 State Responsibility and Liability

Environmental harm occurs through intentional or negligent conduct and as the consequence of an accident. In order to sanction and remedy wrongful conduct, law must determine appropriate enforcement actions and remedies. Legal systems must also decide who should bear the loss when accidental harm occurs. In making such determinations, those drafting and enforcing norms have to address such questions as the degree or amount and kind of harm that may lead to legal action, who is entitled to instigate the action, before what forum or tribunal, and what appropriate orders, sanctions, or compensation may be foreseen. International action is generally inter-state, based on doctrines of state responsibility or liability. State responsibility requires a state that breaches an international obligation to repair harm caused to another state. This responsibility based on fault may be distinguished from imposition of liability for the deleterious effects of lawful acts, that is, without fault. In environmental law, the latter concept can be seen as an application of the polluter pays principle, requiring that the operator or actor who benefits from a lawful activity bear the risk of loss when harm is done to others.

The legal consequences of environmental harm encompass both state responsibility for breaches of international law and liability for harm resulting from an activity permitted under international law, that is, strict or absolute liability over activities attributable to the state. Responsibility is thus a question of duty while liability addresses the allocation of risk.[225] The terms are not always consistently used. UNCLOS distinguishes the two terms in Article 139, seemingly describing liability as the consequence of a failure of state responsibility:

1. States Parties shall have the responsibility to ensure that activities in the Area, whether carried out by States Parties, or state enterprises or natural or juridical persons which possess the nationality of States Parties or are effectively controlled by them or their nationals, shall be carried out in conformity with this Part …
2. Without prejudice to the rules of international law and Annex III, article 22, damage caused by the failure of a State Party or international organization to carry out its responsibilities under this Part shall entail liability; States Parties or international organizations acting together shall bear joint and several liability.

A similar distinction is made in the Convention on International Liability for Damage Caused by Space Objects.[226] In some bilateral treaties, reference is made to liability rather than to responsibility of the states parties.[227]

In contrast, the Institut de Droit International adopted a resolution on September 4, 1997 clearly distinguishing responsibility and liability under international law for environmental damage.[228] It maintains state responsibility as the consequences of breach of an international law obligation, while liability is identified as the duty to re-establish the original position or to pay compensation on the basis of harm alone.[229] It calls for the development of specific rules on responsibility and liability in order to ensure the effectiveness of preventing environmental harm and providing restoration and compensation if harm occurs. Strict responsibility should result from the definition of environmentally-hazardous activities that demand such result, taking into account the nature of the risk involved and the financial implications of such definition. In general, environmental law should assign primary liability to operators, without prejudice to the question of international responsibility should the state concerned fail to establish and implement civil

225 Louis F.E. Goldie, 'Transfrontier Pollution--From Concepts of Liability to Administrative Conciliation' (1985) 12 SYR.J. INT'L L. & COM, 185–86.

226 Convention on International Liability for Damage Caused by Space Objects (March 29, 1972) arts I and XII.

227 *See, e.g.* Frontier Treaty between Germany and the Netherlands (April 8, 1960) art 63(1).

228 Institut de Droit International, 'Responsibility and Liability under International Law for Environmental Damage' (Strasbourg, September 4, 1997).

229 ibid, arts 1–5.

liability mechanisms or adequate insurance schemes, compensation funds or other safeguards.[230]

3.1 *Overview*

According to international law, its subjects are responsible for international law violations that can be attributed to them.[231] In 2001, the UN International Law Commission (ILC) completed work on its Draft Articles on the law of state responsibility and presented its work to the General Assembly,[232] reaffirming that as a matter of customary international law, the breach of an international obligation gives rise to an independent and automatic duty to cease the wrongful act and to make reparation.

Although traditional norms of state responsibility mainly concern the treatment of aliens and their property, the *Trail Smelter* arbitration recognized that principles of state responsibility are applicable in the field of transfrontier pollution, and consequently states may be held liable to private parties or other states for pollution that causes significant damage to persons or property.[233] The principle of state responsibility for environmental harm is contained in numerous international texts. Principle 21 of the Stockholm Declaration declares that states have the responsibility to ensure that activities under their jurisdiction or control do not cause damage to the environment of other states or to areas beyond national jurisdiction and refers to responsibility for transfrontier pollution in Principle 22.[234] Principle 13 of the Rio Declaration calls on states to develop national law regarding liability and compensation for victims of pollution and other environmental damage, providing that '[s]tates shall also cooperate in an expeditious and more determined manner to develop further international law regarding liability and compensation for adverse effects of environmental damage caused by activities within their jurisdiction

230 ibid, art 6.

231 *Chorzow Factory (Indemnity) Case* (1928) PCIJ Ser A No 17, 29.

232 Draft Articles on Responsibility of States for Internationally Wrongful Acts, in Report of the International Law Commission on the Work of Its Fifty-third Session, UNGAOR, 56th Sess., Supp. No. 10, at 45, UN Doc A/56/10 (2001), approved by the General Assembly in GA Res. 56/83 (December 12, 2001). For a history of the ILC's work and commentary on the articles, see James Crawford, 'The ILC's Articles on Responsibility of States for Internationally Wrongful Acts: A Retrospect' (2002) 96(4) *The American Journal of International Law*) 874.

233 See earlier Chapters for discussion of the *Trail Smelter* case.

234 UN General Assembly, 'United Nations Conference on the Human Environment', UN Doc A/RES/2994 (1972).

or control to areas beyond their jurisdiction'.[235] Article 13 of the Helsinki Convention on the Transboundary Effects of Industrial Accidents of March 17, 1992 also contains only a vague call to the parties to 'support appropriate international efforts to elaborate rules, criteria and procedures in the field of responsibility and liability'. The 1979 Convention on Long-Range Transboundary Air Pollution utilizes a procedure virtually unknown in international law to go further and exclude the issue of responsibility from its coverage: a footnote to Article 8(f) on the exchange of information on the effects of long-range transboundary air pollution and the extent of damage which can be attributed to such pollution provides that '[t]he present Convention does not contain a rule of State liability as to damage'.[236]

The principle of state responsibility is recognized more widely than it is detailed or applied. Article 63(1) of the Boundary treaty between the Netherlands and the Federal Republic of Germany (April 8, 1960) proclaims that if one of the contracting parties violates its obligation concerning the protection of boundary waters against pollution, it will be responsible for damage subsequently caused to the other contracting party. Conventions concerning regional seas make the same proclamation and provide that more precise rules shall be elaborated, without, however, always making a distinction between damages to be awarded to states and damages for harm to individuals.[237] A positive example is found in Article XIII of the 1978 Kuwait Regional Convention for Cooperation on the Protection of the Marine Environment from Pollution:[238]

The Contracting States undertake to cooperate in the formulation and adoption of appropriate rules and procedure for the determination of:

a. civil liability and compensation for damage resulting from pollution of the marine environment, bearing in mind applicable international rules and procedures relating to those matters; and
b. liability and compensation for damage resulting from violation of obligations under the present Convention and its protocols.

---

235 UN General Assembly, 'Report on the United Nations Conference on the Environment and Development', Resolution No. A/CONF.151/26, Vol. I (1992).

236 Geneva, November 13, 1979.

237 See Convention on the Protection of the Baltic Sea Area (March 22, 1974) art 17; Convention for the Protection of the Mediterranean Sea Against Pollution (February 16, 1967) art 12; Convention for Cooperation in the Protection and Development of the Marine and Coastal Environment of the West and Central African Region (March 23, 1981) art 15; Convention for the Protection and Development of the Marine Environment of the Wider Caribbean Region (March 23, 1983) art 14.

238 Kuwait Regional Convention for Cooperation on the Protection of the Marine Environment from Pollution (Kuwait, April 24, 1978).

Invocation of the principle of responsibility in international texts and agreements since 1972 led the International Court of Justice (ICJ) to assert in the Advisory Opinion on the *Legality of the Use by a State of Nuclear Weapons in Armed Conflict* and in the *Gabčíkovo-Nagymaros* case that it now forms part of the corpus of customary international law.[239] It also is included in the Restatement (Third) of the Foreign Relations Law of the United States, where state responsibility for environmental harm is found to be 'rooted in customary international law'.[240]

3.2 *Implementation of State Responsibility*

Discussions of state responsibility and liability far outstrip the actual number of cases. One major handicap is time; the *Trail Smelter* case began with the first claims presented by pollution victims in 1926, claims taken up by the government a year later. Only in 1941 was the final arbitral award rendered, in spite of the readily identifiable and attributable international harm. In addition to time, there often are special problems of defining the author and the cause of the injury, especially in complex situations such as acid rain. Perhaps for this reason, most of the precedents are bilateral cases. In addition to the time and cost involved in any type of litigation, aggravated in an international case, there are disadvantages to an adversary system in which the environment is the victim but never a party.

In order to successfully impose an obligation to cease a harmful activity or repair harm caused, the legal basis or degree of fault on which the obligation is premised must be determined. In general, international responsibility is founded on fault imputable to the acting state. Fault should not be confused

---

239 *Legality of the Use by a State of Nuclear Weapons in Armed Conflict*, Advisory Opinion, [1996] ICJ Rep 66; *Gabčíkovo-Nagymaros Project (Hungary/Slovakia)*, Judgment, Merits, [1997] ICJ Rep. 7. See also *Pulp Mills on the River Uruguay (Argentina v Uruguay)*, Judgment, ICJ Rep 14 [273].

240 Introductory Note, Part VI: The Law of the Environment, Restatement (Third) Foreign Relations Law of the United States (1986). Section 601, *Restatement (Third) of the Foreign Relations Law of the United States* (1986). Section 601 maintains that a state is responsible for any significant injury resulting from a violation of its obligations (1) to conform to generally accepted international environmental rules; and (2) to conduct its activities so as not to cause significant injury to the environment of another state or of the commons. Section 602 adds that the responsible state must afford general inter-state remedies to prevent, reduce, or terminate the activity threatening or causing the violation, and to pay reparation for injury caused. Where private individuals are injured, the state of origin is obligated to accord to the person injured or exposed to significant risk of injury access to the same judicial or administrative remedies as are available in similar circumstances to persons within the state.

with intent; it is not necessary that a state intentionally or maliciously violates an international obligation. It is necessary, however, to show that an obligation was violated and that harm resulted from the violation. Fault exists if the actor fails to perform a duty or observe a standard. Generally, the applicable international rules and standards do not hold a state responsible when it has taken necessary and practicable measures, i.e. exercised due diligence.

3.2.1 Causation

The link of causality between a culpable act and the damage suffered must be established and the damage must not be too remote or speculative. Pollution poses specific problems for several reasons. First, the distance separating the source from the place of damage may be dozens or even hundreds of miles, creating doubts about the causal link even where polluting activities can be identified. Second, the noxious effects of a pollutant may not be felt until years or decades after the act. Increase in the rate of cancers as a consequence of radioactive fallout, for example, can be substantially removed in time from the polluting incident. This problem was highlighted by the 1986 Chernobyl accident, which immediately caused twenty-nine deaths, but which directly or indirectly may have produced thousands of cases of cancer over the long term. Intervening factors may play a role as well.

Third, some types of damage occur only if the pollution continues over time. This is true of the deterioration of buildings and monuments, for example, or, in certain circumstances, vegetation. Proof of causation also is made difficult by the fact that some substances cause little harm in isolation but are toxic in combination. Imputing responsibility to one source rather than another is difficult.

Finally, the same pollutant does not always produce the same effects due to the important role played by physical circumstances. Thus, dumping polluting substances in a river will not cause the same damage during times of drought as it will during periods where water levels are high. Similarly, wind or the lack of it, fog, or sunlight can modify the impact of air pollution or even the nature of pollution. For example, urban smog, a harmful combination of persistent fog and pollutants, is exacerbated by atmospheric inversions (layers of warm, still air held below a cold air mass) that block elimination of the air pollutants. The latter derive from several sources, including industry, domestic heating, and motor vehicles. In such a situation it appears impossible to impute injury to a single precise cause in order to impose responsibility. Long-distance pollution, especially long-range air pollution, poses unique problems in identifying the author of the harm and precludes relying on state responsibility in the traditional sense of the term.

3.2.2 Attributing the Pollution

Even at a short distance, proving the identity of the polluter can pose problems. For example, gas emissions from motor vehicles are harmful, including the fumes of each individual automobile. Yet it is difficult to apply rules of responsibility and demand reparations from each driver because the numbers are too great and the effects produced by each unit are relatively limited. Nonetheless the cumulative effects are significant due to the part played by nitrous oxide (NO_2) and burned hydrocarbons (HC) in the formation of ozone at medium altitudes during sunny periods; they are factors in the depletion of forests.

The extent to which states are accountable for the actions of private parties under their jurisdiction or control is another issue of state responsibility. Many, if not most, of the activities causing environmental harm are those of private persons, in particular multinational corporations. Although the ILC's Draft Articles on State Responsibility provide that, in general, states are not responsible for private activities,[241] this view does not appear to be accepted for environmental matters. The rule seems rather to be that the state whose territory serves to support the activities causing environmental damage elsewhere or under whose control it occurs is responsible for the resulting harm. This is the sense of the *Trail Smelter* decision, the Stockholm Declaration, Principle 21 and Rio Declaration, Principle 2. Even under traditional principles, the necessary element of an act or omission by state agents is generally present, because the large majority of domestic activities capable of causing serious environmental harm outside the country now require prior approval or licensing under domestic legislation. Such approval normally will suffice to engage the responsibility of the competent territorial authority.

---

241 Draft Articles on Responsibility of States for Internationally Wrongful Acts, with Commentaries (December 12, 2001), Commentary to Article 3, paragraphs 2 and 3 provide that 'In theory, the conduct of all human beings, corporations or collectivities linked to the State by nationality, habitual residence or incorporation might be attributed to the State, whether or not they have any connection to the Government. In international law, such an approach is avoided, both with a view to limiting responsibility to conduct which engages the State as an organization, and also so as to recognize the autonomy of persons acting on their own account and not at the instigation of a public authority. Thus, the general rule is that the only conduct attributed to the State at the international level is that of its organs of government, or of others who have acted under the direction, instigation or control of those organs, i.e. as agents of the State' and that 'As a corollary, the conduct of private persons is not as such attributable to the State'.

3.2.3 Reparations

The issue of reparations is also difficult. In the *Chorzów Factory* case, the Permanent Court of International Justice, finding the obligation to make reparations to be a principle of international law and even resulting from a general conception of law, indicated the scope and purpose of reparations:

> Reparation must, in so far as possible, wipe out all the consequences of the illegal act and re-establish the situation which would, in all probability, have existed, if that act had not been committed. Restitution in kind, or, if that is not possible, payment of a sum corresponding to the value which a restitution in kind would bear, the award, if need be, of damages for loss sustained which would not be covered by restitution in kind or payment in place of it ....[242]

Of course, damage suffered must be measurable in the absence of restitution in kind, the application of which is more problematic in environmental matters than in other domains. In international practice, various conventions, and drafts state that harm to the environment requires that the state of origin restore the environment to its *status quo ante* and that anyone who carries out the necessary work is entitled to reimbursement if the operation is reasonable. If it is impossible to fully restore the prior conditions, the parties must agree on compensation. However, while restitution in kind might involve restoring living resources to a polluted river or cleaning up a toxic site, often the damage may not be easily remediable, if at all. There is no restitution in kind for a species made extinct. In evaluating or measuring damages, a great deal of uncertainty exists because the elements of the environment often are not viewed as having economic value when they remain outside the marketplace. For example, there may be wide divergence in valuing seabirds killed by an oil spill or the aesthetic value of a clean coastline. In other cases, damages may be estimated according to accepted case law from other fields, including such items as lowered property values due to pollution or lost business due to smoke or noise.

3.2.4 Procedural Issues

A final issue in state responsibility is to obtain diplomatic protection when an individual suffers harm due to activities taking place in another state. The victim of such pollution can seek local remedies to obtain satisfaction, and if

242 *Case Concerning the Factory at Chorzów* (*Germany v Poland*) (*Indemnity*), PCIJ. (Judgement of September 13, 1928) Ser A No 17, 29.

this does not succeed, can subsequently request their national government to take up the case. If the complaint is taken, the complainant's government will present an international claim to the government on whose territory the activities have taken place. According to international law, diplomatic protection is exercised by states in order to ensure respect for international law vis-a-vis their nationals.[243] However, it is arguable whether the traditional conditions for the exercise of diplomatic protection must be fulfilled and whether the usual procedures must be followed in order to obtain reparation for damage caused by acts of transfrontier pollution.

The exercise of diplomatic protection generally requires the presence of two conditions: the claimant must have the nationality of the state taking up the claim and local remedies must be exhausted.[244] Recourse to any international procedure, from a simple protest through negotiations to submission of the case to an international tribunal, normally depends upon fulfillment of these prerequisites. It is not clear, however, that the victim of extraterritorial environmental injury must be a national of the State from which he claims protection. Basically, although the quality of 'victim' derives from the fact that the person or his goods have suffered measurable harm, on the international plane this quality is not dominant. According to the accepted formula of the ICJ, states demand reparation by exercising diplomatic protection in order to obtain respect for international law towards their subjects.[245] In the typical case, the wrongful act is directed at the victim and occurs within the territory of the acting state. However, in cases of environmental injury, usually the acts of pollution attack the individuals incidentally or fortuitously outside the boundaries of the acting state. All who are situated on the territory or territories where the injury occurs, including human beings and their movable and immovable goods, whether private property or public domain of the state, are similarly situated. Moreover, even if no individual complains, even if there is no victim among the inhabitants of the territory of the state, the latter suffers damage because of acts of pollution originating in the other state. It is clear that the injured state has the right to assert the responsibility of the state under whose jurisdiction or control the polluter is found. The claimant state will proceed in order to protect its territorial sovereignty violated by the acts of

---

243 *Mavrommatis Case*, PCIJ (Judgment of August 30, 1924), Ser A, No. 2, 12.

244 See *Nottebohm* Case (Liechtenstein v. Guatemala), [1955] ICJ Rep 4.

245 '... by taking up a case on behalf of its nationals before an international tribunal, a State is asserting its own right – that is to say, its right to ensure in the person of its subject, respect for the rules of international law', *Serbian Loans*, PCIJ Ser A, Nos. 20/21, 17.

pollution and not its personal competence exercised in favor of one of its subjects. Thus, an injured individual may be an alien in the state presenting the claim or even have the nationality of the accused State. In demanding reparations, the state enforces international law respecting its territory rather than in regard to its subjects.

With territory rather than nationality, the usual basis for claims of state responsibility for environmental harm, diplomatic protection will maintain its traditional function only when the victims of polluting activities are found in places where the sole link between them and their state is personal: the high seas and air space above, Antarctica, and outer space.

If these conclusions are valid, it is not necessary to examine whether the second condition for the exercise of diplomatic protection, that of exhaustion of domestic remedies, is fulfilled or not. Nonetheless, when a state exercises its right of diplomatic protection to intervene on behalf of victims of transfrontier pollution within its territory, the latter need not exhaust internal remedies offered by the polluting state. Without entering into detailed considerations concerning private international law, it is useful to look at the basis of the rule of exhaustion of domestic remedies. The requirement is justified largely because there exists a link between the individual claiming reparations and the state to whom the claim is addressed. This link may be tenuous or temporary: the individual visited the territory of the state or concluded a contract with it or implicitly accepted its jurisdiction in a contract with another private persons. In all these cases, a voluntary act on the part of the claimant establishes willing contact with the legal system of the foreign state and submission to it, at least to some extent. In these conditions, it is to be expected that the foreign state's legal system will provide a remedy for violations of the law of which the alien found itself victim. The rule of prior exhaustion of domestic remedies is thus justified on consensual individual links with the wrong-doing state.

A completely different situation is presented when an individual has suffered damages without manifesting any willingness to enter into contact with the foreign state or to submit to its legal system. The acting state is extending its reach into the territory of another sovereign to cause harm to those with whom it has no links. Persons remaining within the boundaries of their country are entitled to feel secure from outside intervention. Due to the burden the pollution would impose on the victim who has sought no benefit from the polluting state, nor availed themselves of its jurisdiction, exhaustion of domestic remedies in the polluting state should not be required in order to claim damages for harm caused.

3.2.5 Harm to the Global Commons

The problem of harm to the global commons, including the environment itself, presents particular legal problems. First, harm to the environment *per se* is a developing legal concept and meets resistance in application, as demonstrated by the *Amoco Cadiz* damages award.[246] The difficulties are exacerbated where it cannot be established with certainty that harm to the global commons would result in identifiable harm to human beings. Second, the threshold of harm impacting the global commons cannot easily be measured with sufficient precision to enable a liability regime to be established. Finally, attribution of the harm is extremely difficult because the effects are dispersed generally and there are multiple contributors.

In the case of transfrontier pollution, the injured state will be able to claim reparations for damages suffered by it. On the contrary, when the damage is caused to the environment of an area outside territorial jurisdiction, such as the high seas and deep seabed, international air space, outer space and Antarctica, no state may be able to present a claim on behalf of all humanity, which is the true victim of environmental damage. UNCLOS provides a solution for the deep seabed. Article 145 confers on the Authority the duty to assure protection of the ocean environment in regard to activities taking place in the Zone. This would seem to encompass the ability to present claims of state responsibility for violations of the treaty, the more so as Article 139 declares that a state party or an international organization is responsible for damages resulting from a breach of the obligations imposed on it by the Convention. It also may be claimed that norms protecting the global commons constitute obligations *erga omnes* that may be enforced by any state.[247]

Outside of conferred representation of the general interests of humanity, responsibility for damage caused to the *res communis*, or common heritage of humanity, can only be engaged in an indirect manner, in the case where there exist conventional rules protecting a given sector. Under general rules of international law, each contracting party to a treaty has the right to supervise application of the treaty by other contracting parties. Thus, a contracting

246 Discussed in this Chapter 7.

247 See *Barcelona Traction, Light and Power Co. Case* (*Belgium v. Spain*), [1970] ICJ Rep 3, [33]-[34]; Advisory Opinion OC-23/17 of November 15, 2017 requested by the Republic of Colombia, 'The Environment and Human Rights' (November 15, 2017). See also Restatement (Third) Foreign Relations Law of the United States, section 601; ILC Third report on State responsibility, by Mr. James Crawford, Special Rapporteur, A/CN.4/507 and Add. 1–4 [92]; Dinah Shelton, 'Common Concern of Humanity', (2009) 5 *Iustum Aequum Salutare* 33, 34, 39; Jutta Brunnée, 'International Legal Accountability through the Lens of the Law of State Responsibility', (2005) 36 *Netherlands Yearbook of International Law* 21, 32.

party that discovers a violation by another treaty party can make a claim in this respect, whether or not the claimant state directly suffered damage. One example would be the dumping of wastes in the ocean in violation of conventional obligations. It is not clear, however, that a state intervening to uphold the treaty can demand damages when it has not suffered any direct injury but instead represents the common interest. Its intervention may be limited to a protest or declaration of non-compliance.

3.2.6 Jurisprudence

In general, international practice has not shown enthusiasm for remedying environmental damage through use of traditional rules of state responsibility, but the law seems to be developing. Importantly, the ICJ rendered its first decision on environmental damage and compensation in 2018 in the case *Certain Activities Carried Out by Nicaragua In the Border Area.*[248] In addition, some examples may be found of inter-state claims presented even prior to the ecological era. Most of the claims arose from nuclear testing. First, following a 1954 United States nuclear test off the Marshall Islands, the Japanese fishing boat *Fukuryu Maru*, its crew and equipment were exposed to nuclear fallout, seriously injuring several people. The Japanese government demanded reparations of nearly six million dollars. In the end, the United States government agreed to pay two million dollars, without formally admitting its responsibility. It was a matter of a 'sovereign act' leaving aside the question of state responsibility.[249] It should be noted, however, that the domestic legal authority under which the United States executive branch may settle foreign claims generally limits the settlement power to 'meritorious' claims.[250]

Environmental damage measurement was a key issue in the later Marshall Islands Nuclear Claims Tribunal.[251] The People of Enewetak filed a class action on July 16, 1990 for damages to land resulting from the United States nuclear testing program conducted between 1946 and 1958. The territory is a low-lying coral atoll in the Marshall Islands, consisting of about 40 islands surrounding a lagoon of about 3888 square miles. After the United States captured the area

---

248 *Certain Activities carried out by Nicaragua in the Border Area* (*Costa Rica v. Nicaragua*) and *Construction of a Road in Costa Rica along the San Juan River* (*Nicaragua v. Costa Rica*), [2015] ICJ Rep 665.

249 Jacques Ballenegger, 'La Pollution en Droit International', 213.

250 10 U.S.C. sec. 2734 (1964); 22 U.S.C. sec. 2669(f) (Supp. 1989), 28 U.S.C. sec. 2672, 2674 (1964). See Linda Malone, '*The Chernobyl Accident: A Case Study in International Law Regulating State Responsibility for Transboundary Nuclear Pollution*' (1987) 12 (203) COL.J. ENV'L L, 222.

251 *In the Matter of the People of Enewetak*, NCT No. 23–0902, decided April 13, 2000, 39 ILM 1214 (2000).

from the Japanese during World War II, the United States began conducting nuclear testing. The people of the atoll were relocated in December 1947, being told that it was for a period of 3–5 years. Instead, they returned only in 1980 to find that the approximate acreage of the atoll had declined from 1919.40 to 815.33 useable acres. In the Compact of Free Association that concluded the United Nations Strategic Trust administered by the United States, the United States government and the government of the Marshall Islands agreed to settle claims resulting from the nuclear testing program.[252] A separate agreement required the establishment of a Claims Tribunal to make a final determination of all claims based on the nuclear testing program, applying the laws of the Marshall Islands, including traditional law, and international law, and in the absence of domestic or international law, the law of the United States. The agreement specified a goal of full compensation for loss or damage to person or property.[253]

The damage award granted by the Marshal Islands Nuclear Claims Tribunal included amounts for loss of use for a specific period of years, using as a measure 'the rental that probably could have been obtained' during the period. Appraisers, agreed to by both sides, offered a joint appraisal report that sought to measure the value of the loss by multiplying the relevant annual rental value times the affected acreage times the period of years use of the land was lost. The period of loss included past loss and future loss, from the date of valuation until return of the property in usable condition. The parties agreed that the latter period would be thirty years from the date of valuation or May 17, 2026. Adjustment was also made for the deferred nature of the compensation for past loss and a discount for future loss.

Annual rental value proved difficult because of the customary system of collective land tenure that does not include the concept of market value. Ownership of land by foreigners is forbidden by law. Instead, the relationship to the land is close to that of other traditional or indigenous peoples who 'have always maintained a deep emotional attachment to their home islands and ancestral land'.[254] In this society, every member of the community is born with a collective right to the lagoon and its resources and this right is passed from

252 The Compact of Free Association between the United States and the Republic of the Marshall Islands was renewed with the signature of a new Memorandum of Understanding on January 12, 2023 between the two governments.

253 Agreement Between the Government of the United States and the Government of the Marshall Islands for the Implementation of Section 177 of the Compact of Free Association.

254 *In the Matter of the People of Enewetak*, NCT No. 23-0902, decided April 13, 2000, 39 ILM 1214 (2000), 1216.

generation to generation. Land is regarded as sacred. Despite this context, the appraisers developed a database of comparable transactions, viewing the highest and best use of the islands as agricultural and residential. They found that rates did not vary according to size of parcel or location. The total amount for past lost use adjusted for prior compensation came to $140,000,000, while the value for lost future use was set at $50,154,811.

A key issue in the case was whether the damages should be set according to the difference in the value of land before and after the harm occurred, or at the cost of restoration. The Tribunal held that the cost of restoration, rather than the difference in value before and after the injury, is the appropriate measure of damage in the case. In part, the Tribunal returned to the lack of market value in finding it not an appropriate measure of damage. In addition, the Tribunal relied upon earlier cases where restoration was deemed appropriate if 'there is a personal reason for the cost of repair'. Relying on an expert, the Tribunal found that land is a part of the identity of the people in question and deeply embedded in a particular parcel of land on a particular atoll. Land is valued because it is scarce, but also because it represents ancestral collective labor over generations.

The Tribunal gave attention to the question of what radiation standard should apply to restoration with reference to the position of the IAEA calling for non-discrimination: 'As a basic principle, policies and criteria for radiation protection of populations outside national borders from releases of radioactive substances should be at least as stringent as those for the population within the country of release'.[255] Using this standard, the Tribunal adopted the United States Environmental Protection Agency standard of 15 millirem per year effective dose equivalent as the maximum dose limit for humans. It then analyzed the soil and food intake of the area. The parties were in relatively close agreement on the results, but presented alternative approaches on how to meet the standard, ranging from removal of contaminated soil, application of potassium to the soil to reduce plant uptake, to phytoremediation (using plants to strip radioactive contaminants from the soil). The Tribunal rejected the last because its application to cleanup radioactive contaminants has not been demonstrated in the environment of a coral atoll and no basis exists for estimating the costs. While potassium works to limit cesium uptake, it does not work at higher concentrations. In the end, the Tribunal found soil removal, despite the attendant ecological disruption, a necessary component of the cleanup. Taking these two elements together, as well as the material costs of

255 ibid 1220.

radiological surveys, contaminated soil disposal through causeway construction,[256] and soil rehabilitation and revegetation, the Tribunal came to a total restoration cost of $101,710,000, from which was deducted $10,000,000 as the amount in the Enjebi Trust Fund.

A final element in the damages claim filed by the People of Enewetak concerned the hardship of relocation in especially bleak conditions, particularly from the early 1950s to the 1970s. Testimony reported famine, near starvation and death from illness, including polio and measles epidemics, food shortages and environmental limitations, including a rat infestation. The Nuclear Claims Tribunal took into account the maximum award for a claimant under its personal injury program, determined the appropriate annual amount for the period of greatest suffering ($4500) and for the later period ($3000), acknowledging both to be somewhat arbitrary and inadequate. Based upon the annual population figures for the thirty-three years between 1947 and 1980, the damages for the relocation hardships were deemed to total $34,084,500. In all, the Tribunal determined the amount of compensation due the People of Enewetak to be $324,949,311.

Through Security Council action, the United Nations created the United Nations Compensation Commission (UNCC) to provide reparations for environmental and other harm caused by Iraq's invasion of Kuwait in 1991. The Security Council made clear Iraq's state responsibility for the environmental harm.[257] The work of the UNCC is discussed in Chapter 16.

In 2018, the ICJ rendered its first environmental compensation award under the international law of state responsibility in the case *Certain Activities Carried Out by Nicaragua In the Border Area*.[258] The case arose from a territorial dispute between Costa Rica and Nicaragua over a 3-kilometer wetland area bordering two countries. In 2010, Costa Rica initiated proceedings before the ICJ against Nicaragua for unlawful incursion, occupation, and use of Costa Rican territory, including environmental damage resulting from the excavation by Nicaragua of a channel for navigational purposes in the disputed area.[259] Nicaragua also

256 The Tribunal considered other alternatives, including dumping in the Marianas Trench and shipping the soil to Nevada for storage. It chose the causeway alternative as one that would enhance the productivity of the community and more fully protect the residents than other local disposal alternatives. Off-site dumping was rejected for legal and political reasons.

257 UNSC, Resolution 687 (1991) of April 3, 1991 (1991) UN Doc S/RES/687.

258 *Certain Activities carried out by Nicaragua in the Border Area* (*Costa Rica v. Nicaragua*) and *Construction of a Road in Costa Rica along the San Juan River* (*Nicaragua v. Costa Rica*), Judgement [2015] ICJ Rep 665.

259 ibid 66.

brought proceedings against Costa Rica for violations of its sovereignty and environmental damage caused by the construction of a road along the disputed area.[260] The ICJ joined the two cases in 2013 and rendered its judgment on the territorial dispute in 2015 in favor of Costa Rica, resulting in Nicaragua's obligation to provide reparation for the damage caused by the violation of its international obligations. The failure of the parties to agree on compensation within the time limit set by the Court led to the institution of new proceedings before the ICJ for compensation. Costa Rica claimed compensation for quantifiable environmental damages caused by Nicaragua through the excavation of channels, as well as for the costs and expenses incurred due to Nicaragua's activities. On the other hand, Nicaragua argued that Costa Rica was only entitled to 'material damages', which included damage to property or other interests of Costa Rica that could be assessed in financial terms.[261] In its judgment on compensation, the ICJ began by recalling the well-established principle of state responsibility according to which the breach of an international obligations gives rise to an obligation to make reparation in an adequate form.[262] Importantly, the Court provided that 'damage to the environment, and the consequent impairment or loss of the ability of the environment to provide goods and services, is compensable under international law. Such compensation may include indemnification for the impairment or loss of environmental goods and services in the period prior to recovery and payment for the restoration of the damaged environment'.[263] Through this statement, the Court clearly indicated that the compensable damage to the environment includes both direct and indirect services rendered by the ecosystem. To evaluate the scope of the compensable damage, the two parties relied on different methodologies, with Costa Rica using the 'ecosystem services approach' and Nicaragua referring to the 'replacement value' of the lost environmental services.[264] The Court noted that international law does not prescribe any specific method of valuation for the compensation of environmental damage and stressed the importance of taking into account the specific circumstances of each case.[265] Therefore, rather than choosing between these two methodologies proposed by the parties, the Court borrowed elements from both approaches

260 ibid 145.

261 *Certain Activities carried out by Nicaragua in the Border Area* (*Costa Rica v. Nicaragua*), *Compensation owed by the Republic of Nicaragua to the Republic of Costa Rica* [2018], paras. 36 and 37.

262 ibid 29.

263 ibid 42.

264 ibid 44–51.

265 ibid 52.

and developed its own approach. In the present case, the Court considered it 'appropriate to approach the valuation of environmental damage from the perspective of the ecosystem as a whole, by adopting an overall assessment of the impairment or loss of environmental goods or services prior to recovery, rather than attributing values to specific categories of environmental goods and services and estimating recovery periods for each of them'.[266] Based on this overall valuation approach, taking into account the removal of trees, wetlands, and the capacity of the area for natural regeneration,[267] the Court awarded US$120,000.00 for the impairment or loss of environmental goods and services of the disputed area.[268] This case is notable for explicitly recognizing that environmental damage, including ecosystem services, is compensable under the international law of state responsibility and for discussing the challenges of valuing environmental damage. With respect to the latter, the Court insisted on the importance of the special circumstances of each case and developed an 'overall assessment' approach. However, the description of this approach in broad terms has left a certain ambiguity with regard to the valuation methodologies for environmental damage.

Thus, despite the reluctance of states generally to demand or accept statements of responsibility, they clearly do pay compensation for damage caused, although they avoid or sometimes deliberately exclude admissions of responsibility, at least on the inter-state level. A much more common technique in international environmental law is for states to agree to transfer the problem of compensation to the private international law realm of civil actions. In other words, international state responsibility is replaced by direct compensation between polluter and victim. UNCLOS Article 235 characterizes this approach:

1. 'States are responsible for the fulfillment of their international obligations concerning the protection and preservation of the marine environment. They shall be liable in accordance with international law.
2. States shall ensure that recourse is available in accordance with their legal systems for prompt and adequate compensation or other relief in respect of damage caused by pollution of the marine environment by natural or juridical persons under their jurisdiction.
3. With the objective of assuring prompt and adequate compensation in respect of all damage caused by pollution of the marine environment, States shall cooperate in the implementation of existing international law and the further development of international law relating to

266 ibid 78.
267 ibid 78–85.
268 ibid 157.

> responsibility and liability for the assessment of and compensation for damage and the settlement of related disputes, as well as, where appropriate, development of criteria and procedures for payment of adequate compensation, such as compulsory insurance or compensation funds'.

After affirming the principle of responsibility, this provision orients states towards civil liability in private international law, while encouraging them to find the means to assure compensation for victims.

3.3 *State Liability for Injurious Consequences of Lawful Acts*

The Convention on International Liability for Damage Caused by Space Objects is one of the few treaties to establish a clear rule of state liability without fault. Subject to exceptions set out in Arts. VI and VII, a state which launches a space object is 'absolutely liable to pay compensation for damage caused by its space object on the surface of the earth or to aircraft in flight'.[269] Damage is defined as 'loss of life, personal injury or other impairment of health; or loss of or damage to property of states or of persons, natural or judicial, or property of international intergovernmental organizations'.[270] The definition is broad enough to include claims for harm to the environment. Canada presented a claim under the Convention in 1979 to the former USSR for damage caused by the crash of Cosmos 954, a nuclear-powered satellite which disintegrated over Canada. Canada claimed that:

> 'The principle of absolute liability applies to fields of activities having in common a high degree of risk. It is repeated in numerous international agreements and is one of the general principles of international law recognized by civilized nations. ... Accordingly, this principle has been accepted as a general principle of international law'.[271]

The claim exceeded $6 million, covering costs of restoring Canadian territory, to the extent possible, to the condition which would have existed if the intrusion had not occurred. The matter was settled in 1981 when the USSR agreed to pay $3 million in full and final compensation.

Since 1978, the ILC has considered the topic of international liability for injurious consequences arising out of acts not prohibited by international

---

269 March 29, 1972, art II.

270 ibid, art I(a).

271 18 ILM 907, para 22.

law.[272] It originated in the discussions on state responsibility. In 1994–95, the Commission provisionally adopted several Articles on first reading. In 1996 a new Working Group submitted draft Articles containing a complete discussion on prevention and liability for compensation or other relief. In 1997, the ILC decided to divide the matter into two topics, prevention and liability, and to first concentrate on prevention. The Third Report of the Special Rapporteur, delivered in May 2000, contained revised draft Articles on prevention. In 2001, the ILC adopted on second reading the draft Articles on prevention of transboundary harm from hazardous activities and recommended that the entire topic be drafted in the form of a framework convention.[273] It submitted the Articles on prevention, recommended them to the General Assembly for consideration, and resumed its work on the international liability in the case of transboundary harm arising out of hazardous activities. In 2006, the ILC adopted on second reading the draft principles on the allocation of loss in the case of transboundary harm arising out of hazardous activities, with commentaries.[274] Since 2006, the UN General Assembly has adopted multiple resolutions commending the draft Articles on prevention and the draft principles on allocation of loss to the attention of governments and inviting governments to submit comments on any future action. The ILC's draft Articles on prevention describe 'prevention' in its draft Article 3 as an obligation of due diligence, that is, as conduct that is appropriate and proportional to the degree of risk of transboundary harm in any particular instance. The state must inform itself of factual and legal elements that relate in a foreseeable manner to the contemplated procedure and must take appropriate responsive measures in a timely fashion. While economic capacity may be taken into account in determining the level of diligence that is due, it cannot exempt a state from its obligations entirely. Activities within the territory of a state must be monitored and a necessary degree of vigilance and infrastructure must obtain. The operator of

272 *International Liability for Injurious Consequences Arising from Activities Not Prohibited by International Law, First Report on a Legal Regime for Allocation of Loss in Case of Transboundary Harm Arising out of Hazardous Activities*, by Mr. Pemmaraju Sreenivasa Rao, Special Rapporteur, A/CN.4/531, March 21, 2003, Int'l L. Commn, 55th Sess 2003 [hereafter the Rao Report]. The first special rapporteur saw the issue as one of developing principles of prevention as part of due diligence, but also of providing for a regime of compensation based on equitable principles. See *Preliminary Report on Liability*, YBILC, 1980, vol. II (Part One), UN Doc A/CN.4/334 (1980); *Second Report on Liability*, YBILC, 1981, vol. II (Part One), UN Doc A/CN.4/346; *Third Report on Liability*, YBILC, 1982, vol. II (Part One), UN Doc A/CN.4/360.

273 Y.B.Int'l L.Comm'n (2001), II-2, UN Doc A/56/10, paras. 91, 92, 94, 97 and 98.

274 Y.B.Int'l L.Comm'n (2006), II-2, UN Doc A/61/10.

an activity is expected to bear the cost of prevention to the extent that he is responsible for the operation.

The obligations of the state of operation are set forth in draft Articles 6 to 11. First, the state must authorize any hazardous activity prior to its commencement. The authorization should be based on a prior assessment of the risk involved. If the consequences could involve significant transboundary harm, the state of origin is required to provide notification and information to states likely to be affected. Draft Articles 9 to 13 provide for discussions between the state of origin and the states likely to be affected. The result could be conditions imposed on the activity or joint management of the risk and the project itself. Draft Article 13 provides for an obligation to inform the population likely to be exposed to the risk involved and to ascertain their views, without regard to boundaries. Draft Article 15 requires protection or other appropriate redress to all persons in accordance with the judicial or other procedures and the legal system of the state of origin, without discrimination on the basis of nationality or residence or place of injury. Draft Article 19 provides for compulsory fact-finding in case of a dispute between the states concerned, in the absence of another applicable mechanism of peaceful dispute settlement. For the most part, the Articles are considered progressive development of international law rather than a codification of existing norms.

On the issue of liability, the approach approved by the ILC Working Group in 2002 proceeds on the basis that the issue is one of allocation of loss, not liability in the sense of state responsibility for wrongdoing. It thus separates the issue of compensation from the fields of torts and strict liability. To delimit the scope of the topic, the ILC has agreed to define transboundary damage as involving three criteria: (1) activities must take place in the territory or control or jurisdiction of the source state (thus leaving out the global commons); (2) they must have a risk of causing significant transboundary harm; (3) harm must be caused by the 'physical consequences' of such activities or be determinable by clear direct physical effect and causal connection between the activity and the harm or injury suffered (leaves aside pollution not attributable to any one source or that emerges gradually). The requirement of significant harm was seen by the ILC as reflecting state practice; because the activities are lawful, they are not subject to the requirement in the law of state responsibility of cessation or restitution. 'Significant' harm is seen as being more than detectable and appreciable, but less than serious or substantial. Such harm must be measurable by factual and objective standards.[275]

---

275 *Rao Report* para 31.

The ILC 1996 Working Group agreed on three broad policy considerations for liability: (a) each state must have as much freedom of choice within its territory as is compatible with the rights and interests of other States; (b) the protection of such rights and interests requires the adoption of measures of prevention and if injury nevertheless occurs, measures of reparations; and (c) the innocent victim should not be left to bear his or her loss or injury.[276] On the third point, the ILC recognizes that full and complete compensation may not be possible in every case because of lack of proof of loss, limits to the definition of damage or other limitations. The major objectives are to provide incentives to prevent harm through requiring the operator to bear the loss in case of harm resulting from hazardous activities, to compensate damage caused to a victim; and to internalize all the environmental costs. Treaties so far reflect the view that the direct accountability of the polluter in national law is the best means of compensating for loss.

The ILC's draft principles on the allocation of loss in the case of transboundary harm arising out of hazardous activities adopted in 2006 aim to ensure prompt and adequate compensation to victims of transboundary damage as well as preserve and protect the environment in the event of transboundary damage.[277] For these purposes, draft principle 4 provides for the obligation of states to impose liability for transboundary damage caused by hazardous activities located within its territory or otherwise under its jurisdiction or control on the operator of the activity, without requiring proof of fault. Draft principle 5 lays down response measures to be taken by states upon the occurrence of an incident involving a hazardous activity which results or is likely to result in transboundary damage, such as notifying all states affected or likely to be affected of the incident and the possible effects of the transboundary damage and cooperating with them to mitigate the effects of transboundary damage and if possible, eliminate them. Under draft principle 6, states must make prompt, adequate and effective remedies available at the domestic level in the event of transboundary damage caused by hazardous activities and must ensure that victims have access to these remedies. Draft principle 7 encourages states to take all efforts to conclude global, regional, or bilateral agreements in respect of particular categories of hazardous activities where these agreements would provide effective arrangements concerning compensation, response measures and international and domestic remedies.

Finally, it is necessary to mention the problem of abatement. One of the requirements arising from breach of a rule of international environmental law

276 ibid 43.

277 Y.B.Int'l L.Comm'n (2006), II-2, UN Doc A/61/10, principle 3.

is that the activity causing environmental harm should cease. Lawful activities may continue, however, even if they cause harm, because their benefits outweigh the risks of harm.[278] In such a case, compensation still must be provided to the victims of any substantial harm that occurs.[279] The risk-creating conduct is permitted, but the victim does not bear the burden of the injury which results. Instead, a social responsibility is imposed upon the actor to compensate the victims for harm which occurs even though the activity is legal.

4 International Dispute Settlement Procedures

Disputes over alleged breaches of international environmental norms may be settled through a variety of mechanisms, including mediation, arbitration, and judicial proceedings. Although recourse to formal procedures is not common, it appears to be increasing, perhaps reflecting a maturation of the normative framework.

4.1 *Arbitration*

While there are some early arbitrations involving environmental questions, most notably the *Trail Smelter* case,[280] there are also a few modern arbitrations. In 1986, France and New Zealand asked the Secretary General of the United Nations to act as an arbitrator in the *Rainbow Warrior Case*,[281] but the case concerned the French sinking of the Greenpeace vessel in Auckland Harbour and the future of the two French intelligence agents who were serving prison sentences in New Zealand for carrying out the action. Underlying issues about the environmental consequences of French nuclear testing was not in issue. A number inter-state arbitration awards involve claims of harms caused to the marine environment, including the 1999 the *Eritrea/Yemen* case and the 2007

278 See *e.g.* Agreement Concerning Frontier Rivers between Finland and Sweden (September 16, 1971), 825 UNTS 191, 282: 'Where the construction would result in a substantial deterioration in the living conditions of the population or cause a permanent change in natural conditions such as might entail substantially diminished comfort for people living in the vicinity or a significant nature conservancy loss or where significant public interests would be otherwise prejudiced, the construction shall be permitted only if it is of particular importance for the economy or for the locality or from some other public standpoint'. Chapter III, art 3(2).

279 See art 11, *Environmental Protection and Sustainable Development: Legal Principles and Recommendations*, (1986).

280 Arbitral Award in the *Trail Smelter Case*, (March 11, 1941), 3 U.N.R.I.A.A. 1905, 1965.

281 See *Ruling Pertaining to the Differences between France and New Zealand Arising from the Rainbow Warrior Affair* (1986), 74 Int'l L. Rep 241, 81 AJIL 325 (1987), 26 ILM 1346.

Guyana v. Suriname case.[282] In the 2005 *Iron Rhine* arbitration award, the arbitration tribunal discussed the sources of international environmental law and held that ICJ case law and Article 31(3)(c) of the 1969 Vienna Convention on the Law of Treaties support the proposition that 'an evolutive interpretation, which would ensure any application of the treaty that would be effective in terms of its object and purpose, will be preferred to a strict application of the intertemporal rule'.[283] This reasoning is consistent with the approach taken by the Court of Arbitration, in the 2013 *Kishenganga* case, concerning a dispute between India and Pakistan on a hydroelectric project. In its 2013 award, the Court of Arbitration held that: 'It is established that principles of international environmental law must be taken into account even when (unlike the present case) interpreting treaties concluded before the development of that body of law'.[284] Importantly, the 2016 *South China Sea* award[285] clarified the interpretation of marine protection obligations under UNCLOS. The dispute arose between China and the Philippines with respect to several issues in South China Sea, including claims of harms caused to the marine environment by China's construction activities and fishing practices. In its award, the arbitration tribunal interpreted the general obligation to protect and preserve the marine environment in Article 192 of UNCLOS in light of the 'corpus of international law relating to the environment' and noted that it includes a 'due diligence obligation to prevent the harvesting of species that are recognized internationally as being at risk of extinction and requiring international protection'.[286] Procedurally, the *South China Sea* arbitration is also notable for having appointed experts to provide an independent opinion on environmental damages. This practice might inform future international environmental disputes, where scientific evidence is of special importance.[287]

---

282 *Agreement to Arbitrate Dated October 3, 1996 between Eritrea and Yemen*, PCA Case No. 1996–04, Award of the Arbitral Tribunal in the Second Stage (Maritime Delimitation) (December 17, 1999); *Guyana v. Suriname*, PCA Case No. 2004–04, Award (September 17, 2007).

283 *Arbitration Regarding the Iron Rhine Railway* (Belgium/Netherlands), PCA Case No. 2003–02, Award (May 24, 2005) para. 58; May 23, 1969; ibid, para. 80.

284 *Indus Waters Kishenganga Arbitration* (Pakistan v. India), PCA Case No. 2011–01, Partial Award (February 18, 2013) para. 452.

285 *South China Sea Arbitration* (Philippines v. China), PCA Case No. 2013–19, Award (July 12, 2016).

286 ibid, paras 941, 956.

287 See further Yoshifumi Tanaka, 'The South China Sea Arbitration: Environmental Obligations under the Law of the Sea Convention' (2018) *Review of European, Comparative & International Environmental Law* 27, 90.

In 2001, the Permanent Court of Arbitration (PCA) adopted by consensus Optional Rules for Arbitration of Disputes Relating to Natural Resources and/or the Environment.[288] The Rules were adopted at an Extraordinary Meeting of the ninety-four member states of the PCA, based upon the UNCITRAL Arbitration Rules. The participants identified as a problem the absence of a unified forum where states, international organizations, non-governmental organizations, businesses, and other private parties could seek resolution of disputes over environmental protection or conservation of natural resources. According to the PCA, over half the inquiries made in 2001–2 concerned these issues. The Optional Rules for Arbitration of Disputes Relating to Natural Resources and/or the Environment are intended to govern disputes between all actors and to provide rapid expertise to resolve the dispute, because time may be of the essence. They provide for the establishment of a list of specialized arbitrators for environmental disputes, as well as for the optional use of a panel of expert arbitrators with legal background and a panel of environmental scientists who can provide technical assistance to the parties and the arbitral tribunal.[289]

4.2 *The International Court of Justice*

Agenda 21, Chapter 39.10 encourages states to have recourse to the ICJ to resolve environmental disputes.[290] The UN Charter gives the Court the power to decide cases that states submit to it, which could include environmental disputes.[291] Article 36(1) of the Statute of the ICJ confirms that the jurisdiction of the Court comprises, *inter alia*, all cases that the parties refer to it and all matters specially provided for in treaties and conventions in force. Several dozen multilateral environmental agreements contain provisions providing for the submission of disputes arising from their interpretation or application to the ICJ.[292]

The Court has indicated its readiness to accept environmental cases. In a statement to UNCED, Sir Robert Jennings, then President of the Court, declared that '[t]he function of the established "principal judicial organ of the United Nations" must include not only the settlement of disputes but also the scientific development of general international law'. He noted that international

288 June 19, 2001, 40 ILM 202 (2001), also available at http://www.pca-cpa.org.

289 ibid, art 8; ibid, art 27. The current lists of specialized arbitrators and specialized experts for environmental disputes are available on the website of the PCA, at https://pca-cpa.org/en/about/panels/panels-of-arbitrators-and-experts-for-environmental-disputes/.

290 Rio, 'Agenda 21' (Rio de Janerio, June 3–14, 1992).

291 United Nations Charter (June 26, 1945); arts 33(1) and 36(3).

292 For the list of treaties and other instruments notified to the ICJ's Registry which contain clauses relating to the jurisdiction to the ICJ, see ICJ, 'Treaties', https://icj-cij.org/treaties.

environmental law constitutes a new field of law and 'that new international law for the protection of the environment needs urgently to be developed cannot be a matter of doubt'.[293] Another expression of the ICJ's willingness to address the environmental aspects of international law was its decision to establish a seven-member chamber for environmental matters, whose first members were elected in July 1993.

While the Chamber for Environmental Matters has not been used to date and is no longer an active chamber of the ICJ,[294] the ICJ received several submissions in the past decades concerning environmental protection. Three of these cases concerned the impact of nuclear weapons or weapons testing on the environment and are discussed in Chapter XIV. The case *Certain Activities Carried Out By Nicaragua In the Border Area* was analyzed in Section C.2.f of Chapter VII with respect to reparation under state responsibility and is further discussed in Chapter X. The five following cases raised more general issues of environmental harm.

In the *Case of Certain Phosphate Lands in Nauru (Nauru v. Australia)*, Nauru filed its application in 1989 asserting Australian governmental liability for environmental damages permitted to occur while Australia governed the island of Nauru. The application requested that Australia be directed to pay compensation for the rehabilitation of lands which were severely degraded through phosphate mining prior to Nauru's independence in 1968, for the artificially low royalties paid by the mining consortium, and for 'aggravated or moral damages'. Nauru asserted that a general principle of international law obligates a state administering a Territory to not bring about changes in the condition of the Territory that will cause irreparable damage to, or substantially prejudice, the existing or contingent interest of another state in respect to that territory. In a judgment of June 26, 1992, the Court accepted jurisdiction over the case even though the environmental damages claimed in the case occurred over a period of seventy years prior to 1968. The case was subsequently settled by the parties, with the payment of substantial damages by Australia, and removed from the Court's docket.

In the most significant environmental matter, the *Gabčíkovo-Nagymaros Project* case,[295] the ICJ developed important environmental concepts and

293 Speech by Sir Robert Jennings, President of the International Court of Justice to the UN General Assembly (October 15, 1993).

294 The Chamber for Environmental Matters is no longer in operation following the decision of the ICJ not to hold elections for the Chamber for Environmental Matters in 2006 due to the lack of requests for the Chamber to handle a case since its establishment.

295 *Gabčíkovo-Nagymaros Project (Hungary/Slovakia)*, Judgment, Merits, [1997] ICJ Rep 7.

norms. In particular, the Court recognized the fundamental importance of environmental protection in the modern world. In both the *Nuclear Weapons Advisory Opinion* and in the *Gabčíkovo* case, the Court declared that the environment is not an abstraction, but represents the living space, the quality of life and the very health of human beings. As a consequence, the Court found that states have the obligation to respect and protect the natural environment.[296] In this regard, the Court recognized the temporal dimension inherent in environmental protection:

> Throughout the ages, mankind has, for economic and other reasons, constantly interfered with nature. In the past, this was often done without consideration of the effects upon the environment. Owing to new scientific awareness and a growing awareness of the risks for mankind – for present and future generations – of pursuit of such interventions at an unconsidered and unabated pace, new norms and standards have been developed, set forth in a great number of instruments during the last two decades. Such new norms have to be taken into consideration, and such new standards given proper weight, not only when States contemplated new activities but also when continuing with activities in the past.[297]

This statement articulates the guiding principle that past and present activities should be governed by evolving international legal norms.[298] Among the norms and principles that the Court applied are the needs or rights of future generations.[299] Judge Weeramantry reminds readers in his separate opinion in the *Gabčíkovo* case that the rights of future generations have woven themselves into international law through major treaties, through juridical opinions, and through general principles of law recognized by civilized nations.[300] The Court also makes it clear that the natural environment constitutes an 'essential interest' of each state.[301]

296 Order of 22 September 1995 in the *Request for an Examination of the Situation in Accordance with Paragraph 63 of the Court's Judgment of December 20, 1974 in the Nuclear Tests Case*, ICJ Reports 1995, 306, para 64.

297 *Gabçikovo* case para 140.

298 See also Vice-President Weeramantry's statement on the inter-temporal aspect of all treaties dealing with projects impacting on the environment, Separate opinion, 22.

299 *Gabçikovo* case para 29.

300 Diss Op, 17.

301 *Gabçikovo* case para 53.

On these bases, the Court reiterated the basic international law rule stemming from the Stockholm and Rio Declarations, announcing that the existence of a general obligation of states to ensure that activities within their jurisdiction and control respect the environment of other states or of areas beyond national control is now part of the corpus of international law relating to the environment.[302] Reinforcing this view, Judge Weeramantry stresses that customary international law prohibits environmental damage and requires continuing environmental impact assessment,[303] and application of the precautionary principle.[304] The Court itself expresses its understanding that in the field of environmental protection, vigilance and prevention are required on account of the often irreversible character of damage to the environment and of the limitations inherent in reparation of this type of damage.[305]

The ICJ also affirmed key customary rules international environmental law, in its judgement on the *Pulp Mills* case in 2010.[306] This case arose from a dispute over Uruguay's alleged unilateral authorization for the construction of two pulp mills on the River Uruguay, which, according to Argentina, was likely to impair water quality and cause significant transboundary damage, and was in contravention of the Statute of the River Uruguay between Argentina and Uruguay. The Court found that Uruguay had breached its procedural obligations to inform, notify, and negotiate under the Statute of the River Uruguay, but concluded that Argentina has not demonstrated that the industrial activities authorized by Uruguay had, or would have, an adverse impact on water quality or caused transboundary damage in contravention of Uruguay's substantive obligations under the Statute of the River Uruguay. In its judgement, the Court highlighted the due diligence aspects of the customary principle of prevention, noting that: 'A State is thus obliged to use all the means at its disposal in order to avoid activities which take place in its territory, or in any area under its jurisdiction, causing significant damage to the environment of another State'.[307] Importantly, the Court observed that the practice of conducting an environmental impact assessment had in recent years 'gained so much acceptance among States it may now be considered a requirement under general international law to undertake an environmental impact assessment where there is a risk that the proposed industrial activity

302 Advisory Opinion para 29.
303 Diss Op, 49–52; Sep Opinion, 20.
304 Diss Op, 50–52.
305 *Gabçikovo* case para 140.
306 *Pulp Mills on the River Uruguay (Argentina v Uruguay)*, Judgment, [2010] ICJ Rep 2010, 14.
307 ibid 101.

may have a significant adverse impact in a transboundary context, in particular, on a shared resource'.[308] With respect to reparation, the Court recalled the customary international law rule that 'where restitution is materially impossible or involves a burden out of all proportion to the benefit deriving from it, reparation takes the form of compensation or satisfaction, or even both'.[309]

In the *Aerial Herbicide Spraying* case, Ecuador alleged that Colombia had sprayed toxic herbicides at locations near, at, and across the border with Ecuador, which caused serious damage to people, to crops, to animals, and to the natural environment on the Ecuadorian side of the frontier, and poses a grave risk of further damage over time. This case was discontinued in 2013 pursuant to an agreement between the Parties to establish an exclusion zone where Colombia would not conduct aerial spraying operations and created a Joint Commission to ensure that spraying operations outside that zone had not caused herbicides to drift into Ecuador.[310]

In *Whaling in the Antarctic*,[311] Australia contended that Japan's continued pursuit of a large-scale program of whaling by Japan breached its obligations under the International Convention for the Regulation of Whaling ('Whaling Convention') and other international obligations for the preservation of marine mammals and the marine environment. Article VIII(1) of the Whaling Convention authorizes whaling under certain conditions for the purposes of scientific research. The ICJ found that the evidence did not establish that the special permits granted by Japan for the killing, taking, and treatment of whales as part of its whaling program were 'for the purposes of scientific research'. As a result, the Court declared that Japan had breached certain of its international obligations and ordered it to revoke any authorization, permit or license to kill, or take or treat whales in relation to its whaling program, and to refrain from granting any further permits.

States could more frequently avail themselves of the opportunities which they have created to submit environmental disputes to the ICJ. It can be concluded that the Court has applied the terms of the declaration made by its President, Sir Robert Jennings, at the Conference of Rio de Janeiro, by contributing to the development of international environmental law, as often as it

308 ibid 204.

309 ibid 273.

310 *Case concerning Aerial Herbicide Spraying* (*Ecuador v. Colombia*), Order (September 13, 2013), ICJ Rep 2013, 278.

311 *Whaling in the Antarctic* (*Australia v. Japan: New Zealand intervening*), Judgement (March 31, 2014), ICJ Rep 2014, 226.

had been given the possibility to do so.[312] This trend is also visible in the advisory role of the ICJ. Pursuant to a resolution adopted by consensus by the UN General Assembly requesting an Advisory Opinion, the ICJ has been invited to clarify the international obligations of states with respect to climate change.[313] As of May 2024, these proceedings remain pending before the Court.

4.3 *The Law of the Sea Tribunal*

UNCLOS proceeds from the basic principle that the states parties shall settle any dispute between them concerning its interpretation or application by peaceful means in accordance with the United Nations Charter and should proceed expeditiously to an exchange of views on the means of settlement to be adopted.[314] States may make a written declaration accepting to refer disputes to one or more of the following tribunals: the International Tribunal for the Law of the Sea, the ICJ, an arbitral tribunal, or a special arbitral tribunal, the last two constituted in accordance with UNCLOS. Where both parties have accepted the same procedure, that procedure is to be used, otherwise arbitration will be applied.[315]

Special arbitration is one of the binding methods of dispute that can be accepted in advance by declaration and may be chosen whenever a technical issue arises for which specialist qualifications may be necessary. Annex VIII of UNCLOS establishes that this procedure may be used for fisheries, the marine environment, scientific research, vessel source pollution or dumping. Lists of experts in each of the four fields are to be maintained by the FAO, UNEP, the Inter-Governmental Oceanographic Commission, and the International Maritime Organization. Each state may nominate two experts from the list 'whose competence in the legal, scientific or technical aspects' is established and who enjoy the highest reputation for fairness and integrity.[316]

The International Tribunal for the Law of the Sea (ITLOS) is one of the judicial bodies designated by UNCLOS among the 'compulsory procedures entailing binding decisions' in disputes over the interpretation or application of the Convention.[317] The Tribunal, whose seat is in Hamburg, has twenty-one

312 Speech by Sir Robert Jennings, President of the International Court of Justice to the UN General Assembly (October 15, 1993).
313 UN General Assembly, 'Request for an advisory opinion of the International Court of Justice on the obligations of States in respect of climate change', UN Doc A/77/L.58 (March 29, 2023).
314 UNCLOS, art 283(1).
315 ibid, art 287.
316 ibid, Annex VIII, art 3.
317 ibid, art 287.

members elected for a nine-year term. Its members are 'persons enjoying the highest reputation for fairness and integrity and of recognized competence in the field of the law of the sea'.[318] The Tribunal has jurisdiction where two states to a dispute have recognized its competence, when any agreement so provides, or when all the parties to any treaty in force concerning the law of the sea agree to refer.[319] It is open to international organizations in certain circumstances and to states which are not parties to UNCLOS.[320] A Sea-Bed Disputes Chamber of eleven members is established within the Tribunal.[321] Its jurisdiction covers disputes between states, between a state and the Authority, between the Authority and a prospective contractor; and between parties to a contract, including state enterprises and natural or juridical persons.[322]

The Law of the Sea Tribunal has broad jurisdiction. Article 288 of UNCLOS provides for the reference of disputes concerning the interpretation or application of the UNCLOS and any international agreement 'related to the purposes' of the UNCLOS, except that disputes involving coastal states' rights over marine research and fisheries shall be submitted to conciliation.[323] One important function of the Tribunal is to settle disputes between states parties regarding the environmental protection provisions of UNCLOS. One of the disputes that may be submitted to the Tribunal is when 'it is alleged that a coastal state has acted in contravention of specified international rules and standards for the protection or preservation of the marine environment which are applicable to the coastal state and which have been established by (or in accordance with) this Convention …'.[324]

Article 289 of UNCLOS allows the appointment of scientific or technical experts and, in accordance with Article 290, the Tribunal may prescribe provisional measures upon request of a party to a dispute. An admissibility provision allows the Tribunal to determine whether a *prima facie* case is set out or whether the case should be immediately dismissed as frivolous. Exhaustion of local remedies is a condition of admissibility for certain claims.

Several contentious environmental claims have been submitted to ITLOS, with many early cases highlighting the problem of overlapping jurisdictions between UNCLOS and regional marine or environmental agreements. For

318 ibid, Annex VI (Statute of the International Tribunal for the Law of the Sea) art 2(1).
319 ibid, art 24.
320 ibid, art 20(2).
321 ibid, art 36.
322 ibid, art 37.
323 See A.O. Adede, *Settlement of Disputes arising under the Law of the Sea Convention*, 69 AJIL 798 (1975).
324 UNCLOS, art 297.

example, the *Southern Bluefin Tuna Case* between Australia and New Zealand against Japan was brought before an Arbitral Tribunal constituted under Annex VII of UNCLOS.[325] Japan objected to the jurisdiction of ITLOS and the Arbitral Panel, but in an Order of August 27, 1999, ITLOS found that the Arbitral Tribunal had *prima facie* jurisdiction and prescribed certain provisional measures.

Southern Bluefin Tuna (SBT) is a migratory species of pelagic fish listed in UNCLOS Annex I. The main market is Japan where the fish is used for sashimi. By the early 1980s, the fish stock was overexploited and Australia, Japan, and New Zealand agreed in 1982 to set a total annual catch, with national allocations. In 1993, the three countries concluded the Convention for the Conservation of Southern Bluefin Tuna,[326] which purpose is to ensure the conservation and optimum utilization of the species, and under which a Commission for the Conservation of Southern Bluefin Tuna was established. Article 4 of the Convention provided that 'nothing in this Convention nor any measures adopted pursuant to it shall be deemed to prejudice the positions or views of any Party with respect to its rights and obligations under treaties and other international agreements to which it is party or its positions or views with respect to the law of the sea'.

As early as 1994, Japan sought to introduce an Experimental Fishing Program (EFP) whereby it would fish for SBT in areas where they were no longer fished, in order to study the status of the stock. By 1998, the Commission was unable to agree on any total allowable catch. That year, Japan announced it would adhere to its quota, but would begin a unilateral three-year EFP in the summer. Urgent consultations among the Parties failed to resolve disagreements over the EFP and Japan continued its unilateral program.

In filing their claims under UNCLOS, Australia and New Zealand invoked UNCLOS Articles 64 and 116–119. They argued that Japan is obliged as a distant water state to cooperate with them, as coastal states, in the conservation of SBT. The 1993 Convention implements the obligations of UNCLOS, but does not override it. Japan argued that the 1993 Convention is the basis of the claim and hence the Arbitral Tribunal has no jurisdiction. ITLOS found that the provisions of UNCLOS appeared to provide a basis for jurisdiction and the existence of the 1993 Convention does not preclude recourse to UNCLOS dispute settlement procedures.

---

325 Arbitral Tribunal, *Australia and New Zealand v. Japan,* (*Award on Jurisdiction and Admissibility*) (August 4, 2000) (hereinafter *Southern Bluefin Tuna Case*).

326 Convention for the Conservation of Southern Bluefin Tuna (Canberra, May 10, 1993) 1819 UNTS.

Subsequently, however, the Arbitral Tribunal found it clear that the most acute elements of the dispute between the parties turn on their inability to agree on a revised total allowable catch and the related conduct by Japan of unilateral experimental fishing in 1998 and 1999, as well as Japan's announced plans for such fishing thereafter. According to the Arbitral Tribunal: 'It is plain that all the main elements of the dispute between the Parties had been addressed within the CCSBT and that the contentions of the parties in respect of that dispute related to the implementation of their obligations under the 1993 Convention'.[327]

The Arbitral Tribunal indeed found no dispute over that fact, only over whether UNCLOS also applies. The Arbitral Tribunal accepted that *lex specialis* may govern general provisions of an antecedent treaty or statute, but also that more than one treaty may bear upon a particular dispute. Noting frequent parallelism, the Arbitral Tribunal says that a single act may violate more than one treaty. In sum, the Arbitral Tribunal found that while centered in the 1993 Convention, the dispute also arises under UNCLOS. In the end, however, UNCLOS itself returned the matter to the regional body because UNCLOS defers to other dispute settlement procedures agreed upon between parties to a dispute. Article 16 of the 1993 Convention contains such a procedure and thus removes the dispute from the reach of the UNCLOS compulsory procedures unless all parties agree. The Arbitral Tribunal noted the conclusion of many treaties post-UNCLOS that exclude unilateral reference of a dispute to compulsory adjudicative or arbitral procedures. However, it does not exclude the possibility that there might be instances in which the conduct of a State Party to UNCLOS and to a fisheries treaty implementing it would be so egregious, and risk consequences of such gravity, that a Tribunal might find that the obligations of UNCLOS provide a basis for jurisdiction, having particular regard to the provisions of Article 300 of UNCLOS, but this was not held to be that case.

The second environmental dispute before ITLOS resulted from authorization by the United Kingdom (UK) of a new facility to reprocess spent nuclear fuel into a new fuel, i.e. mixed oxide fuel (MOX), combining reprocessed plutonium and uranium. The Irish government protested that the plant would contribute to pollution of the Irish Sea and emphasized the potential risks involved in transporting radioactive material to and from the plant. On October 5, 2001, the government of Ireland requested the UK government to agree to submit the dispute to an arbitral tribunal established under Annex VIII of UNCLOS on special arbitration. Ireland in turn asked the Arbitral Tribunal to

327 *Southern Bluefin Tuna Case, para 31.*

declare that the UK has breached its obligations under Articles 192–3 and/or Article 194 and/or Article 207 and/or Articles 211 and 213 of UNCLOS in relation to the MOX plant, including by failing to take the necessary measures to prevent, reduce and control pollution of the marine environment from intended or accidental discharges of radioactive materials and or wastes from the plant and/or international movements of materials and wastes associated with the MOX plant, and/or discharges resulting from a terrorist act. Part of the allegations concerned the failure to undertake risk assessment and prepare a response strategy. With regard to the marine environment, Ireland asserted that the UK failed to undertake a proper environmental impact assessment or share information, but instead proceeded with authorization while the dispute on access to information was pending. Under Article 206 of UNCLOS, Ireland asserted that the UK 1993 Environmental Statement failed to properly assess the effects of the operation of the MOX plant on the marine environment of the Irish Sea and that the UK failed to take into consideration subsequent factual and legal developments.

The ITLOS delivered an Order respecting provisional measures in the *MOX Plant Case* (*Ireland v. United Kingdom*) on December 3, 2001.[328] The jurisdiction of ITLOS allows it to prescribe provisional measures if it considers them appropriate to 'preserve the respective rights of the parties to the dispute or to prevent serious harm to the marine environment', provided that it finds that the arbitral tribunal being constituted has *prima facie* jurisdiction and that the situation urgently requires the measures requested.[329] The ITLOS found that the dispute concerns the interpretation and application of UNCLOS, rejecting the UK's argument that the main elements of the dispute are governed by regional treaties. The ITLOS found, however, that the urgency of the situation did not require that provisional measures be issued prior to constitution of the arbitral tribunal.[330] Nevertheless, the ITLOS did consider that 'the duty to cooperate is a fundamental principle in the prevention of pollution of the marine environment under Part XII of the Convention and general international law and that rights arise therefrom which the ITLOS may find appropriate to preserve under Article 290 of the Convention'.[331] The ITLOS indicated that prudence and caution require Ireland and the UK to cooperate in exchanging information concerning risks or effects of the MOX plant's operations. The ITLOS thus unanimously issued provisional measures mandating cooperation between the two

328 41 ILM 405 (2002).

329 UNCLOS, art 290.

330 *MOX Plant Case* (*Ireland v. United Kingdom*) para 81.

331 ibid 82.

parties to exchange further information about the environmental consequences of the MOX plant, monitor risks, and devise measures to prevent pollution of the marine environment. All other requests for measures were denied.[332]

Once the Arbitral Tribunal was constituted, it had to consider whether it had jurisdiction not only *prima facie* but also in a definitive sense.[333] The UK raised two categories of objections to jurisdiction and admissibility. The first category concerned UNCLOS itself and other instruments invoked by Ireland such as the Convention for the Protection of the Marine Environment of the North-East Atlantic ('the OSPAR Convention').[334] The Tribunal rejected the UK's objections in this respect, finding that the OSPAR Convention did not cover the field as to invoke Articles 281 or 282 of UNCLOS which would have precluded the Tribunal's jurisdiction. The second category of the UK's objections concerned certain European Community law issues. The Tribunal found it unclear whether 'the provisions of the Convention on which Ireland relies are matters in relation to which competence has been transferred to the European Community and, indeed, whether the exclusive jurisdiction of the European Court of Justice, with regard to Ireland and the UK as Member States of the European Community, extended to the interpretation and application of the Convention as such and in its entirety'.[335] The Tribunal held that if this were the case, the jurisdiction of the Tribunal would be precluded by Article 282 of the Convention. The Tribunal recognized that these matters have to be determined within the institutional framework of the European Communities and therefore held that until these issues are definitely resolved, it could not firmly establish jurisdiction in respect of all or any of the claims of the dispute. The Arbitral Tribunal thus decided unanimously that further proceedings on jurisdiction and merits would be suspended until no later than December 1, 2003.

In addition to potentially competing jurisdiction under UNCLOS and Community law, Ireland also submitted the MOX dispute under the 1992 OSPAR Convention, the first case submitted pursuant to this treaty. Ireland asserted that the Convention guaranteed it access to information about the MOX plant and claimed that the UK had breached its obligations under Article 9 of the OSPAR Convention by refusing to disclose information from two reports

332 ibid 89. Text of the Order and opinions are available at www.itlos.org.

333 Arbitral Tribunal, *The MOX Plant Case (Ireland v. United Kingdom)*, Order n°3, Suspension of Proceedings on Jurisdiction and Merits and Request for Further Provisional Measures (June 24, 2003).

334 September 22, 1992.

335 Arbitral Tribunal, *The MOX Plant Case (Ireland v. United Kingdom)* (June 24, 2003) para 21.

prepared as part of the approval process for the MOX plant.[336] The UK argued that the information was deleted for reasons of commercial confidentiality. The Tribunal, in its final award, found by majority decision that Ireland's claim for information did not fall within Article 9(2) of the Convention.[337]

The Tribunal had to decide, *inter alia,* whether the reference of 'applicable international regulations' in Article 9(3) of the OSPAR Convention would include, as contended by Ireland, the Aarhus Convention on Access to Information, Public Participation in Decision-making and Access to Justice in Environmental Matters ('the Aarhus Convention', June 25, 1998) which neither Ireland nor the UK had ratified. By a majority, the Tribunal found that it could only consider current international law and practice insofar as such law and practice are admissible under Article 31 of the Vienna Convention and held that it could not apply the Aarhus Convention.[338]

On the OSPAR Convention itself, the UK argued that Article 9(1) did not establish a direct right to receive information but rather required Parties to establish a domestic framework for the disclosure of information. The UK asserted that Ireland therefore only had a cause of action for breach of Article 9 if the UK had failed to provide a regulatory framework for disclosure of information. The UK maintained that it had taken the required legislative and administrative measures. The Tribunal rejected the UK's arguments and found by majority that 'upon its proper construction Article 9(1) requires an outcome of result, namely that information falling within the meaning or Article 9(2) (and not excluded under Article 9(3)) is in fact disclosed in conformity with the Article 9 obligation imposed upon each Contracting Party'.[339]

---

336 The relevant sections of Article 9 of the OSPAR Convention read: '9.1. The Contracting Parties shall ensure that their competent authorities are required to make available the information described in paragraph 2 of this Article to any natural or legal person, in response to any reasonable request, without that person's having to prove an interest, without unreasonable charges, as soon as possible and at the latest within two months. 9.2. The information referred to in paragraph 1 of this Article is any available information in written, visual, aural or data base form on the state of the maritime area, on activities or measures adversely affecting or likely to affect it and on activities or measures introduced in accordance with the Convention. 9.3. The provision of this Article shall not affect the right of Contracting Parties, in accordance with their national legal systems and applicable international regulations, to provide for a request for such information to be refused where it affects: (d) commercial and industrial confidentiality'.

337 OSPAR Arbitral Tribunal, *Ireland v. United Kingdom, Dispute Concerning Access to Information Under Article 9 of the OSPAR Convention* (July 2, 2003).

338 ibid 104.

339 ibid 148.

The Tribunal rejected, however, Ireland's argument for a broad interpretation of Article 9(2) and held that information has to be related to the state of the maritime area, and, focusing on the second of the three categories of Article 9(2), further held that such information has to be on activities and measures 'adversely affecting or likely to affect' the maritime area. It found that Ireland had failed to demonstrate that the fourteen categories of information which it desired to obtain were 'information on the state of the maritime area' or on 'activities and measures adversely affecting or likely to affect it'.[340]

In addition to issuing decisions on contentious environmental cases, the ITLOS has made substantial contributions to international environmental law in its advisory role.

In 2011, the Seabed Disputes Chamber of ITLOS unanimously adopted an Advisory Opinion on the *Responsibilities and obligations of States sponsoring persons and entities with respect to activities in the Area.*[341] The opinion dealt with the conduct of activities in the seabed area beyond national jurisdiction (the 'Area'). In order to be eligible to carry out activities in the Area, it is required, under the Article 153(2) of UNCLOS, to be a national of a State Party (or effectively controlled by it or its nationals) and be sponsored by this state. According to the Seabed Disputes Chamber, the obligations of sponsoring states with respect to activities in the Area include an obligation of due diligence as well as direct obligations. First, the due diligence obligation to ensure that activities in the Area are carried out in conformity with Part XI of UNCLOS requires the sponsoring state to take 'reasonably appropriate' measures within its legal system to achieve this result.[342] The Seabed Disputes Chamber clarifies that the standard of due diligence may change over time, for instance in light of new scientific or technological knowledge, and that, as a consequence, a precautionary approach should be adopted as part of the obligation of due diligence.[343] Second, the direct obligations to be implemented by sponsoring states include, but are not limited to, applying a precautionary approach, applying best environmental practices, and conducting environmental impact assessments. The Seabed Disputes Chamber observed that: 'the precautionary approach has been incorporated into a growing number of international treaties and other instruments, many of which reflect the formulation of Principle 15 of the Rio Declaration', which has therefore 'initiated a trend towards

340 ibid 182.

341 *Responsibilities and obligations of States sponsoring persons and entities with respect to activities in the Area,* Advisory Opinion (February 1, 2011) ITLOS Rep 2011, 10.

342 ibid 110, 120.

343 ibid 117, 131.

making this approach part of customary international law'.[344] In addition, it stressed that the obligation to conduct an environmental impact assessment is a general obligation under customary international law.[345]

In 2013, the Permanent Secretary of the Sub-Regional Fisheries Commission (SRFC), a fisheries cooperation organization comprising seven West African states, requested an advisory opinion from the ITLOS on illegal fishing obligations. With regards to jurisdiction, Article 21 of the ITLOS Statute and Article 138 of the ITLOS Rules of Procedure respectively provide that the ITLOS has jurisdiction to hear 'all matters specifically provided for in any other agreement which confers jurisdiction on the Tribunal',[346] that it 'may give an advisory opinion on a legal question if an international agreement related to the purposes of the Convention specifically provides for the submission to the Tribunal of a request for such an opinion',[347] and that the 'request for an advisory opinion shall be transmitted to the Tribunal by whatever body is authorized by or in accordance with the agreement to make the request to the Tribunal'.[348] The ITLOS found that, in the present case, the Convention on the Determination of the Minimal Conditions for Access and Exploitation of Marine Resources within the Maritime Areas,[349] entered into by the seven member states of the SRFC, authorizes the Permanent Secretary of the SRFC to request an advisory opinion to the ITLOS and that the objective of this Convention is closely related to the purpose of UNCLOS.[350] The ITLOS concluded that it could hear the request submitted by the SRFC. With respect to substantive issues, ITLOS clarified the obligations of flag states concerning illegal, unreported, and unregulated fishing activities, and coastal states, with regards to certain fish stocks. Importantly, it held that while the coastal state has primary responsibility for taking the necessary measures with respect to illegal, unreported, and unregulated fishing, this does not relieve the flag state of its responsibility to ensure that vessels flying its flag do not conduct illegal, unreported, and unregulated fishing.[351] In particular, it noted that the responsibility of the flag state 'to ensure' constitutes

344 ibid 135.

345 ibid 145.

346 UNCLOS, Annex VI (Statute of the International Tribunal for the Law of the Sea), art 21.

347 ITLOS, Rules of the Tribunal (March 17, 2009), art 138(1).

348 ibid, art 138(2).

349 Convention on the Determination of the Minimal Conditions for Access and Exploitation of Marine Resources within the Maritime Areas under the Jurisdiction of the Member States of the Sub-Regional Fisheries Commission (June 8, 2012).

350 *Request for Advisory Opinion submitted by the Sub-Regional Fisheries Commission*, Advisory Opinion (April 2, 2015) ITLOS Rep 2015, 4, para 62.

351 ibid 124.

a due diligence obligation and that the liability of a flag state arises only if it fails to satisfy its due diligence obligations.[352] Lastly, the ITLOS clarified the various obligations of SRFC member states to ensure the sustainable management of shared fish stocks, and, in particular, observed that management measures should be based on the best scientific evidence available and, when such evidence is insufficient, the precautionary approach should be used.[353]

Informed by the findings of the ITLOS on jurisdiction in the above mentioned *SRFC* Advisory Opinion, the Commission of Small Island States (COSIS) submitted a request for an Advisory Opinion to the ITLOS in December 2022, on the basis of Article 21 of the ITLOS Statute and Article 138 of its Rules.[354] The Agreement establishing the COSIS provides for the competence of COSIS to request advisory opinions from the ITLOS 'on any question within the scope' of UNCLOS.[355] In its request, the COSIS asked ITLOS to clarify the specific obligations of State Parties to UNCLOS (a) to prevent, reduce and control pollution of the marine environment in relation to the deleterious effects that result or are likely to result from climate change; and (b) to protect and preserve the marine environment in relation to climate change impacts.[356]

In its unanimous Advisory Opinion of May 21, 2024, the Tribunal found that, *inter alia*, anthropogenic GHG emissions into the atmosphere constitute pollution of the marine environment within the meaning of Article 1(1)(4) of UNCLOS; under Article 194(1), States Parties have the specific obligations to take all necessary measures to prevent, reduce and control marine pollution from anthropogenic GHG emissions, taking into account the best available science and the global temperature goal contained in the UNFCCC and the Paris Agreement of limiting the temperature increase to 1.5 degrees Celsius above pre-industrial levels; Article 192 encompasses the specific obligation to protect and preserve the marine environment from climate change impacts and ocean acidification; and obligations under Article 192 are subject to a stringent standard of due diligence, given the high risks of serious and irreversible harm to the marine environment from these impacts and acidification. This Advisory Opinion clearly has the potential to have a significant impact on the implementation of environmental obligations under Part XII of UNCLOS, and will

352 ibid 125; ibid 146.

353 ibid 208.

354 COSIS, Request for Advisory Opinion (December 12, 2022).

355 Agreement for the establishment of the Commission of Small Island States on Climate Change and International Law (Edinburg, October 31, 2021), art 2(2).

356 COSIS, Request for Advisory Opinion (December 12, 2022).

likely inform parallel advisory proceedings ongoing before the ICJ on climate change obligations.

4.4 *World Trade Organization*

The Agreement Establishing the World Trade Organization came into force in January 1995 together with the Dispute Settlement Understanding (DSU) which is Annex 2 to the Agreement.[357] The DSU is an integral part of the WTO Agreement and legally binding. It utilizes processes of consultation, good offices/conciliation/mediation, and arbitration, together with a process of panels and appellate review. Various disputes between states involving trade restrictions for environmental purposes have been heard by WTO panels. These decisions are discussed in Chapter 17.

5 International Criminal Law

In addition to its work on liability and the law of state responsibility, the ILC has undertaken to draft a code of crimes against the peace and security of mankind, international crimes committed by private actors. In 1991, the ILC adopted on first reading a new version of the draft which had been sent to the UN General Assembly in 1954.[358] The 1991 draft included two provisions concerning crimes against the environment. In draft Article 22, 'exceptionally serious war crimes' include 'employing methods or means of warfare which are intended or may be expected to cause widespread, long-term and severe damage to the natural environment'. The other provision, draft Article 26, criminalized the act of 'an individual who wilfully causes or orders the causing of widespread, long-term and severe damage to the environment'. Criticism by states of the expansive list of crimes led the ILC Special Rapporteur to propose reducing the number of crimes, in particular eliminating the provisions regarding environmental crimes. The ILC instead decided to create a working group 'to examine the possibility of covering in the draft Code the issue of wilful and severe damage to the environment'.[359] The working group decided the 'time was not yet ripe' for declaring attacks on nature as such crimes against the peace and security of mankind and it thus recommended that damage to

357 Marrakesh Agreement establishing the World Trade Organization (Marrakesh, April 15, 1994) 1867 UNTS.

358 Y.B.Int'l L.Comm'n 94, II-2.

359 ILC, *Report of the International Law Commission on the Work of its Forty-Seventh Session May 2 – July 21, 1995*, GAOR 50th Sess., Supp. No. 10, A/50/10, 67 para 141.

the environment be constituted either a war crime or a crime against humanity only when it is so severe 'that the health or survival of a population will be gravely prejudiced'.[360] The working group continued to view attacks on the environment 'as an indispensable element' of the draft Code.[361] The plenary sent the text on war crimes to the drafting committee, but in an equally divided vote, the committee declined to send the draft on environmental damage as a crime against humanity. The drafting committee changed the working group text on war crimes to require an intent to cause damage to the environment with the aim of prejudicing the health or survival of a population, as reflected in draft Article 20(g) of the draft Code adopted by the ILC in 1996. It will prove virtually impossible to prove such double intent.

The work of the ILC on international crimes, initiated in 1954, led to the adoption of the Rome Statute of the International Criminal Court (ICC) in 1998.[362] The Rome Statute gives the ICC jurisdiction over war crimes, defined as grave breaches of the 1949 Geneva Conventions on the Laws of Armed Conflict or 'other serious violations of the laws and customs applicable in international armed conflict, within the established framework of international law'. Among the list of enumerated offenses is 'intentionally launching an attack in the knowledge that such attack will cause incidental loss of life or injury to civilians or damage to civilian objects or widespread, long-term, and severe damage to the natural environment which would be clearly excessive in relation to the concrete and direct overall military advantage anticipated' (Art. 8(2)(b)(IV)). It applies only to international armed conflicts, as does Protocol I which contains similar language. While the Office of Prosecutor of the ICC indicated in 2016 that it would 'give particular consideration to prosecuting Rome Statute crimes that are committed by means of, or that result in, *inter alia*, the destruction of the environment, the illegal exploitation of natural resources or the illegal dispossession of land',[363] this does not include the prosecution of environmental crime as a separate international crime.

In recent years, discussions have gained momentum on amending the Rome Statute to include the most serious offences against the environment as an international crime under the jurisdiction of the ICC, alongside genocide, crimes against humanity, war crimes, and aggression. A draft definition

360 C Tomuschat, *Crimes Against the Environment*, 26 EPL 242 (1996).

361 ibid.

362 United Nations, Rome Statute of the International Criminal Court, UN Doc No. A/CONF.193/9 (July 17, 1998), 37 ILM 999 (1998).

363 ICC, Office of the Prosecutor, 'Policy Paper on Case Selection and Prioritisation', (The Hague, September 15, 2016).

of this crime, referred to as 'ecocide', has been drafted by a panel of independent experts in June 2021 as follows: 'unlawful or wanton acts committed with knowledge that there is a substantial likelihood of severe and either widespread or long-term damage to the environment being caused by those acts'.[364] The panel of independent experts proposes to use this definition as a basis for an amendment to the Rome Statute to make 'ecocide' the fifth international crime under the jurisdiction of the ICC. In addition to recognizing the gravity of the most egregious offences against the environment, this amendment aims to extend the scope of environmental harm that can be prosecuted by the ICC as a war crime under Article 8(2)(b)(IV) and enable the ICC to prosecute environmental harm inflicted in times of peace.[365]

Bibliography

Bergkamp, L., *Liability and Environment: Private and Public Law Aspects of Civil Liability for Environmental Harm in an International Context* (2001).

Bowman, M. and Boyle, A., *Environmental Damage in International and Comparative Law: Problems of Definition and Valuation* (2002).

Brown Weiss, E. and Jacobson, H.K., eds., *Engaging Countries – Strengthening Compliance with International Accords* (1998).

Cameron, J. and othes, Improving Compliance with International Environmental Law (1996).

Ebbesson, J., *Compatibility of International and National Environmental Law* (1996).

Environnement Sans Frontiere, *Vers l'application renforcée du droit international de l'environnement – Towards Strenghtening Application of International Environmental Law* (1999).

Francioni, F. and Scovazzi, T., et al. eds., *International Responsibility for Environmental Harm* (1991).

Grubb, M. and others, *Greenhouse Gas Emissions Trading* (Geneva: UNCTAD, 1998).

Handl, G., '*Compliance Control Mechanisms and International Obligations*', (1997) 5 Tul J. Int'l & Comp. L. 29.

Haas, M. et al., eds., Institutions for the Earth: Sources of Effective International Environmental Protection (1993).

364 Independent Expert Panel for the Legal Definition of Ecocide, Commentary and Core Text (June 2021).

365 Liana Georgieva Minkova, 'The Fifth International Crime: Reflections on the Definition of "Ecocide"', (2023) 25(1) *Journal of Genocide Research* 62.

Imperiali, C., L'effectivité *Du droit international de l'environnement: contrôle de la mise en oeuvre des conventions internationales* (1998).

Improving Compliance with International Environmental Law (James Cameron et al. Eds. 1996).

Lammers, J., *'International Responsibility and Liability for Damage Caused by Environmental Interferences'*, 30 E.P.L 42 (2001).

Maljean-Dubois, *S., L'éffectivite du droit européen de l'environnement, côntrole de la mise en oeuvre et sanction du non-respect*, (2000).

O'Connell, M.E., 'Symposium: Enforcement and the Success of International Environmental Law', 3 *Ind. J. Global Leg. Stud.* (1995).

OECD, *Dispute Settlement in Environmental Conventions* (1994).

Rehbinder, E., 'Environmental Regulation Through Fiscal and Economic Incentives in a Federalist System', 20 *Ecol. L.Q.* 57 (1993).

Rest, A., 'New Legal Instruments for Environmental Prevent, Control, and Restoration in Public International Law', 23 *E.P.L.* 260 (1993).

Romano, Cesare, *The Peaceful Settlement of International Environmental Disputes* (2000).

Rosenzweig, R. et al., *The Emerging International Greenhouse Gas Market* (2002).

Victor, D.G. et al., *The Implementation and Effectiveness of International Environmental Commitments – Theory and Practice* (1998).

Wetterstein, P., *Harm to the Environment: The Right to Compensation and the Assessment of Damages* (1997).

Wolfrum, R, 'Means of Ensuring Compliance with and Enforcement of International Environmental Law', 272 *RCADI* 9 (1998).

Wolfrum, R. and Langenfeld, C., *Environmental Protection by Means of International Liability Law* (1999).

PART 2

Sectoral and Trans-Sectoral Regulation

CHAPTER 8

Protection of Biological Diversity

Introduction

The interaction of humans with other living organisms has been the subject of discussion, debate, and regulation throughout history. Belief in human dominion over the earth and all its living resources, common in many cultures and religions, has often led to exploiting or conserving other species only insofar as they are seen to have immediate utilitarian value to human well-being. A more ecological ethic accepts that living organisms may be utilized, but argues that humans have a moral obligation of stewardship or trusteeship towards nature that implies restraint in the use of and respect for all life. Legal scholars and philosophers as well as religious leaders have begun to adopt this view. In his 2015 Encyclical *Laudato Si*, Pope Francis remarked that 'It is not enough … to think of different species merely as potential "resources" be exploited, while overlooking the fact that they have value in themselves'.[1] He explicitly rejected the traditional theology of unrestrained human dominion over the natural world, stating that 'nowadays we must forcefully reject the notion that our being created in God's image and given dominion over the earth justifies absolute domination over other creatures'.[2] Going further, an ecocentric approach adopted by animal rights activists among others contends that living creatures should not be exploited except where unavoidable to fulfill basic human needs.

The tension between exploitation and conservation is evident in most international and national legal instruments. Sustainable harvesting has proved to be an elusive goal and, in many instances, populations have declined irretrievably before measures to stabilize them have been taken or become effective. Until recently, the law on the subject was comprised largely of *ad hoc* approaches addressing specific commercially-valuable wildlife. Non-binding

---

1 Encyclical Letter of Pope Francis, *Laudato Si: On Care for Our Common Home* (2015), para. 39. Similar views have emerged in the Orthodox Church. See: John Chryssavgis, *On Earth as in Heaven: Ecological Vision and Initiatives of Ecumenical Patriarch Bartholomew* (Bronx, NewYork, 2012).

2 The Encyclical explained: 'The earth was here before us and it has been given to us. This allows us to respond to the charge that Judaeo-Christian thinking, on the basis of the Genesis account which grants man "dominion" over the earth (cf. Gen 1:28), has encouraged the unbridled exploitation of nature by painting him as domineering and destructive by nature. This is not a correct interpretation of the Bible as understood by the Church'. ibid, para. 67.

 | DOI:10.1163/9789047440802_010

instruments such as the Stockholm Declaration, the 1980 World Conservation Strategy of the International Union for Conservation of Nature (IUCN) and the 1982 World Charter for Nature articulated the first broad principles that were subsequently embodied in the framework United Nations Convention on Biological Diversity (CBD) (June 5, 1992). The Convention establishes limited guidelines for conduct towards all life on the planet, guidelines that are elaborated in national conservation strategies and plans of action, and the obligations contained in other international agreements.

This chapter examines the global and regional legal instruments that attempt to protect the earth's biological diversity. After discussing basic concepts and definitions, it describes some of the major threats to biological diversity and the evolution of legal approaches to the question. It then discusses the Convention on Biological Diversity and other general conventions. In the second section, it reviews legal instruments designed to regulate specific aspects of the problem, such as habitat protection and limiting trade or specific means of harvesting. The third part looks at instruments to protect specific species or other taxonomic groups. The issues of biotechnology and bio-engineering are discussed in Chapter 13.

1 Concepts and Definitions

Conservation of biological diversity has replaced nature conservation as the primary term used in regulating human actions towards other components of the living world. The new term encompasses all genes, species, habitats and ecosystems on earth, thus becoming a unifying principle that denotes all living organisms and their intricate interdependence. Biological diversity is defined in Article 2 of the Convention on Biological Diversity as

> The variability among living organisms from all sources including, inter alia, terrestrial, marine and other aquatic ecosystems and the ecological complexes of which they are part; this includes diversity within species, between species and of ecosystems.

The broad definition includes wild and domesticated animals and wild and cultivated plants found on land and seas, whether within or outside areas under national sovereignty or jurisdiction. The Convention and other sources generally distinguish three levels of biological diversity: genetic diversity, species diversity and ecosystem diversity. Between them they encompass the components of life, different life forms and the interrelationships of all of them. The first Conference of the Parties decided, however, that the definition excludes human beings, their organs, and genetic material.

Genetic diversity refers to the variability of the genetic makeup within a single species. Flowering plants contain over 400,000 genes and even bacteria have more than 1000.[3] In general, no two organisms are genetically identical. The smaller the number of individuals within a species, the less internal genetic diversity the species retains. Inbreeding may result in reduced fertility and increased susceptibility to disease or negative mutation. The threat to the future is particularly pronounced in agriculture, where food security rests on a few grain species with consequent loss of variable characteristics. Of the 75,000 or so edible plant species, only around 150 are widely cultivated, just three of which provide 50 percent of the world's food.[4] Maintenance of genetic and species diversity among plants is also critical to human health as a source of medicines: As many as 50 percent of prescription drugs are based on a molecule that occurs naturally in a plant and between 50,000 and 70,000 plant species are known to be used in traditional and modern medicinal systems throughout the world.[5] According to a recent study conducted by the Intergovernmental Science-Policy Platform on Biodiversity and Ecosystem Service (IPBES), 'an estimated 4 billion people rely primarily on natural medicines for their health care and some 70 per cent of drugs used for cancer are natural or are synthetic products inspired by nature'.[6] Some 80 percent of people in developing countries depend on herbal medicines and remedies for their health care.[7]

Species diversity means the diversity between species of living organisms within a specific habitat or ecosystem; by definition, species cannot breed with other species. The number of species on earth is not known. While more than one and one-half million species have been described by scientists, the total number is estimated to be at least five to ten million and some estimates are as high as fifty million.[8] Vertebrates are the least numerous – about 6,400

3 Katrina Brown and others., *Economics and the Conservation of Global Biological Diversities* (GEF 1993) 3.

4 WWF, *2010 and Beyond: Responding to the Biodiversity Challenge* (Gland, 2008) 10.

5 ibid 11.

6 IPBES, *Summary for Policymakers of the Global Assessment Report on Biodiversity and Ecosystem Services of the Intergovernmental Science-Policy Platform on Biodiversity and Ecosystem Services* (2019).

7 WWF, *2010 and Beyond.*

8 IUCN estimates that some 8.7 million species exist worldwide, of which only 2.16 million have been described and less than one percent of those have been evaluated. Of the species that have been evaluated, nearly 28 percent are threatened with extinction. For up-to-date

mammal species and 11,000 species of birds have been described, compared to 250,000 species of higher plants, but the most studied order. Least well-known are lichens, bacteria, and fungi. New species are still being found. Nearly one-third of the 11,500 reptile, 34,000 fish, and 8,300 amphibian species have been identified in the past twenty years. The numbers of undiscovered species, especially insects, plants, and micro-organisms undoubtedly run to the millions.

All these living resources are unevenly distributed throughout the world, with the highest concentration of terrestrial species in humid tropical zones and the greatest marine diversity in coastal areas and coral reefs. Also, generally, diversity decreases with altitude on land and depth in the oceans; however, little is known about the deep-sea-bed species. Islands like Madagascar and Hawaii are rich in endemic species, as are the lakes of Africa, and the countries of the Amazon forest. Overall, thirty-six biodiversity hotspots have been identified globally. These hotspots collectively comprise just 2.5 percent of the Earth's land surface yet hold especially high numbers of species that occur nowhere else – half the world's plant species and 43 percent of all terrestrial vertebrate species. They are also home to 75 percent of the planet's most threatened mammals, birds and amphibians. This unevenness creates problems for international regulation to protect biological diversity due to the disproportionate impact on hotspot countries and their concern with maintaining their sovereign rights.

Ecosystem diversity denotes the range of natural habitats, biotic communities and ecological processes within which species variety has evolved and to which they are uniquely adapted. Each species depends upon the surrounding environment for its survival and reproduction: temperature, humidity, water, soil and nutrition. Ecosystems contain a complex interrelationship of species and functions leading towards equilibrium, governed by natural rules. The diversity of ecosystems is itself an essential part of biological diversity. Some species, such as frogs and some other amphibians, may be identified as sentinel species because they are sensitive to environmental change and thus important indicators of the health of an ecosystem.

---

data, consult the IUCN Red List. Best estimates of percentage of threatened species for each group are: cycads 62% (62–63%); amphibians 41% (31–56%); chameleons 36%; conifers 34% (34–35%); reef-forming corals 33% (27–44%); cacti 31% (28–37%); sharks and rays 37%; freshwater crabs and shrimps 31% (16–65%); mammals 26% (22–37%); groupers 18% (12–43%); birds 13% (13–14%); cone snails 8% (6–20%); blennies 7% (6–15%); pufferfishes, etc. 7% (6–20%); wrasses 4% (4–18%); lobsters <1% (0–35%). For a discussion of the uncertainties in estimating the number of species, see Mark J. Costello, Robert M. May, and Nigel E. Stork, 'Can We Name the Earth's Species before they Go Extinct?' (2013) 339 Science 413.

2 Loss of Biological Diversity

Extinction of species, although part of the natural order, has reached alarming proportions since the beginning of the industrial revolution. It is estimated that in less than two centuries, one hundred twenty-eight species of bird and ninety-five species of mammals have disappeared. Approximately fifteen percent of all known plant species disappeared during the twentieth century. In some regions, over half the endemic species have become extinct since 1950. The rate of extinction is now thought to be 1000 times the natural rate of nine percent of species every million years.[9] Nearly one-fifth of higher plant species are threatened with extinction or survive only in small populations. Some two-thirds of all bird species are in decline worldwide. The problem of species loss is acute in tropical rain forests. Although they cover only six percent of the Earth's land surface, they contain at least half the earth's species, perhaps as much as ninety percent. A United States (US) National Academy of Science report estimates that four square miles of Amazonian forest typically contains 125 species of mammals, 400 species of birds, and 100 species of reptiles. The impoverishment this represents for humanity and the biosphere is not only biological, but also scientific, cultural and undoubtedly economic.

This loss of biological diversity can be attributed to exploitation, the destruction of habitats, pollution, the introduction of invasive species, and other human activities that negatively impact the environment. Over-exploitation was the original problem to which legal regulation responded, but other activities have considerable direct and indirect impact, from fishing by-catch to destruction of habitats due to urbanization. Pollution and the introduction of alien species upset the natural balance, as does climate change. Even agriculture contributes to the depletion of the genetic heritage. Cultivation, often of single products over large areas, replaces the genetic richness of the prairies, just as forests of a single type of tree displace natural woods. Moreover, agricultural techniques are creating new varieties of plants or domestic animals that are particularly detrimental to varieties that are closer to their wild origin.

The immediate causes of biodiversity loss mask complex economic and social factors, from population growth to lack of economic incentives to conserve natural resources. The lack of land tenure for indigenous or other local communities undermines efforts to maintain traditional and sustainable land

9 Stuart Pimm and others, 'The biodiversity of species and their rates of extinction, distribution, and protection' (2014) 344(6187) Science 987.

management practices. A view of plants and animals as a form of property subject to individual appropriation has resulted in a lack of regulation and consequent overexploitation. Poverty is also linked to unsustainable uses of natural resources. Markets fail to ascribe economic value to the ecological services of biological resources, also leading to unsustainable patterns of economic growth and consumption. Foreign debt and other international economic pressures similarly undermine conservation efforts.

Impoverishment of the global genetic heritage can have dangerous long-term consequences. Genetic variability contributes billions a year in agriculture, medicine and industry; current trade in wildlife alone may amount to over $10 billion a year. A species that disappears may take with it forever a currently unknown biological process or substance of great importance. Moreover, crossing of domestic with wild species may become necessary either to halt the degeneration of overly cultivated species, adapt them to different environments or even to create new varieties. Thus, reserves of non-cultivated varieties are indispensable not only to develop species on which human life depends, but to maintain them over the long term at a high level. In sum, conservation of wildlife is linked with sustainable development and the general interests of humanity.

While there are many reasons why the rate of extinction should produce unease, most international expressions of concern about biodiversity loss focus on utilitarian values: that biodiversity underpins the functioning of ecosystems which provide a wide range of services to human societies, with major implications for current and future human well-being.[10] Other human-centered services mentioned include cultural services such as spiritual and religious values, educational services, with opportunities for knowledge and education, and recreational and aesthetic values.

According to a 2020 report of the Convention on Biological Diversity secretariat,[11] most future scenarios project continuing high levels of extinctions and loss of habitats throughout this century stemming from, *inter alia*, further clearing of tropical forests in favour of crops and pastures, and biofuel production; overfishing; climate change, the introduction of invasive alien species, pollution and dam construction. The geographical distribution of species and vegetation types is projected to shift radically towards the poles due to climate

10 The provision of food, fibre, medicines and fresh water, pollination of crops, filtration of pollutants, and protection from natural disasters are among those ecosystem services potentially threatened by declines and changes in biodiversity.

11 Convention on Biological Diversity, *Global Biodiversity Outlook* 5 (2020).

change, by the end of the 21st century, while both boreal and temperate forests face widespread dieback at the southern end of their existing ranges.

3 Development of Legal Norms

In international law, the exploitation or conservation of living things traditionally has been considered part of state sovereignty over natural resources. In turn, within most states, until recent decades, wild animals and plants generally were protected, if at all, by regulations imposing hunting and fishing limits on specified species or in specific places, such as protected areas or royal forests. Absent such regulations, wild animals and plants historically were considered free for taking and utilization by the first to take or kill specimens. Domestic plants and animals were the property of their owners, who were only limited in how they exploited and used them by the adoption of animal anti-cruelty statutes.[12]

The first treaties aimed at protecting specific species of wild animals appeared at the end of the nineteenth century, reflecting two concerns. Firstly, migratory species required cooperative efforts among range states to ensure conservation of the stocks. Secondly, commercially-harvested species or stocks on the high seas had to be protected from competitive unsustainable exploitation. More recently, it has been recognized that non-migratory species whose range or habitat extends into the territory of more than one state require cooperative efforts to ensure the species' survival. It is still the case that without some transboundary element, most species have little protection under international law.

The first multilateral conventions aimed at protecting non-exploited species reflected an undeniable utilitarian perspective. The Paris Convention of March 19, 1902 protected a limited list of birds 'useful to agriculture' while the second annex to the Convention listed unprotected bird 'pests', including most predators, grain-eating and fish-eating birds. New concepts appeared after World War II, reflecting the emergence of a global environmental consciousness. The International Convention for the Protection of Birds (Paris, October 18, 1950),

12 In 1822, the United Kingdom (UK) passed Martin's Act, the first animal-cruelty law in the UK See Steven M. Wise, *Rattling the Cage: Toward Legal Rights for Animals* (Perseus Bks. 2000) 43. A 1867 New York anti-cruelty law recognized that animals can suffer pain. NY Rev Stat § 375.2 *et seq.* (1867). The law continues to restrict the use of animals by humans in order to prohibit the infliction of unnecessary pain, suffering, or death. See MCL 750.50b(2).

articulated a general principle that all birds should be protected, with a few exceptions set forth in the Convention and specific derogations permitted to states. Birds of prey became among the most protected species. Despite new attitudes towards conservation, however, measures of protection were scattered among international rules that addressed the problem in a fragmentary fashion. The methods of protection that were adopted also were incomplete; most often they forbade taking examples of protected species but failed to adopt measures to ensure habitat conditions sufficient to support the survival of the species. Subsequent agreements expanded the focus to consider the role of species in the ecosystem in which they occur and the need to preserve genetic diversity in the light of new threats, including inadvertent or accidental harm from pollution due to oil spills, pesticides and other harm to wildlife habitats. An ecosystem approach that looks beyond protecting specific species has been coupled with efforts to develop improved compliance techniques and increased participation of non-governmental actors.

A fundamental change of the utilitarian attitude towards wildlife is reflected in Principle 4 of the 1972 Stockholm Declaration:

Man has a special responsibility to safeguard and wisely manage the heritage of wildlife and its habitat, which are now gravely imperiled by a combination of adverse factors. Nature conservation, including wildlife, must therefore receive importance in planning for economic development.

The idea that plants and animals constitute a heritage developed late, and even now the international community remains far from accepting all its implications, preferring instead to refer to biological diversity as a common 'concern' of humanity. In 1980, the World Conservation Strategy, prepared by IUCN in cooperation with the United Nations Environment Programme (UNEP), the World Wildlife Fund (WWF), the Food and Agriculture Organization (FAO), and the United Nations Educational, Scientific and Cultural Organization (UNESCO), defined three major conservation goals: maintain essential ecological processes; preserve genetic diversity; and sustainably use species and ecosystems.

The World Charter for Nature of October 28, 1982 reaffirmed these goals. After proclaiming in its preamble that 'every form of life is unique, warranting respect, regardless of its worth to man', the Charter declares in Principles 2 and 3:

2 The genetic viability of the earth shall not be compromised; the population levels of all life forms, wild and domesticated, must be at least sufficient for their survival, and to this end necessary habitats shall be safeguarded.

3 All areas of the earth, both land and sea, shall be subject to these principles of conservation; special protection shall be given to unique areas, to representative samples of all the different types of ecosystems and to the habitats of rare or endangered species.

These principles appeared to open a new era in conservation policy, reflecting awareness of the planetary dimension of the issues, but it confronted the then-emerging emphasis on permanent sovereignty over natural resources. Conservation of species and of their habitat were nonetheless integrated into the broader conceptual framework of safeguarding the genetic heritage of the planet, a new, immense problem extending beyond the dimensions of conservation in its usual sense. The progression towards identification, regulation and management of processes that adversely affect biological diversity represents one aspect of a shift away from sectoral administration towards more integrated approaches to protecting the biosphere.

Increased recognition of the need for comprehensive norms to protect biological diversity led to the adoption of the CBD at Rio de Janeiro in June 1992. The Convention sets forth a general framework or normative umbrella, tempered by an emphasis on state sovereignty and the use of biological resources. The CBD is reinforced by other legal instruments relating to particular species, areas, and means of protection. These international agreements can be grouped into three main categories. First, there are treaties that aim to protect biological diversity in general. Second, some conventions aim to protect broad categories, e.g. endangered or threatened species, through use of a particular legal technique such as habitat protection or restrictions on international trade. Third, a series of treaties, both multilateral and bilateral, aim at conserving a single endangered species or higher taxonomic group: whales, bats, seals, migratory birds.

In general, the texts safeguard the individuals that comprise the species. Thus, individual rhinoceros are protected, not the species as an abstraction apart from the individual animals. Nonetheless, the abstraction exists, because the characteristic genes of each species confer a range of different qualities to each of its individual members. It is this genetic fund which should be protected and transmitted to future generations to ensure the variability within each species. A major task of international environmental law is to assure the conservation and transmission of this fund, in reality, the greatest material resource of the earth.[13]

---

13 See Cyril de Klemm, 'Conservation of Species, the Need for a New Approach' (1982) 9 EPL 117.

International treaties for the protection of living organisms contain many common obligations, such as the duty to adopt regulatory measures for nature conservation. Older treaties promoted the creation of protected areas and several more recent ones mandate the protection of specific sites (e.g. the February 2, 1971 Ramsar Convention on the Conservation of Wetlands, the November 23, 1972 Convention on the World Cultural and Natural Heritage, and protocols on specially protected areas of regional seas) although states remain free to nominate or remove the names of particular areas from the international lists. The CBD goes beyond these measures to require identification and management of destructive activities a primary obligation.

As a final introductory note, the various conventions discussed in this chapter are not mutually exclusive, but instead often work together to mutually reinforce the guarantees and obligations set forth in each instrument. An example from Europe illustrates this point: in early 2004, Ukraine began construction of a shipping canal in the Danube delta's Bystroe estuary, near the Ukraine/Romanian border. Opponents claimed that this canal would negatively affect important Ukrainian wetlands as well as the entire Danube delta, with transboundary effects in Romania and Moldova. Ukraine not only had obligations under the CBD, but also the Bern Convention on the Conservation of European Wildlife and Natural Habitats, the Ramsar Convention on Wetlands of International Importance, the Espoo Convention on Environmental Impact Assessment in a Transboundary Context, and the Aarhus Convention on Rights to Information, Public Participation and Access to Justice. In 2004, the Bern Convention's Standing Committee tasked with monitoring compliance called on Ukraine to suspend construction of Phase II of the Bystroe Canal. It subsequently opened a case file on the project, issuing a full report in 2012.[14] Additionally, a joint UNESCO-Ramsar mission went to the Ukraine to examine the impact of the project on Ramsar registered wetlands and a UNESCO Biosphere Reserve and World Heritage Site. The Implementation Committee of the Espoo Convention also visited Ukraine and thereafter prepared a Report calling on Ukraine to conduct an environmental assessment. The Compliance Committee of the Aarhus Convention became involved, finding violations of the Aarhus Convention which it called on Ukraine to correct. Finally, the Parliamentary Assembly of the Council of

14 Standing Committee, Convention on the Conservation of European Wildlife and Habitats, Application of the Convention: Complaints and Case Files, T-PVS (2012) 11 (September 19, 2012).

Europe received a report on the matter in 2005[15] and adopted Resolution 1444 (2005) with recommendations to the Ukrainian government. In response to the various findings and recommendations of the different treaty bodies, Ukraine temporarily suspended the project, but resumed it in 2006, prepared an environmental assessment and made several changes in the project that it said mitigated the environmental damage. Ukraine also provided information on the works to the public and its neighbors and established cooperation with Romania and Moldova. Ukraine is not a member of the EU or additional environmental obligations would have applied. The following section looks in more detail at the range of obligations to protect biological diversity.

4 General International Instruments

4.1 *Global Instruments*

4.1.1 The Convention on Biological Diversity

The United Nations Conference on Environment and Development (UNCED) opened for signature the Convention on Biological Diversity,[16] the first global comprehensive instrument on the earth's biological resources. The Convention entered into force on December 29, 1993 and has been ratified by 196 states and the European Union; only the Holy See and the United States are not party to the treaty. The Convention has three broad purposes: (1) the conservation of biological diversity, (2) the sustainable use of its components, and (3) access to genetic resources, including the fair and equitable sharing of benefits arising from the use of genetic resources, and access to technology, including biotechnology. Among the three stated purposes as implemented by the parties, the priority seems to be placed on assuring that developing countries benefit from the natural resources within their territories, through their use and the provision of access to others. The assumption is that benefit-sharing will provide an appropriate incentive to preserve biological diversity.

The Convention primarily concerns the rights and responsibilities of states at the national level. The general obligation imposed on states parties is to take effective national action to halt the destruction of species, habitats and ecosystems, including the adoption of regulations on conservation of biological

15 Protection of European Deltas, Explanatory Memorandum (Mr. Platvoet), Parliamentary Assembly of the Council of Europe, Documents: Working Papers, 2005 Ordinary Session, Vol. IV, Doc. 10452.

16 Convention on Biological Diversity (CBD), adopted May 22, 1992, opened for signature June 5, 1992, in force December 29, 1993.

resources, legal responsibility, regulation of biotechnology, and norms on access to and compensation for use of genetic materials. The states parties are to apply the Convention requirements inside the territorial limits of their national jurisdiction, as well as to processes and activities under their jurisdiction or control wherever located.

The Convention contains several innovative features. Biological diversity is recognized for the first time in a global treaty as a common concern of humankind. Negotiators rejected proposals to label it as the common heritage of mankind because of concern for national sovereignty. Further reflecting this concern, the Convention reverses a traditional principle of free access to genetic resources, making it clear that 'the authority to determine access to genetic resources rests with the national governments and is subject to national legislation'. Developing countries insisted on this extension of the norm of permanent sovereignty over natural resources and the correlative requirement of prior informed consent by the party providing the genetic resource (Art. 15.5). It may be viewed as the counterpart to developed country efforts to ensure intellectual property rights over industrial development of products derived from biological resources, including living material itself. The Convention takes a positive stance on the flow of genetic resources, calling on states parties to facilitate access for environmentally-sound uses and not to impose restrictions that are counter to the objectives of the Convention. It also requires states parties to take measures to share 'in a fair and equitable way' the results of research and development of uses of genetic resources with the state providing those resources.

The emphasis on national sovereignty is balanced by the inclusion of broad state duties and an affirmation of Stockholm Principle 21 in the operative paragraphs of the Convention, the first treaty to do so. The preamble provides that states 'are responsible for conserving their biological diversity and for using their biological resources in a sustainable manner', although it is not clear that this is a reference to the law of state responsibility. The specific requirements of the Convention impose an obligation on states parties to identify important components of biological diversity and priorities that may need special conservation measures, as well as to identify and monitor processes and activities that may have significant adverse effects on biological diversity (Art. 7). With this information, they must develop national strategies and plans, integrating conservation of biological diversity into relevant sectoral plans and programs and decision-making (Art. 6). The planning requirement is reinforced by the requirement in Article 10(a) that parties integrate consideration of the conservation and sustainable use of biological resources into national decision-making. Annex 1 contains indicative lists for the identification and monitoring of ecosystems and habitats, species and communities, and genomes and genes of social, scientific and economic importance.

After long debate among the negotiators, the Convention established a preference for *in situ* conservation, with *ex situ* conservation called for as a complement to *in situ* measures. *In situ* conservation is defined as 'conservation of ecosystems and natural habitats and the maintenance and recovery of viable populations of species in their natural surroundings and, in the case of domesticated or cultivated species, in the surroundings where they have developed their distinctive properties' (Art. 2). Conservation measures range from establishment of protected areas to rehabilitation of degraded ecosystems, and protection of natural habitats (Art. 8). Most importantly, states parties are to protect ecosystems and regulate or manage biological resources important for the conservation of biological diversity whether they are within or without protected areas. The Convention also contains a provision intended to counter the widespread destruction of native species that can occur through the introduction of exotic species against which local ones have little or no protection.[17]

Sustainable use is a major theme of the Convention and is defined as 'the use of components of biological diversity in a way and at a rate that does not lead to the long-term decline of biological diversity, thereby maintaining its potential to meet the needs and aspirations of present and future generations' (Art. 2). Parties agree to regulate or manage harvested biological resources, developing sustainable methods and minimizing adverse impacts on biological diversity. States must institute research, training and public education, as well as techniques like environmental impact assessment. Special emphasis is given to protecting and encouraging traditional cultural practices if compatible with sustainable use and to the adoption of incentives for the conservation and sustainable use of components of biological diversity.

As with all the documents adopted in connection with UNCED, the Biodiversity Convention contains qualifying language indicating that there are differentiated responsibilities among the states parties, depending upon their capacities. Most obligations must be fulfilled when 'possible', 'practicable', or 'appropriate'. States parties are asked to respect, preserve and maintain knowledge, innovations and practices of indigenous and local communities relevant to biological diversity, but only 'subject to national legislation' (Art. 8(j)).[18]

17 Other recent international agreements include provisions to the same effect. See Chapter 8.

18 A Working Group on Article 8(j) of the CBD has been established in 1998. In this context, Parties to the CBD have adopted several voluntary guidelines, including the Akwé: Kon Voluntary Guidelines, Tkarihwaié:ri Code of Ethical Conduct, the Mo'otz Kuxtal

Some provisions make explicit distinctions between developed and developing countries (e.g. Arts. 6 and 20).

In other respects, the CBD reiterates the general principles of international environmental law, including responsibility for, and redress of, transfrontier damage (Arts. 3, 14), cooperation (Art. 5), access to information (Arts. 14, 17), and prevention. The specific development agenda of UNCED is also reflected in various articles that prescribe specific rules of identification and monitoring, access to genetic resources (Art. 15), access to and transfer of technology (Art. 16), and technical and scientific cooperation (Art. 18).

For the first time in a global conservation agreement, there is a legal relationship between the conservation obligations of developing countries and the financial obligations of developed countries. The latter group of countries is required to provide 'new and additional financial resources' to a financial mechanism for the use of developing countries. The Convention specifies that the funding is to be applied to meet the full incremental costs deriving from measures needed to implement the Convention's obligations. The amount is set through bilateral negotiations between each developed country party and the institution chosen to handle the financial mechanism. There is explicit recognition that the implementation of obligations under the Convention is linked to and dependent upon adequate funding being supplied. In addition, implementation must take into account 'the fact that economic and social development and eradication of poverty are the first and overriding priorities of the developing country Parties'. The Conference of the Parties (COP) designated the Global Environment Facility as the financial mechanism. A Memorandum of Understanding (MOU) was concluded between the CBD Executive Secretary and the Global Environment Facility (GEF) Council in 1996 to govern the financial mechanism.

The Conference of the Parties has held regular sessions at which it has adopted important decisions and recommendations on environmental impact assessment, introduction of alien species, transboundary cooperation and the involvement of local and indigenous communities. COP decisions also address agricultural biological diversity, forests, and sustainable tourism. The Jakarta Mandate (Decision II/10), calls for the establishment and reinforcement of arrangements for integrated management of marine and coastal ecosystems and the integration of plans and strategies for such areas. A COP also adopted the Bonn Guidelines on Access to Genetic Resources and Fair and Equitable Sharing of the Benefits Arising out of Their Utilization, a precursor to the

---

Voluntary Guidelines; the Rutzolijirisaxik Voluntary Guidelines and the Glossary of relevant key terms and concepts.

Nagoya Protocol on Access to Genetic Resources and their Fair and Equitable Sharing of Benefits Arising from their Utilization to the Convention on Biological Diversity, adopted October 29, 2010, discussed in Section G. A second protocol, the Cartegena Protocol on Biosafety was adopted January 20, 2000, governing the movements of living modified organisms (LMOs) resulting from modern biotechnology from one country to another. It has been strengthened by the Nagoya-Kuala Lumpur Supplementary Protocol, adopted October 15, 2010, on Liability and Redress relating to living modified organisms. These are addressed in Chapter 13D. In 2016, The Mo'otz Kuxtal Voluntary Guidelines were adopted by the Parties to the CBD under Decision XIII/18, and aim to support the implementation of Article 8(j) and related provisions of the Convention. These guidelines provide a framework for the development of mechanisms, legislation, or initiatives to ensure the prior informed consent (PIC), free, prior and informed consent (FPIC), or approval and involvement of indigenous peoples and local communities when accessing their traditional knowledge, innovations, and practices.

To monitor compliance with CBD obligations, Article 26 calls for the presentation of state reports on measures taken for the implementation of the provisions of the Convention and their effectiveness in meeting the objectives of the Convention. The first reports focussed on Article 6, the general measures and information acquired during national studies on biological diversity. The COP guidelines suggested a structure consisting of an executive summary, an introduction, background, goals and objectives, the strategy chosen, partners involved, action for implementation, budget, monitoring and evaluation and sharing of national experience. In 2014, the Conference of the Parties established the Subsidiary Body on Implementation (SBI) to replace the Ad Hoc Open-ended Working Group on Review of Implementation of the Convention, with the terms of reference contained in the annex to decision XII/26. The main function of the Subsidiary Body is to review relevant information on progress in the implementation of the Convention, including in the provision of support for the implementation of the Convention, as well as of any strategic plans and other relevant decisions adopted by the Conference of the Parties, and on progress in the achievement of targets established under the Convention. It also assists the Conference of the Parties in preparing decisions on enhancing the implementation of the Convention and identifies and develops recommendations to overcome, obstacles encountered in implementing the Convention and any strategic plans adopted under it, as well as recommendations on how to strengthen mechanisms to support implementation of the Convention, and any strategic plans adopted under it. Finally, it reviews the impacts and effectiveness of existing processes under the Convention and identify ways and means that increase efficiencies, including an integrated approach to the implementation of the Convention and its Protocols, including matters such as resource mobilization, guidance to the financial mechanism, capacity-building, national reporting, technical and scientific cooperation and the clearing-house mechanism, and communication, education and public awareness.

In decision X/2, the tenth meeting of the Conference of the Parties, held from 18 to 29 October 2010, in Nagoya, Japan, adopted a revised and updated Strategic Plan for Biodiversity, including the Aichi Biodiversity Targets, for the 2011–2020 period. The plan provides an overarching framework for the entire United Nations system and all other partners engaged in biodiversity management and policy development. States parties agreed to translate the framework into revised and updated national biodiversity strategies and action plans within two years. Additionally, in decision X/10, the Conference of the Parties decided that the fifth national reports, due by March 31, 2014, should focus on the implementation of the 2011–2020 Strategic Plan and progress achieved towards the Aichi Biodiversity Targets. COP15, held in 2022, saw the adoption of the Kunming-Montreal Global Biodiversity Framework. This new framework sets ambitious targets for the period up to 2030, aiming to halt biodiversity loss and ensure ecosystem resilience. The framework builds on the lessons learned from the Aichi Targets and incorporates updated goals and targets to address current global biodiversity challenges.

4.1.2 Convention on the Conservation of Migratory Species of Wild Animals

The Bonn Convention on the Conservation of Migratory Species of Wild Animals, concluded June 23, 1979,[19] is also a treaty of global scope. It was adopted as a follow-up to Recommendation 32 of the Stockholm Action Plan[20] and constitutes a recognition that the conservation and efficient management of migratory species require concerted action by all states within whose national jurisdiction the species spend part of their lives and through which they

19 For further discussion of the Convention, see Clare Shine, 'Selected Agreements Concluded Pursuant to the Convention on the Conservation of Migratory Species of Wild Animals', in Dinah Shelton, ed., *Commitment and Compliance: The Role of Non-Binding Norms in the International Legal System* (Oxford University Press 2000) 196.

20 Recommendation 32 called on governments to take into consideration 'the need to enact international conventions and treaties to protect species inhabiting international waters or those which migrate from one country to another'. The Federal Republic of Germany prepared a preliminary draft in 1974.

transit. Legal measures must broadly address threats to habitats, excessive hunting along migration routes and degradation of feeding sites.

The Convention provides a framework within which range states of migratory species take individual and cooperative action to conserve the species and their habitats. The Preamble states that wild animals in their innumerable forms are an irreplaceable part of the earth's natural system which must be conserved for the good of mankind. Further, it states that each generation holds the resources of the earth for future generations and has an obligation to ensure that this legacy is conserved and utilized wisely. Each party is to adopt strict protection measures for endangered migratory species, conclude multilateral agreements for the conservation and management of migratory species that have an unfavorable conservation status or would benefit significantly from international cooperation, and undertake joint research activities.

For purposes of the Convention, the term 'migratory species' is defined as the entire population or any geographically separate part of the population of a species of wild animals which habitually and predictably cross one or more national jurisdictional boundaries. This obviously includes not only birds, but both land and sea mammals, reptiles and fish. Other definitions, given in Article 1, are rendered necessary by the complexity of the subject. Thus, 'endangered' signifies that the migratory species is in danger of extinction throughout all or a significant portion of its 'range', meaning all the areas of land or water that a migratory species inhabits, stays in temporarily, crosses or overflies at any time on its normal migration route. Another important element is the concept of a 'conservation status', the sum of the influences acting on a migratory species that may affect its long-term distribution and abundance. According to Article 1(1), the conservation status is considered as favorable when:

1. population dynamics data indicate that the migratory species is maintaining itself on a long-term basis as a viable component of its ecosystems;
2. the range of the migratory species is neither currently being reduced, nor is likely to be reduced, on a long-term basis;
3. there is, and will be in the foreseeable future, sufficient habitat to maintain the population of the migratory species on a long-term basis; and
4. the distribution and abundance of the migratory species approach historic coverage and levels to the extent consistent with wise wildlife management.

The favorable or unfavorable conservation status of a migratory species serves as a criterion for determining the applicable rules of the Bonn Convention. For example, one of the fundamental obligations of states is to pay special attention to migratory species whose conservation status is unfavorable and take individually or in cooperation the necessary steps to conserve such species and their habitats.[21]

Like other conservation conventions, the Bonn treaty uses a system of lists. Immediate protection is accorded to endangered migratory species, listed in Appendix I. Range states of species listed in Appendix I are to conserve and, where possible, restore the habitats of these species; eliminate, prevent or minimize impediments to their migration; prevent, reduce, or control factors endangering them; and prohibit the taking of animals belonging to such species except under strictly defined conditions.[22]

Appendix II lists migratory species that have an unfavorable conservation status and thus require international agreements for their conservation and management. Formal agreements are encouraged in Article IV(3) and Guidelines for the content of such Agreements are provided in Article V. Formal agreements should cover the whole of the migratory range and should be open to accession by all range states of that species, whether or not they are Parties to the Bonn Convention. The agreement's contents should identify the migratory species, describe the range and migration route, allow for designation of a national authority to implement the agreement, and establish institutional machinery to assist in achieving its objectives and monitoring its effectiveness. In relation to a migratory species of cetacean, it should, at a minimum, prohibit any taking of whales not permitted by whaling conventions. Where feasible, agreements also should provide for periodic reports of the conservation status of the migratory species concerned, coordinated conservation and management plans, research and exchanges of information on the species, conservation and restoration of habitats, and maintenance of a network of suitable habitats along the migration routes, elimination of or compensation for activities and obstacles which hinder or impede migration, prevention of pollution in habitats of the species, coordinated action to suppress illegal taking, and, finally, provide measures of public awareness.[23]

In addition to concluding treaties governing migratory species listed in Appendix II, states parties are encouraged to enter into other agreements concerning one or more migratory species that are not listed in Appendix II (Art. IV.4). Any population that periodically crosses one or more national jurisdictional boundaries may be subject to such agreement. The Convention does not specify the form or content of the agreements. Some agreements have been

21 Art. II(1).
22 Art. III.
23 Art. VI.

treaties applying the Article V guidelines,[24] while others have been Memoranda of Understanding[25] that are not legally binding but are intended to coordinate short term administrative and scientific measures between range states in collaboration with international non-governmental organizations having expertise on the subject. The MOUs concluded list specific conservation undertakings of each state in an annexed Action Plan.

The Convention provides for three organs: the Conference of States Parties, a Scientific Council, and a Secretariat. The first is the decision-making organ of the Convention, and it meets at least once every three years. It monitors the conservation status of migratory species, makes recommendations to Parties for improving the conservation status of species, reviews the progress being made under agreements, and recommends convening meetings of range states of a migratory species for which there is no agreement in order to improve its conservation status.[26] The Scientific Council, established by the Conference of the Parties, provides advice on scientific matters to the Conference, the Secretariat, any state party, or in appropriate cases any body set up under the Convention or an agreement. It can recommend research and make recommendations on migratory species listed in Appendices I and II and recommend specific conservation and management measures to be included in agreements.[27] The Secretariat's functions include maintaining and publishing a list of range states of all migratory species included in the two Appendices and promoting the conclusion of agreements.[28] Article XI provides that amendments to the Appendices may be adopted at any session, ordinary or extraordinary, of the Conference of the Parties. Amendments are adopted by a two-third's majority of members present and voting and enter into force in regard to all states parties 90 days after the meeting, except for those that file a

24 See the Agreement on the Conservation of Seals in the Wadden Sea (October 16, 1990), Agreement on the Conservation of Small Cetaceans of the Baltic and North Seas (September 13, 1991 opened for signature March 17, 1992), and Agreement on the Conservation of Cetaceans of the Black Sea, Mediterranean Sea and Contiguous Atlantic Area (November 24, 1996).

25 Memorandum of Understanding concerning Conservation Measures for the Siberian Crane (July 1, 1993); Memorandum of Understanding concerning Conservation Measures for the Slender-billed Curlew (September 10, 1994).

26 Art. VII.

27 Art. VIII.

28 Art. IX. The Secretariat is provided by UNEP and has its offices in Bonn, Germany along with the Secretariat of the UN Framework Convention on Climate Change. A Standing Committee provides policy and administrative guidance between regular meetings of the COP. The Standing Committee consists of representatives of the five geographic regions, the Depositary state (Germany) and the host states of the last and next meetings of the COP.

written reservation within the 90 day period.[29] COP14, which took place from February 12–17, 2024, led to the addition of new species to the Convention Appendices, significantly extending international protection to various threatened animals. In total, 14 new species, subspecies, and populations were added to the Convention Appendices following COP14, reflecting a concerted effort to enhance conservation measures and ensure the survival of these species through international cooperation and legal framework.

Parties to the Convention have concluded 26 agreements to 2023, of which seven are formal treaties pursuant to Article IV(3) and nineteen are Memoranda of Understanding. The seven formal agreements concern the conservation of seals in the Wadden Sea, bats in Europe, small cetaceans of the Baltic and North Seas, African-Eurasian waterbirds, and cetaceans of the Black Sea, Mediterranean Sea and contiguous area, the conservation of albatrosses and petrals, and the African gorillas. The more numerous MOUs concern conservation of various birds, such as the Siberian crane and the slender-billed curlew; marine species, including turtles, sharks and cetaceans; and land species such as the Bukhara deer and West African elephants. The contents of the different instruments are discussed later in the chapter in regard to the protection of specific species. There are also three regional initiatives. One, the Sahelo-Saharan initiative was adopted in 1998 by all 14 range states in order to restore and maintain gazelle and antelope populations in the Sahara and the Sahel. It provides a framework for governments, non-governmental organizations (NGOs), scientists, local people and the wider international community to collaborate in the conservation of the most threatened antelope and gazelle populations in Northern Africa. The other two initiatives address Central Asian birds and mammals.

Although states parties to the Bonn agreement initially concluded more formal agreements, the MOU has become increasingly popular. One reason for this shift may be seen in the list of signatories to MOUs: nearly all of them include intergovernmental and non-governmental organizations among the signatories. The Siberian Crane MOU has been signed by three organizations: the UNEP/CMS secretariat, the International Crane Foundation, and the Wild Bird Society of Japan. The Great Bustard MOU was signed by four entities: UNEP/CMS secretariat, IUCN, BirdLife International and the International Council for Game and Wildlife Conservation and all of these except IUCN also signed the MOU on the slender-billed curlew.

29 Art. XI.

4.2 *Regional Instruments*

Regional conventions and other legal instruments regulate a large part of the planet: the Americas, Africa, Western Europe, South-East Asia and the Pacific.

4.2.1 Africa

Africa was the first region to have a convention on nature protection, signed in London on May 19, 1900, for the Preservation of Wild Animals, Birds and Fish in Africa. It was adopted by those European powers having colonies in Africa: Germany, Spain, France, Italy, Portugal, and the United Kingdom. Despite characteristics that were progressive for the time, such as protecting certain species and recommending creation of protected zones, it encouraged the destruction of animals considered nuisances or harmful, such as crocodiles and venomous snakes, and the reduction in numbers of others such as lions, panthers and predatory birds (see Art. II(13) and (15)).

In 1933, the colonial powers and several independent African States concluded a new Convention that insisted on the creation of protected zones and eliminated reference to harmful or nuisance species. This Convention relative to the Preservation of Fauna and Flora in their Natural State, concluded November 8, entered into force January 14, 1936 and led to the creation of many of the existing national parks in Africa.

As African countries achieved independence after the Second World War, it became obvious that a further convention was needed. The Organization of African Unity, now the African Union, recommended that its members make efforts in this direction. As a result, African states adopted the 1968 African Convention on the Conservation of Nature and Natural Resources (Algiers, September 15, 1968), the first of the major modern conservation treaties. On July 11, 2003, the General Assembly of the African Union meeting in Maputo adopted a revised Convention. Its provisions make it the most modern and comprehensive of agreements concerning living resources.

Like its predecessor, the 2003 instrument covers all aspects of environmental conservation and resource management. The Preamble proclaims the conservation of the global environment to be a common concern of humankind and the conservation of the African environment a primary concern of all Africans. States are responsible for protecting and conserving their environment and natural resources and for using them in a sustainable manner in order to satisfy human needs according to the carrying capacity of the environment. The preamble makes reference to the Stockholm Declaration, to the Rio Declaration and to Agenda 21, but not to the instruments adopted by the 2002 Johannesburg Summit on Sustainable Development.

Article III formulates the principles which should guide the action of states, beginning with the right of all peoples to a satisfactory environment favorable to the enjoyment of the right to development, using language from the African Charter of Human and Peoples Rights. Article XVI complements Article III by proclaiming procedural rights and requiring the parties to adopt legislative and regulatory measures necessary to ensure timely and appropriate dissemination of environmental information, access of the public to such information, participation in decision-making and access to justice in matters related to protection of environment and natural resources.

The obligations of the parties are progressive and unusual. The Convention advocates preventive measures and the application of the precautionary principle, 'with due regard to ethical and traditional values as well as scientific knowledge in the interest of present and future generations'. Article XVII on the traditional rights of local communities and indigenous knowledge, Article XVIII on research and Article XIX on development and transfer of technology further develop such principles. It is noteworthy that Article XVII submits access to indigenous knowledge and its use to the prior informed consent of the concerned communities and to specific regulations recognizing their rights to, and appropriate economic value of, such knowledge. In this respect, the African Convention is more favorable to local communities than the Convention on Biological Diversity, which places its emphasis on the sovereign rights of states.

Due to the role played by IUCN in the preparation of the Convention, nature conservation and management form an important part of the text. Article V para. 6 lists six conservation areas for which Article XII enunciates general rules with the aim of conserving the most representative ecosystems and ensuring the conservation of all species. Annex 2 contains rules for each of the specified areas. Even outside conservation areas, species and genetic diversity of plants and animals, whether terrestrial, fresh-water or marine, shall be maintained and enhanced, in particular by the conservation of their habitats within the framework of land-use planning and of sustainable development (Art. IX). Parties shall also take all necessary measures for the protection, conservation, sustainable use and rehabilitation of the vegetation cover (Art. VIII). A more selective approach targets the species which must be identified and protected (Art. X and Annex 1), in part by regulating trade in specimens and products thereof (Art. XI). Annex 3 lists prohibited means of taking.

Conservation measures are to be replaced in a more general approach. On the one hand, the parties shall take effective measures to prevent land degradation and to that effect adopt long-term integrated strategies for the conservation and sustainable management of land resources, including soil, vegetation and related hydrological processes (Art.VI). On the other hand, parties shall manage their water resources by maintaining, *inter alia*, water-based essential ecological processes, by adopting policies for the planning, conservation, management, utilization and development of underground and surface water. Parties sharing surface or underground water resources shall act in consultation and if the need arises, set up inter-state commissions for their rational management and equitable utilization (Art. VII).

Article XIII complements the conservation aspect by adding rules to prevent environmental harm from processes and activities affecting the environment and natural resources. It advocates the adoption of specific national standards, including for ambient environmental quality, emission and discharge limits, as well as process and production methods and products quality. Economic incentives and disincentives shall also be used in this regard. Military and hostile activities should avoid harm to the environment (Art. XV).

The Convention establishes a Conference of the Parties which can consider any matter within its scope (Art. XXVI). It should develop and adopt rules, procedures and institutional mechanisms to promote and enhance compliance with the provisions of the Convention (Art. XXIII); it can also adopt additional annexes to the Convention. Like the first African Convention at the beginning of the 'ecological era', the new instrument can be considered a model for the necessary holistic approach to integrated protection of the environment.

Environmental agreements also have been concluded in Africa at the sub-regional level and some of these contain progressive enforcement measures. A short agreement on the Conservation of Common Natural Resources (Khartoum, January 24, 1982) entered into between Uganda, the Sudan, and Zaire, contains only four substantive Articles. The contracting states agree to devote special attention to common natural resources (Art. 1), to forbid taking of specimens of protected species on their territories (Art. 2), and to prosecute all those who trade without permit in objects coming from protected species, in applying territorial law but restoring the objects seized to the state of origin (Art. 4). Article 3 provides that a certificate of origin issued by one state pursuant to the Convention on International Trade in Endangered Species of Wild Fauna and Flora (CITES) will be accepted by the other contracting states. Institutionally, the Protocol envisages creation of a commission on the black market and contraband. This organ is to meet twice a year, to study the problems posed and to formulate recommendations which it deems necessary (Art. 5). Another example, discussed in Chapter 7, is the Protocol on Wildlife Conservation and Law Enforcement.[30]

30 Maputo, August 13, 1999. See also the discussion of the Southern Africa Ivory agreement in section E.2 of this chapter.

At COP14 of the CBD, which took place in November 2018 in Sharm El-Sheikh, Egypt, the African Ministerial Declaration on Biodiversity was adopted. This declaration emphasizes the importance of biodiversity conservation in Africa and outlines commitments and actions that African countries and stakeholders agreed upon to enhance biodiversity protection and sustainable development on the continent. The 2021 COP13 of the Abidjan Convention (officially known as the Convention for Cooperation in the Protection, Management and Development of the Marine and Coastal Environment of the Atlantic Coast of the West, Central and Southern Africa Region) focused on marine biodiversity conservation and sustainable use, particularly addressing marine species and ecosystems within the context of the Convention's mandate. During COP13, which was likely influenced by ongoing concerns over biodiversity loss and environmental degradation in the region, a resolution was passed emphasizing several key aspects related to marine biodiversity.

4.2.2 The Americas

The Convention on Nature Protection and Wild Life Preservation in the Western Hemisphere (Washington D.C., October 12, 1940) was adopted through efforts led by the Pan-American Union and inspired by the 1933 London Convention on Africa.[31] At the time, it was an advanced instrument containing the principal means of modern conservation, but with weak obligations. It refers to establishment of protected areas, protection of migratory and endangered species, monitoring and regulation of international trade in wild plants and animals. One interesting aspect of the Convention is the series of definitions in Article I for different categories of protected zones and the legal regimes governing them. For example,

- *National parks* are areas placed under public control for the protection and preservation of superlative scenery and wildlife of national significance. No hunting, killing or capturing of fauna or destruction or collection of flora is permitted.
- *National reserves* are regions established for the conservation and utilization of natural resources. Under government control, protection is afforded in so far as consistent with the primary purpose of the reserves.
- *Nature monuments* benefit from strict protection. The purpose is to set aside as inviolate an area, object or species of flora or fauna, due to aesthetic, historic, or scientific interest.

31 In 1933, the African States and colonial powers concluded the Convention relative to the Preservation of Fauna and Flora in their Natural State. See above, section 2.a.

- *Strict wilderness reserves* are placed under public control. In such areas, charaterized by primitive conditions, motor vehicles and all commercial developments are excluded. Only scientific investigation or government inspection is permitted.

States parties to the Convention are required only to explore the possibility of establishing such zones and to notify the Pan-American Union – today the Organization of American States – of their establishment (Art. II). Once established, however, the resources of national parks cannot be exploited for commercial profit and boundaries can only be altered by legislation. In addition, the Convention calls upon states to adopt laws and regulations to protect and preserve all flora and fauna within their territories whether or not in protected areas, as well as natural scenery, striking geological formations, and regions and natural objects of aesthetic interest or historic or scientific value (Art. V). International cooperation and assistance also are foreseen by Article VI. Special measures must be adopted to protect migratory birds (Art. VII) and certain other species listed in an Annex to the Convention. Finally, states parties must take measures to control and regulate the importation, exportation and transit of protected flora and fauna or any part thereof. A system of export certificates is established by Article IX of the Convention.

The Convention has suffered from insufficient implementation due to lack of an institutional structure, although the Organization of American States has organized a few technical meetings. Of great potential, it lacks current effectiveness.

The 1978 Treaty on Amazon Cooperation[32] aims to promote the harmonious development of Amazonian territories and ensure that the joint actions of the parties produce equitable and mutually beneficial results and achieve 'the preservation of the environment, and the conservation and rational utilization of the natural resources of those territories'. Its measures are limited to research and exchange of information, but it creates institutional machinery in meetings of the Ministers of Foreign Affairs and annual meetings of the Amazonian Cooperation Council. The Treaty also creates a secretariat and envisages Permanent National Commissions and special Commissions to study specific problems or matters.

Sub-regional treaties and border agreements have been adopted as well.[33] In Central America, they are: the June 5, 1992 Managua Convention on the

32 Entry into force February 2, 1980. The states parties are Bolivia, Brazil, Colombia, Ecuador, Guyana, Peru, Suriname, and Venezuela.

33 For a discussion of this region, see Michelle-Ann Williams, 'Regional Environmental Agreements and Initiatives in the Americas' (2007) 18 YB Int'l Envtl L 65.

Conservation of the Biodiversity and the Protection of Wilderness Areas in Central America, the October 29, 1993 Guatemala Convention on the Management and Conservation of Natural Forest Ecosystems and Forest Plantation Development, and the 1996 Agreement on the Mesoamerican Biological Corridor. A broader framework was provided in the Environmental Cooperation Agreement signed by the governments of Costa Rica, the Dominican Republic, El Salvador, Guatemala, Honduras, Nicaragua, and the United States of America. Its major focus is on capacity-building. The 1983 Convention for the Protection and Development of the Marine Environment for the Wider Caribbean (Cartagena Convention) has a protocol specifically dedicated to the protection of wildlife, the Protocol Concerning Specially Protected Area and Wildlife (June 18, 2000) or SPAW agreement. The protocol requires each party to take 'the necessary measures to protect, preserve and manage in a sustainable way, within areas of the Wider Caribbean Region in which it exercises sovereignty, or sovereign rights or jurisdiction … threatened or endangered species of flora and fauna'. The protocol requires parties to establish, when necessary, protected areas to sustain the natural resources of the wider Caribbean region and makes provisions for, *inter alia*, protection measures, a planning and management regime for protected areas, a cooperation program for, and the listing of, protected areas, the establishment of buffer zones, national measures for the protection of wild flora and fauna, and cooperative measures for the protection of wild flora and fauna.

4.2.3 Europe

The Bern Convention on the Conservation of European Wildlife and Natural Habitats (September 19, 1979), prepared within the Council of Europe, represents major progress compared to earlier regional efforts, if only because it establishes an institution charged with ensuring its functioning and implementation. It also creates substantive obligations for the contracting parties instead of merely expressing goals and encouraging their fulfillment.

The preamble reflects modern concepts regarding conservation. Wild flora and fauna are said to constitute a natural heritage having intrinsic value which must be preserved and handed on to future generations. The resources also are recognized as playing an essential role in maintaining biological balances. Finally, the importance of conserving natural habitats is seen as one of the essential elements of conservation.

The fundamental purpose of the Convention is to conserve wild flora and fauna and their natural habitats, 'especially those species and habitats whose conservation requires the cooperation of several States' (Art. 1). States parties have an obligation, however, to conserve wild flora and fauna in all circumstances, whether the problems posed are transfrontier or not.

Article 2 provides that the contracting parties will take requisite measures to maintain the population of wild flora and fauna or at a level which corresponds in particular to ecological, scientific and cultural requirements, while taking account of economic and recreational requirements and the needs of sub-species, varieties or forms at risk locally. This provision is undoubtedly vaguer that the criterion of 'optimal sustainable yield' but it may have an advantage in subordinating the economy and tourism to ecological, scientific, and cultural considerations. Contracting parties must take steps to promote national policies for the conservation of wild flora, fauna and natural habitats, with particular attention to endangered and vulnerable species, as well as endangered habitats (Art. 3). A first step is thus taken towards conserving the world genetic heritage 'in vivo' – that is in natural sites and not in museums and laboratories.

The inescapable links between the habitats, flora and fauna are reflected in Article 4 which calls for protecting the habitats of all wild species, whether endangered or not. It gives particular emphasis to those that are considered as needing special protection, listed in two Appendices. Similarly, attention is given to migratory species in protecting zones of importance for migratory routes, as wintering, staging, feeding, breeding or moulting areas.

The heart of the Convention is Chapter III, Articles 5–9, devoted to the protection of species. The importance of conserving flora is underlined, a noteworthy development for something that often appears to be included as an afterthought to the protection of animals. Article 5 is entirely dedicated to this conservation and Appendix I lists those species strictly protected, for which picking, collecting, cutting, or uprooting is prohibited. Prohibition of sale or possession is left to the discretion of the contracting parties.

The provisions relative to protection of wild animals also make use of lists. The second Appendix list species which the Convention, Article 6, protects from deliberate capture and killing, damage to or destruction of breeding or resting sites, deliberate disturbance during particularly vulnerable times (breeding, rearing and hibernation), the deliberate destruction or taking or possession of eggs from the wild, even if empty, and the possession of and internal trade in these animals, alive or dead, and any recognizable part or derivative of them. The listed animals include the wolf, the lynx, and dolphins, as well as numerous bird species.[34] Special provisions in Article 10 respecting migratory species add a duty on range contracting parties to coordinate their

34 The majority of the bird species listed in Appendix II to the Bern Convention also appear in Annex I to the EC Directive of April 2, 1979 concerning conservation of wild birds. O.J. No. L 103, April 25, 1979.

efforts to protect these species and in particular to coordinate protective measures, such as closed seasons.

A third Appendix to the Convention protects vulnerable species, whose exploitation must be regulated pursuant to Article 7. The measures that should be adopted include closed seasons, temporary or local prohibition of exploitation, and restrictions on trade in specimens. In all cases, Article 8 forbids indiscriminate means of capture and killing or means capable of causing local disappearance or disturbance.

Article 9 of the Convention generally permits contracting parties to make exceptions to its provisions, but only if there is no other satisfactory solution and the exception will not be detrimental to the survival of the population concerned. Thus, exceptions can be adopted for the protection of flora and fauna, for public health and security, air safety or other overriding public interests, to prevent serious damage to crops, livestock, forests, fisheries, water and other property, for purposes of research and education, repopulation, reintroduction and breeding, and for the taking, keeping or 'judicious exploitation' of certain wild animals and plants. The number of reasons justifying exceptions is large, but Article 9(2) provides a form of international supervision because contracting parties must submit biannual reports on the exceptions they invoke.

Another aspect of the conservation measures merits attention. Article 11 requires each contracting party to encourage the reintroduction of native species of wild flora and fauna and strictly control the introduction of non-native species. Finally, Article 12 permits contracting parties to adopt stricter measures for conservation than those provided under the Convention.

Currently the Bern Convention has the most complete institutional structure of all regional conservation conventions. Article 13 institutes a Standing Committee composed of representatives of the contracting parties, including the EEC. Any member state of the Council of Europe that is not a contracting party may send an observer and any state which is not a Council of Europe member can be invited by unanimous vote of the Committee to send an observer. International organizations, at their request, also may participate unless one-third of the contracting parties object. The Committee meets at least every two years (Art. 13).

The Committee is responsible for monitoring the application of the Convention. In particular, it makes recommendations to contracting parties on measures to be taken to implement the Convention, makes proposals for improving its effectiveness, including proposals for the conclusion with third states of agreements which would enhance the effective conservation of species or groups of species, and keeps under review the Convention and its Appendices, to examine whether modifications are necessary (Art. 14).

Regarding the last function, there are two distinct procedures for modification set forth in Articles 16 and 17. The first concerns amendments to the Convention itself. Any proposal for amendment coming from a contracting party is examined by the Standing Committee. After decision by a three-quarters majority of the votes cast, the Committee submits the proposal either for acceptance by the contracting parties, or, if it is a procedural change, to the Committee of Ministers of the Council of Europe for approval. All amendments enter into force thirty days after all the contracting parties have informed the Secretary General of the Council of Europe that they have accepted it.

In contrast to this classic amendment procedure, Article 17 provides a simplified 'opt out' means of amending the Appendices. The necessity to adapt the list of threatened or endangered species to changing conditions is obvious. The Convention provides for proposals coming from either a contracting party or the Committee of Ministers to be examined by the Standing Committee, which may adopt them by a two-thirds majority. Unless one-third of the contracting parties submit objections, the amendment enters into force for the non-objecting states three months after adoption of the proposal by the Standing Committee.

The Natura 2000 network is today a cornerstone of the European Union's biodiversity policy, established to ensure the long-term survival of Europe's most valuable and threatened species and habitats. It consists of protected areas designated under two main directives: the Birds Directive (Directive 2009/147/EC), which aims to conserve all wild bird species naturally occurring in the EU, including their habitats. It mandates the establishment of Special Protection Areas (SPAs) for birds across Europe; and the Habitats Directive (Directive 92/43/EEC), which focuses on the conservation of natural habitats and wild fauna and flora in the EU. It requires member states to designate Special Areas of Conservation (SACs) for habitats and species listed in its annexes.

4.2.4 Asia and the Pacific

The Apia Convention on the Conservation of Nature in the South Pacific (June 12, 1976) was modest both in its content and in its geographic scope. It entered into force June 26, 1990 among five states parties. While referring to safeguarding representative samples of natural ecosystems and the heritage of wildlife and its habitat, its preamble also speaks of the production of essential renewable natural resources and underlines their nutritional, scientific, educational, cultural, and aesthetic importance. It also recognizes the importance of indigenous customs and traditional cultural practices. The main focus of the Convention is the creation of protected areas. Each contracting party shall, 'to the extent that it is itself involved, encourage the creation of protected areas' to safeguard, along with existing protected areas, representative samples of natural ecosystems, important natural features and regions or objects 'of aesthetic interest or historic, cultural or scientific value'. Article 2 requires the contracting parties to notify the South-Pacific Commission, the organ responsible for ensuring the secretariat functions for the Convention, of the establishment of any protected area, as well as any legislative or administrative measures or methods of control it adopts. The secretariat functions of the South Pacific Commission are limited to receiving notifications and disseminating information and documents furnished by the contracting states (Art. 8). The Convention leaves it to each state party to establish and maintain a list of indigenous species threatened with extinction, and to communicate the list to the South Pacific Commission. The rather limited obligations are further weakened by Article 6 which permits a contracting party to 'make appropriate provision for customary use of areas and species in accordance with traditional cultural practices'. Despite its modest objectives, the Eighth Meeting of the Parties in 2006 decided to suspend operation of the Convention.

The 1985 ASEAN Convention on the Conservation of Nature and Natural Resources contains substantial obligations in every domain where environmental problems can arise. It is one of the most complete nature protection agreements in existence, but has not entered into force forty years after its conclusion. The states parties agree to adopt the measures necessary to maintain essential ecological processes and life-support systems, to preserve genetic diversity, and ensure the sustainable utilization of harvested natural resources, in order to achieve sustainable development. Article 2 of the Convention requires the contracting states to ensure that conservation and management of natural resources are treated as an integral part of development planning at all stages and at all levels.

The Convention's general framework includes provisions relating to the conservation of species and ecosystems (Chapter II), to ecological processes (Chapter III) and to measures of ecological planning (Chapter IV). These chapters reflect a comprehensive approach to protecting living natural resources, particularly, chapter II (Arts. 3–9) which addresses genetic diversity, sustainable use of harvested species, endangered species, vegetation cover and forest resources, soil, water, and air. The Convention calls for creating protected areas, regulating the taking of species, prohibiting unselective taking methods, and regulating or prohibiting the introduction of exotic species. Article 3 further invites the states party to establish gene banks and other documented collections of animal and plant genetic resources. It also requires the development and implementation of management plans for harvested species based on scientific studies. The Convention applies equally to plant and animal species. Article 6, devoted to vegetation cover and forest resources and their roles in the ecosystems, requires controlling clearance, preventing fires and overgrazing, regulation of mining operations, creation of reserves, reforestation and afforestation, and the conservation of forests, particularly mangroves. Similarly, the protection of the air (Art. 10), soil, and water resources is viewed from the perspective of their functions in natural ecosystems (Art. 7). The regulation and control of water utilization includes maintaining systems supporting aquatic flora and fauna (Art. 8). Article 14 requires the preparation of environmental impact assessment for any proposed activity which may significantly affect the natural environment. When the activities are undertaken, efforts must be made to minimize or overcome any assessed adverse effects. The effects are also monitored in order to take appropriate remedial action.

5 Addressing Specific Threats

The conventions in this category protect wildlife habitats, or impose trade restrictions or means and methods of taking living resources, such as the utilization of driftnets in the marine environment.

5.1 *Habitat Protection*

While protected areas may only afford temporary relief in transitory places for a particular species, other measures may complete the protection by ensuring the conservation of the habitat of particular species. The definition given by Article 1(1)(g) of the Bonn Convention on the Conservation of Migratory Species of Wild Animals is a good example:

> "Habitat" means any area in the range of a migratory species which contains suitable living conditions for that species.

Certain instruments, such as the Oslo Convention on Polar Bears (November 15, 1973), provide greater specificity by referring to areas of hibernation and feeding, as well as migration routes.

Conventions may be entirely oriented towards protecting the habitat of protected species. This is the objective of the 1971 Ramsar Convention on Wetlands of International Importance, whose original title added, 'particularly as waterfowl habitat'. In other treaties, the protection of species of plants and animals can be one of the objectives in the creation of protected areas. For example, the 1982 Geneva protocol relating to the establishment of special areas in the Mediterranean provides in Article 3(2) that such areas are created with the aim of safeguarding genetic diversity of species as well as satisfactory population levels, areas of reproduction and their habitats. The system of the UNESCO Convention concerning the World Cultural and Natural Heritage similarly permits the inscription on an international register of areas when the principal interest is to serve as the habitat of specific species. Numerous regional conventions generally invite the contracting parties to establish protected areas, such as national parks or natural reserves, in the framework of more comprehensive protective measures. Taken together, the different conventions increasingly converge to protect endangered or vulnerable species by conserving their habitats, through reducing pollution and other encroachments, including prohibiting takings of specimens within the area. The limitation this implies is that once an animal leaves the protected habitat, it is subject to killing or capture.

5.1.1 Convention on Wetlands of International Importance (Ramsar, February 2, 1971)

The Ramsar Convention was the first treaty based on the idea that the habitat of particular species should be the focus of protection. As a relatively early conservation treaty, it is rather simple in structure and has been amended twice to strengthen its procedural clauses. It is based on a recognition that wetlands are among the most productive sources of ecological support on earth, acting as the habitat for myriad species, as flood control regions, and as a resource of great economic, cultural, scientific and recreational value, the loss of which would be irreparable. Wetlands are defined in Convention Article 1 as being areas of marsh, fen, peatland or water, whether natural or artificial, permanent or temporary, with water that is static or flowing, fresh, brackish or salt, including areas of marine water whose depth does not exceed six meters at low tide. Waterfowl, whose protection was the original purpose of the Convention, are defined as birds ecologically dependent on wetlands.

Apart from providing a habitat for waterfowl, wetlands play a vital role in the water cycle, helping to refill water-tables and maintain water quality. They are highly productive ecosystems inhabited by large numbers of plant and animal species. In addition, many marine species depend on coastal wetlands for their reproduction, growth or nutrition during part or all of their life cycle. Due to their importance to the global environment, the Ramsar Convention has a significance that today far transcends its original objective of protecting waterfowl. Unfortunately, for decades, state-sanctioned or even mandated drainage operations, as well as drought and landfill, have considerably reduced the extent of the global wetlands. The Ramsar 4th Strategic Plan identified the largest causes of loss of wetlands as unsustainable agriculture, forestry and extractive industries, especially oil, gas and mining, the impacts of population growth (including migration and urbanization) and changes in land use that override environmental considerations.

The purpose of the Convention is based on three pillars: to stop the loss of wetlands through conservation and management, including the designation of wetlands of international importance; to develop and implement national plans for the wise use of wetlands; and to encourage international cooperation on transboundary wetlands and shared species.[35] States parties are required to formulate and implement planning to promote as far as possible the wise use of wetlands in their territory (Art. 3.1). The Convention requires each state party upon becoming such to designate at least one suitable wetland within its territory for inclusion on the List of Wetlands of International Importance, which is maintained by IUCN. The boundaries of each wetland are established in a precise manner; they may incorporate riparian and coastal zones adjacent to the wetland, and islands or bodies of marine water of importance as waterfowl habitats.[36] As of 2022, the Ramsar Sites network constitutes the largest network of officially recognized internationally important areas in the world, comprising 2,439 Ramsar Sites covering more than 254 million hectares.[37]

The meetings of Ramsar state parties have formulated detailed criteria to help in selecting wetlands of international importance.[38] The choice of listed wetlands originally was based on their international importance to waterfowl at any season, as well as their significance for ecology, botany, zoology, limnology or hydrology. The criteria today provide that a wetland should be considered to be of international importance when, *inter alia*, it is a particularly good representative example of a natural or near-natural wetland or a wetland that plays a substantial hydrological, biological or ecological role in the natural functioning of a major river basin or coastal system, or supports an appreciable assemblage of rare, vulnerable or endangered plant or animal species; or is of special value for maintaining the genetic and ecological diversity of a region, or as the habitat of plants or animals at a critical stage of their biological cycle, or for one or more endemic plant or animal species or communities. A wetland usually holding 20,000 waterfowl or one percent of the total population of a water bird species or sub-species should be considered to be of international

35 Preamble, para. 4; see the 4th Strategic Plan for 2016–2024, adopted by the 12th Meeting of the Conference of the Parties at Punta del Este, Uruguay, June 1–9, 2015, through Resolution XII.2 (hereafter Ramsar 4th Strategic Plan).

36 Art. 2(1) and 2(4).

37 Resolution XIV.13 (2022).

38 Recommendation 1.5 (Cagliari, 1980); Recommendation 3.1 (Regina, 1987); Recommendation 4.2 (Montreux, 1990); Recommendation VI.3 (Brisbane, 1996).

importance. In 1996, efforts began to develop criteria based on the importance of the wetland to natural hydrological functions such as groundwater recharge or water quality improvement.[39]

Inclusion of a site on the list does not prejudice the sovereign rights of the territorial state, but according to Article 2(6), the state must conserve, manage and use wisely the listed wetland and migratory stocks of waterfowl. Promotion of conservation includes establishing nature reserves and providing adequately for their wardening (Art. 4). The states parties have given wide meaning to the requirement of 'wise use' contained in the Convention. Article 2(6) defines 'wise use of wetlands' as 'the maintenance of their ecological character, achieved through the implementation of ecosystem approaches, within the context of sustainable development'. Wise use, therefore, has at its heart the conservation and sustainable use of wetlands and their resources, for the benefit of people and nature. Sustainable use, in turn, is defined as the use by man of a wetland in such a way that present generations draw from it the maximum sustainable benefits whilst maintaining its capacity to satisfy the natural needs and aspirations of future generations.

States parties maintain the right to add wetlands to the list, and extend the boundaries of those already included. In case of urgent national interests, a state may also delete a wetland from the list or restrict its boundaries (Art. 2(5)) but then should compensate for the loss by creating additional nature reserves for waterfowl either in the same area or elsewhere (Art. 4(2)). A state without a listed wetland would cease to be a party to the Convention.

The Ramsar Convention provides for cooperation between states parties. They must consult with each other about implementing obligations arising from the Convention, especially where a wetland extends across the territories of more than one state or where there is a shared water system. At the same time, Article 5 requires them to endeavor to coordinate and support present and future policies and regulations concerning conservation of wetlands and their flora and fauna. The International Court of Justice (ICJ) had the opportunity to clarify the content and extent of the obligation under Article 5 of the Convention in the 2015 judgment in the joined *Costa Rica/Nicaragua* cases, involving allegations of transboundary environmental harm concerning a border area containing wetlands that each state had designated as wetlands of international importance under the Convention's List. Concerning Article 5, the ICJ found that, while this provision imposes a general obligation to consult 'about implementing obligations arising from the Convention', it does not

39 Conference of the Parties, Resolution VI.3 (Brisbane, 1996).

specifically require Nicaragua to consult with Costa Rica regarding a particular project, such as the dredging of the Lower San Juan River. Consequently, Nicaragua was not obligated under the Ramsar Convention to notify or consult with Costa Rica before beginning its dredging project.[40]

An international register, known as the Montreux Record identifies priority sites for national and international conservation attention and is intended to guide the allocation of available funding resources. The Record is supported by a Management Guidance Procedure, adopted in 1990, to provide states parties with advice and assistance on measures to preserve threatened Ramsar sites. It usually involves an on site visit by experts and member of the Ramsar Bureau.

The Convention contains few institutional provisions, but they are important in practice and have been supplemented by protocols and decisions of the parties. A protocol adopted in Paris on December 3, 1982 established an amendment procedure and a 1987 protocol that entered into force in 1994 formally established a Conference of the Parties as the primary Convention institution, by amendment to Article 6. The COP by majority vote may adopt general or specific recommendations to the states parties regarding the conservation, management and wise use of wetlands and their flora and fauna. In its first six conferences, the states parties adopted some 120 decisions to give greater precision to the definition of wetlands of international importance and standardize the information form to describe the sites. They also produced a global classification system for all types of wetlands and guidelines on application of the concept of sustainable development and management of wetlands, established the Montreux Record, and adopted the Management Guidance Procedure. In addition, the COP s produced texts on EIA, participation, public awareness, climate change, and other issues affecting wetlands.

Monitoring functions have been conferred on the Bureau and on a Standing Committee. COP4 recommendation (C.4.7) 'endorse[d] the measure taken by the Standing Committee to establish a Ramsar Monitoring Procedure and instructs the Bureau to continue to operate this procedure when it receives information on adverse, or likely adverse changes in ecological character at Ramsar sites'. It also determined 'that Monitoring Procedure reports shall be public documents once the Contracting Party concerned has had an opportunity to study the reports and comment on them'. This last provision strengthened the ability of other Parties and non-governmental organizations to comment on the shortcomings and bring pressure to bear where it is helpful.

---

40 *Certain Activities Carried Out by Nicaragua in the Border Area* (*Costa Rica v. Nicaragua*) *and Construction of a Road in Costa Rica along the San Juan River* (*Nicaragua v. Costa Rica*), Judgment, I.C.J. Reports 2015, para. 110.

The Monitoring Procedure itself was set out in an annex to the recommendation. The Bureau may collect information and collaborate with the party concerned to provide a solution. The Bureau may offer advice and assistance to the party as well. The Bureau shall inform the Standing Committee of any action it has taken in this connection or if it appears that an acceptable solution cannot be achieved. The Standing Committee, acting through the Chairman and Secretary, provided by the Bureau, may pursue the matter, in direct contact with the Party or Parties concerned and, where appropriate, with other responsible agencies or bodies, with a view to helping to find a solution. In the event of alterations to the List or changes in ecological character in wetlands included therein, the Standing Committee shall arrange for the information to be circulated for discussion at the next Meeting of the Conference of the Contracting Parties in accordance with Article 8.2(d) of the Convention.

The Secretariat of the Convention, known as the Ramsar Bureau, is financed by the parties and supervised by a nine-member Standing Committee, established in 1987, to carry out any necessary activities between meetings of the COP, provide the Bureau with guidance on implementing the Convention, and prepare COP meetings. In 1993, the states parties created a permanent Scientific and Technical Review Panel composed of seven experts to provide advice to the other Convention institutions. Finally, in 1990, the COP established a fund, now known as the Ramsar Small Grants Fund for Wetland Conservation and Wise Use. It provides developing states parties with financial support for wetlands conservation activities.

The Ramsar Convention is generally considered to be a success.[41] No state has withdrawn a site from the List. A large number of the sites are threatened, however, and many sites remain unprotected because they are in states that are not party to the Convention. The states parties have taken measures to address these problems and especially to encourage participation by developing countries. In 1993, the COP called on multilateral development banks and agencies to give greater priority to the formulation and adoption of coherent wetland development policies, procedures and practices directed at sustainable utilization, wise management and conservation of wetlands.[42] Other measures have been taken to develop cooperation with other treaty systems or conservation programs, including the Convention on Biological Diversity, the Convention to Combat Desertification, and the GEF. In 1997, the Bureau signed

---

41 For a more detailed discussion of the Ramsar Convention and its operation, see Geoffrey V.T. Matthews, *The Ramsar Convention on Wetlands: Its History and Development* (Ramsar Convention Secretariat, 1993, reissued 2013).

42 Recommendation 5.5 (1993).

a Memorandum of Understanding with the secretariat of the Convention on Migratory Species to improve cooperation in the fields of implementation covered by both Conventions. In the context of the Convention on Biological Diversity, the Ramsar Convention is recognized as the lead on all activities related to wetlands. As such, it has a responsibility to offer political, technical and scientific advice and guidance to the CBD and enhance cooperation between the two conventions at all levels.

Recently, a major focus has been placed on the many services that wetlands can provide. The Millennium Ecosystem Assessment, which was a comprehensive scientific assessment coordinated by the United Nations and conducted between 2001 and 2005, recognized wetlands as providing a wide range of ecosystem services (Millennium Ecosystem Assessment Resolution IX.1 (2005), Appendix A). The Ramsar Strategic Plan 2016–2025 builds upon the principles and findings of the Millennium Ecosystem Assessment and aims to guide the actions of Ramsar Convention Contracting Parties in the conservation and wise use of wetlands. In particular, the Ramsar Strategic Plan underscores the various benefits, or 'services', provided by wetlands to both biodiversity and human communities. It emphasizes the importance of integrating these ecosystem services into national and regional policies and management plans. The plan also promotes the sustainable development of wetlands by recognizing and enhancing their contributions to economic development, food security, water supply, climate change adaptation, and disaster risk reduction. Finally, it encourages Contracting Parties to mainstream wetland conservation and management into broader environmental, social, and economic policies. This includes promoting the value of wetlands and their services to stakeholders and decision-makers.

5.1.2 UNESCO World Heritage Convention

One of the most complete international instruments that exists in the field of habitat conservation, UNESCO's Convention for the Protection of the World Cultural and Natural Heritage (Paris, November 23, 1972) is based on a recognition that parts of the cultural or natural heritage of various nations are of outstanding universal interest and need to be preserved as part of the world heritage of humankind as a whole.[43] The Convention also affirms that cultural and natural heritage are increasingly threatened with destruction, not only by traditional causes of decay, but also by changing social and economic conditions. In spite of the dangers, the national protection of heritage sites often

43 Significantly the Convention adopts the approach that the global heritage constitutes 'property'.

remains incomplete because of the insufficient economic, scientific, and technical resources of the country where the property is situated. Given the global interest in the world heritage, the international community must participate in its protection by granting collective assistance to complement individual state action.

For purposes of the Convention, Article 2 defines 'natural heritage' to include:

- natural features consisting of physical and biological formations or groups of formations, which are of outstanding universal value from the aesthetic or scientific point of view;
- geological and physiographical formations and precisely delineated areas which constitute the habitat of threatened species of animals and plants of outstanding universal value from the point of view of science or conservation;
- natural sites or precisely delineated natural areas of outstanding universal value from the point of view of science, conservation or natural beauty.

As such, the Convention takes protects places and not species. Although it falls upon each state party to identify and delineate the different natural areas situated on its territory (Art. 3), an international system of protection is nonetheless provided. It consists of three parts. First, cultural and natural sites which form part of the world heritage remain subject to the legislation of the state where they are located. The World Heritage resources can continue to belong to public or private establishments or even to individuals as the national law provides. Thus, territorial sovereignty and property rights over elements of the world natural heritage are respected.

Second, in determining the different parts of the world natural heritage, the jurisdiction of the territorial state includes both rights and obligations. Article 4 requires each state party to ensure the identification, protection, conservation, presentation and transmission to future generations of the natural heritage situated in its territory.[44] According to Article 5(a), the state also shall endeavor, as appropriate, to adopt a general policy to give the heritage a function in the life of the community and to integrate the protection of that heritage into comprehensive planning programs. Other legal, scientific, technical, administrative and financial measures must be taken, including the creation of special services for the protection, conservation and presentation of this

44 In the case of *Commonwealth of Australia v. The State of Tasmania*, No. C6 of 1983, 46 A.L.R. 625, 68 I.L.R. 266, the High Court of Australia considered whether these duties contained legal obligations to protect sites. In a 4–3 ruling, the Court decided the Convention obligations were legal in nature.

heritage, and research and training (Art. 5). Article 29 requires states parties to submit periodic reports to a specially created committee on the measures which they have taken to implement the Convention.

The final level of protection is international assistance. The entire international community has a duty to cooperate in the protection of the world cultural and natural heritage (Art. 6(1)). According to Article 6(3), this duty includes an obligation not to take 'any deliberate measures which might damage directly or indirectly the cultural or natural heritage'. The broad prohibition of indirect harm could apply to development assistance programs that affect the environment or to local activities causing transboundary pollution which results in harm to a site. Where appropriate to preserve part of the world cultural and natural heritage, a state party may have recourse to international assistance and cooperation (Art. 4). For their part, other states parties undertake to support the requesting state in the identification, protection, conservation, and the presentation of cultural and natural heritage, recognizing that it constitutes a universal heritage. Thus, Article 7 establishes the concept of international protection of the world cultural and natural heritage, including establishment of a system of cooperation and international assistance supporting states parties in their conservation and identification efforts.

International mechanisms are established in the Convention, based on creation of an Intergovernmental Committee for the Protection of the Cultural and Natural Heritage of Outstanding Universal Value. Better known as the World Heritage Committee, it consists of twenty-one members elected by the General Assembly of States Parties that meets during the General Conference of UNESCO.[45] Elected representatives must be persons qualified in the field of natural or cultural heritage (Art. 9).

Representatives of international intergovernmental and non-governmental organizations may attend meetings of the World Heritage Committee in an advisory capacity and even public or private organizations or individuals may be invited to participate or may be consulted on particular problems.[46] The Committee also may create such consultative bodies as it deems necessary to perform its functions. According to Article 14(1), the Director General of UNESCO provides the Secretariat for the Committee.

One of the principal tasks of the Committee is the establishment, publication and dissemination of the 'World Heritage List'. For this purpose, Article 11 requires every state party to the Convention to submit an inventory including documentation on the location and significance of property forming part of

45 Art. 8. The membership of the Committee was expanded from 15 to 21 in 1976.

46 Arts. 8(2) and 10(2).

the cultural and natural heritage situated on its territory and which it considers of outstanding universal value. Sites are listed by the Committee on the basis of criteria which it establishes, but only with the consent of the territorial state. If the listed property is claimed by more than one state, the competing rights to the property are deemed not to be prejudiced by inclusion on the list.[47] The World Heritage Committee also has the power to remove properties from the World Heritage List if they no longer meet its criteria. The possibility of de-listing acts as an incentive to compliance with the Convention's requirements.

As of June 2024, 195 states are parties to the World Heritage Convention and are therefore eligible to nominate sites for inclusion on the List. ICOMOS (International Council on Monuments and Sites) evaluates nominations and management of cultural sites while IUCN evaluates natural heritage sites proposed for addition to the World Heritage List. The List is heavily tilted in favor of cultural heritage; of the 1199 World Heritage sites listed in 2024 in 168 states parties, 933 are cultural and only 227 are natural sites, with 39 being designated as mixed sites (e.g. Machu Picchu in Peru). The listed natural sites include Australia's Great Barrier Reef; the Grand Canyon, Yellowstone and the Everglades in the United States; the Galapagos Islands (Ecuador), and the Serengeti Park (Tanzania).

When a state party proposes a natural site for inclusion, IUCN prepares a technical report. The process can often raise the level of the site protection, by extending boundaries of those considered too small to be adequately protected and therefore not eligible to be entered on the list or by recommending improved site management. To protect sites, the treaty relies in large part on the prestige associated with having sites included on the list and the enhanced international profile that results from it.

The threshold for inclusion on the World Heritage List is that the site be of Outstanding Universal Value according to criteria described in the Operational Guidelines in effect since the end of 2004. New Operational Guidelines have been adopted in 2016 and in September 2023. The latest Operational Guidelines have merged the criteria for natural and cultural sites (which were previously in two separate lists). The criteria that are most relevant for natural sites require that areas (para. 77):

47 Despite this provision, disputes arose over Jordan's nomination of the Old City of Jerusalem and its Walls and Argentina's proposal of Los Glaciares National Park. Both nominations were eventually approved. World Heritage Committee, First Extraordinary Session, UNESCO Doc. CC-81/CONF.008/2 Rev., Annex IV, para. 7; World Heritage Committee, Fifth Session, UNESCO Doc. CC-81/CONF/003/6, Annex III.

1. Contain superlative natural phenomena, exceptional beauty or aesthetic importance;
2. be outstanding examples representing major stages of earth's history, including the record of life, significant on-going geological processes in the development of landforms, or significant geomorphic or physiographic features;
3. be outstanding examples representing significant on-going ecological and biological processes in the evolution and development of terrestrial, fresh water, coastal and marine ecosystems and communities of plants and animals;
4. contain the most important and significant natural habitats for in situ conservation of biological diversity, including those containing threatened species of outstanding universal value from the point of view of science or conservation.

It is possible to have a 'serial nomination' that consists of two or more physically unconnected areas that are related in some manner, e.g. they belong to the same geological, geomorphologic formation or the same ecosystem type. The total series should be of outstanding universal value, but not necessarily each component taken individually. Serial nominations are inscribed as a single entry on the World Heritage List, but the nominations can come in phases. Transboundary nominations are areas that span an international boundary and they also are listed as a single property. Finally, transboundary serial nominations combine both categories. They must be nominated as a single entry and should be managed jointly. Small island states in the Pacific, for example, could propose to link atolls and reefs in a larger ecosystem site.

In addition to the criteria listed above, a site must meet certain standards of integrity to be inscribed, i.e. it should have a management plan or at least an operational plan describing how the site is managed pending a finalized management plan. Moreover, 'bio-physical processes and landform features should be relatively intact'. However, the Operational Guidelines recognize that 'no area is totally pristine and that all natural areas are in a dynamic state, and to some extent involve contact with people. Biological diversity and cultural diversity can be closely linked and interdependent and human activities, including those of traditional societies, local communities and indigenous peoples, often occur in natural areas' (para. 90, Decision 43 COM 11A). Also, the nominating state or states must submit information on available resources to ensure implementation of the plan.

Once a site is reviewed, IUCN's recommendation is given to the World Heritage Bureau, a seven-member executive body of the World Heritage Committee. The Committee itself makes the final decision to inscribe sites on the list.

Periodic reporting is a part of the process. After inscription and monitoring, such reports can lead the state to act to avoid a site being listed as in danger. In 1994, UNESCO initiated a Global World Heritage Strategy to further protect World Heritage sites. The Strategy helps design adaptive regional action plans and themes to provide guidance on maintaining the integrity of WH sites. As part of this process, in 1997, IUCN and the World Heritage Center collaborated on an inventory of all the world's wetlands, coastal and marine sites.

The World Heritage Committee also establishes and publishes a 'List of World Heritage in Danger' that includes property threatened by serious and specific dangers such as the threat of disappearance caused by accelerated deterioration, large-scale public or private projects or rapid urban or tourist development projects, destruction caused by changes in the use or ownership of the land, major alterations due to unknown causes, abandonment, armed conflict, calamities and cataclysms, such as serious fires, earthquakes, landslides, volcanic eruptions, etc. (Art. 11.4). As this enumeration indicates, the territorial state itself may be the cause of the danger, or at least unable or unwilling to cope with natural or human threats, although inscription on the endangered list normally is subject to a request for assistance by the territorial state.[48] In case of urgent need, the Committee may make a new entry in the List of World Heritage in Danger and publicize such entry immediately.

The second principal function of the Committee, according to Article 13, is to receive and study requests for international assistance formulated by states parties to the Convention for protection, conservation, presentation or rehabilitation of any part of the world cultural or natural heritage, i.e., property included or potentially suitable for inclusion on one of the Lists. Article 11 also permits requests to be submitted for purposes of identifying cultural or natural property. The Committee decides on action to be taken in response to the requests and determines an order of priorities for its operations, taking into account both the intrinsic value of the property to be protected and the ability of the state concerned to safeguard such property by its own means. The Committee maintains and publicizes a list of property for which international assistance has been granted.

The financial means to carry out assistance is provided through an international Trust Fund for the Protection of the World Cultural and Natural Heritage of Outstanding Universal Value, called the 'World Heritage Fund', as set forth in Article 15. The resources of the Fund derive from various sources.

---

48 However, in 1983 the World Heritage Committee itself recommended to Senegal and Tanzania that they propose listing two sites facing dangers. World Heritage Committee, Seventh Session, UNESCO Doc. SC/83/CONF/009/8, para. 43.

States parties have mandatory contributions, the amount of which is decided by the General Assembly of the States Parties to the Convention according to a uniform percentage applicable to all states, but which cannot exceed 1 percent of the contribution to the regular budget of UNESCO.[49] Article 15 provides that in addition to these sums both states parties and other states can make voluntary contributions or gifts, as can international intergovernmental and non-governmental organizations, public or private bodies, and individuals. The Committee may use the contributions only for defined purposes and may accept contributions limited to a particular program or project, provided no political conditions are attached.

A state that seeks international assistance must submit a formal request together with information and documentation as required by the Committee. This information, supported by experts' reports whenever possible, should define the operation contemplated, the work that is necessary, the expected costs, the degree of urgency and the resources of the state. Requests based upon natural disasters are given priority. Before deciding on a request, the Committee carries out such studies and consultations as it deems necessary. It takes its decision by the normal majority provided for in Article 13(8), that is, two-thirds of the members present and voting.

The assistance granted can take various forms, including studies, provision of experts, technicians and skilled laborers, training of staff and specialists, supply of equipment, low-interest or interest-free loans, and, in exceptional cases and for special reasons, non-repayable grants (Art. 22). As a general rule, only part of the cost of the necessary work is borne by the international community. The contribution of the state being assisted normally must be substantial (Art. 25).

The project or program for which assistance is furnished is defined in an agreement between the World Heritage Committee and the recipient state. This agreement also sets forth the conditions under which the project or program operates. Finally, Article 29 provides for a measure of international supervision through establishment of a state reporting system. Each state party submits reports to the General Conference of UNESCO containing information on the legislative and administrative provisions which it has adopted and other action which it has taken to apply the Convention. These reports are communicated to the World Heritage Committee.

The World Heritage Convention contains important legal principles. It encompasses the idea that certain property found under the sovereignty of

49 Art. 16(1). Art. 16(2) allows a state to make a reservation to this provision at the time of ratification or accession.

a state has an interest beyond territorial frontiers and concerns all humanity, leading to the conclusion that such property must be conserved in the name and interest and by the care of the entire international community. As a counterpart to the responsibility of the territorial government, it is recognized that the international community itself has obligations and must assist the territorial state in the accomplishment of international objectives. The relevant legal concept which emerges is that of common heritage of mankind, a trust or a mandate exercised in the interest of present and future generations. Some advocates thus recently have aimed to expand the scope of the Convention to allow the designation of certain species as World Heritage Species, enabling their protection whether they are within or outside protected areas.[50]

5.1.3 Protected Areas Protocols to Regional Seas Agreements

Four regional seas agreements have adopted protocols for the creation of marine and coastal protected areas and the protection of threatened or vulnerable species. These agreements concern the Mediterranean (1982/1995), East Africa (1985), the South-East Pacific (1989), and the Caribbean (1990).

The 1976 Barcelona Convention for the Protection of the Mediterranean Sea against Pollution mainly concerned pollution, but the contracting parties complemented it with a Protocol Concerning Mediterranean Specially Protected Areas, adopted April 3, 1982 and replaced in 1995. The 1995 revision extended the scope of the Convention to coastal areas and modify the definition of pollution to include harm to marine flora and fauna. A new Article 10 provides for the conservation of biological diversity.

The 1995 Protocol implements the concepts and definitions of the Convention on Biological Diversity through creating specially protected areas. They serve to safeguard representative types or coastal and marine ecosystems of adequate size to ensure their long-term viability and to maintain their biological diversity, habitats which are in danger of disappearing in their natural area of distribution, habitats critical to the survival, reproduction and recovery of endangered, threatened or endemic species of flora or fauna and of sites of particular importance for their scientific, aesthetic, cultural or educational interest (Art. 4). Each party may establish specially protected areas in the marine and coastal zones subject to its jurisdiction and cooperation is encouraged between neighboring states (Art. 5). The protective measures include, *inter alia,* a prohibition on dumping or discharge of wastes and other

50 See The International Environmental Law Project of Lewis & Clark Law School, 'World Heritage Species: A New Legal Approach to Conservation' (Discussion Paper, 2005).

substances likely directly or indirectly to impair the integrity of the specially protected area, regulation of the passage of ships and any stopping or anchoring, regulation of the introduction of any non-indigenous species, regulation or prohibition of the exploration of the soil or the exploitation of the subsoil, the regulation of any scientific research activity, of fishing, hunting, taking of animals and harvesting of plants or their destruction. In sum, any activity or act likely to harm or disturb or which might endanger the state of conservation of the ecosystems or species is to be regulated and if necessary prohibited (Art. 6). The Parties also should use planning and management of the specially protected areas. A list of such areas (SPAMI) is drawn up and the party or parties concerned may submit proposals for inclusion (Arts. 8, 9). The Protocol, Articles 11–17, lists national and cooperative measures for the protection and conservation of species and prescribes the preparation of inventories of areas that contain rare or fragile ecosystems and species of fauna and flora that are endangered of threatened, preparation of guidelines and common criteria, and it imposes environmental impact assessments for planning processes concerning activities that could significantly affect protected areas. The parties shall give appropriate publicity to the establishment of SPAMIs, their boundaries, applicable regulations, and to the designation of protected species and their habitats. They also are to cooperate in different fields and report on their implementation of the Protocol. The parties to the Protocol meet every two years to review implementation or management measures, make recommendations concerning scientific, administrative and legal information and decide on designation of SPAMI. The sessions also examine recommendations proposed by the meetings of national authorities, as well as the reports of state parties on application of the Protocol.

The Protocol on Protected Areas and on Wild Fauna and Flora in the East African Region supplements the Convention for the Protection, Management and Development of the Marine and Coastal Environment of the Eastern African Region. The Convention and the Protocol were both adopted in Nairobi, on June 21, 1985. Parties must take 'all appropriate measures to maintain essential ecological processes and support systems, to preserve genetic diversity, and to ensure the sustainable utilization of harvested natural resources under their jurisdiction'. The parties must develop national conservation strategies and may establish protected areas and marine reserves. They also must prohibit the intentional or accidental introduction of alien or new species that may cause significant or harmful changes to the region. Four Appendices list protected plant and animal species.

Similar Protocols have been adopted for the South-East Pacific (Paipa, Colombia, September 21, 1989) and for the Wider Caribbean Region (Kingston,

Jamaica, January 18, 1990). Both contain provisions on the establishment of protected areas, while the latter also refers to protected species. The conservation measures required are similar to those contained in the previously-discussed Protocols.

5.2 *Regulation of Trade*

Unlike the prior conventions, the Convention on International Trade in Endangered Species of Wild Fauna and Flora or CITES,[51] is not based on a spatial concept of protection, but on a given activity endangering wildlife: international trade. One of the most powerful motives for the exploitation of plant and animal species is income-production, especially in poor countries lacking other major resources. Trade in wildlife is mostly from southern to northern countries and is estimated to have a value of up to $50 billion annually, most specimens imported for the production of luxury goods and products such as fur coats.[52] In addition, pharmaceutical companies seek wild plants for the production of medicines and animals for bio-medical research. States sometimes impose quotas or duties to counter trade in animals, plants and their derivatives, but no measure of this type can be truly effective without international cooperation between exporting, transit, and importing states. The principal instrument in this regard is CITES, to which the majority of states in the world are party.

The aim of CITES is to protect endangered species by banning their trade and to regulate trade in other commercially-exploited species in order to ensure sustainable trade and economic benefits for exporting countries. CITES applies the technique of lists, in this case distinguishing three situations. Criteria for listing are reviewed periodically. In 1994, the 'Everglades Criteria' affirmed the special role of range states of species in the listing process and provided specifics regarding the biological and statistical information to be taken into account.[53]

Appendix I contains all species[54] threatened with extinction that are or may be affected by trade, including such well-known animals as the tiger, leopard,

---

51 Washington, D.C., March 3, 1973. For a comprehensive discussion of the drafting history and interpretation of CITES, see David S. Favre, *International Trade in Endangered Species: a Guide to CITES* (Springer 1990).

52 Peter Sand, 'Commodity or Taboo? International Regulation of Trade in Endangered Species' (1997) Green Globe Yearbook 19.

53 CITES Conference Resolution 9.24 (1994) on 'Criteria for Amendment of Appendices I and II'.

54 The term 'species' is not used in its scientific sense. For purposes of the Convention, it includes sub-species and any higher taxon, such as a genus, family or order. Some Appendix listings include entire orders of mammals, such as all primates, and all birds.

whale, and many types of parrots. When the Convention entered into force on July 1, 1975, there were 450 species on the list. Since that date, the number has nearly doubled with the addition of many plants close to extinction. These species benefit from particularly strict regulation and states parties can authorize trade only in exceptional circumstances. The ban extends to any readily recognizable part or derivative of a specimen of listed plant or animal (Art. I(b)).[55] Convention Article III provides that the export of a specimen of any species included in Appendix I requires prior grant and presentation of an export permit issued only upon satisfaction of the following conditions:

- A Scientific Authority of the exporting state has advised that the export will not be detrimental to the survival of the species;
- A Management Authority is satisfied that the specimen was not obtained in contravention of the laws of the state for the protection of fauna and flora;
- The same Authority must be satisfied that any living specimen will be prepared and shipped in ways minimizing the risk of injury, damage to health or cruel treatment; and, finally,
- The Management Authority must be satisfied that an import permit has been granted for the specimen by the country of destination.

Importing states bear some of the burden to ensure the effective protection of endangered species. Before a state may allow the importation of any Appendix A specimen, Article III(3) requires the issuance of an import permit which may be granted only after a Scientific Authority attests that the importation is for purposes that are not detrimental to the survival of the species. The Scientific Authority also must be satisfied that the proposed recipient is suitably equipped to house and care for any living specimen. Finally, the Management Authority of the importing state must be satisfied that the specimen is not to be used for primarily commercial purposes.

The re-exportation of a specimen belonging to an Appendix I species also requires a permit confirming that the specimen was imported into the state in accordance with the provisions of the Convention, that its transportation will be safe, and that an import permit has been granted for any living specimen. Finally, Article III provides that the introduction of any specimen of a marine species requires the authorization of the importing state, based on a finding that the introduction will not be detrimental to the species, that the recipient

55 The Conference of the Parties (COP) has adopted several resolutions to clarify what is meant by 'readily recognizable'. In particular, if a label, mark, or name indicates that a product is part of or derivative from a CITES protected species, the identification will be taken as true even if it is mistaken or intentionally misleading. Conf. 9.6.

has the facilities to care for any living specimen and that the specimen is not to be used for primarily commercial purposes.

Each state party must designate one of more Scientific Authorities to give the required opinions, and one or more Management Authorities competent to grant permits or certificates.[56] Article IX requires the designation of the Management Authority at the time of ratification or accession, and provision of the name and address of the Authority to all other Parties.

Trade in Appendix II species, those which are not currently threatened with extinction but which may become so and species upon which they are dependent, is regulated by Article IV. The requirements are less strict than those of Article III. The conditions of export, like those for Appendix I specimens, require a permit based upon an opinion of the Scientific Authority that the export will not be detrimental to the survival of the species, proof to the Management Authority's satisfaction that the specimen was not obtained in violation of the State's laws for the protection of fauna and flora, and evidence that the specimen will be properly transported. The Scientific Authority monitors both the granting of permits and the actual exports. If this Authority determines that the export should be limited to maintain the species at a level within the ecosystem above the Appendix I level, it advises the Management Authority of suitable measures to take to limit the grant of export permits.

The import of an Appendix II specimen requires only prior presentation of either an export permit or a re-export certificate. Re-export, however, requires certification of the Management Authority that the specimen was imported in accordance with the Convention and that any living specimen will be properly transported, to minimize the risk of injury, damage to health or cruel treatment. For importation of marine species, the Management Authority can grant a permit based upon annual quotas established on advice of the Scientific Authority in consultation with other national or international scientific authorities.

It is clear that for species appearing on Appendix II, strict limitations on imports do not exist and specimens can be brought in for commercial purposes. However, the aim of the Convention is to control the latter. Over time, the number of species contained in Appendix II has become extremely high, especially after adoption of subsequent modifications to the list. There are

56 On the amount of evidence required in order to determine whether or not export of a specimen will be detrimental to the survival of the species, see *Defenders of Wildlife, Inc. v. Endangered Species Scientific Authority*, 659 F.2d 168 (D.C.Cir.), *cert. denied*. 454 U.S. 963 (1981).

thousands of items listed, including nearly all 330 species of parrots and 30,000 species of orchids.

Appendix III lists those species that one state party identifies as being subject to regulation within its jurisdiction in order to prevent or restrict exploitation, and for which it needs the cooperation of other parties to control trade. Article V provides that export of a specimen of any species from a state that listed the species in Appendix III requires the prior grant and presentation of an export permit. Permits are subject to virtually identical conditions to those required for Appendix II specimens. Import of a specimen of an Appendix III species requires prior presentation of a certificate of origin, and, if the specimen comes from a state that listed the species, an export permit.

Appendix III thus allows each state to obtain the aid of other states, potential importers of the specimens that the exporting state seeks to protect and conserve. Canada listed the moose, signaling to other states that it is illegal to import a moose or products made from it without a permit issued by the Canadian authorities. This procedure has not been utilized widely. In the first decade of the Convention's application, only a dozen states listed approximately 150 species on Appendix III. The reason for this may lie in the extensive listings already contained in the first two appendices. Although Article VI provides for a standard export permit according to a model in Appendix IV, controlling trade in the tens of thousands of species listed by CITES is difficult at best. In addition, listing is not appropriate if domestic legislation is adequate to protect the species. Finally, states may be unwilling to lose unilaterally the income derived from trade in a particular species without similar measures being taken by other exporting states. This would be reflected in a preference for listing a species in one of the first two Appendices rather than the third.

It is clear that enforcement measures which state parties must take and exceptions to them are particularly important to achieve the purposes of the Convention. In this regard, Article VII contains a series of flexible provisions and authorizes exemptions for specimens of certain species that were raised in captivity as household pets, or plants artificially propagated for commercial purposes. Exemptions also are granted for non-commercial loans, donations or exchanges of certain plants between scientists or scientific institutions, as well as for the movement of specimens which form part of a zoo, circus, menagerie, or exhibition. However, conditions are imposed, principally relating to the humane treatment of the specimens. In contrast, Article XIV specifically permits a state party to take stricter measures through domestic legislation or international regulation. To enforce the Convention, Article VIII requires states to take measures penalizing prohibited trade and providing for confiscation or return to the state of export of any specimens illegally imported, with specified protection for living specimens.

The CITES controls apply to all trade in listed specimens, even to trade conducted between CITES parties and non-parties. Article X provides that CITES states may accept 'comparable documentation' on import or export issued by the competent authorities in non-party states, provided that it conforms to CITES requirements to a substantial degree. The applicability of CITES to non-parties has encouraged adherence to the treaty because non-compliance procedures have been applied to parties and non-parties alike. States, therefore, have sought to participate in discussions that concern them.

The Convention institutions are a Conference of States Parties (Art. XI) and a Secretariat (Art. XII). The first meets every two years to examine progress in the restoration and conservation of protected species.[57] It receives and examines any report presented by the Secretariat or by a state party. Its role is particularly important in adapting the Convention to evolving conditions, especially in amending Appendices I and II. Amendments, which may involve transferring a species from one list to another as it becomes more or less endangered, are adopted by a two-thirds majority of parties present and voting at a Conference of the parties. The amendments enter into force ninety days after the session for all Parties, except those that file a reservation with respect to the amendment within ninety days from notification. In 1994, the COP adopted a system of classifying its rules as 'resolutions', 'revised resolutions' and 'decisions'. Although none of the categories of resolutions are legally binding, they are authoritative and influential.

A Standing Committee of the Conference, established in 1979, operates between meetings of the Conference. It has been instrumental in developing methods of collective action against non-compliance, based on Article XIV(1), which allows parties to take stricter domestic measures than those provided by the treaty. In a number of cases, the Committee has recommended that all parties apply the article collectively, if temporarily, against individual countries found to be in persistent non-compliance,[58] including non-parties.[59]

57 The meetings are open to observers from the United Nations, non-party states, specialized agencies and IAEA as well as non-governmental organizations and other intergovernmental bodies.

58 United Arab Emirates, 1985–1990; Thailand, 1991–2. CITES Secretariat (1991), Notification to the Parties No. 636 (April 22) (recommending the ban) and No. 673 (April 2, 1992) (lifting the ban). Italy, 1992–3, CITES Secretariat (1992), Notification to the Parties No. 675 (June 30) (recommending the ban), and No. 842 (April 18,1995) (lifting the ban).

59 El Salvador, 1986–7, and Equatorial Guinea, 1988–92. In both cases the ban was lifted after the countries became CITES states parties.

Unilateral action also has been taken by states parties to enforce CITES protections.[60]

The Secretariat of the Convention, provided by the Executive Director of UNEP in Geneva, has extensive powers and functions. In addition to the normal duties of multilateral international organizations, the Secretariat undertakes scientific and technical studies, reviews the reports of states parties, and may request further information as necessary to ensure implementation of the Convention. It periodically publishes and distributes to the Parties the lists contained in the Conventions Appendices and makes recommendations for implementing the aims and provisions of the Convention. The role of the Secretariat is particularly important in monitoring compliance with the agreement. Each state party must maintain records of trade in specimens of species listed in the different Appendices to the Convention and must prepare periodic reports on enforcement of the Convention. When the Secretariat considers, in light of the information received, that a species listed in Appendix I or II is affected adversely by trade or that provisions of the Convention are not being effectively implemented, it communicates the information to the Management Authorities of the state or states concerned. In turn, the states must inform the Secretariat of any relevant facts and, where appropriate, propose remedial action. The Secretariat also may authorize an inquiry. The information provided or acquired by an inquiry is reviewed by the next Conference of the Parties, which can make recommendations that it deems appropriate.

Commentators are divided over the effectiveness of CITES.[61] Critics note that few states have enacted the full panoply of national measures required to give effect to all aspects of the Convention and resolutions and decisions of the Conferences. The record of national reporting also is mixed. In contrast, however, many early reservations have been withdrawn and COP interpretations have narrowed exceptions while allowing flexibility to accommodate short term special needs. The flexibility of CITES has been demonstrated by the action of parties to CITES in adopting an innovative approach to shifting species from Appendix I to II, in part to respond to controversy over the listing of the African

60 See Sand, at 22 (discussing, inter alia, US actions against Singapore and Taiwan and EU actions against Indonesia).

61 See e.g. Holly Dublin, Tom Milliken, and Richard Barnes, *Four Years After the CITES Ban: Illegal Killing of Elephants, Ivory Trade and Stockpiles*, Report of the IUCN/SSC African Elephant Specialist Group (1995); Patty Storey, 'Development vs. Conservation: The Future of the African Elephant' (1994) 18 William & Mary J. Envtl L. 375; Andrew Heimert, 'How the Elephant Lost His Tusks' (1995) 104 Yale L.J. 1473; James Barnes, 'Changes in the Economic Use Value of Elephants in Botswana: The Effect of International Trade Prohibitions' (1996) 18 Ecological Econ. 215.

elephant. The use of 'annotations' to the listing provides added protection by imposing specific restrictions to types of trade when a species is moved from Appendix I to Appendix II. Three well-known examples may be cited: the 1987 transfer of certain populations of vicuna included an annotation permitting only trade in wool sheared from live animals; the South African population of white rhinoceros appeared on Appendix II with an annotation allowing trade in live animals and sport hunted trophies. Finally, the African elephant populations of Zimbabwe, Botswana and Namibia were transferred to Appendix II, subject to an annotation for trade in ivory stockpiles and skins. These measures help induce wider cooperation by tolerating a measure of deviation from strict treaty norms. The combination of incentives and disincentives help achieve some of the Convention goals, but create major enforcement problems.

As a result of concerns about annotations undermining the overall effectiveness of CITES, the 2000 CITES meeting adopted Conference Resolution 11.21 regulating their use. The resolution calls on parties to specify the conditions for import, export and re-export of species whose listing is annotated and directs the Secretariat and the Standing Committee to investigate reports of illegal trade in such species. If the Standing Committee finds illegal trade, it can request parties to suspend trade in that species and ask the Depository Government to submit a proposal to return the species to Appendix I.

Debate over the economics of banning trade and the rising populations of listed species have led to controversy and alternative legal arrangements, exemplified by actions in regard to the African elephant. Throughout the 1980s, elephant populations declined drastically, principally due to trade in ivory. The 1989 CITES Conference placed the elephant in Appendix I, despite the concerns of some states with significant elephant populations.[62] Elephant herds soon began to increase and beginning in 1992, southern African states sought to remove the species from Appendix I in order to engage in managed trade. In 1997, the CITES conference moved to Appendix II the African elephant populations of Namibia, Zimbabwe and Botswana, but kept all other populations in Appendix I. The Appendix II listing was annotated to permit only an experimental sale of one consignment to Japan and it was subject to a number of conditions. In particular, CITES required that the ivory not be the product of poaching and that revenue from the sale be used for elephant conservation.[63] South Africa's elephant population was moved to Appendix II

62 Japan reserved the right to import raw ivory from African CITES parties.

63 Tenth Meeting of the Conference of the Parties, 1997, Decisions 10.1, 10.2. The sale of the ivory produced revenues of approximately $5 million. See Hunter and others, *International Environmental Law and Policy* (6th ed., Foundation Press 2022).

at the 2000 Conference. In exchange, all four African states agreed to a two-year zero quota in sales. In 2016, a proposal to bring elephant populations in Namibia, Zimbabwe and Botswana to Appendix I was put to vote but failed to reach the necessary majority, despite the support of Botswana, which hosts the world's largest elephant population.

Even before CITES moved the elephant populations from Appendix I to Appendix II, southern African states took action to resume marketing of ivory. In mid-1991, five southern cone states signed an Agreement to Establish a Southern African Center for Ivory Marketing (SACIM).[64] Although the title refers only to ivory, the preamble recognizes the advantages of controlling within the region the trade in elephant ivory and other wildlife products, in order to acquire the maximum revenues from sales of wildlife products. Moreover, Article XVIII provides that the Board of the Center may extend the agreement to other wildlife populations and products. The Center, located in Botswana, is created to establish, monitor and control a simple system for the marketing of ivory and other elephant products and a central facility to receive, store, inventory, mark and sell elephant products (Art. III). It also acts to strengthen elephant product manufacturing and processing industries and markets and facilitate the sale of elephant products. The Center is the repository for information on all aspects of elephant management and conservation, population statistics, movements and behavior, as well as relationships between elephants and their habitats. It assists in determining the optimum elephant populations for the member countries and assist in elephant population management and conservation.

Pursuant to Article IV, elephant product sales are centralized. Each country agrees to monitor elephant populations and market ivory only through the Center, except for hunting trophies and small processing by nationals. The country will not exceed the annual ivory production determined for it by the Center. In turn, the Center remits to each member the proceeds generated by the sale of products which originated from that member, less fees for the Center (Art. III(e)). All importation of elephant products and the exportation of commercial shipments of worked ivory are prohibited until the Center decides otherwise (Art. 4(f)). Whole ivory tusks can be exported only to the Center, which shall determine the annual ivory production for each member state. The states will maintain a register and mark the ivory. No private dealing in or resale of unworked ivory is permitted. States are not only to take legislative, administrative or other measures necessary according to the Agreement or

64 June 20, 1991 (Lilongwe, Malawi). The states that signed the agreement are Botswana, Malawi, Namibia, Zambia and Zimbabwe.

recommended by the Center, but shall consider increasing penalties for poaching and smuggling.

The Center is governed by a Board, made up of one representative of each member state selected from senior officers of the Department of Wildlife. It meets twice each year and decisions are taken by consensus. The Board appoints a director who is the chief executive of the Center. To ensure that the Center can function, each state contributes to the Capital Fund for its establishment and operation. An Elephant Conservation Fund, generated by the sale of ivory and other elephant products, was designated for the promotion of elephant conservation and management. Despite this, and the efforts of CITES, poaching of elephants reached new highs in 2015; in a major development in the latter part of the year, China banned the importation of ivory.

Regarding implementation and enforcement, CITES relies mainly on the proper functioning of national management and effective border control. In some countries, illicit wildlife trafficking is poorly controlled because of inadequate enforcement of laws or because the penalties for such crimes are not sufficiently severe. In this regard, the UN General Assembly adopted a resolution in 2015 titled 'Tackling illicit trafficking in wildlife'. This resolution urged states to strengthen enforcement and criminal justice responses and called for enhanced measures against such crimes under the UN Convention against Transnational Organized Crime. This resolution was adopted shortly after the 2030 Agenda for Sustainable Development, which under Sustainable Development Goal (SDG) 15 (target 15.7), specifically calls for urgent action 'to end poaching and trafficking of protected species of flora and fauna and address both demand and supply of illegal wildlife products'. At COP18, in 2017, the 11.3 Resolution on Compliance and Enforcement was revised, directing the CITES Secretariat to 'pursue closer international liaison between the Convention's institutions, regional and subregional wildlife enforcement networks and national enforcement agencies, and to work in close cooperation with ICPO-INTERPOL, the United Nations Office on Drugs and Crime, the World Bank and the World Customs Organization'.[65]

5.3 *Driftnet Fishing*

Several legal measures on both global and regional levels attempt to combat large scale pelagic driftnet fishing. At the beginning of the regulatory efforts, more than one thousand fishing vessels used large-scale pelagic driftnets of up to 48 kilometers (30 miles), nets that were often referred to as 'walls of death'

65 COP18 Com. II. 27.

because they captured everything in their path. On November 24, 1989, twenty-one countries adopted the International Convention for the Prohibition of Fishing with Long Driftnets in the South Pacific. Open to members of the South Pacific Forum and states responsible for territories within the Convention area, it attached additional instruments for signature by distant-water fishing nations and by all Pacific rim countries who wished to express their solidarity with the objectives of the Wellington Convention.

The Convention requires each party to take measures to prohibit the use of driftnets more than 2.5 kilometers long and the trans-shipment of driftnet catches. Each party may take more stringent measures against driftnet fishing activities, such as prohibiting the landing of driftnet catches within its territory, the processing of driftnet catches in facilities under its jurisdiction, or the importing of fish or fish products caught by means of driftnets. States parties also may restrict port access and port servicing facilities for driftnet fishing vessels and prohibit the possession of driftnets on board any fishing vessel within areas under its fisheries jurisdiction. More generally, each party agrees to take measures consistent with international law to restrict driftnet fishing in the Convention area and to take measures leading to the withdrawal of good standing of registered vessels engaging in driftnet fishing activities. All Parties undertake to collaborate in surveillance and enforcement and consult on matters relating to driftnet fishing activities.

United Nations General Assembly resolution 46/215 of December 20, 1991, adopted upon the entry into force of the Wellington Convention, called for a ban on driftnet fishing as of December 31, 1992 and specifically called for individual and collective measures to prevent driftnet fishing operations on the high seas. On April 14, 1991, New Zealand adopted legislation to prohibit driftnet fishing activities in its Exclusive Economic Zone (EEZ) and implement the Wellington Convention. The law is more stringent than the Convention, targeting driftnets more than one kilometer in length and giving broad powers of search, arrest and seizure to enforcement officers. Persons convicted of an offense under the act are subject to fines. The United States adopted similar legislation, called the High Seas Driftnet Fisheries Enforcement Act, on November 2, 1992. The Act denies port privileges and establishes sanctions for high seas driftnet fishing. The President also is required to consult with the government of countries whose fishing fleets still engage in driftnet fishing. If the consultations are not satisfactorily concluded within 90 days, the President must direct the Secretary of the Treasury to prohibit the importation into the United States of fish and fish products and sport fishing equipment from that nation. The denial of port privileges and sanctions remain in effect until certification to the President and Congress that such nation has terminated driftnet fishing.

The South Pacific Forum Fisheries Agency took similar action when it adopted a Treaty on Cooperation in Fisheries Surveillance and Law Enforcement in the South Pacific Region at its 23rd session.[66] The objective of the Treaty is to promote maximum effectiveness in regional surveillance and enforcement through cooperation between countries on a reciprocal or joint basis. The Agreement, Article IV, provides for the implementation of harmonized minimum terms and conditions of fisheries access. The Parties agree they will not license any fishing vessel that is not registered by the South Pacific Forum Fisheries Agency and they agree to exchange information to the extent permitted by the national laws on the location and movement of fishing vessels, licensing and fisheries surveillance and law enforcement activities (Art. V). Article VI provides for a Subsidiary Agreement on mechanisms of cooperation in surveillance and enforcement, allowing reciprocal enforcement in the territorial seas and archipelagic waters of the parties. Extradition procedures and other criminal procedure matters also may be detailed in further agreements (Art. VII, VIII).

The Council of Fisheries Ministers of the EC in 1998 agreed to ban driftnet fishing in EU waters by all vessels flying the flags of EU states as of January 1, 2002, when intended to capture highly migratory species like tuna and swordfish.[67] An earlier regulation permitted driftnets of up to 2.5 km had proven impossible to enforce. A further ban was adopted for the Baltic Sea from January 1, 2008, in order to protect dolphins and porpoises. A lack of consistent enforcement of the rules forbidding using driftnets to catch certain migratory fishes, meant the practice has continued to be a cause of concern due to the incidental catching of marine mammals, sea turtles and sea birds which are mostly protected under EU legislation. To fight circumvention, the European Commission proposed in May 2014[68] a full ban of driftnets fishing in the EU as well as the prohibition of keeping driftnets on board of fishing vessels. Furthermore, to avoid ambiguity, the proposal provided a detailed definition of a driftnet.

66 Niue, July 9, 1992.

67 Council Regulation 1239/98 of June 8, 1998 amending Regulation 894/97 laying down certain technical measures for the conservation of fishery resources, O.J. L 171 (6/17/98), 1–4.

68 Proposal for a Regulation of the European Parliament and of the Council laying down a prohibition on driftnet fisheries, amending Council Regulations (EC) No 850/98, (EC) No 812/2004, (EC) No 2187/2005 and (EC) No 1967/2006 and repealing Council Regulation (EC) No 894/97/* COM/2014/0265 final – 2014/0138 (COD).

6 Protection of Species or Groups of Species

A large number of treaties aim at protecting specific animal species, such as polar bears, or at conserving groups of species, like whales, seals, and birds.[69] The treaties often are concluded on a regional basis because of the localization of the species, but states that are not habitat states sometimes adhere to the agreements for reasons of principle. The European Union also has enacted regulations and directives on this subject.

6.1 *Marine Living Resources*

In recent years, marine biodiversity has become increasingly threatened due to pollution from land-based and other sources, over-exploitation, the introduction of alien species, coastal development, and global climate change and ozone depletion.[70] The 1958 Convention on Fishing and Conservation of the Living Resources of the High Seas addressed only a few of the problems, being focused on commercial fishing, and it has been largely superseded by the 1982 United Nations Convention on the Law of the Sea (UNCLOS) and other agreements. At UNCED, Agenda 21 called for a commitment to conserve and sustainably use the marine living resources, to maintain biological diversity and productivity, cooperate on information exchange and data requirements, and to provide support to developing countries (Chapter 17.46).

The problem of over-fishing has received far more attention than the problem of marine biodiversity because of the global importance of fisheries and the urgency of the threat to them. In 2019, FAO reported that over 35 percent of the world's capture fish stocks were classified as overfished, as measured by SDG Indicator 14.4.1 on the sustainability of fish stocks. The decreasing number of fish has led to conflicts between the approximately seventy coastal states and ten long-range fishing states competing for the resources. In fact, twenty countries account for eighty percent of the world marine catches, nearly all of which occurs in areas under national jurisdiction. The first Report of the UN Secretary General in March 2000 on Oceans and the Law of the Sea called illegal, unregulated and unreported fishing as one of the most severe problems

---

69 To date, there are no instruments devoted to specific species of wild plant life, although tropical timber in general is increasingly regulated.

70 Endangered marine species include: Mediterranean monk seal, trembling sea mat, blue whale, blue fin tuna, Stellers sea cow, Caribbean monk seal, black coral, giant claim, Northern right whale, estuarine crocodile, starlet sea anemone, Christmas frigate bird, Galapagos flightless cormorant, Spot billed pelican, Townsend's shearwater.

facing global fisheries.[71] Further reports eventually resulted in a General Assembly resolution 69/109 of December 9, 2014 adopting a program for sustainable fisheries.

The interdependence of over-exploited fishing resources with non-target species and ecosystems has led to the conclusion of international legal instruments of broader scope, including within them new principles, norms, decision-making procedures, and institutional arrangements to address marine biodiversity generally, from bans on driftnet fishing to codes of conduct for responsible fishing.

UNCLOS, adopted December 10, 1982 in Montego Bay, contains important provisions relating to conservation of marine living resources. Its general rule affirms coastal state authority to ensure the conservation of biological resources in the zones over which it exercises jurisdiction, i.e., the territorial sea, the exclusive economic zone, and the continental shelf.[72] The exclusive economic zone, because of its size and above all because of its objectives, is of primary importance in conservation of the marine living resources. In this region the coastal state has sovereign rights to explore and exploit, conserve and manage the natural resources, but it also has the duty to ensure, through proper conservation and management, that the maintenance of the living resources is not endangered by over-exploitation.[73] UNCLOS Article 61 requires the coastal state to cooperate in appropriate cases with international organizations to achieve the goal of maintaining or restoring populations of harvested species at levels that can produce the maximum sustainable yield. An important innovation reflecting a broad ecological perspective is the requirement that the coastal state take into consideration the effects of its measures on species associated with or dependent upon harvested species, in order to maintain or restore these populations above levels at which their reproduction may become seriously threatened.

The extent of the zones under coastal state jurisdiction creates problems with respect to marine animals that traverse more than one nation's zones. The Convention designates five categories:

a. Stocks of species that occur within the exclusive economic zones of several coastal states or within the economic zone of one and an area adjacent to that zone, are regulated by conservation measures agreed

71 Report of the Secretary-General, Oceans and the Law of the Sea: U.N.G.A. 55th Sess, U.N. Doc. A/55/61 (2000) at 26.

72 Arts. 21(1)(d), 56(1), 61–65, 73(1) and 77.

73 Arts. 56(1) and 61(2).

upon by the concerned states either directly or through appropriate international organizations (Art. 63).

b. For highly migratory species, such as tuna, whales, and sharks, the coastal state and other states whose nationals fish in the adjacent regions, shall seek agreement on the measures necessary to conserve and develop these species (Art. 64).

c. Marine mammals can be regulated more strictly by the coastal state or a competent international organization. Measures may include prohibition, limitation or regulation of the exploitation of such animals (Art. 65).

d. Anadromous species, those fish such as salmon, which reproduce in rivers and live in the sea, pose complex legal problems. Article 66 provides as its basic principle that states in whose rivers these stocks originate have the primary interest in and responsibility for them. They must ensure their conservation by establishing appropriate regulatory measures for fishing in all waters to the outer limits of the exclusive economic zone. For fishing outside the exclusive economic zone, the states concerned consult in order to establish the terms and conditions of such fishing, giving due regard to the conservation requirements and the needs of the state of origin. In effect, the treaty discourages fishing for these species on the high seas. When the stocks of anadromous species migrate into or through the waters of a state other than the state of origin, both states shall cooperate with regard to conservation and management of the species.

e. Catadromous species, such as eels, reproduce in the sea and live in other environments. According to Article 67, the coastal state in whose waters these species spend the greater part of their life cycle has responsibility for their management and shall ensure their ingress and egress. These species may not be harvested on the high seas and fishing for them within the exclusive economic zone is regulated by the general regulations governing the zone. Where such species migrate through the waters of more than one state, rational management must be assured by agreement between the states.

The rules adopted by the coastal state to ensure the conservation and management of the marine living resources in its exclusive economic zone can be enforced through boarding, inspection, arrest and judicial proceedings. However, the measures cannot include imprisonment or any other form of corporal punishment (Art. 72).

On the continental shelf, the Convention considers only the exploration and exploitation of natural resources and not their conservation. 'Natural resources' includes living organisms belonging to sedentary species which are either immobile on or under the seabed or are unable to move except in constant physical contact with the seabed or subsoil (Art. 77). However, considering the objectives of the Convention regarding marine living resources, stated in the Preamble, and the conservation measures required for all other marine zones, including the high seas, it seems that the coastal state also should take conservation measures with regard to these species.[74]

Conservation of marine living resources may be seen, therefore, as a general obligation, in particular, as concerns the high seas. Since no territorial jurisdiction can be exercised on the high seas because of the freedoms which exist in this area, all states have the obligation to take measures applicable to their nationals, which may be necessary for the conservation of the living resources of the high seas, and to cooperate with each other in this regard.[75] Measures must be designed, on the best scientific evidence available, to maintain or restore populations at levels which can produce the maximum sustainable yield, qualified by relevant environmental and economic factors. The interdependence of stocks must be taken into consideration in order not to threaten associated or dependent species (Art. 119). Finally, Article 120 affirms that measures taken to protect marine mammals in the exclusive economic zone may also apply to the high seas.[76] In 2006, the UN General Assembly established an ad-hoc open-ended informal working group dedicated to studying issues concerning marine biodiversity beyond national jurisdiction. The group's mandate encompassed a comprehensive examination of scientific, technical, legal, and policy-related matters pertinent to marine biodiversity beyond national jurisdiction. From 2006 to 2015, the working group convened numerous sessions, fostering discussions that explored diverse facets of marine biodiversity beyond national jurisdiction, aiming to address gaps in governance and promote international cooperation. On June 19, 2023, the Agreement under UNCLOS on the Conservation and Sustainable Use of Marine Biological Diversity of Areas beyond National Jurisdiction (BBNJ Agreement) was adopted by the Intergovernmental Conference on Marine Biodiversity of Areas Beyond National Jurisdiction convened under the auspices of the United Nations. The BBNJ Agreement, which represents the third implementing agreement to UNCLOS, aims to achieve the conservation and sustainable use of marine

74 This view is supported by Article 5 of the 1958 Convention on the Continental Shelf, which provides that the exploration of the continental shelf and the exploitation of its natural resources must not result in any unjustifiable interference with conservation of the living resources of the sea.

75 Arts. 117 and 118.

76 On the problem of protection marine living resources, see Cyrille de Klemm, 'Living Resources of the Oceans', in *the Environmental Law of the Sea* (IUCN 1981).

biological diversity in areas beyond national jurisdiction, both presently and in the long-term.

6.1.1 Fisheries

In 1999, scientists estimated that fish is the primary source of protein for close to 950 million people and is the source of employment for about one quarter of that number. Fish resources are a major component of international trade, with world exports of aquatic products (excluding algae) totaling 151 billion US$ in 2020. In some developing countries fish represent up to 80 percent of the total exports. From 1950 to 1970, fisheries production increased by approximately 6 percent annually, trebling from 18 to 56 million tons. During the 1970s, the rate of increase declined to about 2 percent and in the 1990s fell to zero. Declining catches have led to job losses and higher prices for fish.

Efforts to enforce fishing limits have been undermined by the re-flagging of fishing vessels under the flags of states that are not parties to international high seas fisheries agreements. On November 24, 1994, the 27th FAO Conference approved an Agreement to Promote Compliance with International Conservation and Management Measures by Fishing Vessels on the High Seas. The Agreement is designed to deal with re-flagging by reinforcing the responsibility of states in respect to vessels fishing on the high seas. It also aims to promote the free flow of information on high seas fishing operations. States are required to take such measures as are necessary to ensure that fishing vessels entitled to fly their flag do not engage in any activity that undermines the effectiveness of international conservation and management measures (Art. III) which are defined as measures to conserve or manage one or more species of living marine resources that are adopted and applied in accordance with rules of international law reflected in UNCLOS (Art. 1(b)). States parties are required to provide the FAO with basic information on each fishing vessel entered in the record of fishing vessels entitled to fly its flag and authorized for use on the high seas. The FAO must circulate and provide the information to any fisheries organization. The Agreement has the potential to provide a data bank on fishing operations for all vessels authorized to fish on the high seas.

The 1995 UN Straddling Stocks Agreement[77] includes the protection of marine biodiversity as one of its objectives, but maintains a concern with utilization of the resources, referring specifically to maximum sustainable yield.

---

77 Agreement for the Implementation of the Provisions of the United Nations Convention on the Law of the Sea of December 10, 1982 relating to the Conservation and Management of Straddling Fish Stocks and Highly Migratory Fish Stocks, New York, adopted August 4, 1995, opened for signature December 14, 1995.

Article 7 is characteristic, entitled 'compatibility of conservation and management measures'. The Agreement is concerned primarily with stocks that are beyond the limits of national jurisdiction, but several principles apply generally, including the precautionary principle, as well as the obligation to coordinate conservation and management measures (Art. 7). The Agreement does not specify such measures, leaving them to be agreed at regional or sub-regional levels, but there is considerable emphasis on gathering and sharing scientific, technical and statistical information (Art. 14). The text also details the duties of flag states, which is understandable given the focus on high seas activities. In many respects, the text follows the prior FAO Agreement in requiring that states parties ensure that flag ships do not engage in any activity that might undermine the effectiveness of conservation and management measures. States are not to authorize or license high seas fishing unless they can ensure compliance with applicable national, regional and international regulations. The Agreement foresees a system of boarding and inspections within the regional or sub-regional framework, followed by sanctions imposed by the flag state, although it requires states parties to exercise their rights in a manner that would not constitute an abuse of right (Art. 34). Finally, Article 33 reveals a concern about the problem of 'free riders', requiring states parties to encourage non-parties to join the Agreement and mandating states parties to take measures consistent with the Agreement and international law 'to deter the activities of vessels flying the flag of non-parties which undermine the effective implementation of this Agreement'.

Numerous regional instruments adopted throughout the twentieth century aim at proper management of fish stocks.[78] Twenty-five Pacific states adopted a Convention on the Conservation and Management of Highly Migratory Fish Stocks in the Western and Central Pacific Ocean in Honolulu on September 5, 2000. Its objective is to ensure, through effective management, the long-term conservation and sustainable use of such stocks in accordance with UNCLOS and the Agreement of August 4, 1995, relating to the conservation and management of straddling fish stocks and highly migratory fish stocks. Its principles include application of the precautionary approach, the protection of biodiversity in the marine environment, prevention and elimination of over-fishing and implementation and enforcement of conservation and management measures through effective monitoring, control and surveillance. Article 9 establishes a Commission which can determine the total allowable

78 One of the earliest agreements is the US – Great Britain Convention for Preservation of the Halibut Fishery (March 22, 1923). The Convention was replaced by a new agreement in 1959.

catch or total level of fishing efforts within the Convention area, adopt conservation and management measures and establish cooperative mechanisms for effective monitoring, control, surveillance and enforcement. A Technical and Compliance Committee receives reports from each member of the Commission relating to measures taken to monitor, investigate and penalize violations. In addition, a regional observer program allows to board independent and impartial observers authorized by the secretariat of the Commission. The activities of observers include collecting catch and scientific data, monitoring the implementation of conservation and management measures adopted by the Commission and reporting of their findings in accordance with procedures developed by the Commission. An Annex of the Convention determines the terms and conditions for fishing.

Beginning in 1992, the European Community regulated fishing through Community policy on fisheries and aquaculture, which governs the conservation, management and exploitation of living aquatic resources. The common fisheries policy aims to ensure the long-term viability of the fisheries sector through sustainable exploitation of living aquatic resources based on sound scientific advice and the precautionary approach. A Regulation of December 20, 2002[79] seeks to achieve sustainable exploitation in the waters under the jurisdiction of the member states through managing fisheries on a multi-annual basis within safe biological limits. Multi-annual management plans should establish targets and provide for coherent measures that include limiting the environmental impact of fishing. The EC Council is to adopt, as a priority, recovery plans for fisheries which are exploiting stocks above safe biological limits. Member states shall put in place measures to adjust the fishing capacity of their fleets in order to achieve a stable and enduring balance between fishing capacity and fishing opportunities. They also shall take the inspection and enforcement measures necessary to ensure compliance with common fishery policy norms in the waters subject to their jurisdiction, as well as enforcement measures relating to ships flying their flag and their nationals relating to fishing activities outside Community waters. They shall ensure that appropriate measures are taken, including administrative action or criminal proceedings, against natural or legal persons who violate the rules of the common fisheries policy. Such measures may include fines, seizure of prohibited fishing gear and catches, sequestration or temporary immobilization of the vessel, suspension or withdrawal of the license. An annex of the Regulation determines the conditions of the access to coastal waters of different member states.

79 Regulation EC No 2371/2002, O.J. L 358 (12/31/02).

Another EC Regulation, adopted December 16, 2002,[80] establishes specific access requirements and associated conditions applicable to fishing for deep-sea stocks in specified waters. It provides for a special fishing permit to be issued to vessels fishing for deep-sea species and for limiting fishing efforts in order to secure precautionary management of the stocks in the deep sea.

On May 15, 2014, the European Maritime and Fisheries Fund (EMFF) Regulation was adopted. The EMFF plays a crucial role in promoting sustainable fishing practices by helping fishers adapt to more sustainable methods. It supports coastal communities in diversifying their economies and finances projects that create new jobs and improve the quality of life along European coasts. Additionally, the fund backs sustainable aquaculture developments and simplifies access to financing for applicants. Furthermore, the EMFF supports the implementation of the EU's maritime policy, ensuring comprehensive and integrated management of maritime activities.

As discussed in previous chapters, most of the cases before the International Tribunal on the Law of the Sea have concerned illegal fishing and the requirement of prompt release of seized vessels. One of the more important cases, the *Case on the Conservation and Sustainable Exploitation of Swordfish Stocks in the South-Eastern Pacific Ocean* (Chile v. EC) was discontinued after the parties reached agreement. Another, *The Grand Prince Case* (Belize v. France) ended when it was discovered that Belize was not the flag state of the seized ship. Other examples include the *Southern Bluefin Tuna* cases (New Zealand v. Japan and Australia v. Japan) as well as the *Request for an Advisory Opinion Submitted by the Sub-Regional Fisheries Commission.*

In the southern oceans, the Convention for the Conservation of Antarctic Marine Living Resources (CCAMLR) devotes considerable efforts to protecting the Patagonian toothfish which is illegally fished throughout the area. Several ships have been arrested, while data received under the toothfish catch documentation scheme suggests that data is being misreported and the actual catch levels in CCAMLR waters may be four times higher than CCAMLR estimates.

Regimes for fisheries have been created rapidly in recent years with growing recognition of the threats to sustainability.[81] The conclusion of UNCLOS and the Straddling Stock Convention also stimulated action regionally and according to fish stock. In addition to the agreements discussed above, fisheries treaties include:

---

80 Regulation No 2347/2002, O.J. L 351 (12/28/02).

81 A complete list and texts of fisheries agreements is available at <http://www.oceanlaw.net>.

- Convention for the Conservation of Southern Bluefin Tuna (Canberra, May 10, 1993)
- International Convention for the Conservation of Atlantic Tuna (Rio de Janeiro, May 14, 1966)
- Convention for the Establishment of an Inter-American Tropical Tuna Commission (Washington D.C., May 31, 1949)
- Convention concerning Fishing in the Black Sea (Varna, July 7, 1959); and Convention on Fishing and Conservation of the Living Resources in the Baltic Sea and Belts D[82]
- Agreement for the Establishment of the Indian Ocean Tuna Commission (FAO, March 27, 1996)[83]
- Convention on the Conservation and Management of Pollack Resources in the Central Bering Sea (Washington D.C., June 16, 1994)
- Convention for the Conservation of Salmon in the North Atlantic (Reykavik, October 1, 1983)[84]
- Convention for the Future Multilateral Cooperation in North-East Atlantic Fisheries (London, November 18, 1980)
- Convention for the Conservation of Anadromous Stocks in the North Pacific Ocean (Moscow, February 11, 1992)[85]
- Convention on the Conservation of Living Marine Resources of the High Seas of the South Pacific (Santiago, August 14, 2000).
- Convention on the Conservation of Highly Migratory Fish Stocks in the Western and Central Pacific Ocean (Honolulu, September 5, 2000)

---

82 Gdansk, September 13, 1973. The Baltic Sea Fisheries Commission focuses on more selective taking methods for cod, allowing juveniles to escape nets. It adopted a joint inspection program on an experimental basis whereby inspectors from all Baltic Sea coastal states participated in testing a uniform sea and port inspection scheme.

83 This agreement contains an inspection and control scheme with non-discriminatory at-port inspections and vessel monitoring.

84 The Organization bases its work on scientific evidence that Atlantic salmon is in danger of extinction. It created an International Cooperative Salmon Research Program to identify and explain the causes of increased mortality and countermeasures that may be taken. It has a Plan of Action for the Application of the Precautionary Approach to Protection and Restoration of Atlantic Salmon Habitat which aims to produce a consistent, rational approach to the protection and restoration of habitat and provide a reporting procedure to monitor progress. Each contracting party was to establish a comprehensive salmon habitat protection and restoration plan and report by 2002.

85 Created in 1992, it has a Committee on Enforcement that uses patrols in the convention area through joint arrangements between the parties. Through the use of overflight, patrols were able to identify illegal driftnet fishing in the Russian EEZ. The ships were caught and escorted to port for further action.

- Convention on the Conservation and Management of High Seas Fishery Resources in the South Pacific Ocean (Auckland, November 14, 2000)
- Convention on the Conservation and Management of Fishery Resources in the South-East Atlantic (Windhoek, April 2001)

The World Summit on Sustainable Development (Johannesburg, 2002) called for a representative network of marine protected areas by 2012 and restoration of depleted fish stocks by 2015. It also noted that it is critical to protect breeding and spawning sites to permit stocks to multiply. At the same meeting, Costa Rica, Panama, Colombia, and Ecuador agreed to establish such a network, by creating a marine conservation and sustainable development corridor in the marine waters of the four countries. IUCN, UNESCO, UNEP, ITTA, and NGOs like Conservation International all supported the initiative. The area, geographically known as the Panama Bight, contains four marine national parks, two of them World Heritage Sites. The initiative seeks to strengthen regional and international cooperation, capacity-building, trading and education, marine and coastal biodiversity assessments, and to create a unique cluster of marine World Heritage Sites. The Corridor is defined by its oceanography, topography of the seabed, and ecological interconnectedness. It is an area in which three tectonic plates merge as well as several ocean currents and various undersea mountain ranges. The Corridor also includes the Galapagos islands.

Agenda 2030 for Sustainable Development, adopted in 2015, focuses its SDG14 on the conservation and the sustainable use of oceans, seas and marine resources for sustainable development. Two Targets are especially relevant in the context of fisheries:

> 14.4. By 2020, effectively regulate harvesting and end overfishing, illegal, unreported and unregulated fishing and destructive fishing practices and implement science-based management plans, in order to restore fish stocks in the shortest time feasible, at least to levels that can produce maximum sustainable yield as determined by their biological characteristics
>
> 14.6. By 2020, prohibit certain forms of fisheries subsidies which contribute to overcapacity and overfishing, eliminate subsidies that contribute to illegal, unreported and unregulated fishing and refrain from introducing new such subsidies, recognizing that appropriate and effective special and differential treatment for developing and least developed countries should be an integral part of the World Trade Organization fisheries subsidies negotiation.

To fulfil these Targets, the Agreement on Fisheries Subsidies was adopted in 2022 under the auspices of the World Trade Organization, as discussed in Chapter 17.

6.1.2 Marine Turtles

There are seven species of sea turtles, all of them listed on Appendix I of CITES. The three main threats to sea turtles are incidental taking, direct hunting, and habitat loss. Like marine mammals, sea turtles must breathe at the surface, so when they are trapped in longlines, gill nets, and shrimp trawls, sea turtles drown. Since the 1970s, the incidental take of turtles in shrimp trawls has been identified as the single greatest cause of sea turtle mortality in commercial fisheries.[86] Most sea turtle species also have been hunted for their carapace to be used in making jewelry and ornaments. CITES protection has reduced the turtle market for these purposes, but the consumption of sea turtles for food has increased. Efforts to revive endangered populations of sea turtles have been hampered by the loss of nesting beaches. Sea turtles lay their eggs above the high tide line of beaches. Coastal development has eliminated many traditional sites.

In the early 1980s, the US National Marine Fisheries Service developed a Turtle Excluder Device (TED), a device inserted into fishing gear to provide an escape hatch allowing turtles caught in a trawl net to be released, without, at the same time, releasing a significant amount of intended catch. Slanted bars guide sea turtles and other large objects out of a net through a trap door, while smaller fish swim through the bars on the device to escape the net. Early TEDs excluded 97 percent of the entrapped sea turtles, retained most shrimp, increased trawling efficiency, and reduced fish by-catch by 50–60 percent as well. The use of TEDs has resulted in significantly fewer dead sea turtles washing up on beaches. Some foreign governments have shown an interest in acquiring TED technology and in developing national TED programs and US agencies have provided training and promoted the transfer of TEDs technology. A 1989 amendment to the US Endangered Species Act requires the US government to negotiate with other countries for agreements promoting the conservation of sea turtles and, in particular, mandating the use of TEDs by their fleets if they may endanger sea turtles species protected by US legislation.[87] Moreover, the US introduced an import restriction of foreign shrimp and shrimp products precisely to ensure the protection of sea turtles: to export shrimp to the US, as of May 1996, all countries in whose waters shrimps and sea turtles coexist had to be certified by the US State Department as having and enforcing legislation requiring turtle excluder devices on commercial shrimp trawlers. This measure triggered a dispute at the WTO (*US – Shrimp*) because it is trade restrictive (see Chapter 17).

86 Karen A. Bjorndal, (ed) *Biology and Conservation of Sea Turtles* (1982) 489.

87 Pub. L. No. 101–162, 609(a)(1)(2), 103 Stat. 1037 (1989), codified at 16 U.S.C. 1537.

In 1996, the first international treaty to address the conservation of sea turtles was signed. The Inter-American Convention for the Protection and Conservation of Sea Turtles (Caracas, December 1, 1996) establishes national sea turtle conservation programs in the signatory countries. It applies to land and maritime zones of the parties and to vessels on the high seas which they register. Complementing the CITES prohibition on international trade, parties to the Inter-American Convention are required to prohibit the intentional capture, retention, or killing of sea turtles as well as the domestic trade in sea turtles, their eggs, parts or products. Parties are required, to the extent practicable, to restrict human activities that could seriously affect sea turtles, especially during the periods of reproduction, nesting and migration, as well as protect and restore sea turtle habitat and nesting areas. Most important, in reducing to the greatest extent practicable the incidental harm and taking of sea turtles through fishing activities, parties must require the use of appropriate gear including the use of Turtle Excluding Devices. Shrimp trawl vessels subject to a party's jurisdiction must use TEDs or other measures that are equally effective to protect sea turtles. If a party permits measures other than the use of TEDs, it must provide scientific evidence demonstrating the lack of risk to sea turtles.

The Convention creates two bodies. The Consultative Committee reviews country reports and information relating to the protection and conservation of sea turtles and their habitats, including the environmental, socio-economic and cultural impacts of conservation measures on affected communities. It recommends changes to the Convention which may be adopted at the biennial Meeting of the Parties. All decisions must be adopted by consensus. The Scientific Committee, playing a similar role to the Whaling Scientific Committee, reviews the status of sea turtle conservation efforts and proposes recommendations for enhanced protection to the Consultative Committee based on scientific data. The Convention accepts that highly migratory species can only be protected on the international level.

In the same vein, the Protocol concerning Specially Protected Areas and Wildlife (SPAW Protocol) to the Convention for the Protection and Development of the Marine Environment of the Wider Caribbean Region complements the Inter-American Convention. All six species of Caribbean sea turtle are listed in Annex II of the SPAW Protocol. On a sub-regional level, the International Agreement for the Conservation of Caribbean Sea Turtles (Tripartite Agreement), deals specifically with the Caribbean coasts of Costa Rica, Nicaragua and Panama, signed by the presidents of the three nations on May 8, 1998. Two Memoranda of Understanding adopted in the context of the Bonn Convention on Migratory Species also concern sea turtles: the Memorandum of Understanding concerning Conservation Measures for Marine Turtles on the

Atlantic Coast of Africa[88] and the MOU on Conservation and Management of Marine Turtles and Their Habitats of the Indian Ocean and South East Asia.[89]

6.1.3 Marine Mammals

Of all the marine species exploited by man, the 80 species of cetacean, especially large whales, were the first to be over-exploited; as early as the 13th century they had practically disappeared from the Bay of Biscay.[90] By the 1930s it was clear that whale stocks needed international protection. The technical means placed at the disposition of whale hunters – in particular factory ships – accelerated the process and today the majority of species of whales are threatened with extinction.

The international community has made somewhat belated efforts to remedy this situation, but the measures have been opposed by those countries particularly attached to whaling for reasons of history, culture and economy. In 1931 the first Convention for the Regulation of Whaling[91] attempted to limit the destruction by protecting two particularly endangered species, right whales and bowhead whales, and in seeking to regulate hunting.[92] The Convention forbade killing young whales and nursing mothers, and required utilization of as much of the entire killed whale as possible. However, no quota was established. Even so, several leading whaling states refused to accept the convention.

Initially, the International Convention for the Regulation of Whaling (Washington D.C., December 2, 1946) represented a considerable advance in the situation. It was not drafted as a conservation convention, but as a fishing treaty regulating whaling in order to prevent over-exploitation and conserve and develop whale stocks. The goal was to safeguard whales for future generations as a 'great natural resource'. However, dramatic and continued depletion in the number of whales and the adherence of numerous states that have ceased whaling or have never engaged in it have combined to alter the approach of the regulatory organ which the Convention created, the International Whaling Commission (IWC). The Commission is composed of one member from each Contracting Government, assisted by a Technical Committee and Scientific Committee which meets prior to the meeting of the full Commission. The Commission undertakes its main activities during the annual sessions where

88 Abidjan, May 29, 1999, in force July 1, 1999, reprinted in 39 ILM 1 (2000).

89 June 23, 2001, in force September 1, 2001. Fifteen range states have signed: Australia, Cambodia, Comores, Iran, Kenya, Madagascar, Mauritius, Myanmar, Philippines, Seychelles, Sri Lanka, United Kingdom, Tanzania, United States and Vietnam.

90 Simon Lyster, *International Wildlife Law* (Cambridge University Press 1985) 17.

91 155 L.N.T.S. 349, in force January 16, 1935.

92 Indigenous whaling remained exempt from limitations.

it adopts recommendations, organizes studies and inquiries on whales and whaling, collects and analyses statistical information on the current condition and trend of whale stocks and the effects of whaling activities on these populations.[93]

The Convention applies to all whale catchers including aircraft under the jurisdiction of states parties and to 'all waters' in which whaling takes place. Article 1(2) 'Whale' is not defined. Although the IWC initially regulated only larger whales, since 1976 it has taken limited steps toward including smaller cetaceans such as killer and pilot whales.[94] An annexed Schedule to the Convention contains regulations on whaling. The Commission has the power to modify the Schedule according to Article 5 of the Convention:

> By adopting regulations with respect to the conservation and utilization of whale resources, fixing (a) protected and unprotected species; (b) open and closed seasons; (c) open and closed waters, including the designation of sanctuary areas; (d) size limits for each species; (e) time, methods, and intensity of whaling (including the maximum catch of whales to be taken in any one season); (f) types and specifications of gear and apparatus and appliances which may be used; (g) methods of measurement; and (h) catch returns and other statistical and biological records.

Any modification, which must be adopted by a three quarters majority of the Parties, enters into force 90 days after the date on which the Commission notifies the contracting states. However, each government present can submit an objection to a modification within the 90-day period; the modification thereafter enters into force only for non-objecting states (Art. 5). The procedure has been used by whaling states in the past to override decisions of the IWC.

Two other escape clauses exist and limit protection for whales. First, Article 8 authorizes governments of states parties to grant a special permit to any of their nationals authorizing them to kill, capture, and treat whales for purposes of scientific research. All authorizations granted must be brought to the attention of the Whaling Commission whose Scientific Committee is responsible for reviewing proposed permits before they are issued. However, the Convention establishes neither the number nor the conditions for issuance of permits, leaving this to the determination of states Parties. In fact, not all states have respected the Scientific Committee recommendations. The other exemption from the Convention's regulatory obligations is the permission generally

---

93 Art. 4. The Rules of Procedure allow non-parties, international organizations and non-governmental organizations to observe under certain conditions.

94 Whaling Convention Schedule para. 26.

accorded to indigenous populations to continue whaling. At its July 1985 session, the Commission for the first time gave a quota to the Inuits of Alaska and Greenland which could not be exceeded.

In any case, the Commission's modifications of the regulatory scheme of the Schedule have multiplied since 1949. For many years, the Commission experimented with different management schemes for whales, but failed to halt the progressive disappearance of certain species and reduction of the overall numbers. Consequently, the regulations issued at the 37th annual session of the Commission, held in 1985, brought considerable changes. First, the Commission declared a definitive end to commercial whaling of certain species, notably blue and gray whales, and narwhals. Second, the Indian Ocean was declared off limits to whaling, being declared a sanctuary. Third, whaling by certain particularly cruel methods was prohibited. Finally, undoubtedly the most important decision was to institute a moratorium, a suspension of all commercial whaling, beginning with the 1985–1986 season and the following period, until the Commission reexamined the situation of whales in 1990.[95] Some whaling states remained opposed to these measures and refused to adhere to them.

The Convention and Schedule provide for both national enforcement and international supervision of the obligations they impose. National inspectors have been required on whalers since 1949 and a scheme of international observers was established in 1971. The international observers are appointed by the IWC, but nominated and paid by governments.[96] They may be placed on ships or land stations of whaling countries. In addition to these measures, states must report and prevent violations of the Convention (Art. 9) and supply information on its registered ships.[97]

Strong national measures to implement the Convention have been taken by various states including the United States, which prohibits US nationals or vessels from whaling on the high seas.[98] In addition, legislation authorizes and, in some cases, requires the US government to take economic sanctions against states which violate the IWC.[99]

In 2001, a major dispute arose over Iceland's bid to rejoin the International Whaling Commission. Iceland quit in 1992 in protest over the international whaling ban. It sought readmission while announcing that it did not intend

95 ibid, para. 10(e). See EPL 8 (1985).

96 Whaling Convention, Schedule, para. 21(c).

97 ibid, para. 28.

98 Marine Mammal Prot. Act of 1972 as amended, 16 USC §1361-2, 1371–84, and 1401–07.

99 Fisherman Protective Act of 1967, 22 U.S.C. §1978 (Supp. V 1981) and the Fishing Convention and Management Act of 1976, 16 U.S.C. 1821(e)(2) (Supp. V 1981).

to comply with the ban on commercial whaling. The Commission, by a vote of 19–18, with one nation abstaining, decided that it had the competence to decide on the legality of Iceland's reservation and thus determine Iceland's status. Nineteen states then voted in favor of a resolution declaring that the Commission rejected Iceland's reservation, 3 abstained, while 16 refused to take part on the basis that the vote was illegal. Iceland rejected the vote as illegal and announced that it would not abide by it.

The 2003 meeting of the International Whaling Commission produced a major change in policy. On July 19, the 'Berlin Initiative' created a Conservation Committee and effectively redefined the role of the Whaling Commission away from managing stocks to addressing the multiple threats to their survival. The primary objective is now to conserve whales for present and future generations. Incidental catches of marine mammals, marine pollution, heavier and faster shipping, and rising ocean temperatures due to climate change are threats today as much as the deliberate taking of whales. Pollution is especially a problem for creatures at the top of the food chain who ingest the accumulated pollutants of the ocean. While the IWC reached agreement on the creation of the Conservation Committee, the three remaining whaling states (Japan, Norway and Iceland) announced continuation of 'scientific takings' permitted by the Convention.

After years of controversy over the Japanese whaling program, Australia filed an application at the International Court of Justice (ICJ) in 2010, asking the ICJ for a declaratory judgment that Japan's program, known as JARPA II, was not a program for purposes of scientific research within the meaning of Article VIII of the Convention. In Australia's view, it followed from this that Japan had breached and continued to breach: (1) the obligation to respect the moratorium setting zero catch limits for the killing of whales from all stocks for commercial purposes (para. 10 (e)); (2) the obligation not to undertake commercial whaling of fin whales in the Southern Ocean Sanctuary (para. 7 (b)); and (3) the obligation to observe the moratorium on the taking, killing or treating of whales, except minke whales, by factory ships or whale catchers attached to factory ships (para. 10 (d)). Moreover, according to Australia's final submissions, when authorizing JARPA II, Japan also failed to comply with the procedural requirements set out in paragraph 30 of the Schedule for proposed scientific permits. Australia also sought a declaration that Japan must halt its whaling program. New Zealand intervened in support of Australia. The Court issued its judgment on March 31, 2014,[100] upholding Australia's claims.

100 Whaling in the Antarctic (Australia v. Japan: New Zealand intervening), Judgment, I.C.J. Reports 2014, p. 226.

Taking into account the Preamble and other relevant provisions of the Whaling Convention, the ICJ observed that programs for purposes of scientific research should foster scientific knowledge and they may pursue an aim other than either conservation or sustainable exploitation of whale stocks. This is reflected in the Guidelines issued by the IWC for the review of scientific permit proposals by the Scientific Committee. The applicable Guidelines referred not only to programs that 'contribute information essential for rational management of the stock' or those that are relevant for 'conduct[ing] the comprehensive assessment' of the moratorium on commercial whaling, but also those responding to 'other critically important research needs'. The current Guidelines, Annex P, list three broad categories of objectives. Besides programs aimed at 'improv[ing] the conservation and management of whale stocks', they envisage programs which have as an objective to 'improve the conservation and management of other living marine resources or the ecosystem of which the whale stocks are an integral part' and those directed at 'test[ing] hypotheses not directly related to the management of living marine resources'.

An important aspect of the case involved whether the standard of review should focus on good faith or an objective analysis of the program. The Court decided on the latter: 'When reviewing the grant of a special permit authorizing the killing, taking and treating of whales, the Court will assess, first, whether the program under which these activities occur involves scientific research. Secondly, the Court will consider if the killing, taking and treating of whales is "for purposes of" scientific research by examining whether, in the use of lethal methods, the program's design and implementation are reasonable in relation to achieving its stated objectives' (para. 67). In deciding these issues, the Court declined to adopt criteria for determining what constitutes scientific research. Instead, it focused on whether Japan's program was 'for purposes of' such research, examining whether the design and implementation of the program was reasonable in light of its four stated research objectives. Taken as a whole, the Court concluded that JARPA II involved activities that could broadly be characterized as scientific research, but that the evidence did not establish that the program's design and implementation were reasonable in relation to achieving its stated objectives. The Court therefore concluded that the special permits granted by Japan for the killing, taking and treating of whales in connection with JARPA II are not 'for purposes of scientific research' pursuant to Article VIII(1) of the Convention. It also found violations of some of the obligations under the Schedule. Perhaps most importantly, because the program was an on-going one, the Court found it appropriate to order 'that Japan shall revoke any extant authorization, permit or license to kill, take or treat whales in relation to JARPA II, and refrain from granting any further permits under

Article VIII, paragraph 1, of the Convention, in pursuance of that program' (para. 245). Japan announced it would comply with the judgment and did not conduct Antarctic whaling during 2014, although it took 30 whales in the Pacific. The government announced in September 2015, that it would resume taking whales in the Antarctic for 'scientific research' under a new plan that reduced the quota for minke whales taken from 855 to 333. The IWC was not scheduled to meet until 2016.

In addition to the regulations in the Whaling Convention, the CITES prohibits trade in certain kinds of whales, such as the blue whale and the narwhal, by placing them on its Appendix I list. In addition, the Bern Convention establishes strict protection for several kinds of whale. The Agreement on the Conservation of Small Cetaceans of the Baltic and North Sea (New York, March 17, 1992), concluded in the framework of the Convention on Migratory Species, is based upon recognition 'that small cetaceans are and should remain an integral part of marine ecosystems'. Primarily concerned with harbor porpoises, it recognizes that by-catches, habitat deterioration and disturbance may adversely affect these populations. The parties agree to cooperate to achieve and maintain a favorable conservation status for small cetaceans, according to obligations of conservation, research and management prescribed in an Annex to the Convention. The Annex contains provisions on habitat conservation and management, surveys and research, reporting and retrieving stranded specimens, legislation to prohibit intentional taking and killing of small cetaceans, and information and education of the general public. The treaty itself requires that each party submit an annual report on the progress made and difficulties experienced in implementing the agreement. Each party may take stricter conservation measures.

Institutional mechanisms include a secretariat and an advisory committee. The secretariat summarizes national reports and facilitates the exchange of information and monitoring, as well as organizes meetings and coordinates and circulates proposals for amendments to the agreement and its Annex. The Advisory Committee provides expert advice and information on the conservation and management of small cetaceans. Each party can appoint one member of the advisory committee. A Meeting of the parties is foreseen once every three years to review progress made and difficulties encountered in implementing the agreement. A lengthy list is provided in Article 6.2.1 of organizations entitled to send observers to the meetings of the parties. These include representatives of secretariats of other treaties concerned with species conservation (e.g. CITES, the Bonn and Berne Conventions, the Wadden Sea agreement, the International Whaling Commission), or with marine pollution (the Baltic Sea Marine Environment Protection Commission, the London

Dumping Convention), as well as non-party range states, the European Union, and various non-governmental organizations (IUCN). Any other body qualified in cetacean conservation and management may request to be represented by observers and can attend unless one-third of the states parties object.

A similar Agreement on the Conservation of Cetaceans of the Black Sea, Mediterranean Sea and Contiguous Atlantic Area (Monaco, November 24, 1996) calls on parties to cooperate in creating and maintaining a network of specially protected areas to conserve cetaceans within the framework of the regional seas agreements, to prohibit any taking of cetaceans, to regulate fisheries activities to minimize the incidental taking of cetaceans specifically by prohibiting the use of long driftnets; to require environmental impact assessments for specific activities; and to take measures for research, monitoring, training and emergency planning.

In 1992, states continuing to whale signed the Agreement on Cooperation in Research, Conservation and Management of Marine Mammals in the North Atlantic (April 9, 1992). The Agreement created a regional organization North Atlantic Marine Mammal Conservation Organization (NAMMCO) in response to the actions of the IWC. NAMMCO consists of four organs: a plenary Council, management committees, a Scientific Committee, and a secretariat. The Council is a forum to exchange information regarding North Atlantic marine mammals; to form, coordinate and direct the management committees and coordinate requests for scientific advice; negotiate and cooperate with other organizations and non-party states. The management committees are to propose to their members measures for conservation and management and make recommendations to the Council on scientific research. The management committees can only propose action. Decisions of the Council and the management committees are to be made by unanimous vote of those present. The Agreement provides no supervisory mechanisms for monitoring implementation or verifying compliance. As a coalition of pro-whaling states, it challenges the authority of the IWC.

6.1.4 Seals

Like whales, seals were exploited very early and on a massive scale. From the end of the 19th century conflicts arose among different states whose nationals were engaged in hunting seals. In 1893, in a case involving seals of the Bering Sea, an arbitration between the United States and British Colombia, Canada, led to a series of hunting rules helping to preserve seals from extinction. Several multilateral instruments followed, including a treaty signed in 1911 between Japan, the United States, the United Kingdom and Russia. However, these instruments were concerned with conservation of the species for strictly commercial reasons. Effective measures were taken, however, in particular the prohibition of pelagic (open sea) hunting during migration – a cause of large numbers of un-retrieved dead or wounded animals – and the limitation on the taking of numerous reproducing females. Like many other wildlife treaties, this one excluded aboriginal hunting from its ban on pelagic hunting. When the 1911 Treaty was drafted, the initial numbers of three to four million seals had been reduced to 300,000 animals; by 1950 the numbers had risen again to more than two million.

The Treaty of 1911 expired in 1941 and was replaced by the Interim Convention on Conservation of North Pacific Fur Seals (Washington, D.C., February 9, 1957). It entered into force in October 1957 between the signatory states of Canada, Japan, the United States and the Soviet Union. Concluded for an initial period of six years, it has been periodically renewed. Several times, the agreements renewing the Convention contained modifications, but as a whole the structure of the instrument has remained intact.

The objective is the national exploitation of the fur seals' resource. The preamble of the Convention states clearly the states' desire:

> To take effective measures towards achieving the maximum sustainable productivity of the fur seal resources of the North Pacific Ocean so that the fur seal populations can be brought to and maintained at the levels which will provide the greatest harvest year after year, with due regard to their relation to the productivity of other living marine resources of the area.

The same language reappears in Article 2, setting forth the aims of scientific research and in particular coordination of research programs. These activities play a considerable role: they cover the size of fur seal herds, migration routes, eating habits. In spite of its strong commercial focus, the Convention also serves the cause of conservation. Article VII forbids pelagic hunting, except for limited research purposes and by Indians, Ainu, Aleutes and Eskimo inhabiting the coasts, who hunt seals in canoes without firearms, and on condition that the furs they take not be sold.

One of the interesting characteristics of the instruments concerning North Pacific fur seals is the sharing of the animals taken supplemented by a system of 'royalties' among the contracting parties. This scheme is related to the ban on pelagic hunting, which results in clear benefits for states in whose territory breeding grounds are located, chiefly the US and USSR to compensate the parties suffering loss due to the ban, according to Article IX(1) at the end of each season, Canada and Japan receive 15 percent each of the gross number or value thereof of the seals taken by the USSR and the United States.

Article V of the Convention establishes a North Pacific Fur Seal Commission composed of one member from each party. The Commission formulates and coordinates research programs, studies the data obtained from implementation of such programs, and above all recommends appropriate measures to the Parties based on the research, including measures regarding the size and composition, by sex and age, of the seals taken, and the impact on the herd. The Protocol of May 7, 1976, adds a further element to this article in allowing the Commission to suspend the taking of seals on an island or group of islands where the number of specimens falls below the level of maximum sustainable productivity. An exception is permitted in certain cases for indigenous populations. In any case, states must report annually to the Commission the number of seals they have taken (Art. II(4)).

Another unusual aspect of the convention is that it provides for enforcement on the high seas by authorized officials of the states parties, who may board and search vessels of any other state party, if the officials have reasonable cause to believe that the prohibition on pelagic hunting has been violated. After searching, if the official continues to have reasonable cause to believe that the violation has occurred, he may seize or arrest the vessel or person. However, the vessel or individual must be delivered to the national state, which has sole prosecutorial jurisdiction.[101] Finally, each state party agrees to prohibit use of its ports or harbors for any purpose in violation of the Convention.[102] The furs acquired in violation of the Convention cannot be imported or traded, with certain limited exceptions which must be marked and certified.[103] An inter-State complaint procedure is created by Article XII, which provides that if any state considers that another party is not complying with its obligation, it may notify the other states parties and they must then meet within three months to discuss remedial measures. Seals living at the opposite end of the earth are protected by the Convention for the Conservation of Antarctic Seals within the framework of Antarctic regulation.[104]

Numerous treaties protect marine resources by establishing closed hunting and fishing seasons, especially those aimed at the conservation of particular species. Bilateral agreements, such as the Norwegian-USSR agreement

101 Art. VI.
102 Art. VIII(1).
103 Art. VIII(2).
104 See Chapter 17.

regulating hunting of seals in the North-East Atlantic (Oslo, November 22, 1957) and the Canada-Norway agreement on seal hunting and conservation of the population of the North-East Atlantic (Ottawa, July 15, 1971) often foresee closed seasons. Analogous norms are inserted also in multilateral conventions like the 1972 London Agreement for the Protection of Antarctic Seals, whose annex prohibits killing or capturing seals between March 1 and August 31.

The EEC has adopted a legal instrument specifically concerned with protecting baby seals. The massacre of young seals, in particular by Canadian hunters, was graphically exposed by photographs and provoked a strong movement of public opinion in Europe, demanding governments to act. As a result, the Council of the EEC adopted a resolution on January 5, 1983[105] followed by a Directive[106] concerning the importation into member states of furs of young seals and derivative products. According to the Directive, member states must take or maintain all necessary measures to ensure that the white furs of young harp seals and blue furs of capuchon as well as objects made from these furs are not imported for commercial purposes into their territories. The directive does not apply to products derived from traditional hunting practices by indigenous populations. In 2008, the European Commission presented the first draft of a Regulation banning seal products to the European Parliament. In May 2009, the European Parliament and the Council adopted Regulation (EC) No 1007/2009 on Trade in Seal Products which was followed, a year later, by an implementing regulation. Together, these regulations are commonly known as the 'EU Seal Regime' or the 'EU Seal Ban'. The EU Seal Regime imposes a comprehensive ban on the trade, import, and export of all seal products. The EU Seal Ban triggered a trade dispute brought by Norway against the EU to the WTO in 2011 (*EC – Seals*) (see later Chapter 17).

Also in Europe, Denmark, Germany and the Netherlands have established a treaty for the Conservation of Seals in the Wadden Sea (Bonn, October 16, 1990). Taking the most modern approach to conservation, the treaty regards the seals not only as irreplaceable natural resources, but also as important indicator species of the condition of the sea. Their protection thus requires treating the sea as a single unit, and addressing various issues apart from the taking of seals, i.e. habitat protection and pollution of the marine waters and coastal area. The Agreement was adopted within the context of the Bonn Agreement on the Conservation of Migratory Species of Wild Animals (June 23, 1979).

The Convention applies to the habitat of the seals, meaning any part of the seas, sandbanks, and shore areas of the North Sea coasts of the three countries,

---

105 O.J. C 14 (1/18/83).

106 83/129/EEC, O.J. L 91 (4/9/83).

essential to the maintenance of the vital biological functions of seals, including breeding, whelping, nursing, feeding or resting. The parties agree to cooperate to achieve and maintain a favorable conservation status for the seal population, developing a conservation and management plan for the seal population on the basis of scientific knowledge. The plan is to be kept under review and amended when necessary on the basis of scientific research. In addition, the parties shall coordinate their research and monitoring of the seal population.

The agreement calls for each party to prohibit the taking of seals from the Wadden Sea. Permits for takings may be granted to institutions performing scientific research into seal conservation or conservation of the Sea. To avoid abuse, the agreement provides that such takings are permitted 'insofar as the information required for such research cannot be obtained in any other way'. Diseased, weakened or abandoned suckling seals can be taken by designated institutions for nursing and later released and representatives of such institutions may kill seals which are clearly suffering and cannot survive. Any party granting exemptions must notify the other parties as soon as possible and provide them with an opportunity for review and comment. Appropriate action must be taken to suppress illegal hunting and taking of seals.

Habitat protection includes the possibility of creating protected areas and the preservation of habitats from adverse effects of human activities within or without the area of the agreement. The parties also agree to explore the possibility of restoring degraded habitats. Pollution control measures include identifying the sources of pollution, coordinating research projects on the effects on seals of certain substances, and monitoring levels of substances affecting the conservation status of the seal population. Finally, measures to increase public awareness are foreseen, as is the possibility of stricter domestic measures for the conservation of seals.

There also exist bilateral treaties concerning seal hunting, such as the agreement between Norway and the Soviet Union and the one between Canada and Norway, both regarding the North Atlantic region. Each treaty creates a mixed Commission which provides certain limits on hunting harp and hooded seals and walrus. These measures include quotas and regulation of scientific research. The practical application of these agreements has declined with the extension of national jurisdiction over marine resources to 200 miles.

Finally, it must be recalled that seals, or at least certain kinds of them, can be protected by the general multilateral conventions concerned with endangered species, principally CITES and the Bern Convention. Similarly, as a migratory species, seals benefit from the 1979 Bonn Convention and the provisions of UNCLOS. Finally, their habitats can be protected through application of the 1972 UNESCO World Heritage Convention. The appendix to the 1972 London

Convention for the Protection of Antarctic Seals also establishes areas where it is forbidden to kill or capture seals.

6.1.5 Polar Bears

Little reliable information exists on the Arctic polar bear; its population is thought to have seriously declined since the 1950s. This situation provoked the five circumpolar States – Canada, Denmark (including Greenland), Norway, the United States, and the USSR – to sign an Agreement on Conservation of Polar Bears in Oslo, November 15, 1973. The Convention entered into force on May 26, 1976 and by January 25, 1978 had been ratified by all five states.

The preamble recalls that the states of the Arctic Region have special responsibilities and special interests in relation to the protection of the fauna and flora of the region. The polar bear is a significant resource of the region which should benefit from this protection.

The Agreement not only provides for cooperation and certain common actions, but also contains concrete and precise obligations. For example, Article I prohibits the taking of polar bears, including hunting, killing, and capturing. Nonetheless, it permits taking for *bona fide* scientific purposes, by local people using traditional methods in the exercise of their traditional rights and in accordance with the laws of the party, to prevent serious disturbance of the management of other living resources, and for conservation purposes. However, in the last two cases, the skins and other objects of value resulting from the taking cannot be made available for commercial purposes (Art. III). Even when takings are authorized, it is forbidden to utilize aircraft and large motorized vessels, except where the prohibition would be inconsistent with local law.

The Agreement, Article V, also forbids all international trade in polar bears taken in violation of its provisions, but CITES, in force for all five parties to the Agreement, already provided this means of protection because the polar bear is listed among the threatened species in Appendix II.

Article II also requires action to protect the ecosystems of which the polar bears are a part, with special attention to their habitats. The management of polar bear populations, based upon national research programs, is another obligation of states parties. According to Article VII of the Agreement, research shall be conducted on management problems and coordinated, especially concerning migratory polar bear populations. The effects of long-range pollution on polar bears certainly deserves to be studied, in addition to problems caused by oil and gas drilling.

An October 16, 2000, US-Russia bilateral Agreement on the Conservation and Management of the Alaska-Chukotka Polar Bear Population seeks to further the goals of the 1973 Agreement on the Conservation of Polar Bears. The parties agree to undertake all necessary efforts to conserve polar bear habitats, particularly denning areas and those in which bears concentrate to feed or migrate (Art. IV). The agreement prohibits all taking of polar bears inconsistent with either the 1973 treaty or this agreement. According to the bilateral treaty, bears may be taken only for scientific research, for rescuing or rehabilitating orphaned, sick or injured animals, or when human life is threatened. Bears may be put on public display if they are maintained in captivity for rehabilitation and either party determines that they cannot be released into the wild.

The Agreement takes into account the subsistence needs of native peoples while affording further protection to polar bears. Native taking excludes taking of females with cubs, as well as taking cubs less than a year old and bears entering, leaving or occupying dens. The treaty also prohibits the use of aircraft or large motorized vessels or vehicles and the use of poisons, traps or snares (Art. VI.1). The Agreement does not authorize taking polar bears for commercial purposes, but allows native people, when permitted by domestic law to create, sell and use traditional articles associated with native harvest of polar bears.

A US-Russia Polar Bear Commission is to coordinate measures for the conservation and study of bears, promote cooperation between the parties and with native peoples, and determine annual taking limits not to exceed the sustainable harvest level (Art. VIII). Each party must monitor polar bear harvests in its territory and may take more protective measures. The Commission further enhances the role of native peoples, by requiring that in the two sections of the Commission, one Russian and the other US, one of the two members of each section shall be a representative of the native people and the other a representative of the government. Each section has one vote and both sections must agree on action.

At COP15 of CITES in 2010, the US tabled a proposal to uplist the polar bear from Appendix II to Appendix I. The objective was to completely prohibit the international trade of polar bear products. Although some countries and NGOs supported the proposal, it was unsurprisingly opposed by Canada, Greenland, and Norway, with backing from Iceland and the EU.

6.2 *Terrestrial Species*

6.2.1 Forests

Forests are categorized as tropical, temperate, and boreal. Temperate and boreal forests constitute about half the world's forest cover, but most international attention has been given to the rapid loss of the world's tropical forests.

In all, about one quarter of the world's land area outside Greenland and Antarctica are covered in forests and forests are home to between 50 and 90 percent of all terrestrial species. Forests also serve as sinks for greenhouse gases and produce oxygen for the planet. These ecological services of forests are difficult to value and to contrast with the revenues produced when trees are cut.

The demand for forest products has grown rapidly in recent years, from the production of lumber and paper to collection and burning for fuelwood and charcoal. About half the wood cut worldwide is used for subsistence purposes in developing countries where poverty precludes use of other fuel sources. In many tropical areas industrial logging is also a major threat to forests. One of the greatest increases in use of wood is in the production of paper, which by the end of the twentieth century was consumed at five times the level it was in 1950.[107] Seventy percent of this output is used in the industrialized northern countries that account for twenty percent of the world's population.

The sustainable management of forests is crucial for maintaining biodiversity, regulating climate, and supporting the livelihoods of millions of people worldwide. As FAO noted in its 2022 report on State of the World's Forests, trees, forests, and sustainable forestry have the potential to aid global recovery from the COVID-19 pandemic and address pressing environmental issues like climate change and biodiversity loss. However, achieving this requires societies to better acknowledge the significant value of forests and their essential roles in creating inclusive, resilient, and sustainable economies.

A first Tropical Timber Agreement, adopted on November 18, 1983, established an International Organization of Tropical Woods and recognized the necessity to preserve and protect tropical rain forests in order to ensure their optimal exploitation, while maintaining ecological equilibrium in the concerned areas and the biosphere. A decade later, a new International Tropical Timber Agreement, also adopted in Geneva, on January 21, 1994, replaced the former. It gives recognition to the need to promote and apply comparable and appropriate guidelines and criteria for the management, conservation and sustainable development of all types of timber producing forests and notes the commitment of all members of the former organization, made in May 1990, to achieve exports of tropical timber products from sustainably-managed sources by the year 2000 (Preamble).

The Agreement itself has two principal characteristics. First, it is predominately institutional in that almost all its provisions concern the International Tropical Timber Organization (ITTO), its structures and its functioning. Second, sustainable development and management of forest resources have an

107 Janet Abramovitz, *State of the World* (1998) 22–24.

important place in the Organization's objectives as determined in Article 1. In addition, Article 1(l) encourages the members of the Organization to develop national policies aimed at sustainable utilization and conservation of timber-producing forests and their genetic resources and at maintaining ecological balance in the regions concerned, in the context of tropical timber trade. Another provision encourages members to support and develop industrial tropical reforestation and forest management activities as well as rehabilitation of degraded forest land, with due regard for the interest of local communities dependent on forest resources. It is clear that the institutions have to find the balance between opposed interests and that the world's public opinion cannot forget the importance of tropical forests when opposed to trade interests.

The Non-Legally Binding Authoritative Statement of Principles for a Global Consensus on the Management, Conservation and Sustainable Development of All Types of Forests, adopted by the Rio Conference in June 1992, also reveals these conflicting interests. Its title indicates the difficulties that arose during the negotiations. As controversial as it was, it represents the first global instrument on forests. Its preamble situates the discussion in the context of 'the right to socio-economic development on a sustainable basis'.

The Declaration's guiding objective is to contribute to the management, conservation and sustainable development of forests and to provide for their multiple and complementary functions and uses. The first principle repeats verbatim principle 21 of the Stockholm Declaration, placing it in quotation marks to emphasize the reference. However, the first paragraph of the second principle of the forest declaration restates the beginning of principle 21 in much stronger terms:

> States have the sovereign and inalienable right to utilize, manage and develop their forests in accordance with their development needs and level of socio-economic development and on the basis of national policies consistent with sustainable development and legislation, including the conversion of such areas for other uses within the overall socio-economic development plan and based on rational land-use policies.

This statement is somewhat balanced in the second paragraph, which states that forest resources and forest lands should be sustainably managed to meet the needs of present and future generations.

The Declaration calls for integrated and comprehensive environmental protection and refers to the vital role of all types of forests in ecological processes. Each of the functions that forests fulfill are described and measures recommended to sustaining those functions. All countries are recommended to take action towards reforestation, afforestation and forest conservation. In particular, national policies should include protection of ecologically viable representative or unique examples of forests, including primary or old growth forests, cultural, spiritual, historical, religious and other unique and valued forests of national importance. Access to biological resources of the forests is to be regulated with regard to the sovereign rights of the forest countries, with mutual agreements on technology and profits from biotechnology products derived from these resources. Reference is made to international financial and technical assistance and to traditional mechanisms of environmental protection such as impact assessments. The primary focus is development and poverty, including international indebtedness, but it also foresees transfer of technology, new financial resources, scientific research, education, and international exchange of information. Trade should be non-discriminatory, consistent with and facilitating open and free international trade in forest products. Trade barriers are to be removed, but environmental costs and benefits are to be incorporated into market forces. In particular, unilateral measures to restrict and/or ban international trade in timber or other forest products should be removed or avoided. Finally, principle 15 refers to controlling pollution responsible for damage to forests. The document is far more an international timber trade agreement than an environmental protection statement.

Despite the very timid language of the Forest Declaration, Agenda 21 calls for its effective implementation. Specific activities should include increasing cooperative actions to reduce pollutants and transboundary impacts affecting the health of trees and forests and conservation of representative ecosystems (11.16). The timidity of the Declaration and the subordination of environmental considerations to short term economic goals are reflected in 11.25 where cooperation and assistance of the international community are requested in technology transfer, specialization and promotion of fair terms of trade, without resorting to unilateral restrictions and/or bans on forest products contrary to the General Agreement on Tariffs and Trade (GATT) and other multilateral trade agreements, and the application of appropriate market mechanisms and incentives.

The forest principles declaration was originally intended to be a binding treaty. The FAO first proposed in 1990 to adopt an International Convention on Conservation and Development of Forests.[108] A year later, the Japanese government proposed an International Charter for the World's Forest to the International Tropical Timber Organization. Extensive and often hostile discussions

108 COFO-90/3/a.

resulted only in 'elements for a global consensus'. Southern timber-producing countries fought hard against mandatory multilateral regulation in the field, due to perceived threats to sovereignty. This was in part a response to claims that, like Antarctica and the high seas, tropical rain forests could constitute part of the common heritage of mankind. No agreement was reached even on the need for further action other than promotion of international cooperation. Compared to the response to desertification, the 'progress' has been limited.

The UN created a Forum on Forests (UNFF) in October 2000, with a five-year mandate, in order to give a higher political profile to the issue. Division remains over many questions, including financing, trade, technology-transfer, underlying causes of deforestation, governance and illegal trade. Competing economic interests are pervasive in the forestry sector and movement in favor of protection is extremely slow. The 2007 FAO report on the State of the World's Forests showed deforestation and forest degradation continue to increase, especially in developing countries.

On a regional level, on July 23, 1992, the EC adopted two regulations concerning forests. The first is to protect European forests against air pollution (Reg. 2157/92, amending regulation 3528/86), the second to protect them against fires (Reg. 2158/92). During the same decade, outside the EC law-making process, the Alpine states negotiated a Protocol on the implementation of the 1991 Alpine convention in the field of mountain forests.[109] The objective of the Protocol is the conservation of mountain forests as ecosystems, to develop and, if necessary, extend them and improve their stability (Art. 1). Parties undertake to assure the natural regeneration of the forest, repopulate forests with native plants and prevent erosion and soil compacting. They agree to incorporate these objectives in other policies, such as those on air pollution, wildlife, pasturage, recreation, and logging (Art. 2) and to give priority to the protective function of forests (Art. 6) while also recognizing their ecological and social functions (Art. 8). Where forests are exploited, it should be for the benefit of local communities (Art. 7). Specific forests should be set aside as nature reserves, sufficient in size and number to guarantee their natural dynamic and to be representative of the various ecosystems (Art. 10). A Protocol on Sustainable Forest Management was also adopted for the Carpathians in Bratislava on May 27, 2011. In recent years, states have been incorporating forest-related provisions into Free Trade Agreements (FTAs) (see Chapter 17). These forest annexes (a notable example is the Forest Annex to the US-Peru FTA) aim to

109 February 27, 1996, EMuT 991:83/E.

ensure that trade and economic growth do not come at the expense of forest conservation and sustainable management.

On March 17, 1999, the heads of state of six Central African states[110] signed the Yaounde Declaration on the Conservation and Sustainable Management of Tropical Forests, expressing their desire to promote the rational use and sustainable development of forest resources through the conservation of the entire biodiversity. They agreed to set up transborder protected areas, develop a forestry tax system and attendant measures to support the conservation, sustainable development of and research on forest ecosystems. They also concurred on harmonizing forestry policies and certification systems, involving the rural population and economic operators in sustainable management and conservation, and integrating forest ecosystem protection with other sectors such as transport and agriculture. They specifically mention making concerted efforts to stamp out large-scale poaching and other non-sustainable exploitation in the sub-region. Institutionally, they agreed to revive the Organization for Wildlife Conservation in Central Africa and to create lasting mechanisms for financing forest development, using revenues generated by the forestry sector and international cooperation. An East Asian Ministerial Conference on Forest Law Enforcement and Governance, held in September 2001, adopted an unprecedented Declaration on combating illegal logging, associated illegal trade, and other forest crimes.

Finally, efforts to combat anthropogenic sources of climate change recognize the value of forests as sinks for greenhouse gases. The United Nations Framework Convention on Climate Change (UNFCCC) and the Kyoto Protocol specifically encourage afforestation and reforestation and permit states party to meet their obligations under the Protocol in part by such actions.[111] The 19th COP of the UNFCCC, which took place in Warsaw in 2013, adopted REDD+, commonly known as the Warsaw Framework for REDD+ (WFR).[112] 'REDD+' stands for 'Reducing Emissions from Deforestation and Forest Degradation' with the 'plus' referring to the role of conservation, sustainable management of forests and enhancement of forest carbon stocks in developing countries. The WFR provides comprehensive methodological and financing guidance for REDD+ activities and is recognized in Article 5 of the Paris Agreement. REDD+ primarily aims to reduce human pressures on forests that lead to greenhouse gas emissions at the national level, although it also acknowledges subnational

110 Cameroon, Congo, Gabon, Equatorial Guinea, Central African Republic, and Chad.

111 Kyoto Protocol (December 11, 1997), Art. 3(3). See further, Chapter 12.

112 Work Programme on Results-based Finance to Progress the Full Implementation of the Activities Referred to in Decision 1/CP.16, para. 70 (Decision –/CP.19).

implementation as an interim measure. The implementation of REDD+ is voluntary and dependent on each developing country's circumstances, capacities, capabilities, and the level of support received.

Pursuant to the Convention on Biological Diversity, meanwhile, the Sixth Conference of the Parties, held in The Hague, April 2002, adopted a strategic plan and action plan on forest biodiversity. In 2010, the 10th COP of the CBD in Nagoya, Japan, adopted the Strategic Plan for Biodiversity 2011–2020, which included specific targets related to forests. The Aichi Biodiversity Targets are part of this Strategic Plan for Biodiversity 2011–2020 and Target 7 specifically addresses the conservation of forest biodiversity, aiming to ensure that by 2020, areas under agriculture, aquaculture, and forestry are managed sustainably, ensuring conservation of biodiversity.

6.2.2 Vicuna

The vicuna, a native animal of the Andean range in South America, is hunted for its fine wool. It became threatened with extinction during the 1960s, with its numbers said to be as low as 6000 in 1965 from a pre-Colombian population of over one million. It is listed in Appendix I of CITES. On August 16, 1969, the five Andean countries, Argentina, Bolivia, Chile, Ecuador, and Peru, signed in La Paz a Convention for the Conservation of Vicuna. The agreement requires the contracting states to prohibit and repress vicuna hunting and trade in the wool, meat, and skins, as well as in articles made from these materials, both internally and internationally. The Convention also provided for the establishment and maintenance of reserves and breeding centers.

The results were positive. The population of vicuna recovered, so much that a second agreement permitting some exploitation replaced the La Paz Convention. Bolivia, Chile, Ecuador and Peru signed in Lima a new Convention for the Conservation and Management of the Vicuna on December 7, 1979. Argentina did not sign because it preferred to maintain the strict prohibition on taking vicuna and concluded that the new agreement was insufficiently protective. It subsequently entered into a bilateral agreement with Bolivia (February 16, 1981) on the protection and conservation of vicuna.

The Lima Convention provides for the conservation and management of vicuna taking into account the experience acquired through application of the previous agreement. It prohibited exploitation and trade in vicuna and its products until December 31, 1989. Thereafter, if the population of vicuna attains a high enough level that production of meat, bones, and transformation of skin and wool into products could be envisaged, the state party concerned may authorize trade under strict controls. Skins and cloth must be marked in a way to be recognizable on the international market. These marks are registered according to an agreement between the Parties in coordination with CITES. Export of fertile vicunas or other reproductive material, except to other member countries, for research and/or for repopulation efforts, is forbidden.

The Convention also requires states parties to establish national parks, reserves, and other protected areas for vicuna. It is agreed to continue research undertaken on the vicuna and to exchange information concerning this subject. A Technical-Administrative Commission is established and called upon to meet annually in order to evaluate the implementation of the Convention and to recommend solutions to problems arising from its application. The Commission began meeting in 1981 and publishes reports on the state of the vicuna population and research on the species.

6.2.3 European Bats

On another more limited subject, European countries adopted an Agreement on the Conservation of Bats in Europe (London, December 4, 1991), derived from the Bonn Convention on Migratory Species, and specifically based upon it. The fundamental obligations are similar: each party shall prohibit the deliberate capture, keeping or killing of bats except under permit and shall take action to conserve bat habitats. Research, public education, and measures to promote the conservation of bats are required. An unusual feature is the requirement that states consider the potential effects of pesticides on bats when assessing pesticides for use and must seek safer alternatives to timber treatment chemicals currently in use. The Convention is open to all European bat range states and the European Union.

6.2.4 Birds

It has been noted already that the first major multilateral convention in the field of conservation was that of birds 'useful to agriculture' signed March 19, 1902. Since that date great progress has been made not only in abandoning the strictly utilitarian point of view which characterizes this first instrument, but also regarding techniques of conservation. The protection of habitats has become an essential element of conservation and those of migratory birds occupy an important place in the designation of protected areas.

Today, birds are widely protected, sometimes by overlapping conventions and also by an important EC directive. The legal instruments may involve the creation of protected zones, such as foreseen in the UNESCO Convention and the Ramsar Convention, or have a more general scope, such as the regional instruments of Africa, Europe, and ASEAN. Finally, it is clear that birds are at the heart of the 1979 Bonn Convention on the Protection of Migratory Species and that their place also is marked in CITES.

Other instruments which are specifically and solely concerned with the conservation of birds. The Paris Convention for the Protection of Birds Useful to Agriculture of March 19, 1902, in spite of its utilitarian character and its exclusion or condemnation of 'harmful birds' contains certain precedential elements. In particular, Article 2(1) forbids the taking of nests and eggs and the capturing and destroying clutches. Article 3 also prohibits the placing and use of traps, cages, nets, and other means designed to capture or destroy birds en masse. Importing, transit, transporting, and selling nests, eggs, and the young of protected species are banned (Art. 2(2)). The period between March 1 and September 15 of each year is closed to hunting and capture of birds, with a prohibition on all sales (Art. 5). However, the Convention provides numerous exceptions and derogations, for example, exempting from coverage birds whose presence may be a nuisance, and the capture and sale of birds to be kept in cages. A broad escape clause in Article 4 permits parties to avoid being bound by any of the Convention provisions if they wish.

An International Convention for the Protection of Birds (Paris, October 18, 1950) was drafted nearly half a century later in order to replace the earlier Convention. However, a dozen of the contracting parties to the first Paris Convention have not adhered to the more recent instrument, so that the substitution is only partial. The second Paris Convention is more in conformity with modern ecological thinking. The narrowly utilitarian view of 1902 and the condemnation of certain species disappeared. The provisions also are more protective. Article 4 maintains the protection of nests, eggs, and the young, while Article 5(k) retains the prohibition on using means for mass destruction or capture of birds. The list of other prohibited methods of killing and capture is extended in Article 5, including, for example, the use of spring traps and motor vehicles during hunting. One element in the evolution is that states can no longer offer rewards for the killing or capture of birds (Art. 5(i)). Finally, with certain exceptions all birds are protected during their breeding periods and migratory birds during their transit. The concept of endangered species also appears, in Article 2(b) although the protection is not absolute.

Three other favorable aspects characterize the 1950 Convention. The states parties agree to regulate trade in protected birds (Art. 9); they support the creation of land or water reserves (Art. 11); and they agree to study and adopt the proper means to prevent the destruction of birds by waste oil and other water pollution, by lighthouses, electric cables, insecticides, poisons, or any other cause (Art. 10). Finally, each state party agrees to prepare a list of birds which may be killed or captured lawfully on its own territory, providing the conditions established by the Convention are met (Art. 8). This is an innovative attempt to introduce lists from the opposite perspective, it being understood that any bird which does not appear on the list is protected. The method has certain advantages for the identification of specimens, because obviously species which can be hunted or captured are far less numerous than those which must be protected.

One of the weak points of the Convention is its exceptions. The first category grants each state party the option of derogating. Individual authorizations can be accorded to destroy birds in case of massive damage to agriculture, game, or fish, or when one or several species whose conservation is desirable are threatened with extinction or with the simple reduction in numbers. However, buying or selling birds thus killed and transporting them out of the region where they were destroyed are illegal (Art. 6). Similarly, an exception can be accorded in the interests of science and education, as well as to restock and reproduce game birds and falcons (Art. 7). Finally, Article 9 provides that each state has the possibility of establishing a list of bird species permissible to be kept in captivity by individuals, while determining the methods of capture and the conditions of detention.

Specific exceptions may be accorded individual states parties to the Convention, a rare phenomenon in international treaty law. The prohibition on harvesting eggs does not apply to lapwing eggs in the Netherlands. Other countries are named for specific exceptions, but of them only Sweden has become party to the Convention.

The Agreement on the Conservation of African-Eurasian Migratory Waterbirds (The Hague, June 16, 1995) is the most extensive developed so far under the Convention on Migratory Species.[113] The agreement extends to 119 countries in Europe, Asia, North America, the Middle East and Africa. The AEWA covers 254 species of birds ecologically dependent on wetlands for at least part of their annual cycle, including many species of divers, grebes, pelicans, cormorants, herons, storks, rails, ibises, spoonbills, flamingos, ducks, swans, geese, cranes, waders, gulls, terns and the South African penguin. The Agreement provides for coordinated and concerted action to be taken by the range states throughout the migration system of waterbirds to which it applies. Parties to the Agreement are called upon to take conservation actions which are described in a comprehensive Action Plan (2003–2005) that addresses such key issues as species and habitat conservation, management of human activities, research and monitoring, education and information, and implementation.

The second Session of the Meeting of the Parties, which took place in September 2002 in Bonn, Germany, added 65 species of migratory waterbirds to

113 The Convention entered into force November 1, 1999 after obtaining the required minimum ratifications by fourteen Range States, comprising seven from Africa and seven from Eurasia.

the existing listed species. The relevant Resolution 2.1 was adopted because it had become clear that the list of species excluded some species with an unfavorable conservation status and included others with a favorable conservation status. In early 2000, the Global Environment Facility (GEF) decide to grant $350,000 for the drafting of a brief for a full-size African-Eurasian Flyway project. The goal of the project is to develop transboundary strategic measures necessary to conserve the network of critical wetlands on which migratory waterbirds depend throughout the Agreement area.

In 2014, the Convention on the Conservation of Migratory Species adopted a resolution focused on the prevention of illegal killing, taking, and trade of migratory birds. This resolution aims to address the threats faced by migratory bird species due to illegal activities such as hunting, capturing, and trading.

Several treaties and other instruments concluded pursuant to the Convention on Migratory Species protect specific species of bird. The MOU has been growing in popularity because of its flexibility and because it permits inter-governmental and non-governmental organizations to sign the understanding. An MOU on the Siberian Crane was signed by nine range states and three cooperating organizations on July 1, 1993 and revised January 1, 1999. Eighteen range states and three cooperating organizations signed an MOU which came into effect on September 10, 1994 to protect the slender-billed curlew. A treaty, the Convention on the Conservation of Albatrosses and Petrels, was opened for signature in Canberra, Australia on June 19, 2002. The agreement is a cooperative framework to restore albatrosses and petrels to a favorable conservation status, support coordinated action to mitigate known threats to populations, coordinate data collection, analyze and disseminate information; assess international and regional conservation status of the species and threats to them, and communicate the conservation status to relevant international and regional bodies to promote action. Central and Eastern European states and four cooperating organizations signed an MOU the Conservation and Management of Middle-European Populations of the Great Bustard.[114]

Finally, a few states have adopted bilateral treaties protecting migratory birds, particularly in North America and the Pacific. The United States or Japan concluded a series of treaties with other states between 1916[115] and 1976.[116] The

114 Opened for signature October 5, 2000, entered into force June 1, 2001. The signatory states are Hungary, Macedonia, Romania, Moldova, Bulgaria, Greece, Austria, Slovakia, Ukraine, Albania, Croatia and Germany.

115 Agreement between the United States and Great Britain (August 1916), T.S. 628, 39 Stat. 1702.

116 Agreement between the U.S. and the U.S.S.R. (November 1976), 29 U.S.T. 4647, T.I.A.S. No. 9073, entered into force October 13, 1978. The other treaties are US – Mexico (February 7,

treaties reflect the same evolution from utilitarian to broader ecological concerns, with the earlier ones referring to the great value of birds as a source of food and in protecting agriculture, while the more recent treaties note the aesthetic and scientific qualities of birds and their significance to the environment. The bilateral agreements rely upon lists to designate coverage of species and, except for the earliest treaty, contain amendment procedures. The treaties after 1916 all prohibit trade in specimens of covered species and their eggs and regulate takings.

7 Access to Biological Resources

The Convention on Biological Diversity asserts the rights of states over genetic resources in animals and plants under their jurisdiction, creating a complex relationship of rights and duties. On the one hand, authority to determine access to genetic resources rests with the national governments and is subject to national legislation (Art. 15.1). On the other hand, each state party must endeavor to create conditions to facilitate access to genetic resources for environmentally sound uses by other parties and should not impose restrictions that run counter to the Convention's objectives. When access is granted, it shall be on mutually agreed terms and be subject to prior informed consent by the party providing the genetic resource, unless that party determines otherwise. Permits may be required and it is likely that contractual access agreements will become the primary method by which public and private entities gain access and negotiate a share of the benefits upon a payment of collection fees, royalties or other form of benefit-sharing. Such arrangements will need to take into account, as well the needs and rights of indigenous and local communities from whose land genetic resources or traditional technologies are acquired.

Even prior to the conclusion of the Convention on Biological Diversity, gene banks had become a means of protecting genetic diversity, particularly of plants. Institutions in several countries have collected germplasm, mostly of crops, since the 1970s. Difficult legal issues over safety of the material, ownership, development of national laws restricting availability of the germplasm, and intellectual rights over development of new strains, led the United Nations Food and Agriculture Organization to propose a Global System for the Conservation and Utilization of Plant Genetic Resources. The System, in place

1936), T.S. No 912, 178 L.T.S. 309; supplemented by an exchange of notes March 10, 1972, 837 U.N.T.S. 125. U.S. – Japan (March 1972), 25 U.S.T. 3329, T.I.A.S. No. 7990; U.S.S.R. – Japan, October 1973 (not in force); and Japan – Aust. (February 1974), A.T.S. 1981 No. 6.

since 1983, aims to ensure the safe conservation, and promote the unrestricted availability and sustainable utilization of plant genetic resources for present and future generations, by providing a flexible framework for sharing the benefits and burdens. The System covers the conservation (*ex situ* and *in situ*) and utilization of plant genetic resources at molecular, population, species and ecosystem levels. It is based upon a framework agreement, the International Undertaking which creates an intergovernmental Commission and International Fund for Plant Genetic Resources. By the end of 1991, 128 countries were participating in the System.

The Understanding is now effectively incorporated in the November 2001 FAO International Treaty on Plant Genetic Resources for Food and Agriculture. Unlike the Understanding, the Treaty recognizes the sovereign rights of states over plant genetic resources while seeking conservation and sustainable use of such resources by (a) encouraging farming systems that enhance the sustainable use of agrobiodiversity and other natural resources; (2) maximizing intra- and inter-specific variation for the benefit of farmers, especially those who apply ecological principles in maintaining soil fertility and combating diseases, weeds and pests; (3) broadening the genetic base of crops and increasing the range of genetic diversity available to farmers; and (4) promoting increased world food production in a manner compatible with sustainable development. The treaty includes provisions on access to information, public participation (Arts. 13, 17), and farmers' rights (Art. 9). The Treaty provides in Articles 10–14 a system of facilitated access to an agreed list of over 60 plant genera, including 35 crops. The list is established on the basis of the interdependence and importance of listed plants for food security. The benefits accruing from the use of the material accessed is to be shared fairly and equitably through a variety of actions. There is a conceptual breakthrough in respect to the sharing of monetary benefits: anyone who obtains a commercial profit from the use of genetic resources administered multilaterally is obliged, by a standard Material Transfer Agreement, to share these profits fairly and equitably and pay a royalty to the multilateral mechanism for use as part of the funding strategy for benefit sharing.

After lengthy preparatory studies and negotiations in an Ad Hoc Working Group,[117] the Sixth Conference of the Parties to the CBD adopted the Bonn Guidelines on Access to Genetic Resources and Fair and Equitable Sharing of the Benefits Arising out of their Utilization as a first step in implementing the related provisions of the CBD, in particular Articles 8(j), 10(c), 15, 16, and 19.

---

117 UNEP/CBD/COP/6/6.

The Guidelines in turn provided the basis for negotiating the Nagoya Protocol on Access to Genetic Resources and their Fair and Equitable Sharing of Benefits Arising from their Utilization to the Convention on Biological Diversity (Nagoya, October 29, 2010). The Protocol preamble acknowledges that equitable benefit-sharing is one of the three core objectives of the Convention and reaffirms the sovereign rights of states over their natural resources. It also expresses one of its foundational assumptions, that public awareness of the economic value of ecosystems and biodiversity, as well as benefit-sharing, are key incentives for the conservation and sustainable use of biological diversity. In the preamble, the Nagoya Protocol also becomes the first treaty to refer to the 2007 UN Declaration on the Rights of Indigenous Peoples, affirming that nothing in the Protocol shall be construed as diminishing or extinguishing the existing rights of indigenous and local communities.

The operative parts of the Protocol appear to reduce to some extent the CBD's pro-access approach, calling merely for 'appropriate access to genetic resources'. Article 6 supplements this by establishing an obligation of prior informed consent of the state of origin for access to and utilization of genetic resources. 'Appropriate' measures in accordance with domestic law are also required with the aim of ensuring prior informed consent or approval and involvement of indigenous and local communities for access to their resources. The Protocol calls for clarity and transparency in legislation, rules and procedures governing access, including those establishing mutually agreed terms.

The Protocol's objective stated in Article 1 is to produce fair and equitable sharing of the benefits that arise from utilization of such resources when access is provided, 'thereby contributing to the conservation of biological diversity'. The Protocol extends its coverage to traditional knowledge associated with genetic resources and the benefits arising from its utilization (Art. 3). For all resources and knowledge, the benefits arising from their utilization are to be shared in a fair and equitable way between the party of origin and the party of acquisition, 'upon mutually agreed terms', as well as with any indigenous and local communities with rights over the resources. One of the most important parts of the Protocol is the annex that contains a non-exclusive list of the types of monetary and non-monetary benefits that may be provided.

To facilitate implementation, each party is to designate a national focal point and one or more competent national authorities on access and benefit-sharing. An international Access and Benefit-sharing Clearing-House is also established as a means for sharing information related to access and benefit-sharing. Obligations of enforcement are provided in Articles 15 and 16, along with measures to monitor and enhance transparency, set forth in Article 17. Several provisions specifically concern private parties. Article 18 concerns including provisions in mutually agreed terms on dispute resolution and access to justice, while Article 19 calls on each party to encourage the development of model contractual clauses. Article 20 further encourages the development of voluntary codes of conduct, guidelines and best practices or standards in relation to access and benefit-sharing. The Conference of the Parties is tasked with monitoring these measures and to consider the adoption of its own international standards. It is also to monitor periodic state reports and create procedures and mechanisms to promote compliance. To further facilitate adherence and compliance, the Protocol has a lengthy article devoted to setting forth its relationship to other relevant international agreements, giving priority to specialized instruments where they exist. The Protocol entered into force on October 12, 2014.

On the regional level, on July 2, 1996, the Andean Pact,[118] through its Commission, decided to adopt a Common Regime on Access to Genetic Resources (Decision 391).[119] The states form an eco-region where biodiversity is shared and, because of this, cooperation through harmonized rules helps avoid competitive disadvantage. Decision 391 recognizes that the member countries are sovereign in the use and exploitation of their resources but Article 5 provides that they are to use their sovereign rights to determine access conditions to their genetic resources in conformity with the Decision, which eliminates the possibility of unrestricted access to genetic resources.

Article 1 defines access as the obtaining and utilization of genetic resources conserved in *ex situ* and *in situ* conditions and their derivatives or their intangible components for research, biological prospecting, conservation, industrial application or commercial exploitation purposes. Genetic resources are defined as any material of a biological nature containing genetic information of actual or potential value. According to Article 4, human genetic resources and derivatives are excluded, an exclusion consistent with Decision II/11(2) of the Second COP of the Convention on Biological Diversity. Indigenous exchanges within communities for their own consumption and based on customary practices also are excluded.

Decision 391 extends the requirement of prior informed consent to all parties involved in an access procedure, particularly to indigenous and local communities. No access can be granted without their prior consent. In case of infringement the access contract will be deemed void and the violation could be a criminal offense.

---

118 The member states are Bolivia, Colombia, Ecuador, Peru and Venezuela.

119 See Monica Rosell, 'Access to Genetic Resources: A Critical Approach to Decision 391 'Common Regime on Access to Genetic Resources' of the Commission of the Cartagena Agreement' (1997) 6 RECIEL 274.

The procedure requires an application made to a competent national authority within the Andean Pact countries. The application shall be admissible if it complies with formal requirements and shall be approved if it meets the substantive conditions in the Decision. The procedure requires an application be filed with a competent national authority within the Andean Pact countries. The application shall be admissible if it complies with formal requirements and shall be approved if it meets the substantive conditions in the Decision. The application must provide an outline of the project, its purpose and feasibility. Once approved, the national authority and applicant negotiate the terms and conditions of a contract, including payments, technology transfer, confidentiality, ownership, etc. After the contract is signed, a resolution approves it and it is registered for transparency. Information regarding patents or other intellectual property rights must be provided. Any person who conducts access activities without being authorized infringes the law. National legislation may provide for civil and criminal sanctions and contracts may be suspended or terminated for violation and compensation sought, including for damage to the environment. Article 12 also provides that member countries will not recognize any rights, including intellectual property rights over genetic resources, derivatives, synthesized or intangible assets obtained and/or developed from an access activity not in compliance with the decision. Article 6 declares that genetic resources are the national patrimony or goods of the state of the Andean countries.

8 Invasive or Alien Species

One of the long-standing but intensifying threats to biodiversity comes from the accidental or deliberate introduction of invasive or alien species into a new habitat. Some species, like the desert locust, are not alien, but periodically appear to decimate plants species, including crops. Other plants, animals or micro-organisms travel through modern means of transportation and trade, in the ballast water or on the hull of ships or in the cargo of airplanes for example, to areas where native species have little or no resistance to them or ability to compete for resources. The invasive and alien species often reproduce rapidly and lack their usual predators, allowing them to transform entire ecosystems.

Several invasive species have caused enormous damage in recent years,[120] including the zebra mussel which arrived to the Great Lakes from the Caspian

120 See, *Invasive Species: Status, Impacts and Trends of Alien Species that Threaten Ecosystems, Habitats and Species*, UNEP/CBD/SBSTTA/6/INF/11, February 26, 2001.

or Black Sea. Lacking its usual predators, the mussels have covered piers, rocks and water supply tunnels, costing the US and Canada millions of dollars every year to control them. Pacific islands have also suffered from the introduction of several alien species. The brown tree snake has caused the loss of nearly all native bird and bat species on Guam, as well as half the native lizard species; officials in Hawaii have had to combat non-native fruit flies and ground termites coming from other islands. A toxic underwater plant, the caulerpa taxifolia, poses serious problems in Europe where it has invaded the Mediterranean Sea to kill native marine plants and animals. The West Nile virus arrived from the Middle East and Africa to New York in 2000, killing birds and spreading to humans and other animals through mosquitos. Within three years it was present in all fifty United States causing sickness and death each summer. According to a 2023 report published by IPBES, the annual global economic impact of invasive alien species surpassed $423 billion in 2019, marking a quadrupling of costs approximately every decade since 1970.

Several international legal instruments attempt to control invasive or alien species. Based on earlier efforts to combat locusts, the FAO Council approved in November 2000 the Agreement for the Establishment of a Commission for Controlling the Desert Locust in the Western Region.[121] Membership in the Commission is open to FAO Member Nations that constitute the Region defined under Article III ('... the western region of the invasion area of the desert locust ... comprises Algeria, Chad, Libya, Mali, Morocco, Mauritania, Niger, Senegal and Tunisia ...') and that accept the Agreement. The Commission may, by a two-thirds majority of its members, admit to membership other states who submit an application to this effect.

More generally, Decision VI/23 of the Sixth Conference of the Parties to the Convention on Biological Diversity expands on Convention Article 8(h), which calls on states parties to 'prevent the introduction of, control or eradicate those alien species which threaten ecosystems, habitats or species'. Based on the work of the Convention's Scientific Body, Decision VI/23 urges parties, other governments and relevant organizations to promote and implement the Guiding Principles it drafted to prevent the introduction or mitigate the impact of invasive or alien species. States parties and other governments are urged to ratify the revised International Plant Protection Convention while major international organizations with relevant mandates (e.g. the Office International des Epizooites, the FAO, the IMO, and the World Health Organization) should consider the problems posed by invasive alien species as these organizations

121 Resolution No. 1/119.

elaborate further standards and agreements, or revise existing standards and agreements, including those on risk assessment/analysis.

In their past several conferences, the Ramsar Convention parties also have adopted recommendations on combating invasive species that detrimentally impact wetlands. Resolution VIII.18, adopted at the Eighth Conference of the Parties in November 2002, calls invasive species a 'major threat to the ecological character of wetlands worldwide'. Noting the link to global climate change, which brings with it movement of species into new areas, the Resolution urges parties to address the problem of invasive species in wetland ecosystems 'in a decisive and holistic manner', including undertaking risk assessments of alien species which may pose a threat to the ecological character of wetlands. The resolution asks parties to transmit information to the Ramsar Bureau about the presence on Ramsar sites of invasive alien species, the threats they pose, the risk of invasions by species not yet present, and actions underway or planned for their prevention, eradication or control. The Bureau, in turn, is asked to develop its website as a source of information and to collaborate with other secretariats to assess the impact of invasive species and make this information available. States that share wetland ecosystems, both marine and inland, are asked to cooperate in the prevention, early warning, eradication and control of invasive species.

Conclusions

It has several times been noted that the legal methods to ensure conservation of wildlife have evolved significantly since the first international instruments addressed this matter. From establishing closed hunting and fishing seasons, through a general prohibition on taking specimens and habitat protection, to the complete management of a population of wild animals, great progress has been made. However, the older methods of conservation have not completely disappeared. Today, a wide variety of means are at the disposal of public entities seeking to protect wild plants and animals, although many of the means concern only animals. The protection of plants, while not less important or difficult, may not necessitate the same variety of measures. In most cases, several techniques are combined.

Detailed measures are contained in some treaties favoring particular species. The Bern Convention on the Conservation of European Wildlife and Natural Habitats is one of the most explicit and most complete examples in this regard. It forbids the deliberate picking, collecting, cutting or uprooting of protected plants, and, in regard to protected wild animals, prohibits:

a. all forms of deliberate capture and keeping and deliberate killing;
b. the deliberate damage to or destruction of breeding or resting sites;
c. the deliberate disturbance of wild fauna, particularly during the period of breeding, rearing and hibernation, insofar as disturbance would be significant in relation to the objectives of this Convention;
d. the deliberate destruction or taking of eggs from the wild or keeping these eggs even if empty;
e. the possession of and internal trade in these animals, alive or dead, including stuffed animals and any readily recognizable part or derivative thereof, where this would contribute to the effectiveness of the provisions of this Article (Article 6).

Exceptions can be granted to this general Article, but the cases where they can be introduced are specified and strict. States which adopted them must submit biennial reports to the permanent Committee established by the Convention.

Based upon a number of national legislative measures, some international agreements prohibit certain means of killing or capturing specimens of wildlife. Here again, the Bern Convention appears to be the most complete and reflecting most generally accepted rules. As a whole, it prohibits utilizing non-selective means of killing and capture and means capable of causing local disappearance of or serious disturbance to populations of a species. A special Appendix lists means which are prohibited for mammals (snares, live animal decoys, tape recorders, electrical devices, explosives, nets, traps, poison, etc) and for birds (snares, limes, hooks, explosives, nets traps, poisons). Annex IV of the EC Directive concerning Wild Birds is comparable, containing even more detail as far as the prohibited use of motor vehicles is concerned.

Increasingly, efforts to protect wild fauna and flora are using a comprehensive integrated or ecosystem approach aiming, for example, at flowing bodies of water, wetlands, dry, or unfertilized grasslands. The integrated approach to nature protection is supported by international understanding of the threats to biodiversity. In some cases, various types of property 'set-aside' or conservation measures are used to protect plants and animals. EC directive 92/43 on the conservation of natural habitats and of wild fauna and flora specifically aims to protect biodiversity by conserving natural habitats.[122] It calls for a coherent European ecological network of special conservation areas, called Natura 2000. Each member state must contribute to the creation of Natura 2000 in proportion to the representation within its territory of natural habitat types and the habitats of species listed in annexes to the directive.

122 Directive on the Conservation of Natural Habitats of Wild Fauna and Flora, 92/43/EEC, O.J. L 206 (5/21/92), p. 7.

One of the growing problems in protecting biological diversity stems from the proliferation of agreements and institutions. Specific areas or species are likely to be covered by the Convention on Biological Diversity and may also be encompassed by the World Heritage Convention, the Ramsar Convention, the Convention on Migratory Species, and a particular species agreement. If marine areas are involved, additional legal regulation may stem from UNCLOS, regional seas agreements, and fisheries bodies. The need for coordination is increasingly recognized and efforts are underway among parties to the Convention on Biological Diversity, the Convention on Migratory Species, Ramsar and the World Heritage Convention to harmonize state reporting requirements. The Convention on Migratory Species secretariat has taken the lead in establishing cooperative arrangements with other bodies concerned with biodiversity by concluding Memoranda of Understanding with UNESCO, CITES, UNFCCC, and IUCN. The Conference of the Parties of the CBD also decided to integrate its work on inland water ecosystems with the Ramsar Convention on wetlands, adopting a Work Programme on the biological diversity of such ecosystems. In this regard, parties are encouraged to adopt integrated land and watershed management approaches for the protection, use, planning and management of inland water ecosystems. Such arrangements are increasingly necessary to ensure coordination and consistency in monitoring the many legal obligations of states.

Bibliography

Askin, R.A. et al., *Saving Biological Diversity: Balancing Protection of Endangered Species and Ecosystems* (Springer, 2008).

Bodansky, D., '*International Law and the Protection of Biological Diversity*' (1995) 28 *Vand J. Transnat'l L.* 623.

Bourrinet, J. and Maljean Dubois, S., *Le Commerce International Des Organismes Génétiquement Modifiés* (2002).

Bowman, M. and Redgwell C., *International Law and the Conservation of Biological Diversity* (1996).

Brown, K., et al., *Economics and the Conservation of Global Biological Diversities* (1993).

Castree, N., *Nature* (London: Routledge, 2005).

Cooper, H.D., 'The International Treaty on Plant Genetic Resources for Food and Agriculture', (2002) 11 *RECIEL* 1.

De Klemm, C. and Shine, C., *Guidelines For Legislation to Implement Cites* (2d ed. 1998).

Favre, D., *International Trade in Endangered Species* (1989).

Freese, *Harvesting Wild Species: Implications for Biodiversity Conservation* (1997).

Glennon, M.J., 'Has International Law Failed the Elephant' (1990) 84 *AJIL*. 1.

Glowka, L., *A Guide to Designing Legal Frameworks to Determine Access to Genetic Resources*, (IUCN Policy and Law Paper No. 34 1998).

Grifo, F. and Rosental, J., eds, *Biodiversity and Human Health* (1997).

Guruswamy, L. and Mcneely, J., *Protection of Global Biodiversity – Converging Strategies* (1998).

Hanna, S., Folke, C., and Maler K.G., *Rights to Nature : Ecological, Economic, Cultural, and Political Principles of Institutions for the Environment* (1996).

Houck, O., 'On The Law of Biodiversity and Ecosystem Management' (1997) 81 *Minn L. Rev.* 869.

Lyster, S., 'The Convention on the Conservation of Migratory Species of Wild Animals (the Bonn Convention' (1989) 29 *Nat. Res. J.* 903.

Lyster, S., *International Wildlife Law* (1985).

Oberthür, S. and Rosendal, K, *Global Governance of Genetic Resources: Access and Benefit Sharing after the Nagoya Protocol* (Routledge, 2013).

Ramakrishna, K. and Woodwell, G., *World Forests for the Future* (1993).

Ramsar Convention Bureau, *The Ramsar Convention Manual* (2d ed. 1997).

Reid, W., et al., eds., *Biodiversity Prospecting: Using Genetic Resources for Sustainable Development* (1993).

Richerzhagen, C. *Protecting Biological Diversity: The Effectiveness of Access and Benefit-sharing Regimes* (Routledge, 2013).

Schiffman, H.S., 'The Protection of Whales in International Law: A Perspective for the Next Century' (1996) 22 *Brooklyn J. Int'l L.* 303.

Schrijver, N., *Sovereignty over Natural Resources – Balancing Rights and Duties* (Cambridge: CUP, 1997).

Secretariat to the CBD, *Handbook to the Convention on Biological Diversity* (2014).

Snape, W., *Biodiversity and the Law* (1996).

Stokke, Olav, ed., *Governing High Seas Fisheries: The Interplay of Global and Regional Regimes* (2001).

Van Heijnsbergen, P., *International Legal Protection of Wild Fauna and Flora* (1997).

CHAPTER 9

Soil

Soil is the part of the Earth between its surface and its bedrock. It performs two types of ecological functions. On the one hand, it contains the nutrients necessary for the maintenance of life and constitutes a habitat for humans, as well as for flora and fauna.[1] On the other hand, it protects other sectors of the environment: first, it acts to filter pollutants before they reach subterranean water sources or enter the food chain and, second, it helps avoid flooding by absorbing considerable amounts of water. Only six to eight inches of topsoil stands between much of the world and starvation.

Degraded soils have lowered global agricultural yields significantly since World War II.[2] Soil erosion greatly exceeds rates of production in many agricultural regions: an estimated 35 billion tonnes of soil are lost each year due to erosion.[3] Nitrogen is headed toward possible scarcity, creating problems for ecosystems.[4] Land degradation negatively impacts 3.2 billion people worldwide.[5] One soil scientist has called land degradation 'the root of all socioeconomic problems' in developing nations.[6]

Soil naturally erodes and degrades, and erosion is a principal threat to soil fertility. Erosion occurs naturally due to the ordinary flow of water, but is exacerbated due to flooding and strong winds. Throughout most of the Earth's history, soil formation exceeded soil erosion. Now a combination of overplowing, overgrazing, and deforestation has reversed that relationship. The principal cause of erosion today is loss of plant cover, which can be caused by incorrect management of forests and agricultural lands.[7] With soil erosion exceeding soil formation, many areas of the Earth are slowly being drained of their inherent

1 A study of soil organisms in one acre of a pasture in Denmark revealed some 50,000 small earthworms, an equal number of mites and other insects, and nearly 12 million roundworms. A gram of soil contains an estimated 30,000 protozoa, 50,000 algae, 4000,000 fungi and billions of bacteria. Gretchen Daily, 'Introduction: What Are Ecosystem Services?' *in* Gretchen Daily (ed) *Nature's Services: Societal Dependence on Natural Ecosystems* (1997) 3.

2 Ronald Amundson and others, 'Soil and Human Security in the Twenty-first Century' (2015) 348 SCIENCE no. 6325.

3 FAO and UNEP, *Global Assessment of Soil Pollution: Summary for Policy Makers* (2021) 15.

4 Rachel Mason and others, 'Evidence, causes and consequences of declining nitrogen availability in terrestrial ecosystems' (2022), Science Vol. 376:6590 1.

5 IPBES, *The assessment report on land degradation and restoration* (2018) IV and xx.

6 *State of the Planet: A World Transformed,* (National Geographic, 2002).

7 IPBES, *supra* n 5 at 225.

 | DOI:10.1163/9789047440802_011

fertility.[8] UNEP estimates that a third of the Earth's land surface is degraded, affecting more than 2,6 billion people globally.[9]

Soil also is degraded by excess demands on it. Overuse of soil depletes the nutrients and leads to desertification. Grazing lands cover more than a third of the world's land surface.[10] As herds and flocks grow in response to increased demand for meat, milk, leather and other livestock products, overgrazing has become a widespread problem. Agriculture also has intensified in many areas, increasing crop and livestock yields, but increasing chances of land degradation.[11] The increase in the human population in the past century and changed consumption patterns of much of the world population have greatly increased the demand for land-based resources.[12]

Legal protection for soil is rather recent, although some forestry laws protected trees at least in part to avoid erosion and consequent flooding. Part of the neglect was due to a general perception of soil as an inexhaustible resource in view of its use for food production. At the international level, cooperation started later than in other sectors of environmental protection, because it was generally considered that the soil conservation was mainly a domestic problem without international implications. Non-binding regional instruments played an early role in developing the international dimension of soil conservation. In Europe, for example, the Committee of Ministers of the Council of Europe adopted the European Soil Charter on May 30, 1972.[13] Globally, the UN Food and Agriculture Organization proclaimed a World Soil Charter on November 25, 1981, which was revised in 2015.[14] The soil charters both contain non-binding guidelines for action and basic principles. They proclaim the responsibility of governments to develop land-use programs that include measures aimed at the best possible utilization of the land, ensuring long-term maintenance and improvement of its productivity, and avoiding losses of productive soil. The two charters focus on the need for land-use policies that create incentives for people to participate in soil conservation. These policies require technical, institutional and legal frameworks. In order to ensure optimum land use, a country's land resources should be assessed in terms of their suitability at different levels of inputs for different types of land use, including agriculture, grazing and forestry. Land having the potential for a wide range of uses

8 Lester R. Brown, *The Future of Growth* (State of the World 3, 1998) 9.
9 UNEP, *Land Degradation – Factsheet* (2017) 1.
10 IPBES, *supra* n 5 at XXIV.
11 ibid XXIV.
12 ibid XXXVIII.
13 Resolution (72)19.
14 Weston V.G.2; FAO, Revised World Soil Charter (2015).

should be employed so that future options for other potential functions are not denied. Utilization of land for non-agricultural purposes should be organized in such a way as to avoid, as much as possible, the occupation or permanent degradation of good quality soils. The World Charter for Nature also declares that the productivity of soils shall be maintained or enhanced through measures that safeguard their long-term fertility and the process of their organic decomposition, and prevent erosion and all other forms of degradation.[15]

In 1983, UNEP developed environmental guidelines for the formulation of national soil policies.[16] FAO contributed a partial, but important, approach to the problem of soil conservation by adopting an International Code of Conduct on the Distribution and Use of Pesticides on November 28, 1985. It was amended in 1989[17] was in part a predecessor of the Convention on Prior Informed Consent signed in September 1998.[18] It has also, more recently, put out other non-binding instruments to provide guidance on soil management. Some examples of this are the Voluntary guidelines for sustainable soil management in 2017, and the International Code of Conduct for the Sustainable Use and Management of Fertilizers in 2019.[19] In addition, it has provided multiple guides on good agricultural practices for various crops.[20]

Several days before the opening of the United Nations Conference on Environment and Development, on May 18, 1992, the Council of Europe Committee of Ministers adopted Recommendation 92(8) on Soil Protection. It calls for action by governments of member states to combat soil loss, soil degradation, reduction of ecological habitats and species biodiversity, and for national surveys of soils to monitor changes. Suggested mechanisms for international cooperation include harmonization of methods for quantifying and assessing soils and implementation of a concerted research program. The recommendation stresses the need to take soil protection into consideration in all other policies such as, for example, agriculture, forestry, industry, transportation, town planning and regional planning policies.

15 UN General Assembly, 1982, Weston, V.B 11, para. 10 (b).

16 *Environmental Management Guidelines* (No.7, UNEP, 1983).

17 Weston, V.H.17.

18 Convention on the Prior Informed Consent Procedure for Certain Hazardous Chemicals and Pesticides in International Trade (Rotterdam, September 10, 1998), 2244 UNTS 337.

19 *Voluntary guidelines for sustainable soil management* (FAO, ITPS & Global Soil Partnership, 2017); FAO, ITPS & Global Soil Partnership, International Code of Conduct for the Sustainable Use and Management of Fertilizers (2019).

20 See for example, recently: FAO, the Good Agricultural Practices (GAP) on Chickpeas (2023), the Good Agricultural Practices (GAP) on Groundnut (2024) and the Good Agricultural Practices (GAP) on Green Gram (2024).

Agenda 21, adopted at the 1992 Rio Conference, echoes this approach by devoting five chapters to different aspects of soil conservation. Chapter 10 discusses an integrated approach to the planning and management of land resources, Chapter 11 addresses action to combating deforestation, Chapter 12 is devoted to the problem of desertification, Chapter 13 concerns sustainable mountain development and Chapter 14 discusses sustainable agriculture and rural development. More recently, the UN Sustainable Development Goals (SDGs) also refer to soil; connections therein will be discussed below.

There has been one majorly relevant convention concerning soil, namely the UN Convention to Combat Desertification (UNCCD).[21] This is therefore discussed in Section A of this chapter. Other binding legal instruments on the subject are discussed in Section B. Wetlands, and more specifically, the 1971 Ramsar Convention on Wetlands are discussed in Chapter 8.E.1, in connection to protection of habitats of living organisms.

1 The UN Desertification Convention

Desertification is not a new phenomenon: old empires collapsed thousands of years ago as a result of severe drought that induced desert-like conditions.[22] Today, desertification affects 2.7 billion people worldwide, influencing, for example, the rate of migration.[23] Groundwater depletion is a real danger, which more than doubled between the years 1960 and 2000.[24] Desertification, therefore, had to be regulated.

As a direct consequence of the crisis due to drought in the African Sahel in the 1970s, the UN General Assembly convened a conference on desertification in 1977, which adopted a Plan of Action to Combat Desertification calling for national and regional efforts through an integrated program of land management assessment, implementation of corrective measures, and strengthening of scientific and technological infrastructures in

21 United Nations Convention to Combat Desertification in those Countries Experiencing Serious Drought and / or Desertification, Particularly in Africa (adopted 1994, entry into force 1996) 1954 UNTS 3 (UNCCD, or Desertification Convention).

22 William C. Burns, 'The International Convention to Combat Desertification: Drawing a Line in the Sand?' (1995) 16 Mich. J. Int'l L 831.

23 IPBES, *supra* n 5, XXXVI.

24 ibid 257; Yoshihide Wada and others, 'Global Depletion of Groundwater Resources' (2010) 37(29) Geophysical Research Letters 1. For more on groundwater, see Chapter 10.

dryland nations.[25] Effective progress was made, however, only in the aftermath of the 1992 Rio Conference. An international negotiating committee was established[26]and on June 17, 1994 the UN Convention to Combat Desertification in Those Countries Experiencing Serious Drought and/or Desertification, Particularly in Africa, was adopted.[27]

The Convention defines desertification as land degradation in arid, semiarid, and dry sub-humid areas resulting from various factors, including climatic variations and human activities (Art. 1(a)). To combat desertification and mitigate the effects of drought in the affected countries, the Convention advocates effective action in the form of action programs (Arts. 9–11). This involves long-term integrated strategies that focus simultaneously, in affected areas, on improved productivity of land and the rehabilitation, conservation and sustainable management of land and water resources (Arts. 2(2), 10). Accordingly, the Parties shall adopt an integrated approach addressing the physical, biological and socio-economic aspects of the processes of desertification and drought (Arts. 4(2)(a), 10(4)).

The Convention adopts an original approach to the desertification problem, which is a global issue but with direct effects experienced differently among regions, states and local areas. Recognizing this variation, the Convention consists of a general treaty and five annexed regional agreements. It also emphasizes the principle of common but differentiated responsibilities and provides for cooperation at national, subregional and regional levels, including public participation, in particular, during the elaboration and the implementation of action programs. Finally, it creates mechanisms, both administrative and financial, in order to monitor and ensure compliance.

The Convention's preamble insists on the global dimensions of desertification and drought and the need for joint action of the international community to combat it. At the same time, it notes the high concentration of developing countries, notably the least developed ones, among those experiencing serious drought and/or desertification. Each Annex to the Convention concerns a specific geographic region, setting out guidelines for the preparation of action programs and their exact focus (Art. 15). The first annex addresses Africa, Annex II is for Asia, while Latin America and the Caribbean are covered by Annex III.

---

25 Report of the UN Conference on Desertification, UN Doc. A/CONF.74/36 (1977). See also Kyle W. Danish, 'International Environmental Law and the "Bottom-up" Approach: a Review of the Desertification Convention', 3(1) Indiana J. of Global Legal Studies 141.

26 On the history of the negotiating process, see Burns supra n 22 at 11.

27 Weston V.G.4 (entry into force 1996).

Annex IV addresses the Northern Mediterranean. A fifth annex, adopted by the Conference of the Parties in December 2000, applies to Central and Eastern Europe.[28] Annex I is more than twice the length of the other annexes, indicating the importance of the topic to Africa, where desertification is linked to poverty and subsistence agriculture. The Convention (Arts. 7, 13(2)) explicitly grants priority to Africa in the quest to halt desertification.

The Convention advocates cooperation and coordination at subregional, regional and international levels (Arts. 3(b), 4(2)(e)). The Parties should implement their obligations individually or jointly, either through existing or prospective bilateral and multilateral arrangements (Art. 4.1) and they must strengthen sub-regional, regional and international cooperation and cooperate within relevant international organizations (Art. 4.2 (e)(f)). Actions programs, which constitute the main mechanism to implement the Convention, should also be elaborated at subregional and regional levels (Art. 11), when possible, through relevant intergovernmental organizations (Art. 14.1). Cooperation also is specified in the fields of information collection, analysis and exchange (Art. 16), research and development (Art. 17), capacity building (Art. 19), and in the implementation of the Convention (Art. 12). The Convention also calls for coordinating activities carried out under it and under other relevant international agreements, in particular, under the Framework Convention on Climate Change (Art. 8.1).

The principle of common but differentiated responsibilities, proclaimed in the Rio Declaration and previously reflected in the Ozone Treaties and the Convention on Climate Change, is largely applied in the Desertification Convention. Article 5, containing the obligations of affected country parties, requires them to give due priority to combating desertification and mitigating the effects of drought, and to allocate resources in accordance with their circumstances and capabilities. According to Article 6, developed countries shall actively support such efforts and provide substantial financial resources and other forms of support to assist affected countries and promote the mobilization of new and additional funding including funding from the private sector (Arts. 6, 20). In addition, developed countries shall promote and facilitate access by affected countries to appropriate technology, knowledge and know-how (Arts. 6, 12, 18, 20, 2(c)). The different forms of assistance provided by developing countries shall give priority to supporting national, sub-regional and regional action programs of affected developing countries (Art. 9.2).

28 See 31 EPL 14 (2001).

An additional important feature of the Convention is that its implementation involves many levels of cooperation, with an emphasis on public participation. The need for effective action at all levels of government, supported by international cooperation and partnership arrangements (Art. 2.1) is a basic requirement. Affected countries must create an enabling environment at higher levels to facilitate action at local levels (Art. 3(a)). Cooperation should be developed in a spirit of partnership between the government, communities, non-governmental organizations, and landholders, to establish a better understanding of the nature and value of land and scarce water resources in affected areas and to work towards their sustainable use (Art. 3(c)). One of the main elements of the Convention is the participation of populations and local communities in decisions concerning the design and implementation of programs to combat desertification (Art. 3(a)). National action programs should be prepared and updated through a continuing participatory process (Art. 9.1, 10.2(f)). A necessary complement of public participation is capacity building, education and public awareness (Art. 19).

Finally, the Convention calls for the development of institutional mechanisms (Art. 4.2(g)), including operational mechanisms at the national and field levels (Art. 14.2) and promotes the use of existing bilateral and multilateral financial mechanisms and arrangements (Art. 4.2(h)). Article 22 establishes a Conference of the Parties assisted by a Permanent Secretariat (Art. 23) and a Committee on Science and Technology (Art. 24). Article 21 foresees a financial mechanism, while Article 26 institutes a reporting system. According to the latter, each party shall transmit to the Conference of the Parties reports on the measures it has taken to implement the Convention. Affected countries shall provide a description of the strategies and programs established and of any relevant information on their implementation. Any group of affected countries may make a joint communication on measures taken at the sub-regional and/or regional levels in the framework of action programs. The Conference of the Parties is to facilitate the provision to affected developing countries, on request, of technical and financial support in compiling and communicating such information. Developed countries shall report on measures taken to assist in the preparation and implementation of action programs, including information on the financial resources they have provided, or are providing, under the Convention.

Many of the states parties submitted their National Actions Plans in 2000, and in 2010, the Secretariat of the CCD launched a program to integrate these National Action Plans with UNFCCC National Adaptation Plans of Action

(NAPAS).[29] The rationale for such an approach being that a collaborative approach would contribute more effectively towards achieving the desired results, rather than working separately, sometimes in competition with each other or duplicating efforts, translating into wasted resources and less than optimal results.

The UNCCD annexes describe the particular conditions of each concerned region and outline the recommended contents of national, sub-regional and regional action programs. All the annexes include provisions for the coordinating the different programs. Article 9 of Annex IV relating to the Northern Mediterranean expressly precludes affected developed countries of the region from receiving financial assistance under the Convention.

Commentators on the Convention have stressed two of its characteristics. The first is its recognition of the importance of public participation at the local level in affected nations,[30] also called 'bottom-up' approach'.[31] The second is the innovation of confronting problems of harmful patterns of land use, which underlies the whole instrument.[32]

In general, the COP for the UNCCD has discussed the SDGs on multiple occasions, striving to implementation of the UNCCD in accordance with these goals.[33] It mainly discusses Goal 15. It encourages parties to formulate voluntary land degradation neutrality targets, and to implement measures to accelerate their achievement, in accordance with goal 15.3: to by 2030, 'combat desertification, restore degraded land and soil, including land affected by desertification, drought and floods, and strive to achieve a land degradation-neutral world'.[34]

---

29 Synergistic Implementation, *Integration of UNCCD National Action Programmed (NAP) with UNFCCC National Adaptation Plans of Actions (NAPA s)* (UNCCD/UNFCCC2010).

30 Burns, *supra* n 22 at 877.

31 Danish *supra* n 25 at 161, 173.

32 *Id.* at 172.

33 See: UNCCD Decision 2/COP.13 (9th Plenary Meeting, September 14, 2017) ICCD /COP(13)/21/Add.1 ; UNCCD Decision 3/COP.13 (10th Plenary Meeting, September 15, 2017) ICCD/COP(13)/21/Add.1 ; UNCCD Decision 3/COP.14 (14th Plenary Meeting, September 13, 2019) ICCD/COP(14)/23/Add.1 ; UNCCD Decision 3/COP.15 (5th Plenary Meeting, May 19, 2022) ICCD/COP(15)/23/Add.1.

34 UNCCD Decision 3/COP.15, preamble, para. 1–2 ; UN a/RES/70/1, adopted September 25, 2015, 24.

2 General Norms on Soil Protection

It is generally recognized that protecting soil fertility is essential to international efforts to promote food security and conservation and sustainable use of plant genetic resources. The FAO's International Treaty on Plant Genetic Resources for Food and Agriculture has as its objective conservation, sustainable use and equitable benefit sharing of plant resources.[35] The obligations of the contracting parties include developing and maintaining appropriate policy and legal measures that promote sustainable use of plant genetic resources (Art. 6.1); these measures may include strengthening research to enhance and conserve biological diversity for the benefit of farmers, especially those who generate and use their own plant varieties and 'apply ecological principles in maintaining soil fertility and in combating diseases, weeks and pests' (Art. 6.2(b)).

The first international treaty exclusively dedicated to soil was adopted October 16, 1998 as a protocol to the 1991 framework Convention on the Protection of the Alps. The Convention itself designates soil conservation as an objective, which it defines as 'to reduce quantitative and qualitative soil damage, in particular by applying agricultural and forestry methods which do not harm the soil, through minimum interference with soil and land, control of erosion and the restriction of soil sealing' (Art. 2(2)(d)). The Protocol of Application of the Convention in the Field of Soil Protection has been ratified by three of the eight signatories and entered into force on December 18, 2002. The Preamble reiterates the Convention's objective and goes on to express the parties' recognition of the fact that soil occupies a particular place in ecosystems and that its reconstitution and regeneration occur extremely slowly. The parties also recognize that erosion is a particular problem in the Alpine region because of the topography and that the concentration of pollutants in the soil can thus be carried to other ecosystems and present a risk to humans, flora and fauna. The Protocol notes the need for an integrated approach because of the impacts on soil of industrialization, urbanization, mining, tourism, agriculture, forestry, and transport.

Article 1(2) acknowledges the multiple functions of soil as a vital base and space for biological diversity; a notable element of nature and the countryside; a part of ecosystem functioning, especially with water cycles and soil nutrients;

35 Rome, November 3, 2001.

a milieu to transform and regulate substances, notably through its filtration capacity in protecting underground aquifers; as a habitat; and as a source of natural and cultural history. The functions of the soil, particularly the ecological functions, should be guaranteed and preserved over the long term, both in quantity and in quality. The restoration of degraded soils is encouraged. The measures states parties should take must aim at utilizing soil appropriately according to location, economizing surface use, preventing erosion and structural damage to soil, as well as minimizing the transfer of polluting substances to soil. Special measures should be taken to preserve and promote the diversity of soil typical of the Alpine region and its characteristic places. In this context, prevention includes guaranteeing the functional capacity as well as the possibility of different utilizations of soil by future generations with a view towards sustainable development.

The basic obligations of the parties are to take legal and administrative measures necessary to protect soil and to monitor the application of these measures. Where there is a risk of grave and persistent danger to the functional capacity of soil, protection should have priority over utilization as a general rule. The protocol also provides that soil should be a factor in delimiting protected areas and in particular that characteristic formations or areas of particular interest for geology and understanding the evolution of the earth should be preserved. The parties agree to look into the application of financial and fiscal measures to protect soil. Article 3 adds an obligation to apply an integrated approach that incorporates soil protection into all aspects of land management. Assignment of responsibility to different levels of governance is encouraged, as is international cooperation. (Arts. 4, 5). Chapter II of the Protocol details the specific measures to be taken. One of these calls for including consideration of soil impacts in environmental impact assessments for major projects. The contracting parties agree on the need for cartography to identify zones at risk from erosion, avalanches or other earth movements, earthquakes, or flooding and to delimit zones at risk. Preference is to be given to natural techniques to respond to threats (Arts. 10, 11). As for contaminated soil, the parties agree to inventory these sites and evaluate the risk they present, as well as to take further measures of waste management to prevent further contamination.

The comprehensive obligations contained in the Protocol are supplemented by requirements of permanent observation and monitoring, with state reports to be submitted to the Alpine Conference. The permanent committee of the Conference is to examine the reports to verify compliance with the Protocol. The committee may request additional information from the states parties or have recourse to other sources of information. A non-compliance procedure is also foreseen.

In Africa, the 2003 revised African Convention on Conservation of Nature and Natural Resources reflects the Desertification Convention and other developments concerning protection of soil. Its Art. VI provides:

1. 'The Parties shall take effective measures to prevent land degradation, and to that effect shall develop long-term integrated strategies for the conservation and sustainable management of land resources, including soil, vegetation and related hydrological processes.
2. They shall in particular adopt measures for the conservation and improvement of the soil, to, *inter alia*, combat its erosion and misuse as well as the deterioration of its physical, chemical and biological or economic properties.
3. To this end:
    a. they shall establish land-use plans based on scientific investigations as well as local knowledge and experience and, in particular, classification and land-use capability;
    b. they shall, when implementing agricultural practices and agrarian reforms,
        i. improve soil conservation and introduce sustainable farming and forestry practices, which ensure long-term productivity of the land,
        ii. control erosion caused by land misuse and mismanagement which may lead to longterm loss of surface soils and vegetation cover,
        iii. control pollution caused by agricultural activities, including aquaculture and animal husbandry;
    c. they shall ensure that non-agricultural forms of land use, including but not limited to public works, mining and the disposal of wastes, do not result in erosion, pollution, or any other form of land degradation;
    d. they shall, in areas affected by land degradation, plan and implement mitigation and rehabilitation measures.
4. Parties shall develop and implement land tenure policies able to facilitate the above measures, *inter alia* by taking into account the rights of local communities'.

With their detailed and integrated approach to protecting soil as an essential component of ecosystems, the Alpine Convention Protocol and the African Convention provide models which could be adapted to other regions. In the EU, efforts have been undertaken for the EU Soil Strategy for 2030, with the aim of achieving healthy soils by 2050.[36] However, as of May 2024, binding regulations have yet to materialize.

Protection of soils has been referred to in other regimes such as the 2011 Protocol on Sustainable Forest Management to the Framework Convention for the Protection and Sustainable Development of the Carpathians. Its Article 2 requires that the parties 'develop and implement policies and strategies in their national territory aimed at sustainable management of the Carpathian forests …'. In Article 3, it further requires Parties to take into consideration the objectives of the Protocol in other policies, including soil protection. This integrated approach is also taken by the post-2015 Sustainable Development Agenda which, in Goal 15 commits UN Members, by 2030, to 'combat desertification, restore degraded land and soil, including land affected by desertification, drought and floods, and strive to achieve a land degradation-neutral world'.[37] Other goals also relate to soil, such as 'implementing resilient agricultural practices that increase productivity and production',[38] and reducing the release of chemicals and other wastes into, amongst others, soil.[39]

There remains a school of thought – led by the IUCN specialist group on soils – that there is a need for either an Annex or Protocol to the UN Convention on Desertification, or a more broadly-based Convention, to cover all aspects of land degradation, not just those relating to drylands.[40] However, there seems to be no serious efforts to make this a legal reality yet.

Bibliography

Boer, B. and Hannam I., 'Legal Aspects of Sustainable Soils: National and International' (2003) 12(1) *RECIEL* 149.

Boer, B. and Hannam I., 'Developing a Global Soil Regime' (2015) 1 *International Journal of Rural Law and Policy* 1.

Burns, W.C., 'The International Convention to Combat Desertification: Drawing a Line in the Sand?' (1995) 16 *Mich.J. Int'l L.* 831.

36 European Union (European Commission) 'EU Soil Strategy for 2030: Reaping the benefits of healthy soils for people, food, nature and climate' (2021) COM 699 final 2.

37 UN a/RES/70/1, adopted September 25, 2015, 24–25.

38 ibid 15.

39 ibid 22.

40 The possible elements of such an instrument have been elaborated by Boer and Hannam: Ben Boer and Ian Hannam 'Developing a Global Soil Regime' (2015) International Journal of Rural Law and Policy 1.

Danish, K.W., 'International Environmental Law and the "Bottom-up" Approach: A Review of the Desertification Convention' (1995) 3 *Indian J. Global Leg. Stud.* 1.

Desertification Control Bulletin.

Dregne, H.E., *Desertification of Arid Lands* (1983).

FAO, *Law and Sustainable Development since Rio: Legal Trands in Agriculture and Natural Resources Management* (2002).

Ginzky, H. et al., *International Yearbook of Soil Law and Policy* 2019 (2021).

Grainger, A., *The Threatening Desert* (1990).

Heathcote, R.l. *the Arid Lands: Their Use and Abuse* (1983).

IPBES, *The assessment report on land degradation and restoration* (2018).

Ruppel, O., 'Overview of International Soil Law' in *Soil Security*. (6 2022) 100056.

UNCCD, Desertification Convention: <https://www.unccd.int/>.

UNEP, Desertification Control Bulletin.

CHAPTER 10

Fresh Waters

Inland or fresh water accounts for only 2.5 percent of the earth's water, and over two-thirds of this limited quantity is frozen in glaciers and ice caps at the two poles and on high mountains. Another 30 percent is located in underground aquifers, leaving just 1.2 percent of all water as surface fresh water. The demand for water is rising with increasing population, higher living standards, and the extension of water-utilizing industries such as mining and metal-processing, cement production, wood processing and irrigation-based agriculture. Over the past century, water consumption has been increasing at more than double the rate of population growth.[1] This is a critical problem because the water cycle is essentially a closed one – the only water is existing water.

The 2019 UN Water Development Report, referring to a study by Mekonnen and Hoekstra in 2016, indicated that about two thirds of the world population, about 4 billion people, experience severe water scarcity at least one month of the year.[2] While water demand rises with the global population growth, water supply does not, causing the freshwater supply to be overdrawn in more and more areas. Chronic shortages have existed for a few decennia in many areas where precipitation is low or unreliable and/or where withdrawals have been significantly increased to meet additional demand from irrigation, industry or urban populations.[3] The replenishment of many freshwater sources around the world cannot keep up with the rate at which they are being pumped.[4] This is, for example the case in North Africa and West Asia, where some regions withdraw up to 1000 percent of their renewable water resources.[5] The UN predicts that in 2050, more than half of the world population, 40 percent of global

1 UN Water, Water Scarcity Factsheet (2014).

2 Mesfin Mekonnen and Arjen Hoekstra, 'Four Billion People Facing Severe Water Scarcity' (2016) 2(2) SA 1.

3 See, generally, Edward H.P. Brans, and others, *The Scarcity of Water, Emerging Legal and Political Responses* (Kluwer Law International BV 1997).

4 Sandra Postel, 'Entering an era of water scarcity: The challenges ahead' (2000) 10(4) EA 941; Arjen Hoekstra and others, 'Global Monthly Water Scarcity: Blue Water Footprints versus Blue Water Availability' (2012) 7(2) PLoS ONE 1.

5 UN-Water, *Summary Progress Update 2021: SDG 6 – water and sanitation for all* (2021) 8.

 | DOI:10.1163/9789047440802_012

grain production and 45 percent of the global gross domestic product will be put at risk due to stress put on global water resources.[6]

The legal issues that arise concerning access to and use of water are largely international. There are 310 transboundary river basins in the world (68 transboundary river basins in Africa, 66 in Asia, 88 in Europe, 49 in North America and 39 in South America) and 468 transboundary aquifers have also been identified.[7] In fact, nearly half of all land and 40 percent of the world's population are found within international river basins.[8] Rivers may constitute the border between two countries, traverse the frontier, or even combine the two characteristics, as with the Danube, the Rhine and the Rio Grande. International regulation thus must adapt itself to multiple situations, resulting in a variety of regulatory schemes, often influenced by factors other than environmental.

For more than half of all great rivers, the volume, timing and geography of water flow is controlled by some 62,000 large dams built to secure water resources for food production, energy generation, flood control and domestic use.[9] At the same time, dams are very disruptive of aquatic habitats, leading to declining fish stocks and significant and irreversible losses in biological diversity. Retreating deltas result in the loss of productive land, a problem that could be compounded by climate change and rising sea levels. An example of concerns how a dam can disrupt the normal flow of water is found in the Grand Ethiopian Renaissance Dam (GERD), built for hydroelectric reasons, which for years has been the topic of heated discussions between Ethiopia, Sudan and Egypt about the water flow of the Nile. Even though Ethiopia holds the standpoint that the power generation will be hugely beneficial for the Ethiopian population and its building of the dam is fully legitimized, downriver Sudan and Egypt are concerned the changes to the water flow will be disastrous, endangering the livelihood of a major part of its population living downstream of the GERD along the Nile.[10]

---

6 UN-Water, *Sustainable Development Goal 6: Synthesis Report 2018 on Water and Sanitation* (2018) 10.

7 Melissa McCracken and Aaron Wolf, 'Updating the Register of International River Basins of the world' (2019) 35(5) IJWRD 732; For a map, see UN IGRAC (International Groundwater Resources Assessment Centre), *Transboundary Aquifers of the World* [map] (2021).

8 UN, *The Economic Commission for Europe Water Convention and the United Nations Watercourses Convention: An analysis of their harmonized contribution to international water law* (2015) UN Doc. ECE/MP.WAT/42, preface.

9 For up-to-date statistics, see the website of ICOLD (International Commission on Large Dams) at <www.icold-cigb.net/GB/world_register/general_synthesis.asp>.

10 See for the respective position of these states for example: Letter dated September 12, 2023 from the Permanent Representative of Egypt to the United Nations addressed to the President of the Security Council (UN Doc. S/2023/664); Letter dated April 12, 2021 from

Legal issues concerning freshwater resources are not only quantitative but also qualitative ones. In 2022, approximately 2.2 billion people in developing countries lacked safe water supplies and 3.5 billion lacked access to safely managed sanitation services.[11] Safe drinking water and sanitation have been a priority issue on the international agenda, appearing in the Millennium Development Goals, the 2002 Johannesburg Summit, and the post-2015 Sustainable Development Agenda, as well as in the work of human rights bodies.

Threats to freshwater quality are varied and complex. Sewage disposal is a classic use of flowing water and has been linked to epidemics of plague and cholera. The disposal of chemicals and hazardous wastes, the use of pesticides and fertilizers, also affect water quality. Freshwater resources are threatened by deforestation as well; for example, the very existence of China's Lijiang River is in jeopardy, not in the least due to destruction of highland forests[12] and countries in Asia have suffered major flooding as a result of upland deforestation.[13]

Although most of the waters of the earth are linked, the legal regimes applicable to them differ widely in response to geographic, economic, social and political factors. The sea receives a large part of its pollution from rivers, but specific rules are needed to resolve the latter problem. Groundwater is closely connected with surface waters, but their legal regimes are often distinct.[14]

---

the Chargé d'affaires a.i. of the Permanent Mission of the Sudan to the United Nations addressed to the President of the Security Council (S/2021/350); Letter dated September 18, 2023 from the Permanent Representative of Ethiopia to the United Nations addressed to the President of the Security Council (S/2023/684); For an in-depth discussion, see Wossenu Abtew & Shimelis Behailu Dessu, *The Grand Ethiopian Renaissance Dam on the Blue Nile* (Springer 2019) and Harry Verhoeven, 'The Grand Ethiopian Renaissance Dam: Africa's Water Tower, Environmental Justice & Infrastructural Power' 150(4) Daedalus 159.

11 UN, *The Sustainable Development Goals Report: Special Edition* (2023) 24.

12 *China's Lijiang River Could Dry Up*, International Herald Tribune, July 24, 1990, 2; Coco Liu, 'What Happens When Asia's Water Tower Dries Up?' (*Scientific American*, April 16, 2013) <https://www.scientificamerican.com/article/what-happens-when-asias-water-tower-dries-up/>.

13 See Cahyadi Ramadhan, Ruslanjari Dina and Emilya Nurjani, 'Spatial and temporal based deforestation proclivity analysis on flood events with applying watershed scale (case study: Lasolo watershed in Southeast Sulawesi, Central Sulawesi, and South Sulawesi, Indonesia)' (2023) 92 IJDRR 103745; Jen Feng Khor and others, 'Assessing the Impact of Deforestation on Decadal Runoff Estimates in Non-Homogeneous Catchments of Peninsula Malaysia' (2023) 15 Water 1162.

14 Few international agreements are addressed exclusively to groundwater. Relevant provisions can be found, however, in multilateral agreements applicable to a continent (e.g. Art. 5 of the African Convention on the Conservation of Nature and Natural Resources, November 15, 1968) or a region (e.g. Art. 4 of the May 17, 1980 Protocol to the Barcelona Convention for the Protection of the Mediterranean (February 16, 1976); for an overview of treaties and other legal instruments related to groundwaters specifically or more broadly

Moreover, even the same type of water source may be regulated differently, according to the use to which the waters are put (e.g., domestic, agricultural and industrial purposes). The different uses are a function of population density, the level of economic development and cultural traditions and they affect the economic and environmental values of water.[15]

The physical unity of an integrated water network should lead naturally to addressing water problems for an entire hydrographic basin. The legislation of certain countries adopts this approach, but it is a recent development at the international level. For the most part, conventions concerning the protection of rivers traditionally have applied only to isolated rivers, or even certain portions of rivers.[16] The Rhine, for example, is protected by conventional international provisions only between its exit from Lake Constance and its mouth, while waters in the lake are governed by a separate treaty.[17] In addition, most instruments governing boundary waters concern only the surface waters in the zone regulated by these treaties. Care must be taken to identify the geographic scope of international instruments; some refer to watercourses, others to water systems,[18] and still others to frontier waters,[19] international basins,[20] or water resources.[21]

The 1997 UN Convention on the Law of the Non-Navigational Uses of International Watercourses made an important contribution to international

---

until 2005, see Stefano Burchi and Kerstin Mechlem for the FAO Legal Office, *Groundwater in international law: Compilation of treaties and other legal instruments* (Food and Agriculture Organization of the United Nations 2005).

15 See H.L.F. Saeijs and M.J. van Berkel, *The Global Water Crisis, the Major Issue of the Twenty-first Century, a Growing and Explosive Problem,* in *The Scarcity of Water, supra* n 3, at 3.

16 As early as the 14th Century, disputes arose over riparian rights along the Isar River, leading to a ducal verdict of 1430, an inter-state treaty in 1624, and later lawsuits. Most of these were decided or settled on the basis of Roman law transferred from the private realm to the inter-state level. See Karl Neumeyer, 'A Contribution to International Water Law' ['Ein Beitrag zum Internationalen Wasserrecht'], (1915) Festschrift für Georg Cohn, Zürich, Switzerland: Orell Füssli 143, translated from German by Peter H. Sand (2014) in P. Sand (ed) *The History and Origin of International Environmental Law* (Edward Elgar Publishing 2015).

17 See respectively: Convention on the Protection of the Rhine (Bern April 12, 1999) and Agreement on the Protection of Lake Constance against Pollution (Steckborn, October 27, 1960).

18 E.g. Yugoslavia-Hungary Agreement of August 8, 1955, UN Doc. ST/LEG/SER.B/12 at 830.

19 E.g. Poland-Czechoslovakia agreement of March 21, 1958, 538 UNTS 108; Poland-USSR of July 17, 1964, 552 UNTS 177.

20 E.g. the Statute of the Lake Chad Commission of August 22, 1964, III IUWR 964. See also the ILA Helsinki Rules on the Use of the Waters of International Rivers (1966).

21 Recommendations 51–55 of the Stockholm Action Plan.

environmental law by defining a 'watercourse' as 'a system of surface waters and groundwaters constituting by virtue of their physical relationship a unitary whole and normally flowing into a common terminus'.[22] This definition reflects the approach taken by Rio Conference Agenda 21 (1992). According to Chapter 18 para. 36, the complex and interconnected nature of freshwater systems demands that freshwater management be holistic, taking a 'catchment' approach, and must be based on a balanced consideration of the needs of people and the environment. Agenda 21 declares that three objectives need to be pursued concurrently to integrate water quality and water resource management: the maintenance of ecosystem integrity of the drainage basin, public health protection, and human resources development for implementing water quality management.[23]

The legal treatment of water pollution may be complicated by differences between identifiable 'point' sources and 'diffuse' pollution sources. The latter category includes emissions that individually or separately are responsible for possibly insignificant amounts of pollution, such as small, often continuous discharges of wastes and utilization of pesticides and fertilizers in agriculture. Taken together, however, they may result in considerable contamination and harm to the environment.

1 Overview

It is impossible in this text to analyze all the regimes that have developed concerning different types of waters, even those of a single region, but it is necessary to give a general outline of the evolution that has occurred.[24] Early inter-state cooperation concerning rivers and lakes generally addressed utilization of a watercourse for navigation or irrigation, or concerned the management of risks, such as flooding. Environmental aspects began to be included toward the beginning of the twentieth century, but cooperation generally was limited to neighboring states sharing all or part of a river or a lake. In addition, deterioration of water quality was not seen a matter of common concern

22 May 21, 1997, Art. 3(a).

23 Para. 18.38.

24 For a history of the development of international law in this field, see James L. Wescoat Jr., 'Main Currents in Early Multilateral Water Treaties: A Historical-Geographic Perspective, 1648–1948' (1996) Colorado J Int Environmental Law & Policy.

because it did not affect all riparian states in similar manner, downstream states suffering more harm than the upstream riparians.[25]

International water law has to take into account, among other factors, the geography, meteorology, society, history, politics and economics of each region. For almost a century, local and sub-regional regulations have been tailored to a specific watercourse or an area. At first, particular water pollution problems were addressed when harmful activities originated in neighboring countries, applying general precedents and norms of transboundary pollution. Later, the development of international environmental law led to the adoption of global rules and principles to govern the conduct of states in respect to the conservation and harmonious utilization of natural resources shared by two or more states. Inland waters perhaps best illustrate the problems of shared natural resources which need integrated protection of their complex ecosystems.

The legal status of rules on shared resources has been debated but their regular inclusion in different global and regional conventions and in other forms of state practice leads to the conclusion that they constitute customary international law or at least emerging customary norms. The judgments of the International Court of Justice in the cases concerning the Gabčíkovo-Nagymaros Project on the Danube, the Costa Rica – Nicaragua cases about the San Juan river and its surrounding area, and the construction of Pulp Mills on the River Uruguay confirmed the creation of a coherent corpus of environmental principles governing shared water resources.[26] This evolution also has been supported by principles announced in non-binding texts adopted by international organizations such as the United Nations, the Council of Europe, and the UNECE. Special attention must be given to European Union action governing or at least harmonizing member state legislation.

The present chapter examines general global and regional rules protecting fresh waters before reviewing specific regional and subregional developments. Concrete cases are included to illustrate the law of international watercourses. The international rivers involved have economic, political, and ecological

25 Johan G. Lammers, *Pollution of International Watercourses* (Brill 1984); Albert E. Utton and Ludwik A. Teclaff, *Transboundary Resources Law* (Avalon Publishing 1987). For a review of groundwater law, see Julio A. Barberis, *International Groundwater Resources Law* (Food & Agriculture Org. 1986); A. Nollkaemper, *the Legal Regime for Transboundary Water Pollution: Between Discretion and Constraint* (Springer Netherlands 1993).

26 ICJ, *Gabčíkovo-Nagymaros Case (Hungary v Slovakia)*, Judgment of September 25, 1997; ICJ, *Certain Activities Carried Out by Nicaragua in the Border Area (Costa Rica v Nicaragua) and the Construction of a Road in Costa Rica along the San Juan River (Nicaragua v Costa Rica)*, Judgment, ICJ Reports 2015; ICJ, *Pulp Mills on the River Uruguay (Argentina v Uruguay)*, Judgment, ICJ Reports 2010.

importance and are international boundaries. The chapter also briefly examines efforts to protect freshwaters through human rights law and through the innovative approach of declaring a river to be a legal person.

1.1 *General Rules*

1.1.1 Global Norms

A holistic approach considers all water resources without regard to the existence of international borders. The 1966 'Helsinki Rules'[27] of the non-governmental International Law Association are among the first and most-often-cited norms related to international fresh waters. Article 4 contains the basic principle that each state within an international drainage basin has the right to a reasonable and equitable part of the beneficial use of the basin waters. Article 10 adds that, conforming to the principle of equitable utilization, each state should refrain from causing any new form of pollution of the waters or any increase in the level of actual pollution of the waters in the international drainage basin, likely to cause serious damage on the territory of another state in the basin. The state also should take all reasonable measures in order to reduce actual pollution of all kinds so that no serious damage is caused on the territory of another state in the basin.

After adoption of the Helsinki Rules, the 1972 Stockholm Action Plan called for international cooperation to protect inland waters and water resources against pollution (Recommendations 51 to 55). A United Nations water conference, held in 1977 at Mar del Plata, Argentina, recommended the study of methods that could be used for the management of shared water resources, the elaboration of common programs, and the implementation of mechanisms and institutions necessary for the coordinated utilization of water resources. The Principles of Conduct in the Field of Environment for the Guidance of States in the Conservation and Harmonious Utilization of Natural Resources Shared by Two or More States, approved on May 1979 by the Governing Council of UNEP, were modeled on the prior texts on shared water resources.[28] Agenda 21, Chapter 18, goes further, calling for 'protection of the quality and supply of

27 See ILA, Report of the Committee on the Uses of the Waters of International Rivers, Report of the Fifty-Second Conference, Helsinki, 1966, at 484 (1966). In 1982, the ILA adopted the Montreal Rules on Water Pollution in an International Drainage Basin to update the Helsinki Rules 'taking into account developments in theory and practice since 1966'. ILA, Report of the Sixtieth Conference (Montreal, 1982), pp. 1–3, 13, 535 et seq.

28 UN Doc. UNEP/IG 12/2 (1978), 17 ILM 1097 (1978).

freshwater resources' by 'application of integrated approaches to the development, management and use of water resources'.[29]

The United Nations International Law Commission, in its mandate to develop and codify international law, began work on the law of non-navigational uses of international watercourses in 1971. In 1990, at its forty-second session, it adopted Articles devoted to the environmental protection of international waters.[30] The United Nations General Assembly accepted the Articles and adopted a Convention on the Law of the Non-Navigational Uses of International Watercourses on May 5, 1997.

The framework UN Convention includes four categories of provisions: general norms applicable to all international watercourses (Arts. 5–10), procedural rules to implement such norms (Arts. 11–19 and 29–32), substantive provisions concerning the fresh water protection, preservation and management (Arts. 20–28), and clauses concerning agreements between watercourse states (Arts. 3–4).

The Convention mandates that watercourse states, in their respective territories, utilize an international watercourse in an equitable and reasonable manner and with a view of obtaining optimal and sustainable utilization thereof consistent with adequate protection of the watercourse (Art. 5(1)). In addition, such states shall participate in the use, development and protection of the watercourse in an equitable and reasonable manner, with the duty to cooperate in the protection and development thereof (Art. 5(2)). Article 6 lists the factors relevant to deciding whether a use is equitable and reasonable: natural factors (geography, hydrology, climate, ecology); social and economic needs; dependent populations; existing and potential uses of the watercourse; conservation, protection, development and economy of use of the water resources and the costs of measures taken to that effect; and the availability of alternatives of comparable value to a particular planned or existing use. In determining what is a reasonable and equitable use, all relevant factors must be considered together. Article 10 adds, somewhat contradictorily, that in the absence of agreement or custom to the contrary, no use enjoys inherent priority over other uses, but in the event of a conflict, special regard must be given to the requirements of human needs.

Article 7 is important to the question of whether a use is equitable and reasonable. The text obliges states to take all appropriate measures to prevent

---

29 See: Eyal Benvenisti, 'Collective Action in the Utilization of Shared Freshwater: the Challenges of International Water Resources Law' (1996) 90 AJIL 384.

30 International Law Commission, Report of the International Law Commission on the Work of its Forty-Second Session, May 1-July 20, 1990, UN GAOR Supp. 10, A/45/10 (1990).

significant harm to other watercourse states. Any state causing such harm 'having due regard for the provisions of Articles 5 and 6' must consult with the affected state and eliminate or mitigate such harm and, where appropriate, discuss the question of compensation. Upstream states, whose long-standing uses may be harmful to downstream states, may argue that Article 7 is subordinate to Articles 5 and 6 according to its own terms, and thus harm to downstream states is only one factor to weigh in deciding on the equity or reasonableness of uses, to be balanced against costs, benefits, and prior uses. Downstream states may view or contend that Article 7 is an independent obligation that necessarily renders uses unreasonable if there is significant harm. The Convention does not resolve this problem clearly, and disputes are likely to arise, which will require judicial interpretation or arbitration.

The Convention confirms the general rules of international environmental law by requiring transmission of information about planned measures that could have a transboundary impact (Arts. 11–16), consultations and negotiation concerning such measures (Art. 17) and emergency situations (Art. 25). It also affirms the duty of non-discrimination on the basis of nationality or residence in granting access to judicial or other procedures to any person who has suffered appreciable harm as a result of an activity related to an international watercourse or is exposed to a threat thereof (Art. 32). The term 'appreciable' indicates that the threshold for individual remedies is lower than that prompting the preventive and other interstate obligations, which only arise if the threatened harm is 'significant' or 'serious'.

The most innovative provisions are those particularly relevant for international environmental law. The Convention obliges watercourse states to protect, preserve and manage international watercourses and their waters (Art. 1(1)) and specifically to protect and preserve watercourse ecosystems (Art. 20). The latter provision echoes the duty imposed by UNCLOS Article 192 in respect of marine waters.[31] Watercourse states also must prevent the introduction of alien or new species into the watercourse if the species may have detrimental effects on the ecosystem of the watercourse resulting in significant harm to other watercourse states (Art. 22). The pollution of an international watercourse is defined broadly as 'any detrimental alteration in the composition or quality of the waters … which results directly or indirectly from human conduct'. Watercourse states shall prevent, reduce and control pollution, in

---

31 Interestingly, the Watercourses Convention also addresses the protection and preservation of the marine environment, requiring watercourse states to take all measures that are necessary to this effect, if appropriate in cooperation with other states, taking into account generally accepted international rules and standards (Art. 23).

particular by harmonizing their policies. The measures advocated include setting joint water quality objectives and criteria, establishing techniques and practices to address pollution from point and non-point sources, and establishing lists of substances whose introduction is to be prohibited, limited, investigated or monitored (Art. 21).

Albeit the entire Convention focuses on cooperation among watercourse states, Articles 3 and 4 promote formalized cooperation by encouraging the conclusion of watercourse agreements that further apply and adjust the provisions of the Convention. Even without concluding such an agreement, consultations shall be undertaken at the request of a watercourse state concerning the management of the watercourse, including the possible establishment of a joint management mechanism (Art. 24(1)). 'Management', as used in this provision, 'refers, in particular, to (a) planning the sustainable development of an international watercourse and providing for the implementation of any plans adopted; and (b) otherwise promoting the rational and optimal utilization, protection and control of the watercourse' (Art. 24(2)).

The UN Convention, which entered into force on August 17, 2014, now constitutes the essential basis of international law on fresh waters. As a codification convention, it generally expresses customary international law, although elements in the Convention also reflect compromises between upstream and downstream riparian interests and the progressive development of international environmental law. The International Court of Justice, in its judgment of September 25, 1997 in the Gabčíkovo-Nagymaros case, explicitly recognized the obligatory nature of the principle of equitable utilization contained in Article 5(2) of the Convention.[32]

The requirement of equitable utilization has inevitably given rise to a trend favoring the conclusion of joint management agreements which create institutions and procedures for allocating shared water resources, establishing priorities and determining equitable use. Examples of such cooperation are discussed below with respect to the US-Mexican boundary waters agreements and the agreement between Uruguay and Argentina to govern the Uruguay River.[33]

1.1.2 Regional Regulation

Regional bodies have adopted general principles regarding fresh water. The Council of Europe announced fundamental principles in the 1968 European

32 *Gabčíkovo-Nagymaros, supra n 26*, para. 147.

33 *Pulp Mills, supra* n 26.

Water Charter,[34] a non-binding instrument adopted two years after the ILA Helsinki Rules and more broadly addressing all fresh waters. The Charter calls water an indispensable resource which is not inexhaustible. It proclaims that water quality must be preserved at the levels necessary for the use foreseen, that water is a heritage whose value must be recognized by all, that water knows no boundary, and that its regulation demands international cooperation.

Other regional instruments concern specific forms or sources of pollution. In 1968, the Council of Europe adopted the European Agreement on the Restriction of the Use of Certain Detergents in Washing and Cleaning Products.[35] The United Nations Economic Commission for Europe has made several recommendations through its Committee on Water Problems, including a 1970 recommendation on the protection of ground and surface waters against pollution by oil and oil products.[36] Paragraph 3 called on member governments to designate 'protection zones' in areas needing to be preserved from pollution in view of their utilization; issue regulations concerning the storage, transport and disposal of oil, oil products and effluents from oil industries in order to avoid water pollution; and immediately report all spillage of oil and oil products likely to contaminate either ground or surface waters.

The OECD adopted a recommendation in 1989 on Water Resource Management Policies: Integration, Demand Management, and Groundwater Protection.[37] This instrument recommends review by member countries of existing institutional arrangements in the field of water resources to improve the integrated management of their policies. Comprehensive policies should exist for the efficient, sustainable development of groundwater resources and for their long-term protection from pollution and over-use. Particular attention should be paid to establishment and enforcement of pollution control programs and research to better understand pollution processes. Legislation on water should include environmental protection. The recommendation notes that the slow movement of groundwater and high cost of assessing its quality make it particularly vulnerable to long-term cumulative pollution and raise substantial uncertainties regarding its current and future condition. An important aspect of water resources management is thus to reduce pollution from diffuse and small point sources. Therefore, the production, sale and use of chemicals,

34 May 6, 1968. Consultative Assembly Recomm. 493 (1967), adopted April 28, 1967; Committee of Ministers Res. (67) 10, adopted May 26, 1967, reprinted in UN Doc. A/CN.4/274, para. 373.

35 September 16, 1968.

36 E/ECE/WATER/7, annex I.

37 Council Recommendation C(89)12(Final), March 31, 1989.

emissions into the atmosphere, and dumping of wastes must be controlled. Finally, 'because currently available information will rarely resolve all uncertainties in decision-making for groundwater management, policies should encourage precautionary decisions'.

In the decade between 1980 and 1990, the Committee on Water Problems of the UNECE drafted a series of general texts on cooperation in the field of transboundary waters.[38] They start from the accepted principle that states must take measures not to cause environmental damage outside national jurisdiction. As a consequence, the protection of transboundary waters cannot be national, but requires cooperation among riparian countries. Riparian states should conclude treaties, notably on matters concerning pollution, where they should jointly define water quality standards and objectives. Supervision, monitoring and observation of water quality and pollution should be jointly undertaken and states should exchange facts and information on pollution. This needs the creation of efficient alert systems in cases of serious accidental pollution and, in appropriate cases, the organization of mutual aid for emergency situations. Finally, institutional arrangements are deemed necessary including the creation of commissions and mixed working groups.

In 1990, the UNECE adopted a lengthy Code of Conduct on Accidental Pollution of Transboundary Inland Waters[39] applicable to hazardous activities resulting or likely to result in significant impairment of the quality of transboundary inland waters and/or significant damage to aquatic ecosystems in the territory of other countries. In the same regional framework, a Convention on the Protection and Use of Transboundary Watercourses and International Lakes was drafted and adopted in Helsinki, on March 17, 1992, covering Europe, Canada and US.

The Helsinki Convention aims to protect watercourses against harmful transboundary environmental impacts. Although the treaty was originally regional, it was amended in 2013 and it is now open to all UN Member States.[40] Since 2016, numerous states, primarily from the African continent, have acceded to it.[41] As well as being amended in this way, a protocol on civil liability

38 Res. 1(42), April 10, 1987, E/1987/33, E/ECE/1148 65. See also the ECE Declaration of Policy on Prevention and Control of Water Pollution, Including Transboundary Pollution, Res. B(XXXV) of April 26, 1980, U.N. Doc. E/1980/28, E/ECE 1008, 92.

39 Decision C(45), UN Pub. E/ECE/1225, ECE/ENVWA/16 (1990).

40 UNECE Convention on the Protection and Use of Transboundary Watercourses and International Lakes as amended (amended on November 28, 2003, entry into force February 6, 2013) ECE/MP.WAT/14, Art. 25(3).

41 As of May 2024, these states are (in order of accession): Chad (2018), Senegal (2018), Ghana (2020), Guinea-Bissau (2021), Togo (2021), Cameroon (2022), Nigeria (2022), The Gambia (2023), Iraq (2023), Namibia (2023) and Panama (2023).

and compensation was adopted in 2003.[42] The impact of the 2003 protocol is so far of little note: although 24 states signed it, only Hungary has become a State Party and it does not come into effect until sixteen states have acceded to the protocol.[43] Besides that, building on the Helsinki Convention, in 2006 the model provisions on transboundary flood management were adopted, which serve, as a soft law instrument, the purpose of guiding states on how to work cooperatively in situations of flooding.[44]

The Helsinki Convention is not formally a framework treaty because it does not provide for the conclusion of additional protocols for signature by all the contracting parties. While adopting some common solutions, it takes into account the variety of situations pertaining to different river systems: its preamble recites that cooperation between states parties shall be implemented primarily through the elaboration of agreements between countries bordering the same waters. Article 2(6) adds that such agreements should develop harmonized policies, programs and strategies covering the catchment areas or parts thereof. Article 9, entirely devoted to bilateral and multilateral cooperation, contains indications concerning the fields and the functioning of such cooperation.

Several aspects of the regional Convention are similar to those of the UN Convention, including the definition of transboundary waters as surface or ground waters and the call for ecologically sound and rational water management. The parties shall take appropriate measures to prevent, control and reduce pollution of waters causing or likely to cause transboundary impact and to ensure conservation and, where necessary, restoration of ecosystems (Art. 2(2)).

The Helsinki Convention, however, also includes additional elements such as prevention, precaution and the polluter pays principle which must guide the states parties (Arts. 2(3) and (5)), and the obligation to avoid the transfer of pollution from one to another part of the environment (Art. 2(3)). Article 3 lists

---

42 Protocol on civil liability and compensation for damages caused by the transboundary effects of industrial accidents on transboundary waters (adopted in Kiev, May 21, 2003, entry into force pending).

43 ibid, Art. 29(1).

44 UNECE Model Provisions on Transboundary Flood Management (adopted August 29, 2006) ECE/MP.WAT/2006/4; See for an in-depth discussion of the 2003 and 2006 protocol (1) Phani Dascalopoulou-Livada and Alexandros Kolliopoulos, 'The 2003 Kiev Protocol on Civil Liability and Compensation for Damage Caused by the Transboundary Effects of Industrial Accidents on Transboundary Waters' and (2) Alexandros Kolliopoulos, 'The UNECE Model Provisions on Transboundary Flood Management' in *The UNECE Convention on the Protection and Use of Transboundary Watercourses and International Lakes: Its Contribution to International Water Cooperation* (Hotei Publishing 2015).

measures which the parties are to develop, adopt and implement. They include, *inter alia*, the prior licensing of waste-water discharges, stricter requirements when the quality of the receiving water or the ecosystem so requires, the reduction of nutrient inputs, environmental impact assessment, monitoring the state of the watercourses, and the development of contingency planning.

In implementing the agreement, states shall use the best available technology, which Annex I to the Convention defines as 'the latest stage of development of processes, facilities or methods of operation which indicate the practical suitability of a particular measure for limiting discharges, emissions and waste'. The text elaborates the criteria to which special consideration shall be given: comparable processes, technological advances and changes, economic feasibility, time limitations, the nature and volume of the discharges and effluents concerned, low and non-waste technology. Annex II proposes guidelines for developing 'best environmental practices' including public information and education, product labeling, recycling, recovery and reuse, and licensing.

Primary obligations of the contracting parties include setting emission limits for discharges from point sources into surface waters (Art. 3(2)) and, where appropriate, defining water quality objectives and adopting water quality criteria (Art. 3(3)). Annex III to the Convention proposes guidelines for developing such objectives and criteria. Other provisions repeat and confirm more general international environmental law obligations such as monitoring (Arts. 4, 11), cooperation in the conduct of research (Arts. 5, 12), exchange of information (Arts. 6, 13), consultations (Arts. 6, 10) and public information. States parties are to set up and operate coordinated or joint alarm systems (Art. 14) and provide mutual assistance upon request in emergencies (Art. 14). A Meeting of parties reviews the implementation of the Convention.

The Protocol on Water and Health to the Helsinki Watercourses Convention (London, June 17, 1999) aims to promote the protection of human health and well-being at all appropriate levels, nationally as well as in transboundary and international contexts. The Convention notes from the outset that water is essential to sustain life and that water quality and quantity must be assured to meet basic human needs, 'a prerequisite both for improved health and for sustainable development'. The general provisions oblige parties to take all appropriate measures to prevent, control and reduce water-related disease within a framework of integrated water management systems, aimed at sustainable use of water resources, ambient water quality which does not endanger human health, and protection of water ecosystems. (Art. 4(1)). In particular, parties shall take measures to ensure and protect adequate supplies of wholesome drinking water free from dangers to human health and provide sanitation

(Art. 4(2)). Article 5 includes all the modern principles of international environmental law: polluter pays, precaution, prevention, duty not to cause transboundary harm, rights of future generations, and subsidiarity. Rights to information and public participation in decision-making are emphasized 'in order to enhance the quality and the implementation of the decisions, to build public awareness of issues, to give the public the opportunity to express its concerns and enable public authorities to take due account of such concerns' (Art. 5). Information and participation are to be supplemented by access to justice for review of relevant decisions when appropriate.

The European Union has made efforts to address the problem of water pollution in all its aspects. As a quasi-federal entity, its approach goes beyond the consideration of transboundary waters to include the internal water resources of its member states. The EC's water law was developed initially in the mid-1970s to address specific substances, sources, processes and uses of water, as well as its function in habitat protection. The measures lacked integration because of their piecemeal nature and because they were occasionally inconsistent or conflicting. For this reason, the Water Framework Directive (WFD) that was adopted in 2000 established a comprehensive framework for Community Action in the field of water policy.[45] The Directive also has two daughter-directives. The Groundwater Directive, drafted in 2006, is concerned with the quality and quantity of groundwater, and the Environmental Quality Standards Directive, drafted in 2008, with the quality of surface waters.[46] These two Directives set out more precise procedures for the requirements in the Water Framework Directive. Not related to the Water Directive, but also policing the quality of fresh water in Europe, is the Bathing Water Directive.[47] The Water Directive also covers floods, which is elaborated on in the 2007 Directive on the Assessment and Management of Flood Risks.[48]

The Water Directive aims to introduce a strategic framework, providing more holistic and integrated approaches to water management and conservation.

45 Directive 2000/60/EC, OJ L 327 of December 22, 2000. A decision of November 20, 2001 amended and complemented the framework directive by establishing a new list of priority substances in the field of water policy. Decision No 2455/2001/EC, OJ L 331 of December 15, 2001.

46 Directive 2006/118/EC, OJ L 327 of December 27, 2006 and Directive 2008/105/EC, OJ L 348 of December 24, 2008, amended by Directive 2013/39/EU, OJ L 226 of August 24, 2013. The EU also continuously puts out new updates for the Watch List of substances that are of concern. The most recent of these is the Commission Implementing Decision C/2022/5098, OJ L 197 of July 26, 2022.

47 Directive 2006/7/EC, OJ L 64 of March 4, 2006.

48 Directive 2007/60/EC, OJ L 288 of November 6, 2007.

The underlying aims are (1) to use hydrological catchments rather than political or administrative boundaries as the basis for action; (2) to set environmental objectives to ensure that all waters achieve good status and do not deteriorate; (3) to introduce a combined approach to pollution control and encourage sustainable water use; (4) to contribute to mitigating the effects of floods and droughts and (5) to ensure active stakeholder and community involvement. Europe was divided into a series of river basin districts, some of which traverse international boundaries. River Basin Management Plans established a program of measures to meet specific environmental objectives for each river basin. Water management issues and the measures to be taken are developed through public consultation.

The basic principle of the Directive is that water is not a commercial product like any other but, rather, a heritage which must be protected, defended and treated as such. The supply of water is a service of general interest. Further, protection and sustainable management of water must be integrated into other Community policy areas such as energy, transport, agriculture, fisheries, regional policy and tourism. The Directive itself aims to maintain and improve the aquatic environment in the Community by contributing to the progressive reduction of emissions of substances presenting a significant risk to or via the aquatic environment, including risks to waters used for the abstraction of drinking water. As minimum requirements and using a combined approach for point and diffuse pollution sources, the Community is to adopt common environmental quality standards and emission limit values for certain groups or families of pollutants, in order to prevent further deterioration of aquatic ecosystems, protect and enhance their status, and promote sustainable water use based on long-term protection of available water resources.

The Directive innovated by covering inland surface waters and groundwater, as well as by adding the categories of 'transitional waters' and 'coastal waters'. Transitional waters are bodies of surface water in the vicinity of a river mouth which are partly saline but which are substantially influenced by freshwater flows.[49] Coastal water means surface water on the landward side of a line, every point of which is at a distance of one nautical mile on the seaward from the baseline, which means a portion of the territorial sea.[50]

The Directive sets out distinct environmental objectives for basin management plans for surface waters, for groundwater and for protected areas (Art. 4). In 2015, the European Court of Justice made the clarification that member states are required to refuse authorization of a project where that project

49 Art. 2(6) Water Framework Directive.
50 ibid, Art. 2(7).

jeopardizes the attainment of good surface water status (unless there is a derogation), and it explains the definition of deterioration of the quality of surface waters in a very strict manner.[51] The Directive thus has binding effects for the EU Member States when the status of the surface water has been determined, and the quality of the water is not allowed to deteriorate from this point on as a result of any projects.

Furthermore, specific provisions apply to waters used for the abstraction of drinking water (Art. 7). Article 9 affirms the principle that the costs for water services, including environmental and resource costs, should be recovered from the user. The Directive encourages the active involvement of all interested parties in its implementation, by ensuring that each river basin district makes available or publishes information for public comment and consultation on significant water management issues (Art. 14). The eleven annexes of the Directive list detailed technical data corresponding to the different types of aquatic environment. Annex VI lists the categories measures to be taken, including legislative, administrative and economic instruments. Annex VII provides the elements which river basin management plans shall cover, while Annex VIII contains an indicative list of the main pollutants. Annex XI maps 25 European 'eco-regions for rivers and lakes', significantly including the territory of states which are not members of the European Union.

The Directive set up for the water quality to be rated as high, good, fair, poor or bad based on a range of ecological, chemical and hydrological criteria. By 2015 all surface waters should have been classified as 'good'.[52] However, states could extend the deadline for meeting environmental objectives for up to twelve years if there were valid technical problems, cost implications or natural constraints, as long as the water quality did not deteriorate in the meantime.[53] Other loopholes contained in the Directive were that less stringent environmental objectives could be set for artificial and heavily modified water bodies, and objectives also could be set aside to benefit human health or sustainable development if the benefits outweigh the loss of the environmental objectives. The challenge was to integrate ecological indicators with traditional water quality and quantity objectives. The Directive says that ecological status would be assessed through measuring biological, hydromorphological and chemical elements, including pollution levels. Special protection zones could to be established to protect special habitats, conserve drinking water or

---

51 Bund für Umwelt und Naturschutz Deutschland e.V. v. Federal Republic of Germany, July 1, 2015, C-461/13, para. 71.

52 Art. 4(1)(a)(ii) Water Framework Directive.

53 ibid, Art. 4(4).

protect bathing water. States were required to prevent or limit groundwater contamination, monitor groundwater, and impose measures to reverse significant pollution caused by human activity.

In 2018, the classification 'good' regarding the chemical status had been granted to 74 percent of the groundwater, and 89 percent received the classification 'good' regarding the quantitative status. Concerning surface waters, 40 percent were in good ecological status or potential and 38 percent were in good chemical status.[54] Even though it is clear that the goals of the Directive have not been reached yet, the Directive has given rise to many national measures to reach the 'good' status.[55]

In North America, Mexico and the United States have had a contentious relationship concerning freshwater resources in the border region. The two-thousand-mile border between the United States and Mexico extends from the Pacific Ocean across the Sonora Desert to the Gulf of Mexico. The border region includes many freshwater bodies, which fall under the jurisdiction of six Mexican and four US states, although they constitute a single geographic region of shared air and water resources, both surface and groundwater. Unlike the land around many other rivers, virtually the entire area is desert, with attendant shortage and poor quality of both underground and surface waters. Population growth, unplanned urbanization and rapid industrialization, including the enormous increase in 'maquiladora',[56] have added to the pressures on transboundary water resources.[57] As a result, both countries are turning to groundwaters to satisfy their needs. However, these exhaustible resources can become depleted irreversibly if pumping exceeds the natural rate of renewal.

Historically, due to water scarcity in the arid borderlands, competition between Mexico and the United States focused on the use of the Colorado and Rio Grande River systems for agricultural irrigation. While both the US and

54 European Environment Agency, *European waters: Assessment of status and pressures 2018* (EEA Report No. 7/2018) 6.

55 2021 Report from the Commission to the Council and the European Parliament on the implementation of the Water Framework Directive (2000/60/EC), the Environmental Quality Standards Directive (2008/105/EC amended by Directive 2013/39/EU) and the Floods Directive (2007/60/EC) 3.

56 Maquiladora are Mexican-based border industries, largely U.S. and other foreign-owned, which take advantage of significant savings in labor, services and other operational costs, while remaining close to the United States. See Roberto A. Sanchez, 'Health and Environmental Risks of the Maquiladora in Mexicali' (1990) 30 NATRESJ 63.

57 See, Stephen P. Mumme, *Managing Acute Water Scarcity on the U.S. Mexico Border: Institutional Issues Raised by the 1990's Drought,* 1998 Transboundary Resources Report 6.

Mexico have strong domestic environmental legislation, enforcement along the border has been weak. International cooperation to protect the environment of US-Mexican boundary waters has been slow in coming. Early on, two treaties resolved some of the allocation disputes between Mexico and the United States: the 1906 Rio Grande Irrigation Convention[58] and the 1944 Treaty Relating to the Utilization of Waters of the Colorado and Tijuana Rivers and of the Rio Grande.[59] However, many issues of water quality remained unsettled by the treaties. The Water Utilization Treaty failed to include any guarantees of water quality, although Article 3 provided that both nations 'hereby agree to give preferential attention to the solution of all border sanitation problems'. The Treaty also provided a list of priority uses for the waters, with highest priority given to domestic and municipal uses, followed by agriculture and stock-raising, then electric power, other industrial uses, navigation, fishing and hunting. However, the 1944 Treaty also established an International Boundary and Water Commission (IBWC), replacing an earlier International Boundary Commission. The IBWC, although an international agency, has specific authority to address boundary water pollution problems. The Treaty authorizes the Commission to plan, build, and manage water works; to enter into further agreements relating to international waters; and to settle disputes between the two countries involving interpretation of the Treaty. The Commission also has authority to initiate investigations and to make decisions involving utilization of the international waters. The decisions, known as Minutes, are binding on the two nations unless one of the governments objects within thirty days.[60] The jurisdiction of the IBWC is, however, limited to surface waters at the boundary.

Given the date of the 1944 Treaty, it is not surprising that it contains no substantive obligations or principles for water quality protection or regulation of border pollution problems. Perhaps because of this and because there was little pressure from the respective governments, the IWBC initially did not pay much attention to environmental protection. Later, several Minutes and agreements expanded protection and focused attention on environmental issues.

Minute 242 was adopted in 1973 as a 'Permanent and Definitive Solution to the International Problem of the Salinity of the Colorado River'.[61] Beginning in the 1960s, Mexico protested that United States water deliveries included highly

58 May 21, 1906.

59 February 3, 1944, 3 UNTS, 59 Stat. 1219, TS No. 994.

60 In the United States, the Minute has the legal status of an executive agreement. See Stephen P. Mumme, 'The US-Mexican Conflict over Transboundary Groundwaters: Some Institutional and Political Considerations' (1980) 12(3) Case W. Res. J. Int'l L. 505.

61 IBWC Minute No. 242, August 30, 1973, Mexico-United States, 24 UST 1971, TIAS No. 7708.

saline drainage waters which caused severe damage to Mexico's agriculture. For its part, Mexico began extracting large quantities of groundwater from the border near Yuma, Arizona. In Minute 242, the United States recognized an obligation to deliver good quality water to Mexico. In return, Mexico agreed to control its groundwater mining near Yuma. However, the agreement applies only to one aspect of water quality, salinity, and only to one water source, the Colorado. No comprehensive agreement on boundary groundwater or salinity exists.

The role of the IBWC was expanded in 1979 by Minute 261 which gave the IBWC authority to solve any water quality problems 'that present a hazard to the health and well-being of the inhabitants of either side of the border or impair the beneficial uses of the waters. Emphasis was placed on the need for preventive measures. With Minute 261, the IBWC obtained the authority to determine when a water pollution problem exists.

The first major use of the IBWC expanded powers came with Minute 264 which adopted specific water quality objectives and standards for the New River.[62] The goal of Minute 264 was the complete elimination of all domestic and industrial waste waters in the New River at the boundary through action by Mexico. Mexico also agreed to improve the Mexicali sewage treatment system to achieve specific water quality standards within established time limits. The water quality standards adopted are based upon US standards and act to harmonize the laws of the two countries. IBWC is responsible for monitoring Mexico's implementation of Minute 264.

In 1983, the United States and Mexico adopted a new framework agreement to cooperate on border environmental issues.[63] The two states agreed to strengthen and expand both individual and cooperative efforts to address pollution at the border, implicitly recognizing the ecological unity of the region. In Article 2, for the first time, both countries acknowledged their obligations to prevent transboundary pollution, as they agreed to adopt appropriate measures to prevent, reduce and eliminate sources of pollution that affect the border area of the other and agreed to cooperate to solve environmental problems of mutual concern. The Agreement also requires each party to monitor polluting activities, to consult on the measurement and analysis of pollution sources,

62 IBWC, Minute 264, Recommendations for Solution of the New River Border Sanitation Problem at Calexico, California - Mexicali, Baja California Norte (Ciudad Juarez, Chihuahua, August 26, 1980).

63 Agreement between the United States of America and the United Mexican States on Cooperation for the Protection and Improvement of the Environment in the Border Area (August 14, 1983, in force February 16, 1984), TIAS 10827, 23 ILM 1025 (1983).

and to share all information obtained from monitoring. Article 7 requires assessment of projects that may have significant impacts on the environment of the border area. Perhaps most importantly, Article 3 requires the drafting of implementing annexes to address specific issues.

The parties have adopted four annexes to the 1983 agreement, two of which directly concern boundary waters.[64] Annex I, adopted July 18, 1985, concerns solving sanitation problems in the Tijuana-San Diego border region. Annex II, adopted the same day, addresses pollution of the environment due to the discharge of hazardous substances. Annex II also establishes a Joint Contingency Plan regarding polluting incidents (a discharge or threat of discharge of any hazardous substance on one side of the boundary which causes or threatens to cause imminent and substantial adverse effects on the public health, welfare, or the environment) caused by hazardous substances. In Article III, the parties agree to develop response plans to detect sewage spills.

The Annex also concerns cooperation to expand and improve drinking water and the sewage system of Tijuana and calls on the states to determine the measures necessary to preserve environmental conditions and ecological processes. The Annex specifically anticipates US assistance to Mexico in case of a breakdown or interruption in service and calls for a consideration of the existence or threat of polluting incidents and adoption of measures to eliminate the threat posed by such incidents and to minimize any adverse effects on the environment and the public health and welfare. The parties agree to consult and exchange information and to implement agreed upon joint responses to a polluting incident. Appendices establish the joint contingency plan and the joint response team that has the responsibility for determining the hazardous substances covered by the Annex. As with similar agreements, appendices may be added or amended through flexible procedures. Minute 311 (2004) adds to this arrangement other measures to address secondary treatment of sewage in the Tijuana River area.

In the 1990s, a drought caused severe impacts in northern Mexico. Ranching and agricultural drought-based losses were estimated at upwards of US$ 1.1 billion. Acknowledging the evidence of serious Mexican conservation and mitigation efforts in the face of the persistent drought, the US consented to loan water, up to the amount of 81,000 acre-feet over a period of 18 months, beginning in November 1995. IBWC Minute 293 expresses this arrangement. According to an author, 'this agreement may be taken as *de facto* recognition by both parties, but particularly by the US, of the need, indeed the obligation,

64 All four annexes are reprinted in 26 ILM 18, 19, 25 and 33 (1987).

to assist its treaty partner in times of acute water scarcity'[65] Minute 317 (2010) created a more long-term framework for discussions of cooperative actions concerning the Colorado River. These and other recent agreements and activities reflect growing concern with environmental protection of US-Mexican boundary waters, indeed with the entire boundary region.

Meanwhile, across the Atlantic, an Interim Agreement was concluded on September 28, 1995 between Israel and the Palestine Liberation Organization, which mainly focused on the sharing of water resources in the West Bank and Gaza Strip. Article 40 of Annex III speaks abstractly of preventing the deterioration of water quality, of using the water resources in a manner that will ensure sustainable use in the future, of preventing any harm to water resources as well as to water and sewage systems, and of treating, reusing or properly disposing of all domestic, urban, industrial, and agricultural sewage.[66] For the same region the Declaration on Cooperation on Water-related Matters, adopted February 13, 1996, by Israel, Jordan, and the Palestine Liberation Organization is more explicit by stating that new and additional water resource projects will be based on environmentally-sound principles. Each party is responsible for protecting water against environmental pollution originating within its jurisdiction as well as for the preservation of water quality. The Declaration also proposes cooperation in sustainable water-related natural resources management and desertification control as well as the development of norms, standards and specifications for water devices.[67]

A Protocol on Shared Watercourse Systems was adopted on August 28, 1995 in the framework of the Southern African Development Community,[68] and revised by a new agreement adopted on August 7, 2000. The Revised Protocol is largely based on the principles of the 1997 UN Convention. Its objective is to foster closer co-operation for judicious, sustainable and coordinated management, protection and utilization of shared watercourses. The State Parties recognize the unity and coherence of each shared watercourse and undertake to respect the existing rules of customary or general international law relating to the utilization and management of shared watercourses. They agree to exchange available information and data regarding the hydrological, water quality and environmental condition of shared watercourses and utilize

---

65 Mumme, *supra* n 57 at 7.

66 36 ILM 551 (1997) at 624.

67 36 ILM 761 (1997), at 768 and 769. See also: Stephen McCaffrey, 'Middle East Water Problems, the Jordan River' in *The Scarcity of Water*, *supra* n 3 at 158.

68 The Community was created on August 17, 1992 by the Treaty of Windhoek adopted by ten states of Southern Africa.

a shared watercourse in an equitable and reasonable manner, with a view to attaining optimal and sustainable utilization for the benefit of current and future generations (Art. 3).

The Protocol follows the definitions and rules of the UN Convention on various points, such as the definition of equitable and reasonable utilization, the procedure to be followed for planned measures, for environmental protection and preservation and for the management of shared watercourses. The term 'environmental use' is defined as the use of water for the preservation and maintenance of ecosystems, while 'significant harm' is characterized as 'non-trivial harm capable of being established by objective evidence without necessarily rising to the level of being substantial' (Art. 1). Using the existing framework of the Southern African Development Community, the Protocol establishes different Water Sector Organs such as a Committee of Water Ministers, and a Committee of Water Senior Officials which have the task to oversee and monitor the implementation of the Protocol and advise State Parties on matters pertaining to the Protocol (Art. 5).

2 From Transboundary Pollution Control to Shared Resource Management

Concern for water pollution in an international context has been expressed since the beginning of the industrial era, with legal instruments addressing the topic concluded as early as 1868.[69] Two categories of relevant international instruments may be distinguished. First, until the 1960s, most anti-pollution provisions were included in conventions of more general purpose, for example, those regulating boundary matters between neighboring states. Since that time, a growing number of sub-regional or regional treaties have been concluded to combat the pollution of international watercourses or lakes. More recently, holistic agreements address all the environmental problems of managing fresh waters. The examples discussed below may therefore be distinguished from the legal frameworks discussed in Section A(1)(b) above, which are not limited to a specific watercourse or freshwater body.

69 An agreement between France and Spain on the international frontier of the Pyrenees provided in section 1(6) that 'The discharge of foul or harmful water into the bed of the said river by riparian or other proprietors shall also be prohibited'. UN Doc. A/CN.4/4122 add 1, 9.

2.1 *Europe*

Although the Rhine river is not among the longest or widest rivers of the world, it has exceptional economic, political, and cultural importance as the principal international watercourse of western Europe. It constitutes the direct and essential source of water for a region of close to fifty million inhabitants in one of the most industrialized areas of the world.[70] As such, the Rhine serves many purposes, from drinking and industrial water supply, navigation and the production of electricity, to a dumping ground for many kinds of waste.

The legal status of the Rhine is regulated by a complex network or juxtaposition of norms and institutions. Two international bodies, in particular, are concerned with the use of its waters. First, the Central Commission for Navigation of the Rhine, created in 1868 in order to ensure free navigation, has become concerned with Rhine pollution and has taken preventive measures concerning pollution of the waters by hydrocarbons.[71] It also has prohibited or regulated the transportation of certain hazardous products. Although limited in scope, these measures are successful because the regulations of the Central Commission are binding. In addition, the Central Commission adopted, on September 9, 1996, a Convention on the collection and disposal of wastes in the navigation of the Rhine.

The International Commission for the Protection of the Rhine against Pollution is the primary organ of international action to protect the river. Created by an agreement signed in Bern on April 29, 1963, its member states are France, Luxembourg, the Netherlands, the Federal Republic of Germany, and Switzerland. Luxembourg, a non-riparian state, is also a member of the Commission due to the presence in its territory of the Mosel, which flows into the Rhine. In 1976, the Commission of the European Community joined the Rhine Commission. A Convention on the Protection of the Rhine (Bern, April 12, 1999) reorganized the Commission, which became an international institution invested with legal personality. Concerned non-governmental organizations can be recognized as observers at the Commission and, as such, they can express opinions in discussions, submit information or reports, attend meetings of the Commission and be consulted (Art. 14).

The Commission prepares international programs for monitoring the ecosystem of the Rhine, makes proposals for individual actions, coordinates alarm plans and systems of the river states, and assesses the effectiveness of the measures adopted, largely on the basis of reports which the parties submit to it (Art. 8). The Commission adopts decisions by unanimous vote, addressed

70 See the TWAP River Basins map – Rhine basin at <http://twap-rivers.org/indicators/>.

71 Art. 1.15, Reglement de police pour la navigation du Rhin.

to member states in the form of recommendations for specific action and for broader programs (Art. 10). Recommendations can include implementation deadlines and provide for coordinated compliance procedures (Art. 11(1) and (2)).

A compliance control system is foreseen: the Commission can decide that the parties shall submit regular reports on the legislative, regulatory or other measures that they have taken in order to comply with the provisions of the Convention and the decisions adopted, on the problems they raise and on the results of such measures. If a contracting party cannot implement a Commission decision, it can report this fact within a prescribed period of time, explaining the cause of the non-compliance. Any other party can ask for consultation, which then shall be held within two months. If no state requests consultations, the Commission can decide on measures to be taken on the basis of the reports of the contracting parties or whether to organize consultations in order to enhance the implementation of the decisions (Art. 11(3)-(5)).

The 1999 Rhine Convention is based on a holistic vision with a view towards the sustainable development of the Rhine ecosystem, considering the river itself, its banks and its alluvial zones. It also takes into account the April 9, 1992 Helsinki Convention on the Protection and Use of Transboundary Watercourses and Lakes as well as the Convention on the Protection of the Marine Environment of the North-East Atlantic (Paris, September 22, 1992). As a consequence, the new Convention has an extensive scope, in contrast with that foreseen by the prior regime. While the Rhine itself is defined as including the river with its exit from Lake Constance, and its side arms system in the Netherlands, the Convention is to be applied not only to the Rhine, but also to the underground waters which are in connection with it, the aquatic and terrestrial ecosystems which are or which could be connected to it, and the catchment area as far as the pollution originating from it affects the Rhine or plays an important role in the prevention and protection of floods along the Rhine (Art. 2).

Between 1976 and 1999, the main legal instrument for controlling Rhine pollution was the Convention for the Protection of the Rhine against Chemical Pollution (Bonn, December 3, 1976), an instrument directly inspired by EEC directive 76/464 concerning pollution caused by certain dangerous substances discharged into the aquatic environment of the Communities. It thus provided for emission standards of listed substances, including substances which should not be discharged into the water and substances which could only be discharged upon prior authorization. The 1976 Convention, which entered into force on February 1, 1979, represented a step forward in dealing with freshwater pollution when compared to former regulations. While previous instruments most often failed to include the relevant hydrographic basin, several provisions of this Convention have a larger territorial applicability. The concept of a hydrographic basin, the modern framework for water management, is found in the treaty and confirmed by the presence of Luxembourg in the International Commission. The 1999 Rhine Convention, discussed above, explicitly adopts and systematizes this concept.

The years following adoption of the Bonn Convention saw an improvement of water quality in the Rhine, until a 1986 accident in the Swiss company Sandoz located near Basel, demonstrated that accident prevention needed improvement. As a result of a fire in the Sandoz factory, chemicals entered the Rhine, causing serious damage to living organisms and endangering the water supply along the river in France and in Germany. In less than a year, the question of damages was settled by negotiations between the company and the victims. The company agreed to fund the establishment of a measuring station on the Rhine, a station to alert populations and inform border towns, and contribute to the restoration of the Rhine ecosystem. At the interstate level, Rhine riparians decided to improve the emergency alert system, to address the problem of compensating victims by providing for strict liability, and to elaborate a program of action in three stages, aimed at improving the water quality of the Rhine to allow the reintroduction of species formerly present, such as salmon, and the utilization of the waters for drinking purposes.

The 1999 Rhine Convention further develops these concerns. Its objectives are the preservation and improvement of Rhine water quality, including underground water, protection against suspended substances and sediments, protection of living organisms and of species diversity, and the preservation and restoration of the natural functions of the river system, including its function as the habitat of fish. The Convention prescribes water resource management that respects the environment and takes into account ecological requirements when planning technical measures for flood protection, for navigation, and for the production of electricity. The Convention also aims at the production of drinking water and improvement in the quality of sediments as well as to contribute to controlling the pollution of the North Sea (Art. 3).

Article 4 of the Convention lists as guidelines all the principles and norms which have emerged in international environmental law: the precautionary principle, prevention, control of polluting emissions at the source, polluter pays, nuisance abatement and compensation for unavoidable nuisances, sustainable development, use of best available technologies and best environmental practices, and non-transfer of pollution from one sector to others. The contacting parties are obliged to execute Commission decisions on programs of study and measurement and to transmit the results to the Commission, to endeavor to identify the causes of, and the responsibility for pollution of the water, to establish a system of permits for waste water, to progressively reduce the emission of hazardous substances, to monitor general regulations and permits, to reduce the risks of accidental pollution and immediately to inform other states of emergencies (Art. 5).

On the same day the treaty was concluded, the contracting parties adopted guidelines for a program of sustainable development of the Rhine. The program provides for ensuring a high level of protection, for an integrated approach to the protection of the Rhine, for the use of modern tools in the management of the river and for the systematic dissemination of information and knowledge of environmental problems and solutions.

Other European conventions create similar mechanisms for controlling the pollution of international watercourses. The political changes which started in the late 1980s in Central and Eastern Europe, where cooperation generally had been achieved through bilateral treaties between neighboring river states, made possible new, multilateral forms of co-operation. On October 8, 1990, Germany, Czechoslovakia and the European Community established an International Commission for the Protection of the Elbe. The aims of the agreement were to enable the river to be used, in particular for obtaining supplies of drinking water from bank-filtered waters and for agricultural purposes; to achieve as natural an ecosystem as possible with a diversity of species; and to reduce substantially the pollution of the North Sea from the Elbe area (Art. 1(2)). The Commission's mandate is to prepare surveys of pollution, to propose limit values for the discharge of effluents, and to propose specific quality objectives (Art. 2(1)).

The adoption of the Convention on Cooperation for the Protection and Sustainable Use of the Danube River (Sofia, June 29, 1994) by eleven Central and Eastern European countries and the European Community marked a particularly important step in the development of regional approaches to environmental protection of inland waters. The treaty is modeled after the 1992 Helsinki Convention on the Protection and Use of Transboundary Watercourses and International Lakes, applying it in a concrete project of cooperation. It is the most advanced treaty on environmental protection of inland waters, because of its integrated approach.

The objective of the Danube Convention is sustainable and equitable water management, including the conservation, improvement and the rational use of surface and ground waters in the catchment area, as far as possible. One of the innovative features of the Convention is the breadth of its territorial scope, which is the catchment area of the Danube, defined as the hydrological river basin. The target countries, called Danubian States, are defined as sovereign states having a share exceeding 2,000 km^2 of the total hydrological catchment area (Art. 1(a) and (b)). The impact and the significance of the Convention are enhanced by Article 2(1), which provides that the parties shall endeavor to contribute to reducing the pollution loads of the Black Sea from sources in the catchment area, thus addressing land-based marine pollution in the region. Finally, the Convention mandates specific preventive water resources measures, primarily concerning groundwater pollution caused by nitrates, plant protection agents, and pesticides, in particular, and measures to reduce the risks of accidents (Art. 6).

France, the Netherlands and the three Belgian regions (Wallonia, Flanders, and Brussels-Capital regions) adopted two parallel agreements of more limited territorial scope for the Meuse and the Scheldt.[72] The agreements are much shorter and less developed than the Danube Convention, although all are based on the 1992 Helsinki Convention on the Protection of Transboundary Watercourses and International Lakes.[73] They make a distinction between the river basin, including all the waterways and canals which directly or indirectly run into the main river, where situated on the territory of the contracting parties, and the drainage area, the waters of which run into the Meuse (Scheldt) or its tributaries (Art. 1). The second definition appears wider than the first in the sense that the 'river basin' is defined as a hydrological network, while the 'drainage area' refers not to the water itself, but the territorial area on which this water flows.[74] Cooperation between parties must be guided by the polluter pays and the precautionary principles, as well as by the principles of preventive action, containment, and pollution reduction. The contracting states shall act in a comparable way throughout the drainage area in order to avoid distortions of competition and shall take appropriate measures to achieve an integrated management of the drainage area (Art. 3). Article 4 provide for mutual information on and coordination of policies regarding the management of sediments and for limiting dumping and discharges of dredged material and its movement downstream. Such provisions were necessary for the areas covered by the two agreements, which are heavily industrialized and receive large amounts of polluting substances, in particular, heavy metals, from sediments carried by the rivers.

Both agreements have strong institutions, international commissions composed of the delegations of the parties (Arts. 2(2), 5 and 6). They have the usually-conferred tasks of collecting and evaluating data provided by the parties,

---

72 Charleville Mézières, France, April 26, 1994, reprinted in 34 ILM 851 (1995).

73 See Nicolette Bouman, 'A New Regime for the Meuse' (1996) 5(2) RECIEL 161.

74 Axel Gosseries, 'The 1994 Agreements Concerning the Protection of the Scheldt and Meuse Rivers' (1995) 4(1) EELR 9.

drawing up inventories and programs of action, and promoting the exchange of information. In addition, they also may issue advisory opinions and recommendations regarding cooperation under the agreements (Art. 5). They also draw up annual reports of their activities, made available to the public, and any other type of report deemed necessary.

Finally, the Czech Republic, the EU European Commission, Germany and Poland created an International Commission for the Protection of the Oder[75] by a Convention concluded April 11, 1996. Its aim is broad, to prevent pollution not only of the Oder River, but also of the Baltic Sea. The Commission, which consists of the delegates of the contracting parties, draws up joint action programs with timetables for their implementation, propose limit values and water quality objectives, and prepare surveys of point sources of pollution.

2.2 *North America*

In North America two treaty regimes have been established, one for boundary waters shared by the United States and Canada and one for the United States-Mexico boundary waters. This subsection only focuses on the Great Lakes, and thus only on the United States-Canada border, as the United States-Mexico border has been discussed in depth above in section A.1.b. The Treaty relating to Boundary Waters and Questions Arising between the United States and Canada,[76] signed by the United Kingdom and the US in Washington on January 11, 1909, contained in Article IV(2) the obligation not to pollute waters forming or crossing the US-Canadian boundary. This provision had little effect, however, and the Great Lakes – which contain ten percent of the world's available fresh water – became extremely polluted, despite the investigations and recommendations of the International Joint Commission created by the treaty. In the 1960s renewed efforts were made to implement the obligation contained in Article IV(2). The Great Lakes Water Quality Agreements of 1972 and 1978[77] reaffirmed and elaborated the provisions of the Great Lakes system.

Particularly detailed regulations are found in the November 22, 1978 Agreement between the United States and Canada on Great Lakes Water Quality. The purpose of the agreement is 'to restore and maintain the chemical, physical, and biological integrity of the waters of the Great Lakes Basin Ecosystem' (Art. II). The parties agree to control pollutants and to comply with both general and specific objectives set forth in the treaty. General objectives are defined as broad descriptions of water quality conditions consistent with the

75 Wroclaw, April 11, 1996, EMuT, 996:28.

76 AJIL.(1910) Suppl. 239.

77 Johan G. Lammers, *Pollution of International Watercourses* (Brill 1984).

protection of the beneficial uses and the level of environmental quality sought by the parties and which will provide overall water management guidance. Specific objectives are the precise concentration or quantity of a substance or level of effect that is allowable. Annex I to the agreement contains the specific objectives and lists chemical, physical, microbiological and radiological pollutants. While the specific objectives establish minimum water quality standards, Article IV of the agreement provides that if higher water quality exists, such quality must be maintained and improved.[78] In 2012, the 1978 Agreement was last renewed. In addition to adding several new regulations, the value of this new version lies in the fact that it named climate change at various points as having great impact on, and being a threat to the Great Lakes.[79]

Concern for the Great Lakes system has also developed on issues of water quantity. Trade in water is becoming economically viable in water-rich countries and could pose problems for the future if water, which is often considered a public good, is subject to private appropriation for export. In 1998 a Canadian company proposed to export 158 million gallons from Lake Superior to Asia, raising concerns about potential water loss in the Great Lakes. In 2001 US state governors and Canadian provincial premiers in areas surrounding the Great Lakes agreed to negotiate a binding instrument setting forth standards for reviewing proposals to withdraw water from the region. Such standards are to be based upon the principles of (1) preventing or minimizing water loss to the Great Lakes basin through return flow and implementation of environmentally sound and economically feasible water conservation measures; (2) no significant adverse individual or cumulative impacts to the quantity or quality of the waters and water-dependent natural resources of the Great Lakes; (3) an improvement to the waters and water-dependent natural resources of the basin and (4) compliance with applicable state, provincial, federal and international laws and treaties.[80] In 2005, the Great Lakes – St. Lawrence River Basin Sustainable Water Resources Agreement and The Great Lakes – St. Lawrence

78 The 1972 and 1978 Agreements were strengthened by a 1985 protocol. On the new trend to initiate an ecosystem approach to the management of the international river basins shared by the two countries across the entire boundary, see L. B. Dworsky, *News Notes from the International Joint Commission Canada-United States*, 1988 TRANSBOUNDARY RESOURCES REPORT 2.

79 The Great Lakes Water Quality Protocol of 2012 – Protocol Amending the Agreement Between Canada and the United States of America on Great Lakes Water Quality, 1978, As Amended on October 16, 1983 and on November 18, 1987 (ISBN: 978-1-100-21204-3) (Catalog No.: En14-73/2012E-PDF).

80 Great Lakes Charter Annex: A Supplementary Agreement to the Great Lakes Charter, Directive No. 3 (June 18, 2001).

River Basin Water Resources Compact were signed, continuing to litigate the issue of water quantity in the region and putting emphasis on transboundary cooperation in these matters.[81]

2.3 *South America*

The Amazon is the largest river in South America, its output of freshwater being approximately 210,000m2 per second.[82] It is therefore of major importance for there to be cooperation on preservation of the river basin. In 1978, its eight riparian states created the Amazon Cooperation Treaty, to begin working in 1980.[83] The goal of this treaty was not solely environmental protection, but also to balance out environmental protection and economic progress equally for all riparian states.[84] Under its core principles are conservation of the environment, equality amongst member states, cooperation between member states and sovereignty.[85] The agreement does not contain any definitive numbers or concrete goals, but its value lay in providing the basis for international cooperation between the riparian States. It was fifteen years later, in 1995, that a Permanent Secretariat was created which had legal authority, and not long after, in 1998, the member states created the Amazonian Cooperation Treaty Organization (ACTO).[86] This organization still works under the core principles named in the preamble of the ACT, and it deals with any questions that may arise under it.

However, the ACTO is not a story of unlimited success in harmonious cooperation. Policy-making has been difficult in the past for many reasons, and the body has had many issues including financial difficulties. It almost came to a standstill in 2007 when trying to select a new Secretary-General.[87] Luckily,

81 For an in-depth discussion of these two agreements, see Bradley C. Karkkainen, 'The Great Lakes Water Resources Compact and Agreement: Transboundary Normativity Without International Law' (2013) 39(3) William Mitchell Law Review 997.

82 OAS: Office for Sustainable Development & Environment, *Amazon River Basin: Integrated and Sustainable Management of Transboundary Water Resources in the Amazon River Basin* (2005) 1.

83 Treaty for Amazonian Co-operation (adopted July 3, 1978, entry into force October 30, 1980) 1202 UNTS 51 (Amazon Cooperation Treaty, ACT); The riparian States are Bolivia, Brazil, Colombia, Ecuador, Guyana, Peru, Suriname and Venezuela.

84 ACT, Art. 1.

85 ACT, Preamble.

86 Protocol of Amendment of the Amazon Cooperation Treaty (adopted December 14, 1998, entry into force August 2, 2002) 2199 UNTS 163.

87 See for some of these issues the English translation of the Minutes of the meeting of July 2, 2007: Extraordinary Session of the Amazon Cooperation Council (Brasília July 2, 2007) DOC/III.-EXTRAORDINARY SESSION-ACC-ACTO-06.

since then, things have improved. In 2009, ACTO issued a declaration to '[e] ndow ACTO with a new and modern role as a cooperation, exchange, knowledge and joint visibility forum to face the new and complex international challenges that lie ahead', assuring that ACTO would be renewed to perform its duties.[88] Indeed, it launched a Strategic Agenda, in which it made clear that sustainable development was a priority.[89] It currently has multiple ongoing projects, of which one is the revising of its Amazonian Strategic Cooperation Agenda (ASCA).[90] It seems that the renewal of ACTO after its internal struggles, though ACTO is limited in its effectiveness, has only proven to benefit the granted importance to cooperation for sustainability in the Amazon.[91]

Furthermore, Argentina and Uruguay adopted a Statute of the Uruguay River in 1975 in order to coordinate, through a commission established by the treaty, 'appropriate measures to prevent the alteration of the ecological balance, and to control impurities and other harmful elements in the river and its catchment area'.[92] The parties also agreed to conserve and preserve living resources of the river and to 'protect and preserve the aquatic environment'.[93] In subsection C.2 below, a conflict that arose between these two states about the river will be discussed. Two decades later, in 1995, Argentina, Bolivia and Paraguay established a Tripartite Commission for the Development of the basin of the Rio Pilcomayo. This body is to monitor water quality and to propose emission standards for specific polluting substances. It also has the task of coordinating necessary national measures in order to avoid deterioration of the biological balance and the propagation of diseases.[94]

---

88 Declaration of Heads Of State on the Amazon Cooperation Treaty Organization (Manaus, November 26, 2009) para. 1.

89 ACTO, *Amazonian Strategic Cooperation Agenda* (Approved at the X Meeting of the TCA's Ministers of Foreign Affairs, November 2010).

90 For more on the current undertakings of the ACTO, see their website: <https://otca.org/en/>.

91 For a more elaborate explanation of the (failings of the) ACTO, see (1) Maria Antonia Tigre, *Regional Cooperation in Amazonia: A Comparative Environmental Law Amalysis* (Brill 2017) (2) Joana Pereira and Eduardo Viola, 'Close to a Tipping Point? The Amazon and the Challenge of Sustainable Development under Growing Climate Pressures' (2020) 52(3) Journal of Latin American Studies 467 (3) Viviane Passos Gomes and Francisco Delgado Piqueras, 'The Role of the Amazon Cooperation Treaty for Shared Water Management' (2016) 53 Actualidad Jurídica Ambiental 1.

92 Statute of the Uruguay River, Uruguay, Ministerio de Relaciones Exteriores, *Actos Internacionales Uruguay-Argentina, 1830–1980* (1981) 593, Article 36.

93 Arts. 37, 41.

94 Agreement of La Paz, February 9, 1995, I.E.L. 995:12.

2.4 *Africa*

The Niger Basin Agreement of October 26, 1963, provides that the riparian states will cooperate regarding the study and execution of any project likely to have an appreciable effect on certain features of the regime of the river, its tributaries and sub-tributaries, the sanitary conditions of their waters, and the biological characteristics of their fauna and flora.[95] In 2008, the Niger River Water Charter was drafted, with the purpose 'to encourage cooperation based on solidarity and reciprocity for a sustainable, equitable and coordinated use of the Niger Basin hydrographic catchment area'.[96] As well as including provisions on, for example, the polluter-pays principle and the precautionary principle, it includes an in-depth Article on preservation and protection of the environment.[97]

The 1978 Gambia River Agreement[98] provides in Article 4 that '[n]o project which is likely to bring about serious modifications of the characteristics of the river's regime, ... the sanitary state of the waters, the biological characteristics of its fauna and its flora... will be implemented without prior approval of the contracting states'. The Agreement on the Preparation of a Tripartite Environmental Management Program for Lake Victoria, adopted August 5, 1994, by Kenya, Tanzania and Uganda, provides for the establishment of a Regional Policy and Steering Committee, to be assisted by a Regional Secretariat, and two regional Task Forces. The Management Program includes fisheries management and control of water hyacinth and other invasive weeds, as well as the management of water quality and land use, including wetlands.[99] In 2003, Kenya, Uganda and Tanzania agreed on a Protocol for Sustainable Development of Lake Victoria Basin as well, recognizing that water is a delicate resource 'essential to sustain life, development and the environment and must be integrated in a holistic manner, linking social and economic development with protection and conservation of natural ecosystems'.[100]

---

95 Article 4, Act Regarding Navigation and Economic Cooperation between the States of the Niger Basin, October 26, 1963, 567 U.N.T.S. 9. The states parties are Burkina Faso, Cameroon, Chad, Dahomey, Guinea, Ivory Coast, Mali, Niger, and Nigeria. One month later the states established the Niger River Commission, November 25, 1964.

96 Niger Basin Water Charter (signed in Niamey, April 30, 2008) (Water Charter) Art. 2.

97 ibid, art. 12.

98 Convention relating to the Status of the River Gambia (Gambia, Guinea, Senegal, June 30, 1978), reproduced in Natural Resources/Water Series No. 134, ST/ESA/141 (1984), 39.

99 See also: Charles O. Okidi, 'International Law and Water Scarcity in Africa' in *The Scarcity of Water, supra* n 3 at 166.

100 Protocol for Sustainable Development of Lake Victoria Basin (adopted in Arusha, November 29, 2003).

In Southern Africa, the Zambezi Watercourse Commission (ZAMCOM), regarding the Zambezi River, was established through an agreement in 2004 which entered into force in 2011.[101] Currently, the agreement involves Angola, Botswana, Malawi, Mozambique, Namibia, Tanzania, Zambia and Zimbabwe.[102] Its objective is to 'promote the equitable utilization of the water resources of the Zambezi watercourse as well as the efficient management and sustainable development thereof'.[103] The agreement puts great emphasis on sustainable development and the preventing of pollution of the Zambezi River. More recently, in 2014, Angola and Namibia created CUVECOM, a Commission for the management of the Cuvelai River Basin on their territories in a sustainable manner.[104]

2.5 *Asia*

Several Asian treaties concerning international rivers and lakes focus on the utilization of waters rather than their conservation. The principal objective of the 1992 Treaty on Sharing of the Ganges Waters at Farakka between Bangladesh and India[105] and the February 12, 1996 Treaty Concerning the Integrated Development of the Mahakali River between India and Nepal is to determine the quantity of water to which the contracting parties are entitled. The first agreement aims to make 'optimum utilization' of the waters of the region, applying the principles of 'equity, fair play and no harm to either party' (Arts. I, IX and X), while the second makes only limited reference to similar principles (Art. 9(1)). With regard to another relationship between India and its neighbors concerning freshwater resources, the Indus Waters Kishenganga Arbitration is discussed in Section C.4 of this chapter.

One of the most significant Asian treaties on the protection of inland waters is the 1995 Agreement on Cooperation for the Sustainable Development of the Mekong River Basin, adopted by Cambodia, Laos, Thailand and Vietnam. It

101 Agreement on the Establishment of the Zambezi Watercourse Commission (adopted in Kasane July 13, 2004, entry into force June 19, 2011) (ZAMCOM Agreement).

102 ibid.

103 ibid, art. 5.

104 Agreement Between the Government of the Republic of Angola and the Government of the Republic of Namibia on the Establishment of Cuvelai Watercourse Commission (CUVECOM) (adopted in Windhoek, September 16, 2014) (CUVECOM Agreement).

105 December 12, 1992, reprinted in 36 I.L.M. 519 (1997). See Salman M.A. Salman, 'Sharing the Ganges Waters between India and Bangladesh: an Analysis of the 1996 Treaty' in Salman M.A. Salman and L. Boisson de Chazournes (eds.), *International Watercourses, Enhancing Cooperation and Managing Conflict. Proceedings of a World Bank Seminar* (World Bank 1998).

adopts the river basin approach and thus has a comprehensive territorial aim, but it lacks participation by upstream state China. It defines 'environment' as 'the conditions of water and land resources, air, flora and fauna that [exist] in a particular region'[106] and it aims at 'protecting the environment from pollution or other harmful effects resulting from any development plans and uses of water and related resources in the basin'.[107] Every effort shall be made to avoid, minimize and mitigate harmful effects that might occur to the environment, especially the water quantity and quality, the aquatic eco-system conditions and the ecological balance of the river system. It also mentions the responsibility for damage caused by a state, without, however, going into details. A Mekong River Commission is given the mandate of ensuring the implementation of the Convention.[108] In 2015, the Lancang-Mekong Cooperation (LMC) was established at the initiative of China, between China and the other riparian states of the Mekong.[109] The agreement included the proposition of cooperating on issues of climate change and environmental problems, even going so far as to include 'economic and sustainable development' as one of the three pillars for cooperation and cooperation on water resources was one of the five 'key priority areas during the initial stage of the LMC', as was declared in the Sanya Declaration in 2016.[110] Since then, cooperation has continued, boding well for the future of cooperation on the Mekong, with all riparian states involved.

3 Case Studies

Where the above section focused on cooperation, this section illustrates the topic of fresh waters and international environmental law with several cases. Certain recent major judicial proceedings concerning specific lakes or rivers are highlighted. These recent case studies invariably build upon earlier judicial precedents such as the PCIJ's judgment in the River Oder Commission and the award of the Arbitral Tribunal in Lake Lanoux (France v. Spain).[111]

---

106 Chapter II 1995 Agreement on Cooperation for the Sustainable Development of the Mekong River Basin (April 5, 1995).

107 Art. 3 1995 Agreement.

108 Chiang Mai, Thailand, April 5, 1995, *reprinted in* 34 ILM 864 (1995).

109 Cambodia, Laos, Myanmar, Thailand and Vietnam.

110 Sanya Declaration of the First Lancang-Mekong Cooperation (LMC) Leader's Meeting, Xinhua, March 23, 2016, at <http://www.lmcchina.org/eng/2016-03/23/content_41449864.html> accessed November 18, 2023.

111 *Territorial jurisdiction of the International Commission of the River Oder* (October 28, 1928) PCIJ Rep Series A No. 23; *Lake Lanoux Case* (France v Spain) (November 19, 1957), 12

3.1 *The Danube*

The dispute over a project to construct a hydroelectric dam system on the Danube River illustrates the potential for conflicts between neighboring states raised by competing uses of water resources.[112] In 1920, the Treaty of Trianon made the Danube River part of the boundary between Hungary and the newly created state of Czechoslovakia. The 1947 Peace Treaty of Paris transferred to Czechoslovakia three Hungarian villages facing Bratislava, on the south, or Hungarian, bank of the river near the Austrian border. Since that time, the Danube has flowed through Slovak territory for 22.5 km. For the next 142 km, the Danube forms the boundary between Slovakia and Hungary until its junction with the Ipoly river, where the boundary turns north and separates from the river. The Danube flows east within Hungary before making a sudden bend to the south to pass through Budapest and the rest of Hungary.

At the end of the 1940s both Czechoslovakia and Hungary came under Soviet domination and communist regimes. Like other states in the region, they became members of the Warsaw Pact and the Council for Mutual Economic Co-operation (COMECON). The ruling communist parties maintained close relations under the surveillance of Moscow. Negotiations began in 1951 concerning the construction of a system of hydroelectric plants, inspired by the Soviet construction of huge canals, dams, industrial sites and similar projects. In 1958 the governments decided to proceed with the system and, five years later, government committees of the two countries agreed to draw up a joint investment program. The two sides signed a treaty on the construction and operation of the system on September 16, 1977.[113]

The Treaty envisaged a system of dams in order to serve four purposes: electricity production, navigation, flood protection, and regional development. It included provisions on the protection of the water quality (Art. 15), maintenance of navigation (Art. 18), the protection of nature (Art. 19) and protection of fishing interests (Art. 20). According to the preamble of the Treaty, however, another of its aims was to further strengthen the fraternal relations of the two states and significantly contribute to bringing about the socialist integration of the state's members of COMECON. Hungarian opinion later held that political

---

UNRIAA 281 (1957).

112 See Georg M. Berrisch, 'The Danube Dam Dispute under International Law' (1994) 46 Austrian J. Pub. Int'l L. 231; Maurizio Arcari, 'La controversia tra Slovacchia ed Ungheria circa la costruzione di un sistema di dighe sul Danubio' (1993) 8 Rivisto Giuridico Dell'ambiente 951.

113 Treaty concerning the construction and operation of the Gabčíkovo-Nagymaros system of locks (Signed at Budapest on September 16, 1977) 1109 UNTS 211.

considerations played a large part in the adoption of a project that was economically and environmentally unsound from the beginning.

The project involved the creation of a reservoir beginning at the south-east end of Bratislava, at river km 1,860, covering 60 km^2 and having a total capacity of 200 million cubic meters. Forty-nine million cubic meters were to be used to generate electricity at a power plant situated at Gabčíkovo, 17 km downstream at the end of a canal that ran from the reservoir.[114] A large part of the reservoir, the power canal, and the Gabčíkovo power plant were to be constructed entirely on Slovak territory, while the old bed of the Danube remained the boundary between the two states. The power plant was intended to operate in 'peak mode', meaning it would utilize the accumulated water for several hours a day, depending on the discharge of the Danube. Except for the morning and evening peak hours of production, the flow of the Danube would have virtually stopped, with little water coming through the power plant into the 8.2 km long tail race canal[115] joining the Danube. The average discharge of the Danube, calculated on an annual basis, is 2,000 cubic meters per second. At river km 1843, the major part of the water was to be channeled into the thirty-one km long diversion system[116] so that the water in the main riverbed would have fallen to a mere fifty cubic meters per second.

The operation of the Gabčíkovo power plant in peak mode made it necessary to dam the Danube water to regulate the water flow. This was the objective of a second dam, situated 113 km downstream at Nagymaros, at river km 1,696, where the Danube flows between two mountain ranges. At this site, another, smaller hydroelectric plant was to be built.

A joint investment plan and national investments were to finance the project. The two governments, negotiating with the participation of their two communist parties, agreed to share the cost of the operation and the benefits of the electricity produced. The latter contributed only a small part – less than 3 percent – to the energy needs of the two countries. Furthermore, until 2015, Hungary would be obliged to use its share of the electricity produced to pay back the foreign loans which were necessary to finance its part of the construction.

As the planning continued, doubts emerged on the Hungarian side concerning the environmental impact. There were three main concerns: (1) the potential pollution of a large underground water reserve near the upstream

114 The canal is referred to as a 'head-race' canal.

115 A 'tail race' canal runs from the power plant back to the river.

116 The diversion system consisted of the head race canal, the power plant, the ship locks and the tail race canal.

reservoir by infiltration from the reservoir's sediments, (2) damage to Szigetköz, a unique wetland area south of the Danube, by the lowering of the level of the subsurface water, and (3) potential pollution of the underground water north of Budapest, due to the Nagymaros dam. In 1981, the Hungarian Academy of Sciences appointed an *ad hoc* interdisciplinary committee to investigate the project. It concluded that the ecological effects and consequences of the system had not been considered in any comprehensive way and it proposed postponing the construction work in order to make changes in the plans, or to cancel the construction plans. The report was ignored and the government then in power prohibited its publication.

Despite the ban, public opinion became aware of the potential problems. As a result, both Hungarian and foreign environmental movements mounted challenges. Street demonstrations took place in Budapest against the project, the first demonstrations in Hungary since the 1956 insurrection. Rapid political changes permitted the Hungarian Parliament to adopt a resolution on October 7, 1988 submitting the continuation of the construction to strict rules of environmental protection and, on May 13, 1989, the Hungarian government suspended the works at Nagymaros. It also announced its intention to suspend the execution of its part of the works near Gabčíkovo until the environmental consequences of the project were fully assessed. Several days later, Hungary proposed to Czechoslovakia further studies and a joint analysis of the ecological risks arising from the operation of the system. On June 2, 1989, the Hungarian Parliament authorized the initiation of preliminary negotiations to amend the 1977 Treaty. When independent experts confirmed the ecological risks of the project, the Hungarian government proposed to amend the Treaty after a thorough scientific investigation. The Czechoslovak government rejected the doubts and scientific findings and expressed its conviction that monitoring and subsequent technical corrections would suffice to preserve the natural resources. It agreed only to begin negotiations with a view to putting the Gabčíkovo part of the project into operation by 1991.

The following one and a half years were dominated by the total transformation of the political situation in both countries. On March 25, 1990, Hungary held its first free elections since 1945. The new Parliament requested the government to cease state investments in the Danube project. The international context changed as well, as Soviet troops withdrew from Hungary and both COMECON and the Warsaw Pact dissolved. While negotiations continued between Czechoslovakia and Hungary, Czechoslovak authorities began the construction of a 'provisional solution' called 'Variant C' which involved the completion of the Gabčíkovo upstream reservoir entirely on Slovak territory. Variant C called for a diversion of almost all the water of the Danube, the construction of the head-race plant with ship locks, and of the tail race canal. Peak production was, however, abandoned, as a consequence of the suspension of the work on the Nagymaros part of the project.

Czechoslovak authorities notified Hungary of the decision to proceed with the construction of 'Variant C' on July 30, 1991, one day after Czechoslovakia began pumping water from the Danube into the diversion canal. The Hungarian Ministry of Foreign Affairs protested and Parliament authorized the government to terminate the 1977 Treaty if the Czechoslovak government did not cease the construction works. The protest was rejected and, on May 19, 1992, the Hungarian government issued a declaration stating that the Treaty was terminated. On October 27, 1992, Czechoslovakia completed the closure of the Danube, after having rejected a Hungarian proposal to submit the dispute to the International Court of Justice and expressing preference for trilateral negotiation with EC involvement. Hungary sought urgently to ensure the discharge of water into the Danube. An agreement reached on October 28, 1992 provided for a discharge level not less than ninety-five percent of the former volume, but the agreement was not implemented by Czechoslovakia or, later Slovakia. Instead, they proposed a fifty percent flow rate. Slovakia became an independent state on January 1, 1993 and claimed that the Gabčíkovo plant produced between eight and ten percent of the state's electricity.

On April 7, 1993 Hungary and Slovakia signed a Special Agreement on the submission of the dispute to the ICJ.[117] The agreement requested the court to decide, on the basis of the 1977 Treaty and 'rules and principles of general international law, as well as such other treaties as the court may find applicable':

1. Whether Hungary was entitled to suspend and subsequently abandon, in 1989, the works on the Nagymaros Project and on its part of the Gabčíkovo Project;
2. Whether Czechoslovakia was entitled to proceed, in November 1991, to the 'provisional solution' and to put this system into operation from October 1992 (this meant damming the Danube at river kilometer 1,851.7 on Czechoslovak territory); and
3. What are the legal effects of the notification of the termination of the Treaty by Hungary?

The parties also asked the court to determine the legal consequences, including the rights and obligations for the parties, arising from its judgment. Pending the final judgment, the two states agreed to establish and implement a temporary water-management regime for the Danube. They also agreed to enter

117 *Gabčíkovo-Nagymaros Case* (*Hungary v Slovakia*), Special Agreement of July 2, 1993.

into negotiations, immediately after the transmission of the judgment, on the modalities of its execution. If the parties failed to reach agreement within six months, either party could request the Court to render an additional judgment to determine the modalities for executing its judgment.

The memorials, counter-memorials and replies submitted to the ICJ totaled some twenty-five volumes containing 8,500 pages and the Court held forty-two hours of oral hearings. Between two sets of hearings, the entire Court made unprecedented on-site visits to Slovakia and Hungary. The lengthy judgment is accompanied by two declarations, three separate opinions and seven dissenting opinions, indicating the complexity of the case and the difficulty of the Court's task, including analysis and understanding of extensive scientific documents and presentations.

The multiplicity of international legal issues in the case included questions of the suspension and abrogation of treaties, the role of new rules in the interpretation of treaties, state succession, state responsibility and the place of environmental law in the international system. Summarizing the position of the parties, it can be stated that the arguments of Slovakia affirmed the validity of the 1977 Treaty and the text which complemented it and the duty of the parties to fulfill the obligations therein, while Hungary asserted the need to protect the environment and in particular to safeguard natural resources in the context of the Treaty and in customary international law.

The judgment comprises four parts.[118] The first part summarizes the facts and data of the case and the positions of the two parties. The second part has a declaratory character in reference to the lawfulness or unlawfulness of the conduct of the parties between 1989 and 1992, and the effect of that conduct on the continued existence of the 1977 treaty. In the third part, the Court determines, on the basis of its prior findings, the present and future legal rights and obligations of the parties. This prescriptive part of the judgment has to be implemented through an agreement on the modalities to execute the judgment. The final part consists of one paragraph in which the Court answers the questions formulated in the Special Agreement.

The Court addresses the law of international watercourses and, in particular, environmental protection of them, in several sections of the second part of the judgment. Notably, the Court accepted the duty not to cause transboundary

118 *Gabčíkovo-Nagymaros, supra* n 26. For an in-depth discussion of the case, see Serena Forlati, Makane Moïse Mbengue and Brian McGarry, *The Gabčíkovo-Nagymaros Judgment and Its Contribution to the Development of International Law* (Brill 2020).

harm as part of general international law and recognized the existence of ecological necessity as a legal excuse for an otherwise illegal act.

Hungary alleged that there was, in 1989, a state of necessity created by the threats to the environment, including pollution of the underground water resource, drying-out of an ecologically- important alluvial plain, and potential harm to the supply of drinking water to Budapest, that justified its suspension and abandonment of the works. The Court evaluated the doctrine of a state of necessity according to the criteria laid down by the International Law Commission in Article 33 of the Draft Articles on the International Responsibility of States.[119] The Court acknowledged that the concerns expressed by Hungary for its natural environment related to an essential interest in the meaning of that provision. It also recalled its advisory opinion on the *Legality of the Threat of Use of Nuclear Weapons,* where it recognized the general obligation of states to ensure that activities within their jurisdiction and control respect the environment of other states or of areas beyond national control is now part of the corpus of international law relating to the environment.[120] The Court was not convinced, however, by the Hungarian argument on the state of necessity, because the government did not prove that a real grave and imminent peril existed in 1989 and that the measures taken by Hungary were the only possible response to it (paras. 49–54). Instead, the Court found that the dangers ascribed to the upstream reservoir at Nagymaros 'were mostly of a long-term nature and, above all ... they remained uncertain' (para. 55). The Court's analysis indicates the limits of juridical intervention in environmental cases, where deterioration of the environment has very often a long-term nature and cannot be proven in the present.

The second question submitted to the Court concerned the legality of Hungary's termination of the 1977 Treaty as a response to the construction and the operation of the system unilaterally by Czechoslovakia, exclusively under its own control and for its own benefit. The termination of the 1977 Treaty by Hungary also was based, *inter alia,* on a state of necessity. The Court did not accept this argument, holding that necessity does not allow a treaty to be terminated, but will only exonerate the state from responsibility for not having executed the agreement.

Hungary also sought to justify terminating the 1977 Treaty on the basis that it was impossible to perform the obligations flowing from it. Hungary contended that it could not be 'obliged to fulfil a practically impossible task, namely to

---

119 The Articles were completed and presented to the UN General Assembly in December 2002.

120 ICJ Reports 1996 at 241–242, para 29.

construct a system of dams on its own territory that would have caused irreparable environmental damage'. The Court held, however, that the 1977 Treaty – and in particular Articles 15, 19 and 20 – actually made available to the parties the necessary means to proceed at any time, by negotiation, to the required readjustments between economic and ecological imperatives (para. 103).

Hungary further argued that it was entitled to invoke a number of events that, cumulatively, constituted a fundamental change of circumstances, allowing it to escape the Treaty. One of the circumstances cited was the progress of environmental knowledge and the development of new norms and prescriptions of international environmental law. The Court answered that such new developments could not be said to have been completely unforeseen. In addition, the treaty provisions relating to the quality of water in the Danube and the protection of nature could accommodate change, allowing the parties to take account of developments when implementing those treaty provisions.

One of the most important elements of the case was Hungary's claim that it was entitled to terminate the 1977 Treaty because new requirements of international law for the protection of the environment precluded performance of the Treaty. The Court once more referred to the treaty's environmental provisions, Articles 15, 19 and 20, in pointing out that new environmental norms are relevant for the implementation of the Treaty and that the parties could, by agreement, incorporate them into the Treaty (para. 112). Significantly, by inserting those dynamic provisions in the Treaty, the parties recognized the potential necessity to adapt the Project. Consequently, the Treaty allows reference to emerging norms of international law. In this context, the Court recalled its statement in the Advisory Opinion on the *Legality of the Threat or Use of Nuclear Weapons* that 'the environment is not an abstraction but represents the living space, the quality of life and the very health of human beings, including generations unborn'. It added that awareness of the vulnerability of the environment and recognition that environmental risks have to be assessed on a continuous basis have become much stronger in the years since the Treaty's conclusion (para. 112). The result enhances the importance of Articles 15, 19 and 20.

Respecting riparian rights on the river, the Court held that Hungary's unlawful termination of the treaty did not mean that it had forfeited its basic right to an equitable and reasonable sharing of the resources of the watercourse. Czechoslovakia, by putting Variant C, the so-called 'provisional solution', into operation, and appropriating between eighty and ninety percent of the Danube waters, had violated this provision (para. 78).

The third part of the judgment contains particularly important *dicta* for the protection of the environment, in particular three statements of the Court.

First, after holding that the 1977 Treaty is still in force and consequently governs the relationship between the parties, the Court said it could not disregard the fact that the Treaty had not been fully implemented by either party for years and that their acts of commission and omission contributed to the present factual situation. What might have been the correct application of the law in 1989 or 1992, could be a miscarriage of the justice in 1997. The Court pointed out that the Slovak reservoir was significantly smaller than what was planned, that the plant was operated in a run-of-the-river mode and not in a peak hour mode, and that Nagymaros had not been built. As both parties appeared to have abandoned the peak operation mode, there was no longer any point in building the second dam.

Second, the Project's implementation and environmental impact were necessarily a key issue. According to the Court, the parties must take into account current standards in evaluating environmental risks, as implicitly prescribed by Treaty Articles 15 and 19 concerning water quality and nature protection. On this point, the Court proclaimed its concern for the environment:

> ... (I)n the field of environmental protection, vigilance and prevention are required on account of the often irreversible character of damage to the environment and of the limitations inherent in the very mechanism of reparation of this type of damage.
>
> Throughout the ages, mankind has, for economic and other reasons, constantly interfered with nature. In the past, this was often done without consideration of the effects upon the environment. Owing to new scientific insights and to a growing awareness of the risks for mankind – for present and future generations – of pursuit of such intervention at an unconsidered and unabated pace, new norms and standards have been developed, set forth in a great number of instruments during the last two decades. Such new norms have to be taken into consideration, and such new standards given proper weight, not only when States contemplate new activities but also when continuing with activities begun in the past.[121]

As a consequence, the parties should look afresh at the environmental effects of the operation of the power plant and, in particular, find a satisfactory solution regarding the volume of water to be released into the old bed of the Danube and into the side-arms on both sides of the river. Such solution should

121 *Gabčíkovo-Nagymaros, supra n 26*, para. 140.

take account of the objectives of the Treaty, as well as the norms of international environmental law and the principles of the law of international watercourses (para. 141). The parties should participate in the use and the benefits of the system of locks in equal measure (para. 146) and the re-establishment of the joint regime must optimally reflect the concept of common utilization of shared water resources. The Court mentions with approval Article 5(2) of the 1997 UN Convention on the Law of the Non-Navigational Uses of International Watercourses, which states '[w]atercourse states shall participate in the use, development and protection of an international watercourse in an equitable and reasonable manner. Such participation includes both the right to utilize the watercourse and the duty to cooperate in the protection and development thereof, as provided in the present Convention'.

On the whole, although the International Court of Justice did not take into account several aspects of environmental protection, such as avoiding long-term effects of present activities, and did not apply the precautionary principle, its judgment will certainly be among the most quoted ones and constitutes a major development in international environmental law.

3.2 *The River Uruguay*

An agreement was concluded in 1975 between Uruguay and Argentina to govern the Uruguay River.[122] The bilateral treaty requires both parties to inform the other of any project that might affect the river. Beginning in 2003, Argentina claimed that projects in Uruguay to construct very large pulp mills alongside the river was governed by the agreement and should be halted. On May 4, 2006, Argentina filed an application with the ICJ and requested provisional measures to halt the project while the court considered the case. Argentina argued that suspending construction of the pulp mills was necessary to preserve its rights because the potential consequences of the mills' operational harm to public health and the river environment could not be made good with financial compensation. The measures were denied.[123]

On the merits, Argentina argued the project would harm the river's environment due to pollution. It also claimed that the Uruguayan government had wrongfully failed to request permission to build the mills. Uruguayan authorities counter that the treaty did not require that permission be obtained, but merely that the other part be appropriately informed. It affirmed that conversations had indeed been held, without objections being raised by the

122 Statutes of the River Uruguay (adopted February 26, 1975, entered into force September 18, 1976) 1295 UNTS 331 (1975 Statute).

123 *Pulp Mills on the River Uruguay* (*Argentina v Uruguay*), Provisional Measures May 4, 2006.

Argentinians. In addition, they claim that the technology used in the mills would avoid polluting the river to the extent claimed by Argentinians. Indeed, it asserted that the mills would have a positive impact on the river's waters as the factory included state-of-the-art wastewater treatment equipment that would also treat previously untreated local sewage.

On April 20, 2010, the International Court of Justice (ICJ) announced its judgment.[124] The Court held that Uruguay was obligated by treaty to notify and consult with Argentina before authorizing the pulp mills and letting construction start; and that Uruguay breached this obligation. The Court considered that its declaration of Uruguay's breach was a sufficient remedy for this breach. The Court examined Argentina's additional claim that Uruguay breached substantive treaty obligations to coordinate with Argentina through a bilateral river management agency, and to monitor and prevent pollution of the water and riverbed. The Court scrutinized factual evidence from both sides in detail, and found no breach had occurred. The Court rejected all other claims in light of these two decisions.

The Court made several important statements of law on shared watercourses and international environmental law in general. First, it recognized environmental impact assessment as a practice that has become an obligation of general international law in these situations. It further found that general international law does not prescribe the scope or content of such assessments. The Court also gave more detail to the principles of sustainable development and equitable and reasonable uses of shared transboundary watercourses. In this respect the ICJ highlighted the importance of ensuring environmental protection of shared natural resources while allowing for sustainable economic development. A bilateral mechanism established by the 1975 Statute, the Administrative Commission of the River Uruguay (CARU), existed to provide joint management of the river and achieve this balance. In interpreting the principle of equitable and reasonable use of the River, Argentina argued that account must be taken of pre-existing legitimate uses of the river, including recreational and tourist uses. In Uruguay's view, new and pre-existing uses should be on an equal footing. The Court stated that a balance must be struck between the rights and needs of each riparian State to use the river for economic and commercial purposes and their obligation to protect it from environmental damage. The Court called on both parties to coordinate their regulatory activities to preserve the ecological balance of the river, as required by Article 36 of the 1975 Statute. The role of CARU in coordination and rulemaking was

124 *Pulp Mills, supra* n 26 at 14.

particularly relevant here, reflecting the common interest expressed in the 1975 Statute. After reminding the parties of their customary international law obligation to ensure that activities within their jurisdiction and control respect the environment of other States or of areas beyond national control, the Court found that Article 41 of their bilateral agreement requires the parties to adopt domestic pollution prevention regulations and measures that meet international standards.

3.3 *Costa Rica v. Nicaragua*

In 2010, a dispute arose between Costa Rica and Nicaragua in response to infrastructure projects undertaken around the same time by both states. Nicaragua began conducting dredging activities in a long-disputed border region (Isla Portillos or Harbor Head), which it considered part of its territory, in order to clear an overgrown channel and to restore the natural flow of the San Juan River. It also sent its troops to be part of these operations and ultimately excavated two more canals in 2013.[125] Combined, Nicaragua's projects led to the removal of approximately 300 trees and 6.19 hectares of vegetation in the disputed area.[126] In the same period, Costa Rica started construction work in its territory on a road alongside the San Juan River. Both states accused the other of violating international law, including substantive and procedural obligations of international environmental law, and separately instituted proceedings before the International Court of Justice in 2010 and 2011. The cases were joined by the Court in 2013 and resulted in one judgment on the merits and a separate judgment on compensation (in addition to provisional measures orders). Both of these judgments provided numerous important contributions to international environmental law.

In terms of the case's substantive and procedural environmental law components, the parties' allegations included violations of the obligations to prevent transboundary harm and to carry out EIAs. Costa Rica argued that Nicaragua's dredging and excavation projects had caused harm to Costa Rican lands as well as to the Colorado River (by seriously affecting the flow of water to it), and that Nicaragua had erroneously neglected to conduct an EIA.[127] Nicaragua, on its part, asserted that Costa Rica's construction work along the San Juan River had resulted in large amounts of sediment, which it considered to be a pollutant,

---

125 *Certain Activities Carried Out by Nicaragua in the Border Area* (Costa Rica v Nicaragua) (December 16, 2015), Merits, ICJ Rep 15 (II), para. 66.

126 *Certain Activities Carried Out by Nicaragua in the Border Area* (Costa Rica v Nicaragua) (February 2, 2018), Compensation, ICJ GL No. 150, para. 75.

127 Certain Activities, Merits, para. 114.

dumped into the river, and that Costa Rica had similarly failed to conduct an EIA for this.[128] The ICJ issued a judgment on the merits in 2015, in which it agreed that Costa Rica had violated this procedural obligation.[129] The other environmental claims were rejected, but the Court did find that Nicaragua's excavation projects had violated Costa Rica's territorial sovereignty, as well as its navigational rights, and the provisional measures ordered. As a result, Nicaragua was obliged to compensate Costa Rica for the material damages caused by its unlawful activities on Costa Rican territory.

The Court's decision on the merits had various implications for international environmental law. It reaffirmed the due diligence obligation of states under customary international law to prevent transboundary harm from activities occurring within their territories and jurisdictions. The Court also provided guidance on and clarification of the related responsibility to conduct transboundary EIAs, including that such an obligation exists with regard to all activities that may entail a significant adverse impact in a transboundary context.[130] Further, the Court held that a preliminary assessment could help determine whether a significant risk exists.[131] Factors that merit consideration include the nature and magnitude of the project and the context in which it is to be carried out.[132]

The ICJ's judgment on the merits did not signal the end of the case (or its contribution to international environmental law). In its decision, the Court had left it to the parties to come to an agreement on compensation. However, new proceedings were eventually instituted because they were unable to do so. On the question of compensation, the parties agreed that environmental damage qualified as compensable damage. Their dispute instead related to the scope of compensable environmental damage and to the methodology that was to be employed to calculate the value of the impairment or loss of environmental goods and services. Regarding the scope of compensation, Costa Rica claimed compensation for two categories of damage: the quantifiable environmental damages caused by the excavation of two of the canals, and the costs and expenses incurred as a result of Nicaragua's unlawful activities, including expenses it made to monitor or remedy the environmental damage caused.[133] Nicaragua argued that Costa Rica was merely entitled to material damages,

128 ibid, paras. 177, 146.
129 ibid, para. 162.
130 ibid, para. 104.
131 ibid, para. 154.
132 ibid, para. 155.
133 Certain Activities, Compensation, para. 36.

which included damage to property and other interests that can be assessed in financial terms.[134]

In terms of the appropriate methodology, Costa Rica proposed an 'ecosystem services approach', according to which both the direct and indirect use values of environmental goods and services had to be taken into account.[135] Nicaragua instead argued that the proper method is to determine the replacement costs of the environmental services that have been lost or that may be lost prior to the recovery of the impacted area.[136]

The ICJ issued its judgment concerning compensation in 2018, which marked the first time the Court had ever decided an environmental compensation case. The decision provided a valuable contribution to international environmental law by offering a clarification of the scope of compensable damage. Moreover, it set out a methodology in broad terms for calculating the value of the impairment or loss of environmental goods and services. With regard to the scope of compensable environmental damage, the Court sided with Costa Rica and recognized that this includes loss of both direct and indirect ecosystem services. The Court also affirmed that this could not be valued as a one-time loss.[137] In addition, the Court confirmed that the assessment of compensation requires a link between the wrongful act and the injury suffered, and recognized that environmental claims may have their own particular issues in this respect, in light of concurrent causes or the state of science.[138] The Court emphasized that, in any case, a lack of certainty regarding the extent of damage need not frustrate the ability to award compensation.[139] In terms of the appropriate methodology for valuation, the Court held that this must be decided on a case-by-case basis.[140] There is, in that sense, no single methodology.[141] Still, the Court opined that it is appropriate to approach the valuation of environmental damage from the perspective of the ecosystem as a whole. This entails adopting an overall assessment of the impairment or loss of environmental goods and services prior to recovery, rather than attributing values to specific categories and estimating recovery periods for each of them.[142]

134 ibid, para. 37.
135 ibid, para. 47.
136 ibid, para. 49.
137 ibid, para. 85.
138 ibid, para. 34.
139 ibid, para. 35.
140 ibid, para. 52.
141 ibid, para. 44.
142 ibid, para. 78.

3.4 *Indus Waters*

In 1960, India and Pakistan concluded a treaty on the Indus River Basin: the Indus Water Treaty.[143] Under this treaty, the Jhelum river – of which Kishenganga is a part – falls under the control of Pakistan, but India is allowed to make use of the water flow for the production of hydro-electric power.[144] In 2010, Pakistan instituted arbitral proceedings against India because of the construction of the Kishenganga Hydro-Electric Project (KHEP) that India was building. The KHEP would constitute of a dam on the Kishenganga and a 23.5 kilometer long tunnel through which its water was to be diverted into the Bonar Nallah, another tributary to the Jhelum.[145] The fear of Pakistan was that in the drier season, this dam would effectively cut off the water flow downstream, which would be harmful to for example agricultural activity.[146] Relevant for this concern was also that Pakistan had started their own hydro-electric project: the Neelum-Jhelum Hydro-Electric Project (NJHEP) downriver shortly after India started the KHEP, and without water flow, this would be naturally fruitless. An Arbitral Tribunal was constituted to rule on two substantive issues. The first was whether the KHEP's inter-tributary diversions were permissible under the Treaty, and the second was whether India was permitted to use drawdown flushing to counter the accumulation of sedimentation. Pakistan also filed for interim measures to halt the KHEP's construction. The Tribunal granted this request, though only with respect to any permanent features of the KHEP.

The essence of the first issue concerned the interpretation of Paragraph 15(III) of Annexure D of the Treaty, which allows India to divert water only to the extent that the *then existing* Agricultural Use or hydro-electric use by Pakistan on the former tributary would not be adversely affected. Pakistan asserted that its NJHEP was a 'then existing use' because these terms should be understood in a dynamic manner and thus call for regular reassessments of the existing uses. This was referred to as the 'ambulatory approach'. India argued for a static approach, according to which Pakistan's existing uses were frozen after a critical period, namely, when India communicated its firm intention to proceed with the project. The Tribunal did not fully adopt either of these interpretations, suggesting instead that existing uses become static when a high degree of certainty that a project will actualize is demonstrated. Based on these criteria, the KHEP preceded the NJHEP, which thus did not constitute a 'then

143 Indus Waters Treaty (signed September 19, 1960, entered into force January 12, 1961) 419 UNTS 126 (Indus Waters Treaty).

144 IWT Annexure D.

145 Partial Award, para. 155.

146 ibid, paras. 129, 249.

existing use'. Accordingly, the Tribunal ruled that India had a right to divert the waters of the Kishenganga, though it also emphasized that this right was not absolute. India was allowed to proceed with the construction (and operation) of the KHEP under the condition that it did this in a way that maintained a minimum flow of 9 cubic meters of water per second in the River. Each of the parties could request the reconsideration of this figure after seven years.

On the second issue, Pakistan asserted that the 'drawdown flushing' sediment control technique violated the Treaty because it would reduce the reservoir level of the KHEP below Dead Storage Level, which would provide India with control over the amount of water flowing further downstream.[147] By contrast, India argued that the Treaty was purposefully drafted to take full advantage of advances in technical knowledge, thus permitting the use of drawdown flushing.[148] On this matter, the Tribunal ultimately sided with Pakistan and prohibited India from using drawdown flushing at the KHEP and any future projects.

Although the decision in this case was largely based on the interpretation of a bilateral treaty, it also contributed to the development of the international law on watercourses and international environmental law more generally. Perhaps most notable is the Tribunal's proposed method for distinguishing between existing and potential uses of a watercourse. The Tribunal also reaffirmed various (customary) international environmental law principles, including the obligation to avoid transboundary harm, and demonstrated that these may give rise to a minimum flow requirement in shared watercourses. It merits mentioning that the determined rate of 9 cubic meters was decidedly not grounded in a precautionary approach, which the Tribunal considered inappropriate.[149] In general, the Indus Waters Arbitration also illustrated the possibility of resolving disputes on international watercourses peacefully, with the caveat that the source of the settlement continued to be a matter of contention afterwards. Pakistan initiated new arbitration proceedings in 2016, which was ongoing as of May 2024.[150]

3.5 *Silala River*

The Silala River dispute before the International Court of Justice provided insights on the status and permitted uses of the Silala River and also had (albeit more limited) broader implications regarding the customary international law

147 ibid, para. 492.
148 ibid, para. 492.
149 Final Award, para. 11.
150 PCA Case No. 2023-01.

on watercourses. The Silala River has its source in Bolivia and flows across the border into Chile, where it discharges into the San Pedro River.[151] Though both states granted concessions for the use of the Silala from the early 1900s on, by 1999 the status and use of the Silala had become a point of contention between them.[152] Bolivia claimed that the River only flowed into Chile because of artificial channels and that it was thus not an international watercourse. Accordingly, Chile allegedly had no rights to it and was obliged to compensate Bolivia for its use of the waters. Chile rejected this. The two states attempted to come to an agreement, but were unable to, which led Chile to institute proceedings before the Court in 2016.

The case involved five claims of Chile, and three counterclaims of Bolivia. Chile requested the Court to determine that: (1) the Silala River is an international watercourse governed by international law, (2) Chile is entitled to equitable and reasonable utilization of the waters of the Silala River system, (3) Chile is entitled to its current use of the waters, (4) Bolivia is obliged to take all appropriate measures to prevent and control pollution and other forms of harm to Chile resulting from its activities in the vicinity of the Silala River system, and (5) Bolivia is under an obligation to notify and consult with respect to measures that may have adverse effect on the River system.

In its counterclaims, Bolivia asked the Court to affirm its sovereignty over the artificial channels and drainage mechanisms installed in its territory, as well as its sovereignty over the artificial flow of the Silala waters engineered, enhanced or produced in its territory. It also sought the Court's opinion on the need for the parties to conclude an agreement for any future delivery to Chile of the 'enhanced flow' of the Silala.

Since neither of the states were parties to the United Nations Watercourses Convention, the questions posed to the Court required analyses of customary international law.[153] Remarkably, the Court found that it was not called upon to issue a decision on six of the eight claims. It considered that there was ultimately no dispute between the parties concerning most of the issues that were raised, and that the claims thus had no object. For instance, during the proceedings, the parties had come to agree that the Silala was in fact an international watercourse under customary international law after evidence presented by independent experts indicated that the River would have also

151 *Dispute over the Status and Use of the Waters of the Silala* (Chile v Bolivia) (December 1, 2022), Merits, ICJ Rep 22, para. 28.

152 ibid, para. 32.

153 ibid, para. 54.

flowed into Chile naturally (without the artificial channels).[154] The two surviving claims were Chile's claim that Bolivia had breached its procedural obligations under customary international law to notify and consult with Chile, and Bolivia's claim regarding the need to conclude an agreement relating to future deliveries to Chile of 'enhanced flow' of the Silala. Both of them were rejected by the Court, the former because Chile had neglected to demonstrate a (significant) risk of harm, and the latter because it concerned a hypothetical scenario.

One of the judges in this case observed that the Court's judgment curiously decided almost nothing.[155] Others voiced similar criticisms.[156] Still, the rendered decision had a number of important implications. Firstly, although the Court did not make use of the opportunity to clarify whether the definition of international watercourses in the United Nations Watercourses Convention reflects customary international law, it did confirm the status of the Silala River. Namely, it accepted the unity of the Silala water system and affirmed that it is governed by customary international law in its entirety.[157] It also asserted that modifications which increase the surface flow of a watercourse have no bearing on its characterization as an international watercourse.[158] Moreover, the decision reaffirmed the customary right of riparian parties to equitable and reasonable use of the waters of an international watercourse.[159] It further reaffirmed the customary obligation to prevent transboundary harm and the accompanying procedural obligations to conduct an EIA and to notify and consult (including the latter's contingency upon the risk of significant harm).[160] This case also demonstrated the role that science and independent experts can play in proceedings before the Court.

4 Beyond the Banks of the River

Fresh water does not limit itself to waterways and lakes, and neither does the law on it. This section discusses some other fresh water sources, forms water can take, and regulation in these situations.

Groundwater and aquifers are often connected to other fresh water resources, but have not always received the same kind of attention. The 1997

154 ibid, para. 53.
155 Silala River Dispute, Separate Opinion of Judge ad hoc Simma, para. 2.
156 Silala River Dispute, Declaration of Judge Tomka, Declaration of Judge Charlesworth.
157 Silala River Dispute, para. 54.
158 ibid, para. 93.
159 ibid, para. 97.
160 ibid, paras. 83, 118.

Watercourses agreement defines a watercourse as a system of surface waters and groundwaters constituting by virtue of their physical relationship a unitary whole and normally flowing into a common terminus (Art. 2(a)).[161] This definition gives only limited protection to groundwaters, excluding as it does those that are confined and do not flow into common terminus, even if they are transboundary. The International Law Commission took up the more general issue in 2006, and in 2008 adopted Draft Articles on the Law of Transboundary Aquifers.[162] Domestic aquifers are excluded, but if they are linked to an international watercourse, the 1997 Convention would apply.

The 2008 Draft Articles affirm principles of sovereignty, equitable and reasonable utilization, and the duty not to cause harm. The recognition that each state has sovereignty over the portion of a transboundary aquifer or aquifer system located within its territory is balanced by the requirement that such sovereignty be exercised in accordance with the draft Articles. In particular, aquifer states must utilize the waters in a manner that is consistent with the equitable and reasonable accrual of benefits therefrom to that state (Art. 4(a)) taking into account all relevant factors (Art. 5(1)). The latter include consideration of populations that rely on the aquifer; present and future social and economic needs of the aquifer states concerned; natural characteristics of the aquifer or aquifer system; the impact of the utilization on the formation and recharge of the aquifer; the current and potential utilization of the aquifer; the impact of the utilization on other concerned aquifer states; the development and protection of the aquifer and the cost of related action; and the role of the aquifer in the surrounding ecosystem (Art. 5). Article 6 adds that states must take all appropriate steps to prevent causing transboundary harm, while Article 9 requires states to take all appropriate measures to protect ecosystems dependent on aquifers.

On December 11, 2008, the UN General Assembly by resolution 63/124 took note of the ILC draft Articles on the law of transboundary aquifers and commended them to the attention of Governments 'without prejudice to the question of their future adoption or other appropriate action'. It encourages states to make appropriate bilateral or regional arrangements for the proper management of their transboundary aquifers, taking into account the provisions of

161 Convention on the Law of the Non-Navigational Uses of International Watercourses (adopted 21 May 1995, entered into force 17 August 2014) 2999 UNTS (Watercourses agreement).

162 The International Law Association adopted its Berlin Rules on Water Resources in 2004, calling for the integrated management of all aquifers.

these draft Articles, while leaving open the question of the form that might be given to the draft Articles in the future.

The Water Convention (Helsinki 1992) was, as previously stated, amended in 2013 and thereby opened to all UN Member States for accession.[163] The 2014 UNECE Model Provisions on Transboundary Groundwaters were drafted to elaborate on the Water Convention on the topic of groundwater, facilitating a move towards more transboundary cooperation in the management of groundwater by requiring states to draw up specific agreements addressing the sustainable use, management and protection of those groundwaters.[164] Throughout the years, numerous small-scale agreements on transboundary aquifers have been concluded, showing that, over time more cooperation in the management of these fresh water resources has emerged.[165]

On the margins of discussions of fresh water, iced water resources nevertheless warrant serious attention. Due to water scarcity, eyes have been turning for decades toward the exploitation of water in ice-form, found in the polar regions, but the idea has so far not been put into practice on a significant scale. However, the potential harvesting of these resources is not without its environmental concerns, and there is no international law specifically pertaining to the matter. At present, pursuing this option on a significant scale thus raises questions concerning responsibility for any resulting environmental harm.[166]

---

163 See for a discussion of the Water Convention section A.1.b of this chapter.

164 UNECE Model Provisions on Transboundary Groundwaters (January 2014) ECE/MP.WAT/40, 1.

165 For example, there is the Arrangement on the protection, utilization, and recharge of the Franco-Swiss Genevese aquifer (June 9, 1977, revised in January 2008); the Joint Authority (1992) created by Chad, Egypt, Libya and Sudan; the establishment of a consultation mechanism approved in 2008 by Algeria, Libya and Tunisia; and the Agreement on the Guarani Aquifer System concluded by Argentina, Brazil, Paraguay, and Uruguay (2010); For a more in-depth summary and discussion of legislation on transboundary aquifers, see Francesco Sindico, 'Transboundary Aquifer Agreements and Arrangements' in Francesco Sindico (ed.), *International Law and Transboundary Aquifers* (Edward Elgar Publishing 2020).

166 See, throughout the decades, interest in the possibility of harvesting icebergs: John L. Hult and Neill C. Ostrander, *Antarctic Icebergs as a Global Freshwater Resource* (Rand 1973); Frank Pallone, 'Resource Exploitation: The Threat to the Legal Regime of Antarctica' (1978) 12(3) International Lawyer 547; Bryan S. Geon, 'A Right to Ice?: The Application of International and National Water Laws to the Acquisition of Iceberg Rights' (1997) 19 Michigan Journal of International Law 277; Cory Lewis, 'Iceberg Harvesting: Suggesting a Federal Regulatory Regime for a New Freshwater Source' (2015) 42(2) Boston College Environmental Affairs Law Review 439; Ruth Morgan, 'Dry continent dreaming: Australian visions of using Antarctic icebergs for water supplies' (2018) 4(1) International Review of Environmental History 145.

The agricultural concept of 'virtual' water reflects another understudied topic in international water law. Virtual water measures the amount of water needed for a given product. Due to climate change, there exists a risk that areas in which water is scarce will have to increase their import of products which, in turn, require more water to produce. In economic terms, such areas are thus importing water.[167] Since this topic bears particular relevance for international trade in water-intensive produce, it will be further discussed in Chapter 17.

5 Conclusions

There is general recognition that freshwater is fundamental to all forms of life and, at the same time, crucial to many human activities. The protection of this vital resource needs a holistic approach, taking into account the interrelationships among different forms of water resources (surface and groundwater, atmospheric water, ice) over a large geographic area (water basins, interfaces between continental waters and sea) and the multiple uses of water (basic human needs, irrigation, industrial uses, energy production). Water usage also must respect the integrated nature of resources within ecosystems. It also must be remembered that water quality and quantity cannot be separated.

The law of water resources and, in particular, international cooperation must be based on such complex analysis. In addition, it is necessary to recognize that while access to water is a fundamental human need, water is also an economic good whose distribution requires infrastructure that sometimes necessitates massive investment and good governance. Left as a public good, water can be subject to the 'tragedy of the commons', because there are no incentives to conservation. Proper use of economic instruments with pricing reflecting the quantities of water appropriated by consumers can help to reduce waste and ensure long-term protection of water quantity and quality.

Two principles are increasingly asserted. The first is that despite the reluctance of many agreements to prioritize uses of water, the fulfillment of basic needs (drinking and sanitation) should be generally given the highest priority as a substantive element of the right to environment. Second, as a general framework, water may be looked upon as a heritage to be shared among all users, including ecosystems, in a reasonable and equitable way, in a spirit of solidarity and in a manner consistent with the needs of sustainable development.

167 See Edith Brown Weiss and Lydia Slobodian, 'Virtual Water, Water Scarcity, and International Trade Law' (2014) 17(4) Journal of International Economic Law 717.

There are situations in which the law on fresh water intersects with other fields of international law. This can be the case for, for example, the human right to water, access to fresh water in armed conflict, and economic development issues relating to fresh water. These topics will be discussed in their respective chapters in Part III of this book, which concerns transversal issues.

Bibliography

Benvenisti, E., 'Collective Action in the Utilization of Shared Freshwater: The Challenges of International Water Resources Law' (1996) 90 *AJIL* 384.

Boisson de Chazournes, L., *Fresh Water in International Law* (2021).

Bruhacs, F., *The Law of Non-Navigational Watercourses* (1993).

Clarke, R., *Water: The International Crisis* (1993).

Francis, G., 'Binational Cooperation for Great Lakes Water Quality: A Framework for the Groundwater Connection' (1989) 65 *Chi-Kent L. Rev.* 359.

Heller, L., *The Human Rights to Water and Sanitation* (2022).

Kiss, A., 'The Protection of the Rhine Against Pollution' (1985) 25 *Nat. Res. J.* 613.

Lammers, J., *Pollution of International Watercourses* (1984).

Leroy, P., 'Troubled Waters: Population and Water Scarcity' (1995) 6 *Colo. J. Int'l L. & Pol'y* 299.

McCaffrey, S., *The Law of International Watercourses* (2002).

Nollkaemper, A., *The Legal Regime for Transboundary Water Pollution: Between Discretion and Constraint* (1993).

Sette-Camara, J., 'Pollution of International Rivers' (1984) 186 *RCADI* 117.

Sohnle, J., *Le droit international des ressources en eau douce: solidarité contre* souveraineté (2002).

Tanzi, A. and others, *The UNECE Convention on the Protection and Use of Transboundary Watercourses and International Lakes* (2015).

Tanzi, M.A., *The United Nations Convention the Law of International Watercourses: A Framework for Sharing* (2001).

Teclaff, L.A. and Teclaff, E., 'Transboundary Toxic Pollution and the Drainage Basin Concept' (1985) 25 *Nat. Res. J.* 589.

Tignino, M. and Bréthaut, C., *Research Handbook on Freshwater Law and International Relations* (2018).

Trevin, J.O. and Day, J.C., 'Risk Perception in International River Basin Management: The Plata Basin Example' (1990) 30 *Nat Res. J.* 87–105.

Wescoat, Jr., J.L., 'Main Currents in Early Multilateral Water Treaties: A Historical-Geographic Perspective, *1648–1948*' (1996) 7 *Colo. J. Int'l Envtl. L. & Pol'y* 39.

CHAPTER 11

Protection of the Marine Environment

1 Overview

Maritime waters cover over seventy percent of the planet's surface area and a vast majority of the total volume that is known to sustain life.[1] Despite the importance of the marine environment, human activities everywhere are depleting marine and coastal living resources and degrading ecosystems in sometimes irreversible ways. The oceans possess great natural capacity for self-purification, but there are limits to this process that are being reached and exceeded as the amounts of harmful substances flowing directly or indirectly into the seas have increased along with growing world population and expanding industrialization. In fact, the many threats to the health, productivity, and biodiversity of the marine environment result from human activities that take place on land, in coastal areas, and even further inland.[2] 'Dead zones' in the oceans have increased from about 400 in 2008 to more than 700 in 2019 as a result of human activity, with the most affected areas being the North of the Gulf of Mexico, the Baltic Sea, the North Sea, the Bay of Bengal, the South China Sea and the East China Sea.[3]

The traditional uses of the sea have intensified and diversified, also threatening the marine environment. The sea has always played a particularly important role in the transport of products. This is still its principal role, and today, the vast number and size of ships provokes great concern about the heightened risk of marine pollution. Another traditional use of the sea, fishing, equally has seen an unprecedented expansion. Practiced since time immemorial, ocean fishing has been transformed into an industry which today impacts on biological resources in the farthest and most inhospitable ocean reaches. The UN indicates that 33 percent of the world's fish stocks are being depleted, due to fishing at unsustainable levels.[4] Overfishing is not the only cause for concern about the preservation of marine living resources. Fish have been showing signs of contamination and damage from pollution since at least the 1970s, including concentrations of carcinogens, tumors, wounds, and malformations,

1 United Nations, *The Second World Ocean Assessment: World Ocean Assessment II* vol I (2021) 5.
2 ibid 273–274.
3 ibid 8.
4 ibid 17; On fisheries law, see Chapter 8.

 | DOI:10.1163/9789047440802_013

which render them unsuitable for consummation and which threaten their ability to reproduce.[5]

Besides the intensification and transformation of traditional uses of the seas, new activities increase ocean pollution. The discovery of polymetallic nodules on the ocean floor has not led to massive exploitation thus far, but since the turn of the century the International Seabed Authority has approved numerous exploration contracts.[6] It is currently undertaking steps to create exploitation regulations, but as of May 2024, this process remains ongoing.[7] Tourism also plays an important role in uses of the sea. Although transoceanic liners almost disappeared with the development of mass air transport, pleasure cruises are increasingly popular and create numerous sources of pollution that are difficult to control.[8] Massive utilization of the sea as a dumping ground for waste means thousands of tons of matter that must be disposed of can be dumped by a single ship in one voyage. Since the beginning of the Industrial Revolution, humankind has been altering the pH balance of the oceans by emitting more CO_2, causing ocean acidification.[9] Ocean fertilization has been proposed as a solution for this issue, but poses its own environmental concerns and its effectiveness has been called into question.[10] Finally, the amount of plastic littering in the oceans grows every day and is showing no signs of stopping. Estimations of the amount of plastic in the oceans are between 75 and 199 million tons – an inconceivable number.[11]

International environmental law must respond to this evolution, despite two distinct but converging problems. First, while the oceans share homogeneous characteristics such as ocean currents, salt, and contiguity, their geophysical

5 See, Ulrich Förstner and Gottfried Wittman, *Metal Pollution in the Aquatic* (1977) ; Matt Landos, Mariann Lloyd Smith and Joanna Immig, *Aquatic Pollutants in Oceans and Fisheries* (IPEN 2021) 9.

6 For a current list of permit-holders, see the website of the ISA at <www.isa.org.jm/exploration-contracts/>.

7 Earth Negotiations Bulletin, 'Summary Report 30 October – 8 November 2023: 3rd Part of the 28th Annual Session of the International Seabed Authority,' vol 25 No. 254 (November 11, 2023).

8 Constance Dijkstra and Valentin Simon, *The Return of the Cruise: How Luxury Cruises Are Polluting European Cities* (Transport & Environment 2023) 3.

9 Jean-Pierre Gattuso and Lina Hansson, 'Acidification: Background and History' in Jean-Pierre Gattuso and Lina Hansson (eds.), *Ocean Acidification* (OUP 2011) 2.

10 See Long Cao and Ken Caldeira, 'Can Ocean Iron Fertilization Mitigate Ocean Acidification? A Letter' in *Climatic Change* vol 99 (2010) 303–311; Elise Johansen, 'Ocean Fertilization' in *The Law of the Sea and Climate Change: Solutions and Constraints* (Signe Veierud Busch and Ingvild Ulrikke Jakobsen, CUP 2021) 186.

11 UNEP, *From Pollution to Solution: A Global Assessment of Marine Litter and Plastic Pollution* (2021) 14.

situation differs widely in the various regions of the world. It seems clear that the problem of maritime pollution requires measures be taken on both the regional and the global level, with local variation being resolved through appropriate specific regulations at the same time that universal norms are formulated.

Secondly, the origins of the pollutants that affect the marine environment differ greatly one from the other. They can be intentional, for example the dumping of wastes whose disposal is difficult or more expensive on land and the cleaning of oil tanker hulls on the high seas followed by discharge of the residue of oils into the ocean waters. Pollution also can be accidental, resulting from tanker grounding or loss of containers of toxic or dangerous products. It may be necessary to utilize various regulatory techniques which take into account these differences.

Five categories of pollution can be distinguished: vessel-based pollution coming from normal utilization of the oceans; pollution transported by air; pollution arising from exploration or exploitation of the sea bed; deliberate and large, mostly industrial, dumping of wastes; and, finally, land-based pollution whether coming from direct discharges into the ocean or carried into it by rivers.[12]

Legal norms must be flexible to deal with this diversity of situations. International legal rules affirming state responsibility for environmental damage caused by pollution are a beginning, but they have tended to lack concrete standards and means of implementation.[13] International responsibility for marine pollution is clearly recognized in principle (UNCLOS Art. 235), but the development of more precise rules is necessary. In the meantime, compensation must be assured by other means, primarily through internal legal proceedings, for damage caused by pollution of the marine environment.

International environmental law places its emphasis on prevention. Numerous standards prohibit certain deliberate or intentional acts or strictly regulate them. To minimize accidental environmental harm, other legal principles must be applied, such as strict rules governing the construction of tankers, navigation, and the training of crews. It is clear that marine environmental pollution due to accidents can only be combated through international cooperation. In this regard, a 1969 Convention permits intervention on foreign-flag vessels on the high seas in case of accidents that involve or threaten marine

12 These kinds of pollution are discussed in-depth in section E of this chapter.

13 See Chapter 7.C.

environmental pollution.[14] Part of the task of international law is to further develop international cooperation.

2 Historical Evolution

Marine pollution is a relatively long-standing concern, although initial efforts to regulate it were unsuccessful. A 1926 international conference, convened by the United States, elaborated a convention to limit discharges of oil and gas into the sea, but the treaty was never signed. A second draft, prepared under the auspices of the League of Nations in 1935, contained many of the same provisions but also failed to gain acceptance. Not until 1954 was an International Convention for the Prevention of Pollution of the Sea by Oil adopted to prohibit the deliberate discharge of oil in specified zones.[15]

In the meantime, two of the 1958 United Nations Conventions on the law of the sea contained prohibitions relating to pollution of the sea by oil or pipelines as well as by radioactive wastes and wastes resulting from oil drilling on the continental shelf.[16] The 1958 Convention on the High Seas obligates all states to adopt regulations to prevent pollution of the seas by the discharge of oil from ships or pipelines or resulting from the exploitation and exploration of the seabed and its subsoil, 'taking account of existing treaty provisions on the subject';[17] to take measures to prevent pollution of the seas from the dumping of radioactive waste, 'taking into account any standards and regulations which may be formulated by the competent international organizations';[18] and 'to cooperate with the competent international organizations' in taking measures for the prevention of pollution of the seas resulting from 'any activities with radioactive materials or other harmful agents'.[19] Although these provisions are general, they established several important precedents. First, the goal of universality is reflected in the Preamble's statement of intent to 'codify the rules of international law relating to the high seas'. Second, the numerous references to

14 International Convention Relating to Intervention on the High Seas in Cases of Oil Pollution Casualties (Brussels, November 29, 1969).

15 London, May 12, 1954. The Convention was amended several times: in 1962, extending the protected zones; in 1969, enacting a general prohibition on oil pollution; and finally in 1971.

16 Arts. 24, 25, Convention on the High Seas (Geneva, April 29, 1958); Art. 5, Convention on the Continental Shelf (Geneva, April 29, 1958).

17 Art. 24, Convention on the High Seas.

18 ibid, Art. 25(1).

19 ibid, Art. 25(2).

existing treaty provisions and organizations emphasize that states must comply with internationally-developed standards and cooperate with competent international organizations in implementing such standards.

A rise in general environmental awareness, coupled with the 1967 *Torrey Canyon* tanker accident, which spilled over 100,000 tons of crude oil into the English Channel causing black tides and damage to both the French and English coastlines, led to further serious consideration of the problem of marine environmental pollution regionally and globally. Soon after the disaster, the UN General Assembly passed Resolution 2414 (XXIII) on 'international cooperation in problems related to the oceans', inviting member states and organizations to promote the adoption of effective international agreements in the prevention and control of maritime pollution.[20] Another resolution, on prevention of pollution of the marine environment by seabed development, requested that the Secretary General study the problem of pollution resulting from undersea development.[21] Two years later, the General Assembly, in a recommendation concerning effective measures for the prevention and control of marine pollution, requested the Secretary General to prepare a review concerning harmful substances affecting the ocean and activities of member nations and international agencies dealing with the prevention and control of marine pollution, and also to seek the views of member nations on the desirability and feasibility of an international treaty on this subject.[22]

During this period, global efforts centered on finding a solution to the problems posed by accidents causing serious pollution. The *Torrey Canyon* spill revealed the difficulty of resolving the numerous claims for compensation and liability issues under then-existing law. As a result, the International Maritime Consultative Organization (now International Maritime Organization) drafted two Conventions in 1969, one concerning civil responsibility for oil pollution damage and the other relating to intervention on the high seas in cases of oil pollution casualties.[23] These agreements were supplemented in 1971 with adoption of a Convention creating an international fund for compensation for oil pollution damage.[24]

In 1972, the Stockholm Conference gave new impetus to the development of international environmental norms. The Conference Declaration contains a general principle regarding pollution, providing that the discharge of toxic

---

20 A/RES/2414 (XXIII) of December 17, 1968.

21 A/RES/2467 B (XXIII) of December 21, 1968.

22 A/RES/2566 (XXIV) of December 13, 1969.

23 Brussels, November 29, 1969.

24 Brussels, December 18, 1971.

substances or of other substances and the release of heat in quantities or concentrations that exceed the capacity of the environment to render them harmless must be halted in order to ensure that serious or irreversible damage is not inflicted on ecosystems.[25] Following this general provision, Principle 7 specifically addresses marine pollution, declaring that states shall take all possible steps to prevent pollution of the seas by substances that are liable to create hazards to human health, harm living resources and marine life, damage amenities or interfere with other legitimate uses of the sea. In addition, Recommendations 86–94 of the Stockholm Action Plan address marine pollution. Most of the measures concern scientific research and monitoring the state of the environment, but Recommendation 86 urges states to adhere to and implement existing instruments combating marine pollution, and to develop norms, national as well as international, to more effectively prevent further deterioration of the marine environment.

Before the end of 1972, a conference in London created a new global international instrument, with the states present signing the Convention on the Prevention of Marine Pollution by Dumping of Wastes and other Matter.[26] One year later, also in London, a conference convoked by IMCO (now IMO) adopted a treaty that aimed at all pollution caused by ships.[27] The same year saw the beginning of the Third United Nations Conference on the Law of the Sea, whose work resulted in the Law of the Sea Convention (UNCLOS).[28]

UNCLOS, whose provisions generally reflect customary international law, provides the overall legal framework for ocean activities.[29] Its comprehensive regulation addresses the protection and preservation of the marine environment in Part XII.[30] In addition, Article 145 specifically aims to prevent pollution resulting from exploration and exploitation of the deep seabed. The Convention recognizes the competence of the coastal state to combat pollution in the territorial sea and also proclaims its competence in the UNCLOS-created exclusive economic zone.[31] On the other hand, UNCLOS contains no new

25 Principle 6.

26 London, December 29, 1972.

27 International Convention for the Prevention of Pollution by Ships (MARPOL) (London, November 2, 1973).

28 Montego Bay, December 10, 1982, entry into force 1994, A/CONF.62/122, reprinted in 21 I.L.M. 1261 (1982). As of 2023, UNCLOS has 169 states parties.

29 WSSD, Plan of Action, para. 38(d): referring to UNCLOS as 'the overall legal framework for ocean activities' and inviting all states to become party to and implement it.

30 Arts. 192–237.

31 Arts. 21, 56(1)(b)(iii).

substantive rules to combat pollution of the high seas, although there are rules to protect marine living resources.

Marine environmental law has been evolving towards comprehensive regulation for some time. The 1992 Rio Conference built on the norms contained in UNCLOS, with Chapter 17 of Agenda 21 attempting an integrated approach in its reference to all matters that concern the sea. The formulation of the title, *Protection of the oceans, all kinds of seas, including enclosed and semi-enclosed seas and coastal areas and the protection, rational use and development of their living resources*, announces the three main areas of interest: the sea itself, the coastal areas and living resources.

While protection of the marine environment against pollution and protection of the living resources of the sea against depletion are traditionally related and included within international environmental law, broad extension of international norms to coastal areas is an innovation. Until UNCED, the management of coastal areas and of waters under national jurisdiction generally was considered a national concern: the Principles Concerning Coastal Management adopted by OECD on October 12, 1976,[32] exceptionally focused on coastal land areas. Agenda 21 also linked the problem of marine pollution and of the management of coastal zones for two obvious reasons. First, coastal areas play a major role in human settlements. In 2020, more than 2 billion people are living within 100 km of the coast and this number could rise in the coming years.[33] At the same time, many of the world's poor are crowded in coastal areas, and the development of such areas is a problem of growing importance. Linked to the concentration of people, more than 80 percent of the pollution of the oceans results from land-based sources.[34]

Agenda 21, including Chapter 17, was not a treaty setting detailed rules of conduct for states. Rather, the commitment of states is to cooperate in taking action. Section 17.30 of Agenda 21 established a list of measures which should be taken to address degradation of the marine environment. Such measures include, *inter alia*, cooperation in monitoring marine pollution from ships, especially from illegal discharges, and enforcing MARPOL discharge provisions more rigorously; assessment of the state of pollution caused by ships in particularly sensitive areas and implementation of applicable measures; respect of

32 C(76)161(Final).

33 Lena Reimann, Athanasios T. Vafeidis and Lars E. Honsel, 'Population development as a driver of coastal risk: Current trends and future pathways' in *Cambridge Prisms: Coastal Futures* 1(14) (2023) 1, 3.

34 UNEP, '2006 Annual Report' (March 18, 2007) 56; Delia Paul, *Protecting the Marine Environment from Land-based Activities* (January 2021) 2.

areas designated by coastal states, within their exclusive economic zones, in order to protect and preserve rare or fragile ecosystems, such as coral reefs and mangroves; adoption of stricter international regulations to further reduce the risk of accidents and pollution from cargo ships and the development of an international regime governing the transportation of hazardous and noxious substances carried by ships. The present section discusses only the protection of the marine environment against pollution; the conservation of living resources is contained in Chapter 8.

Paragraph 17.22 of Agenda 21 confirms that the main rules of international law in this realm are those formulated in the United Nations Convention on the Law of the Sea, Part XII:

> States, in accordance with the provisions of the United Nations Convention on the Law of the Sea on protection and preservation of the marine environment, commit themselves, in accordance with their policies, priorities and resources, to prevent, reduce and control degradation of the marine environment so as to maintain and improve its life-support and productive capacities ....

The Convention for the Protection of the Marine Environment of the North-east Atlantic recognized the applicability of at least some of Part XII of UNCLOS even before the latter entered into force.[35] In fact, all international treaties concerning the oceans adopted since 1989, and even the Convention on Biological Diversity, follow the general principles set forth in UNCLOS and many specifically cite it. The international common law of the environment thus applies to specifically protecting the marine environment.

After Agenda 21, in 2000, the Millennium Development Goals were established, which although not addressing the oceans directly, entailed a promise to respect nature.[36] In 2012, at Rio+20, the UN Member States decided to begin the process of developing the Sustainable Development Goals (SDGs), which the UN General Assembly accepted in 2015.[37] Sustainable Development Goal 14 is the goal to 'conserve and sustainably use the oceans, seas and

---

35 'Recalling the relevant provisions of customary international law reflected in Part XII of the United Nations Law of the Sea Convention and, in particular, Article 197 on global and regional cooperation for the protection and preservation of the marine environment ...' Preamble, Convention for the Protection of the Marine Environment of the North-east Atlantic (Paris, September 22, 1992), EMuT, 992:71.

36 A/RES/55/2 of September 18, 2000.

37 A/RES/70/1 of October 21, 2015.

marine resources for sustainable development'.[38] This goal, like all other SDGs, is divided up into smaller, more concrete targets. After more than a decade of negotiation, on June 19, 2023 the UN General Assembly adopted the Treaty of the High Seas (also known as the BBNJ).[39] The BBNJ is a long-awaited treaty, which provides for action on several issues in marine environmental law. Its purpose is 'to ensure the conservation and sustainable use of marine biological diversity of areas beyond national jurisdiction, for the present and in the long term'.[40] It also emphasizes international cooperation and coordination.[41] The Treaty contains a chapter on marine genetic resources (Part II), a chapter on Marine Protected Areas (MPAs) and other area-based management tools (Part III), environmental impact assessments (Part IV) and capacity-building and the transfer of marine technology (Part V).[42]

The law of marine environmental protection also developed regionally, following the main directions of UNCLOS. First, states of different maritime regions of the Northern hemisphere, i.e., the Baltic Sea, North East Atlantic and Black Sea, concluded general treaties on these waters. Second, UNEP initiated its 'regional seas program' resulting in treaty systems, each consisting of a main convention, additional protocols, and, often, action plans for the development of the region.

Eight European states signed in Bonn on June 9, 1969, the first regional convention dedicated to the problem of marine pollution.[43] The states parties, clearly responding to the *Torrey Canyon* accident in 1967, developed the means of cooperation to combat pollution of the North Sea by oil. Two years later, Denmark, Finland, Norway and Sweden signed another regional agreement concerning regional marine pollution.[44] In 1972, twelve European States bordering the Atlantic or the North Sea signed a Convention to address the

38 A/RES/70/1 of October 21, 2015 at 23.

39 Agreement under the United Nations Convention on the Law of the Sea on the Conservation and Sustainable Use of Marine Biological Diversity of Areas Beyond National Jurisdiction (adopted June 19, 2023, not in force as of December 6, 2024) (A/CONF.232/2023/4) (BBNJ).

40 BBNJ Art. 2.

41 ibid, Art. 2, 8.

42 For more on the BBNJ, see Sarah Louise Lothian, *Marine Conservation and International Law: Legal Instruments for Biodiversity Beyond National Jurisdiction* (Routledge 2023) and Wen Duan, *The International Legal Regime Relating to Marine Protected Areas in Areas beyond National Jurisdiction: Identifying and Addressing Gaps* (Brill 2022).

43 Agreement of Cooperation in Dealing with Pollution of the North Sea by Oil (Bonn, June 9, 1969).

44 Agreement Concerning Cooperation in Taking Measures Against Pollution of the Sea by Oil (Copenhagen, September 16, 1971).

previously ignored problem of marine pollution caused by dumping of wastes from ships and aircraft.[45] The agreement only concerned a part of the Atlantic and the Arctic oceans, however, to the exclusion of the Baltic and Mediterranean Seas. The same maritime zone was the subject of another convention, signed by the same European countries on June 4, 1974, aimed at preventing marine pollution from land-based sources.[46]

In 1974, the Helsinki Convention on the Protection of the Marine Environment of the Baltic Sea Area initiated another advance in international legal mechanisms to protect the marine environment.[47] For the first time, the seven littoral states (Denmark, Finland, the then-two Germanies, Poland, Sweden and the USSR) agreed to comprehensively address all forms of marine pollution. A 1992 convention for the Baltic Sea replaced the 1974 Helsinki Convention.[48] Similarly, a 1992 Paris Convention comprehensively regulates all sources of marine pollution that may affect the North Sea and the North-East Atlantic, replacing both the 1972 Oslo Convention to prevent the dumping of wastes and the 1974 Paris Convention regulating the prevention of land-based pollution.[49] A third convention, equally adopted in 1992, although somewhat less developed, concerns the Black Sea.[50] Given the importance of the three instruments, they will be analyzed later in detail.

As international environmental law has expanded, it is increasingly recognized that treaties have overlapping mandates and may apply to regulate the same geographic area. Coastal areas, for example, may be regulated not only according to the provisions of UNCLOS and a regional sea agreement, but also the Convention on Biological Diversity, the Ramsar Convention on Wetlands, the UNESCO World Heritage Convention, and treaties and other rules governing freshwaters. The consequence is a considerable network of law and institutions that are not always coordinated. The Convention on Biological Diversity is one of the few to reference and give deference to UNCLOS (Art. 22). For the rest, it is unclear how competing rules will be reconciled.

---

45 Oslo, February 15, 1972.

46 Convention for the Prevention of Marine Pollution from Land-Based Sources (Paris).

47 March 22, 1974.

48 Convention on the Protection of the Marine Environment of the Baltic Sea Area, Helsinki, April 9, 1992, EmuT, 992:28.; See S. Mahmoudi, '*The Baltic and the North Sea*' in Alexandre Kiss and Dinah Shelton (eds) Manual Of European Environmental Law (2nd ed. 1997) 360.

49 Convention for the Protection of the Marine Environment of the North-East Atlantic, Paris, September 22, 1992, EMuT, 992: 55. See also Mahmoudi, ibid.

50 Convention on the Protection of the Black Sea against Pollution, Bucharest, April 21, 1992, EMuT, 992:20.

3 Rights and Duties of States in Maritime Areas

The environmental provisions of UNCLOS have a dynamic character, not only building on prior instruments, but adding structure and establishing the means for incorporating future developments. The Convention covers the three major sources of marine pollution: land-based sources, vessel-source pollution, and atmospheric pollution. The provisions apply to all ocean surfaces, not only the high seas, but also to areas under the jurisdiction of coastal states. They also seek to combat marine pollution by various preventive measures, including the duty to notify states of any imminent danger of pollution, to develop contingency plans for responding to incidents, to monitor the risks of pollution, and to assess potential effects of planned activities that may cause substantial pollution or significant changes in the marine environment and to communicate such assessments.

As previously noted, UNCLOS Article 192 proclaims that states have a general obligation to protect and preserve the marine environment. The primary concern seems to be the prevention of pollution, given that Article 192 figures first among a series of provisions relating to marine pollution. In contrast, clauses relating to the preservation of marine biological resources are contained in the sections of the Convention regulating each of the established marine zones.[51]

The Convention enunciates only broad principles respecting pollution prevention, such as the requirement in Article 194(1) that states take, individually or jointly as appropriate, all measures consistent with the Convention that are necessary to prevent, reduce, and control pollution of the marine environment from any source. The Convention reaffirms several principles of the Stockholm Declaration. For example, Article 191, like Principle 21, confirms the sovereign right of each state to exploit natural resources pursuant to its environmental policies. Similarly, UNCLOS Article 194 reaffirms the duty expressed in Principle 21 for states to respect the environment of others. More precisely, states must combat pollution of the marine environment from all sources.[52] At the same time, they must take care to avoid cross-media pollution, *i.e.*, transfer, directly or indirectly, of damage or hazards from one area to another or one type of pollution to another.[53]

The Convention uses a now classic definition of pollution by stating that it consists in 'the introduction by man, directly or indirectly, of substances or energy into the marine environment, including estuaries, which results or

51 The protection of marine living resources is treated in Chapter 8.

52 Art. 194(3).

53 Art. 195.

is likely to result in such deleterious effects as harm to living resources and marine life, hazards to human health, hindrance to marine activities, including fishing and other legitimate uses of the sea, impairment of quality for use of sea water and reduction of amenities'.[54]

Article 196 expands the scope of the definition in an unexpected way by calling for preventing, reducing and controlling pollution of the marine environment resulting from the 'use of technologies', without specifying what technologies are envisaged. It additionally prohibits 'the intentional or accidental introduction of species, alien or new, to a particular part of the marine environment, which may cause significant and harmful changes thereto'.

International cooperation both regionally and globally is presented as an obligation, explicitly with the aim of formulating and elaborating international rules and standards and 'recommended practices and procedures'.[55] Specific provisions govern cooperation in emergency situations.[56] States also are required to continuously monitor the risks or effects of pollution. In particular, they must 'keep under surveillance' the effects of any activities that they permit or in which they engage, in order to determine whether these activities are likely to pollute the marine environment.[57] The results obtained from such surveillance must be communicated to international organizations which should make them available to all states.[58] In addition, states should assess the potential effects of any activities that may cause substantial pollution and communicate the results of such assessments.[59] As a final element in the framework of international cooperation, the Convention foresees assistance to developing states in the fields of science and technology and preferential treatment for these states by international organizations.[60]

In 2016, the South China Sea Arbitration contributed to the interpretation of the environmental provisions of UNCLOS by confirming that their content is informed by other rules of international law (thus also alluding to their evolving character). Notably, the Tribunal interpreted the general obligation of Article 192 in light of subsequent provisions of Part XII (in particular Article 194(5)), the Convention on Biodiversity and the Convention on International Trade in Endangered Species of Wild Fauna and Flora. It concluded that the obligation to protect and preserve the marine environment extends to rare

54 Art. 1(4).
55 Art. 197.
56 Arts. 198–99.
57 Art. 204.
58 Art. 205.
59 Art. 206.
60 Arts. 202–03.

and fragile ecosystems, and to species that are internationally recognized as depleted, threatened, or endangered as well as their habitats.[61] Moreover, the Tribunal emphasized the importance of the duties to cooperate and coordinate for marine protection and preservation, which are embedded in Article 197 and Article 123, respectively. It alluded to a link between this responsibility and the communication of environmental impact assessments, and concluded that the latter is an absolute obligation under Article 206.[62]

More recently, the Commission of Small Island States on Climate Change and International Law (COSIS) has brought a request for an Advisory Opinion before ITLOS. It has requested what the specific obligations of State Parties to UNCLOS are, especially under Part XII, (1) to prevent, reduce and control pollution of the marine environment, and (2) to protect and preserve the marine environment as a result of climate change, such as ocean warming, sea level rise and ocean acidification, caused by greenhouse gas emissions into the atmosphere.

In its unanimous Advisory Opinion of May 21, 2024, the Tribunal found that, *inter alia*, anthropogenic GHG emissions into the atmosphere constitute pollution of the marine environment within the meaning of Article 1(1)(4) of UNCLOS; under Article 194(1), States Parties have the specific obligations to take all necessary measures to prevent, reduce and control marine pollution from anthropogenic GHG emissions, taking into account the best available science and the global temperature goal contained in the UNFCCC and the Paris Agreement of limiting the temperature increase to 1.5 degrees Celsius above pre-industrial levels; Article 192 encompasses the specific obligation to protect and preserve the marine environment from climate change impacts and ocean acidification; and obligations under Article 192 are subject to a stringent standard of due diligence, given the high risks of serious and irreversible harm to the marine environment from these impacts and acidification. This Advisory Opinion clearly has the potential to have a significant impact on the

---

61 *The South China Sea Arbitration* (The Republic of Philippines v. The People's Republic of China) (July 12, 2016) Award, para. 945.

62 ibid, para. 986. For an in-depth discussion of the South China Sea Arbitration and its impact on the interpretation of Chapter XII UNCLOS, see Yoshifumi Tanaka, 'The South China Sea arbitration: Environmental obligations under the Law of the Sea Convention' (2018) 27 RECIEL 90–96; See Chie Kojima, 'South China Sea Arbitration and the Protection of the Marine Environment: Evolution of unclos, Part XII Through Interpretation and the Duty to Cooperate' in *Asian Yearbook of International Law* (21 Brill 2015) 166. For a discussion of the possible consequences of the case, see Guanping Huo, Wangiang Li and Haoyu Tian, 'The Climate Advisory Opinion: A Medicine with Side-Effects?' in *Marine Policy* vol 156 (2023) 1–8.

implementation of environmental obligations under Part XII of UNCLOS, and will likely inform parallel advisory proceedings ongoing before the ICJ on climate change obligations.

UNCLOS identifies three states competent to exercise jurisdiction over matters of marine pollution: flag states, port states, and coastal states. One aspect common to the jurisdiction of all is the repeated obligation to take into account or enact and enforce internationally agreed rules and standards. In some cases, the Convention requires that national laws and measures 'shall be no less effective than international rules, standards and recommended practices and procedures',[63] whether the international rules, standards and recommended practices have been established before or after the adoption or entry into force of UNCLOS. Finally, states 'shall adopt laws and regulations and take other measures necessary to implement applicable international rules and standards established through competent international organizations or diplomatic conference to prevent and control pollution of the marine environment' from various sources.[64] The unusual feature of these obligations is that the state's duty to adopt laws and regulations conforming to the international rules and standards does not depend on its ratification of a particular agreement or its actual participation in the adoption of a rule or standard; it is enough that the international rules and standards be 'generally accepted'.[65] The process is thus one of elaboration and incorporation under the umbrella of UNCLOS, of a veritable code of rules and standards for the protection of the marine environment.

3.1 *Flag State Jurisdiction*

Pursuant to the detailed provisions of UNCLOS Article 217, states must ensure that ships under their jurisdiction and control comply with applicable international rules and standards and with flag state laws and regulations adopted in accordance with the Convention. They also shall take appropriate measures to ensure that ships they register or which fly their flag are prohibited from sailing unless they are in compliance with international rules and standards. Ships shall carry any certificates required by international law and be periodically inspected. In case of any violation, the flag state shall investigate and where appropriate institute proceedings regardless of where the violation or pollution occurred. Penalties must be adequate in severity to discourage violations wherever they occur. The 1993 Agreement to Promote Compliance with

---

63 Arts. 207(4), 208(5), 210(4), 211(1), 212(3).
64 Arts. 213–14, 216–20, 222.
65 Art. 211(2).

International Conservation and Management Measures by Fishing Vessels on the High Seas approved by the FAO Conference on November 24, 1993[66] reinforces the obligation of flag states to take such measures as may be necessary to ensure that fishing vessels entitled to fly their flag do not engage in any activity that undermines the effectiveness of international conservation measures (Article III (1)(a)). In particular, no state shall allow any fishing vessel entitled to fly its flag to be used for fishing on the high seas unless it has been authorized to do so by the appropriate authority of that state (Article III(2)).[67]

3.2 *Port State Jurisdiction*

Port states have jurisdiction, confirmed in Article 218, in cases where ships voluntarily enter a port or off-shore terminal. The state may undertake investigations and, where the evidence warrants, institute proceedings against the ship for any discharge on the high seas in violation of applicable international rules and standards. For discharges in the internal waters, territorial sea or exclusive economic zone of another state, the port state may open a proceeding only if requested by the other state or if the violation has caused or is likely to cause pollution of its own waters. Port states should respond also to requests from any state for investigation of pollution caused in its waters as well as requests from the flag state. Finally, the port state may prevent from sailing any foreign ships in violation of international rules and standards relating to seaworthiness that could thereby threaten damage to the environment, until the violations have been cured.

Port state exercise of this jurisdiction (port state control) is a crucial step towards the reinforcement of flag state responsibilities to comply with international rules and standards and the elimination of sub-standard ships. In effect, by allowing the inspection of foreign-flagged vessels, it can act as a safety net when shipowners, classification societies, insurers, or flag state administrators have in one way or another failed to comply with legal and technical regulations. As noted above, all countries have the right to inspect ships visiting their ports to ensure that they meet IMO requirements regarding safety and marine pollution prevention standards. Port authorities of different countries have concluded Memoranda of Understanding (MOUs) to improve and harmonize port state inspections and avoid distorting competition among ports. Such agreements also preempt unilateral approaches that could lead to

66 33 I.L.M. 968 (1994).

67 See also Lan Ngoc Nguyen, 'Flag States' Rights and Obligations under the Law of the Sea' in *The Development of the Law of the Sea by UNCLOS Dispute Settlement Bodies* (CUP 2023).

international conflict.[68] IMO has been fully involved in encouraging the establishment of these agreements.

Experience has shown that port state control works best when it is organized on a regional basis. MOUs generally require each maritime authority which is a signatory to the agreement to establish and maintain an effective system of port state control and set an annual required total of inspections of at least 10 percent of the estimated total number of foreign merchant ships entering the ports during the year. MOUs encourage exchange of information so that ships that have been inspected by one port state and found to be in compliance with all safety and marine pollution prevention rules are not subject to too frequent inspections, while ships presenting a hazard and those ships which have been reported by another port state as having deficiencies which need to be rectified will be targeted.

Western European national port authorities adopted the first Memorandum of Understanding on the Surveillance of Ships by Port States in 1982,[69] covering Europe and the North Atlantic. The primary objective of the fourteen signatories was to dissuade dangerous ships that could pollute the marine environment from frequenting European ports and adjacent waters. The contracting authorities agreed to enforce within their ports a body of international conventions regarding the security of ships and the prevention of pollution,[70] even if the flag state was not a contracting party. The parties harmonized their supervisory mechanisms both as to the means of control and the number of regulated ships, the target being 25 percennt of the ships frequenting European ports. In addition, the contracting maritime authorities agreed to exchange information and evidence regarding breaches of maritime rules and of pollution.

The first results from application of the Memorandum were very encouraging. During the initial four years following its entry into force, authorities inspected 38,000 ships or 21.5 percent of those entering European ports. Of these, they held 1500 in port because of infractions. Nearly one quarter (23.6 percent) were held for violation of norms concerning pollution and 13 percent

68 See Lee Kimball, Introductory Note, 'Memorandum of Understanding on Port State Control in the Caribbean Region' (1997) 36 I.L.M. 231.

69 This agreement, known as the 'Paris MOU' was signed on January 26, 1982 between national port authorities. It is thus not considered as an international treaty, but as a soft law instrument.

70 For example, the November 1, 1974 International Convention for the Safety of Human Life at Sea (SOLAS) and the November 2, 1973 MARPOL Convention (see n 27).

for irregular documents, more than half of which related to the 'international certificate' on oil pollution.[71]

The system of port state control expanded to other parts of the world and since 1992 the inspections cover not only technical requirements but also operational requirements. At present ships may be subject to a review of relevant certificates and documents on board the vessel, a cursory survey that may lead to more detailed inspection if clear grounds exist for doing so, and possible detention of the vessel until serious deficiencies are rectified. If the defects cannot be remedied in the port of inspection, the ship may proceed to another port, subject to appropriate conditions determined by the inspecting state's authorities to ensure that the vessel does not pose unreasonable danger to safety, health or the environment.[72]

Since the beginning of the 1990s, many regions have adopted MOUs on port state control. A Latin American Agreement (Acuerdo de Viña del Mar) was signed in 1992; an Asia-Pacific Memorandum of Understanding (Tokyo) in 1993; a Caribbean Memorandum of Understanding in 1996; a Mediterranean Memorandum of Understanding in 1997; an Indian Ocean Memorandum of Understanding on Port State Control in 1998; a Memorandum of Understanding for West and Central Africa in 1999, and an MOU on Port State Control in the Black Sea (Istanbul, 2000). In 2004, the Riyadh MOU was established between the United Arab Emirates, Bahrain, Saudi Arabia, Oman, Qatar and Kuwait. With this, the coverage of all areas of the world was completed.[73]

The process of elaborating an MOU can be illustrated by the process followed in West and Central Africa. In 1997, nineteen nations in the region agreed to work towards establishing a Port State Control (PSC) regime in the shortest possible time in order to eradicate sub-standard ships from the region. They agreed on a preliminary draft text of a Memorandum of Understanding (MOU) and a draft Training Programme. They also agreed to make every effort to put in place or strengthen competent maritime administrations in order to implement an effective PSC regime. International bodies such as IMO, the International Labour Organization (ILO), the United Nations Development Programme (UNDP), the Economic Commission for Africa (ECA), the International Association of Classification Societies (IACS), the International Transport

71 Jean-Luc Prat, 'Le Système Specifique de l'Europe du Nord-Ouest,' in *Droit de l'Environment Marin D* (SFDE, 1988) 92.

72 Kimball, *supra* n 68 at 232.

73 For a more in-depth discussion of port state jurisdiction in the context of pollution, see Robin Churchill, 'Port State Jurisdiction Relating to the Safety of Shipping and Pollution from Ships – What Degree of Extra-territoriality?' (2016) 31 The International Journal of Marine and Coastal Law 442.

Workers Federation (ITF), the Communauté Economique et Monétaire de l'Afrique Centrale (CEMAC) and other regional organizations supported this initiative, which resulted in final agreement on the MOU in 1999.

In 2016, an Agreement on Port State Measures (PSMA) entered into force, enacted out of concern for the 'detrimental effect on fish stocks, marine ecosystems and the livelihoods of legitimate fishers, and the increasing need for food security on a global basis'.[74] The PSMA is the first binding international agreement that attempts to combat illegal, unreported and unregulated (IUU) fishing, which it does by preventing vessels engaged in such activities from mooring in member states' ports and landing their catch.[75] The goal is to prevent IUU fishing at the beginning of the chain and thereby, in the long term, promoting the sustainable use and conservation of marine ecosystems and living marine resources.[76]

3.3 *Coastal State Jurisdiction*

Coastal states are granted extensive jurisdiction by UNCLOS Article 220 to combat pollution of the marine environment in their territorial seas and exclusive economic zones, supplementing the general grant of coastal state jurisdiction over these zones proclaimed by Article 21(1) and Article 56(1)(b)(iii). The legislative power of the coastal state to combat pollution by ships is affirmed for the territorial sea by Article 211(4) and for the exclusive economic zone by Article 211(5). The scope of authority over the two zones differs. For the more distant exclusive economic zone, the coastal state must adopt laws and regulations that conform and give effect to generally accepted international rules and standards. No such limitation appears on the jurisdiction of the coastal state for the more proximate twelve-mile territorial sea, except that laws and regulations governing the territorial sea must not hamper innocent passage of foreign vessels (Article 211(4)).

The interplay between coastal state regulation of environmental protection and innocent passage is not entirely clear. Article 19(2)(h) provides that any act of wilful and serious pollution contrary to the Convention shall be considered prejudicial to the peace, good order, or security of the coastal state and therefore is not innocent passage. It thus seems that the coastal state may enact the

---

74 Agreement on Port State Measures to Prevent, Deter and Eliminate Illegal, Unreported and Unregulated Fishing (adopted November 22, 2009, entered into force June 5, 2016) (PSMA) Preamble.

75 PSMA Art. 3.

76 PSMA Preamble; For a practical look at the PSMA, see Lonna Bethel, Henning Jessen and Johan Hollander, 'Implementing the Port State Measures Agreement to combat illegal, unreported and unregulated fishing in the Caribbean' (2021) 132 Marine Policy 1.

strictest possible measures against ships which engage in wilful and serious pollution and may enact other stringent local rules and regulations to prevent, reduce and control pollution, preventing non-innocent passage or taking other enforcement measures. It is less clear what measures a coastal state may take to reduce the risk of pollution by ships passing through the territorial sea. The Convention allows the coastal state to require use of sea lanes and traffic separation schemes by tankers, nuclear-powered ships and ships carrying nuclear or other inherently dangerous or noxious substances or materials. The implication is that the coastal state cannot bar such ships from the passage through the territorial sea regardless of the hazardous nature of the cargo being carried, provided there is no willful pollution. On the other hand, passage is defined as innocent if it is not prejudicial to, *inter alia*, the security of the coastal state. With the emergence of the concept of environmental security, coastal states may find objectionable the passage of ships carrying ultra-hazardous cargos.

Article 220 distinguishes several possibilities respecting the enforcement of norms against pollution. These follow the general approach in UNCLOS of diminishing coastal state competence the further the maritime zone is from the coast,[77] while other rules in the Convention are common to the exercise of jurisdiction by any of the interested states. Article 224 provides that the powers of enforcement against foreign vessels is a government function, to be exercised by officials or by warships, military aircraft, or other government ships or aircraft. Moreover, the exercise of enforcement powers must not endanger the safety or navigation.[78]

When the ship is voluntarily within a port of a state whose territorial waters or exclusive economic zone it is suspected of having polluted in violation of laws and regulations adopted in accordance with the Convention or applicable international rules and standards, the state may institute proceedings.[79] If the ship is navigating the territorial sea and there are clear grounds to believe that it has violated applicable norms against pollution, the coastal state may subject it to physical inspection, detention, and proceedings, where the evidence so warrants.[80]

Where the offense concerns the exclusive economic zone and the ship is navigating in the territorial sea or in the exclusive economic zone of the coastal state, the state may require the vessel to give information regarding its identity and port of registry, its last and its next port of call and other relevant

77 See Dinah Shelton and Gary Rose, 'Freedom of Navigation' (1977) 17 Santa Clara L. Rev. 523.

78 Art. 225.

79 Art. 220(1).

80 Art. 220(2).

information required to establish whether a violation has occurred. The laws, regulations and other measures adopted by all states shall require their registered ships to comply with requests from other states for information regarding suspected violations.[81]

If the coastal state has clear grounds for believing that a violation has resulted in a substantial discharge causing or threatening significant pollution to the marine environment, Article 220(5) permits the state to undertake physical inspection of the vessel. The following paragraph provides that if the discharge causes major damage or threat of major damage to the coastline or related interests of the coastal state, the state may institute proceedings, including detention of the vessel, in accordance with its laws. The vessel can be authorized to proceed, however, if there exist procedures foreseen in advance to assure compliance by a bond or other appropriate financial security.[82]

The provisions of Article 226 also apply where foreign vessels are the object of an investigation or an enforcement action, whether these occur in ports or on the sea. Physical inspection of a foreign vessel is limited to an examination of such certificates, records or other documents the vessel is required to carry; further inspection may be undertaken only when there are clear irregularities or omissions. Even in case of violation, a vessel cannot be detained unless it presents an unreasonable threat of damage to the marine environment. In such case, the flag state must be promptly notified. In no case may states discriminate in form or in fact against the vessels of any other state.[83]

The Convention also seeks to guarantee the interests of the flag state in cases where the coastal state institutes proceedings. Article 231 requires that the measures taken must be reported to the flag state. If the flag state itself institutes proceedings to impose penalties, the coastal state must suspend its proceedings, unless the violation took place within the territorial sea or relates to a case of major damage to the coastal state or, finally, if the flag state has failed repeatedly to enforce applicable international rules and standards.[84]

As regards the rules of liability, the Convention distinguishes between civil, criminal, and international liability. States are liable for damage or loss attributable to them arising from unlawful or excessive measures taken to apply the provisions of the Convention relating to protection of the marine environment. This liability falls within the internal legal order; it is explicitly provided that states shall allow recourse to their courts for actions in respect of such damage

---

81 Art. 220(3) and 220(4).

82 Art. 220(7).

83 Art. 227.

84 Art. 228.

or loss.[85] While this provision aims to deter over-reaching by the coastal state, its interests are also protected: nothing in the Convention may affect the ability to institute civil proceedings in respect of any claim for loss or damage resulting from pollution of the marine environment.[86] Criminal liability is foreseen in rules that distinguish the place of the harm: only monetary penalties may be imposed on foreign vessels for violations outside the territorial sea, but within the territorial sea criminal sanctions are permitted for willful and serious acts of pollution.[87]

International responsibility is governed by Article 235, which affirms that states shall be liable in accordance with international law for failure to fulfill their international obligations concerning the protection and preservation of the marine environment. States also must ensure the availability within their legal systems of procedures for prompt and adequate compensation or other relief in respect of damage caused by pollution by natural or juridical persons under their jurisdiction, being understood that states are to cooperate in the implementation and further development of international law in this field.

Finally, UNCLOS contains concessions to state sovereignty. By the terms of Article 236, the provisions of the Convention regarding the protection and preservation of the marine environment do not apply to any warship, naval auxiliary, or other vessels or aircraft being used by the government in non-commercial service. This serious derogation is not only irreconcilable with the rest of the Convention, it is incompatible with the usual principles of immunity which provide only for exemption from enforcement procedures, not from applicability of the law. Logically and according to general international law, there is no reason why government ships and aircraft should be exempt from marine pollution rules, even though they may be immune from otherwise applicable enforcement procedures. Undoubtedly, the drafters of the Convention sought to remedy this loophole by inserting the final sentence of Article 236 which requires states to take 'appropriate measures not impairing operations or operational capabilities of such vessels or aircraft owned or operated by it, that such vessels or aircraft act in a manner consistent, so far as is reasonable and practicable, with this Convention'. It is difficult to see in this tortured phraseology anything other than a reaffirmation of state sovereignty and an

85 Art. 232.

86 Art. 229.

87 Art. 230.

invitation to military or other state actors to ignore applicable environmental norms.[88]

Protection through creation of marine protected areas (MPAs) is a form of protection that has steadily covered more regions of the oceans, and which are predominantly found in EEZs. There is no singular definition of MPAs in international law, but one often used is 'a geographically defined area, which is designed or regulated and managed to achieve specific conservation objectives'.[89] The authority to create MPAs under national jurisdiction is not expressly stated in UNCLOS, but states have the power to create them in their territorial waters pursuant to their sovereign rights under Part II. They also have this authority in their EEZ under Part V of UNCLOS, since their states also have sovereign rights to conserve and manage their natural resources.[90]

The *Chagos Marine Protected Area Arbitration* contributed to the clarification of the obligations that states have when they declare MPAs. This case involved competing claims to coastal state status, which in turn called into doubt the authority to create an MPA. Although this issue was not resolved, an Arbitral Tribunal clarified that the power to establish MPAs is coupled with obligations under UNCLOS in relation to states whose rights and interests are affected by the MPA.[91] In particular, Article 2(3), Article 56(2) and Article 194(4) oblige states declaring MPAs to act in good faith and have due regard to these rights and interests. At minimum, this requires both adequate consultation and balancing between competing rights, based on an evaluation of the extent of the interference, the availability of alternatives, and the importance of the rights and policies at issue.[92] States declaring MPAs must also endeavour to harmonize their policies with the affected states under Article 194(1), though the Tribunal considered that this merely requires 'best efforts' and has no particular deadline.[93]

88 See also Lan Ngoc Nguyen, 'Coastal State's Rights and Obligations under the Law of the Sea' in *The Development of the Law of the Sea by UNCLOS Dispute Settlement Bodies* (CUP 2023).

89 Art. 2, Convention on Biological Diversity.

90 For a discussion of MPAs on the High Seas, see Wen Duan, *The International Legal Regime Relating to Marine Protected Areas in Areas beyond National Jurisdiction: Identifying and Addressing Gaps* (Brill 2022) ; for a discussion on the circumstances relevant for the establishment of MPAs, see Justin Alger, *Conserving the Oceans: The Politics of Large Marine Protected Areas* (OUP 2021).

91 *Chagos Marine Protected Area Arbitration* (Mauritius v. UK) (March 18, 2015), Award, para. 521.

92 ibid, para. 534.

93 ibid, para. 539.

4 Comprehensive Regional Treaties

The United Nations Environment Program launched its program for 'regional seas' in 1974, aiming to create a treaty system for each targeted area. The systems consist of a plan and a framework convention for the protection of the marine environment, accompanied by special protocols devoted to problems such as the dumping of wastes and cooperation in case of accident or land-based pollution. The earliest of these treaty systems concerns the Protection of the Mediterranean Sea against Pollution.[94] It has since been amended and renamed Convention for the Protection of the Marine Environment and the Coastal Region of the Mediterranean. The main treaty is accompanied by two protocols signed the same day, one concerning dumping from ships and aircraft,[95] the other concerning cooperation in combating pollution by oil and other harmful substances in cases of emergency.[96] Five additional protocols, subsequently concluded, relate to land-based pollution,[97] to Mediterranean specially protected areas[98] – replaced by another instrument[99] – to pollution resulting from exploration and exploitation of the seabed,[100] and to pollution by transboundary movements of hazardous wastes.[101] The Protocol on land-based pollution was amended March 7, 1996 (Syracuse) and its title changed significantly into Protocol for the Protection of the Mediterranean Sea against Pollution from Land-Based Sources and Activities. The modified text notes the increasing environmental pressures resulting from human activities in the Mediterranean Sea Area, particularly from industrialization

94 Barcelona, February 16, 1976.

95 Protocol for the Prevention of Pollution of the Mediterranean Sea by Dumping from Ships and Aircraft, Barcelona, February 16, 1976, EMuT 976:14.

96 Protocol concerning Co-operation in Combating Pollution of the Mediterranean Sea by Oil and other Harmful Substances in Cases of Emergency, Barcelona, February 16, 1976, EMuT 976:15.

97 Protocol for the Protection of the Mediterranean Sea against Pollution from Land-Based Sources, Athens, May 17, 1980, EMuT, 976:13/C.

98 Protocol concerning Mediterranean Specially Protected Areas, Geneva, April 3, 1982, EMut, 982:26/D.

99 Protocol concerning Specially Protected Areas and Biological Diversity in the Mediterranean, Barcelona, June 10, 1995, EmuT: 976:13/F.

100 Protocol for the Protection of the Mediterranean Sea against Pollution resulting from Exploration and Exploitation of the Continental Shelf and the Seabed and its Subsoil, Madrid October 14, 1994, EMuT, 976:13/E.

101 Protocol on the Prevention of Pollution of the Mediterranean Sea by Transboundary Movements of Hazardous Wastes and their Disposal, Izmir, October 1, 1996, UNEP(OCA)/MED/IG.4/4, October 11, 1996.

and urbanization, as well as the seasonal increase in the coastal population due to tourism.

The original Barcelona Convention was revised and amended by an agreement of June 10, 1996,[102] which expands its scope to coastal areas, integrates principles such as the precautionary principle, the polluter-pays principle, and public information and introduces into it the obligation to prepare environmental impact assessments as well as to adopt integrated management for coastal areas. The amendments also oblige the contracting parties to submit reports on the implementation of the Convention. In sum, the Barcelona Convention was revised substantially, taking into account developments in international environmental law.

By now, a large part of the world's oceans has been covered by UNEP-sponsored treaty systems.[103] Taken together more than 146 states today cooperate in UNEP's regional seas program. The details of the regional conventions diverge although there are commonalities. All the systems address emergency situations due to their importance. The Barcelona system has seven protocols, making it the most detailed regulatory system, while the regional convention for the South-East Pacific provides the most precise rules concerning land-based pollution.

Besides the regional seas programme, several important regional agreements were concluded after 1990. The Convention for the Protection of the Marine Environment in the North-East Atlantic replaced both the 1972 Oslo Convention on dumping and the 1974 Paris Convention on land-based pollution, following a 1990 decision of the state parties.[104] The earlier agreements had a similar geographic coverage, an established commission that met annually, and a joint secretariat based in London. The other significant conventions protect the Baltic Sea against pollution, replacing a 1974 instrument, and the Black Sea. The first of the three Conventions is of particular importance, however, not only because of the large area covered, but also because it incorporates many modern trends of international environmental law.

The Convention on the North-East Atlantic, adopted in Paris on September 22, 1992, proclaims in its preamble two important principles. The first recognizes the inherent value of the marine environment of the North-East Atlantic;

---

102 Doc. UNEP(OCA)/Med.IG.6/7.

103 For a list of which regions are covered by which kind of UNEP-treaties, visit <www.unep.org/topics/ocean-seas-and-coasts/regional-seas-programme/regional-seas-programme>.

104 Between 1984 and 1990, the North Sea coastal states organized three ministerial conferences to update the two instruments (Bremen, 1984; London 1987; and The Hague, 1990). Not all states parties participated in the meetings.

this implies that it should be protected independently of all direct utility for the contracting states. The second principle, already mentioned, recognizes that UNCLOS Part XII contains norms of customary international law.

Several environmental principles are incorporated in the body of the Convention, including the polluter pays principle (Art. 2(2)(b)) and the precautionary principle. As previously noted, the 1990 Declaration of the International North Sea Conference contained the first international formulation of the precautionary principle. Article 2(2)(a) of the Paris Convention defines it.[105] The Convention definition, like that of the Rio Declaration, focuses on the uncertainty of a causal relationship between inputs and effects, establishing a test of 'reasonable grounds for concern' as the basis for action. 'Reasonableness' may require some objective evidence, but no conclusive proof is required. The latter would be particularly difficult to obtain where an area as vast as the marine environment is involved, or when new products or substances are being dumped in a river far upstream.

The Convention defines two widely used terms. The first, 'best available techniques' is 'the latest stage of development (state of the art) of processes, of facilities or of methods of operation which indicate the practical suitability of a particular measure for limiting discharges, emissions and waste'. Special consideration is given to comparable processes, facilities, or methods, to technological advances and changes in scientific knowledge and understanding, to the economic feasibility, to the characteristics of plants and to the nature and volume of the discharges and emissions (Appendix I).

The term 'best environmental practice' is defined as the application of the most appropriate combination of environmental control measures and strategies, ranging from education and information to establishing a system of licensing. Here again, particular consideration should be given to specific criteria, such as the environmental hazard of the product or activity and its ultimate disposal, the scale of use, the substitution by less polluting activities or substances and benefit to the environment and social and economic implications (Appendix I).

The body of the Convention outlines the obligations of contracting parties regarding pollution from land-based and offshore sources, dumping, incineration, installations and pipelines from which substances or energy reach the maritime area. Two land-locked countries, Luxembourg and Switzerland, have become party to the Convention, taking into account their contribution to the pollution carried by the Rhine River to the North Sea.

105 See Chapter 4.B.2.

Detailed regulations are found in four annexes. Annex I, related to the prevention and elimination of pollution from land-based sources, provides that the parties shall adopt programs and measures using best available techniques for point sources and best environmental practices for point and diffuse sources. Point source discharges into the maritime area and releases into water or air which reach and may affect the maritime area, shall be strictly subject to authorization or regulation by the competent national authorities, implementing relevant decisions of the Commission. The Commission also draws up plans for the reduction and phasing out of hazardous substances and for the reduction of inputs of nutrients from urban, municipal, industrial and other sources.

Annex II concerns the prevention and elimination of pollution by dumping or incineration. When compared to the Oslo Convention, the main innovation is the prohibition on the dumping of all wastes or other matter, with specified exceptions (dredged material, inert materials of natural origin, fish waste, etc.). Permitted dumping is subject to prior authorization or regulation by the competent authorities, in accordance with the relevant rules of the Commission. The dumping of low and intermediate level radioactive substances, including wastes, is prohibited.

Annex III prohibits any dumping of wastes or other matter from offshore installations. The use of substances on offshore sources or any discharge or emission which may reach and affect the maritime area are strictly subject to authorization or regulation by the competent national authorities in conformity with the Convention and the rules which may be adopted under it.

Each of the two former Conventions created a commission (OSCOM for the convention on dumping and PARCOM for that on land-based pollution). The 1992 Paris Convention set up another Commission to supervise the implementation of the Convention and generally review the condition of the maritime area, the effectiveness of the measures being adopted, the priorities and the need for any additional or different measures (Art. 10). It can adopt amendments to the Convention and its Annexes and Appendices. The contracting parties report to it at regular intervals on the measures they have taken to implement the Convention, including, in particular measures taken to prevent and punish conduct in contravention of its provisions (Art. 22). The Commission assesses compliance by contracting parties on the basis of their periodic reports. When appropriate, it decides upon and calls for steps to bring about full compliance with the Convention and the decisions adopted thereunder, and promotes the implementation of recommendations, including measures to assist a contracting party to carry out its obligations (Art. 23).

The Convention on the Protection of the Marine Environment of the Baltic Sea Area (Helsinki, April 9, 1992) is the second instrument to replace a former one. The earlier Convention was considered as particularly advanced when adopted in March 1974. Nevertheless, progress in knowledge concerning marine pollution made it necessary to adopt a replacement treaty. Initially, the states adopted a Baltic Sea Declaration (1990) with a Joint Comprehensive Program aiming to restore the Baltic Sea Area to a sound ecological balance.

The Convention is similar to the treaty on the North-East Atlantic: it concerns all forms of pollution; it announces the principles of precaution (Art. 3(2)) and polluter pays (Art. 3(4)) in comparable terms; it prescribes the use of the Best Environmental Technology and of the Best Environmental Practice (Art. 3(3)) defining them as well as the criteria for their use (Annex II). It also provides that information shall be made available to the public, but limits accessible information to permits issued, the conditions required to be met, the results of water and effluent sampling, and water quality objectives. The means of obtaining such information also are restricted to all reasonable times, with reasonable facilities, on payment of reasonable charges (Art. 17). Information related to intellectual property including industrial and commercial secrecy or national security and confidential personal data may be withheld (Art. 18).

The 1992 Baltic Sea Convention contains several innovations. It stresses the need to prevent and eliminate pollution in order 'to promote the ecological restoration of the Baltic Sea Area and the preservation of its ecological balance' (Art. 3(1)). It reflects the importance of the catchment area of this sea: measures relevant to combating the pollution from land-based sources shall be taken by each contracting party in the catchment area (Art. 6) and in particular, they are obliged to ban listed substances or groups of substances not only from the sea, but also from its catchment area. The use of such substances, including pesticides, must be minimized and, whenever possible, banned in the same zone (Annex I, parts 2 and 3). Permits for industrial plants also are determined for the entire catchment area (Annex II), as is the scope of information to be made available to the public (Art. 17(1)).

Article 24 is noteworthy as a step forward in the definition of international law rules for environmental responsibility. The contracting parties undertake jointly to develop and accept rules concerning responsibility for damage resulting from acts or omissions in contravention of the Convention including, *inter alia*, limits of responsibility, criteria and procedures for the determination of liability, and available remedies (Art. 25). This approach is useful in identifying the source of responsibility as duties owed under the Convention. Damage caused by the breach of Convention obligations gives rise to responsibility.

In its remaining provisions, the Convention regulates the usual sources of marine environmental harm, although its approach is often different from that of the other treaties concerning regional seas. In addition to rules concerning vessel-source pollution (Art. 8 and Annex IV), it foresees special measures to combat harm caused by pleasure craft (Art. 9). It prohibits incineration in general, not specifying wastes and dumping of wastes and other matter in the sea (Art. 11). Disposal of dredged materials at sea is permitted if a prior special permit has been obtained in accordance with specified conditions (Annex V).

The Baltic Marine Environment Protection Commission (HELCOM), established by the 1974 Convention, is maintained. It meets at least once a year, and its functions follow the pattern of international bodies rather than the more innovative North-East Atlantic Commission. The Baltic Commission continuously observes the implementation of the Convention, makes recommendations, and promotes cooperation (Arts. 19–20). The contracting parties report to it at regular intervals on the legal, regulatory and other measures taken for the implementation of the Convention and of recommendations adopted thereunder, on their effectiveness and on the problems encountered in their implementation (Art. 16). No specific review of the reports is foreseen, however, except that the Commission can ask the parties to provide information on discharge permits, emission data or data on environmental quality, as far as available (Art. 16(2)). The most important task of the Commission is to define pollution control criteria, objectives for the reduction of pollution, and objectives concerning measures taken (Art. 29(1) and Annex III). An example of the way HELCOM does this is the Baltic Sea Action Plan, adopted in 2007, to restore the environmental status of the Baltic Sea. It has four distinct goals: improve biodiversity, lessening eutrophication, lowering the amounts of hazardous substances and litter and using environmentally sustainable sea-based activities. It has been updated since and aims to have all measures be implemented at the latest by 2030.

Six coastal states adopted the Convention on the Protection of the Black Sea against Pollution at Bucharest on April 21, 1992. It follows the pattern established by the UNEP regional seas program – consisting of a framework convention completed by three protocols – without being integrated into that program. The general undertaking is to prevent, reduce and control pollution in order to protect and preserve the marine environment of the Black Sea. The area of application includes the territorial sea and the exclusive economic zone of each contracting party in the Black Sea (Art. 1), but the adverse effects of pollution within the internal waters on the marine environment also must be taken into account (Art. 5(1)).

The Convention's principles that aim to protect the Black Sea marine environment against pollution and polluting activities derive, in large part from the rules of UNCLOS and comparable regional sea treaties (Arts. 6–12), but two original provisions are added. The first concerns pollution by hazardous substances and matter: each contracting party shall prevent in the Black Sea any introduction of substances or matter listed in the annex to the Convention (mercury, cadmium, persistent carcinogenic substances, organohalogen compounds) (Art. 6). Secondly, states parties must combat pollution by wastes in transboundary movement (Art. 14).

Some of the terminology used by formerly communist regimes appears in the Convention: Article 3 speaks of full equality in rights and duties, respect for national sovereignty and independence, non-interference in internal affairs and mutual benefit (Art. 3). The weak institutional mechanisms set up by the Convention may be another heritage of the previous era. The Convention defines the functions of the Commission and of the Meeting of the parties only vaguely and provides no real supervision of implementation. In addition, decisions and recommendations of the Commission must be adopted unanimously (Art. 18).

The first of the three Protocols, adopted on the same day, concerns the protection of the Black Sea marine environment against pollution from land-based sources. It aims to prevent, reduce and control pollution caused by discharges from rivers, canals, coastal establishments, other artificial structures, outfalls or run-off, as well as pollution transported by the atmosphere (Art. 1). It applies to the waters landward of the baseline and in the case of fresh-water courses, to the fresh-water limit.

The protocol uses the technique of lists: the parties undertake to prevent and eliminate pollution caused by hazardous substances and matter listed in Annex I, while reducing and, whenever possible, eliminating, pollution from land-based sources by substances listed in Annex II. Annex III determines the conditions under which states parties may issue permits for the discharge of wastes containing substances and matter included in both lists. Thus, the Protocol contains no prohibitions on discharges: it only submits them to authorization. Uniform emission standards and timetables for the implementation of the programs and measures will be fixed by the contracting parties, who also will define pollution prevention criteria (Art. 6).

The second additional instrument to the Black Sea Convention is the Protocol on Cooperation in Combating Pollution of the Black Sea Marine Environment by Oil and Other Harmful Substances in Emergency Situations. Like other earlier agreements, it provides for the preparation of contingency plans, the reporting of accidents and the notification of other states. Its Annex contains detailed prescriptions, to be given to the masters of vessels and the pilots of aircraft, concerning the reports to be made.

The third Protocol, on the Protection of the Black Sea Marine Environment Against Pollution and Dumping, is also similar to earlier international instruments. It prohibits dumping of wastes or other matter listed in Annex I and mandates that national authorities issue a prior special permit for dumping of wastes or other matter listed in Annex II and a prior general permit for the dumping of all other wastes or matter. Annex III adds prescriptions which should be applied in issuing permits for dumping at sea, relating to the characteristics and composition of the matter and those of the dumping site and disposal method.

In sum, maritime pollution agreements increasingly show uniform patterns based upon UNCLOS. The primary concerns, revealed by a comparison of their provisions, are accidental pollution and prevention of pollution at source, including land-locked states through which watercourses flow that may carry pollution to maritime areas. The result is a holistic approach to maritime pollution linked to a more general integrated approach to environmental protection.

5 Different Forms of Pollution

5.1 *Vessel Source Pollution*

Certain longstanding and formerly-accepted practices on the part of maritime vessels are among the main sources of marine pollution: dumping of wastes in the ocean, the discharge of various forms of oil, including used oil, rinsing of tanker containers, and the release of sea water serving as ballast in empty tankers. When accidental pollution is added, coming from grounded oil tankers or the loss of cargoes containing dangerous substances, the result is a shocking amount of discharge into the oceans. In 2022, just the amount of oil ending up in the ocean from oil spills was 15,000 tonnes.[106]

The general framework of international norms concerning this problem is outlined by UNCLOS Articles 194(3)(b), 211, and 217–221. The provision first cited summarizes the problem, providing that the measures taken to enforce the Convention should include those designed to minimize to the fullest possible extent ‘pollution from vessels, in particular measures for preventing accidents and dealing with emergencies, ensuring the safety of operations at

106 ITOPF, *Oil Tanker Spill Statistics 2022* (ITOPF Ltd. 2023) 4.

sea, preventing intentional and unintentional discharges, and regulating the design, construction, equipment, operation and manning of vessels'.

Article 211 entirely concerns vessel-source pollution. It reaffirms the legislative mandate and obligation of states to prevent, reduce, and control pollution of the marine environment. Paragraph one emphasizes the role of international rules and standards which states shall establish, 'acting through the competent international organization or general diplomatic conference'. States also should promote the adoption, as appropriate, of routing systems designed to minimize the threat of accidents which might cause pollution.

The remaining parts of Article 211 mandate state laws and regulations to combat pollution by vessels registered by them or flying their flag. The same rules can be imposed on foreign vessels entering coastal state ports or internal waters. Similarly, coastal states can adopt laws and regulations to prevent, reduce and control pollution of the marine environment by foreign vessels within their territorial sea and their exclusive economic zone. However, for the exclusive economic zone, these norms shall conform to and give effect to generally accepted international rules and standards. Those applicable to their flag ships may be stricter, but they shall 'at least have the same effect' as international rules. When the international rules and standards are inadequate to meet special circumstances in an exclusive economic zone or part of it, the coastal state that exercises jurisdiction over the zone may enact special measures to prevent pollution from vessels. In such case, the competent international organization shall be consulted and may decide if the situation in the zone corresponds to the claimed oceanographic and ecological conditions. Local laws and regulations do not become applicable to foreign vessels until fifteen months after submission of the communication to the organization.[107]

The various provisions of UNCLOS relating to jurisdiction over vessel violations of environmental norms have been supplemented by a global convention and by several conventions applying to regional seas. The general instrument, the International Convention for the Prevention of Pollution by Ships (MARPOL) has as its objective 'the complete elimination of intentional pollution of the marine environment by oil and other harmful substances and the minimization of accidental discharge of such substances'.[108] MARPOL and its 1978 protocol replaced an earlier 1954 Convention which also has been amended several times. Together, the current law makes up an impressive body of the main conventions, protocols, annexes which are accompanied by appendices and many resolutions. Several of the resolutions contain important

107 Art. 211(6)(a).

108 November 2, 1973, amended by Protocol adopted February 17, 1978.

recommendations directed at the International Maritime Organization and its participating states.

MARPOL applies to ships, the term being defined in Article 2(4) as a vessel of any type whatsoever operating in the marine environment, including hydrofoil boats, air-cushion vehicles, submersibles, floating craft and fixed or floating platforms. Pollution itself is not defined, but its elements are found in the definition of discharge. This term means any release from a ship, whatever its cause, including escape, disposal, spilling, leaking, pumping, emitting or emptying.[109] Dumping is excluded,[110] however, as is the release of harmful substances directly arising from the exploration, exploitation and processing of sea-bed mineral resources or legitimate scientific research into pollution abatement or control.[111] Article 3(3) of the Convention also excludes government, non-commercial vessels from its coverage, in language identical to that found in the later-adopted UNCLOS.

The primary obligation of states parties to the MARPOL Convention, contained in Article 1, is to give effect to its provisions and its annexes, an obligation which exists under general international law even without an explicit statement to that effect. Article 4 adds that any violation of the requirements of the Convention shall be prohibited and sanctioned by legislation enacted by the authority over the ship, that is, the flag state. This competence is exclusive on the high seas; in other zones, either the flag state or the coastal state may exercise jurisdiction. In case the coastal state chooses not to institute proceedings, it must furnish the flag state with the information and evidence in its possession regarding the violation. In all cases, the sanctions specified by local law shall be adequate in severity to remedy violations of the Convention and equally severe irrespective of where the violations occur. MARPOL also reaffirms the police powers of the port state where a ship is found: its authorities can inspect the ship not only to verify its documentation, but to determine whether it discharged harmful substances in violation of the Convention. If a violation is uncovered, a report is forwarded to the flag state in order for appropriate action to be instituted pursuant to Article 4.[112] Whenever an incident occurs involving the actual or probable discharge into the sea of a harmful substance or containing such a substance, MARPOL requires the master of the

109 Art. 2(3).

110 Art. 2(3)(a), adding in subparagraph (b) that '... discharge does not include (i) dumping within the meaning of the Convention on the Prevention of Marine Pollution by Dumping of Wastes and Other Matter ...'.

111 Art. 2(3)(b).

112 Art. 6(2).

ship which is involved or other person having charge of the ship to prepare a report for the state administering the vessel as well as any other state that could be affected by the incident.[113] Other rules are deferred for inclusion in the annexes, no doubt because of their highly technical nature and because there is a simplified procedure for their modification.[114]

The governing scheme of MARPOL is the use of Annexes containing regulations according to the type of pollutant. Thus, Annex I governs oil, Annex II concerns control of pollution by noxious liquid in bulk (e.g. acetone, acrylic acid, ammonia, benzene, formaldehyde), Annex III applies to 'harmful substances carried by sea in packaged forms or in freight containers, portable tanks or road and rail tank wagons', Annex IV controls sewage, Annex V regulates garbage and Annex VI governs air pollution from ships. Annexes III, IV, V and VI are optional.

Annex I is by far the most complex and detailed. The general principle established is that discharge into the sea of oil or oily mixtures is prohibited except under strictly controlled conditions. The conditions vary depending upon whether the vessel is or is not an oil tanker; if it is not, its size is determinative. Discharges are prohibited everywhere, but in specially threatened areas (such as the Mediterranean, the Baltic, the Black, and the Red Seas, the Gulf areas and several others) they are even stricter. However, all prohibitions may be suspended when necessary to secure the safety of a ship or save life at sea. Furthermore, numerous provisions that have been modified by an Amendment to the Annex,[115] concern the construction of oil tankers, the construction of facilities for loading and discharge of oil, and the retention of oil on board ships. In 2010, a chapter was added to protect the Antarctic from heavy grade oils, by prohibiting certain (crude) oils from being transported in bulk in the area as cargo. Of course, this does not apply to vessels engaged in the securing of ships or in a search and rescue operation.[116] The Convention was amended again in 2021, including the Arctic region in the prohibition of these fuels from July 1, 2024 or July 1, 2029, depending on whether the Polar Code applies to the ships in question.[117]

113 Art. 8 and Protocol I.

114 Arts. 16(2)(f)(II) and (III).

115 September 7, 1984.

116 Amendments to the Annex of the Protocol of 1997 to Amend MARPOL 73/78 (adopted March 26, 2010) Resolution MEPC.189(60) Regulation 43.

117 Amendments to the Annex of the Protocol of 1997 to Amend MARPOL 73/78 (adopted June 17, 2021) Resolution MEPC.329(76) Regulation 43A.; For more on the Polar Code, see the end of this subsection.

The regulations of Annex II regarding transportation of noxious liquid in bulk divide the substances into four categories. Those found in category A present a major hazard to either marine resources or human health or could cause serious harm to amenities or other legitimate uses of the sea. In principle they should not be discharged. Annex II establishes specific conditions for the discharge of substances classified in categories B, C and D and particularly severe conditions are imposed to protect the Baltic and Black Seas. The appendices to this Annex list the noxious liquid substances and the category for each. A revised Annex on Bulk Liquids and Gas (2003) incorporates all amendments that have been adopted on this topic since the MARPOL Convention entered into force in 1983 and deletes outdated requirements.

The optional Annexes III to V, concerning container cargo, sewage and garbage, contain technical prescriptions for combating pollution from these sources; special zones also are established where discharge of garbage is not permitted and the discharge of sewage and plastics generally is prohibited.

Under the optional Annex VI, Emission Control Areas can be established, such as, for example, will be the case for the whole of the Mediterranean Sea starting from May 1, 2025.[118] In Emission Control Areas (ECAS), the permitted levels of sulfur and/or nitrogen oxides are restricted. Outside of these ECAS, Annex VI still only allows for 0.5 percent sulfur content in fuel oils. Besides providing for the possibility of establishing Emission Control Areas, Annex VI contains other measures added in 2011 on energy efficiency of large ships to reduce the amount of greenhouse gas emissions from vessels.[119]

Amendments to MARPOL 73/78 adopted in 1992 require the application of the double hull or equivalent design standards to existing single hull oil tankers when they reach a certain age. Other rules, adopted April 27, 2001, provide for an accelerated phasing-out scheme for single hull oil tankers.[120] Seriously concerned by shipping accidents involving oil tankers and the associated pollution of its coast-lines, the EC decided to support the IMO actions by upgrading and/or phasing out existing ships.[121]

In the context of MARPOL, the IMO Assembly has adopted Guidelines for the Designation of Special Areas. A 'Particularly Sensitive Sea Area' is one that

118 Amendments to the Annex of the Protocol of 1997 to Amend MARPOL 73/78 (adopted December 16, 2022) Resolution MEPC.361(79) MEPC 79/15/Add.1 Annex 3.

119 Amendments to the Annex of the Protocol of 1997 to Amend MARPOL 73/78 (adopted July 15, 2011) Resolution MEPC.203(62) MEPC 62/24/Add.1 Annex 19.

120 Adopted by the 46th session of the Marine Environment Protection Committee of the International Maritime Organization by Resolution MEPC 95(46), in force September 1, 2002.

121 Regulation No 417/2002 of February 18, 2002, O.J. L 64 (3/7/02).

needs special protection through the IMO because of its significance for ecological, socio-economic, or scientific reasons and that may be vulnerable to damage by shipping activities. It took some years before any areas were identified after the adoption of the guidelines in 1991, but between 1997 and now the number of areas with this definition has steadily grown.

Further measures to combat vessel source pollution were adopted by the IMO on October 5, 2001, when it concluded the International Convention on the Control of Harmful Anti-Fouling Systems.[122] This convention aims to protect the marine environment from toxic paint or other means of preventing marine organisms from attaching to ships' hulls. Preventing the encrustation of ships' hulls with marine life, such as barnacles, is necessary to ensure that ships can move smoothly and quickly through the water. Such encrustation or fouling will slow down the ship and cause it to use more fuel, thereby causing both commercial and environmental problems. The primary obligation of States Parties to the Convention is to prohibit or restrict the use of the harmful anti-fouling systems listed in Annex I, which were leaching into the water and causing serious harm to marine life and possibly to humans eating affected seafood. The only item on the initial list was fouling systems with organotins acting as biocides, banned in systems as of January 1, 2003, but in 2021, anti-fouling systems containing the biocide cybutryne were added to the list, being outlawed as of January 1, 2023.

The Convention on the Protection of the Marine Environment of the Baltic Sea, March 22, 1974, was the first regional marine treaty to be adopted. A large part of its regulations concern pollution from vessels. The 1992 Convention on the Protection of the Marine Environment of the Baltic Sea Area which replaced it,[123] includes special provisions (Art. 8 and Annex IV) relating to vessel pollution. Article 8 provides that the contracting parties shall develop and apply uniform requirements for the provision of reception facilities for ship-generated wastes. Annex IV invites the parties to promote the development of international rules including the promotion of the use of Best Available Technology and Best Environmental Practice. The Convention refers to the annexes of MARPOL 73/78, with the exception of specific provisions concerning sewage which are included in Regulation 5.

Safety at sea, especially with regard to ships carrying hazardous cargoes, is a major topic within the IMO. In January 2001, amendments to the IMO SOLAS Convention made mandatory an International Code for the Safe Carriage of

---

122 International Convention on the Control of Harmful Anti-Fouling Systems (adopted October 5, 2001, entered into force September 17, 2008) 3356 UNTS.

123 Helsinki, April 9, 1992, EMuT 992:28.

Packaged Irradiated Nuclear Fuel,[124] Plutonium, High-Legal Radioactive Waste on Board Ships. Its provisions include shipboard emergency plans, notification in the event of an incident, training, cargo securing arrangements, and damage stability. Shortly thereafter, the *Castor*, a fully laden oil tanker, discovered structural damage while in the Mediterranean Sea and sought shelter to transfer its cargo and conduct repairs. Fear of potential harm caused states to refuse entry into various ports and waters. IMO has thus placed the issue of providing shelter for stricken vessels on its agency as a priority matter.

In contrast to the Baltic Sea Convention, the regional sea conventions drafted under the auspices of UNEP do not contain rules additional to those set out in MARPOL 73/78. Instead, they generally declare that the states parties shall take all appropriate measures conforming to international law to prevent, abate, combat and control pollution caused by ships and ensure effective implementation for the zones in question of applicable international rules relating to this type of pollution.[125] The 1981 Lima Convention for the Protection of the Marine Environment and Coastal Area of the South-East Pacific notably contained this obligation in Article 4(b), although formulated differently. It adds that the measures to be taken by the states parties shall aim, in particular, at preventing accidents, managing emergency situations, and assuring the safety of operations at sea by preventing intentional discharges, as well as by regulating the design, construction, crew, utilization and equipment of ships in conformity with international rules and standards.

In 2017, the International Code for Ships Operating in Polar Waters (the Polar Code) came into force, covering all matters relating to safety of ships in the polar regions. It concerns persons on board, the environment, and the ship itself. The Polar Code is based on MARPOL and SOLAS, and expressly recognizes the fact that more safety on board will have a positive impact for the protection of the environment.[126] The Polar Code therefore takes a holistic approach to protection on all fronts in the polar regions.[127] Part I-A and part II-A respectively deal with safety measures and pollution prevention. These

124 International Convention for the Safety of Human Life at Sea, November 1, 1974.

125 Such provisions are, for example, found in: Article 6 of the 1976 Barcelona Convention for the Mediterranean Sea; Article 4 of the 1978 Kuwait Convention for the Gulf; Article 5 of the 1981 Abidjan Convention on West and Central Africa; Article 4 of the 1982 Jeddah Convention on the Red Sea; Article 5 of the 1983 Cartagena Convention on the Caribbean; Article 6 of the 1986 Noumea Convention on the South Pacific Region.

126 International Code for Ships Operating in Polar Waters (adopted November 21, 2014 and May 15, 2015, entered into force January 1, 2017) Resolution MSC.385(94) and MEPC.264(68) (Polar Code) Preamble para. 5.

127 ibid, preamble para. 6 and introduction para. 1.

parts are binding. Parts I-B and II-B deal with the same subjects, but merely contain recommendatory provisions.

5.2 *Marine Pollution Transported by Air*

Beyond the principles governing the protection of the atmosphere and climate detailed in Chapter 12, it should be noted here that basic rules relative to air pollution generally apply to the marine environment as well as to land. Nonetheless, UNCLOS contains two provisions directed towards combating air-borne pollution. According to Article 212, states shall take the measures necessary to prevent, reduce and control atmospheric pollution. These measures shall include the adoption of laws and regulations applicable to the air space under their sovereignty and to vessels flying their flag or vessels or aircraft of their registry. Internationally, they shall act to establish global and regional rules, standards and recommended practices and procedures. Article 222 provides that states shall enforce within their air space or with regard to flag state or registered ships or aircraft the laws and regulations they adopt, including applicable international rules and standards. Besides this, Annex VI to MARPOL regulates the prevention of air pollution from ships and the carbon intensity of global shipping. It is updated regularly to limit harmful effects on the marine environment through pollution of the air.[128]

Certain regional seas treaties also provide that states should take all appropriate measures to prevent, abate and control atmospheric pollution. The obligation is contained in Article 9 of the 1981 Abidjan Convention on West and Central Africa, Article 4(a)(ii) of the 1981 Lima Convention on the South-East Pacific, Article 9 of the 1983 Cartagena Convention on the Caribbean, and Article 9 of the 1986 Noumea Convention on the South Pacific. Atmospheric pollution is assimilated to land-based pollution in instruments relating to the Mediterranean and to the Gulf.[129] This solution also appears in the Montreal Guidelines on the Protection of the Marine Environment against Land-Based Pollution (April 19, 1985), adopted by a group of experts under the auspices of

128 See for an up-to-date list of amendments and updates to MARPOL Annex VI the website of the IMO: <www.imo.org/en/OurWork/Environment/Pages/Index-of-MEPC-Resolutions-and-Guidelines-related-to-MARPOL-Annex-VI.aspx>.

129 See the 1978 Kuwait Convention for the Gulf and the Protocol of Athens (May 17, 1980) supplementing the Barcelona Convention for the Protection of the Mediterranean (Art. 6). Article 4(1)(b) of the 1996 Amendments to the Athens Protocol (EmuT 976:13/1) applies to inputs of polluting substances transported in the Mediterranean Sea Area from land-based activities within the territories of the Contracting Parties under conditions defined in Annex III to the Protocol.

UNEP.[130] The same idea is contained in the 1992 Convention for the Protection of the Marine Environment of the North-East Atlantic,[131] Article 1(e) of which defines land-based sources of pollution as point and diffuse sources on land from which substances or energy reach the maritime area by water, through the air, or directly from the coast.

Another form of marine pollution transported by air, even if only for short distances, stems from the incineration of wastes on board ships. Incineration with the aid of special vessels was used, primarily by the Netherlands in the North Sea, to eliminate chemical substances, especially organohalogen compounds. Importantly, UNCLOS did not include incineration in the issue of dumping of wastes, and for quite a significant period of time no international text directly addressed the question (although basic regulations that could apply to incineration were included in the Convention for the Prevention of Marine Pollution by Dumping from Ships and Aircraft).[132] A Protocol, opened for signature March 2, 1983, added to the Convention a fourth annex setting forth 'rules on incineration at sea'.[133] In addition, other treaties have developed specific norms on this topic. The 1992 Conventions relating to the Baltic Sea Area (Art. 10) and to the North-East Atlantic (Art. 4 and Annex II) formally prohibit incineration, defined by the former as 'the deliberate combustion of wastes or other matter at sea for the purpose of their thermal destruction. Activities incidental to the normal operation of ships or other man-made structures are excluded from the scope of this definition', (Art. 2(5)). On the global level, a 1996 Protocol to the London Dumping Convention bans all incineration of wastes at sea (Art. 5).[134] More recently, Annex VI to MARPOL regulates incineration when done on ships.[135]

5.3 *Dumping of Wastes*

According to the definition given by UNCLOS, dumping means any deliberate disposal of wastes or other matter from vessels, aircraft, platforms or other man-made structures at sea. Dumping does not include the disposal of wastes or other matter arising from the normal operations of vessels, aircraft,

130 See the text in EPL 77 (1985).

131 Paris, September 22, 1992, EMuT 992: 71.

132 Oslo, February 15, 1972.

133 Protocol Amending the Oslo Convention for the Prevention of Marine Pollution by Dumping from Ships and Aircraft, EMuT 972:12/A.

134 For science-based research on the effectiveness of policies, see Stefan Gössling, Christiane Meyer-Habighorst and Andreas Humpe, 'A Global Review of Marine Air Pollution Policies, their Scope and Effectiveness' (2021) 212 *Ocean and Coastal Management* 1.

135 Regulation 16 MARPOL Annex VI.

platforms or other man-made structures at sea or placement of matter for a purpose other than disposal.[136]

Use of the sea as a universal waste disposal site is tempting for those who seek to avoid or reduce the high costs of eliminating industrial wastes. Dumping of radioactive wastes has been widespread in the past, and has posed serious problems.[137] In some cases, dumping of toxic wastes at sea has given rise to strong protests. The incident of the 'boues rouges', where specially-constructed ships dumped waste off the island of Corsica in the early 1970s, is one example.[138] The dumping was followed by a judgment holding the director of the company liable.

States began to take measures to reduce or resolve the problem of dumping rather rapidly after the beginning of the ecological era. UNCLOS declares at the beginning of Part XII that states should take measures, individually or jointly, including those which are designed to minimize to the fullest possible extent the release by dumping of toxic, harmful or noxious substances, especially those which are persistent.[139] Article 210 provides that states shall adopt laws and regulations to prevent, reduce and control pollution of the marine environment by dumping. In particular, no dumping shall take place without the permission of the competent authorities of the state. For the territorial sea, the exclusive economic zone and the continental shelf, the coastal state should deliver an authorization and regulate and control dumping, taking due consideration of the matter with other states which by reason of their geographical situation could be adversely affected. It is also necessary to adopt global and regional rules, standards and recommended practices and procedures to prevent, reduce, and control such pollution. National laws, regulations and measures must be no less effective than the global rules and standards. Article 216 relating to enforcement of laws and regulations with respect to pollution by dumping, reaffirms the jurisdiction of the coastal state within its territorial sea, exclusive economic zone, or continental shelf. It adds that the flag state also has jurisdiction with regard to its vessels and aircraft. Finally, any state may exercise jurisdiction in response to acts of loading of wastes or other matter occurring within its territory or at its off-shore terminals.

---

136 UNCLOS, Art. 1(5).

137 UN, 'The First Global Integrated Marine Assessment: United Nations World Ocean Assessment I,' (2015) 28.

138 See, Alexandre Kiss, 'Un Cas de Pollution Internationale: L'Affaire Des Boues Rouges' (1975) 102 Journal du Droit International 207.

139 Art. 194(3).

International law concerning dumping of wastes at sea was already in place well before the adoption of UNCLOS. Like vessel-source pollution, the regulatory scheme consisted of a global instrument and several treaties or conventional instruments of a regional nature. The first global treaty on this subject, the Convention on the Prevention of Marine Pollution by Dumping of Wastes and other Matter was opened for signature simultaneously in London, Mexico, City, Moscow and Washington on December 29, 1972. It clearly has a preventive purpose, underlined both in its preamble and in its first two articles: the states parties shall take all practicable steps to prevent the pollution of the sea by dumping of wastes and other matter that is liable to create hazards to human health, to harm living resources and marine life, to damage amenities or to interfere with other legitimate uses of the sea. The Convention initially permitted the dumping of wastes except those on the 'black list' contained in Annex I, which included such substances as organohalogenic compounds, mercury and its compounds, and persistent plastics. Annex II established a 'gray list', those products containing significant amounts of, *inter alia*, lead, arsenic, copper, zinc, cyanides, fluorides, pesticides and their by-products.

Following developments at the regional level, a 1996 Protocol to the Convention reversed the listing process to prohibit all dumping except for those substances specified in Annex I, which may be dumped, but only with a permit delivered by the appropriate authority of the contracting party in according with Annex II.[140] The Protocol prohibits the incineration at sea of waste and other matter and the export of waste or other matter to other countries for dumping or incineration at sea. Each state must designate one or several authorities competent to issue the required permits in respect of matter intended for dumping and loaded in its territory, as well as that loaded by a vessel or aircraft registered in its territory or flying its flag if the loading occurs in the territory of a state not party to the Convention.[141] The nature and the quantities of all matter to be dumped as well as the location, time and method of dumping must be recorded and communicated to other parties.

The Convention and the Protocol require each state party to enforce the Convention by ensuring that the measures are applied by vessels and aircraft registered in its territory or flying its flag, as well as by those who are found under its jurisdiction, notably in its territorial waters, and those who load matter which is to be dumped.[142] International measures are only outlined:

---

140 Protocol to the Convention on the Prevention of Marine Pollution by Dumping of Wastes and Other Matter (adopted November 7, 1996, entered into force 2006) (London Protocol).

141 Art. 6.

142 Convention, Art. 7; Protocol, Art. 10.

states agree to cooperate in the development of procedures for the effective application of the Convention, particularly on the high seas, including procedures for the reporting of vessels and aircraft observed dumping in contravention of the Convention. Vessels and aircraft entitled to sovereign immunity are excepted from coverage of the rules.[143]

The London Dumping Convention also invites the conclusion of regional accords addressing the same problem. One such agreement, the Oslo Convention for the Prevention of Marine Pollution by Dumping from Ships and Aircraft was in fact adopted before the London conference and may have provided a model for the authors of the London Convention ten months later.[144] The 'reverse listing' procedure was first introduced in another regional agreement, the 1974 Helsinki Convention on the Protection of the Marine Environment of the Baltic Sea,[145] which forbids all dumping except as specified in Annex 5. The 1992 Convention on the Protection of the Marine Environment of the Baltic Sea Area applies the same principle: dumping is prohibited in the Baltic Sea Area, subject to exemptions which can be given for dredged material when a prior special permit is issued by the appropriate national authority (Art. 11).[146] Annex v to the Convention specifies the conditions under which such permits can be delivered. Compliance with the provisions of Article 11 shall be ensured by each contracting state respecting ships and aircraft registered in its territory or flying its flag, loading within its territory or territorial sea matter which is to be dumped, or believed to be engaged in dumping within its internal waters and territorial sea.

The 1992 Paris Convention for the Protection of the Marine Environment of the North-East Atlantic follows the same method by prohibiting the dumping of all wastes or other matter, but admits the dumping of dredged material and inert materials of natural origin, i.e., solid, chemically-unprocessed, geological material, the chemical constituents of which are unlikely to be released into the marine environment.[147] Fish waste from industrial fish processing operations also can be dumped, as can scuttled vessels and aircraft, until the end of 2004 and under specified conditions (Arts. 3(1) and (2)). In each case the competent authorities must authorize the dumping (Art. 4). Each contracting party shall keep, and transmit to the Commission of the Convention, records of the nature and quantities of wastes or other matter dumped in accordance

143 ibid.

144 Oslo, February 15, 1972.

145 Helsinki, March 22, 1974, EMuT 974:23.

146 Helsinki, April 9, 1992, EMuT 992:28.

147 Paris, September 22, 1992, EMuT 992:71.

with the Convention's provisions, and of the dates, places and methods of dumping (Art. 4).

The regional treaties elaborated under the auspices of UNEP call on states parties to take all appropriate measures to prevent and reduce, in the relevant areas, pollution of the sea due to dumping carried out by their vessels and aircraft.[148] More detailed regulation of this problem appeared first in the framework of the Barcelona Convention, followed by the Noumea Convention. A special protocol to the former, signed at the same time as the principal Convention, relates to 'the prevention of pollution of the Mediterranean Sea by dumping by vessels and aircraft'. Its contents are similar to those of the model 1972 London Convention. A permit regime based on three categories is set out: matter on a black list cannot be dumped (Art. 4); substances or matters appearing on the gray list can only be dumped after receiving in advance a special permit (Art. 5); any other dumping requires a prior general permit (Art. 6). Annex III sets out the factors which must be considered before a permit is authorized. UNEP, designated as the secretariat for the Convention, receives information relating to the permits delivered. A Protocol for the Prevention of Pollution in the South Pacific by Dumping, signed the same day as the general Noumea Convention contains provisions comparable to the Barcelona treaty.

The pressure of public opinion has led to significant progress in restricting the dumping of radioactive wastes. During the 1958 effort to codify the international law of the sea, the question of dumping, primarily the dumping of radioactive wastes on the high seas, was raised. At the time, states accepted that coastal states could take the measures they deemed necessary to take in their territorial seas. Agreement was reached on including a specific provision respecting the commons area in the 1958 Convention on the High Seas: 'Every state shall take measures to prevent pollution of the seas from the dumping of radioactive waste, taking into account any standards and regulations which may be formulated by the competent international organizations'.[149]

Over time, a norm emerged forbidding the dumping of radioactive wastes, with the result that the issue has been largely resolved. The 1972 London Convention, Annex I, enumerates those substances for which dumping is

148 These include: - Article 6 of the Barcelona Convention for the Mediterranean (February 16, 1976); Article 5 of the Kuwait Convention for the Gulf (April 24, 1978); Article 6 of the Abidjan Convention on West Africa (March 23, 1981); Article 4(a)(iii) of the Lima South-East Pacific Convention (November 20, 1981); Article 5 of the Jeddah Convention on the Red Sea (February 14, 1982); Article 6 of Cartagena Convention on the Caribbean (March 24, 1983); Article 5(3) of the Noumea Convention on the South Pacific (November 24, 1986).

149 Art. 25(1).

prohibited and includes 'high-level radio-active wastes or other high-level radio-active matter, defined on public health, biological or other grounds, by the competent international body in this field, at present the International Atomic Energy Agency, as unsuitable for dumping at sea'.[150] In 1977, the International Agency for Atomic Energy itself established a multilateral mechanism for consultation and monitoring of dumping of radioactive wastes at sea. The European Agency of Nuclear Energy established technical criteria and procedures on the topic.

Further progress led towards the eventual prohibition on dumping all radioactive wastes. First, twenty member states of the OECD unilaterally renounced any dumping of such wastes. Subsequently, the contracting parties to the London Dumping Convention adopted a ten-year moratorium on the dumping of nuclear waste at sea. Finally, the moratorium was replaced by a permanent ban approved November 12, 1993, by a vote of 37–0 with five abstentions (Britain, France, Russia, China and Belgium). Each state had 100 days to file an objection refusing to be bound by the ban. The same meeting also banned dumping industrial waste and outlawed incineration of industrial waste at sea.[151]

Regionally, strong provisions were placed in the 1974 Baltic Sea Convention which forbid any dumping not authorized by Annex V. The Annex enumerated limited exceptions to the general prohibition on dumping and did not include radioactive wastes among them. The 1976 Protocol Additional to the Barcelona Convention relating to the Mediterranean Sea also forbids dumping of 'wastes and other matters highly, partly, or slightly radioactive'.[152] Finally, Article 3(3) of the Convention for the Protection of the North-East Atlantic explicitly prohibits the dumping of low and intermediate level radioactive substances, including wastes.

Although not necessarily intentional dumping, sunken vessels and shipwrecks pose a serious danger to the marine environment when they are left to disintegrate. It is for this reason that they are salvaged. The 1989 Salvage Convention was drafted to take environmental issues into consideration, which were lacking from the 1910 Convention for the Unification of Certain Rules of Law relating to Assistance and Salvage at Sea.[153] Under the 1989 Convention, salvors are compensated for preventing or minimizing damage to the environment, even when a ship or its cargo cannot be salvaged, as well as deprived

150 Annex I(6).

151 By the end of the 100 days, only Russia had opted out.

152 Art. IV and Annex I, No. 7.

153 International Convention on Salvage (adopted April 18, 1989, entered into force July 14, 1996) (Salvage Convention).

of special compensation if they fail to prevent or minimize environmental damage.[154] This provides an incentive for salvors to take the environment into consideration when performing their duties. Recycling is considered to be the most environmentally conscious way of disposing of ships at the end of their life, but it is a dangerous undertaking in the current circumstances. In 2009, the IMO drafted the Hong Kong Convention to combat this problem, for environmental protection, but also not in the least because of the incredibly dangerous working circumstances in the industry.[155] The Convention aims to 'effectively address, in a legally-binding instrument, the environmental, occupational health and safety risks related to ship recycling, taking into account the particular characteristics of maritime transport and the need to secure the smooth withdrawal of ships that have reached the end of their operating lives'.[156] The Convention will enter into force in 2025, hopefully contributing effectively to the lessening of polluting materials entering the marine environment.

5.4 *Exploration and Exploitation of the Sea-Bed*

Paralleling other provisions relating to marine pollution, UNCLOS provides that states should take measures individually or jointly to minimize to the fullest possible extent:

> Pollution from installations and devices used in exploration or exploitation of the natural resources of the sea-bed and sub-soil, in particular measures for preventing accidents and dealing with emergencies, ensuring the safety of operations at sea, and regulating the design, construction, equipment, operation and manning of such installations or devices.[157]

Other provisions of the Convention distinguish between pollution resulting from activities taking place in the Area – i.e., the seabed, declared to be the common heritage of mankind – and those resulting from activities relating to underwater areas falling under national jurisdiction. The relevant principles for the Area are contained in Article 145, located in UNCLOS Part VI rather

154 Art. 13(1)(b), 14(1) and (5).

155 Hong Kong International Convention for the Safe and Environmentally Sound Recycling of Ships (adopted May 15, 2009, entry into force June 26, 2025) SR/CONF/45 (Hong Kong Convention). The Convention was meant to be a supplement to the 1989 Basel Convention on Shipping of Hazardous Materials.

156 Hong Kong Convention, Preamble.

157 Art. 194(3)(c).

than in the section devoted to protection of the marine environment. Article 145 reads:

> Necessary measures shall be taken in accordance with this Convention with respect to activities in the Area to ensure effective protection for the marine environment from harmful effects which may arise from such activities. To this end the Authority shall adopt appropriate rules, regulations and procedures for, *inter alia*:
>
> a. the prevention, reduction and control of pollution and other hazards to the marine environment, including the coastline, and of interference with the ecological balance of the marine environment, particular attention being paid to the need for protection from harmful effects of such activities as drilling, dredging, excavation, disposal of waste, construction and operation or maintenance of installations, pipelines and other devices related to such activities;
>
> b. the protection and conservation of the natural resources of the Area and the prevention of damage to the flora and fauna of the marine environment.

Article 209, containing the environmental protections of Part XII, refers back to Article 145 to affirm that international rules, regulations and procedures shall be established to prevent, reduce and control pollution of the marine environment from activities in the Area. Article 215 confers responsibility for implementation of this obligation on the Authority. Nonetheless, all states must adopt laws and regulations governing activities in the Area by their vessels, installations, structures and other devices flying their flag or of their registry or operating under their authority. National laws and regulations shall not be less effective than the international rules.[158]

In 2000, the International Seabed Authority (ISA) drafted and adopted Regulations on Prospecting and Exploration for Polymetallic Nodules in the Area.[159] These were revised in 2013.[160] Part V of the Regulations, adopted by the Council and approved by the Assembly on July 13, 2000, concern protection and preservation of the marine environment. Both the Authority and holders of contracts for exploration are to ensure effective protection of the marine environment from harmful effects which may arise from activities in the Area. The term 'marine environment' is defined in an inclusive way as 'the physical,

158 Art. 209(2).

159 See 30 EPL 174–177(2000).

160 ISBA/19/C/17.

chemical, geological and biological components, conditions and factors which interact and determine the productivity, state, condition and quality of the marine ecosystem, the waters of the seas and oceans and the airspace above those waters as well as the seabed and ocean floor and subsoil thereof'.[161]

The Regulations mandate the Authority to establish and keep under periodic review environmental rules, regulations and procedures to ensure effective protection for the marine environment. The regulations are supplemented and revised regularly by the Authority as more knowledge and experience is gained. The Authority, sponsoring States and, indirectly, the contractors, are required to apply the precautionary approach.

Under the regulations, contractors applying for exploitation rights must propose areas to be set aside and used exclusively as impact reference zones (areas used to assess the effects of mining activities on the marine environment and which are representative of the environmental characteristics of the Area) and preservation reference zones (areas in which no mining shall occur to ensure representative and stable biota of the seabed in order to assess any changes in the flora and fauna of the marine environment). Contractors also must submit contingency plans and promptly report to the Authority any incident arising from activities that has caused or is likely to cause serious harm to the marine environment.[162]

On July 4, 2001, the Legal and Technical Commission of the International Seabed Authority approved the Recommendations for the Guidance of Contractors for the Assessment of Possible Environmental Impacts Arising from the Exploration for Polymetallic Nodules in the Area.[163] These recommendations were adopted pursuant to Regulation 38 of the Mining Code. The recommendations specify the data the contractor should gather on natural conditions before exploration begins (baseline data), what information should be provided by the contractor to the ISA, and what observations and measurements should be made by the contractor while performing a specific activity as well as following its performance. Baseline data falls into six groups: physical oceanography, chemical oceanography, sediment properties, biological communities, bioturbation, and sedimentation. The information is required to allow the Legal and Technical Commission to carry out its responsibilities to ensure the protection of the marine environment.

161 Regulation 1(3)(c) Amended Regulations 2013 (ISBA/19/C/17).

162 For more, see Joanna Dingwall, *International Law and Corporate Actors in Deep Seabed Mining* (Oxford Academic 2021).

163 Doc. ISBA/7/LTC/1/Rev.1 of July 10, 2001.

Under the regulations and recommendations, EIAs are not required for: gravity and magnetometric observations and measurements; bottom and sub-bottom acoustic or electromagnetic profiling or imaging without the use of explosives; water and biotic sampling and mineral samplings of a limited nature such as those obtained using core, grab, or basket samplers to determine seabed geological or geotechnical properties; meteorological observations and measurements, including the setting of instruments; oceanographic, including hydrographic, observations and measurements, including the setting of instruments; television and still photographic observation and measurements; shipboard mineral assaying and analysis; and positioning systems, including bottom transponders and surface and sub-surface buoys filed in notices to mariners.

List 2 includes activities that require an EIA and monitoring: dredging to collect nodules for on-land studies for mining and/or processing; the use of special equipment to study the reaction of the sediment to disturbances made by collecting devices or running gears; and testing of collection systems and equipment.

The Legal and Technical Commission admitted that while 'current knowledge of the deep-sea environment is insufficient to predict the real impacts of tests of [actual technology yet to be developed], the environmental disturbances, based on the experience and knowledge gathered from previous activities carried out by the registered pioneer investors and by the scientific community, may be forecast to some extent. The main impacts are expected to occur at the seafloor, with minor impacts expected at the tailings-discharge depth. The nodule collector will disturb the semi-liquid sediment-surface layer and will create a near-bottom plume. The nodule collector will compress, breakup and squeeze the harder underlying sediment layer'.[164] This statement still holds true more than twenty years later: the environmental impact of deep-sea mining is still unclear, and many experts have warned against it due to fear of environmental damage.[165]

The adoption of the Mining Code and recommendations allowed the ISA to proceed with signing contracts for exploration starting at the beginning of the 21st Century.[166] Contracts for exploitation have not been granted yet, because

164 Doc. ISBA/7/C/7 of July 12, 2001, para. 9.

165 See Rahul Sharma (ed.), *Environmental Issues of Deep-Sea Mining: Impacts, Consequences and Policy Perspectives* (Springer 2019); Lisa Levin and others, 'Defining "Serious Harm" to the Marine Environment in the Context of Deep-Seabed Mining' (2016) 74 Marine Policy 245.

166 See Doc. ISBA/7/C/4 of June 22, 2001; For a current list of permit-holders, see the website of the ISA at <www.isa.org.jm/exploration-contracts/>.

the legal framework for doing so in the Mining Code is not yet complete. This process was scheduled to have been finalized on July 9, 2023, but the ISA was not able to meet this deadline. The process remains ongoing as of May 2024.

While the earlier known sources of minerals are thus regulated, scientific explorations have revealed other sources of metals in the deep sea: polymetallic sulphides and cobalt-rich crusts. The former are linked to vents from underwater volcanos where the tectonic plates meet. They contain copper, lead, zinc, silver and gold in varying amounts. Cobalt crusts usually occur as hard encrustations on the sides of islands and on seamounts. They are widely distributed in the Pacific Ocean. The characteristics of these other sources make application of the rules developed for nodules inappropriate. Therefore, in 2010 and 2012 respectively, the ISA adopted regulations on the exploration for polymetallic sulphides and cobalt-rich ferromanganese crusts.[167] For the future, there is also a need to consider the legal relationship between the biodiversity and UNCLOS because of bio-prospecting of genetic resources on seabed, especially surrounding the thermal vents.

Pollution from sea-bed activities subject to national jurisdiction is governed by UNCLOS Article 208. It requires coastal states to adopt laws and regulations, no less effective than international rules, for activities subject to their jurisdiction, while endeavoring to harmonize their policies in this connection at the regional level. States shall also act through international organizations or conferences to establish global or regional rules which they shall then implement.[168]

The obligations and liability of states sponsoring sea-bed activities were clarified by the Seabed Disputes Chamber in its unanimously adopted Advisory Opinion in 2011. Under UNCLOS and related instruments, sponsoring states have obligations with respect to the activities included in Article 145, and these obligations are generally the same for developed and developing nations.[169] The Chamber distinguished between due diligence and 'direct' obligations, the former being a responsibility to make the best possible efforts to ensure compliance by sponsored contractors with the terms of their contract, and with UNCLOS and related instruments.[170] To this end, sponsoring states must adopt domestic laws and regulations, and take administrative measures

167 ISBA/16/A/12/Rev.1 of November 15, 2010; ISBA/18/A/11 of October 22, 2012.

168 Art. 208, 214.

169 *Responsibilities and Obligations of States Sponsoring Persons and Entities with Respect to Activities in the Area* (February 1, 2011) Advisory Opinion, ITLOS Rep. 11, paras. 85, 158.

170 ibid, paras. 117–121.

that are reasonably appropriate.[171] Notably, the Chamber affirmed that the required standard of due diligence may vary over time and depends on the level of risk and on the activities involved.[172] The important direct obligations of sponsoring states include: assisting the International Seabed Authority, applying a precautionary approach, applying the best environmental practices, adopting measures to ensure the provision of guarantees in the event of an emergency order by the International Seabed Authority for protection of the marine environment, and the obligation to provide recourse for compensation.[173] Moreover, the Chamber affirmed that sponsoring states are liable for their failure to fulfil their responsibilities under UNCLOS and related instruments if damage occurs as a result of this failure.[174] They may, however, be exempt from liability if they have taken all necessary and appropriate measures to secure effective compliance by the sponsored contractor with its obligations (even if damage has occurred).[175] Such an exemption does not exist for their direct obligations.[176]

The 2002 UNESCO Convention on the Protection of the Underwater Cultural Heritage aims to protect the historical and archaeological resources represented by shipwrecks and other human artifacts on the sea floor.[177] In general, the Convention requires that activities directed at underwater cultural heritage are conducted in conformity with an Annex containing rules and standards for underwater archaeology. Parties to the Convention must regulate the activities of their nationals and flagged vessels. When a find is made, the coastal state becomes the 'coordinating state' for activities on its continental shelf, in effect controlling access in conformity with the Convention. The Convention itself has a strong preference for *in situ* conservation and requires efforts to prevent trade in illegally taken artifacts. Many states, including France, Germany, the Netherlands, Norway, Russia, the US and the UK, opposed the treaty or withheld approval, contending that the Convention fails to adequately protect flag states of warships and extends coastal state jurisdiction beyond the provisions of UNCLOS, despite the 'without prejudice' clause of Article 3, which requires the Convention be interpreted and applied consistent with UNCLOS. Although many shipwrecks are associated with fragile coral reefs, the environment is not mentioned in the Convention itself, but is included in the Rules annexed to the

171 Activities in the Area, paras. 119–120.
172 ibid, paras. 117–121.
173 ibid, paras. 124–140.
174 ibid, paras. 176, 184.
175 ibid, para. 186.
176 ibid, para. 207.
177 41 ILM 37 (2002).

treaty. Part II of the Rules requires a project design be developed and submitted to the appropriate authorities prior to any activity directed at underwater cultural heritage and mandates that all activities be conducted in conformity with the project design. Rule 10 specifies that the project design include, *inter alia*, an environmental policy while Rule 29 adds the rather weak statement that the environmental policy shall be adequate 'to ensure that the seabed and marine life are not unduly disturbed'.

Many regional seas treaties reaffirm the UNCLOS principles,[178] but two regional seas agreements include specific rules in additional protocols, due to the potential for harm from this source in their regions. The Kuwaiti system added a Protocol Concerning Marine Pollution Resulting from Exploration and Exploitation of the Continental Shelf.[179] Article II requires contracting states to take all appropriate measures to prevent, abate and control marine pollution from offshore operations in those areas within their jurisdiction, as well as to take action individually and jointly to combat such pollution. According to the Protocol, any offshore operation must be licensed. Article IV requires a prior assessment of the potential environmental effects before the licensing of any offshore operation which could cause significant risks of pollution in the Protocol Area. Moreover, no license shall be granted until the competent state authority is satisfied that the operation will entail no unacceptable risk of environmental damage in the Area. The regional organization establishes guidelines for the environmental impact statements and states must transmit to the organization a summary of the environmental effects reported in the assessments submitted to them. Within four days of receiving the assessment summaries, the organization sends them to all other contracting states who are allowed to submit representations through the organization within a stated reasonable time. States must consider any such representations before licensing an operation.

Once an operation is licensed, Article IX prohibits most discharges from any offshore installation and establishes limits for the oil content of permitted discharges. Dumping of plastics and garbage are prohibited or regulated by Article X. In one of the most advanced measures, Article XI requires that each operator

---

178 See for example: Article 10, Helsinki Convention on the Baltic Sea (March 22, 1974); Article 7, Barcelona Convention for the Mediterranean (February 16, 1976); Article 7, Kuwait Convention for the Gulf (April 24, 1978); Article 8, Abidjan Convention for West Africa (March 23, 1981); Article 4(c), Lima Convention for South-East Pacific (November 20, 1981); Article 7, Jeddah Convention for the Red Sea (February 14, 1982); Article 8, Cartagena Convention for the Caribbean (March 24, 1983); Article 9, Noumea Convention for the South-Pacific (Novemer 24, 1986).

179 ROMPE, 'Fourth Legal/Technical Expert Meeting,' Kuwait, December 11-12, 1988, reprinted in 19/1 Envtl Pol. and L 32 (1989).

of an offshore installation prepare a 'Chemical Use Plan' for approval by the competent state authority. Except in case of emergency, the operator must amend the plan any time he wishes to use a chemical outside the approved plan and that chemical may escape into the marine environment. The state authority has the power to prohibit, limit or regulate the use of a chemical or product and to impose conditions on its storage and its use, for the protection of the marine environment. In exercising its power, the authority shall have regard to any guidelines issued by the regional organization. Remaining articles establish stringent requirements for the disposal of all other wastes.

The treaty system, founded in Barcelona in 1976 also has been enriched by a Protocol for the Protection of the Mediterranean Sea against Pollution resulting from Exploration and Exploitation of the Continental Shelf and the Seabed and its Subsoil, which similarly introduces an authorization system for exploration or exploitation.[180] Article 5 lists the requirements for such authorization, including an environmental impact assessment, evidence of the qualification of the candidate operator and personnel of the installation, safety measures, a contingency plan, plans for the removal of installations, precautions for specially-protected areas and insurance or other financial security to cover liability. Each country is obliged to prescribe sanctions for breach of obligations arising out of the Protocol (Art. 7). The parties also must impose a general obligation upon operators to use the best available, environmentally-effective and economically-appropriate techniques and to observe internationally-accepted standards regarding wastes, as well as the use, storage and discharge of harmful or noxious substances and material. (Arts. 8 and 9). Common standards shall be adopted for the disposal of oil and oily mixtures from installations (Art. 10) and the discharge of sewage shall be prohibited from installations permanently manned by ten or more person. (Art. 11) The disposal in the Protocol area of specified products and materials is also prohibited (Art. 12). The contracting parties agree to cooperate in promoting studies and research, in establishing common rules, standards and recommended practices and procedures (Arts. 22 and 23) and also in formulating and adopting appropriate rules and procedures for the determination of liability and compensation for damage resulting from activities dealt with in the Protocol (Art. 27).

At a global level, UNEP has contributed to this field by formulating a certain number of 'conclusions' addressed to states. A group of experts in environmental law adopted forty-two principles which should govern operations relating to the seabed and subsoil within the limits of national jurisdiction. These

180 Madrid, October 14, 1994, EMuT 976:13/E.

principles generally establish permit systems based on prior impact assessments and statements concerning the ecological consequences of exploitation, a monitoring system in the interest of the environment, procedures of information and consultation between states when damage could result from operations outside the limits of national jurisdiction, security measures to apply to the operations, prior measures to take to remedy emergency situations and, finally, international responsibility and in particular compensation for victims.[181] In fact, most states having a maritime zone or where activities relating to the deep seabed and its subsoil can be envisaged have enacted legislation requiring prior authorization.

A detailed global treaty in this field concerns civil responsibility for damage from pollution by oil resulting from the research and exploitation of mineral resources of the seabed. The Convention (London, May 1, 1977) establishes a regime parallel to that of the 1969 Brussels Convention, to permit compensation for damage caused by an installation at sea placed under the jurisdiction of a state party, for damage suffered on the territory or in the waters of a state party, as well as safeguard measures designed to prevent or to limit such damage by pollution, wherever it might be (Art. 2). The owner of the installation at the moment of the accident is strictly liable (Art. 3), but has the right to limit responsibility if he has established a fund. (Art. 6). A state party can set a liability limit higher that provided by the Convention or even abolish limits, on condition that no discrimination based on nationality is exercised (Art. 15). The competent courts are those of the state where the damage has been suffered (Art. 11) and their decisions must be executed in the other states parties (Art. 12).[182]

5.5 *Land-Based Pollution*

Land-based pollution can be defined as pollution of maritime zones due to discharges by coastal establishments or coming from any other source situated on land or artificial structures, including pollution transported by rivers into the sea. The majority of marine pollution comes directly from land-based sources. Land-based pollution is logically particularly severe in heavily-populated regions, such as along the Mediterranean and the Baltic Sea coastlines, as well as in regions where seasonal tourism may greatly increase the number of inhabitants. Plastic is by far the most commonly found material amongst

181 See the text published in English in EPL 50–52 (1981).

182 See on deep-sea mining and its environmental concerns Julia Guifang Xue and Xiangxin Xu, 'Deep Seabed Mining: Environmental Concerns and Improvement of Regulations' in *Global Commons and the Law of the Sea* (Brill Leiden Boston 2018) 168.

ocean debris, and most plastic that ends up in the oceans stems from land-based sources.[183]

The diversity of origins of land-based pollution makes it difficult to combat. Such pollution can occur directly, by dumping or discharges along the coast, or indirectly, by the intermediary of rivers or streams or subterranean waters. Applicable rules should in principle include all waters that flow into the sea, thus governing the entire aquatic environment in certain regions. As such, in addition to the 'traditional' techniques of forbidding discharge or requiring prior authorization of certain discharges, cooperation between states plays a great role, notably in establishing programs to progressively reduce pollution throughout an entire water basin.

UNCLOS regulates land-based pollution by the methods it applies to other pollution sources. Article 194 provides that states should take the necessary measures tending to limit as much as possible 'the release of toxic, harmful or noxious substances, especially those which are persistent, from land-based sources, from or through the atmosphere or by dumping'.[184] Article 207 provides that states shall adopt laws and regulations as well as all other measures that may be necessary to prevent, reduce and control this pollution. Article 213 requires states to ensure their application.

Apart from UNCLOS, existing conventional sources regulating land-based pollution are largely regional. The United Nations Environment Program studied the problem during 1984–85 and a group of experts adopted guidelines to combat it.[185] However, the legal effect of the guidelines remains limited because they are not contained in a treaty or government document. Regionally, all regional seas treaties proclaim the principle of combating land-based pollution. The most precise regulations are those for the North-East Atlantic, the Baltic, the Mediterranean and the South-East Pacific. There are also several European Union directives that concern, in one manner or another, pollutants originating on land.

The first convention to address land-based pollution was adopted in 1974,[186] and replaced in 1992 by the Convention for the Protection of the Marine Environment of the North-East Atlantic.[187] According to Article 3 of the 1992 treaty,

---

183 United Nations, *The First World Ocean Assessment: World Ocean Assessment I* vol I (2015) summary 5; United Nations, *The Second World Ocean Assessment: World Ocean Assessment II* vol II (2021) 154.

184 Art. 194(3)(a).

185 Montreal, April 19, 1985. For the text see EPL 77 (1985).

186 Convention for the Prevention of Marine Pollution from Land-Based Sources, Paris, June 4, 1974.

187 Paris, September 22, 1992, EMuT 992:71.

the contracting parties shall take, individually and jointly, all possible steps to prevent and eliminate pollution from land-based sources as provided in Annex I, in particular by adopting programs and measures for the prevention and elimination of this type of pollution. The large number of recommendations and agreements adopted under the former Convention continue to be applicable, unaltered in their legal nature, according to Article 31.[188]

The 1992 Convention obliges the contracting parties to set priorities and assess the nature and extent of the programs and measures and their time scales, using the criteria given in Appendix 2 to the Convention. These criteria are, *inter alia*, persistency, toxicity or other noxious properties, tendency to bioaccumulation, radioactivity, risk of eutrophication, risk of undesirable changes in the marine ecosystem and irreversibility or durability of effects, and non-fulfillment of environmental quality objectives. The criteria identify substances that must be subject to programs and measures, including heavy metals and their compounds, organohalogen compounds, biocides, and radioactive substances. Point source discharges to the maritime area, and releases into water or air which reach and may affect the maritime area are strictly subject to authorization or regulation by the competent authorities of the contracting parties, taking into account relevant decisions of the Commission. The states parties also are to establish systems of regular monitoring and inspection to assess compliance with such authorizations and regulations. This system seems more flexible than the former one which also required the use of best available techniques for point sources and best environmental practice for point and diffuse sources.

The 1992 Convention on the Protection of the Marine Environment of the Baltic Sea Area includes detailed rules relating to land-based pollution (Art. 6 and Annex III).[189] The main principle is that harmful substances from point sources originating from the catchment area of the Baltic Sea shall not, except in negligible quantities, be introduced directly or indirectly into the marine environment of the Baltic Sea Area, without a prior special permit, subject to periodic review and issued by the appropriate national authority (Art. 6). Convention Annex III describes detailed criteria and measures to prevent pollution from land-based sources. It also refers to the best environmental practice, recommended for eliminating pollution from diffuse sources including agriculture, and the best available technology, described in Annex II. Like the

188 See, Philippe Sands, 'Principles of International Environmental Law' (1994) 321–323.

189 Helsinki, April 9, 1992, EMuT 992:28. The treaty replaced the Convention for the Protection of the Marine Environment of the Baltic Sea, March 22, 1974.

Convention for the North-East Atlantic, the Baltic Sea treaty shows the same trend toward flexibility in efforts to control land-based pollution.

All the regional marine pollution conventions elaborated under the auspices of UNEP contain agreement in principle to combat land-based pollution. Three of them, the Barcelona Convention for the Mediterranean,[190] the Lima Convention for the South-East Pacific,[191] and the Convention for the Protection and Development of the Marine Environment of the Wider Caribbean Region,[192] have adopted more precise measures which are contained in Protocols additional to the Conventions. The Barcelona Convention is supplemented by the Protocol for the Protection of the Mediterranean Sea against Pollution from Land-Based Sources and Activities.[193] The text notes the increasing environmental pressures resulting from human activities in the Mediterranean Sea Area, particularly from industrialization and urbanization, as well as the seasonal increases in coastal population due to tourism. The general obligations of the Parties include controlling discharges from rivers, coastal establishments or outfalls, and pollution emanating from any other land-based sources and activities, giving priority to the phasing out of inputs from substances that are toxic, persistent and liable to bioaccumulate. Reflecting developments in the law of international watercourses, the Protocol covers the hydrologic basin of the contracting parties, defined as the entire watershed area within their territories, and draining into the Mediterranean Sea Area.[194] Non-party states whose territories include part of the hydrologic basin of the Mediterranean Sea are invited to cooperate in the implementation of the Protocol.[195] The Protocol also applies to discharges originating from land-based and point sources and activities within the territories of the contracting parties that may affect directly or indirectly the Mediterranean Sea Area.[196]

The parties generally undertake to eliminate pollution deriving from land-based sources and activities, in particular, to phase out inputs of the substances listed in Annex I that are toxic, persistent and liable to bioaccumulate. The

190 Barcelona, February 16, 1976.

191 Lima, November 12, 1981.

192 Cartagena de Indias, March 24, 1983. The parties adopted the Protocol concerning Pollution from Land-Based Sources and Activities in Oranjestad, Aruba on October 6, 1999, EmuT 983:23/C.

193 The Protocol was originally adopted in Athens in 1980 as the Protocol for the Protection of the Mediterranean Sea against Pollution from Land-Based Sources. It was amended and its title changed in Syracuse, March 7, 1996.

194 Art. 2(d).

195 Art. 4(3).

196 Art. 4(1)(a).

Annex lists thirty sectors of activities, including energy production, petroleum refining, animal husbandry, and tourism, as well as thirteen characteristics of polluting substances (e.g. persistence, health effects and risks, effects on the smell, colour, transparency or other characteristics of sea water) and categories of hazardous substances, such as organohalogen compounds and substances, heavy metal, biocides. Article 4 (1)(b) and Annex III add concern for atmospheric pollution from land-based sources or activities within the territories of the parties, taking into account to prevailing meteorological conditions.

Article 6 of the amended Protocol provides for an authorization or regulation system: the competent authorities of the parties are to strictly regulate point source discharges into the Protocol area and releases into water or air that reach and may affect the Mediterranean area. A revised Annex II lists the elements to be taken into account in the issue of the authorizations for discharges of wastes. It distinguishes the characteristics and composition of the discharges according to their harmfulness and the characteristics and composition of discharge site and the receiving environment. According to Article 8, the parties shall carry out monitoring activities and give public access to the findings in order to systematically assess the levels of pollution along their coasts and to evaluate the effectiveness of action plans, programmes and measures implemented to eliminate to the fullest possible extent pollution of the marine environment.

The Protocol establishes a reporting system providing for bi-annual reports from the parties about measures taken, results achieved and difficulties encountered in the application of the Protocol (Art. 13). Meetings of the parties shall take place in conjunction with ordinary meetings of the parties to the Barcelona Convention. Such meetings shall adopt the short-term and medium-term regional action plans and programs containing measures and timetables for their implementation (Art. 15).

The Quito Protocol relating to Protection of the South-East Pacific against Pollution from Land-Based Sources,[197] supplements the Lima Convention. Article 3 of the Protocol, indicating the general obligations of the states parties, is directly inspired by UNCLOS. Two methods are used to combat land-based pollution: a system of lists and a program to eliminate or reduce pollution. The agreement has two annexed lists that are the same as those attached to the Athens Protocol, but the legal obligations respecting them differ because the Quito Protocol states agreed only to endeavor to eliminate discharge of substances contained in Annex I and to endeavor progressively to reduce those

197 July 22, 1983.

contained in Annex II.[198] States parties also are obliged to cooperate in application of the provisions of the instrument and their meetings monitor implementation of the rules adopted.

The sixteen states parties to the Convention for the Protection and the Development of the Marine Environment of the Wider Caribbean Region adopted a Protocol Concerning Pollution from Land-Based Sources and Activities on October 6, 1999 at Oranjestad, Aruba.[199] It calls for the preparation of environmental impact assessments for planned land-based activities or planned modifications to such activities which are subject to regulatory control and which are likely to cause substantial pollution of or significant harmful changes to the Convention area (Art. VII). The parties are to promote public access to relevant information concerning pollution of the Convention area as well as public participation in decision-making processes concerning the implementation of the Protocol (Art. XI). Annexes to the Protocol list source categories, activities and associated pollutants of concern, but also factors to be used in determining effluent and emission source controls and management factors. A very detailed Annex relates to domestic wastewater and the last Annex proposes plans for the prevention, reduction and control of agricultural non-point pollution sources. Finally, the Protocol calls for reporting by the Parties on measures adopted and results obtained, as well as on the state of the environment of the Convention area (Art. XII).

The Regional Convention for the Conservation of the Red Sea and Gulf of Aden Environment was created in 1982, while in 2005 the Protocol Concerning the Protection of the Marine Environment from Land-Based Activities in the Red Sea and Gulf of Aden was added.[200] It contains Annexes, focusing on which priorities need to be taken into consideration and which areas need to be given particular attention. The Third annex indicates that air-borne pollution from land-based sources is also covered by the Protocol. Similar protocols have been added to the Black Sea Convention, the Nairobi Convention and most recently, to the Tehran Convention.[201]

---

198 Art. 4.; Art. 5.

199 Cartagena de Indias, March 24, 1983.

200 Jeddah, September 25, 2005.

201 Addition of: Protocol on the Protection of the Black Sea Marine Environment Against Pollution from Land-based Sources and Activities (adopted April 7, 2009, entry into force pending) to the Convention on the Protection of the Black Sea against Pollution (adopted April 21, 1992 in Bucharest, entered into force January 15, 1994); Protocol for the Protection of the Marine and Coastal Environment of the Western Indian Ocean from Land-Based Sources and Activities (adopted March 31, 2010, entry into force August 3, 2011) to the Amended Nairobi Convention for the Protection, Management and Development

The EC also has adopted several directives in this field. In particular, the directive of May 4, 1976 relating to the protection of the aquatic environment explicitly applies to the territorial seas of member states.[202] This text contains a system of prohibition and authorization based on lists of harmful discharges, but it also envisages quality standards. Programs to reduce pollution and improve water quality had to be implemented within time limits fixed by the European Commission. A series of EC directives to preserve the water quality of the Community applies to inland waters as well as the marine environment. Although they primarily aim at protecting fresh waters from pollution, their effect can lessen marine pollution from land-based sources. Similarly, a Directive of October 30, 1979 which applies to coastal waters and brackish waters designated by the states members as needing protection or improvement in order to support shellfish, sets the applicable limits which member states should take into account in fixing the standards for the designated waters.[203] In 2000, the EC issued the Water Framework Directive (WFD) which covers fresh waters, but also extends to coastal waters up to a nautical mile from the coast.[204] In 2008, the EU issued the Marine Strategy Framework, which just like the WFD aimed to make the marine environment reach 'good environmental status' by the year 2020, but this target was largely not reached.[205] In addition to this, the EU adopted a directive dedicated to maritime spatial planning in 2014. It is 'aimed at promoting the sustainable growth of maritime economies, the sustainable development of marine areas and the sustainable use of marine resources.'[206] However, the Directive states clearly that its purpose is

---

of the Marine and Coastal Environment of the Western Indian Ocean (adopted March 31, 2010 in Nairobi, entered into force March 31, 2010); Protocol for the Protection of the Caspian Sea against Pollution from Land-based Sources and Activities (adopted December 12, 2006, entered into force November 23, 2023) to the Framework Convention for the Protection of the Marine Environment of the Caspian Sea (adopted November 4, 2003 in Tehran, entered into force August 12, 2006).

202 76/464/EEC, O.J L 129 (5/18/76).

203 79/923/EEC, O.J. L 281 (11/10/79).

204 Art. 1, 2(7) Water Framework Directive; For a discussion of the Water Framework Directive, see Chapter 10.

205 Art. 1(1) MSFD ; DIRECTIVE 2008/56/EC 17 June, 2008; EC, 'Report from the Commission to the European Parliament and the Council assessing Member States' programmes of measures under the Marine Strategy Framework Directive SWD (2018) 393 final (July 31,2018) 9; See for more Suvi-Tuuli Puharinen, 'Achieving Good Marine Environmental Status in the EU – Implications of the Marine Strategy Framework Directive for Member States and Blue Economic Activities' (2023) 155 Marine Policy 1.

206 Directive 2014/89/EU, Art. 1(1).

not to impose any new obligations on State Parties, but that it rather aims to contribute to the planning process of policies.[207]

Many rivers carry pollution into the sea and it is thus useful to add international treaties protecting fresh watercourses against pollution to this summary. Review of the developments concerning inland waters is necessary to give a complete picture of international regulation concerning land-based pollution.[208] The 1997 UN Convention on the Law of the Non-Navigational Uses of International Watercourses, confirms in Article 23 that:

> Watercourse States shall, individually and, where appropriate, in cooperation with other States, take all measures with respect to an international watercourse that are necessary to protect and preserve the marine environment, including estuaries, taking into account generally accepted international rules and standards.[209]

6 Prevention and Remediation of Environmental Harm

After having discussed the different forms of pollution, this section sets out the legal framework in cases of environmental emergencies, such as oil spills. Emergencies can be defined as those where the presence or danger of hydrocarbons or other dangerous polluting substances constitute a serious and imminent danger for the coasts or related interests of a state. In part due to the harm caused by accidents in the 20th Century involving the tankers *Torrey Canyon, Amoco Cadiz, Exxon Valdez,* this is one of the most developed parts of international law relating to marine pollution. On the global level it is governed by general principles set out in UNCLOS,[210] and by the International Convention on Oil Pollution Preparedness, Response and Cooperation, complemented in 2000 by a Protocol on Preparedness, Response and Cooperation to Pollution by Hazardous and Noxious Substances.[211] The Protocol expands the scope of cooperation between the Parties to include spills of hazardous and noxious substances, The Convention is elaborated in the framework of the International Maritime Organization.[212] Before its conclusion, only regional

207 ibid, preamble para. 9.
208 See Chapter 10.
209 New York, May 21, 1997, EMuT 997:39.
210 Arts. 189, 204 and 211(7).
211 See 31 EPL 145 (2001).
212 London, November 30, 1990, 5 WESTON V.F.28.

instruments handled this matter, such as the 1969 Bonn Agreement which concerned pollution only by oil and was replaced by the 1983 Bonn Agreement for Cooperation in Dealing with Pollution of the North Sea by Oil and Other Harmful Substances.[213] Several additional protocols to regional seas conventions also provided for co-operation in emergencies.

In the regional context, several additional protocols are attached to UNEP-sponsored regional seas conventions.[214] Each convention contains a provision envisaging adoption of the protocol. All except the Caribbean instrument are directed towards oil pollution as well as other harmful substances. In fact, it is surprising that even one of the agreements is limited to oil, because the general trend has been to extend these instruments to regulate all polluting substances.

Jurisdictional considerations are different on the high seas. In the past, in case of an accident that causes pollution, only the flag state could intervene since they had sole jurisdiction, even if it was a question of taking absolutely

---

213 Bonn, September 13, 1983; EMuT 983:68.

214 See: – Protocol Concerning Cooperation in Combating Pollution of the Mediterranean Sea by Oil and Other Harmful Substances in Cases of Emergency (February 16, 1976), supplementing the Barcelona Convention on the Mediterranean; replaced by the Protocol Concerning Cooperation in Preventing Pollution from Ships and, in Cases of Emergency, Combating Pollution of the Mediterranean Sea (January 25, 2002); – Protocol Concerning Regional Cooperation in Combating Pollution by Oil and other Harmful Substances in Cases of Emergency (April 24, 1978), supplementing the Kuwait Convention on the Gulf; – Protocol Concerning Cooperation in Combating Pollution in Cases of Emergency (March 23, 1981), supplementing the Abidjan Convention on West-Africa; – Agreement on Regional Cooperation in Combating Pollution of the South-East Pacific by Hydrocarbons or Other Harmful Substances in Cases of Emergency (November 12, 1981), supplementing the Lima Convention on the South-East Pacific; – Protocol Concerning Regional Cooperation in Combating Pollution by Hydrocarbons or Other Harmful Substances in Cases of Emergency (February 14, 1982), supplementing the Jeddah Convention on the Red Sea; – Protocol Concerning Cooperation in Combating Oil Spills in the Wider Caribbean Region (March 24, 1983), supplementing the Cartagena Convention on the Caribbean; – Protocol Concerning Co-operation in Combating Marine Pollution in Cases of Emergency in the Eastern African Union (June 21, 1985), supplementing the Nairobi Convention on the Eastern African region which is since 2010 the Amended Nairobi Convention for the Protection, Management and Development of the Marine and Coastal Environment of the Western Indian Ocean; - Protocol Concerning Cooperation in Combating Pollution Emergencies in the South Pacific Region (November 25, 1986), supplementing the Noumea Convention on the South Pacific; – Protocol on Joint Action in the Case of Accidents (Such as Oil Spills) (April 21, 1992), supplementing the Bucharest Convention on the Black Sea; – Protocol Concerning Regional Preparedness, response and Co-operation in Combating Oil Pollution Incidents (August 12, 2011) supplementing the Aktau Convention on the Caspian Sea.

indispensable measures to stop the pollution. Soon after the 1967 *Torrey Canyon* catastrophe, IMO adopted the International Convention Relating to Intervention on the High Seas in Cases of Oil Pollution Casualties.[215] It establishes that each of the state parties can take such measures on the high seas as may be necessary 'to prevent, mitigate or eliminate grave and imminent danger to their coastline or related interests from pollution or threat of pollution of the sea by oil, following a casualty or acts related to such a casualty, which may reasonably be expected to result in major harmful consequences'.[216] In 1973, the provisions of this Convention were extended by a protocol, to cover substances other than oil. [217] Since the applicable area of the two conventions has considerably shrunk due to the establishment of EEZs under UNCLOS, the practical consequences of the two conventions on intervention on the high seas have been diminished.

The issues of responsibility and damages for harm are also important. Although this question is treated in detail in Chapter 7, relevant in this context are the 1969 Brussels Convention from Oil Pollution Damage with its 1971 treaty creating a compensation fund, which was later amended; the 1977 London Convention on Civil Liability for Oil Pollution Damage Resulting from Exploration for and Exploitation of Seabed Mineral Resources; certain principles of UNCLOS and in 2001, the International Convention on Civil Liability for Bunker Oil Pollution Damage.

Having discussed all of this, we will now look at the prevention and remediation of environmental emergencies, which may arise in a number of frameworks already discussed. Generally speaking, the provisions relating to emergencies caused by oil pollution fall into two categories. One part aims at organizing advance cooperation before the existence of an emergency situation. The second part becomes applicable when an emergency arises and concerns the actions which must be taken.

6.1 *Preventive Actions*

The fundamental requirement is that states maintain the ability to react efficiently to emergency situations. Article 2(2) of the Kuwait Protocol provides a good example:

> The Contracting States shall endeavor to maintain and promote, either individually or through bilateral or multilateral cooperation, their con-

215 Brussels, November 29, 1969.
216 Art. 1(1).
217 London, November 2, 1973.

> tingency plans and means for combating pollution in the Sea Area by oil and other harmful substances. These means shall include, in particular, available equipment, ships, aircraft and man power prepared for operations in cases of emergency.[218]

An initial obligation is to transmit to other states parties information necessary to respond to any potential action: information regarding national authorities responsible for combating pollution, including their structure and operation, and designating the authorities who should receive information concerning marine pollution and implement measures of assistance between parties.[219] States parties may also be required to provide each other with their laws, regulations, and other legal instruments relating generally to combating pollution of the sea by hydrocarbons and other harmful substances.[220] Some also request transmission of information on the existing national methods of responding to pollution, which could be useful in international emergencies.[221] A few provisions require that new techniques to combat, prevent and limit the effects of pollution be shared. This is especially the case in regional instruments whose states parties include both industrialized and developing countries.[222] Finally, in certain cases it is required that states transmit and centralize a list of experts who can be called upon in case of emergency.[223]

One of the most important tasks among the anticipatory measures is to assure that communications will function at the moment an emergency arises. Article 8 of the Barcelona Convention's Valletta Protocol Concerning Cooperation in Preventing Pollution from Ships and, in Cases of Emergency, Combating Pollution of the Mediterranean Sea codifies this need: 'The Parties undertake to coordinate the utilization of the means of communication at their disposal in order to ensure, with the necessary speed and reliability, the reception, transmission and dissemination of all reports and urgent information which relate to the occurrences and situations referred to in Article 1 ….'[224]

---

218 See also Art. 2, Helsinki Convention; Art. 4, Protocol of Barcelona; Art. 9, Protocol of Abidjan; Art. 2(2), Protocol of Jeddah; Art. 3 Protocol of Nairobi; Art. 9 Protocol of Aktau.

219 Art. 9(1), Helsinki; Art. 6(a), Barcelona; Art. 5, Kuwait; Art. 5(a) Abidjan; Art. 7, Lima; Art. 5, Jeddah; Art. 4, Cartagena; Art. 4(a),(b), Bonn; Art. 5(1)(b) Aktau.

220 Art. 1(b), Helsinki; art. 3(3), 5, Kuwait; Art. 5(b), Abidjan; Art. 5(b), Jeddah; and Art. 4, Cartagena.

221 Art. 4(c), Bonn; Arts. 3(3)(III), 12; Kuwait; Art. 1(a), Quito; Art. 13 Bucharest.

222 Art. 6(1)(c), Barcelona; Arts. 3(3)(II), 6, Kuwait; Art. 6(a) Jeddah.

223 E.g., Art. 3(3)(III), Kuwait.

224 Valletta, January 25, 2002. See also Art. 5, Helsinki; Art. 9, Abidjan; Art. 8, Lima; Art. 5(3), Bonn; Art. 3 Bucharest.

It is obvious that the most reliable means of alerting states in case of major marine environmental pollution is to exercise systematic monitoring. Article 204 of UNCLOS summarizes this:

1. 'States shall, consistent with the rights of other States, endeavor, as far as practicable, directly or through the competent international organizations, to observe, measure, evaluate and analyze, by recognized scientific methods, the risks or effects of pollution of the marine environment.
2. In particular, States shall keep under surveillance the effects of any activities which they permit or in which they engage in order to determine whether these activities are likely to pollute the marine environment'.

Article 205 adds that states shall publish reports of the results obtained in applying Article 204 or provide such reports, at appropriate intervals, to the competent international organizations.

A number of regional treaties provide for the organization of ocean monitoring to detect pollution.[225] The 1983 Bonn Agreement best accomplishes this in an annex which divides the North Sea region into zones.[226] The Convention designates one or several states to be responsible for each zone. In case of emergency, the responsible state evaluates the nature and importance of the accident or, if appropriate, the type and approximate quantity of hydrocarbons or other dangerous substances, as well as the direction and speed of its movement. The state is to immediately inform all other states parties, transmitting to them its evaluations. It also must maintain its surveillance of the pollution for as long as it remains within the zone.[227]

UNCLOS Article 199 invites states to jointly develop and promote contingency plans for responding to pollution incidents in the marine environment. Several protocols concerning regional seas provide for the preparation on the national level of such contingency plans,[228] and some require that these plans be communicated to other states parties.[229]

Another anticipatory measure on the international level is the establishment of mutual aid centers in case of emergency at sea as provided for in several regional protocols.[230] The Malta center, established within the framework of the Barcelona Convention for the Mediterranean Sea, serves as a model for other comparable initiatives. Article 3 of the Kuwait protocol has the most

---

225 Art. 3, Helsinki; Art. 4, Barcelona; Art. 5, Lima; Art. 11 Bucharest.
226 Referring in turn to Article 6 of the Agreement.
227 Art. 6.
228 Art. 4, Lima; Art. 2, Quito; Art. 2 Bucharest; Art. 5 Aktau.
229 Art. 5, Kuwait; Art. 5(c), Abidjan.
230 Arts. 6–11, Barcelona; Arts. 3, 8 Kuwait; Art. 3, Jeddah; Art. 9, Cartegena.

complete provision in this regard, granting numerous functions to its regional Marine Emergency Mutual Aid Center: gathering and disseminating information, assisting states parties in developing laws and regulations, preparing marine emergency contingency plans, establishing procedures for transport of personnel, equipment and materials, transmitting reports concerning marine emergencies, and promoting and developing training programs for combating pollution. In addition, in emergency situations, the Center must be immediately informed and transmit this information to states parties as soon as possible.

6.2 *Responsive Actions*

Obviously, the first task of states who learn of an emergency at sea is to inform the states exposed to it as well any competent international organizations.[231] This general obligation is reaffirmed and detailed in all the instruments specially concerned with international cooperation in case of emergencies. Thus, information should be addressed without delay to the competent authorities of any state which could be affected by the pollution. Moreover, according to the terms of the Valletta Protocol, the maritime authorities of the states parties should instruct the captains of vessels flying their flag and aircraft pilots registered on their territory to signal a state participating in the regional center, by the most rapid and adequate means, information regarding all accidents causing or likely to cause pollution of the sea by oil or other harmful substances. They must also notify of the presence, characteristics and extent of spillage of such substances observed at sea which are likely to present a serious and imminent threat to the marine environment or to the coast or related interests of one or more states parties.[232] The information thus received is communicated to other states susceptible of being affected by the pollution, either directly by the state which received the information or by the regional center.[233]

An Annex to the Protocol sets out the precise contents of the report to be made pursuant to Article 9. Each report must contain, as far as possible, the identification of the source of pollution, the geographic position, time and date of the occurrence, the prevailing wind and sea conditions, relevant details concerning the ship, and a clear indication or description of the harmful substances involved. Supplementary information should be furnished where

231 Arts. 198, 211(7), UNCLOS.
232 Art. 9(1).
233 Art. 9(7).

appropriate. Several other protocols contain similarly detailed provisions,[234] while other instruments contain the same principles, but are less detailed.[235]

The states parties to such treaties also have financial or material obligations. They must not only observe and evaluate polluting incidents, but intervene. In case of a release or loss overboard of harmful substances in packages, freight containers, portable tanks or road and rail tank wagons, they shall cooperate to salvage and recover such substances in order to reduce the danger of pollution of the marine environment.[236] The principal types of assistance required by the different regional instruments, are first, furnishing of personnel, material, and equipment, as well as means of monitoring and control; and second, facilitating the transfer of personnel, material, and equipment into, out of, and through the territories of the contracting states.[237]

A complete picture of obligations in emergency situations is found in Article 7 of the Cartagena Protocol, titled *Operational Measures*:

> Each contracting party shall, within its capabilities, take steps including those outlined below in responding to an oil spill incident:
>
> a. make a preliminary assessment of the incident, including the type and extent of existing or likely pollution effects;
> b. promptly communicate information concerning the incident pursuant to Art. 5;
> c. promptly determine its ability to take effective measures to respond to the incident and the assistance that might be required;
> d. consult as appropriate with other contracting parties concerned in the process of determining the necessary response to the incident;
> e. take the measures necessary to prevent, reduce or eliminate the effects of the incident, including monitoring of the situation.

Financing assistance is explicitly discussed only in the protocol of Quito,[238] the protocol of Aktau,[239] and the 1983 Bonn Agreement. Article 9 of the last of these states that unless otherwise agreed between the interested states, when action is undertaken by a state at the express request of another state party, the latter should reimburse the first for the costs incurred because of its assistance.

234 Art. 7 and Annex A, Kuwait; Art. 7 and Annex, Abidjan; Art. 9 and Annex, Lima; Art. 7 Nairobi.

235 Art. 5(2)–(5), Helsinki; Art. 7, Jeddah; Art. 5, Cartagena; Art. 5(2)-(3), Bonn.

236 Art. 5, Barcelona; Art. 4, Helsinki; Art. 6, Lima.

237 Art. 10, Abidjan and Art. 11(2), Kuwait. See also, Art. 8, Helsinki; Art. 10, Barcelona; Art. 11, Lima; Art. 1(b), Quito, Art. 11, Jeddah; Art. 6, Cartagena; Art. 7, Bonn.

238 Art. 1(c).

239 Art. 11.

When the action is undertaken at the sole initiative of a state, it accepts the costs incurred by reason of its action. Finally, when the state having solicited the assistance terminates its request – which can occur at any time – it pays the expenses already incurred by the assisting state party. In all cases, unless otherwise agreed, the costs incurred by an action undertaken by a state at the demand of another are calculated according to the legislation and practices in force in the assisting country.[240]

The use of regional centers has already been discussed.[241] It must be added that the same regional instruments frequently provide for regular meetings of the states parties to exercise a general monitoring of the implementation of the treaty obligations, to examine regularly the efficiency of the measures taken by virtue of the agreement, and to exercise any other function which might be necessary.[242]

Conclusions

Throughout the past few decades, the sources of pollution have become increasingly varied, while the ways in which humanity makes use of the world's oceans have become increasingly diverse. These forms and sources of pollution are regulated by numerous instruments, which are intended to work together to create a coherent approach for the control of marine pollution. In this regard, increasing recognition of the mutual impacts of land and marine areas and the activities on them has produced a trend towards integrated ecosystem management, including integrated management of coastal areas, coral reefs and their associated mangroves and sea grasses, wetlands, and freshwater systems. Chapter 14. further addresses integrated environmental management of coastal and marine ecosystems. However, as the UNEP regional seas programme illustrates, environmental legal frameworks may be designed to provide for regional jurisdiction and membership, in order to protect and preserve resources in specific areas without the flexibility required to manage, on a global scale, the vastly different marine ecosystems found on our planet.

240 Art. 10, Bonn.

241 See infra.

242 Arts. 12, 14, Bonn; Art. 12, Barcelona; Art. 13, Kuwait; Art. 11, Abidjan; Art. 12, Lima; Art. 10, Cartagena.

Bibliography

Brown, E.D., *The International Law of the Sea* (1994).

Brubaker, D., *Marine Pollution and International Law* (1993).

Beurier, J-P, Kiss, A. Ch. and Mahmoudi, S., *Nouvelles Technologies et Droit de l'Environnement Marin* (2000).

Churchill R.R., Lowe, A.V. and Sander A., *The Law of the Sea* (2022).

Churchill R.R. and Oude Elferink A., *New Knowledge and Changing Circumstances in the Law of the Sea* (2020).

Kasoulides, G.C., *Port State Control and Jurisdiction: Evolution of the Port State Regime* (1993).

Khodjet El Khil, L., *La Pollution De La Mer Méditerranée du Fait du Transport Maritime De Marchandises* (2003).

Kuribayashi, T., and Miles, E.L. (eds), *The Law of the Sea in the 1990s: A Framework for Further International Cooperation* (1992).

Mitchell, R.B., *Intentional Oil Pollution at Sea: Environmental Policy and Treaty Compliance* (1994).

Molenaar, E.J., *Coastal State Jurisdiction over Vessel-Source Pollution* (Kluwer, 1998).

Nandan, S. and Rosenne, B., *United Nations Convention on the Law of the Sea 1982: A Commentary* (1995).

Nordquist, M.H., Moore, J.N. and Long, R., *The Marine Environment and United Nations Sustainable Development Goal* 14 (2018).

Peet, G., 'The MARPOL Convention: Implementation and Effectiveness' (1992) 7 J. *Estuarine & Coastal L.* 290.

Rayfuse, R., *Research Handbook On International Marine Environmental* Law (2015).

Van Dyke, J., and others, *Freedom for the Seas in the 21st Century* (1993).

CHAPTER 12

Atmosphere and Climate

The earth is surrounded by a cover of gases that condition life, protect all living things from harmful solar radiation, and regulate the global climate. The chemical composition of the atmosphere has been quite stable for 600 million years, with four gases comprising 99.99 percent of dry air: nitrogen (78.08%), oxygen (20.95%), argon (0.93%) and carbon dioxide (0.03%).[1] The proportion of these gases remains almost identical up to an altitude of approximately 25 kilometers.[2] The atmosphere is also composed of several layers where inputs of pollutants may have very different impacts. In order from the earth to outer space, these are the troposphere, stratosphere, mesosphere, thermosphere and exosphere. The lowest level, the troposphere, contains about 80 percent of the air mass, the other 20 percent being found in the stratosphere.[3]

The introduction of pollutants into the atmosphere creates multiple effects, because the air is essentially a place of transit: gases or particles remain there temporarily and manifest many of their impacts only after returning to the soil, plants, marine waters, lakes or rivers. Poisonous air also directly damages living creatures and objects. Three of the most widely known and serious ecological catastrophes of the 20th Century – Bhopal, India; Chernobyl, Ukraine; and the Indonesian forest fires – produced most of their victims as a result of direct contact with polluting elements in the atmosphere. Pollutants often undergo modifications in their composition once they enter the atmosphere. Finally, and significantly, air pollutants move quickly and cover greater distances than pollutants do in watercourses or the marine environment. The atmosphere is in fact the planet's largest single shared resource consisting of several large air basins.

Numerous sources emit pollution into the atmosphere, including energy-production facilities, industrial processes, waste incinerators, transportation vehicles, and even animal farms. The amounts of pollutants vary from one area to another, depending on the type and concentration of human activities and on the measures taken to reduce emissions. Data from the World Resource

1 Marvin Soroos, *The Endangered Atmosphere: Preserving a Global Commons* (South Carolina University Press 1997), 24.

2 ILC, 'Report of the International Law Commission on the Work of its 72nd Session' (April 26–June 4 and July 5–August 6, 2021) UN Doc A/76/10, 24.

3 ibid.

 | DOI:10.1163/9789047440802_014

Institute shows that the top three greenhouse gas emitters were responsible for fifteen times the emissions of the bottom hundred.[4] The data further illustrates that the countries responsible for emissions are changing; half of the top 10 emitters were developing countries. Per capita emissions continue to evidence inequality, but the US, EU (treated as one emitter), Russia and Japan all show a declining trend in per capita emissions.[5]

Legal regulation of other environmental issues can have an impact on air pollution. Efforts to clean up water or soil, for example, including the tendency to incinerate wastes instead of depositing them on the ground or dumping them into the sea or into inland waters, can aggravate air pollution. Similarly, the siting of industrial facilities is important, because when pollutants are emitted into the atmosphere, the amount and direction of their dispersion plays a significant role in determining the extent of damage they cause. Efforts to reduce atmospheric pollution must not only set emission and air quality standards, but should address the use of fuels that are rich in sulfur, lead or other pollutants, and control combustion processes. With sulfur oxide and nitrous oxide being the main causes for acid rain, reducing acid rains means reducing the sulfur content of combustion gases, either by using low-sulfur fuels or by removing sulfur before or during the combustion process. Although acid rain is still an issue, the phenomenon has greatly decreased in the past few decades in the west, with emissions most responsible for causing acid rain dropping by around 80% in Europe and North America in the 1980s and 1990s due to effective policies on air pollution.[6] However, the issue remains in for example India, China and Brazil.[7] Although this is still concerning, and the

---

4 See World Resources Institute, 'This Interactive Chart Shows Changes in the World's Top 10 Emitters' (March 2, 2023) available at < https://www.wri.org/insights/interactive-chart-shows-changes-worlds-top-10-emitters> (accessed January 22, 2024).

5 ibid. According to the Global Carbon Budget for 2015, in 2014 China had the highest contribution to global CO_2 emissions at 27%, with the United States making the second largest contribution at 15%. However, the United States had considerably higher CO_2 emissions per capita, with 4.8 tons of carbon per person, per year compared to 1.9 for China and 1.3 globally, see Le Quéré et al, '*Global Carbon Budget*' (2915) 7(2) *Earth System Science Data* 349, 375.

6 Peringe Grennfelt e.a., 'Acid rain and air pollution: 50 years of progress in environmental science and policy' (2020) 49 *Ambio* 849–864; USEPA, *2015 Program Progress – Cross-State Air Pollution Rule and Acid Rain Program* (2015) 6; Sulfur dioxide (SO_2) is a primary cause of acid rain. The major sources are coal and oil combustion and the major effects are acidification of water and soil. Acid rain has no uniform definition, but most scientists regard pH readings below 4.5 to be highly acidic. This level is ten times that of normal rain. Some areas of Europe and North American have in the past regularly received precipitation that is forty times the normal level.

7 Jigyasa Prakash, Shashi Bhushan Agrawal, and Madhoolika Agrawal, 'Global Trends of Acidity in Rainfall and Its Impact on Plants and Soil' (2023) 23(1) *Journal of Soil Science and Plant Nutrition* 398, 413.

remaining issue is still deserving of attention, it can be seen as a success story of the influence of legal regulation on air pollution over a relatively short term.

This chapter, like Agenda 21, Chapter 9, addresses the three main international legal issues concerning the atmosphere: transboundary pollution, protection of the ozone layer, and climate change, the last of which comprises a transversal body of norms (rather than being restricted to rules of general international or an isolated *lex specialis* regime). The three problems first will be described, then the legal aspects of each of them will be analyzed separately.

1 Overview

Air pollution has been defined as

> the introduction by man, directly or indirectly, of substances or energy into the air, resulting in deleterious effects of such a nature as to endanger human health, harm living resources and ecosystems and material property, and impair or interfere with amenities and other legitimate uses of the environment.[8]

This definition adapts the general concept of pollution, focusing on risk or harm resulting from changes in the environment.

Atmospheric pollution appears in multiple forms. Domestic and international regulation have evolved as the impacts of each form of pollution have become known. Pollutants, principally nitrous oxides (NO_x) and hydrocarbon emissions such as carbon dioxide combine with sulfuric gases to produce ozone (O_3) or smog during sunny periods.[9] Ozone harms the needles of conifers, particularly the membrane which supports photosynthesis. These lie at the source of the serious damage caused above all on western and southern slopes at an altitude near 800 meters. Ground level ozone is also particularly harmful to those who have vulnerable respiratory systems, including children, the elderly and the sick.[10] The major sources of ozone pollution are motor vehicles, power stations, and industries utilizing fossil fuels. Particulates are

---

8 art 1(a), Convention on Long-Range Transboundary Air Pollution (Geneva, Nov. 13, 1979).

9 Nitrous oxides, emitted by many industrial processes, are a precursor to smog. They are also a source of acid rain; Carbon dioxide (CO_2) is the largest contributor to anthropogenic climate change. Carbon dioxide is released by the combustion of fossil fuels, largely by automobiles and other motor vehicles.

10 In contrast, stratospheric ozone is a necessary component of the atmosphere because it acts to filter harmful ultraviolet radiation.

larger than a single molecule and consist of matter such as ash and bits of heavy metal. Particulates corrode buildings, monuments, and other objects and harm vegetation. Among the other substances entering the atmosphere, the impact of persistent organic pollutants (POPs) and chlorofluorocarbons (CFCs) in the atmosphere has become a major concern.[11]

Air pollution led to international disputes relatively early. From the end of the 19th century, fumes emitted by a zinc and lead smelter situated in Trail, Canada, some dozen kilometers from the United States border, posed the problem of transboundary pollution and reparation for the harm it caused. Slightly more than forty years later, an arbitral decision rendered in the *Trail Smelter* case became the first major decision of international jurisprudence announcing the obligation of each state not to cause or allow transboundary pollution damage to other states.[12]

To combat deterioration in air quality, initial measures sought to disperse the pollutants through increasing the height of factory smokestacks. The 'solution' created new environmental problems: emissions taken to higher atmospheric levels traveled considerable distances on air currents, causing long-range pollution damage. As a result, air pollution was no longer solely a local phenomenon concerning large cities and industrial zones, but by the 1970s, it was a matter that affected non-industrial countries and agricultural areas often far from the source of the emissions. The effects were particularly felt in Scandinavian countries, even though their air quality was not considered unacceptable. The rivers and lakes of Scandinavia showed disquieting symptoms, due to the increase in sulfuric substances, transformed into sulfuric acid. The increased presence of acid in freshwaters reached a point where it endangered fish, micro-decomposers, algae, and other aquatic life.[13]

While acidification of Scandinavian lakes by sulfuric rain originating from afar was at the heart of discussions during the 1970s, by 1980 public opinion in Central and Eastern Europe and in Canada turned to the disappearance of forests due to pollution. In 1995–1997, a survey of European forests, taking into account 116,000 hectares in twenty-nine countries, revealed that one in every four trees was suffering from abnormal thinning of the crown, with only slight

---

11 POPs are organochlorides that are released as chemical byproducts of industrial production. They do not decompose easily and can travel great distances, and bioaccumulate, resulting in high concentrations in animals at the top of the food chain. Some of them have been linked to cancer, immune deficiencies and loss of fertility; CFCs deplete stratospheric ozone. See below in this chapter, section C.

12 Arbitral Award in the *Trail Smelter Case*, (March 11, 1941), 3 U.N.R.I.A.A. 1905.

13 George P. Smith, 'Acid Rain: Transnational Perspectives' (1983) 4 *N.Y.U. Int'l & Comp. L.* 459, 463.

differences between conifers and broad-leaved trees.[14] Multiple causes for the destruction have been suggested, including successive drought years, viral diseases, and fungi; atmospheric pollution is still considered the primary factor, either as principal agent or as contributing to the weakening of trees, making them less resistant to the lack of water or disease.

In the 1980s scientists discovered two other problems related to the emission of substances into the atmosphere: the depletion of the stratospheric ozone layer and the threat of a major, anthropogenic change of the global climate.

Ozone is a form of oxygen, containing one more atom than the oxygen breathed in the atmosphere. While ground-level ozone in the form of 'smog' produces harmful consequences, especially to plants, stratospheric ozone, whose strongest concentrations are found between twenty and twenty-five kilometers above earth, filters a part of the sun's ultraviolet radiation which otherwise would injure life forms on earth. The absorption of ultraviolet rays by stratospheric ozone is also a source of climatic energy. According to a 2022 study prepared under the aegis of UNEP, UV-radiation exposure (which occurs more as a result of the depletion of the ozone layer) can harm human health by causing skin cancer, inflammatory skin disorders, sunburn and eye disorders.[15] Besides this, it has also been proven that a reduction in ozone in the stratosphere influences biological factors such as the weather, which in turn changes the growth of plants, and ecosystems, such as the speed of decomposition of plant litter.[16]

The anthropogenic source of ozone depletion was clear by the late 1970s.[17] The utilization of chlorofluorocarbons (CFCs), contained in aerosol sprays and to a lesser extent in solvents and refrigeration, was identified as a major contributing cause. When first developed, CFCs were viewed favorably because they are nontoxic, nonflammable, noncorrosive and stable. It is the very stability of CFCs that is the source of the problem because they migrate over long distances and survive for many years. When they reach the stratosphere intact, solar radiation breaks the molecules apart to free reactive chlorine atoms, catalyzing

14 The surveys were carried out by the UN Economic Commission for Europe and the European Union. See, Martin Lorenz et al., 'Forest Conditions in Europe, Results of the 1996 Crown Conditions Survey: 1997 Technical Report', (1997)14–15.

15 UNEP, *Environmental Effects of Stratospheric Ozone Depletion, UV Radiation, and Interactions with Climate Change: 2022 Assessment Report* (2022) 4.

16 Janet Bornman et al., 'Solar ultraviolet radiation and ozone depletion-driven climate change: effects on terrestrial ecosystems' (2015) 14(1) *Photochemical & Photobiological Sciences* 88, 88.

17 The first publication linking CFCs and their role in the destruction of the ozone layer appeared in 1974. See Mario Molina and F. Sherwood Rowland , 'Stratospheric Sink for Chlorofluoromethanes: Chlorine Atoms-Catalyzed Destruction of Ozone' (1974) 249 *Nature* 810.

chain reactions that destroy ozone; even if CFC production and use are phased out, ozone depletion will remain for some time, because of the substances already released. By 1985 it was understood that most depletion of the ozone layer occurs on a seasonal basis above Antarctica and the Arctic region.[18] The Antarctic ozone hole has recently been showing signs of recovery as a result of effective policies on the regulation of CFCs and other similar substances.[19]

The third major problem of the atmosphere is climate change, meaning a change in the climate attributed directly or indirectly to human activity that alters the composition of the global atmosphere and is in addition to natural climate variation observed over a comparable time period.[20] The adverse effects from this change have been characterized as changes in the physical environment or biota which have significant deleterious effects on the composition, resilience or productivity of natural and managed ecosystems or on the operation or socio-economic systems or on human health and welfare.[21]

Since the 1960s scientists have expressed concern that a generalized warming of the planet's atmosphere might lead to changes in the global climate. The global average temperature between 1866 and 1996 increased by more than one degree.[22] The Intergovernmental Panel on Climate Change (IPCC), a network established in 1988 of more than 2,000 scientists and policy experts advising governments on climate policy, states with high confidence that the global surface temperature between 2011 and 2020 reached 1.1°C above the 1850–1900 period.[23] The accumulation of gases such as carbon dioxide, nitrous oxide, methane, chlorofluorocarbons and tropospheric ozone is viewed as at least partly responsible for the warming. The IPCC also states that the carbon dioxide concentration in the atmosphere in 2019 was higher than at any time in at least 2 million years.[24]

---

18 The European Commission reported that the Arctic stratosphere may have lost up to 60% of its ozone during the 1999–2000 winter and that average ozone concentrations over Europe were 15% less than those of the early 1970s. See David Hunter, James Salzman, and Durwood Zaelke, *International Environmental Law and Policy* (2nd edn, Foundation Press 2002) 530.

19 WMO, *Executive Summary. Scientific Assessment of Ozone Depletion: 2022* (GAW Report No 278, 2022) 33; see the end of section C for more on this topic.

20 U.N. Framework Convention on Climate Change (adopted 9 May 1992, enteres into force 21 March 1994) 1771 U.N.T.S. 107, art 1(2).

21 ibid, art 1(1).

22 See Lester R. Brown et al., *State of the World* 2001 (New York: W.W. Norton &. Company. 2001), 168.

23 IPCC, 'Summary for Policymakers' in *Climate Change 2023: Synthesis Report. Contribution of Working Groups I, II and III to the Sixth Assessment Report of the Intergovernmental Panel on Climate Change* (IPCC 2023) 4.

24 ibid.

Carbon dioxide is a basic by-product of the combustion of fossil and other natural fuels such as wood, coal, oil and gasoline. Other significant greenhouse gases are chlorofluorocarbons, which also contribute to the depletion of the ozone layer, methane and nitrous oxide. Chlorofluorocarbons are discussed later in this chapter. Methane is a metabolic by-product of animals (including humans) and is produced in significant quantities by domestic cattle. It is also a byproduct of petroleum production and often used as burning fuel. Nitrous oxide has various industrial applications as an aerosol propellant, and is used as an anesthetic gas. The accumulation of these gases acts as an insulating blanket that traps the energy of sunlight and prevents it from radiating back into outer space. The accumulation of solar energy causes a gradual increase in the average temperature of the earth's surface.

The trend towards increasing temperatures has resulted in rising sea levels – between 2006 and 2018, the sea level has steadily risen with 3.7 mm per year, with human influence being the main cause for sea level rise since at least 1971.[25] In 2015, the IPCC found that the global mean sea level has risen by approximately 0.17m to 0.21m and stated with high confidence that 'the rate of sea level rise since the mid-19th century has been larger than the mean rate during the previous two millennia'.[26] According to some projections, many small islands would be submerged or become unsafe and huge areas of heavily-populated countries such as Bangladesh or Indonesia could become partly uninhabitable.[27]

Climate change also would modify the world's agriculture: some areas would become arid, while other regions that are presently too cold would become able to grow cereals, corn or fruit and other products needing a warmer climate. Increased water temperatures would disrupt aquatic ecosystems and further burden already distressed fisheries. A particularly sinister consequence of global climate change is the multiplication of violent weather patterns, including severe drought, tropical storms, hurricanes, unusually heavy rainfalls, and the consequential floods and landslides. In addition, a slight rise in average annual air temperature could greatly increase the risk of insect outbreaks,

25 ibid 5.

26 IPCC, *Climate Change 2014: Synthesis Report. Contribution of Working Groups I, II and III to the Fifth Assessment Report of the Intergovernmental Panel on Climate Change* (2014), 42.

27 See The World Watch Institute, State of the World 2013 (Island Press 2013) 346–347.

resulting in pests damaging agriculture.[28] It could, however, also reduce other insect populations, influencing pollination in a negative fashion.[29]

The global warming issue exemplifies the ecological principle that all activity in an ecosystem is interrelated and interdependent. In addition to industrial and automotive emissions from developed countries, a large part of global warming results from agricultural and resource activities in developing countries. Tropical deforestation is a serious problem that concerns more than loss of renewable resources and biological diversity; two aspects of deforestation contribute significantly to global warming. First, much of the deforestation that occurs in tropical countries results from land-clearing for agriculture. Soils in most tropical countries are so poor that they cannot sustain crops for more than one or two seasons. The farmers then move and clear still more forest, typically by means of the 'slash and burn' technique. The trees are chopped down or bulldozed, followed by the burning of all the native vegetation and the unusable wood that remains. Industrialized logging practices increase the destruction through burning large areas to clear roads; in 1997 and 2001, forest fires in Indonesia created a thick layer of smoke that covered a large part of South-east Asia. This problem and its aftermath are discussed later in this chapter.[30]

Unsustainable exploitation of tropical forests also contributes to greenhouse effects. Forests and oceans are natural 'sinks' that remove greenhouse gases by absorbing carbon dioxide, although it is difficult to know the exact proportion of such absorption. Deforestation hinders the process and thus enhances global warming. The greenhouse effect can also be slowed down by the storage of greenhouse gases by components of the climate system which then constitute 'reservoirs'.

2 International Efforts to Control Air Pollution

2.1 *Initial Legal Approaches*

Although air pollution was traditionally considered a local problem, the leading early case in international environmental law concerns transboundary pollution caused by fumes. The pollution resulted from the activities of a smelter,

28 Cheikh Mbow et al., *Food Security. In: Climate Change and Land: an IPCC special report on climate change, desertification, land degradation, sustainable land management, food security, and greenhouse gas fluxes in terrestrial ecosystems* (2019), 459.

29 ibid.

30 See Section B.2.

located in Trail, Canada, and the resulting dispute was decided by an arbitral award on March 11, 1941.[31] Beginning in 1896, fumes from the smelter damaged agricultural lands in the United States by releasing into the air up to 350 tons of sulfurous smoke daily. Some victims were indemnified, but in 1925, it became necessary to undertake a collective action. Two years later, the United States government officially began negotiations with Canada, resulting in an agreement to submit the dispute to an international arbitral tribunal. The latter delivered its final judgment on March 11, 1941, concluding that

> under the principles of international law ... no State has the right to use or permit the use of its territory in such a manner as to cause injury by fumes in or to the territory of another or the properties or persons therein, when the case is of serious consequence and the injury is established by clear and convincing evidence.[32]

The first international regulations addressing air pollution were aimed at resolving a different problem. In 1958 the Economic Commission for Europe of the United Nations sought to facilitate international trade by establishing uniform standards for automobile equipment and parts, which are accepted in all European countries today. Several of the measures adopted aimed at creating 'cleaner' exhaust by imposing engine standards concerning carbon monoxide (CO), nitrous oxides, and unburned gasoline emissions.[33]

The Council of Europe took a major step forward when it adopted a regional Declaration of Principles on Air Pollution Control, on March 8, 1968.[34] The text sets forth very general but still relevant principles such as the demand that national legislation should require contributors to air pollution to reduce the pollution. Regulations applying one or more methods should be based on the principle of prevention, which may differ according to the nature of the

31 Arbitral Award in the *Trail Smelter Case*, (March 11, 1941), 3 U.N.R.I.A.A. 1905, 1965.

32 ibid 1965.

33 See for example, amongst others: Regulations 15, 24, 47, and 49 annexed to the Geneva Accord of March 20, 1958; affirmed by EC Directive 70/220 of March 20, 1970, O.J. L 76 (4/6/70). Regulation 15 concerns the Approval of Vehicle Equipment with a Positive-Ignition Engine with regard to Emission of Gaseous Pollutants by the Engine; Regulation 24 concerns the Approval of Vehicles Equipped with Diesel Engines with regard to the Emission of Pollutants by the Engine; Regulation 47 the Approval of Mopeds equipped with a Positive Ignition Engine with regard to the Emission of Gaseous Pollutants by the Engine; and Regulation 49 the Measures to be Taken against the Emission of Gaseous and ParticulatePollutants from Compression-Ignition Engines and Positive-Ignition Engines.

34 Resolution (68)4.

source of pollution. In the first method, fixed installations capable of causing a significant increase in air pollution should be subject to individual authorization specifying the conditions of construction and operations in order to limit emissions. Installations not presenting a risk of significantly increasing air pollution may be the object of general operational specifications if the density of such operations may provoke a significant concentration of pollutants in the neighborhood. Finally, motor vehicles and mass-produced fuel-burning appliances should be subject to general provisions. The Declaration takes into account urbanization and regional growth: planning for urban and industrial development should consider the effect of development on air pollution.

During the same year, WMO established a global network to monitor atmospheric chemical components related to climate change and environmental issues. This network, the Background Air Pollution Monitoring Network (BAPMON), merged with Global Ozone Observing System to form the Global Atmosphere Watch (GAW).[35] As of 2024, the GAW comprises 30 global stations, more than 400 regional stations and around 100 contributing stations.[36] The functions of these stations include measuring the atmospheric content of a variety of chemical pollutants. OECD first adopted a strategy of proposing rules for the control of the emission of specified pollutants, then in 1974 recommended measures for 'further air pollution control'.[37] It simultaneously adopted guidelines for action to reduce emission of sulfur oxides and particulates from stationary fuel combustion sources. The following step was the adoption of a recommendation on the control of air pollution from fossil fuel combustion.[38] The annex to this recommendation proposed guiding principles such as the development of innovative regulatory schemes to improve efficiency or flexibility of compliance while achieving existing emission control regulations; regulations to ensure availability and use of clean fuels or against use of polluting fuels where emission controls are not usually feasible (e.g. small central heating boilers); the implementation of emission standards by an effective program of control measures for large stationary installations; and incentives (tax, investment, loan or grant) for timely retirement of modernization of older, more polluting installations.

---

35 Ed Dlugokencky, John Miller and Johannes Staehelin, 'The Global Atmosphere Watch: a history of contributing to climate monitoring' (2010) 59(1) *WMO Bulletin*.

36 See the website of the WMO at <https://community.wmo.int/en/activity-areas/gaw/research-infrastructure/gaw-stations>.

37 OECD, Resolution of November 14,1974, C(74)219.

38 OECD, Guidelines adopted June 20, 1985, C(85)101.

2.2 *International Treaties to Combat Air Pollution*

There are few global rules concerning air quality. The first binding rules of a global nature concerning atmospheric pollution are found, perhaps unexpectedly, in UNCLOS (December 10, 1982). According to Article 212, states must adopt laws and regulations to prevent, reduce and control pollution of the marine environment from or through the atmosphere. The laws and regulations should apply to the states' airspace, and to vessels and aircraft flying their flag or under their registry. States also must take other measures as necessary to prevent, reduce and control such pollution. On the international level, they must endeavor to establish global and regional rules and procedures. Within the limits of their jurisdiction, they must enforce the laws and regulations they adopt.[39]

Significant progress in air pollution control has been achieved at the regional level, primarily within Europe. The Final Act of the Helsinki Conference on Security and Cooperation in Europe (August 1, 1975) gave the UNECE the task of preparing an international treaty concerning air pollution, which became the Geneva Convention on Long-Range Transboundary Air Pollution (LRTAP).[40] Adopted on November 13, 1979, by all European states as well as US and Canada, the Geneva Convention is a framework convention. It is primarily concerned with cooperation and its character is essentially programmatic; it contains almost no precise rule aimed at reducing air pollution which could be implemented as such. The definition given to long-range transboundary air pollution suggests why there are difficulties in developing legal techniques to achieve results in this field:

> Long-range transboundary air pollution means air pollution whose physical origin is situated wholly or in part within the area under the national jurisdiction of one State and which has adverse effects in the area under the jurisdiction of another State at such a distance that it is not generally possible to distinguish the contribution of individual emission sources or groups of sources.[41]

Obviously, this definition excludes any idea of individual responsibility of the polluter because that person or entity cannot be identified.

---

39 United Nations Convention on the Law of the Sea (adopted 10 December 1982, entered into force 16 November 1994) 1833 U.N.T.S. 3, Art. 222.

40 Convention on Long-Range Transboundary Air Pollution (adopted 13 November 1979, entered into force 16 March 1983) 1302 U.N.T.S. 217.

41 ibid, Art. 1 lit. (b) para. B. It aims to control transboundary harm caused by human activity.

The general obligation of the states parties is to protect humans and the environment against air pollution, and to endeavor to limit and, as far as possible, gradually reduce and prevent it (Art. 2). The article is cautiously drafted and includes no duty to limit pollution to a given level. The parties are to develop policies and strategies to serve as a means of combating the discharge of air pollutants, using the best available, economically feasible technology. They are also to exchange information concerning national policies, scientific activities, and technical measures aimed at combating the risks of pollution. The principle of consultation is an important element of the Convention. According to the terms of Article 5, consultations shall be held at an early stage between contracting parties that are affected by, or exposed to, a significant risk of long-range transboundary air pollution and parties within which, and subject to whose jurisdiction, a significant contribution to this pollution originates or could originate in connection with activities carried on or contemplated therein.

More systematic cooperation is called for in Article 7 of the Convention, primarily concerning the conduct of research and/or development in areas of science and nature, but also with regard to economic, social and ecological assessment of measures that might be envisaged and the elaboration of teaching and training programs concerning pollution. Article 9 provides for implementing a cooperative program for monitoring and evaluating long-range transmission of air pollutants in Europe, including continuous monitoring of sulfur dioxide and related substances not only in the air, but also in other media such as water, soil and vegetation, utilizing comparable or standardized procedures, and establishing a monitoring program and exchange of data on emissions.

The main organ of the Convention, called the Executive Body, consists of representatives of the contracting states, within the framework of the Senior Advisers to the UNECE Governments on Environmental Problems. This organ meets at least once annually to review the implementation of the Convention. By decision 1997/2 the Executive Body established an Implementation Committee to carry out such reviews and report to the Parties. The Executive Secretary of UNECE provides the secretariat.

A cooperative program for monitoring and evaluating the long-range transmission of air pollutants in Europe (EMEP) provides a framework for fulfilling the Convention's obligations.[42] Notably, when the Convention was signed, EC

42 Protocol to the 1979 Convention on Long-Range Transboundary Air Pollution on Long-Term Financing of the Cooperative Programme for Monitoring and Evaluation of the Long-Range Transport of Air Pollutants in Europe (EMEP) (adopted 28 Sepetmber 1984, entered into force 28 January 1988) 27 I.L.M. 701.

member states participating in the conference adopted a resolution deciding to provisionally apply the Convention and execute as fully as possible the obligations.[43] Thus, EMEP was initiated rather rapidly for the observation and study of long-range air pollution. In a relatively short time, a bank of more than ninety monitoring stations was set up in twenty-four countries. States parties submitted documents to the UNECE indicating numerous other national measures as well, including the establishment of licensing systems for polluting activities, adoption of stricter emission and quality standards, energy conservation, and controls on lead and nitrous oxide emissions from motor vehicles.

Regulatory priority has been given to the reduction of sulfur emissions. In 1984, ten states, meeting at a ministerial conference in Ottawa, agreed to reduce the 1980 emission levels of sulfurous substances by at least thirty percent by 1990. A protocol to this effect was adopted by 21 countries July 8, 1985, in Helsinki,[44] becoming the first international treaty to contain precise and verifiable objectives to combat air pollution. It entered into force on September 2, 1987. The Protocol required states to reduce their national sulfur emissions by at least thirty percent as soon as possible and at the latest by 1993, using 1980 levels as the basis for calculation. Implementation is controlled by EMEP utilizing its monitoring system,state reporting on national annual sulfur emissions, and the basis on which they have been calculated.

By 1986, ten countries had already achieved the thirty percent reduction. It appeared, however, that the reductions were counterbalanced by sulfur increases in countries not party to the Protocol. Rio Conference Agenda 21 included as a topic for future action the control of transboundary atmospheric pollution.[45] Conforming to this aim and drawing upon the principles of the Rio Declaration, the parties to the Geneva Convention adopted a new Protocol on Further Reduction on Sulfur Emissions.[46] The preamble of the instrument refers to the precautionary principle and expresses a new preoccupation in stating that measures to control emissions of sulfur and other air pollutants should also contribute to protecting the sensitive Arctic environment.

The main obligation of the parties was to ensure, as far as possible without entailing excessive costs, that the presence or deposition of oxidized sulfur

---

43 For the text of the resolution, *see* O.J. L 171 (6/27/81).

44 The 1985 Helsinki Protocol on the Reduction of Sulphur Emissions or Their Transboundary Fluxes by at Least 30 Per Cent (adopted 8 July 1985, entered into force 2 September 1987) 1480 U.N.T.S. 215.

45 U.N. Doc A/CONF.151/26 Nr. 9.1–9.35.

46 Protocol to the 1979 Convention on Long-Range Transboundary Air Pollution on Further Reduction of Sulphur Emissions (adopted 14 June 1994, entered into force 5 August 1998) 2030 U.N.T.S. 122.

compounds in the long term do not exceed critical loads for sulfur represented on a map of Europe in Annex I (Art. 2(1)). This approach is more flexible, but also more technical, than attacking the problem by limiting emissions. Article 1 of the Protocol defines critical sulfur deposition and critical load. The first is a quantitative estimate of the exposure to oxidized sulfur compounds, below which significant harmful effects on specified sensitive elements of the environment do not occur, according to present knowledge. Critical load is a quantitative estimate of an exposure to one or more pollutants below which significant harmful effects on specified sensitive elements of the environment do not occur, according to present knowledge. Annex I presents a table that shows the critical sulfur depositions for different zones of Europe.

Emission limits were not abandoned, however. As a first and minimum step, the parties agreed to reduce and maintain their annual sulfur emissions in accordance with the timing and levels specified in Annex II. The Annex specified the obligations of each of the twenty-nine contracting states and the European Union, with a table determining the emission levels in 1980 and 1990, the sulfur emission ceilings per year in 2000, 2005, and 2010 and the percentage emission reductions in 2000, 2005, and 2010 taking the year 1980 as a base year. The greatest burden was imposed on the United Kingdom which had to reduce its emissions calculated on the base of 1980 by fifty percent by 2000, seventy percent by 2005, and eighty percent by 2010. In contrast, Greece could keep the level of its 1980 emissions to 2000 and had to only reduce it by three percent in 2005 and four percent by 2010. Annex III designated southeast Canada as a Sulfur Oxides Management Area (SOMA), where annual sulfur emissions at a minimum should be reduced and maintained according to the timing and levels specified in Annex II. This means that different sulfur emission ceilings were fixed for Canada in general and for the SOMA which is a part of its territory.

Article 2(4) listed the most effective measures for the reduction of sulfur emissions, for new and existing sources. The measures included increasing energy efficiency, utilizing renewable energy, reducing the sulfur content of particular fuels, and applying the best available technology not entailing excessive costs. Annex V listed emission limit values for major stationary sources, while Annex IV proposed control technologies for sulfur emissions from stationary sources.

Several articles of the Protocol show the evolution of the treaty system to more developed regulation in the 1990s, in particular those provisions that apply legal techniques aimed at ensuring compliance with environmental treaty obligations. The provisions stress the importance of the Executive Body established by the Convention of 1979. In particular, the Protocol requires that each party periodically report to this body on its implementation measures to control and reduce sulfur emissions and on the levels of national annual sulfur emissions.[47] Moreover, the Implementation Committee reports to the parties at sessions of the Executive Body and may make recommendations.[48] The parties, after considering the report and any recommendations made by the Implementation Committee, may decide upon and call for action to bring about full compliance with the Protocol, including measures to assist partiess' compliance with the Protocol.

The problem of nitrogen oxides has been more difficult to solve, not only because, as Russia has pointed out, these substances originally were not mentioned by the Convention, but also because a principal source of this pollution is motor vehicles, a politically-sensitive issue in many countries as the Kyoto Protocol has further evidenced. Nonetheless, in the wake of Community directives and alarming reports by EMEP, the parties signed a Protocol on October 31, 1988 calling for the reduction of emissions and transboundary fluxes of nitrogen oxides (NOx) from fixed or mobile sources, with the aim of stabilizing them at the 1987 level by the year 1995.[49] The agreement entered into force on February 14 1991. Twelve of the twenty-five signatory states also made a Declaration undertaking to reduce NOx emissions by at least thirty percent by 1988, as compared with any year between 1980 and 1986.

A fourth Protocol Concerning the Control of Emissions of Volatile Organic Compounds (VOC) or their Transboundary Fluxes was signed in Geneva on November 18, 1991.[50] In the presence of sunlight, VOCs react with nitrogen oxides to form ground-level ozone, which is harmful to health and the environment. The Protocol generally obliges the parties to control and reduce their emissions of VOCs in order to reduce their transboundary fluxes and the fluxes of the resulting secondary photochemical oxidant products (Art. 2(1)). The aim could be achieved in two ways. The first option is to reduce national annual emissions of VOCs by at least thirty percent by the year 1999, using 1988 levels as a baseline or any annual level during the period 1984 to 1990. The second method could be used by countries whose VOC emissions causing transboundary pollution originated only from specified areas. These areas, called Tropospheric Ozone Management areas (TOMAS), are designated in Annex I to the Protocol. Two are found in Canada and one exists in Norway. Annual emissions in TOMAS were

47 Art. 5(1) and (2).

48 Art. 7(1).

49 Protocol to the 1979 Convention on Long-Range Transboundary Air Pollution Concerning the Control of Emissions of Nitrogen Oxides or Their Transboundary Fluxes (adopted 31 October 1988, entered into force 14 February 1991) 1591 U.N.T.S. 234.

50 Protocol to the 1979 Convention on Long-Range Transboundary Air Pollution Concerning the Control of Emissions of Volatile Organic Compounds or Their Transboundary Fluxes (adopted 18 November 1991, entered into force 29 September 1997) 2020 U.N.T.S. 89.

also required to be reduced by at least thirty percent but, in addition, the total national annual emissions of the countries who designate TOMAS were not to exceed the 1988 levels by the year 1999. An exception was foreseen for Central and Eastern European countries with economies in transition: no reduction of their emissions of VOCs was required immediately, but they had to ensure that their emissions did not exceed the 1988 levels by (Art. 2(2)(c)).

The Protocol specified incremental obligations. No less than two years after the entry into force of the instrument, the Parties were to apply emission standards to new stationary sources and to new mobile sources, in each case using control measures foreseen in Protocol Annex II (Art. 2(3)). The same techniques should apply in those areas in which national or international tropospheric ozone standards were exceeded or where transboundary flux originated.

Each party has to foster public participation in emission control programs through public announcements, encouraging the best use of all modes of transportation, and promoting traffic management schemes (Art. 2(3)(a)(IV)). A mechanism for monitoring compliance was foreseen (Art. 3(3)) and the parties were required to report annually on national programs, policies and strategies, and on progress in applying national or international emission standards and control techniques (Art. 8). Finally, the Protocol foresaw negotiations on further steps to reduce VOC emissions and proposes a work program in this regard (respectively Art. 2(6) and (7)).

A Meeting of the European Ministers for Environment held in Aarhus in June 1998 adopted two further protocols to the 1979 Geneva Convention. First, the Protocol on Persistent Organic Pollutants (POPs) addresses pollutants that resist degradation under natural conditions and have been associated with adverse effects on human health and the environment.[51] POPs can biomagnify in upper trophic levels to concentrations that could affect the health of exposed wildlife and humans. The Arctic ecosystems and especially its indigenous people, who subsist on Arctic fish and mammals, are particularly at risk. Article 3 lists the basic obligations of the contracting parties: eliminate the production and use of the substances listed in Annex I and ensure that the destruction or disposal is undertaken domestically in an environmentally sound manner.[52] Each Party also shall reduce its total emissions of each of the

51 Protocol to the 1979 Convention on Long-Range Transboundary Air Pollution on Persistent Organic Pollutants (adopted 24 June 1998, entered into force 23 October 2003) 2230 U.N.T.S. 79.

52 The terms waste, waste disposal, and environmentally sound are to be interpreted in a manner consistent with the use of those terms in the 1989 Convention on the Control of Transboundary Movements of Hazardous Wastes and their Disposal (Basel, March 22, 1989). See Chapter 13B.2.

substances listed in Annex III, shall adopt limit values that are at least as stringent as those specified in Annex IV for each existing stationary source,[53] and shall take effective measures to control emissions from mobile sources. Eight highly technical Annexes treat in detail the substances scheduled for elimination, substances scheduled for restrictions on use, limit values for emissions from stationary sources, and the best available techniques to control emissions of persistent organic pollutants from such sources. Amendments to the POPs Protocol were adopted in 2009 and came into force in 2022 and 2023.[54] These amendments included removing conditions to the elimination of some Annex I substances, adding several substances to Annex I and Annex II, increasing flexibility for countries with transitioning economies and adding guidance on best available technologies.[55]

A parallel Protocol to the Convention on Long-Range Transboundary Air Pollution on Heavy Metals,[56] adopted the same day as the POPs Protocol, contains many corresponding provisions. Each party commits itself to reduce its total annual emissions into the atmosphere of each of the heavy metals listed in Annex I, applying the best available techniques (Annex III). Limit values are specified for the listed stationary sources of emission (Annexes V and II). Other regulations provide for product control measures and product management measures (Annexes VI and VII). Amendments to the Heavy Metals Protocol were adopted in 2012 and entered into force in 2022.[57] The amendments centered on allowing flexibility for new parties to accede to the Protocol.[58] Guidance on best available technologies in Annex III was updated and Annex V was amended to include separate provision for the United States of America and other parties.

The parties to the 1979 Convention adopted a further Protocol in Gothenburg on November 30, 1999 in order to apply a multi-effect, multi-pollutant approach to prevent or minimize exceeding critical loads and levels.[59] This

---

53 A fixed stationary sources, according to art 1(10) is 'any fixed building, structure, facility, installation or equipment that emits or may emit any persistent organic pollutant directly or indirectly into the atmosphere.'

54 December 18, 2009, art 14(3). The amendments to Annexes V and VII (removed from the Protocol) entered into force on 13 December 2010 (art 14(4)).

55 December 18, 2009, Annexes I, II, V and VI.

56 Protocol to the 1979 Convention on Long-Range Transboundary Air Pollution on Heavy Metals (adopted 24 June 1998, entered into force 29 December 2003) 2237 U.N.T.S. 4.

57 13 December 2012, art 13(3). The amendments to Annex II entered into force on January 9, 2014 (art 13(4)).

58 December 13, 2012, Annex IV.

59 Protocol to the 1979 Convention on Long-Range Transboundary Air Pollution to Abate Acidification, Eutrophication and Ground-level Ozone (adopted 30 November 1999, entered into force 17 May 2005) 2319 U.N.T.S. 81.

Protocol is the first agreement under the Convention to deal specifically with reducing nitrogen compounds. According to Article 2, the objective of the Protocol is to control and reduce emissions of sulphur, nitrogen oxides, ammonia and volatile organic compounds that are caused by anthropogenic activities and are likely to cause adverse effects on human health, natural ecosystems, materials and crops. For most parties the critical loads of acidity, nutrient nitrogen, and ozone are described in Annex I to the Protocol. Article 3 specifies that each Party having an emission ceiling in a table in Annex II shall reduce and maintain the reduction in its annual emissions in accordance with that ceiling and the timetable specified in that Annex. Specific limit values are applied to stationary sources under specified conditions (Annexes IV to VII). Annex VIII establishes the limit values for fuels and new mobile sources while Annex IX foresees ammonia control measures. State parties are to promote public awareness by giving information to the general public on annual emissions, deposits and concentrations of the relevant pollutants, as well as strategies and measures applied or to be applied and means to minimize emissions.[60] Each Party shall report on a periodic basis information on the measures that it has taken to implement the Protocol as well as on levels of emissions of the substances to be controlled.[61] The Implementation Committee established by a 1997 decision of the Executive Body for the 1979 Convention reviews the information supplied by the parties, the data on the effects of concentrations and depositions of determined pollutants. Reviews shall take into account the best scientific information on the effects of such pollutants (Art. 10). The 1999 Gothenburg Protocol was amended in 2012 and the amendments entered into force in 2019.[62] Significantly, the 2012 amendments introduced reductions for fine particulate matter, including black carbon, for the first time. The amendments acknowledge the adverse effects particulate matter has on human health and the environment and the potential transboundary risks.[63] Amendments reflecting this inclusion were made throughout the Protocol, including to both the objectives (Art. 2) and the basic obligations (Art. 3). This inclusion is important not only for reducing air pollution but also for mitigating climate change.[64] The 2012 amendments also introduce flexible transitional arrangements for new parties to the Protocol,[65] and a mechanism for existing Parties

60 Art. 5.
61 Art. 7.
62 May 4, 2012, Arts. 13 bis (3) and (4).
63 May 4, 2012, Preamble.
64 May 4, 2012, Art. 2(2).
65 May 4, 2012, Art. 3 bis.

to propose adjustments to their emission reduction commitments contained in Annex II.[66] Any adjustments must be adopted by consensus at a session of the Executive Body.[67] Annex II was amended to set out the Parties' emissions ceilings up to the year 2020 and beyond,[68] and Annexes IV–VIII are updated.

The protocols and their amendments demonstrate the aptitude of the treaty system established by the 1979 LRTAP Convention to evolve and develop new techniques. They are also a good example of the permanent negotiations carried on through the conferences of the parties, which have become a necessary part of international environmental law. Finally, they show the increasing place of detailed technical approaches to international environmental protection. The bodies created by the 1979 LRTAP Convention also illustrate these factors. The Executive Body continues to meet on an annual basis and makes decisions guiding parties in meeting their obligations,[69] reviewing, supporting and recognizing the compliance of parties,[70] and facilitating information sharing and research into emerging issues and new technology.[71]

Outside the region of the LRTAP Convention system, the Stockholm Convention on Persistent Organic Pollutants was signed in May 2001 by over 90 states and came into force in 2004.[72] There are now 152 signatories, the majority of whom have ratified, accepted or approved the Stockholm Convention.[73] The Stockholm Convention's objective is to 'protect human health and the environment from persistent organic pollutants',[74] through regulating how parties can produce, use, import and dispose of certain chemicals.[75] The Convention also

66 May 4, 2012, Art. 13.

67 May 4, 2012, Art 13(5).

68 May 4, 2012, Annex II.

69 See for example, Decision 2014/1 Improving the guidance for adjustments under the 1999 Protocol to Abate Acidification, Eutrophication and Ground-level Ozone to emission reduction commitments or to inventories for the purposes of comparing total national emissions with them, ECE/EB.AIR/127/Add.1 and Decision 2012/2 Reporting on strategies, policies and other measures to implement obligations under the Convention and its Protocols, ECE/EB.AIR/122/Add.1.

70 Executive Body, Decision 2013//7 Concerning compliance by Spain with the Protocol concerning the Control of Emissions of Volatile Organic Compounds or their Transboundary Fluxes, ECE/EB.AIR/122/Add.1.

71 See for example Decision 2014/2 Establishment of the Task Force on Techno-economic Issues, ECE/EB>AIR/127/Add.1.

72 Stockholm Convention on Persistent Organic Pollutants (adopted May 22, 2001, entry into force May 17, 2004) 2256 U.N.T.S. 119 (Stockholm Convention).

73 See UNEP, Stockholm Convention: Status of Ratification available at <http://chm.pops.int/Countries/StatusofRatifications/Glossary/tabid/3485/Default.aspx>.

74 Stockholm, May 22, 2001, Art. 1.

75 Art. 3.

seeks to regulate unintentional releases of the chemicals and emissions from waste.[76] Similarly to the LRTAP Convention, the Stockholm Convention provides for the exchange of information and technical assistance, research obligations, monitoring and reporting obligations and promoting public awareness.[77] Annexes A and B list chemicals to be eliminated and restricted, respectively, and country specific exemptions. Annex C concerns unintentional production of certain chemicals and guidance on preventing their production. Annexes D to F concern the process for adding a chemical to the previous annexes, including requiring information on risk and socio-economic considerations. Amendments have regularly been made to the convention, including adding dispute resolution procedures and including additional chemicals in the Annexes,[78] of which most have entered into force.[79] The Stockholm Convention has been described as breaking new ground, particularly with accounting for parties' specific circumstances, for example through inviting countries to share any objections on individual substances early in the negotiation process and the creation of a register under Article 4 for parties with specific exemptions to the Annexes, to be subject to a review process and open to any new party.[80] It is also interesting to note that unlike the LRTAP Convention, the Stockholm Convention does not set a timeline for emission reductions.[81]

Turning to other sources of pollution, it may be recalled that forest fires devastated areas of Brunei and Indonesia in the closing years of the twentieth century, producing a heavy haze that polluted the atmosphere and caused serious health problems not only in the originating countries, but also in Malaysia, Myanmar, Singapore and Thailand. In 1997, in response to the problem, ASEAN adopted a Regional Haze Action Plan followed in 2002 by an Agreement on Transboundary Haze Pollution.[82]

The Agreement defines haze pollution as smoke resulting from land and/or forest fire which causes deleterious effects of such a nature as to endanger

76 Arts. 5–6.

77 Arts. 9–12, 14.

78 Punta Del Este, May 2005, Annex G; Geneva, May 2009, Annexes A, B and C; Geneva, April 2011, Annex A; Geneva, May 2013, Annex A; Geneva, May 2015, Annex A and C.

79 UNEP, Amendments to Annexes to the Stockholm Convention, available at <http://chm.pops.int/Countries/StatusofRatifications/Amendmentstoannexes/tabid/3486/Default.aspx> (last accessed March 10, 2024).

80 Art. 4; Peter L. Lallas, 'The Stockholm Convention on Persistent Organic Pollutants', (2001) 95(3) *The American Journal of International Law* 692, 699–700.

81 ibid 703–704.

82 ASEAN Agreement on Transboundary Haze Pollution (adopted 10 June 2002, entered into force 25 November 2003).

human health, harm living resources, ecosystems and material property, and impair or interfere with amenities and other legitimate uses of the environment.[83] The Agreement aims at preventing and monitoring such pollution which should be mitigated through concerted national efforts and intensified regional and international cooperation.[84] To that effect, precautionary and preventive measures should be taken, when necessary by developing and implementing international measures aiming at controlling sources of fires, identifying fires, creating monitoring, assessment and early warning systems, exchanging information and technology and providing mutual assistance.[85] The Parties shall take appropriate measures to monitor all fire prone areas, land and/or forest fires, the environmental conditions conducive to such fires and haze pollution arising from them[86] as well as the necessary preventive measures.[87] Technical co-operation should include relevant training, education and awareness raising campaigns, in particular relating to the promotion of zero-burning practices and the impact of haze pollution on human health and the environment. Markets should be developed for the utilization of biomass and appropriate methods to treat agricultural wastes.[88]

An ASEAN Co-ordinating Center for Transboundary Haze Pollution Control works on the basis that the national authorities will act first to put out the fires. If a Party needs assistance in the event of land and/or forest fires or haze pollution arising from such fires within its territory, it may request such assistance from any other Party, directly or through the ASEAN Centre.[89] Unless otherwise agreed, the requesting Party shall exercise the overall direction, control, co-ordination and supervision of the assistance within its territory. It shall provide, to the extent possible, local facilities and services for the proper and effective administration of the assistance and ensure the protection of personnel, equipment and materials brought into its territory by or on behalf of the assisting Party for such purposes.[90] The requesting or receiving Party shall accord to personnel of the assisting Party the necessary exemptions and facilities for the performance of their functions. Indonesia was the last to ratify the Agreement on Transboundary Haze Pollution in 2014, following considerable

83 Art 1.(6).
84 Art. 2.
85 Art. 4.
86 Art. 7.
87 Art. 9.
88 Art. 16.
89 Art. 12.
90 Art. 13.

diplomatic tension,[91] and serious forest fires in 2013. Since the creation of the Agreement, ASEAN has continued to address haze pollution through soft law,[92] and through increasing co-operation on monitoring fires and haze.[93]

In bilateral relations, systematic cooperation between Canada and the United States has existed since the January 11, 1909 Treaty Respecting Boundary Waters Between the United States and Canada which created the International Joint Commission for the protection of boundary waters.[94] The Commission has been invoked in several instances of air pollution, notably in the Trail Smelter case.[95] In 1978, the two states established a bilateral research group on the long-range transport of atmospheric pollutants. On August 5, 1980, a memorandum of intent was signed in Washington,[96] establishing joint working groups to prepare a formal agreement. At the same time the memorandum called for national measures and a procedure for notification and consultation in regard to projected activities which could cause significant increases in air pollution. The two countries concluded a special agreement in Ottawa on August 23, 1983 concerning research into the effects of weather on long-range transboundary air pollution.[97] Subsequently, the Great Lakes Water Quality Agreement was amended to include air pollution among the regulated subjects.[98] Finally, on March 13, 1991 the two countries signed an Agreement on Air Quality whose general objective to control transboundary air pollution.[99] They commit themselves to establish specific objectives for emission limitations or reductions of specific air pollutants (Art. 4). Annex I sets such objectives

91 See Koh Kheng-Lian, 'Transboundary and Global Environmental Issues: The Role of ASEAN' (2012) 1(1) *Transnational Environmental Law* 67 and Laely Nurhidayah, Shawkat Alam and Zada Lipman, 'The Influence of International Law upon ASEAN Approaches in Addressing Transboundary Haze Pollution in Southeast Asia' (2015) 37(2) *Contemporary Southeast Asia* 183.

92 For example, instruments concerning burning and peatland management, see Laely Nurhidayah, Shawkat Alam and Zada Lipman, 'The Influence of International Law upon ASEAN Approaches in Addressing Transboundary Haze Pollution in Southeast Asia' (2015) 37(2) *Contemporary Southeast Asia* 183, 191.

93 ibid 190.

94 36 Stat.2448, T.S. No 548, UN Doc ST/LEG/SER.B12.261.

95 See *Trail Smelter* (n 14).

96 Memorandum of Intent between Canada and the United States Concerning Transboundary Air Pollution (Aug. 5, 1980), 32 U.S.T. 2521, 20 I.L.M. 690 (1981).

97 Memorandum of Understanding between Canada and the United States on the Cross Appalachian Tracer Experiment (Aug. 23, 1983) 22 I.L.M. 1017 (1983).

98 See also Chapter 10.

99 30 I.L.M. 676 (1991).

for sulfur dioxide and nitrogen oxides separately and differently for the US and for Canada.

The Agreement applies customary environmental law rules, such as the prior assessment of proposed actions, activities, and projects if they are likely to cause significant transboundary air pollution, the duty to notify the other state concerning such activities or projects as well as those that create a potential risk of significant transboundary harm, and to consult on request of the other party. Consultation also can be sought if changes to laws, regulations, or policies of a party are foreseen. Pursuant to the agreement, the International Joint Commission has oversight of a permanent bilateral Air Quality Committee which is to report on the progress of the parties in meeting the specific objectives of the agreement. The process involves soliciting public comments on the report and recommendations to the parties.[100] In 2000 the Agreement was amended to include the Ozone Annex, which intended to 'reduce the transboundary flow of tropospheric ozone and precursor emissions (NOx and VOC)'.[101] The Ozone Annex amends the Agreement to reiterate the specific objectives for the reduction of sulphur dioxide and nitrogen oxides in Annex 1 and also adds specific objectives for volatile organic compounds and nitrogen oxides in the new Annex 3.[102] Annex 3 provides that each party designate a 'Pollution Emission Management Area' which the specific emissions obligations apply to.[103] The possibility of adding an annex on particulate matter was raised and assessed by both parties, but the International Joint Commission reports that joint analyses did not support doing so.[104]

More generally, UNEP has been expanded and strengthened through the United Nations Environment Assembly (UNEA), with a renamed UNEP Governing Council after universal membership was permitted.[105] At its first session,

---

100 The progress reports are publicly available and invite public comment. See the USEPA website, at <https://www.epa.gov/airmarkets/us-canada-air-quality-agreement-progress-reports> (last accessed March 10, 2024). In the 2014 report, both states were reported as meeting emissions targets and, in most cases, exceeding them. See Canada – United States Air Quality Agreement Progress Report (2014).

101 Canada – US Air Quality Agreement – Ozone Annex (2000) amending the 'Agreement between the Government of Canada and the government of the United States of America on Air Quality' (adopted December 7, 2000, entry into force December 7, 2000).

102 ibid, Art. II.

103 ibid, Annex 3, Part II.

104 Canada – United States Air Quality Agreement Progress Report, 58 (2014).

105 UN Doc A.RES/66/288, 88(a); UN Doc A/RES/67/213; see Donald Kaniaru, 'First United Nations Environment Assembly: Some Highlights and Challenges' (2014) 44(4) *Environmental Law and Policy* 342, 342.

the UNEA passed a resolution calling for the role of UNEP to be strengthened in promoting air quality.[106]

The International Court of Justice (ICJ) has also upheld and reiterated the principle of prevention – the duty one state has to prevent activities in its territory causing damage in another State – as a customary rule, independent of any specific treaty obligation.[107] Significantly, the ICJ has also found that 'it may now be considered a requirement under general international law to undertake an environmental impact assessment' where there is a risk of transboundary damage.[108]

2.3 *Legislation of the European Union*

As a pioneer in regionally legislating air pollution, it is worth recalling that as the European Union evolved from the Common Market and the European Community, it adopted three types of legislation concerning air pollution. Several directives have a general scope, others concern specific forms and sources of pollution, and the third establishes ambient air quality objectives.

Following the 'discovery' at the beginning of the 1980s of damage to the forests of central Europe, the EC adopted a general directive relating to air pollution produced by industrial installations.[109] This directive introduced the obligation to obtain specific authorization for new industrial installations that emit pollutants into the air, including energy (mines, oil refineries), production and working of metals and minerals, chemical industries, waste treatment, and certain paper mills. Authorities were not allowed to deliver licenses unless the enterprise has adopted appropriate measures to prevent air pollution and respects the limit values for emissions and air quality. The license should require utilization of the best available technology not involving excessive costs and, in addition, take into account existing value limits. Member states also are required to develop strategies and programs to progressively adapt existing industrial facilities to the requirements of the best available

---

106 UNEA, Resolution 1/8 (adopted June 27, 2014).

107 *Pulp Mills on the River Uruguay (Argentina v Uruguay)* ICJ Reports 2010, 14 at 101, citing *Corfu Channel (United Kingdom v Albania), Merits Judgement,* ICJ Reports 1949, 22 and *Legality of the Threat or Use of Nuclear Weapons Advisory Opinion,* ICJ Reports 1996(I) 242; see Ilias Plakokefalos, '*Prevention Obligations in International Environmental Law*' (2012) 23(1) Yearbook of International Environmental Law 3.

108 *Pulp Mills on the River Uruguay (Argentina v Uruguay)* ICJ Reports 2010, 14 at 204; see Xiaoqin Zhu and Jinlong He, 'International Court of Justice's Impact on International Environmental Law: Focusing on the Pulp Mills Case', (2012) 23(1) *Yearbook of International Environmental Law* 151, 120.

109 Directive 84/360 of June 28, 1984, O.J. 1984 L 188 (7/16/84), end of validity October 29, 2007.

technology. Specially protected zones can be established. Demands for authorization and decisions of competent authorities should be placed before the affected public and environmental impact statements can be required. When pollution is capable of affecting other EC states, they should be informed and can request consultations. Following the lead of this directive, the Council adopted, in 1988, a directive on installations of combustion of 50 megawatt or more.[110] Each new installation must respect the emission norms fixed by the directive for sulfur dioxide, particulates and nitrogen oxides. For existing plants, member states create and implement programs aimed at progressively reducing their annual emissions of these elements. The reductions in relation to 1980 and up to the year 2003 are indicated in absolute quantities and in percentages. Parallel directives provided for emission limit values for municipal waste-incineration plants and for the incineration of hazardous wastes.[111] All these above-named directives were updated and bundled in one overarching directive, the current version of which was implemented in 2010.[112] General EC directives, such as directive 85/337/EEC of June 27, 1985 concerning the assessment of the effects of certain public and private projects,[113] and the *Seveso* directive,[114] relating to the risks of major accidents of certain industrial activities, apply to activities that risk causing major air pollution.

In addition to efforts to reduce air pollution by directives of general scope, EC measures aim to reduce emissions from specific sources. Directive 70/220,[115] modified several times, concerns polluting emissions from automobiles; a 1975 directive fixed the limit of sulfur in diesel fuel;[116] another directive limited the amount of lead in gasoline.[117] These laws began by establishing uniform rules, but the directive relating to the sulfur content of diesel fuel introduced flexibility by providing that states should establish zones in which the permissible amount of sulfur differs according to local conditions. More recently, there

110 Directive 88/609 of November 24, 1988, O.J. L 336 (7/12/88), end of validity November 26, 2002.

111 Directives 89/369 and 89/429, O.J.1989 L 163 p. 32 and O.J.1989 L 203, p. 50, later amended. End of validity for both Directives December 27, 2000; Directive 94/67, O.J.1994 L 365 p. 34, end of validity December 27, 2000.

112 Directive 2010/75/EU of November 24, 2010, O.J. L 334 17.12.2010, p. 17.

113 O.J. L 175 (7/5/85), end of validity February 16, 2012. The current version is Directive 2011/92/EU of December 13, 2011.

114 82/501/EEC of June 24, 1982, O.J. L 230 (8/5/82), modified by Directive 87/216 of March 19, 1987, O.J. L. 85 (3/28/87). This was replaced by the *Seveso II* Directive (Directive 96/82/EC) which in turn was repealed by *Seveso III* (Directive 2012/18/EU).

115 Directive 70/220, O.J. 1970, L 76, p. 1.

116 Directive 75/716, O.J. 1975, L 307, p. 22.

117 Directive 78/611 of Feb. 20, 1978, O.J. 1978, L 197, p. 19.

has been a directive concerning road transport by heavy vehicles,[118] Directive 2010/75/EC, which was mentioned above, also recasting several directives concerning specific industries,[119] and Directive 2008/1/EC,[120] which requires stricter limits for nitrogen oxide and sulphur dioxide.

Other environmental directives aimed at air pollution control established quality objectives for the entire Community. Such objectives were fixed for sulfur dioxide and particulates,[121] lead,[122] and nitrogen dioxide under the Directive of Ambient Air Quality and Cleaner Air for Europe of 2008.[123] Community legislation has evolved away from quality objectives, however, because adequate environmental protection is difficult to attain by this method. Throughout the last few decades, several directives have shown a preference for an 'at source' approach that limits polluting emissions. This technique also has its limits, given that the notion of the 'best available technology not involving excessive costs' is viewed in a different manner from one member state to another, so that a permanent coordination at the Community level is required to assure harmonized implementation.

The 1996 Ambient Air Quality Assessment and Management (Air Quality Framework Directive) led to increased European legislation,[124] including its daughter directives setting limit values,[125] and Directive 2001/81/EC on National

118 Directive 2011/76/EC, O.J. L 269, p. 1.

119 Directive 78/176/, Directive 82/883/ and Directive 92/112/ concerning the titanium dioxide industry, Directive 1999/13/EC concerning the use of organic solvents, Directive 2000/76/EC on the incineration of waste, and Directive 2001/80/EC on large combustion plants.

120 Directive 84/306 (above) was expanded upon by the 1996 Directive 96/61/EC Concerning Integrated Pollution Prevention and Control built upon the 1984 Directive, to include emissions into water and soil (O.J. 1996 L 257, p. 26). The 1996 Directive and its amendments were then codified by the Integrated Pollution Prevention and Control Directive, (Directive 2008/1/EC, O>J> L 24, p. 8) which continued to provide a framework for the prevention of pollution from industrial sources. The Directive was amended by Directive 2009/31/EC.

121 Directive 80/779, O.J. 1980, L 229, p. 30, end of validity January 1, 2005.

122 Directive 82/884, O.J. 1982, L 378, p. 15, end of validity January 1, 2005.

123 Directive 85/203, O.J. 1985, L 87, p. 1, end of validity December 31, 2009. As discussed below, the new Directive is Directive 2008/50/EC of May 21, 2008, O.J. L 152, 11.6.2008, p. 1. For other recent EU frameworks relevant to air pollution, see the Renewable Energy Directive (Directive (EU) 2023/2413) <https://energy.ec.europa.eu/topics/renewable-energy/renewable-energy-directive-targets-and-rules/renewable-energy-directive_en>.

124 Directive 96/62/EC, O.J. 1996, L 296, pg. 55; see Adam Byrne, 'The 1979 Convention on Long-Range Transboundary Air Pollution: Assessing its Effectiveness as a Multilateral Environmental Regime after 35 Years' (2015) 4(1) *Transnational Environmental Law* 37, 42.

125 Including Directive 2004/107/EC relating to arsenic, cadmium, mercury, nickel and polycyclic aromatic hydrocarbons in ambient air, O.J. 2004, L 23, 3.

Emission Ceilings for Certain Atmospheric Pollutants.[126] In 2008, replacing the Air Quality Framework Directive among others, the Directive on Ambient Air Quality and Cleaner Air for Europe was enacted.[127] This directive concerns assessment of ambient air quality and managing the quality of ambient air, by requiring member states to ensure limit values for specified pollutants are not exceeded.[128] In 2022, the Commission proposed revising the Ambient Air Quality Directives to bring them into closer alignment with recommendations made by the WHO in 2021, as part of the European Green Deal.[129] As of May 2024, this plan is currently no more than a proposal.

3 The Protection of the Ozone Layer

The present section outlines the international legal regime of the ozone layer, illegal trade in ozone-depleting substances, and the effects of protective measures in this context. The discovery that widely-used chemical substances were destroying stratospheric ozone induced a number of countries in the early 1980s to ban the use of CFCs for aerosol sprays. At the same time, their general use made it obvious that the problem could not be solved unilaterally or even regionally. Thus, UNEP made the protection of the stratospheric ozone a priority item in its legal action plan and after several years of effort, succeeded in negotiating the Convention for the Protection of the Ozone Layer (Vienna Convention).[130]

The treaty is a framework convention, providing the basis for systematic cooperation among the states parties to respect the protection of stratospheric ozone. The general obligation of states parties is to take appropriate measures to protect human health and the environment against adverse effects resulting or likely to result from human activities that modify or are likely to modify the ozone layer (Art. 2). Annex I of the Convention details the duty to cooperate in research and scientific assessments, set out in Article 3. Article 4 and Annex II require cooperation in the legal, scientific and technical fields, including the exchange of information. The parties define the information to exchange

126 O.J. 2001 L 309, 22.

127 Directive 2008/50/EC, O.J. 2008, L 152, 1.

128 Arts. 12–22, Annexes XI, XIV.

129 Proposal for a Directive of the European Parliament and of the Council on ambient air quality and cleaner air for Europe, October 26, 2022 (COM/2022/542 final). Visit for an overview of the process the website of the European Commission, <https://environment.ec.europa.eu/topics/air/air-quality/revision-ambient-air-quality-directives_en> (last accessed March 7, 2024). As of May 2024, this plan is currently no more than a proposal.

130 Convention for the Protection of the Ozone Layer (adopted 22 March 1985, entered into force 22 September 1988) 1513 U.N.T.S. 323.

through their regular meetings in conferences (Art. 6 and Annex II) within the boundaries of the Convention, which recognizes the need to protect intellectual property rights. States parties generally are to make known their laws, their national administrative measures and legal research relevant to protection of the ozone layer, as well as relevant methods and terms of licensing and availability of patents.

According to Convention Article 8, the Conference of the Parties may adopt protocols to the Convention. Two months after the conclusion of the Vienna Convention, a British Antarctic Survey team published its findings indicating a forty percent loss of stratospheric ozone over Antarctica.[131] This ozone 'hole' stimulated UNEP and the World Meteorological Organization to issue a comprehensive international assessment, which concluded that CFC production trends would lead to dangerous ozone depletion. A subsequent meeting of the parties to the Vienna Convention adopted the Montreal Protocol on Substances that Deplete the Ozone Layer.[132] At the time the Protocol was adopted, scientific uncertainty remained about global ozone loss and increases in UV radiation reaching the earth. The action taken in adopting the Protocol thus represents the first significant application of the precautionary principle.

The Montreal Protocol foresaw the control of various forms of chlorofluorocarbons and halons, and their progressive elimination. Industrial countries agreed to cut production and use of CFCs in half by 1998, and by 1992 to freeze production and use of halons.[133] Countries with an annual consumption of CFCs under 0.3 kilograms per capita, which were mainly developing countries, were given a ten-year period to comply. The Protocol also restricted trade between states parties and non-parties, addressing the 'free rider' problem.

The Montreal Protocol came into force on January 1, 1989. The parties to it have met regularly, as foreseen by the agreement. At the first meeting (Helsinki, May 1989), new information indicated that ozone losses were two to three times more severe than had been predicted. Participating states thus adopted a declaration that called for accelerating the phase-out of substances that destroy stratospheric ozone. The meeting also initiated a major revision of the Montreal Protocol.[134]

The second meeting (London, June 1990) considerably tightened the reduction schedule, again in light of scientific findings: it decided on new and shorter

---

131 Joe Farman, Brian Gardiner and Jonathan Shanklin, 'Large losses of total ozone in Antarctica reveal seasonal ClO_x/NO_x interaction' (1985) 315 *Nature* 207.

132 Montreal Protocol on Substances that Deplete the Ozone Layer (adopted 16 September 1987, entered into force 1 January 1989) 1522 U.N.T.S. 3.

133 Halons are a bromine-containing chemical used in fire-fighting.

134 Report of the First Meeting of the Parties to the Montreal Protocol, UNEP/OzL.Pro.1/5.

deadlines for the complete phaseout of substances. This made even more necessary the effective participation of all significant producers and consumers of ozone depleting substances, in particular countries like China, Brazil and India. In a breakthrough, the London amendments endorsed a financial mechanism and an interim international fund consisting of voluntary contributions from the industrialized nations in order to assist developing countries in meeting the costs of compliance with the Convention and Protocols. For the first time an international environmental treaty called for financial transfers from industrialized to developing countries.[135]

The Fourth Meeting of the parties (Copenhagen, November 1992) completed the task of adapting the Montreal Protocol and of making it operational.[136] The meeting advanced the phase-out dates for industrial countries to 1994 for halons and to 1996 for CFCs, methyl chloroform, and carbon tetrachloride. It also took up the question of hydrochlorofluorocarbons (HCFCs), a proposed substitute for CFCs that is still ozone-depleting but less so than CFCs. The agreement called for their complete phase-out by 2030. A 1995 meeting in Vienna added a phase-out for methyl bromide, to the year 2010 for industrial countries.[137] The meeting also strengthened requirements for industrialized country use of HCFCs, and added a complete phase-out by 2040 for developing countries. Subsequently in the San José, Costa Rica, meeting held from November, 1996,[138] the states parties adopted new reduction schedules for a number of ozone-depleting substances as well as decisions on illegal trade in such substances and on financial issues.

With the various actions taken by the states parties, the 1985 Vienna Convention for the Protection of the Ozone Layer has grown into an international treaty system composed of the Convention itself, the Montreal Protocol, and its amendments (London 1990, Copenhagen 1992, Vienna 1995, San Jose 1996, Beijing 1999, Kigali 2016). It is managed by the Conference of the Parties to the Vienna Convention, the Meeting of the Parties to the Montreal Protocol, a Financial Mechanism,[139] and a secretariat. The Ninth Meeting of the Parties

135 Amendment to the Montreal Protocol on Substances that Deplete the Ozone Layer (adopted 29 June 1990, entered into force 10 August 1992) 1852 U.N.T.S. 337.

136 Amendment to the Montreal Protocol on Substances that Deplete the Ozone Layer (adopted 25 November 1992, entered into force 14 June 1994) 1785 U.N.T.S. 517.

137 Report of the Seventh Meeting of the Parties to the Montreal Protocol on Substances that Deplete the Ozone Layer (Vienna, 5–7 December 1995) UNEP/OzL.Pro.7/12.

138 Report of the Eighth Meeting of the Parties to the Montreal Protocol on Substances that Deplete the Ozone Layer (San José, 25–27 November 1996) UNEP/OzL.Pro.8/12.

139 See Chapter 4.

(Montreal, September 15 to 17, 1997) further strengthened control measures and dealt with improving treaty implementation compliance.[140]

The Meeting of the Parties (and more infrequently, the Conference of the Parties) have taken periodic decisions that affect the implementation of the Protocol.[141] The Vienna Convention and the Montreal Protocol have achieved universal ratification, along with almost all amendments.[142] Since 2002, the majority of these decisions have related to implementation, non-compliance and administrative matters. There have consistently been decisions and adjustments on more significant issues, however. Overwhelmingly, the key issues faced by the Montreal Protocol centered on the regulation of methyl bromide and hydrofluorocarbons.

The conflict over methyl bromide came to a head at the 2003 Meeting of the Parties in Nairobi, where the control schedule and critical use exemptions were tabled for discussion.[143] Conflict over this issue continued for many years, with extraordinary Meetings of the Parties required to be held in 2004 and 2005. Progress was made after this point, with the parties able to agree on a control schedule for methyl bromide in 2004,[144] and decisions on critical use exemptions made at the annual Meeting of the Parties from 2006 onward, with a downtrend in nominations of exemptions observable.[145] This conflict had residual effects on developing nations phasing out methyl bromide; many were unwilling to commit to new targets where developed nations had high

140 Amendment to the Montreal Protocol on Substances that Deplete the Ozone Layer (adopted 17 September 1997, entered into force 10 November 1999) 2233 U.N.T.S. 256.

141 See, e.g., the Beijing Amendment, in force Feb. 2002, which is contained in Annex V of the Report of the Eleventh Meeting of the Parties to the Montreal Protocol on Substances that Deplete the Ozone Layer.

142 Report of the Twenty-Seventh Meeting of the Parties to the Montreal Protocol on Substances that Deplete the Ozone Layer (Montreal, 1–5 November 2015) UN Doc UNEP/OzL.Pro.27/13. Only the Kigali agreement has not (yet) achieved universal ratification.

143 Report of the Fifteenth Meeting of the Parties to the Montreal Protocol on Substances that Deplete the Ozone Layer (Nairobi, 10–14 November 2003) UN Doc UNEP/OzL.Pro.15/9. See Hugo -Maria Schally, Hermann E. Ott and Tilman Santarius, '*11.* Air and Atmosphere' (2004)14(1) *Yearbook of International Environmental Law* 269 .

144 Report of the First Extraordinary Meeting of the Parties to the Montreal Protocol on Substances that Deplete the Ozone Layer, UN Doc UNEP/OzL.Pro.ExMP/1/3. See Hugo Maria Schally and Hermann E. Ott, '11. Air and Atmosphere' (2005) 15(1) *Yearbook of International Environmental Law* 243.

145 The downtrend in nominations for critical use exemptions since 2005 was noted at the 21st Meeting of the Parties, see UN DOC UNEP/OzL.Pro.21/8.

critical use exceptions,[146] and the critical use exemptions for methyl bromide continue to be discussed at the Meeting of the Parties.[147]

Another key issue has been the regulation of hydrofluorocarbons (HFCs), substances which do not deplete ozone, but are greenhouse gases, which have been substituted for hydrochlorofluorocarbons (HCFCs, ozone depleting substances regulated by the Protocol). Amendments had been tabled at Meetings of the Parties to include HFCs under the Montreal Protocol, on the basis that though not ozone depleting substances, the Protocol should be utilized to address the side effects of its control measures. The opposition was that HFCs are simply outside the scope of the Convention and the Protocol.[148] At the 27th Meeting of the Parties, held from November 1–3, 2015, Decision XXVII/1 was made. This Decision paved the way for the latest amendment to the Montreal Protocol in 2016 in Kigali, which regulates the consumption and production of HFCs. This is a landmark accomplishment, since as noted, HFCs are not ozone-depleting substances, but rather powerful greenhouse gases developed to replace ozone-depleting substances banned by the Montreal Protocol. This implies that the 1985 Vienna Convention for the Protection of the Ozone Layer and all its subsequent protocols and amendments do not only serve to protect the ozone layer anymore, but now have a widened scope to also address climate change.

The ozone regime is administered, in principle, by three secretariats: one for the Vienna Convention, one for the Montreal Protocol and one for the Multilateral Fund. In fact, the two first are joined in a small body and all of them are affiliated with UNEP. The core of the international structure is the annual Meeting of the Parties to the Montreal Protocol which allows the participating states to decide collectively when there is a conflict concerning the interpretation of or the compliance with the treaty obligations accepted. The main organ of the Fund is an Executive Committee of 14 members of whom seven are selected by the group of developing country states parties to the Protocol and seven others by the industrialized states. It develops and monitors the implementation of specific operational policies, guidelines, and administrative arrangements, including the disbursement of resources; develops the plan and the budget for the Fund, as well as criteria for project eligibility; and approves, where appropriate, country programs for compliance with the Protocol. Decisions are taken

146 See Hugo Maria Schally and Hermann E. Ott, '11. Air and Atmosphere' (2006) 16(1) *Yearbook of International Environmental Law* 391.

147 For example, see Report of the Twenty-Seventh Meeting of the Parties to the Montreal Protocol on Substances that Deplete the Ozone Layer, UN Doc UNEP/OzL.Pro.27/13.

148 Cornelius Rhein, 'Air and Atmosphere: 2. Ozone Layer' (2014) 24(1) *Yearbook of International Environmental Law* 224.

by consensus; a two-third majority of the parties present and voting, including majority of both groups is needed. One of the most interesting features of the Financial Mechanism is the noncompliance procedure, established by annex IV of Decision IV/18, and discussed in detail in Chapter 4.

Unless effectively halted, illegal trade in ozone-depleting substances could undermine the Montreal Protocol's key achievements. While the consumption of ozone-depleting substances has been greatest in Europe and in North America in the past, the fastest growing use has been in developing countries. The illegal trade of these substances has been attributed to the Protocols staged phase outs, with different control measures for developing countries.[149] In 2008, UNEP found that India was both the largest producer of CFCs and the greatest source of smuggling.[150] Estimates of the amount of the illegal trade vary, but the chemical industry has in the past suggested that as much as twenty percent of the CFCs in use worldwide were illegally traded.[151] Across Europe and Asia, 60 tons of smuggled ozone depleting substances were seized between July 2010 and August 2012.[152] In China in 2014, it was discovered that a banned CFC was being sold under a false label, with estimates that over 80% of automobile air conditioning products sold may have contained the banned CFC.[153] NGOs have recommended that developing countries be given greater funding to assist with the accelerated phaseout of harmful substances. An amendment to the Montreal Protocol, adopted on September 17, 1997 aims at remedying the situation, at least in part.[154] It requires that when, after the phase-out date applicable to it for a controlled substance, a party is unable, despite having taken all practicable steps to comply with its obligation under the Montreal Protocol, to cease production of that substance for domestic consumption, other than for uses agreed by the parties to be essential, it shall ban the export of used, recycled and reclaimed quantities of that substance, other than for the purpose of destruction. As a complementary measure, by January

---

149 OECD, *Illegal Trade in Environmentally Sensitive Goods* (OECD Trade Policy Studies 2012).

150 Armin Rosencranz and Siddharth Johar, 'Illegal Smuggling of Ozone-depleting Substances' (2015) 45(2) *Environmental Policy and Law* 73.

151 Jim Vallette, *Deadly Complacency: US CFC Production, the Black Market, and Ozone Depletion,* (Ozone Action 1995); Duncan Brack, International Trade and the Montreal Protocol (Routledge 1996).

152 Lorraine Elliot, 'Fighting Transnational Environmental Crime' (2012) 66(1) *Journal of International Affairs* 87.

153 Armin Rosencranz and Siddharth Johar, 'Illegal Smuggling of Ozone-depleting Substances' (2015) 45(2) *Environmental Policy and Law* 73.

154 Montreal Amendment to the Montreal Protocol on Substances that Deplete the Ozone Layer (adopted 17 September 1997, entered into force 10 November 1999) 2054 U.N.T.S. 522.

1, 2000, each party had to establish and implement a system for licensing the import and export of new, used, recycled and reclaimed controlled substances. From 2002, each Meeting of the Parties recorded how many parties had licensing systems and encouraged their introduction, leading to a steady increase in their use.[155] In 2007, the Meeting of the Parties made a decision that encouraged all parties to fulfill their obligation on establishing a licensing system and to enforce existing systems.[156]

International efforts to protect the ozone layer have had substantial impact. Every four years, an assessment report on ozone depletion is released by the Scientific Assessment Panel to the Montreal Protocol. The most recent one, published in 2022, reports that the ozone layer has overall gradually been recovering since the banning of ozone-depleting substances and expects the ozone layer to be recovered to the levels of 1980 completely around 2066.[157] Besides this, the report states that the implementation of the Montreal Protocol, which caused ozone-depleting substances to be outlawed, has had the effect of avoiding an additional increase of 0.5-1 degrees Celsius by the middle of the century compared to an extreme scenario without regulation of ozone-depleting substances.[158] Although the task is not complete, the international community has responded clearly to the issue. The Kigali Amendment of 2016 is a positive development concerning the compatibility between the ozone and climate change regimes, effectively bringing the two legal regimes closer.

The Implementation Plan of the 2002 WSSD in Johannesburg agreed to enhance cooperation in the field of air pollution and ozone depletion.[159] States agreed to take actions to facilitate the implementation of the Montreal Protocol by ensuring adequate replenishment of the Multilateral Fund by 2003/2005 and to further support the regime for protection of the ozone layer established by the convention system. They pledged to improve access by developing countries to alternatives to ozone-depleting substances by 2010

155 OECD, *Illegal Trade in Environmentally Sensitive Goods* (OECD Trade Policy Studies 2012).

156 See Report of the Nineteenth Meeting of the Parties to the Montreal Protocol on Substances that Deplete the Ozone Layer UN Doc UNEP/OzL.Pro.19/7, Decision XIX/12; see for more Armin Rosencranz and Siddharth Johar, 'Illegal Smuggling of Ozone-Depleting Substances' (2015) 45(2) *Environmental Policy and Law* 73 and Ning Liu, Vira Somboon, and Carl Middleton, 'Illegal trade in ozone-depleting substances' in Lorraine Elliott and William Schaedla (eds.) *Handbook of Transnational Environmental Crime* (Edward Elgar2016) 212.

157 WMO, Executive Summary n 25, 33.

158 ibid 20.

159 Implementation Plan of the 2002 of the World Summit on Sustainable Development (A/CONF.199/L.7) Annex, para. 37.

and assist them in complying with the phase-out schedule under the Montreal Protocol. In a significant phrase, the WSSD text recognizes the scientific and technical interrelationship between ozone depletion and climate change. Finally, participating states agreed to take measures to address illegal traffic in ozone-depleting substances. As discussed above, the Parties to the Vienna Convention and the Montreal Protocol – now universally ratified – have continued to work towards these commitments. In 2014, 507 million US dollars was pledged to the Multilateral Fund to assist developing nations phase out ozone depleting substances for the period of 2015–2017 alone.[160]

4 Anthropogenic Climate Change

4.1 *International Cooperation and Governance on Anthropogenic Climate Change*

4.1.1. Regulation before the UNFCCC

Early signs of international concern over climate change appeared in a series of international conferences on CO_2 between 1985 and 1987.[161] The rather disappointing results of these meetings led to an international Conference on the Atmosphere in Evolution and its Implications for the Safety of the Globe, held in Toronto from 27 to 30 June 1988.[162] At that time, UNEP joined its efforts with those of WMO and ICSU in order to study the scientific aspects of the problem. In November 1988, the IPCC was created, made up of scientific and political experts, and given the task of exploring possible measures to be taken in order to protect the atmosphere.

On December 6, 1988, The UN General Assembly adopted Resolution 43/53 on the conservation of the global climate for present and future generations of mankind.[163] It stated that climate change is a 'common concern of mankind' and that it was necessary to adopt promptly the necessary measures to deal with it within a global framework. It approved a World Climatological Program

160 Report of the Tenth Meeting of the Conference of the Parties to the Vienna Convention for the Protection of the Ozone Layer and the Twenty-Sixth Meeting of the Parties to the Montreal Protocol on Substances that Deplete the Ozone Layer UN Doc UNEP/OzL.Conv.10/7; UNEP/Oz:.Pro.26/10, Decision XXVI/10; for more on the international legal regime concerning the ozone layer, see Osamu Yoshida, *The International Legal Régime for the Protection of the Stratospheric Ozone Layer: Second Revised Edition* (Brill 2019).

161 Villach Conference (PNUE/OMM/ICSU) 1985, Brussels Symposium (CEE) 1986, Bellagio and Villach Seminars 1987.

162 See WMO/OMM, nº 70, 1989.

163 28 I.L.M 1326 (1989).

to be set up by UNEP in collaboration with WMO and ICSU, and it supported the work of the IPCC. It requested the institutions to carry out an overall study on the matter and to examine in particular those aspects that might be addressed in a possible international convention on the climate.

Two months later, an International Assembly of Political and Legal Experts met in Ottawa, charged with working out elements for an international agreement for the protection of the atmosphere. The Hague Conference of March 10 and 11, 1989, convened by France, Norway and the Netherlands, went still further; its Final Declaration, adopted by twenty-four states, proclaimed the fundamental duty to do all that can be done in order to preserve the quality of the atmosphere for present and future generations. It also called for the development of new principles of international law and new and more effective decision-making and enforcement mechanisms, including a new institutional authority within the framework of the United Nations which would be responsible for defining protection standards, the respect for which would be under the control of the International Court of Justice.[164]

Resolution 15/36, adopted by the UNEP Executive Council on May 25, 1989 reaffirmed the idea of a framework convention on the climate.[165] The Council of the European Communities adopted a June 21, 1989, resolution on the greenhouse effect and the Community, declaring the need to conclude an international agreement on climate change, to promote action with a view to reducing emissions of other greenhouse gases (CO_2 in particular), to protect forests and engage in reforestation.[166] On December 22, 1989 the UN General Assembly adopted a new resolution on the subject, emphasizing the urgent need to work out a general convention on climate change issues as well as the to set up international mechanisms for financing and to guarantee access of developing countries to the technologies required.

The Second World Climate Conference, held in Geneva from October 29 to November 7, 1990, was attended by delegations from more than 100 states, in some cases led by their Heads of State or Government. The Conference had before it the IPCC report which, although less dramatic than some had imagined, was explicit regarding the need to adopt immediate precautionary measures in order to reduce emissions of gases having a greenhouse effect, as well as other measures aimed at stabilizing the climate such as reforestation. The Final Declaration of the Conference contained a compromise solution requesting developed countries to establish either reduction objectives

164 28 I.L.M. 1308 (1989).
165 28 I.L.M. 1330 (1989).
166 28 I.L.M. 1306 (1989).

by specific dates, or 'feasible national programs and strategies', which should have a significant effect on the limitation of emissions of CO_2 and other gases having a greenhouse effect.

On December 21, 1990, the UN General Assembly adopted another resolution on the protection of the world climate for present and future generations.[167] The Resolution reflected a desire for an Intergovernmental Negotiating Committee (INC) to prepare a general and effective convention on climate change.[168]

4.1.2 1992 United Nations Framework Convention on Climate Change

The UN Framework Convention on Climate Change was adopted on May 8, 1992 in New York and opened for signature during the Rio de Janeiro Conference. It defines climate change as a modification of the climate which is attributed directly or indirectly to human activity that alters the composition of the global atmosphere, and which is in addition to natural climate variability observed over comparable time periods (Art. 1(2)). The stated objective is to stabilize the concentrations of all greenhouse gases in the atmosphere at a level that will prevent dangerous anthropogenic interference with the climate system (Art. 2). In this regard, precautionary measures must be taken to anticipate, prevent, or minimize the causes of climate change and mitigate its adverse effects (Art. 3(3)).

The obligations of all parties are mainly contained in Articles 4 and 12: developing, periodically updating, publishing, and making available national inventories of anthropogenic emissions and sinks; formulating and implementing national and regional programs containing measures to mitigate climate change; promoting the application of processes that control emissions including transfer of technologies; promoting sustainable management of sinks and reservoirs of all greenhouse gases; elaborating integrated plans for coastal zone management and cooperation in research (Art. 4(1)).

The Convention recognizes the necessity of returning to earlier levels of anthropogenic emissions of carbon dioxide and other greenhouse gases (Art. 4(2)(a)), but sets no specific timetables and targets for limiting such emissions, establishing only that the parties' obligations differ. Applying the principle of common but differentiated responsibilities and respective capabilities, the

167 UNGA, *Protection of Global Climate for Present and Future Generations of Mankind* (21 December 1990) UNGA Res 45/212, UN Doc A/RES/45/212.

168 See: José Juste, 'Protection of the Atmospheric Environment by International Law', *in* Alexandre Kiss and Dinah Shelton, *Manual of European Environmental Law* (CUP 1997) 394, 403–404.

Convention provides that its developed country parties should take the lead in combating climate change and its adverse effects (Art. 3(1)). The Convention divides countries into three groups: Annex I parties, Annex II parties and non-Annex I parties. Annex I parties are industrialized parties which were members of the OECD in 1992 and countries with economies in transition (EITs) to a market economy. Annex II parties are the OECD countries minus the EIT Parties. Non-Annex I parties are mostly developing countries. Annex I parties pledge to adopt national and regional policies and take corresponding measures to mitigate climate change by limiting their emissions of greenhouse gases and protecting and enhancing their greenhouse sinks and reservoirs. They recognize the need for equitable and appropriate contributions to the global effort. To this end, each is obliged to communicate, within six months of the entry into force of the Convention for it, and periodically thereafter, detailed information on its policies and measures. This information is reviewed by the Conference of the Parties. Each of the developed parties shall coordinate with other such parties, as appropriate, relevant economic and administrative instruments developed to achieve the objective of the Convention (Art. 4(2)).

EIT parties have a special status under the Convention which grants them some flexibility to enhance their ability to address climate change (Art. 4(6)). Annex II parties are to provide new and additional financial resources to meet the agreed full costs incurred by developing countries in complying with their obligations relating to the communication of national inventories and the measures taken or envisaged to implement the convention. The most developed states also must assist developing countries that are particularly vulnerable to adverse effects of climate change in meeting costs of adaptation to those adverse effects (Art. 4(2)(a)). The transfer of environmentally sound technologies is particularly stressed, but the development and enhancement of endogenous capacities and technologies should also be supported (Art. 4(5)). The Convention explicitly provides that the extent to which developing countries will implement their commitments depends on the effective implementation by developed countries of their commitments related to financial resources and transfer of technology (Art. 4(7)).

The instrument deserves its title: it constitutes a framework for which concrete and specific obligations must be elaborated. This is the task of the institutions established by it: the Conference of the Parties (Art. 7), the Secretariat (Art. 8), and two subsidiary bodies – one for scientific and technological advice (Art. 9), the other for implementation (Art. 10). A Financial Mechanism is also defined (Art. 11).

The Conference of the Parties (COP) is the supreme body of the Convention. In addition to duties comparable to those of bodies created by other treaties – facilitation of information exchanges, coordination of measures adopted to address climate change, elaboration of recommendations, organization of its own work – it has three broad categories of functions:

a. Adoption of protocols to the Convention. Article 17, which foresees such instruments, is not very developed, but it is clear that these instruments are intended to inject substance into the framework convention.
b. Supervision of the implementation. According to Article 12(1), information concerning national inventories of emissions and sinks and steps taken or envisaged to implement the Convention should be communicated by all states parties. Developed states also should furnish a detailed description of their policies and measures on the mitigation of climate change and on the assistance they grant developing countries (Art. 12(2)). Such information shall be considered by a subsidiary body on implementation in order to assess the overall aggregated effects of the steps taken by the parties (Art. 10). The COP then assesses the implementation of the Convention by the parties, taking into account the environmental, economic, and social effects of the measures taken, as well as their cumulative impacts (Art. 7(2)).
c. The COP must mobilize financial resources (Art. 7(2)(h)), the amount of which should be determined in a predictable and identifiable manner. The COP also decides on the policies, program priorities, and eligibility criteria related to financial assistance to developing countries. Under its guidance, the Financial Mechanism, established on the basis of the principle of an equitable and balanced representation of all parties, has the task of providing financial resources on a grant or concessional basis (Art. 11(1)(2)). Arrangements must be agreed upon, including modalities, to ensure that the funded projects are in conformity with the policies, program priorities and eligibility criteria established by the COP. The weakness of the commitments contained in the Convention thus had to be balanced by the strength of the institutions established. The rules agreed upon primarily served as the basis of future negotiations both inside and outside these institutions.

The parties to the UNFCCC could choose from a range of policy options to counter anthropogenic climate change, some of the policies having important impacts on national economies. Measures could include improving energy efficiency, forest management, air pollution control, fuel switching and restructuring transportation. Many environmental economists support carbon taxes as a way to establish appropriate incentives away from polluting fuels. Reforestation and other measures to expand carbon sinks are also possible. The debates that have taken place since adoption of the Climate Change Convention have largely centered on determining the appropriate measures to be taken.

At its first session, held in Berlin from March 28 to April 7 1995,[169] the COP had to consider the establishment of a multilateral consultative process regarding questions on the implementation of the Convention (Art. 13). It was decided that any body or agency, whether national or international, governmental or non-governmental, qualified in matters covered by the Convention, may be represented at a session of the COP. Such presence can be useful when the implementation of the Convention is discussed on the basis of national reports. The importance of the meeting was enhanced by an interim report released by the Intergovernmental Panel on Climate Change (IPCC) at the end of 1994, which pointed out that even with a stabilization of current global CO_2 emissions, atmospheric concentrations of this most important greenhouse gas would continue to rise for at least two centuries.[170] The presence of around 4000 participants, including 2000 journalists at this 'Berlin Summit' demonstrated the interest raised by the problem of climate change.

Taking into account the rising emission trends of industrialized countries and of developing countries, it appeared that the commitments in the UNFCCC were too weak. Several mainly oil-exporting countries opposed negotiating further commitments, however. As a compromise, the COP adopted the 'Berlin Mandate' in which the parties agreed to begin a process that could lead to the conclusion of a 'protocol or another legal instrument' based on an analysis and assessment identifying appropriate policies and measures. It was also aimed to sett 'quantified limitation and reduction objectives within specified time-frames' for greenhouse gas emissions.

The first COP also adopted institutional arrangements. The restructured Global Environmental Facility continued the international entity entrusted with the operation of the Convention on an interim basis. The two subsidiary organs foreseen by Articles 9 and 10 were established,[171] both as plenary organs open for all parties and observers from other states, international organizations

169 For the full texts of decisions adopted by the Conference of the Parties at its first through fifth sessions, see documents FCCC/CP/1995/7/Add.1, FCCC/CP/1996/15/Add.1, FCCC/CP/1997/7/Add.1, FCCC/CP/1998/16/Add.1 and FCCC/CP/1999/6/Add.1. See also Sebastian Oberthür and Hermann Ott, 'UN/Convention on Climate Change, the First Conference of the Parties' (1995) 25 *EPL* 144–156.

170 John Houghton et al., *Climate Change 1994: Radiative Forcing of Climate Change and An Evaluation of the IPCC IS92 Emission Scenarios* (IPCC 1994) 13.

171 The two organs are called the "Subsidiary Body for Scientific and Technological Advice" (SBSTA) and the "Subsidiary Body for Implementation" (SBI).

and NGOs. Finally, the Berlin COP decided to install the secretariat of the Convention in Bonn.[172]

The Second COP, convened in July 1996 in Geneva, adopted a Declaration recording the belief of the ministers representing more than 100 states that the findings of the IPCC's second assessment report indicate 'dangerous interference with the climate system'. They also stressed the need for accelerating negotiations on a legally binding protocol and outlined the directions of future action. The Third COP, held in Kyoto on December 1–10 1997, concluded the negotiations by adopting the Kyoto Protocol, moving forward in the development of precise rules to mitigate the greenhouse effect (as discussed below).

4.1.3 The 1997 Kyoto Protocol

The Kyoto Protocol to the UN Framework Convention specifies different goals and commitments for developed and developing countries concerning future emission of greenhouse gases. The complexity of the text increases the risk of disagreement over interpretation and thus of implementation. The main features of the protocol are the reduction targets accepted by the industrialized countries, without corresponding obligations for developing countries; acknowledgment of the role of sinks of greenhouse gases (seas, forests) and their inclusion in the targets; the possible creation of 'bubbles' and trading emissions as means for reducing their aggregate emissions and joint implementation agreements with countries that only emit small amounts of greenhouse gases, in principle developing countries.

Articles 2 to 8 of the Protocol concern the states listed in Annex I of the Framework Convention.[173] Article 3(1) adopts a 'big bubble approach': these countries must, individually or jointly, cut their aggregate anthropogenic carbon dioxide equivalent emissions of greenhouse gases listed in Annex A by at least five percent (averaging 5.2 percent) below 1990 levels by the first commitment period of 2008–2012. These reductions cover six greenhouse gases: carbon dioxide, methane, nitrous oxide, hydrofluorocarbons (HFCs), perfluorocarbons (PFCs) and sulfur hexafluoride (SF6). Thus, if a state party is able to limit emissions of greenhouse gases other than carbon dioxide, restrictions on the use of fossil fuels may be correspondingly relaxed. Each state of this group shall, by 2005, have made demonstrable progress in achieving its commitments under the Protocol. Countries in transition benefit from a certain degree of flexibility in the implementation of their commitments (Art. 3(6)).

172 On the aftermath of the Berlin Conference see 26 EPL158 (1996).

173 Bulgaria, Croatia, Czech Republic, Estonia, Hungary, Latvia, Poland Romania, Russia, Slovakia, Slovenia and Ukraine.

They may use, for example, a different base year to determine the reduction of their emission (Art. 3(5)).

Article 2 lists methods that may be used in order to achieve quantified emission limitation and reduction: enhancement of energy efficiency, protection and enhancement of sinks and reservoirs of greenhouse gases, promotion of sustainable forms of agriculture, increased use of new and renewable forms of energy and of environmentally sound technologies, reduction or phasing out of market imperfections, the use of economic instruments, limitation and reduction of emissions of greenhouse gases in the transport sector and limitation and/or reduction of methane through recovery and use in waste management.

Annex I parties are allowed to join together in the establishment of 'bubbles' and thereby attain their emission reduction commitments jointly. Countries doing this will be deemed to have met their reduction requirements provided that their total aggregate emissions do not exceed the total of their combined amounts set out in Annex B. In the event of failure to achieve the aggregated target, each of the countries concerned will still be held responsible for their respective individual commitments in Annex B (Art. 4).[174]

Another specific form of cooperation in the reduction of the emission of greenhouse gases is emissions trading. According to Article 6(1), any developed country, for the purpose of meeting its commitments, may transfer to or acquire from, any other party emission reduction units resulting from projects aimed at reducing emissions. It also can enhance anthropogenic removals by sinks of greenhouse gases in any sector of the economy. The condition is that any such project provides a reduction in emission by sources or an enhancement of removal by sinks, that is additional to any that would otherwise occur. The acquisition of emission reduction units thus shall be supplemental to domestic actions for the purposes of meeting commitments under Article 3. A developed country may also authorize legal entities to participate, under its responsibility, in actions leading to the generation, transfer or acquisition of emission reduction units (Art. 6(3)). The COP defines the relevant principles, modalities, rules and guidelines, in particular for the verification, reporting and accountability for emission trading (Art. 16bis).

Any emission reduction units, or any part of an assigned amount, that a party acquires from another party shall be added to the assigned amount for that party (Art. 3(10)). Parallel to this provision, Article 3(11) foresees that any emission reduction units, or any part of an assigned amount, that a party

174 James H. Searles, 'Analysis of the Kyoto Protocol to the U.N. Framework Convention on Climate Change' (1998) 21 *Int'l Envtl. Rep.* 132.

transfers to another party shall be subtracted from the assigned amount for that party.

Article 12 outlines a 'clean development mechanism' the task of which is to assist developing countries in achieving sustainable development and in contributing to the ultimate objective of the convention and also to assist developed countries in achieving compliance with their quantified emission limitation and reduction commitments. Emission reductions resulting from each project activity shall be certified on a voluntary basis approved by each party involved, by operational entities to be designated by the COP (Art. 12(5)). Developing countries will benefit from project activities resulting in certified emission reductions while developed countries may use the certified emission reductions accruing from such project activities to contribute to compliance with part of their quantified emission limitation and reduction commitments (Art. 12(3)(b)). The clean development mechanism will assist in arranging funding of certified project activities as necessary. Certified emission reductions obtained during the period 2000 to 2008 can be used by developed countries to assist in achieving compliance in the commitment period 2008 to 2012.

Monitoring of greenhouse gases plays an important role in the Kyoto Protocol. Developing countries must establish national systems to estimate anthropocentric emissions by sources and removals by sinks (Art. 5) as well as annual inventories to incorporate the supplementary information necessary to demonstrate compliance with the commitments accepted under the Protocol (Art. 7). Such information will be reviewed by teams composed of experts nominated by parties to the Framework Convention and, as appropriate, by intergovernmental organizations, and coordinated by the secretariat. The information submitted by the parties and the reports of the expert reviews shall be submitted to the COP which can take decisions on any matter required for the implementation of the Protocol (Art. 8).

Articles 10 and 11 of the Protocol concern in particular developing countries. Their emissions are not limited, but they should formulate, where relevant, cost-effective national and where appropriate regional programs to improve the quality of local emission factors, formulate, implement, publish and regularly update national or regional programs to mitigate climate change, taking into account all relevant economic activities. Cooperation with developing countries shall include the transfer of, or access to, environmentally sound technologies, know-how, practices and processes pertinent to climate change as well as capacity building. Article 11 foresees that new and additional financial resources should be provided to meet the agreed full costs incurred by developing country parties in advancing the implementation of existing commitments.

The COP of the Convention serves as the Meeting of the Parties to the Protocol. It keeps under regular review the implementation of the Protocol and shall make the decisions necessary to promote its effective implementation. It assesses, on the basis of the information made available to it, the overall effects of the measures taken and makes recommendations on any matters necessary for the implementation of the Protocol (Art. 13). The COP approves appropriate and effective procedures and mechanisms to determine and address cases of non-compliance with the provisions of the Protocol (Art. 17). Any body or agency, whether national or international, governmental or non-governmental that is qualified in matters covered by the Protocol may be admitted as an observer, unless at least one third of the parties present at the meeting objects (Art. 13). The secretariat and the subsidiary bodies established by the Framework Convention shall be used for the Protocol (Arts. 14 and 15).

The Fourth Conference of Parties to the UNFCCC was held in Buenos Aires from November 2–14, 1998 and adopted the Buenos Aires Mandate. Its results were modest. In spite of the insistence of the US delegation, the developing countries did not accept any obligation to reduce their emissions of greenhouse gases, which would have been necessary to satisfy the US private sector demand for the rapid creation of a pollution trading market. European countries stressed the need for industrialized countries to reduce their emissions within the limits of their jurisdiction, while the developing countries asked for the transfer of clean technologies. In the end, the 161 countries present adopted an action plan listing issues for future discussion including the elaboration of rules on emission trading, the Clean Development Mechanism (CDM) and joint implementation.

In 2000 the Sixth Conference of the Parties to the UNFCCC met at the Hague and failed to reach agreement on implementing the Kyoto Protocol. Soon thereafter, the United States administration announced it would not proceed to ratify the Kyoto Protocol which it had signed, following which Europe, Japan and other countries resumed COP-6 in Bonn. At Bonn, they established an international regulatory framework to make Kyoto operational; this was translated into the Marrakech Accords at COP-7 at the end of 2001. The Marrakech Accords, at 218 pages, represent the detailed legal framework for implementing the Kyoto Protocol.

The most important controversy at COP-6 was over whether or not there should be an absolute cap to the use of emissions trading, Joint Implementation and the Clean Development Mechanism (CDM) to fulfil Kyoto commitments, thus keeping the pressure on states to reduce national emissions. The final agreement, contained in Decision 15 of COP-7 is that 'the use of the mechanisms shall be supplemental to domestic action and domestic action shall thus constitute a significant element' of implementing Article 3.1 of the protocol.[175] Nuclear power is banned from the CDM and Joint Implementation. In Article 12 of the Kyoto Protocol, the parties agreed on a prompt start to the CDM. According to Decision 17/CP.7, projects that started from 2000 onwards may be credited retroactively. The determination of whether a CDM project is sustainable lies with the host country. Parties also may use afforestation and reforestation activities in the CDM up to a ceiling of 1 percent of a party's 1990 emissions.[176] An Executive Board of ten members oversees the CDM. Five of them come from the five regional groups, one from a small island state, and one each from Annex I and non-Annex I countries. Since the Executive Board may take decisions only with a 3/4 majority, the four Annex I countries could block action. Joint implementation has its own supervisory committee to be elected immediately after the entry into force of the protocol, also composed of 10 members: 3 from EIT countries, three from other annex I countries, three from developing countries and one from a small island developing country. In this body, the 4 developing countries could potentially block action.

Following the Marrakesh Accords, the Kyoto Protocol was ratified by over 100 counties by 2002.[177] Also in 2002, the Plan of Implementation of the World Summit on Sustainable Development strongly urged states that had not done so to ratify the Kyoto Protocol in a timely manner and recalled the U.N. Millennium Declaration in which heads of state and government resolved to embark on the required reduction of emissions of greenhouse gases in conformity to the Framework Convention on Climate Change. The Plan of Implementation calls the Convention 'the key instrument for addressing climate change, a global concern'.[178] Following the Summit, although most industrialized countries had ratified the Kyoto Protocol, the number was insufficient to account for enough of a percentage of the 1990 CO_2 emissions for the Protocol to enter into force. The United States refused to ratify which caused Russia's ratification to become vital to the Protocol's operation.[179]

175 UNFCCC, 'Report of the Conference of the Parties on Its 7th Session' (October 29–November 10 2001) FCCC/CP/2001/13/Add.2, Decision 15/CP.7, para. 1.

176 UNFCCC, 'Modalities and Procedures for a Clean Development Mechanism as Defined in Article 12 of the Kyoto Protocol' (10 November 2001) Decision 17/CP.7, FCCC/CP/2001/13/Add.2, para. 7.

177 See UNFCCC, *Status of Ratification of the Kyoto Protocol* (2014) available at <http://unfccc.int/kyoto_protocol/status_of_ratification/items/2613.php>; and Hugo M. Schally and Herman E. Ott, 'II. Air and Atmosphere' (2003) 13(1) *Yearbook of International Environmental Law* 258, 261

178 Plan of Implementation of the World Summit on Sustainable Development (n 166), para. 38.

179 Hugo M. Schally and Herman E. Ott, '*II.* Air and Atmosphere' (*2003*) 13(1) *Yearbook of International Environmental Law* 258, 262; Art. 25(1).

Despite successes, challenges remained, including securing Russia's ratification, the conduct of the United States, tension between developing and industrialized countries, and issues arising from the Marrakesh Accords that needed expansion.

The United States began to act in opposition of the Kyoto Protocol, giving rise to the potential for other states to be discouraged from ratifying.[180] This included preventing dialogue on the second commitment phase (beyond 2012) of the Protocol and pursuing bilateral arrangements.[181] Tension arose between developing and industrialized states, exacerbated by the United States who, despite previously calling for commitments for developing nations,[182] contributed to blocking EU efforts to discuss this very issue.[183] This tension was encapsulated in the Delhi Declaration,[184] which enabled those who had ratified the Protocol to call for the ratification of those who had not and recognized the need to urgently work towards emissions reductions. However, it also set out overcoming poverty and economic and social development as the 'overriding priorities' for developing countries; two somewhat opposing focuses requiring significant compromise to reach.[185]

Another point of tension, between industrialized states that had ratified and both developing nations and the United States, was the discussion of the second commitment period under the Kyoto Protocol. In 2004 Argentina proposed to conduct two seminars in 2005 as a preliminary discussion of views before any negotiations on the second commitment period. This was opposed, including by the United States who would only support one seminar discussing past efforts only with no reporting to the 2005 COP. Developing Countries also opposed this, concerned about negotiations happening too quickly when Parties had not yet implemented their current commitments.[186] The Decision reached provided for only one seminar, which was to focus on present efforts,

180 ibid 261.

181 See ibid; and Hugo M. Schally and Herman E. Ott, '11. Air and Atmosphere' (*2005*) 15(1) *Yearbook of International Environmental law* 243.

182 See footnote 173 above.

183 See Hugo M. Schally and Herman E. Ott, '11. Air and Atmosphere' (*2003*) 13(1) *Yearbook of International Environmental Law* 258, 263.

184 UN DOC FCCC/CP/2002/7Add.1 Report of the Conference of the Parties on its Eighth Session, Decision 1/CP.8, perambulatory paragraphs, paragraphs (a), (b).

185 See Hugo M. Schally and Herman E. Ott, '11. Air and Atmosphere' (*2003*) 13(1) *Yearbook of International Environmental Law* 258, 264.

186 Hugo M. Schally and Hermann E. Ott, '11. Air and Atmosphere' (2005) 15(1) *Yearbook of International Environmental Law* 243, 251.

and specifically stated that 'this seminar does not open any negotiations leading to new commitments'.[187]

The Parties also were required to expand upon several aspects of the Marrakesh Accords, including the operation of the funds established by it,[188] deciding what 'reforestation' and 'afforestation' projects would be incorporated and determining the limit of greenhouse gas removals by sinks under the CDM.[189] Capacity building for non-Annex I Parties was also a key issue, including the disputed measure of using funds for developing countries to aid in economic diversification for oil producing countries.[190] In this period, the European Commission legislated a trading scheme for greenhouse gas emission, the largest ever to be established, designed to cover approximately half of the European Community's 1990 emissions.[191] The United States inaction on climate change has in part resulted in pressure on the European Community not to take any further steps without other major state actors.[192]

Russia finally ratified the Kyoto Protocol in late 2004, just before COP10,[193] and the Kyoto Protocol was able to enter into force in 2005. The first Conference of the Parties serving as the Meeting of the Parties of the Kyoto Protocol (CMP), run simultaneously with COP11 in Montreal, formally adopted many of the decisions forwarded by the COP that made up the Marrakesh Accords.[194] Some decisions were cause for discussion, for example Decision 24/CP.7 on compliance. It was ultimately adopted by CMP1, but with the *proviso* that amendments would be considered due to differences in legal interpretation.[195] No agreement was reached on the Special Climate Change Fund

187 UNFCCC, *COP 10 conclusion on the seminar of governmental experts*, available at <http://unfccc.int/files/meetings/cop_10/adopted_decisions/application/pdf/seminar_final.pdf> (2004).

188 UN Doc FCCC/CP/2002/7/Add.1 Report of the Conference of the Parties on its Eighth Session, Decision 7/CP.8 and Decision 8/CP.8; UN Doc FCCC/CP/2003/6/Add.1 Report of the Conference of the Parties on its Ninth Session, Decision 5/CP.9 and 6/CP.9.

189 UN Doc FCCC/CP/2004/10/Add.2 Report of the Conference of the Parties on its Tenth Session, Decision 13/CP.10, Decision 14/CP.10 and Decision 15/CP.10.

190 UN Doc FCCC/CP/2004/10/Add.1 Report of the Conference of the Parties on its Tenth Session, Decision 1/CP.10, Part II Impact of the implementation of response measures.

191 Directive 2003/87/EC and Directive 2004/101/EC.

192 Hugo M. Schally and Hermann E. Ott, 'II. Air and Atmosphere' (*2005*) 15(1) *Yearbook of International Environmental Law* 243, 252.

193 ibid 243.

194 UN Doc FCCC/KP/CMP/2005/8/Add.1 and UN Doc FCCC/KP/CMP/2005/8/Add.3 Report of the Conference of the Parties Serving as the Meeting of the Parties to the Kyoto Protocol on its First Session.

195 UN Doc FCCC/KP/CMP/2005/8/Add.1 Report of the Conference of the Parties Serving as the Meeting of the Parties to the Kyoto Protocol on its First Session, Decision 27/CMP.1;

established under the Accords, due to continued disagreement on economic diversification for oil producing states.[196] There was also difficulty with the Adaptation Fund, due to the influence of the United States in decision making for that fund.[197] Progress was made on the post-2012 commitment period, with COP11 establishing a dialogue on long term cooperative action to address climate change,[198] and CMP1 establishing an *ad hoc* working group to consider post-2012 commitments for Annex I Parties pursuant to Article 3 of the Protocol.[199] Reaching agreement on any part of the process of creating the second commitment period would be turbulent.

After the first CMP, the end of the first commitment period was just seven years away, and the overriding issue became the post 2012 commitments. A work program was established by the CMP1 working group in 2006,[200] and in 2007, the Bali Roadmap was adopted by the Conference of the Parties.[201] The Roadmap sets out a process to implement the convention in the present and after 2012, to be undertaken by a subsidiary body, the Ad Hoc Working Group on Long-term Cooperative Action under the Convention. The process includes reaching agreement and adopting a decision by COP15, through considering enhanced actions on various issues to achieve the overall objective of the Convention. The Bali working group was to meet at the latest by April 2008. The Roadmap does differentiate between industrialized and developing nations, but importantly includes a pathway for commitments for developing nations to be considered. The success of COP13 in 2007 has been attributed to the willingness of developing countries to take on commitments.[202]

Hugo M. Schally and Hermann E. Ott, '*11. Air and Atmosphere*' (2006) 16(1) Yearbook of International Environmental Law 391, 395.

196 Hugo M. Schally and Hermann E. Ott, '*11. Air and Atmosphere*' (2006) 16(1) Yearbook of International Environmental Law 391, 396.

197 ibid.

198 UN Doc FCC/CP/2005/5/Add.1 Report of the Conference of the Parties on its Eleventh Session, Decision 1/CP.11.

199 UN Doc FCCC/KP/CMP/2005/8/Add.1 Report of the Conference of the Parties Serving as the Meeting of the Parties to the Kyoto Protocol on its First Session, Decision 1/CMP.1.

200 UN DOC FCCC/KP/CMP/2006/10 Report of the Conference of the Parties Serving as the Meeting of the Parties to the Kyoto Protocol on its Second Session, p. 10.

201 UN Doc FCCC/CP/2007/6/Add.1 Report of the Conference of the Parties on its Thirteenth Session, Decision 1/CP.13.

202 Hermann E. Ott, '11. Air and Atmosphere' (2018) 18(1) *Yearbook of International Environmental Law* 201.

However, progress under the Roadmap was stagnant in 2008,[203] and in 2009 at COP15 an agreement was not able to be reached by the Parties. Instead, the mandate of the working group established under the Bali Roadmap was extended to COP16,[204] and likewise the working group established by CMP1 was requested to deliver its work at CMP6.[205] The main outcome of COP15 was the Copenhagen Accord, which is described as political only.[206] At COP16, in 2010, the Cancun Agreements were created.[207] The legal form of the continuation of the Protocol was not decided upon, but the Agreements provided that a global goal for reducing emissions by 2050 should be identified and considered at COP17 and reaffirmed the aim for the increase in global temperature to remain under two degrees Celsius (Decision 1/CP.16, Part II). It also provided for enhanced reporting for both Annex I and non-Annex I Parties (Decision 1/CP.16 Part III) and considers, adaptation, mitigation, technology, deforestation and financing in detail. Following on from COP15, Decision 1/CP.16 included a commitment by developed country Parties to jointly mobilize USD 100 billion per year by 2020 to address the needs of developing country Parties in meaningful mitigation and implementation.[208] There is however, a lack of provision for implementation and financing for these new measures.[209]

At CMP7 in 2011 it was decided that the second commitment period of the Kyoto Protocol would commence on January 1 2013.[210] However, the length of this second period was not decided upon and nor were any specific reduction

203 Leonardo Massai, Hugo-Maria Schally, and Hermann E. Ott, 'II. Air and Atmosphere' (2009) 19(1) *Yearbook of International Environmental Law* 225.

204 UN Doc FCCC/CP/2009/11/Add.1 Report of the Conference of the Parties on its Fifteenth Session, Decision 1/CP.15.

205 UN Doc FCCC/KP/CMP/2009/21/Add.1 Report of the Conference of the Parties Serving as the Meeting of the Parties to the Kyoto Protocol on its Fifth Session, Decision 1/CMP.5.

206 UN Doc FCCC/CP/2009/11/Add.1 Report of the Conference of the Parties on its Fifteenth Session, Decision 2/CP.5. See Leonardo Massai and Wolfgang Sterk, 'II. Air and Atmosphere' (*2010*) 20(1) *Yearbook of International Environmental Law* 263.

207 UN Doc FCCC/CP/2010/7/Add.1 Report of the Conference of the Parties on its Sixteenth Session, Decision 1/CP.16; UN Doc FCCC/KP/CMP/2010/12/Add.1 Report of the Conference of the Parties Serving as the Meeting of the Parties to the Kyoto Protocol on its Sixth Session, Decision 1/CMP.6 and 2/CMP.6.

208 UN Doc FCCC/CP/2010/7/Add.1 Report of the Conference of the Parties on its Sixteenth Session, Decision 1/CP.16, para. 98; UN Doc FCCC/CP/2009/11/Add.1 Report of the Conference of the Parties on its Fifteenth Session, Decision 2/CP.15, para. 8.

209 Wolfgang Sterk, Christof Arens, Urda Eichhorst, Florian Mersmann, and Hanna Wang-Helmreich, '*3. Global Climate*' (*2011*) 21(1) Yearbook of International Environmental Law 206.

210 UN Doc FCCC/KP/CMP/2011/10/Add.1 Report of the Conference of the Parties Serving as the Meeting of the Parties to the Kyoto Protocol on its Seventh Session, Decision 1/CMP.7.

targets. Instead, Annex I Parties were to submit their quantified emission limitation or reduction objectives for the second commitment period for consideration by the CMP1 Working Group and adoption at CMP8. This decision was made at a time where the Parties to the convention had different priorities and visions for the second phase of the Kyoto Protocol; some were focused on the participation of the United States and developing countries that were fast industrializing, some on industrialized states continuing to bear responsibility, and the United States pressed for the creation of a new instrument that operated in a 'bottom up' manner, rather than Kyoto's 'top down'.[211] In the end, COP17 agreed to establish the Ad Hoc Working Group on the Durban Platform for Enhanced Action, as a process to develop 'a protocol, another legal instrument or an agreed outcome with legal force under the Convention applicable to all Parties'.[212] The inclusion of the words 'with legal force' and 'applicable to all Parties' were subject to some debate,[213] as was the timeline for the working group, which is to complete its task not later than 2015, with the instrument to be in effect from 2020. Several Parties did not agree, with Canada, Russia and Japan refusing to accept commitments in the second period and Canada ultimately announcing its intention to withdraw from the Kyoto Protocol.[214] New Zealand also refused to participate in the second period.[215] COP18 in 2012 was an intermediary step in negotiating the new agreement, with decisions made on the agreed outcome pursuant to the Bali Action Plan and on Advancing the Durban Platform.[216] Decision 2/CP.18 provides that the working group established in Durban is to consider a draft negotiating text to be made available before May 2015. Significantly, CMP8 amended the Kyoto Protocol to include 37 Annex 1 countries emission pledges for the second commitment period, 2012–2020.[217]

---

211 See Wolfgang Sterk, and others '3. *Global Climate*' (*2012*) 22(1) Yearbook of International Environmental Law 193.

212 Un Doc FCC/CP/2011/9/Add.1 Report of the Conference of the Parties on its Seventeenth Session, Decision 1/CP.17.

213 See Wolfgang Sterk, and others, '3. *Global Climate*', (2012) 22(1) Yearbook of International Environmental Law 193.

214 See Schatz et al, 'International Environmental Law' (2012) 46(1) *The International Lawyer* 419.

215 Wolfgang Sterk, and others, '3. *Global Climate*' (2013) 23(1) Yearbook of International Environmental Law 236.

216 Un Doc FCCC/CP/2012/8/Add.1 Report of the Conference of the Conference of the Parties on its Eighteenth Session, Decision 1/CP.18 and Decision 2/CP.18.

217 UN Doc FCCC/KP/CMP/2012/13/Add.1 Report of the Conference of the Parties Serving as the Meeting of the Parties to the Kyoto Protocol on its Eight Session, Decision 1/CMP.8.

4.1.4 The 2015 Paris Agreement

Finally, and surprisingly,[218] COP 21 in 2015 saw the adoption of the Paris Agreement,[219] the first binding agreement to firmly set a goal restricting the rise in global temperature and set it as a goal for all Parties to the agreement.[220] The objective of the Paris Agreement, set out in Article 2, is to enhance the implementation of the Convention and its objectives by holding the rise in global average temperature to 'well below' two degrees Celsius and aiming for 1.5 degrees, increasing adaptability and providing finance consistent with these goals. Article 2 also enshrines the principle of common but differentiated responsibility. Article 3 sets out how the Agreement will operate – which is in stark contrast to the Kyoto Protocol. Instead of a specified timeline of targets, the Paris Agreement provides that contributions to the global response to climate change are to be nationally determined, with all Parties required to 'undertake and communicate ambitious efforts' (Art. 3). It is intended that there should be a progression of efforts over time and allowance for developing Parties for the Agreement to be effective. The efforts are defined in Articles 4, 7, 9, 10, 11 and 13 and Parties should act with the overall purpose of achieving the objectives in Article 2.

Article 4 of the Paris Agreement covers a number of matters relating to the achievement of the objectives in Article 2. These include the aim of reaching peak greenhouse emissions as soon as possible, and the need for rapid

218 Like its predecessors, COP19 in 2013 and COP20 in 2014 were not very constructive, achieving little in the way of progress on the new agreement. This was due to the same tensions and differences that had been playing out between the Parties, particularly the divide between industrialized and developing nations: see Wolfgang Obergassel, and others, '*3. Global Climate*' (2015) 25(1) Yearbook of International Environmental Law 201 and Annalisa Savaresi, 'The Paris Agreement: a New Beginning?' (2016) 34(1) *Journal of Energy & Natural Resources Law* 16. Throughout these tense negotiations leading to the Paris Agreement, the COP and the CMP also addressed the general workings of the climate regime, including the Clean Development Mechanism, the operation of the funds of the convention and Protocol, continued financing of the regime, deforestation and loss and damage as a result of climate change.

219 UN Doc FCCC/CP/2015/10/Add.1 Report of the Conference of the Parties on its Twenty-First Session, Decision 1/CP.21; The Paris Agreement (adopted December 12, 2015, entered into force November 4 2016) 3156 U.N.T.S. 79 (Paris Agreement).

220 See for more Geert van Calster and Leonie Reins, *The Paris Agreement on Climate Change: A Commentary* (Edward Elgar 2021); Daniel Klein et al., *The Paris Agreement on Climate Change: Analysis and Commentary* (OUP 2017); Vegard Tørstad, 'Participation, Ambition and Compliance: can the Paris Agreement solve the effectiveness trilemma?' (2020) 29(5) *Environmental Politics* 761; Silvia Bacchetta, 'Reasons for Agreeing, Reasons for Complying: The Paris Agreement and the Compliance Issue' (2020) 75(75) *Rivista di estetica* 72.

reductions in emissions to achieve a balance between anthropogenic emissions by sources and removals by sinks. There is also recognition for the position of developing countries and the need for a context of sustainable development and the eradication of poverty. Article 4 goes on to cover Parties preparing successive nationally determined contributions every five years, with each to represent a progression beyond that Party's current contribution. Domestic mitigation action must be undertaken by Parties. Industrialized Parties are to continue to bear the most responsibility, with developing country Parties to focus on enhancing mitigation and moving towards emissions reductions. The support to be provided, the manner of communication of determined contributions and the adjustment of time frames for those contributions is also covered. Provision is made for Parties intending to act jointly under Article 2. Article 7 establishes a goal on adaptation, contributing to sustainable development and the objective of the Agreement. Article 9 concerns the provision of financial resources by industrialized Parties to support developing country Parties. Article 10 covers the importance of technology development and transfer. Capacity building (Art. 11) and a transparency framework concerning the reporting required of the Parties and a review process (Art. 13) is also provided for.

Article 5 concerns the conservation and enhancement of sinks and reservoirs of greenhouse gases. Article 6 establishes a mechanism for the mitigation of greenhouse gas emissions and the support of sustainable development that includes incentives for participation by both public and private entities. In particular, Article 6(2) allows for a cooperative approach where Parties may trade mitigation outcomes, or carbon credits, amongst one another. Article 6(4) establishes the successor to the Kyoto Protocol's Clean Development Mechanism, the Sustainable Development Mechanism, and sets rules for emissions reduction credits for certified climate mitigation projects. Article 8 concerns loss and damage associated with climate change. Article 14 concerns the monitoring of the implementation of the Paris Agreement through a "global stocktake", which first assesses the collective progress in 2023 and every five years thereafter. Article 16 establishes that the Conference of the Parties shall serve as the Meeting of the Parties to the Paris Agreement, and makes provision for the conduct of meetings. The secretariat of the Convention shall serve as the secretariat for the Paris Agreement (Art. 17). Articles 18 and 19 concern the subsidiary bodies of the Convention, and Article 20, the signature and ratification of the Agreement. Article 21 prescribes when the Agreement shall enter into force; similarly to the Kyoto Protocol, 55 Parties to the Convention must have deposited their instruments of ratification and in addition, those 55 Parties must account for 55% of global greenhouse gas emissions.[221] Articles 22–24 concern articles of the Convention which shall apply to the Agreement and Article 25 sets out the voting procedure.

In addition to adopting the Paris Agreement, Decision 1/CP.21 also established the Ad Hoc Working Group on the Paris Agreement, giving it the task of preparing for the Agreement's entry into force and for the first Conference of the Parties serving as the Meeting of the Parties to the Paris Agreement. In regard to the nationally determined contributions, the Decision invited all Parties to communicate their determined contributions to the secretariat. The disparity between the goal of a temperature rise of less than two degrees, the predicted levels of greenhouse gas emissions, and the intended contributions is also noted. The Decision also provides for enhanced action prior to the commencement of the Paris Agreement in 2020.

The Agreement provides Parties with a large scope to determine how they will comply with their commitments, having moved away from the strict targets set by the Protocol. This has caused concern; however, the review process has been identified as a particularly useful mechanism – but questions of whether it will effectively govern the achievement of pledged contributions, and facilitate the action needed to achieve the Agreement's objectives, have plagued it since its adoption.[222]

4.1.5 Cooperative Efforts beyond the Paris Agreement

Following the adoption of the Paris Agreement, the implementation phase commenced. By the end of COP21, most Parties submitted their intended NDCs while various aspects on the implementation of the Paris Agreement still remained uncertain. At COP21, Parties launched the Paris Agreement Work Programme specifically to address these issues, which saw to continued negotiations over the next few years.

In 2018, in advance of COP24, the IPCC had released a special report on global warming of 1.5 °C. This report found that at the current rate of CO_2 emissions, global warming is likely to reach 1.5 °C between 2030 and 2052.[223]

221 These conditions were met in 2016, and subsequently the Paris Agreement entered into force on November 4 2016.

222 For example, see Annalisa Savaresi, 'The Paris Agreement: a New Beginning?' (2016) 34(1) *Journal of Energy & Natural Resources Law* 16; and Raymond Clémençon, 'The Two Sides of the Paris Agreement: Dismal Failure or Historic Breakthrough?' (*2016*) 25(1) *Journal of Environment & Development* 3.

223 IPCC, Summary for Policymakers in *Global Warming of 1.5°C. An IPCC Special Report on the impacts of global warming of 1.5°C above pre-industrial levels and related global greenhouse gas emission pathways*, 2018, available at <https://www.ipcc.ch/sr15/>.

The report further assessed and compared the climate change impacts between the global warming projections of 1.5°C and 2°C above pre-industrial levels. The report noted significant disparities in the loss of biodiversity, sea-level rise, food security, and adaptive capacity between a global warming projection of 1.5°C and 2°C. Significantly, at a temperature increase of 1.5°C, coral reefs are estimated to further decline by 70–90% compared to >99% at 2°C.[224] The report also outlined model pathways for the reduction of greenhouse gases to limit global warming to 1.5°C. This would require clear emission reductions by 2030.[225] The report also noted with medium confidence that the currently level of nationally stated mitigation ambition is "broadly consistent with cost-effective pathways that result in a global warming of about 3°C by 2100, with warming continuing afterwards".[226]

The special report set the scene for the negotiations at COP24. The report was presented during COP24, leading vulnerable States, such as Small Island Developing Nations, to call for increased climate ambition.[227] During COP24, the Parties delivered the Katowice Climate Package. The package provided various procedures and guidance on the implementation of the Paris Agreement.[228] For instance, Decision 4/CMA.1 provides further guidance for the content of nationally determined contributions to increase their clarity and transparency.[229] Nonetheless, the Katowice Climate Package was still left incomplete, with further clarification required on Article 6 of the Paris Agreement establishing market-based and non-market-based mechanisms to reduce greenhouse gas emissions. These were subsequently addressed at COP26.

---

224 IPCC, Summary for Policymakers in *Global Warming of 1.5°C. An IPCC Special Report on the impacts of global warming of 1.5°C above pre-industrial levels and related global greenhouse gas emission pathways*, 2018, available at <https://www.ipcc.ch/sr15/>, para. B.4.2. This is noted with very high confidence.

225 IPCC, Summary for Policymakers in *Global Warming of 1.5°C. An IPCC Special Report on the impacts of global warming of 1.5°C above pre-industrial levels and related global greenhouse gas emission pathways*, 2018, available at <https://www.ipcc.ch/sr15/>, para. D.1.1.

226 IPCC, Summary for Policymakers in *Global Warming of 1.5°C. An IPCC Special Report on the impacts of global warming of 1.5°C above pre-industrial levels and related global greenhouse gas emission pathways*, 2018, available at <https://www.ipcc.ch/sr15/>, D.1.1.

227 Secretariat of the Pacific Regional Environment Programme, 'The battle for 1.5 at the UN Climate Conference in Poland' (2018) available at <https://www.sprep.org/news/the-battle-for-15-at-the-un-climate-conference-in-poland>.

228 Lavanya Rajamani and Jacob Werksman, 'Climate Change' in Lavanya Rajamani and Jacqueline Peel (eds.) *The Oxford Handbook of International Environmental* Law (Oxford University Press 2021), 504–505.

229 UN Doc FCCC/PA/CMA/2018/3/Add.1, Report of the Conference of the Parties serving as the meeting of the Parties to the Paris Agreement on the third part of its first session, /PA/CMA/2018/3/Add.1, Decision 4/CMA.1.

By the time the Parties met for COP26, significant geopolitical shifts had occurred. Amidst the COVID-19 pandemic, COP26 was deferred from 2020 to November 2021, which also led to a delay in the preparation process of NDCs.[230] Further challenges to the implementation were foreseen when the US, under President D. Trump, announced its intention to withdraw from the Paris Agreement on 4 November 2019, leading to the official withdrawal a year later at the end of 2020.[231] The withdrawal from the Paris Agreement was, however, short-lived with the Biden administration elected in the same year and rejoining the agreement in February 2021.

In 2021, the IPCC released the contributions of Working Group I to the Sixth Assessment Report, which informed subsequent COP negotiations.[232] The report of Working Group I warned that "[g]lobal surface temperature will continue to increase until at least mid-century under all emissions scenarios considered".[233] Global warming will also exceed the 1.5°C and 2°C temperature goals in the 21st century unless "deep reductions" occur.[234]

Ahead of COP26 Parties submitted their second generation NDCs, with most Parties having strengthened their commitment to emission reductions beyond their existing contributions.[235] These negotiations made a breakthrough through the adoption of the Glasgow Climate Pact. Under this Pact, Parties recognized the different climate change impacts of holding the global temperature increase to 1.5°C compared to 2°C, and resolved to pursue efforts to limit the temperature increase to 1.5°C.[236] The Parties further recognized that

---

230 UN Doc FCCC/PA/CMA/2021/8, Nationally determined contributions under the Paris Agreement Synthesis report by the secretariat, 2021, para. 1.

231 US Department of Justice, On the U.S. Withdrawal from the Paris Agreement, 2019, available at <https://2017-2021.state.gov/on-the-u-s-withdrawal-from-the-paris-agreement>.

232 See for instance, UN Doc FCCC/CP/2021/12/Add.1, Report of the Conference of the Parties on its twenty-sixth Session, Decision 1/CP.26, paras. 2–5. The reports of the Working Groups I-III formed the basis of the IPCC Synthesis Report of the Sixth Assessment Report, released on 20 March 2023.

233 IPCC, Summary for Policymakers in *Climate Change 2021: The Physical Science Basis. Contribution of Working Group I to the Sixth Assessment Report of the Intergovernmental Panel on Climate Change*, 2021, available at <https://www.ipcc.ch/report/ar6/wg1/downloads/report/IPCC_AR6_WGI_SPM.pdf>, para. B.1.

234 IPCC, Summary for Policymakers in *Climate Change 2021: The Physical Science Basis. Contribution of Working Group I to the Sixth Assessment Report of the Intergovernmental Panel on Climate Change*, 2021, available at <https://www.ipcc.ch/report/ar6/wg1/downloads/report/IPCC_AR6_WGI_SPM.pdf>, para. B.1.

235 UN Doc FCCC/PA/CMA/2021/8, Nationally determined contributions under the Paris Agreement Synthesis report by the secretariat, 2021, para. 5.

236 UN Doc FCCC/CP/2021/12/Add.1, Report of the Conference of the Parties on its twenty-sixth Session, Decision 1/CP.26, para. 21.

this requires a 45% reduction of greenhouse gas emissions by 2030 relative to the 2010 level and reaching net zero around the mid-century.[237] The Pact called upon Parties to accelerate their efforts towards the phasedown of coal power and the phase-out of fossil fuel subsidies.[238] Parties also noted with "deep regret" the failure to meet the target of developed country Parties to jointly mobilize USD 100 billion each year to support developing country Parties.[239] They further urged Parties to meet this goal.[240] COP26 also delivered on the Paris Rulebook. Among other provisions, the Paris Rulebook further clarified rules on the Sustainable Development Mechanism under Article 6(4) of the Paris Agreement.[241]

In 2022, COP27 saw a shift in focus to climate finance. Parties established the Loss and Damage Fund, a new arrangement assisting those developing countries vulnerable to climate change's adverse effects in responding to loss and damage.[242] The decision was influenced by Working Group II to the Sixth Assessment Report, which was released in early 2022.[243] This report found that climate change impacts are increasingly becoming difficult to manage.[244] It also found with high confidence that approximately 3.3–3.6 billion people are living in regions highly vulnerable to climate change.[245] In parallel to the negotiations at the COP, States had taken further action at the UN General Assembly regarding the impact of climate change on the effective enjoyment

237 UN Doc FCCC/CP/2021/12/Add.1, Report of the Conference of the Parties on its twenty-sixth Session, Decision 1/CP.26, para. 22.

238 UN Doc FCCC/CP/2021/12/Add.1, Report of the Conference of the Parties on its twenty-sixth Session, Decision 1/CP.26, para. 36.

239 UN Doc FCCC/CP/2021/12/Add.1, Report of the Conference of the Parties on its twenty-sixth Session, Decision 1/CP.26, para. 44.

240 UN Doc FCCC/CP/2021/12/Add.1, Report of the Conference of the Parties on its twenty-sixth Session, Decision 1/CP.26, para. 46.

241 UN Doc FCCC/PA/CMA/2021/10/Add.1, Report of the Conference of the Parties serving as the meeting of the Parties to the Paris Agreement on its third session, Decision 3/CMA.3.

242 UN Doc FCCC/CP/2022/10/Add.1, Report of the Conference of the Parties on its twenty-seventh session, Decision 2/CP.27, para. 2.

243 UN Doc FCCC/CP/2022/10/Add.1, Report of the Conference of the Parties on its twenty-seventh session, Decision 2/CP.27, second and third preambular paragraphs.

244 IPCC, Summary for Policymakers in *Climate Change 2022: Impacts, Adaptation and Vulnerability. Contribution of Working Group II to the Sixth Assessment Report of the Intergovernmental Panel on Climate Change*, 2022, para. B.5.

245 IPCC, Summary for Policymakers in *Climate Change 2022: Impacts, Adaptation and Vulnerability. Contribution of Working Group II to the Sixth Assessment Report of the Intergovernmental Panel on Climate Change*, 2022, para. B.2.

of human rights: in 2022, they adopted a resolution formally recognizing the right to a clean, healthy and sustainable environment as a human right.[246]

In 2023, the UNFCCC also released the synthesis report by the co-facilitators on the technical dialogue of the first global stocktake in line with Article 14(1) of the Paris Agreement. This synthesis report made some important findings regarding the implementation of the Paris Agreement. While the Paris Agreement has driven climate ambition and action, it finds that 'much more is needed now on all fronts'.[247] The report analyzed the global mitigation response and concluded that 'global emissions are not in line with modelled global mitigation pathways consistent with the temperature goal of the Paris Agreement'.[248] The report identified two gaps in implementation: a lack of mitigation ambition of NDCs, which is insufficient in achieving the temperature goal, and a lack of enacted policies implementing the NDCs.[249] In addition, the report observes global adaptation efforts as 'fragmented, incremental, sector-specific and unequally distributed across regions'.[250] This leaves the 'window of opportunity to secure a liveable and sustainable future […] rapidly closing'.[251] The report also calls for the 'scaling up' of finance for climate action in developing countries, noting that the goal of jointly mobilize USD 100 billion per year by 2020 had not been met.[252]

The first global stocktake was later adopted in a decision by the Parties at COP28 in December 2023.[253] This decision also called upon Parties to transition away from fossil fuels in energy systems to achieve net zero by 2050.[254] At COP28, the Parties further finalized and operationalized the Loss and Damage

246 UN Resolution A/RES/76/300, Resolution adopted by the General Assembly on 28 July 2022, The human right to a clean, healthy and sustainable environment, 2022.

247 UN Doc FCCC/SB/2023/9, Technical dialogue of the first global stocktake, 2023, available at <https://unfccc.int/documents/631600>, p. 4.

248 UN Doc FCCC/SB/2023/9, Technical dialogue of the first global stocktake, 2023, available at <https://unfccc.int/documents/631600>, p. 5.

249 UN Doc FCCC/SB/2023/9, Technical dialogue of the first global stocktake, 2023, available at <https://unfccc.int/documents/631600>, p. 16.

250 UN Doc FCCC/SB/2023/9, Technical dialogue of the first global stocktake, 2023, available at <https://unfccc.int/documents/631600>, p. 24.

251 UN Doc FCCC/SB/2023/9, Technical dialogue of the first global stocktake, 2023, available at <https://unfccc.int/documents/631600>, p. 24.

252 UN Doc FCCC/SB/2023/9, Technical dialogue of the first global stocktake, 2023 available at <https://unfccc.int/documents/631600>, p. 33.

253 UN Doc FCCC/PA/CMA/2023/L.17UNFCCC, Outcome of the first global stocktake, Draft decision -/CMA.5, 2023, available at <https://unfccc.int/documents/636608>.

254 UN Doc FCCC/PA/CMA/2023/L.17UNFCCC, Outcome of the first global stocktake, Draft decision -/CMA.5, 2023, available at <https://unfccc.int/documents/636608>, para. 28.

Fund.[255] Developed economies and the United Arab Emirates initially pledged almost USD 700 billion to the fund.[256]

The focus of negotiations on finance and funding continued at COP29 in Azerbaijan in 2024. Parties agreed on a New Collective Quantified Goal on Climate Finance by increasing their commitment of jointly mobilize USD 100 billion per year by 2020 to USD 300 billion per year by 2035.[257] The decision calls on "all actors to work together to enable the scaling up of financing to developing country Parties for climate action from all public and private sources to at least USD 1.3 trillion per year by 2035".[258] COP29 also issued further guidance for carbon markets for the Sustainable Development Mechanism under Article 6(4) of the Paris Agreement.[259] Looking ahead to COP30 held in Brazil, the submission of third generation of NDCs is expected in 2025.

4.2 *Domestic and International Litigation on Anthropogenic Climate Change*

4.2.1 Domestic Climate Change Litigation

Since the adoption of the Paris Agreement, States' international obligations and commitments on anthropogenic climate change are increasingly tested and enforced in domestic courts. Individuals, organizations, and groups have brought a wave of domestic cases against governments and private actors for their failure to take sufficient mitigation and adaptation action. The total number of reported domestic climate change litigation cases has doubled from 884 in 2017 to 2,180 in 2022.[260] These developments are occurring globally, with 17% of cases being heard in developing States.[261] In addition to relying on

255 UN Doc FCCC/CP/2023/11/Add.1, Report of the Conference of the Parties on its twenty-eighth session, Decision 1/CP.28.

256 UN Doc FCCC/CP/2023/11/Add.1, Report of the Conference of the Parties on its twenty-eighth session, Decision 1/CP.28, para. 14.

257 UN Doc FCCC/PA/CMA/2024/L.22, New collective quantified goal on climate finance, Draft decision -/CMA.6, para. 8.

258 UN Doc FCCC/PA/CMA/2024/L.22, New collective quantified goal on climate finance, Draft decision -/CMA.6, para. 7.

259 UNFCCC, COP29 UN Climate Conference Agrees to Triple Finance to Developing Countries, Protecting Lives and Livelihoods, 2024, available at <https://unfccc.int/news/cop29-un-climate-conference-agrees-to-triple-finance-to-developing-countries-protecting-lives-and>.

260 UNEP, *Climate litigation more than doubles in five years, now a key tool in delivering climate justice* (2023), available at <https://www.unep.org/news-and-stories/press-release/climate-litigation-more-doubles-five-years-now-key-tool-delivering>.

261 ibid.

domestic legislation, claims raised in these cases have made widespread use of the principles in the UNFCCC, the Paris Agreement, and those established under international environmental law and international human rights law.

These cases are predominantly brought on the North American continent, notably in the US. In as early as 2007, the US Supreme Court found that the Environmental Protection Agency was under an obligation to regulate the emission of greenhouse gases in accordance with domestic law.[262] In *Juliana v. United States* of 2020, the plaintiffs claimed the US government violated their constitutional rights for the failure to mitigate climate change.[263] While the claim was dismissed for lack of standing, cases aiming to incite State mitigation and adaptation action in the US continue.[264]

Domestic climate change litigation gained traction in Europe with the landmark case of *Urgenda Foundation v. State of the Netherlands* of 2019.[265] Relying on the European Convention of Human Rights (ECHR) and the Dutch constitution and civil code, the Urgenda Foundation sought a court order directing the State to reduce emissions by at least 25% compared to 1990 levels by the end of 2020 in line with IPCC assessment reports. The Dutch Supreme Court decision was unprecendented in recognizing that the obligation to protect the right to life and the right to private life under Articles 2 and 8 of the ECHR encompassed climate action. According to the Court, 'no other conclusion can be drawn but that the State is required pursuant to Articles 2 and 8 ECHR to take measures to counter the genuine threat of dangerous climate change'.[266] The Court interpreted Articles 2 and 8 in light of the UNFCCC, the Paris Agreement, COP decisions, the no harm principle, and Article 47 of the Draft Articles on Responsibility of States for Internationally Wrongful Acts to justify the 'partial responsibility' of each State for its part in preventing climate change.[267] The Court further relied on the IPCC's fourth and fifth assessment reports, COP decisions, and the precautionary principle in concluding that the State, as an Annex I country, is required to reduce emissions at least 25% by 2020.[268] In its reasoning, the Court took particular regard to the fact that the Netherlands

262 *Massachusetts v. Environmental Protection Agency* (EPA), 549 U.S. 497 (2007).

263 *Juliana v. United States*, 947 F. 3d 1159, 1167 (9th Cir. 2020).

264 *Genesis B. v. U.S. Environmental Protection Agency*, First Amended Complaint for Declaratory and Injunctive Relief, 2:23-cv-10345, 20 May 2024.

265 *Urgenda Foundation v. the Netherlands*, Judgment of 20 December 2019, No. 19/00135, ECLI:NL:HR:2019:2007 (Supreme Court of the Netherlands) (hereafter '*Urgenda Foundation v. Netherlands*').

266 *Urgenda Foundation v. Netherlands*, para. 5.6.2.

267 *Urgenda Foundation v. Netherlands*, para. 5.7.1–5.7.5.

268 *Urgenda Foundation v. Netherlands, paras. 7.2.1–7.2.5, 7.4.6–7.5.3.*

has a 'very high per capita emissions of greenhouse gases' and that a postponement in emissions reductions after 2020 would be more far-reaching, costly, and risky.[269]

The *Urgenda Foundation v. State of the Netherlands* was groundbreaking in finding a legal obligation on the State to take increased climate action. It marked a turn for climate change litigation on the continent and paved the way for exploring possible legal avenues to address climate change before European courts. Shortly thereafter in *Neubauer et al. v. Germany*, the German Federal Constitutional Court found Germany's climate legislation to be partially incompatible with the constitution because it lacked specific emission targets beyond the year 2030. The Court found that the government is required to take climate action in order to protect fundamental rights under the constitution. This obligation is not invalidated by the worldwide nature of global warming.[270] On the basis of the Paris Agreement, keeping global warming to below 2°C and preferably to 1.5°C was found to be the 'constitutionally relevant target'.[271] Notably, when setting specific emission reduction targets to meet the temperature goal, the State is required to consider the intertemporal distribution effects of climate legislation to prevent the losses of freedoms of future generations by leaving them with a disproportionate reduction burden.[272]

Similar cases have proliferated on the continent. In 2021 in *Notre Affaire à Tous and Others v. France*, the Administrative Court of Paris ordered the French government to remedy the ecological damage caused by its failure to meet its commitments to reduce emissions under the Paris Agreement, the constitution, and domestic climate legislation.[273] In 2023, the Court of Appeal of Brussels also made an evolutionary interpretation of Articles 2 and 8 of the ECHR in light of the UNFCCC and other international agreements and unanimously agreed scientific studies. It thus found a violation by the Belgian government for failing to revise emission reduction targets and meeting those targets.[274]

269 *Urgenda Foundation v. Netherlands, paras. 7.3.4, 7.4.2–7.4.3.*

270 *Neubauer et al. v Germany*, Judgment of 2021, Case No. BvR 2656/18/1, BvR 78/20/1, BvR 96/20/1, BvR 288/20 (German Federal Constitutional Court) (hereafter '*Neubauer et al. v. Germany*'), paras. 197–198.

271 *Neubauer et al. v. Germany*, para. 246. *See also*, paras. 203–212.

272 *Neubauer et al. v. Germany*, paras. 190–192.

273 *Notre Affaire à Tous and Others v. France*, Judgment of 14 October 2021, No. 1904967, 1904968, 1904972, 1904976/4-1 (Administrative Tribunal of Paris, France).

274 *VZW Klimaatzaak v. Kingdom of Belgium & Others*, Judgment of 17 June 2021, 2015/4585/A (Brussels Court of First Instance in Belgium), paras. 152, 156, 176–183. See also, Climate Litigation Network, Successful Climate Change Litigation in Belgium, 2024, available at <https://climatelitigationnetwork.org/wp-content/uploads/CLN-REPORT-Successful-Climate-Litigation-in-Belgium-2024.pdf>.

Recent years are seeing to further cases striking down government climate change legislation, holding them accountable to more stringent greenhouse gas emission targets as understood in international agreements and scientific consensus.[275]

The enforcement of international climate change commitments in domestic courts is not limited to the European continent, but the phenomenon can be increasingly observed globally. For instance, the South Korean National Human Rights Commission ordered the Korean government to set additional targets for the reduction of greenhouse gas emissions "considering the proportionality of the burden of GHG reduction for current and future generations and the responsibility of Korea as a developed country".[276] In its opinion, the Commission considered recent global developments, including the Paris Agreement; the appointment Special Rapporteur on climate change by the Human Rights Council in Resolution 48/14; the *Urgenda* and *Neubauer* judgments; and the IPCC's Sixth Assessment Report of 2022.[277] Similarly, the Supreme Court of India has also recognized the constitutional right to be free from the adverse effects of climate change, taking India's obligations under international law into account.[278] In particular, the Supreme Court acknowledged the interpretation of human rights in the climate change context in other international forums, referencing for instance, the preamble to the Paris Agreement and the 2017 advisory opinion of the Inter-American Court of Human Rights on State responsibility for environmental harm.

Equally on the African continent, in *Earthlife Africa Johannesburg v Minister of Environmental Affairs*, the South African government was required to make a climate change impact assessment to ensure that a project for a proposed coal-fired power station fits South Africa's emission reduction commitments as outlined in its NDC.[279] In its reasoning, the High Court interpreted national

---

275 *Friends of the Irish Environment v. Ireland*, Judgment of 19 September 2019, No. 793 JR (Irish Supreme Court).

276 National Human Rights Commission (Korea), Opinion to the government of the Republic of Korea (President) on the climate crisis and human rights, 2023, unofficial English translation available at <https://climatecasechart.com/wp-content/uploads/non-us-case-documents/2023/20230101_19555_opinion-1.pdf>, p. 23.

277 ibid p. 13–18, 23.

278 *MK Ranjitsinh et al. v. Union of India et al.*, Judgment of 21 March 2024, 2024 INSC 280 (Supreme Court of India), paras. 19–35.

279 *Earthlife Africa Johannesburg v Minister of Environmental Affairs*, Judgment of 8 March 2017, Case No 65662/16 (South Africa High Court), para. 90.

environmental legislation consistently with international law, namely the precautionary principle and Article 4(1)(f) of the UNFCCC.[280]

International environmental law has also been applied by domestic courts to address climate change in South America. In *Future Generations v. Ministry of the Environment and Others* (*Colombia*), the Supreme Court of Colombia used various international agreements and instruments as guiding criteria for national legislation.[281] The Court held that the current situation of deforestation in Colombia 'constitutes a serious ignorance' of the obligations under the Paris Agreement.[282] In finding that the Colombian Amazon is a 'subject of rights' entitled to protection, conservation, maintenance and restoration led by the State', the Court referred to the Rio Declaration and the principles of precaution, intergenerational equity, and solidarity.[283] These examples are merely representative of a growing body of domestic jurisprudence holding governments accountable for the international climate change commitments.

4.2.2 International Climate Change Litigation

In light of these developments in domestic courts, States, particularly those most vulnerable to the adverse effects of climate change, are increasingly bringing their concerns to regional international courts, tribunals, and committees. Looking for greater climate ambition and action, States have started to bring claims or request the clarification of their obligations under international law as well as regional human rights conventions. One of the earliest requests was made by Colombia and Costa Rica to the Inter-American Court of Human Rights (IACHR) on 14 March 2016. These two countries requested an advisory opinion on the potential impact of the development of new infrastructure projects in the Wider Caribbean Region on the marine environment and inhabitants of coastal areas.[284] The request concerned the interpretation of the American Convention of Human Rights (ACHR) and the Cartagena Convention regarding State responsibility for environmental harm.

280 *Earthlife Africa Johannesburg v Minister of Environmental Affairs*, Judgment of 8 March 2017, Case No 65662/16 (South Africa High Court), para. 83.

281 *Future Generations v. Ministry of the Environment and Others* ("Demanda Generaciones Futuras v. Minambiente"), Judgment of 5 April 2018 (Colombia Supreme Court), para. 6.

282 ibid, para. 11.3.

283 ibid, para. 14.

284 Embassy of Colombia in Costa Rica, Request for an Advisory Opinion, 14 March 2016, available at <https://www.corteidh.or.cr/solicitudoc/solicitud_14_03_16_ing.pdf> para. 8.

The landmark advisory opinion was delivered on 15 November 2017 making various contributions to States Parties' human rights obligations with respect to environmental harm including climate change. Significantly, it marks the first regional human rights tribunal to consider States' obligations on transboundary environmental harm.[285] In defining the ACHR's jurisdiction, the Court accepted that the activities within the jurisdiction of a State Party can impact the human rights of individuals outside of their territory.[286] It further noted the obligation of State Parties to refrain from causing transboundary environmental damage. Significantly, the Court considered that transboundary environmental damage could violate rights of persons under the ACHR 'if there is a causal link between the act that originated in its territory and the infringement of the human rights of persons outside its territory.'[287] The Court further indicated that under the rights to life and personal integrity, State Parties must comply with certain environmental obligations, including the precautionary principle and the obligations to prevent significant environmental damage, cooperate, and ensure the right of access to information, public participation, and justice. Although not expressly mentioned in the ACHR, the Court additionally considered the economic, social and cultural rights protected by Article 26 to include the right to a healthy environment.[288]

This advisory opinion was shortly followed by a further request from the governments of Chile and Colombia on 9 January 2023 to clarify State obligations to respond to the climate emergency.[289] The request posits various questions under six broader themes. These questions concern: (1) duties of prevention in light of the Paris Agreement and the 1.5°C temperature goal; (2) obligations under the ACHR to preserve the right to life and survival; (3) differentiated obligations of States in relation to the rights of children and new generations; (4) procedural obligations, such as providing consultations and effective judicial remedies to redress human rights impacted by the climate

285 Maria L. Banda, Inter-American Court of Human Rights' Advisory Opinion on the Environment and Human Rights (2018) 22(6) American Society of International Law, available at <https://www.asil.org/insights/volume/22/issue/6/inter-american-court-human-rights-advisory-opinion-environment-and-human>.

286 Inter-American Court of Human Rights, Advisory Opinion OC-23/17 of 15 November 2017, Requested by the Republic of Colombia (hereafter 'IACHR Advisory Opinion'), para. 101.

287 ibid, para. 101.

288 ibid, para. 57.

289 Request for an advisory opinion on the Climate Emergency and Human Rights submitted to the Inter-American Court of Human Rights by the Republic of Colombia and the Republic of Chile, 9 January 2023, available at <https://www.corteidh.or.cr/docs/opiniones/soc_1_2023_en.pdf>.

emergency; (5) obligations to protect territorial and environmental defenders, women, indigenous peoples, and Afro-descendant communities; and (6) shared and differentiated human rights obligations and responsibilities of States. Hearings on these questions were held in April and May of 2024, in which the Court heard more than 150 interventions from States, international organizations, and further stakeholders.[290] As of the end of 2024, the Court's opinion remains expected.

On 9 April 2024, the regional human rights court on the European Continent, the European Court of Human Rights (ECtHR), also saw to significant climate change-related human rights developments. The Grand Chamber of the ECtHR, for the first time, delivered two decisions and one judgment regarding climate change. In these cases, the applicants argued that various European countries had violated their rights under the European Convention of Human Rights for failing to take sufficient climate action. Two of the decisions, *Carême v. France* and *Duarte Agostinho v. Portugal and 32 other states*, for were dismissed at early stages on the grounds of inadmissibility.[291]

The case of *KlimaSeniorinnen v Switzerland*, however, delivered a breakthrough judgment on the linkage between human rights and climate change obligations. This case was initially brought to the Swiss government on the 25 November 2016 by *KlimaSeniorinnen*, an association of over 2,000 of women of an average age of 73, and four individuals of the association.[292] In light of Swiss constitutional duties and Articles 2 and 8 of the ECHR, the applicants initially requested the government to take all necessary actions to reduce emissions to meet Switzerland's contribution in holding the increase in global average temperature to well below 2°C above pre-industrial levels.[293] Among other reasons, the Swiss government rejected the initial request on grounds that the requested action had to affect rights and obligations, and considered no individual legal positions to be affected.[294] Appeals before the Swiss Federal

290 Organization of American States, 'In historic hearing process with the participation of REDESCA, I/A Court an Advisory Opinion will issue an advisory opinion on state obligations on climate emergency', Press Release, 5 June 2024, available at <https://www.oas.org/fr/CIDH/jsForm/?File=/en/iachr/media_center/PReleases/2024/125.asp>.

291 *Case of Carême v. France*, Judgment of 9 April 2024, Application no. 7189/21 (European Court of Human Rights Grand Chamber); *Case of Duarte Agostinho and Others v. Portugal and 32 Others*, Judgment of 9 April 2024, Application no. 39371/20 (European Court of Human Rights Grand Chamber).

292 *Case of Verein Klimaseniorinnen Schweiz and Others v. Switzerland*, Judgment of 9 April 2024, Application no. 53600/20 (European Court of Human Rights Grand Chamber) (hereafter '*KlimaSeniorinnen v Switzerland*'), para. 10.

293 ibid, para. 22.

294 ibid, paras. 29–31.

Administrative Court and the Federal Supreme Court were also subsequently dismissed in May 2017 and May 2020 for lack of standing, before the matter was brought to the ECtHR[295]

In April 2024, the ECtHR delivered its decision. It rejected the standing of the four individual applicants but affirmed the standing of the association *KlimaSeniorinnen*.[296] From the outset, the Court relied on State obligations under the Paris Agreement, including the principle of CBDR, subsequent COP decisions, and the Draft Articles on Responsibility of States for Internationally Wrongful Act, to establish that each State has its share of responsibility to take mitigation measures in line with their capabilities.[297]

In examining Article 8 of the ECHR concerning the right to private life, the Court found the obligation to extend to the effective protection from the adverse effects caused by climate change.[298] The ECtHR noted that the States' duties to mitigate the effects of climate change flow from the 'causal relationship between climate change and the enjoyment of Convention rights'.[299] In line with scientific evidence provided by the IPCC and member States' international commitments, notably under the UNFCCC and the Paris Agreement, Article 8 of the Convention requires States to 'undertake measures for the substantial and progressive reduction of their respective GHG emission levels, with a view to reaching net neutrality within, in principle, the next three decades.'[300] This requires 'immediate action' to set adequate reduction goals, including targets and timelines for the period leading to net neutrality.[301] While the margin of appreciation afforded to States under Article 8 is reduced when it comes to the setting of objectives, they enjoy a wide margin of appreciation regarding the choice of means to pursue these objectives. In assessing whether a State has remained within this margin of appreciation, the ECtHR considered whether it had: (a) adopted measures specifying a target timeline for achieving carbon neutrality and the overall remaining carbon budget;

---

295 ibid, paras. 34, 52.

296 In the climate change context, the victim status of an applicant under Article 6 of the Convention 'must be interpreted in an evolutive manner'. Therefore, 'without undermining the exclusion of *actio popularis* from the Convention system', the ECtHR affirmed the standing of KlimaSeniorinnen on the basis that they (i) are subject to a high intensity of exposure to the adverse effects of climate change, and (ii) have a pressing need to ensure their protection. *See KlimaSeniorinnen v Switzerland*, paras. 481–482 and 487.

297 ibid, paras. 442–443.

298 ibid, para. 544.

299 ibid, para. 545.

300 ibid, para. 548.

301 ibid, para. 549.

(b) set out immediate carbon reduction targets; (c) provided evidence demonstrating compliance; (d) updated the relevant targets with due diligence and based on the best available science; and (e) acted appropriately, consistently, and in good time when devising and implementing measures.[302] The ECtHR concluded that Switzerland had exceeded in margin of appreciation in that it failed to (i) quantify limitations to national greenhouse gas emissions (*e.g.*, through a carbon budget); (ii) meet prior greenhouse gas emission reduction targets; and (iii) act appropriately, consistently, and in good time when developing and implementing a relevant framework.[303]

In addition to claims brought to regional human rights bodies, climate change litigation has also made its way to international courts, tribunals, and committees. In 2019, sixteen children brought a request to the United Nations Committee on the Rights of Child to declare that Argentina, Brazil, France, Germany and Turkey had violated their rights under the Convention on the Rights of the Child by failing to prevent and mitigate climate change.[304] In its decision of 2021, the Committee adopted the test for jurisdiction developed by the IACHR for which States can violate human rights of persons outside their territory if there is a causal link.[305] In light of the principle of common but differentiated responsibilities, the Committee further noted that the 'collective nature of the causation of climate change does not absolve the State party of its individual responsibility' for the harm of children by the emission of greenhouse gases.[306] Nonetheless, the claims were still found to be inadmissible for the applicants' failure to exhaust domestic remedies.[307]

In 2019, a further campaign was initiated by a grassroots movement of students from the University of the South Pacific to bring an advisory opinion on climate justice before the ICJ.[308] By 2021, the Government of Vanuatu commenced a diplomatic process, garnering support for a resolution at the UN General Assembly to request an advisory opinion on the obligations of States with respect to climate change. With 132 States as co-sponsors of the resolution, UN General Assembly Resolution A/Res/77/276 was adopted on

302 ibid, para. 550.
303 ibid, para. 573.
304 CRC/C/88/D/104/2019, Decision adopted by the Committee under the Optional Protocol to the Convention on the Rights of the Child on a communications procedure, concerning communication No. 104/2019, para. 3.8.
305 ibid, para. 10.7–10.8.
306 ibid, para. 10.10.
307 ibid, para. 10.18.
308 Pacific Islands Students Fighting Climate Change, 'Our Journey' (PISFCC 2019) <https://www.pisfcc.org/ourjourney>.

the 29 March 2023.[309] The resolution requested the Court to clarify (i) the obligations of States under international law to ensure the protection of the climate system from greenhouse gas emissions, and (ii) the legal consequences for States having caused significant harm to the climate system, with respect to States injured, specially affected, or particularly vulnerable and peoples and individuals of the present and future generations. The judicial proceedings are currently ongoing. 79 States and 12 international organizations filed written statements, which were followed by written comments by 55 States and 7 international organizations.[310] The advisory opinion is expected to clarify the rights and obligations of States with respect to climate change across different regimes in international law, including international environmental law.

In parallel, on 31 October 2021, the eve of COP26, Antigua and Barbuda and Tuvalu concluded the Agreement for the establishment of the Commission of Small Island States on Climate Change and International Law. This agreement has a mandate 'to promote and contribute to the definition, implementation, and progressive development of rules and principles of international law concerning climate change'.[311] Notably, it authorizes the Commission to request an advisory opinion from the International Tribunal for the Law of the Sea (ITLOS).[312] It was later acceded by further Small Island Developing States (SIDS): Palau, Niue, Vanuatu, St. Lucia, St. Vincent and the Grenadines, St. Kitts and Nevis, and the Bahamas. '[A]larmed by the catastrophic effects of climate change'[313] that threaten their survival combined with the 'inaction' and 'failure of political will' to mitigate greenhouse gas emissions, SIDS launched a process to request an advisory opinion from the ITLOS.[314]

On 12 December 2022, the Commission submitted its formal request to the ITLOS to render an advisory opinion to clarify State Parties' specific obligations under the United Nations Convention on the Law of the Sea of 1982 (UNCLOS)

309 A/RES/77/276, Resolution adopted by the General Assembly on 29 March 2023; United Nations, Landmark climate change hearings represent largest ever case before UN world court (2024), available at <https://www.ungeneva.org/en/news-media/news/2024/12/100905/landmark-climate-change-hearings-represent-largest-ever-case-un>.

310 International Court of Justice, Public Sitting on the Obligations of States in respect of Climate Change, Verbatim Record CR 2024/35, p. 93–94.

311 Agreement for the Establishment of the Commission of Small Island States on Climate Change and International Law, Article 1(3).

312 ibid, Article 2(2).

313 ibid, first preambular paragraph.

314 International Tribunal for the Law of the Sea, Public Sitting on the Request for an Advisory Opinion Submitted by the Commission of Small Island States on Climate Change and International Law, ITLOS/PV.23/C31/1/Rev.1, p. 4.

to (i) 'prevent, reduce and control pollution of the marine environment' and (ii) 'protect and preserve the marine environment', in relation to the deleterious effects resulting from climate change.[315] The language of the two questions posed to the Tribunal reflect that of Articles 194(1) and 192 of Part XII of the UNCLOS on the protection and preservation of the marine environment. The UNCLOS was adopted in 1982, prior to various international cooperative efforts regarding anthropogenic greenhouse gas emissions, and thus for the first time, State Parties' law of the sea obligations were assessed with respect to greenhouse gas emissions. After a round of written statements and oral pleadings given by 35 State Parties and four Intergovernmental Organizations, the Tribunal delivered a unanimous opinion on 21 May 2024.

As a preliminary matter, the Tribunal clarified that the definition of 'pollution of the marine environment' under Article 1(1)(4) of the UNCLOS includes the adverse effects of climate change caused by greenhouse gas emissions.[316] In addressing the first question, the Tribunal found that under Article 194(1), State Parties are required to 'take all necessary measures with a view to reducing and controlling existing marine pollution from such emissions and eventually preventing such pollution from occurring at all.'[317] Article 194(1) is a due diligence obligation, the standard of which is 'stringent' in the context of climate change.[318] According to the Tribunal, 'necessary measures' must be determined objectively and three factors become relevant.[319] First, science 'undoubtedly plays a crucial role',[320] in which the best available science is that of the IPCC, reflecting scientific consensus.[321]

Second, international rules and standards, which include the UNFCCC, Paris Agreement, Annex VI to MARPOL, volumes III and IV of Annex 16 to the Chicago Convention, and the Montreal Protocol with its Kigali Amendment are also relevant in determining necessary measures.[322] This includes the global temperature target of limiting temperature increases to 1.5°C above pre-industrial levels and the timeline for emission pathways to achieve the target.[323]

315 Commission of Small Island States on Climate Change, Request for an Advisory Opinion, 12 December 2022, p. 2.

316 International Tribunal for the Law of the Sea, Request for an Advisory Opinion Submitted by the Commission of Small Island States on Climate Change and International Law, Advisory Opinion No. 31, 21 May 2024 (hereafter 'ITLOS Advisory Opinion'), paras. 178–179.

317 ibid, para. 199.

318 ibid, para. 241.

319 ibid, paras. 206–207.

320 ITLOS Advisory Opinion, para. 212.

321 ibid, para. 208.

322 ibid, para. 214.

323 ibid, para. 243.

While the Tribunal found that the UNFCCC and the Paris Agreement are relevant in interpreting and applying the UNCLOS, State Parties cannot satisfy Article 194(1) 'simply by complying' with these agreements.[324]

Third, 'necessary measures' is also determined by the means available to State Parties and their capabilities. Although the UNCLOS does not make reference to the principle of common but differentiated responsibilities as reflected in Article 3 of the UNFCCC and Article 4(4) of the Paris Agreement, it comprises 'elements common to this principle'.[325] In line with Article 194(1) in which State Parties must take necessary measures 'using for this purpose the best practicable means at their disposal and in accordance with their capabilities', State Parties with greater means and capabilities must do more to reduce emissions than those with less means and capabilities.[326]

The Tribunal also identified other specific obligations of State Parties to prevent, reduce and control pollution of the marine environment under Part XII of the UNCLOS. For instance, the Tribunal stressed State Parties' obligations to cooperate meaningfully and in good faith to prevent, reduce and control marine pollution from greenhouse gas emissions under Articles 197–201. Articles 202–203 of the UNCLOS further envisage obligations to assist developing States, in particular those vulnerable to the adverse effects of climate change.[327] Under Articles 204–206, State Parties are required to conduct an environmental impact assessment for any planned activity, public or private, that may cause harm to the environment through greenhouse gas emissions.[328]

In addressing the second question posed by the Commission, the Tribunal found that the State Parties' obligation under Article 192 to protect and preserve the marine environment is one of due diligence[329] and of 'dual significance'.[330] The obligation to protect the marine environment relates to the duty to prevent or at least mitigate environmental harm.[331] The obligation to preserve the marine environment requires maintaining ecosystem health and the natural balance of the marine environment, which may include its restoration.[332] Thus, the obligation entails the mitigation of anthropogenic

324 ibid, para. 223. The Tribunal further noted that '[i]f a State fails to comply with this obligation, international responsibility would be engaged for that State.'

325 ibid, para. 229.

326 ibid, para. 227.

327 ibid, para. 339.

328 ibid, para. 367.

329 The standard of due diligence is also 'stringent'. ITLOS Advisory Opinion, para. 400.

330 ITLOS Advisory Opinion, para. 390.

331 ibid, para. 385.

332 ibid, paras. 385–386.

greenhouse gas emissions as well as promoting the conservation and resilience of living marine resources.[333] The Tribunal placed an emphasis on resilience and adaption measures as described in the climate change treaties.[334] These requests to clarify State obligations on climate change to regional and international bodies, such as the ITLOS, demonstrate the increasing dissatisfaction with the implementation of international commitments and the pressing need for urgent action to be taken at the global level, particularly for States vulnerable to the adverse effects of climate change.

Bibliography

Anderson, D & Grubb, M., eds., Controlling Carbon and Sulphur: Joint Implementation and Trading Initiatives (1997).

Benedict, R.e., Ozone Diplomacy: New Directions in Safeguarding the Planet (1991).

Bodansky, D., Brunnée, J. & Rajamani, L., International Climate Change Law (2017).

Calster, G. van & Reins, L., The Paris Agreement on Climate Change: A Commentary (2021).

Fermann, G., ed., International Politics of Climate Change: Key Issues and Critical Actors (1997).

Flinterman, C. et al., Transboundary Air Pollution (1986).

French, H., 'Learning from the Ozone Experience', in Lester R. Brown, et al., State of The World (1997).

Goldberg, D., A Legal Analysis of the Kyoto Protocol, CIEL (1998).

Goldberg, D.M., 'As the World Burns: Negotiating the Framework Convention on Climate Change', 5 Geo.envtl L.rev. 239 (1993).

IPPC, Climate Change 2001: Impacts, Adaptation, and Vulnerability (2001).

Jepsen, H. et al., Negotiating the Paris Agreement: The Insider Stories (2021).

Lang, W., 'Trade Restrictions as a Means of Enforcing Compliance with International Environmental Law: Montreal Protocol on Substances that Deplete the Ozone Layer', in R. Wolfrum, ed. Enforcing International Standards: Economic Mechanisms as Viable Means? 265–283 (1996).

Mackenzie J. & El-ashry, M., Air Pollution's Toll on Forests and Crops (1989).

Makhijani, A. & Gurney, K., Mending the Ozone Hole (1995).

Mayer, B., The International Law on Climate Change (2018).

Mintz, J.A., 'Keeping Pandora's Box Shut: A Critical Assessment of the Montreal Protocol on Substances that Deplete the Ozone Layer, 20 U. Miami Inter-Am. L. Rev. 565–578 (1989).

333 ibid, para. 390.

334 ibid, paras. 391–394.

Nagle, O.E., Stratospheric Ozone: United States Regulation of Chlorofluorocarbons', 16 B.C. Envt'l Aff. L. Rev. 531–80 (1989).

Nanda, V., 'Stratospheric Ozone Depletion: A Challenge for International Environmental Law and Policy', 10 Mich. J. Int'l L. 482 (1989).

Ott, H.E., 'The Kyoto Protocol, Unfinished Business', 40 Environment No 6, 17–45.

Peters, R. & Lovejoy, T., Global Warming and Biological Diversity (1993).

Read, J., 'The Trail Smelter Dispute', Canadian Y.b. Int'l l. 213 (1963).

Sarma, K.M. 'The Montreal Protocol's First 10 years: The United Nations Environment Program's Perspective', Int'l Envtl Rep. Sept. 3, 1997, 853.

Smelofff, E.A., 'Global Warming: The Kyoto Protocol and Beyond', 28 E.P.L. 63 (1998).

Soroos, M., The Endangered Atmosphere: Preserving a Global Commons (1997).

UNEP, Environmental Effects of Ozone Depletion (1994).

Vellinga, P. and Grubb, M., eds., the Climate Change Policy in the European Community (1993).

Wexler, P., 'Protecting the Global Atmosphere: Beyond the Montreal Protocol', 14 Md. J. Int'l L & Trade 1–19 (1990).

Yoshida, O., The International Legal Régime for the Protection of the Stratospheric Ozone Layer: Second Revised Edition (2019).

CHAPTER 13

Regulating Threats to the Environment

Human activities introducing hazardous or toxic substances into the environment may cause irremediable harm to natural, cyclical phenomena such as the life cycle (birth, life, death, decomposition and environmental fertilization assisting birth), the water cycle or the carbon cycle. Non-cyclical phenomena are exceptional and often arise in catastrophic circumstances such as volcanic eruptions, earthquakes, landslides. Toxic substances similarly introduce a non-cyclical element because these substances do not return, at least in the short term, to their original state, and thus may accumulate and produce synergistic effects with other substances leading to irreversible harm. Radioactive matter provides an example: the longevity of some radioactive substances is measured in thousands or millions of years. The environmental impacts of utilizing radioactive materials are thus practically irreversible.

Since the end of the 1970s, rules increasingly have regulated the substances and human activities that produce or can produce harmful environmental consequences and that transfer from one sector to another. Such 'beginning of the pipeline' regulation addresses hazardous and toxic products and wastes, radioactivity and nuclear wastes, and dangerous industrial and other activities. Their consequences in producing long-term or irreversible harm were taken into account by international environmental law from the beginning of the 1990s with the formulation of the precautionary principle.[1]

Non-industrialized countries have often willingly imported chemical products without local authorities knowing or having the means to know their nature and what effects they can have on human health and on the environment. In order to remedy this situation, if only partially, UNEP established an International Register of Potentially Toxic Chemicals (IRPTC) as early as 1976. A legal catalogue in the Register contained important information on the national and international regulations concerning more than 6000 chemical substances.[2] Similarly, in response to General Assembly Resolution 37/137 of December 17, 1982, the United Nations secretariat initiated periodic listing of products whose consumption and/or sale have been banned, withdrawn,

1 The precautionary principle is discussed in detail in Chapter 4.

2 *International Register of Potentially Toxic Chemicals (IRPTC) Legal File 1994–1995: Regulations and Guidelines on Pesticides – An Extract of the IRPTC Data Bank* (Volume 1, UNEP and IRPTC 1995).

 | DOI:10.1163/9789047440802_015

severely restricted or not approved by governments.[3] A year later, the General Assembly began publishing the list annually. In 1985, in cooperation with the World Health Organization and UNEP/IRPTC, the UN Secretariat carried out the first review of the list to determine criteria for the inclusion and treatment of commercial data. The three entities entered into a memorandum of understanding to allocate responsibilities. In 1997, the agencies decided to divide the reports into two parts to be published in alternate years, one part concerning pharmaceuticals and the other part chemicals.

More recently, the 'Globally Harmonized System of Classification and Labelling of Chemicals' (GHS) was created under the auspices of the UN.[4] Efforts for the establishment of this GHS took more than a decade, effectively reaching back to 1992 UNITED NATIONS CONFERENCE ON ENVIRONMENT AND DEVELOPMENT, and the need for a harmonized system are reflected in Agenda 21.[5] The creation of the GHS was based on the premise that harmonization was necessary on a larger scale than done at that point.[6] 2008 was originally set as the target year for implementation, but this target was not reached.[7] Efforts for harmonization continue. In addition, the Strategic Approach to International Chemicals Management (SAICM) was created, with the aim to achieve, by 2020, that chemicals are used and produced in ways that minimize significant adverse effects on human health and the environment, as the Johannesburg Plan of implementation aims.[8] Efforts have continued beyond 2020.[9] These, in turn, serve the fulfilment of UN Sustainable Development Goals (SDGS) such as Goal 12.4 ('[A]chieve the environmentally sound management of chemicals and all wastes throughout their life cycle […] and significantly reduce their release to air, water and soil in order to minimize their adverse impacts on human health and the environment').

3 See Report of the UN Secretary General on Products Harmful to Health and the Environment, A/53/156, 29 June 1998.

4 UN, *Globally harmonized system of classification and labelling of chemicals* (8th rev edn, UN 2019).

5 United Nations Conference on Environment and Development, Agenda 21: Programme of Action for Sustainable Development (UN 1992), para. 19.27.

6 UN, *Globally harmonized system of classification and labelling of chemicals* (8th rev edn, UN 2019), III.

7 UN, *Report of the world summit on sustainable development* (2002); For more on the implementation of the GHS, see Goh Choo Ta, 'GHS Implementation to Strengthen Global Chemical Hazard Communication: Will We Ever Get There?' (2021) *ACS Chemical Health & Safety* 153.

8 ICCM (1st Session) Resolution I/1: Implementation arrangements (Dubai 4–6 February 2006), preamble.

9 ICCM, 'Report on the International Conference on Chemicals Management on the work of its 15th session' (2023).

The structure of the present chapter is as follows. All regulation of hazardous products must take into account their production, trade (including transportation), use, and elimination. After identifying and addressing the former aspects of the present chapter addresses this last aspect separately, in light of the particular problems presented by the objective of eliminating such products.

In this context, it is important to note that the separate parts of the lifecycle of hazardous products are increasingly being regulated through an integrated approach, thus making the separation between these sections increasingly less clear. This is illustrated by the fact that the Basel, Rotterdam and Stockholm Conventions (all discussed separately below), which encompass the whole lifecycle of hazardous products together, at this point in time, for example, share a website.[10] In general, more and more interlinkages of the different legal fields relating to hazardous products are identified, as illustrated by the 2021 document 'Chemicals, waste and climate change: Interlinkages and potential for coordinated action' by UNEP, the Secretariats of the previously discussed conventions, and the Minamata Convention on Mercury.[11] However, many documents still only regulate part of the cycle or only certain products, which is why this chapter maintains a segmented approach. Other specialized concerns are then addressed.

1 Toxic and Hazardous Products

The production and utilization of chemical substances in the world have undergone unprecedented growth in the course of the past century. 40,000 to 60,000 different chemicals can be found in commerce, although only 6,000

10 Basel Convention on the Control of Transboundary Movements of Hazardous Wastes and their Disposal (adopted 22 March 1989, entry into force 5 May 1992) 1673 UNTS 57 (Basel Convention) ; Rotterdam Convention on the Prior Informed Consent Procedure for Certain Hazardous Chemicals and Pesticides in International Trade (adopted 10 September 1998, entry into force 24 February 2004) 2244 UNTS 337 (Rotterdam Convention, PIC Convention) ; Stockholm Convention on Persistent Organic Pollutants (adopted 22 May 2001, entry into force 17 May 2004) 2256 UNTS 119 (Stockholm Convention, POP Convention); See <https://www.brsmeas.org/> for the synergy page of the three linked websites.

11 UNEP, Basel/Rotterdam/Stockholm Conventions & Minamata Convention on Mercury, *Chemicals, waste and climate change: Interlinkages and potential for coordinated action* (2021).

of these make up 99% of the use in commerce globally.[12] In 2017, the industry in chemicals was worth more than 5 trillion USD, and it is growing steadily, expected to be double that by 2030.[13] Cross-border trade of chemicals is growing, and it is getting increasingly complex.[14] Millions of tons of manufactured chemicals are released into the environment every year, and in many areas this release of hazardous materials is increasing.[15] It is clear that this poses a serious risk to the environment.

Some substances travel long distances and affect populations who have never sought access to or used the products containing them. The Inuit of the Canadian Arctic, for example, have been found to have the highest known concentrations of PCBs in their bodies.[16]

International instruments devoted to hazardous substances have been adopted mostly since the second half of the 1980s, although the regulation of toxic or dangerous products appeared earlier and continues to appear in instruments addressing sectoral problems, such as rules relating to discharges into the marine environment and inland waters. The SDGs are certainly concerned with hazardous products, although there is not one goal specific to them. Instead, they are alluded to across the SDGs. With general regard to chemicals, SDG 3 (ensuring healthy lives and promoting well-being for all at all ages) includes the goal to 'by 2030, substantially reduce the number of deaths and illnesses from hazardous chemicals and air, water and soil pollution and contamination'.[17]

1.1 *Production and Use*

The potential effects of chemical substances on humans and the environment, including the long-term risks, should be evaluated before and during production. Reliable testing and sharing of resulting data was an early concern of the OECD, which adopted a 1974 recommendation on assessing the potential environmental effects of chemical compounds (eco-toxicity)[18] supplemented by a 1977

12 WHO, 'Compendium of WHO and other UN guidance on health and environment 2022 update' (2022) 63.
13 UNEP, *Global Chemicals Outlook II: From Legacies to Innovative Solutions. Implementing the 2030 Agenda for Sustainable Development* (2019).
14 ibid, VI and 2.
15 ibid, 92.
16 David Hunter and others, *International Environmental Law and Policy* (2d ed. 2002).
17 UN A/RES/70/1 of 21 October 2015, 16.
18 OECD Res. C(74)215 of Nov. 14, 1974.

resolution[19] recommending a procedure for anticipating the potential effects of chemical products on man and the environment. A series of decisions from 1981[20] to 1983 set forth guidelines for good laboratory practices and testing, the mutual recognition of data and the minimum pre-marketing data requirements.

A major step in the control of hazardous chemicals occurred when 154 states and the European Union adopted the Stockholm Convention on Persistent Organic Pollutants (POPs).[21] POPs possess toxic properties, resist decay, bioaccumulate and are transported through air, water and with migratory species across international boundaries, where they accumulate in terrestrial and aquatic ecosystems. They create risks to health, especially in developing countries and the polar ecosystems. Using the precautionary approach and advocating the polluter pays principle, the Convention insists on the responsibility of POPs' manufacturers to reduce adverse effects caused by their products and provide information to users, governments and the public at large on the hazardous properties of these chemicals.

The Convention makes a distinction between releases from intentional production and use (Arts. 3 and 4) and from unintentional production (Art. 5). The first category of chemicals, listed in Annex A, includes certain insecticides and PCBs. Each Party shall prohibit and/or take the legal and administrative measures to eliminate their production and use and regulate their import and export. Each Party also shall take measures concerning the unintentional production of the chemicals listed in Annex C (primarily PCBs and dioxins), such as developing and implementing an action plan designed to identify, characterize and address their release by using the best available techniques and best environmental practices. Parties may make proposals for listing a chemical in one of the Annexes (Art. 8). Article 6 suggests measures to reduce or eliminate releases from stockpiles and wastes, such as identification of stockpiles and the adoption of appropriate measures so that such wastes, including products and articles becoming wastes, are handled, collected, transported and stored in an environmentally sound manner and finally disposed in such a way that the POP content is destroyed or irreversibly transformed so that it represents no environmental danger. Cooperation with the appropriate bodies of the Basel Convention on the Control of Transboundary Movements of Hazardous Wastes and their Disposal is foreseen. Article 10 of the Convention invites the Parties to promote and facilitate public information, awareness and education.

---

19 OECD Res. C(77)97 of July 7, 1977.

20 OECD Res. C(81)30 of May 12, 1981, OECD Res. C(82)196 of Dec. 8, 1982, OECD Res. C(83)95 of July 26, 1983.

21 May 22, 2001, EMuT 2001:3; see also Chapter 12.

Convention provisions seek to promote and facilitate compliance by foreseeing technical and financial assistance mainly to developing countries (Arts. 12 and 13) and also by imposing reporting obligations on the states parties concerning the measures they have taken to implement the provisions of the Convention and on their effectiveness (Art. 15). A Conference of the Parties (Art. 19) assisted by a secretariat (Art. 20) is charged with evaluating the effectiveness of the Convention (Art. 16) and developing procedures and institutional mechanisms to determine and respond to non-compliance with the provisions of the Convention (Art. 17).

The importance of the POPs Convention lies in the fact that most other international instruments related to chemicals or to dangerous wastes concern international trade or transboundary movements of such substances. The exceptions are the Chemical Weapons Convention and the Montreal Protocol which prohibits the production and use of ozone-depleting substances.[22] The Stockholm Convention now imposes a global ban on a wider range of toxic and environmentally hazardous chemicals, a ban that could be extended to other materials.

ILO Convention No. 184 Safety and Health in Agriculture Convention, adopted one month after the POPs Convention,[23] covers agricultural and forestry activities (including crop production, forestry activities, animal husbandry and insect raising), the primary processing of agricultural and animal products by or on behalf of the operator of the undertaking as well as the use and maintenance of machinery, equipment, appliances, tools, and agricultural installations, including any process, storage, operation or transportation in an agricultural undertaking, which are directly related to agricultural production. The Convention does not cover subsistence farming, industrial processes that use agricultural products as raw material and the related services, or the industrial exploitation of forests.

The aim of the Convention is to have ILO Members formulate, carry out and periodically review a coherent national policy on safety and health in agriculture with the aim of preventing accidents and injury to health by eliminating, minimizing or controlling hazards in the agricultural working environment. National laws and regulations should designate a competent authority

---

22 Convention on the Prohibition of the Development, Production, Stockpiling and Use of Chemical Weapons and on their Destruction (adopted 3 September 1992, entry into force 29 April 1997) 1975 UNTS 45 (Chemical Weapons Convention); Montreal Protocol on Substances that Deplete the Ozone Layer (adopted 16 September 1987, entry into force 1 January 1989) 1522 UNTS 3 (Montreal Protocol).

23 International Labour Organization, Safety and Health in Agriculture Convention, 2001 (No. 184) (adopted 21 June 2001, entered into force 20 September 2003).

responsible for implementing and enforcing relevant national laws and regulations. A specific section of the Convention governs chemicals. Article 12 requires the competent authority to take measures to ensure that (a) there is an appropriate system establishing specific criteria for the importation, classification, packaging and labeling of chemicals used in agriculture and for their banning or restriction; (b) those who produce, import, provide, sell, transfer, store or dispose of chemicals used in agriculture comply with national or other recognized safety and health standards, and provide adequate and appropriate information to the users in the appropriate official language or languages of the country and, on request, to the competent authority; and (c) there is a suitable system for the safe collection, recycling and disposal of chemical waste, obsolete chemicals and empty containers of chemicals so as to avoid their use for other purposes and to eliminate or minimize the risks to safety and health and to the environment. Article 13 adds that there must be preventive and protective measures for the use of chemicals and handling of chemical waste at the level of the undertaking. The measures must cover, *inter alia*, the preparation, handling, application, storage and transportation of chemicals; agricultural activities leading to the dispersion of chemicals; the maintenance, repair and cleaning of equipment and containers for chemicals; and the disposal of empty containers and the treatment and disposal of chemical waste and obsolete chemicals.

On a general basis, the regulation of hazardous industrial activity is carried out through risk assessment and environmental impact assessment procedures, as well as licensing and permitting. These subjects are dealt with in Chapter 4 above. Industrial activities involving hazardous substances must also be subject to strict security measures.

The risk of major accident hazards involving certain industrial activities was the subject of a well-known series of EC and EU directives[24] on industrial accidents, of which the first was created on June 24, 1982. They are called the 'Seveso directives', named for the Italian town where the most serious industrial accident in European history occurred on July 10, 1976. The earlier Seveso Directives were repealed in 2012 and EU regulation on the topic is currently laid down in Seveso III.[25] The Directive highlights the fact that major accidents often have serious consequences, also transboundary, meaning that precautionary action is vital for protection.[26] It therefore lays down rules for

24 82/501/EEC, O.J. L 230 (8/5/82); 96/82/EC, O.J. L 10 (14/01/1997) and 2012/18/EU (Seveso-III) O.J. L 197 (24/07/2012).

25 ibid.

26 ibid preamble para. 2.

the prevention of major accidents involving dangerous substances, and for the limitation of their consequences for human health and the environment.[27]

Another highly relevant treaty in this context is the 2013 Minamata Mercury Convention, which specifically regulates the production and use of mercury.[28] The Convention is named after the Japanese city of Minamata, whose inhabitants experienced widespread mercury poisoning beginning in 1956, due to seafood poisoning caused by the release of methylmercury into the Minamata Bay.[29] The instrument, which entered into force in 2017, has the objective to protect not only human health, but also the environment from anthropogenic emissions of mercury and mercury compounds.[30]

1.2 *Trade and Transport*

Specific international conventions regulate the transport of hazardous substances according to the different means of transport.[31] Historically, the requirements of these agreements have often been highly technical and focused on packaging, handling, insurance, and liability.

The marketing of chemical products in particular, has been regulated by the EC since the end of the 1960s, as a response to the necessities of the common market. One directive,[32] of June 27, 1967 which was modified many times, aimed at harmonizing the legislative, regulatory and administrative measures in force in the member states as far as the classification, packaging and handling of dangerous substances is concerned. It established methods for determining

27 Art. 1.

28 Minamata Convention on Mercury (adopted 10 October 2013, entry into force 16 August 2017) 3202 UNTS (Minamata Convention). See also the website: <https://minamataconvention.org/en>. See also the UNECE Convention on the Transboundary Effects of Industrial Accidents (Helsinki, 17 March 1992).

29 Hisachi Yokoyama, *Mercury Pollution in Minamata* (Springer Nature 2018) 1.

30 Minamata Convention, Art. 1.

31 See, e.g., European Agreement Concerning the International Carriage of Dangerous Goods by Road (1957); Convention Concerning International Carriage by Rail (1924) and its annex; the Regulations Concerning the International Carriage of Dangerous Goods by Rail, 1924/1985; International Convention for Safety at of Human Life at Sea (SOLAS, Nov. 1, 1974); Convention on Liability and Compensation, for Damage in Connection with the Carriage of Hazardous and Noxious Substances by Sea (May 3, 1996); Convention on International Civil Aviation (1944), Annex 18; and Technical Instructions for the Safe Transport of Dangerous Goods by Air; International Convention for the Prevention of Pollution by Ships (MARPOL Nov. 2, 1973, Feb., 17, 1978); Regulation of the Carriage of Dangerous Substances on the Rhine (1970).

32 67/548/EEC, O.J. L 196 (8/16/6)7. This Directive is no longer in force, end of validity: 31 May 2015. See currently Regulation (EC) No 1272/2008, O.J. L 353 31 December 2008, 1, which includes all specific regulations previously in separate directives.

the physico-chemical properties as well as the toxicity and eco-toxicity of substances and preparations and the characteristics which should be taken into account in evaluating the danger, real or potential, which the substances can pose to the environment. It also established a notification system. Three other directives contained specific regulations for particular products: solvents,[33] paints, varnishes, printing inks, glues and related products,[34] and pesticides.[35] The EC as well as OECD have in the past also adopted special rules for phytopharmaceutical products,[36] polychlorinated biphenyls (PCBs),[37] polychlorinated terphenyls (PCTs)[38] and mercury.[39]

The safe use of chemicals supposes that the user knows their characteristics and their potential danger. For this reason, international instruments put the accent on notification and consultation, and detail the modalities of trade. OECD was one of the first to take action concerning trade, and largely to protect commerce, by suggesting advance notification and consultation concerning proposed measures concerning hazardous substances, when those measure could have significant impact on the economies of other countries.[40]

In 1985, the FAO adopted the first International Code of Conduct on the Distribution and Use of Pesticides to reduce the hazards associated with the use of pesticides.[41] The Code established voluntary standards for use by countries without existing pesticide regulation. It allocated shared responsibility among government, industry and the public. In November 1989, the FAO amended the Code to adopt the principle of prior informed consent (PIC) and subsequently produced

33 73/173/EEC of June 4, 1973, O.J. L 189 (7/11/73); most recent modification June 10, 1982 by Directive 82/473/EEC, O.J. L 213 (7/21/82). This Directive is no longer in force, end of validity: 7 June 1992.

34 77/728/EEC of Nov. 7, 1977, O.J. L 303 (11/28/77), modified by Directive 82/265/EEC of May 16, 1983, O.J. L 147 (6/6/83). This Directive is no longer in force, end of validity: 7 June 1992.

35 78/631/EEC of June 26 1978, O.J. L 206 (7/29/78), modified by directive 81/187/EEC of March 26, 1981, O.J. L 88 (4/2/81). This Directive is no longer in force, end of validity: 29 July 1999.

36 Directive 79/117/EEC of Dec. 21, 1978, O.J. L 33 (2/8/79). This Directive is no longer in force, end of validity: 13 June 2011. See currently Regulation (EC) No 1107/2009, O.J. L 309 24 November 2009, 1.

37 OECD decisions C(73)1 of Feb. 13, 1973 and C(87)2 of Feb. 13, 1987. Decision C(73)1 was abrogated in 1992. Decision C(87)2 is still in force.

38 Directive 76/769/EEC of July 27, 1976, O.J. L 262 (9/27/76) and L 197 (8/3/79). This Directive is no longer in force, end of validity: 31 May 2009. See currently Regulation (EC) No 1907/2006, O.J. L 396 30 December 2006, 1.

39 OECD Res. C(73)172 of Sept. 18, 1973.

40 OECD Res. C(71)73 of May 18, 1971.

41 FAO Code of Conduct on the Distribution and Use of Pesticides, UN Doc. M/R8130, E/8.86/1/5000 (1986).

operational procedures for PIC and guidelines on its process. Under the PIC provision, a pesticide that is banned or severely restricted in an exporting country because of its threat to human health or the environment should not be shipped to an importing country over that country's objection. It requires relevant information to be provided by each country so that it can determine the risks and benefits associated with the chemical. The Code was updated last in 2013, incorporating for example public health pesticides, thereby effectively broadening the scope of the Code beyond agriculture.[42] Because of the more recent adoption of binding legislation on the subject (which is discussed below), the Code is meant to complement these legally-binding instruments at this point in time.[43]

UNEP also adopted guidelines to address trade in hazardous chemicals, including but not limited to pesticides. The 1987 London Guidelines for the Exchange of Information on Chemicals in International Trade[44] aimed to provide access to information on hazardous chemicals in order to facilitate informed choices on importation, handling and use. The London Guidelines Prior Informed Consent procedure was added in 1989 as a voluntary procedure implemented through the FAO/UNEP Joint Program for the Operation of the PIC.

Prior informed consent became increasingly required for trade in hazardous substances and products. In 1983, the United Nations General Assembly declared that

> products that have been banned from domestic consumption and/or sale because they have judged to endanger health and the environment should be sold abroad by companies, corporations or individuals only when a request for such products is received from an importing country or when the consumption of such products is officially permitted in the importing country.[45]

Finally, in 1998, the FAO sponsored the adoption of the Rotterdam Convention on the Prior Informed Consent Procedure for Certain Hazardous Chemicals and Pesticides in International Trade (PIC Convention),[46] incorporating

---

42 FAO and WHO, *The International Code of Conduct on Pesticide Management* (4th version, 2013).

43 ibid, VI.

44 London Guidelines for the Exchange of Information on Chemicals in International Trade, UN Doc. UNEP/GC, 14/17, Annex IV (1987).

45 UNGA Res. 37/137 (1983) para. 1.

46 Rotterdam Convention on the Prior Informed Consent Procedure for Certain Hazardous Chemicals and Pesticides in International Trade (adopted 10 September 1998, entered into force 24 February 2004)

the various voluntary arrangements into a legally binding instrument. The preamble expresses the desire of the states parties to ensure that hazardous chemicals that are exported from their territory are packaged and labeled in a manner that is adequately protective of human health and the environment. Similarly, the objective of the Convention expressed in Article 1 is

> to promote shared responsibility and cooperative efforts among Parties in the international trade of certain hazardous chemicals in order to protect human health and the environment from potential harm and to contribute to their environmentally sound use, by facilitating information exchange about their characteristics, by providing for a national decision-making process on their import and export and by disseminating these decisions to Parties.

The PIC Convention relies in large part on private actors to ensure that information on chemical and pesticide hazards is made available to the public. Each party is to require that exported Annex III chemicals as well as chemicals banned or severely restricted in its territory are subject to labeling requirements that ensure the provision of information about risks and/or hazards to human health or the environment, taking into account relevant international standards. The Convention thus implicitly places the primary duty to provide information on the manufacturer or packager of the export. Whenever a customs code has been assigned to a chemical by the World Customs Organization, each state party also must require that the shipping document for that chemical bears the code when exported.[47] Article 13 requires that exporting parties include for the importer a safety data sheet following an internationally-accepted format with the most up-to-date information available on the listed chemicals. Article 15, which concerns implementation, requires each

47 Art. 13(1)(a) calls on the Conference of the Parties to encourage the World Customs Organization to assign specific Harmonized System customs codes to the individual chemicals or groups of chemicals listed in Annex III, as appropriate. At UNCED in 1992, a group of participating states launched an initiative to develop a common set of chemical hazard symbols, terms, data sheets and classification techniques. The proposed Globally Harmonized System (GHS) has been coordinated by the UN Inter-Organizational Program for Sound Management of Chemical with the cooperation of OECD and the participation of companies, labor representatives and environmental groups. Harmonized criteria were completed at the end of 1998 for classifying chemicals for their various physical, environmental, and health hazards, coordinated by the United Nations and the OECD at the Intergovernmental Forum on Chemical Safety. Industry strongly favors harmonization because wide variation in classification and labeling requirements have negative impacts on trade.

state party to ensure, to the extent practicable, that the public has appropriate access to information on chemical handling and accident management and on safer alternatives to the chemicals listed in Annex III to the Convention. The list of chemicals has been continuously updated through the years through amendments.[48]

2 Wastes

As stated in Goal 12.5 of the SDGs, the international community has undertaken to 'substantially reduce waste generation through prevention, reduction, recycling and reuse' in our time. Yet the problem of waste is of course extraordinarily long, and has changed and increased with the industrial age and the growth and concentration of human populations. In pre-industrial Europe and in China there was little waste product, other than human sewage, because the bulk of substances and objects were reutilized in some way. Domestic animals consumed some waste, another part was used as agricultural fertilizer, and most metal was recycled. Today, the constant increase of waste has become a major concern. The activities of mass production in agriculture and in industry have created an accumulation of garbage. Moreover, the current economic system is based upon obsolescence and a 'throw-away' culture designed to sell a larger number of products. All these factors accelerate waste accumulation. UNEP estimates that more than 400 million tons of hazardous waste is generated annually throughout the world.[49] Most of this amount is treated within the country that produces it; historically, only about 4% of the hazardous waste generated by OECD countries is shipped across an international border.[50] In total amount, however, this still represents a considerable hazard to human health and the environment, because OECD countries generate the largest amount of waste in the world. In addition, transboundary movements have increased because of the economic advantages involved in shipping waste for disposal to poorer countries where the costs are much lower.[51]

48 Amended in 2004, 2008, 2011, 2013, 2015, 2017 and 2019. See for a current update on amendments the website at <https://www.pic.int/TheConvention/Overview/Textofthe-Convention/tabid/1048/> (last accessed 8 May 2024).

49 Victor Akpan and David Olukanni, 'Hazardous Waste Management: An Overview' (2020) 5(15) *Recycling* 1.

50 OECD, 'Practical Information for the Implementation of the OECD Control System: Transfrontier Movements of Wastes Destined for Recovery Operations' (1997).

51 Disposal of hazardous waste may cost $2000 per ton in a developed country compared to $40 per ton in Africa. See Jennifer R. Kitt, 'Waste Exports to the Developing World: A

There is general agreement that the best means to control waste is the reduction of the quantity of waste produced. Those that are produced can be eliminated by different methods: discharge into surface dumps, burial in the earth, submersion into the oceans or lakes, and incineration. More ecological methods consider waste as much as possible as primary derived material which should be reutilized or recycled. This concept is badly expressed in legal instruments, however, which generally are based upon the notion of waste as *res derelicta* (abandoned property).

The problem of toxic or dangerous waste is a serious concern. Many dump sites are found to contain toxic products. Sometimes these sites are clandestine and result in severe consequences. As a result, the Council of Europe's Convention on Civil Liability for Damage Resulting from Activities Dangerous to the Environment[52] includes in its definition of dangerous activity '(c) the operation of an installation or site for the incineration, treatment, handling or recycling of waste … provided that the quantities involved pose a significant risk for man, the environment or property; and (d) the operation of a site for the permanent deposit of waste'.[53]

One of the legal problems raised by this topic results from the difficulty of defining 'waste'. The initial tendency in international regulation was to turn to national legislation for the definition of waste. Thus, the OECD defined waste as 'any material considered as waste or legally defined as waste in the country where it is situated or through or to which it is conveyed'.[54] The Governing Council of UNEP[55] approved a decision utilizing the same terms. The framework EC directive[56] of July 15, 1975 declares that 'waste' is 'any substance or object which the holder disposes of or is required to dispose of pursuant to the provisions of legislation', unfortunately failing to take into account recycling.[57]

In two cases, the European Court of Justice attempted to clarify the EC definition of waste and to establish criteria to determine whether waste is destined

Global Response' (1995) *Geo. Int'l Envr'l L. Rev.* 485; European Union (European Commission) 'A New Circular Economy Action Plan for a cleaner and more competitive Europe' (2020) 14.

52 Council of Europe, Convention on Civil Liability for Damage Resulting from Activities Dangerous to the Environment (adopted 21 June 1993).

53 ibid art. 2(1)(c) and (d).

54 OECD Rec. C(83)180 of Feb. 1, 1984.

55 Art. 1(a), Decision 14/30 of June 17, 1987.

56 75/442/EEC, O.J.L 194/39 (7/25/75). This directive is no longer in force. End of validity: 16 May 2006. See currently Directive 2008/98/EC, O.J. L 312 22 November 2008, 3.

57 Art. 1(a). Current EU directive 2008/98/EC of 19 November 2008 defines it as 'any substance or object which the holder discards or intends or is required to discard' in art. 3(1), being very similar to the 1975 definition.

for recovery or disposal.[58] Also at issue in the first case was the question of who determines whether waste is shipped for disposal or recovery, a significant issue because the rules governing waste vary according to whether it is for disposal or recovery.[59] The Court permitted the authorities of the destination to scrutinize the initial classification of the shipping state, but also held that the decision in favor of 'recovery' must be based on whether the operation serves a 'useful purpose' in replacing other materials which would have been used for that purpose. Waste might be bound for recovery if 'its principal objective is that the waste serve a useful purpose in replacing other materials which would have had to be used for that purpose'.[60] In the second case, the issue of stone as waste arose. The Court held that the test of waste is whether a substance constitutes a production residue not sought for subsequent use and whether it is likely that the substance will be reused without any further processing prior to its reuse. Where, as here, the stone was likely to be stored for an indefinite period of time to await possible reuse, it was considered discarded and therefore waste.

The problem of toxic or dangerous waste involves other legal problems. There is considerable overlap in regulation: e.g. specific rules regulate waste and rules aimed at protecting the seas and continental waters from pollution indirectly regulate them as well. There are also general rules concerning chemical products and norms for the protection of workers that affect waste policies.[61] Transport regulations, norms of transboundary pollution, rules relating to territorial management, regimes of prior authorization, and environmental impact procedures also are relevant. Two particular aspects are of special concern and have led to direct international regulation of toxic or dangerous wastes: their management and transboundary shipments of them.

2.1 *Waste Management*

Three international institutions have addressed the problem of waste management: OECD, UNEP, and the EU. The first two have elaborated texts which for

58 See Case C-6/00, Abfall Service AG (ASA) v. Bundeminister für Umwelt, Jugend und Familie (2002) and Case C-9/00, Palin Granit OY and Vehmassalon kansanterveystyon huntayhtyman hallitus (2002).

59 The most important difference concerns the grounds on which various competent authorities concerned may oppose the proposed shipment. Waste for recovery is subject to less stringent rules.

60 Case C-6/00 ASA v Bundesminister für Umwelt, Jugend und Familie (2002) (N 58)para. 69.

61 See e.g., ILO Convention No. 170 Concerning Safety in the Use of Chemicals at Work (June 1990), and Convention No. 162 on Asbestos (1986).

the most part are not obligatory. Those of the EU are in the form of mandatory directives.

On the global level, UNEP has taken measures to avoid environmental harm from toxic or dangerous wastes. Following discussions within the Governing Council, UNEP added to its legal program the question of limiting production and international transport of toxic or dangerous wastes as a priority matter[62] leading to the adoption of the Cairo Guidelines of December 10, 1985 which were endorsed by the Governing Council of UNEP.[63] The Cairo Guidelines inspired the Basel Convention on the Control of Transboundary Movements of Hazardous Wastes and their Disposal, discussed below, but are broader in their focus on management.[64]

The Cairo Guidelines recognize that differences exist among countries of the world in their ability to safely manage toxic and hazardous wastes and they seek to establish a general framework for administrative action aimed at the good management of dangerous wastes, especially in developing countries. The text is very general, perhaps because it was primarily aimed at countries that had not yet regulated the problem of dangerous wastes. It calls on states to take legislative or other measures to assure the protection of health and the environment against dangers posed by the production and management of dangerous wastes. States should cooperate to attain this objective, notably in elaborating and implementing technologies that produce the least wastes and, where appropriate, in transferring applicable technology.

Principle 7 of the Cairo Guidelines insists on prevention and contributes an important principle: the production of wastes should be reduced to a minimum and even the pollution that is permitted by the Guidelines should be avoided as much as possible. Each state should designate a special authority to plan, authorize and monitor the management of dangerous wastes. This authority should ensure that hazardous wastes are collected, transported and separately eliminated from other garbage. Lists of international waste treatment and elimination installations are foreseen. As for the effects that these installations may produce in other countries, the state which grants the authorization for a plant should furnish to any state potentially affected by such a facility all necessary information and enter into consultation with it as needed. In the granting of authorizations and in all administrative or judicial procedures relative to these grants, states must ensure equality of access and

62 Conference of Montevideo, 1981.

63 UNEP Governing Council, Cairo Guidelines and Principles for the Environmentally Sound Management of Hazardous Wastes, Decision 14/30 (June 17, 1987).

64 See Section B.2.

treatment of nationals and those from states that could be affected by nuisances coming from treatment plants or other discharges.

The Guidelines also announce principles related to monitoring of activities concerning dangerous wastes. They emphasize that appropriate authorities should maintain registers of operating authorities and that the public should have free access to information relating to the number and type of authorizations delivered as well as the details of the measures which accompany them. Several principles are devoted to the training of personnel employed in operations relating to dangerous wastes, emergency plans and the provision of information to other states in case of emergency. The problem of transport is addressed only in recalling applicable international rules on the subject and in foreseeing systems to assure that dangerous wastes will be accompanied by appropriate documents from the place of their production until they are eliminated. The final principle concerns responsibility for damage caused by dangerous wastes, inviting states to adopt domestic rules concerning liability, insurance and compensation for damage caused by dangerous wastes. These rules should be harmonized with international norms.

The texts adopted by the OECD in this field are different and more numerous. Alongside one general recommendation, specific instruments concern particular products, e.g. beverage containers and waste paper. The general recommendation envisages state development and implementation of a comprehensive waste management policy.[65] Such a policy involves 'a coherent system of measures concerning the design, manufacture and use of products as well as the reclamation and disposal of wastes aiming at the most efficient and economic reduction of the nuisances and costs generated by waste'.[66] Protection of the environment should be one objective of this policy.[67]

The principles of a comprehensive waste management program should include reduction at the source of waste, especially measures concerning the design and marketing of products, their rational use and, where appropriate, the extension of product life. Changes in manufacturing processes, the re-use of products or their reclamation and recycling and, eventually, the use of alternative products are also addressed. The operations should not increase the risk of pollution transfer, however. Application of the 'polluter pays' principle should encourage waste prevention and recycling. Appropriate measures should be taken in order to permit the appropriate authorities to receive all necessary information to assure that waste disposal or reclamation is realized

65 Recommendation C(76) 155 of Sept. 28, 1976.

66 ibid Art. 1.

67 ibid Art. 2.

in the most economic and judicious way with regard to environmental protection. Finally, the recommendation foresees the adoption of administrative arrangements designed to organize waste management: reducing the types and quantities of wastes to be disposed of, the promotion of research on minimal-waste technology, and encouraging the creation of markets for recycled products.

Recommendations relating to the reuse and recycling of beverage containers[68] and to waste paper recovery[69] provide the most detailed indications on the practical implementation of the principles, envisaging a general policy of waste management. The OECD also has adopted a classification scheme for hazardous wastes based on the chemical components of the wastes and the reasons why the materials are intended for disposal operations.[70]

The EU legal framework for waste management includes two approaches: general regulations and specific measures focused on particular types of wastes or on methods of disposal. General regulations could previously be found in Directive 91/689[71] which prescribed measures of adequate waste management based on a twofold objective: to protect human health against noxious influences caused by the collection, transport, treatment, storage and disposal of waste and to promote the recovery, recycling and reuse of waste in order to preserve natural resources. Both objectives established a permit system to ensure the coherence of waste management, using waste disposal plans, and to control all establishments or undertakings that carry out the main waste operations. The Directive has since been replaced by the EU Waste Framework Directive of 2008, which has roughly the same objectives, but also names protecting the environment, not only human health, by preventing or reducing the generation of waste and the adverse impacts of the generation and management of waste, and by reducing overall impacts of resource use and improving the efficiency of such use.[72] It also emphasizes the need for a transition to a circular economy.[73] An amendment proposed July 5, 2023, specifically concerning textiles, remains unadopted as of May 2024.

The general framework was complemented by Regulation 259/93 on the Supervision and Control of Shipments of Waste Within, Into and Out of the EU[74] which established a notification and control procedure for all shipments

68 Recommendation C(78)8, Feb. 3, 1978.

69 Recommendation C(79)218, Jan. 30, 1980.

70 C(88)90(Final), May 27, 1988.

71 Dec. 20, 1991, O.J. L 377 (12/31/91).

72 Directive 2008/98/EC, O.J. L 312 (22 November 2008) 3, art. 1.

73 ibid.

74 Feb. 1, 1993, O.J. L 30 (6/2/93).

of waste. The competent authorities may object to certain movements of waste or impose special requirements for environmental, safety, public policy or health protection. Currently, this is regulated by a more up-to-date EU Regulation which has been regularly amended.[75]

Other international organizations have become involved in the question of toxic or hazardous wastes, although they are not generally concerned with environmental protection. The International Labor Organization (ILO) adopted a Convention Concerning Safety in the Use of Chemicals at Work in June 1990.[76] Over the objections of the employer members, this Convention includes a provision that hazardous chemicals and contaminated empty containers 'shall be handled or disposed of in a manner which eliminates or minimizes the risk to safety and health and to the environment, in accordance with national law and practice'. The worker members insisted that this language be retained, and also insisted on the inclusion of other provisions in the Convention that were not directly applicable to worker health and safety, but rather to public health and environmental protection.

The Protocol on Environmental Protection to the Antarctic Treaty[77] contains a general obligation for the states parties to reduce as much as possible the amounts of wastes produced or disposed in the Antarctic Treaty Area. Annex III includes provisions on waste disposal by removal from the area, by incineration, by disposal on land and in the sea. It also provides for waste management planning and recommends management practices. Even before the adoption of the Protocol, the 1989 Basel Convention on the Control of Transboundary Movements of Hazardous Wastes and Their Disposal, discussed in the next section, prohibited the export of hazardous wastes or other wastes for disposal within the area south of 60 degrees South latitude (Art. 4(6)).

2.2 *Transboundary Movements*

The transport of toxic or dangerous substances from one country to another in order to eliminate, recycle or dispose of it is one of the most common forms of exporting pollution. Several reasons may motivate the producer of waste to seek to dispose of it in another country. First, the regulations of the producing country may make disposal there difficult. The wastes will thus be sent towards a country

75 Regulation (EC) No 1013/2006, O.J. L 190 (12 July 2006) 1. As of May 2024, the prospect of replacing or more thoroughly updating this Regulation has been discussed, but has not materialized.

76 International Labour Organization, Chemicals Convention, 1990 (No. 170) (adopted 25 June 1990, entered into force 4 November 1993).

77 Madrid, Oct. 4, 1991, 30, ILM 1455 (1991).

where regulation is less strict or the monitoring of compliance is less effective. The most targeted countries obviously are those that offer protection against claims and accept the wastes without always being concerned with the dangers they pose.

A second reason that could motivate a producer to export waste is lower disposal costs, even if the operation conforms to the law. The 'importing' country could offer inexpensive possibilities of storage, for example in abandoned mines, or waste treatment plants less costly than those in the producing country. It is also evident that installations capable of treating certain types of waste do not exist in all countries. Finally, a multinational enterprise might have a foreign subsidiary specialized in the elimination of certain types of dangerous wastes. The enterprise will transport its wastes to the foreign subsidiary to be treated and disposed of, even if borders must be crossed.

These factors led to an increasing movement of hazardous wastes across boundaries in the 1980s. According to OECD estimates for European countries, the volume of dangerous wastes crossing boundaries in 1983 was approximately 2.2 million tons.[78] The content of the waste being transported and the attendant hazards became as much a concern as the rising quantity of the transboundary movement.

The transport of hazardous wastes from developed countries to developing countries, which acquired the title 'garbage imperialism', led at least thirty-nine states to adopt and implement national legislation entirely prohibiting the importation into or transshipment through their territories of all foreign wastes.[79] In addition, by the end of the 1980s a general opposition to transboundary movements of hazardous wastes led to international regulation, first at a global level, then regionally. Transboundary disposal of waste also may be controlled by norms dealing with chemicals or transboundary pollution.[80]

At the global level, UNEP first developed the Cairo Guidelines and Principles for the Environmentally Sound Management of Hazardous Wastes, adopted by the Governing Council.[81] The Guidelines aimed to assist states in prepar-

---

78 United Nations Environment Programme, *1989 The State of the World Environment*, (UNEP/GC.15/7/Add.2, 1989).

79 States that have adopted such prohibitions include, e.g. Algeria, Barbados, Belize, Benin, Burundi, Comoros, Congo, Dominican Republic, Gabon, Gambia, Ghana, Guatemala, Guinea, Guinea-Bissau, Guyana, Haiti, Indonesia, Ivory Coast, Jamaica, Kenya, Liberia, Libya, Niger, Nigeria, Peru, Philippines, Saint Lucia, Senegal, Sierra Leone, Solomon Islands, Tanzania, Togo, Trinidad & Tobago, Turkey, Vanuatu, Venezuela, Yugoslavia, Zambia, and Zimbabwe.

80 In addition to the measures discussed in this chapter, see the work of the United Nations Human Rights Commission discussed in Chapter 15.

81 Decision 14/30, June 17, 1987.

ing appropriate bilateral, regional and multilateral agreements and national legislation for the environmentally sound management of hazardous wastes. They were followed by the Basel Convention on the Control of Transboundary Movements of Hazardous Wastes and their Disposal,[82] adopted on March 22, 1989 by 116 states. This instrument establishes a global framework for international regulation, although it has been criticized as not going far enough. Indeed, it does not ban all transboundary movements of hazardous waste. One of its objectives is to make the movements of hazardous waste so costly and difficult that industry will find it more profitable to cut down on waste production.

The Convention defines wastes as substances or objects that are disposed of or are intended to be disposed of or are required to be disposed of by the provisions of national law.[83] The hazardous character of wastes is defined by combined approaches of Annexes I, II and III. Annex I lists categories of wastes to be controlled (e.g. chemical wastes from medical care in hospitals, and waste from different products such as pharmaceuticals, or production of specified substances such as biocides, organic solvents). Annex II contains two categories of wastes that require special consideration: wastes collected from households and residues arising from the incineration of household wastes. Annex III adds a list of hazardous characteristics of wastes, such as explosive, flammable, oxidizing, poisonous, infectious, corrosive, toxic and eco-toxic. This combined method is now increasingly used in international regulation, since the simple listing of polluting substances is inadequate.

Some of the important provisions in the Basel Convention are:

- the generation of hazardous wastes and other wastes and their transboundary movement should be reduced to a minimum consistent with the environmentally sound and efficient management of such wastes (Art. 4(2)(a) and (d));
- a signatory state cannot send hazardous waste to another signatory state that bans importation of it (Art. 4(1)(b)), to another signatory state if the importing country does not have the facilities to dispose of the waste in an environmentally sound manner (Art. 4(2)(b)(e) and (g)), or to any non-party state (Art. 4(5));
- every country has the sovereign right to refuse to accept a shipment of hazardous wastes (Art. 4(1)(a)) and (12);
- before an exporting country can start a shipment on its way, it must have the importing country's consent in writing (Art. 4(1)(c));

82 28 ILM 657 (1989).

83 Art. 2(1).

- when an importing country proves unable to dispose of legally imported waste in an environmentally sound way, then the exporting state has a duty either to take it back or to find some other way of disposing of it in an environmentally sound manner (Art. 8);
- the parties consider that 'illegal traffic in hazardous wastes is criminal' (Art. 4(3));[84]
- shipments of hazardous waste must be packaged, labeled, and transported in conformity with generally accepted and recognized international rules and standards (Art. 4(7)(b) and accompanied by a movement document from the point at which a transboundary movement commences to the point of disposal (Art. 4(7));
- bilateral agreements may be made, but they must conform to the terms of the Basel Convention and be no less environmentally sound (Art. 11);
- parties should cooperate in the training of technicians, exchange of information and transfer of technology (Arts. 10 and 13).

The Convention established a Conference of the Parties and a secretariat to supervise and facilitate its implementation. The secretariat plays, in particular, an important role in receiving and conveying information to and from the parties and in handling the notification system provided for by the convention.

Decision II/12 adopted by the Conference of Parties to the Basel Convention in September 1995[85] phased out and prohibited by December 31, 1997 all transboundary movements of waste for disposal, recovery and recycling from OECD member states, the European Community and Liechtenstein to all other states. However, because the decision was not incorporated in the text of the Convention itself, the question arose as to whether or not it was legally binding. Therefore, at COP-3, it was proposed that the ban be formally incorporated in the Basel Convention as an amendment. Decision III/1 bans hazardous wastes exports for final disposal and recycling from Annex VII countries (EU and OECD member states plus Liechtenstein) to non-Annex VII countries (all other parties to the Convention). In order to enter into force, the Ban Amendment required ratification by three-fourths of the Parties who were present at the time of the adoption of the Amendment (62 Parties).

The Fourth Conference of the Parties, meeting in February 1998, adopted lists of hazardous (List A) and nonhazardous (List B) wastes. The first list

84 For more on international illicit waste trafficking, see Serena Favarin and Alberto Aziani, 'The Global Waste Trafficking and Its Correlates' (2020) 36(3) *Journal of Contemporary Criminal Justice* 351.

85 Conference of the Parties to the Basel Convention, Decision II/12: The Based Ban Amendment (adopted March 1994) UNEP/CHW.2/30.

comprises wastes that may not be sent by Annex VII countries to other states. List B, contained in Annex IX, includes materials that are not subject to the shipment ban unless they contain constituents at a level that causes them exhibit hazardous characteristics, such as flammability or toxicity. Even prior to the entry into force of the annexes, the European Union adopted a regulation giving effect to it.[86]

Starting in 1998, parties to the Basel Convention turned their attention to elaborating a liability protocol, concluded December 10, 1999 and discussed in Chapter 7A.2, and drafting guidelines on environmentally sound management of particular categories of hazardous wastes, e.g. lead acid batteries, plastic wastes, decommissioned ships to be dismantled. These guidelines may include technical specifications for recycling and reclamation and specific strategies for implementation. In January 2002, a working group of the Basel Convention adopted a set of technical guidelines to protect human health and the environment from the improper management and disposal of plastic wastes.[87] The guidelines address a range of waste management issues such as sorting for mechanical recycling, health and safety mechanisms, shipping and transport services, feedstock recycling, compaction, energy recovery, and final disposal.

More recently, at the Fourteenth Meeting of the Conference of the Parties in 2019, the Basel Convention was amended to enhance the control of the transboundary movements of plastic waste and clarify the scope of application of the Convention to such waste.[88] At the subsequent meeting of the Conference of the Parties in 2022, parties adopted amendments to the Convention with the objective of enlarging control over transboundary movements of e-wastes, and making all of this waste subject to the PIC procedure. As of May 2024, these amendments on e-waste are scheduled to enter into force on January 1, 2025.[89]

In June 2001, the OECD revised its texts on the transboundary movement of wastes to harmonize its work with the Basel Convention. It adopted Council Decision C(2001)107 on Control of Transboundary Movements of Wastes Destined for Recovery Operations.

Several regional conventions and EU rules also have been adopted in order to regulate transboundary movements of hazardous wastes. The EU has very

---

86 Regulation 2408/98, O.J. Nov. 7, 1998.

87 Conference of the Parties to the Basel Convention, Technical Guidelines for the Identification and Environmentally Sound Management of Plastic Wastes and for Their Disposal (adopted Dec 2002) UNEP/CHW.6/21.

88 Decision BC-14/12 and BC-14/13; See also Eva Romée van der Marel, 'Trading Plastic Waste in a Global Economy: Soundly Regulated by the Basel Convention?' (2022) 34(3) *Journal of Environmental Law* 477.

89 Decision BC-VI/31, BC-VIII/2, BC-VIII/5, BC-IX/6 and BC-IX/9.

recently made great progress in waste shipments, through a new regulation which entered into force on May 20, 2024.[90] It was created as a result of the EU's New Circular Economy Plan, as part of the Green Deal.[91] The Regulation aims to prevent the export of waste challenges, for example banning the export of plastic wastes to non-OECD countries from November 2026 on.[92] Furthermore, it also aims to better address illegal shipments of waste and facilitate recycling and re-use.[93] To address the issue of illegal waste shipping, the EU waste shipment enforcement group was created, which facilitates and improves cooperation and coordination between the member states of the EU in order to prevent and detect illegal shipments.[94] They meet at least once a year to share information relevant for the prevention and detection of illegal shipments.[95]

African states generally did not consider the original Basel Convention satisfactory and wanted to ban the importation of all hazardous wastes on their continent. They concluded, in the framework of the Organization of African Unity, a Convention on the Ban of the Import of Hazardous Wastes into Africa and on the Control of their Transboundary Movements within Africa (Bamako Convention).[96] The Convention, which advocates inter-African cooperation (Art. 10), is based on two principles: (1) states have the sovereign right to ban, for human health and environmental reasons, the transportation of hazardous wastes and substances into and across their territory and (2) hazardous wastes should, as far as is compatible with environmentally sound and efficient management, be disposed of in the country where they were generated.

Most of the provisions of the Bamako Convention correspond to those of the Basel Convention, but the regional Convention differs in some important respects from the global instrument. First, the definition of waste is broader and includes those radioactive wastes that are subject to any international control system (Art. 2(3)). Second, the parties must strive to apply the precautionary approach (Art. 4(3)(f)). Most importantly, it prohibits the import of hazardous wastes for any reason into Africa from outside the continent

90 Regulation (EU) 2024/1157 (11 April 2024) <https://environment.ec.europa.eu/topics/waste-and-recycling/waste-shipments_en>.

91 European Union (European Commission) 'The European Green Deal' (Brussels, 11 December 2019) COM(2019) 640 final; European Union (European Commission) 'A new Circular Economy Action Plan for a cleaner and more competitive Europe' (Brussels, 11 March 2020) COM(2020) 98 final.

92 Art. 31(1)(d) and 86(3)(c) Regulation EU 2024/1157.

93 Regulation (EU) 2024/1157 (11 April 2024) (n 90), preamble para. 3.

94 ibid Art. 66(1).

95 ibid Art. 66(4) and (3).

96 Bamako, Jan. 29, 1991, 30 ILM 773 (1991) and 31 ILM 163 (1992).

and from non-contracting states and declares such movement a criminal act (Art. 4(1)). It prohibits dumping hazardous waste at sea, including incineration. Finally, the Convention requires the parties to impose unlimited and joint and several liability on hazardous waste generators in Africa (Art. 4(3)(b)). Like the Basel Convention, the Bamako Convention establishes a Conference of the Parties and a secretariat.

In conformity with the Bamako Convention, the Treaty Establishing the African Economic Community[97] declares that member states undertake, individually or collectively, to take every appropriate step to ban the importation and dumping of hazardous wastes in their respective territories and to cooperate in the transboundary movement, management and processing of such wastes produced in Africa (Art. 59).

The Bamako Convention also corresponded to Article 39 of the Fourth Lomé Convention between the EU and African, Caribbean and Pacific (ACP) countries.[98] According to this text the contracting parties undertake to make every effort to ensure that international movements of hazardous waste and radioactive waste are generally controlled, with the Community agreeing to prohibit all direct or indirect export of such waste to the ACP states while the ACP states undertake to prohibit the direct or indirect import into their territory of such waste from the Community or from any other country. On June 23, 2000, the EC-ACP states signed a new Partnership Agreement in Cotonou, Benin. In Article 32(1)(d), the parties agree to cooperate on questions relating to the transport and elimination of hazardous wastes.

Even before the Basel Convention, the problem of the transboundary movements of hazardous wastes was envisaged in the Convention for the Protection of the Natural Resources and Environment of the South Pacific Region,[99] a convention of large scope containing general obligations. Articles 10 and 11 of this instrument speak of measures that the states in the region should take to prevent, reduce and monitor, in the area covered by the Convention, pollution which could be caused by the immersion in the sea or by dumping of toxic or hazardous wastes.

Other regional treaties were adopted after the Basel Convention and are inspired by it. The Regional Agreement on the Transboundary Movement of Hazardous Wastes[100] adopted in 1992 by six Central-American countries prohibits the transboundary transport as well as the import and transit of

---

97 Abuja, June 3, 1991, 30 ILM 1241(1991).
98 Fourth ACP-CEE Convention, Dec. 15, 1989, EMuT 989:93.
99 Noumea, Nov. 24, 1986, 26 ILM 38 (1987).
100 Panama, Dec. 11, 1992, EMuT 992:91.

hazardous wastes. A 1995 Convention to Ban the Importation into Forum Island Countries of Hazardous Wastes and Radioactive Wastes and to Control the Transboundary Movement and Management of Hazardous Wastes within the South Pacific[101] further expanded the geographic area where movements of hazardous waste should be controlled. Within the Convention area, developing Pacific Island states shall ban the import of all hazardous wastes and radioactive wastes from outside that Area. Any other party – in fact Australia and New Zealand – shall ban the export of all hazardous wastes and radioactive wastes to all Forum Island countries. Finally, in 1996 the treaty system elaborated for the protection of the Mediterranean Sea was supplemented by a specific Protocol for the Prevention of the Pollution of the Mediterranean Sea by Transboundary Movements of Hazardous Wastes and their Disposal.[102] It is framed on the principles and approaches of the Basel Convention, but is integrated in the structures of the Mediterranean treaty system.

Examples of bilateral agreements are the agreement between Canada and the United States on Transfrontier Movements of Hazardous Wastes[103] and Annex III to the Agreement of Cooperation for the Protection and Amelioration of the Environment in the Frontier Region Between Mexico and the United States.[104] The American – Canadian agreement provides that the two countries are obliged not only to promulgate all the necessary regulations to apply the agreement, but they should also transmit them to the other party by diplomatic note when they enter into force.[105] Annex III to the United States – Mexico agreement insists on the obligation of the contracting states to apply their own legislation regarding hazardous wastes to shipments which leave their territory.[106] It adds to this the obligation to inform the other contracting party of any measure prohibiting a pesticide or other chemical substance or restraining its utilization.[107]

Several points deserve particular attention in the problem of transporting hazardous wastes beyond national borders. The obligation of states relating to the transboundary movement of hazardous wastes is based on the rule of international law formulated first in Principle 21 of the Stockholm Declaration, now recognized as customary law: States have the obligation to ensure that activities carried out within the limits of their jurisdiction – in this case the

101 Waigani, September 16, 1995, EmuT, 995:69.
102 Izmir, Oct. 1, 1996, Doc. UNEP(OCA)MED/IG.4/4.
103 Ottawa, Oct. 28, 1986.
104 Washington, Nov. 12, 1986, 26, ILM 16 (1987).
105 Art. 5, para. 3.
106 Art. 2, para. 2.
107 Art. 5.

production and export of hazardous wastes – do not cause damage to the environment of other states.[108] Equally in the spirit of Principle 21 of the Stockholm Declaration and respectful of the sovereignty of states, the Preamble of the Basel Convention on the Control of Transboundary Movements of Hazardous Wastes and their Disposal reaffirms the right of states to refuse to accept on their territory hazardous wastes produced elsewhere. The fundamental principle in the field is that a state should only permit the export of hazardous wastes to a receiving state if that state consents to the importation by an explicit act in writing.[109] Similarly, Article 9 of the Basel Convention provides that the exporting country will accept the return of any transport of hazardous waste that was not legally imported into the other country.

3 Radioactivity

The use of radioactive substances constitutes one of the most urgent but technically and politically difficult areas of environmental protection. In addition to the problem of nuclear weapons, which nuclear states jealously guard,[110] nuclear energy production has become a major industry. There are currently more than 400 nuclear power plants in operation around the world.[111] Nuclear power makes up about 9% of total global electricity generation.[112] To these issues must be added the problem of illicit trafficking in nuclear materials. The International Atomic Energy Agency (IAEA) identified 146 such incidents in 2022.[113]

The IAEA, headquartered in Vienna, has been given broadest responsibility in the field.[114] The IAEA negotiates international treaties providing the struc-

108 Declaration on the Human Environment, Stockholm, June 16, 1972. See UN General Assembly Res. 2994/XXVII, 2995/XXVII and 2996/XXVII of Dec. 15, 1972.

109 Basel Convention on the Control of Transboundary Movements of Hazardous Wastes and Their Disposal (adopted 22 March 1989, entered into force 5 May 1992) 1673 U.N.T.S- 57, Art. 4.

110 In addition to the acknowledged nuclear powers, (U.S., France, UK, Russia, China, India, Pakistan), approximately another dozen posess or control separated plutonium for military or commercial use. See Barry Kellman, 'Protection of Nuclear Materials' in Dinah Shelton (ed.), *Commitment and Compliance: The Role of Non-Binding Norms in the International Legal System* (Oxford University Press 2000).

111 See for the current status IAEA, <https://pris.iaea.org/pris/home.aspx> (last accessed 10 April 2024).

112 IAEA, Energy, Electricity and Nuclear Power Estimates for the Period up to 2050 (2023).

113 IAEA, Incident and Trafficking Database (ITDB) 2023 Factsheet (2023) 2.

114 Two regional organizations also work on the topic: the European Agency for Nuclear Energy, created in 1957 within the OECD framework; and Euratom, also created in 1957 by the European Community.

ture of the nuclear safety system, supplemented by recommendations that set forth the detail of protective measures. The IAEA Statute was adopted in 1957, authorizing the organization to sponsor atomic energy research and development[115] and to have international regulatory authority over nuclear materials and technologies. In addition, states parties to the Nuclear Non-Proliferation Treaty accept IAEA verification of their non-proliferation commitments. The structure and functioning of the IAEA are described in Chapter 5.

International regulations on radiation aim to safeguard human health and life. For nuclear weapons, the most general international text is the Treaty Banning Nuclear Weapons Tests in the Atmosphere, in Outer Space, and Underwater.[116] Nearly all states in the world are parties to it. Five years later, the Nuclear Non-Proliferation Treaty (NPT)[117] obliged each non-nuclear weapon state to ensure that nuclear materials, equipment, facilities, and information are not used to advance military purposes. The treaty requires these states to accept international safeguards under IAEA supervision, including reporting requirements, installation of monitoring equipment, and on-site inspections. (NPT Art. III). Most states have entered into bilateral safeguards agreements with the IAEA pursuant to the NPT and according to an IAEA internal guidance document, INFCIRC/153.[118] These agreements are themselves supplemented by subsidiary agreements containing more detailed operating procedures. The package of commitments allows the IAEA to verify through state reporting and on-site inspections the security of nuclear materials and the features of nuclear facilities. In 1997, the IAEA Board of Governors proposed a new model Additional Protocol to safeguards agreements (INFCIRC/540) which aims at obtaining more information about nuclear facilities, including the collection of environmental samples.

The Antarctic Treaty goes further in forbidding not only nuclear explosions, but also eliminating all weapons and radioactive wastes in the Antarctic region.[119] Placing objects carrying nuclear arms on the moon or in orbit around

115 Statute of the International Atomic Energy Agency, Oct. 26, 1956, 8 UST 1093, 276 U.N.T.S. 3.

116 Treaty Banning Nuclear Weapon Tests in the Atmosphere, in Outer Space and Under Water (adopted 5 August 1963, entered into force 10 October 1963) 480 U.N.T.S. 43.

117 Treaty on the Non-Proliferation of Nuclear Weapons, July 1, 1968, 21 UST 483, TIAS No. 6839, 719 U.N.T.S. 161, 7 ILM 809. The treaty has over 175 states parties.

118 The Structure and Content of Agreements Between the Agency and States Required in Connection with the Treaty on the Non-Proliferation of Nuclear Weapons, IAEA Doc. INFCIRC/153 (May 1971).

119 Antarctic Treaty (adopted 1 December 1959, entered into force 23 June 1961) 402 U.N.T.S. 71, Art. 5. Several regions of the world have similarly declared themselves nuclear weapons free zones. See the Treaty of Tlatelolco for the Prohibition of Nuclear Weapons in

the moon is equally forbidden by the Agreement Governing the Activities of States on the Moon and Other Celestial Bodies.[120] Finally, in 1996 the Nuclear Test Ban Treaty of 1963 was expanded to ban all categories of nuclear tests by a Comprehensive Nuclear Ban Treaty and a Protocol which complements it.[121]

3.1 *Security of Nuclear Materials*

In addition to the IAEA Statute and the NPT, several other treaties address the protection of nuclear materials. The most important is the 1980 Convention on the Physical Protection of Nuclear Material, but other agreements also add protective norms, especially the 1994 Convention on Nuclear Safety and the 1997 Convention on the Safety of Spent Fuel Management and on the Safety of Radioactive Waste Management. To these must be added the IAEA recommendations which are linked to the treaties and provide specifications and details of necessary measures. The recommendations can be incorporated into a binding treaty, but even without this they are widely followed.

Separate instruments govern matters of transport and radiological emergencies. Regulations on the transport of nuclear material are contained within general conventional norms concerning transport by road, rail, sea[122] and air, supplemented at the request of the United Nations Economic and Social Council (ECOSOC), by an IAEA Regulation on the safe transport of radioactive materials, drafted in 1961 and periodically updated since that time. A separate Code of Practice governs the transboundary movement of radioactive waste and is discussed later in this chapter.[123] The general IAEA transport code contains recommendations formulated so that they can be easily incorporated into the domestic legislative provisions of member states. The recommendations set appropriate technical criteria (e.g. packaging, handling, and other aspects of transport) but also contain provisions relating to the institution of administrative procedures (e.g. verifications, procedures in case of accident).

Latin America, Feb. 14, 1967; South Pacific Nuclear Free Zone Treaty, Aug. 6, 1985; African Nuclear Weapon Free Zone Treaty, April 11, 1996; South-East Asia Nuclear Free Zone Treaty, Dec. 15, 1996.

120 December 5, 1979, Art. 3, para. 3; G.A. Res. 34/68; UNGAOR Supp. No. 46 at 77, UN Doc. A/34/46, 18 ILM 1434 (1979).

121 Comprehensive Nuclear-Test-Ban Treaty (adopted 10 September 1996) UN Doc A/50/1027.

122 See e.g., the IMO Code for the Safe Carriage of Irradiated Nuclear Fuel, Plutonium, and High-Level Radioactive Waste in Flasks on Board Ships, IMO Assembly Res. A. 748 (18) (Nov. 4, 1993).

123 See IAEA Code of Practice on the International Transboundary Movement of Radioactive Waste (Dec. 11, 1991), 30 ILM 556.

In 1972 the IAEA issued its first recommendations for the physical protection of nuclear materials, aimed at avoiding theft or sabotage. To strengthen the normative base on this issue, the member states subsequently negotiated the Convention on the Physical Protection of Nuclear Material.[124] The treaty establishes a framework for international cooperation to protect civilian nuclear material while in storage and transport. Its aims are to avert the potential dangers of unlawful taking and use of nuclear materials; adopt appropriate and effective measures to ensure the prevention, detention and punishment of such offenses; establish effective measures for the physical protection of nuclear material; and facilitate its safe transfer.[125] The provisions focus on the obligations of states during the transport of nuclear material to ensure a minimum level of physical protection. In 2005, the Convention was amended.[126] The most important addition of the amendment is that it extends the scope of the Convention significantly, now also covering the physical protection of nuclear facilities and including the use of nuclear material for peaceful purposes in domestic use, storage and transport.[127] Additionally, it criminalizes acts of sabotage or trafficking of nuclear facilities or nuclear materials.[128] The amendment entered into force on May 8, 2016.

With the dissolution of the Soviet Union and rising threat of terrorist attacks, the IAEA revised its recommendations based an expert proposal entitled 'Physical Protection Objectives and Fundamental Principles'.[129] The objectives are to (1) protect against unauthorized removal of nuclear material in use and storage, and during transport, (2) implement rapid and comprehensive measures to locate and recover missing or stolen nuclear material, (3) protect against the sabotage of nuclear facilities or of nuclear material in use and storage, and during transport, and (4) mitigate or minimize the radiological consequences of sabotage. Each state is responsible for the establishment, implementation and maintenance of its own effective physical protection regime, which should be based upon a legislative and regulatory framework, designate a competent authority, establish the responsibility of the licence holders, and elaborate contingency plans.

124 Convention on the Physical Protection of Nuclear Material (adopted 26 October 1979, entered into force 8 February 1987) 1456 U.N.T.S. 246.

125 ibid preamble.

126 Amendment to the Convention on the Physical Protection of Nuclear Material (adopted 8 July 2005, entry into force 8 May 2016) 3132 U.N.T.S. 136.

127 ibid para. 4 and 5.

128 ibid para. 3 and 6.

129 IAEA, GOV/2001/41, August 15, 2001, 41 ILM 737 (2002).

As for operations using nuclear materials, the IAEA has carried out a program aimed at establishing codes of good practices and guidelines relating to the safety of nuclear facilities. These texts form a body of regulation in five chapters concerning government, siting of facilities, construction, operation and quality controls[130] and are designed to lead to the elaboration of consistent national regulations. Each chapter is introduced by a 'code of good practice' and contains a number of safety standards. Current recommendations for strengthening physical protection systems include making standards mandatory for domestic uses, raising standards, and requiring international inspections or enforcement mechanisms to provide verification of compliance.

THE IAEA further developed the law by sponsoring the adoption in Vienna, on June 17, 1994, of a Convention on Nuclear Safety. It entered into force after only two years on October 24, 1996, probably due to the awareness of the danger posed by some unsafe conditions in nuclear installations in former parts of the Soviet Union. Its objective is to achieve and maintain a high level of nuclear safety worldwide through the enhancement of national measures and international co-operation including safety-related technical co-operation (Art. 1(i)). The Convention reaffirms that the responsibility for nuclear safety rests with the state having jurisdiction over a nuclear installation. It entails a commitment to apply fundamental safety principles for such installations (Preamble).

The general obligation of the contracting parties is to establish and maintain effective defenses in nuclear installations against potential radiological hazards (Art. 1(ii)), in particular by reviewing as soon as possible the safety of existing nuclear installations (Art. 6). The Convention stresses the importance of the legislative and regulatory framework which each party shall establish and maintain to govern the safety of nuclear installations, including a system of licensing and inspection and assessment to ascertain compliance with applicable regulations and the term of licences (Art. 7). The licence holder has primary responsibility for the safety of the installation (Art. 9). A regulatory body shall be established or designated in each contracting party (Art. 8) and adequate financial resources made available to support the safety of each nuclear installation throughout its life (Art. 11(1)). States parties must establish and implement quality assurance programs for satisfying specified requirements for all activities important to nuclear safety throughout the life of a nuclear installation (Art. 11).

130 IAEA, 'International Atomic Energy Agency, Regulation of Nuclear Activities' (1986), 13.

In addition to the general safety norms the Convention includes specific prescriptions concerning the siting (Art. 17), the design and construction (Art. 18), and the operation (Art. 19) of nuclear installations. States parties must periodically report (Art. 5) and hold meetings for reviewing the reports that are filed (Art. 20). The IAEA provides the secretariat for the meetings (Art. 28).

3.2 *Nuclear Accidents*

THE IAEA elaborated directives concerning the procedures to be followed in case of nuclear accident. These directives were published in 1969; they were further developed in 1981 and in 1985, but not implemented as they should have been, as the Chernobyl accident demonstrated.

On April 26, 1986, at 1:23 in the morning, an explosion occurred in reactor Number 4 of the Chernobyl nuclear power plant, near Prypiat, a town of 25,000 inhabitants situated 130 km north of Kiev, Ukraine, in the Soviet Union. An investigation which took place after the accident established that negligence led to the explosion. The procedure to stop the reactor for routine maintenance had begun at the time of the accident, but before it was completed, management at the plant had decided to proceed with tests without obtaining the authorization of the responsible authority. They also declined to wait for the properly prepared team which would have been present the following night. The tests were insufficiently monitored and the necessary safety measures were not taken, with the result that overheating caused a chemical explosion. The resulting fire melted a portion of the uranium fuel. Although there was no nuclear explosion and the core of the reactor did not melt, the fire which engulfed the reactor was serious and released a large quantity of radioactive material into the air.

Large amounts of fallout occurred near the plant and spread beyond. Between April 27 and May 8, nearly 50,000 persons were evacuated from towns located within a 30 kilometer radius of the plant. Two persons were immediately killed by the explosion, 29 died shortly after, and 203 were afflicted with radiation poisoning. The foreign consequences were also severe, even though no deaths were immediately attributed to the accident. Following rapid changes in the wind direction, the radioactive cloud which had formed crossed the airspace of a series of countries beginning with those of Scandinavia. Four days after the incident, radiation measurements along the Swedish coast were ten times higher than normal.

The radioactive cloud moved south, crossing Germany, Austria, Switzerland, Yugoslavia and Italy. Preliminary studies showed that about half the radioactive material consisted of iodine, but other more persistent elements, like cesium, were detected. On May 4, unusually high levels of radioactivity were found in the milk on farms in Austria, Hungary, Italy, Sweden and Yugoslavia, and relatively high values of Cesium-137 in milk on farms in Switzerland, the United Kingdom, Austria and Germany. The radioactive half-life of Iodine-131 is only about 8 days, while the half-life of Cesium-137 is approximately thirty years, meaning the latter could persist in the environment at significant levels for well over a century after the Chernobyl release.

No conventional international regulation applied at the time the accident occurred in the Soviet Union. The interpretation then given to the Convention on Long-Range Transboundary Air Pollution[131] excluded pollution by radioactive elements. The USSR was not a contracting party to the Vienna Convention on Civil Liability for Nuclear Damage.[132] Indeed, among the states that suffered effects from the radioactive cloud, only Yugoslavia had signed and ratified the Convention. There remained, therefore, only the recourse to general rules of international environmental law.

The IAEA took action after being requested to assist in fact-finding concerning the circumstances of the accident and to prepare a text transforming certain principles of international environmental law into obligatory rules applicable in cases of nuclear accidents of international scope. The Governing Council of the Agency decided, in an extraordinary session held May 21, to convoke a group of governmental experts in order to elaborate measures to reinforce international cooperation in the field of nuclear security and radioactive protection. This meeting took place in Vienna from July 21 to August 15, 1986, and resulted in two conventions which were subsequently adopted by the IAEA General Conference, meeting in extraordinary session from September 24 to 26. The Convention on Early Notification of a Nuclear Accident, signed September 26, entered into force on October 27; the Convention on Assistance in the Case of a Nuclear Accident or Radiological Emergency was signed the same day and also rapidly ratified by the signatories.

The first of the two conventions, relating to rapid notification of nuclear accidents, expresses and gives concrete application to the duty to inform other states that may be affected by an accident causing environmental harm. While making this obligation explicit, the Convention remains a cautious text. It does not speak to the problems of liability and reparation for damage, but instead of the necessity for states to furnish pertinent information on nuclear accidents as soon as possible. The drafters rejected Germany's proposal for an explicit

131 Convention on Long-Range Transboundary Air Pollution (adopted 13 November 1979, entered into force 16 March 1983) 1302 U.N.T.S. 217.

132 Vienna Convention on Civil Liability for Nuclear Damage (adopted 21 May 1963, entered into force 12 November 1977) 1063 UNTS 265.

proclamation that all states have a responsibility to see that their nuclear activities are carried out in such a manner as to protect the health and security of the public and the environment.

The essential obligation of states parties is to notify without delay of any nuclear accident and to rapidly furnish pertinent available information in order to limit as much as possible the radioactive consequences in other countries.[133] The types of information to be furnished are detailed in Article 5. They should include, to the extent the notifying state knows: the exact time, location and the nature of the accident, the installation or activity concerned, the presumed or known cause, the likely evolution of the accident, and the general characteristics of the radioactive discharge. The state should also provide information on the current meteorological conditions, and protective measures taken or projected outside the site. This information should be supplemented as new data become available. The states affected can demand further information or consultations in order to limit as much as possible the radioactive consequences within the limits of their jurisdictions.[134] Information furnished confidentially should not be released to the public.[135] Each state should indicate to the Agency in Vienna – which should also receive the information and transmit it to each state that requests it – the responsible authorities and the points of contact capable of furnishing and receiving the notification.[136]

Contrary to other provisions of the Convention adopted without great difficulty, Article 1, which determines when notification is required, gave rise to serious disagreement. Its first paragraph was finally approved as follows:

> This Convention shall apply in the event of any accident involving facilities or activities of a state party or of persons or legal entities under its jurisdiction or control, referred to in paragraph 2 below, from which a release of radioactive material occurs or is likely to occur and which has resulted or may result in an international transboundary release that could be of radiological safety significance for another state.[137]

According to paragraph two, the obligation to notify applies to all accidents from any nuclear reactor to any nuclear fuel cycle facility, radioactive waste

133 Convention on Early Notification of a Nuclear Accident (adopted 26 September 1986, entered into force 27 October 1986) 1439 U.N.T.S. 275, Art. 2.

134 ibid, Art. 2.

135 ibid, Art. 5, para. 3.

136 ibid, Arts. 4, 7.

137 Art. 1.

management facility, the transport and storage of nuclear fuels, as well as any operation involving the manufacture, use, storage, disposal or transport of radioisotopes, including the use of nuclear-powered spacecraft. Nuclear arms are not mentioned, and the *travaux préparatoires* and the terms of Article 3 indicate that this omission is in fact an exclusion. Article 3 envisages that 'other nuclear accidents' may be the subject of notification on a voluntary basis, but notification in these situations is not required by the Convention. In fact, all nuclear powers have declared themselves ready to notify of such accidents.

The Convention on Assistance in the Case of a Nuclear Accident or Radiological Emergency, also adopted on September 26, 1986, similarly corresponds to rules already existing in international law. However, even if customary international law imposes on states a general obligation to cooperate, it does not indicate the means and methods of the assistance, which must be explicitly detailed by conventional law. The Vienna Convention on Assistance reinforces the duty to aid states that are victims of catastrophes, and expands it in particular to radiological catastrophes, developing the implications of this expanded norm. The Convention still remains, however, a framework treaty which explicitly calls for the conclusion of bilateral or multilateral arrangements and action of the Agency to promote, facilitate and encourage cooperation between the states parties.

The instrument on assistance traces a general framework for cooperation between states on the one hand, and between the states and the IAEA on the other, in the case of nuclear accident or other radiological emergency. It seems that the last term can be interpreted as covering any danger caused by radiation, whatever the cause, and includes nuclear arms testing. Any state which is exposed can claim assistance, whether or not the origin of the accident or emergency is found within its territory, under its jurisdiction or under its control.[138] Thus, in the case of the Chernobyl accident, the states affected by the radioactive cloud could have demanded the aid of other states or of the IAEA. It is clear, however, that states parties do not accept any obligation other than cooperating between themselves and with the Agency in order to facilitate early response.[139]

When there is a question of mutual assistance in response to an emergency, two types of measures are foreseen by the Convention: preventive measures and those to be undertaken when the situation is actually presented. In the first category, the Convention provides for identifying and notifying the IAEA of experts, equipment and materials which could be made available to provide

138 Art. 2, para. 1.

139 Art. 1, para. 1.

assistance, as well as the terms, notably financial, under which such assistance could be furnished,[140] the authorities competent to intervene and points of contact,[141] the emergency plans and implementation of programs of assistance and monitoring of radioactivity.[142] When a crisis arises, the state party to the Convention that requires assistance should indicate the scope and type of assistance required and should furnish all information which could be necessary.[143] Each state may request assistance relating to medical treatment or the temporary relocation of persons involved in a nuclear accident or radiological emergency into the territory of another state.[144]

The state requiring assistance has direction, control, coordination and supervision of all assistance on its territory. Within possible limits, it should furnish the equipment and local services necessary for the proper and effective administration of assistance. On the other hand, measures which occur on the territory of the state which furnishes the assistance are under the latter's control.[145]

The Convention also addresses the issue of reimbursement of costs. If the state which furnishes the assistance does not offer its services freely, the state having requested the assistance should reimburse the assisting state, as well as any persons or organizations acting on its behalf, for all costs incurred for the services rendered and for any other costs of assistance.[146] Article 8 provides that privileges and immunities are accorded to personnel who furnish assistance to a foreign state – immunity from arrest, detention, and legal process in the jurisdiction – and also exemption from taxation, duties, or other charges.

The Convention grants a large role to IAEA in the organization and coordination of assistance operations. The Agency should facilitate cooperation with and between states;[147] it receives information relating to the capacities of intervention of different states;[148] it should itself respond to certain requests for assistance;[149] it centralizes information concerning the responsible authorities and the points of contact different states;[150] it collects and disseminates

140 Art. 2, para. 4.
141 Art. 4.
142 Art. 5b.
143 Art. 2, para. 2.
144 Art. 2, para. 5.
145 Art. 3.
146 Art. 7.
147 Art. 1, para. 1.
148 Art. 2, para. 4.
149 Art. 2, para. 6(a).
150 Art. 4.

all information regarding available resources and emergency situations, and helps with the elaboration of emergency plans, etc.[151]

On the whole, it can be said that the tragedy of the Chernobyl accident significantly influenced the development of international environmental law, and demonstrated the inevitable character of international institutions at a moment when these organizations were the object of serious criticism. States recognized the gravity of the accident and above all, that similar situations that could arise in the future.

Finally, it is interesting to note that it seems that no government pushed to conclude rules on state responsibility for accidental environmental harm. Negotiations would no doubt have been lengthy and perhaps unsuccessful over such matters (e.g. standard of care (strict liability or negligence), proximate harm, and mitigation of damages). The difficulty of evaluating the cost of the consequences of the Chernobyl accident, especially the precautionary measures taken by the affected countries, also may have been a determinant factor in avoiding the issue of state responsibility. It also seems, however, to be consistent with the general reticence displayed towards rules imposing international responsibility or liability on states for damages caused by that state or its citizens. There remains a preference for preventative rather than remedial measures.

The world was reminded of this history on March 11, 2011, when the Fukushima Daiichi nuclear power plant was damaged as a result of an earthquake and tsunami that had cut the power supply. This took away the possibility for controlling and cooling the reactors. The accident is considered the worst nuclear accident since Chernobyl, leading as well to a release of radioactive material into the environment.[152] Concern over environmental impacts of the Fukushima incident was aggravated when in 2021, Japan announced its plan to release into the Pacific purified waste water that had been used to cool down Fukushima's nuclear reactors following the accident.[153] It followed through on this plan in 2023, over numerous concerns raised by surrounding

---

151 Art. 5.

152 WHO, *Health Risk Assessment from the nuclear accident after the 2011 Great East Japan Earthquake and Tsunami based on preliminary dose estimation* (2013); For a comparison of the environmental impacts of Chernobyl and Fukushima, see Georg Steinhauser, Alexander Brandl and Thomas Johnson, 'Comparison of the Chernobyl and Fukushima nuclear accidents: a review of the environmental impacts' (2014) 470(471) *Science of the Total Environment* 870.

153 Chie Kobayashi, Blake Essig and Nectar Gan, 'Japan to start releasing treated Fukushima water into sea in two years' (2021) CNN <https://edition.cnn.com/2021/04/12/asia/japan-fukushima-water-intl-hnk/index.html> last accessed 19 April 2024.

states such as China and Russia.[154] These critics have called into question the safety of this waste water discharge, regardless of the IAEA's assurance that it aligns with global safety standards.[155] Despite this global and regional attention, the Fukushima incident has not given rise to a surge in international law-making on the scale of Chernobyl.[156]

3.3 *Radioactive Wastes*

One of the principal problems posed by nuclear activities is the disposal of radioactive wastes. It is therefore important to regulate the discharge of nuclear matter into the environment. In many cases the disposal of radioactive wastes is accomplished within a state's borders, but international shipments of radioactive wastes are a concern. The principal questions in international law level thus concern transport and the immersion of radioactive waste in areas beyond national jurisdiction.

Several international conventions contain provisions aimed at the dumping of radioactive wastes. The most important of them is the London Convention on the Prevention of Pollution by Dumping of Wastes and Other Matter ('London Dumping Convention') of December 29, 1972. Article IV of this convention, combined with Annex I, forbids the dumping of 'high-level radioactive wastes or other high level radioactive matter'.[157] In 1983, the Seventh Consultative Meeting adopted a non-binding resolution establishing a moratorium on all dumping at sea of radioactive materials pending scientific studies. Several states publicly opted not to comply, including many of the nuclear weapons states. In 1994, the IMO made the ban mandatory and this was accepted by all states parties except Russia. Annex I paragraph 3 now provides that materials containing more than the *de minimis* levels of radioactivity shall not be considered eligible for dumping; the ban is subject to a 25 year scientific review. An international evaluation process approved by the 21st Consultative Meeting of

154 Ministry of Foreign Affairs of the People's Republic of China, 'Remarks by Director-General of the Department of Arms Control of the Foreign Ministry Sun Xiaobo at the "Linjia 7 Salon – Press Conference on Japan's Disposal of the Fukushima Nuclear Contaminated Water"' (2023); China Aerospace Studies Institute, 'In their own words: Joint Statement of the Russian Federation and the People's Republic of China on the International Relations Entering a New Era and the Global Sustainable Development' (2022).

155 IAEA, 'Comprehensive Report on the Safety Review of the Alps-Treated Water at the Fukushima Daiichi Nuclear Power Station' (2023).

156 This does not mean that there was no impact at all: for example, the IAEA Action Plan on Nuclear Safety was endorsed by IAEA member states in September 2011.

157 Defined on public health, biological or other grounds by the competent international body in this field (at present the International Atomic Energy Agency).

the London Convention defines the *de minimis* level of radioactivity.[158] In 2013, at its 60th Plenary Meeting, the UN General Assembly also adopted a resolution on the prohibition on the dumping of radioactive wastes.[159]

As to transport, the IAEA adopted a Code of Practice on the International Movement of Radioactive Waste in 1991. These recommendations have been adopted by the UN and all other international organizations concerned with the transport of hazardous goods, as well as by a large number of states. In general, the regulations hold the shipper responsible for design safety and for the correct assembly of the package, as well as for labeling and marking. The carrier is responsible for providing the necessary control measures during transport and storage in transit. Access to packages should be restricted. As noted above, the 1997 Spent Fuel Management treaty also contains safety measures for the transport. States parties must develop programs to ensure that transboundary movement is properly authorized and transpires with prior notification and consent of the receiving state. The latter may consent only if it has the technical and administrative capacity as well as regulatory structure to manage the spent fuel or radioactive waste.

4 Biotechnology

Throughout history, farmers have used selective breeding to alter their livestock and crops for qualities sought by the farmers or consumers. They have also applied biological fermentation to produce new products and increase the period of conserving food. These techniques rely on genetic variation, including mutations, already present in species and populations of flora and fauna. All major crops and farm animals are the product of some degree of human intervention.

Genetic modification or biotechnology differs from the directed but natural processes of selective breeding. Genetic engineering isolates genes from an organism and transfers one or more to another organism, across populations or across species or phyla. Animal genes may be inserted into plants and vice versa. Once inserted, the genes may be transmitted to subsequent generations.

The 1992 UN Convention on Biological Diversity defines biotechnology to include any technological application that utilizes biological systems, living organisms, or derivations of them, to create or modify products or processes to

158 UN, Report of the Secretary-General, March 2000, UN A/55/61.

159 UN, Resolution adopted by the General Assembly, 11 December 2013, A/RES/68/53.

a specific use.[160] One of the most controversial subjects concerning this science is the scope of potential risks associated with the handling and introduction into the environment of living modified organisms (LMOs) or, as they were first referred to, genetically-modified organisms. The need to promote biosafety has centered on two related issues: first, the handling of LMOs at the laboratory level, in order to protect workers and prevent the accidental liberation of such organisms into the surrounding ecosystem ('contained use'); second, the need for regulatory systems to govern the deliberate release of LMOs into the environment, either for testing or commercial purposes.

Genetic engineering has reached the point where living organisms can be adapted and created in the laboratory. Many of these LMOs are not intended to stay in the laboratory, however. Genetically altered corn and soybean seeds are widely used in for example North America, and legal in various countries across the world.[161] Biotechnology is applied in many fields, but its use to raise crop yields has received the most publicity and been the most controversial, including efforts to broaden the germplasm basis from which new genetic combinations can be created and improving and speeding up the propagation of plants. The most widely used and commercially successful application of plant biotechnology is the rapid and large-scale multiplication of plants through clones produced in tissue culture.

Many scientists see biotechnology as permitting them to pursue plant breeding efforts, with favorable impact on food supplies, international trade in agricultural products, the environment and existing plant resources. Aware of possible benefits, a substantial number of scientists nonetheless urge caution in releasing genetically engineered organisms, because of the possibility that such organisms might have an unfavorable impact upon the environment and because considerable scientific uncertainty exists about the scope and degree of the environmental risks. There is a fear that genetically altered genes may naturally transfer to wild-grown relatives, with unforeseeable consequences. Early on, this major negative impact was already illustrated by the harm to monarch butterflies caused by the protein used in genetically altered corn to repel certain pests.[162]

160 Convention on Biological Diversity (adopted 5 June 1992, entry into force 29 December 1993) 1760 U.N.T.S. 79 (CBD) art. 2.

161 ISAAA, 'Executive Summary: Global Status of Commercialized Biotech/GM Crops in 2019: Biotech Crops Drive Socio-Economic Development and Sustainable Environment in the New Frontier' (2019) ISAAA Brief 55.

162 See 'Monarch Larvae Killed by Bt-Dusted Leaves, Iowa State University Researchers Report' (2000) BNA In'tl Evnt'l Rep 682.

Particular concerns arise over the release of LMOs in or close to a center of genetic diversity of that crop. Mass production of identical plant materials introduces greater danger of genetic destruction because all specimens are equally vulnerable to a single disease or pest. No resistant varieties remain as alternative sources. The widespread use of cloned crops or artificial seeds to replace sexually reproducing crops thus likely increases crop vulnerability. Finally, the release of genetically modified micro-organisms (bacteria and fungi) could pose particular problems for the environment for the reasons stated above.

THE OECD was one of the first organizations to act on genetic modifications. In 1986, the OECD published an extensive report identifying safety considerations associated with LMOs but finding that the development of international guidelines was premature.[163] A report in 1992, Safety Considerations for Biotechnology, contained general principles for the design and safety assessment of small scale-field testing of LMOs that have low or negligible risk. In terms of important subsequent developments, it may be noted that the 'OECD Conference on Genome Editing: Applications in Agriculture – Implications for Health, Environment and Regulation' was held at the OECD headquarter in Paris in June 2018. The conference 'aimed to provide a clearer understanding of the regulatory considerations raised by products of genome editing, pointing towards a coherent policy approach to facilitate innovations involving genome editing'.[164] This suggests that the OECD is, at this point in time, much more willing to consider the benefits of genome editing than it has been in the past.

Uncertainty surrounding the environmental impacts of LMOs is recognized in the Convention on Biological Diversity (CBD) which does not define the term 'living modified organism' but calls on the contracting parties to consider the need for a protocol setting out procedures for the safe transfer, handling and use of any living modified organism resulting from biotechnology that may have adverse effect on the environment (Art. 19(3)). The Convention itself obligates parties to 'provide any available information about the use and safety regulations required by th[e] contracting party in handling such organisms, as well as any available information on the potential adverse impact of the

163 OECD, 'Recombinant DNA Safety Considerations--Safety Considerations for Industrial, Agricultural and Environmental Applications of Organisms Derived by Recombinant DNA Techniques' (1986).

164 Steffi Friedrichs et al., 'Meeting report of the OECD conference on "Genome Editing: Applications in Agriculture – Implications for Health, Environment and Regulation"' (2019) 28 *Transgenic Research* 419.

specified organisms to concerned' to any party into which those organisms are introduced.

In respect to *in situ* conservation, the CBD requires the parties to establish or maintain means to regulate, manage or control the risks associated with the use and release of living modified organisms resulting from biotechnology which are likely to have adverse environmental impacts that could affect the conservation and sustainable use of biological diversity, taking into account the risks to human health. The Convention also calls for implementing the rights of countries of origin of genetic resources or countries providing genetic resources, particularly developing countries, to benefit from the biotechnological development and the commercial utilization of products derived from such resources (Art. 15.4(j)).

While thus expressing some concerns over the risks of biotechnology, both the CBD and UNCED's Agenda 21 encourage such technology in order to increase benefits from biological resources. Agenda 21, chapter 16, 'Environmentally Sound Management of Biotechnology' states that its goal is to foster international principles for the environmental management of biotechnology, as well as to promote sustainable applications of biotechnology.[165] In addition to increasing the availability of food and improving human health, the program calls for enhancing protection of the environment and 'establishing enabling mechanisms for the development and the environmentally sound application of biotechnology'. States are to consider the need for and feasibility of internationally agreed guidelines on safety in biotechnology releases, including risk assessment and risk management, and consider studying the feasibility of guidelines which could facilitate national legislation on liability and compensation. In national legislation governments are encouraged to promote rights associated with intellectual property and informal innovations, including farmer's and breeder's rights.

Decision II/5, adopted by the Conference of the Parties in 1995, expressed concern about the significant gaps that remain in knowledge about between LMOs and the environment and called for application of the precautionary principle pending further scientific findings.[166] The same meeting authorized

165 Chapter 16 at 218. Other sections of Agenda 21 containing references to biotechnology are Chapter 14 on sharing of research and plant genetic resources; Chapter 19, risk management of hazardous products; and Chapter 15, conservation of biological diversity.

166 *A Call to Action: Decisions and Ministerial Statement from the Second Meeting of the Conference of the Parties to the Convention on Biological Diversity, Jakarta, Indonesia, Nov. 6–17, 1995* (UNEP/CBD 1996).

an Ad hoc Working Group to begin negotiations on a biosafety protocol to the Convention.

After extensive negotiations, the parties to the Convention on Biological Diversity adopted a Protocol on Biosafety on January 29, 2000.[167] The objective of the Protocol is to contribute to ensuring an adequate level of protection in the safe transfer, handling and use of living biotechnology-modified organisms that may have adverse effects on the conservation and sustainable use of biological diversity, taking into account risks to human health and specifically focusing on transboundary movements.[168] The Protocol does not apply to the transboundary movement of living modified organisms which are pharmaceuticals for human use and that are addressed by relevant international agreements or organizations, nor to the transit and contained use of living modified organisms. These exceptions do not preclude a Party from subjecting such actions to prior risk assessment.[169]

The Protocol institutes an 'advance informed agreement' procedure which mirrors prior informed consent procedures contained in other international treaties. Thus, the state of export must notify or require the exporter to notify, in writing, the competent national authority of the state of import prior to the intentional transboundary movement of a living modified organism. Annex I of the Protocol specifies the information which must be transmitted. It requires technical data and a risk assessment report consistent with the conditions set forth in Annex III. The Party of import is to acknowledge the notification in writing, but failure to do so does not imply consent to the shipment.[170] The importing state has 270 days from the date of notification to make a decision on permitting or denying the importation and must transmit the decision to the notifying party and to a Biosafety Clearing House established by the Protocol (Arts. 10 and 20). A special procedure is foreseen for domestic use of LMOs, including marketing a living modified organism that may be subject to transboundary movement for direct use as food or feed or for processing (Art. 11). Annex II lists the information required for such use, which may include a risk assessment report.

Apart from the intentional movements of LMOs, each Party shall take appropriate measures to notify affected or potentially affected states, the Biodiversity

167 Although the Protocol was adopted in Montreal, it is known as the Cartagena Protocol because of the importance of the prior negotiations which took place in Cartagena, Colombia.

168 Preamble, Arts. 1 and 4.

169 Arts. 5 and 6.

170 Art. 9.

Clearing House and, when appropriate, relevant international organizations, when it knows of a release that leads or may lead to an unintentional transboundary movement of a living modified organism that is likely to have significant adverse effects on the conservation and sustainable use of biological diversity or creates risks to human health.[171] States parties also must prevent and, if appropriate penalize illegal transboundary movements of living modified organisms.[172] Generally states parties are to promote and facilitate public awareness, education, consultation and participation, encompassing access to information on living modified organisms that may be imported, but the notifier is permitted to identify information to be treated as confidential.[173] Finally, compliance monitoring procedures are foreseen. Parties to the Protocol shall, at intervals to be determined by the Conference of the Parties to the Biodiversity Convention, report to that Conference on measures that they have taken to implement the Protocol and the states parties should develop additional cooperative procedures and institutional mechanisms to promote compliance and address cases of non-compliance.[174]

Because the CBD does not contain a reference to the precautionary principle it was a focus of debate during negotiations for the Biosafety Protocol, especially on the extent to which measures could be taken by states to exclude LMOs either on scientific or socio-economic grounds. In the end, it was agreed that parties must undertake a process of scientific risk assessment that conforms to the Protocol's requirements (carried out 'in a scientifically sound and transparent manner', on a case-by-case basis, according to the provisions of Annex III, Art. 15). Perhaps best reflecting the divergence of views, Annex III(4) provides that the 'lack of scientific knowledge or scientific consensus should not necessarily be interpreted as indicating a particular level of risk, an absence of risk, or an acceptable risk'.

Another area of disagreement centered on the inclusion of products made of LMOs or processed materials of LMO origin. In the end, such products and materials were not included, although they are encompassed in the risk assessment procedures of Article 23(3)(c), Annex I(1) and Annex III(5). As discussed in Chapter 17, the Protocol has a complex relationship with the international trade agreements of the WTO that is reflected in an explanatory note accompanying its Preamble, which states that it 'is not intended to subordinate this Protocol to other international agreements'.

171 Art. 17.
172 Art. 25.
173 Arts. 21, 23.
174 Arts. 33 and 34.

The Protocol is open for signature only by states that are party to the CBD. As is increasingly common in regard to international environmental agreements, the CBD Conference of the Parties decided to establish an Inter-Governmental Committee for the Cartagena Protocol on Biosafety to take action pending entry into force of the protocol. In particular it was charged with preparing decisions to be adopted at the first meeting of the parties to the Protocol.[175] The Committee met in three sessions between 2001–2003. The protocol entered into force in September 2003. Since then, it has accumulated a more recent Protocol: the Nagoya-Kuala Lumpur Supplementary Protocol on Liability and Redress, which serves exactly the purposes for which it was named.[176] It also contains provisions on civil liability.

On the regional level, the European Community issued directives in 1990 creating lengthy series of control procedures both for laboratory research and for release of LMOs. The first Directive,[177] on Contained Use of Genetically Modified Microorganisms (GMM), was amended in 1998 to establish four classes of contained uses and the restrictions that apply to each.[178] Although this directive is no longer in force, the current directive of 2009 uses the same classes.[179] The four classes are: Class 1, activities of 'no or negligible risk' to human health or the environment; Class 2, 'low risk' activities; Class 3, 'moderate risk' activities; and Class 4, 'high risk' activities. Any user of a GMM in a contained use must follow procedures set forth in Annex III of the predecessor Directive and its future amendments for determining the class to which a particular activity belongs. This includes an assessment of the risks to human health and the environment that the contained uses may incur, including the question of waste disposal. The directive requires the users to maintain a record of the assessment and make it available to the competent national authority.

The precautionary principle has been incorporated by requiring that 'where there is a doubt as to which class is appropriate for the proposed contained use, the more stringent protective measures shall be applied' unless there is sufficient evidence according to the competent authority that less stringent

175 Conference of the Parties to the Convention on Biological Diversity, 'Decision EM-I/3: Adoption of the Cartagena Protocol and Interim Arrangements' (29 January 2000) UNEP /CBD/ExCOP/1/3, Annex.

176 Nagoya-Kuala Lumpur Supplementary Protocol on Liability and Redress to the Cartagena Protocol on Biosafety (adopted 15 October 2010, entry into force 5 March 2018).

177 Community Directive 90/219/EEC of April 23, 1990, O.J. L 117 (8/5/90).

178 Directive 98/81/EC, O.J. L. 330 (12/12/98), amends and substantially revises Directive 90/212/EEC on the Contained Use of Genetically Modified Microorganisms.

179 Directive 2009/41/EC, O.J. L 125 (21 May 2009) 75, art. 4(3).

measures are justified. Any use in classes 2–4 requires prior notification of the competent authority and prior written authorization of the authority if the use is in class 3 or 4. Further notification is required for any relevant new information or modifications that could have significant consequences for the risks posed. Users must develop and make available to the public contingency plan for emergencies. Member states are required to notify annually the European Commission of all Class 3 and 4 uses.

Cultivation of GMOs in the territory of member states is regulated in Directive (EU) 2015/412. It is for example obligatory for GMOs to undergo an individual risk assessment before being allowed on the EU market, taking into account the direct, indirect, immediate and delayed effects, as well as the cumulative long-term effects, on human health and the environment.[180] Member states that allow GMOs to be cultivated, shall take appropriate measures in border areas to avoid cross-border contamination.[181]

Directive 2001/18/EC, replacing Directive 90/220/EEC,[182] concerns the voluntary release of genetically modified organisms into the environment. The precautionary principle is explicitly incorporated into several provisions. In particular, Article 4 provides that member states, 'in accordance with the precautionary principle, shall ensure that all appropriate measures are taken to avoid adverse effects on human health and the environment which might arise from the deliberate release or the placing on the market of GMOs'. Applicants for release must carry out an environmental risk assessment of the GMO being proposed for authorization. Environmental risk assessment means that 'direct or indirect, immediate or delayed risks' shall be evaluated by the national authorities. Assessors may not discount any potential adverse effect on the basis that it is unlikely to occur. (Annex II, C(2)(1)). The authorization system has a ten year limit and renewal is only permitted if monitoring carried out during the period shows no negative results. Labelling of products is also required.

Finally, it should be recalled that the 1993 Council of Europe Convention on Civil Responsibility for Damage Resulting from the Exercise of Activities Dangerous for the Environment specifically covers damage caused by genetically modified organisms.[183] GMOs are defined in the Convention as an organism

180 Directive (EU) 2015/412 O.J. L 68 (13 March 2015) 1, amending Directive 2001/18/EC, preamble and para. 2.

181 ibid Art. 1.

182 Council directive 90/220/EEC of April 23, 1990 (O.J. L 117, May 8, 1990).

183 See supra, Chapter 7

in which the genetic material has been altered in a way which does not occur naturally by mating and/or natural combination.[184]

5 Noise

Society has increasingly recognized excessive noise as a form of pollution. It is both a nuisance and a threat to health.[185] In the EU, at least twenty percent of the population is exposed to levels of noise considered harmful to health.[186] Excessive noise also has severe impact on the environment, for example interfering with sound detection, altering animals' temporal patterns which can impede sleep patterns, and impairing foraging and provisioning rates.[187] The non-binding Stockholm Action Plan addressed the elaboration of norms to combat noise as early as 1972. In addition, as discussed in Chapter 15, several cases submitted to the European Court of Human Rights have alleged that levels of airport noise constitute a violation of their right to privacy and home life guaranteed in the European Convention on Human Rights, Article 8.

International environmental law primarily regulates two forms of noise pollution: airport noise and urban noise. In 1983, the International Civil Aviation Organization (ICAO) established a Committee on Environmental Protection, a technical committee reporting to the ICAO Council, charged with addressing the main environmental problems of civil aviation: pollution caused by aircraft engine emissions and aircraft noise. The main approaches to controlling or reducing aircraft noise seek to reduce the noise at source, use noise abatement operating measures, and adopt land use planning for the siting of airports. The ICAO has also established a noise certification standard in Annex 16 to the Convention on International Civil Aviation.[188]

EU legislation also regulates noise generated by air traffic. An EC Directive adopted in 2002 established rules and procedures with regard to the introduction of noise-related operating restrictions at Community airports in order to limit or reduce the number of people significantly affected by the harmful

184 See for more on the environmental law on biotechnology Matthias Herdegen, *GMOs, Crops and Precaution: biotechnology and international protection of the environment* (The International Law on Biotechnology, Elgar 2023).

185 UNEP, *Noise, Blazes and Mismatches – Emerging Issues of Environmental Concern* (2022).

186 Eulalia Peris, *Environmental noise in Europe 2020* (EEA 2022).

187 See for this and more examples Clinton Francis and Jesse Barber, 'A framework for understanding noise impacts on wildlife: an urgent conservation priority' (2013) 11(6) *Frontiers in Ecology and the Environment* 305.

188 Vol. 1, Pt II, Ch. 4. See, further, the discussion of ICAO in Chapter 5.

effects of noise.[189] The directive has since been replaced by a similar, but more up-to-date regulation.[190]

A growing number of international and regional rules aim to reduce noise from other sources. The EU Environmental Noise Directive[191] aims to define a common approach to prevent or reduce the harmful effects of exposure to noise. 'Environmental noise' is defined as unwanted or harmful outdoor sound created by human activities, including noise emitted by means of transport, road, rail or air traffic and from sites of industrial activity.[192] Noise indicators are proposed and States should make and approve noise maps and action plans for urban areas and major roads, railways and airports. The Directive applies to noise emitted by road and rail vehicles and infrastructure, aircraft, outdoor and industrial equipment and mobile machinery. It applies in noise-sensitive areas such as in public parks and near schools and hospitals. Specific categories of noise emissions are also regulated by EC legislation: motor vehicles,[193] agricultural or forestry tractors[194] and two or three-wheel motor vehicles.[195]

Conclusions

The shift from regulating each sector of the environment to addressing the sources of harm has led to recognition of the interrelated impacts of various human activities. Combining concern over sources of harm and resulting impacts has given rise to broader ecosystem approaches to environmental protection. These approaches are discussed in the following chapter, while Part III of this book applies these integrated approaches to contemporary interfaces between international environmental law and other specialized fields.

189 Directive 2002/30/EC of March 26, 2002, O.J. L 85/40 (3/28/02). The Member States had to implement the Directive by Sept. 28, 2003.

190 EU Regulation No. 598/2014, O.J. L 173 (12 June 14) 65.

191 Directive 2002/49/EC, O.J. L. 189/12 (7/18/02).

192 Art. 3(a).

193 Directive 70/157/EEC of Feb. 6, 1970, O.J. L 42 (2/23/70).

194 Directive 77/311/EEC of March 29, 1977, O.J. L 105 (4/28/77). This Directive is no longer in force, end of validity: 31 December 2009. See currently Regulation (EU) No 167/2013, O.J. L 60 2 March 2013, 1.

195 Directive 92/61/EEC of June 30, 1992, O.J. L 225 (8/10/92) and 2002/51/EC of July 19, 2002, O.J. L 252 (9/20/02). These Directives are no longer in force, end of validity: 8 November 2003 and 31 December 2015. See currently Regulation (EU) No 168/2013, O.J. L 60 2 March 2013, 52.

Bibliography

Baender, M., 'Pesticides and Precaution: The Bamako Convention as a Model for an International Convention on Pesticides Regulation', 24 N.Y.U. J. Int'l L.& POL. 557 (1991).

Colborn, T., Dumanoski, D., & Myers, J., Our Stolen Future (1996).

Colopy, J., 'Poisoning the Developing World: The Exportation of Unregistered and Severely Restricted Pesticides from the United States', 13 UCLA J. Envt'l L. & Pol'y 167 (1995).

Donald, J., 'The Bamako Convention as a Solution to the Problem of Hazardous Waste Exports to Less Developed Countries', 17 Colum. J. Envt'l L. 419 (1992).

Hilz, C., The International Toxic Waste Trade (1992).

Kiss, A., 'The International Control of Transboundary Movement of Hazardous Waste', 26 Texas Int'l L. J. 521 (1991).

Kummer, K. and Rummel-Bulska, I., The Basel Convention on the Control of Transboundary Movement of Hazardous Wastes and Their Disposal (1990).

Kwiatowska, B., and Soons, A. (eds), Transboundary Movements and Disposals of Hazardous Waste in International Law: Basic Documents (1993).

Le Droit Europeen Des Consommateurs et La Gestion Des Dechets – European Consumer Law and Waste Management (Boucqey, N., ed..1999).

Louka, E., Overcoming National Barriers to International Waste Trade (1995).

Mackenzie, R., et al, An Explanatory Guide to the Cartagena Protocol on Biosafety (IUCN, 2003).

OECD, Practical Information for the Implementation of the Oecd Control System: Transfrontier Movements of Wastes Destined for Recovery Operations (1997).

Perez Martin, M.T., Que Fait Le Village Planetaire De Ses Dechets Dangereux? (2001).

Shearer, C., 'Comparative Analysis of the Basel and Bamako Conventions on Hazardous Waste', 23 Envt'l L. 141 (1993).

Uram, C., 'International Regulation of the Sale and Use of Pesticides', 10 NW. J. INT'L & BUS. 460 (1990).

PART 3

Inclusive Environmental Protection

CHAPTER 14

Integrated Environmental Protection

New approaches to achieving effective environmental protection derive from greater knowledge and understanding of the biosphere and its components. Some changes may also be attributed to a greater involvement of non-state actors in the international legal system and a stronger role for international institutions, particularly financial institutions, in developing and applying international environmental law. Increased recognition of the global and multidimensional character of environmental problems and potential remedies is clear. Most states now accept that holistic international efforts are required to address many aspects of environmental deterioration, such as ocean pollution, depletion of stratospheric ozone, the greenhouse effect, and threats to biodiversity. Concern for ecosystems has been broadened due to integrated approaches to safeguarding the planet's environment. The aim of protecting wild fauna and flora is now incorporated in the larger goal of maintaining biological diversity. This means that domesticated species in all their varieties also must survive, as well as insects, moss and microbes. The expanded vision includes efforts to reverse the trend towards monocultural agriculture and stock-breeding, and devotes increased attention to the potential contributions of and threats posed by biotechnology. Climate change is another environmental issue that requires a holistic and integrated approach. As a multifaceted global issue, climate change presents a significant environmental, ecological, and socio-economic challenge. It disrupts natural ecosystems, threatens biodiversity, and exacerbates the degradation of both terrestrial and marine environments. Climate change is not only an environmental problem but also a complex challenge that intersects with various aspects of human life and global governance, requiring integrated, holistic approaches and international cooperation to effectively address its far-reaching impacts.

The evolution of international environmental law has thus led to emphasizing the integration of environmental considerations into policies and institutions concerned with a wide range of human activities. The integrated approach is being applied to activities through 'mainstreaming' environmental protection.[1] Tourism, for example, has risen in the last 60 years from 25

1 Some of the major activities are discussed in the following chapters: human rights, armed conflict, trade and investment.

 | DOI:10.1163/9789047440802_016

million persons a year to 1.3 billion.[2] More than 212 million persons around the world are employed in tourism-related activities. The impact of tourism on the environment can be enormous. On the one hand, tourism raises awareness of the beauty of wilderness areas and landscapes and of the need to protect the environment. On the other hand, it puts pressure on the environment due to the massive utilization of resources needed (water, energy, land) and the emissions produced (waste, used water, noise, air pollution). In many areas, there are too many visitors for the carrying capacity of the area. The need for a holistic approach involving a partnership between tourism, local populations and the environment has led to a new theory of Integrated Total Quality Tourism Management which integrates socio-cultural, economic and environmental aspects in a global fashion.[3]

The Hague Declaration on Tourism (1989) Principle III notes the intrinsic interrelationship between tourism and the environment and sets out measures to ensure an unspoilt natural, cultural and human environment as a condition for the development of tourism. Since the Manila Declaration on World Tourism (1982), the World Tourism Organization has adopted a series of measures concerning relationships. In 1997, the Maldives Declaration on Sustainable Tourism was adopted by tourism and environment ministers of the Asia Pacific region. Essential requirements for sustainable tourism are the promotion of ethics in tourism, reduction of unsustainable patterns of consumption of resources and reduction of wastes; conservation of natural, social and cultural diversity; integration of tourism planning; promotion of the local economy and the participation of the local population, the groups of tourists affected and the general public; the development of responsible tourism marketing; assessment of the impacts of tourism on natural and cultural heritage; and the special role of the private sector. Similar principles are contained in the Manila Declaration on the Social Impact of Tourism (May 22, 1997). The United Nations Environment Programme (UNEP) also has adopted draft principles on sustainable tourism, endorsed in February 1999 by the UNEP Governing Council. The Global Code of Ethics for Tourism, adopted by the Summit of the World Tourism Organization October 1, 1999, is the most recent and perhaps the most important of these declarations. It consolidates and reinforces previous recommendations on sustainable tourism with the aim of preserving the world's natural resources and cultural heritage from disruptive tourist activities and ensuring a fair and equitable sharing of benefits. Article 3 of the

2 UN Tourism, 'International Tourism to Reach Pre-Pandemic Levels in 2024', Jan. 19, 2024.

3 Proposed by Hoffman, id., in cooperation with the World Travel & Tourism Environment Research Centre (Oxford 1995).

Code refers specifically to sustainable development and includes the most progressive legal principles and environmental methods. The World Committee on Tourism Ethics enforces the mechanism which involves private and intergovernmental conciliation. The Committee of twelve independent experts is able to consider disputes between states and other entities involved in tourist development. The Committee does fact-finding, hears the parties and renders a recommendation to resolve the dispute.

At the 26th Conference of the Parties (COP) of the United Nations Framework Convention on Climate Change (UNFCCC), which took place in Glasgow in 2021, the Glasgow Declaration on Climate Action and Tourism was adopted. Over 850 organizations have become signatories. By becoming signatories, organizations agree to implement the commitments detailed in the Glasgow Declaration, notably supporting the global commitment to halve emissions by 2030 and reach net zero as soon as possible before 2050. They commit to delivering climate action plans within 12 months of becoming a signatory (or updating existing plans) and implementing them. These plans must align with the five pathways of the Declaration – Measure, Decarbonize, Regenerate, Collaborate, Finance – to accelerate and coordinate climate action in tourism. Signatories also pledge to report publicly on an annual basis on progress against interim and long-term targets, as well as on actions being taken.

On the regional level, the Parliamentary Assembly of the Council of Europe in Recommendation 810(1977) called for European Cooperation in the Field of Tourism. It recommended that the member states make an appropriate and detailed analysis of the effects on the environment and the socio-cultural situation before developing tourist facilities.

In a different sphere of activity, the Baltic Marine Environment Protection Commission (HELCOM)[4] has taken measures to ensure integrated action to protect the Baltic. Its actions indicate the potentially broad reach of regulation to protect the marine environment, discussed in more detail below in 'coastal and marine ecosystems'. Recommendation 22/4 of March 2001 on the Proper Handling of Solid Waste/Landfill, relating to Article 13(b) of the Convention, applies to all landfill sites built after January 1, 2001. It has a large geographic scope, applying to existing sites within ten kilometers of the Baltic Sea or 5 kilometers from a river bank zone where the zone is within 50 kilometers of the mouth of the river and the river discharges into the Baltic Sea and has a catchment area of more than 200 square kilometers. Parties are to reduce the quantities of waste going into landfill and to decrease the hazardousness of

4 HELCOM is established by the Convention on the Protection of the Marine Environment of the Baltic Sea Area (Helsinki, Apr. 9, 1992).

disposed waste. Environmental risks posed by existing closed landfills should be assessed and pollution prevention measures implemented. The recommendation also indicates what constitutes a proper landfill over the life-cycle of the site, taking into account the location, design, and construction of the site and its operation, closure, aftercare. The operational techniques and management practices are at the same level as EC Directive 1999/31 on the Landfill of Waste.

The 1996 EC Directive Concerning Integrated Prevention of Environmental Pollution lays down measures designed to prevent or, where that is not practicable, to reduce emissions in the air, water, and land from activities listed in an Annex to the Directive. The Directive is, however, limited to pollution prevention and control.

In 2007, the European Commission adopted Communication 2007/621 titled 'Agenda for a sustainable and competitive European tourism', which outlines the EU's strategy to enhance the tourism sector's sustainability and competitiveness. The agenda advocates for a holistic and integrated policy approach, involving all stakeholders in sustainable destination management and business practices. Effective planning, community involvement, and continuous monitoring are essential to achieving long-term sustainability. Moreover, raising tourist awareness about sustainable options can drive the industry toward more responsible practices, ultimately enhancing the quality of the tourist experience and ensuring that tourism continues to be a force for local development and conservation. The agenda calls for collaborative efforts to align economic, social, and environmental objectives, ensuring that tourism in Europe remains competitive and sustainable.

An ecosystem approach to environmental protection considers the totality of environmental impacts on the functioning of an entire ecosystem, even when it crosses international boundaries. Both integrated protection and an ecosystem approach are stressed in the current work of international bodies concerned with environmental protection. Early legal measures for the joint or common management of shared resources are thus being extended to ecosystem management.

1 Shared Resource Management

The concept of joint management of shared resources began with commercially exploited species and to international watercourses.[5] Establishment

5 See UNEP, *The Principles of Conduct in the Field of the Environment for the Guidance of States in the Conservation and Harmonious Utilization of Nature Resources Shared by Two or More*

of permanent institutions or rules for joint management allows treating the resource as an integrated whole, reflecting the ecological reality. Common or joint management is not a new technique – it was utilized as early as the last century in Convention for the Navigation of the Rhine River and later in the 1911 Treaty for the Preservation and Protection of Fur Seals – but it is increasingly applied to international watercourses and to shared ecosystems such as the Alps and the Arctic. Almost half the Earth's land surface lies within 263 international river basins, i.e. those that traverse political boundaries.[6] The Congo, Niger, Nile, Rhine, and Zambesi, for example, are each shared by more than nine countries. The essential need for water and potential conflicts that can arise from competition over it makes it important that countries reach agreement on sharing water resources. State practice demonstrates awareness of this fact: the first known international water agreement dates back to the settlement of a water dispute over the Tigris River between the Sumerian city-states of Lagash and Umma (2500 B.C.).[7] The Food and Agriculture Organization (FAO) has identified more than 3600 international water treaties concluded between 805 and 1984.[8] Between 1948 and 2012, states have adopted some 300 international water agreements.

Early agreements mostly aimed to regulate navigation and demarcate boundaries, but the development of hydropower and large-scale irrigation development in the twentieth century shifted the focus to reconciling non-navigational uses. Now better knowledge and understanding of ecosystems and their natural processes lead states to conclude more comprehensive agreements protecting freshwater resources as hydrographic units rather than as individual watercourses. These agreements recognize the difficult problem of balancing competing demands and differences between upstream and downstream states and their varied interests, including agriculture, industry, recreation, flood control, hydropower, environmental protection and human health. The physical, economic and social disparities between riparian nations can make management complex. An integrated approach offers a legal framework to reconcile differences and make choices. When coupled with joint or shared management and monitoring, water basin agreements may provide the

---

States, May 9, 1978; and Alexandre Kiss, 'Can We Speak of the Protection and Management of Shared Natural Resources?' (1998–98) IV *Juridisk Tidskrift* 1.

6 A 'river basin' is the area which contributes hydrologically to surface and groundwater of a first order stream. The latter discharges into the ocean or a closed lake or inland sea. River basin is thus similar in concept to watershed or catchment area.

7 Aaron T. Wolf, 'Conflict and Cooperation Along International Waterways' (1998) 1 *Water Policy* 251.

8 UNEP, *Atlas Of International Freshwater Agreements* (2002), UNEP/DEWA/DPDL/RS.02/4, at 3.

structure for effective environmental protection in the context of sustainable development.

The 1987 Agreement on the Action Plan for the Environmentally Sound Management of the Common Zambezi River System was one of the first to adopt a holistic approach to water resources management through the entire river system. Although the Action Plan is not legally binding, it provides the framework for action for the riparian states. The use of a 'soft law' instrument may reflect the fact that basin conditions and priorities may change considerably over time, necessitating flexibility in provisions and institutions. Water allocation, in particular, may vary according to availability, changing needs and values. In contrast to the approach of the Zambezi states, the newly independent countries around the Aral Sea adopted a series of binding agreements between 1993 and 1999 on water-related activities, improving the environment and economic development of the region.[9] Similarly, the Southern African Development Community (SADC) countries adopted a Protocol on shared water systems in the Southern African Development Community on August 28, 1995 and revised it on August 7, 2000. Another notable example is the series of treaties adopted by the riparian states of the Senegal River Basin, including the Convention Concerning the Status of the Senegal River (March 11, 1972), the Convention Establishing the Organization for the Development of the Senegal River (March 11, 1972), the Convention Concluded Between Mali, Mauritania and Senegal Concerning the Legal Status of Common Works (Dec. 21, 1978) and the Charter of the Senegal River Waters (May 28, 2002).

Despite the large number of positive developments, many international water basins lack a cooperative management framework.[10] In addition, many of the older agreements lack provisions on water quality management, monitoring, public participation, flexible allocation and dispute resolution. Future agreements may be developed within the legal framework of the 1997 UN Convention on the Non-Navigational Uses of International Watercourses, which adopts the principles of 'equitable and reasonable utilization' and the

9 E.g. Agreement on Joint Activities in Addressing the Aral Sea and the Zone around the Sea Crisis, Improving the Environment, and Ensuring the Social and Economic Development of the Aral Sea Region (March 26, 1993); Agreement between the Government of the Republic of Kazakhstan, the Government of the Kyrgyz Republic, and the Government of the Republic of Uzbekistan on Cooperation in the Area of the Environment and Rational Nature Use (March 17, 1998); Agreement on the Use of Water and Energy Resources of the Sry Darya Basin (March 17, 1998); Protocol to the Agreement on the Use of Water and Energy Resources of the Syr Darya Basin (May 7, 1999).

10 United Nations Environment Programme, Atlas of International Freshwater Agreements (UNEP 2002), 7.

'obligation not to cause significant harm'. These principles, together with an adaptable management structure and flexible criteria for maintaining water quality and quantity, can promote holistic water management (see Chapter 10).

In the context of international agreements, the environmental unity of international watercourses has led to a recognition of the need for common management with the active participation of all concerned states. Article 24 of the 1997 UN Convention on International Watercourses stops short of mandating the establishment of joint management, but provides that watercourse states must enter into consultations concerning management, including the possible creation of a joint management mechanism, at the request of any of the concerned states. In this regard, management means planning the sustainable development of the watercourse and implementation of any plans adopted. It also means promoting the rational and optimal utilization, and protection and control of the watercourse. Such joint management has been adopted in many regions of the world. The Great Lakes, which contain one-fifth of the world's freshwaters, are jointly managed by the United States and Canada pursuant to a 1909 Boundary Waters Treaty through the International Joint Commission, an independent bilateral agency. The Commission today also addresses transboundary air pollution. Namibia and South Africa also have created a permanent water commission. The Senegal River Basin provides another notable example. The 1978 Convention Establishing the Organization for the Development of the Senegal River led to the creation of the Organisation Pour la Mise en Valeur du Fleuve Senegal (OMVS), with which the riparian States 'relinquished their sovereign control and even their ownership of the land and the river works to the OMVS',[11] designing a unique legal regime that, exceptionally, goes beyond any of the four major theories of watercourses law.[12] The importance of joint management through a joint water commission has also been emphasized by the International Court of Justice (ICJ) in the *Pulp Mills* case. In its judgment, the Court praised the parties' 'long-standing and effective tradition of co-operation and co-ordination through [the Administrative Commission of the River Uruguay] CARU', by means of which they 'have established a real community of interests and rights in the management of the River Uruguay and in the protection of its environment'.[13]

11 Margaret J. Vick, 'The Senegal River Basin: A Retrospective and Prospective Look at the Legal Regime' (2006) 46 *Natural Resources Journal* 211, 215–16.

12 Makane M. Mbengue and Elena Cima, 'Environmental Diplomacy. The Elements' in Margaret E. McGuinness and David P. Stewart (eds.), *Research Handbook on Law and Diplomacy* (Edward Elgar 2023).

13 *Pulp Mills*, ICJ Rep. 14, para. 281.

Agreements among interested states call for the common management of the Niger, the Mekong, the Danube, the Meuse, the Scheldt the Zambezi, the Mosel, the Mahakali (Nepal-India), the Ganges (India-Bangladesh) and La Plata rivers, and the Lake Chad basin. A declaration of principles between Jordan, the Palestine Liberation Organization and the state of Israel seeks cooperation in regard to the Jordan River. The Agreements on the rivers Meuse and Scheldt, signed in 1994, call for integrated management of the drainage area of the two rivers and the need for measures of management and cooperation in regard to the sediments in the bed of the rivers. The agreements create an international commission to facilitate international cooperation.

The Convention on Cooperation for the Protection and Sustainable Use of the Danube River (Sofia, June 29, 1994) establishes an International Commission to coordinate consultation and joint activities for the sustainable and equitable management of surface and ground waters in the Danube catchment area. It looks to joint or harmonized programs in part because its aim is regional and includes the reduction of the pollution loads of the Black Sea from sources in the catchment area. According to Article 4a, the states parties should engage in consultations and joint activities in the framework of the International Commission. Other provisions call for harmonized domestic regulations for emission limits and standards (Art. 7(5)(a)), harmonized monitoring and assessment methods (Art. 9(1)) joint monitoring systems and programs (Art. 9), joint research (Art. 15) and joint warning systems (Art. 16).

2 Transboundary Protected Areas and Landscapes

On a bilateral or even multilateral basis, transboundary protected areas are being created. Recently, the governments of Argentina, Paraguay and Brazil agreed to link state and private reserves in the Parana jungle region, thus creating a green corridor. Since 1972, the Gran Paradiso National Park in the Italian Alps has been paired with the Vanoise National Park in France, nearly tripling the protected area and providing year-round protection to the ibex. On the regional level, the Waddenzee National Park covers all the natural range of seals along the tidal flats of Denmark, Germany and the Netherlands. In 1987, the three coastal states entered into an administrative agreement on a common secretariat to set out their duties to cooperate in research and management of the Waddenzee ecosystem as a whole. Similarly, Spain and France coordinate signposts, visitor centers and tourist information for the French

Pyrenees Occidentales National Park and the Spanish Ordesa National Park. On November 30, 1999, Kenya, Tanzania and Uganda signed in Arusha a Treaty for the Establishment of the Eastern African Community. Chapter 19 of the treaty provides for co-operation in environment and natural resources management providing, in this framework *inter alia,* for irrigation and water catchment management, food security, and wildlife management (Arts. 109, 110 and 116). It also advocates for the integration of environmental management and conservation measures in all developmental activities such as trade, transport, agriculture, industrial development, mining and tourism in the Community (Art.112, 1(e)).

The Council of Europe member states adopted the European Landscape Convention on October 20, 2000 (amended by the 2016 Protocol), with the objective of promoting landscape protection, management and planning and organizing European cooperation on landscape issues. 'Landscape' is defined in the Convention as an area, as perceived by people, whose character is the result of the action and interaction of natural and/or human factors. Landscape protection means action to conserve and maintain the significant or characteristic features of a landscape justified by its heritage value derived from its natural configuration and/or from human activity. These definitions place the Convention fully in the approach of integrated protection, reinforced by Article 2 which provides an extensive scope of application including the entire territory – land, inland waters and marine areas – of the parties and covers natural, rural, urban and peri-urban areas.

The general measures parties should take include the recognition of landscapes in law as an essential component of peoples' surroundings, an expression of the diversity of their shared cultural and natural heritage and a foundation of their identity. This formulation indicates an understanding that humans throughout the world have altered the natural environment in diverse ways, that today are part of the cultural identity of the group. This is expressed in the preamble which notes that developments in agriculture, forestry, industrial and mineral production techniques and the regional planning, town planning, transport, infrastructure, tourism and recreation and, at a more general level, changes in the world economy are in many cases accelerating the transformation of landscapes.

Specific obligations include identifying, assessing and developing quality objectives for landscapes, with public participation. There should also be education and awareness-raising of the general public. Article 9 calls on parties to encourage transfrontier cooperation on local and regional levels and whenever necessary to prepare and implement joint landscape programs.

3 Ecosystem Protection and Management

The integrated approach plays a particularly important and growing role in protecting large ecosystems of the planet: the polar regions, mountains, and marine ecosystems.

3.1 *The Polar Regions*

Antarctica, while almost entirely ice and snow covered, nonetheless supports abundant wildlife. It also plays critical roles in the global climate, ocean currents, the marine food chain, and sea temperatures and levels. Approximately 70% of all freshwater is located in Antarctica. It is increasingly popular as a tourist site and its waters have been the target of considerable illegal and unreported fishing.

The foundations of the Antarctica Treaty System (ATS) emerged from the International Geophysical Year 1957–1958, proclaimed by the International Council of Scientific Unions, a non-governmental organization supporting open scientific research. The 1959 Antarctic Treaty, concluded outside the auspices of the United Nations, de-militarized the continent and established that it be set aside for peaceful purposes in the interest of all humanity. The Treaty guarantees freedom of scientific investigation and promotes the exchange of scientific information. All issues respecting state claims to portions of Antarctica are frozen for the period the Treaty is in force.[14] State compliance with the treaty obligations is ensured through a system of mutual inspections. The Antarctic Treaty parties are also, according to Article X, to 'exert appropriate efforts consistent with the Charter of the United Nations, to the end that no one engages in any activity in Antarctica contrary to the principles or purposes of the ... Treaty'. The language of Article X has given rise to many debates over whether or not it is intended to ensure that the activities of non-parties conform to the treaty within Antarctica and its surrounding waters.[15] Article IX foresees regular meetings of the Contracting Parties[16] who are given authority

14 Seven nations had made sometimes overlapping territorial claims on Antarctica by 1950: Argentina, Australia, Chile, France, New Zealand, Norway, and the United Kingdom. The United States and Russia, among others, have rejected these territorial claims.

15 The provisions of the Antarctic Treaty and the Environmental Protocol apply to the area south of 60 deg. South Latitude, including all ice shelves (Art. VI). The CCAMLRA applies to the area within the 'Antarctic convergence', an area of marine waters that changes with the seasons.

16 The parties to the treaty do not all have the same rights of participation. Fully participating states are those which demonstrate their interest in Antarctica 'by conducting substantial scientific research activity there, such as the establishment of a scientific station

to adopt measures regarding, *inter alia*, the preservation and conservation of living resources in Antarctica. Thus, although the word environment does not appear in the Treaty, there is a juridical base for considering and acting on environmental issues. The Scientific Committee on Antarctic Research attends meetings of the parties regularly and has considerably influence.

The Antarctic Treaty (Dec. 1, 1959) has been progressively complemented by conservation measures and by two conventions, one adopted June 1, 1972, on the Conservation of Antarctic Seals, the second May 20, 1980, on the Conservation of Antarctic Marine Living Resources (CCAMLR) in the area. While CCAMLR was negotiated largely in response to over-fishing in the waters off Antarctica, the treaty is one of the first international agreements to adopt an ecosystem approach because it considers the interrelationship between all species and their particular physical environment. Its coverage is uniquely based upon a biological boundary, because it extends to ocean waters that are south of the 'Antarctic convergence', the cold waters favorable to nutrients and phytoplankton growth and to the proliferation of krill, one of the bases of the marine food chain. The parties to CCAMLR meet regularly to adopt conservation measures, including on the maximum sustainable yield for target species, which they do by consensus on the basis of recommendations by the scientific advisory committee and regulatory commission (see Chapter 8).

CCAMLR envisages the creation of a system to observe and supervise compliance with the Convention, including procedures relating to on-site visits to, and inspections of, ships operating within the treaty area. These inspections are undertaken by observers and inspectors designated by members of an international Commission established by the Convention.[17] The major problem has been unreported and illegal catches, most of them made by non-parties to the agreement.[18] In order to strengthen its effectiveness, the CCAMLR Commission created a documentation scheme[19] in 1999 and a monitoring system at the end of 2000.

In 1991, the parties to the Antarctic Treaty negotiated a Protocol to the Antarctic Treaty on Environmental Protection that includes principles and rules

---

or the dispatch of a scientific expedition'. These are the Antarctic Treaty Consultative Parties (ATCP) who meet in the Consultative Meeting (ATCM).

17 May 20, 1980, Art. 24, U.K.T.S. 48 (1982), Cmd. 8714, T.I.A.S. 10240, A.T.S. 3 (1982), 19 I.L.M. 837 (1980).

18 Greenpeace estimates that over half of the Patagonian toothfish catch is taken by illegal fishing conducted from countries that are not party to CCAMLR.

19 Although the Catch Documentation Scheme is intended to ensure that all toothfish are legally procured, in practice the captain of a vessel need only state that the fish were caught outside the Convention area to circumvent the restrictions.

concerning all activities in the Antarctic Treaty area. The Madrid Protocol designates Antarctica as 'a natural reserve, devoted to peace and science' (Art. 2). It invests the Antarctic Treaty System Consultative Meetings with the task of defining the general policy for the comprehensive protection of the Antarctic environment (Art. 10) and creates a Committee for Environmental Protection to assist it in this task (Art. 11). The Committee provides advice and formulates recommendations to the Parties in connection with the implementation of the Protocol. In particular, it provides advice on the effectiveness of implementation measures, on the state of the Antarctic environment, on the need for scientific research, and on procedures for situations requiring urgent action (Art. 12). The Treaty foresees opening all areas of Antarctica, including stations, installations and equipment and all ships and aircraft within this area, to inspection by observers designated by the Consultative Parties (Art. 7). Article 12 of the Madrid Protocol mandates that the Committee for Environmental Protection provide advice on inspection measures, including formats for inspection reports and checklists for the conduct of inspections in application of Article 7 of the 1959 Treaty. Article 14 adds more details on the inspection.

Activities shall be planned and conducted so as to

- limit adverse impacts on the Antarctic environment and dependent and associated ecosystems, in particular on climate and weather patterns and on air or water quality;
- avoid significant changes in the atmospheric, terrestrial, glacial or marine environment;
- avoid detrimental changes in the distribution, abundance or productivity of species or populations of species of fauna and flora;
- avoid jeopardy to endangered or threatened species or degradation of, or substantial risk to, areas of biological, scientific, historic, aesthetic or wilderness significance (Art. 3).

Unless an activity is determined to have less than a minor or transitory impact, a Comprehensive Environmental Evaluation shall be prepared and procedures shall be put in place to assess and verify the impact of any activity that proceeds following the completion of the evaluation (Art. 6 and Annex I).

As of the end of 2023, twenty-nine states conducted activities in Antarctica sufficient to be recognized as Antarctic Treaty Consultative Parties. Twenty-eight more states are non-consultative parties. Also in 2001, a permanent secretariat was established in Buenos Aires after years of traveling according to the site of the bi-annual meeting. Most recently, the Committee on Environmental Protection has begun to designate historic sites.

At the northern extreme of the earth, eight Arctic countries adopted in 1991 a detailed instrument on environmental protection. Called the Arctic Environmental Protection Strategy, it is based on the principle that management, planning and development activities shall provide for the conservation, sustainable utilization and protection of Arctic ecosystems and natural resources for the benefit and enjoyment of present and future generations, including indigenous peoples. The use and management of natural resources shall be based on an approach which considers the value and interdependent nature of ecosystem components. Management, planning and development activities which may significantly affect the Arctic ecosystems shall

- be based on informed assessments of their impact, including cumulative impact, on the Arctic environment;
- provide for the maintenance of the region's ecological system and biodiversity;
- respect the Arctic's significance for, and influence, on the global climate;
- be compatible with the sustainable utilization of Arctic ecosystems;
- take into account the results of scientific investigations and the traditional knowledge of indigenous peoples; and
- develop a network of protected areas.

The Arctic Strategy identifies six specific pollution issues that require attention: persistent organic contaminants, oil pollution, heavy metals, noise, radioactivity, and acidification. Potential disturbance from noise also is taken into account, which is quite exceptional in the field of international co-operation. The Strategy identifies existing international mechanisms and proposes actions for each identified nuisance. Separate chapters relate to the protection of the Arctic marine environment, emergency prevention, preparedness and response, and the conservation of Arctic fauna and flora.

In order to implement the Arctic Environmental Strategy, the eight Arctic countries agreed to hold regular meetings. A 1996 Declaration, also a legally non-binding text, created the Arctic Council as a multilateral forum in order to serve as a permanent high-level intergovernmental framework in which the eight Arctic nations can oversee existing Arctic multilateral activities, as well as develop new initiatives. In addition to the eight member States, three organizations representing the majority of indigenous peoples in the circumpolar Arctic are Permanent Participants in the Council. The Council meets on a biennial basis, with meetings of senior officials taking place more frequently. Responsibility for hosting meetings of the Arctic Council, including provision of secretariat support functions, rotates sequentially among the Arctic States.

The Arctic Council oversees and coordinates programs originally established under different instruments: the Arctic Environmental Protection Strategy, the Arctic Monitoring and Assessment Program, the Conservation of Arctic Flora and Fauna, the Protection of the Arctic Marine Environment, and Emergency Prevention, Preparedness and Response. Other developments include the adoption of an International Code of Safety for Ships in Polar Waters and a Circumpolar Protected Areas network.

The Arctic Council has established a number of working groups: Arctic Monitoring and Assessment Program (scientific assessments of POPs, heavy metals, radioactivity, human health); Conservation of Arctic Flora and Fauna (overview completed on June 11, 2001); Circumpolar Seabird Working Group, which has published several technical reports on management and harvesting; and Emergency Prevention, Preparedness and Response, a forum for information exchange in regard to national activities relating to contingency planning and emergency response. In 2001 the working group agreed to a timetable for completing a circumpolar map of resources at risk from oil spills in the Arctic, and continued to develop a standardized approach to shoreline cleanup assessment technology. The Protection of the Arctic Marine Environment Working Group has prepared amendments and additions to the 1997 Offshore Oil and Gas Guidelines. The Sustainable Development Working Group has given special attention to Arctic Council health initiatives, the future of children in the region, culture and eco-tourism, and prevention and control of infectious disease.

The Arctic States have negotiated three legally binding agreements through the Arctic Council: the Agreement on Cooperation on Aeronautical and Maritime Search and Rescue in the Arctic (signed in 2011), the Agreement on Cooperation on Marine Oil Pollution Preparedness and Response in the Arctic (signed in 2013), and the Agreement on Enhancing International Arctic Scientific Cooperation (signed in 2017). These agreements focus on bolstering international cooperation concerning maritime search and rescue, marine oil pollution preparedness and response, and Arctic scientific collaboration.

3.2 *Mountain Ecosystems*

Mountains and uplands constitute about half of the terrestrial landmass of the earth and exist in over three-quarters of the world's countries. Mountain areas contain all the environmental milieu and human activities that have been part of international environmental regulation. They are places of unique and rich biodiversity, cultural diversity within largely traditional lifestyles, freshwater, pristine landscapes, tourism (eco- and industrial) and forest and mineral resources. They are also areas of poverty, erosion, natural disasters, desertification, and industrial development. They have a significant impact on other ecosystems and areas, being important water towers and sensitive indicators of global climatic and environmental change. Some of the activities most destructive to mountain areas, such as extractive mining and large-scale dams, have few or no international norms governing them. Further, it has been argued that

> [a]pplying laws and policies that were enacted with lowland environments in mind to mountain areas can have disastrous effects. Developing mountain-specific approaches requires an understanding of what characteristics of mountains are unique. These characteristics include economic and legal marginalization, isolation, transboundary location, diversity of livelihood strategies, cultural diversity, and environmental sensitivity and diversity.[20]

On the global level no single treaty for mountain areas exists; only Chapter 13 of Agenda 21 offers a blueprint for mountain resources. Chapter 13, together with Commission on Sustainable Development (CSD) progress reports, United Nations Economic and Social Council (ECOSOC) resolution 1997/45, a 1997 FAO report on Chapter 13 of Agenda 21, and the 2030 Agenda for Sustainable Development (2015) identify the importance of law in the promotion of mountain conservation and development.[21] As to Agenda 2030, Sustainable Development Goal (SDG) 15.4 calls on Parties to 'ensure the conservation of mountain ecosystems, including their biodiversity, to enhance their capacity to provide benefits which are essential for sustainable development'. A study by the Mountain Institute found that legal, regulatory, and enforcement structures are perhaps the most important contributing factors to promoting conservation and sustainable development, particularly when utilizing the principle of subsidiarity to enhance local participation.[22]

The UN exercised efforts in connection with the International Year of the Mountains and International Year of Eco-Tourism in 2002. Other institutions

20 Owen J. Lynch and Gregory F. Maggio, 'Mountain Laws and Peoples: Moving Towards Sustainable Development and Recognition of Community-Based Property Rights' (2002) *CIEL* 6.

21 FAO, *Task Manager's Report on Chapter 13, Agenda 21, Report of the Secretary-General*, E/CN.17/1997/2/Add.12, January 22, 1997. The report refers to the need for new or reinforced legal mechanisms (charters, conventions, national legislation etc.) to protect fragile mountain ecosystems and promote sustainable development in mountain regions.

22 Lynelle Preston (ed.), *Investing in Mountains: Innovative Practices and promising Examples for Financing Conservation and Sustainable Development* (The Mountain Institute 1997).

also took action during this period, including the program Environment for Europe and the Work Program on mountain ecosystems adopted by the states parties to the Convention on Biological Diversity. Indeed, most treaties for the protection of nature developed projects on mountain ecosystems during 2002.

The Convention on the Protection of the World Cultural and Natural Heritage (Nov. 23, 1972) has more than 40 mountain areas around the world on the World Heritage list, including Virunga National Park (DRC), Mount Kenya, Simen National Park (Ethiopia), Prinin National Park (Bulgaria) and Yosemite National Park (USA). In New Zealand, the sacred peaks of Tongariro National Park became the first national park to be created from a gift of land by an indigenous people and a World Heritage site in 1992 and the first to be granted that status on both landscape and cultural grounds. Listing increases international recognition for the importance of the sites, but measures are largely left to national authorities.

The treaty system established for the protection of the Alps is the most extensive and explicit corpus concerning mountain areas. It aims at protecting one of the largest continuous and relatively unspoilt natural regions in Europe. A Convention Concerning the Protection of the Alps adopted Nov. 7, 1991 by seven countries of the region and the EU,[23] proclaimed a set of principles covering virtually every aspect of human activities which produce direct or indirect impacts on the environment. The Convention is a framework treaty which lists the main fields where specific protocols are to be drafted (Art. 2). It also establishes the foundations of legal, scientific, economic and technical cooperation and creates a Conference of Contracting Parties, called the Alpine Conference, charged with elaborating the Protocols. The Conference also has established a Compliance Mechanism providing for reporting procedures.

The first Protocol, adopted in 1994, aimed to implement the Alpine Convention in the Field of Town and Country Planning and Sustainable Development.[24] Its specific objectives are to ensure the rational use of land and the harmonious development of the whole region, to avoid the under- and overuse and the conservation and rehabilitation of natural habitats by means of a clarification and evaluation of land-use requirements, and the development of foresighted integral planning and coordination of the measures taken. The protocol stresses both international cooperation and the importance of the participation of local communities.

23 Salzburg, November 7, 1991, EMuT 991/83.

24 Chambéry, December 20, 1994, EMuT 991:83/B.

A second instrument, the Protocol for the Implementation of the Alpine Convention in the Field of Mountain Agriculture,[25] insists on the use of agricultural methods of production which are respectful of nature and environment. It also advocates for the integration of agricultural considerations into other policies and has a particular importance for land conservation and management. The aim of the Protocol on Nature Protection and Landscape Conservation[26] is not only to protect, but also the manage and, if necessary, restore landscapes and nature in the Alpine region. It recommends cooperation, in particular transboundary cooperation, in the preparation of inventories, and the creation and the monitoring of protected areas. Here again, local communities should participate.

After this first series of Protocols, the Alpine States adopted a further instrument in 1996, relating to mountain forests.[27] It insists on protecting the main functions of the forests as well as urban areas and agricultural land and maintaining the productivity of forests and their social and ecological functions.

On October 16, 1998, parties to the Alpine convention adopted three more Protocols. The first of them, on the protection of soils,[28] is analyzed in Chapter 9. The Protocol concerning Energy[29] invites the parties to harmonize their plans related to energy with their general management scheme for the Alpine region, to optimize energy production, transport and distribution taking into account the needs of environmental protection, and to limit the impact of the uses of energy on the environment including that of negative effects on the landscapes. The Protocol also advocates for the energy-saving and the use of renewable sources of energy. Parties shall exchange information on the use and surveillance of nuclear energy sources. All new projects related to energy and all modification of existing installations should be submitted to an environmental impact assessment. The third Protocol adopted on the same day[30] is no less creative: its objective is to ensure sustainable development of the Alpine region through tourism which respects the environment. The influx of tourists should be controlled within the natural limits of the development of

25 Chambéry, December 20, 1994, EMuT 991:83/C.

26 Chambéry, December 20, 1994, EmuT 991:83/D.

27 Protocol for the Implementation of the Alpine Convention in the Field of Mountain Forests, Brdo, February 27, 1996, EMuT 991:83/E.

28 Protocol for the Implementation of the Alpine Convention in the Field of Soil Protection, Bled, October 16, 1998, EMuT 991:83/F.

29 Bled, October 16, 1998, EMuT 991:83/G.

30 Protocol for the Implementation of the Alpine Convention in the Field of Tourism, October 16, 1998, EMuT, 991:83/H.

the region. This principle should be applied to different aspects of tourism: housing, transport, sports, use of aircraft, coordination of the dates of vacation, cooperation with agriculture, forestry and local handcraft. Quiet areas should be created and the use of ski-lifts and of ski-slopes should be in conformity with environmental requirements.

Two more Protocols were adopted on October 31, 2000. The objective of the first, related to transport,[31] is to adopt a sustainable policy in this field by reducing nuisances and risks, avoiding or minimizing danger for biodiversity and using means of transport which respect as much as possible the environment and natural resources. Such objectives should also be taken into account in other policies. As with all the Protocols, participation of local populations is encouraged. The second Protocol concerns dispute settlement[32] and aims to reach such settlement by consultation and by arbitration.

On November 19, 2002 the 7th Alpine Conference meeting in Merano passed a resolution establishing a compliance mechanism called Reviewing Committee. Each party is to provide the Committee every four years with a country report concerning compliance which will be sent to the other Alpine Convention contracting parties and observers. The Secretariat is to make the reports public, except for the information that the relevant party has classified as confidential. The report is to contain information on compliance with protocol-specific obligations, which includes: measures of compliance taken and an assessment of the effectiveness of the measures; problem areas, such as divergent interests concerning the use of natural resources, as well as measures which relate to these areas; measures taken in cooperation with other contracting parties; and the implementation of resolutions and recommendations of the Alpine Conference. Each relevant contracting party has the right to participate in the entire proceedings,seed all relevant documentation, and comment on the work of the Reviewing Committee. As regards matters dealt with by a specific protocol, only contracting parties to that protocol are entitled to vote. With the agreement of the relevant contracting party, the Reviewing Committee can undertake enquiries on that party's territory. Information that has been described as confidential is to be treated confidentially and discussions during the entire mechanism are confidential. In certain situations, observers can be excluded from discussion during the proceedings.

Based on the reports adopted by the Reviewing Committee, the Alpine Conference can pass resolutions or recommendations by consensus. These

---

31 Protocol for the Implementation of the Alpine Convention of 1991 in the Field of Transport, Lausanne, October 31, 2000, EMuT, 991:83/I.

32 Lausanne, October 31, 2000, EMuT, 991:83/J.

resolutions and recommendations encompass advice and support of contracting parties; support in the setting up of a compliance strategy; assistance of experts to assist the relevant party; enquiries on the spot if the party agrees, in order to identify compliance problems and possible solutions; demands that the concerned party set up a compliance strategy; and requirements for a timetable on compliance. The reports of the Reviewing Committee as well as the resolutions of the Alpine Conference are published.[33]

The Alpine Conference has adopted a set of Declarations on several topics, including the Declaration on Population and Culture and the Declaration on Climate Change (IX Alpine Conference, 2006), the Declaration on Fostering a Sustainable Economy in the Alps (XIV Alpine Conference, 2016), the Declaration of Innsbruck: Climate-neutral and Climate-resilient Alps 2050 (XV Alpine Conference, 2019), the Declaration on Integrated and Sustainable Water Management in the Alps, and the Declaration on the Protection of Mountain Biodiversity and its Promotion at International Level (XVI Alpine Conference, 2020).

Finally, the Framework Convention on the Protection and Sustainable Development of the Carpathians was adopted in Kiev on May 23, 2003 by the fifth ministerial conference 'Environment for Europe' and signed by five countries: Hungary, Romania, Serbia and Montenegro, Slovakia and Ukraine. It follows the model of the Alpine conventional system but so far no protocol has been adopted, although the possibility of Protocols is foreseen by Article 18 therein. The Convention itself includes all the aspects of protecting the environment of mountain areas. Detailed provisions concern the conservation, sustainable use and restoration of biological and landscape diversity including the protection of endangered species, endemic species and large carnivores. It also aims at preventing the introduction of alien invasive species and release of genetically modified organisms threatening ecosystems, habitats or species, and their control or eradication. Article 6 also has a particular importance in the light of heavy pollution accidents which caused major environmental effects. The provision invites states parties to ensure sustainable and integrated water/river management, including land-use planning. It also calls on them to adopt policies aiming at conserving natural watercourses, springs, lakes and groundwater resources, recognizing the importance of pollution and flood management, prevention and control. States parties should also preserve and protect wetlands and wetland ecosystems. An early warning system for transboundary impacts on the water regime or flooding and accidental water

33 33 E.P.L. 179 (2003).

pollution should also be further developed. Other provisions concern an integrated approach to land resource management, spatial planning, sustainable agriculture and forestry, sustainable transport and infrastructure, sustainable tourism, cultural heritage and traditional knowledge. The Parties shall apply, where necessary, risk assessments and environmental impact assessments and shall consult on projects of transboundary character. Awareness raising, education and public information and participation are also imposed by the Convention.[34] All the obligations of the Convention are to be applied on the basis of general principles listed in Article 2(2): precaution and prevention, polluter pays, public participation and stakeholder involvement, transboundary cooperation, integrated planning and management of land and water resources, a programmatic approach and the ecosystem approach.

The Convention establishes a Conference of Parties which also should define the geographical scope of the Carpathian region, and which can adopt protocols to the Convention. It is assisted by a secretariat. This first result of the UN General Assembly declaring 2002 International Year of Mountains is likely to be followed by other developments concerning different mountain areas in the world. Starting in 2006, the UN General Assembly has adopted several resolutions on Sustainable Mountain Development (the most recent one was adopted in 2019), and declared 2022 as the International Year of Sustainable Mountain Development.

3.3 *Coastal and Marine Ecosystems*

Efforts to protect the marine environment increasingly take an ecosystem approach, recognizing that coastal areas, mangroves, sea grasses, coral reefs and other marine living and non-living resources combine to produce complex ecosystems demanding integrated management. There are several definitions of what integrate coastal and marine management means. Agenda 21, chapter 17 defines integrated coastal management as a system that: (a) provides for an integrated policy and decision-making process, including all involved sectors, to promote compatibility and a balance of uses; (b) identifies existing and projected uses of coastal areas and their interactions; (c) concentrates on well-defined issues concerning coastal management; (d) applies preventive and precautionary approaches in project planning and implementation, including prior assessment and systematic observation of the impacts of major projects; (e) promotes the development and application of methods, such as national resource and environmental accounting, that reflect changes in value

34 Parties to this agreement are also parties to the June 24, 1998 Aarhus Convention on information, participation and access to remedies in environmental matters.

resulting from uses of coastal and marine areas, including pollution, marine erosion, loss of resources and habitat destruction; and (f) provides access, as far as possible, for concerned individuals, groups and organizations to relevant information and opportunities for consultation and participation in planning and decision-making at appropriate levels.

The Ramsar states parties also have defined integrated coastal zone management by adopting principles and guidelines for incorporating wetland issues into Integrated Coastal Zone Management (ICZM).[35] According to Appendix I of the Recommendation VIII.4, integrated coastal zone management is a mechanism for bringing together the multiplicity of users, stakeholders, and decision-makers in the coastal zone in order to secure more effective ecosystem management while achieving economic development and equity within and between generations through the application of sustainability principles. This, like most other definitions, recognizes that ICZM is a continuous, pro-active and adaptive process of resource management for sustainable development of coastal zones. Its goals must be achieved within the constraints of physical, social, economic and environmental conditions.

The purposes of integrated management are generally recognized to be to guide uses so as not to exceed the carrying capacity of the resource base; respect natural dynamic processes; reduce risks to valuable resources; ensure ecosystem biodiversity; encourage complementary activities; ensure that environmental, social and economic objectives are achieved at an acceptable cost; protect traditional uses and rights and equitable access to resources; and resolve sectoral issues and conflicts. All of these goals require full participation of local communities based upon a 'bottom-up' approach.

The Jakarta Mandate on Marine and Coastal Biological Diversity adopted by the second Conference of the Parties to the Convention on Biological Diversity (CBD) in 1995, and supplemented by a program of work adopted in 1998,[36] also has a focus on integrated marine and coastal area management, sustainable use of living resources, protected areas, mariculture and alien species. The five key program areas are chemical pollution and eutrophication, fisheries operations, global climate change, alterations of physical habitat, and invasion of exotic species.

---

35 Resolution VIII.4, Principles and Guidelines for Incorporating Wetland Issues into Integrated Coastal Zone Management, 8th Meeting of the Conference of the Parties, Valencia, Spain, Nov. 18–26, 2002.

36 Conference of the Parties to the Convention on Biological Diversity, 'Conservation and Sustainable Use of Marine and Coastal Biological Diversity, including a Programme of Work' (1998) Decision IV/5, UNEP/CBD/COP/4/27.

The Jakarta Mandate identifies key operational objectives and priority activities within the five areas and as a general element, looks to coordinate and collaborate with other organizations and experts. It also solicits from states a list of experts from scientific, technical, technological, social, management, economic, policy, legal and indigenous and traditional knowledge.

The Mandate calls integrated marine and coastal area management 'the most suitable framework' for addressing human impacts and promoting conservation and sustainable use of biodiversity. The basic principle of the Program of Work is that 'The ecosystem approach should be promoted at global, regional, national and local levels'. In addition, 'protected areas should be integrated into wider strategies for preventing adverse effects to marine and coastal ecosystems from external activities and take into consideration, *inter alia*, the provisions of Article 8 of the Convention [on Biological Diversity]'. The precautionary approach should be used as guidance for all activities with science providing knowledge on key processes and influences in the marine and coastal ecosystems, which are critical to the structure, function and productivity of biological diversity.

The Jakarta Mandate supports the involvement of relevant stakeholders in protecting marine ecosystems: 'The primary basis for this program of work is action at national and local levels'. Regional bodies should be invited to coordinate activities when relevant, while global organizations should be encouraged to implement the CBD.

Coral reefs exemplify the need for integrated coastal zone management. Reefs are animals that evolved some 200 million years ago.[37] They cover a tiny fraction of the ocean floor (less than 0.1%) but healthy reefs are the most biologically diverse of all known ecosystems, containing more species than tropical rainforests, perhaps as many as two million species.[38] Coral reef ecosystems are highly integrated with sea grasses and mangroves. The latter bind soft sediments and help keep waters clear enough for corals to grow. Corals in

37 While the simplest may consist of a single tube-like polyp, with a mouth surrounded by a ring of tentacles, the polyps may form colonies. Other corals lay down a 'skeleton'; soft corals and fan corals have protein skeletons, while reef-builders lay down skeletons of calcium carbonate or limestone. Most corals obtain their food in a unique symbiosis with thousands of microscopic algae (zooxanthellae), which derive their energy from photosynthesis. Corals get most of their energy and oxygen from the zooxanthellae, while the latter utilize the carbon dioxide produced by the corals in their metabolic processes.

38 Coral reefs are distributed off the coasts of 101 countries, where they provide a habitat for up to 10% of the global fisheries and up to 20–25% of the fish catch of developing countries. There are some 800 known species of scelereactinian (reef-building) corals alone, more than three-fourths of which are located in the Asia-Pacific region.

turn buffer the impacts of waves and storms, allowing grasses and mangroves to flourish and thus protect the coastal areas from erosion and flooding.

Many human communities, especially in the tropics, live near reefs, because they depend upon them for food and livelihood. In addition, coral reefs are a focus of medical research.[39] Some ten percent of the world's reefs are already seriously degraded and 30% are seriously threatened.[40] Scientists estimate that without preventative action up to 70% of the world's coral reefs will disappear within 40 years. The slow growth rate of coral reefs compounds the severity of these many threats. Coral reefs grow no more than 12 meters every 1,000 years, provided the waters remain at the appropriate temperature, are clean and allow light to pass through.

The environmental threats to coral reef ecosystems are numerous. Corals are sensitive to water quality that is often affected by marine pollution, including land-based agricultural run-off and untreated sewage. This type of pollution causes eutrophication that stimulates algae growth, covering the coral and blocking light. The movement of topsoil into coastal waters due to erosion linked to coastal development also blocks sunlight from reaching the corals. When the algae die, covered by sediment, so do the corals. Corals are also extremely sensitive to changes in water temperature and clarity, making global warming and climate change a potential threat. Overheated corals release their algae, exposing the white of the coral skeletons. Many 'bleached' reefs can return to their previous state over time if the water cools down, but they die if the stress is not relieved. During the 1998 'El Nino' phenomenon, some 40% of the world's coral reefs suffered bleaching. Some reefs are damaged by destructive fishing methods such as those that rely on dynamite blasts or poison. Overfishing of herbivores such as parrot fish causes damage because no protection is left against fast-growing seaweed that can engulf reefs. The complexity of a reef ecosystem makes it particularly vulnerable to overexploitation of individual species. Vessel anchoring, marine archaeology, the use of coral for souvenirs and jewellery, and sports diving also threaten reefs.

Few international instruments mention coral reefs, although the general protection of regional seas agreements can apply to them. Recent international activity has focused on raising awareness of the issues and promoting local and regional initiatives. One reason for the lack of regulation to date may be the mistaken view that coral reefs present no transboundary issues, being located

39 AZT, a treatment for HIV/AIDS, is derived from a Caribbean reef sponge.

40 The rate of loss varies widely. 85–90% of the reefs of Indonesia and the Philippines are threatened with destruction despite their economic value of approximately $1.1 billion and $1.6 billion respectively.

for the most part within coastal state jurisdiction. In fact, coral reefs have a juvenile stage when larvae migrate on ocean currents to rebuild and replenish existing reefs. Restoring degraded reefs and maintaining existing ones depends upon the genetic flow and repopulation that comes from migration of the larvae. Thus, coral reefs present issues of regional, if not global, concern.

Coral reefs received some attention at the 1992 Earth Summit, particularly in Chapter 17 of Agenda 21. Chapter 17.30 calls on states, acting individually or internationally and within the framework of the International Maritime Organization (IMO) and other relevant international organizations to assess the need for additional measures to address the degradation of the marine environment. In particular they should take action to ensure respect of areas designated by coastal States, within their exclusive economic zones 'in order to protect and preserve rare or fragile ecosystems, such as coral reefs and mangroves'. Section 17.85 recommended that states identify:

> marine ecosystems exhibiting high levels of biodiversity and productivity and other critical habitat areas and should provide necessary limitations on use in these areas, through, *inter alia*, designation of protected areas. Priority should be accorded, as appropriate, to:
> a. Coral reef ecosystems;
> b. Estuaries;
> c. Temperate and tropical wetlands, including mangroves;
> d. Seagrass beds;
> e. Other spawning and nursery areas.

In 1994, Australia, France, Jamaica, Japan, the Philippines, Sweden, the United Kingdom (UK) and the United States (US) created the International Coral Reef Initiative (ICRI), in cooperation with the United Nations Development Programme (UNDP), UNEP, and the United Nations Educational, Scientific and Cultural Organization (UNESCO), regional organizations (e.g., the South Pacific Regional Environment Program), the World Bank, the Inter-American Development Bank and the International Union for Conservation of Nature (IUCN) as well as other non-governmental organizations (NGOs). The aims of the group are to strengthen the commitment of governments and international organizations and implement programs at the local, national, regional, and international levels to conserve, restore and promote sustainable use of coral reefs and associated environments. In addition, each country and region should incorporate into existing local, regional, and national development plans, management and provisions for protection, restoration, and sustainable use of the structure, processes and biodiversity of coral reefs and associated environments. ICRI also seeks to strengthen capacity for the development and implementation of policies, management, research and monitoring of coral reefs and associated environments; and establish and maintain coordination of international, regional and national research and monitoring programs, including the Global Coral Reef Monitoring Network, in association with the Global Ocean Observing System, to ensure efficient use of scarce resources and a flow of information relevant to management of coral reefs and associated environments. ICRI has developed a Framework for Action to provide governments and other interested parties a framework for effective measures to protect coral reef ecosystems. A Global Coral Reef Monitoring Network aims to surveythe earth's estimated 400,000 square miles of reef.

Eight reefs have been listed as World Heritage Sites under the UNESCO World Heritage Convention, including the Great Barrier Reef in Australia and Tubbataha Reefs Ocean National Park in the Philippines. UNESCO's Man and the Biosphere program also lists ten biospheres that have coral reefs under local community control. In total, some eight percent of all reefs are within protected areas. Finally, the Global Environment Facility (GEF) and the EU financed a regional monitoring group with Indian Island states following the 1998 coral bleaching due to El Niño. The network assists the Comoros, Madagascar, Mauritius, Reunion and Seychelles to manage their reef resources within the Regional Environment Program of the Indian Ocean Commission. Some 43 stations provide continuous monitoring to strengthen national capacity for resource management.

Conclusions

The developments described in this chapter represent the emergence of a holistic approach to environmental protection that corresponds to the nature of the environment, but which also poses considerable legal difficulties. Concrete integrated action is effective, but more difficult to achieve than the narrower sectoral or source-based approach that was seen in prior decades. Many international instruments contain vague directives calling for integrated participatory action, but the provisions lack specificity. This may partly be responsible for the proliferation of 'case studies' to illustrate best practices as a starting point for action. Such studies are increasingly published by treaty bodies to accompany guidelines and action plans.

The concept of adaptive management has become central to an ecosystem approach to conservation of living resources. An eco-system approach is defined as the 'strategy for the integrated management of land, water and living resources that promote conservation and sustainable use in an equitable way'. CBD Decision V/6 emphasizes the role of adaptive management and stresses the necessity of flexibility of management systems of biological resources. The lack of knowledge about ecosystems requires that 'management must be adaptive in order to be able to respond to such uncertainties and contain elements of "learning-by-doing" or research feedback'. The Decision recognizes the necessity of measures based on the precautionary principle. The latter is described as measures needed 'even when some cause-and-effect relationships are not yet fully established scientifically'. Monitoring is in fact key to adaptive management because it helps reduce uncertainties and allows quick responses to changes in the ecosystem.

An ecosystem approach to environmental protection still requires the incorporation and balance with other societal goals, including economic and social development. The WSSD refers to the 'three pillars' of sustainable development: economic development, social development and environmental protection. The participating states called for a collective responsibility to advance and strengthen these three interdependent and mutually reinforcing social goals, at local, national, regional and global levels. The problem remains to determine the bases and procedures for balancing the sometimes competing, although interdependent aspects.

Bibliography

Francioni, F. & Scovazzi, T. (eds.), *International Law for Antarctica* (Martinus Nijhoff 1987).

Joyner, C. & Chopra, S. (eds.), *The Antarctic Legal Regime* (Martinus Nijhoff 1988).

Mccaffrey, S., *The Law of International Watercourses* (Oxford University Press 2002).

Rothwell, D., 'The Antarctic Treaty: 1961–1991 and Beyond', 14 *Sydney L. Rev.* 62 (1992).

Sohnle, J., *Le Droit International des Ressources en Eau: Solidarité contre souveraineté* (2002).

Triggs, C. (ed.), *The Antarctic Treaty Regime* (Cambridge University Press 1987).

Wouters, P., *Codification and Progressive Development of International Water Law* (Oxford University Press 2000).

Zang, D., 'Frozen in Time: The Antarctic Minerals Convention', 76 *Cornell L. Rev.* 722 (1991).

CHAPTER 15

Human Rights and the Environment

Protecting human rights and safeguarding the environment, along with achieving peace and security, are fundamental values of modern international society. The first two topics emerged as matters of international concern several decades apart and the earlier development of human rights law[1] encouraged international lawyers and activists as early as the 1972 Stockholm Conference on the Human Environment to explore and attempt to understand the interrelationship human rights and environmental protection. As this understanding has grown, the two fields have increasingly interacted.

Human rights emerged fully as an international concern at the close of the Second World War, although specific human rights issues, e.g., slavery, labor rights, and the protection of religious minorities, were addressed far earlier.[2] The primary objective of human rights law is to protect individuals from abuse of power by state agents, including legislative representatives of the democratic majority. Each state is also obliged to exercise due diligence to ensure that human rights are not violated by non-state actors. Due diligence requires action to prevent abuses where possible, investigate violations that occur, sanction the perpetrators, through criminal prosecution as appropriate, and provide redress for victims.

The first stage in modern international human rights law consisted of enumerating the internationally guaranteed human rights, along with the state duties to respect and ensure them. After the United Nations (UN) adopted the International Covenants on Economic, Social and Cultural Rights (ICESCR) and Civil and Political Rights (ICCPR) in 1966, many human rights activists turned their attention to developing effective compliance and enforcement procedures to supervise state implementation of human rights. Other individuals and groups have continued to devote their attention to the articulation of new norms or the further elaboration of existing ones in response to new problems that detrimentally impact human dignity and well-being. The issue of

1 The United Nations and the Organization of American States both adopted international declarations of human rights in 1948. Universal Declaration of Human Rights, Dec. 10, 1948, and American Declaration of the Rights and Duties of Man, April 30, 1948. Most of the major global and regional human rights treaties, discussed in this chapter, were adopted before the emergence of environmental protection as an international issue.

2 See Paul Gordon Lauren, *Visions Seen: The Evolution of Human Rights* (University of Pennsylvania Press 1998).

 | DOI:10.1163/9789047440802_017

environmental degradation impairing or undermining human rights emerged in this context.

From the environmental perspective, human rights law initially provided the only international legal recourse available to individuals seeking to prevent or remedy environmental harm. At the time of the 1972 Stockholm Conference, international environmental law was undeveloped, although environmental issues had clearly emerged on the international agenda. Significantly, preparations for the Stockholm Conference coincided with the United Nations convening the 1968 Teheran Conference on Human Rights,[3] the first international conference organized by the United Nations, to mark the twentieth anniversary of the adoption of the Universal Declaration of Human Rights. The Teheran Conference, overcoming a long-standing political debate that led to the adoption of two human rights covenants[4] rather than a single instrument, proclaimed all human rights to be interdependent and indivisible, opening the door for consideration of complex issues like environmental rights. Human rights language also provided an inducement to developing countries to participate in the emerging environmental movement. While developing states largely viewed environmental degradation as a problem of rich, industrialized countries, they were vitally concerned with human rights, particularly decolonization, self-determination and economic development. The Teheran Conference addressed concerns about economic development and human rights, proclaiming the interdependence of peace, development and human rights. Resource depletion fit within this agenda and stimulated interest among developing states in the forthcoming Stockholm Conference. Nonetheless, from Stockholm to the present, most advances in considering the relationship between human rights and environmental protection have occurred first, if not only, at the national and regional levels.

3 Also in 1968, a wave of student-led demonstrations throughout Europe and North America represented a rejection of many then-dominant social values, including conspicuous consumption. Public awareness of environmental threats expanded considerably after the Torrey Canyon oil spill in 1967. See, further, Chapter 2.

4 The two Covenants divide human rights into categories of civil and political rights, on one hand, and economic, social and cultural rights, on the other hand. See International Covenant on Civil and Political Rights, Dec. 16, 1966, 999 U.N.T.S. 171, 6 I.L.M. 368 (1967); International Covenant on Economic, Social and Cultural Rights, Dec. 16, 1966, 993 U.N.T.S. 3, 6 I.L.M. 360 (1967).

1 Introduction: Inter-Relating Human Rights and Environmental Protection

Four principal and complementary approaches have emerged to characterize the relationship between human rights and the environment. The approaches are outlined below, before a detailed analysis of the international instruments and state practice that reflect the first three approaches:

1. International environmental law incorporates and utilizes those human rights guarantees deemed necessary or important to ensuring effective environmental protection, such as the right to information, public participation in decision-making, and the right of access to justice.
2. Human rights law re-casts or interprets internationally-guaranteed human rights to include an environmental dimension when environmental degradation prevents full enjoyment of the guaranteed rights, such as the right to life, right to health, and right to an adequate standard of living.
3. International environmental law and international human rights law merge with the articulation of a specific right to a specific (high) quality environment.
4. International environmental law contains ethical and legal duties of individuals that include environmental protection and human rights.

The first approach selects from among the catalogue of human rights those rights most relevant to the aims of environmental protection, independent of the utility of environmental protection to the enjoyment of the full human rights catalogue. The approach thus emphasizes procedural rights such as freedom of association, which permits the existence and activities of non-governmental environmental activists and organizations, and the right of access to information concerning risks and existing environmental harm, which may be used for nature protection not necessarily related to human health and well-being. The potential for improving environmental protection through effective guarantees of procedural rights is solid, but the general absence of complaint mechanisms in international environmental agreements is a limiting aspect.[5]

The second approach, which uses global and regional human rights norms and institutions, is clearly anthropocentric and supported by indications of the public health impacts of environmental deterioration. The United Nations

---

5 Note, however, that procedural rights, such freedom of association and access to information also appear in human rights instruments and thus in appropriate instances complaints of their violation may be filed with human rights bodies.

Conference on Sustainable Development (UNCSD or Rio+20) indicated in its outcome document *The Future We Want*, that 'health is a precondition for and an outcome and indicator of all three dimensions of sustainable development', that is, the social, environmental and economic dimensions. A World Health Organization (WHO) report found that environmental risk factors play a role in more than 80% of the diseases regularly reported by it. Globally, nearly one quarter of all deaths and of the total disease burden can be attributed to environmental degradation. In children, however, environmental risk factors can account for slightly more than one-third of the disease burden.[6] The environmental burden per capita of diarrhoeal diseases and lower respiratory infections is significantly greater in certain developing country subregions as compared to developed country subregions, due to variations in exposure to environmental risks and in access to health care.[7] More than one billion people in developing countries lack clean and safe drinking water, with the result that waterborne infections account for 80 percent of all infectious diseases worldwide and unclean water the second largest cause of death among children.[8] In many areas, industrial and household wastes are dumped directly into rivers and lakes. Air pollution adversely affects the health of several billion people. Globally some three billion people use solid fuel (e.g., wood, agricultural residue, coal) to generate energy. It is estimated that these activities are responsible for two million deaths each year related to chronic-obstructive pulmonary disease (COPD), primarily among the poor, women and children.[9]

Moreover, according to a 2024 WHO Report:

> As much as 24% of deaths are estimated to be attributable to environmental risks to health that are largely preventable. Acting on these environmental risks can be key to reducing many communicable and noncommunicable diseases and injuries. As much as 31% of deaths from ischaemic heart disease, 25% of strokes, 20% of lung cancers, 43% of acute respiratory infections and 33% of cases of chronic obstructive

6 Annette Prüss-Üstün and Carlos Corvalán, *Preventing Disease Through Healthy Environments: Towards and Estimate of the Environmental Burden of Disease* (WHO 2006), 6, 9.

7 ibid at 14.

8 UNDP, *Human Development Report 2006. Beyond Scarcity: Power, Poverty and the Global Water Crisis*, 1. In Latin America and the Caribbean alone, 40 million people lack access to improved sources of water for human consumption, 117 million do not use improved sanitation structures and 36 million still practice open defecation WHO/UNICEF, Joint Monitoring Programme.

9 PAHO, Health, Environment and Sustainable Development: Towards the Future We Want (PAHO, 2012), 5.

> pulmonary disease (COPD) could be prevented by reducing air pollution. In addition, 69% of diarrhoeal diseases could be prevented through providing safer water, sanitation and hygiene (WASH); 40% of road traffic injuries could be reduced by changing the built environment and land use, and increasing occupational safety and traffic regulations; and 73% of unintentional poisonings could be prevented by improving the management of chemicals and restrictions regarding their use.[10]

In general, human rights law can be invoked when environmental conditions deteriorate to the point where the right to life, the right to health, the right to a family and private life, the right to culture, and other nationally and internationally-guaranteed human rights are seriously impaired. As Judge Weeremantry of the International Court of Justice expressed it:

> The protection of the environment is … a vital part of contemporary human rights doctrine, for it is a *sine qua non* for numerous human rights such as the right to health and the right to life itself. It is scarcely necessary to elaborate on this, as damage to the environment can impair and undermine all the human rights spoken of in the Universal Declaration and other human rights instruments.[11]

The General Assembly has called the preservation of nature 'a prerequisite for the normal life of man'.[12]

With a focus on the consequences of environmental harm to existing human rights, this approach serves to address the most serious cases of actual or imminently-threatened pollution. The primary advantage over the procedural approach is that existing human rights complaint procedures may be employed against states that allow the level of environmental protection to fall below what is necessary to maintain any of the guaranteed human rights. Using human rights law has had its limits, however.

For a long time, because of its anthropocentric focus, human rights law has not been easily invoked to counter threats to other species, nature as a whole, or to ecological processes. The European Court of Human Rights (ECtHR) has

---

10 WHO, UNDP, UNICEF, UN Environment, *Compendium of WHO and Other UN Guidance on Health and Environment. 2024 Update* (2024), 1.

11 *Gabčíkovo-Nagymaros Case* (Hungary-Slovakia), I.C.J., Judgment of Sept. 25, 1997 (Sep. Op. Judge Weermantry) p. 4.

12 UNGA, *Historical Responsibility of States for the Preservation of Nature for Present and Future Generations* (30 October 1980) UNGA Res 35/8, UN Doc A/RES/35/8.

stated that 'no right to nature preservation is as such included among the rights and freedoms guaranteed by the Convention'. As such, it has been difficult to meet the admissibility standard that requires applicants to be 'victims' of a violation when the issue is one of protecting elements of nature or the environment in general.[13] It appears that the Court has somewhat relaxed its admissibility standards in this respect,[14] although subsequent merits determinations have not always been favorable.[15] A recent judgment of the ECtHR, the first one dealing specifically with climate change, has confirmed a more flexible approach regarding admissibility. In the *Verein Klimaseniorinnen Schweiz and Others v. Switzerland*, the Court confirmed that 'the issue of victim status must be interpreted in an evolutive manner in the light of conditions in contemporary society and that any excessively formalistic interpretation of that

---

13 See *Athanassoglou and Others v. Switzerland*, ECtHR [GC] 27644/95 Judgment (April 6, 2000) holding Articles 5 and 13 inapplicable where applicants complained of the extension of a license for a nuclear power plant in the absence of allegations of specific and imminent danger in their personal regard, but instead raised concerns about a general danger in relation to all nuclear power plants. According to the Court, 'how best to regulate the use of nuclear power is a policy decision for each Contracting State to take according to its democratic processes'.

14 See, e.g. *Lizarraga and Others v. Spain*, ECtHR 62543/00 Judgment (April 27, 2004) (applicant members of an environmental association were victims in challenging plans to build a dam that would result in three nature reserves and a number of small villages being flooded). According to the Court, having regard to the particular circumstances of the case, and especially the fact that the applicant association had been set up for the specific purpose of defending its members' interests before the courts and that those members were directly concerned by the dam project, the first five applicants could claim to be victims, within the meaning of Article 34 of the Convention.

15 In *Lizarraga,* no violation was found. But see *L'Erablière asbl v. Belgium*, ECtHR 49230/07 Judgment (February 24, 2009) allowing a non-profit association campaigning for the protection of the environment to complain against the granting of planning permission to expand a waste collection site. The Court reiterated that for Article 6 of the ECHR to be applicable there must be a dispute with a sufficient link to a civil right and that, in order to exclude applications concerning the mere existence of a law or a court decision affecting third parties, the Court did not allow an actio popularis. It has, however, previously held that this Article was applicable in cases brought by an association that, whilst of general interest, also defended the specific interest of the members. The Court considered that increasing the capacity of the waste collection site could directly affect the private life of the members of the applicant association, and stressed that the aim of the association was limited to the protection of the environment in Marche-Nassogne (Province of Luxembourg). Consequently, the Court found that the applicant association's action could not be regarded as an actio popularis and held that Article 6 of the Convention was therefore applicable. In this case, the Court held that there had been a violation of Article 6 § 1, finding that the limitation on the right of access to a court imposed on the applicant association had been disproportionate to the requirements of legal certainty and the proper administration of justice.

concepts would make protection of the rights guaranteed by the Convention ineffectual and illusory'.[16]

A second problem with reliance on human rights law is that complaints procedures are reactive to violations that occur and are more difficult to invoke to prevent foreseeable risks of a medium- or long-term nature. Even where existing harm can be shown, many human rights bodies are limited to making recommendations or providing compensation and lack the power to halt environmental harm. With regard to this problem, the recent ECtHR judgment in the *Klimaseniorinnen* case has adopted a more flexible approach in the context of climate change and, in particular, with regard to a possible violation of Article 8 of the European Convention on Human Rights (Right to respect for private and family life). The Court in fact found that, in the context of states' obligations under Article 8, 'the state's primary duty is to adopt, and to effectively apply in practice, regulations and measures capable of mitigating the existing and potentially irreversible, *future* effects of climate change'.[17]

The third possibility is to formulate a new human right to an environment that is not defined in purely anthropocentric terms, an environment that is safe not only for humans, but one that is ecologically-balanced and sustainable in the long term. At the national level, rights to an environment of a specified quality are increasingly recognized, and today more than 100 national constitutions explicitly recognize a right to a healthy environment.[18] Similarly, regional human rights conventions increasingly feature a right to a healthy environment, starting with the African Charter on Human and Peoples' Rights, adopted in 1981 which, at Article 24, explicitly protects the right of all peoples to 'a general satisfactory environment favorable to their development'. The notion of a right to environmental quality initially met resistance from those who claim that the concept cannot be given content and who assert that no justiciable standards can be developed to enforce the right, because of the inherent variability of environmental conditions,[19] but subsequent adminis-

16 *Verein Klimaseniorinnen Schweiz and Others v. Switzerland* ECtHR [GC] 53600/20 Judgment (Apr. 9, 2024), para. 482. The Court relies on a previous judgment: *Lizarraga and Others v. Spain*.

17 ibid para. 546 (emphasis added).

18 As discussed in part C, more than 100 constitutions presently proclaim a right to an environment of a specified quality or impose duties on the government to protect the environment.

19 See e.g. Gunther Handl, 'Human Rights and Protection of the Environment: A Mildly 'Revisionist' View' in Antônio Augusto Cancado-Trindade (ed.), *Human Rights and Environmental Protection* (Routledge 1992); Alan Boyle and Michael Anderson (eds.), *Human Rights Approaches to Environmental Protection* (Oxford University Press 1996).

trative and judicial enforcement of environmental rights has reduced if not overcome many of the objections. In 2021, the Human Rights Council adopted a Resolution (48/13) recognizing the existence of a right to a clean, healthy and sustainable environment, followed, in July 2022, by a Resolution of the UN General Assembly (A/76/L.75).

Finally, the fourth approach prefers to address environmental protection as a matter of human responsibilities rather than rights. Many proponents of this approach posit ecological rights or rights of nature as a construct to balance human rights, attempting to reconcile human rights and ecology by introducing ecological limitations on human rights. It has been suggested that 'the objective of these limitations is to implement an eco-centric ethic in a manner which imposes responsibilities and duties upon humankind to take intrinsic values and the interests of the natural community into account when exercising its human rights'.[20]

The concept of nature's rights has been proposed in a variety of formulations, from legally enforceable rights, to 'biotic rights' as moral imperatives, to human responsibilities and duties. Some suggest giving legal recognition to the intrinsic value of nature, by adding new 'subjects' of law: '[i]f it is possible to grant rights to people [in international law], and to future generations, then it is arguably possible to grant rights to animals and to the environment itself, and thus confer upon them limited subject status'.[21] Others point out that this has already occurred,[22] while some object that the ascription of rights to nature anthropomorphizes it to its detriment.[23] Still others view rights-conferring as one tool to enhance the value of nature. In practice, an example of this innovative approach is the 2008 amendment to the Constitution of Ecuador, which not only guarantees the right of people to live in a healthy and ecologically-balanced environment (Art. 14), but in Article 71, provides that nature is entitled to the full respect, existence, and the maintenance and regeneration of its vital cycles, structure, functions and evolutionary processes. Moreover, 'Any person, community, nation or nationality may require the public authority to

---

20 Prudence Taylor, 'From Environmental to Ecological Human Rights: A New Dynamic in International Law' (1998) 10 *Georgetown Int'l Envt'l L. Rev* 309, 310. See also Catherine Redgwell, 'Life, the Universe and Everything: A Critique of Anthropocentric Rights', in Alan E. Boyle & M. Anderson (eds.), *Human Rights Approaches to Environmental Protection* 71 (Oxford University Press 1996).

21 ibid, 373.

22 See Anthony D'Amato & Sudhir K. Chopra, 'Whales: Their Emerging Right to Life' (1991) 85 *AJIL* 21.

23 See Cynthia Giagnocavo & Howard Goldstein, 'Laws Reform or World Re-Form' (1990) 35 *McGill L.J.* 346 (1990).

comply with the rights of nature'. Article 72 adds that nature is entitled to restoration and article 73 requires the state to apply precautionary and restrictive measures to activities that could lead to species extinction, destruction of ecosystems, or the permanent alteration of natural cycles.

A legal system in which the environment is said to have rights will evolve differently from one in which such rights do not exist. A system of biotic rights for nature had been described as 'morally justified claims or demands on behalf of nonhuman organisms, either individuals or aggregates (populations and species), against all moral agents for the vital interests or imperative conditions of well-being for nonhumankind'.[24] The same author posits a Bill of Biotic Rights that includes claims or demands for participation in the natural competition for existence; healthy and whole habitats; reproduction without artificial distortions; no human-induced extinctions; freedom from human cruelty, flagrant abuse or frivolous use; restoration of natural conditions disrupted by human abuse and the right to a fair share of the goods necessary for sustainability. At present, no international legal instrument takes this approach, albeit the World Charter for Nature had proclaimed the intrinsic value of nature and a non-governmental Universal Declaration of Animal Rights was proclaimed at the United Nations Education, Scientific and Cultural Organization (UNESCO).[25]

The remainder of this chapter addresses the interface between the international protection of human rights and international environmental law from the perspective of the first three approaches. It looks at the efforts in environmental law to use procedural human rights to improve environmental protection. It then discusses how human rights law redresses the negative consequences of environmental degradation on the enjoyment of human rights. The merger of the two fields through elaborating a human right to the environment is then considered, as well as the special recognition given the rights of indigenous and tribal peoples.

2 Human Rights in International Environmental Law

States and non-state actors participating in the Stockholm Conference initiated the enduring process of appraising the relationship between environmental

24 James A. Nash, 'The Case for Biotic Rights' (1993) 18 *Yale J. Int'l L.* 235.

25 Jean-Marc Neumann, 'The Universal Declaration of Animal Rights or the Creation of a New Equilibrium Between Species' (2013) 19 *Animal L.* 91 (2013). For further discussion, see Chapter 8.

protection and human rights, an appraisal that has continued in particular through the UN special procedures created by the Human Rights Council.[26] The United States delegation submitted the most far-reaching proposal at Stockholm, seeking to proclaim:

> Every human being has a right to a healthful and safe environment, including air, water and earth, and to food and other material necessities, all of which should be sufficiently free of contamination and other elements which detract from the health or well-being of man.

The proposal was supported by non-governmental organizations, but participating states preferred the formulation of what became the frequently quoted Principle 1 of the Final Declaration:

> Man has the fundamental right to freedom, equality and adequate conditions of life, in an environment of a quality that permits a life of dignity and well-being, and he bears a solemn responsibility to protect and improve the environment for present and future generations.

This complex sentence stops short of proclaiming a right to the environment, but it clearly links human rights and environmental protection. It sees human rights as a fundamental goal and environmental protection as instrumental to achieve the 'adequate conditions' required for the guaranteed 'life of dignity and well-being'.

The lack of state support for a substantive right to an environment like that proposed by the United States,[27] led scholars and activists during the following

26 See e.g. the Reports of the Independent Expert on the issue of human rights obligations relating to the enjoyment of a safe, clean, healthy and sustainable environment, John H. Knox, A/HRC/25/43 (preliminary report, 2013); A/HRC/25/53 (mapping report, 2014); and A/HRC/28/61 (good practices, 2015). Knox was appointed in August 2012 to a three-year term as the first Independent Expert on human rights obligations relating to the enjoyment of a safe, clean, healthy and sustainable environment. His mandate was extended in March 2015 for another three years as a Special Rapporteur on the topic. In March 2018, the Human Rights Council extended the mandate (resolution 37/8) and appointed Mr. David R. Boyd as the Special Rapporteur for a three-year term. In March 2021, the Council renewed the mandate for another three years (resolution 46/7). On April 3, 2024, the mandate was extended once more, and the title was revised to Special Rapporteur on the human right to a clean, healthy, and sustainable environment (A/HRC/RES/55/2). Other relevant UN rapporteurships are discussed infra section C.

27 See e.g., Alexandre Kiss, 'Peut-on définir le droit de l'homme à l'environnement?' (1976) Rev. Juridique de l'environnement 15; Alexandre Kiss, 'Le droit à la conservation de

decade to consider human rights in a more instrumental fashion that gives content to environmental rights by identifying those rights whose enjoyment could be considered a prerequisite to effective environmental protection. They focused in particular on the procedural rights of information, public participation in decision-making, and remedies in the event of environmental harm. Various international instruments, particularly in Europe, built upon this concept to give content to Stockholm Principle 1.

Almost twenty years later, in resolution 45/94, the UN General Assembly recalled the language of Stockholm, stating that it:

> Recognizes that all individuals are entitled to live in an environment adequate for their health and well-being; and calls upon Member States and intergovernmental and non-governmental organizations to enhance their efforts towards ensuring a better and healthier environment.[28]

The texts adopted in connection with the United Nations Conference on Environment and Development (UNCED) contain few references to human rights. No right to environment is declared and there is almost no discussion of the interrelationship of human rights and environmental protection. Working Group III of the UNCED Preparatory Committee considered numerous proposals to include a right to environment in the Rio Declaration. The consolidated draft Declaration contained several provisions referring to a human right to a healthy environment. In the final meetings prior to Rio, however, the participants failed to reach consensus on including such a right.

The resulting text changes the formulation of the Stockholm Declaration. The Rio Declaration states that human beings are 'entitled to a healthy and productive life in harmony with nature'. Unlike the Stockholm Declaration, the Rio Declaration proclaims only the sovereign right of states to exploit their resources (Principle 2) and the right to development (Principle 3). The Rio Declaration accepts the importance of a role for the public, but – consistent with its avoidance of rights language – calls for including it on the ground of efficiency: 'Environmental issues are best handled with the participation of all concerned citizens at the relevant level' (Principle 10). Principle 10 adds that individuals

---

l'environnement' (1990) 2 Rev. Univ. des Droits de l'homme 445; Alexandre Kiss, 'An introductory note on a human right to environment', in Edith Brown Weiss (ed.), *Environmental Change and International Law* (UNU Tokyo 1992) 551.

28 UNGA, *Need to Ensure a Healthy Environment for the Well-Being of Individuals* (14 December 1990). UNGA Res45/94, UN Doc A/RES/45/94.

> shall have appropriate access to information concerning the environment that is held by public authorities, including information on hazardous materials and activities in their communities, and the opportunity to participate in decision-making processes. States shall facilitate and encourage public awareness and participation by making information widely available. Effective access to judicial and administrative proceedings, including redress and remedy, shall be provided.

Numerous environmental instruments now contain the three procedural rights, discussed in turn in the following sub-sections. What follows is an analysis of the universal instruments dealing with the aforementioned procedural environmental rights. It should be noted, however, that there exist also regional instruments that expressly address the rights (see later Section 4).

2.1 *The Right to Environmental Information*

Access to environmental information is a prerequisite to public participation in decision-making and to monitoring governmental and private sector activities. It also can assist enterprises in planning for, and utilizing, the best available techniques and technology. Environmental deterioration, which can arise only long after a project is completed and be irreversible, compels early and complete data to make informed choices. Transboundary impacts also produce significant demands for information across borders.

A 'right to information' can mean, narrowly, the freedom to seek information, or, more broadly, a right to access information, or even a right to receive it. Corresponding duties of the state can be limited to abstention from interfering with public efforts to obtain information from state agents or private entities, or expanded to require the state to obtain and disseminate all relevant information concerning both public and private projects that might affect the environment. If the government's duty is limited to abstention from interfering with the ability of individuals or associations to seek information from those willing to share it, then little may actually be obtained. A governmental obligation to release information about its own projects can increase public knowledge, but fails to provide access to the numerous private-sector activities that can affect the environment. Information about the latter may be obtained by the government through licensing or environmental impact requirements. Imposing upon the state a duty to disseminate this information in addition to details of its own projects provides the public with the broadest basis for informed decision-making.

As noted above, Rio Principle 10 calls for states to provide environmental information. Similarly, Chapter 23 of Agenda 21, on strengthening the role of major groups, proclaims that individuals, groups and organizations should have access to information relevant to the environment and development, held by national authorities, including information on products and activities that have or are likely to have a significant impact on the environment, and information on environmental protection matters.

Informational rights are widely found in environmental treaties, in weak and strong versions.[29] The United Nations Framework Convention on Climate Change (UNFCCC), through Article 6, exemplifies the weak approach. It provides that its parties 'shall promote and facilitate at the national and, as appropriate, sub-regional and regional levels, and in accordance with national laws and regulations, and within their respective capacities, public access to information and public participation'. The Convention on Biological Diversity (CBD) similarly does not oblige states parties to provide information, but refers in its preamble to the general lack of information and knowledge regarding biological diversity and affirms the need for the full participation of women at all levels of policy-making and implementation. Article 13 calls for education to promote and encourage the understanding of the importance of the conservation of biological diversity. Article 14 provides that each contracting party, 'as far as possible and as appropriate', shall introduce 'appropriate' environmental impact assessment procedures and 'where appropriate', allow for the public participation in such procedures. The provisions of the CBD on access to information were strengthened with the adoption of the the Nagoya Protocol on Access to Genetic Resources and the Fair and Equitable Sharing of Benefits Arising from their Utilization (October 29, 2010, Nagoya, Japan). The Protocol continues the

29 E.g. Convention for the Protection of the Marine Environment of the North-East Atlantic (Paris, September 22, 1992) Art. 9; Convention on Civil Liability for Damage Resulting from Activities Dangerous to the Environment (Lugano, June 21, 1993), Arts. 13–16; North-American Agreement on Environmental Co-operation (September 13, 1993), Art. 2(1)(a); International Convention to Combat Desertification in those Countries Experiencing Serious Drought and/or Desertification, particularly in Africa (Paris, June 17, 1994), Preamble, Arts. 10(2)(e), 13(1)(b), 14(2), 19 and 25; Convention on Co-operation and Sustainable Use of the Danube River (Sofia, June 29, 1994), Art. 14; Energy Charter Treaty, Lisbon (December 17, 1994), Arts. 19(1)(i) and 20; Amendments to the 1976 Barcelona Convention for the Protection of the Mediterranean Sea against Pollution (Barcelona, June 10, 1995), Arts. 15 and 17; Protocol concerning Specially Protected Areas and Biological Diversity in the Mediterranean (Barcelona, June 10, 1995), Art. 19; Rotterdam Convention on the Prior Informed Consent Procedure for Certain Hazardous Chemicals and Pesticides in International Trade (September 10, 1998), Art. 15(2); Protocol on Water and Health to the 1992 Convention on the Protection and use of Transboundary Watercourses and International Lakes (London, June 17, 1999), Art. 5(i); Cartagena Protocol on Biosafety to the Convention on Biological Diversity (Montreal, January 29, 2000), Art. 23; International Treaty on Plant Genetic Resources for Food and Agriculture (Nov. 3, 2001).

instrumentalist approach to the access to information, not seeing it as a right, but recognizing 'that public awareness of the economic value of ecosystems and biodiversity and the fair and equitable sharing of this economic value with the custodians of biodiversity are key incentives for the conservation of biological diversity and the sustainable use of its components, provides a strong basis for greater legal certainty and transparency for both providers and users of genetic resources'. Nonetheless, the Protocol emphasizes the importance of the full participation of women and also acknowledges and reaffirms the rights of indigenous peoples and local communities. Specific provisions aim to ensure that access to traditional knowledge held by indigenous and local communities is done with their prior informed consent[30] and strengthens the ability of these communities to benefit from the use of their knowledge, innovations and practices.

Broader guarantees of public information are found in regional agreements, including the 1992 Helsinki Convention on the Protection and Use of Transboundary Watercourses and International Lakes (Art. 16), the 1992 Espoo Convention on Environmental Impact Assessment in a Transboundary Context (Art. 3(8)), and the 1992 Paris Convention on the North-East Atlantic (Art. 9). The one last mentioned requires the contracting parties to ensure that their competent authorities make available relevant information to any natural or legal person, in response to any reasonable request, without the person having to prove an interest, without unreasonable charges and within two months of the request.

The provisions of the Rotterdam Convention on the Prior Informed Consent Procedure for Certain Hazardous Chemicals and Pesticides in International Trade (Sept. 11, 1998) vaguely encourage parties to ensure that information on chemical and pesticide hazards is made available to the public. The prior informed consent referred to in the title is that of the government of the importing state; there are few direct references to the duty to inform. The only provision imposing a direct duty on states parties to make information available to the public is Article 15 on implementation. Paragraph 2 requires each state party to ensure, 'to the extent practicable' that the public has 'appropriate' access to information on chemical handling and accident management and

30 Article 7 defers to domestic law on this issue, however. 'In accordance with domestic law, each Party shall take measures, as appropriate, with the aim of ensuring that traditional knowledge associated with genetic resources that is held by indigenous and local communities is accessed with the prior and informed consent or approval and involvement of these indigenous and local communities, and that mutually agreed terms have been established'.

on alternatives that are safer for human health or the environment than the chemicals listed in Annex III to the Convention. Nonetheless, the objectives of the Convention cannot be carried out in the absence of informed persons.

Other treaties require states parties to inform the public of specific environmental hazards. The International Atomic Energy Agency (IAEA) Joint Convention on the Safety of Spent Fuel Management and on the Safety of Radioactive Waste Management[31] is based to a large extent on the principles contained in the IAEA document 'The Principles of Radioactive Waste Management'. The Preamble of the treaty recognizes the importance of informing the public on issues regarding the safety of spent fuel and radioactive waste management. This is reinforced in Articles 6 and 13, on siting of proposed facilities, which require each state party to take the appropriate steps to ensure that procedures are established and implemented to make information available to members of the public on the safety of any proposed spent fuel management facility or radioactive waste management facility. Similarly, Article 10(1) of the Convention on Persistent Organic Pollutants[32] specifies that each Party shall, within its capabilities, promote and facilitate provision to the public of all available information on persistent organic pollutants and ensure that the public has access to public information and that the information is kept up-to-date (Art. 10 (1)(b) and (2)).

Regionally, the European Community generally guarantees the right of individuals to be informed about the environmental compatibility of products, manufacturing processes and their effects on the environment, and industrial installations. Two general directives address rights of information. First, Council Directive 85/337 Concerning the Assessment of the Effects of Certain Public and Private Projects on the Environment[33] made explicit the duty to provide information in connection with mandatory environmental assessment projects. Second, the EC adopted in 1990 a Directive on Freedom of Access to Information on the Environment,[34] replaced in January 2003.[35] The 2003 Directive insists that the disclosure of information should be the general rule, making information more accessible than was required under the 1990 directive. Public authorities should be authorized to refuse requests for environmental

31 Vienna, September 5, 1997, *reprinted in* 36 I.L.M. 1431 (1997).

32 Stockholm Convention on Persistent Organic Pollutants (POP s Convention) (Stockholm, May 22, 2001), U.N.T.S. 119..

33 Council Directive 85/337/EEC of June 27, 1985, O.J. L 175/40 (7/5/85).

34 Council Directive 90/313/EEC of June 7, 1990 on the freedom of access to information on the environment, O.J. L 158 (6/23/90).

35 Directive 2003/4/EC of Jan. 28, 2003 on public access to environmental information and repealing Council Directive 90/313/EEC, O.J. L 041 (14/02/2003) 26–32.

information only in specific and clearly defined cases. Environmental information means any information in written, visual, aural, electronic or any other material form on the state of the elements of the environment; factors affecting or likely to affect those elements; measures, including administrative ones; policies, legislation, plans, programs, environmental agreements and activities affecting or likely to affect the environment; and reports on the implementation of environmental legislation; relevant economic analyses and the state of human health and safety. 'Public authority' means the government or other public administration, at national, regional or local level, any natural or legal person performing public administrative functions or having public responsibilities, excluding bodies or institutions acting in a judicial or legislative capacity.

Public authorities shall make available environmental information held by or for them to the public. The latter means one or more natural or legal persons and, in accordance with national legislation or practice, their associations, organizations or groups. Environmental information shall be made available to the applicant as soon as possible. Article 7 of the Directive provides for the dissemination of environmental information, in particular by means of computer telecommunication and/or electronic technology. The information shall include texts of international treaties and of Community, national, regional or local legislation on the environment or relating to it as well as progress reports on the implementation of such texts. Public authorities may charge a reasonable fee for supplying such information, while access to any public registers or lists and examination *in situ* of the information requested shall be free of charge. Authorities may refuse a request for environmental information in conditions similar to those foreseen by the Aarhus Convention, discussed below in section 2.4.

The Directive does not mention public participation. The scope of its Article 6 on access to justice is limited to situations where a request for information has been ignored, wrongfully refused, inadequately or not dealt with in accordance with the provisions related to the access to information. EU guarantees of public participation in environmental procedures, following Aarhus, was transposed by Directive 2003/35/EC. A Regulation adopted in 2006 is intended to guarantee the application of the provisions and principles of the Aarhus Convention by Community institutions and bodies. Access to information is also generally guaranteed by Article 42 of the Charter of Fundamental Rights of the European Union, made binding by the Treaty of Lisbon.[36] The European Green Deal and the EU Biodiversity Strategy for 2030 also emphasize

36 OJ C 83 (30.3.2010), 389–403.

transparency, public participation, and access to environmental information as part of the EU's broader environmental and sustainability goals.

Other organizations have issued non-binding declarations proclaiming a right to environmental information. The World Health Organization's European Charter on the Environment and Health states that 'every individual is entitled to information and consultation on the state of the environment'.[37] The states participating in the Organization for Security and Cooperation in Europe (OSCE) have confirmed the right of individuals, groups, and organizations to obtain, publish and distribute information on environmental issues.[38] The Bangkok Declaration, adopted October 16, 1990, affirms similar rights in Asia and the Pacific[39] while the Arab Declaration on Environment and Development and Future Perspectives of September 1991 speaks of the right of individuals and non-governmental organizations to acquire information about environmental issues relevant to them.[40]

2.2 *Public Participation in Environmental Decision-Making*

The process by which rules emerge, how proposed rules become norms and norms become law, is highly important to the legitimacy of the law, and legitimacy in turn affects compliance. To a large extent, legitimacy is a matter of participation: the governed must have and perceive that they have a voice in governance through representation, deliberation or some other form of action. Participation may take place through elections, grass roots action, lobbying, public speaking, hearings, and other forms of governance whereby various interests and communities participate in shaping the laws and decisions that affect them.

The major role played by the public in environmental protection is the participation in decision-making, especially in environmental impact assessments

---

37 European Charter on Environment and Health, adopted 8 December 1989 by the First Conference of Ministers of the Environment and of Health of the Member States of the European Region of the World Health Organization.

38 Conference on Security and Cooperation in Europe, Sofia Meeting on Protection of the Environment (October-November 1989), (CSCE/SEM.36, November 2, 1989).

39 Ministerial Declaration on Environmentally Sound and Sustainable Development in Asia and the Pacific (Bangkok, October 16, 1990), A/CONF.151/PC/38. Paragraph 27 affirms 'the right of individuals and non-governmental organizations to be informed of environmental problems relevant to them, to have the necessary access to information, and to participate in the formulation and implementation of decisions likely to affect their environment'.

40 Arab Declaration on Environment and Development and Future Perspectives, adopted by the Arab Ministerial Conference on Environment and Development (Cairo, September 1991), A/46/632, U.N. Doc E/CN.4/Sub.2/1992/7, 20.

or other permitting procedures. Public participation is based on the right of those who may be affected, including foreign citizens and residents, to have a say in the determination of their environmental future.

The preparation of the Rio Conference was itself an important step in encouraging the participation of non-governmental organizations and the representatives of economic interests. The Global Forum of Rio, a meeting of non-governmental organizations parallel to the official conference, represented world public opinion in favor of conserving the world's ecosystems. The Rio Declaration reflects and confirms the importance of this opinion. In addition to Principle 10, the Declaration includes provisions on the participation of different components of the population: women (Principle 20), youth (Principle 21), and indigenous peoples and local communities (Principle 22).

Public participation is also emphasized in Agenda 21. The Preamble to Chapter 23 states:

> One of the fundamental prerequisites for the achievement of sustainable development is broad public participation in decision-making. Furthermore, in the more specific context of environment and development, the need for new forms of participation has emerged. This includes the need of individuals, groups, and organizations to participate in environmental impact assessment procedures and to know about and participate in decisions, particularly those that potentially affect the communities in which they live and work. Individuals, groups and organizations should have access to information relevant to environment and development held by national authorities, including information on products and activities that have or are likely to have a significant impact on the environment, and information on environmental protection measures.

Section III identifies major groups whose participation is needed: women, youth, indigenous and local populations, non-governmental organizations, local authorities, workers, business and industry, scientists, and farmers.

The right to participate has two components: the right to be heard and the right to affect decisions. Most multilateral and many bilateral agreements contain references to, or guarantees of, public participation.[41] The UNFCCC,

41 In addition to the treaties discussed in the text, other agreements referring to public participation are the: Protocol to the 1979 Convention on Long-Range Transboundary Air Pollution Concerning the Control of Emissions of Volatile Organic Compounds or Their Transboundary Fluxes (Geneva, November 18, 1991), Art. 2(3)(a)(4); Convention on the Protection and Utilization of Transboundary Rivers and Lakes (Helsinki, March

Article 4(i), obliges Parties to promote public awareness and to 'encourage the widest participation in this process including that of non-governmental organizations'. The Paris Agreement similarly emphasizes the importance for the Parties to 'enhance public and private sector participation in the implementation of nationally determined contribution' (Art. 6(8)(b)). The Convention on Biological Diversity allows for public participation in environmental impact assessment procedures in Article 14(1)(a). Outside the UNCED context, the 1991 Espoo Convention on Environmental Impact Assessment in a Transboundary Context requires states parties to notify the public and to provide an opportunity for public participation in relevant environmental impact assessment procedures regarding proposed activities in any area likely to be affected by transboundary environmental harm. In a final decision on the proposed activities, the state must take due account of the environmental impact assessment, including the opinions of the individuals in the affected area. The Desertification Convention goes furthest in calling for public participation, embedding the issue throughout the agreement. Article 3(a) and (c) begins by recognizing that there is a need to associate civil society with the actions of the state. The treaty calls for an integrated commitment of all actors – national governments, scientific institutions, local communities and authorities, and non-governmental organizations, as well as international partners, both bilateral and multilateral.[42]

The trend towards including rights of public participation is not followed in all multilateral environmental agreements. The United Nations Convention on the Law of the Non-Navigational Uses of International Watercourses[43] and

17, 1992), Art. 16; Convention on the Transboundary Effects of Industrial Accidents (Helsinki, March 17, 1992), Art. 9; Convention for the Protection of the Marine Environment of the Baltic Sea (Helsinki, April 9, 1992), Art. 17; Convention for the Prevention of Marine Pollution of the North-East Atlantic (Paris, September 22, 1992), Art. 9; Convention on Civil Responsibility for Damage resulting from Activities Dangerous to the Environment (Lugano, June 21, 1993), Arts. 13–16; North American Convention on Cooperation in the Field of the Environment (Washington, D.C., September 14, 1993), Arts. 2(1)(a), 14; Convention on Cooperation and Sustainable Development of the Waters of the Danube (Sofia, 29 June 1994), Art. 14; Protocol to the 1975 Barcelona Convention on Specially Protected Zones and Biological Diversity in the Mediterranean (Barcelona, June 10, 1995), Art. 19; Joint Communique and Declaration on the Establishment of the Arctic Council (Ottawa, September 19, 1996), Preamble and Arts.s 1(a), 2, 3(c); Kyoto Protocol to the United Nations Framework Convention on Climate Change (December 11, 1997), Art. 6(3); Convention on Persistent Organic Pollutants (Sept. 22, 2001), Art.10(1)(d), 40 I.L.M. 532 (2001).

42 See also, Arts. 10(2)(e), 13(1)(b), 14(2), 19, and 25.

43 United Nations Convention on the Law of the Non-Navigational Uses of International Watercourses (adopted 21 May 1997, entered into force 17 August 2014) 2999 U.N.T.S. 77.

recent regional agreements for water management provide for interstate cooperation, but do not refer to public participation in decisions regarding the uses and management of international watercourses.[44] An exception to this omission is the 1909 US – Canada Boundary Waters Agreement and the work of its International Joint Commission. The Boundary Waters Treaty requires that the Commission give all interested parties a 'convenient opportunity to be heard' on matters under consideration. The Commission invites public participation and advice when it undertakes studies under References, when it deals with Orders of Approval, and when it prepares reports to Governments. In many instances, citizens, both specialists and non-specialists, also serve on Commission boards and task forces. The Commission is specifically authorized to develop a public information program under the Great Lakes Water Quality Agreement.

Other bilateral agreements also provide for public participation. The 1991 Canada-United States Agreement on Air Quality[45] provides that the International Joint Commission established pursuant to an earlier agreement, shall invite comments, including through public hearings as appropriate, on each progress report prepared by the Air Quality Committee established to assist in implementing the agreement. A synthesis of public views and, if requested, a record of such views shall be submitted to the Parties. After submission to the Parties, the synthesis shall be released to the public. The Parties agree to consult on the contents of the progress report based in part on the views presented to the Commission. Further, in Article XIV, the Parties shall consult with State or Provincial Governments, interested organizations, and the public, in implementing the Agreement. The Agreement on Environmental Cooperation between Canada and Chile[46] lists among its objectives to promote transparency and public participation in the development of environmental law, regulations and policies. The obligations of the parties include periodically preparing and making publicly available reports on the state of the environment. In more detail, Article 4 provides that each party shall ensure that its laws, regulations, procedures and administrative rulings of general application respecting any matter governed by the agreement are promptly published or otherwise made available to enable interested persons and the other party to

44 See e.g. Kenya-Tanzania-Uganda, Final Act of the Conference of Plenipotentiaries on the Establishment of the Lake Victoria Fisheries Organization (Kisumu, Kenya, June 30, 1994); Bangladesh-India Treaty on Sharing of the Ganges Waters at Farakka (New Delhi, December 12, 1996); India-Nepal, Treaty Concerning the Integrated Development of the Mahakai River (New Delhi, February 12, 1996).

45 Agreement between the Government of Canada and the Government of the United States of America on Air Quality (entered into force 13 March 1991) 30 I.L.M. 676.

46 Ottawa, February 6, 1997, *reprinted in* 26 I.L.M. 1193 (1997).

become acquainted with them. To the extent possible, each party is to publish in advance any such measure that it proposes to adopt and provide interested persons and the other party a reasonable opportunity to comment on the proposed measures.

Finally, the 1993 North American Agreement on Environmental Cooperation (NAAEC), also known as the North American Free Trade Agreement (o) side agreement, similarly contains institutional arrangements for public participation. It creates a permanent trilateral body, the Commission for Environmental Cooperation, composed of a Council, a Secretariat and a Joint Public Advisory Committee (Art. 8). The Joint Public Advisory Committee includes fifteen members from the public, five from each member country, and advises the Council as well as provides technical, scientific, or other information to the secretariat. The Committee also may advise on the annual program and budget as well as reports that are issued. NAAEC was also the first environmental agreement to establish a procedure which allows individuals, environmental organizations and business entities to complain about a state's failure to enforce its environmental law, including those deriving from international obligations.

2.3 *The Right to a Remedy for Environmental Harm*

Principle 10 of the Rio Declaration provides that 'effective access to judicial and administrative proceedings, including redress and remedy, shall be provided'. Agenda 21 calls on governments and legislators to establish judicial and administrative procedures for legal redress in order to remedy actions affecting the environment that may be unlawful or infringe on rights under the law. They should provide such access to justice to individuals, groups and organizations with a recognized legal interest. The United Nations Convention on the Law of the Sea (UNCLOS) also provides that states shall ensure that recourse is available for prompt and adequate compensation or other relief in respect of damage caused by pollution of the marine environment by natural or juridical persons under their jurisdiction (Art. 235(2)).

Some instruments make it explicit that the right to a remedy is not limited to nationals of a state, e.g. the Organisation for Economic Cooperation and Development (OECD) Recommendation on Equal Right of Access in Relation to Transfrontier Pollution.[47] International agreements may contain obligations to grant a potential or *de facto* injured person a right of access to any administrative or judicial procedure equal to that of nationals or residents. Equal

47 May 11, 1976, C(76)55(Final).

access to national remedies has been considered one way of implementing the polluter pays principle. Implementing the right of equal access to national remedies requires that states remove jurisdictional barriers to civil proceedings for damages and other remedies in respect of environmental injury. Both the Feb. 25, 1991 Espoo Convention and the March 17, 1992 Helsinki Convention on the Transboundary Effects of Industrial Accidents call for equality of access. The 1997 UN Convention on the Non-Navigational Uses of International Watercourses, Article 32, formulates the same principle under the title 'nondiscrimination'.

More general guarantees of the right of access to justce and to redress are found in human rights law.

2.4 *Regional Agreements*

International efforts to promote procedural rights in environmental instruments produced a landmark agreement on June 25, 1998, when thirty-five states and the European Community signed a Convention on Access to Information, Public Participation and Access to Justice in Environmental Matters (Aarhus).[48] As of July 2023, there are 47 Parties to the Convention, 38 Parties to the Protocol on Pollutant Release and Transfer Registers (PRTRs), and 32 Parties to the amendment concerning public participation in decisions regarding the deliberate release into the environment and the placing on the market of genetically modified organisms (GMOs). The Convention builds on prior texts, especially Principle 1 of the Stockholm Declaration and Principle 10 of the Rio Declaration. The Preamble expressly states that 'every person has the right to live in an environment adequate to his or her health and well-being, and the duty, both individually and in association with others, to protect and improve the environment for the benefit of present and future generations.' The following paragraph adds that to be able to assert the right and observe the duty, citizens must have access to information, be entitled to participate in decision-making and have access to justice in environmental matters. Article 1 also refers to the right of every person of present and future generations to live in an environment adequate to his or her health and well being. In order to contribute to the protection of this right, states parties agree to guarantee the rights of access to information, public participation, and access to justice. The Convention acknowledges its broader implications as well, expressing a

48 The Convention was sponsored by the United Nations Economic Commission for Europe and is open for signature by the 55 members of the UNECE, which includes all of Europe as well as the United States, Canada, and states of the former Soviet Union. States having consultative status with the UNECE may also participate.

conviction that its implementation will 'contribute to strengthening democracy in the region of the UNECE.'

The Convention obliges states parties to collect and publicly disseminate information, and respond to specific requests (Art. 4–5). Each party is to prepare and disseminate a national report on the state of the environment at three- to four-year intervals. In addition, it must disseminate legislative and policy documents, treaties, and other international instruments relating to the environment. Each party must ensure that public authorities, upon request, provide environmental information to a requesting person without the latter having to state an interest. Public authorities means, in addition to government bodies, any natural or legal person having public responsibilities or functions or providing public services. The information has to be made available within one month, or in exceptional cases up to three months. In addition to providing information on request, each state party must be pro-active, ensuring that public authorities collect and update environmental information relevant to their functions. This requires that each state party establish mandatory systems to obtain information on proposed and existing activities which could significantly affect the environment. This provision is clearly aimed at the private sector and is supplemented by Article 5(6) which requires states parties to encourage operators whose activities have a significant impact on the environment to inform the public regularly of the environmental impact of their activities and products, through eco-labeling, eco-auditing or similar means. States parties are also to ensure that consumer information on products is made available.

To enhance the effectiveness of the Convention, the states parties must provide information about information, i.e. the type and scope of information held by public authorities, the basic terms and conditions under which it is made available and the procedure by which it could be obtained. The Convention also foresees the establishment of publicly-accessible electronic sites that should contain reports on the state of the environment, texts of environmental legislation, environmental plans, programs and policies, and other information that could facilitate the application of national law.

Article 4(4) provides numerous exceptions to the duty to inform, reflecting other political, economic and legal interests. A state may refuse to provide the information if the information is not in its possession; the request is manifestly unreasonable or too general; concerns material not completed or internal communications of a public authority; or if the disclosure would adversely affect:

> the confidentiality of public proceedings;
> international relations, national defense or public security;
> criminal investigations or trials;

commercial and industrial secrets (however, information on emissions relevant to the protection of the environment shall be disclosed);
intellectual property rights;
privacy;
the interests of a third party;
the environment, such as the breeding sites of rare species.

The Convention demands that all exceptions be read restrictively and provides that the state may provide broader information rights. In addition, where non-exempt information can be separated from that not subject to disclosure, the non-restricted information must be provided. Despite these interpretive provisions, some environmental groups expressed concern that the exceptions could result in state officials withholding extensive or crucial information.

Any refusal to provide information must be in writing and with reasons given for the refusal. Reasonable fees may be charged for supplying information. The government has special disclosure obligations in case of any imminent threat to human health or the environment.

Public participation, guaranteed in Articles 6–8, is required for all decisions on whether to permit or renew permission for industrial, agricultural and construction activities listed in an Annex to the Convention, as well as other activities which may have a significant impact on the environment. The public must be informed in detail about the proposed activity early in the decision-making process and given time to prepare and participate in the decision-making. During the process, the public must have access to all relevant information on the proposal including the site, description of environmental impacts, measures to prevent and/or reduce the effects, a non-technical summary, an outline of the main alternatives, and any reports or advice given. Public participation can be through writing, hearings or inquiry. All public comments, information, analyses or opinions shall be taken into account by the party in making its decision. All decisions shall be made public, along with the reasons and considerations on which the decision is based.

In addition to providing for public participation regarding decisions on specific projects, the Convention calls for public participation in the preparation of environmental plans, programs, policies, laws and regulations. Further, states parties are to promote environmental education and to recognize and support environmental associations and groups.

The provisions of Article 9 on access to justice mirror many human rights texts in requiring proceedings before an independent and impartial body established by law. Each state party must provide judicial review for any denial of requested information, and a remedy for any act or omission concerning the permitting of activities and 'acts and omissions by private persons and public authorities which contravene provisions of its national law relating to the environment'. Standing to challenge permitting procedures or results is limited to members of the public having a sufficient interest or maintaining impairment of a right; however, the Convention provides that environmental non-governmental organizations 'shall be deemed' to have sufficient interest for this purpose. The public has standing to challenge violations of environmental law as do nongovernmental organizations (NGOs), 'where they meet the criteria, if any, laid down in national law' (Art. 9(3)).

The Convention's topic induced the drafters to take steps towards creating compliance procedures and public participation on the international level. Primary review of implementation is conferred on the Meeting of the Parties (MOP), at which non-governmental organizations 'qualified in the fields to which this Convention relates' may participate as observers if they have made a request and not more than one-third of the parties present at the meeting raise objections (Art. 10). The Convention provision on compliance review (Art. 15) also directs the MOP to create a 'non-confrontational, non-judicial and consultative' optional arrangement for compliance review, which 'shall allow for appropriate public involvement and may include the option of considering communications from members of the public on matters related to this Convention'. This tentative language marked the first time an open compliance procedure has been contemplated in an international environmental agreement.

The first Aarhus MOP, held in 2002, adopted Decision 1/7 on review of compliance,[49] establishing a Compliance Committee composed of independent experts and creating a complaints procedure. The Committee may consider issues brought to its attention of non-compliance by a Party with any provision of the treaty and make recommendations to the MOP on response measures. It also may take certain interim measures and can make its own recommendations if and as appropriate about matters of compliance. The Secretariat acts as the administrative body in the handling of non-compliance cases.

Complaints of non-compliance may be brought by a state party against another state party (or the filing state may self-report that despite its efforts it is unable to comply with the Convention). The Secretariat also has the power to trigger the process if it becomes aware through publicly-available information, including from NGOs, of non-compliance by a party and consultations fail to resolve the matter. Finally, members of the public are permitted to file

49 UNECE Doc. ECE/MP.PP/2/Add.8.

communications, whether or not they are personally affected. Parties may opt out of the public standing to file communications, but not for more than four years.

The communications procedure is similar to that of human rights bodies. Once registered, the communication is circulated to Committee members to review according to a list of admissibility criteria. The Committee normally appoints a rapporteur who is not a national of the state concerned and if it appears that the admissibility criteria are met, a file is opened and the communication is transmitted to the state concerned, together with any points or questions the committee wishes to present. The state has five months to submit written explanations or statements clarifying the matter. The Aarhus Committee considers the information submitted by the applicant and the state party, but may also seek or consider information from experts and advisors, including NGOs, scientists, and international financial institutions. It also may hold a public hearing or, with the consent of the state, undertake an on sit visit to gather information. On the merits, the Committee determines in closed session whether or not the state is in non-compliance with the Convention and may make recommendations to transmit along with its findings to a meeting of the parties.

By 2024, the Committee had received only two inter-state complaints. In contrast, no state had reported on its own non-compliance while more than 130 communications had been filed by the public.[50] The communications concern nearly two dozen states parties and the European Community, which is also a party to the treaty.

Finally, the Protocol to the Aarhus Convention on Pollutant Release and Transfer Registers[51] requires each party to establish a publicly accessible and user-friendly Pollutant Release and Transfer Register, based on a mandatory scheme of annual reporting. The Register covers information on 86 pollutants including greenhouse gases, acid rain pollutants, heavy metals and cancer-causing chemicals such as dioxins. States must report on any significant levels of a wide range of activities, including refineries, thermal power stations, chemical and mining industries, waste incinerators, wood and paper production and

---

50 A compilation of all findings adopted by the Compliance Committee to date is available in a searchable format at https://unece.org/sites/default/files/2023-08/Compilation_of_CC_findings_14.08.2023_eng.pdf (last accessed June 3, 2024).

51 Protocol on Pollutant Release and Transfer Registers to the Convention on Access to Information, Public Participation in Decision-Making and Access to Justice in Environmental Matters (adopted 21 May 2003, entered into force 8 October 2009) 2626 UNTS 119 The Protocol was developed under the auspices of the UN Economic Commission for Europe, but is open to accession by any member state of the UN.

processing and intensive agriculture and aquaculture. The Protocol also provides a framework for reporting on pollution from diffuse sources such as traffic, agriculture and small and medium-sized enterprises. Some of the reported information may be kept confidential, for example, where disclosure could affect commercial confidentiality, national defense or public security, but such examples should be interpreted in a restrictive way, taking into account the public interest served by disclosure. The public should be able to find out about the annual pollution of a given source when it is covered by the Protocol. In what will probably become common in future agreements on public information, the Protocol provides that the Register should be accessible by Internet.

The Escazú Agreement, officially known as the Regional Agreement on Access to Information, Public Participation and Justice in Environmental Matters in Latin America and the Caribbean, aims to ensure the implementation of rights of access to environmental information, public participation in the environmental decision-making process, and access to justice in environmental matters across the region. The Agreement originated from the 2012 United Nations Conference on Sustainable Development, making it the only binding treaty adopted as a result of the conference. Drafted between 2015 and 2018, with the UN Economic Commission for Latin America and the Caribbean (ECLAC) serving as the technical secretariat, the agreement was adopted in Escazú, Costa Rica, on March 4, 2018. It was opened for signature on September 27, 2018 and obtained the required eleven ratifications to enter into force on January 22, 2021. Consequently, the agreement came into effect on April 22, 2021. Like the Aarhus Convention, the Escazú Agreement builds on Principle 1 of the Stockholm Declaration and Principle 10 of the Rio Declaration. Its stated objective is to 'guarantee the full and effective implementation in Latin America and the Caribbean of the rights of access to environmental information, public participation in the environmental decision-making process and access to justice in environmental matters, and the creation and strengthening of capacities and cooperation, contributing to the protection of the right of every person of present and future generations to live in a healthy environment and to sustainable development'.

3 Environmental Protection in International Human Rights Law

This section reviews environmental protection in human rights law and practice. In general, the human rights community now views environmental protection as an appropriate part of the human rights agenda. International complaints procedures are used as an accepted means to achieve the ends of environmental protection when deterioration threatens human well-being. In fact, the dearth of international environmental complaints procedures means human rights tribunals currently provide the main international venues to challenge government action or inaction respecting the environment, at least when the deleterious consequences have an impact on the enjoyment of human rights.

The rights to life, health, adequate standard of living, association, expression, information, property, political participation, personal liberty, equality and remedies, all contained in international legal instruments, can and have been invoked to further environmental goals. The right of minorities to maintain their traditional cultures is also pursued. International courts and other treaty bodies[52] have expanded or reinterpreted these guarantees in the light of environmental concerns, despite the lack of explicit reference to environmental rights in many human rights instruments. The former UN Commission on Human Rights and present Council, the UN Human Rights Committee, the Inter-American Commission and Court of Human Rights, the European Commission and Court of Human Rights, and the African Commission and Court of Human Rights, have developed jurisprudence that recognizes and enforces rights linked to environmental protection. Members of the Committees on the Elimination of Racial Discrimination and Elimination of Discrimination against Women have questioned states parties on environmental matters related to the guarantees of the treaties they monitor. The UN Committee on the Rights of the Child has called for better compliance with Article 24(2)(c), which concerns safe drinking water, sanitation, and nutrition. In 2023, the same Committee adopted General Comment No. 26 on 'Children's Rights and the Environment with a Special Focus on Climate Change'.

Among UN Charter-based organs, most of the human rights work was done in the past by two subsidiary organs: the UN Commission on Human Rights and its Sub-Commission on the Promotion and Protection of Human Rights. The mandates of these bodies extended to all member states of the United Nations and have been taken over by a new body, the Human Rights Council, created in 2006. The UN Commission and, later, the Human Rights Council have adopted several resolutions on aspects of the issue. Res. 2005/60 of April 20, 2005, for example, was entitled 'Human rights and the environment as part

52 International human rights courts exist in the European, Inter-American and African regional systems. The main global treaty bodies are the Human Rights Committee, Committee on Economic, Social and Cultural Rights, Committee on the Elimination of All Forms of Racial Discrimination, Committee on the Elimination of Discrimination against Women, Committee on the Rights of the Child, and Committee against Torture.

of sustainable development'. The resolution noted that environmental damage can have potentially negative effects on the enjoyment of human rights and on a healthy life and a healthy environment, and that protection of the environment and sustainable development can contribute to human well-being and potentially to the enjoyment of human rights. The General Assembly has also spoken to specific issues. General Assembly Resolution 64/292 of 26 July 2010, for example, proclaims that 'health is a fundamental human right indispensable for the exercise of other rights. Every human being should be entitled to the highest attainable standard of health to live on. And since there can be no health without water and sanitation, the right to health thus includes the right of access to safe water and basic sanitation'.

United Nations human rights organs began annually considering environmental issues in the late 1980s, when African countries expressed concern about transboundary movements of hazardous and toxic wastes. In 1988, the UN Sub-Commission on Prevention of Discrimination and Protection of Minorities adopted resolution 1988/26 (Sept. 1) which referred to the right of all peoples to life and the right of future generations to enjoy their environmental heritage. It noted that the movement and dumping of toxic and dangerous products endangers basic human rights, such as the right to life, the right to live in a sound and healthy environment, and consequently the right to health. To help remedy these problems, the resolution called for a ban on the export of toxic and dangerous wastes and a global convention on that subject. In 1989, the Commission approved this text.[53]

During its 1989 session, the Sub-Commission added the topic of human rights and the environment to its agenda and recommended appointment of a special rapporteur on the topic. A rapporteur was appointed and presented a series of reports until 1994, when the final report included a draft declaration on human rights and the environment.[54] The declaration was held for comments each year and no action was taken before the demise of the Commission.

In 1995, a divided Commission decided to appoint a special rapporteur to study the adverse effects of the illicit movement and dumping of toxic and dangerous products and wastes on the enjoyment of human rights.[55] In addition to investigating the human rights effects of illegal dumping of toxic and

53 E/CN.4/1989/42 (Mar. 6, 1989).

54 E/CN.4/Sub.2/1999/9 (July 4, 1994).

55 Res. 1995/81. The vote was 32 to 15, with six abstentions. The division was geographic, with all developing countries of the South voting in favor of the proposal and all Northern states expressing opposition. France, on behalf of the European Union, argued that the question could be dealt with much more effectively through instruments such as the Basel Convention on the Control of Transboundary Movements of Hazardous Wastes and

dangerous products and wastes in developing countries, the Special Rapporteur was given authority to receive and examine communications and undertake fact-finding concerning illicit traffic and dumping, in effect creating an individual complaints procedure. The rapporteur may make recommendations to states on measures to be taken and must produce an annual list of the countries and transnational corporations engaged in illicit dumping, as well as a census of persons killed, maimed or otherwise injured in the developing countries due to the practice. Unlike many international human rights procedures, the mechanism generated a relatively large number of complaints or communications from states as well as NGOs and individuals. The mandate has been continued by the Human Rights Council. The latest renewal was in 2020, ensuring that the Special Rapporteur continues to monitor and report on the issues related to toxic and dangerous products and wastes.

The mandates of other special rapporteurs also extend to environmental matters, including the special rapporteur on the right of everyone to the enjoyment of the highest attainable standard of physical and mental health, the rapporteur on the right to food, and the rapporteur on the right to housing. Each of them has examined environmental degradation as it has an impact on the enjoyment of the rights in question. Such issues include desertification as a contribution to food insecurity, environmentally-hazardous activities as they negatively impact the right to housing, and the siting of residences on or near toxic waste sites.

More recently, special rapporteurs have been appointed to address specific environmental matters. The mandate of the Special Rapporteur on the rights to water and sanitation was established by the Human Rights Council in 2011 (replacing the mandate of the Independent Expert on the human rights to water and sanitation). On the same topic, in 2002, the Committee on Economic, Social and Cultural Rights had adopted General Comment No. 15 on 'The Right to Water', which builds on Articles 11 and 12 of the ICESCR and clearly states that 'the human right to water entitles everyone to sufficient, safe, acceptable, physically accessible and affordable water for personal and domestic uses'.

The first special rapporteur on the promotion and protection of human rights in the context of climate change was appointed by the Human Rights Council in 2022. The Human Rights Council, led by small island states, initially turned to the impact of climate change on the enjoyment of human rights in 2008 when it adopted Council resolution 7/23 on the topic. The resolution

their Disposal. Consequently, the study 'would lead to needless duplication of international mechanisms and to dissipation or wastage of resources'.

recognized that climate change 'poses an immediate and far-reaching threat to people and communities around the world and has implications for the full enjoyment of human rights'. The Council called for a study by the Office of the High Commissioner for Human Rights (OHCHR), a study completed and presented in January 2009.[56] Following consideration of the study, the Council adopted a second resolution on human rights and climate change, resolution 10/29 (Mar. 20, 2009), in which it noted that 'climate change-related effects have a range of implications, both direct and indirect, for the effective enjoyment of human rights' especially for those people who are already in vulnerable situations. Since then, the Council has stressed the link between climate change and human rights in a number of subsequent resolutions.[57]

Several years later, the Council took up again the broader question of the impact of environmental conditions on the enjoyment of human rights, appointing an independent expert on the topic in 2012 and renewing the mandate with the title special rapporteur on the human right to a healthy environment in 2015. The mandate of this special rapporteur was then extended several times, lastly on April 3, 2024, when the title changed to Special Rapporteur on the human right to a clean, healthy and sustainable environment (A/HRC/RES/55/2).

Regional human rights tribunals and national courts increasingly interpret guaranteed human rights by applying environmental law, principles and standards to adjudicate human rights claims related to the environment and to judge whether or not States have complied with their international and domestic obligations (rule of law). Thus, the European Court has indicated that the scope of guaranteed rights is affected by the 'growing and legitimate concern both in Europe and internationally about offenses against the environment'.[58] In the specific case before it, the Court concluded that governments

56 Office of the U.N. High Comm'r for Human Rights, Report of the Office of the U.N. High Commissioner for Human Rights on the Relationship between Human Rights and Climate Change, U.N. Doc. A/HRC/10/61 (Jan. 15, 2009).

57 See e.g. HRC 'Resolution 10/4, Human Rights and Climate Change' UN Doc A/HRC/RES/10/4 (March 25, 2009).

58 See *Mangouras v. Spain*, ECtHR 12050/04 Judgment (January 8, 2009), para. 41 (referred to a Grand Chamber June 5, 2009). Increased concern with the environment has also proved important in cases where states have taken measures to protect the environment and the actions are resisted on the grounds that they interfere with the right to property. In *Fredin v. Sweden* the applicant argued that nature protection was an inadequate reason to revoke a license to extract gravel on his property and therefore was a violation of Article 1, Protocol 1. The Court found no violation, noting that the protection of the environment is an increasingly important consideration. *Fredin v. Sweden*, ECtHR 12033/86 Judgment (February 18, 1991). The Court similarly found no violation of the same provision in *Pine Valley*

may adjust the amount of permissible bail that can be demanded and the length of pre-trial detention allowable according to the particular circumstances of an environmental disaster.[59] In reaching this conclusion, the Court took into account the 1982 Convention on the Law of the Sea and its provisions on offenses against the marine environment, the International Convention for the Prevention of Pollution from Ships (MARPOL),[60] and European law on environmental crimes and liability.[61] In its *Öneryıldız v. Turkey* judgment, the European Court referred to the Convention on Civil Liability for Damage resulting from Activities Dangerous to the Environment[62] and the Convention on the Protection of the Environment through Criminal Law[63] despite the fact that the majority of member States, including the respondent State, had neither signed nor ratified the two Conventions. In the *Taşkın and Others v. Turkey* case, the Court built on its case-law concerning Article 8 of the Convention in matters of environmental protection, largely on the basis of principles enshrined in the Aarhus Convention on Access to Information, Public Participation in Decision-making and Access to Justice in Environmental Matters.[64] Turkey had not signed the Aarhus Convention, but its provisions were deemed to reflect the emerging consensus within Europe on the procedural obligations of parties to the European Convention on Human Rights. Recently, the European Court has been confronted with the question of the applicability of the Convention to climate change. In its first judgment

---

Developments Ltd v. Ireland, where permission to carry out construction in a green belt area was revoked on grounds of environmental protection. *Pine Valley Devs. Ltd. v Ireland,* ECtHR 12742/87 Judgment (November 29, 1991). The most difficult and contentious cases in this respect have concerned travellers or gypsies, whose lifestyle may bring them into contact with modern land use planning. The European Court has repeatedly refused to override local zoning restrictions, especially the creation of green belts, in order to ensure a permanent home for this minority group. See *Buckley v. United Kingdom,* ECtHR 20348/92 Judgment (September 29, 1996), and the four recent cases: *Smith v. United Kingdom,* ECtHR 25154/94 Judgment (January 18, 2001); *Lee v. United Kingdom,* ECtHR 25289/94 Judgment (January 18, 2001); *Chapman v. United Kingdom,* ECtHR 27238/94 Judgment (January 18, 2001); *Beard v. United Kingdom* (GC), ECtHR [GC] 24882/94 Judgment (January 18, 2001).

59 ibid, *Mangouros v. Spain.*

60 International Convention for the Prevention of Pollution from Ships, Nov. 2, 1973 (MARPOL 73/78) and the Protocol thereto adopted Feb. 17, 1978.

61 The Court cited two European Community directives, Directive 2004/35/CE of April 21, 2004 on environmental liability with regard to the prevention and remedying of environmental damage; and Directive 2005/35/EC of 7 Sept. 2005 on ship-source pollution and on the introduction of penalties for infringements.

62 ETS no. 150 – Lugano, June 21, 1993.

63 ETS no. 172 – Strasbourg, November 4, 1998.

64 *Taşkın and Others v. Turkey,* ECtHR 49517/99 Judgment (December 4, 2003), paras. 99 and 119..

on the matter, *Klimaseniorinnen v. Switzerland*, the European Court held that the Swiss Confederation had failed to comply with its duties under the Convention concerning climate change and had therefore violated Article 8 of the European Convention (right to respect for private and family life).[65]

National courts often have jurisdiction to adjudicate complaints about governmental action or inaction with reference to environmental laws and standards. Environmental protection laws in many, if not most states, provide for citizen lawsuits as a means of enforcing legislative and regulatory standards. Such suits have played a significant role in enforcing clean air and water acts,[66] endangered species laws, as well as climate laws.[67] As with human rights litigation, citizens sue the government to secure its performance of mandatory duties under the law;[68] in addition, suits may be brought against regulated industries and other polluters in order to halt environmental harm. Courts have upheld citizen suit provisions and enforced substantive limits on permissible activities. In a significant number of these cases, the primary issue is one of the rule of law – ensuring that properly enacted laws, treaties, and regulations are implemented and enforced.

In general, government officials are held to a due diligence standard.[69] The criteria used to assess whether or not due diligence has been exercised are

---

65 *Verein Klimaseniorinnen Schweiz and Others v. Switzerland*, ECtHR [GC] 53600/20 (Apr. 9, 2024). The European Court also found a violation of Article 6§1 of the Convention (Access to court).

66 The US Clean Air Act of 1970, 42 U.S.C. § 7604, was the first of some twenty environmental statutes in the US to provide for citizen enforcement by allowing suit to be brought for injunctive relief to force compliance and to require the Environmental Protection Agency (EPA) to perform mandatory duties imposed on it by the statute. See Michael D. Axline, *Environmental Citizen Suits* (Butterworth Legal Publishers 1995); James R. May, 'Now More than Ever: Recent Trends in Environmental Citizen Suits' (2004) 10 Widener Law Review 8. The 1972 Clean Water Act, 33 U.S.C. § 1365 is similar, but also authorized citizens to sue polluters for civil penalties. Similar provisions exist in nearly all statutes under the authority of the EPA.

67 See e.g. *Urgenda Foundation v. State of the Netherlands* (2020), *Neubauer et al v. Germany* (2021), *Massachusetts v. Environmental Protection Agency* (2007), *Leghari v. Federation of Pakistan* (2015), *Save Lamu et al v. National Environmental Management Authority and Amu Power CVo. Ltd.* (2019), *Barrick Exploraciones Argentinas S.A. and others v. National Government* (2021), and *Milieudefensie et al v. Royal Dutch Shell Plc.* (2021).

68 See e.g. *Friends of the Earth v. United States EPA*, 2006 U.S. App. LEXIS 10264 (D.C. Cir. 2006) (successfully challenging the EPA determination that pollution caps under the Clean Water Act could be done on a seasonal or annual basis and not as daily loads).

69 Where the agency is engaged in appropriate enforcement of the law through judicial action, citizen suits are inadmissible. See *Baughman v. Bradford Coal Co.*, 592 F.2d 215, 219 (3rd Cir. 1979), cert denied 441 U.S. 961 (1979); *PIRG of N.J. v. Fritzsche, Dodge & Olicott, Inc.*, 759 F.2d 1131 (3rd Cir. 1985).

also applied in many human rights cases to decide whether or not a government has taken the requisite measures to respect and ensure environmental rights. In general, due diligence is tested by whether or not the government sought compliance from the polluter through an enforcement action; whether or not the government monitored the polluter's activities after conclusion of the enforcement action; and whether or not the penalties assessed provided adequate deterrence against repetition of the violation.[70]

Assessing whether rights have been violated involves not only determining the mandated environmental quality, but also assessing whether or not the government has taken the requisite actions to achieve that quality. Human rights tribunals have specified that the state may be responsible whether pollution or other environmental harm is directly caused by the state or whether the state's responsibility arises from its failure to regulate properly private-sector activities.[71] Human rights instruments require states not only to respect the observance of rights and freedoms (duty to respect) but also to guarantee their existence and the free exercise of all of them against private as well as state actors (duty to protect). Thus, any act or omission by a public authority which impairs guaranteed rights may violate a state's obligations.[72] This is particularly important in respect to the environment, where most activities causing harm are undertaken by the private sector.

Regional human rights jurisprudence and country studies have specified that governments must enact appropriate laws and regulations, and then fully enforce them. Governments must regulate industrial and other activities that potentially could result in environmental conditions so detrimental that they create risks to health or life.[73] Furthermore, the government must enforce the laws that it enacts as well as any constitutional guarantee of a particular quality of environment.[74] The state must also comply with and enforce the

---

70 In Citizens for a Better Environment v. Laidlaw Environmental Services (TOC), Inc., 890 F. Supp. 470 (D.S.C. 1995), rev'd on other grounds, 149 F.3d 303 (4th Cir. 1998); rev'd on other grounds, 528 U.S. 167 (2000), a civil penalty of $100,000 was considered inadequate and a citizen suit for additional penalties was allowed to proceed.

71 See: *Hatton and Others v. the United Kingdom*, ECtHR [GC] 36022/97 Judgment (July 8, 2003), VIII; *Moreno Goméz v. Spain*, ECtHR 4143/02 Judgment (November 16, 2004). para 55; *Giacomelli v. Italy*, ECtHR 59909/00 Judgment (November 2, 2006), paras. 78–79; *Surugiu v. Romania*, ECtHR 48995/99 Judgment (April 20, 2004).

72 *Case of Velásquez-Rodríguez v. Honduras*. IACtHR Judgment (July 29, 1988), para. 155. (concerning disappearance of civilians perpetrated by the Honduran army); *Case of Godínez Cruz v. Honduras*. IACtHR Judgment (January 20, 1989), paras. 152–53.

73 Inter-Am.C.H.R., *Report on the Situation of Human Rights in Ecuador*, OEA/Ser.L/V/II.96, doc. 10 rev. 1 (1997) [hereinafter *Report on Ecuador*], p. v.

74 ibid.

international agreements to which it is a signatory, whether these are human rights instruments or ones related to environmental protection.[75]

The European Court requires at a minimum that the state subject to a complaint should have complied with its domestic environmental standards.[76] The issue of compliance with domestic law is particularly important when there is a domestic constitutional right to environmental protection. The European Court will review governmental actions in the light of the domestic law. Beyond ensuring that any domestic environmental rights are enforced, the European Court scrutinizes the adequacy of the domestic law, to see if the State has ensured a fair balance between the interests of the community and the rights of those affected. The Court accords the state a wide margin of appreciation, noting that national authorities 'are in principle better placed than an international court to assess the requirements' in a particular local context and to determine the most appropriate environmental policies and individual measures while taking into account the needs of the local community,[77] especially in such a technical sphere.[78] The wide margin of appreciation afforded governments in this sphere means that the Court will only find a violation if there is a 'manifest error of appreciation' by the national authorities in striking a fair balance between the competing interests of the different private actors.[79] The final evaluation as to whether the justification given by the State is relevant and sufficient remains subject to review by the Court[80] but 'only in exceptional circumstances' will the court look beyond the procedures followed to disallow the conclusions reached by domestic authorities.[81] Beyond this conclusion, the Court will not determine exactly what should have been done to reduce

---

75 In the Ecuador report, the Commission noted that the state is party to or has supported a number of instruments 'which recognize the critical connection between the sustenance of human life and the environment', including: the Additional Protocol to the American Convention in the Area of Economic, Social and Cultural Rights, the ICCPR and the ICESCR, the Stockholm Declaration, the Treaty for Amazonian Cooperation, the Amazon Declaration, the World Charter for Nature, the Convention on Nature Protection and Wildlife Preservation in the Western Hemisphere, the Rio Declaration on Environment and Development, and the Convention on Biological Diversity. Through the standard-setting and enforcement process, the State must 'take the measures necessary to ensure that the acts of its agents ... conform to its domestic and inter-American legal obligations'.

76 ibid; see also *Ashworth and Others v. the United Kingdom*, ECtHR 39561/98 Admissibility (January 20, 2004); *Moreno Goméz v. Spain*.

77 *Giacomelli*, para. 80.

78 *Fadayeva v. Russia* ECtHR 55723/00 Judgment (June 9, 2005), citing *Hatton*, para. 122.

79 ibid.

80 ibid paras. 102–103.

81 ibid para. 105, citing *Taşkın*.

the pollution in a more efficient way.[82] In the *Klimaseniorinnen v. Switzerland* decision, the European Court made a clear distinction between the scope of the margin of appreciation as regards the setting of climate change mitigation objectives and the choice of means designed to achieve those objectives. The Court reached the following conclusion:

> As regards the former aspect, the nature and gravity of the threat and the general consensus as to the stakes involved in ensuring the overarching goal of effective climate protection through overall GHG reduction targets in accordance with the Contracting Parties' accepted commitments to achieve carbon neutrality, call for a reduced margin of appreciation for the States. As regards the latter aspect, namely their choice of means, including operational choices and policies adopted in order to meet internationally anchored targets and commitments in the light of priorities and resources, the States should be accorded a wide margin of appreciation.[83]

3.1 *Right to Life and Right to Health*

In the context of the periodic state reporting procedure established by the International Covenant on Civil and Political Rights,[84] the Human Rights Committee makes concluding observations and recommendations to the state. In addition, the Committee issues General Comments to all states parties about the scope of rights and obligations contained in the Covenant. In the latter context, the Committee has indicated that state duties to protect the right to life can require positive measures designed to reduce infant mortality and

---

82 In particular, the Court says it would be going too far to assert that the State or the polluting undertaking were under an obligation to provide the applicant with free housing (para. 133). It is enough to say that the situation called for a special treatment of those living near the plant.

83 *Klimaseniorinnen v. Switzerland*, para. 203.

84 The eighteen independent experts on the UN Human Rights Committee supervise state implementation of and compliance with the International Covenant on Civil and Political Rights, primarily through a system of state reporting. Each state party submits periodic reports on the measures taken to give effect to the rights in the Covenant, and sends a representative to answer questions of the Committee members when the report is considered in public session. A study published in 1990 surveyed 36 states whose periodic reports had been considered by the Committee. Of these 32 reported changes in their laws or practices in response to the review procedure. See C. Cohn, *1990 Human Rights Quarterly*.

protect against malnutrition and epidemics, matters related to environmental protection.[85]

The Human Rights Committee may hear individual complaints against a state party to the International Covenant on Civil and Political Rights if the state has accepted the first Optional Protocol to the Covenant. The Committee has received several complaints concerning environmental damage as a violation of one or more civil and political rights. A group of Canadian citizens, for example, alleged that the storage of radioactive waste near their homes threatened the right to life of present and future generations. The Committee found that the case raised 'serious issues with regard to the obligation of states parties to protect human life', but declared the case inadmissible due to failure to exhaust local remedies.[86]

The Committee on Economic, Social and Cultural Rights supervises implementation of the Covenant guaranteeing these rights, also by means of periodic reporting. In this context, states often report on environmental issues as they affect guaranteed rights. The Ukraine reported on the environmental situation consequent to the explosion at Chernobyl, in regard to the right to life. Committee members also sometimes request specific information about environmental harm that threatens human rights. Poland, for example, was asked to provide information about measures to combat pollution in upper Silesia.[87] The Committee may pose questions and make recommendations in response to the state report.

On November 8, 2000, the Committee on Economic, Social and Cultural Rights issued General Comment No. 14 on 'Substantive Issues Arising in the Implementation of the International Covenant on Economic, Social and Cultural Rights' (Art. 12).[88] The Comment states in paragraph 4 that 'the right to health embraces a wide range of socio-economic factors that promote conditions in which people can lead a healthy life, and extends to the underlying determinates of health, such as … a healthy environment'. General Comment 14 adds that '[a]ny person or group victim of a violation of the right to health should have access to effective judicial or other appropriate remedies at both national and international levels and should be entitled to adequate

85 See the General Comment on Article 6 of the Civil and Political Covenant, issued by the United Nations Human Rights Committee, in *Compilation of General Comments and General Recommendations adopted by Human Rights Treaty Bodies*, UN Doc. HRI/GEN/1/Rev.3 (1997) 6–7 [hereinafter *Compilation*].

86 Communication No. 67/1980, *EHP v. Canada*, 2 Selected Decisions of the Human Rights Committee (1990), 20.

87 E/1989/4/Add.12.

88 U.N. CESCR, General Comment 14, U.N. Doc. E/C.12/2000/4 (2000).

reparation'.[89] Thereafter, General Comment No. 15[90] set forth a detailed discussion of the right to water implicit in the Covenant's Articles 11 and 12.

Regional human rights bodies in Europe, the Americas and Africa have all examined cases alleging violations of the right to life due to environmental harm. In the Inter-American system, the Commission established a link between environmental quality and the right to life in response to a petition brought on behalf of the Yanomani Indians of Brazil. The petition alleged that the government violated the American Declaration of the Rights and Duties of Man[91] by constructing a highway through Yanomani territory and authorizing the exploitation of the territory's resources. These actions led to the influx of non-indigenous people who brought contagious diseases which remained untreated due to lack of medical care. The Commission found that the government had violated the Yanomani rights to life, liberty and personal security guaranteed by Article 1 of the Declaration, as well as the right of residence and movement (Art. VIII) and the right to the preservation of health and well-being (Art. XI).[92]

Apart from receiving and examining individual complaints, the Inter-American Commission on Human Rights has the authority to study the human rights situation generally or in regard to specific issues within an OAS member state. The Commission devoted particular attention to environmental rights in reports on Ecuador[93] and Brazil.[94] In the first instance, the Commission responded to claims that oil exploitation activities were contaminating water, air and soil, thereby causing the people of the region to become sick and to have a greatly increased risk of serious illness.[95] In addition, many inhabitants

89 ibid Para. 59.

90 General Comment No. 15 (2002), E/C.12/11, Jan. 20, 2003, the Right to Water (Arts. 11 and 12 of the International Covenant on Economic, Social and Cultural Rights.

91 Pan American Union, Final Act of the Ninth Conference of American States, Res. XXX, at 38 (1948), reprinted in OAS, *Basic Documents Pertaining to Human Rights in the Inter-American System* (1996).

92 Case 7615 (Brazil), Inter-Am.Ch.R., 1984–1985 Annual Report 24, OEA/Ser.L/V/II.66, doc. 10, rev. 1 (1985).

93 Inter-Am.C.H.R., *Report on the Situation of Human Rights in Ecuador*, OEA/Ser.L/V/II.96, doc. 10 rev. 1 (1997).

94 Inter-Am.C.H.R., *Report on the Situation of Human Rights in Brazil*, OEA/Ser.L/V/II.97, doc. 29, rev. 1 (1997). Among the problems discussed are those of environmental destruction leading to severe health and cultural consequences. In particular indigenous cultural and physical integrity are said to be under constant threat and attack from invading prospectors and the environmental pollution they create. State protection against the invasions is called 'irregular and feeble' leading to constant danger and environmental deterioration.

95 *Report on Ecuador.* The Commission first became aware of the situation in the Oriente through a petition filed on behalf of the indigenous Huaorani people in 1990. The Com-

claimed that pollution of local waters contaminated fish and drove away wildlife, threatening food supplies.

The Commission identified relevant human rights law and emphasized the right to life and physical security. It stated that

> [t]he realization of the right to life, and to physical security and integrity is necessarily related to and in some ways dependent upon one's physical environment. Accordingly, where environmental contamination and degradation pose a persistent threat to human life and health, the foregoing rights are implicated.[96]

States parties may be required therefore to take positive measures to safeguard the fundamental and non-derogable rights to life and physical integrity, in particular to prevent the risk of severe environmental pollution that could threaten human life and health, or to respond when persons have suffered injury.

The Commission directly addressed concerns for economic development, noting that the Convention does not prevent nor discourage it, but rather requires that it take place under conditions of respect for the rights of affected individuals. Thus, while the right to development implies that each state may exploit its natural resources, 'the absence of regulation, inappropriate regulation, or a lack of supervision in the application of extant norms may create serious problems with respect to the environment which translate into violations of human rights protected by the American Convention'.[97] The Commission returned to the procedural dimension, concluding that

> [c]onditions of severe environmental pollution, which may cause serious physical illness, impairment and suffering on the part of the local populace, are inconsistent with the right to be respected as a human being … The quest to guard against environmental conditions which threaten human health requires that individuals have access to: information, participation in relevant decision-making processes, and judicial recourse.[98]

---

mission decided that the problem was more widespread and thus should be treated within the framework of the general country report.

96 ibid, 88.

97 ibid, 89.

98 ibid, 92, 93. The Commission also stated that the right to seek, receive and impart information and ideas of all kinds is protected by Article 13 of the American Convention. According to the Commission, information that domestic law requires be submitted as part of environmental impact assessment procedures must be 'readily accessible' to potentially

The Commission called on the government to implement legislation enacted to strengthen protection against pollution, clean up activities by private licensee companies, and take further action to remedy existing contamination and prevent future recurrences. In particular it recommended that the State take measures to improve systems to disseminate information about environmental issues, enhance the transparency of and opportunities for public input into processes affecting the inhabitants of development sectors.

The Inter-American Court of Human Rights provided a significant interpretation of the right to life in its 2017 Advisory Opinion OC-23/17. This opinion addresses environmental protection and its impact on human rights, specifically focusing on the right to life under Article 4 of the American Convention on Human Rights. In particular, the Court clarified that, regarding transboundary environmental harm, the obligations to 'respect' and 'ensure' the rights to life and personal integrity must be interpreted in light of international environmental law – with particular regard to the duty to prevent environmental harm, the precautionary principle, the duty to cooperate with potentially affected states, and procedural environmental rights.

Within Europe, there have been several significant right to life cases concerning environmental harm.[99] In *Oneryildiz v. Turkey*,[100] the European Court of Human Rights made reference to several environmental texts, both binding and non-binding in holding the Turkish government responsible for the loss of life and property resulting from a methane explosion in a waste site. The binding texts deemed relevant were the Lugano Convention on hazardous

---

affected individuals. Public participation is viewed as linked to Article 23 of the American Convention, which provides that every citizen shall enjoy the right 'to take part in the conduct of public affairs, directly or through freely chosen representatives'. Finally, the right of access to judicial remedies is called 'the fundamental guarantor of rights at the national level'. The Commission quotes Article 25 of the American Convention that provides everyone 'the right to simple and prompt recourse, or any other effective recourse, to a competent court or tribunal for protection against acts that violate his fundamental rights recognized by the constitution or laws of the state concerned or by th[e] Convention'.

99 See e.g. at ECtHR : *Oneryildiz v. Turkey*, App. No. 48939/99, Judgment (November 30, 2004), paras. 89–90; *Kolyadenko and Others v. Russia*, App. Nos. 17423/05, 20534/05, 20678/05, 23263/05, 24283/05 and 35673/05, Judgment (February 28, 2012), paras. 157–61; *Vilnes and others v. Norway*, App. No. 52806/09, Judgment (December 5, 2013), paras. 219–20; *Brincat and others v. Malta*, App. Nos. 60908/ 11, 62110/11, 62129/11, 62312/11, and 62338/11, Judgment (July 24, 2014), paras. 59, 79–85, 101; *Özel and others v. Turkey*, App. Nos. 14350/05, 15245/05, and 16051/05, Judgment (November 17, 2015), paras. 170–2.

100 *Oneryildiz v. Turkey* (GC), Rep. 2004-VI.

activities[101] and the Strasbourg Convention on Protection of the Environment through Criminal Law.[102] The European Court used the Lugano Convention to define 'dangerous activity' and 'damage' incurring the liability of public authorities. It noted the duty under the Strasbourg Convention for authorities to establish criminal offenses for loss of life involving the disposal or treatment of hazardous wastes.

The Court also made reference in particular to non-binding Council of Europe texts, including Parliamentary Assembly Resolution 587 (1975) on problems connected with the disposal of urban and industrial waste; Resolution 1087 (1996) on the consequences of the Chernobyl disaster, and Recommendation 1225 (1993) on the management, treatment, recycling and marketing of waste. In addition to Parliamentary Assembly texts, the Court cited the Committee of Ministers Recommendation No. R(96) 12 on the distribution of powers and responsibilities between central authorities and local and regional authorities with regard to the environment.

On the merits of this case, the Court explained that the right to life provision, Article 2 of the European Convention 'must be construed as applying in the context of any activity, whether public or not, in which the right to life may be at stake, and a fortiori in the case of industrial activities, which by their very nature are dangerous, such as the operation of waste–collection sites'. According to European standards, waste disposal is a hazardous activity, therefore Article 2 applies. The resulting duty of care depends on several factors: the harmfulness of the phenomena inherent in the activity; the contingency of the risk to the applicant; the status of those involved in creating the risk, and whether or not the conduct was deliberate. The court merged procedural rights into the substantive evaluation, finding that 'particular emphasis' should be placed on the public's right to information concerning the risks to life and the duty to investigate when loss of life occurs.[103] Assessing the evidence, the Court found that the authorities must have known of the risk and of the need to take preventive measures 'particularly as there were specific regulations on the matter'.[104] As such they had an obligation as well under Convention Article

101 Convention on Civil Liability for Damage resulting from Activities Dangerous to the Environment, Lugano, June 21, 1993, E.T.S. No. 150.

102 Convention on Protection of the Environment through Criminal Law, Strasbourg, Nov. 4, 1998, E.T.S. No. 172. The Court noted that the Strasbourg Convention was not in force, but found it 'very much in keeping with the current trend towards harsher penalties for damage to the environment'.

103 ibid para. 90.

104 ibid para. 101.

2, 'to take such preventive measures as were necessary and sufficient to protect those individuals ….'[105] The government failed in its duty.

Like *Oneryildiz*, the case of *Budayeva and Others v. Russia*,[106] concerned governmental knowledge of hazards and the failure to act upon that knowledge. The difference was that the latter case involved repeated natural disasters rather than hazards originating in human activities. The standard of care did not differ appreciably, however. Governmental authorities aware of mudslide hazards in a mining district failed to take reasonable precautions, with resulting deaths in a village and loss of property. They pleaded violations of Article 2 (right to life) and Protocol 1, Article 1 (right to property). They claimed that the domestic authorities were responsible for failing to take appropriate measures to mitigate the risks to their lives against the natural hazards, also that they were negligent in maintaining a dam intended to prevent mudslide damage, and were negligent in monitoring the hazardous area. The Court held the government responsible for the loss of life, but found that the causal link was not established in respect of the latter claims. The applicants could not demonstrate that 'but for' the official failures to act, their property would have been safe. The mudslide in question, which took place in July 2000, was of unprecedented severity.

Looking at the substantive aspect of the government's obligations respecting dangerous activities, the Court placed special emphasis on the adoption of regulations geared to the special features of the activity in question, particularly with regard to the level of the potential risk to human life.[107] Such regulations must govern the licensing, setting up, operation, security and supervision of the activity and must make it compulsory for all those concerned to take practical measures to ensure the effective protection of citizens whose lives might be endangered by the inherent risks.[108] Supervision and monitoring are also required. The choice of particular practical measures is in principle a matter within the State's margin of appreciation and the Court will seek to avoid placing an impossible or disproportionate burden on authorities.[109] In this case, the Court requested the government to provide information on its regulatory framework, land-planning policies and specific safety measures implemented at the relevant time to respond to natural hazards. The Court

105 ibid.

106 *Budayeva and Others v. Russia*, ECtHR 15339/02, 21166/02, 20058/02, 11673/02 and 15343/02, Judgment (March 20, 2008).

107 ibid para. 132.

108 ibid.

109 ibid para. 135.

found that the measures were limited to a mud-retention dam and collector that were not adequately maintained. The Court found no justification for the failure to act regarding foreseeable mortal risks to the residents of the town and found a causal link between that failure and the death and injuries suffered in the mudslide. Accordingly, there was a violation of Article 2.

The wide margin of appreciation afforded in environmental matters, due to their technical complexity, and the state's priorities and resources, is given even greater weight in the sphere of emergency relief in relation to weather events. In respect to protecting property, the Court held that the State's positive obligation is less in the context of natural disasters, 'which are as such beyond human control', than in the sphere of dangerous activities of a man-made nature. The right to peaceful enjoyment of possessions, which is not absolute, requires only that the state do what is reasonable in the circumstances.[110] As for Article 2, the positive obligations require the state to do everything within the authorities' power in the sphere of disaster relief for the protection of the right to life. The origin of the threat and the extent to which one or another risk is susceptible to mitigation are factors to be evaluated in determining the scope of the state's positive obligations.[111] Despite this highly deferential standard, the Court found that the authorities had been given warnings about the risks, including the state of disrepair of the dam, and had failed to provide resources for strengthening the defense infrastructure – resources that became available immediately after the mudslide. The government provided no explanation and the Court concluded that the restoration of the defense infrastructure between 1999 and 2000 was 'not given proper consideration by the decision-making and budgetary bodies prior to the hazardous season of 2000'.[112] Nor were any alternative land-planning policies being implemented or monitoring stations set up. The Court noted that the public's procedural right of information can only be implemented if the government obtains the relevant information, which in this case was indispensable for ensuring the residents' safety. The authorities' failure to ensure the functioning of an early warning system was thus also unjustified.

There is no right to health in the European Convention, but cases concerning privacy and home life often assert that environmental conditions are such

---

110 ibid para. 174. While the Court found that the measures taken by the state were negligent, it found the causal link was not well-established. The mudslide of 2000 being exceptionally strong, the Court said it was unclear whether a functioning warning system or proper maintenance of the defence infrastruction would have mitigated the damage.

111 ibid para. 137.

112 ibid para. 149.

that health and well-being are negatively affected. These cases are discussed infra in the section on the right to privacy and home life.

The cases submitted in the African system initially invoked the right to health, protected by Article 16 of the African Charter, rather than the right to environment contained in the same document. In *Communications 25/89, 47/90, 56/91 and 100/93 against Zaire* the Commission held that failure by the Government to provide basic services such as safe drinking water constitute a violation of Article 16. More recently, applicants successfully alleged a violation of the right to environment by Nigeria, as described in the section on the right to a healthy environment (*Ogoni* case).

3.2 *Right to an Adequate Standard of Living and the Fulfillment of Basic Needs*

UN human rights treaty and Charter-based bodies have taken up the relationship between environmental protection and the enjoyment of human rights in the context of economic, social and cultural rights. A Special Rapporteur on the right to food has paid specific attention to the issue of safe drinking water,[113] with resolutions specifically linking implementation of the right to food with sound environmental policies and noting that problems related to food shortages 'can generate additional pressures upon the environment in ecologically fragile areas.'

The Committee on Economic, Social and Cultural Rights has pursued similar questions in monitoring state reports, including asking about measures to prevent degradation of natural resources, particularly erosion, and measures to prevent contamination of food.[114] The Committee also referred to environmental issues in its General Comments on the Right to Adequate Food[115] on the Right to Adequate Housing, and on the Right to Water. In the first, the Committee interpreted the phrase 'free from adverse substances' in Article 11 of the Covenant to mean that the state must adopt food safety and other protective measures to prevent contamination through 'bad environmental hygiene'. The Comment on housing states that 'housing should not be built on polluted sites nor in proximity to pollution sources that threaten the right to health of the inhabitants'.[116] General Comment No. 15 on the Right to Water states that *inter*

113 Resolution 2001/25, The Right to Food, E/CN.4/RES/2001/25 of 20 April 2001. For further discussion of the right to water, see Chapter 7.

114 E/1986/3/Add.9.

115 General Comment 12, E/C.12/1999/5.

116 General Comment 4 of Dec. 13, 1991, United Nations, *Compilation,* HRI/GEN/1/Rev.3, 63, para. 5.

alia 'the water required for each personal or domestic use must be safe, therefore free from micro-organisms, chemical substances and radiological hazards that constitute a threat to a person's health'.

The limited number of communications procedures with respect to economic, social and cultural rights has hampered the development of jurisprudence on these issues. The European Committee on Social Rights does receive collective complaints, however, alleging violations of the 1961 European Social Charter. Complaint No. 30/2005, *Marangopoulos Foundation for Human Rights v. Greece* was the first to concern environmental conditions. It claimed violations of Article 11 (right to protection of health), and other articles addressing unhealthy working conditions. The complaint alleged and the Committee found that in the main areas where lignite is mined, the State had not adequately prevented negative environmental impacts nor had it developed an appropriate strategy in order to prevent and respond to the health hazards for the population. The Committee on Social Rights transmitted its findings to the Council of Europe's Committee of Ministers which stated that the right to health had been violated in part because of a failure to take action against excessive greenhouse gas emissions and to provide for public information and participation as required by national legislation.

3.3 *Right to Privacy, Home and Family Life*

In Europe, those who have suffered from environmental harm have complained most often that the resulting conditions violate the right to privacy and home guaranteed by the 1950 European Convention on Human Rights and Fundamental Freedoms. Article 8(1) provides that 'everyone has the right to respect for his privacy, his home and his correspondence'. The second paragraph of Article 8 sets forth the permissible grounds for limiting the exercise of the right.[117]

The former European Commission on Human Rights[118] and the European Court have held that environmental harm attributable to state action or inaction which has significant injurious effect on a person's home or private and family life constitutes an interference with Article 8(1). The harm may be

117 Paragraph 2 provides: 'There shall be no interference by a public authority with the exercise of this right except such as is in accordance with the law and is necessary in a democratic society in the interests of national security, public safety or the economic well-being of the country, for the prevention of disorder or crime, for the protection of health and morals, or for the protection of the rights and freedoms of others'.

118 With the entry into force of Protocol 11 to the European Convention on Human Rights, the former Commission and the European Court were merged into a new permanent European Court which was inaugurated on November 1, 1998.

allowable, however, under Article 8(2) if it results from an authorized activity of economic benefit to the community in general, as long as there is no disproportionate burden on any particular individual; *i.e.* the measures must have a legitimate aim, be lawfully enacted, and be proportional. To make a claim under Article 8, an individual's home life must be directly affected; harm to the surrounding environment, even protected areas, is not sufficient. According to the European Court, Article 8(1) extends only to protection against 'a harmful effect on a person's private or family sphere and not simply the general deterioration of the environment'.[119]

Many of the European privacy and home cases involve noise pollution, with early ones being resolved through friendly settlement.[120] Settlement of the cases left unresolved numerous issues, some of which were addressed by the Court in *Powell & Raynor v. United Kingdom*[121] in which the Court found that aircraft noise from Heathrow Airport constituted a violation of Article 8, but was justified under Article 8(2) as 'necessary in a democratic society' for the economic well-being of the country.[122] The Court revisited the question of noise at Heathrow in *Hatton and Others v. The United Kingdom.* The initial Chamber judgment of October 2, 2001, found that the noise from increased flights at Heathrow airport between 4 a.m. and 6 a.m. violated the rights of the applicants to respect for their home and family life. This judgment was overturned by a Grand Chamber decision (12–5) on July 8, 2003. The Grand Chamber's lengthy decision continues to accept that 'where an individual is directly and seriously affected by noise or other pollution, an issue may arise under Article 8'[123] and the Court will assess the government's actions both on the substantive merits, to ensure that it is compatible with Article 8, and procedurally, 'to ensure that due weight has been accorded to the interests of the

---

119 *Kyrtatos v. Greece*, App. No. 41666/98, 40 EHRR 390 (2003) (finding no violation of Article 8 due to the destruction of a protected wetland adjacent to the applicant's property).

120 Application 7889/77, *Arrondelle v. United Kingdom*, 19 D. & R. 186 (1980) and 26 D. & R. 5 (1982); Application 9310/81, *Baggs v. United Kingdom*, 44 D. & R. 13 (1985); 52 D. & R. 29 (1987).

121 *Powell and Rayner v. United Kingdom*, 172 Eur.Ct.H.R. (ser.A)(1990).

122 Noise was acceptable under the principle of proportionality, if it did not 'create an unreasonable burden for the person concerned', a test that could be met by the state if the individual had 'the possibility of moving elsewhere without substantial difficulties and losses'. In a subsequent case, the Commission found that the level and frequency of the noise did not reach the point where a violation of Article 8 could be made out and the application was therefore inadmissible. Application 1281/87, *Vearncombe et al. v. United Kingdom and Federal Republic of Germany*, 59 D. & R. 186 (1989).

123 Judgment of July 8, 2003, para. 96.

individual'.[124] It pays particular attention to the compatibility of the state's actions or inactions with domestic law.[125] In all environmental cases, however, the state enjoys a wide margin of appreciation 'because it would not be appropriate for the Court to adopt a special approach in this respect by reference to a special status of environmental human rights'.[126] Applying its 'fair balance' test with deference to the government, the Court assessed the economic contribution of the flights and the harm to the individuals.[127] On the procedural side, the Court agreed that the government must undertake appropriate investigations and studies in order to allow them to strike a fair balance between the various conflicting interests.[128] Looking at the studies done, the Court found that the government did not exceed its margin of appreciation in striking the balance and following the procedures it did to allow more night flights at Heathrow. Thus, there was no violation of Article 8.[129] The Grand Chamber did uphold the Chamber's judgment finding a violation of Article 13 (right to a remedy) and awarded some costs and fees to the applicants.

Subsequent noise cases have made clear the importance of domestic law. In *Moreno Gomez v. Spain* (Nov. 16, 2004) the applicant succeeded in his claim of noise pollution under the 'fair balance' test. The Court unanimously held that noise levels from bars, pubs and discotheques near the applicant's home amounted to a breach of Article 8, noting in particular that the city council did not enforce its own noise abatement measures. The applicant was awarded damages, as well as costs and expenses.

Lopez-Ostra v. Spain[130] was the first major decision of the Court finding air pollution to be a breach of the right to private life and the home. The applicant and her daughter suffered serious health problems from the fumes of an

---

124 ibid para. 99.

125 The Grand Chamber notes that the Hatton case is unlike either *Lopez Ostra* or *Maria Guerra*, discussed infra, because in the latter two cases the government's actions were irregular or incompatible with domestic law or procedures. ibid, para. 120.

126 ibid para 122.

127 ibid para. 127. It notes as an additional 'significant' factor that the 2–3% of the population specially affected can 'if they choose, move elsewhere without financial loss'. As several applicants in the case had moved away from Heathrow by the time the Court heard the case, the record may have included information on the economic impact of the moves.

128 The dissent points out that the report on the economic well-being of the country was prepared for the government by the aviation industry and no attempt was made to assess the impact of the aircraft noise on the applicants' sleep.

129 See also, *Ashworth and others v. UK*, finding inadmissible a claim of noise pollution from a private airport. Adm. Dec. 20 2004.

130 *Lopez-Ostra v. Spain*, 303C Eur.Ct. Hum. Rts. (ser. A) (1994).

illegally-operating tannery waste treatment plant which operated alongside the apartment building where they lived. The plant malfunctioned when it began operations, releasing gas fumes and contamination that caused health problems and nuisance to people living in the district. Despite this, the authorities allowed the plant to resume partial operation and the problems continued. The European Court's judgment was significant for several reasons. First, the Court did not require the applicant to exhaust administrative remedies to challenge operation of the plant under the environmental protection laws, but only to complete remedies applicable to enforcement of basic rights. Secondly, the European Human Right Court held that Article 8 was violated because severe environmental pollution may affect individuals' well-being and prevent them from enjoying their homes in such a way as to affect their private and family life adversely, even if it does not seriously endanger their health. It held Spain had exceeded its margin of appreciation in balancing the individual interests and those of the community. It awarded Mrs. Lopez damages, court costs, and attorneys fees. This judgment opened the door to several further cases.[131] In *Maria Guerra and Others v. Italy*,[132] the basis of the complaint was the government's failure to provide environmental information, not pollution and the Court found a positive obligation in this respect under Article 8, thus expanding the obligations of the state to disseminate environmental information.

The Court further explained the *Lopez Ostra* standard in *Fadayeva v. Russia*,[133] noting that because 'no right to nature preservation is as such included among the rights and freedoms guaranteed by the Convention', the adverse effects of environmental pollution must attain a certain minimum level if they are to fall within the scope of Article 8. The requisite effects or interference need not reach the level of proven injury to health; it is enough if there are serious risks posed. In *Fadayeva*, the applicant succeeded on her claim because she was made more vulnerable to various diseases, even though quantifiable

131 *Bacila v. Romania*, Judgment of March 30, 2010, Eur. Ct. Hum. Rts.; *Dubetska and Others v Ukraine*, Judgment of Feb. 10, 2011, Eur. Ct. Hum. Rts.; *Di Sarno and Others v. Italy*, Judgment of Jan. 10, 2012, Eur. Ct. Hum. Rts.

132 *Guerra and Others v. Italy*, Judgment of February 19, 1998, 1998–I Eur. Ct. Hum. Rts.

133 *Fadayeva v. Russia*, no. 55723/00, judgment of June 9, 2005, 2005/IV Eur. Ct. Hum. Rts.. 255 (2005). See also *Dubetska and Others v. Ukraine*, finding a violation of Article 8 due to the failure of the Ukrainian authorities – who had been aware of the adverse environmental effects of a local coal mine and factory – to either resettle the applicants or find another solution to diminish pollution to levels that were not harmful to people living in the vicinity of the industrial facilities.

harm to her health was deemed not proved; in addition, the Court found that her quality of life at her home was adversely affected.[134]

In deciding the merits of cases, the Court increasingly cites to national constitutional guarantees and international instruments that guarantee environmental quality. In *Taskin and Others v. Turkey*,[135] which involved challenges to the development and operation of a gold mine, the Court referred to Rio Principle 10 and the Aarhus Convention, as they set forth procedural rights. In addition, the Court quoted from a Parliamentary Assembly resolution on environment and human rights[136] that addressed the substantive issues in the case. The Assembly resolution recommended that member states ensure appropriate protection of life, health, family and private life, physical integrity and private property, taking particular account of the need for environmental protection, and that member states recognize a human right to a healthy, viable and decent environment. Given this recommendation and the domestic Turkish Constitutional guarantees, the Court found a violation despite the absence of any accidents or incidents at the mine. It was enough that the mine presented an unacceptable risk. In *Tatar v. Romania*, the European Court relied on the right to a healthy environment and the precautionaty principle, both enshrined in Romanian law, to justify its finding of a violation of Article 8 of the Convention.[137]

Some applicants have complained that environmental protection measures themselves violate their property or privacy rights. In response, the European Court has made clear that Article 8 rights may be interfered with for environmental purposes. In *Chapman v. The United Kingdom* (January 18, 2001), the European Court of Human Rights considered a conflict between Art. 8 and planning restrictions imposed to preserve natural areas. A Grand Chamber of the Court decided 10–7 that prohibiting a gypsy family to occupy its own land

---

134 Compare *Smaltini v. Italy*, March 24, 2015, declaring inadmissible a case in which applicants (husband and children) claimed local steelworks caused the death of the first applicant (deceased wife/mother) from leukaemia. The Court declared the application manifestly ill-founded. Examining the decedent's complaint under the procedural aspect of Article 2 of the Convention, the Court held that the decedent had had the benefit of adversarial proceedings in the course of which investigations had been carried out at her request. In the Court's view, the first applicant had not demonstrated that, in the light of the scientific data available at the time of the events, there had been a breach of the procedural aspect of her right to life.

135 No. 46117/99, Nov. 10, 2004.

136 Parliamentary Assembly Recommendation 1614 (2003) of June 27, 2003. See also as in *Okyay and Others v. Turkey*, No. 36220/97, judgment of July 12, 1996, Rep. 2005–VII 43 Eur. H.R. Rep 788 (2006).

137 *Tâtar v. Romania*, Judgment of Jan. 27, 2009, Eur. Ct. Hum. Rts., para. 109.

in its caravans did not violate Article 8 of the European Convention on Human Rights. The Court afforded considerable deference to the government, finding that 'the judgment in any particular case by the national authorities that there are legitimate planning objections to a particular use of a site is one which the Court is not well equipped to challenge'. Consequently, the Court will look for 'a manifest error of appreciation by the national authorities' and will be especially cognizant of the procedural safeguards available to the individual applicant. The majority of the Court spoke to the appropriate balance between individual rights and the protection of the environment, holding that '[t]he Court will be slow to grant protection to those who, in conscious defiance of the prohibitions of the law, establish a home on an environmentally protected site. For the court to do otherwise would be to encourage illegal action to the detriment of the protection of the environmental rights of other people in the community'.

For a long time, given the anthropocentric nature of human rights law, Article 8 has been essentially limited to cases of pollution. Issues of resource management and nature conservation or biological diversity have proven extremely difficult to bring before human rights tribunals.[138] Recently, the European Court found a violation of Article 8 with regard of climate change. In fact, in *Klimaseniorinnen v. Switzerland,* the Court found that Article 8 includes the right for individuals to receive effective protection from State authorities against the severe negative impacts of climate change on their lives, health, well-being, and quality of life. In this context, a states' primary responsibility is to establish and implement regulations and measures that can mitigate both current and potentially irreversible future effects of climate change. This obligation arises from the causal relationship between climate change and the enjoyment of Convention rights, as well as the Convention's purpose as a human rights protection instrument.

3.4 *Freedom of Association*

The protections of European Convention Article 11, guaranteeing freedom of association, have been sought to assure civil society the ability to take action in favor of the environment. In the *Case of Zeleni Balkani v. Bulgaria*,[139] the government was found to have unduly restricted the work of environmental associations by refusing to allow peaceful protests. In the case of *Koretsky and Others v. Ukraine*,[140] the Court found a violation of Article 11 due to the

138 Eur. Comm'n H.R., Case 68/25/74, 5 D. & R. 86.

139 App. No. 63778/00, judgment of April 12, 2007.

140 App. No. 40269/02, judgment of April 3, 2008.

government's refusal to register an environmental association as a non-governmental organization. In *Marie Cassagnou and Others v. France*[141] the European Court found a violation of the right to freedom of association due to a French law that required certain owners of small areas of land to belong to a hunting association and permit hunting on their property.

3.5 *Right to Property*

Article 1 of Protocol 1 of the European Convention ensures that 'every natural or legal person is entitled to the peaceful enjoyment of his possessions'. Pollution or other environmental harm may result in a breach of Article 1 of Protocol 1, but only where such harm results in a substantial reduction in the value of the property and that reduction is not compensated by the state; in effect it is treated as an issue of expropriation. On the other hand, environmental regulations restricting property use will be upheld, so long as they are according to law and proportionate to the legitimate aim pursued. Thus, restriction on fishing rights[142] or development projects[143] have been deemed justified. In contrast, in the *Case of Pialopoulos and Others v. Greece*, judgment of February 15, 2001, planning restrictions that prevented applicants from building a shopping center on their land for over ten years without compensation was found to be a violation. The Court accepted that the impugned measures aimed at environmental protection, but held that the applicants were entitled to compensation. Similarly in *Papastavrou and Others v. Greece*,[144] public authorities were found not to have struck a fair balance in restricting the applicant's use of land.

In the Inter-American system, the right to property has been of special importance in the claims of indigenous peoples to their ancestral lands and resources. Those cases are discussed later. Here it may be noted that, as in Europe, there must be an individualized property right at stake to invoke Convention Article 21. In the case of *Metropolitan Nature Reserve v. Panama*[145] the petitioners charged the Government of Panama with violations of the

141 Eur. Ct. Hum. Rts, 1999–III Reports of Judgments and Decisions.

142 *Alatulkkila v. Finland*, App. No. 335438/96, 43 EHRR 737 (2006).

143 *Pine Valley Developments Ltd. and Others v. Ireland*, 14 EHRR 319 (1991); *Kapsalis and Nima-Kapsali v. Greece*, inadmissible Sept. 23, 2004.

144 App. No. 46372/99, 2003–IV Eur. Ct. H.R. 257 (10 Apr.). See also *Housing Ass'n of War Disabled and Victims of War of Attica and Others v. Greece*, App. No. 35859/02, July 13, 2006, holding property rights of applicants were violated because the government failed to strike a fair balance between the public interest and private rights in re-classifying land for reforestation.

145 Inter-American Human Rights Commission, Rep. Nº 88/03, Case No. 11.533 (Inadmissibility), Oct. 22, 2003.

Panamanian people's right to property. The violation was alleged to have resulted from the adoption of Public Law 29 on June 23, 1995 which authorized construction of a public roadway through the Nature Reserve, designated by law in 1985 as a protected area of environmental, scientific, and cultural value. The State pointed out that it acted under color of constitutional law to relieve Panama City's heavy traffic congestion, and that it properly consulted public and private institutions during the environmental impact study it commissioned. The State added that the aim of building the North Corridor project was to cut pollution in the city and therefore it had met its duty to promote environmentally sound development. The IACHR concluded that the petition was inadmissible since no individual victims had a property right to the preservation of the nature preserve.

3.6 *Freedom of Information and Expression*

Human rights texts generally contain a right to freedom of information or a broader state duty to provide information. Freedom of information is included in the Universal Declaration of Human Rights (Art. 19), the International Covenant on Civil and Political Rights (Art. 19(2)), the Inter-American Declaration of the Rights and Duties of Man (Art. 10), the American Convention on Human Rights (Art. 13), and the African Charter on the Rights and Duties of Peoples (Art. 9). European states are generally bound by Article 10 of the European Convention on Human Rights, which guarantees 'the freedom to receive information'. In the case of *Leander v. Sweden*, the applicant alleged violation of Article 10 after he was refused access to a file that was used to deny him employment. The Court unanimously stated:

> the right to receive information basically prohibits a Government from restricting a person from receiving information that others wish or may be willing to impart to him. Article 10 does not, in circumstances such as those of the present case, confer on the individual a right to access to a register containing information on his personal position, nor does it embody an obligation on the Government to impart such information to the individual.[146]

146 *Leander v. Sweden*, 116 Eur. Ct. H. R. (ser. A) (1987) para. 74. See also *Gaskin v. United Kingdom*, 160 Eur. Ct. H. R. (ser. A) (1987) (government did not breach Convention in failing to allow access to a personal file of former foster child).

The Court has adhered to this view of Article 10 in environmental cases.[147]

The Court has considered the extent to which a state may extend defamation laws to penalize the dissemination of environmental information. In the case of *Bladet Tromsø and Stensaas v. Norway*,[148] a Grand Chamber of the European Court held 13–4 that Norway had violated the rights of a newspaper and its editor by fining them both for defamation after they published extracts of a highly critical report by a governmental seal hunting inspector.[149] The names of the crew were deleted from the publication but they successfully sued for defamation. The European Court found that the reporting appeared in the wider context of the newspaper's coverage of the controversial seal hunting issue, a matter of public interest and conveyed an overall picture of balanced reporting. The Court also was influenced by the fact that the report was an official one.

In the Inter-American system, the Court addressed access to environmental information in the case of *Claude Reyes et al v. Chile*. The applicants, NGOs and individuals, alleged that the state violated Article 13 of the American Convention (Freedom of Expression and Information) when the Chilean Committee on Foreign Investment omitted to release information about a deforestation project the petitioners wanted to evaluate. The state argued that the requested information must be considered confidential as part of the economic guarantees for foreign investors. In 2006, the Court found violations of the right to information and the right to judicial remedies, citing a wide range of environmental instruments as well as human rights texts, including the Rio Declaration and the Aarhus Convention. The Court directed the government to devise a means to ensure access to the information sought by the applicants.

3.7 *The Right of Public Participation*

As with the right to information, the right to public participation is widely expressed in human rights instruments. Article 21 of the Universal Declaration of Human Rights affirms the right of everyone to take part in governance of his or her country, as does the American Declaration of the Rights and Duties of Man (Art. 20) and the African Charter (Art. 13). Article 25 of the International Covenant on Civil and Political Rights provides that citizens have the right,

---

147 See Stefan Weber, 'Environmental Information and the European Convention on Human Rights' (1991) 12 Hum. Rts. L. J. 177. See also *Anna Maria Guerra and Others v. Italy*.

148 *Bladet Tromsø et Stensaas v. Norway*, Judgment of May 20, 1999. See also *Thoma v. Luxembourg* (March 29, 2001) overturning the defamation conviction of a journalist who suggested bribery was occurring in forest management.

149 The government decided, based on Norwegian law, to not publish the report because the contents alleged violations of law.

without unreasonable restrictions 'to take part in the conduct of public affairs, directly or though freely chosen representatives …'. The American Convention contains identical language in Article 23. In a 1997 report on the situation of human rights in Ecuador, the Inter-American Commission indicated that public participation in environmental decision-making is linked to Article 23 as well as to the right to receive and impart information.[150]

3.8 *The Right to a Remedy*

The right to a remedy when a right is violated is itself a right expressly guaranteed by universal and regional human rights instruments. The Universal Declaration of Human Rights affirms that '[e]veryone has the right to an effective remedy by the competent national tribunals for acts violating the fundamental rights granted him by the constitution or laws'.[151] The International Covenant on Civil and Political Rights also obliges states to provide remedies.[152] The Human Rights Committee, established pursuant to the Covenant, has identified the kinds of remedies required, depending on the type of violation and the victim's condition. The Committee has indicated that the state which has engaged in human rights violations, in addition to treating and financially compensating the victim, must undertake to investigate the facts, take appropriate action, and bring those found responsible for the violations to justice. The International Labor Organisation (ILO) Convention concerning Indigenous and Tribal Peoples in Independent Countries[153] specifically refers to 'fair compensation for damages' (Art. 15(2)), 'compensation in money' (Art. 16(4)) and full compensation for 'any loss or injury' (Art. 16(5)). Several other treaties refer to the right to legal protection for attacks on privacy, family, home or correspondence, or attacks on honor and reputation.[154]

---

150 Inter-Am. Comm'n H.R., Report on the Situation of Human Rigths in Ecuador, OEA /Ser.L/V/II.96, Doc. 10 rev. 1, Apr. 24, 1997.

151 Universal Declaration of Human Rights, Art. 8.

152 According to Article 2(3), 'Each State Party to the … Covenant undertakes: (a) To ensure that any person whose rights or freedoms as … recognized [in the Covenant] are violated shall have an effective remedy notwithstanding that the violation has been committed by persons acting in an official capacity. (b) To ensure that any person claiming such a remedy shall have the right thereto determined by competent judicial, administrative or legislative authorities, or by any other competent authority provided for by the legal system of the State, and to develop the possibilities of judicial remedy; (c) To ensure that the competent authorities shall enforce such remedies when granted'.

153 Convention Concerning Indigenous and Tribal Peoples in Independent Countries, I.L.O. No. 169, June 27, 1989, *in force* Sept. 5, 1991, 28 I.L.M. 1382 (1989).

154 See Universal Declaration on Human Rights, Art. 12; International Covenant on Civil and Political Rights, Art. 17; Convention on the Rights of the Child, Art. 16; American Decla-

Declarations, resolutions and other non-treaty texts also proclaim or discuss the right to a remedy. The third General Comment of the Committee on Economic, Social and Cultural Rights, concerning the nature of state obligations pursuant to Article 2(1) of the Covenant, states that appropriate measures to implement the Covenant might include the provision of judicial remedies with respect to rights which may be considered justiciable. It specifically points to the non-discrimination requirement of the treaty and cross-references to the right to a remedy in the Covenant on Civil and Political Rights. A number of other rights are cited as 'capable of immediate application by judicial and other organs'.[155]

Regional instruments also contain provisions regarding legal remedies for violations of rights. Article XVII of the American Declaration of the Rights and Duties of Man guarantees every person the right to resort to the courts to ensure respect for legal rights and protection from acts of authority that violate any fundamental constitutional rights. The American Convention entitles everyone to effective recourse for protection against acts that violate the fundamental rights recognized by the constitution 'or laws of the state or by the Convention', even where the act was committed by persons acting in the course of their official duties (Art. 25).[156] The states parties are to ensure that the competent authorities enforce remedies that are granted.

Article 6 of the European Convention on Human Rights[157] guarantees a fair and public hearing before an international tribunal for the determination of rights and duties.[158] Applicability of Article 6 depends upon the existence of a dispute concerning a right recognized in the law of the state concerned, including those created by licenses, authorizations and permits that affect the use of property or commercial activities.[159] In *Oerlemans v. Netherlands*[160] Article 6 was deemed to apply to a case where a Dutch citizen could not challenge a ministerial order designating his land as a protected site. In *Zander v.*

---

ration of the Rights and Duties of Man, Art. V; American Convention on Human Rights, Art. 11(3); European Convention on Human Rights, Art. 8; African Charter on Human and Peoples Rights, Art. 5.

155 United Nations, *Compilation of General Comments and General Recommendations Adopted by Human Rights Treaty Bodies,* HRI/GEN/1/Rev.3, 63, para. 5.

156 American Convention on Human Rights (Nov. 22, 1969), Art. 25.

157 Art. 6, para. 1 states: 'In the determination of his civil rights and obligations or of any criminal charge against him, everyone is entitled to a fair and public hearing within a reasonable time by an independent and impartial tribunal established by law'.

158 *Golder v. United Kingdom,* 18 Eur. Ct. H. R. (ser. A) (1975); *Klass v. Germany,* 28 Eur. Ct. H. R. (ser. A) (1978).

159 *Benthem v. Netherlands,* 97 Eur. Ct. H. R. (ser. A) (1985).

160 *Oerlemans v. Netherlands,* 219 Eur. Ct. H. R. (ser. A) (1991).

Sweden,[161] the European Court held that Article 6 applied and was violated because the applicants' claim concerned the environmental conditions of their property and they 'could arguably maintain that they were entitled under Swedish law to protection against the water in their well being polluted as a result of VAFAB's activities on the dump'.[162]

The rights of access to justice and fair trial are particularly important in respect to those countries in which the domestic constitution contains a right to environmental quality or other guarantees. In the *Kyrtatos* case, for example, although the European Court denied that Article 8 had been violated when a wetland was taken by local authorities to build tourist facilities, the Court found a breach of Article 6 because the government failed to enforce its constitutional provisions on environmental protection and ignored court decisions against the development. In a series of cases involving Turkey, the European Court found violations of Article 6 because the domestic authorities failed to provide a remedy for violations of the domestic constitutional right to a healthy environment.[163] In *Klimaseniorinnen v. Switzerland*, the European Court determined that Swiss national courts did not offer persuasive reasons for deeming it unnecessary to examine the merits of the complaints. They neglected to consider the substantial scientific evidence on climate change and did not take the association's complaints seriously. Since there were no additional legal avenues or safeguards available to the applicant association or its individual members, the European Court concluded that there had been a violation of Article 6 § 1 of the European Convention.

The right to a remedy extends to compensation for pollution. In *Zimmerman and Steiner v. Switzerland*,[164] the Court found Article 6 applicable to a complaint about the length of proceedings for compensation for injury caused by noise and air pollution from a nearby airport. Article 6 does not, however, encompass a right to judicial review of legislative enactments. In *Braunerheilm v. Sweden*,[165] the Commission denied a claim that Article 6 was violated when the applicant could not challenge in court a new law that granted fishing

161 *Zander v. Sweden*, 279B Eur. Ct. H. R. (ser. A) (1993).

162 ibid para. 24.

163 See e.g., *Taskin and Others v. Turkey*, App. No. 46117/99, Eur. Ct. H. R. (Nov. 10, 2004); *Okyay and Others v. Turkey*, App. No. 36220/97, Eur. Ct. H. R. (July 12, 2005).

164 *Zimmerman and Steiner v. Switzerland*, 66 Eur. Ct. H. R. (ser. A) (1983).

165 *Braunerheilm v. Sweden*, App. No. 11764/85 (Mar. 9, 1989). See Maguelonne Déjeant-Pons, 'Le Droit de l'homme a l'environnement, droit fondamental au niveau europeen dans le cadre du Conseil de l'Europe, et la Convention europeenne de sauvegarde des droit de l'homme et des libertes fondamentales' (1994) 4 Rev. Jur. De L'environnement.

licenses to the general public in waters where the applicant previously had exclusive rights.

The European Court has restricted the use of procedural limits on access to justice in cases where harm emerges long after exposure to the environmental cause. In *Howald Moor and Others v. Switzerland* (March 11, 2014) a worker was diagnosed in May 2004 and died in 2005 from malignant pleural mesothelioma caused by his exposure to asbestos in the course of his work in the 1960s and 1970s. The worker's wife and two daughters complained that their right of access to a court had been breached when the Swiss courts dismissed as time-barred their claims for damages against the deceased's employer and the national authorities. The Court considered that the application of the limitation period breached Article 6 § 1 of the Convention because the systematic application of the statute of limitations rule to persons suffering from diseases, which could not be diagnosed until many years after the triggering events, deprived those persons of the chance to assert their rights before the courts. The Court therefore considered that in cases where it was scientifically proven that a person could not know that he or she was suffering from a certain disease, that fact should be taken into account in calculating the limitation period.

The African Charter contains a broad right to a remedy in Article 7, supplemented by 'the right to adequate compensation for the spoliation of resources of a dispossessed people'.[166] Article 26 also imposes a duty on states parties to the Charter to guarantee the independence of the courts and to allow the establishment and improvement of appropriate national institutions entrusted with the promotion and protection of rights and freedoms guaranteed by the Charter.

3.9 *Cultural and Minority Rights*

Indigenous groups have invoked provisions of the Covenant on Civil and Political Rights to protect their land and culture from environmental degradation.[167] The United Nations Human Rights Committee has interpreted the right of minority groups to their culture, contained in Article 27[168] of the Covenant on Civil and Political Rights, in a broad manner to encompass resource and

166 African Charter on Human and Peoples Rights, Art. 21(2).

167 For specific recognition of indigenous rights apart from the recognition of indigenous peoples as minority groups under CCPR Art. 27, see the section on this topic below in this chapter.

168 CCPR Art. 27 provides that members of minority groups 'shall not be denied the right, kin community with other members of their group, to enjoy their own culture, to profess and practice their own religion, or to use their own language'. CCPR, art. 27.

land rights.[169] Yet, most environmental cases have been rejected as inadmissible for failure to exhaust local remedies or on other grounds. On the merits, the Committee held in one case that Article 27 was not violated by the extent of stone-quarrying permitted by Finland in traditional lands of the Sami,[170] finding that measures which simply have a 'certain limited impact on the way of life of persons belonging to a minority' will not necessarily violate the treaty. The Committee noted that the group was consulted, their views were taken into account in the government's decision, and measures were taken to minimize the impact on reindeer herding activity and on the environment. In regard to future activities, 'if mining activities in the Angeli area were to be approved on a large scale and significantly expanded', then it might constitute a violation of Article 27. According to the Committee, '[t]he State party is under a duty to bear this in mind when either extending existing contracts or granting new ones'.[171]

The interplay of procedural and substantive rights was also a major factor in *Apirana Mahuika et al v. New Zealand*.[172] The petitioners claimed violations of several Covenant rights, including Article 27, as a result of New Zealand's efforts to regulate fishing after dramatic growth in the fishing industry. The government and the Maori, whose rights are guaranteed by the Treaty of Waitangi, executed a Deed of Settlement in 1992 to regulate all fisheries issues between the parties. The authors of the communication represented tribes and sub-tribes that objected to the Settlement. The government acknowledged its duty to ensure recognition of the right to culture, but argued that the Settlement met the obligation because the system of fishing quotas reflected the need for effective measures to conserve the depleted inshore fishery, carrying out the government's 'duty to all New Zealanders to conserve and manage the

169 General Comment 23 paras. 7, 9 in *Compilation* at 41. *See Kitok v. Sweden*, Comm. 197/1985, *II Official Records of the Human Rights Committee 1987/88*, UN Doc. CCPR/7/Add.1, at 442 (Swedish 1971 Reindeer Husbandry Act held not to violate rights of an individual Sami as a reasonable and objective measure necessary for the continued viability and welfare of the minority as a whole); Bernard Ominayak and the *Lubicon Band v. Canada*, Communication No. 167/1984, Decisions of the Human Rights Committee, UN Doc. CCPR /C/38/D/167/1984 (1990) (oil and gas exploitation threaten the way of life and culture of the Band and thus violate Article 27).

170 Communication No. 511/1992, *Ilmari Lansman et al. v. Finland*, Human Rights Committee, Final Decisions, 74, CCPR/C/57/1 (1996).

171 Other cases involving Sami reindeer breeders include Communication No. 431/1990, *O.S. et al. v. Finland*, decision of March 23, 1994, and Communication No. 671/1995, *Jouni E. Lansmann et al. v. Finland*, decision of 30 October 1996.

172 *Communication No. 547/1992, Apirana Mahuika et al v. New Zealand*, CCPR/C/70/D/547/1993, views issued November 16, 2000.

resource for future generations' 'based on the reasonable and objective needs of overall sustainable management'. The Human Rights Committee held for the government and emphasized 'that the acceptability of measures that affect or interfere with the culturally significant economic activities of a minority depends on whether the members of the minority in question have had the opportunity to participate in the decision-making process in relation to these measures and whether they will continue to benefit from their traditional economy'. The process of consultation undertaken by the government complied with this requirement, because the government paid special attention to the cultural and religious significance of fishing for the Maori.

4 The Right to a Safe and Healthy Environment

The concept of a right to a healthy and safe environment has generated debate since the first discussions of the topic at the Stockholm Conference on the Human Environment. The debate grows when claims are formally proposed for addition to the list of guaranteed human rights. Nonetheless, the recognition that human survival depends upon a safe and healthy environment has placed the claim of a right to environmental quality fully on the human rights agenda. Moreover, recognizing a right to an ecologically-balanced environment could encompass elements of nature protection not generally protected under human rights law because of its anthropocentric focus.

An immediate, practical objective of international human rights law is to elevate the legal protection afforded the interests included. Successfully placing personal entitlements within the category of human rights law preserves them from the ordinary political process.[173] Denominating rights thus limits the political will and discretion of a democratic majority, as well as a dictatorial minority. Even to attain a widely accepted policy goal, a representative democracy is barred from adopting legislation that e.g. limits or abolishes the individual right to be free from slavery or torture. This limitation on political decisions is potentially an important consequence of elaborating a right to environmental quality, particularly given the high shortterm costs involved in many environmental protection measures and the resulting political disfavor they may experience.

The issue of a right to an environment of a certain quality is complicated by both temporal and geographic elements absent from other human rights

173 In most legal systems, human rights are of constitutional status and override ordinary legislative or executive acts.

protections. While most human rights violations affect only specific and identifiable victims in the present, environmental degradation may cause harm to many currently living and future generations of humanity as well. The harm can take various forms. First, an extinct species and whatever benefits it would have brought to the global ecosystem are lost forever. Second, economic, social, and cultural rights cannot be enjoyed in a world where resources are inadequate due to the waste of prior generations. Third, the very survival of future generations may be jeopardized by sufficiently serious environmental problems. A right to a healthy environment thus implies significant and constant duties toward persons not yet born.

The other problematic aspect of a right to a healthy environment is the potentially vast territorial scope of state obligations. Human rights instruments typically require each state to respect and ensure guaranteed rights 'to all individuals within its territory and subject to its jurisdiction'. This geographic limitation reflects the reality that a state normally will have the power to protect or the possibility to violate human rights only of those within its territory and jurisdiction. Nature recognizes no political boundaries, however. A state polluting its coastal waters or the atmosphere may cause significant harm to individuals thousands of miles away. States that permit or encourage depletion of the tropical rain forest can contribute to global warming that threatens the entire biosphere.

Ultimately, the definition of a right to a healthy environment would have to include substantive environmental standards to restrict harmful air pollution and other types of emissions. Although establishing quality standards requires extensive international regulation of environmental sectors based upon impact studies, such regulation is by no means impossible. Adoption of quality standards demands extensive research and debate involving public participation, but substantive minima are a necessary complement to the procedural rights leading to informed consent. Otherwise, a human rights approach to environmental protection would be ineffective in preventing serious environmental harm.

Establishing the content of a right through reference to independent and variable standards is often used in human rights, especially with regard to economic entitlements, and need not be a barrier to recognition of the right to a specific environmental quality. Rights to an adequate standard of living and to social security are sometimes defined in international accords such as the European Social Charter or Conventions and Recommendations of the International Labor Organization. States implement these flexible obligations according to changing economic indicators, needs, and resources. The human rights treaties provide a 'framework' containing the basic guarantees on which international, national and local laws and policies are elaborated.

A similar approach can be utilized to give meaning to a right to a healthy environment. Both the threats to humanity and the resulting necessary measures are subject to constant change based on advances in scientific knowledge and conditions of the environment. Thus, it is impossible for a human rights instrument to specify precisely what measures should be taken, i.e., the products which should not be used or the chemical composition of air which must be maintained. These technical requirements can be negotiated and regulated through international environmental norms and standards, giving content to the right to environment by reference to independent environmental findings and regulations capable of rapid amendment. The variability of implementation demands imposed by the right to environment in response to different threats over time and place does not undermine the concept of the right, but merely takes into consideration its dynamic character.

More than 150 of the constitutions in the world today guarantee a right to a clean and healthy environment, impose a duty on the state to prevent environmental harm, or mention the protection of the environment or natural resources.[174] Many of them explicitly recognize the right to a clean and healthy environment.[175] Within federal systems, including those whose federal constitution lacks mention of the environment, state or provincial constitutions contain environmental rights.[176] These provisions vary in the chosen description

---

174 Examples include: Angola ('all citizens shall have the right to live in a healthy and unpolluted environment'. Art. 24–1); Argentina ('all residents enjoy the right to a healthy, balanced environment which is fit for human development ...' Art. 41); Azerbaijan ('everyone has the right to live in a healthy environment'.); Brazil ('everyone has the right to an ecologically balanced environment, which is a public good for the people's use and is essential for a healthy life'. Art. 225).

175 See e.g. Angola, Argentina, Azerbaijan, Belarus, Belgium, Benin, Brazil, Bulgaria, Burkina Faso, Cameroon, Cape Verde, Chad, Chechnya, Chile, China, Colombia, Congo, Costa Rica, Croatia, Cuba, Ecuador, El Salvador, Equatorial Guinea, Eritrea (draft), Finland, Georgia, Germany, Ghana, Greece, Guatemala, Guyana, Haiti, Honduras, Hungary, India, Iran, Kazakhstan, Kuwait, Laos, Latvia, Lithuania, Macedonia, Madagascar, Malawi, Mali, Malta, Mexico, Micronesia, Mongolia, Mozambique, Namibia, Nepal, Netherlands, Nicaragua, Niger, Palau, Panama, Papua New Guinea, Paraguay, Peru, Philippines, Poland, Portugal, Romania, Russia, Sao Tome and Principe, Saudi Arabia, Seychelles, Slovakia, Slovenia, South Africa, South Korea, Spain, Sri Lanka, Suriname, Switzerland, Taiwan, Tajikistan, Tanzania, Thailand, Togo, Turkey, Turkmenistan, Uganda, Ukraine, Uzbekistan, Venezuela, Vietnam, Yugoslavia, Zambia.

176 The Constitution of the State of Pennsylvania, for example, in Article 1, Sec. 27 provides: 'The people have a right to clean air, pure water, and to the preservation of the natural,

of the environmental quality that is protected. While many of the older provisions refer to a 'healthy' or 'healthful' environment, more recent formulations add references to ecology and/or biodiversity to the guarantee, although the right may be stated in a limited manner. The Quebec provincial Charter, for example, provides that 'Every person has a right to live in a healthful environment in which biodiversity is preserved, to the extent and according to the standards provided by law'.[177] The French Constitution, was amended to add a Charter of the Environment in 2005,[178] affording French citizens the right to live in a 'balanced environment, favorable to human health'.[179] The French *Conseil Constitutionnel* has used the Charter to review legislative enactments,[180] finding that the Charter constitutes a 'fundamental freedom' of constitutional value allowing for the suspension of an administrative decision under French procedural law.[181] Eastern European countries have also altered or changed their constitutions since the fall of the Soviet Union to include a substantive right to the environment and courts have found these rights justiciable.[182] In Latin America, Article 19 of the 1980 Constitution of Chile provides for a 'right to life' and a 'right to live in an environment free of contamination' and establishes that certain other individual rights may be restricted to protect the environment.[183] The Government of Chile is required to 'ensure that the right to

---

scenic, historic and esthetic values of the environment. Pennsylvania's public natural resources are the common property of all the people, including generations yet to come. As trustee of these resources, the Commonwealth shall conserve and maintain them for the benefit of all the people'. For a commentary see John C. Dernbach, 'Taking the Pennsylvania Constitution Seriously When it Protects the Environment: Part II: Environmental Rights and Public Trust' (1999) 104 *Dickenson L. Rev.* 97; 'Part I An Interpretative Framework for Art. 1, Section 227' (1999) 103 Dickenson L. Rev. 693.

177 Quebec Charter of Human Rights and Freedoms, R.S.Q., c. C-12, s. 46.1.

178 Charter for the Environment, Art. 1. See generally Ole Pedersen, 'European Environmental Human Rights and Environmental Rights: A Long Time Coming?'; David Marrani, 'The Second Anniversary of the Constitutionalisation of the French Charter for the Environment: Constitutional and Environmental Implications' (2008) 10 *Env. L. Rev.* 9; James R. May, 'Constituting Fundamental Environmental Rights Worldwide' (2005–2006) 23 *Pace Envtl. L. Rev.* 113, 113–14.

179 Legifrance, Charter for the Environment, Art. 1.

180 *See e.g.* Conseil Constitutionnel decision no. 2005–514DC, Apr. 28, 2005, R. 305 (*Loi relative à la création du registre international français*).

181 *See Marrani,* (n 179), at 21–22.

182 The Hungarian Constitution, for example, states 'Hungary recognizes and implements everyone's right to a healthy environment'. A Magyar Küztársaság Alkotmánya [Constitution] Art. 18 (Hung.), *translated in* Constitutions Of The Countries Of The World; *see also* Gyula Badni, 'The Right to Environment in Theory and Practice: The Hungarian Experience' (1993) 8 Conn. J. Int'l L. 439.

183 Chile Const, Art. 19 §§ 1, 8.

live in an environment free of contamination is not violated' and to 'serve as a guardian for and preserve nature/the environment'.[184]

The constitutional rights granted are increasingly being enforced by courts.[185] In India, for example, a series of judgments beginning in 1996 responded to health concerns caused by industrial pollution in Delhi.[186] In some instances, the courts issued orders to cease operations.[187] The Indian Supreme Court has based the closure orders on the principle that health is of primary importance and that residents are suffering health problems due to pollution. In Argentina, the right is deemed a subjective right entitling any person to initiate an action for environmental protection.[188] Colombia also recognizes the enforceability of the right to environment.[189] In Costa Rica, a

184 ibid, Art. 19, § 8. In 1988, the Supreme Court of Chile held that the constitutional-environmental provisions established a substantive right. Residents of the village of Chanaral filed suit against a government-run copper mine to restrain the company from continuing to discharge tailings on local beaches and coves. Based on a site visit, the Court found much of the shore and local waters inert and enjoined further dumping within one year. *Pedro Flores y Otros v. Corporacion Del Cobre, Codeloco*, Division Salvador. Recurso de Proteccion, (1988) 12.753.FS. 641 (Chile).

185 For a discussion of African cases, see Carl Bruch et al, 'Constitutional Environmental Law: Giving Force to Fundamental Principles in Africa' (2001) 26 Colum. J. Envtl L. 131. For up-to-date information on climate litigation, see the Climate Change Litigation Databases managed by the Sabin Center for Climate Change Law at Columbia Law School, accessible at https://climatecasechart.com/ (last accessed June 3, 2024).

186 As early as 1991, the Supreme Court interpreted the right to life guaranteed by Article 21 of the Constitution to include the right to a wholesome environment. See *Charan Lal Sahu v. Union of India*, AIR 1990 SC 1480 (1991). In a subsequent case, the Court observed that the 'right to life guaranteed by Art. 21 includes the right of enjoyment of pollution-free water and air for full enjoyment of life'. Subhash *Kumar v. State of Bihar*, AIR 1991 SC 420, 1991 (1) SCC 598.

187 See, e.g., *M.C. Mehta v. Union of India & Others*, JT 1996, reprinted in 1 The Environmental Activists' Handbook at 631.

188 *Kattan, Alberto and Others v. National Gov't*, Juzgado Nacional de la Instancia en lo Contenciosoadministrativo Federal. No. 2, ruling of May 10, 1983, La Ley, 1983–D, 576; *Irazu Margarita v. Copetro S.A.*, Camara Civil y Comercial de la Plata, ruling of May 10, 1993 (the right to live in a healthy and balanced environment is a fundamental attribute of people. Any aggression to the environment ends up becoming a threat to life itself and to the psychological and physical integrity of the person ...).

189 *Funde publico v. Mayor of Bugalagrande and Others*, Juzgado Primero superior, Interlocutorio # 032, Tulua, Dec. 19, 1991 ('It should be recognized that a healthy environment is a *sine qua non* condition for life itself and that no right could be exercised in a deeply altered environment'.).

court stated that the right to health and to the environment are necessary to ensure that the right to life is fully enjoyed.[190]

South African courts also have deemed the right to environment to be justiciable.[191] The South African Constitutional Court relied on the international environmental principles in giving substantive content to the country's Constitutional guarantee. In *Fuel Retailers Association of Southern Africa v Director-General Environmental Management, Department of Agriculture, Conservation and Environment, Mpumalanga Province, and Others*[192] the Court characterized the case as one that required the integration of the need to protect the environment with the need for social and economic development. In the Court's view, the international principle of sustainable development provided the applicable framework for reconciliation.[193] Sustainable development 'recognises that socio-economic development invariably brings risk of environmental damage as it puts pressure on environmental resources' but it envisages that decision-makers 'will ensure that socio-economic developments remain firmly attached to their ecological roots and that these roots are protected and nurtured so that they may support future socio-economic developments'.[194] In the Court's view, the National Environmental Management Act (NEMA), which was enacted to give effect to section 24 of the Constitution, embraces the concept of sustainable development, defined to mean 'the integration of social, economic and environmental factors into planning, implementation and decision-making for the benefit of present and future generations'. In turn, this broad definition of sustainable development incorporates both the internationally recognised principle of integration of environmental protection and socio-economic development, and the principles of inter-generational and intra-generational equity.[195]

---

190 *Presidente de la Sociedad Marlene S.A. v. Municipalidad de Tibas*, Sala Constitucional de la Corte Supreme de Justicia. Decision No. 6918/94 of Nov. 25, 1994.

191 S. Afr. Constt. ch. IV, § 24 provides: 'Everyone has a right to (a) to an environment that is not harmful to their health or well being; and (b) to have the environment protected, for the benefit of present and future generations, through reasonable legislative and other measures that (i) prevent pollution and ecological degradation; (ii) promote conservation; and (iii) secure ecologically sustainable development and use of natural resources while promoting justifiable economic and social development'.

192 Case no CCT 67/06; ILDC 783 (ZA 2007). The case arose out of a decision by the Department of Agriculture, Conservation and Environment, of a South African province to grant private parties permission to construct a filling station.

193 ibid paras. 56–57.

194 ibid paras. 58.

195 ibid paras. 59. In addition, NEMA sets out some of the factors that are relevant to decisions on sustainable development. These factors largely reflect international experience. But as

The Court saw a second objective inherent in the Constitutional and legislative guarantees: to identify and predict the actual or potential impact of development and to consider ways of minimising negative impacts while maximising benefits. Thirdly, and finally, the Court pointed out that NEMA requires the application of the precautionary approach, 'a risk averse and cautious approach', that takes into account the limitation on present knowledge about the consequences of an environmental decision. This precautionary approach was seen to be especially important because NEMA requires the cumulative impact of a development on the environmental and socio-economic conditions to be investigated and addressed.[196] The precautionary principle required the authorities to insist on adequate precautionary measures to safeguard against the contamination of underground water: 'This principle is applicable where, due to unavailable scientific knowledge, there is uncertainty as to the future impact of the proposed development. Water is a precious commodity; it is a natural resource that must be protected for the benefit of

---

NEMA makes it clear, these factors are not exhaustive. The Court quoted the factors set forth in the domestic National Environmental Management Act, Section 2(4)(a):

Sustainable development requires the consideration of all relevant factors including the following:

i. That the disturbance of ecosystems and loss of biological diversity are avoided, or, where they cannot be altogether avoided, are minimised and remedied;
ii. that pollution and degradation of the environment are avoided, or, where they cannot be altogether avoided, are minimised and remedied;
iii. that the disturbance of landscapes and sites that constitute the nation's cultural heritage is avoided, or where it cannot be altogether avoided, is minimised and remedied;
iv. that waste is avoided, or where it cannot be altogether avoided, minimised and re-used or recycled where possible and otherwise disposed of in a responsible manner;
v. that the use and exploitation of non-renewable natural resources is responsible and equitable, and takes into account the consequences of the depletion of the resource;
vi. that the development, use and exploitation of renewable resources and the ecosystems of which they are part do not exceed the level beyond which their integrity is jeopardised;
vii. that a risk-averse and cautious approach is applied, which takes into account the limits of current knowledge about the consequences of decisions and actions; and
viii. that negative impacts on the environment and on people's environmental rights be anticipated and prevented, and where they cannot be altogether prevented, are minimised and remedied.

196 Section 24(7)(b) of NEMA provides: 'Procedures for the investigation, assessment and communication of the potential impact of activities must, as a minimum, ensure ... investigation of the potential impact, including cumulative effects, of the activity and its alternatives on the environment, socio-economic conditions and cultural heritage, and assessment of the significance of that potential impact'.

present and future generations'.[197] The Court thus set aside the decision of the environmental authorities and required reconsideration consistent with the judgment. As to the role of the courts in giving effect to environmental rights, the Court was clear:

> The role of the courts is especially important in the context of the protection of the environment and giving effect to the principle of sustainable development. The importance of the protection of the environment cannot be gainsaid. Its protection is vital to the enjoyment of the other rights contained in the Bill of Rights; indeed, it is vital to life itself. It must therefore be protected for the benefit of the present and future generations. The present generation holds the earth in trust for the next generation. This trusteeship position carries with it the responsibility to look after the environment. It is the duty of the court to ensure that this responsibility is carried out.[198]

Domestic litigation has also shown some inherent limitations. This limitation of a constitutional right to a healthy environment was illustrated by the Norwegian Supreme Court's decision in *Nature and Youth Greenpeace Nordic v. the Government of Norway*. The Court found that while Article 112 of the Norwegian Constitution, which enshrines the right to a healthy environment, implies an obligation for the State, it does not establish a fundamental right.[199]

At present no global human rights treaty proclaims a general right to environment.[200]

On the regional level, the African Charter on Human and Peoples Rights was the first international human rights instrument to contain an explicit guarantee of environmental quality (Art. 24). Subsequently, the Protocol on Economic, Social and Cultural Rights to the American Convention on Human Rights included the right of everyone to live in a healthy environment (Art. 11), but did not list it among the rights in the Protocol about which complaints may be filed.[201] Article 38 of the 2004 Arab Charter on Human Rights specifies the

197 Case no CCT 67/06; ILDC 783 (ZA 2007), para. 98.

198 ibid para. 102.

199 *Nature and Youth et al. v Norway*, HR-2020-2472-P (Case No 20–051052SIV-HRET), December 22, 2020, para. 92

200 United Nations Convention on the Rights of the Child, Nov. 20, 1989, Art. 24, 28 I.L.M. 1457 (1989).

201 As an extension of the American Convention on Human Rights, Nov. 22, 1969, 1144 UNTS 123 (entered into force July 18, 1978), the Organization of American States adopted the Additional Protocol to the American Convention on Human Rights in the Area of Eco-

right to a healthy environment and other articles ensure rights to information and public participation. Article 39 expressly commits states parties to combat environmental pollution and take measures to provide proper sanitation and safe drinking water. Article 28 of the 2012 ASEAN Declaration of Human Rights similarly guarantees not only the right to a safe, clean and sustainable environment, but also the right to safe drinking water and sanitation. In Europe, neither the European Convention for the Protection of Human Rights and Fundamental Freedoms[202] nor the European Social Charter[203] contain a right to environmental quality and the former European Commission on Human Rights held that such a right cannot be directly inferred from the Convention. The Committee of Ministers reaffirmed on June 19, 2010, its view that adoption of a protocol to add such a right, which had been requested by the Parliamentary Assembly, is unnecessary, although it recognizes the importance of a healthy, viable and decent environment.[204]

On a sub-regional level, according to the terms of the Memorandum of Understanding between Kenya, Tanzania and Uganda for Cooperation on Environment Management of October 22, 1998, the three states agree to cooperate in developing, enacting and harmonizing their national environmental laws on the rights of their peoples to a clean, decent and healthy environment.

Given the innovations in Africa, it is not surprising that the African Commission on Human and Peoples' Rights was the first international human rights body to decide a contentious case involving violation of the right to a general satisfactory environment. The case is a landmark not only in this respect, but also in the Commission's articulation of the duties of governments in Africa to monitor and control the activities of multinational corporations. Acting on a petition filed by two non-governmental organizations on behalf of the people of Ogoniland, Nigeria, the African Commission on Human and Peoples Rights found Nigeria had breached its obligations to respect, protect, promote, and fulfill rights guaranteed by the African Charter on Human and Peoples

nomic, Social and Cultural Rights (OASTS No. 69), Nov. 17, 1988, 28 ILM 156 (1989) (entered into force Nov. 16, 1999). The Protocol guarantees the right to a healthy environment in Art. 11 ('(1) Everyone shall have the right to live in a healthy environment and to have access to basic public services. (2) The States Parties shall promote the protection, preservation, and improvement of the environment'.). See Dinah Shelton, 'Environmental Rights', in *Peoples' Rights* 185 (Philip Alston ed., 2001).

202 European Convention for the Protection of Human Rights and Fundamental Freedoms (Nov. 4, 1950), E.T.S. No. 5, 213 U.N.T.S. 221.

203 European Social Charter (Oct. 18, 1961), E.T.S. No. 35, 529 U.N.T.S. 89.

204 Committee of Ministers, Doc. 12298, June 19, 2010.

Rights.[205] The Commission held that Nigeria had violated the right to enjoy Charter-guaranteed rights and freedoms without discrimination (Art. 2), the right to life (Art. 4), the right to property (Art. 14), the right to health (Art. 16), the right to housing (implied in the duty to protect the family (Art. 18(1)), the right to food (implicit in Arts 4, 16, and 22), the right of peoples to freely dispose of their wealth and natural resources (Art. 21), and the right of peoples to a "general satisfactory environment favorable to their development" (Art. 24). Most of the violations stemmed from actions taken by or involving the Nigerian National Petroleum Development Company (NNPC) in a consortium with Shell Petroleum Development Corporation (SPDC).[206]

Assessing the claimed violations of the rights to health (Art. 16) and to a general satisfactory environment (Art. 24), the Commission found that the right to a general satisfactory environment imposes clear obligations upon a government, requiring the state to take reasonable and other measures to prevent pollution and ecological degradation, to promote conservation, and to secure an ecologically sustainable development and use of natural resources.[207] Moreover, '[g]overnment compliance with the spirit of Articles 16 and 24 of the African Charter must also include ordering or at least permitting independent scientific monitoring of threatened environments, requiring and publicizing environmental and social impact studies prior to any major industrial development, undertaking appropriate monitoring and providing information to those communities exposed to hazardous materials and activities and providing meaningful opportunities for individuals to be heard and to participate in the development decisions affecting their communities'.[208] Applying these obligations to the facts of the case, the Commission concluded that although Nigeria had the right to produce oil, it had not protected the Article 16 and Article 24 rights of those in the Ogoni region. The Commission found numerous other rights violated, as well, and concluded its analysis by emphasizing that collective rights, environmental rights, and economic and social rights are essential elements of human rights in Africa.[209] The Commission's final comment is that all rights in the Charter may be applied and enforced; there is not

205 Decision regarding Communication 155/96 (*Social and Economic Rights Action Center /Center for Economic and Social Rights v. Nigeria*), Case No. ACHPR/COMM/A044/1 (Afr. Comm'n Hum. & Peoples' Rts. May 27, 2002).

206 For a lawsuit directed against Shell for its involvement in these activities see *Wiwa v. Royal Dutch Petroleum*, 226 F.3d 88 (2d Cir. 2000), cert. denied, 121 S.Ct. 1402 (2001) and the discussion in Chapter 6,.

207 Decision regarding Communication 155/96, para. 52.

208 ibid para. 53.

209 ibid para. 68.

right that cannot be made effective. The Commission gives the right to environment meaningful content by requiring the state to adopt various techniques of environmental protection, such as environmental impact assessment, public information and participation, access to justice for environmental harm, and monitoring of potentially harmful activities.[210]

In its 2017 Advisory Opinion on the Environment and Human Rights, requested by Colombia, the Inter-American Court of Human Rights stated that the right to a healthy environment, enshrined in the Protocol of San Salvador at Article 11, is essential for the realization of other human rights. It emphasized that environmental degradation can directly and indirectly affect the enjoyment of human rights, including the rights to life, health, and personal integrity. The Court also asserted that States have obligations to prevent significant environmental harm, regulate activities that may cause such harm, and provide effective legal remedies for environmental damage. The Court also clarified that the right to a healthy environment presents both individual and collective connotations and that, 'in its collective dimension', it 'constitutes a universal value that is owed to both present and future generations'.[211]

In March 2010, that the UN General Assembly, by a divided vote (127–54 with 5 abstentions) adopted a resolution affirming that a just and equitable international order requires, *inter alia*, the realization of 'the right of every person and all peoples to a healthy environment and to enhanced international cooperation that responds effectively to the needs for assistance of national efforts to adapt to climate change, particularly in developing countries, and that promotes the fulfilment of international agreements in the field of mitigation …;'.[212]

In 2011, the Human Rights Council requested the OHCHR to study the relationship between human rights and the environment. After reviewing the

210 The Inter-American Commission on Human Rights has adopted a similar approach in the context of countrywide studies of the human rights performance of OAS member states. See Inter-Am. Comm'n on Hum. Rts., *Report on the Situation of Human Rights in Ecuador*, OAS Doc. OEA/Ser.L/V/II.96, doc. 10, rev. 1 (1997); Inter-Am. Comm'n on Hum. Rts., *Report on the Situation of Human Rights in Brazil*, OAS Doc. OEA/Ser.L/V/II.97, doc. 29, rev. 1 (1997).

211 IACtHR, *The Environment and Human Rights* (*State Obligations in Relation to the Environment in the Context of the Protection and Guarantee of the Rights to Life and to Personal Integrity – Interpretation and Scope of Articles 4*(*1*) *and 5*(*1*) *of the American Convention on Human Rights*), Advisory Opinion OC-23/17, Inter-American Court of Human Rights Series A No 23 (November 15, 2017), para 59. Elena Cima 'The Right to a Healthy Environment: Reconceptualizing Human Rights in the Face of Climate Change' (2022) 31(1) *RECIEL*.

212 UNGA, Promotion and Protection of Human Rights: Human Rights Defenders (18 December 2009) UNGA Res 64/157, UN Doc A/RES/64/157, para. 4(l).

study, the Human Rights Council recognized the need for further examination and appointed an independent expert to delve deeper into the subject. Over the years, the Human Rights Council has facilitated significant discussions and provided a framework for the independent expert, and later, the Special Rapporteur, to define and clarify this area. In 2018, the Special Rapporteur developed the *Framework Principles on Human Rights and the Environment*,[213] which outline states' procedural and substantive obligations under human rights law as they relate to the enjoyment of a healthy environment. The term 'enjoyment of a safe, clean, healthy, and sustainable environment' – as used in the Framework Principles – has been a crucial step towards recognizing a healthy environment as a human right. In October 2021, following the Special Rapporteur's recommendations, the Human Rights Council rephrased this to 'enjoyment of the *right to* a safe, clean, healthy, and sustainable environment' in adopting a Resolution on the matter (Res. 48/13).[214] The Human Rights Council Resolution also encouraged States 'to adopt policies for the enjoyment of the right to a safe, clean, healthy and sustainable environment'.[215] One year later, in July 2022, the United Nations General Assembly adopted Resolution 76/300, which

1. Recognizes the right to a clean, healthy and sustainable environment as a human right;
2. Notes that the right to a clean, healthy and sustainable environment is related to other rights and existing international law;
3. Affirms that the promotion of the human right to a clean, healthy and sustainable environment requires the full implementation of the multilateral environmental agreements under the principles of international environmental law;
4. Calls upon States, international organizations, business enterprises and other relevant stakeholders to adopt policies, to enhance international cooperation, strengthen capacity-building and continue to share good practices in order to scale up efforts to ensure a clean, healthy and sustainable environment for all.[216]

---

213 *Framework Principles on Human Rights and the Environment*, in 'Report of the Special Rapporteur on the Issue of Human Rights Obligations Relating to the Enjoyment of a Safe, Clean, Healthy and Sustainable Environment' UN Doc A/HRC/37/59 (January 24, 2018).

214 HRC Res. 48/13 (Oct. 8, 2021).

215 ibid.

216 UNGA, *The Human Right to a Clean, Healthy and Sustainable Environment* (28 July 2022) UNGA Res 76/300, UN Doc A/RES/76/30.

5 Indigenous Populations

There are over 200 million indigenous people in the world and many of them live in some of the world's most vulnerable ecosystems. Despite the attention devoted to environmental protection in recent decades, indigenous ancestral territories have come under severe pressure as governments, development banks, transnational corporations and entrepreneurs search out resources to supply a growing global demand. The territories used and occupied by indigenous peoples often are seen only as important repositories of unexploited riches due to their mineral deposits, hydroelectric potential, hardwoods and biodiversity.

Indigenous peoples[217] are particularly affected by environmental harm, because the loss of land and resources can destroy the very basis of the cultural and physical existence of such groups. Deforestation, desertification, and climate change all threaten to extinguish indigenous peoples who are often isolated and marginalized. As found by the special rapporteur on human rights and the environment:

> indigenous peoples have a special relationship with the land and the environment in which they live. In nearly all indigenous cultures, the land is revered; 'Mother Earth' is the core of their culture. The land is the home of the ancestors, the provider of everyday material needs, and the future held in trust for coming generations. According to the indigenous view, land should not be torn open and exploited – this is a violation of the Earth – nor can it be bought, sold or bartered. Furthermore, indigenous peoples have, over a long period of time, developed successful systems of land use and resource management. These systems, including nomadic pastoralism, shifting cultivation, various forms of agro-forestry, terrace agriculture, hunting, herding and fishing, were for a long time considered inefficient, unproductive and primitive. However, as world opinion grows more conscious of the environment and particularly of the damage being done to fragile habitats, there has been a corresponding interest in

217 There is no clear definition of the term 'indigenous peoples', but a certain number of criteria emerged in the course of discussions in the Working Group on Indigenous Populations. Indigenous peoples are the descendants of the original inhabitants of territories since colonized by foreigners; they have distinct cultures which set them apart from the dominant society; many have, until comparatively recently, had a high degree of control over their development; indigenous peoples have a strong sense of self-identity. ILO Convention 169 relies on self-identification, while the 2007 UN Declaration does not attempt to define the term.

> indigenous land-use practices. The notion of sustainability is the essence of both indigenous economies and their cultures.[218]

Where there is unrestrained deforestation, forest-dwelling indigenous peoples may be forced from their traditional homelands, may thereby be denied a means of livelihood, may be driven to take refuge among strangers and, in the most extreme cases, may fall victim to diseases against which they have no immunity. Similarly, desertification, a phenomenon which is as much man-made as it is an act of nature, has led many self-sufficient pastoralists to an impoverished existence in refugee camps. Even smaller scale environmental sacrifices – the inundation caused by dam-building, mining, prospecting and so on – have affected indigenous peoples all over the world, causing them to leave lands they have occupied for generations, often without their willing consent or any compensation.

The normative framework respecting the rights of indigenous peoples has substantially changed in recent years. None of the major international human rights instruments mentions specifically the rights of indigenous peoples. The Covenant on Civil and Political Rights has two relevant provisions, Article 1 (self-determination of peoples) and Article 27 (minority rights). The definition of racial discrimination in the Convention on the Elimination of All Forms of Racial Discrimination is also broad enough to include indigenous peoples. Given their unique situation as peoples claiming sovereignty and subject to massive historical injustices, however, indigenous groups for many years have pressed for legal instruments devoted exclusively to their rights. The International Labor Organization (ILO) first adopted a convention in 1957, subsequently criticized for its assimilationist tenor, then replaced the 1957 agreement in 1989 with ILO Convention No. 169 concerning Indigenous and Tribal Peoples in Independent Countries, which

218 E/CN.4/Sub.2/1990/12, 33 and n. 9. For other reports of the special rapporteur discussing indigenous peoples and the environment, see: E/CN.4/Sub.2/1991/8; E/CN.4/Sub.2/1992/7; E/CN.4/Sub.2/1992/7/Add.1; E/CN.4/Sub.2/1993/7. For further reading, see: James Anaya, *Indigenous Peoples in International Law* (2d edn. 2004); James Anaya & Robert A Williams, Jr., 'The Protection of Indigenous Peoples' Rights Over Lands and Natural Resources Under the Inter-American Human Rights System' (2001) 14 Harv. Hum. Rts. J. 33. Robert K. Hitchcock, 'International Human Rights, the Environment, and Indigenous Peoples' (1994) 1 Colo. J. Int'l Envtl. L. & Pol'y 1; William Andrew Shutkin, 'International Human Rights Law and the Earth: The Protection of Indigenous Peoples and the Environment' (1991) 31 Va. J. Int'l L. 479; Lee Swepston, 'A New Step in the International Law on Indigenous and Tribal Peoples: ILO Convention 169 of 1989' (1990) 15 Okla. City U. L. Rev. 677; Mario Ibarra, 'Traditional practices in respect of the sustainable and environmentally sound self-development of indigenous people', E/CN.4/Sub.2/1992/31/Add.1. 219 UN Declaration on the Rights of Indigenous Peoples, A/RES/61/25, adopted September 13, 2007.

to date has been ratified by only a small number of countries. Subsequently, on September 13, 2007, the United Nations completed a two-decade long negotiating process by adopting the UN Declaration on the Rights of Indigenous Peoples. Four countries which contain large indigenous populations (Australia, Canada, New Zealand, and the United States) originally declined to support the resolution, but all of them later announced support for the Declaration. The OAS also spent years negotiating a declaration on the rights of indigenous peoples, which was finally adopted in 2016 (American Declaration on the Rights of Indigenous Peoples, June 15, 2016, AG/RES. 2888 (XLVI-O/16). For its part, the European system adopted a Framework Convention on National Minorities on November 10, 1994. It is a programmatic treaty that envisages national laws and policies to give effect to its principles. The treaty does not define the term national minorities and supervises implementation solely by a system of periodic state reports.

The UN Declaration guarantees the right of self-determination, as well as respect for the individual human rights of indigenous peoples. In addition, the Declaration contains many rights linked to environmental protection, including cultural rights, land and resource rights, development rights, procedural rights (information, participation, and remedy), religious rights, and environmental rights. In particular, Article 29 specifies that:

1. Indigenous peoples have the right to the conservation and protection of the environment and the productive capacity of their lands or territories and resources. States shall establish and implement assistance programmes for indigenous peoples for such conservation and protection, without discrimination.
2. States shall take effective measures to ensure that no storage or disposal of hazardous materials shall take place in the lands or territories of indigenous peoples without their free, prior and informed consent.
3. States shall also take effective measures to ensure, as needed, that programmes for monitoring, maintaining and restoring the health of indigenous peoples, as developed and implemented by the peoples affected by such materials, are duly implemented.

The United Nations Human Rights Committee has addressed the rights of indigenous peoples primarily through the minority rights provision, Article 27. The Committee has explicitly held that it has no jurisdiction to hear cases asserting 'peoples rights, such as the right to self-determination.[219] Most of the communications under Article 27 have come from the Sami, traditional reindeer herders in Scandinavia.

219 See CCPR, General Comment 12, the Right to Self-Determination (1984) and General Comment 23, the Rights of Minorities (1994).

The member states subject to the Inter-American human rights system extend from the Arctic to Patagonia and each State in the region includes descendants of 'pre-contact' indigenous populations who overwhelminingly continue to suffer exclusion, poverty, and loss of their lands and resources. In deciding cases concerning indigneous and tribal peoples, the Inter-American Commission and the Inter-American Court have evolved a doctrine of unique rights for indigenous and tribal peoples and articulated special obligations states have towards them.

The petitioners in *Awas Tingni Mayagna (Sumo) Indigenous Community v. Nicaragua* sought protection from deforestation of lands they traditionally owned and occupied. The government had granted logging concessions to a foreign company without consulting the Awas Tingni community. On August 31, 2001, the Inter-American Court declared that the state violated the petitioners' right to judicial protection (Art. 25) and the right to property (Art. 21). It unanimously declared that the state must adopt domestic laws, administrative regulations, and other necessary means to create effective surveying, demarcating and title mechanisms for the lands of the indigenous communities, in accordance with customary law and indigenous values, uses and customs. Pending the demarcation, the state must abstain from realizing acts or allowing the realization of acts by its agents or third parties that could affect the existence, value, use or enjoyment of those properties located in the Awas Tingni lands. The Court also ordered the state to invest US$50,000 in public works and services of collective benefit to the Awas Tingni as a form of reparations for non-material injury. On December 18, 2008, the Commission announced that the government had complied with the Court's judgment.

Indigenous land and resource claims were increasingly brought to the Inter-American Commission and Court following the *Awas Tingni* decision. On June 17, 2005, the Court decided the case of the *Indigenous Community Yakye Axa v. Paraguay.*[220] Nine months later, the *Case of the Sawhoyamaxa Indigenous Community v. Paraguay*[221] addressed the difficult issue of returning indigenous lands long after they have been sold to and occupied by others. The Court summed up its earlier jurisprudence: 1) traditional possession of their lands by indigenous people has equivalent effects to those of a state-granted full property title; 2) traditional possession entitles indigenous people to demand official recognition and registration of property title; 3) the members

220 Merits, Reparations and Costs, Inter-Am. Ct. Hum. Rts, Ser. C, No. 125.

221 Inter-Am. Court Hum. Rts., Ser. C, No. 146 (March 29, 2006), For an earlier discussion, see the Commission's Third Report on the Situation of Human Rights in Paraguay. OEA /Ser.L/V/II.110, Doc. 52, March 9, 2001.

of indigenous peoples who have unwillingly left their traditional lands, or lost possession therof, maintain property rights thereto, even though they lack legal title, unless the lands have been lawfully transferred to third parties in good faith; and 4) the members of indigenous peoples who have unwillingly lost possession of their lands, when those lands have been lawfully transferred to innocent third parties, are entitled to restitution thereof or to obtain other lands of equal extension and quality. Consequently, possession is not a requisite conditioning the existence of indigenous land restitution rights.

The Inter-American Court significantly extended the property guarantees afforded indigenous peoples in its 2007 judgment in the case of the *Saramaka People v. Suriname*.[222] Like prior cases, this one concerned land and resource claims stemming from concessions granted by the state for the exploration and extraction of natural resources, in this case oil and gemstones. The Court extended its prior case law[223] on indigenous peoples to protect a non-indigenous tribal group[224] declaring that the jurisprudence regarding indigenous land and resource rights applies to tribal peoples, requiring special measures under international human rights law to protect their physical and cultural existence. The Court easily concluded that resources related to traditional agricultural, hunting and fishing activities are protected as subsistence activities, but it also considered the impact that other activities might have on subsistence resources, attempting to strike a balance between the state's concern with economic development and indigenous land and resource rights. The Court held that the protection of the right to property is not absolute and cannot be read to preclude all concessions for exploration and extraction in the Saramaka territory[225] since Article 21 itself provides for the limitation of property rights under certain circumstances. The Court itself will assess and give crucial weight to the question of 'whether the restriction amounts to a denial of the [indigenous and tribal peoples'] traditions and customs in a way that endangers the very survival of the group and its members'.[226] The Court set forth three safeguards it deems essential: (1) the state must ensure the effective participation of the members of the Saramaka people, in conformity with

222 *Case of the Saramaka People v. Suriname*, IACtHR Judgment of Nov. 28, 2007.

223 In particular, the Court cited the Case of the Moiwana Community v. Suriname, Preliminary Objections, Merits, Reparations and Costs, Judgment of June 15, 2004, Inter-Am.Ct. Hum. Rts, Ser. C No. 124, paras 132–133.

224 The Court found that the Saramaka maintain "a strong spiritual relationship" with their traditional lands, which constitute a source of life and cultural identity for the people. Id. para. 82.

225 ibid paras. 125–126.

226 ibid para. 128.

their customs and traditions, regarding any development, investment, exploration or extraction plan within Saramaka territory; (2) the state must guarantee that the Saramakas will receive a reasonable benefit from any such plan within their territory; and (3) the state must ensure that no concession will be issued within Saramaka territory unless and until independent and technically capable entities, with the state's supervision, perform a prior environmental and social impact assessment.[227] The Court viewed benefit-sharing as inherent to the right of compensation recognized under Article 21(2) of the Convention.[228] This right to compensation extends to any deprivation of the regular use and enjoyment of property.

The first duty requires the state both to compile and to disseminate information and entails constant good faith consultations, through culturally appropriate procedures and with the objective of reaching an agreement. The Court also stated that "the state must also ensure that members of the Saramaka people are aware of possible risks, including environmental and health risks, in order that the proposed development or investment plan is accepted knowingly and voluntarily'.[229] Most importantly, the Court added an obligation of result to the obligation of process in respect to certain activities. It held that large-scale development or investment projects that would have a major impact within Saramaka territory can only proceed with the free, prior, and informed consent of the people, according to their customs and traditions.

The jurisprudence of the Inter-American Court was adopted within the African context by the African Commission on Human and Peoples' Rights, which held that the denial of land and resources rights to the Endori people of Kenya violated their rights under the African Charter.[230] Notably, the case was not in response to government-sponsored extractive industrial activity, but to the creation of a game park for tourism. The Commission held that the Endoris constitute an indigenous people who could not be barred from access to and use of the park. The High Court of Botswana decided a similar case with a similar result.[231]

227 ibid para. 129.

228 Article 21(2) provides that '[n]o one shall be deprived of his property except upon payment of just compensation, for reasons of public utility or social interest, and in the cases and according to the forms established by law'.

229 *Case of the Saramaka People*, para. 133. See also *Case of the Indigenous Communities of the Lhaka Honhat (Our Land) Association v Argentina* I-A Ct Hum.Rts, Judgement of 6 February 2020 (Merits Reparations and Costs).

230 Case 276/2003, *Center for Minority Rights Development (Kenya) and Minority Rights Group International on Behalf of Endoris Welfare Council v. Kenya*, Afr, Comm'n H.P.R

231 *Sesana and Others v Attorney General*, High Court, Misc. No 52 of 2002; ILDC 665 (BW 2006), Judgment of Dec. 13, 2006.

Among environmental agreements, the most innovative in regard to indigenous rights and responsibilities is the Declaration on the Establishment of the Arctic Council.[232] A major feature of the Council is the involvement of indigenous peoples as Permanent Participants, based on 'recognition of the special relationship and unique contributions to the Arctic of indigenous peoples and their communities' (Preamble). Three organizations, the Inuit Circumpolar Conference, the Sami Council and the Association of Indigenous Minorities of the North, Siberia and the Far East of the Russian Federation, are specifically included in the Declaration. Other groups may participate, up to one less than the number of member states, if they meet the criteria set forth in Article 2 of the Declaration including having a majority Arctic indigenous constituency. The category of Permanent Participation is created, according to the Declaration 'to provide for active participation and full consultation with the Arctic indigenous representatives within the Arctic Council'.

The Conference of the Parties to the Convention on Biological Diversity (CBD) have addressed indigenous rights in the context of implementing Article 8 of the Convention, initially adopting the Bonn Guidelines, Decision VI/1 of the sixth Conference of the Parties, followed by conclusion of the 2010 Nagoya Protocol on Access to Access To Genetic Resources And The Fair And Equitable Sharing Of Benefits Arising From Their Utilization. Like the CBD itself, the Protocol aims to facilitate access to genetic resources, but it also recognizes the interests and rights of indigenous peoples and local communities who have been stewards of these resources and the repositories of traditional knowledge about them. The preamble notes the interrelationship between genetic resources and traditional knowledge, their inseparable nature for indigenous and local communities, the importance of the traditional knowledge for the conservation of biological diversity and the sustainable use of its components, and for the sustainable livelihoods of these communities. Yet, the Protocol remains deferential to local law. Article 5 provides that each Party shall take legislative, administrative or policy measures, 'as appropriate', with the aim of ensuring that benefits arising from the utilization of genetic resources and knowledge about those resources that are held by indigenous and local communities, 'in accordance with domestic legislation regarding the established rights of these indigenous and local communities over these genetic resources', are shared in a fair and equitable way with the communities concerned, based on mutually agreed terms. Similarly, Article 6 provides

232 Canada-Denmark-Finland-Iceland-Norway-the Russian Federation-Sweden-United States, Declaration on the Establishment of the Arctic Council, Ottawa, September 19, 1996, *reprinted in* 35 I.L.M. 1382 (1996).

that again 'in accordance with domestic law', each Party shall take measures, 'as appropriate', with the aim of ensuring that the prior informed consent or approval and involvement of indigenous and local communities is obtained for access to genetic resources where they have the established right to grant access to such resources. Article 7 provides a similar requirement of 'appropriate' prior informed consent for access to indigenous traditional knowledge 'in accordance with domestic law'. Article 12 provides further detail about support for indigenous and local communities, while Annex 1 provides illustrative lists of monetary and non-monetary benefits.

On a regional level, in the context of the North American Agreement on Environmental Cooperation, on November 6, 2001, the Secretariat decided to accept and transmit to Mexico a case alleging that Mexico denied indigenous communities of the Sierra Tarahumara access to environmental justice by failing to enforce its environmental laws regarding citizen complaints, environmental crimes and forest resources. As part of its case, the applicants invoked ILO Convention 169 concerning indigenous peoples. The regional body indicated that it would have jurisdiction over the Convention if it forms part of the domestic law of a state party, but that proper procedures had not been followed in the case to allow it to be considered.

6 Farmers' Rights

The issue of protecting traditional knowledge and local resources is one that goes beyond indigenous peoples to encompass local communities in general, particularly farmers that have been instrumental in conserving, improving and contributing to plant genetic resources. Farmers' Rights are crucial to food security in providing an incentive for the conservation and development of plant genetic resources.

The international community was initially divided over whether intellectual property rights or other equitable considerations should apply to farmers' developments of plant genetic resources or whether plant genetic resources constitute part of the common heritage of mankind or the natural resources of sovereign states. The FAO Global System for the Conservation and Utilization of Plant Genetic Resources attempted to reconcile competing interests by providing in an International Undertaking that such resources are the common heritage, but subject to the overriding sovereign rights of nations over their genetic resources. FAO Resolution 5/89 also accepted the concept of farmers' rights arising from their contributions, rights it sees as vested in the international community as trustee for present and future generations of farmers, for the purpose of ensuring full benefits to farmers and supporting the continuation of their contributions.

The FAO's International Treaty on Plant Genetic Resources for Food and Agriculture concluded in 2002 provides for access to information (Arts. 13 and 17) and public participation. Farmers' rights are formally endorsed by this legally binding instrument at the global level, for the first time (Art. 9). The treaty provides in Articles 10–14 a system of facilitated access to an agreed list of over 60 plant genera, including 35 crops, chosen on the basis of interdependence and importance of those listed for food security. The benefits accruing from the use of the material accessed is to be shared fairly and equitably through a variety of actions. There is a conceptual breakthrough in respect to the sharing of monetary benefits: anyone who obtains a commercial profit from the use of genetic resources administered multilaterally is obliged, by a standard Material Transfer Agreement, to share these profits fairly and equitably and pay a royalty to the multilateral mechanism for use as part of the funding strategy for benefit sharing.

India was one of the first countries to pass legislation specifically protecting plant breeders' rights.[233] The African Union also drafted a model law on biological resources in 2000.

Conclusions

The enjoyment of human rights depends upon environmental protection, and environmental protection depends upon the exercise of certain human rights such as the right to information and the right to political participation. Despite this common core, the two topics remain distinct. Environmental protection probably cannot be wholly incorporated into the human rights agenda without deforming the anthropocentric concept of human rights. Also, some human rights are not directly affected by environmental considerations, e.g. the right to a name or to be free from *ex post facto* laws.

A right to environmental quality must still be balanced with other human rights. The General Assembly has pronounced many times on the indivisibility, interdependence, interrelatedness, and universality of all human rights.[234] Yet, the possibility of collision or conflict between rights cannot be avoided. For example, internationally guaranteed rights include the right of each family

233 The Protection of Plant Varieties and Farmer's Rights Act No. 53 of August 31, 2001.

234 See the Vienna Declaration and Program of Action, adopted by the World Conference on Human Rights, June 25, 1993, U.N. Doc. A/CONF.157/24 (Part I).

to decide on the number and spacing of their children. Demographic pressures have been recognized as a threat to environmental quality and economic development, leading to demands that national birthrates be lowered to achieve sustainable development.[235] Who decides on the appropriate balance is an important issue of governance.

On a theoretical level, human health can be seen as a bridge between human rights and environmental protection, being a primary objective of both areas of regulation. Human rights exist to promote and protect human well-being, to allow the full development of each person and the maximization of the person's goals and interests, individually and in community with others. This cannot occur without basic conditions of health, which the state is to promote and protect. Among the pre-requisites for health are safe environmental milieu, i.e. air, water, and soil. Pollution destroys health and kills and thus not only destroys the environment, but infringes human rights as well. From the perspective of the law of state responsibility, there may be little difference between a state that arbitrarily executes persons and a state that knowingly allows drinking water to be poisoned by contaminants. In both instances, the state can be responsible for depriving individuals of their life in violation of human rights law; in the second case, international environmental law is also implicated. Implementing and enforcing the latter will also help protect the former. Thus, the goal of human health provides the basis for reinforcing both areas of law.

The recognition of a right to a clean, safe and healthy environment represents a crucial step in advancing the synergetic relationship between human rights and environment protection. It reflects the view that mankind is part of a global system, which may reconcile the aims of human rights and environmental protection, since both ultimately seek to achieve the highest quality of sustainable life for humanity within the existing global ecosystem.

Further Reading

Alfredson, G. & Ovsiouk, A., 'Human Rights and the Environment', 60 *Nordic J. Int'l L.* 19 (1991).

Anaya, S.J, 'Indigenous Rights Norms in Contemporary International Law', 8 *Ariz J. Int'l & Comp. L.*1 (1991).

---

235 See Report of the International Conference on Population and Development, Cairo, September 5–13, 1994, U.N. Pub. E.95.XIII.18.

Anton, D. & Shelton, D., *The Environment and Human Rights* (Cambridge University Press 2011).

Boyd, D. R. *The Environment Rights Revolution* (UBC Press 2012).

Boyle, A., 'Human Rights or Environmental Rights? A Rassessment', 18 *Fordham Envtl L. Rev.* 471–511 (2007).

Boyle, A & M. Anderson (eds.), *Human Rights Approaches to Environmental Protection* (Oxford University Press 1996).

Cullet, P. 'Definition of an Environmental Right in a Human Rights Context', 13 *Neth. Q. Hum. Rts.* 25 (1995).

Dejeantpons, Má. & Pallemaerts, M., *Droits De L'homme et Environnement* (2002).

Desgagne, R., 'Integrating Environmental Values into the European Convention on Human Rights', 89 *AJIL* 263 (1995).

Eaton, J.P., 'The Nigerian Tragedy, Environmental Regulation of Transnational Corporations and the Human Right to a Healthy Environment', 15 *B.U.I.L.J.* 261 (1997).

Factoran, F.S., 'A Reaction to the Right to a Balanced and Healthful Ecology: The Oddesy of a Constitutional Policy', 157–163 (1994).

Handl, G., 'Human Rights and Protection of the Environment: A Mildly "Revisionist" View', in *Human Rights and Environmental Protection* (A. A. Cancado Trindade (ed). 1992).

Hayward, Tim, *Constitutional Environmental Rights* (2005).

Kane, M.J., 'Promoting Political Rights to Protect the Environment', 18 *Yale J. Int'l L.* 389 (1993).

Kiss, A., 'Le Droit a la Conservation de l'environnement', 1 *Rev. Universelle Des Droits De L'homme* 445 (1990).

Knox, J. H & R. Pejan, *The Human Right to a Healthy Environment* (Cambridge University Press 2018).

May, J.R. 'Constituting Fundamental Environmental Rights Worldwide', 23 *Pace Envtl L.Rev.* 113–82 (2005/2006).

Meltz, Robert, *Right to a Clean Environment Provisions in State Constitutions as to a Federal Counterpart* (Congressional Research Service, Library of Congress 1999).

Shelton, D., 'Human Rights, Environmental Rights, and the Right to Environment', 28 *Stan. J. Int'l L.*103 (1991).

Shelton, D., 'The Benefits and Limitations of a Human Rights Approach to Environmental Protection', *Hungarian Yearbook of International Law and European Law* 120–132 (2014).

Shelton, D., 'Developing Substantive Environmental Rights', 1 *Journal of Human Rights and the Environment* 89–121 (2010).

Swepston, L., 'A New Step in the International Law on Indigenous and Tribal Peoples: ILO Convention 169 of 1989', 15 Okla City U. L. Rev. 677 (1990).

CHAPTER 16

Environmental Protection and Military Activities

Throughout history, militaries have harmed the environment incidentally or deliberately as a wartime strategy.[1] Examples from armed conflicts since the end of the Second World War include widespread use of defoliants during the Vietnam War that destroyed entire ecosystems and led to public health concerns in the United States and Vietnam[2]; two decades later, while the United Nations (UN) was preparing for the 1992 Rio Conference on Environment and Development,[3] Iraqi forces invading Kuwait set oil fires and caused major environmental harm.[4] Perhaps in reaction to these and similar acts, states participating in the Rio Conference adopted Principle 24 of the concluding Declaration on Environment and Development, in which they affirmed that 'warfare is inherently destructive of sustainable development' and further issued a call to states 'to respect international law concerning the environment in times of armed conflict and to cooperate in its further development, as necessary'.[5]

---

1 See generally Eric Talbot Jensen, 'The International Law of Environmental Warfare: Active and Passive Damage during Armed Conflict' (2005) 38 *Vanderbilt Journal of Transnational Law* 145, 147; Alexandre Kiss and Dinah Shelton, *Guide to International Environmental Law* (Brill 2007) at 253.

2 Aspen Institute, 'History: Agent Orange/Dioxin in Vietnam', *available at* http://www.aspeninstitute.org/policy-work/agent-orange/history (last accessed June 1, 2024). See generally, Richard A. Falk, 'Environmental Warfare and Ecocide: Facts, Appraisal & Proposals' (1973) 9 Review Belge de Droit International [Belgian Review of International Law] 1 (commenting that the Vietnam War was a major example of purposeful wartime environmental damage).

3 The UN General Assembly convened the world conference by G. A. Res. 44/228 of December 22, 1989. Three preparatory committee meetings took place during 1990 and 1991 before the conference met in Rio de Janeiro from June 3–14, 1992.

4 Kelly Ann Furr, 'Note: Environmental Degradation In The Mesopotamian Marshlands: A Case Study In Legal Deficiencies' (2011) 19 *South Eastern Environmental Law Journal* 271. Luan Low and David Hodgkinson, 'Compensation for Wartime Environmental Damage: Challenges to International Law after the Gulf War' (1995) 35 *Virginia Journal of International Law* 405, 405. For an assessment of the damage in Southern Iraq, see generally United Nations Environmental Programme, Support for Environmental Management of the Iraqi Marshlands 2004–2009 (2009).

5 United Nations Conference on Environment and Development, Rio de Janeiro, June 3–14, 1992, Rio Declaration on Environment and Development, A/CONF.151/26 (Vol. 1), 31 ILM 874 (Aug. 12, 1992) [hereinafter Rio Declaration] ('Warfare is inherently destructive of sustainable development. States shall therefore respect international law providing protection for the environment in times of armed conflict and cooperate in its further development, as necessary'.).

 | DOI:10.1163/9789047440802_018

Principle 24's assertion about the environmental consequences of armed conflict was borne out by the United Nations Environment Programme's (UNEP) environmental assessments of more than twenty conflicts between 1999 and 2009. The study found that armed conflict causes significant harm to the environment and communities that depend on natural resources: '[d]irect and indirect environmental damage, coupled with the collapse of institutions, lead to environmental risks that can threaten people's health, livelihoods and security, and ultimately undermine post-conflict peacebuilding'.[6]

International and internal armed conflicts throughout the world continue to cause damage[7] to the environment;[8] in recent conflicts, this damage has included the deliberate looting of the natural wealth of conflict zones.[9] This environmental damage is not only committed by official military forces, but is often caused by rebel forces and insurgents, as has occurred in the Democratic Republic of the Congo (DRC).[10] During the conflict in Syria and Iraq, reports suggest that the self-proclaimed Islamic State of Iraq and Syria has set out to

---

6 UNEP, 'Protecting the Environment during Armed Conflict: An Inventory and Analysis of International Law' (2009), 4 [hereinafter UNEP Inventory and Analysis].

7 'Damage' is considered in accordance with the definition adopted by the International Law Commission (ILC) in its Draft Principles on the Allocation of Loss in the Case of Transboundary Harm Arising out of Hazardous Activities. Report of the International Law Commission on Its Fifty-eighth Session, UNGAOR, 60st Sess. Supp. No. 10, U.N. Doc. A/61/10 (2006, principle 2 (a) (III)–(V), at pp. 121–22 ('"Damage" includes loss or damage by impairment of the environment; the costs of reasonable measures of reinstatement of the environment, including natural resources; and the costs of reasonable response measures'). See paragraph 10 of the commentary to principle 2 on the protection of cultural property in times of war. ibid, at p. 127.

8 For the purpose of damages, the environment includes 'natural resources, both abiotic and biotic, such as air, water, soil, fauna and flora and the interaction between the same factors; and the characteristic aspects of the landscape'. ibid, 410.

9 Trade in so-called 'conflict diamonds' during the Liberian civil war is perhaps the most widely-known example. Luke Whittemore, 'Intervention and post-conflict natural resource governance: lessons from Liberia' (2008) 17 *Minnesota Journal of International Law* 387–433; Melvin, Neil, and Ruben De Koning, 'Resources and Armed Conflict' (2011) in SIPRI Yearbook 2011: Armaments, Disarmament and International Security. See also *D. R. Congo v. Burundi, Rwanda and Uganda*, African Commission on Human and Peoples' Rights, Communication No. 227/99 (2003) (addressing alleged grave and massive violations of human and peoples' rights committed by the armed forces of these three countries in the Congolese provinces where there have been rebel activities since August 2, 1998, including 'systematic looting of the underground riches of the regions controlled by their forces'). The case is discussed below.

10 See e.g. Reports of the Group of Experts Submitted through the Security Council Committee Established Pursuant to Resolution 1533 (2004) Concerning the Democratic Republic of the Congo.

appropriate fresh water and use dams as weapons in its military campaign.[11] The expansion of UN peacekeeping since the end of the Cold War has also led to consideration of how to protect the environment during UN missions. In May 2012, UNEP released a report that discusses the important role of missions in avoiding injurious environmental consequences and suggested actions such as ensuring that the sanitary conditions at the United Nations stabilization missions are adequate to avoid contamination of local waterways.[12] The UN could also help reduce deforestation and illicit trade in natural resources.[13]

These events have led to renewed interest in examining the state of the law on environmental protection in the context of military activities. The International Committee of the Red Cross (ICRC) published a comprehensive study of customary international humanitarian law[14] and asserted that environmental law remains generally applicable during armed hostilities. For its part, at its sixty-fifth session, in 2013, the International Law Commission (ILC) decided to include the topic 'Protection of the environment in relation to armed conflicts' in its work program.[15] The ILC rapporteur for the topic, Marie Jacobbson, took a temporal approach to examining the issue, looking at international obligations before, during and subsequent to an armed conflict.[16] In this framework, her 2014 preliminary report had as its main focus an introductory overview of the environmental rules and principles applicable to military activities during peacetime.[17] The preliminary report noted that environmental harm is often long-term and irreparable and can therefore be an obstacle to the effective rebuilding of societies after a conflict.[18] The focus of the 2015 report was to

---

11 Peter Schwartstein, 'Amid Terror Attacks, Iraq Faces Water Crisis,' National Geographic News, Nov. 4, 2014.

12 David Jensen and Silja Halle, eds., *Greening the Blue Helmets: Environment, Natural Resources and U.N. Peacekeeping Operations* (UNEP 2012), 8 and 33.

13 ibid, p. 37.

14 Some commentators disagree, concluding that environmental agreements may be suspended during wartime. See Arthur Westing, 'Environmental Protection from Wartime Damage: The Role of International Law', in Nils Petter Gleditsch (ed.), *Conflict and the Environment* (1997), 535, 538. On customary international law, see: Jean-Marie Henckaerts and Louise Doswald-Beck (eds.), *Customary International Humanitarian Law, vols. I and II* (Cambridge University Press 2005).

15 International Law Commission, Report on its Sixty-Fifth Session, (May 6 to June 7 and July 8 to August 9, 2013). General Assembly Official Records, Sixty-eighth Session, Supplement No. 10, U.N. Doc. A/68/10.

16 Preliminary Report of the Special Rapporteur, para. 59.

17 ibid.

18 International Law Commission, Protection of the Environment in Relation to Armed Conflicts, Preliminary report of the Special Rapporteur, Ms. Marie G. Jacobsson (66th session of the ILC (2014)) [hereinafter Preliminary Report of the Special Rapporteur]; Report

identify existing rules of armed conflict that are directly relevant to the protection of the environment in relation to armed conflict, while also containing draft principles.[19] In one demonstration of the connection between international peace and security and protection of the environment and natural resources, the ILC Rapporteur identified 2,195 UN Security Council resolutions adopted as of December 31, 2014, of which 242 (or 11 per cent) addressed natural resources in some manner.[20]

In 2022, at its 73rd Session, the ILC adopted the Draft Principles on Protection of the Environment in relation to armed conflicts, together with commentaries.[21] The draft principles are mainly addressed to states but also encompass international organizations and non-state actors. Draft principles 10 and 11 regulate corporate environmental conduct in conflict areas, while principles 13 and 14 address the environment during armed conflicts, applying to both international and non-international armed conflicts. The ILC chose not to differentiate between international and non-international armed conflicts in the draft principles themselves but made distinctions in the commentaries. Environment-specific provisions in international humanitarian (IHL) law apply differently to international and non-international armed conflicts, which the ILC clarifies in its commentaries. The draft principles integrate rules from various fields of international law, such as the UN Declaration on the Rights of Indigenous Peoples, the law of State responsibility, and international environmental law. These principles reflect the comprehensive approach of the ILC in addressing environmental protection in armed conflicts. Draft principle 12 extends the Martens clause (see later in this Chapter) to environmental protection. Draft principles 13 and 14 affirm that the environment is a civilian object

---

of the International Law Commission on its Sixty-Sixth Session (May 5 to June 6 and July 7 to August 8, 2014), U.N. Doc. A/CN.4/674 and Corr.1, para. 1.

19 International Law Commission, Protection of the Environment in Relation to Armed Conflicts, Report of the Special Rapporteur, Ms. Marie G. Jacobsson (67th session of the ILC (2015), UN Doc. A/CN.4/685 (May 28, 2015).

20 International Law Commission, Protection of the Environment in Relation to Armed Conflicts, Report of the Special Rapporteur, Ms. Marie G. Jacobsson (67th session of the ILC (2015), UN Doc. A/CN.4/685 (May 28, 2015), para. 79. The Security Council has on several occasions condemned the targeting of oil installations, pipelines and other facilities. Numerous resolutions address the use of natural resources (gold, diamonds, minerals, charcoal and opium poppy, among others) in financing armed conflict. Afghanistan stands out as a particular case. Although many resolutions are framed in the context of terrorism and violence, they are an indication of the role that natural resources play in the context of financing terrorism and/or armed conflict. ibid, paras. 82–3.

21 United Nations General Assembly, Protection of the environment in relation to armed conflicts (7 December 2022) UNGA Res 77/104, UN Doc A/RES/77/104.).

under IHL and must be protected accordingly. Draft principle 14 mandates that IHL principles, such as distinction, proportionality, and precautions, apply to environmental protection during armed conflict. Draft principle 17 prohibits the hostile use of environmental modification techniques, reflecting the Environmental Modification Convention. The ILC's occupation-related draft principles reflect an evolutionary interpretation of the law of occupation regarding environmental protection, integrating IHL, international environmental law, and international human rights law.

As the ILC reports indicated, the normative framework governing military activities derives from a complex interplay of international environmental law, human rights law and international humanitarian law, along with special rules governing particular weapons systems. Many multilateral environmental agreements are silent[22] on their application during armed conflict, but some contain specific provisions indicating their continued applicability. The United Nations Educational, Scientific and Cultural Organization (UNESCO)'s World Heritage Convention (WHC), for example, contains a provision that armed conflict suffices to place a site on the list of WHC sites in danger, suggestion that the drafters intended the treaty to continue to apply during armed conflict.[23] The drafters of the ILC commentary to the 1997 Convention on the Law of the Non-navigational Uses of International Watercourses,[24] specified that the obligation of watercourse States to protect and use international watercourses and related works in accordance with the articles remains in effect during armed conflict.[25] More generally, the 2011 ILC Articles on the effects of

22 See e.g., the 1992 Convention on Biological Diversity, 1760 U.N.T.S. 142; 1993 Convention on International Trade in Endangered Species of Wild Fauna and Flora, 993 U.N.T.S. 243; and the 1979 Convention on Migratory Species, 19 ILM 15 (1980), among others.

23 Article 11(4), 1972 UNESCO Convention Concerning the Protection of the World Cultural and Natural Heritage, See Britta Sjöstedt, 'The Role of Multilateral Environmental Agreements in Armed Conflict: Green-keeping in Virunga Park. Applying the UNESCO World Heritage Convention in the Armed Conflict of the Democratic Republic of the Congo' (2013) 82 *Nordic Journal of International Law* 129,53.

24 1997 Convention on the Law of the Non-navigational Uses of International Watercourses, 36 ILM 700 (1997). Article 29 of that Convention provides that 'international watercourses and related installations, facilities and other works shall enjoy the protection accorded by the principles and rules of international law applicable in international and internal armed conflict and shall not be used in violation of those principles and rules'.

25 The commentary gives examples of applicable rules and principles drawn from the Hague Convention of 1907 Concerning the Laws and Customs of War on Land; Protocol I additional to the Geneva Conventions of 12 August 1949; and the Martens clause ibid, at para. 3 of the commentary to draft article 29. The ILC Commentary also suggested that the duty to give special consideration to 'the requirements of vital human needs' represents an expression of the Martens Clause. Yearbook of the International Law Commission,

armed conflicts on treaties[26] presume that the existence of an armed conflict does not *ipso facto* terminate or suspend the operation of treaties (Art. 3). The ILC provided an indicative list of treaties 'the subject matter of which involves an implication that they continue in operation, in whole or in part, during armed conflict' and included this list of treaties in the annex to the draft articles.[27] This list includes treaties concerning environmental protection.[28] For other types of agreements, the nature of the treaty, its subject matter, its object and purpose, its content and the number of its parties are factors to be considered as well as the characteristics of the armed conflict, such as its territorial extent, its scale and intensity, its duration and, in the case of non-international armed conflict, also the degree of outside involvement.

Human rights law more systematically specifies the extent to which it continues during periods of emergency, including international and internal armed conflicts. Although much of the corpus of the law of war predates human rights law and was designed specifically to protect persons who are not (or are no longer) participating in hostilities and to restrict the means and methods of warfare, it is now widely recognized that human rights obligations generally continue to apply in these situations as well. The scope of guaranteed rights may be limited through properly declared and implemented temporary suspensions according to the terms of derogations clauses, but human rights treaties as a whole are not suspended during armed conflicts, including those provisions relevant to environmental protection. Any derogation is subject to strict requirements: a public emergency that threatens the life of the nation; the measures taken must be 'strictly required by the exigencies of the situation', consistent with other obligations under international law, as well as necessary and proportional, temporary, non-discriminatory, and subject to judicial guarantees. In its Advisory Opinion on *the Wall*, the International Court of Justice (ICJ) supported the continuity of human rights obligations:

> More generally, the Court considers that the protection offered by human rights conventions does not cease in case of armed conflict, save through

---

1994, vol. II, Part Two, draft article 10, paras. 2–3 on the law of the non-navigational uses of international watercourses, p. 132.

26 International Law Commission, 'Report on the Work of Its Sixty-Third Session' (26 April–3 June and 4 July–12 August 2011) UN Doc A/66/10, ch VI.

27 ibid.

28 ibid. In addition to treaties concerning the law of armed conflict itself, the annexed list includes treaties relating to the international protection of the environment, international watercourses and related installations and facilities, aquifers and related installations and facilities, human rights, and international criminal law.

> the effect of provisions for derogation of the kind to be found in Article 4 of the International Covenant on Civil and Political Rights. As regards the relationship between international humanitarian law and human rights law, there are thus three possible situations: some rights may be exclusively matters of international humanitarian law; others may be exclusively matters of human rights law; yet others maybe matters of both these branches of international law. In order to answer the question put to it, the Court will have to take into consideration both these branches of international law, namely human rights law and, as *lex specialis*, international humanitarian law.[29]

International humanitarian law itself contains principles that can be specifically invoked to limit harm to the environment. These principles are found in customary international law and codified in The Hague Conventions of 1899 and October 18, 1907 and the Geneva Conventions of August 12, 1949. In 1976, states adopted the first treaty specifically aimed at protecting the environment against military assault: the Environmental Modification Convention, (Dec. 10, 1976).[30] The following year, Additional Protocol I to the 1949 Geneva Conventions added additional guarantees.

To determine the applicable rules among these three bodies of law requires identifying whether or not an armed conflict exists and if so how it should be classified, as well as investigating whether or not the state involved has or has not derogated from its human rights obligations.[31] Not all rules applicable to an international armed conflict are considered applicable during non-international armed conflict, although fundamental principles, such as the principles of distinction and proportionality, reflect customary law and apply during all types of armed conflict.

Outside the context of armed conflict, international law has been slow to recognize that all military activities may cause serious and widespread environmental harm. Weapons testing, training missions, and occupation of military bases and other installations may result in spilled fuel, dumping of hazardous wastes, and unexploded ordnance are some examples.[32] Military

29 *Advisory Opinion of the International Court of Justice on the Legal Consequences of the Construction of a Wall in the Occupied Palestinian Territory*, para. 106, July 9, 2004.

30 G. A. Res. 31/72 of Dec. 10, 1976 approved the ENMOD Convention and opened it for signature on May 18, 1977. The text is reprinted at 16 I.L.M. 90 (1977).

31 See Elizabeth Wilmshurst (ed.), *International Law and the Classification of Conflicts* (Oxford University Press 2012).

32 See generally, Steven Dycus, *National Defense and the Environment* (1996) at 4–5 (explaining that military operations affect the environment in a variety of ways, such as discharging

exercises may harm local flora and fauna, including endangered species.[33] The departure of foreign forces can leave the territorial government with massive, long term, and often-undetected environmental harm.[34] This chapter examines first the norms concerning environmental protection in armed conflict and then examines the problems arising from peacetime military activities.

1 Protection of the Environment during Armed Conflict

1.1 *Treaty and Customary International Law*

State practice and religious traditions have long prohibited deliberate attacks on certain features of the environment. Jewish and Muslim texts, for example, enjoin the destruction of trees during war.[35] Grotius, in his classic *On the Law of War and Peace*, contended that the law of nations forbid the poisoning of water[36] and in a chapter on 'moderation in laying waste' promoted the principle of military necessity.[37] Until the United States civil war (1861–1864), however, states had not approved any agreement defining the laws of war. During that conflict, the US army adopted the Lieber Code of 1863 which imposed rules on the treatment of civilians and prisoners of war and limited the means and methods of warfare. Four principles emerged from the Lieber Code to become generally accepted in state practice and international agreements: the principles barring unnecessary damage (the principle of military necessity); requiring proportionality (actions should not cause excessive or indiscriminate damage in relation to the military advantage); prohibiting the infliction of unnecessary suffering; and requiring discrimination between civilian and military targets. These principles have been elaborated in many treaties establishing the law of armed conflict, including agreements on treatment of

---

'wastes into lakes and streams, groundwaters, the ocean, and the air'); see also Richard A. Phelps, 'Environmental Law for Overseas Installations' (1996) 40 *Air Force Law Review* 49, 74.

33 See e.g. the allegations and evidence concerning loss of flora and fauna in *D. R. Congo v. Burundi, Rwanda, and Uganda.*

34 See generally, Jean-Marie Cadiou, 'The Environmental Legacy of the Cold War' (1993) 41 NATO Review 33; Philippe Rekacewicz, 'Environmental Disaster in Eastern Europe', Le Monde Diplomatique, July 2000. See also the NATO-sponsored study 'Cross-Border Environmental Problems Emanating From Defence-Related Installations and Activities (Phases 1 and 2)'.

35 Deuteronomy 20:19-20 prohibits during a siege the cutting of trees that yield food, while the Qur'an contains a prohibition on harming trees or other plants during war, except in case of grave military necessity.

36 Hugo Grotius, *On the Law of War and Peace* (F.W. Kelsey, trans., 1925), Bk. III, ch. XI.

37 ibid, Bk. III, ch. XII.

civilians and prisoners of war, bans on certain weapons, specifying the obligations of occupying powers, and establishing rules for different theaters of conflict (land, air, sea).

Specific rules in the law of armed conflict aimed at protecting the environment during wartime remain few, not surprising given the relatively recent emergence of international environmental law.[38] Older treaties made no reference to the environment and the only protection offered was to property rights and certain natural resources. Most texts did not explicitly mention the environment, but did contain general principles and provisions that may be applied in order to promote environmental protection. The St. Petersburg Declaration on explosive projectiles, for example, proclaims that '[t]he only legitimate object which States should endeavor to accomplish during war is to weaken the military forces of the enemy'. Thus, any action lacking a military purpose would be unlawful.

The 1907 Hague Convention with its detailed and annexed regulations prohibits the use of poison or poisoned weapons and requires occupying states to refrain from over-exploiting resources such as forests.[39] These rules emerged from a general agreement of the parties that 'the right of belligerents to adopt means of injuring the enemy is not unlimited'.[40] Several customary international norms enshrined in the Hague Convention could provide potentially far-reaching environmental protection, including the fundamental principles of necessity, proportionality and discrimination between military and civilian targets.

Perhaps most importantly, the Preamble to the Convention recites the well-known Martens Clause. That clause recites:

> [u]ntil a more complete code of the laws of war has been issued, the High Contracting Parties deem it expedient to declare that, in cases not included in the Regulations adopted by them, the inhabitants and the belligerents remain under the protection and the rule of the principles of the law of nations, as they result from the usages established among

---

38 See 1976 Convention on the Prohibition of Military or Any Other Hostile Use of Environmental Modification Techniques, 1108 UNTS 151 [hereinafter ENMOD], and the 1977 Protocol additional to the Geneva Conventions of 12 August 1949, and relating to the protection of victims of international armed conflicts (Protocol I), 1125 U.N.T.S. 3 [hereinafter Protocol I].

39 Convention (No. IV) Respecting the Laws and Customs of War on Land, with Annex of Regulations (The Hague, Oct. 18, 1907), Arts. 23(a), 55, 36 Stat. 2277 (1911).

40 Hague Convention (IV) Respecting the Laws and Customs of War on Land, Art. 22 Annex, sec. 2, ch. I.

> civilized peoples, from the laws of humanity, and the dictates of the public conscience.

The wording of the clause has been echoed in a number of subsequent treaties, including the 1949 Geneva Conventions, the 1977 Additional Protocols I and II, and the 1980 Convention on Certain Conventional Weapons. In the aftermath of the 1991 Gulf War, the ICRC and the General Assembly asserted the relevance of the Martens Clause to environmental protection. The International Union for Conservation of Nature (IUCN)'s Amman Congress also recommended that states apply the clause.[41]

Although the 1925 Geneva Protocol on gas and bacteriological warfare does not mention the environment, the UN General Assembly invoked it in 1969 during the conflict in Vietnam. The General Assembly declared that the Protocol prohibits the use of any chemical agents of warfare which might be employed because of their direct toxic effects on man, animals or plants and any biological agents intended to cause disease and death in man, animals or plants.[42]

The Geneva Conventions of 1949 built on the provisions of the 1907 Hague Regulations and like them protects property, including property owned collectively or by the State or other public authorities. Article 147 of Geneva Convention (IV) on the protection of civilians includes among 'grave breaches' of the Convention any extensive destruction and appropriation of property not justified by military necessity and carried out unlawfully and wantonly. Whether or not the term 'property' includes public goods such as water resources, public lands, and air, remains debated.

Other treaties include specific measures relating to the environment, *inter alia*, Article I of the ENMOD Convention; Articles 35(3) and 55(1) of the 1977 Additional Protocol I to the Geneva Convention; and Article 2 of Protocol III

---

41 At its Second World Conservation Congress (Amman, Oct. 4–11, 2000), IUCN urged UN Member States to endorse the following policy: 'Until a more complete international code of environmental protection has been adopted, in cases not covered by international agreements and regulations, the biosphere and all its constituent elements and processes remain under the protection and authority of the principles of international law derived from established custom, from dictates of the public conscience, and from the principles and fundamental values of humanity acting as steward for present and future generations'. While inspired by the Martens Clause, this formulation is not limited to the context of armed conflict, but applies as an overarching principle to all human activities. See, 30 E.P.L. 285 and 313(2000); Alexandre Kiss, 'International Humanitarian Law and the Environment' (2001) 31 E.P.L. 223.

42 UNGA, *Question of Chemical and Bacteriological (Biological) Weapons* (16 December 1969) UNGA Res 2603A (XXIV), UN Doc A/RES/2603(XXIV). (80 in favor, 3 against, 36 abstentions).

to the United Nations Conventional Weapons Convention. The ENMOD is primarily concerned with the use of nature as a weapon of war. Article 1 prohibits all 'hostile use of environmental modification techniques having widespread, long-lasting or severe effects as the means of destruction, damage or injury' to the opposing side. Environmental modification, defined in Article II, means 'any technique for changing – through the deliberate manipulation of natural processes – the dynamics, composition or structure of the Earth, including its biota, lithosphere, hydrosphere and atmosphere, or of outer space'. A contemporaneous understanding of the Conference of the UN Committee on Disarmament defined widespread to mean an area on the scale of several hundred square kilometers. Long-lasting means a period of months, approximately a season, while severe is defined as 'involving serious or significant disruption or harm to human life, natural and economic resources or other assets'.

Additional Protocol I to the 1949 Geneva Convention significantly advanced environmental protection during warfare. It reflects two aims of environmental protection: protection of the environment itself, which is contained in Article 35(3) of the Protocol, and protection of the human population from environmental harm, which is contained in Article 55. Article 35(3) prohibits employing methods or means of warfare 'which are intended, or may be expected, to cause widespread, long-term and severe damage to the natural environment' without mentioning potential impacts on humans. Article 55(1) repeats that care should be taken to avoid such harm, but adds that 'this protection includes a prohibition of the use of methods or means of warfare which are intended or may be expected to cause such damage to the natural environment and thereby to prejudice the health or survival of the population'. Article 55(2) further specifies that attacks against the natural environment by way of reprisals are prohibited.

Without mentioning the environment specifically, other provisions of Protocol I may provide additional protection. Article 52, which concerns the general protection of civilian objects, prohibits attacks on objects indispensable to the survival of the civilian population, such as food, agricultural areas, crops, livestock, drinking water installations and supplies and irrigation works. Article 56 affords protection to works and installations containing dangerous forces, namely dams, dykes and nuclear electrical generating stations. These protections were notably referred to in the 1997 UN Convention on International Watercourses,[43] Article 29 of which refers to the protection afforded to

43 May 21, 1997, 36 I.L.M. 700 (1997).

international watercourses and related installations, facilities and other works during international and non-international armed conflicts.

Protocol I applies only to land warfare and to sea or air warfare that affects the land. The Protocol does not protect the atmosphere generally or the air above the land if the land below is not affected. In addition, Article 35(3) and Article 55 set a high threshold for prohibited acts, only banning those which cause 'widespread, long-term and severe damage'. Protocol I defines 'long-term' to be a period of decades, in contrast to the ENMOD, and uses the conjunctive 'and' instead of the ENMOD's 'or'. The Conference Committee clearly stated that the terms of Protocol I must be interpreted in accordance with the meaning specified in the Protocol, and not in the light of similar terms contained in other instruments, such as the ENMOD. On the other hand, as noted by the US Army's Operational Law Handbook, 'once the degree of damage to the environment reaches a certain level, Geneva Protocol I does not employ the traditional balancing of military necessity against the quantum of expected destruction. Instead, it establishes this level as an absolute ceiling of permissible destruction'.[44]

The large majority of states are parties to Protocol I,[45] but it has not attracted support among several key states, including the United States and India. The rules embodied in the Protocol can only be binding on non-signatories if the rules constitute or become customary international law. A further limiting factor arises from the fact that Protocol I applies only to international armed conflicts. Additional Protocol II to the Geneva Conventions specifically applies to non-international armed conflicts but contains no provision concerning the environment.

The Convention on the Prohibition of the Development, Production, Stockpiling and Use of Chemical Weapons and on their Destruction[46] contains far-reaching provisions on the control of national chemical production facilities and international verification of state obligations. Contracting states must destroy all chemical weapons and all production facilities within ten years of the agreement's entry into force. Each state party must provide access to any chemical weapons destruction facility for the purpose of on-site systematic verification and monitoring.

---

44 US Army, Operational Law Handbook, 2st rev. ed. JA 422 (1997) at 5. The 1998 Rome Statute of the International Criminal Court, Art. 8 concerns war crimes within the jurisdiction of the ICC and appears to reintroduce a proportionality analysis by referring to 'widespread, long-term and severe damage to the natural environment which would be clearly excessive in relation to the concrete and direct overall military advantage anticipated'.

45 As of June 2024, there are 174 States Parties to Protocol I.

46 Convention on the Prohibition of the Development, Production, Stockpiling and Use of Chemical Weapons and on their Destruction (adopted 3 September 1992, entered into force 29 April 1997) 1975 U.N.T.S. 45.

The treaty covers all toxic chemicals and their precursors, listed in three schedules or annexes. Schedule 1 chemicals, including all nerve and mustard gases now in existence, cannot be produced in excess of 10 kilograms per year, and production must be done at a single specially designated facility. Schedules 2 and 3 list chemicals which can be used for both civilian and military purposes. States may produce these chemicals without production limits, but production above a range from one kilogram to one ton triggers a reporting obligation in regard to the producing facility. In addition, there may be on-site inspections. For schedule 3 chemicals, states are required to submit reports for each facility that produces amounts over limits ranging from 30 to 200 tons per year.

Within thirty days of the entry into force of the agreement on April 29, 1997, each state party had to submit to the Organization for the Prohibition of Chemical Weapons (OPCW), a treaty monitoring group based in the Hague, a declaration on its ownership or possession of chemical weapons, the precise location, quantity and detailed inventory of such weapons, and information on the import or export after January 1, 1946 of weapons-producing equipment. Each state also had to provide a general plan for destruction, closure, or conversion of any chemical weapons production facility it owns or possesses or is within its jurisdiction or control. Contracting states must also forward annual data on the national production, import and export of listed chemicals and provide to the Technical Secretariat, for each of its chemical weapons destruction facilities, plant operations manuals, safety and medical plans, laboratory operations and quality assurance and control manuals, and the environmental permits that have been obtained.

The Convention is the first agreement to apply verification procedures to the civilian chemicals industry. All locations at which chemical weapons are stored or destroyed are subject to systematic verification through on-site inspection and monitoring with on-site instruments. The procedures allow international inspectors to examine chemical facilities on request of another signatory state. More detailed measures concerning the elimination and disposal of chemical reserves are dealt with by the Organization.

Implementation of the agreement raises significant environmental problems due to the number of weapons and technical difficulties involved. Environmentally sound implementation of the Convention is costly. Article IV, para. 12, obligates states parties to cooperate and provide information and assistance regarding methods for the safe and efficient destruction of chemical weapons. The Convention includes some specific obligations regarding the environmental implications of the destruction of chemical weapons. Article VII(3) provides that each state party shall assign the highest priority to ensuring the safety of people and to protecting the environment as the treaty is implemented. Thus, a state party may not refuse to implement the Convention on environmental grounds, but must reconcile environmental protection with the goals of the Convention to the fullest extent possible. A similar provision is included in the Convention on the Prohibition of the Development, Production and Stockpiling of Biological and Toxic Weapons and Their Destruction of April 10, 1972.[47] The latter provides that 'in implementing the provisions of this Article all necessary safety precautions shall be observed to protect populations and the environment' (Art. II(2)).

The Chemical Weapons Convention refers to national standards for safety and emissions in regard to the destruction of chemical weapons (Art. IV(10)). In principle each state party may decide how it shall destroy chemical weapons consistent with its obligation to place safety and environmental protection at the forefront. The weapons must be destroyed, however, in designated facilities suited for the task and states may not eliminate agents through dumping in water, land burial or open-air burning. Old chemical weapons, i.e. those produced before 1925 and those produced between 1925 and 1946 which have deteriorated to such extent that they can no longer be used as chemical weapons are to be treated as toxic waste under national and international regulation according to Paragraph B.6 of Part IV (B) of the Verification Annex.

Finally, the Convention indicates that a state party bears responsibility for all chemical weapons it abandoned on the territory of another state party. The explicit obligations are, however, limited. Paragraph C.15 of Part IV(B) of the Verification Annex provides that for the purpose of destroying abandoned chemical weapons, the abandoning state party shall provide all necessary financial, technical, expert, facility, as well as other resources. The territorial state on which the abandoned weapons are located must provide appropriate cooperation. The Convention specifies that the weapons are to be destroyed in accordance with Article IV of the Convention and Part IV (A) of the Verification Annex. This means that destruction of the weapons has to be carried out in conditions that do not result in significant damage to the environment. The interplay with environmental conventions such as the Basel and Bamako Conventions dealing with the transboundary transport of hazardous wastes means that in general the transboundary shipment of war materials in order to destroy them is permitted only in very limited circumstances. Other conventions, such as the Geneva Convention on Long-Range Transboundary Air Pollution, may limit the disposal of weapons inland and abroad.

---

47 1015 U.N.T.S. 163.

Several bilateral agreements have been concluded that also may contribute to the environmentally sound destruction of chemical weapons. In the United States-Russian Agreement Concerning the Safe, Secure and Ecologically Sound Destruction of Chemical Weapons (July 30, 1992), the United States agreed to provide up to $55 million to assist Russian chemical weapons destruction. An agreement of December 1992 between Russia and Germany enabled the construction of a plant to destroy specific materials. Similarly, Sweden agreed to assist Russia by examining the risks associated with the storage and destruction of the Russian chemical stockpile, and the US signed an agreement with Albania in 2004 concerning the safe, secure and ecologically sound destruction of chemical weapons.

Other specific weapons systems have been restricted because of their indiscriminate effects or the excessive injuries they cause. In particular, nuclear weapons and anti-personnel land mines have been targeted by the international community. In 1996, the conference of state parties to the Convention on Prohibitions or Restrictions on the Use of Certain Conventional Weapons adopted a protocol on the use of mines, booby-traps and other devices.[48] The Protocol applies to international and to internal armed conflicts. It limits the types of weapons that can be used and calls on each contracting party to clear, remove, or destroy all mines, booby-traps and similar devices.

Another weapons treaty, the Convention on the Prohibition of the Use, Stockpiling, Production and Transfer of Anti-Personnel Mines and on Their Destruction,[49] mentions the environment, although its purpose is to end the casualties caused by land mines. According to Article 5 of the Convention, each state party must clear all mines in areas under its jurisdiction or control at the latest within ten years following the entry into force of the Convention. Within that time, if a state party believes it cannot destroy or ensure the destruction of all anti-personnel mines by the end of ten years, it may submit a request for an extension to a meeting of the States parties or a review conference. The request must contain, *inter alia*, a reference to the environmental implications of the extension (Art. 5(4)(c)). The meeting of the States parties or the review conference decides by majority vote whether to grant the request, taking into consideration the factors mentioned in the agreement, including the environmental implications. The Convention does not require an environmental impact assessment prior to mine clearance activities, although this may be

48 Protocol II to the Convention on Prohibitions on the Use of Certain Conventional Weapons which may be Deemed to be Excessively Injurious or to have Indiscriminate Effects, Geneva, May 3, 1996, *reprinted in* 35 I.L.M. 1206 (1996).

49 Oslo, Sept. 18, 1997, 36 I.L.M. 1507 (1997).

necessary pursuant to other international agreements or national law. Each state party is required to report to the Secretary General of the United Nations within 180 days of the entry into force of the Convention for that party on numerous matters related to mines and mined areas. Included in the reporting obligation is information regarding the status of programs for the destruction of anti-personnel mines, including details of the methods which will be used in destruction, the location of all destruction sites and the applicable safety and environmental standards to be observed (Art. 7(1)(f)).

Throughout the 1990s, various international organizations attempted to consider the impacts of armed conflict on the environment and to propose new rules. The International Atomic Energy Agency (IAEA) General Conference adopted a resolution on September 21, 1990 recognizing that attacks or threats of attack on nuclear facilities devoted to peaceful purposes could jeopardize the development of nuclear energy, affirmed the importance and reliability of its safeguard procedures, and emphasized the need for the Security Council to act immediately should such a threat or attack occur.[50]

The UN General Assembly supported the IAEA with its own Resolution 45/581 (Dec. 4, 1990) in which it referred to the IAEA resolution and expressed its conviction of the need to prohibit armed attacks on nuclear installations. It expressed its awareness of the danger that such an attack could result in radioactive releases with grave transboundary consequences. On November 25, 1992, the General Assembly again adopted a resolution on the protection of the environment in times of armed conflict,[51] affirming that environmental considerations constitute one of the elements to be taken into account in implementing the principles of law applicable in armed conflict. In referring to the Iraqi occupation of Kuwait, it condemned the destruction of hundreds of oil-well heads and the release and waste of crude oil into the sea and noted that existing provisions of international law prohibit such acts. It stressed that destruction of the environment, not justified by military necessity and carried out wantonly, is clearly contrary to existing international law. The Resolution invited the International Committee of the Red Cross to report on activities undertaken by the Committee and other relevant bodies with regard to the protection of the environment in times of armed conflict. In 1994, the ICRC issued its first *Guidelines for Military Manuals and Instructions on the Protection of the Environment in Times of Armed Conflict* to support the instruction and

50 IAEA GC, 'Resolution GC(XXXIV)/RES/533' (21 September 1990) IAEA Doc GC(34)/RES/533.

51 UNGA, Protection of the Environment in Times of Armed Conflict (25 November 1992) UNGA Res 47/37, UN Doc A/RES/47/37.

training of armed forces on IHL related to the protection of the natural environment. In 2020, the ICRC published an updated version of the *Guidelines* as a collection of IHL rules and recommendations on the protection of the environment during armed conflict.

In 1994, UNEP established a Working Group on Liability and Compensation or Environmental Damage Arising from Military Activities as part of its Montevideo Program for the Development and Periodic Review of Environmental Law (II–1993). According to the Report, a state which has committed an act of aggression cannot rely on the rules of international law allowing for exclusions or exemptions of responsibility and liability, but will be fully liable for damage to the environment.[52] The Working Group also proposed a comprehensive definition of environmental damage and methods of valuation.

The Security Council has on numerous occasions addressed protecting the natural heritage and natural resources in the context of the conflicts in the Central African Republic and the Democratic Republic of the Congo. In Resolution 2121 (2013), it condemned the devastation of natural heritage and noted that poaching and trafficking of wildlife were among the factors that fueled the crisis in the Central African Republic. In Resolution 2127 (2013), adopted some months later, it condemned the illegal exploitation of natural resources in the Central African Republic which contributed to the perpetuation of the conflict.[53] Moreover, its Resolution 2134 (2014) contains provisions on sanctions for individuals that have been providing support for armed groups or criminal networks through the illicit exploitation of natural resources, including diamonds and wildlife and wildlife products, in the Central African Republic.[54] Lastly, in Resolution 2149 (2014), the Council concluded that one of the prioritized tasks within the mandate of the United Nations Multidimensional Integrated Stabilization Mission in the Central African Republic should be to advise the transitional authorities on efforts to keep armed groups from exploiting natural resources.[55] With regard to the Democratic Republic of the Congo, it adopted a number of resolutions that relate to natural resources and the environment.[56]

From February 2001 onwards, the tone of resolutions concerning the country increasingly focused on the plunder (or pillage) of its natural resources

52 UNEP/ENV.LAW/3/info.1, October 15, 1996, *reprinted in* 27 EPL 134 (1997).

53 Security Council resolution 2127 (2013), para. 16.

54 Security Council resolution 2134 (2014), para. 37 (d).

55 Security Council resolution 2149 (2014), para. 31 (d).

56 For example, Security Council resolutions 1291 (2000), 1304 (2000), 1323 (2000), 1332 (2000), 1376 (2001), 1991 (2011), 2021 (2011) and 2053 (2012) all relate to the country's natural resources and express the Council's concern at their exploitation.

during armed conflict.[57] The linkage between natural resources and armed conflicts has also been emphasized in Security Council resolutions on Liberia,[58] Libya,[59] Sierra Leone[60] and Somalia.[61] On specific topics, resolutions on the Kimberley Process,[62] as well as those concerning the linkages between the illegal exploitation of natural resources and the proliferation and trafficking of arms,[63] have underscored the importance of natural resources and protection of the natural environment during armed conflict. In 2005, the Security Council adopted Resolution 1625, which underlined the Security Council's effectiveness in conflict prevention, emphasizing the necessity of a comprehensive strategy that addresses the root causes of armed conflict, including the promotion of sustainable development.

This network of obligations suggests a generalized concern with environmental protection, given the often irreversible and widespread harm caused human activities, especially during wartime. National and intergovernmental military forces are increasingly recognizing the developments that have taken place in environmental laws and policies over the past four decades. The North Atlantic Treaty Organization (NATO), for example, has adopted Military Principles and Policies for Environmental Protection,[64] noting the increased concern with environmental protection globally.[65] Strategic Commands are responsible for integrating these Principles and Policies in agreement with states[66] and NATO status-of-forces agreements and other similar arrangements have begun to contain provisions on the protection of the environment. NATO also has Standardization Agreements related to various areas of environmental

57 See e.g. Security Council resolutions 1341 (2001), 1355 (2001), 1457 (2003), 1499 (2003), 1533 (2004), 1565 (2004) and 1592 (2005). It should be noted in this context that such pillaging and plundering, although not noted by the Security Council specifically in the resolution, is a war crime; see e.g. the Nuremberg Charter, article 6(b), the Statute of the International Criminal Tribunal for the Former Yugoslavia, article 3(e) and Geneva Convention IV, article 33.

58 Security Council resolutions 1343 (2001), 1408 (2002) and 1478 (2003).

59 See Security Council resolution 2146 (2014), concerning banning of illicit crude oil export and safeguarding of the country's national resources, and resolution 2174 (2014), regarding sanctions against individuals providing support for armed groups through illicit export of crude oil or any other natural resources.

60 Security Council resolution 1306 (2000).

61 Security Council resolutions 2036 (2012), 2060 (2012), 2111 (2013) and 2124 (2013).

62 Security Council resolution 1459 (2003), which observes that diamonds fuel conflict.

63 Security Council resolution 2117 (2013).

64 NATO Military Principles and Policies for Environmental Protection (MC 0469/1), October 2011.

65 ibid para. 1.

66 ibid para.9.

protection.[67] In June 2024, climate change envoys and representatives from 23 Allied nations convened for the first time in Reykjavik, Iceland. The meeting focused on enhancing cooperation to better understand and adapt to the security impacts of climate change. One months later, NATO released the Secretary General's annual Climate Change and Security Impact Assessment. The report highlights that accelerating climate change has 'a profound impact on Allied security' and emphasizes the importance of NATO remaining capable and effective in an environment undergoing rapid change.

Finally, another treaty that contains a directly relevant provision on the protection of the environment during armed conflicts is the Rome Statute. Its Article 8, Paragraph 2 (b)(iv), includes among serious violations of the laws and customs applicable in international armed conflict within the established framework of international law, the act of: (iv) Intentionally launching an attack in the knowledge that such attack will cause incidental loss of life or injury to civilians or damage to civilian objects or widespread, long-term and severe damage to the natural environment which would be clearly excessive in relation to the concrete and direct overall military advantage anticipated. In 2016, the ICC made a significant step by prosecuting its first case related to the destruction of cultural heritage sites. This case (*The Prosecutor v. Ahmad Al Faqi Al Mahdi*) concerning the destruction of cultural sites, was brought under Article 8(2)(e)(iv) of the Rome Statute, which classifies such acts as war crimes. This marked a notable development in international law, emphasizing the protection of cultural heritage during armed conflicts.

In September 2016, the Prosecutor of the ICC adopted the Policy on Case Selection and Prioritization, which provides a framework for how cases are chosen and prioritized, taking into account various factors such as the gravity of the crimes, the degree of responsibility of alleged perpetrators, and the potential impact of investigations and prosecutions. According to the Policy on Case Selection and Prioritization, the impact of the crimes may be assessed in light of

> *inter alia*, the increased vulnerability of victims, the terror subsequently instilled, or the social, economic and environmental damage inflicted on the affected communities. In this context, the Office will give particular consideration to prosecuting Rome Statute crimes that are committed by means of, or that result in, *inter alia*, the destruction of the environment, the illegal exploitation of natural resources or the illegal dispossession of land (Para. 41).

---

67 For more information on the environmental protection policy of NATO, see www.nato.int/cps/en/natolive/topics_80802.htm (last accessed June 1, 2024).

1.2 *Claims for Environmental Damage Stemming from Armed Conflicts*

The Gulf War raised numerous questions about the law applicable to environmental protection during armed conflicts. In January, 1991, the Iraqi military occupying Kuwait detonated more than 700 Kuwaiti oil wells, igniting more than 600 of them. Smoke from the fires affected not only Kuwait, but Iran, Turkey, Jordan and Saudi Arabia, while oil that spilled into the desert seeped into the underground aquifer. Iraq also opened valves at several oil terminals and pumped large quantities of crude oil into the Gulf, perhaps as much as 11 million barrels. Subsequent allied bombing of the terminals halted the flow of oil. Other oil slicks appeared, apparently caused by damage to tankers and oil-storage facilities. Oil refineries, oil gathering stations and power and water desalination plants were all damaged or destroyed.[68]

The United Nations Security Council reacted to the Iraqi destruction in Resolution 687 which affirmed that Iraq:

> is liable under international law for any direct loss, damage, including environmental damage and the depletion of natural resources, or injury to foreign Governments, nationals and corporations, as a result of Iraq's unlawful invasion and occupation of Kuwait (para. 16).

Paragraph 18 of the Resolution created a fund for the payment of claims and established a commission to administer the fund. A portion of the export sales of Iraqi oil was used for the fund. This action represented the first time that an international body has been charged with compensating for wartime environmental damage.

The United Nations Compensation Commission (UNCC) established its procedures regarding claims in a series of decisions taken by its Governing Council. Council Decision 7 provides that payments were to be made available with respect to direct environmental damage and the depletion of natural resources, including losses or expenses resulting from:

a. Abatement and prevention of environmental damage, including expenses directly relating to fighting oil fires and stemming the flow of oil in coastal and international waters;
b. Reasonable measures already taken to clean and restore the environment or future measures which can be documented as reasonably necessary for that purpose;
c. Reasonable monitoring and assessment of environmental damage for the purpose of evaluating and abating harm and restoring the environment;

68 Letter of July 12, 1991 from the Chargé d'affaires of the Permanent Mission of Kuwait to the United Nations to the Secretary-General, July 15, 1991; U.N. Doc. A/45/1035, S/22787, at 2.

d. Reasonable monitoring of public health and performing medical screening for the purposes of investigation and combating increased health risks as a result of the environmental damage; and
e. Depletion of or damage to natural resources.[69]

The list is not exhaustive, but the word 'direct' limited the extent of liability for environmental damage, excluding indirect and remote harm. It appears that the two terms 'environmental damage' and 'depletion of or damage to natural resources' were included to provide comprehensive relief, in order to ensure that components of the natural environment having no commercial value as well as those primarily commercial in nature would be encompassed in the claims process. Given the potentially large claims, Decision 7 required documentary and other appropriate evidence sufficient to demonstrate the circumstances and the amount of the claimed loss.

Following completion of earlier categories of cases, such as those concerned with individual personal injuries, the UNCC turned to the question of environmental claims. In 1996, the UNCC approved a payout of US$ 610,048,547 to the Kuwait Oil Company on behalf of the public oil sector as a whole for the well blowout.[70] In December 1998, the Governing Council of the UNCC appointed a three-member panel to review other claims for losses resulting from environmental damage and the depletion of natural resources submitted by governments and by public sector enterprises. Before the Panel began consideration of the environmental claims, the Governing Council decided to 'consider the special circumstances pertaining to successful environmental monitoring and assessment claims and, in this context, to consider addressing the level and priority of payments to be made in respect of such claims'.[71] Two years after establishing a template for claims, the UNCC decided to provide technical assistance to Iraq in defending the environmental claims.[72] The Governing Council, observing the complexity and limited amount of international practice relevant to environmental losses, noted that this category of claims, unlike the others, would be conducted through written and oral proceedings. As a result, pursuant to the decision, Iraq was permitted to select experts to assist in developing the facts and technical issues, with the UNCC compensating the experts.

69 UNCC, Governing Council Decision 7, para. 35, revised March 16, 1992, S/AC.26/1991/7/Rev.1.

70 See Decision Concerning the Well Blowout Control Claim, Governing Council of the UNCC, 66th meeting, Dec. 17, 1996, S/AC.26/Dec. 40 (1996), Dec. 18, 1996.

71 Dec. 73, S/AC.26/Dec. 73 (1999), June 25, 1999.

72 S/AC.26/Dec. 124 (2001), June 22, 2001.

On June 22, 2001, the UNCC delivered its first set of awards[73] on 107 claims for monitoring and assessment of environmental damage, depletion of natural resources, monitoring of public health, and performing medical screenings for the purposes of investigation and combating increased health risks (the 'monitoring and assessment claims'). The total amount of the claims exceeded US$ 1 billion ($1,007,412,574), with Kuwait and Saudi Arabia each claiming close to $500 million.

In its report, the Commission noted that its mandate required it to apply Security Council Resolution 687 and other relevant Security Council resolutions, Governing Council criteria and decisions, and 'where necessary ....other relevant rules of international law'.[74] The Commission reaffirmed its status as a fact-finding body whose function was to examine claims, verify their validity, evaluate losses, assess payments and resolve disputed claims.

The environmental claims reported in the first installment concerned monitoring and assessment related to damage from air pollution; depletion of water resources and damage to groundwater; damage to 'cultural heritage resources;' oil pollution to the Persian Gulf; damage to coastlines; damage to fisheries; damage to wetlands and rangelands; damage to forestry, agriculture and livestock; and damage or risk of damage to public health. In addition to the claims that were expected to be filed related to oil fires and released oil from destroyed wells, claims were filed over disruption of desert and coastal ecosystems due to the movement of military vehicles, personnel, and ordnance, as well as adverse impacts on the environment resulting from the transit and settlement of persons who departed Iraq and Kuwait as a result of the invasion.

The claims for monitoring and assessment presented special problems because they were heard before any substantive claims were considered, although the latter were needed to demonstrate that environmental damage or depletion of nature resources occurred. The Panel accepted that the claims for monitoring and assessment should be determined first, however, because the results of the monitoring and assessment could be critical in enabling claimants to establish the existence of damage and evaluate the quantum of compensation to be claimed. The claims for monitoring and assessment were thus permitted in order to generate evidence of substantive harm. At the same time, the Panel sought to avoid accepting claims for monitoring and assessment activities of a purely theoretical nature. It sought a 'nexus between the

73 See UNCC, *Report and Recommendations Made by the Panel of Commissioners Concerning the First Instalment of "F4" Claims*, UN Doc. S/AC.26/2001/16, June 22, 2001.

74 ibid, para. 17.

activity and environmental damage or risk of damage that may be attributed directly to Iraq's invasion and occupation of Kuwait'.[75]

In assessing the nexus and reasonableness of the monitoring and assessment activity, the Panel considered:

- the possibility of causality, i.e. the plausibility that pollutants released during the invasion and occupation could have impacted the territories of the claimants;
- whether the areas or resources in question could have been affected by pollutants resulting from the conflict.
- whether there is evidence of environmental damage or risk of damage; and
- whether the monitoring and assessment might produce results that could assist the panel in determining substantive claims.

It concluded that the mere fact that monitoring and assessment activity did not establish conclusively that environmental damage had occurred was not necessarily a valid reason for rejecting a claim for expenses of the monitoring activity, because it could be of benefit even if no evidence of war-caused damage was found. The same result would be obtained if the results show that damage has occurred but no restoration or remediation is possible or feasible.

To be within the UNCC mandate, any proven damage had to be attributable to Iraq's invasion and occupation. As in other liability proceedings, identifying causation was a difficult matter, particularly in the absence of baseline information. Monitoring and assessment to determine causality thus were compensable even if the results ultimately demonstrated the cause was other than the Iraqi invasion.

In assessing each claim, the panel considered the circumstances of the claim, including the nature of the damage to be assessed and the location and purpose of the monitoring and assessment activity and the appropriateness of the activity by reference to generally accepted scientific criteria and methodologies. Where supporting evidence and documentation was lacking, the Panel rejected claims.[76] On June 21, 2001, the Governing Council rejected the claim of Turkey and awarded compensation to Iran, Jordan, Kuwait, Saudi Arabia, and Syria, but with a lower assessment of damages than asserted. The lower amounts and rejected claims appear to have been based on a lack of evidence.

75 ibid para. 31.

76 See e.g. Iran's claim for a preliminary monitoring study to evaluate possible damage to cultural relics by pollutants from the oil fires. The claim was rejected because no reports or other evidence were submitted to show that any work had been undertaken. Claim No. 5000331, paras. 79–83.

The successful claimant states must submit periodic progress reports on environmental monitoring and assessment.

The Panel reported a second installment of environmental claims in late 2002.[77] In addition to receiving eleven new claims from Iran, Kuwait and Saudi Arabia, the Panel received nineteen claims from states outside the region (Australia, Canada, Germany, the Netherlands, United Kingdom, and United States). The thirty claims totaled some US $872,760,534 for expenses incurred for measures to abate and prevent environmental damage, to clean and restore the environment, to monitor and assess environmental damage, and to monitor public health risks alleged to have resulted from Iraq's invasion and occupation of Kuwait.

Iran, Kuwait and Saudi Arabia sought compensation in the amount of USD 829,458,298 for measures to respond to environmental damage and human health risks from:

a. Mines, unexploded ordnance and other remnants of war;
b. Oil lakes formed by oil released from damaged wells in Kuwait;
c. Oil spills in the Persian Gulf caused by oil released from pipelines, offshore terminals and tankers; and
d. Pollutants released from oil well fires in Kuwait.

Australia, Canada, Germany, the Netherlands, the United Kingdom and the United States asked US $43,302,236 for expenses incurred in providing assistance to countries in the Persian Gulf region to respond to environmental damage, or threat of damage to the environment or public health, resulting from Iraq's invasion and occupation of Kuwait.

The second installment claims involved some novel issues and by Procedural Order Nos. 7 and 8, both dated February 1, 2002, the Panel informed Iraq and the Regional Claimants that oral proceedings would be held to focus on: (a) whether compensation would be awarded for environmental damage or depletion of natural resources even if such damage or depletion may not have been caused solely as a result of Iraq's invasion and occupation of Kuwait; (b) where environmental damage or depletion of natural resources may not have resulted solely from Iraq's invasion and occupation of Kuwait, what factors should the Panel take into account in determining that: (i) a portion of the damage or depletion is compensable, or (ii) no portion of the damage or depletion is compensable; (c) whether the phrase 'environmental damage and the depletion of natural resources' under Security Council Resolution 687 (1991) and Governing Council decision 7 include loss or damage to elements such

77 UNCC, *Report and Recommendations Made by the Panel of Commissioners Concerning the Second Instalment of "F4" Claims*, UN Doc. S/AC.26/2002/26, October 3, 2002.

as cultural property, human health, aesthetic values of landscapes, etc.; and (d) to what extent, if any, should the procedure and criteria used for selecting contractors to undertake the removal of mines and ordnance affect compensability of expenses arising from these activities?

After oral and written proceedings, the Panel gave an expansive reading to Governing Council decision 7 on the meaning of environmental damage. As the Panel noted, some of the losses or expenses for which compensation was sought were not included in the list of specific losses or expenses in paragraph 35 of Governing Council decision 7. The Panel noted, however, that paragraph 35 of Governing Council decision 7 did not purport to give an exhaustive list of the activities and events that could give rise to compensable losses or expenses and thus should be considered as providing guidance regarding the types of activities and events that can result in compensable losses or expenses, rather than as a limitative enumeration of such activities or events. In the view of the Panel, the term 'environmental damage' in paragraph 16 of Security Council Resolution 687 (1991) similarly is not limited to losses or expenses resulting from the activities and events listed in paragraph 35 of Governing Council decision 7, but can also cover direct losses or expenses resulting from other activities and events. A loss or expense may be compensable even if does not arise under any of the specific subparagraphs of paragraph 35 of Governing Council decision 7. For example, expenses incurred due to measures undertaken to prevent or abate harmful impacts of airborne contaminants on property or human health could qualify as environmental damage, provided that the losses or expenses are a direct result of Iraq's invasion and occupation of Kuwait.

On the second issue, the Panel found that the question of Iraq's liability for environmental damage resulting from parallel or concurrent causes was not an issue that needed to be addressed in relation to the claims being made, because the claims were principally for losses or expenses allegedly incurred by the Claimants in undertaking measures to respond to the oil spills and oil fires or to remove and dispose of mines, unexploded ordnance and other remnants of war. According to the Claimants, these measures were all the direct result of Iraq's invasion and occupation of Kuwait. The Panel agreed, finding that there was well-documented evidence showing that massive quantities of oil were released into the marine environment of the Persian Gulf and onto the territories of Kuwait and other countries of the region as a result of Iraq's invasion and occupation of Kuwait. The evidence also showed that numerous oil fires which were deliberately caused by Iraqi forces in Kuwait resulted in the release of large volumes of contaminants into the atmosphere of the entire region. Finally, the Panel found it 'undeniable' that a large number of mines and unexploded ordnance remained in the territory of Kuwait as a result of Iraq's invasion and occupation of Kuwait. On compensable losses, the Panel also agreed with the claimants that expenses resulting from activities undertaken by military personnel are compensable if there is sufficient evidence to demonstrate that the predominant purpose of the activities was to respond to environmental damage or threat of damage to the environment or to public health in the interest of the general population. For other government employees, salaries and related expenses were not compensable if such expenses would have been incurred regardless of Iraq's invasion and occupation of Kuwait.

Regarding the prevention and abatement claims of states from outside the region, the Panel found that neither Security Council Resolution 687 nor Governing Council decision 7 restricted eligibility for compensation to losses or expenses incurred by the countries in which the environmental damage occurred or by countries located in the Persian Gulf region. In the view of the Panel, expenses resulting from assistance rendered to countries in the Persian Gulf region to respond to environmental damage, or threat of damage to the environment or public health, qualified for compensation. The Panel found that its conclusion on this point was reinforced by the fact that the United Nations had made specific appeals for assistance in dealing with the environmental damage caused by Iraq's invasion and occupation of Kuwait, as did other organizations and bodies of the United Nations system and the affected countries. The Panel cautioned, however, that compensation paid to an assisting country should not duplicate any compensation paid or to be paid to any country in the Persian Gulf region.

The Panel awarded less than claimed in all instances and denied the claim of the Netherlands in its entirety. The Panel found that the latter claim was for services rendered in the military campaign and not for prevention or abatement of environmental harm. In total, the Panel awarded US $711,087,737 in the second installment. Environmental claims awarded by the UN Compensation Commission eventually amounted to over ten percent ($5.26 billion) of the awards made for the damage caused by the illegal Iraqi invasion.[78]

Other institutions also stepped in to assess environmental damage resulting from the Gulf War. At the beginning of the conflict, UNEP's Governing Council expressed concern over destruction of the environment. The Global Resources Information Database of UNEP and the International Maritime Organization (IMO) conducted an extensive preliminary assessment of the impact of the oil

78 UNCC, Status of Processing and Payment of Claims, January 27, 2011.

spill on the coastal waters of Kuwait and Saudi Arabia. The IMO responded to a request of Saudi Arabia and other governments in the region, pursuant to the International Convention on Oil Pollution, Preparedness and Cooperation of 1990, and took action to facilitate and coordinate international assistance.

The UNEP Governing Council decided in May 1991 to recommend:

> that governments consider identifying weapons, hostile devices and ways of using such techniques that would cause particularly serious effects on the environment and consider efforts in appropriate forms to strengthen international law prohibiting such weapons, hostile devices and ways of using such techniques.

It invited the General Assembly to review the 1977 Convention on the Prohibition of Military or Any Other Hostile Use of Environmental Modification Techniques with a view to strengthening and encouraging accession to it and establishing concrete means of verification of its implementation.[79]

The conflicts that marked the breakup of the former Yugoslavia also involved environmental damage, and the precedent of the Gulf War stimulated international organizations and civil society to monitor and document the damage.[80] The 1999 Kosovo conflict allegedly included poisoning of wells, scorched earth tactics and indiscriminate bombing, leading UNEP to establish an expert task force that included NGO representatives to assess the environmental damage.

Other consequences followed the air campaign conducted by members of NATO against Yugoslavia during the Kosovo conflict. Allegations that the environmental and other impacts of the bombing made the attacks illegal under international humanitarian law persuaded the prosecutor for the International Tribunal for the Former Yugoslavia to appoint a committee to advise on whether or not to conduct a formal investigation. The June 14, 2000 Final Report of the Committee Established to Review the NATO Bombing Campaign against the Federal Republic of Yugoslavia,[81] recommended against an investigation. In so doing, the Committee assessed both the law and the available evidence that were relevant to its mandate.

---

79 UNEP/GC.16/L.53, Part B, 'Environmental Effects of Warfare' (May 1991).

80 See e.g. Regional Environmental Center for Central and Eastern Europe, *Assessment of the Environmental Impact of Military Activities during the Yugoslavia Conflict: Preliminary Findings* (June 1999).

81 International Criminal Tribunal for the former Yugoslavia, *Final Report of the Committee Established to Review the NATO Bombing Campaign against the Federal Republic of Yugoslavia* (13 June 2000).

On the first matter, the Committee considered Additional Protocol I's Arts. 35(3) and 55 to state the 'basic' legal provisions applicable to environmental protection during armed conflict. Significantly, the Committee asserted that article 55 'may ... reflect current customary law',[82] despite a suggestion from the International Court of Justice four years earlier that it does not.[83]

Turning to the facts, the Committee found that the bombing campaign did cause some environmental damage through attacks on industrial facilities such as chemical plants and oil installations which released pollutants.[84] But, given the duty to find cumulative conditions fulfilled (long-term, widespread and severe damage) and acknowledging the high threshold set by those conditions, the Committee concluded that it would be difficult to assess whether such a threshold was reached in this case 'even if reliable environmental assessments were to give rise to legitimate concern concerning the impact of the NATO bombing campaign'.[85] The Committee referred to UNEP's Balkan Task Force, established to consider the environmental impacts of the Kosovo conflict and noted that the UNEP assessment was hampered by 'a lack of alternative and corroborated sources regarding the extent of the environmental contamination caused by the NATO bombing campaign'.[86] It also noted that the reliable assessment of long-term effects of such contamination may not yet be practicable. The Committee concluded by expressing its opinion that, according to the information in its possession, 'the environmental damage caused during the NATO bombing campaign does not reach the Additional Protocol I threshold'.[87]

The conclusion did not end the matter because the Committee estimated that the legality of the attacks also had to be tested in light of the principles of military necessity and proportionality. It would appear that there was little debate over the issue of military necessity, because most of the discussion in the report concerns proportionality. The Committee states that in applying this principle 'it is necessary to assess the importance of the target in relation to the incidental damage expected: if the target is sufficiently important, a greater degree of risk to the environment may be justified'.[88] Regretting the lack of concrete guidelines on what constitutes excessive damage, the

82 ibid para. 15.

83 See *Advisory Opinion on the Threat or Use of Nuclear Weapons*, ICJ Rep. 1996, p. 242, para. 31.

84 Final Report (n 81), para. 14.

85 ibid para. 15.

86 ibid para. 17.

87 ibid.

88 ibid.

Committee said that 'at a minimum, actions resulting in massive environmental destruction, especially when they do not serve a clear and important military purpose, would be questionable'.[89] While recommending that no investigation proceed, the Committee considered that independently of the principle of proportionality, there is a duty to take precautionary measures to minimize collateral damage to the environment: 'If there is a choice of weapons or methods of attack available, a commander should select those which are most likely to avoid, or at least minimize incidental damage. In doing so, however, he is entitled to take account of factors such as stocks of different weapons and likely future demands, the timeliness of attack and risks to his own forces'.[90] Thus, the general principles of international humanitarian law play as great a role as do the more recent provisions that specifically mention environmental protection.

Since February 2014, a prolonged conflict between Russia and Ukraine has resulted in significant environmental consequences. In Eastern Ukraine, the conflict exacerbated pollution from around 5,300 industrial enterprises. Military actions caused power outages, halting ventilation and water pumps at industrial sites and coal mines, leading to toxic leaks and accidents. Notable incidents include a methane explosion at the Zasyadko mine and a major coke gas leak at the Avdiivskyi plant. Agricultural lands and waterways were further contaminated by heavy metals and nitrates from military activities. Russian invasion in 2022 has intensified environmental damage across Ukraine. Nuclear safety has become a critical concern, with several electricity supply cuts to the Chernobyl plant and the Russian occupation of the Zaporizhzhia nuclear power plant, Europe's largest. The International Atomic Energy Agency has reported compromised safety at these sites due to ongoing military actions.[91] In 2022, in response to a request from the Ukrainian Government, UNEP published a Report as part of the preparatory process to aid Ukraine's recovery from the ongoing conflict and to support a comprehensive post-conflict assessment.[92] The report offers an initial overview, rather than a detailed account, of the environmental damage in Ukraine and the potential public health impacts, helping to set priorities for further on-site verification. Preliminary data indicate that Ukraine, already dealing with various longstanding environmental

89 ibid para. 22.

90 ibid para. 21. See also para. 17.

91 Update 20 – IAEA Director General Statement on Situation in Ukraine, March 13, 2022.

92 UNEP, *The Environmental Impact of the Conflict in Ukraine: A Preliminary Review* (UNEP 2022).

challenges, is now confronted with a compounded environmental crisis, which has either worsened existing issues or introduced new ones.

More recently, the conflict in Gaza, since its escalation after October 7, 2023, has caused unprecedented environmental harm in the region. As noted by UNEP in a Report published in 2024,[93] direct impacts include the unprecedented destruction to infrastructure, productive assets, and essential services caused by intensive bombardment; the collapse of sewage, wastewater, and solid waste management systems; the devastation of buildings, roads, and other infrastructure, which has produced over 39 million tons of debris, some of which is contaminated with unexploded ordnance, asbestos, and other hazardous materials. Human remains are also buried within the vast amounts of debris. Additionally, there are urgent but less visible environmental challenges, such as land, water, and air contamination from munitions and unexploded ordnance, potential land instability due to extensive tunnel systems, and soil and water contamination from the recent destruction and flooding of these tunnels.

1.3 *Jurisprudence of the International Court of Justice*

In a general effort to determine the scope of legal obligations towards the environment during armed conflict or in weapons testing, the International Court of Justice was asked on three occasions after 1993 to consider the legality of nuclear weapons and weapons testing. First, on September 6, 1993, the World Health Organization (WHO) requested an advisory opinion of the International Court of Justice on whether the use of nuclear weapons is a violation of international law, including the WHO Constitution, 'in view of the health and environmental effects' such use would have. The Court decided in 1996 that the request exceeded the competence of the WHO. It viewed the question as being one within the purview of those organs of the United Nations expressly conferred the responsibility to regulate the use of force and armaments.[94] Perhaps anticipating this result, the United Nations General Assembly presented its own request asking a series of similar questions in 1995.[95] In fact, transnational civil society, in the form of a coalition of non-governmental organizations

93 UNEP, *Environmental Impact of the Conflict in Gaza. Preliminary Assessment of Environmental Impacts* (UNEP 2024).

94 *Legality of the Use by a State of Nuclear Weapons.* For a critical analysis of the Court's opinion, see Burns Weston, 'Nuclear Weapons and the World Court: Ambiguity's Consensus' (1997) 7 *Trans. L. & Contemp. Prob.* 371.

95 *Request for an Advisory Opinion from the International Court of Justice on the Legality of the Threat or Use of Nuclear Weapons*, G.A. Res. 49/75K U.N. GAOR, 49th Sess., Supp. No. 49, at 71, U.N. Doc. A/4949 (1995).

and individuals calling themselves 'the World Court Project', was behind both requests, having successfully exerted pressure on both the WHO and the General Assembly to make the request to the Court. The Court decided it had jurisdiction to answer the General Assembly's questions and did so on July 8, 1996,[96] the same date it rejected the WHO request. A third proceeding before the Court was an effort to reopen a contentious case filed by Australia and New Zealand against France, challenging the legality of nuclear testing in the South Pacific.[97] The Court held that the proceedings were definitively terminated but noted that its conclusion was 'without prejudice to the obligations of states to respect and protect the natural environment'.[98]

The Court was intensely divided on some issues and unanimous in regard to others in the advisory opinion on the legality of nuclear weapons. Given the complexity of the matter, it is perhaps not surprising that for the first time in its history, every judge sitting in the matter issued a separate declaration or opinion. Several holdings were closely linked to international environmental law. First, the Court found by a vote of 11–3 that neither customary nor conventional international law – including international environmental law – prohibits nuclear weapons *as such*.[99] The three dissenting judges found that nuclear weapons in all their probable uses are so devastating that they would be likely to breach human rights and environmental standards and thus are prohibited as such. The Court unanimously agreed that '[a] threat or use of nuclear weapons should ... be compatible with ... the principles and rules of international humanitarian law, as well as with specific obligations under treaties and other undertakings which expressly deal with nuclear weapons'.[100] The Court noted that certain treaties prohibit the use of nuclear weapons in specific geographic areas,[101] but none of them prohibit the threat of use of nuclear weapons.

The Court's final holdings were the most divided. The Court's vote was 7–7, necessitating a deciding vote of the president, in holding that 'the threat or use

---

96 *Legality of the Threat or Use of Nuclear Weapons.* The Court decided to comply with the request by a vote of 13–1, Judge Oda dissenting.

97 See *Request for an Examination of the Situation in Accordance with Paragraph 63 of the Court's Judgment of Dec. 20, 1974 in the Nuclear Tests (New Zealand v. France) Case*, Order of Sept. 22, 1995, I.C.J. Rep. 1995.

98 ibid, at 306, para. 64.

99 *Legality of the Threat of Use of Nuclear Weapons,* at 36, para. 105(2)(B).

100 ibid, 36, para. 105(2)(D).

101 E.g. the Antarctic Treaty (Dec. 1, 1959), the Partial Test-Ban Treaty (Aug. 5, 1963), the Outer Space Treaty (Jan. 27, 1967), the Treaty of Tlatelolco (Feb. 14, 1967), the 1971 Sea-Bed Arms Control Treaty, the Moon Treaty (Dec. 5, 1979), the South Pacific Nuclear Free Zone Treaty (Aug. 6, 1985), the Treaty on an African Nuclear-Weapon-Free Zone (Apr. 11, 1996), and the Treaty on the Southeast Asia Nuclear-Weapon-Free Zone (Dec. 15, 1995).

of nuclear weapons would generally be contrary to the rules of international law applicable in armed conflict and, in particular, the principles and rules of humanitarian law'.[102] The Court went on, however, to say that it could not conclude definitively whether or not extreme self-defense in which the life of the state would be at stake, would allow the threat or use of nuclear weapons.[103]

Some of the twenty-eight states participating in the proceedings argued that any use of nuclear weapons would be unlawful according to international environmental law, making reference to various international treaties,[104] such as Principle 1 of the Stockholm Declaration and Principle 2 of the Rio Declaration. Other states contended that international environmental law principally applies in times of peace. The Court itself recognized that 'the use of nuclear weapons could constitute a catastrophe for the environment', the latter representing 'not an abstraction but … the living space, the quality of life and the very health of human beings, including generations unborn'. Given this, the Court held that states must take environmental considerations into account in assessing what is necessary and proportionate in the pursuit of military objectives. The Court noted that the provisions of Additional Protocol I to the 1949 Geneva Conventions embody a general obligation to protect the natural environment against widespread, long-term and severe environmental damage; the prohibition of methods and means of warfare which are intended, or may be expected to cause such damage; and the prohibition of attacks against the natural environment by way of reprisals. Thus, while no specific provision prohibits the use of nuclear weapons, humanitarian law indicates that important environmental factors should be taken into account in the use of such weaponry in armed conflicts.

Contentious cases about environmental harm related to armed conflict include the dispute between Ecuador and Colombia concerning 'Plan

---

102 *Legality of the Threat of Nuclear Weapons,* at 36, para. 105(2)(E).

103 Note that the three dissenters from the earlier holding also dissented on this point, finding the Court's pronouncement too weak, not too strong. Only four judges, three of them from nuclear power states, felt the Court had gone too far in questioning the legality of the threat or use of nuclear weapons pursuant to international humanitarian law. On the other hand, some of those concurring with the majority clearly seemed to approve mutual deterrence, i.e. the threat of use of nuclear weapons, disagreeing with the view that all threats of use of nuclear weapons are illegal.

104 The instruments referred to included Additional Protocol I of 1977 to the Geneva Conventions of 1949 and the Convention on the Prohibition of Military or Any Other Hostile Use of Environmental Modification Techniques (Dec. 10, 1976), Art. 1.

Colombia.'[105] The Plan included aerial spraying of Monsanto's glyphosate[106] in order to deprive Colombian insurgents of the coca production that was a primary funding source for their armed uprising.[107] Glyphosate, a non-selective herbicide, destroys other plants, including food crops, and can cause significant adverse health effects on people and animals.[108] The aerial spraying allegedly caused transboundary environmental damage. In 2008, Ecuador filed an application against Colombia before the ICJ[109] claiming that from 2000 through 2008, herbicide drift sickened people on the Ecuadorean side of the border, also harming livestock, farmland, and sensitive, ecologically diverse rainforest areas. After five years of litigation, the parties agreed to a settlement, which included an undisclosed amount of compensation, and the case was removed from the Court's docket on 13 September 2013.

In other cases, the ICJ has held that a state's responsibility during an occupation is engaged both for any acts of its military that violate its international obligations and for any lack of vigilance in preventing violations of human rights and humanitarian law by other actors present in the occupied territory, including rebel groups. In the *Armed Activities* case,[110] the ICJ noted that

---

105 See Grace Livingstone, *Inside Colombia: Drugs, Democracy and War* (Latin American Bureau 2003), 71.

106 Monsanto's glyphosate is commercially sold as 'Roundup™' and is said to be the most widely used agricultural chemical in the world.

107 Morgane Landel, 'Are Aerial Fumigations in the Context of War in Colombia a Violation of the Rules of International Humanitarian Law?' (2010) 19 *Transnational Law and Contemporary Problems* 419.

108 Colombia's Council for Human Rights and Displacement alleged that the herbicide program left 75,000 people nationwide displaced due to crop destruction. In addition, residents living inside of spray zones allegedly suffered a variety of skin, respiratory, and other ailments. C.A. Youngers and Eileen Rosen, 'Drugs and Democracy in Latin America: The Impact of U.S. Policy', Washington Office on Latin America (WOLA) at 118. See also E.J.P. Marshall, K.R. Solomon, and G. Carrasquilla, 'Coca (Erythroxylum coca) Control is Affected by Glyphosate Formulations and Adjuvants' (2009) 72 *Journal of Toxicology and Environmental Health* 930.

109 Application Instituting Proceedings, Aerial Herbicide Spraying (Ecuador v. Colombia) (2008), ICJ, March 31, 2008.

110 See Judgment, *Armed Activities on the Territory of the Congo* (*DRC v. Uganda*), ICJ, December 19, 2005 (*Armed Activities*). See also *D.R. Congo v. Burundi, Rwanda and Uganda*, African Commission on Human and Peoples' Rights, Communication No. 227/99 (2003) (addressing alleged grave and massive violations of human and peoples' rights committed by the armed forces of these three countries in the Congo, including 'systematic looting of the underground riches of the regions controlled by their forces'). As concerned the looting of natural resources, which allegedly negatively affected the endangered species in the country, the African Commission found sufficient evidence that the alleged acts did take place and were imputable to the armies and agents of the respondent States. The

Uganda at all times had responsibility for all actions and omissions of its own military forces in the territory of the DRC when these acts were in breach of its obligations under the relevant rules of international human rights law and international humanitarian law.[111] In similar manner, human rights tribunals have judged the legality of military activities, including cases concerning harm to the environment.[112] In the *Armed Activities* judgment, the ICJ found violations of both human rights law and humanitarian law for the same offense of illegal exploitation of natural resources.[113]

2 Peacetime Military Activities

The environmental problems associated with military activities flow from the use and misuse of chemicals and weapons, inappropriate disposal or dumping of toxic and hazardous waste, attacks on protected sites, and the taking or destruction of renewable and non-renewable natural resources. Problems may arise in peacetime when states have foreign military bases or facilities. US bases, many of which date back to the end of World War II, provide an important example, given their large number.[114] In one such instance, the United States negotiated a Military Bases Agreement with the Philippines in 1946, with a termination date of September 16, 1991.[115] In 1998, the two countries concluded a follow-up Status of Forces Agreement.[116] Prior to the 1991

Commission cited UN findings that during the period when the armies of the Respondent States were in effective control over parts of the territory of the Complainant State, there were lootings of the natural resources. The UN report, submitted to the UN Security Council in April 2001, evidenced the involvement of the three respondent states in the illegal exploitation of the natural resources of the DRC. Thus applying the law of armed conflict to interpret the rights in the African Charter, the Commission concluded that the illegal exploitation/looting of the natural resources of the complainant State violated Articles 21 and 22 of the African Charter.

111 *Armed Activities*, at paras. 179–80.

112 See *Social and Economic Rights Centre* (SERAC) *v. Nigeria*, Case No. 155/96, African Commission on Human Rights, October 27, 2001 (finding the government responsible for violations of, *inter alia*, the right to environment due to military activities in the Niger Delta region).

113 *Armed Activities*, at para. 222 *et seq.*

114 A 2010 Pentagon report lists 662 bases in 38 countries, with the most sites in Germany, Japan and the Republic of Korea. Department of Defense, '2010 Base Structure Report'.

115 1947, 61 Stat. 3283. See Kim David Chanbonpin, 'Holding the United States Accountable for Environmental Damages Caused by the U.S. Military in the Philippines, A Plan for the Future' (2003) 4 *Asian-Pacific Law and Policy Journal* 320, 333.

116 1998 Status of Forces Agreement (US-Philippines) TIAS 12931.

expiration date, the countries held no negotiations to address environmental cleanup, nor did the Department of Defense conduct an environmental assessment prior to the US withdrawal from its Philippine bases. No specific agreement governed cleanup of Clark Air Force Base or the Naval Station at Subic Bay.[117] In June of 1991, when the Mt. Pinatubo volcano erupted near Clark Air Force Base, local residents entered the base, using the buildings the United States left behind for immediate shelter.[118] After their villages were destroyed by the eruption, they remained in Clark, digging wells for drinking water and farming the land.[119] Subsequently, local inhabitants reportedly became ill with leukemia, women gave birth to stillborn babies, and others developed cancers and skin diseases,[120] perhaps due to the millions of gallons of sewage, oil, and chemicals that had been dumped into the groundwater during the US tenure at Clark.[121] Similar events occurred at Naval Station Subic Bay, where substantial contamination was left behind.[122]

The issue of environmental protection in the context of military activities cannot be considered exclusively under the law of armed conflict. Peacetime military activities are governed by general international law, including norms related to environmental protection and human rights. Even during an armed conflict, much of the general law and specific peacetime norms remain applicable. International environmental law and human rights law, in particular, contain relevant obligations that largely continue during armed conflict,[123]

---

117 See Adam G. Province, 'You Don't Have to Go Home But You Can't Stay Here: Recent Environmental Violations Lead to Wearing Out Our Welcome in Japan' (2010) 59 *Naval Law Review* 21, 38.

118 See Michael Satchell, 'What the Military Left Behind', U.S. News & World Report, Jan. 24, 2000 (reporting nearby locals entered Clark upon the eruption of Mt. Pinatubo, and then dug wells for drinking water); see also Chanbonpin, at 345 (estimating that 20,000 families moved into Clark because of the eruption of Mt. Pinatubo).

119 ibid.

120 ibid (reporting that medical workers began documenting major health problems, such as a rise of spontaneous abortions, and kidney and nervous system disorders).

121 See US Gen. Acct. Office, 'Military Base Closures: U.S. Financial Obligations in the Philippines' 27–28, GAO/NSIAD-92-51 (Jan. 1992) [hereinafter 1992 GAO Report] (finding, at the request of the US Senate subcommittee on defense, that heavy metals, untreated chemicals, and toxic waste pollution were discharged into the ground at Clark).

122 See e.g., 1992 GAO Report, ibid, at 27–28 (finding that U.S. personnel were discharging sewage and processed waste waters directly into Subic Bay). See also Satchell (citing that Yokosuka Naval Station in Japan was so heavily tainted with soil contaminated with PCBs and heavy metals that it could not be legally disposed of in a landfill).

123 A small set of multilateral environmental agreements specifically state that they are suspended, terminated or inapplicable during armed conflict, but the large majority are either silent on the topic or implicitly indicate their continued applicability. Notably,

although specific norms of international humanitarian law may pre-empt certain obligations as *lex specialis*.[124] In general, however, as the ICJ made clear in its *Nuclear Weapons Advisory Opinion*, 'the international law on the environment does not cease to apply once an armed conflict breaks out'.[125] In that opinion, the Court also noted that states have an obligation 'to take environmental considerations into account in assessing what is necessary and proportionate in the pursuit of legitimate military objectives'.[126]

The International Law Commission, in its work on the effects of armed conflicts on treaties, took as its starting point the presumption that the existence of an armed conflict does not *ipso facto* terminate or suspend the operation of treaties.[127] The Commission's illustrative list of treaties presumed to continue in force includes both human rights and environmental agreements.[128]

Principle 21 of the 1972 Stockholm Declaration restates the norm formulated in the *Trail Smelter* arbitration and *Corfu Channel* case with two important alterations. First, it substitutes the term 'jurisdiction and control' for 'territory' and secondly, it extends the duty to protect the environment to 'areas beyond the limits of national jurisdiction'. The language of 'jurisdiction and control' appears clearly intended to impose a duty on states to protect the environment not only from activities within their territory, but also from those conducted on their flag ships, air and space craft, and areas under their effective control, such as an occupied territory[129] or leased foreign military base. This

---

most of those that are suspended during hostilities are conventions concerning civil liability for environmental harm, whether from activities dangerous to the environment, nuclear activities or oil pollution damage. See UNEP Inventory and Analysis, at 40–46.

124 See *Armed Activities on the Territory of the Congo* (*DRC v. Uganda*), ICJ Rep. 19 (2005).

125 *Legality of the Threat or Use of Nuclear Weapons*, Advisory Opinion, 1996 I.C.J., 226 30, (Jul. 8) [*Nuclear Weapons Advisory Opinion*]. See Christopher Greenwood, 'Jus Ad Bellum and Jus in Bello in the Nuclear Weapons Advisory Opinion', in Christopher Greenwood (ed.), *Essays on War in International Law* (2006) 284–85. The ICJ discussed possible inconsistencies between environmental law and humanitarian law and sought to resolve the discrepancies between protections afforded in environmental treaties and the environmental devastation resulting from the use of nuclear weapons. ibid.

126 *Nuclear Weapons Advisory Opinion*, at 136.

127 The International Law Commission's study of the effects of armed conflict on treaties includes environmental agreements among the categories of those whose subject matter 'involves the implication that they continue in operation' during armed conflict. See ILC, Report on the work of its sixty-third session (April 26 to June 3 and July 4 to August 12, 2011) GAOR 66th Sess., Supplement No. 10 (A/66/10 and Add.1), para. 100.

128 ibid.

129 In its judgment of December 19, 2005 in the case of *Armed Activities on the Territory of the Congo* (*Democratic Republic of the Congo v. Uganda*) the ICJ 'observe[d] that, under customary international law, as reflected in Article 42 of the Hague Regulations of 1907,

interpretation is supported by treaty obligations and case law on the attribution of responsibility for breaches of international law. Treaties concerned with the marine environment, for example, codify Principle 21 in imposing on states parties a duty to protect and preserve the entire marine environment, including through preventing, reducing, and controlling degradation of that environment.[130] Although such treaties generally provide sovereign immunity for warships and other non-commercial government vessels, they nonetheless impose duties on states parties to 'ensure, by the adoption of appropriate measures not impairing operations or operational capabilities of such vessels or aircraft owned or operated by it, that such vessels or aircraft act in a manner consistent, so far as is reasonable and practicable, with the Convention'.[131] Moreover, the express inclusion of such provisions may suggest that government vessels, including warships, would be governed by the substantive provisions of environmental treaties absent the exclusionary language, although enforcement would remain governed by the customary guarantees of sovereign immunity.[132] Whether a state is an occupying power, exercising effective

territory is considered to be occupied when it is actually placed under the authority of the hostile army, and the occupation extends only to the territory where such authority has been established and can be exercised.' *Armed Activities*, at 173–78.

130 See e.g., Part XII of the 1982 United Nations Convention on the Law of the Sea (proclaiming in Article 192 an obligation to protect and preserve the marine environment and establishing in Article 194 obligations to prevent, reduce and control pollution from all sources); 1992 Convention for the Protection of the Marine Environment of the North-East Atlantic; and 1969 Agreement of Cooperation in Dealing with Pollution of the North Sea by Oil, for a few examples. Among non-binding instruments, see para. 17.22 of Agenda 21 ('States, in accordance with the provisions of the United Nations Convention on the Law of the Sea on protection and preservation of the marine environment, commit themselves, in accordance with their policies, priorities and resources, to prevent, reduce and control degradation of the marine environment so as to maintain and improve its life-support and productive capacities.')

131 'Sovereign Immunity', UNCLOS, Art. 236. Similar provisions are found in regional seas agreements and IMO Conventions on marine pollution. Some treaties provide for complete exemption from the convention rather than guaranteeing sovereign immunity. The London Dumping Convention, for example, states that it is not applicable to 'vessels and aircraft entitled to sovereign immunity under international law', but still requires the flag States to 'ensure by the adoption of appropriate measures that such vessels and aircraft owned or operated by it act in a manner consistent with the object and purpose of this Convention' and must 'inform the [International Maritime] Organization accordingly.' 1972 Convention on the Prevention of Marine Pollution by Dumping of Wastes and Other Matter (London Convention), 1046 U.N.T.S. No. 15749, Art. VII, para. 4.

132 The customary law of sovereign immunity applies in both peacetime and during armed conflict. See Jurisdictional Immunities of the State (*Germany v. Italy*: Greece intervening), Judgment, I.C.J. Reports 2012, p. 99.

control over foreign military bases, or conducting military exercises, it could have a duty under general international law to prevent its activities from harming the host state, which continues to exist as a sovereign nation with a right to be free from significant environmental harm caused by activities under the jurisdiction or control of another state.[133]

The general duty to prevent extraterritorial harm has been given more specific content through the development of customary international law principles such as the fundamental principle of prevention. The status of this principle as law is evidenced by its inclusion in nearly all international environmental treaties and judicial recognition of its binding nature, including the ICJ *Pulp Mills*[134] and *Gabčikovo-Nagymaros*[135] cases. The arbitral tribunal in the *Iron Rhine Railway* case also explicitly found that the duty to prevent harm 'has now become a principle of general international law'.[136]

Bilateral Status of Forces Agreements (SOFA) set forth the legal obligations governing the operations of foreign military forces, at least during peacetime. Provisions concerning bases or separate base agreements are normally in the form of leases.[137] As with leases in private property, they provide for divided 'ownership', with the host state retaining territorial sovereignty, coupled with a cession of jurisdiction and control over the base and its personnel to the other party to the agreement.[138] A typical lease includes an agreement by a lessor to turn over specifically-described premises to the exclusive possession to the

---

133 Foreign military bases not the result of armed conflict generally exist pursuant to bilateral Status of Forces or base agreements. Such agreements are often in the form of leases of the areas in which the bases are to be located; they do not result in a full transfer of sovereignty from the host state to the base state. See e.g., *Boumediene v. Bush*, 553 US 723 (2008).

134 *Pulp Mills.*

135 *Gabčíkovo-Nagymaros Project* (*Hungary/Slovakia*), Judgment, I.C.J. Reports 1997, p. 81.

136 ibid, at para. 59. See also *United Kingdom v. Commission of the European Communities* (C-180/96) (1998), ECR I-2265, paras. 99–100. *R. v. Ministry of Agriculture, Fisheries and Food, Commissioners of Customs and Excise* (C-157/96)(1998) ECR I-2211, para. 64.

137 E.g. 1903 Lease to the United States by the Government of Cuba of Certain Areas of Land and Water for Naval or Coaling Stations in Guantanamo and Bahia Honda; in 1941, the United States entered into an agreement with the United Kingdom regarding the lease of naval and air bases in Newfoundland, Bermuda, Jamaica, St. Lucia, Antigua, Trinidad, and British Guiana. 55 Stat. 1560; Executive Agreement Series 235. Other bases are leased through independent Base Lease Agreements, rather than through SOFAs. See, e.g. the 1941 US-Canada Base Lease Agreement, 55 Stat. 1560.

138 For a discussion of the distinction between sovereignty and jurisdiction and control in the context of the U.S. base at Guantanamo, see *Boumediene v. Bush* (accepting the position of the US government that Cuba retains sovereignty over the territory while the U.S. exercises 'complete jurisdiction and control' over the leased areas).

lessee for a definite period of time and for consideration or rent. SOFA provisions regarding bases can specify the substantive and procedural standards governing claims for damage. They rarely speak of the environment, however,[139] although few provide a general exemption of responsibility for restoration of bases when the forces depart. The US-Japan Status of Forces Agreement (Japan-SOFA),[140] for example, contains no provisions expressly mentioning the environment, but in the event of US withdrawal from Japan, Article VI of the agreement explicitly eliminates any responsibility of the United States to clean up its military facilities:

> The United States is not obligated, when it returns facilities and areas to Japan on the expiration of this Agreement or at an earlier date, to restore the facilities and areas to the condition in which they were at the time they became available to the United States armed forces, or to compensate Japan in lieu of such restoration.[141]

The US-Korea SOFA (Korea-SOFA) contains a similar provision.[142] These provisions are not surprising, nor are agreements that do not speak to the issue, because many base agreements were concluded before environmental laws and policies emerged domestically and internationally in the 1960s.

More recent agreements indicate a change. In 1993, Germany successfully negotiated for the inclusion of environmental provisions in its SOFA with the United States as a condition for the continued presence of US bases.[143] The United States agreed to the following language in Article 63:

---

139 See e.g., 1951 North Atlantic Treaty: Status of Forces (US-F.R.G), Art. VIII, s 5, TIAS No. 2846 at 1802–03 [hereinafter North Atlantic Treaty]; 1960 Agreement Under Article VI of the Treaty of Mutual Cooperation and Security: Facilities and Areas and the Status of United States Armed Forces in Japan, US-Japan, art IV, 11 UST, 1652; TIAS No. 4510 at 1654 [hereinafter Japan-SOFA].

140 ibid.

141 ibid Art. 6.

142 The Korean-SOFA provides: '[t]he Government of the United States is not obliged, when it returns facilities and areas to the Government of the Republic of Korea ... to restore the facilities and areas to the condition in which they were at the time they became available to the United States armed forces, or to compensate the Government of the Republic of Korea in lieu of such restoration'. Agreement Under Article IV of the Mutual Defense Treaty Between the United States of America and the Republic of Korea Regarding Facilities and Areas and the Status of United States Armed Forces in the Republic of Korea, US-Korea, July 9, 1966, Art. IV, TIAS No. 6127 at 1680–81.

143 1993 Amendments to Supplement the Agreement Between the Parties to the North Atlantic Treaty Regarding the Status of their Forces with Respect to Foreign Forces Stationed in the Federal Republic of Germany [hereinafter German-SOFA]; see also 1959 Status of

> A force … shall in accordance with this paragraph bear costs arising in connection with the assessment, evaluation and remedying of hazardous substance contamination caused by it and that exceeds then-applicable legal standards … The authorities of the force or of the civilian component shall pay these costs as expeditiously as feasible consistent with the availability of funds and the fiscal procedures of the Government of the sending State.[144]

Under the current US-German SOFA (German-SOFA), the United States and other applicable NATO member states pay 75% of environmental damage claims.[145] The German-SOFA further provides that the United States is to apply German environmental law to all activities on military installation unless they are deemed to have no effect on German nationals or property.[146] The Australian-SOFA similarly contains clean up provisions regarding property damage. If the United States is solely responsible for the property damage in Australia, it shall pay 75% and Australia 25%.[147]

The situation of the Philippines exemplifies the impact of not having environmental provisions in a SOFA.[148] As described earlier, the 1947 US-Philippines Military Base Agreement lacks provisions for environmental remediation.[149] Upon the agreement's expiration in 1991, no environmental clean-up assessments were made for Clark Air Force Base of Subic Bay.[150] It was later discovered that millions of gallons of sewage, oil, chemicals, heavy metals, and other

---

Forces Agreement with Respect to Forces Stationed in the Federal Republic of Germany, 14 UST 531.

144 German-SOFA, at art. 64(8bis.) (b) (emphasis added). See ibid, at Art. 54A(1) (acknowledging the importance of environmental protection with operating in the Federal Republic of Germany), ibid, Art. 54A(2) (requiring NATO forces to conduct an environmental assessment before a military action is taken), and ibid, at Art. 53(5)(g) (requiring forces to recognize the impact of environmental protection).

145 North Atlantic Treaty, at 1802–03.

146 Commander Margaret M. Carlson, 'Environmental Diplomacy: Analyzing why the US Navy still falls short Overseas' (2000) 47 *Naval Law Review* 62, 82.

147 Agreement Concerning the Status of US Forces in Australia, art. 12(7)(e)(i), May 9, 1963, 14 U.S.T. 506.

148 See generally Province, *supra* n 57 (using the environmental harms caused by Clark Air Force Base and Subic Bay as case studies).

149 A 1988 amendment to the US-Philippine Agreement Concerning Military Bases provides that the United States is not under an obligation to return its bases to the Philippines in their original condition. Memorandum of Agreement between the United States and the Philippines: Defense Bases, Oct. 17, 1988, US-Phil., Art. VII(2), TIAS No. 11,633 at 5–6.

150 See e.g., *ARC Ecology v. US Dept. of the Air Force*, 411 F.3d 1092, 1096 (9th Cir. 2005) (discussing the factual background of a claimant's CERCLA petition that the United States failed

hazardous materials left substantial contamination to the ground water and soil.[151]

The United States and the Philippines entered into a new agreement on April 28, 2014.[152] The parties concluded the Enhanced Defense Cooperation Agreement (EDCA) as an executive agreement, obviating the requirement of Senate consent in both countries.[153] Article IX addresses the 'Environment, Human Health, and Safety' and commits the United States to respect Philippine environmental, health, and safety laws, regulations, and standards; to implement the 'most protective environmental compliance standards reflected in United States, Philippines, and international standards'; to not intentionally release any hazardous materials or waste; and to take expeditious action to contain and address environmental contamination in the event of an accidental spill.[154] In turn, the Philippines agreed to enforce relevant laws.[155] The United States and Philippines are to engage in a periodic review to ensure that Philippine standards are accurately applied.[156] Both parties agreed to pursue 'a preventative rather than a reactive approach'.[157] Under Article X, the parties may enter into additional implementation agreements to carry out the EDCA provisions.[158] Such agreements may be necessary, because all US obligations under the EDCA 'are subject to the availability of appropriated funds authorized for these purposes'.[159]

Other host states may lack the strong negotiating power necessary to obtain explicit environmental guarantees in base agreements.[160] If a SOFA is silent on

to conduct an environmental assessment, and concluding that CERCLA does not apply abroad).

151 See US Gen. Acct. Off., Military Base Closures: U.S. Financial Obligations in the Philippines 27–28, GAO/NSIAD-92-51 (Jan.1992) [hereinafter 1992 GAO Report].

152 Carl Thayer, Analyzing the U.S.-Philippines Enhanced Defense Cooperation Agreement, The Diplomat, (May 2, 2014).

153 ibid. For the text of the agreement, see: Document: Enhanced Defense Cooperation Agreement between the Philippines and the United States, Official Gazette (Apr. 29, 2014).

154 ibid Art. IX § 2.

155 ibid Art. IX §§ 2–3.

156 ibid Art. IX § 2.

157 ibid Art. IX § 1.

158 ibid Art. X §§ 2–3.

159 ibid Art. X § 1.

160 US practice is that absent a governing SOFA provision to address environmental harms, the DoD generally negotiates financial responsibility on a case-by-case approach Commentators explain: US negotiators typically begin by asserting a claim for 'current value,' defined as the current value of the improvements made to the facilities to be transferred to host country control at the time of closure, adjusted for inflation and depreciation. The

the duty of the base state to respect the environment of the host state, it may be argued that the agreement should be interpreted consistent with general international law, which as discussed earlier, requires a state to ensure that activities within its jurisdiction and control respect the environment of other states and areas outside national jurisdiction. The Vienna Convention on the Law of Treaties (VCLT) calls for the terms of a treaty to be interpreted in good faith in accordance with their ordinary meaning in the context of the whole agreement and in the light of its object and purpose.[161] VCLT Article 31(3) adds several paragraphs designed to ensure that the treaty as a whole is also placed in context. It requires taking into account subsequent agreements between the parties regarding the interpretation of the treaty or the application of its provisions; any subsequent practice, which establishes an agreement of the parties regarding its interpretation; and 'any relevant rules of international law applicable in the relations between the parties'. Thus, no agreement stands in isolation, but it must always be considered along with other relevant treaties, customary international law and general principles of law.

There is very little international case law on the duty to remediate following occupation or control of foreign territory. The most relevant may be the application of Nauru filed against Australia at the ICJ, which raised issues of the rehabilitation of phosphate mining lands in Nauru, depleted when Australia controlled the territory, first under a League of Nations Mandate and later as a UN Trustee. In its Judgment on the Preliminary Objections filed by Australia, the Court rejected Australia's objections to jurisdiction and found that the application was admissible.[162] Nauru claimed that the failure to rehabilitate the area left it unfit for human habitation or economic activity, meaning that Australia had breached its obligations pursuant to United Nations Charter and Articles 3 and 5 of the Trusteeship Agreement for Nauru of November 1, 1947, as well as obligations under general international law governing the principles of self-determination, abuse of rights, and denial of justice. Nauru also alleged maladministration in violation of applicable international standards in respect of the duties of a predecessor responsible for the territory. Finally, Nauru claimed that there existed a duty of restitution because of the failure to take

---

DoD then seeks to hold the host country liable for the 'residual value' of the facility; residual value is calculated by subtracting host country remediation claims from the current value of the facility. Richard A Wegman and Harold G. Bailey, 'The Challenge of Cleaning up Military Wastes When U.S. Bases are Closed' (1994) 21 *Ecology Law Quarterly* 865, 929.

161 1969 Vienna Convention on the Law of Treaties, 1155 U.N.T.S. 331, Art. 31(1) [hereinafter VCLT].

162 *Certain Phosphate Lands in Nauru* (*Nauru v. Australia*) (Preliminary Objections), ICJ (June 26, 1992).

into account the rights and interests of the Nauruan people in the habitability of Nauru, or of the Republic of Nauru as the successor in respect of the territory. A 1993 Compact of Settlement between the two parties ended the litigation; Nauru obtained cash payment of AUD $57 million and Australia agreed to pay AUD $2.5 million annually for 20 years to be used on development projects.

3 Environmental Security and Conflict Prevention

War is inimical to sustainable development and can lay the seeds for future violence. The aftermath of war can place additional pressures on natural resources as governments struggle for reconstruction and can be as harmful to the environment as war itself.[163] If it is now generally recognized that war causes environmental harm, it is increasingly recognized that environmental degradation has the potential to produce internal and interstate conflict by undermining stability and producing mass migrations. A 2015 UNEP Report acknowledged that 'resolving natural resource conflicts is a defining peace and security challenge of the 21st century'.[164] Given the integrated nature of the environment it is impossible for a state to protect itself entirely against intentional or accidental environmental harm originating in another state. The consequences of that harm may be severe and long-lasting to the receiving state.

An additional concern is the problem of 'environmental refugees' and, more recently, 'climate refugees', many fleeing water scarcity and no longer fertile soil. Their numbers are increasing. In 2022, the United Nations High Commissioner for Refugees (UNHCR) reported that the number of people forced to leave their homes because of events linked to climate change since 2010 years reached 21.5 million. If predictions of rising sea levels due to global climate change are accurate, the number of refugees from low-lying areas can further increase over the coming years. The rapid movement of refugees and the sudden increase in local demand for food, fuelwood and goods for barter can lead to significant degradation of ecosystems and natural spaces.

Given these concerns, traditional visions of state security are expanding to include environmental security. National security law and policy have traditionally focused on protecting the territorial integrity and political sovereignty of the state from military aggression from other states, but now place increasing

163 Jeffrey McNeely, 'War and Biodiversity', in Richard Matthew, Mark Halle, Jason Switzer and Anne Hammill (eds.), *Conserving the Peace: Resources, Livelihoods and Security* (IISD/IUCN 2002).

164 UNEP, *Addressing the Role of Natural Resources in Conflict and Peacebuilding* (2015).

emphasis on the growing array of non-military and non-conventional threats, including economic change, terrorism, population growth and migration. Key environmental threats that have received scrutiny include: resource scarcity, outbreaks of infectious disease, toxic contamination, ozone depletion, global warming, water pollution, soil degradation and loss of biodiversity.

Both 'environment' and 'security' are abstract concepts whose meaning has been extensively debated.[165] In its 1994 Human Development Report, the UNDP described security as an 'integrative' rather than merely a 'defensive' concept. The UNDP definition of human security includes seven categories of threats, ranging from economic and food security to protection of human rights and access to clean water, air and land.

In addition to recognizing that environmental harm can be a threat to state security, an emerging consensus accepts that the object of security policy can no longer be confined to the state, but must range to governance levels above (e.g. regional and international) and below (e.g. sub-regions and individuals) the state. The 1986 nuclear meltdown at Chernobyl and its attendant devastation of neighboring human populations and ecosystems, and the global recognition of the common threat to humanity posed by the declining ozone layer, placed individual health and international environmental governance within the domain of security institutions.

There is also growing agreement that environmental degradation, inequitable access to resources and predation of valuable plants, animals and minerals are among the most important sources of human insecurity. They can in many instances trigger or fuel violence, and increase vulnerability to natural disasters.[166] More sustainable and equitable management of the environment can be a cost-effective means for building social cohesion and reinforce mechanisms for collaboration across social and political boundaries. In sum, environmental protection has become an essential part of conflict prevention.

There are few legal instruments addressing this issue. None of the refugee treaties, for example, defines refugee to include those fleeing environmental harm or devastation. Such individuals do not, therefore, qualify for asylum

---

165 See for example Jessica T. Matthews, 'Redefining Security', Foreign Affairs (Spring 1989), Richard H. Ullman, 'Redefining Security', International Security (Summer 1983), and Daniel Deudney and Richard Matthew (eds.), *Contested Grounds: Security and Conflict in the New Environmental Politics* (SUNY Press 1999).

166 *State of the Art Review of Environment, Security and Development Cooperation* (IUCN/OECD 1999); Mats Berdal & David M. Malone, *Greed and Grievance: Economic Agendas in Civil War* (IPA 2000); and Janet Abramovitz, *Unnatural Disasters* (Worldwatch Institute 2001).

within the territory of another state. UNHCR has expressed strong reservations in its firts report regarding the terminology (2009):

> the use of such terminology could potentially undermine the international legal regime for the protection of refugees whose rights and obligations are quite clearly defined and understood. It would also not be helpful to appear to imply a link and thus create confusion regarding the impact of climate change, environmental degradation and migration and persecution that is at the root of a refugee fleeing a country of origin and seeking international protection.[167]

Similarly, climate law instruments do not define or even mention 'climate refugees'. The first instruments to refer to the phenomenon are the 2010 Cancun Agreements, which invited all Parties to enhance action on adaptation under the Cancun Adaptation Framework, including by adopting 'measures to enhance understanding, coordination and cooperation with regard to climate change induced displacement, migration and planned relocation, where appropriate, at the national, regional and international levels.' The question was then addressed at COP 19 in Warsaw (2013) and in Paris in 2015 in the context of 'loss and damage'. In particular, COP Decision 1/21 states:

> the Executive Committee of the Warsaw International Mechanism to establish, according to its procedures and mandate, a task force to complement, draw upon the work of and involve, as appropriate, existing bodies and expert groups under the Convention including the Adaptation Committee and the Least Developed Countries Expert Group, as well as relevant organizations and expert bodies outside the Convention, to develop recommendations for integrated approaches to avert, minimize and address displacement related to the adverse impacts of climate change.

Despite the absence of legal measures, the issue of environmental security has emerged in national policies and international discussions. In 1996 the United States created a high-level position to focus on international environmental issues that bear on national security.

As an example of conflict prevention, the governments of Colombia and Panama suggested that establishing a series of nature parks along their common

167 UNHCR, *Climate Change, Natural Disasters and Human Displacement: A UNHCR Perspective* (2009), 9.

border could reduce tension there. Earlier, the United States and Mexico established Chamizal National Memorial in 1963 as a key part of the agreement that resolved a hundred-year-old border dispute along the Rio Grande. Another combined environmental/security action can be seen in the Arctic Military Environmental Cooperation (AMEC) Program, a forum for dialogue and joint activities among U.S., Russian, and Norwegian military and environmental officials to ensure that the militaries of the respective nations help assess, preserve, and repair the Arctic environment. The program addresses Arctic environmental issues that are related to the militaries' capabilities and unique activities. Currently, six projects fall under the AMEC, including four radioactive waste projects and projects dealing with military base cleanup and the treatment of shipboard wastes.

UNEP began an initiative for South Eastern European and Central Asian states for presentation to the Kiev Summit in May 2003.[168] UNEP's report maps out the environmental concerns with likely security implications and outlines the environmental policy tools best suited for promoting peace in the regions. A subsequent phase of activities commissioned and verified, through multi-stakeholder consultations, environmental security priorities, and promoted appropriate remedies and implementation strategies.

According to UNEP, principal environmental issues with implications for regional security include:

- Environmentally-induced migration as a consequence of natural resources degradation and exclusion from resources, or transboundary air pollution.
- Increasing water scarcity. Poor water quality as a consequence of pollution and lack of infrastructure is among the major causes of infant mortality in the two regions. Many of the major cities are dependent on and are over-exploiting their groundwater resources. Water pollution and scarcity may worsen in the near term as a consequence of economic recovery.
- Aging and obsolete hydropower and nuclear energy generation facilities, chemical production facilities and infrastructure.
- Land contamination, soil erosion and flawed irrigation schemes creating food insecurity. Of Europe's total land area, 12 per cent is affected by

168 As UNEP reports, 'Regional inequalities figure prominently in local tensions – per capita GDP in Western Europe is ten times that of the rest of Europe, whereas GDP in many countries of Eastern Europe and Central Asia fell (for some by as much as 40%) after 1990 as a consequence of the economic collapse of the East Bloc. Internal economic fragility place great pressure on newly-democratic transition states. Ensuring economic development and responding to governance challenges in the context of deepening regional integration will intensify pressure on natural resources unless mechanisms are put in place in advance to manage the transition'.

water erosion and 4 per cent by wind erosion, generally as a consequence of unsustainable agriculture, salinization and water logging.
- Severe overharvesting of forest resources in Armenia, Georgia and Central Asia, triggering avalanches and diminishing water quality.
- Overfishing of transboundary marine and coastal areas, including the North Sea, Baltic Sea, Mediterranean, Black Sea and Azov Sea. The Caspian Sea, for example, possesses 85 per cent of the world's sturgeon and 90 per cent of its black caviar. Shared between five states, it is increasingly threatened by extensive hydromodifications, growing oil exploration, and overfishing (including illegal traffic in caviar).
- Coupling of environmental and ethnic grievances to fuel political insurgencies.

In 2008, UNEP established the Environmental Cooperation for Peacebuilding programme (ECP), with bilateral support from Finland and Sweden, with the aim to 'strengthen the capacity of countries, regional organizations, UN entities and civil society to understand and respond to the conflict risks and peacebuilding opportunities presented by natural resources and environment'. Between 2008 and 2015, the ECP programme implemented an ambitious workplan focused on three key areas: gathering evidence, developing policy, and initiating innovative pilot projects in the field. These efforts aimed to benefit the UN's peace and security framework. These three interconnected pillars were based on UNEP's mandate, technical expertise, and operational reach, as well as the needs of the UN system.

In sum, environmental degradation and scarcities of resources threaten to undermine the way of life of populations around the world and the stability of internal governance structures. Environmental security calls for action to prevent the degradation and scarcity from leading to internal and international conflict. The concept also implies and requires the maintenance or reestablishment of ecological balance because an emphasis on conflict prevention alone is not effective to secure long-term security. Emphasis on protecting the environment attacks some of the root causes of conflict and, at the same time, highlights the common concern of humanity.

Bibliography

Al-Duaij, N., *Environmental Law of Armed Conflict* (Transnational Publishers 2004).

Austin, J. E. & Bruch, C. E. (eds.), *The Environmental Consequences of War: Legal, Economic, and Scientific Perspectives* (Cambridge University Press 2000).

Bostian, I., 'The Environmental Consequences of the Kosovo Conflict and the NATO Bombing of Serbia' 1999 *Colo. J. Int'l Envtl L. & Pol'y* 230 (2000).

Brunnee, J. & Toope, S., 'Environmental Security and Freshwater Resources: Ecosystem Regime Building', 91 *AJIL* 26 (1997).

Droege, C. & Tougas, M.-L., 'The Protection of the Natural Environment in Armed Conflict – Existing Rules and Need for Further Legal Protection', 82 *Nordic Journal of International Law* 21 (2013).

Gleditsch, N.P. (ed.), *Conflict and the Environment* (Springer 1997).

Henckaerts, J.l-M. & Constantin, D., 'Protection of the Environment' in Clapham, A. & Gaeta, P. (eds.), *The Oxford Handbook on International Humanitarian Law* (Oxford University Press 2014).

Hensen, E.T., 'The International Law of Environmental Warfare: Active and Passive Damage during Armed Conflict', 38 *Vanderbilt Journal of Transnational Law* 145 (2005).

Liebler, A., 'Deliberate Wartime Environmental Damage: New Challenges for International Law', 23 *Cal. W. Int'l L.J.* 67 (1992).

M. A. Lundberg, 'The Plunder of Natural Resources During War: A War Crime', 39 *Georgetown Journal of International Law* 495 (2008).

Mollard-Bannelier, K., *La Protection de L'environnement en Temps de Conflit Armé* (Pedone 2001).

NATO, *Environmental Guidelines for the Military Sector* (June 1996).

Payne, Cymie R. & Sand, Peter, *Gulf War Reparations and the U.N. Compensation Commission: Environmental Liability* (Oxford University Press 2011).

Plant, G., *Environmental Protection and the Laws of War* (1993).

Roberts, A., 'Environmental Destruction in the 1991 Gulf War', 291 *Int'l Rev. Red. Cross* 538 (1992).

Schafer, B., 'The Relationship between the International Law of Armed Conflict and Environmental Protection: The Need to Reevaluate What Types of Conduct are Permissible During Hostilities', 19 *Cal. W. Int'l L.J.* 287 (1989).

Schmidt, Michael, 'Green War: An Assessment of the Environmental Law of International Armed Conflict', 22 *Yale J. Int'l L.* 73 (1997).

Seacor, J.E., 'Environmental Terrorism: Lessons from the Oil Fires of Kuwait', 10 *Am U.J. Int'l L. & Pol'y* 481 (1994).

Stahn, C. et al., *Environmental Protection and Transitions from Conflict to Peace* (Oxford University Press 2017).

Tignino, M., *Water During and After Armed Conflicts: What Protection in International Law?* (Brill 2016).

Westing, A. (ed.), *Environmental Hazards of War* (Sage 1990).

Weston, B., 'Nuclear Weapons and the World Court: Ambiguity's Consensus', 7 *Transnational L & Contemp. Prob.* 371 (1997).

CHAPTER 17

Environmental Protection and Economic Activities

International environmental law does not and cannot develop in isolation, because all human activities have an impact on the environment. Many organized common endeavors have their own laws and procedures with goals specific to them. Previous chapters have discussed some of the problems that arise in interrelating or reconciling environmental protection with the fields of human rights, armed conflict, and various uses of the earth's waters and soils. The present chapter presents an overview of economic activities, especially those that have an international dimension, and the relationship of the laws and institutions governing them with those seeking to protect the environment. The chapter looks first at efforts to address poverty and how this has coalesced with environmental and social concerns to give content to the concept of sustainable development. A second and related problem is external or international debt. Third, the role of foreign investment and the conduct of multinational companies is presented followed by some examples unilateral national laws given extraterritorial effect and the difficulties they pose. Finally, the chapter offers an overview of international trade law, with its emphasis on eliminating barriers to trade, and the conflicts that have emerged between its aims and those of environmental protection.

1 Poverty Eradication and Environmental Protection

As of 2022, the world population is nearly 8 billion people.[1] World population is expected to rise to 9.7 billion by 2050 and 10.4 billion by 2100.[2] Virtually all this future growth will be concentrated in developing countries, especially in Africa and Asia.[3] Using an absolute poverty line of $2.15 a day, the World Bank estimated in October 2023 that over 800 million persons live in extreme poverty.[4] Progress

1 7.951.150, according to the World Development Indicators database of the World Bank (2023).

2 UN, *World Population Prospects 2022* (Summary of Results) UN DESA/POP/2021/TR/NO.3 (2022), 1.

3 More than half of the projected increase will be concentrated in the Democratic Republic of Congo (DRC), Egypt, Ethiopia, India, Nigeria, Pakistan, the Philippines and Tanzania. ibid, 1.

4 The per capita income of $2.15 was adopted in 2022 using the 2017 purchasing power parity (PPP). Before 2022, the poverty line was set at $1.90. UN, *The Sustainable Development Goals Report 2023: Special* Edition (2023).

 | DOI:10.1163/9789047440802_019

has been achieved, however, in part due to an international focus on poverty alleviation and eradication, as exemplified by the 2030 Sustainable Agenda of the United Nations (UN), centered around the eradication of poverty and hunger. In its preamble, the Stockholm Declaration recognized that

> [i]n the developing countries most of the environmental problems are caused by underdevelopment. Millions continue to live far below the minimum levels required for health and sanitation. Therefore, the developing countries must direct their efforts to development, bearing in mind their priorities and the need to safeguard and improve the environment. For the same purpose, the industrialized countries should make efforts to reduce the gap between themselves and the developing countries …

Prior to the Stockholm Conference many poor countries did not accept the necessity of global cooperation to protect the environment,[5] because such problems were considered an ailment of rich, industrialized countries. At Stockholm, developing countries seeking to become industrialized chose to ignore the environmental costs of industrialization. The same countries also suspected that wealthy nations of the north subordinated foreign economic development to environmental protection, considering the former less urgent than pollution and nature protection. Some feared that funds previously dedicated to development would be diverted to fight environmental deterioration. These fears seemed to be borne out several days before the Stockholm meeting, when the Third United Nations Conference on Trade and Development (UNCTAD) produced particularly disappointing results on development aid.[6]

This background explains the parts of the Stockholm Declaration and Action Plan that were dedicated to economic and social development as a condition of environmental protection. The documents promoted transfer of financial and technical aid, stability of prices and adequate remuneration for basic commodities and raw materials, enhancement of the potential for progress of

5 Prior to Stockholm, a General Assembly resolution on development and the environment stated that standards to preserve the environment 'as a general rule will have to be defined at the national level and, in all cases, will have to reflect conditions and systems of values prevailing in each country'. Furthermore 'each country has the right to formulate, in accordance with its own particular situation and in full enjoyment of its national sovereignty, its own national policies on the human environment, including criteria for the evaluation of projects'. G.A. Res. 2849, adopted Dec. 20, 1971, U.N. Doc. A/Res. 2849 (XXVI) (1972), 11 I.L.M. 422 (The vote was 85–2-34, the United States and the United Kingdom opposed).

6 Alexandre C. Kiss and Jean Didier Sicault, 'La Conférence des Nations Unies sur l'environnement' (1972) 18 *Annuaire Français de Droit International* 603, 624.

developing countries, and international assistance to aid developing countries to face costs which can delay incorporation of environmental safeguards in development planning. According to Principle 11:

> The environmental policies of all States should enhance and not adversely affect the present or future development potential of developing countries, nor should they hamper the attainment of better living conditions for all, and appropriate steps should be taken by States and international organizations with a view to reaching agreement on meeting the possible national and international economic consequences resulting from the application of environmental measures.

Principle 23 first expressed the now widely-recognized notion that a distinction may be necessary in applying environmental norms according to the state of development of different countries, a concept reflected in the principle of 'common but differentiated responsibilities'.

In the aftermath of Stockholm, consensus emerged about the need for global cooperation to safeguard the planet. The Charter of Economic Rights and Duties of States, adopted by the United Nations General Assembly on December 12, 1974, proclaims that protection, preservation and management of the environment for present and future generations is the responsibility of all states and that they should strive to halt detrimental policies in environmental matters and develop programs conforming to this responsibility.[7] The Brundtland Commission, appointed in 1983, further integrated development and environment, coining the concept of 'sustainable development.'

By the mid-1980s, developing countries manifested greater concern with environmental issues. In 1989, the Amazon Declaration[8] expressed the support of the states of Amazonia for a new Amazon Special Environmental Commission, created to foster development and conserve natural resources and the environment. While reaffirming the sovereign right of each country to manage freely its natural resources, the Declaration expressed the willingness of the signatories to cooperate and to carry environmental protection and conservation in the region for the benefit of present and future generations. Environmental protection was linked, however, to resolution of the foreign debt crisis, economic development and growth, 'an essential condition for the protection, conservation, exploitation and rational utilization' of the region.

7 G. A. Res. 3281 (XXIX) 'Charter of Economic Rights and Duties of States' (December 12, 1974).

8 May 6, 1989, U.N. Doc. A/44/275, E/1989/79, Annex, May 15, 1989; 28 I.L.M. 1303 (1989).

In June 1989, the Organization of African Unity (OAU) convened a Ministerial meeting in Kampala to assess environmental problems affecting the African region and evolve a common strategy for environmental management and sustainable development. The study evaluated progress made on implementation of the recommendations contained in the Brundtland Report and led to adoption of the Kampala Declaration, which identified several priority areas for achieving environmentally-sound sustainable development: managing demographic change and pressures, achieving food self-sufficiency and food security, ensuring efficient and equitable use of water resources, securing greater energy self-sufficiency, optimizing industrial production, maintaining species and ecosystems, and halting and reversing desertification.

In a more widespread initiative, the European Economic Community (EEC) and some seventy African, Caribbean and Pacific states (ACP) signed the Lomé IV agreement on December 15, 1989[9] which included a chapter specifically devoted to protection of the environment and conservation of natural resources, deemed to be fundamental objectives sought by the ACP States with the support of the EC.[10] The Lomé agreement was reaffirmed in a revised form November 4, 1995 in Mauritius. After challenges by the United States (US), a Green Paper document published by the European Commission in 1996 made it clear that Lomé trade preferences had to be seen in the light of the World Trade Organization (WTO) rules. In 2000, the EEC-ACP states replaced Lomé IV by an Agreement on Partnership between ACP and European Union (EU) states. The agreement called on the states to take into account questions related to the transport and disposal of hazardous waste (Art. 32.1.d), but otherwise did not discuss environmental matters.

The Organization of Economic Cooperation and Development (OECD) also adopted measures to link environmental protection to development assistance. It recommended an environmental checklist for development assistance, calling on member countries to ensure that bilateral and multilateral development assistance takes into account environmental considerations in the identification, planning, implementation and evaluation of those development projects which are proposed for funding.[11] Despite generalized concern with environmental protection, some developing countries continue to view such conditions as constraints on development opportunities and national sovereignty as well as attempts to protect markets rather than the environment.

---

9 Fourth ACP-EEC Convention (Lome IV) 29 I.L.M. 783 (1990); EMuT 989:93

10 15, Article 33, Lome IV.

11 OECD, Doc. C(89)2(Final), March 2, 1989; 28 I.L.M. 1314 (1989).

During the 1980s, several developing countries began to take a leadership role in environmental matters, especially on the issue of transfer of hazardous substances and wastes. They also ratified most global environmental instruments.[12] Zaire initiated the World Charter for Nature in the United Nations General Assembly while Brazil agreed to host the 1992 United Nations Conference on Environment and Development. The title of the Rio Conference reflects the importance given to addressing both topics equally.

Several reasons may explain why many developing countries began to give enhanced attention to environmental protection. First, the link between environmental deterioration and poverty and its consequences became obvious, including the fact that pollution from urban growth, lack of water quality and quantity, and desertification harm developing countries more than industrialized nations. Second, the natural resources of poor countries overwhelmingly bear the cost of unregulated development. Third, health, nutrition, and general well-being of the peoples of developing countries depend on the integrity and productivity of the environment and the compatibility of the development process with the imperatives of conservation. These principles were strictly formulated in the development strategy elaborated for the Third United Nations Development Decade.[13]

Fourth, developing countries increasingly came to realize the dangers of the 'exportation of pollution' by companies or individuals seeking to profit from the weakness of protective legislation or enforcement mechanisms in these countries. Especially acute problems have arisen from exports of dangerous products prohibited or regulated in industrialized states, the dumping of industrial waste products, and the installation of dangerous industrial operations. The accident at an American-owned chemical factory in Bhopal, India, which caused 2,500 deaths in December 1984, emphasized the problem.

Perhaps most importantly, the long-held assumption that conditions for reconciling growth and the attainment of environmental quality involved a tradeoff, with environmental quality reached only at the expense of higher incomes and improved levels of welfare, began to give way to the idea that the development process could be compatible with or even enhanced

12 On the whole, the participation of Third World countries in global instruments is comparable to that of industrialized states. Among the contracting parties to the UNESCO World Heritage Convention are 31 of the 51 African States, 15 of 20 Latin-American States and 22 of 38 Asian States. Still more comprehensive is participation in CITES: 36 African States have ratified or signed it, while all but one Latin-American and half the Asian States (19 out of 38) are parties to it. Most of the UNEP regional seas conventions also include developing countries.

13 G. A. Res. 35/36 of January 20, 1981.

by environmental protection, as reflected in the notion of 'sustainable development'.

Serious issues remain about how to implement and integrate environmental protection and economic development, many centering on the problem of environmental costs. Developing countries often see increased efforts to implement stringent environmental safeguards across boundaries as creating new non-tariff trade barriers or at least as imposing significant costs and constraints on production processes or products, resulting in a loss of competitive advantage.

At the same time, efforts since the Rio Conference on Environment and Development have tried to address poverty reduction and environmental protection through various programs. The United Nations Development Program (UNDP) and the European Commission, for example, are engaged in a joint initiative on poverty and the environment aimed at identifying concrete policy recommendations and practical measures that address the environmental concerns of the poor in developing countries. The programs seek more localized, community-based approaches to natural resource management and sustainable development, informed by an understanding that the various groups in a society often experience environmental problems in very different ways. The goal of the Poverty and Environment Initiative is to provide a forum for practitioners, policy-makers and researchers working in this area to share their experiences and identify solutions.

In September 2000, 147 heads of State and Government, and 189 nations in total endorsed the United Nations Millennium Declaration[14] committing themselves to making the right to development a reality for everyone and to freeing the entire human race from want. They acknowledged that progress is based on sustainable economic growth, which must focus on the poor, with human rights at the center. The objective of the Declaration was to promote 'a comprehensive approach and a coordinated strategy, tackling many problems simultaneously across a broad front'. The Declaration called for halving by the year 2015 the number of people who live on less than one dollar a day; the goal was achieved five years in advance of the deadline. Direct support from the richer countries, in the form of aid, trade, debt relief and investment, was provided to help the developing countries.

To help track progress with the Millennial Development Goals (MDGs), the United Nations Secretariat and the specialized agencies of the UN system, as well as representatives of International Monetary Fund (IMF), the World

---

14 United Nations Millennium Declaration, A/RES/55/2.

Bank and the OECD defined a set of time-bound and measurable goals and targets for combating poverty, environmental degradation and other goals of the program. International experts also selected relevant indicators to be used to assess progress over the period from 1990 to 2015. Each year, the Secretary-General prepared a report on progress achieved towards implementing the Declaration, based on data on the 48 selected indicators, aggregated at global and regional levels. The political framework for achieving the Millennium Development Goals was provided by an agreement between North and South reached in 2002 in Monterrey, Mexico. The *Financing for Development* agreement was reaffirmed at the World Summit for Sustainable Development held in Johannesburg, South Africa, in August 2002, which determined that "poverty eradication, changing consumption and production patterns and protecting and managing the natural resource base for economic and social development are overarching objectives of and essential requirements for sustainable development."[15]

In September 2015, the MDGs expired and were replaced with the 2030 Sustainable Development Goals (SDGs),[16] containing a set of seventeen commitments that begin with ending poverty and hunger. The Preamble recognizes that 'eradicating poverty in all its forms and dimensions, including extreme poverty, is the greatest global challenge and an indispensable requirement for sustainable development'. Health, education, gender equality and reduced inequalities are also included. Environmental goals mentioned relate to clean water and sanitation, affordable clean energy, and action on climate change. The 2030 Agenda also specifically addresses the means of implementation of the SDGs, which include finance, technology transfer and performance review. As far as 'finance' is concerned, the 2030 Agenda refers expressly to another document adopted earlier in 2015 – the Addis Ababa Action Agenda – which establishes a global framework for financing sustainable development.[17] Regional action, particularly in the developing world, soon followed. In the Americas, for example, the Third Meeting of Ministers and High Authorities on Sustainable Development adopted on October 20, 2015, the Tela Declaration for Sustainable Development in the Americas, based on the UN SDGs.[18] The

15 Johannesburg Declaration on Sustainable Development, A/CONF.199/20, para. 11.

16 Transforming our world: the 2030 Agenda for Sustainable Development, A/RES/70/1, Sept. 25, 2015.

17 ibid, para 40. G. A. Res 69/313 'Addis Ababa Action Agenda of the Third International Conference on Financing for Development' (July 27, 2015).

18 Declaration of Tela for Sustainable Development in the Americas, OEA/Ser.K/XL.III.3, CIDI/RIMDS-III/DEC.1 /15 (20 October 2015).

Declaration approved the Strategic Framework for the Inter-American Program for Sustainable Development,[19] which supports action in six key areas:

1. Disaster Risk Management;
2. Sustainable Management of Ecosystems;
3. Sustainable Cities and Communities;
4. Integrated Water Resources Management;
5. Sustainable energy management, prioritizing the promotion of clean, renewable, environmentally sustainable energy and energy efficiency; and,
6. Strengthening and capacity building for efficient, effective, accountable and inclusive institutions for sustainable development.

Climate change has had an unprecedented impact on poverty, especially in developing countries, and this impact has been exacerbated by emerging challenges such as the COVID19 pandemic and increasing conflicts. The World Bank estimates that climate change will drive 68 million to 135 million people into poverty by 2030.[20] Poverty eradication has as a result been at the center of the fight against climate change in the last decades. The 2015 Paris Agreement recognized 'the intrinsic relationship that climate change actions, responses and impacts have with equitable access to sustainable development and eradication of poverty'.[21] In 2018, the Intergovernmental Panel on Climate Change (IPCC) concluded that 'limiting global warming to 1.5°C rather than 2°C above preindustrial levels would make it markedly easier to achieve many aspects of sustainable development, with greater potential to eradicate poverty and reduce inequalities'.[22] The Conference of the Parties (COP) of the United Nations Framework Convention on Climate Change (UNFCCC) accepted the recommendation of the IPCC and stressed in its 2023 Decision on the Global Stocktake the importance of the 1.5°C target and, among other things, to contribute effectively to poverty eradication.[23]

2 International Debt

The environmental damage that results from conditions of poverty is most evident in the case of developing countries burdened with severe foreign debt

19 ibid.

20 World Bank Group, Poverty and Shared Prosperity 2020 (2020).

21 Preamble.

22 IPCC, *Global Warming of 1.5°C. An IPCC Special Report on the impacts of global warming of 1.5°C above pre-industrial levels and related global greenhouse gas emission pathways*, 2018, available at <https://www.ipcc.ch/sr15/>, p. 447.

23 UN Doc FCCC/PA/CMA/2023/L.17UNFCCC, Outcome of the first global stocktake, Draft decision -/CMA.5, 2023, available at <https://unfccc.int/documents/636608>, para. 26.

and dependent on a narrow range of exports to earn the foreign exchange to meet their debt obligations. Policy-makers tend to take less account of environmental consequences when they are faced with short-term financial pressures. This pressure is increased by the fact that the developing countries lack the capacity of the industrialized countries to undertake research on more environmentally desirable technologies and processes.

World indebtedness of low- and middle-income countries (LMICs) increased dramatically between 1982 and 2014, growing from US $838 billion to almost $5.4 trillion.[24] It fell in 2022 for the first time since 2015, decreasing by 3.4 percent from $9.3 trillion in 2021 to $9.0 trillion in 2022.[25] Despite this slight decrease, the external debt stock of LMICs remains at unprecedented high levels.[26]

In 1996, the World Bank and the IMF initiated the Highly Indebted Poor Country (HIPC) Initiative agreed by governments around the world. It was a comprehensive approach to reduce the external debt of the world's poorest, most heavily indebted countries, and represented an important step forward in placing debt relief within an overall framework of poverty reduction. A major review in 1999 resulted in a significant enhancement of the original framework to produce even greater relief. In 2005, to help accelerate progress toward the MDGs, the HIPC Initiative was supplemented by the Multilateral Debt Relief Initiative (MDRI). The MDRI allows for 100 percent relief on eligible debts by three multilateral institutions – the IMF, the World Bank, and the African Development Fund (AfDF) – for countries completing the HIPC Initiative process. In 2007, the Inter-American Development Bank (IaDB) also decided to provide additional ('beyond HIPC') debt relief to the five HIPCs in the Western Hemisphere. Since then, 36 of the 39 eligible countries have reached HIPC completion and have received substantive debt relief through both initiatives (HIPC and MDRI).[27]

To be considered for HIPC Initiative assistance, a country must be eligible to borrow from the World Bank's International Development Agency, which provides interest-free loans and grants to the world's poorest countries, and from the IMF's Poverty Reduction and Growth Trust, which provides loans to low-income countries at subsidized rates. The country must face an unsustainable debt burden that cannot be addressed through traditional debt relief mechanisms and have established a track record of reform and sound policies

24 World Bank Group, *International Debt Statistics 2016* (2016).
25 World Bank, *International Debt Report 2023* (2023).
26 ibid, 3.
27 ibid, xv.

through IMF- and World Bank-supported programs. Finally, it must have developed a Poverty Reduction Strategy Paper (PRSP) through a broad-based participatory process in the country. This initiative and other economic factors between 2007 and 2015 resulted in the proportion of countries at high risk of external debt distress (or in distress) falling from 43 to 26 percent.[28] For states not eligible for the HIPC assistance, the debt ration remained very high.

In May 2020, at the start of the COVID-19 pandemic, the G20 established the Debt Service Suspension Initiative, which suspended $12.9 billion in debt-service owed by the 49 participating countries to their creditors.

3 Private Economic Enterprises

Business associations, like other non-governmental organizations (NGOs), have long been active and have expanded their international presence in recent years. The International Chamber of Commerce (ICC) participated in the League of Nations proceedings and even signed some legal instruments.[29] Today, many multinational corporations have an enormous influence on the global economy and environmental protection, being linked with foreign affiliates throughout the world.[30] Organized business groups participate in the international arena as NGOs, subject to the same requirements and enjoying the same rights as other NGOs. Like other NGOs, business entities often are excluded from international dispute settlement procedures, even when they are the real parties in interest.[31]

Some business associations are organized for specific issues, such as the World Business Council on Sustainable Development that participates in

---

28 International Monetary Fund, *Public Debt Vulnerabilities in Low-Income Countries: The Evolving Landscape* (December 2015), 2.

29 The ICC delegate signed League instruments relating to import/export restrictions and customs formalities. See Lyman C. White, *International Non-Governmental Organizations: Their Purposes, Methods and Accomplishments* (Rutgers University Press 1951) 22.

30 See Eric W. Orts, 'The Legitimacy of Multinational Corporations' in Lawrence E. Mitchell (ed), *Progressive Corporate Law* (Routledge 1995) 247–248. Gerald Epstein, 'The Role and Control of Multinational Corporations in the World Economy' in Jonathan Michie (ed), *The Handbook of Globalisation* (3rd edn, Edward Elgar 2019) 165–177. World Bank Group, *The Effect of Multinational Enterprises on Climate Change: Supply Chain Emissions, Green Technology Transfers and Corporate Commitments* (2023).

31 See G. Richard Shell, 'Participation of Nongovernmental Parties in the World Trade Organization: The Trade Stakeholders Model and Participation by Nonstate Parties in the World Trade Organization' (1996) 17 *University of Pennsylvania Journal of International Economic Law* 359, 368.

multilateral forums relating to the environment and was particularly effective in climate change negotiations. The Global Climate Coalition is a national industry group that represents the interests of fossil fuel and transportation companies in the US.

The role of business entities is particularly important in international environmental law, where regulation most often is aimed at private economic activities, although it is states that sign the agreements. The Energy Charter Treaty (ECT), for example, requires state parties to ensure that state enterprises and other 'privileged' entities conduct their operations in a manner consistent with the Treaty.[32] Each state party is also required to take reasonable measures to ensure observance by regional and local governments and authorities within its area. These obligations likely will bring in private entities acting under governmental authority.

The power of the private sector has expanded considerably with globalization, the integration of markets, communications, and national economies. Policies and laws are being redrafted in many countries in order to provide investment incentives. With growing power comes growing responsibility. International efforts are being made to ensure socially-responsible investment and business conduct, including in respect to the environment. In addition to corporate codes of conduct for self-regulation, described in Chapter 6, international norms are developing through various institutions and transnational litigation is increasingly attempting to hold business enterprises accountable for their environmental and social policies.

Yet, the overall picture is one of relative freedom of economic movement. Although developing countries and environmental activists in particular have sought an international regulatory framework for multinationals at least since 1970, there are few concrete results, apart from the non-binding voluntary declarations discussed herein.[33]

---

32 The Energy Charter Treaty (Dec. 17 1994), 33 I.L.M. 360 (1994).

33 For discussion of the problem and recent efforts to ensure corporate accountability, see generally Larry C. Backer, 'Multinational Corporations, Transnational Law: The United Nations' Norms on the Responsibilities of Transnational Corporations as a Harbinger of Corporate Social Responsibility in International Law' (2006) 37 *Columbia Human Rights Law Review* 287; Ann Marie McLoughlin, 'Comment, International Trend of Multinational Corporate Accountability for Human Rights Abuses and the Role of the United States' (2007) 33 *Ohio Northern University Law Review* 153; Emeka Duruigbo, 'Corporate Accountability and Liability for International Human Rights Abuses: Recent Changes and Recurring Challenges' (2008) 6 *Northwestern Journal of International Human Rights* 222; Debbie Johnston, 'Lifting the Veil on Corporate Terrorism: The Use of the Criminal Code Terrorism Framework to Hold Multinational Corporations Accountable for Complicity in Human Rights Violations Abroad' (2008) 66 *University of Toronto Faculty Law Review*

The OECD has drafted voluntary principles and standards for responsible business conduct, jointly addressed by its member governments to multinational enterprises (OECD Guidelines for Multinational Enterprises on Responsible Business Conduct).[34] First adopted in 1976, the OECD Guidelines were revised several times with the most recent update in 2023. Section VI of the OECD Guidelines affirms that enterprises should take due account of the need to protect the environment, within the framework of laws, regulations and administrative practices in the countries in which they operate and in consideration of relevant international agreements, principles, objectives and standards. This section largely reflects the principles laid out in the Rio Declaration on Environment and Development, such as the duty of diligence, the precautionary principle, and the importance of ensuring access to environmental information and justice. In particular, enterprises should establish and maintain a system of environmental management appropriate to the enterprise, including the collection and evaluation of adequate and timely information regarding the environmental impacts of their activities, the establishment of measurable objectives and where appropriate, targets for improved environmental performance and regular monitoring and verification of progress toward such objectives or targets. They should provide the public and employees with adequate and timely information on the potential environmental impacts of the activities of the enterprise and engage in consultation with the communities directly affected by their environmental policies and by their implementation, as far as this is compatible with concerns about cost, business confidentiality and protection of intellectual property rights. They should assess and address in decision-making the foreseeable environmental impacts associated with the processes, goods and services of the enterprise over their full life cycle and, if necessary, they should prepare an appropriate environmental impact assessment. They should use a precautionary approach where there are threats of serious damage to the environment and maintain contingency plans for preventing serious environmental damage. They also should seek to improve corporate environmental performance by adopting adequate technologies and operating procedures, by developing products or

137; Olga Martin-Ortega, 'Human Rights Due Diligence for Corporations: From Voluntary Standards to Hard Law at Last?' (2013) 31(4) *Netherlands Quarterly of Human Rights* 44–74. Marco Fasciglione, 'The Enforcement of Corporate Human Rights Due Diligence: From the UN Guiding Principles on Business and Human Rights to the Legal Systems of EU Countries' (2016) 10 *Human Rights & International Legal Discourse* 94–116; Elisa Morgera, *Corporate Environmental Accountability in International Law* (Oxford University Press 2020).

34 OECD, Guidelines for Multinational Enterprises (June 27, 2000), 40 I.L.M. 237 (2000).

services that have no undue environmental impact, by promoting higher levels of awareness among customers of the environmental implications of using the products and services of the enterprise and by providing adequate education and training to employees in environmental matters. Finally, enterprises are encouraged to contribute to the development of environmentally meaningful and economically efficient public policy, for example, by means of partnerships. The 2023 edition of the OECD Guidelines provides updated recommendations for responsible business conduct in several key areas such as climate change, biodiversity loss, technology, business integrity and supply chain due diligence. The updated environment chapter reflects all the key environmental instruments, including the most recent ones, and including the 2030 Agenda for Sustainable Development, the UNFCCC and the Paris Agreement, the Convention on Biological Diversity (CBD) and the 2022 Kunming-Montreal Biodiversity Framework, as well as the 2012 International Finance Corporation's Environmental and Social Performance Standards and the 2006 Strategic Approach to International Chemicals Management.[35]

Another important attempt to engage the private sector in more sustainable practices has been the Global Compact, established by the UN in 2000, which advocates good corporate practices and commits enterprises to adhere to a set of principles and values including (i) supporting a precautionary approach to environmental challenges, (ii) undertaking initiatives to promote greater environmental responsibility, and (iii) encouraging the development and diffusions of environmentally friendly technologies.[36]

In 2003, the former Sub-Commission on the Promotion and Protection of Human Rights adopted 'Norms on the Responsibilities of Transnational Corporations and Other Business Enterprises with regard to Human Rights' – a set of human rights, environmental and consumer protection responsibilities of business.[37] Article 24 of the draft states that businesses must respect the rights of local communities by avoiding endangerment of 'the health, environment, culture and institutions of indigenous peoples and communities …'.[38] Businesses are also 'to respect international agreements and standards with regard to the environment as well as human rights;… take due account of the need to protect the environment, public health, and safety, and shall generally conduct their activities in a manner contributing to the wider goal of sustainable

35 ibid, Commentary, para. 66.

36 United Nations Global Compact (2000), Principles 7, 8 and 9.

37 'Introduction to the Human Rights Principles and Responsibilities for Transnational Corporations and Other Business Enterprises, UN Doc E/CN.4/Sub.2/2002/WG.2/WP.1/Add.1.

38 ibid Art. 24.

development'.[39] In its commentary to the draft, the Sub-Commission states 'businesses shall respect the right to a clean and healthy environment in light of the relationship between the environment and human rights'.[40] The accompanying report also indicated that the norms were more than aspirational statements of desired conduct; instead the report ambitiously claimed that they constituted a restatement of international legal principles applicable to companies. The Sub-Commission transmitted the norms to the Commission on Human Rights, which did not endorse them, perhaps because they purported to be obligatory. The Commission passed a short resolution in 2004, stating that the norms had 'not been requested', that the document 'has no legal standing', and that the Sub-Commission 'should not perform any monitoring function in this regard'.[41]

In 2005, the UN Office of the High Commissioner on Human Rights made its own report to the former Commission on Human Rights about the responsibilities of multinational companies. The report reiterated that states are the primary duty bearers in international law, but agreed that businesses can affect significantly implementation of international norms.[42] Although focused on human rights, the report looked to the Global Compact, which includes environmental norms, as a starting point and proposed a tripartite responsibility – to 'respect' norms, to 'support' them, and to 'make sure they are not complicit' in abuses committed by others. The report prompted the UN Secretary-General to appoint a Special Representative on Human Rights and Transnational Corporations and Other Business Enterprises, whose work formed the basis of the Guiding Principles on Business and Human Rights, endorsed unanimously by the Human Rights Council in June 2011.[43]

In 2014, the Human Rights Council adopted Resolution 26/9, by which it decided 'to establish an open-ended intergovernmental working group on transnational corporations and other business enterprises with respect to human rights; whose mandate shall be to elaborate an international legally binding instrument to regulate, in international human rights law, the activities

39 ibid Art. 12.

40 ibid Art. 12, Comment m.

41 UN Commission on Human Rights, Res. No. 2004/116, UN Doc. E/CN.4/2004/L.11/Add.7 (2004).

42 Report of the United Nations High Commissioner on Human Rights and Responsibilities of Transnational Corporations and Related Business Enterprises with Regard to Human Rights, UN Doc E/CN.4/2005/91 (2005).

43 UN OHCHR, 'Guiding Principles on Business and Human Rights: Implementing the United Nations "Protect, Respect and Remedy" Framework' (2011).

of transnational corporations and other business enterprises.'[44] Although the focus is on human rights, the working group has also been taking into account the impact on human rights of environmental degradation caused by corporate conduct.

In the European context, significant progress has been made in regulating the private sector. Article 9 of the 1998 Council of Europe Convention on the Protection of the Environment Through Criminal Law provides specifically for corporate liability and the Explanatory Report notes that the international trend at present seems to support a general recognition of corporate liability in criminal law, even in countries which only a few years ago formally adopted the principle according to which corporations cannot commit criminal offences. The treaty leaves it open to states parties to impose 'criminal or administrative sanctions or measures on legal persons' corresponding to each legal tradition. The 2003 UN Convention against Corruption also addresses the liability of legal persons, requiring parties to hold such persons liable, but leaves states the choice of criminal, civil, or administrative measures to ensure liability.

As part of the European Green Deal, launched in 2019, the European Commission has introduced two proposals that aim to enhance corporate sustainability in Europe: the Corporate Sustainability Reporting Directive (CSRD)[45] and the Corporate Sustainability Due Diligence Directive (CS3D).[46] The former, which entered into force in January 2023, aims to enhance the transparency and comparability of corporate sustainability reporting within the EU. It builds upon the existing Non-Financial Reporting Directive (NFRD) by expanding the scope of reporting requirements, introducing standardized reporting formats, and imposing stricter disclosure obligations on large companies and public interest entities. The CSRD aims to ensure that companies provide comprehensive information on their environmental, social, and governance (ESG) performance, enabling investors, consumers, and other stakeholders to make informed decisions. The CS3D, approved by the European Parliament in April 2024, aims to promote sustainable business practices and prevent negative

44 UN Human Rights Council Res 26/9 'Elaboration of an International Legally Binding Instrument on Transnational Corporations and Other Business Enterprises with Respect to Human Rights' A/HRC/RES/26/9 (2014), para 1.

45 Council Directive 2022/2464 of December 14, 2022 amending Regulation (EU) No 537/2014, Directive 2004/109/EC, Directive 2006/43/EC and Directive 2013/34/EU, as regards corporate sustainability reporting (Corporate Sustainability Reporting Directive or CSRD).

46 Council Directive 2024/0628 of April 24, 2024 amending Directive (EU) 2019/1937 on Corporate Sustainability Due Diligence (Corporate Sustainability Due Diligence Directive or CS3D).

social and environmental impacts throughout the supply chain. It proposes mandatory due diligence obligations for companies operating in the EU, requiring them to identify, prevent, mitigate, and account for adverse impacts on human rights, labor rights, and the environment. The CS3D targets companies that operate within the EU market, regardless of their size or sector, and aims to create a level playing field for responsible business conduct.

Independently of efforts to set international standards for corporate conduct, many states have developed domestic legislation imposing due diligence duties on enterprises and establishing mechanisms for transparency and liability in cases of environmental harm or human rights violations. Moreover, companies engaged in multinational business operations are finding themselves the subject of litigation over their practices. Bhopal was an early instance where the conduct of a company gave rise to litigation in the home state of the company, Union Carbide,[47] as well as in the state where the event took place. More recently, plaintiffs alleging injuries due to pollution – usually linked to human rights violations – have invoked broad jurisdictional provisions to file lawsuits in the country where the company is registered or has its home office. Many of these cases have been filed in the United States pursuant to the federal Alien Tort Claim Act,[48] as well as in several other jurisdictions.[49] An increasing number of cases have been filed against multinational corporations for their significant contribution to climate change and the severe impacts they consequently have both on the environment and on the enjoyment of a vast range of human rights.[50] One of the most emblematic cases has been the one filed by the Dutch NGO *Milieudefensie* against Shell.[51] In its 2021 decision, the District Court of The Hague ruled that Royal Dutch Shell must significantly reduce its carbon emissions by 45 per cent by 2030 compared to 2019 levels. The court found that Shell's current emissions reduction targets were insufficient to

47 In fact, some 145 lawsuits were filed against Union Carbide in the US seeking over $250 billion in damages on behalf of more than 400,000 injured persons. See *In re Union Carbide Corp. Gas Plant Disaster*, 809 F.2d 195 (2d Cir. 1987) (affirming dismissal for forum non conveniens conditioned upon defendant consenting to personal jurisdiction in India).

48 28 USC sec 1350. See e.g., *Jota v. Texaco Inc.*, 157 F.2d 153 (2d Cir. 1998); *Wiwa v. Royal Dutch Petroleum*, 226 F.3d 88 (2d Cir. 2000); *Doe v. Unocal*, 110 F. Supp.2d 1294 (C.D. Cal.2000).

49 See e.g. Samvel Varvastian and Felicity Kalunga, 'Transnational Corporate Liability for Environmental Damage and Climate Change: Reassessing Access to Justice after *Vedanta v. Lungowe*' (2020) 9(2) *Transnational Environmental Law* 323–345.

50 Annalisa Savaresi and Joana Setzer, 'Rights Based Litigation in the Climate Emergency: Mapping the Landscape and New Knowledge Frontiers' (2022) 13(1) *Journal of Human Rights and the Environment* 7–34.

51 *Milieudefensie et al v. Royal Dutch Shell* (2021), Hague District Court, C/09/571932/HA ZA 19–379, 2021. This decision was partially overturned by the Court of Appeal in 2024.

meet the goals of the Paris Agreement and failed to adequately prevent the adverse impacts of climate change. The decision marked the first time a court has ordered a private company to align its emissions reduction targets with the Paris Agreement, holding Shell legally responsible for its contribution to climate change.

4 Foreign Investments and the Environment

The enactment of legislative and regulatory measures by states to safeguard the environment is fundamentally an assertion of state sovereignty, a cornerstone principle in modern international law.[52] This sovereignty encompasses regulatory authority, granting states the freedom and exclusive jurisdiction to legislate within their territories and over their populations. Nevertheless, the regulatory sovereignty of states is inherently constrained by their international obligations,[53] including those undertaken through international investment agreements (IIAs) or contracts with foreign investors. Over several decades, countries have made various commitments with the aim of promoting and protecting foreign investments in their territory, such as the commitment to treat them fairly and equitably or the commitment not to deprive them of their investment unless some conditions are met. All these commitments have necessarily and progressively reduced countries' policy space, and the result is what is generally described as a *regulatory chill*, namely the fear that adopting new laws or measures may trigger an investment dispute.

International investment law was created to protect and promote foreign investments. In 1959, with the entry into force of the first bilateral investment

52 Samantha Besson, 'Sovereignty', in *Max Planck Encyclopedia of Public International Law* (2011), para 1.

53 Negotiating and concluding a treaty, for instance, is both an expression of state sovereignty and a limitation of it. See *S.S. Wimbledon* (U.K. and others v Germany), 1923 PCIJ Series A No 1; *S.S. Lotus* (France v Turkey) PCIJ Series A No 10. These limitations were made clear by the panel in the WTO *China – Raw Materials* dispute: while the respondent (China) tried to justify a series of export restrictions on certain raw materials arguing that 'nothing should interfere with their sovereignty over such natural resources,' the panel responded that 'in joining the WTO, China obtained significant commercial and institutional benefits, including with respect to its natural resources [but] It also committed to abide by WTO rights and obligations'. Report of the Panel, *China – Measures Related to the exportation of Various Raw Materials*, WT/DS394/R (adopted on February 22, 2012), paras 7.356, 6.33, and 7.382.

treaty,[54] States began negotiating treaties with the main or sole purpose of protecting foreign investors, providing them with certain standards of treatment and permitting them to initiate direct actions against the host State for a dispute arising from the state's treatment of their investment.[55]

For a very long time, international investment agreements did not contain any reference to the environment or to the possibility for the host state's right to regulate within its territory (for instance to protect the environment) and arbitral tribunals have long ignored environmental considerations in the interpretation of different standards of treatment or protection, adopting decisions that completely ignored the legitimate environmental objective of state measures that produced an impact on foreign investors operating on their territory. In *CDSE v. Costa Rica*, for instance, the tribunal refused to analyze the detailed evidence submitted by the respondent, pointing to Costa Rica's international obligation to preserve the unique ecological site that is the Santa Elena property. The company argued that 'expropriatory environmental measures – no matter how laudable and beneficial to society as a whole – are, in this respect, similar to any other expropriatory measures that a state may take in order to implement its policies.'[56]

The Rio Declaration on Environment and Development subsumed this notion and made explicit the idea that the economic system and environmental protection are intertwined and should be mutually supportive. References to sustainable development and environmental protection started appearing in the text of the preamble of many investment treaties, as well as many free trade agreements (FTAs) signed from the 1990s. The 1994 North American Free Trade Agreement (NAFTA) mentions in its preamble the importance of promoting sustainable development and of strengthening 'the development and enforcement of environmental laws and regulations'.[57] Within NAFTA, Chapter 11 contains investment rules that operate in parallel with trade rules to regulate investors and foreign investment activities in host countries. Article 1114(1)

54 Treaty for the Promotion and Protection of Investments (Federal Republic of Germany/Pakistan) (adopted 25 November 1959) 28 UNTS 1963. See Giorgio Sacerdoti, 'Bilateral Treaties and Multilateral Instruments on Investment Protection' (1997) 269 *Recueil Des Cours* 255, 299.

55 Barnali Choudhury, 'Recapturing Public Power: Is Investment Arbitration's Engagement to the Public Interest Contributing to Democratic Deficit?' (2008) 41 *Vanderbilt Journal of Transnational Law* 775, 777.

56 *Compañía del Desarrollo de Santa Elena S.A. v. Republic of Costa Rica,* ICSID Case No ARB/96/1, Award (February 17, 2000) para 72.

57 The North American Free Trade Agreement (NAFTA) (adopted December 17, 1992, entered into force January 1, 1994), preamble.

provides: 'Nothing in this Chapter shall be construed to prevent a Party from adopting, maintaining or enforcing any measure otherwise consistent with this Chapter that it considers appropriate to ensure that investment activity is undertaken in a manner sensitive to environmental concerns'. The second paragraph of the same article recognizes that it is 'inappropriate to encourage investment by relaxing domestic health, safety or environmental measures'. Accordingly, a Party should not 'waive or otherwise derogate from, or offer to waive or otherwise derogate from, such measures as an encouragement for the establishment, acquisition, expansion or retention in its territory of an investment of an investor'.

Most of the complaints under Chapter 11 have concerned the requirement of non-discrimination, that each party treat an investor no less favorably than it treats a domestic investor 'in like circumstances'.[58] In these cases the NAFTA tribunals have stated that the phrase 'like circumstances' must take into account NAFTA's concern with the environment. A few matters have found direct conflict between investment activities and environmental protection. The *Metalclad* case, for example, arose from a complaint of alleged indirect expropriation because of government environmental regulation. The Tribunal agreed that Metalclad's investment in a hazardous waste facility was expropriated by the denial of a construction and operating permit contrary to Mexican law and the issuance of an 'Ecological Decree' declaring the site a nature reserve in order to preserve a rare cactus.[59] Similarly, in *Methanex v. USA*, the state argued that the claimant and local competitors could not be considered in 'like circumstances' because, *inter alia*, of the environmental impact of the respective activities, and the tribunal differentiated between methanol and ethanol producers in determining the proper comparison for the analysis, precisely because of their environmental impact.[60]

---

58 See *Pope and Talbot Inc. v. Government of Canada*, UNCITRAL, Award on the Merits of Phase 2 (Apr. 10, 2001) (*Pope and Talbot v Canada*) (imposition of fees by Canada on lumber exports to the US found non-discriminatory); *S.D. Myers, Inc. v. Government of Canada*, UNCITRAL, Partial Award (Nov. 13, 2000) (*S.D. Myers v. Canada*) (Canadian prohibition on export of PCB wastes to US found discriminatory); *In the Matter of Cross-border Trucking Services*, NAFTA Arbitral Panel Established Pursuant to Chapter XX, Final Report of the Panel (Feb. 6, 2001) (finding Mexican and US trucking companies to be in like circumstances and US ban on Mexican trucks to be unjustified).

59 *Metalclad Corporation v. The United Mexican States*, ICSID Case No ARB(AF)/97/1, Award (August 30, 2000). A Canadian Court reviewed the Tribunal's decision and agreed that there had been an expropriation, but only on the second assertion.

60 *Methanex Corporation v. United States of America*, UNCITRAL, Final Award of the Tribunal on Jurisdiction and Merits (August 3, 2005) (*Methanex v. United States*) paras 15–38, part IV, chapter B.

Other Chapter 11 cases have similarly alleged expropriation due to environmental regulations.[61]

Even beyond NAFTA, arbitral tribunals have been increasingly taking into account environmental considerations in interpretating national standards of treatment – such as non-discrimination or the protection against unlawful expropriation. In particular, tribunals have been increasingly accepting the respondents' use of environmental differentiation in defining the condition of 'in like circumstances' in non-discrimination disputes. In *Parkerings v. Lithuania*, for instance, Lithuania argued that the claimant's project and that of another foreign investor were not alike because the claimant's project had a higher impact on Vilnius' old town, which was included on the World Heritage List. The tribunal sided with Lithuania and held that environmental protection could indeed be a ground for the refusal of a project and that the two projects were not in 'like circumstances'.[62] In recent years, arbitral tribunals have also been confronted with the possibility that for the host state may bring environmental counterclaims against the foreign investor.[63]

Over time, the instrumental role of foreign investments in contributing to the sustainability agenda has become increasingly clear. The 2030 Agenda for Sustainable Development emphasizes the important role of foreign investment as a means to achieve several of the SDGs. The goals include, for instance, supporting 'accelerated investment in poverty eradication actions' (1.b), increasing investment 'in rural infrastructure, agricultural research and extension services, technology development and plant and livestock gene banks in order to enhance agricultural productive capacity in developing countries, in particular least developed countries' (2.a) and promoting 'investment in energy infrastructure and clean energy technology' (7.a) The critical role of foreign investment towards climate change mitigation has been also emphasized in the context of several Conferences of the Parties to the UNFCCC.[64] Along the same lines, the latest report of the IPCC acknowledged the important contribution of investment in low-carbon

---

61 See *Ethyl Corporation v. The Government of Canada*, UNCITRAL, Award on Jurisdiction (June 24, 1998); *S.D. Myers v Canada*, Partial Award; *Pope and Talbot v. Canada*, Interim Award (June 26, 2000); *Robert Azinian, Kenneth Davitian, & Ellen Baca v. The United Mexican States*, ICSID Case No ARB(AF)/97/2, Award (November 1, 1999); *Methanex v United States; Waste Management, Inc. v United Mexican States*, ICSID Case No ARB(AF)98/2, Award (April 30, 2004).

62 *Parkerings-Compagniet AS v. Republic of Lithuania*, ICSID Case No. ARB/05/8, Award (September 11, 2007), para 392.

63 See e.g. *Perenco Ecuador Ltd. v. Republic of Ecuador and Empresa Estatal Petróleos del Ecuador (Petroecuador)*, ICSID Case No ARB/08/6, Award (September 27, 2019).

64 See e.g. COP26 in Glasgow in 2021 and COP28 in Dubai in 2023.

technologies and infrastructure, which has been facilitated by appropriate policies and regulations.[65]

In recent years, IIAs have begun to incorporate several references to the environment (so-called 'greening' investment agreements). These references can be found in the preamble, in a stand-alone provision recognizing the host state's right to regulate, or even in environmental exceptions and carve-out, for instance in the provisions dealing with expropriation or non-discrimination. Annex 8-A to the EU-Canada Comprehensive Economic and Trade Agreement (CETA), for instance, clarifies that 'except in the rare circumstance when the impact of a measure or series of measures is so severe in light of its purpose that it appears manifestly excessive, non-discriminatory measures of a Party that are designed and applied to protect legitimate public welfare objectives, such as health, safety and the environment, *do not constitute indirect expropriations*'.[66] Moreover, because FTAs today generally feature a whole chapter devoted to 'environment' or 'sustainable development', tribunals are directly confronted with environmental norms. Even when such norms do not fall under their immediate jurisdiction, if they are part of the same agreement they have a certain weight in the tribunal's decision. A particularly good example is provided by the interpretation of the minimum standard of treatment by the tribunal in *Al Tamimi v. Oman*, an investment dispute raised under the US-Oman FTA.[67] Chapter 17 of the FTA, entitled 'Environment' does not fall directly within the tribunal's jurisdiction.[68] Nevertheless, the tribunal gave substantial weight to this chapter in interpreting the content of the minimum standard of treatment, as it 'provides further relevant context' in which the

65 IPCC, *Climate Change 2022. Mitigation of Climate Change. Summary for Policymakers* (2002) paras. B.5 and E.4.3.

66 EU-Canada Comprehensive Economic and Trade Agreement (CETA) (2016), Annex 8-A. See Pierre-Olivier Savoie, 'Reservations, Corporate Social Responsibility and Other Mechanisms in Support of Sustainable Development in Canada's Model Foreign Investment Promotion and Protection Agreement', in Freya Baetens (ed.), *Investment Law within International Law* (Cambridge University Press 2013) 234. See also the ASEAN-Australia-New Zealand FTA (Annex on Expropriation and Compensation) Art. 4; COMESA Art 20(8); Canada-Colombia FTA, Annex 811.

67 *Adel A Hamadi Al Tamimi v. Sultanate of Oman*, ICSID Case No. ARB/11/33, Award (November 3, 2015) (*Al Tamimi v. Oman*). See Jorge E Viñuales, 'Foreign Investment and the Environment in International Law: The Current State of Play' C-EENRG Working Papers (2016–1).

68 *Al Tamimi v. Oman*, para 388. According to Article 17.8.5, which provides for a consultation mechanism, '[n]either Party may have recourse to dispute settlement under this Agreement for any matter arising under any provision of this Chapter …'

provisions of the investment chapter must be interpreted.[69] In the exact words of the tribunal, '… the very existence of Chapter 17 exemplifies the importance attached by the US and Oman to the enforcement of their respective environmental laws. … When it comes to determining any breach of the minimum standard of treatment under Article 10.5, the Tribunal must be guided by the forceful defense of environmental regulation and protection provided in the express language of the Treaty'.[70]

Traditionally, IIAs do not provide for any obligations for foreign investors. However, the importance of holding corporations accountable for their impact on the environment has been increasingly debated. The Investment Policy Framework for Sustainable Development, released by UNCTAD in 2015, while primarily addressing the role of states in guiding foreign investments towards sustainable development objectives, also acknowledges the potential to harmonize state commitments with investor obligations as part of promoting responsible investment practices.[71] As of today, there are very few examples of IIAs imposing obligations directly on the investor.

5 Extraterritorial Application of National Laws

With increasing awareness of environmental interdependence, states may enact national laws that are intended to promote environmental protection in other countries, promote environmental protection of the global commons, or stimulate the adoption of multilateral agreements by seeking to influence a foreign government to refrain from acting or to compel it to act, either in its domestic policies or towards third states. As reflected in Principle 12 of the Rio Declaration, there is intense debate over unilateral measures applied extraterritorially to raise or enforce environmental standards. States often enact trade restrictions to ensure that domestic environmental goals, such as consumer safety, are attained. A state's ban on the sale of locally-produced products containing a hazardous substance will be ineffective if the same or similar goods can be imported. In other circumstances, local laws may seek to induce or coerce another country to change or better enforce its own national environmental laws or policies. Finally, domestic laws may seek to contribute to international aims such as preservation of the global climate.

---

69 ibid para. 388.

70 ibid para. 389.

71 UNCTAD, *Investment Policy Framework for Sustainable Development* (2015) 77.

Generally, a state has authority to apply its laws with respect to: (1) conduct that takes place within its territory; (2) the status of persons or things within its territory; (3) conduct outside its territory that has a substantial effect within its territory; (4) activities of its nationals both outside and inside its territory; and (5) certain conduct outside its territory by persons other than nationals that is directed against the security of the state. Some environmental agreements require that domestic laws apply to the full range of a state's jurisdiction, e.g. the Biodiversity Convention.[72] Many states now apply all or some of their environmental laws broadly to activities of their nationals wherever they take place.

The US National Environmental Protection Act (NEPA) requires an environmental impact assessment when extraterritorial actions have direct or indirect impacts in the United States.[73] When the environmental impact occurs *only* in foreign countries, NEPA does not apply. However, US Executive Order 12114, signed in January 1979, requires analysis of environmental impacts of any major federal action significantly affecting the environment of the global commons or the environment of a foreign nation, or to major actions outside the United States which significantly affect protected natural or ecological resources of global importance. Exceptions are provided for, *inter alia*, armed conflicts, intelligence activities, arms transfers, disaster and emergency relief action.

Another US domestic law seeking to enhance environmental protection is the so-called 'Pelosi Amendment'.[74] It requires the United States Executive Director for each multilateral development bank (including the World Bank), to refrain from voting in favor of any proposed action by the Bank that would have a significant effect on the human environment unless an environmental assessment has been prepared and circulated to the Bank and other interested organizations at least 120 days before the date of the vote. The assessment analyzing the environmental impacts of the proposed action and its alternatives can be prepared by the borrowing country or the lending institution and must be made available to the board of directors of the institution. Absent compelling circumstances, the assessment must also be made available to the Bank, affected groups and local non-governmental organizations. In practice,

---

72 Article 4 provides that the jurisdictional scope of the Convention applies, in relation to each contracting party, to areas within the limits of national jurisdiction, i.e. land and maritime zones, and to processes and activities carried out under its jurisdiction or control, whether within or beyond the limits of its national jurisdiction.

73 See *Sierra Club v. Adams*, 578 F.2d 389 (DC Cir 1978).

74 22 USCA § 262m-7.

the Pelosi Amendment extends NEPA's broad coverage to multilateral development bank operations.

In a related development, the US Export-Import Bank, a sixty-year-old independent agency that finances overseas sales of US goods and services, has incorporated environmental considerations into its lending policies. The Bank guarantees loans for US exporters and repayment of loans by foreign purchasers of US goods and services and often provides credit for risks commercial banks will not accept. In 1995, as required by the statute, the Bank adopted a detailed set of Environmental Guidelines to consider the environmental consequences of proposed transactions prior to approving export finance.[75] Applicants are required to submit for evaluation information about the project's environmental impacts. The Guidelines establish standards for air quality, water quality, waste management and noise for projects in specific industry sectors (e.g., mining, pulp and paper, energy). Certain transactions that do not raise significant environmental issues are exempt from review procedures. Projects that do not meet all the environmental guidelines are reviewed on a case-by-case basis by the Bank's Board of Directors, taking into account mitigating effects and circumstances. Financing may be conditioned on the implementation of mitigating measures.

The US Congress also directed the United States Overseas Investment Corporation (OPIC) to take account of the environmental effects of projects in determining whether to provide insurance, financing, or reinsurance for a development project. OPIC provides insurance for American investments in new ventures and expansions of existing enterprises, including protection against limits on repatriation of local currency, expropriation, and political violence. Congress has directed OPIC 'to the maximum degree possible', consistent with its development purposes, to refuse to 'insure, reinsure, guarantee or finance any investment in connection with a project which the Corporation determines will pose an unreasonable or major environmental, health, or safety hazard, or will result in the significant degradation of national parks or similar protected areas'.[76] OPIC screens all investment requests to determine whether it meets the environmental standards and major projects will require preparation of an environmental impact assessment.

Other national measures are directed specifically at international trade, including the EC enforcement of CITES trade bans, Austria's brief effort to regulate trade in tropical hardwoods, and the US restrictions on dolphin-unsafe

75 12 USC §635i-5; Export-Import Bank of the United States Environmental Procedures and Guidelines, effective February 1, 1995.

76 22 USCA § 2191(n).

tuna. Agenda 21, based almost entirely on earlier work at UNCTAD, calls for reversing unilateral trade barriers that restrict access to markets, as well as reducing external debt. It insists upon improved access for exports of developing countries and an open, non-discriminatory and equitable multilateral trading system. It provides that particular states should avoid the use of trade restrictions or distortions to offset differences in cost arising from differences in environmental standards and regulations, and should ensure that environmental regulations or standards do not constitute a means of arbitrary or unjustifiable discrimination or disguised restriction on trade. Even when based upon the required international consensus, trade measures necessary to render effective environmental objectives should be non-discriminatory and no more trade-restrictive than necessary to achieve the objectives. Transparency and notification are required, as well as public input in the formation, negotiation and implementation of trade policies. Although setting out general guidelines, the difficult issues involved in reconciling free trade and environmental protection were not settled at Rio nor have they been resolved by later developments.

Recently, in particular in the context of countries' efforts to contribute to climate change mitigation, a number of trade measures have been adopted, which can be perceived as imposing a country's environmental preferences on trading partners. A notable example is the Carbon Border Adjustment Mechanism (CBAM), which is a policy proposed by the EU to address carbon leakage and ensure that imports into the EU are subject to environmental standards comparable to those imposed on EU-based producers. Under CBAM, certain imported goods would be subject to a carbon price equivalent to the cost of carbon emissions associated with their production, based on the EU's carbon pricing system. This mechanism aims to prevent carbon leakage, where industries relocate production to countries with less stringent environmental regulations, and to incentivize global partners to adopt similar climate policies.

6 Trade and the Environment

International trade law is dominated by the desire to eliminate protectionism and promote free trade. The theory underpinning this system is that free trade and investment can increase consumer choice, reduce the expense of manufacturing consumer goods, thus lowering the price of products and producing economies of scale resulting in potentially higher returns on investment for producers in goods and services. In addition, advocates of globalization claim that technological advances are rapidly diffused, with social progress stimulated due to the sharing of ideas and policies, leading to an enhanced prospect of international harmony and peace.[77] Sceptics of the open market express doubts that free trade will lead to environmental protection, based on the conviction that the economic/financial system today operates with an overwhelming reliance on business decisions driven by short-term financial gains, without regard to social costs, unless the latter are imposed through regulation.

The goal of free trade and that of environmental protection may collide, first, because national environmental laws increase production costs for domestic industries. States may seek to avoid the competitive disadvantage that would result for domestic companies if they were forced to implement expensive environmental protection measures. Many fear a race to the bottom in environmental standard setting if the free market approach dominates. This was the original basis for European Community regional action. Without harmonized regional or global norms, domestic countervailing action may be sought against imports not bearing the burden of environmental costs.

Second, states may impose trade restrictions to enforce compliance with international environmental agreements. International environmental treaties have used quantitative restrictions at least since the 1940 Convention on Nature Protection and Wildlife Preservation in the Western Hemisphere. Agreements for the protection of wildlife typically use restrictions on export or import between parties based on a permit system. The Convention on International Trade in Endangered Species of Fauna and Flora (CITES) and the Basel Convention on the Control of Transboundary Movements of Hazardous Wastes and Their Disposal address trade issues directly and as the primary means to achieve the objectives of the agreements.

The Montreal Protocol on Substances that Deplete the Ozone Layer was the first global environmental agreement containing trade restrictions as a subsidiary but necessary measure. The Protocol addresses trade as part of the effort to ensure that non-parties do not benefit from the advantages of the Protocol without accepting its obligations. Its provisions also limit the possibility that parties can circumvent their obligations by ensuring that the production of controlled substances cannot be transferred to the territory of non-parties.[78]

The regulation of trade and the environment began separately, with different aims, but they have increasingly converged, even collided. Free traders fear that environmental regulations will become pretexts to close markets. Environmentalists fear that free trade will eliminate or restrict environmental protection. Both international and unilateral measures have been taken to try and reconcile the differences. Unilaterally, in November 1999, US President

---

77 Cordell Hull, *The Memoirs of Cordell Hull* (Macmillan 1948) 81.

78 See the GATT Secretariat Note of September 18, 1991, Doc L/6899.

Clinton announced Executive Order 13141, requiring the Office of the United States Trade Representative (USTR) and the Council on Environmental Quality within the White House to carry out environmental reviews of all international trade negotiations. The aim was to identify environmental threats and opportunities posed by trade arrangements.

Over the years, and in particular with the introduction of the concept of sustainable development, the relationship between trade and the environment – and between international trade law and international environmental law – has increasingly become more synergetic and mutually supportive. Principle 12 of the Rio Declaration states that 'States should cooperate to promote a supportive and open international economic system that would lead to economic growth and sustainable development in all countries, to better address the problems of environmental degradation'. The idea that trade and trade policies can contribute positively to the sustainable development agenda has been reiterated several times over the years. Agenda 2030, for instance, emphasizes the critical role that trade can play in delivering many of the SDGs. The following sections describe the evolution of the relationship between environment and trade both at the multilateral and at the regional level.

6.1 *GATT/WTO*

6.1.1 The GATT Years

The General Agreement on Tariffs and Trade (GATT)[79] of 1947 provides the legal framework for trade and the limited use of trade restrictions. The GATT was intended to be the normative framework for an international trade organization, a goal that was only achieved in 1994 with the creation of the World Trade Organization (WTO).

The GATT generally accepts customs duties and other charges applied in a non-discriminatory fashion, but Article III requires that imported products be treated no less favorably than 'like' products of national origin with respect to all 'regulations and requirements affecting the internal sale' of such products. Thus, regulations on product safety or quality, such as auto emission standards, applied neutrally to domestic and imported products is permissible under the GATT.

Article XIII requires that import or export restrictions be non-discriminatory. It provides that no prohibition or restriction shall be applied by any contracting party on the importation of any product from the territory of any other contracting party or on the exportation of any product destined for the

79 General Agreement on Tariffs and Trade (GATT) (October 30, 1947) 55 UNTS 194.

territory of any contracting party, unless the importation of the like product of all third countries or the exportation of the product to all third countries is similarly prohibited or restricted. Article XI of the GATT prohibits quantitative restrictions (quotas or bans) on imports and exports. There are no rules regarding trade restrictions on products that are deemed environmentally harmful. Thus, massive importation of products that have a low price due to cheap and highly polluting production methods is not considered dumping by the GATT and therefore may not be countered by countervailing duties, nor may the imports be limited. Further, environmental taxes for goods in transit, such as road use fees to clean-up increased air pollution, may run afoul of GATT Article V(3) which guarantees freedom of transit.

A major issue in many trade disputes is the classification of a state's action as a regulation affecting 'processes and production methods' or PPMs (and in particular non-product-related PPMs or NPR-PPMs) rather than the physical attributes of the traded product. It has been held that PPM measures do not fall under GATT Article III governing the domestic sale of a product, but under Article XI, quantitative restrictions on importation. As such, they violate GATT unless the measure can fall within an exception in Article XX, discussed below. While some commentators argue that Article III should apply,[80] others disagree and contend that the relevant issue is trade discrimination.[81] The WTO has continued to analyze PPMs under Article XI.

PPMs are important to environmental protection, as recognized by the OECD.[82] PPM regulations set standards on pollution emissions or manufacturing techniques and substances used in making product (e.g. Chlorofluorocarbons or CFCs). Product regulations, in contrast, concern the design, characteristics, and uses of particular products. GATT grants governments broad discretion to set product standards and even ban their sale. The characteristics of fuel

80 See Robert Howse and Donald Regan, 'The Product/Process Distinction An Illusory Basis for Disciplining 'Unilateralism' in Trade Policy' (2000) 11 *European Journal of International* Law 249 (arguing that PPM measures are regulations affecting the internal sale of products).

81 David M. Driesen, 'What is Free Trade?: The Real Issue Lurking Behind the Trade and Environment Debate' (2001) 41 *Vanderbilt Journal of International Law* 279; Dale Arthur Oesterle, 'The WTO Reaches Out to the Environmentalists: Is It Too Little, Too Late?' (1999) *Colorado Journal of International Environmental Law & Policy* 1, 19.

82 OECD, *Processes and Production Methods (PPMs): Conceptual Framework and Considerations on Use of PPM-based Trade Measures*, OECD/GD (97) 137 (11 August 1997). See also Richard Parker, 'The Use and Abuse of Trade Leverage to Protect the Global Commons: What We can Learn from the Tuna-Dolphin Conflict' (1999) 12 *Georgetown International Environmental Law Review* 1 (demonstrating the utility of trade measures for environmental protection).

economy of automobiles, for example, is accepted as a legitimate product standard, so long as it is non-discriminatory in application.[83] Access restrictions to limited resources, such as fish, also may be permitted provided foreign nationals are not treated unfairly.[84] PPM trade measures may concern transboundary pollution; management of transboundary living resources; global environmental concerns, like greenhouse gases; or conditions in the affected country or countries. The fourth is the most likely to fail under GATT, because it attempts to impose environmental laws extraterritorially on foreign sovereigns without an international dimension to the issue.

Many common PPMs seek to enforce resource conservation agreements or alleviate global problems like the ozone layer or climate. Given their beneficial aim, but recognizing their harmful impacts on trade, PPM measures have been at the heart of some of the most controversial trade/environment disputes, in particular as far as the application of the General Exceptions contained in GATT Article XX are concerned. An impermissible trade restriction under the GATT may still be justified if it falls within the exception allowing measures 'necessary' to protect human, animal or plant life or health (Article. XX(b)) or measures relating to the conservation of exhaustible natural resources if such measures are made effective in conjunction with restrictions on domestic production or consumption (Article XX(g)). Before the establishment of the WTO, GATT Panels have been reluctant to apply Article XX to environmental measures, in particular considering that the article itself had not been drafted with the environment in mind.[85]

6.1.2 The Establishment of the WTO

The multilateral trading system fundamentally changed in 1994 with the adoption of the Marrakech Agreement establishing the World Trade Organization.[86]

83 The issue most often debated is whether products are 'like' products which must be treated identically. The Report of the Appellate Body in the case involving France's regulations severely limiting the use of certain kinds of asbestos, found that the dangers associated with the particular type of asbestos made it a different product than less hazardous forms of the product or competing materials. See Report of the Appellate Body, *European Communities. – Measures Affecting Asbestos and Asbestos-Containing Products*, WT/DS135/AB/R (March 12, 2001) (*EC-Asbestos*), para. 192.

84 See Sanford E. Gaines, 'Process and Production Methods: How to Produce Sound Policy for Environmental PPM-Based Trade Measures?' (2002) 27 *Columbia Journal of Environmental Law* 383, 393.

85 See e.g. Report of the GATT Panel, *United States – Restrictions on Imports of Tuna*, DS21/R39S/155 (September 3, 1991) (*US – Tuna*).

86 Marrakesh Agreement Establishing the World Trade Organization (WTO Agreement) (April 14, 1994) 1867 U.N.T.S. 187.

Environmental concerns appear in the Preamble where the parties recognize that their relations should be conducted so as to allow 'for the optimal use of the world's resources in accordance with the objective of sustainable development, seeking both to protect and preserve the environment and to enhance the means for doing so in a manner consistent with their respective needs and concerns at different levels of economic development'.

While the text of the GATT was not amended in 1994 to introduce environment-specific provisions, the Uruguay Round led to a considerable expansion of the multilateral rules governing international trade, with the adoption of several new agreements as part of the so-called 'single undertaking'. Some of these agreements contain provisions that are relevant for the environment. The Agreement on Trade-Related Aspects of Intellectual Property Rights (TRIPS), for instance, states that 'Members may, in formulating or amending their laws and regulations, adopt measures necessary to protect human health and nutrition, and to promote the public interest in sectors of vital importance in their socio-economic and technological development, provided that such measures are consistent with the provisions of the Agreement'.[87] They also may exclude from patentability those inventions whose commercial exploitation it is necessary to prevent in order to 'protect *ordre public*, or morality, including the protection of human, animal or plant life or health or to avoid serious prejudice to the environment, provided that such exclusion is not made merely because the exploitation is prohibited by their law'.[88] Members also may exclude from patentability 'plants and animals other than micro-organisms and biological processes for the production of plants and animals other than non-biological and microbiological processes'.[89]

The Agreement on Technical Barriers to Trade (TBT) regulates technical regulations, standards, and conformity assessment procedures applied to products. Many countries use technical regulations and standards to establish environmental requirements for products, including for instance criteria related to energy efficiency, emissions levels, recyclability, and other environmental attributes. The primary objective of the TBT Agreement is to ensure that such measures, which may also include packaging and labeling schemes, do not create unnecessary obstacles to international trade. To this end, technical regulations must not be 'more trade-restrictive than necessary to fulfil a

87 Agreement on Trade-Related Aspects of Intellectual Property Rights (TRIPS Agreement) (April 15, 1994) Marrakesh Agreement Establishing the World Trade Organization, Annex 1C, Art. 8.

88 ibid Art. 27(2).

89 ibid Art. 27(3)(b).

legitimate objective, taking into account the risks non-fulfilment would create'.[90] These 'legitimate objectives' include 'the protection of human health or safety, animal or plant life or health, or the *environment*' and, in assessing the risks for health or the environment, the relevant factors include 'available scientific and technical information, related processing technology or intended end-uses of products', suggesting that both the product characteristics and it production process are relevant.[91]

The WTO Sanitary and Phytosanitary Agreement (SPS) allows countries to apply sanitary and phytosanitary measures to ensure that plants and animals are protected from pests and diseases and that food is safe for consumers. By their nature they act to restrict trade. The purpose of the Agreement is not to limit the right of states to set their own levels of health protection, but to require transparent decision-making to avoid disguised barriers to trade. The Agreement encourages the harmonization of sanitary and phytosanitary measures through the adoption of international standards such as those provided by the Codex Alimentarius Commission. Countries may adopt higher standards provided they are based on a risk assessment consistent with the requirements of the SPS Agreement. To be consistent, it must be applied only to the extent necessary to protect human, animal or plant life or health, be based on scientific principles, and not be maintained without sufficient scientific evidence. A measure also must not arbitrarily or unjustifiably discriminate between WTO Members or constitute a disguised restriction on international trade. Measures should be based on an appropriate risk assessment process, taking into account available scientific evidence as well as relevant economic, ecological and environmental conditions. Finally, any measure which a party does impose should not be more trade restrictive than required to achieve the appropriate level of sanitary or phytosanitary protection.[92]

The Declaration on the Contribution of the Multilateral Trading Order to Achieving Greater Coherence in Global Economic Policymaking proclaims that successful cooperation in each area of economic policy should contribute towards the expansion of trade, sustainable growth and development. Two of the four Declarations adopted at Marrakech had a particular importance for the environment. The Decision on Trade in Services and the Environment acknowledged that measures necessary to protect the environment may

---

90 Agreement on Technical Barriers to Trade (TBT Agreement) (April 15, 1994) 1868 UNTS 120, Art. 2.2.

91 ibid.

92 Agreement on the Application of Sanitary and Phytosanitary Measures (SPS Agreement) (April 15, 1994) 1867 UNTS 493, Arts. 3, 5.

conflict with the provisions of the General Agreement on Trade in Services, but added that because such measures typically have as their objective the protection of human, animal or plant life or health 'it is not clear that there is a need to provide for more than is contained in Article XIV(b)'.

The most important text concerning the environment was the Decision of the Ministers on Trade and Environment. It referred to the relevant paragraph of the preamble of the Agreement establishing the WTO and to other texts adopted at the Conference, but also to the Rio Declaration, to Agenda 21, and to its follow-up in GATT. It declared that there should not be, nor need be, any policy contradiction between the trading system as it should result from the new structures and rules on one hand, and the protection of the environment and the promotion of sustainable development on the other hand. In deciding that the policies in the two fields should be coordinated, the Decision directed the General Council of WTO to establish a Committee on Trade and Environment (CTE) at its first meeting. The terms of reference of the Committee included identification of the relationship between trade measures and environmental measures, enhancement of the positive interaction between trade and environmental measures for the promotion of sustainable development, avoidance of protectionist measures, and the surveillance of trade measures used for environmental purposes as well as environmental measures which have significant trade effects. A list of issues for the Committee to address initially was included, particularly the relationship between the multilateral trading system and trade measures and policies for environmental purposes. The environmental measures that had to be scrutinized were: charges and taxes, requirements relating to products such as standards and technical regulations, packaging, labeling and recycling, exports of domestically prohibited goods, and those with effects on market access. The problem of the relationship between the dispute settlement mechanisms provided for in the multilateral trading system on the one hand and in environmental treaties on the other hand was also mentioned.

6.1.3 Integrating Trade and the Environment in GATT/WTO Jurisprudence

Throughout its history, the GATT and now the WTO have faced questions about reconciling the demands of free trade with concerns for environmental protection. Several cases have been brought against states to challenge their environmental regulations as they affect trade. The GATT exceptions to free trade contained in Article XX cover only human or animal health and the conservation of exhaustible natural resources. They do not mention protection of non-living environmental sectors such as water or air or renewable resources.

The case law has established several criteria for permissible trade-related environmental measures.

As explained by the Appellate Body in *US-Gasoline*, the justification of an otherwise GATT-inconsistent measure requires a two-tiered test: the measure must not only fall within the specific exceptions outlined in paragraphs (a) to (j) of Article XX, but it must also meet the requirements outlined in the *chapeau*. When it comes to measures adopted for environmental reasons, two paragraphs have proven especially relevant: (b) and (g). A state seeking to justify a trade restriction under Article XX(b) (protection of human, animal or plant life or health) needs to demonstrate that: (1) the substance of the policy of the measure in question is the protection of human, animal, or plant life or health; and (2) the measure for which the exception is being invoked is necessary to protect that aim. One GATT panel found that Art. XX(b) can only be used for a measure that is necessary and that 'entails the least degree of inconsistency with other GATT provisions'.[93] The necessity requirement is the primary problem because it has been interpreted to require adoption of the measure least inconsistent with free trade. The approach appears to misread the exception which requires only that the measure be necessary to protect the resource, not that the trade restriction is necessary. As far as the exception contained in Art. XX(g) (protection of exhaustible natural resources) is concerned, sea turtles and clean air have been held to be exhaustible natural resources. The WTO Appellate Body in the *US-Shrimps* case concluded that endangered animal species are capable of falling within this category[94] while in *US-Gasoline*[95] that clean air is an exhaustible natural resource within the meaning of Article XX(g). The legality of environmental measures that restrict trade has been tested by asking (1) whether the law and policy relate to the conservation of exhaustible natural resources; and (2) whether the measures are made effective in conjunction with restrictions on domestic production or consumption. The second step of the analysis under Article XX of the GATT requires to demonstrate that the measure (that is provisionally justified by falling under one of the paragraphs of the provision) respects the conditions set out in the *chapeau* and which relate to the way in which the measure is implemented. In fact, according to the *chapeau*, the measure should not be 'applied in a manner

---

93 Report of the GATT Panel, *United States – Section 337 of the Tariff Act of 1930*, BISD 36th Supp 345 (adopted November 7, 1989), para. 5.26.

94 Report of the Appellate Body, *United States – Import Prohibition of Certain Shrimp and Shrimp Products*, WT/DS58/ABR (October 12, 1998) (*US – Shrimp*).

95 Report of the Appellate Body, *United States – Standards for Reformulated and Conventional Gasoline*, WT/DS2/AB/R (April 29, 1996) (*US – Gasoline*).

which would constitute a means of arbitrary or unjustifiable discrimination between countries where the same conditions prevail, or a disguised restriction on international trade'.

The first trade/environment conflict was the GATT *tuna/dolphin* case, which was first heard after a Mexican complaint concerning the US Marine Mammals Act. The Act forbid importation of tuna caught with nets which injured and killed dolphins in the process. The objective of the US law was the protection of cetaceans, in particularly dolphins, from indiscriminate forms of fishing which were leading to large losses of marine mammal life without regard to the place of the fishing. The action was not pursuant to treaty, but involved unilateral sanctions imposed by the US.

The panel held that the import ban imposed on Mexico violated Article XI of the GATT and was not a permissible exception under Article XX. In particular, the panel refused to accept process standards related to products as exceptions under Article XX(b) and (g) because then

> each contracting party could unilaterally determine the life or health protection policies from which other contracting parties could not deviate without jeopardizing their rights under the General Agreement. The General Agreement would then no longer constitute a multilateral framework for trade among all contracting parties but would provide legal security only in respect of trade between a limited number of contracting parties with identical internal regulations.[96]

The panel also declared that the exceptions cannot be used for extraterritorial measures, i.e. protection of dolphin outside the jurisdictional limits of the state taking the measure.[97] The panel added that the appropriate way to protect such resources is through multilateral negotiation of an environmental agreement, not through unilateral measures threatening market access; however, it is not clear that the Panel would approve measures taken pursuant to CITES against a non-party state. The GATT Council was not asked to adopt the panel report, because Mexico and the United States negotiated an environmental agreement to ensure proper dolphin protection.

In Tuna II, a 1994 case brought by the European Union against the US, the panel stated that in the ordinary meaning of 'necessary', a member could not

96 *US – Tuna*, para. 5.27.

97 This could affect the implementation of the Montreal Protocol. The import prohibitions on chlorofluorocarbons violate GATT requirements if the exporting country is not a party to the Montreal Protocol.

justify a GATT-inconsistent measure if an alternative GATT-consistent measure were available that the member could reasonably be expected to employ. Significantly, *Tuna II* did accept the permissibility of extraterritorial laws affecting the international commons and the US policy to conserve dolphins in the eastern tropical Pacific Ocean was deemed within the range of policies covered by GATT Article XX(g).

In the *US-Gasoline* case, the plaintiff states argued against the United States that a measure could only be 'related to' or 'primarily aimed at' conservation if the measure was both primarily intended to achieve a conservation goal and had a positive conservation effect. The panel found no direct connection between less favorable treatment of imported gasoline that was chemically identical to domestic gasoline and the US objective of improving domestic air quality and thus concluded that the measure was not primarily aimed at the conservation of natural resources. The Appellate Body disagreed with this conclusion, finding that it was the purpose of the measure as a whole that had to be tested.

An important year for the trade/environment nexus was 1998, when the Appellate Body its report in the landmark *US-Shrimp* case. The dispute involved once again a US trade restriction, this time designed to protect endangered sea turtles. As discussed in Chapter 8, all seven species of sea turtles are listed in Appendix I of CITES and on the International Union for Conservation of Nature (IUCN) Red List.[98] The challenged measure was intended to counter the costs for US shrimp trawlers of complying with US environmental regulations and foreign shrimp trawlers who were not. To export shrimp to the US, as of May 1996, all countries in whose waters shrimps and sea turtles coexisted had to be certified by the US State Department as having and enforcing legislation requiring turtle excluder devices on commercial shrimp trawlers. This case was brought to the WTO by India, Malaysia, Pakistan and Thailand, who objected to the measure as being extra-territorial and unilateral.[99] Sixteen countries and the EU joined as third parties. On April 6 a panel ruled that the US had violated its obligations under the GATT and on July 23, 1998, the US appealed.

98 All of the parties to the dispute are signatories to CITES. In the US, CITES is implemented by the Endangered Species Act of 1973, Public Law No. 93–205, 87 Stat. 884 (codified as amended at 16 USC sec 1531–1543 (1988). The Sea Turtle Conservation Act, or Section 609 of Public Law 101–162, requires the US to negotiate with countries whose fleets appear to threaten sea turtle populations after which it may restrict the importation of shrimp harvested with commercial fishing technology which may adversely affect sea turtles.

99 *US – Shrimp*.

The Appellate Body, on October 12, 1998, upheld the decision against the United States, but overturned several aspects of the Panel's decision.[100] Most importantly, the Appellate Body agreed with the US that it had a right to adopt its restrictions for environmental purposes. In looking at the contemporary context, it affirmed that the term 'exhaustible natural resources' is not static in its content but is rather 'by definition, evolutionary'.[101] The words 'must be read … in the light of contemporary concerns of the community of nations about the protection and conservation of the environment'.[102] The Appellate Body relied on a several environmental principles and multilateral environmental agreements (MEAs) to give such an evolutionary interpretation of the phrase 'exhaustible natural resources' and confirming its application to sea turtles. The US failed, however, to demonstrate that the ban had been imposed in a nondiscriminatory manner. The ruling concluded that the measure did not meet the conditions of the *chapeau* of GATT Article XX and set down a number of criteria to ensure that environmental trade measures do not discriminate between WTO members.[103]

On October 23, 2000, Malaysia invoked Article 21.5 of the Dispute Settlement Understanding (DSU) to assert US non-compliance with the decision in the *US-Shrimp* case and requested the Dispute Settlement Body (DSB) to decide whether the US had complied with the recommendations and rulings of the DSB's earlier decision adopting the reports of the original panel and the Appellate Body. The DSB had recommended that the US bring its import prohibition into conformity with its obligations under the WTO. At the DSB meeting held October 23, 2000, Malaysia said it was not satisfied with US compliance. The matter went back to the original panel.[104] Since the report of the Appellate Body was published in 1998, the US had issued Revised Guidelines for the Implementation of Section 609 of Public Law 101–162 Relating to the

---

100 ibid.

101 ibid paras. 129 and 130.

102 ibid para. 129.

103 In several cases involving China, the government argued that its restrictions on the export of certain mineral resources were also for the purpose of conserving exhaustible natural resources. The panel and Appellate Body disapproved of the measures. See Report of the Panel, *China – Measures related to the Exportation of Various Raw Materials*, WT/DS394, 395, 398/R (July 5, 2011); Report of the Appellate Body, WT/DS394, 395, 398/AB/R (January 30, 2012) (*China – Raw Materials*). Report of the Panel, *China – Measures related to the Exportation of Rare Earths, Tungsten, and Molybdenum*, WT/DS431, 432, 433/R (March 26, 2014); Report of the Appellate Body, WT/DS431, 432, 433/AB/R (August 7, 2014) (*China – Rare Earths*).

104 Report of the Panel, *United States – Import Prohibition of Certain Shrimp and Shrimp Products. Recourse to Article 21.5 by Malaysia*, WT/DS58/RW (June 15, 2001).

Protection of Sea Turtles in Shrimp Trawl Fishing Operations, which did not prohibit imports of shrimp that came from harvesting nations 'certified' by the US. The main change was that the legislation now allowed certification of governments whose harvesting programs requires commercial shrimp trawlers to have devices that are 'comparable in effectiveness' to those used in the US and to have a credible enforcement program that includes monitoring for compliance. In other words, the Revised Guidelines allowed countries to apply for certification even if they do not require Turtle Excluder Devices (TEDS), provided they had a comparably effective regulatory program to protect sea turtles. A nation may also be certified if its shrimp fishing environment does not pose a threat of incidental capture of sea turtles because (1) the relevant species of sea turtles do not occur in waters subject to that country's jurisdiction; (2) shrimp is harvested in that country's waters exclusively by means that do not pose a threat to sea turtles, such as by artisanal means; or commercial shrimp trawling operations take place exclusively in waters in which sea turtles do not occur. The rigid application of the ban was one of the reasons why the Appellate Body, in its 1998 ruling, had found that the US measure did not meet the conditions of the *chapeau* of Article XX. Here, the Appellate Body noted that 'comparable in effectiveness' is less rigid than 'essentially the same' and found this flexibility sufficient to avoid the measure being arbitrary or unjustifiable discrimination.

Moreover, according to the Appellate Body, in the first *US-Shrimp* case, the US was found to not have complied with the conditions of the *chapeau* of Article XX of the GATT also because it treated WTO members differently, cooperating with Caribbean and Western Atlantic States to conclude an agreement, while failing to negotiate with other states. The differential treatment was held 'plainly discriminatory'. Yet, while a multilateral approach 'is strongly preferred ... it is one thing to *prefer* a multilateral approach in the application of a measure that is provisionally justified under one of the subparagraphs of Article XX of the GATT 1994; it is another to require the *conclusion* of a multilateral agreement as a condition of avoiding "arbitrary or unjustifiable discrimination" under the chapeau of Article XX. We see, in this case no such requirement'.[105] As the US has attempted, after the first *US-Shrimp* ruling, to cooperate with the four complaining countries, the Appellate Body concluded that the conditions of the *chapeau* of GATT Article XX had been met.

105 Report of the Appellate Body, *United States – Import Prohibition of Certain Shrimp and Shrimp Products. Recourse to Article 21.5 by Malaysia*, WT/DS58/AB/RW (October 22, 2001), para. 124.

Over the years, a number of environmental disputes brought to the WTO have allowed the panel and Appellate Body to clarify the content and scope of both the paragraphs and the *chapeau* of Article XX of the GATT. The Appellate Body Report in *Brazil-Tyres* explicitly referenced measures taken to address environmental issues – specifically climate change and global warming. It concluded that even if a measure's contribution to these objectives is not immediately evident, it can still be justified under Article XX(b) by demonstrating its potential to significantly contribute to achieving its goal.[106] This perspective acknowledges that addressing certain complex public health or environmental problems may require a comprehensive policy involving multiple interacting measures, and that evaluating the results of actions may require time.[107] In *EC-Asbestos*, both the panel and the Appellate Body discussed the application of GATT Article XX(b) to a French ban on asbestos and asbestos-containing products. They started with the premise that countries have the freedom to determine their own level of protection and concluded that assessing the 'necessity' of the ban should be based on the level of protection chosen by France.[108] A noteworthy development in WTO trade and environment jurisprudence was the recognition, in *EC-Seals*, of public morals concerns as a potential justification for imposing trade restrictions related to environmental protection, opening the door the use of Article XX(a) of the GATT to justify trade-restrictive measures to protect wildlife.[109]

In addition to GATT Article XX jurisprudence, the Appellate Body has interpreted and refined the understanding of various provisions of the TBT Agreement and the SPS Agreement, which are crucial for trade-related climate and environmental measures. In its interpretations, the Appellate Body has often shown deference to WTO Members implementing allegedly trade-restrictive measures, particularly regarding the legitimacy of the objective pursued and the level of environmental protection intended to be ensured. For example, in *EC-Hormones*, it emphasized the importance of a Member's right to determine its own appropriate level of sanitary protection, as articulated in the sixth preambular paragraph of the SPS Agreement. Similarly, in *US-Tuna II*, a dispute brought by Mexico against the United States under the TBT Agreement, the Appellate Body showed a deferential attitude toward the WTO member adopting the technical regulation when it comes to reviewing the legitimacy

---

106 Report of the Appellate Body, *Brazil – Measures Affecting Imports of Retreaded Tyres*, WT/DS332/AB/R (December 3, 2007) (*Brazil – Tyres*), para. 151.

107 ibid.

108 Report of the Appellate Body, *European Communities – Measures Affecting Asbestos and Products Containing Asbestos*, WT/DS135/AB/R (March 12, 2001) (*EC – Asbestos*).

109 Report of the Appellate Body, *European Communities – Measures Prohibiting the Importation and Marketing of Seal Products*, WT/DS401/AB/R (May 22, 2014) (*EC – Seals*).

of the objective being pursued.[110] The dispute involved US regulations setting the conditions for use of a 'dolphin-safe' label on tuna products based on the methods for harvesting and fishing tuna. While the measure was found to be discriminatory as the US had failed to demonstrate that this stemmed solely from 'legitimate regulatory distinctions', the Appellate Body disagreed with the Panel's ruling that the measure was more trade-restrictive than necessary to fulfil US legitimate objectives, and found instead that 'the alternative measure proposed by Mexico would contribute to both the consumer information objective and the dolphin protection objective to a lesser degree than the measure at issue'.[111]

SPS disputes are often based on science and they showcase the role played by scientific evidence and the challenges linked to the burden of proof for the country defending the measure. In *EC-Hormones,* the WTO panel directed detailed scientific questions to six experts on the issues raised in the dispute. The scientific evidence submitted by the EU was deemed insufficient to justify the ban[112] in part because, in 1995, the Codex Commission adopted maximum residue limitations for the hormones in question, thus approving their use. Despite the consequential presumption of validity, the WTO panel sought information from the Commission and requested the nomination of experts from the secretariat. Finding that there was no scientific evidence in support of the action, the panel rejected the precautionary principle as inapplicable, instead holding that members must base their actions on a risk assessment adopting the criteria laid down by the SPS Agreement. According to the Panel, unilateral restrictions should be allowed as long as there is a scientific justification, but if there is no scientific evidence, the ban could not be 'based on' science. The Panel rejected the EU scientific interpretations as being 'minority views' in the scientific community. In other recent cases, the panel and the Appellate Body have rejected measures they determine have been adopted without a properly conducted risk assessment. Thus, in rejecting EC measures on the approval and marketing of biotech products,[113] the panel found that

110 Report of the Appellate Body, *United States – Measures Concerning the Importation, Marketing and Sale of Tuna and Tuna Products*, WT/DS381/AB/R (May 16, 2012) (*US – Tuna II (Mexico)*), para 313. See also Report of the Appellate Body, *United States – Certain Country of Origin Labelling* (COOL) *Requirements*, WT/DS384/AB/R (July 23, 2012) (*US – COOL*), para. 372.

111 ibid.

112 Report of the Panel, *–European Communities – Measures Concerning Meat and Meat Products (Hormones)*, WT/DS26/R (Aug. 18, 1997).

113 Report of the Panel, *European Communities – Measures Affecting the Approval and Marketing of Biotech Projects*, WT/DS291, 292, 293/R (Sept. 29, 2006).

the safeguard measures were not based on risk assessments that met trade agreement standards and thus could be presumed to be maintained without sufficient scientific evidence. Similarly, in a case involving Australia's regulations on importation of apples from New Zealand[114] the panel held that sixteen measures taken respecting apple imports were not based on a proper risk assessment and so were inconsistent with trade law, and the Appellate Body agreed.[115]

6.1.4 Recent Developments on Trade and the Environment

The WTO has been criticized for its emphasis on trade and lack of expertise in and understanding of environmental problems. Its panel decisions sometimes have appeared hostile in general to environmental measures. The Committee on Trade and Environment has produced few results of any substance. Its primary recommendation has been the extension of its mandate, something that was approved in 1996 at the Ministerial Meeting held in Singapore. The WTO has improved its transparency, however, by agreeing to release more documents to the public and to set up an internet site to provide greater access. The secretariat has instituted symposia for NGOs and granted observer status at the 1996 and 1998 Ministerial Conferences. An appellate body approved the acceptance of NGO amicus briefs in disputes. Finally, the 2002 Doha Ministerial Meeting adopted a Declaration that contains a renewed commitment to sustainable development, sets goals for the WTO Committee on Trade and Environment and specifically agrees to address fisheries subsidies and to reduce or eliminate tariff and non-tariff barriers to environmental goods and services.

Over the last decade, the WTO Secretariat has been increasingly collaborating with environmental and climate organizations. A notable example of this successful cooperation is the 2009 landmark report on *Trade and Climate Change*, published jointly by the WTO and UNEP. More recently, several plurilateral initiatives have been launched to advance the sustainability agenda at the WTO, including the Trade and Environmental Sustainability Structured Discussions (TESSD), the Dialogue on Plastics Pollution (DPP), and the initiative on Fossil Fuel Subsidy Reform.

The adoption of the Agreement on Fisheries Subsidies, signed in 2022, is another important initative. The Agreement marks a pivotal step in aligning global trade practices with environmental sustainability and development

114 Report of the Panel, *Australia – Measures Affecting the Importation of Apples from New Zealand,* WT/DS367/R (August 9, 2010).

115 Report of the Appellate Body, *Australia – Measures Affecting the Importation of Apples from New Zealand,* WT/DS367R/AB/R (Nov. 29, 2010).

goals. By addressing harmful subsidies that contribute to overfishing and the depletion of marine resources, this agreement underscores the WTO's commitment to promoting responsible and sustainable trade policies. It highlights the organization's openness to integrating environmental considerations into its framework, recognizing that sustainable development is integral to long-term economic prosperity. This agreement not only aids in the preservation of marine ecosystems but also sets a precedent for future trade negotiations to incorporate environmental sustainability, thereby reinforcing the WTO's role in fostering a balanced and forward-looking global trade system.

6.2 *Regional Economic Institutions and Agreements*

Despite questions about the short-term economic impact of environmental protection, developing countries began expressing concern for environmental protection in their economic relations. Taking a cue from the European Community, which began its environmental programs after the Stockholm Conference, other legal instruments of economic integration began to proclaim the need to protect the environment. In Africa, the Treaty of the Southern African Development Community[116] proclaimed among its objectives the promotion of self-sustaining development and the achievement of sustainable utilization of natural resources and effective protection of the environment. More widely, the Constitutive Act of the African Union was adopted July 2000 and came into force on 26 May 2001. The objectives identified in Article 3 include the promotion of sustainable development and cooperation in order to raise the living standards of African peoples; cooperation towards the eradication of disease and the promotion of good health, and the development of common African positions on issues of interest to the continent. The environment is not specifically mentioned, but the Executive Council is given authority to make decisions on a range of issues that include mineral resources, agriculture and forestry; water resources; and environmental protection.

The Treaty Establishing the Common Market for Eastern and Southern Africa[117] provides for cooperation of the contracting parties in the joint and efficient management and sustainable utilization of natural resources within the Common Market, especially in the management of fresh water resources, fisheries resources (Art. 122) and in general in the management of natural resources (Art. 123) and of the environment (Art. 124). The parties also

116 Treaty of the Southern African Development Community (adopted August 17, 1992, entered into force September 30, 1993) 32 ILM 116.

117 Treaty Establishing the Common Market for Eastern and Southern Africa (adopted 5 November 1993, entered into force 8 December 1994) 33 ILM 1067.

undertake to develop a collective and coordinated approach to sustainable development and management, rational exploitation and utilization and the protection of wildlife in the Common Market (Art. 125). These principles are developed in detail so as to provide the states members of the Common Market with precise instructions. The treaty also integrates environmental protection in agricultural development policy (Art. 130).

In the Western Hemisphere, apart from the North American Free Trade Agreement – which will be addressed in the next section – the Caribbean Common Market (CARICOM), established in 1973,[118] and the Mercado Comun del Sur (MERCOSUR)[119] also seek to eliminate trade barriers in their regions in order to stimulate economic development and have expressed interest in environmental matters. MERCOSUR (Mercado Comun del Sur) was established on January 1, 1995 between Brazil, Argentina, Paraguay and Uruguay based on the Treaty of Asuncion in 1991. Bolivia and Chile are associate members. MERCOSUR aims to establish a common market of free movement of goods, services, labor and capital. The Preamble of the MECOSUR Agreement recognizes that the objective of establishing a common market 'must be achieved by making optimum use of available resources, preserving the environment, improving physical links, coordinating macroeconomic policies and ensuring complementarity between the different sectors of the economy, based on the principles of gradualism, flexibility and balance'. Prior to the 1992 Rio Conference, the parties adopted the Declaration of Canela, adopting a common political position on biological diversity, global climate change, water resources, human settlements, forests, soils, international trade, maritime ocean protection, hazardous wastes, and institutional mechanisms for sustainable development. A Special Meeting on Environmental Issues has worked to analyze environmental legislation in the member states and recommend action to assure adequate environmental protection and harmonization of environmental legislation within MERCOSUR. In 1995 a Working Sub-group on environmental issues was assigned the task of developing common policies for the region.

---

118 The member states are Antigua and Barbuda, the Bahamas, Barbados, Belize, Dominica, Grenada, Guyana, Jamaica, Montserrat, St. Kitts and Nevis, St. Lucia, St. Vincent and the Grenadines, and Trinidad and Tobago. Treaty Establishing the Caribbean Community (adopted July 4, 1973, entered into force August 1, 1973) 12 ILM 1033.

119 Treaty of Asuncion, South American Quadripartite Common Market, Argentina, Brazil, Paraguay and Uruguay (March 26, 1991) 30 ILM 1041. See, Daniel C. Esty and Damien Geradin, 'Market Access, Competitiveness, and Harmonization: Environmental Protection in Regional Trade Agreements' (1997) 21 *Harvard Environmental Law Review* 265.

In Asia, the six member states of the Association of Southeast Asian Nations (ASEAN)[120] adopted the Singapore Declaration on political and economic cooperation on January 28, 1992. The Declaration provides that ASEAN member countries shall continue to play an active part in protecting the environment by further cooperating to promote the principle of sustainable development and integrate it into all aspects of development. The Declaration calls for enhanced environmental cooperation, particularly on issues of transboundary pollution, natural disasters, forest fires and 'in addressing the anti-tropical timber campaign'. The Declaration also asks developed countries to commit to assisting developing countries by providing new and additional financial resources as well as the transfer of, and access to, environmentally sound technology on concessional and preferential terms. The framework Agreement on Enhancing ASEAN Economic Cooperation, signed the same day, makes no reference to the environment, however.

Finally, the Central European Free Trade Agreement (CEFTA)[121] provides that its implementation shall not preclude prohibitions or restrictions on imports, exports or goods in transit justified by the conservation of exhaustible natural resources if such measures are made effective in conjunction with restrictions on domestic production or consumption.

Other treaties concerning economic cooperation also stress the importance of environmental protection and of its integration into economic policies. The International Tropical Timber Agreement[122] which tends to promote the expansion and diversification of international trade in tropical timber affirms the will of the contracting parties to contribute to the process of sustainable development and encourages states members of the International Tropical Timber Organization to support and develop not only industrial tropical timber reforestation but also the rehabilitation of degraded forest land and to develop national policies aimed at the sustainable utilization and conservation of timber-producing forests and their genetic resources and at maintaining the ecological balance in the regions concerned, in the context of tropical timber trade.

The European Energy Charter Treaty of December 17, 1994,[123] which intends to establish long-term cooperation in the energy field, includes detailed

---

120 Brunei Darussalam, Indonesia, Malaysia, Philippines, Singapore, Thailand.

121 Central European Free Trade Agreement (Czech Republic, Hungary, Poland and Slovak Republic, Krakow) (adopted December 21, 1992, entered into force March 1, 1993) 34 ILM 3.

122 International Tropical Timber Agreement (adopted January 26, 1994, entered into force January 1, 1997) 33 ILM 1014.

123 Energy Charter Treaty (adopted December 17, 1994, entered into force April 16, 1998) 33 ILM 360.

provisions concerning environmental aspects of such cooperation. Each contracting party shall strive to minimize in an economically efficient manner harmful environmental impacts occurring either within or outside its area from all operations within the energy cycle in its area, striving to take precautionary measures to prevent or minimize environmental degradation. The polluter should, in principle, bear the cost of pollution, including transboundary pollution, with due regard to public interest and without distorting investment in the energy cycle or international trade. Parties should have particular regard to energy efficiency and develop and use renewable energy sources. They also should promote the transparent assessment at any early stage and prior to decision, and subsequent monitoring, of environmental impacts of environmentally significant energy investment projects.

From the experience of the regional economic institutions, it seems clear that attention to environmental concerns improves the performance and political attractiveness of multilateral trade agreements because of the need to ensure internal coherence in managing the world's economic relations. The absence of environmental considerations limits the potential for obtaining the full benefits of trade liberalization because it fails to require internalization of environmental externalities and to prevent the over-exploitation of common resources. Allocative inefficiencies and environmental degradation result from omitting the environment, thereby diminishing the trade-derived gains in social welfare. The greater the degree of economic integration in a trading system, the greater the level of policy coordination and integration required in other realms; otherwise conflicts inevitably arise.

6.3 *NAFTA and a New Generation of Free Trade Agreements*

Since the second half of the twentieth century, countries have also been negotiating bilateral and regional trade agreements – generally known as free trade agreements (FTAs). Starting from the 1990s, and in particular after the Rio Conference in 1992 and the advent of the notion of sustainable development, FTAs have started to feature environmental or sustainable development provisions.

Pioneer in this regard has been the North American Free Trade Agreement (NAFTA) between Canada, Mexico and the United States. Signed at three different places at four different dates in December 1992, NAFTA mentions in its preamble the will of the three contracting governments to promote sustainable development and to strengthen the development and enforcement of environmental laws and regulations. Article 104 and Annex 104.1 state that in the event of any inconsistency between the Agreement and the specific obligations set out in three multilateral and two bilateral environmental treaties[124] the latter obligations prevail to the extent of the inconsistency. The same provision requires, however, that parties implementing these agreements adopt the implementing alternative that is the least inconsistent with other provisions of the Agreement.

An innovative provision is Article 1114 (the so-called *Pollution-Haven Package*), which addresses the concerns of the three countries about a possible 'race to the bottom'. It provides:

> The parties recognize that it is inappropriate to encourage investment by relaxing domestic health, safety or environmental measures. Accordingly, a Party should not waive or otherwise derogate from, or offer to waive or otherwise derogate from, such measures as an encouragement for the establishment, acquisition, expansion or retention in its territory of an investment of an investor. If a Party considers that another Party has offered such an encouragement, it may request consultations with the other Party and the two Parties shall consult with a view to avoiding any such encouragement.

Over the years, inspired by NAFTA, the *Pollution-Haven Package* has become a fundamental and consistent element of FTAs, frequently addressing both trade and investment. Alongside affirming the parties' regulatory sovereignty – the right to set their own levels of environmental protection and to adjust their environmental laws and policies accordingly – the parties also pledge not to lower their environmental standards to attract trade or investment.

Due to concerns about the lack of specificity in NAFTA, an environmental side accord was signed on September 13, 1993, by the three governments – the North American Agreement on Environmental Cooperation or NAAEC,[125] which addressed environmental concerns in more detail. It also established a trilateral North American Commission for Environmental Cooperation (NACEC) designed to (1) facilitate cooperation between NAFTA countries on environmental issues; (2) serve as a forum for regular ministerial-level meetings; (3) provide an independent secretariat to report regularly on significant environmental issues confronting NAFTA parties; (4) ensure that environmental

124 Respectively: CITES, the Montreal Protocol, the Basel Convention on Wastes, a 1986 agreement between Canada and the US on hazardous wastes, and a 1983 agreement between Mexico and the US for the Protection and Improvement of the Environment in the Border Area.

125 North American Agreement on Environmental Cooperation (Sept. 13, 1993) 32 ILM 1480.

enforcement remains a priority in all three countries, including provision for an annual enforcement activity report; (5) coordinate with trade officials in all three countries on any NAFTA related environment issues; and (6) ensure that there are opportunities for public participation in the development and implementation of environmental laws and programs in all three NAFTA countries. The agreement requires each NAFTA country to prepare periodic reports on the state of the environment and make these reports available to the public. Each state party must assess environmental impacts 'as appropriate' and consider stopping exports to NAFTA partners of any pesticide or toxic substance whose use is banned within the exporting nation's borders.[126] In addition, the NAFTA parties commit themselves to guaranteeing their citizens access to national courts to undertake enforcement actions and to seek redress of harm. They also agree to ensure the openness of judicial and administrative proceedings and transparent procedures for the creation of environmental laws and regulations. They further seek to limit trade in toxic substances that they have banned domestically.

In 2020, NAFTA was replaced by a new trade agreement between the three countries, called the United States-Mexico-Canada Agreement, or USMCA.[127] The new text builds on many of NAFTA's provisions and incorporates additional chapters and provisions devoted to the environment and sustainable development. NAFTA remains a pioneer agreement, as most FTAs concluded after 1992 have followed NAFTA's approach and have been increasingly incorporating provisions that clarify and develop the relationship between trade and environment/sustainable development. In fact, most FTAs now include an 'Environment' or 'Sustainable Development' chapter, which encompasses provisions on environmental cooperation, the prohibition of lowering environmental standards to attract foreign trade and investment (*Pollution-Haven Package*), and detailed regulations for specific environmental goods and services.[128] General exceptions in FTAs often clarify that certain sub-paragraphs – especially those mirroring letters (b) and (g) of GATT Article XX

126 On September 21, the United States government proposed banning the export of pesticides that are prohibited in the United States. It also would ban the export of a pesticide if the manufacturer withdrew an application for approval.

127 United States-Mexico-Canada Agreement (adopted December 10, 2019, entered into force July 1, 2020).

128 See e.g. Elena Cima, 'Promoting Renewable Energy Through FTAs? The Legal Implication of a New Generation of Trade Agreements' (2018) 52(4) *Journal of World Trade* 663–696. Ilaria Espa and Gracia Marín Durán, 'Promoting Green Energy Through EU Preferential Trade Agreements: Potential and Limitations' (2020) 47(2) *Legal Issues of Economic Integration* 115–150.

– are intended to apply to environmental measures. Additionally, some of the more recent FTAs feature specific environmental exceptions or carve-outs within individual chapters. Their preambles highlight the mutual supportiveness of trade rules and multilateral environmental agreements, often explicitly referencing specific MEAs, such as the UNFCCC and even the Paris Agreement.

Conclusions

The key to making trade and environmental policies compatible and mutually supportive in a market economy lies in pricing environmental resources properly to reflect their real scarcity and true social value. Undervalued resources pose a particularly difficult case for trade restrictions. Part of the reason for the destruction of tropical rain forests is the undervaluing of them as an international environmental resource. Unilateral restrictions on imports of tropical timber or other reduction of demand reduces the value of the trees at the source. As a result, exploitation may be accelerated in order to maintain income levels or the trees may be cleared to obtain higher income levels from mining or cattle ranching. Restrictions on production and sale need to be taken at the source, as well as at the market, in order to work. GATT will not impede some trade measures, but will question whether they are necessary trade restrictions or create distortion.

While trade negotiations are becoming more ecologically conscious, states parties to environmental agreements based on trade restrictions, like CITES, are questioning the economic and environmental consequences of their policies. There is evidence that a strict prohibition of trade can be counterproductive in discouraging conservation efforts and undervaluing the resource, while encouraging black market activities.

In the meantime, treaty law does not entirely resolve the problem of conflicting norms in trade agreements and environmental instruments. GATT Art. XXV allows its parties to waive any and all obligations under GATT for any specified measures of a contracting party, by a two-thirds majority of those voting of contracting parties. Potentially, this could resolve some of the conflicts. General treaty law provides that later treaties take priority over earlier ones, between the same parties; more specific treaties take priority over general ones. Where a treaty says it is subject to another, the other will prevail. The rules set out in Article 30 of the Vienna Convention on the Law of Treaties (VCLT) apply in the absence of express treaty provisions regulating the issue of priority. One problem is that GATT and environmental treaties deal with different subject matters while the VCLT rules are designed to cope with the problem of successive treaties governing the same subject matter.

While many continue to view trade and environment as hostile and competing policies, there is evidence that they are complementary; increasing world welfare can lead to demands for greater environmental protection. The basic policy underlying GATT/WTO is to liberalize trade across national boundaries and to pursue the benefits of comparative advantage and economies of scale. The theoretical foundation of free trade assumes that when nations specialize, they become more efficient in producing a product or service and can trade with other nations specializing in other goods and services, with the result that everyone is better off. The question is whether the theory is always correct in practice because externalities can distort the picture: a producer who pollutes the air imposes a cost on the world which is not recovered unless the polluter pays principle requires the internalization of the the environmental costs. Much of the debate about trade and the environment concerns how much environmental protection costs should be internalized.

Bibliography

Cameron, J. et al., *Trade and the Environment: the Search for Balance* (WM Gaunt & Sons 1994).

Cima, E., *From Exception to Promotion. Rethinking the Relationship Between International Trade and Environmental Law* (Brill 2022).

Cima, E. & Mbengue, M. M., *A Multifaceted Approach to Trade Liberalisation and Investment Protection in the Energy Sector* (Brill 2021).

Copeland, B. & Taylor, M.S., *Trade and Environment: Theory and Evidence* (Princeton University Press 2005).

Esty, D., *Greening the GATT* (PIIE 1994).

Esty, D. & Geradin, D., 'Market Access, competitiveness, and Harmonization: Environmental Protection in Regional Trade Agreements', 21 *Harv. Envt'l L. Rev.* 265 (1997).

Esty, D., & Ivanova, M. (ed.), *Global Environmental Governance, Options and Opportunities* (Yale 2002).

Gallagher, K, *Free Trade and the Environment: Mexico, NAFTA and Beyond* (Stanford University Press 2004).

Johnson, P.M. & Beaulieu, A., *the Environment and NAFTA* (Island Press 1996).

MacMillan, F., *WTO and the Environment* (Sweet & Maxwell 2001).

Meier, M., 'GATT, WTO, and the Environment: To what Extent do GATT/WTO Rules Permit Member Nations to Protect the Environment when doing so Adversely Affects Trade', 8 *Colo. J. Int'l L. & Pol'y* 241 (1997).

Najam, A., Halle, M. & Melendez-Ortiz R. (eds.), *Trade and the Environment: A Resource Book* (IISD 2007).

Safrin, Sabrina, 'Treaties in Collision? The Biosafety Protocol and the WTO Agreements', 96 *AJIL* 606 (2002).

Schoenbaum, T.J., 'International Trade and Protection of the Environment: The Continuing Search for Reconciliation', 91 *AJIL* 268 (1997).

UNEP, *the Use of Trade Measures in Select Multilateral Environmental Agreements* (1995).

Viñuales, J. E., *Foreign Investment and the Environment in International Law* (Cambridge University Press 2012).

Zaelke, D., et al., *Trade and the Environment: Law, Economics and Policy* (Island Press 2d. ed. 2002).

Index